DISCARD

Encyclopedia of
POPULATION

EDITORIAL BOARD

Encyclopedia of
POPULATION

EDITED BY

PAUL DEMENY

GEOFFREY MCNICOLL

VOLUME

1

A-H

**MACMILLAN
REFERENCE
USA**™

THOMSON

GALE

New York • Detroit • San Diego • San Francisco • Cleveland • New Haven, Conn. • Waterville, Maine • London • Munich

THOMSON
GALE

Encyclopedia of Population

Paul Demeny

Geoffrey McNicoll

Editors in Chief

LIBRARY OF CONGRESS CATALOGING-IN-PUBLICATION DATA

Encyclopedia of population / edited by Paul Demeny, Geoffrey McNicoll.
    p. cm.
        Includes bibliographical references and index.
        ISBN 0-02-865677-6 (hardcover (set))—ISBN 0-02-865678-4 (v. 1)—
        ISBN 0-02-865679-2 (v. 2)
        1. Population—Encyclopedias. I. Demeny, Paul George, 1932- II.
    McNicoll, Geoffrey.
  HB871.E538 2003
  304.6'03—dc21
  2003002712

Printed in the United States of America
10 9 8 7 6 5 4 3 2 1

CONTENTS

EDITORIAL AND PRODUCTION STAFF

Monica M. Hubbard, *Project Editor*

Nicole Watkins *Project Assistant Editor*

Shawn Beall, Mark Drouillard, Jan Klisz, Gloria Lam, Rebecca Marlow-Ferguson, Christine Mauer, Mark Mikula, Kate Millson, Pamela Parkinson, Angela Pilchak, Christine Slovey, Jennifer Wisinski, *Editorial Support*

Mary Jane DeFrosia, Elizabeth B. Inserra, Christine Kelley, Eric Lowenkron, David E. Salamie, *Copy Editors*

John Krol, *Proofreader*

Laurie Andriot, *Indexer*

Tracey Rowans, *Product Design Manager*

Kate Scheible, *Art Director*

Datapage Technologies International, Inc. and GGS, Inc., *Typesetters*

Mary Beth Trimper, *Manager, Composition*

Evi Seoud, *Assistant Manager, Composition*

Rita Wimberley, *Buyer*

MACMILLAN REFERENCE USA

Frank Menchaca, *Vice President*

Jill Lectka, *Director, Publishing Operations*

PREFACE

Population as a field of study is concerned with the membership of human groups and categories in all their variety and with the processes of change in membership. Interest in populations and population change can be found across a wide array of disciplines in the social and biological sciences—from history and economics to epidemiology and genetics. In addition, population issues have numerous political and ethical ramifications.

The Study of Population

The study of population has a history as old as the study of society itself. Its origin as a distinct field, however, is usually traced to the classical era of political economy and in particular to the writings of Thomas Robert Malthus (usually T. R. Malthus, sometimes Robert) in the late eighteenth and early nineteenth centuries. Malthus's prominent place does not derive from his popular (largely unfounded) repute as an anti-populationist but rests on his acute and wide-ranging empirical investigations of comparative demographic regimes, exploring how economic, social, and cultural circumstances influence demographic behavior and outcomes. Separate precursors of the modern-day subject lie in the "political arithmetic" of John Graunt and other scholars a century before Malthus, out of which came the systematic treatment of mortality through life tables and actuarial analysis, and in the mathematics of population change and renewal, dating from the eighteenth century. Additional, later, factors shaping the field came from the domain of public policy: social Darwinism and eugenics (an influence later to be regretted); hygiene and public health; measures toward women's emancipation; and the discourse of human rights.

The core of population studies is the subject (to many practitioners, the discipline) of demography or demographic analysis, focusing on the quantitative dimensions of population change and its explanation—a subject that can readily extend beyond human populations to other animate and even inanimate collectivities. Demographic analysis makes substantial use of applied mathematics and statistical theory. The numbers that make up its feedstock derive from longstanding government concerns with recording "vital" events (births, marriages, deaths), from the periodic complete enumeration of a country's inhabitants through censuses of population, and, in recent decades, from a large and elaborate survey-taking industry.

These threads of theory, analysis, and policy, in various combinations, form the modern tapestry of population studies. The emerging shape of the field can be observed in the proceedings of the successive quadrennial conferences of the International Union for the Scientific Investigation of Population Problems, an organization set up in the 1920s, and its successor, the present-day International Union for the Scientific Study of Population. Various entries in this encyclopedia, notably those treating the history of demography and population thought, offer a fuller description of the evolution of the subject.

Surveys and Appraisals of the Population Field

The first formal stocktaking of the field of population was the volume *Traité de démographie,* by Adolphe Landry and collaborators (Paris, 1945). This important and pioneering treatise was never translated into English. Alfred Sauvy, one of Landry's co-authors, published his two-volume *Théorie*

vii

générale de la population (Paris: Presses universitaires de France) in 1952 and 1954—a study whose ambition was signified by the Keynesian echoes of its title. (A one-volume English translation, *General Theory of Population,* appeared in 1969.) For an English-speaking readership the first large-scale overview of the field was *The Study of Population: An Inventory and Appraisal,* edited by Philip M. Hauser and Otis Dudley Duncan (Chicago: University of Chicago Press, 1959)—a large and impressive work that still repays reading. In some 30 chapters, well-known scholars surveyed the elements of demography, the status of demographic research in major countries, and the place of demography in the various more established social science disciplines.

The scope of demography—concepts, the institutional makeup of the field, and a who's who of demographers—was laid out by William Petersen and Renee Petersen in their 1985 *Dictionary of Demography.* Around the same time, the first specialized encyclopedia on the subject, the *International Encyclopedia of Population,* edited by John A. Ross, was issued (New York: The Free Press, 1982). More recently, a number of assessments of the field of population have been occasioned by anniversaries. Special journal issues comprising articles that survey the state of demographic research appeared on the 50th anniversary of *Population* (the journal of the Institut national d'études démographiques, Paris) in November-December 1995, and of *Population Studies* (Population Investigation Committee, London School of Economics) in November 1996; and on the 30th anniversary of *Demography* (the journal of the Population Association of America) in November 1993.

Population matters have some place in each of the three multi-volume encyclopedias of the social sciences—published in 1930–1935, 1968, and 2001—although perhaps limited by demography's uncertain status as a discipline. (The 2001 encyclopedia accepted it as "possessing a kind of disciplinary integrity.") Various specialized encyclopedias—on aging, bioethics, economics, the environment, and so on—necessarily also give appreciable space to population. In economics, what was once a strong interest in population slowly waned over the course of the twentieth century, typified by the drop from two full chapters on the subject in F. W. Taussig's *Principles of Economics* (1911), the standard university text of the early decades of the century, to a few passing paragraphs in Gregory Mankiw's 1998 *Principles.* Much of the modest population content of *The New*

Palgrave (1987), a current encyclopedic authority on economics, is concerned with the microeconomics of the family.

The Encyclopedia of Population

What is the need for an encyclopedia of population at this time? One answer would be that the world's population growth is far from over, with continuing and far-reaching effects on human society and the natural environment. Even though birth rates have declined quite steeply across much of the world, another two billion people are expected to be added to the existing six billion in the period 2000–2030—almost as many as were added in 1970–2000, the peak period of the "population explosion." Large regions of the world are still characterized by pervasive poverty, poor health conditions, and intractable problems of development—each with significant demographic dimensions.

But the main reason this encyclopedia is called for is the enlargement of the scope of the subject. In the 1980s, population issues seemed to many people to connote little else but rapid population growth and measures to curtail it. Today, population growth is one concern among many. Even a partial listing suggests the breadth of this expanded range of interest: the entrenchment of very low fertility and the growing problems of old-age support; the retreat from marriage and the diversification of family forms; new medical technologies affecting reproduction and longevity; the AIDS epidemic and the resurgence of a number of other infectious diseases; increased South-North migration and refugee movements; the press for women's equality and fuller reproductive rights; a widened array of environmental effects, notably climate change; and global shifts in the relative population sizes of countries. The evolutionary bases of human development and behavior have received renewed attention, with insights drawn from radical advances in genomic research and from comparisons with other species. Many of these topics have ethical debates associated with them—longstanding, like abortion and asylum-seeking, or newfound, like genetic engineering and animal rights. Along with such contemporary issues, research on population history and prehistory has proceeded apace, settling some controversies and raising others. All this is territory staked out by the *Encyclopedia of Population.*

The *Encyclopedia of Population* is directed both to professionals in the population sciences reading outside their immediate areas of expertise and to other social scientists, college students, advanced high school students, and the educated lay reader. Catering to this range of readership is challenging. An effort is made to avoid material and jargon that would require prior specialized knowledge, but without losing significant detail through undue simplification. (Characterizations of persons named in the text of articles by their nationality or profession are included for the same reason, even when such information would be well known to many users.) Where a topic requires technical treatment, it receives it, or the reader is referred to appropriate further sources. However, the Encyclopedia is not intended to serve as a textbook on its field. If it has an ambition beyond the utilitarian it is to push out the boundaries of the subject—an ambition that stands in contrast to that implicitly set by the Population Association of America, whose journal prominently defines its scope as being "the statistical study of human populations."

Not a few topics in population studies are contentious, either in terms of research findings or, more basically, in terms of their political and ethical premises or implications. Unsurprisingly, the various authors writing on matters related to such topics may often take differing positions. We have not sought to suppress those differences, but rather to ensure a rough overall degree of balance among the articles.

The Encyclopedia contains 336 articles by a total of 278 authors. The contributors are all accomplished scholars, their expertise spanning a wide range of fields: biology, demography, economics, geography, history, law, philosophy, political science, public health, sociology. Many of the articles are short entries of 500–1000 words of text; only a relatively few are longer than 3000 words. Within this range, length is roughly dictated by the scope of the topic; the level of technicality is governed by what is required to explain it.

Among the short entries are 60 biographies of persons selected from those whose work has been important in the development of population studies, whether or not they were seen (or saw themselves) as "population" people. Compiling such a list entails many somewhat arbitrary choices and no two lists would be the same. In the present case, contributors to technical demography will be less in evidence in the encyclopedia than persons whose work has been influential in the development of population thought more broadly. Invidious choice among

presently active scholars has been avoided by including only persons born in or before 1930, or deceased.

A thematic overview of the Encyclopedia of Population is given in the Topical Outline, which follows the List of Authors in the frontmatter . The Outline may be particularly helpful to students who wish to find population-related information relevant to their studies in other fields but who do not have in mind a particular topical entry. A student in environmental studies, for example, could narrow his or her search within the sixteen articles listed under the heading Environment and Resources; a political science student might scan the eleven articles listed under Political Demography, and perhaps also the ten under Population Policy.

The Population Tables at the end of the second volume presents four summary tables showing statistics on population size, rates of change, area, and density, by country, for countries of 10 million population and over. (These countries contain over 90% of the world's population.)

We hope readers of the Encyclopedia will find in it much material that is new to them. A test of such a work, in addition to its reference function, is the extent to which it repays browsing and offers the casual serendipitous discovery or insight. Inevitably, occasional gaps in coverage will be found. Some of these may reflect particular editorial decisions; others result from nondelivery of promised articles (the proportion of such defaults, some 7%, is relatively low for enterprises such as this). We would hope, like the editors of The New Palgrave (p. x), that "such errors of omission and commission . . . are unbiased, in almost every sense of the word."

Our main acknowledgment is of the encyclopedia's contributors, for their work and sometimes for their forbearance of editorial intrusiveness. Assistance from members of the committee of Editorial Advisors is also much appreciated. At Macmillan Reference, Jill Lectka, Monica Hubbard, and Nicole Watkins were efficient and congenial counterparts; to them also should go credit for ensuring that the project kept not too far behind its schedule. At the Population Council, Robert Colasacco provided administrative and secretarial assistance. The overall institutional support of the Population Council was an essential factor in the undertaking.

PAUL DEMENY
GEOFFREY MCNICOLL
NEW YORK, MARCH 2003

LIST OF ARTICLES

LIST OF CONTRIBUTORS

John A. Agnew
University of California, Los Angeles
GEOPOLITICS

Dennis Ahlburg
University of Minnesota; University of
Southampton, England
ECONOMIC-DEMOGRAPHIC MODELS

John Alcock
Arizona State University
SOCIOBIOLOGY

Margo Anderson
University of Wisconsin, Milwaukee
CENSUS

Douglas L. Anderton
University of Massachusetts, Amherst
DISEASE, CONCEPTS AND CLASSIFICATION OF

Adria N. Armbrister
Mount Vernon, New York
IMMIGRATION, UNAUTHORIZED

Fred Arnold
ORC Macro, Calverton, Maryland
DEMOGRAPHIC AND HEALTH SURVEYS
GENDER PREFERENCES FOR CHILDREN

Nan Marie Astone
Johns Hopkins University
SOCIAL CAPITAL

Judith Banister
Beijing Javelin Consulting Company; Hong
Kong University
ONE-CHILD POLICY

David B. Barrett
World Evangelization Research Center,
Richmond, Virginia
RELIGIOUS AFFILIATION

Alaka Malwade Basu
Cornell University
CASTE

Eva Bernhardt
Stockholm University, Sweden
COHABITATION

Robert L. Bettinger
University of California, Davis
HUNTER-GATHERERS

Francesco C. Billari
Università Bocconi, Milan, Italy
LIFE COURSE ANALYSIS

Jean-Noël Biraben
Institut National d'Études Démographiques,
Paris
WORLD POPULATION GROWTH

Alain Blum
Institut National d'Études Démographiques,
Paris, France
FAMINE IN THE SOVIET UNION

Barry Bogin
University of Michigan, Dearborn
ANTHROPOMETRY

Donald J. Bogue
University of Chicago
HUMAN ECOLOGY

Jesper L. Boldsen
University of Southern Denmark, Odense
PREHISTORIC POPULATIONS: EUROPE

John Bongaarts
Population Council, New York
FERTILITY, PROXIMATE DETERMINANTS OF

Heather Booth
Australian National University, Canberra
POPULATION DYNAMICS

George J. Borjas
Harvard University
IMMIGRATION, BENEFITS AND COSTS OF

Nick Bostrom
Yale University
EXTINCTION, HUMAN

Patrice Bourdelais
École des Hautes Études en Sciences Sociales
(EHESS), Paris
BERTILLON, JACQUES
FARR, WILLIAM

Christopher R. Browning
Ohio State University
CRIME, DEMOGRAPHY OF

John C. Caldwell
Australian National University, Canberra
DEMOGRAPHY, HISTORY OF
POPULATION ORGANIZATIONS: PROFESSIONAL
ASSOCIATIONS

James R. Carey
University of California, Davis
LIFE SPAN

Bruce A. Carnes
Center on Aging NORC, University of Chicago
AGING AND LONGEVITY, BIOLOGY OF

John B. Casterline
Population Council, New York
DEMOGRAPHIC TRANSITION
FREEDMAN, RONALD

Joseph Chamie
United Nations Population Division, New York
POPULATION ORGANIZATIONS: UNITED NATIONS
SYSTEM

Tony Champion
University of Newcastle upon Tyne, England
CITIES, FUTURE OF
SUBURBANIZATION

Christopher Chase-Dunn
University of California, Riverside
CITIES, SYSTEMS OF

Andrew J. Cherlin
Johns Hopkins University
FAMILY DEMOGRAPHY

Jean-Claude Chesnais
Institut National d'Études Démographiques,
Paris, France
LANDRY, ADOLPHE
SAUVY, ALFRED

John I. Clarke
University of Durham, England
SEX RATIO

Lynda Clark
Centre for Population Studies, London School of
Hygiene and Tropical Medicine, England
GRANDPARENTHOOD

John Cleland
London School of Hygiene and Tropical
Medicine, England
MORTALITY-FERTILITY RELATIONSHIPS
WORLD FERTILITY SURVEY

Samuel Cohn, Jr.
University of Glasgow, Scotland
BLACK DEATH

David Coleman
University of Oxford, England
KEYNES, JOHN MAYNARD
POPULATION DECLINE

Michel P. Coleman
Cancer and Public Health Unit, London School
of Hygiene and Tropical Medicine, England
CANCER

John Connell
University of Sydney, Australia
MICROSTATES, DEMOGRAPHY OF

Rebecca J. Cook
University of Toronto, Canada
REPRODUCTIVE RIGHTS

Eileen M. Crimmins
University of Southern California
DISABILITY, DEMOGRAPHY OF

Gretchen C. Daily
Stanford University
CARRYING CAPACITY

David Dalby
>Linguasphere Observatory, Wales
>LANGUAGES AND SPEECH COMMUNITIES

Herman E. Daly
>University of Maryland
>LIMITS TO GROWTH

Joel Darmstadter
>Resources for the Future, Washington, D.C.
>ENERGY AND POPULATION

Partha Dasgupta
>St. John's College, University of Cambridge,
>England
>COMMON PROPERTY RESOURCES
>EXTERNALITIES OF POPULATION CHANGE

Paul A. David
>Stanford University; All Souls College, Oxford,
>England
>FERTILITY CONTROL, INDIRECT MEASUREMENT OF

Henk A. de Gans
>University of Amsterdam, Netherlands
>PEARL, RAYMOND

Paul Demeny
>Population Council, New York
>BOSERUP, ESTER
>HARDIN, GARRETT
>POPULATION POLICY

Bernard M. Dickens
>University of Toronto, Canada
>REPRODUCTIVE TECHNOLOGIES: ETHICAL ISSUES

Peter J. Donaldson
>Population Reference Bureau, Washington, D.C.
>BERELSON, BERNARD

D. Peter Drotman
>Emory University School of Medicine; National
>Center for Infectious Diseases, Atlanta,
>Georgia
>DISEASES, INFECTIOUS

Tim Dyson
>London School of Economics, England
>FAMINE IN SOUTH ASIA
>FOOD SUPPLY AND POPULATION

Richard A. Easterlin
>University of Southern California
>KUZNETS, SIMON
>THOMAS, DOROTHY SWAINE

Nicholas Eberstadt
>American Enterprise Institute, Washington, D.C.
>COMMUNISM, POPULATION ASPECTS OF

Anne H. Ehrlich
>Stanford University
>ECOLOGICAL PERSPECTIVES ON POPULATION

Paul Ehrlich
>Stanford University
>ECOLOGICAL PERSPECTIVES ON POPULATION

Paula England
>Northwestern University
>FEMINIST PERSPECTIVES ON POPULATION ISSUES

Thomas J. Espenshade
>Office of Population Research, Princeton
>University
>BLAKE, JUDITH

Norman Etherington
>University of Western Australia, Perth
>WAR, DEMOGRAPHIC CONSEQUENCES OF

Malin Falkenmark
>Stockholm International Water Institute, Sweden
>WATER AND POPULATION

Jane Falkingham
>University of Southampton, England
>WELFARE STATE

Griffith Feeney
>Scarsdale, New York
>DATA ASSESSMENT
>LEXIS DIAGRAM
>MOMENTUM OF POPULATION GROWTH

Lois A. Fingerhut
>Centers for Disease Control and Prevention,
>National Center for Health Statistics,
>Hyattsville, Maryland
>ACCIDENTS

Jason L. Finkle
>University of Michigan
>CONFERENCES, INTERNATIONAL POPULATION

Jochen Fleischhacker
>Max Planck Institute for Demographic Research,
>Rostock, Germany
>MARX, KARL

Warwick Fox
>University of Central Lancashire, England
>ENVIRONMENTAL ETHICS

Odile Frank
United Nations, Department of Economic and
Social Affairs, New York
ABSTINENCE

Mary Anne Freedman
National Center for Health Statistics, Hyattsville,
Maryland
VITAL STATISTICS

Gary P. Freeman
University of Texas, Austin
IMMIGRATION POLICIES

Paul K. Freeman
University of Denver
DISASTERS

R. G. Frey
Bowling Green State University
EUTHANASIA

William H. Frey
University of Michigan
INTERNAL MIGRATION

Tom Fricke
University of Michigan
CULTURE AND POPULATION

Frank F. Furstenberg
University of Pennsylvania
FAMILY: FUTURE

Anne H. Gauthier
University of Calgary, Canada
FAMILY ALLOWANCES

Leonid A. Gavrilov
Center on Aging, NORC, University of Chicago
AGING OF POPULATION

Nigel Gilbert
University of Surrey, England
ARTIFICIAL SOCIAL LIFE

Jeanne Gobalet
Lapkoff & Gobalet Demographic Research, Inc.,
Saratoga, California
STATE AND LOCAL GOVERNMENT DEMOGRAPHY

Joshua R. Goldstein
Princeton University
DIVORCE

Jack A. Goldstone
University of California, Davis
NATIONAL SECURITY AND POPULATION

Emily Grundy
Centre for Population Studies, London School of
Hygiene and Tropical Medicine, England
GRANDPARENTHOOD

Thomas Gryn
Ohio State University
LONGITUDINAL DEMOGRAPHIC SURVEYS

Michel Guillot
University of Wisconsin, Madison
EVENT-HISTORY ANALYSIS
LIFE TABLES

John G. Haaga
Population Reference Bureau, Washington, D.C.
POPULATION ORGANIZATIONS: RESEARCH
INSTITUTIONS

Michael R. Haines
Colgate University
TRANS-ATLANTIC MIGRATION

Catherine Hakim
London School of Economics, England
PARENTHOOD

Eugene A. Hammel
University of California, Berkeley
ANTHROPOLOGICAL DEMOGRAPHY

Michael T. Hannan
Stanford University
ORGANIZATIONS, DEMOGRAPHY OF

Henry C. Harpending
University of Utah
ARCHAEOGENETICS

Carl Haub
Population Reference Bureau, Washington, D.C.
FERTILITY MEASUREMENT
MORTALITY MEASUREMENT

Adrian C. Hayes
Johns Hopkins University
ACTION THEORY IN POPULATION RESEARCH

Jacqueline Hecht
Institut National d'Études Démographiques,
Paris, France
ARIÈS, PHILIPPE
SÜSSMILCH, JOHANN

David M. Heer
University of California, San Diego
DAVIS, KINGSLEY

Judith Helzner
John D. and Catherine T. MacArthur
Foundation, Chicago
REPRODUCTIVE HEALTH

Stanley K. Henshaw
Alan Guttmacher Institute, New York
INDUCED ABORTION: LEGAL ASPECTS
INDUCED ABORTION: PREVALENCE

Donald J. Hernandez
State University of New York, Albany
RACIAL AND ETHNIC COMPOSITION

Patrick Heuveline
NORC & Population Research Center, University
of Chicago
AGING OF POPULATION

Allan G. Hill
Harvard School of Public Health
FAMINE IN AFRICA

Kenneth Hill
Johns Hopkins University
BRASS, WILLIAM
ESTIMATION METHODS, DEMOGRAPHIC

Charles Hirschman
University of Washington
FERTILITY TRANSITION, SOCIOECONOMIC
DETERMINANTS OF

Peter Hiscock
Australian National University, Canberra
PREHISTORIC POPULATIONS: AUSTRALIA AND THE
PACIFIC

Dennis Hodgson
Fairfield University
NOTESTEIN, FRANK W.
POPULATION THOUGHT, CONTEMPORARY
THOMPSON, WARREN S.

Dennis Hogan
Brown University
SOCIAL INSTITUTIONS

Robert D. Hoppa
University of Manitoba, Canada
PREHISTORIC POPULATIONS: THE AMERICAS

Shiro Horiuchi
Rockefeller University
MORTALITY, AGE PATTERNS OF

Graeme Hugo
University of Adelaide, Australia
GEOGRAPHIC INFORMATION SYSTEMS
RESETTLEMENT

Serguey Ivanov
United Nations Population Division, New York
FERTILITY, AGE PATTERNS OF

David K. Jesuit
Luxembourg Income Study, Luxembourg
POVERTY AND INCOME

S. Ryan Johansson
University of Cambridge, England
EPIDEMICS
HEALTH TRANSITION

Andrew Jorgenson
University of California, Riverside
CITIES, SYSTEMS OF

Todd M. Johnson
Gordon-Conwell Theological Seminary
RELIGIOUS AFFILIATION

Gavin W. Jones
Australian National University, Canberra
CALDWELL, JOHN C.
URBANIZATION

M.W. Jones-Lee
University of Newcastle upon Tyne, England
VALUE OF LIFE, ECONOMIC

Debra S. Judge
University of Western Australia, Perth
PRIMATE DEMOGRAPHY

Vasantha Kandiah
United Nations Population Division, New York
CONTRACEPTIVE PREVALENCE
FERTILITY, AGE PATTERNS OF

Hillard Kaplan
University of New Mexico
EVOLUTIONARY DEMOGRAPHY

Lynn A. Karoly
RAND
LABOR FORCE

Laura Katzive
Center for Reproductive Law and Policy, New
York
INDUCED ABORTION: LEGAL ASPECTS

Nathan Keyfitz
Harvard University
EULER, LEONHARD
WHELPTON, P. K.

Leslie J. King
McMaster University, Hamilton, Canada
CENTRAL PLACE THEORY

Stephan Klasen
University of Munich, Germany
SEX SELECTION

Herbert S. Klein
Columbia University
AFRICAN-AMERICAN POPULATION HISTORY

Hans-Peter Kohler
University of Pennsylvania
FERTILITY, BELOW-REPLACEMENT

Laurence J. Kotlikoff
Boston University
GENERATIONAL ACCOUNTING

Philip Kreager
Somerville College, Oxford University, England
GRAUNT, JOHN
POPULATION THOUGHT, HISTORY OF

Shepard Krech III
Brown University
ENVIRONMENTAL IMPACT, HUMAN

Lauren J. Krivo
Ohio State University
CRIME, DEMOGRAPHY OF

Steven Kull
Program on International Policy Attitudes,
Washington, D.C.
PUBLIC OPINION ON POPULATION ISSUES

Lewis H. Kuller
University of Pittsburgh
CARDIOVASCULAR DISEASE

David Lam
University of Michigan
BECKER, GARY S.

C. M. Langford
London School of Economics, England
CANNAN, EDWIN
GLASS, DAVID
KUCZYNSKI, R. R.

Ulla Larsen
Harvard University
INFERTILITY

Edward O. Laumann
University of Chicago
SEXUALITY, HUMAN

Jacques Ledent
Université du Québec, Canada
KEYFITZ, NATHAN

Barrett A. Lee
Pennsylvania State University
RESIDENTIAL SEGREGATION

Ronald Lee
University of California, Berkeley
AGE STRUCTURE AND DEPENDENCY
INTERGENERATIONAL TRANSFERS

Jacques Légaré
Université de Montréal, Canada
RYDER, NORMAN B.

Henri Leridon
Institut National d'Études Démographiques,
Paris, France
HENRY, LOUIS
NATURAL FERTILITY

Ron Lesthaeghe
Vrije Universiteit Brussel, Belgium
QUETELET, ADOLPHE
VERHULST, PIERRE-FRANÇOIS

David Levine
OISE; University of Toronto, Canada
FAMILY RECONSTITUTION
LITERACY

Alexandra M. Levitt
National Center for Infectious Diseases, Atlanta,
Georgia
DISEASES, INFECTIOUS

Massimo Livi-Bacci
University of Florence, Italy
PEOPLING OF THE CONTINENTS

Cynthia B. Lloyd
Population Council, New York
EDUCATION

Alan D. Lopez
World Health Organization, Geneva, Switzerland
DISEASE, BURDEN OF
TOBACCO-RELATED MORTALITY

Wolfgang Lutz
International Institute for Applied Systems
Analysis, Laxenburg, Austria
PROJECTIONS AND FORECASTS, POPULATION

Alphonse L. MacDonald
Université René Descartes, Paris, France
FAMINE IN CHINA

POPULATION ORGANIZATIONS: NATIONAL AND
INTERNATIONAL AGENCIES

F. Landis MacKellar
International Institute for Applied Systems
Analysis, Laxenburg, Austria
HOMICIDE AND SUICIDE
SIMON, JULIAN L.

Rainer Mackensen
Technical University of Berlin, Germany
LÖSCH, AUGUST
SOMBART, WERNER

Diane J. Macunovich
Barnard College, Columbia University
CYCLES, POPULATION
EASTERLIN, RICHARD A.

Deborah Maine
Columbia University
MATERNAL MORTALITY

Patrick Manning
Northeastern University
SLAVERY, DEMOGRAPHY OF

Peter Marden
RMIT University, Melbourne, Australia
STATES SYSTEM, DEMOGRAPHIC HISTORY OF

Robert D. Mare
University of California, Los Angeles
SOCIAL MOBILITY

Howard Margolis
University of Chicago
RISK

Douglas S. Massey
University of Pennsylvania
INTERNATIONAL MIGRATION

Luigi Mastroianni, Jr.
University of Pennsylvania
REPRODUCTIVE TECHNOLOGIES: MODERN
METHODS

Pauline M. H. Mazumdar
University of Toronto
EUGENICS

Peter McDonald
Australian National University, Canberra
FAMILY POLICY

C. Alison McIntosh
Melbourne, Australia
CONFERENCES, INTERNATIONAL POPULATION

Roderick J. McIntosh
Rice University
CLIMATE CHANGE AND POPULATION: HISTORY

A. J. McMichael
Australian National University, Canberra
ENVIRONMENTAL HEALTH

Geoffrey McNicoll
Population Council, New York
DEVELOPMENT, POPULATION AND
KING, GREGORY
MILL, JOHN STUART
OPTIMUM POPULATION
PETTY, WILLIAM
POPULATION

Barbara S. Mensch
Population Council, New York
ADOLESCENT FERTILITY

Thomas W. Merrick
World Bank Institute, Washington, D.C.
HEALTH SYSTEMS

France Meslé
Institut National d'Études Démographiques,
Paris, France
CAUSES OF DEATH

Deborah Waller Meyers
Migration Policy Institute, Washington, D.C.
TEMPORARY MIGRATION

Geraldine P. Mineau
University of Utah
GENEALOGICAL RECORDS

Armindo Miranda
Chr. Michelson Institute, Bergen, Norway
BIBLIOGRAPHIC AND ONLINE RESOURCES

S. Philip Morgan
Duke University
BABY BOOM, POST–WORLD WAR II
FAMILY SIZE INTENTIONS

Martina Morris
University of Washington
SIMULATION MODELS

Peter A. Morrison
RAND, Santa Monica, California
BUSINESS DEMOGRAPHY

Stephen S. Morse
Columbia University
EMERGING INFECTIOUS DISEASES

Michael Mortimore
  Dryland Research, Somerset, England
  TECHNOLOGICAL CHANGE AND POPULATION
  GROWTH

Frank Mott
  Ohio State University
  LONGITUDINAL DEMOGRAPHIC SURVEYS

Tim Mulgan
  University of Auckland, New Zealand
  FUTURE GENERATIONS, OBLIGATIONS TO

Rainer Münz
  Humboldt University, Berlin, Germany
  IMMIGRATION TRENDS IN MAJOR DESTINATION
  COUNTRIES

Krishnan Namboodiri
  Ohio State University
  AGE MEASUREMENT

Andrew Noymer
  University of California, Berkeley
  INFLUENZA
  TUBERCULOSIS

Cormac Ó Gráda
  University College Dublin, Ireland
  FAMINE, CONCEPTS AND CAUSES OF
  FAMINE IN IRELAND

Brian C. O'Neill
  International Institute for Applied Systems
    Analysis, Laxenburg, Austria; Brown
    University
  CLIMATE CHANGE AND POPULATION: FUTURE
  PROJECTIONS AND FORECASTS, POPULATION

Philip E. Ogden
  Queen Mary College, University of London,
    England
  DENSITY AND DISTRIBUTION OF POPULATION
  GEOGRAPHY, POPULATION

S. Jay Olshansky
  University of Illinois, Chicago
  AGING AND LONGEVITY, BIOLOGY OF

José Antonio Ortega
  Universidad Autónoma de Madrid, Spain
  FERTILITY, BELOW-REPLACEMENT

Lars Østby
  Statistics Norway, Oslo
  POPULATION REGISTERS

Anthony Paik
  University of Chicago
  SEXUALITY, HUMAN

Alberto Palloni
  University of Wisconsin
  DIFFUSION IN POPULATION THEORY

Demetrios G. Papademetriou
  Migration Policy Institute, Washington, D.C.
  LABOR MIGRATION, INTERNATIONAL

John Parkington
  University of Cape Town, South Africa
  PREHISTORIC POPULATIONS: AFRICA

Jack Parsons
  Population Policy Press, Wales
  LEBENSRAUM

Erin Patrick
  Migration Policy Institute, Washington, D.C.
  REFUGEES, DEMOGRAPHY OF

Anne R. Pebley
  University of California, Los Angeles
  INFANT AND CHILD MORTALITY

Mark Perlman
  University of Pittsburgh
  LEIBENSTEIN, HARVEY

William Petersen
  Carmel, California
  CONDORCET, MARQUIS DE
  GODWIN, WILLIAM

James F. Phillips
  Population Council, New York
  DEMOGRAPHIC SURVEILLANCE SYSTEMS

Gilles Pison
  Institut National d'Études Démographiques,
    Paris, France
  MULTIPLE BIRTHS

Andrejs Plakans
  Iowa State University
  FAMILY: HISTORY

Kari Poikolainen
  Finnish Foundation for Alcohol Studies,
    Helsinki, Finland
  ALCOHOL, HEALTH EFFECTS OF

Robert A. Pollak
  Washington University in St. Louis
  FAMILY BARGAINING

John H. Pollard
  Macquarie University, Australia
  ACTUARIAL ANALYSIS

Geoffrey G. Pope
  William Paterson University
  PREHISTORIC POPULATIONS: ASIA

Dudley L. Poston, Jr.
  Texas A&M University
  CHINESE, OVERSEAS

Joseph E. Potter
  University of Texas, Austin
  MASS MEDIA AND DEMOGRAPHIC BEHAVIOR

David Malcolm Potts
  University of California, Berkeley
  BIRTH CONTROL, HISTORY OF
  SANGER, MARGARET

Mary G. Powers
  Fordham University
  OCCUPATION AND INDUSTRY

Kenneth Prandy
  Cardiff University, Wales
  SOCIAL REPRODUCTION

Samuel H. Preston
  University of Pennsylvania
  FAMILY SIZE DISTRIBUTION

Thomas W. Pullum
  University of Texas, Austin
  FAMILY LIFE CYCLE

Radhika Ramasubban
  Centre for Social and Technological Change,
    Mumbai, India
  WOMEN'S STATUS AND DEMOGRAPHIC BEHAVIOR

Sara Randall
  University College London, England
  NOMADS

Jai Ranganathan
  Stanford University
  CARRYING CAPACITY

Tom Regan
  Culture and Animals Foundation, Raleigh,
    North Carolina
  ANIMAL RIGHTS

Robert E. Ricklefs
  University of Missouri, St. Louis
  ANIMAL ECOLOGY

James C. Riley
  Indiana University, Bloomington
  DISEASE AND HISTORY

Nancy E. Riley
  Bowdoin College
  GENDER

Jean-Marie Robine
  INSERM, Montpellier, France
  EPIDEMIOLOGICAL TRANSITION
  OLDEST OLD

Kim Rodgers
  Redefining Progress, Oakland, California
  SUSTAINABLE DEVELOPMENT

Osamu Saito
  Hitotsubashi University, Tokyo, Japan
  HAYAMI, AKIRA

Warren C. Sanderson
  State University of New York, Stony Brook
  FERTILITY CONTROL, INDIRECT MEASUREMENT OF

Jean-Paul Sardon
  Institut National d'Études Démographiques,
    Paris, France
  CHILDLESSNESS

Italo Scardovi
  Università di Bologna, Italy
  BOTERO, GIOVANNI
  GINI, CORRADO
  PARETO, VILFREDO

Walter Scheidel
  University of Chicago
  ANCIENT WORLD, DEMOGRAPHY OF

Robert Schoen
  Pennsylvania State University
  PARTNER CHOICE

Sheldon J. Segal
  Population Council, New York
  CONTRACEPTION, MODERN METHODS OF
  SPONTANEOUS ABORTION

Peter Selman
  University of Newcastle upon Tyne, England
  ADOPTION

William Seltzer
  Fordham University
  DATA COLLECTION, ETHICAL ISSUES IN
  GENOCIDE
  HOLOCAUST

Harry L. Shipman
University of Delaware
OUTER SPACE, COLONIZATION OF

Vladimir M. Shkolnikov
Max Planck Institute for Demographic Research,
Rostock, Germany
MORTALITY REVERSALS

Susan Short
Brown University
SOCIAL INSTITUTIONS

Lionel Shriver
London, England
LITERATURE, POPULATION IN

John Simons
London School of Hygiene and Tropical
Medicine, England
RELIGIONS, POPULATION DOCTRINES OF

Steven W. Sinding
International Planned Parenthood Federation,
London, England
FAMILY PLANNING PROGRAMS

Susheela Singh
Alan Guttmacher Institute, New York
ADOLESCENT FERTILITY

Timothy M. Smeeding
Syracuse University; Luxembourg Income Study,
Luxembourg
POVERTY AND INCOME DISTRIBUTION

Vaclav Smil
University of Manitoba, Canada
DIETARY REGIMES
NATURAL RESOURCES AND POPULATION
NITROGEN CYCLE

Ken R. Smith
University of Utah
GENEALOGICAL RECORDS

Richard M. Smith
University of Cambridge, England
HISTORICAL DEMOGRAPHY
LASLETT, PETER

Stanley K. Smith
University of Florida
BUSINESS DEMOGRAPHY
SMALL-AREA ANALYSIS

Timothy Snyder
Yale University
ETHNIC CLEANSING

Edward J. Spar
Council of Professional Associations on Federal
Statistics, Alexandria, Virginia
DATABASES, DEMOGRAPHIC

Eric Stallard
Duke University
DISEASES, CHRONIC AND DEGENERATIVE

Katrina Stamas
Columbia University
MATERNAL MORTALITY

Richard H. Steckel
Ohio State University
NUTRITION AND CALORIE CONSUMPTION

Karl Steyaert
Redefining Progress, Oakland, California
SUSTAINABLE DEVELOPMENT

Ross M. Stolzenberg
University of Chicago
RISK

J. Edward Taylor
University of California, Davis
MIGRATION MODELS

John Taylor
Australian National University, Canberra
INDIGENOUS PEOPLES

Lars-Göran Tedebrand
Umeå University, Sweden
WICKSELL, KNUT

Michael S. Teitelbaum
Alfred P. Sloan Foundation, New York
ETHNIC AND NATIONAL GROUPS

Pál Péter Tóth
Hungarian Central Statistical Office,
Demographic Research Institute, Budapest
KŐRÖSI, JÓZSEF

James Trussell
Princeton University
COALE, ANSLEY JOHNSON
FECUNDITY

Shripad Tuljapurkar
Stanford University
BIOLOGY, POPULATION
RENEWAL THEORY AND THE STABLE POPULATION
MODEL

Peter Uhlenberg
University of North Carolina
VALUES AND DEMOGRAPHIC BEHAVIOR

Martin Vaessen
ORC Macro, Calverton, Maryland
DEMOGRAPHIC SURVEYS, HISTORY AND
METHODOLOGY OF

Tapani Valkonen
University of Helsinki, Finland
MORTALITY DIFFERENTIALS, SOCIOECONOMIC

Dirk J. van de Kaa
University of Amsterdam, Netherlands
JOURNALS, POPULATION
SECOND DEMOGRAPHIC TRANSITION

Etienne van de Walle
University of Pennsylvania
CANTILLON, RICHARD
DUMONT, ARSÈNE
INDUCED ABORTION: HISTORY
INFANTICIDE
MOHEAU, JEAN-BAPTISTE

Evert van Imhoff
Netherlands Interdisciplinary Demographic
Institute, The Hague, Netherlands
COHORT ANALYSIS

Bernard M. S. van Praag
University of Amsterdam, Netherlands
COST OF CHILDREN

Joanne van Selm
Migration Policy Institute, Washington, D.C.
ASYLUM, RIGHT OF
FORCED MIGRATION

James W. Vaupel
Max Planck Institute for Demographic Research,
Rostock, Germany
BIODEMOGRAPHY
GOMPERTZ, BENJAMIN
LOTKA, ALFRED J.

Daniel R. Vining, Jr.
University of Pennsylvania
QUALITY OF POPULATION

Kenneth W. Wachter
University of California, Berkeley
STOCHASTIC POPULATION THEORY

Mathis Wackernagel
Redefining Progress, Oakland, California
SUSTAINABLE DEVELOPMENT

Paul E. Waggoner
Connecticut Agricultural Experiment Station,
New Haven
DEFORESTATION
LAND USE

Linda J. Waite
University of Chicago
MARRIAGE

Ingrid Waldron
University of Pennsylvania
MORTALITY DIFFERENTIALS, BY SEX

John Waller
Wellcome Trust Centre for the History of
Medicine, University College London, England
GALTON, FRANCIS

Hartmut S. Walter
University of California, Los Angeles
BIOGEOGRAPHY

Susan Cotts Watkins
University of Pennsylvania
SOCIAL NETWORKS

Michael S. Watson
American College of Medical Genetics, Bethesda,
Maryland
GENETIC TESTING

James A. Weed
National Center for Health Statistics, Hyattsville,
Maryland
VITAL STATISTICS

John R. Weeks
San Diego State University
REMOTE SENSING

Charles F. Westoff
Princeton University
TAEUBER, IRENE B.
UNWANTED FERTILITY

Michael J. White
Brown University
RURAL-URBAN BALANCE

Frans Willekens
University of Groningen, Netherlands
MULTISTATE DEMOGRAPHY

Robert J. Willis
University of Michigan
MICROECONOMICS OF DEMOGRAPHIC BEHAVIOR

John R. Wilmoth
University of California, Berkeley
MORTALITY DECLINE

Chris Wilson
Max Planck Institute for Demographic Research,
Rostock, Germany
HOMEOSTASIS

Donald Winch
University of Sussex, England
DARWIN, CHARLES
MALTHUS, THOMAS ROBERT

Barbara L. Wolfe
University of Wisconsin, Madison
FERTILITY, NONMARITAL

James W. Wood
Pennsylvania State University
PALEODEMOGRAPHY

Robert Woods
University of Liverpool, England
CITIES, DEMOGRAPHIC HISTORY OF

Basia Zaba
Centre for Population Studies, London School of
Hygiene and Tropical Medicine, England
AIDS

Zhongwei Zhao
University of Cambridge, England
HOUSEHOLD COMPOSITION

TOPICAL OUTLINE

The classification of articles that follows provides a thematic view of the encyclopedia's contents, depicting overall coverage in the various familiar divisions of the field of population studies. It is also intended to assist the user, whether researcher or browser, in locating articles broadly related to a given topic. This purpose would be defeated if articles that clearly belong under more than one category were listed only once. For example, Sex Selection might be sought under either Ethical Issues or Reproduction and Birth Control. To prevent the listing from becoming too large, however, only articles where the case for multiple entry is compelling (about one in six) are so treated. Where two categories are closely related, such as Mortality and Health on the one hand and Disease and Disability on the other, articles appear in only one of them. A more detailed means of finding cognate material is through the list of cross-references shown after each article. For finer-grained access to the encyclopedia's contents, the index should be consulted.

Biographies are not included among the articles listed in the substantive classification. They appear in the subsequent list, ordered by date of birth and grouped by the century in which the subject's main work was done.

ABORIGINAL DEMOGRAPHY

See *Indigenous Peoples*

ABORTION

See *Induced Abortion; Spontaneous Abortion*

ABSTINENCE

Abstinence is a state of nonengagement in sexual relations, whether voluntary or involuntary. It applies to a situation prevailing for months or years, or to a recurring situation, as in periodic abstinence. Abstinence can serve to regulate sexual activity per se, or to regulate one of the outcomes of sexual activity: fertility and transmission of disease. Abstinence is typically a function of age, sex, marital status, fecundity status, and fecundability status. Sociocultural factors influence the prevalence of abstinence, either through these characteristics or by direct influence on sexual activity (e.g., observance of celibacy, virginity, cessation of childbearing at grandmotherhood).

Abstinence prevails before sexual maturity. Where sexual maturity precedes regular exposure to intercourse, abstinence depends on customs regulating age at marriage and tolerance of sexual intercourse before marriage. Abstinence before and outside marriage is often related to gender. Women abstain more than men, most often to reduce the risk of pregnancy outside marriage, which is not tolerated in many societies.

In marriage, voluntary abstinence by women tends to occur during menstruation and pregnancy, and after delivery. Otherwise abstinence occurs principally among women for contraceptive reasons, taking three forms: periodic abstinence methodically timed to coincide with ovulation; postpartum abstinence to delay a subsequent pregnancy; and terminal abstinence to cease childbearing. Involuntary abstinence occurs also among women, influenced by their marital status (single, divorced, widowed) and duration of marriage (frequency of sexual relations declines with marriage duration).

Historically, abstinence was practiced in order to confine fertility to marital unions and to regulate marital fertility, often in conjunction with other traditional methods of fertility regulation such as withdrawal (*coitus interruptus*), abortion, or even infanticide. It occurs less for these purposes today, except in Africa. In the 1980s and 1990s, abstinence was recommended, particularly to young persons, as a means of reducing HIV/AIDS transmission, but the extent to which this advocacy has altered behavior is not clear.

Historically, long durations of postpartum abstinence were practiced in Africa. Regardless of reported reasons, abstinence improved survival chances of newborns by protecting breastfeeding from curtailment by a subsequent pregnancy. Long durations of abstinence are still found in West Africa; they have shortened substantially in East Africa, and are intermediate in length in Central and Southern Africa.

Postpartum abstinence makes a contribution to nonsusceptibility to the risk of pregnancy and thus lowers fertility, complementing the effect of lactational amenorrhea (suppression of menstruation). In 22 comparative country surveys in sub-Saharan Africa around 2000, abstinence duration exceeded lactational amenorrhea in only six cases. However, the nonsusceptible period was lengthened by abstinence in all cases, because many women who abstain are not protected by amenorrhea (the reverse also holds). In the surveys, amenorrhea ranged from 8 to 19 months, postpartum abstinence from 2 to 22 months. On average in the 22 countries, an abstinence duration of eight months extended amenorrhea by four months.

Four of ten women reporting current abstinence in African surveys are not practicing abstinence to prevent a subsequent pregnancy: An unknown proportion of this nonspecific abstinence may be involuntary. Similarly, in six national surveys in Europe, among all women 20 years and older, from one in four to three in four women who practice abstinence do so for nonspecific reasons that may be largely involuntary.

See also: *Birth Control, History of; Fertility, Proximate Determinants of.*

BIBLIOGRAPHY

Bongaarts, John, Odile Frank, and Ron Lesthaeghe. 1984. "The Proximate Determinants of Fertility in Sub-Saharan Africa." *Population and Development Review* 10: 511–537.

Demographic and Health Surveys. 2000. *Country Reports.* Calverton: Opinion Research Corporation Company (ORC Macro).

Fertility and Family Surveys in Countries of the ECE Region. 2000. *Standard Country Reports (Economic Studies No. 10).* New York and Geneva: United Nations.

ODILE FRANK

ACCIDENTS

In more precise language, accidents should be referred to as "unintentional injuries." The contention over the use of the word *accident* has to do with the

TABLE 1

Global Incidence of Mortality from Unintentional Injury (UI), by Cause and Sex, 2000				
Type of injury	Males	Females	Total	Percent of total
		(thousands)		
Road traffic accidents	931	329	1,260	37.0
Poisoning	204	112	315	9.3
Falls	170	113	283	8.3
Fires	104	135	238	7.0
Drowning	301	148	450	13.2
Other UI	553	304	857	25.2
Total	2,262	1,141	3,403	100.0

SOURCE: WHO (2001).

issue of preventability. In common usage, the term *accident* implies that the event was random and nonpreventable. But for "accidents," whether resulting in death or lesser injury, such an implication is incorrect, hence the term *accident* is best avoided. In June 2001, the British Medical Journal took the position of "Banning the inappropriate use of 'accident' in our pages" (Davis, p. 1,320). Injuries may be intentional or unintentional. This article focuses on the latter category.

Definition

Injury events are those in which "(1) injury occurs over a relatively short period of time—seconds or, at most, minutes, (2) the harmful outcome was not sought, and (3) the injury resulted either from one of the forms of physical energy in the environment (kinetic, chemical, thermal, electrical, or ionizing radiation) or because normal body mechanisms for using such energy were blocked by external means (such as drowning)" (Waller, p. 8). Unintentional injuries may be described simply as "unforeseen incident(s), where the intent to cause harm, injury or death was absent, but which resulted in injury" (International Classification of External Causes of Injury).

How Injury Is Classified

The World Health Organization's (WHO) International Classification of Diseases (ICD) specifies codes for diseases and injury. Injury, unlike diseases or natural causes, is captured by two distinct sets of codes, those for the nature of the injury and those for the external causes of the injury. For external causes, a single code is assigned that combines both the intentionality or manner of the injury and the

TABLE 2

Age-Adjusted Death Rates per 100,000 Population for Leading Causes of Unintentional Injury in Selected Developed Countries

	United States 1999	France 1998	Canada 1996–98	Denmark 1998	New Zealand 1994–98	Israel 1993–97	Australia 2000
Motor Vehicle and Traffic	14.7	13.3	9.4	8.4	14.7	10.5	9.0
Poisoning	4.3	0.9	2.5	2.5	0.5	0.1	4.1
Falls	3.9	4.8	3.9	16.1	3.5	1.1	2.5
Suffocation	1.8	3.9	1.2	1.0	1.1	1.0	1.1
Drowning	1.3	0.9	1.4	0.6	2.6	0.7	1.2
Fires	1.2	0.7	0.9	0.9	0.9	0.5	0.5
All Unintentional	**33.4**	**36.1**	**26.3**	**32.6**	**26.9**	**20.2**	**25.2**

Note: Rates are age-adjusted to the European Standard 2000 population. In Denmark, the rate for falls is much higher than in other countries because of the inclusion of "fractures, cause unspecified" within the category for falls.

SOURCE: Individual country vital statistics offices.

mechanism or cause of the injury. The intent of injury takes precedence in the classification, with mechanism of injury being coded within an intent category. The manner of the injury can be unintentional or "accidental," intentional (including self-inflicted and assault injuries), or of undetermined intent. For data presentation purposes, a standard framework based on groupings of ICD external cause of injury codes allows for data to be examined separately by intent as well as by mechanism.

The ICD is limited because it is a one-dimensional code system (a single code describing intent and cause) and because external cause codes often lack the specificity needed for designing or monitoring injury prevention and control activities. Hence, injury professionals around the world, under the auspices of the World Health Organization, have worked to develop a new multidimensional system for classification, the International Classification of External Causes of Injury (ICECI). The ICECI has the flexibility of coding in settings where minimal data are available as well as in those settings with great detail.

Scope

WHO estimated that there were 3.4 million unintentional injury deaths worldwide in 2000, accounting for 6 percent of all deaths and for two-thirds of all injury deaths. Deaths of males comprised 2.3 million, or two-thirds, of the unintentional injury deaths. Table 1 shows the main causes of death from unintentional injury, on a global basis and catego-

rized by gender, in 2000. There is relatively little regional variation in unintentional injury mortality, with crude death rates ranging from lows of 44 to 50 deaths per 100,000 population per year in the Americas, the Western Pacific, and the Eastern Mediterranean to highs of 69 in Africa and Southeast Asia. Within-region variation can be much higher, however, and was most pronounced in Europe where mortality ranged from an average of 34 in countries with very low child and adult mortality to 117 where adult mortality was very high. In every region except for Europe, road traffic accidents accounted for 30 to 40 percent of all unintentional injury mortality. In Europe they accounted for 24 percent, with deaths from poisoning accounting for 21 percent.

Table 2 shows the unintentional injury death rates in the United States and selected other developed countries. To facilitate comparisons the rates here and below are age-standardized to remove the effects of differences in age distribution. In each country with the exception of Denmark, motor-vehicle traffic deaths were the leading cause of unintentional injury.

U.S. Fatal Injuries

In 1999, 97,860 persons resident in the United States died as the result of an unintentional injury. The death rate in 1999, 35.9 deaths per 100,000 population, was 23 percent lower than in 1979 and 54 percent lower than in 1950 (see Figure 1). Unintentional injury ranked as the fifth-leading cause of death for all ages in 1999, accounting for 4 percent of all

FIGURE 1

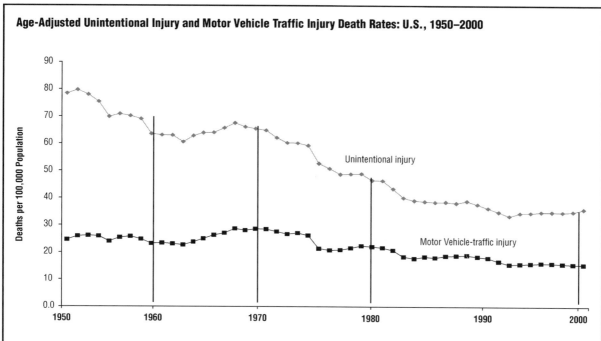

Age-Adjusted Unintentional Injury and Motor Vehicle Traffic Injury Death Rates: U.S., 1950–2000

Note: Vertical lines indicate change in ICD revision which introduce minor changes in the data. Beginning with the 9th revision introduced in 1979, unintentional injury rates exclude deaths from complications of medical and surgical care. Rates are adjusted to the U.S. standard 2000 population.

SOURCE: National Vital Statistics System, NCHS.

FIGURE 2

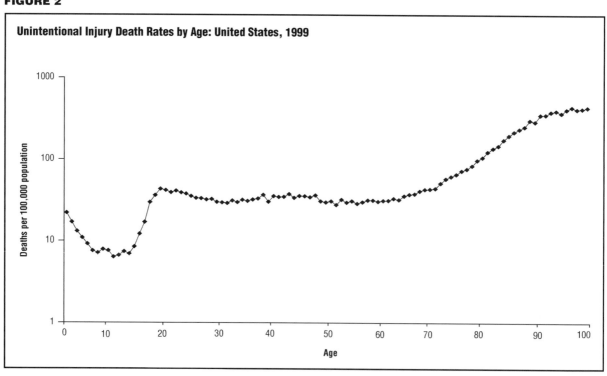

Unintentional Injury Death Rates by Age: United States, 1999

deaths. (The four causes ranked above it were diseases of the heart, malignant neoplasms, cerebrovascular diseases, and chronic lower respiratory diseases.) In contrast, homicide (16,889 deaths) and suicide (29,199 deaths) did not rank in the top ten causes of death.

Among all causes of death in the United States, unintentional injury ranked fourth among males and seventh among females, and third to fifth across racial and ethnic groups. By age, unintentional injury was the leading cause of death for persons 1 to 34 years of age, ranked second for those 35 to 44, and ranked third for persons 45 to 54. As seen in Figure 2, the age distribution of unintentional injury includes three relatively distinct peaks—for infants, for older teens and young adults, and among the elderly.

Motor-vehicle traffic injuries continue to be the leading cause of unintentional injury death for persons 1 to 74 years of age. Between 1979 and 1999, declines in death rates from motor-vehicle traffic injuries were responsible in large part for the overall decline in unintentional injury mortality. For infants, suffocation causes more deaths than other kinds of unintentional injury, and for persons 75 years and older, falls rank highest. For persons 25 to 54, poisoning is one of the leading causes of unintentional injury death.

Nonfatal Injuries

Nonfatal unintentional injuries are more difficult to measure than fatal injuries because, unlike the case of deaths, there is no complete count of them. Usually nonfatal injuries are measured by nationally representative sample surveys, primarily of medical records. Estimates rely on what is written in the patient's medical record, and because health-care providers are often under time pressure, documentation of intent can easily be affected. When intent is not precisely stated, coding often defaults to "unintentional." Thus, estimates of unintentional injury based on surveys are likely to have an upward bias.

In the United States in 1999, there were an estimated 29.3 million visits to emergency departments for unintentional injuries, accounting for about 30 percent of all emergency department visits. In general, visit rates were higher for the younger and older populations than for the middle-aged. Falls were the leading external cause of emergency department visits, followed by motor-vehicle traffic injuries, injuries from being struck by or against an object or person, and injuries from instruments used for cutting or piercing.

Hospital admissions for unintentional injuries are less frequent than emergency department visits. In the United States, during 1998-1999, approximately 6 percent of emergency department visits for an unintentional injury resulted in an admission to the hospital with percentages ranging from about 3 to 4 percent for those younger than 45 years to upwards of 25 percent for those 75 years and older. Falls and motor-vehicle-related injuries are the leading external causes of unintentional injury resulting in hospitalization.

Estimates of the numbers of unintentional injuries and deaths in the United States are produced by the National Center for Health Statistics of the Centers for Disease Control and Prevention (CDC). Additional data on nonfatal injuries are produced by the National Electronic Injury Surveillance System (NEISS) of the U.S. Consumer Product Safety Commission. Prevention of unintentional injuries and deaths falls within the activities of the CDC's National Center for Injury Prevention and Control.

See also: *Causes of Death; Disability, Demography of; Disasters.*

BIBLIOGRAPHY

Anderson, Robert N. 2001. "Deaths: Leading Causes for 1999." *National Vital Statistics Reports* 49(11). Hyattsville, MD: National Center for Health Statistics.

Centers for Disease Control and Prevention. 1997. "Recommended Framework for Presenting Injury Mortality Data." *Morbidity and Mortality Weekly Report* 46(RR–14): 1–30.

Davis, Ronald M., and Barry Pless. 2001. "BMJ Bans 'Accidents': Accidents Are Not Unpredictable" (editorial). *British Medical Journal* 322: 1,320–1,321.

Fingerhut, Lois A., and Elizabeth McLoughlin. 2001. "Classifying and Counting Injury." In *Injury Control: A Guide to Research and Program Evaluation,* ed. Fred P. Rivara, Peter Cummings, Thomas D. Koepsell, David C. Grossman and Ronald V. Maier. New York: Cambridge University Press.

Hoyert, Donna L., Elizabeth Arias, Betty L. Smith, Sherry L. Murphy, and Kenneth D. Kochanek.

2001. "Deaths: Final Data for 1999." *National Vital Statistics Reports* 49(8). Hyattsville, MD: National Center for Health Statistics.

Institute of Medicine. 1999. *Reducing the Burden of Injury: Advancing Prevention and Treatment,* ed. Richard J. Bonnie, Carolyn E. Fulco, and Catharyn T. Liverman. Washington, D.C.: National Academy Press.

McCaig, Linda F., and Cathy W. Burt. 2001. *National Hospital Ambulatory Medical Care Survey: 1999 Emergency Department Summary.* Hyattsville, MD: National Center for Health Statistics.

Pless, Barry 2001. "Banning Accidents: An Addendum." *Injury Prevention* 7: 169–170.

Waller, Julian A. 1985. *Injury Control: A Guide to the Causes and Prevention of Trauma.* Lexington, MA: Lexington Books.

World Health Organization. 1992. *International Statistical Classification of Diseases and Related Health Problems,* 10th rev. Geneva, Switzerland: World Health Organization.

INTERNET RESOURCES.

Centers for Disease Control and Prevention. National Center for Health Statistics. 2002. <http://www.cdc.gov/nchs/>.

Centers for Disease Control and Prevention. National Center for Injury Prevention and Control. 2002. <http://www.cdc.gov/ncipc/>.

Consumer Product Safety Commission. National Electronic Injury Surveillance System (NEISS). 2003. <http://www.cpsc.gov/about/clrnghse.html>.

International Classification of External Causes of Injury. 2002. <http://www.iceci.org/>.

World Health Organization. 2001. "World Health Report 2001: Statistical Annex." <http://www.who.int/whr/2001/main/en/annex/index.htm>.

Lois A. Fingerhut

ACTION THEORY IN POPULATION RESEARCH

Understanding social institutions and social behavior, the province of social theory, is clearly relevant to explaining population dynamics. Demographers, however, make little systematic use of social theory. Conversely, the enormous volume of demographic research conducted since the 1950s has had little impact on the development of social theory. A more fruitful interchange between demography and social theory would benefit both fields. This entry reviews a major part of social theory—action theory—and appraises its relevance to explaining demographic change, in particular, fertility transition.

Action theory is concerned with the role of human agency in the development and maintenance of institutional structures and with the meaning of human action "from the actor's point of view." Its intellectual roots run deep in Western cultural history, but modern approaches derive largely from the seminal work of the German sociologist Max Weber (1864–1920). The following sections focus on the work of more recent theorists in the Weberian tradition: Talcott Parsons, Jürgen Habermas, and Anthony Giddens.

Talcott Parsons

The American sociologist Talcott Parsons (1902–1979) was probably the world's preeminent sociologist during the 1950s and 1960s. His theory of action was intended to provide a basic conceptual framework for unifying the social and behavioral sciences as well as explaining the development of the distinctive organizational features of modern societies.

Parsons defined action as the structures and processes through which human beings form meaningful intentions and, more or less successfully, implement them in specific situations. The basic unit of analysis is the unit act, which involves an actor (an individual or a collective), an end (a future state of affairs to which the action is oriented), a situation consisting of means (aspects over which the actor has some control) and conditions (aspects over which the actor has no control), and a normative orientation (because means and ends typically are not chosen at random but take into account shared meanings and standards).

These elements of action were seen by Parsons as being invariably organized as systems, with subsystems nested within larger systems. Cultural, social, personality, and behavioral systems were viewed as different fundamental types of action systems, each with its own distinctive organizing principles. Patterns of shared meaning—referred to as normative culture—are institutionalized in a society's social systems and internalized in its individual members' personalities.

Parsons claimed that his theory was the culmination of theoretical developments immanent in the major traditions of Western social theory. The Anglo-French positivistic tradition, for instance, privileged scientific knowledge as the only valid way to apprehend reality, with the result that it reduces the subjective meaning of action either to rational-scientific knowledge or to deviations from that standard in the form of error and superstition. The German idealistic tradition, according to Parsons, was better able to deal with the meaning of action in cases where it diverges from rational-scientific knowledge. Parsons's theory, building on Weber, was an attempt to synthesize these insights within a single comprehensive framework.

How might Parsonsian action theory bear on efforts to explain changes in fertility behavior? Classical demographic transition theory, which explains changes in fertility behavior in terms of "adaptive response to the requirements of an age of modern science and technology" and treats normative elements as simply "slowing the process of social change" (Notestein, p. 351), has many of the hallmarks of positivistic-utilitarian theory. The criticism during the 1980s and 1990s of transition theory's unilinear view of social change and neglect of cultural factors is anticipated by Parsons almost point by point in his critique of the positivistic-utilitarian system 50 years earlier in *The Structure of Social Action*, first published in 1937. The cultural theories of fertility change put forth during those decades to overcome these limitations often exhibit what Parsons described as the complementary shortcoming of idealistic theories of action: although they avoid reifying science and technology and treat cultural factors as structuring the choices involved in fertility behavior, they fall short in their treatment of the conditions of action.

Demographers nonetheless need a theory of behavior that goes beyond Parsonsian action theory. Demography lies at the intersection of the social and biological sciences. Fertility outcomes are a result of both biological and behavioral factors acting in combination, and so fertility behavior has to be analyzed in a framework like that developed by Kingsley Davis and Judith Blake (1956), which embraces both intentional behavior and unintentional biological processes. Parsons's theory considers human agency selectively only to the extent that it engages the symbolic or cultural level of representation; it therefore drives a conceptual wedge between social systems composed of meaningful action and population systems composed of discrete biological organisms. Its relevance for developing demographic theory is therefore circumscribed.

Jürgen Habermas

The contemporary German critical theorist Jürgen Habermas (born 1929) offers an alternative action-theoretic approach. Like Parsons, he criticizes positivism for the way it privileges one kind of knowledge and thus reduces the scope of rational action. In his early work (1971) Habermas distinguished three kinds of rational-scientific knowledge: (1) the empirical-analytic sciences, centering on a technical cognitive interest; (2) the historical-hermeneutic sciences, incorporating a practical cognitive interest grounded in communication; and (3) the critically oriented sciences, incorporating an emancipatory cognitive interest (that is, one aimed at overcoming irrational restraints).

Critical theory draws on both empirical-analytic knowledge of nomological (lawlike) regularities in human action and historical-hermeneutical knowledge of cultural meanings. Habermas's concept of an emancipatory cognitive interest is seen as problematic by many commentators, but it has a long intellectual history. Socrates saw self-reflection and dialogue as essential to freedom from tyranny and false beliefs. Habermas examines the conditions and constraints for emancipatory communication that are embedded in social action and modern social institutions.

Habermas's later work (1984, 1987) analyzes the ways in which different types of action can be rationalized and uses this analysis as a foundation for a critical account of the development of modern institutions (and the need for their reconstruction). It is an enormously complex exercise that spans many fields in social science, psychology, linguistics, and philosophy and is widely recognized as one of the most important achievements of late twentieth-century social theory.

What Habermas calls purposive-rational action can be rationalized by choosing more efficient or consistent means, but this is quite distinct from the kind of rationalization appropriate for communicative action. Problems of modernity are seen by Habermas as deriving from the dominance of rationalization processes of the purposive-rational type, which undermines the conditions for effective rationalization of communicative action, especially the institutions needed to support a politically vibrant public sphere. Modern societies are suffering from a "colonization of the lifeworld" by systems of purposive-rational action.

Significant links between demography and critical theory have been most striking in their absence. For example, in the 1990s there was a shift in the ideology and organization of national family planning programs from "instrumental" population control to a client-oriented reproductive health approach grounded in human rights and a more "dialogic" approach to provider–client relationships. Demographers working in this policy field faced a new-found nexus of issues involving sexual reproduction, reproductive rights, power, gender, communication, and individuation. They showed scant awareness that these were issues of central interest to critical theory. A plausible reason for this lack of awareness is the fact that demographers usually focus on increasing people's freedom from traditional institutions (e.g., increasing the autonomy of women), whereas critical theorists focus on the less conspicuous loss of freedom engendered by modern "disciplinary" institutions such as the state, the market economy, and even modern medicine.

Knowledge of critical theory would alert demographers involved with public policy to the ways in which the rationalization of conduct in one sphere of life can undermine the chances of appropriate rationalization in another sphere, particularly if the broader context of power relations is not taken into account. Reproductive rights are described in recent international declarations in terms of "the capability to reproduce and the freedom to decide if, when and how often to do so" (United Nations, paragraph 7.2), yet many women in developed countries (where fertility is below the replacement level) report that they would like more children than they actually have. Their participation in the market economy, which is increasingly rewarded, comes at the cost of time and energy devoted to child rearing. Removing gender inequality and giving people tech-nical control over the number and timing of the children they produce are not sufficient conditions for people to have the number of children they want. This realization may push demographers into the kind of value-driven analysis enjoined by critical theorists, which relates individual behavior to political economy and communication.

Anthony Giddens

The works of Parsons and Habermas are couched in what to many people is impenetrable prose. More accessible are the works of the British sociologist Anthony Giddens (born 1938). In discussing action theory, Giddens adopts a less systematic, more eclectic approach—he calls it structuration theory—several features of which have resonance for demographic research. First, he focuses on the embodied conduct of actors and gives serious attention to the space and time dimensions (acknowledging the contribution of time geographers such as Torsten Hägerstrand). Second, he treats actors as "knowledgeable" (in their practical consciousness) about what they do. Third, he avoids many of the pitfalls associated with the conventional action–structure dualism by arguing, "Structure only exists in so far as people do things knowledgeably and do them in certain contexts that have particular consequences" (Giddens and Pierson, p. 81). Thus, institutions are reproduced through the repeated interactions of everyday life and are both enabling and constraining for human agency. Giddens, however, is of limited help in operationalizing these concepts by, for example, shedding light on the ways in which institutional factors may contribute to falling birthrates.

The Need for an Integrated Theory

None of the versions of action theory to date has integrated causal and interpretive analysis satisfactorily. An important research program in action theory is to develop a perspective on embodied action that would allow one to distinguish the different elements of action in order to clarify which ones are related causally and which ones are related in terms of schemas of meaning. The analysis of fertility behavior not only stands to gain from this program but would provide an ideal empirical case for testing and refining an integrated theory.

Social Theory and Demographic Narratives

As this brief review has tried to show, there are links and potential links between demography and social theory that have been underutilized by both sides. The Dutch demographer Dirk van de Kaa has characterized 50 years of demographic research on fertility as the development of a series of verbal theories from various disciplinary perspectives that attempt to explain some "central action" apparent in the data by locating it in "a setting which allows for an easy interpretation of that action" (van de Kaa, p. 389).

What is striking in many of these "anchored narratives" is the care and precision that go into data collection and analysis and, by contrast, the almost casual manner in which theoretical perspectives and orientations are borrowed and used to fashion interpretive narratives. Theory building in demography has not kept pace with the amassing of data, and what theory there is tends to focus on fragmentary issues and "subnarratives" rather than showing how all the elements fit together. Action theory has no ready-made answers for demographic questions, but it does present a wealth of analytical insight that can be dedicated to that task.

See also: *Culture and Population; Social Institutions.*

BIBLIOGRAPHY

Davis, Kingsley, and Judith Blake. 1956. "Social Structure and Fertility: An Analytic Framework." *Economic Development and Cultural Change* 4: 211–235.

Giddens, Anthony. 1984. *The Constitution of Society.* Berkeley and Los Angeles: University of California Press.

Giddens, Anthony, and Christopher Pierson. 1998. *Conversations with Anthony Giddens.* Cambridge, Eng.: Polity Press.

Habermas, Jürgen. 1971 (1968). *Knowledge and Human Interests.* Boston: Beacon Press.

———. 1979 (1976). *Communication and the Evolution of Society.* Boston: Beacon Press.

———. 1984, 1987 (1981). *The Theory of Communicative Action,* 2 Vols. Boston: Beacon Press.

Hayes, Adrian C. 1985. "Causal and Interpretive Analysis in Sociology." *Sociological Theory* 3(2): 1–10.

McNicoll, Geoffrey. 1994. "Institutional Analysis of Fertility." In *Population, Economic Development,*

and the Environment, ed. Kerstin Lindahl-Kiessling and Hans Lanberg. Oxford: Oxford University Press.

Notestein, Frank W. 1983. "Population Growth and Economic Development." *Population and Development Review* 9: 345–360.

Parsons, Talcott. 1949 (1937). *The Structure of Social Action.* New York: Free Press.

———. 1977. *The Evolution of Societies,* ed. Jackson Toby. Englewood Cliffs, NJ: Prentice-Hall.

Turner, Bryan S., ed. 2000. *The Blackwell Companion to Social Theory,* 2nd edition. Oxford: Blackwell.

United Nations. 1994. *Programme of Action Adopted at the International Conference on Population and Development, Cairo, 5–13 September 1994.* New York: United Nations.

van de Kaa, Dirk J. 1996. "Anchored Narratives: The Story and Findings of Half a Century of Research into the Determinants of Fertility." *Population Studies* 50: 389–432.

Weber, Max. 1978 (1925). *Economy and Society: An Outline of Interpretive Sociology,* eds. Guenther Roth and Claus Wittich. Berkeley and Los Angeles: University of California Press.

ADRIAN C. HAYES

ACTUARIAL ANALYSIS

The origins of the actuarial profession can be traced to the late-seventeenth and early-eighteenth centuries when leading mathematicians were prevailed upon to compute the cost of annuities and life insurances. Many of the early great names of mathematics contributed in this way. The first professional body (the Institute of Actuaries) was established in London in 1848. Since that time, the professional interests of actuaries have widened to include pensions, general (property and casualty) insurance, health insurance, finance, and a wide range of "non traditional" problems, for which their quantitative skills and understanding of risk are readily applicable (e.g., pricing electricity supplied to a national grid).

Mortality

Most very early life tables were used and/or prepared in connection with life annuities and life insurance. The Equitable Assurance Society, which established long-term life insurance on a scientific basis in 1762, for example, used James Dobson's life table (based on London Bills of Mortality between 1728 and 1750) and Richard Price's table of 1783 (based on death records for a parish in Northampton). Price later constructed a life table from the population and deaths in Sweden, the first national life table ever made. The standard life table symbols still used in the twenty-first century were adopted as part of the International Actuarial Notation as early as 1898. Government actuaries continue to prepare the official national life tables of many countries, including Australia, the United Kingdom, and the United States.

Within a national population there is a considerable degree of mortality heterogeneity. Persons accepted for life insurance tend to have mortality that is lower than that of the national population over much of the age span because they are generally better educated, more affluent, and subject to medical scrutiny by the insurer. Purchasers of life annuities have even lower mortality as no one expecting to live only a relatively short time would purchase a life annuity. Because of these and other differences between the mortalities of the various subpopulations, many different types of life tables are regularly prepared, covering, for example, nonsmoker insured lives, smoker insured lives, super-select insured lives, annuitants, members of pension funds, actively employed persons, age retirees, and persons who have retired because of ill health. Large insurance companies often can prepare their own life tables on the basis of their own experience, and those tables reflect their own standards of underwriting. Only a small proportion of life tables are ever published.

Standard tables based on confidential data collected from groups of insurers are prepared and reviewed regularly by the various actuarial professional bodies. More recent standard tables tend to be published on the Internet.

Finding a suitable life table for use in a developing market is a problem faced by many actuaries of the twenty-first century and requires considerable judgment. Actuaries usually have to rely on insurance tables prepared for similar products in another market that is believed to have similar characteristics. If national life tables are available, they may be used as collateral information. The collection of local insurance mortality data is a high priority.

Temporary Initial Selection

The mortality of persons recently selected for life insurance is normally lower than that of other insured lives of the same attained age who were selected in earlier years. For this reason, since the mid-nineteenth century, when the first life tables based on the combined mortality experience of several insurers were constructed, actuaries usually have estimated mortality rates that take account of both age at selection and duration since selection. The mortality rate of persons selected at age x who have been insured for t years and are now aged $x + t$ is denoted by $q_{[x]+t}$ (the +0 is suppressed when $t = 0$).

In theory, therefore, separate life tables are required for each age at selection. The effects of temporary initial selection tend to disappear after several years, however, so that lives the same attained age that are selected at different ages eventually develop mortality rates that are indistinguishable. When the effect of temporary initial selection has worn off, the insured lives are said to be "ultimate lives" and their mortality is given by the "ultimate life table" with mortality rates $[q_y]$, where y is the attained age. In other words, once the temporary initial selection has disappeared (the duration t is greater than or equal to the select period), $q_{[x]+t} = q_{[x-1]+t+1} = q_{[x-2]+t+2} = \ldots = q_y$ where $y = x + t$.

For pragmatic reasons, British actuaries have tended to use very short select periods, whereas their North American colleagues have used longer periods (up to 15 years). If one uses common ultimate (l_y) values for the latter part of all the distinct life tables (corresponding to various ages at selection and durations in excess of the select period) and chooses appropriate radices ($l_{[x]}$), survivorship values can be represented concisely as in Table 1. Based on this table, for example, the probability that a select life aged 47 will die before age 50 is $1 - 32{,}670/32{,}975 = 0.00925$, the probability that a life now aged 47 who was selected at age 46 will die before age 50 is $1 - 32{,}670/33{,}020 = 0.01060$, and the probability that a life now aged 47 who was selected on or before his or her forty-fifth birthday will die before age 50 is $1 - 32{,}670/33{,}045 = 0.01135$.

Temporary initial selection also is observed in other situations. Persons who have retired more recently because of ill health, for example, tend to have mortality that is higher than that of the survivors of those who retired from ill health earlier, but again, the effect wears off with duration since retirement.

The technique is a convenient one that could be applied in a number of demographic situations, such as immigrant mortality, where the mortality of recent immigrants differs from that of the host population but gradually approaches the same level. Other possible applications include the study of the mortality of divorced and widowed persons, with the age at selection being the age at which the person became divorced or widowed.

Effects of Lifestyle and Medical Conditions

A number of life insurance companies formed in the nineteenth century distinguished between persons who abstained from alcohol and nonabstainers. Actuary Roderick Mckenzie Moore (1904), for example, was able to produce separate life tables for the two groups and investigate the effects of transitions between the two classes. Such a distinction normally would not be made in the twenty-first century, although "excessive" consumption might be taken into account at the underwriting stage.

Although the standard insurance life tables referred to above are usually for lives insured on normal terms, persons in less than perfect health can often obtain insurance on special terms. In determining the terms, company actuaries work alongside experienced medical officers, making use of a wealth of international data on the effect on mortality of many different medical conditions, personal habits (tobacco, alcohol, and drug consumption, exercise, etc.), and fitness, including weight to height measures. The data come from a wide range of sources: clinical trials, longitudinal studies of whole communities, special longitudinal studies for particular diseases, surveys, and cancer registries. A two-volume reference work entitled *Medical Risks—Trends in Mortality by Age and Time Elapsed* (Lew and Gajewski 1990), for example, provides an extensive description of many different conditions and advice on the relative mortality of persons suffering from those conditions. The major international life reinsurance companies produce their own electronic rating manuals to advise client insurers on the rating of impaired lives, and special investigations are undertaken from time to time by actuarial professional organizations.

TABLE 1

Extract from a British Insurance Life Table: Select Period Two Years

Select Age [x]	$l_{[x]}$	$l_{[x]+1}$	$l_{[x]+2}$	Age [x]+2
0	34,481	34,461	34,440	2
1	34,457	34,438	34,419	3
2	34,434	34,417	34,399	4
3	34,413	34,397	34,380	5
⋮	⋮	⋮	⋮	⋮
45	33,180	33,122	33,045	47
46	33,084	33,020	32,934	48
47	32,975	32,904	32,810	
48	32,852	32,774	32,670	50
⋮	⋮	⋮	⋮	⋮

SOURCE: Institute of Actuaries and Faculty of Actuaries (1975).

Improvements in Mortality

Improvements in mortality can undermine the financial viability of companies that sell life annuities. For this reason, actuaries have long been interested in measuring mortality improvements and estimating future mortality. Projected generation life tables are required, as annuities will be taken out at different ages in the same calendar year. The simplest commonly used approach has been to observe the annual rates of improvement in q values over time and then to extrapolate the q rates by using improvement factors at each age, although other approaches are also adopted. In most cases the actuaries' assumptions have led to underestimates of improvement.

Variation of Mortality with Age

Since the eighteenth century mathematical "laws" of mortality have been explored in an attempt to facilitate the otherwise very tedious life contingencies calculations essential for pricing and valuing life assurance and annuity contracts. The mathematician Abraham de Moivre was possibly the first to do this (in 1725), but the most celebrated early development was that of mathematician and Fellow of the Royal Society Benjamin Gompertz (1825), modifications of which have been proposed ever since. The model allows many quick approximate calculations that are remarkably accurate even with mortality tables that are not strictly of the Gompertz shape. Actuary T. N. Thiele, in 1872 proposed a model applicable over the whole age span, as did demographer

Larry Heligman and actuary John Pollard (1980). Actuaries David Forfar and David Smith (1987) applied the latter model in 1987 to all 26 English Life Tables to project the English Life Tables for 1991. The projected mortality rates for females turned out to be very good, but those for the males were less satisfactory.

A variety of models were studied by actuary Wilfred Perks in 1932, who noted the effects of heterogeneity, and variants of his models were used to graduate (smooth) British standard tables in the 1950s and 1960s. Other more generalized formulas that have been used in more recent British standard tables are discussed in Forfar et al. (1988).

Mortality Heterogeneity

In recent years some life insurance companies have begun marketing policies to super-select lives, persons with characteristics that tend to make their mortality extremely low even compared with those accepted for life insurance under normal conditions. In doing so, the companies are attempting to exploit the considerable mortality heterogeneity that exists in any national population. Actuaries are therefore becoming very interested in measuring heterogeneity and understanding its underlying causes.

Morbidity

Before the development of the welfare state in the early twentieth century there was little financial security for those who were sick and unable to work; they had to depend on charity or small payments to the destitute from the local parish. "Friendly Societies" began to proliferate, providing small benefits in times of need to members in return for small weekly contributions. In this way workers in particular occupations and regions were able to support each other. Actuaries were soon required to ensure that these mutual institutions were financially viable and, as a result, became involved in sickness investigations. The largest and most thorough of these studies was the Manchester Unity investigation of 1893–1897, and the tables derived by actuary Alfred Watson (1901) showing age-specific proportions sick were used extensively (with adjustments) well into the twentieth century.

Employers in most developed countries of the twenty-first century offer some level of income maintenance for short periods of sickness, for example, a certain number of days of full pay while sick, with the number of allowable days generally increasing with length of service. National sickness schemes also may pay basic income benefits. A need for private sickness and disability insurance remains, particularly for the self-employed, and insurers offer a wide range of products designed for specific markets. As with mortality, the actuarial professional bodies coordinate the collection and analysis of morbidity data and the preparation of standard tables of incidence and recovery. More recent standard tables tend to be published on the Internet. The major international reinsurers also provide underwriting manuals for their clients.

Competing Risks

The first detailed study of competing risks was done by the British actuary William Makeham (1874), although some of the ideas can be traced to eighteenth-century Swiss mathematician Daniel Bernoulli, who attempted to estimate the effect on a population of the eradication of smallpox. Makeham's approach was to extend the concept of the "force of mortality" (which was well known to actuaries of that time) to more than one decrement, and he noted the essential independence between the different decrements implied by his analysis.

Actuaries who have used multiple decrement tables ever since have almost invariably assumed independence between the "competing risks." Important applications include pension schemes, where active employees may be depleted by a number of different decrements (death, resignation, termination, ill-health retirement, and age retirement), and mortality analysis, where mortality rates for certain causes may be changed to take account of trends or to answer "what if" questions about possible future changes in mortality.

The formulas relating the decrement rates in a multiple decrement table to those in the associated single decrement tables or with other multiple decrement tables (e.g., tables with fewer decrements) depend on the manner in which the decrements operate. In cause of death analyses, for example, decrements in the related single cause tables often are assumed to be spread evenly over the year of age. Formulas derived under this assumption may not necessarily be transferable to other situations, such as pension funds, where certain events may be concentrated at birthdays. There is an extensive literature on this topic, and attempts have been made to deal with dependence between decrements.

Multiple decrement tables belong to a very special class of the Markov process, and more general Markov chain processes are often required in morbidity studies, because persons can recover from their illnesses.

Population Modeling: HIV/AIDS

The HIV/AIDS epidemic that started in the 1980s caused considerable alarm in the insurance industry, particularly in respect to policies providing death benefits, those providing income replacement during illness, and medical and health policies. Actuaries in various countries therefore began modeling the development of the disease in the community at large and the numbers at risk or already HIV-positive in the insuring subpopulation.

Crucial to the modeling of the insurance process were assumptions concerning the numbers of existing policyholders at risk and the numbers already infected and the numbers and sizes of new policies that would be issued to persons in those categories once the community and the insurers reacted to the epidemic. A major concern was the possibility of high-risk groups and those already HIV-positive selecting against the insurers (taking out a disproportionate amount of insurance). Because the diffusion of the disease differed from country to country and because legislation controlled the extent to which insurers were permitted to discriminate between different groups in their underwriting, a model developed in one country was not necessarily immediately transferable to another.

Improved community awareness and safer sexual practices in developed countries ultimately caused the spread of HIV/AIDS and the effects on insurers to be less serious than had been projected.

Population Modeling: Genetic Testing

Almost since the dawn of life insurance, insurance companies and their actuarial advisers have sought genetic information from those applying for life insurance by asking details about survivorship and cause of death of family members. With the recent rapid developments in genetics considerably more information about the likely survivorship and morbidity of an individual can be provided by a genetic test. A person who has taken a test may be aware that he or she is more likely to die younger or be subject to increased ill health. Serious ethical questions ensue. Should insurers be permitted to demand ge-

netic tests? If not, should an individual who has taken a genetic test be required to reveal the results to the insurer under the basic insurance principle of utmost good faith (*uberrima fides*)? If such information is available only to the proposer, there is a serious risk of selection against the insurer, to the detriment of the company and others insured with it.

There are also serious privacy issues. Genetic information about an individual also provides information about that individual's relatives. Such indirect genetic information also can be used to select against an insurer. For example, a person may submit to a genetic test and learn that he or she bears an undesirable gene. Knowing this, that person might advise a sibling to take out insurance, and the sibling could justifiably claim not to have undergone a test.

Even in situations where no genetic test has been undertaken, an insured life may take one and, after learning that he or she does not have deleterious genes, discontinue the insurance, leaving the insurer with a higher than average proportion of policyholders with genes associated with increased morbidity and premature death.

Human rights supervisors, privacy officials, insurers, actuaries, insurance regulators and legislators are grappling with these issues, and actuaries are endeavoring to model the underlying genetic processes in the population and in the insuring subpopulation.

See also: *AIDS; Genetic Testing; Gompertz, Benjamin; Life Tables; Lotka, Alfred; Mortality, Age Patterns of; Risk.*

BIBLIOGRAPHY

Benjamin, Bernard, and John H. Pollard. 1993. *The Analysis of Mortality and Other Actuarial Statistics.* Oxford: Institute of Actuaries and Faculty of Actuaries.

Continuous Mortality Investigation Committee, Institute of Actuaries and Faculty of Actuaries. 1998. "The Mortality of Holders of Permanent (Whole Life and Endowment) Policies of Assurance 1991–94." *Continuous Mortality Investigation Reports* 16: 1–34.

———. 1998. "The Mortality of Smokers and Non-Smokers 1991–94." *Continuous Mortality Investigation Reports* 16: 83–94.

————. 1998. "The Mortality of Impaired Insured Lives." *Continuous Mortality Investigation Reports* 16: 95–112.

————. 2000. "An Analysis of the PHI Experience of Individual Companies in the United Kingdom: I. Claim Inception Rates." *Continuous Mortality Investigation Reports* 18: 109–150.

————. 2000. "An Analysis of the PHI Experience of Individual Companies in the United Kingdom: II. Claim Termination Rates." *Continuous Mortality Investigation Reports* 18: 151–180.

Forfar, David O., and David M. Smith. 1987. "The Changing Shape of English Life Tables." *Transactions of the Faculty of Actuaries* 40: 98–134.

Forfar, David O., et al. 1988. "On Graduation by Mathematical Formulae." *Journal of the Institute of Actuaries* 115: 1–149.

Gompertz, Benjamin. 1825. "On the Nature of the Function of the Law of Human Mortality and on a New Mode of Determining the Value of Life Contingencies." *Philosophical Transactions of the Royal Society* 115: 513–585.

Heligman, Larry, and John H. Pollard. 1980. "The Age Pattern of Mortality." *Journal of the Institute of Actuaries* 107: 49–80.

Institute of Actuaries and Faculty of Actuaries. 1975. *A1967-1970 Tables for Assured Lives.* Oxford: Institute of Actuaries and Faculty of Actuaries.

————. 1979. *A(90) Tables for Annuitants.* Oxford: Institute of Actuaries and Faculty of Actuaries.

Lee, Ronald. 2000. "The Lee-Carter Method for Forecasting Mortality, with Various Extensions and Applications." *North American Actuarial Journal* 4: 80–93.

Lew, Edward A., and Jerzy Gajewski. 1990. *Medical Risks: Trends in Mortality by Age and Time Elapsed.* New York: Praeger.

Macdonald, A. S. 1999. "Modelling the Impact of Genetics on Insurance." *North American Actuarial Journal* 3(1): 83–101.

Makeham, William. 1874. "On an Application of the Theory of the Composition of Decremental Forces." *Journal of the Institute of Actuaries* 18: 317–322.

Moore, Roderick M. 1904. "On the Comparative Mortality among Assured Lives of Abstainers and Non-Abstainers from Alcoholic Beverages." *Journal of the Institute of Actuaries* 38: 213–259.

Panjer, Harry H. 1988. "AIDS: Survival Analysis of Persons Testing HIV Positive." *Transactions of the Society of Actuaries* 40: 517–530.

Pollard, John H. 1987. "Projection of Age-specific Mortality Rates." *Population Studies of the United Nations* 21/22: 55–69.

————. 1991. "Fun with Gompertz." *Genus* 47: 1–20.

Subramanian, Krupa, Jean Lemaire, John C. Hershey, Mark V. Pauly, Katrina Armstrong, and David A. Asch. 1999. "Estimating Adverse Selection Costs from Genetic Testing for Breast and Ovarian Cancer: The Case of Life Insurance." *Journal of Risk and Insurance* 66: 531–550.

Watson, Alfred W. 1901. "An Account of an Investigation of the Sickness and Mortality Experience of the I.O.O.F. Manchester Unity Friendly Society, during the Years 1893–1897." Review (Editorial) 369. *Journal of the Institute of Actuaries* 38: 334.

INTERNET RESOURCES.

Faculty and Institute of Actuaries. 2002. <http://www.actuaries.org.uk>.

Society of Actuaries. 2002. <http://www.soa.org>.

JOHN H. POLLARD

ADOLESCENT FERTILITY

In those developed countries where substantial numbers of young women give birth as teenagers, adolescent fertility has been a long-standing concern and is increasingly becoming a concern in the developing world.

To monitor adolescent childbearing, demographers commonly rely on two measures. The adolescent fertility rate is the number of births per 1,000 women aged 15 to 19 and is computed from vital statistics reports or birth history data from fertility surveys. The proportion of women aged 20 or older who have had a child by specified ages, usually 15, 18, and 20, is computed from fertility surveys.

Fertility Rates and Trends

Adolescent childbearing declined in the 1980s and 1990s in much of the world, although substantial numbers of women still gave birth in their teenage years. In sub-Saharan Africa, according to fertility surveys conducted in the 1990s, the percentage of women aged 20 to 24 who gave birth before age 20 ranged from a low of approximately 40 percent in Ghana to a high of around 70 percent in Chad, Mali, Niger, and Uganda with most francophone (French-speaking) countries having elevated rates by comparison to the anglophone (English-speaking) countries. In Latin America and the Caribbean, where data from fertility surveys were available for only nine countries, the percentage ranged from a low of 30 percent in Peru to over 50 percent in Nicaragua. In Asia, in the six countries for which fertility surveys were conducted in the 1990s, Bangladesh stood out: Just over 60 percent of young women in Bangladesh gave birth as teens. This is a considerable decline, however, from the previous generation, when over three-quarters of surveyed women aged 40 to 44 had had a child before age 20. In India and China, of women aged 20 to 24, 49 percent and 14 percent, respectively, reported giving birth as teenagers in surveys from the early 1990s. There were only five Middle Eastern/North African countries for which data were available for the 1990s; in Egypt, just under one-quarter of 20- to 24-year-olds were mothers by age 20, compared with 17 percent in Jordan and Morocco, 26 percent in Turkey, and 45 percent in Yemen.

Within the industrialized world in the 1990s, the percentage of women aged 20 to 24 who had had children as teenagers ranged from 3 percent in Japan to 22 percent in the United States. The latter figure was one of the highest levels in the developed world. The proportion of U.S. women who give birth as teenagers is unusually large in comparison to other wealthy countries—mostly a consequence of less use and less effective use of contraception. It is also worth noting that the U.S. adolescent fertility rate declined less than in Europe between the early 1980s and the late 1990s.

Adolescent fertility rates in the 1990s range from a low of 4 births per year per 1,000 women aged 15 to 19 in Japan to a high of over 200 in Niger and Uganda. Within the industrialized world, there is also considerable variation. In addition to Japan, low rates—under 10—are found in western (Belgium,

Netherlands, and Switzerland), northern (Denmark, Finland, and Sweden), and southern Europe (Italy, Spain, and Slovenia). High rates—over 50—are found in some countries of eastern Europe (Armenia, Georgia, Moldova, and Ukraine) and in the United States. In 2000 the U.S. fertility rate for age 15 to 19 was 56.5 (50 among whites, 93 among blacks, and 99 among Hispanics). Within the developing world, adolescent fertility is highest in sub-Saharan Africa, but there are also countries in South Asia and Latin America with teen birth rates of over 100.

The late-twentieth-century decline in adolescent childbearing was especially pronounced in certain sub-Saharan African countries (namely Cameroon, Kenya, Senegal, and Tanzania), the Middle East/North Africa, Asia, and the industrialized countries. In Latin America, adolescent fertility declined in some countries—notably Bolivia, Guatemala, and Nicaragua—but rose in others, such as Brazil and Colombia. Moreover, where declines occurred in Latin America, they were less rapid than declines in the fertility of older women. This pattern was in contrast to many industrialized countries where the adolescent fertility rate fell faster than the overall fertility rate. In monitoring trends in adolescent childbearing, demographers observed that the reported age-specific fertility rate of women aged 15 to 19 declined more than the proportion giving birth before age 20, indicating that while women in many countries were still becoming mothers at a young age they apparently were having fewer births as teenagers. Indeed, there are countries—for example, Burkina FASO, Central African Republic, Ivory Coast, and Bolivia—where the proportion of women giving birth before age 20 has remained stable or even increased slightly since the 1970s but where the adolescent fertility rate has declined. Potential reasons for this include a rise in the age at first marriage and a delay in the age at first birth, and an increase in contraceptive use after the first birth.

Within Marriage Childbearing

There is a perception that most teenage childbearing takes place prior to marriage. In fact, throughout the developing world—and in contrast to the situation in developed countries—the majority of young women who give birth as teenagers do so within marriage. Indeed, one reason why adolescent childbearing has declined in many developing countries is that the proportion of women marrying during their teenage years has fallen. While substantial proportions of young women give birth out of wedlock in sub-Saharan Africa and Latin America, premarital childbearing has not changed or has increased only slightly in most countries in these two regions. (There are some noteworthy exceptions in sub-Saharan Africa, such as Ivory Coast, Kenya, Namibia, Tanzania, and Zambia.) What has increased in many sub-Saharan countries and in the United States, although not in Latin America, is the percentage of births to teenage girls that are premarital.

Consequences of Adolescent Childbearing

Many observers take it for granted that having a child during the teenage years is problematic. But the research on the health, social, and economic consequences of adolescent childbearing reveals a complex set of associations. Adolescent mothers are at much greater risk of poorer health outcomes than are somewhat older mothers, but this is largely a consequence of teen mothers on average being poorer, less well nourished, and less likely to get adequate obstetric care. Indeed cephalopelvic disproportion, a major cause of obstructed labor in developing countries and a condition that is much more prevalent among young mothers, is extremely uncommon in developed countries even among teen mothers because nutrition is adequate, physical growth is almost completed by the mid-teenage years, and there is access to adequate delivery services, including cesarean section.

Research on the social and economic consequences of teenage childbearing has been conducted almost exclusively in the United States. The findings are still far from definitive, in large part because of the presence of selection bias—namely, that those who give birth as teens differ systematically in many respects from those who delay. Outcome measures that have been focused on by researchers in the United States include earnings, poverty status, completion of high school, employment, and subsequent fertility. There is a consensus that, although early childbearing has a significant effect on some social and economic outcomes, researchers in the past overstated the deleterious effects of teen childbearing.

The social environment in the developing world is quite different from that of the United States, where most teen childbearing is unplanned or unwanted and occurs outside of marriage and where the opportunity costs of teen motherhood are greater. In many poor countries, particularly in rural areas, early childbearing may benefit a young woman because it increases her status within the family. Nonetheless, there is some evidence from the developing world that as levels of schooling and the demand for skilled labor rise, adolescent mothers, who are often less well educated, may become increasingly disadvantaged.

See also: *Fertility, Age Patterns of; Fertility, Nonmarital.*

BIBLIOGRAPHY

Alan Guttmacher Institute. 1998. *Into a New World: Young Women's Sexual and Reproductive Lives.* New York: Alan Guttmacher Institute.

Mensch, Barbara S., Judith Bruce, and Margaret E. Greene. 1998. *The Uncharted Passage: Girls' Adolescence in the Developing World.* New York: Population Council.

Ribar, David C. 1999. "The Socioeconomic Consequences of Young Women's Childbearing: Reconciling Disparate Evidence." *Journal of Population Economics* 12: 547–565.

Singh, Susheela. 1998. "Adolescent Childbearing." *Studies in Family Planning* 29(2): 117–136.

Singh, Susheela, and Jacqueline E. Darroch. 2000. "Adolescent Pregnancy and Childbearing: Levels and Trends in Developed Countries." *Family Planning Perspectives* 32(1): 14–23.

Zabin, Laurie Schwab, and Karungari Kiragu. 1998. "Health Consequences of Adolescent Sexuality and Fertility Behavior in Sub-Saharan Africa." *Studies in Family Planning* 29(2): 210–232.

Barbara S. Mensch
Susheela Singh

ADOPTION

Adoption has been practiced in many societies through the centuries, usually in situations where the birth parents are unable to raise a child or where natural reproduction has failed to provide some desired fertility outcome. This entry focuses on adoption in modern, low-fertility societies.

Adoption is a legal procedure involving the permanent transfer of parental rights and duties in respect to a child from the birth parent(s) to another person. Legal adoption has been introduced in most industrialized societies over the past 150 years (in Massachusetts, legal adoption was introduced in 1851; in England and Wales, in 1926; in Ireland, in 1952). It involves at least three key parties: the adopted child(ren); the birth parent(s); and the adoptive parent(s) (sometimes termed the adoption triangle). Adoption provides a new family for children whose parent(s) are unable or unwilling to care for them, and it also meets the needs of childless adults.

Traditional Baby Adoption

Rising rates of non-marital fertility after World War II led to many unmarried mothers relinquishing their babies for adoption. In England and Wales in 1968, there were 24,831 adoptions—of which 14,461 (58%) involved "illegitimate" children adopted by non-relatives: more than one in five babies born outside marriage were adopted in the 1960s. By 1984 the number of such adoptions had fallen to 2,910. The widespread availability of reliable contraception, the legalization of abortion, and an increased acceptance of single parenthood resulted in few single mothers relinquishing their babies.

In other European countries, within-country adoption of non-relative children had virtually ceased by the end of the twentieth century: in the Netherlands, numbers fell from 747 in 1970 to 54 in 1995; in Norway, from 411 to 90. In Sweden in 1995, there were only 34 non-relative adoptions of Swedish children.

Special Needs Adoption and Permanency

In-country adoption continues in the United Kingdom and the United States, and it has expanded in the cases of older children in the public care system and those with serious physical, intellectual, or emotional problems. In the United States, the term *permanency planning* was widely used in the early 1970s in reference to this kind of adoption. The practice was formalized in the 1980 Adoption Assistance and Child Welfare Act. In 1998 some 36,000 children were adopted from the public care system, and 86 percent of adopters received public subsidies. Adop-

tion allowances were also introduced in the United Kingdom in the 1980s. In both countries, government policy is to increase the number of such adoptions, and this has been accompanied by a rise in contested adoptions where courts have, in some instances, dispensed with the consent of birth parents.

Stepparent Adoption

The increase in divorce rates in many Western countries during the late twentieth century led to a rise in second marriages where stepparents (usually stepfathers) sought to adopt their partner's birth children. In England and Wales, the number of stepparent adoptions peaked in 1974 when there were 14,805 adoptions of children where one partner in the adopting couple was a parent of the adoptee. New legislation (the 1975 Children Act) sought to discourage such adoptions; the Houghton Committee Report, on which much of the act is based, argued that stepparent adoption should not be used as it often involved the birth mother adopting her own legitimate child, removing all parental rights from the birth father. By 1984 the number of stepparent adoptions had fallen to 2,650. Two decades after the 1975 Children Act, stepparent adoptions still accounted for about half of the 5,000 adoptions recorded each year in England and Wales. In the United States in 1982, stepparent adoptions made up 42 percent of the 127,441 adoptions.

Adoption Criteria

In most countries legal adoption is only permitted for married couples, but in the United Kingdom, the Adoption and Children Bill debated in Parliament in 2002 has been amended to allow unmarried couples in a stable union to adopt jointly; this would extend to gay and lesbian couples. Adoption by a single person is becoming more common and, in practice, this has allowed one of a cohabiting couple to adopt with the understanding that a partner would become a caregiver, albeit without (adoptive) parental rights. Prospective adopters must be of a minimum age, and an upper age limit (often as young as 40) is often imposed for those wishing to adopt an infant. Older couples have often turned to intercountry adoption if they did not want an older or handicapped child. Most agencies also have criteria in relation to income and housing conditions.

Transracial Adoption

Transracial adoption (TRA) in the United States and United Kingdom has almost always meant the adop-

TABLE 1

Intercountry Adoptions in Selected Receiving Countries, 1989 and 1998

Country	1989 Total number	1989 Adoptions per 1,000 births	1998 Total number	1998 Adoptions per 1,000 births
United States	7,948	2.0	15,774	4.2
France	2,383	3.0	3,777	5.3
Italy	2,332	3.8	2,263	4.4
Germany	1,088	1.6	1,819	2.4
Sweden	883	9.4	928	10.8
Switzerland	509	6.2	686	8.6
Netherlands	642	3.7	825	4.6
Norway	578	11.0	643	11.2
Denmark	468	9.4	624	9.9
United Kingdom	n/a	n/a	258	0.4

SOURCE: Kane (1993); Selman (2002).

tion of an African-American or West Indian, Asian, Native American, or non-white Hispanic child by a white family. TRA became common in the United States in the 1960s as fewer white babies were available for adoption, but from the mid-1970s opposition to the practice mounted. Adoption of Native American children was subsequently restricted by legislation. Transracial adoption of black children has remained controversial in the United States and the United Kingdom, with both strong supporters and strong opponents of the view that black children should only be adopted by black parents, even if there is a lack of available black adopters and the alternative to being placed with white adopters is to remain in an institution. In the United States, the 1994 Multiethnic Placement Act made consideration of race in adoptive placements impermissible.

Intercountry Adoption

Intercountry adoption, which can be seen as a form of migratory behavior, originated in American philanthropy toward devastated countries after World War II. Later the Korean and Vietnam Wars resulted in many adoptions to the United States, Sweden, and other countries. The decline in infants available for domestic adoption made intercountry adoption an attractive option for childless couples; in Northern Europe, it was often the only option. Reports of child trafficking and large payments for newborn babies led to international concern, culminating in The Hague Convention on Protection of Children and Co-operation in Respect of Intercountry Adoption,

which was concluded and signed by 63 states in May 1993. By 2002 the Convention had been ratified by 37 countries. However, scandals continued—including accusations of child-trafficking in Guatemala and of profiteering by officials in Romania. At the end of the twentieth century, the incidence of intercountry adoption was highest in mainland Europe, although the number of such adoptions was greatest in the United States (see Table 1).

Global numbers of intercountry adoption reached some 20,000 a year in the late 1980s and then began to decline. The fall of the Ceausescu regime in 1989 led to many adoptions from Romania in 1990–1991, and in the mid- and late 1990s a growing number of very young children were adopted from China (almost all of them girls) and Russia. By the end of the century, the total intercountry adoption movement was approaching 35,000 a year. The number of foreign children adopted in the United States rose further from 15,774 in 1998 to 19,327 in 2001. Table 2 shows the major sources of children (a large majority of them infants) in the 1980s and 1998.

Low Fertility Countries as States of Origin

Although intercountry adoption often is characterized as the movement of children from poor, overpopulated countries, some states of origin have had low fertility levels (e.g., Germany after World War II). In the late 1990s, three of the four most important sources of children—Russia, China, and South Korea—had fertility below replacement level, as did Romania, and had fertility rates lower than some states receiving children from these countries. Many other Eastern European countries such as Belarus, Ukraine, and Kazakhstan, which became major providers of infants for the United States from 1998, also have low fertility rates.

In Search of Origins

In most low-fertility countries, legal adoption has been marked by secrecy and stigma. Before the last quarter of the twentieth century, most countries refused adopted persons access to information about their origins. The United States has a long tradition of sealed records, and even in 2000 a majority of its states did not allow the adoptee access to identifying information.

In England and Wales, the 1975 Children Act gave the right of access to their original birth records to all adopted persons over the age of 18. This right

TABLE 2

Intercountry Adoptions to Western Countries by Major Source Countries, 1980–1989 and 1998					
	1980–1989 (annual average)			1998	
Country	Number of adoptions	Adoptions per 1,000 births in 1989	Country	Number of adoptions	Adoptions per 1,000 births
South Korea	6,123	5.4	Russia	5,064	5.4
India	1,532	<0.1	China	4,855	0.24
Colombia	1,484	2.5	Vietnam	2,375	1.4
Brazil	753	0.5	South Korea	2,294	3.4
Sri Lanka	682	1.0	Colombia	1,162	1.2
Chile	524	3.0	Guatemala	1,143	2.9
Philippines	517	0.4	India	1,048	0.04
Guatemala	224	0.8	Romania	891	4.4

SOURCE: Selman (2002)—adoptions to 10 receiving countries; Kane (1993)—adoptions to 13 receiving countries.

has been exercised widely, and it is estimated that a majority of those adopted by non-parents will seek information about their origins over their lifetime. In 1991 an Adoption Contact Register was established, enabling adopted persons and birth relatives to indicate an interest in meeting each other.

In New Zealand, the 1985 Adult Adoption Information Act gave adopted persons the right to their original birth certificate at age 20. Birth parents also have a right to ask for information about their children, although either party can veto the transmission of information.

By the beginning of the twenty-first century, adoption was much more open. In the United States, adoption of infants increasingly involves birth mothers meeting with (and even choosing) their child's adoptive parents. Research by Harold Grotevant and Ruth McRoy indicates that contact between birth parents and adoptees may continue after placement, and appears to have no detrimental effect.

See also: *Infertility; Reproductive Technologies.*

BIBLIOGRAPHY

Altstein, Howard, and Rita Simon, eds. 1991. *Intercountry Adoption: A Multinational Perspective.* New York: Praeger.

Avery, Rosemary, ed. 1997. *Adoption Policy and Special Needs Children.* Westport, CT: Auburn House.

Grotevant, Harold, and Ruth McRoy. 1998. *Openness in Adoption: Exploring Family Connections.* London: Sage.

Howe, David, and Julia Feast. 2000. *Adoption, Search, and Reunion: The Long Term Experience of Adopted Adults.* London: The Children's Society.

Kane, Saralee. 1993. "The Movement of Children for International Adoption: An Epidemiological Perspective." *The Social Science Journal* 30(4): 323–339.

Kirton, Derek. 2000. *"Race," Ethnicity and Adoption.* London: Open University.

Mueller, Ulrich, and Barbara Perry. 2001. "Adopted Persons' Search for and Contact with their Birth Parents." *Adoption Quarterly* 4(3): 5–62.

Selman, Peter, ed. 2000. *Intercountry Adoption: Developments, Trends, and Perspectives.* London: BAAF.

———. 2002. "Intercountry Adoption in the New Millennium: The Silent Migration Revisited." In *Population Research and Policy Review* 21: 205–225.

Simon, Rita J., Howard Altstein, and Marygold Melli. 1994. *The Case for Transracial Adoption.* Washington, D.C.: American University Press.

Triseliotis, John. 1973. *In Search of Origins.* London: Routledge.

Triseliotis, John, Joan Shireman, and Marian Hundleby. 1997. *Adoption: Theory, Policy and Practice.* London: Cassell.

INTERNET RESOURCES.

Hague Conference. 2002. <http://www.hch.net/e/
conventions/menu33e.html>.

National Adoption Information Clearinghouse
(NAIC). 2002. "Adoption: Numbers and
Trends: Adoption from Foster Care."
<http://www.calib.com/naic/index.htm>.

Selman, Peter. 1999. "In Search of Origins: Estimating Lifetime Take-up of Access to Birth Records
in England and Wales." Minneapolis: International Conference on Adoption Research.
<http://fsos.che.umn.edu/mtarp/Papers.htm>.

PETER SELMAN

AFRICAN-AMERICAN POPULATION HISTORY

In the course of four and a half centuries after 1492 some 9.5 million Africans arrived in the Western Hemisphere. Until the 1820s more Africans crossed the Atlantic than did Europeans, and Africans and their descendants outnumbered Europeans and their descendants in most of the new American colonies until the early nineteenth century. The balance would shift with the arrival of over 48 million Europeans in the period from 1830 to the 1920s, although African forced migration continued until the early 1860s.

The Destinations

Africans were not brought in equal numbers to all regions of the Americas but tended to be concentrat- ed in zones that had few American Indian laborers and had rich virgin lands that could be used to grow commercial export products for European con- sumption. In light of the fact that all the Africans were involuntary migrants and were purchased for work purposes, it is no surprise that they were con- centrated in the plantation agricultural zones that produced sugar, cotton, and coffee for European markets. The two biggest centers of African slave res- idence were the West Indies, which absorbed some 4.4 million African slave immigrants—the last arriv- ing in Cuba in the 1860s—and Brazil, which took in some 3.9 million Africans until the slave trade ended

in that region in 1850. North America probably ab- sorbed some 361,000 Africans before the trade ended there in 1808, with most of the forced migrants com- ing in the late eighteenth century. The other 834,000 Africans who arrived in America went to continental Spanish America and the Guyanas.

Despite this concentration of Africans in key ex- port centers, there was no region of the Americas, from Hudson Bay to the Rio de la Plata, that did not contain Africans and their descendants. In colonial Spanish America, which had a competing group of American Indian laborers, Africans tended to be concentrated in urban areas and often made up half the local populations. Everywhere else they lived pri- marily in the rural areas and even worked in gold mines in Brazil and the northeastern South Ameri- can interior.

Population Growth

As a result of the fact that the slave trade carried pri- marily adults and males to the Americas, most resi- dent African populations in the New World experi- enced negative growth rates. As the slave trade declined or was abolished, most of those slave popu- lations finally began to achieve positive growth rates. With fewer adults and males arriving, the native- born populations, with their balanced sex ratios, began to replace themselves in sufficient numbers to cause the resident slave populations to grow. This occurred in the West Indies and in Brazil as well, de- spite the steady out-migration of slave women and children through manumission.

To estimate the population of Africans and their descendants in the Americas at the end of the eigh- teenth century, one must include both slaves and "free persons of color," as manumitted slaves and Africans were called in most American slave socie- ties. Combining these two groups gives a very rough population estimate of over 4.3 million persons of African descent at that time. Slaves numbered close to 3 million persons, of whom 1.1 million lived in the West Indies, another 1 million resided in Brazil, 271,000 in lived in mainland Spanish America, and 575,000 resided in the United States. There were al- most 1.3 million free persons of color at that time, of whom 212,000 resided in the Caribbean, 400,000 in Brazil and 650,000 in Mainland Spanish America, and some 32,000 in the United States

Although all native-born slave populations had positive reproductive rates and those rates became dominant with the end of the slave trade, the United States was unique in the rapidity of the growth of its slave population. By the 1860s the United States had 3.9 million slaves and 488,000 free colored persons. By the time of the first national census of Brazil in 1872 that country had a free colored population of 4.2 million persons along with 1.5 million slaves, for a total of 5.7 million Afro-Brazilians. Cuba and Puerto Rico by then had 412,000 slaves and 474,000 free colored persons. Counting just these three slave regions in the middle of the nineteenth century gives a population of 5.8 million slaves and 5.2 million free persons of color. Clearly these 11 million Afro-Americans do not account for the total number in the Americas, considering that the descendants of slaves in mainland Spanish America probably numbered another million.

Racial Categories

Until the end of slavery or the establishment of republican governments in most regions of the Americas careful records were kept on people of African origin and descent. However, that systematic examination of race changed, with most census takers no longer listing color or race in their enumerations of populations. It thus becomes extremely difficult from the late nineteenth century onward to estimate the size of the African-American populations. Added to the problem of a lack of enumerations is the question of the definition of groups. Miscegenation between the races was common to all American societies from the very beginning. Thus, to the original African group were added mulattoes and other admixtures of whites, Africans, and American Indians. In most American societies it was assumed that this mixed element formed a new racial category, distinct from whites and Africans. Only in the United States were these people of mixed origins exclusively associated with the "black" population.

Therefore, defining who is "black" or of African-American descent has become a complex social and political problem. Are people with mixed origins white or black? Are they European or African-American in origin? Finally, in almost all the American republics that did list color in the census, color is almost always self-defined and is much influenced by local societal definitions of color, class, and local patterns of racial prejudice. Thus, the size of the populations of African origin is almost impossible to determine with precision.

This situation is reflected in the few attempts made to categorize this population throughout the Americas. An estimate for all the Americas in 1992 gave a minimum figure of 64 million persons and a maximum of 124 million persons of African descent, which represented, respectively, 9 percent and 17 percent of the total American hemispheric population. An earlier attempt in 1983 estimated that whites in the Americas made up roughly 36 percent of the total population, Indians some 10 percent, and blacks just 6 percent, with the rest being of persons of mixed origin. Illustrative of this problem is the case of Colombia. A more recent study has argued that "there is no precise data on the size of the Afro-Colombian population. The government tends to minimize the number, putting it at about 30 percent of the total population, or approximately 10.5 million individuals" (Archbold 2000, p. 3).

For the two largest populations of African-Americans there are some reliable data. In the United States, which has the most rigid definition of who is African-American or black, the census of 2000 counted 34.6 million persons of this color, excluding black Hispanics, in the total population. When persons who list more than one race are included, the figure rises to 36.4 million. The National Household Survey of Brazil carried out in 1999 estimated that 39.9 percent of the population of 160 million Brazilians consisted of mulattoes (63.8 million persons) and 5.4 percent (8.6 million) consisted of blacks. Using a U.S. definition of the population of African origin would give Brazil approximately 72.4 million persons of this origin if mulattoes are to be classified as blacks rather than whites or as a class by themselves.

Migration within the Americas

Although the traditional plantation areas were zones with high densities of African populations, the abolition of slavery in most regions led to an out-migration of ex-slaves as early as the beginning of the nineteenth century. As long as there were economic opportunities in the labor market or farming land was available, ex-slaves refused to work on the traditional plantations. In many cases their initial migration was delayed by competition from the foreign-born workers who arrived in large numbers until the 1920s. However, even before the decline of this competitive migration, ex-slaves were moving to new regions and new countries in large numbers. It is estimated that between 200,000 and 250,000 black

West Indians permanently moved to Panama and the United States in the period from 1881 to 1921.

By the twentieth century those migrations would become more common everywhere. In the 1950s and 1960s over 300,000 black West Indians moved to Britain. In the United States the African-American population moved out of the South in large numbers after 1910 in what has come to be seen as a great internal migration. Whereas 90 percent of this African-American population resided in the southern states in 1900 and was 83 percent rural, by 1990 only 53 percent resided in the South and only 13 percent of these people were classified as rural residents. By the census of 1980 over 4 million southern-born blacks were residing outside the states of their birth. There were also migrations within Brazil beginning in the 1910s with major interregional movements of northeastern residents to the central and southern parts of the country, which had an impact on the color ratios in those formerly more European regions.

Conclusions

One can conclude that since abolition, the population of African descent in the New World has become both less concentrated and less rural than it was in the nineteenth century. It can be stated in very broad terms that the majority of the population of the Americas, according to very broad definitions of color, is primarily nonwhite and that a high proportion of that population can claim some relationship with the 9.5 million Africans who were brought to America by the Atlantic slave trade.

See also: *Racial and Ethnic Composition; Slavery, Demography of.*

BIBLIOGRAPHY

Archbold, Julio E. Gallardo. 2000. "Colombian Legislation: Regulations Governing Afro-Colombian Communities." In *Race and Poverty: Interagency Consultation on Afro-Latin Americans*. Washington, D.C.: Inter-American Dialogue, Inter-American Development Bank, World Bank.

Davis, Darién J., ed. 1995. *Slavery and Beyond: The African Impact on Latin America and the Caribbean*. Wilmington, DE: Scholarly Resources.

Eltis, David. 2001. "The Volume and Structure of the Transatlantic Slave Trade: A Reassessment." *William and Mary Quarterly* 58(1): 45.

Ferenczi, Imre, and Walter F. Wilcox. 1919. *International Migrations*. New York: National Bureau of Economic Research.

Gregory, James N. 1995. "The Southern Diaspora and the Urban Dispossessed." *Journal of American History* 83(1): 112.

Henriques, Ricardo. 2001. *Desigualdade Racial no Brasil: Evolução das Condições de Vida na década de 90*. Rio de Janeiro: IPEA, Texto Para Discussao no. 807.

Klein, Herbert S. 1986. *African Slavery in Latin America and the Caribbean*. New York: Oxford University Press.

———. 1999. *The Atlantic Slave Trade*. New York: Cambridge University Press.

Nobles, Melissa. 2000. *Shades of Citizenship: Race and the Census in Modern Politics*. Stanford, CA: Stanford University Press.

Oviedo, Rodolfo Monge. 1992. "Are We or Aren't We?" *NACLA Report on the Americas* 25(4): 19.

Peach, G. C. K. 1967. "West Indian Migration to Britain." *International Migration Review* 1(2): 34.

Tolnay, Stewart E. 1998. "Educational Selection in the Migration of Southern Blacks, 1880–1990." *Social Forces* 77(2): 487–488.

U.S. Bureau of the Census. 2001. *Profiles of General Demographic Characteristics 2000*. Washington, D.C.: Census Bureau.

HERBERT S. KLEIN

AGE MEASUREMENT

In most countries, throughout the year following their seventh birthday a child who was asked "How old are you?" would say he or she is seven years old. In demographic terminology, this response represents the child's age last birthday or age in completed years. Other possible definitions of age include "age

TABLE 1

Age Heaping: Population Counts (in '000) by Age for the Range 52–65 Years, in the 1960 Census of the Philippines													
Age	52	53	54	55	56	57	58	59	60	61	62	63	64	65
Count	129	93	96	163	88	72	93	72	279	31	50	40	34	102

SOURCE: Shryock and Siegel (1971).

at the nearest birthday" and "age next birthday"; these definitions are no longer used in censuses or surveys. The term *exact age* is applied to the time elapsed since birth: an infant born on April 20, 2000, attains age 2.03 years on May 1, 2002. An East Asian practice of reckoning age involves assigning age one at birth and then increasing it by one at each subsequent New Year. The East Asian age, thus calculated using the lunar calendar (the lunar year is shorter than the solar year by a few days), may exceed the corresponding Western age by as much as three years for the elderly beyond the age of 70 years. Given the East Asian age, the animal year of birth, and whether the birthday falls between the New Year's day and the census or survey date, the Western age can be calculated. In situations where a direct question on age is unlikely to produce useful answers, a person's age may be calculated as the difference between the year of the census or survey and the reported year of birth.

The United Nations' recommendation for the 1970 round of population censuses was to use the following definition of age: "the estimated or calculated interval of time between the date of birth and the date of the census, expressed in completed years" (United Nations 1967, p. 41). The recommendation indicates that information on age can be collected by asking a direct question on age, one on the date of birth, or both.

Errors in Age Data

The frequency distribution of age may show irregularities (see Table 1), which may be real, reflecting past patterns of mortality (e.g., age-selective war casualties), fertility (e.g., a baby boom, birth heaping in auspicious years and deficits in inauspicious years), or migration, or may reflect errors in the data resulting from omission, multiple inclusion, or inaccuracy in reported age. Notice the tendency in Table 1 for the counts to peak at ages ending in 0 and 5, and to a lesser extent in ages ending in 2 and 8. Such

heaping patterns reflect digit preference, the tendency to report ages ending in certain digits.

The pattern of digit preference varies among societies, and it also depends on the procedure used in collecting age data. The use of a question on date of birth, in combination with a direct question on age, tends to reduce such irregularities in the age data. When age is estimated as the difference between the census or survey year and the reported year of birth, age heaping occurs because of the preference shown for years ending in certain digits (such as 1900, 1910, 1920, and so on). Similar problems arise when age data are obtained by attempting to pinpoint the year of birth with reference to a list of historical events.

Age heaping has an inverse association with literacy level. The tendency to prefer ages ending in 0 and 5 is, however, widespread. Certain age preferences are no doubt culturally determined (e.g., the tendency found in some countries to avoid the number 13).

The term *age shifting* refers to deliberately giving an inaccurate age or date of birth. The elderly are prone to exaggerate their age, particularly if old age brings with it higher status; young men may understate or overstate their age, if by doing so they stand to benefit in some way (e.g., avoid or, as the case may be, qualify for military duty).

Correction Methods Applicable to Age Data

The importance of obtaining accurate information on age stems partly from the fact that many demographic features—such as reproductive behavior and geographic mobility—show distinct age patterns. Deficiencies in age data may lead to misleading patterns of such characteristics. The use of age groups for cross-classifications partially overcomes the problem.

In choosing age groups, it is advisable to have the "preferred" ages (displaying marked heaping) located toward the middle of each interval rather than at the end points. By centering the age groups at distribution peaks, the adjacent, depleted ages are brought within the interval.

If interest centers on the age distribution itself, rather than in cross-tabulations involving age as one of the variables, then techniques such as graduation can be used to produce age distributions smoothed over the observed irregularities.

Requirements for Improved Age Reporting

There are essentially three requirements for correct age reporting.

1. Availability of information: A respondent unsure of his or her age is unlikely to give the correct response to a query about age. In populations with complete birth registration, the age data tend to be more accurate, other things being the same. Also, the data are of better quality in population segments of higher literacy levels.

2. Use of appropriate methods of data collection: As mentioned, following a direct question on age by one on the date of birth may improve the data quality. Also, when the enumerators are free to adjust the responses (e.g., to hide digit preferences), the final age data may reflect to a large extent variation in the procedures used for adjustment.

3. Use of appropriate data processing and reporting procedures: The quality of the collected data may be excellent, but the reported age distribution still may be inaccurate, if, for example, only the year of birth, not the exact date of birth, is used at the tabulation stage.

See also: *Data Assessment; Estimation Methods, Demographic.*

BIBLIOGRAPHY

Carrier, Norman, and John Hobcraft. 1973. *Demographic Estimation for Developing Societies.* London: London School of Economics.

Prassat, Roland. 1985. *The Dictionary of Demography,* ed. Christopher Wilson. New York: Blackwell.

Scott, Christopher, and George Sabagh. 1970. "The Historical Calendar as a Method of Estimating Age." *Population Studies* 24: 93–109.

Shryock, Henry S., Jacob S. Siegel, and Associates. 1971. *The Methods and Materials of Demography,* Volume 1. Washington, D.C.: U. S. Government Printing Office.

United Nations. 1967. "Manual IV-Methods of Estimating Basic Demographic Measures for Incomplete Data." *Population Studies* 39.

———. 1967. "Principles and Recommendations for the 1970 Population Censuses." *Statistical Papers, Series M,* 44.

KRISHNAN NAMBOODIRI

AGE STRUCTURE AND DEPENDENCY

Every individual is some particular age. Populations are collections of individuals, and rather than being some particular age, populations are characterized by the frequency distribution of the ages of the individuals who constitute them. This is called the population age distribution or age structure. The age structure can be summarized in various ways, for example, by the average or median age of the population. A population with a low median age is called "young," and one with a high median age is called "old." One can also define life cycle stages, such as youth, working age, and old age, and describe the age structure by the percentage of the population in each of these categories, for which various age boundaries are used. Thus one can speak of the proportions of the population below age 15 or 18 or 20; proportions between one of these ages and ages up to 60 or 65; and proportions above ages 60 or 65. With reference to these same life cycle stages, so-called dependency ratios may be calculated. The ratio of the elderly to the working age population is the old age dependency ratio, the ratio of youth to the working age population is the child or youth dependency ratio, and the sum of these two is the total dependency ratio.

Some of these measures are shown in Table 1 for the years 1950 to 2000, along with United Nations projections to the year 2050, for the more developed countries (DC) and the less developed countries (LDC), the countries being classified according to their economic status in 2000. In every year, the DCs have a higher median age than the LDCs, with a smaller proportion of children and a higher proportion of the elderly. Evidently, aging has already affected the LDCs as well as the DCs; the phenomenon is not restricted to the industrial nations. The aging of the DC populations is shown by the projected increase in their median age by about 18 years from 1950 to 2050, and by the corresponding increase for the LDC populations by about 14 years.

Stable Population States

The age structure of a population is shaped by the past history of births, the past age distributions of deaths, and the age characteristics of net migrations. Consider first the case in which net migration is always zero at all ages (a closed population, on net), and age-specific fertility and mortality rates have been unchanging for a long time—about a century or more. In this case, it can be shown that the population will converge to a so-called stable state, in which the percentage age distribution is constant over time, and the population and every age group grow at the same constant exponential rate. Furthermore, this stable population age distribution is independent of the population age distribution that existed a sufficiently long time ago—again, about a century. That is, the particular features and shape of the initial age distribution tend to be forgotten as time passes, and the eventual age distribution depends only on the constant age-specific fertility and mortality rates. Depending on those rates, a stable population can have a constant growth rate within a wide band of particular values, and the rate can be positive, negative, or zero. A stationary population is a stable population with a zero growth rate.

Members of a population who are now age x were born x years ago and have survived for x years. In a stable population, the number of births grows at the exponential population growth rate. In a growing population, the number of births x years ago will be smaller than the number of births today, and the higher the population growth rate, the smaller will be the generation born x years ago relative to the generation born in the current year. The opposite will be true if the growth rate is negative and the population is shrinking. Indeed, the rate of population growth is the most important determinant of the age distribution of a closed, stable population. The age distribution, however, is also affected by mortality, which determines the proportions of

TABLE 1

Age Structure for Developed and Less Developed Countries, 1950–2050

	1950	1975	2000	2025	2050
Median Age (yrs)					
DC	28.6	30.9	37.4	44.1	46.4
LDC	21.4	19.4	24.3	30.0	35.0
Percent less than age 15					
DC	27.3	24.2	18.3	15	15.5
LDC	37.6	41.1	32.8	26	21.8
Percent age 60 and older					
DC	11.7	15.4	19.4	28.2	33.5
LDC	6.4	6.2	7.7	12.6	19.3

SOURCE: United Nations (2002).

births that survive to each age x. The lower the mortality rate, the higher will be the proportions surviving from birth to older ages.

Nonstable and Irregular Population Distributions

For a given level of mortality, higher fertility will always be associated with faster population growth and therefore with a younger stable age distribution in a closed population. Mortality differences, however, have two contradictory effects. On the one hand, lower mortality makes a stable population older by increasing the proportions surviving from birth to older ages. On the other hand, lower mortality tends to make a stable population younger, because it raises the population growth rate (for a given level of fertility). When the initial level of mortality is high, the net outcome of lower mortality is to make a population younger. When the initial level of mortality is low, lower mortality tends to make a population older. For intermediate initial levels, the effects of lower mortality are mixed, sometimes leading to higher proportions of both youth and of elderly and sometimes hardly changing the age distribution at all. These different effects of mortality decline are observed in real-world situations as well as in the hypothetical stable populations. For example, Table 1 shows that the LDC population in 1975 had a younger median age than it did in 1950, as well as a higher proportion of children and lower proportion of elderly. Mortality declined rapidly from 1950 to 1975, illustrating how falling mortality can make a population younger.

Many actual population age distributions are highly irregular rather than smooth and geometric like those of stable populations. Irregular distributions can come about in several major ways. The populations of a number of industrial countries, for example, experienced a baby boom from the late 1940s through the mid-1960s, followed by subsequent baby busts. These changes in fertility created large bulges and hollows in the population age distributions as the affected birth cohorts reached higher ages. The changing relative sizes of cohorts had important consequences for average wages, unemployment rates, and prospects for promotion, and they eventually will exert differential fiscal pressures through public pension and health-care systems. Population age distributions can also be heavily marked by traumatic events such as major wars or, for example, China's disastrous famine resulting from the Great Leap Forward (an economic plan launched in the late 1950s). Such crises cause heavy mortality that is sometimes concentrated at certain age and sex groups, and they also lead to sharp reductions in fertility and therefore in the size of generations born during and immediately after the crisis. When a population age distribution is strongly distorted by influences such as these, the distortions simply age with the population, moving up from younger to older ages as time passes. For example, the effects of both World War I and World War II are still clearly apparent in the age pyramids (as the conventional graphic representation of age distributions are labeled) of many European countries. A third cause of irregular age structure is age-focused patterns of immigration and emigration. These are more frequently seen in a sharp differential at the local rather than the national level. Often such patterns occur in towns with universities, prisons, army bases, or retirement communities. A fourth cause is emigration of the younger population from some rural areas, which leaves behind an elderly population. Some characteristic age pyramids are shown in Figure 1.

Not only do distorted age structures tend to persist over time as the population ages; they also can be transmitted to the stream of new births through the processes of reproduction, as echoes. If some generations are unusually large, because of an earlier baby boom, for example, then when the members of those generations enter their peak reproductive ages they will themselves generate an unusually large number of births, given typical levels of fertility. In this way they create another bulge in the age distribution, albeit a somewhat smaller one than the first. Formal analysis shows that populations with nonstable age distributions but which are subject to constant age-specific fertility and mortality will tend to move in cycles about one generation (25 to 30 years) long as they converge to stability. This result can be generalized to populations that are constantly subjected to random perturbations. Historical time series of baptisms often show evidence of such cycles. Sometimes, however, there is negative feedback in the renewal process, so that large generations of young adults experience adverse economic conditions and consequently have lower fertility and give birth to smaller, rather than larger, generations. In this way cycles longer than one generation may be generated; these are known as Easterlin cycles.

Consequences of Population Age Distributions

In many contemporary societies, there is particular interest and concern about the process of population aging and rising old age dependency ratios, because these factors will affect the cost per worker of supporting the elderly retired populations. Some analysts suggest that governments should seek to raise fertility in order to reduce and postpone population aging. Others propose to alleviate population aging through increased immigration, because immigrants are typically younger than natives and have higher fertility. But analysis shows that any gains from such a policy would be short lived and smaller than most people expect, because immigrants grow old themselves and require support. Only constantly accelerating rates of immigration achieve much effect, and such policies cannot be sustained for long. As an example, the U.S. Bureau of the Census reported the old age dependency ratio and the median age in 1995 to be .21 and 34.3 years, respectively. The Census Bureau projected these quantities to the year 2050 under low and high immigration assumptions that differed by more than a million immigrants per year. With low immigration, the Census Bureau projected that, by 2050, the old age dependency ratio would rise to .38 and the median age to 38.8 years. With a million more immigrants per year, these figures were projected to be only slightly lower at .35 and 37.6 years. The additional 55 million immigrants would have a big effect on population size but only a small effect on population aging.

FIGURE 1

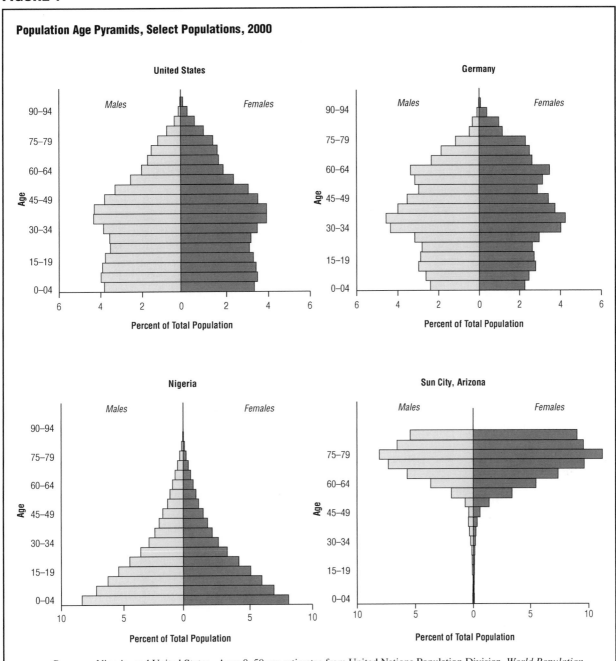

Population Age Pyramids, Select Populations, 2000

SOURCE: Germany, Nigeria, and United States. Ages 0–59 are estimates from United Nations Population Division, *World Population Prospects: The 2000 Revision, Volume II: The Sex and Age Distribution of Populations* (2001), Annex Table 2; Ages 60 and over are estimates from World Population Aging 1950–2050, United Nations Population Division (2002), Annex Table III.2; Sun City, AZ: "American Factfinder," U.S. Census Bureau, table P12. Sex by Age, from Census 2000 Summary File 1.

Population age distributions have a range of socioeconomic consequences, because people's behaviors, abilities, and entitlements all vary with age. These variations reflect biological changes over the life cycle, but in addition they reflect somewhat arbitrary institutional age categories and individual choices in response to various preferences and incentives. On the biological side, it appears that health and vitality at the older ages have been increasing over time, so that working life could be extended to older ages. This option, however, is apparently not commonly viewed as desirable, because actual ages at retirement have declined by five to ten years over the twentieth century in industrial countries. These declines are due in part to the desire for more leisure as incomes rise, pensions becoming more common, and financial institutions making saving easier. It is also clear, however, that the structures of both public and private pensions provide strong incentives for early retirement, and that this has contributed to the decline. This trend slowed or slightly reversed in the 1990s in many countries.

The boundary age for dependency in youth also reflects a number of factors, most notably the length of time spent in formal education, that influence the age at which the workforce is entered. These age boundaries for youth and old age correspond roughly to directions of flows of intergenerational transfers, through the family and through the public sector. The public sector in industrial countries provides pensions and health care for the elderly and education for youth. The size of these public transfer programs for the young and the old swamps the transfers to those of working age. Private transfers in most industrial countries consist mainly of parental support of children and assistance from the elderly to their adult children and grandchildren through transfers made prior to death and through bequests.

As the population age distribution changes, pressure on those who make these transfers is relaxed or intensified. Population aging often goes with reduced fertility, resulting in not only a reduced need for public and private transfers to children but also a greatly increased need for transfers to the elderly for health care and pensions. A generalized fiscal dependency ratio can be calculated as follows. The numerator is determined by weighting each population age group by the costliness of public transfers it receives, with the denominator equal to the level of taxes that age group pays. Holding these weights fixed, one can then see how the fiscal dependency ratio changes over time for demographic reasons alone. For the United States, for example, the federal fiscal support ratio has been projected to increase by 56 percent from 2010 to 2075. This means that in order to provide the same set of age-specific benefits, age-specific tax rates financing intergenerational transfers would have to be raised by 56 percent. Alternatively, if age-specific tax rates financing transfers were held constant, then benefits received as transfers would have to be scaled back by 36 percent.

See also: *Aging of Population; Cycles, Population; Generational Accounting; Intergenerational Transfers; Oldest Old.*

BIBLIOGRAPHY

Coale, Ansley J. 1972. *The Growth and Structure of Human Populations: A Mathematical Investigation.* Princeton: Princeton University Press.

Lee, Ronald. 1994. "The Formal Demography of Population Aging, Transfers, and the Economic Life Cycle." In *The Demography of Aging,* ed. Linda Martin and Samuel Preston. Washington, D.C.: National Academy Press.

United Nations Department of Economic and Social Affairs, Population Division. 2002. *World Population Aging, 1950–2050.* New York: United Nations.

RONALD LEE

AGING AND LONGEVITY, BIOLOGY OF

Most strains of mice live an average of 1,000 days; dogs live approximately 5,000 days; and humans, in low mortality countries, live about 29,000 days (around 80 years). The average duration of life of a species and the age-specific rate of increase in the risk of death is calibrated to each species' unique pattern of growth, development, and reproduction. These linkages between longevity and growth and development are the cornerstone of the scientific understanding of the biology of aging and death and the duration of life of humans and other sexually reproducing species. This entry presents a brief discussion of the biology of aging with emphasis on its implications for human longevity.

Causes of Aging

In its simplest form, aging may be thought of as the accumulation of random damage to the building blocks of life—especially to DNA, certain proteins, carbohydrates, and lipids. The damage begins from conception, occurs in a largely random fashion throughout the body, and accumulates with time, eventually exceeding the body's self-repair capabilities. The damage gradually impairs the functioning of cells, tissues, organs, and organ systems, resulting in the increased vulnerability to disease and a rise in the physical, physiological, and psychological manifestations of aging.

There are many agents of damage including, ironically, the life-sustaining processes involved in converting the food we eat and fluids we drink into usable energy. The primary energy generators of cells are the mitochondria. As they perform their usual function, the mitochondria emit oxidizing molecules known as free radicals that exist for only a fraction of a second. Although free radicals contribute to several important biological processes (e.g., cell communication, immune response), they are also a destructive force. Most of the damage caused by these highly reactive molecules is fixed by the body's impressive mechanisms for surveillance, maintenance, and repair. However, unrepaired damage accumulates and causes injury to the mitochondria and other parts of the cell and extracellular environment.

The process of aging makes us ever more susceptible to the common fatal diseases that we tend to associate with growing older, such as the increased risk of heart disease, stroke, and cancer. Even if medical interventions were to eliminate the major remaining killer diseases, the aging process would continue unabated—making the saved population ever more susceptible to a new set of diseases expressed at even later ages. Aging contributes to a wide variety of non-fatal diseases and disorders such as arthritis, loss of vision and hearing, muscle and bone loss, and a reduction in skin elasticity. It should be noted that aging is not a genetically programmed process that plays itself out along a rigid time frame. Instead, aging can be viewed as an inadvertent by-product of living beyond the biological warranty period for living machines, which in the case of sexually reproducing species means surviving beyond the end of the reproductive life span.

Forecasting Life Expectancy

How much higher can human life expectancy rise? This question has been the subject of debate among actuaries and demographers for centuries; it has taken on a new practical significance in modern times because it affects the future solvency of the age-entitlement programs found in all modern welfare states. There is a wide range of estimates: Their lower bound accords with the view that life expectancy for human populations (males and females combined) is unlikely to exceed the mid to high 80s; others claim that there is no biological reason why life expectancy cannot rise indefinitely in the future. The sections that follow present the basic arguments of the three main schools of thought that have contributed to this debate.

Extrapolation Models

Scientific forecasts of the survival of individuals and populations began with the practical work of actuaries employed by life insurance companies. Benjamin Gompertz (1779–1865), in an article published in 1825, first identified a common age pattern to the dying-out process. The formula developed by Gompertz showed that the force of mortality among humans increases exponentially from about age 20 to 85. Interestingly, Gompertz's formula provides an accurate characterization of the timing of death not just for humans but also for a variety of other species. When the U.S. Social Security program was created in the 1930s, actuaries needed to make forecasts of the annual number of beneficiaries that would draw benefits from the program. They did so by simple extrapolation: If, for example, life expectancy at birth had increased by two years in the previous two decades, it was projected to increase by another two years in the subsequent two decades.

During the next five decades, using this model, the Social Security Administration (SSA) consistently underestimated the speed with which mortality was declining. The SSA actuaries also believed that the average achievable life expectancy was constrained by biological limits to life, and that there was reason to assume that the population of the United States was approaching those limits. This view was supported by the demographic predictions at that time that the rise in life expectancy at birth would soon begin to tail off.

Toward the end of the twentieth century, the opposite problem occurred—the SSA began to overestimate the rise in life expectancy. The actuaries, as before, chose as the basis for their forecast a relatively narrow time period. In the earlier projection this introduced a conservative bias, but in the 1970s declines in death rates at middle and older ages were exceptionally rapid. Extrapolation of such rapid gains turned out to be unrealistic.

The extrapolation model, with its implication that life expectancy for humans will continue to rise far into the future, is frequently used. In a 2002 study, Jim Oeppen and James Vaupel remark that the historic rise in life expectancy is one of the most regular biological events ever observed, and argue that there is reason to believe this trend will continue throughout the twenty-first century. They project that life expectancy for humans in low mortality populations will rise to 100 years by the year 2060.

The advantages of the extrapolation method are that it is parsimonious, observation-based, and easily adjusted to reflect new developments in population health and aging. Ample evidence in the scientific literature suggests that when used over relatively short time frames, it has been a highly reliable predictor of trends in life expectancy.

Extrapolation also has weaknesses. Much of the rise in life expectancy in the twentieth century came from declining death rates before age 50. Future rises will have to come mainly from declining death rates at middle and older ages—the prospects for which may not be soundly gauged based on what happened in the earlier period. The absence of biological information as an input to projecting mortality is another problematic feature of extrapolation.

Biodemographic Views of Aging

An alternative approach to forecasting mortality draws on insights from the biodemography of aging. Biodemography is an effort to merge the scientific disciplines of biology (including evolutionary biology, genetics, and molecular biology) and demography and actuarial science in order to understand the biological forces that lead to consistent and predictable age patterns of death among sexually reproducing species. Although the intellectual roots of biodemography date back to the nineteenth century with the search for the "law of mortality," it is only in modern times that biodemographic reasoning has been used to inform mortality forecasts.

According to evolutionary theory, there is a fundamental link between the force of natural selection and the timing of reproduction among sexually reproducing species. The timing of death in populations is thought to be calibrated to the timing of genetically fixed programs for development, maturation, and reproduction. Further, the onset and length of the reproductive window (i.e., for females, the time between menarche and menopause) is thought to influence the rate of increase in the death rate from biological causes—a theoretical underpin-

ning of evolutionary theory that has since been empirically demonstrated.

The main forces that influence the death rates of humans at high life-expectancy levels are those associated with the regulation and pathogenesis of intrinsic disease processes; biochemical changes that contribute to senescence; and biodemographic forces that influence the speed with which life expectancy rises.

In their 1996 study, Bruce Carnes, S. Jay Olshansky, and Douglas Grahn reasoned that the demonstrated linkage between the timing of reproduction and senescence could be used to inform and improve forecasts of human life expectancy. If each species has fixed programs for growth and development, there should be relatively fixed age patterns of intrinsic (biologically-caused) mortality: a species-specific "intrinsic mortality signature." This biodemographic perspective yields a practical upper bound on human life expectancy of 88 years for females and 82 years for males (85 years for males and females combined). Exceeding that boundary, according to this argument, would require modifying the biological rate of aging itself—a technological feat that, although theoretically possible in the future, is currently beyond the reach of science.

Extreme Forecasts of Life Expectancy

According to some claims, advances in the biomedical sciences will be so dramatic in the coming decades of the twenty-first century that life expectancies of 150 years or higher may be attained in the lifetimes of people living in 2002. It has even been suggested that it is currently possible to modify the rate of human aging, and that immortality is a realistic goal for the twenty-first century. The suggestion that medical science is on the verge of discovering the secret to the fountain of youth and that humanity is about to extend life dramatically has been made repeatedly throughout history, with each proclamation contradicted by subsequent experience. What has encouraged many people in the early years of the third millennium to be newly optimistic about the prospects of greatly extending average human life expectancy is that scientists now have pieced together important elements of the puzzle of aging. Also, investigators can claim legitimately that they have experimentally increased the duration of life of a variety of organisms. If it is possible to extend the life of experimental animals, the argument goes, then it should also be possible to make humans live longer.

Advances in the biomedical sciences may well continue to postpone death ("manufacture survival time") by treating the primary fatal manifestations of aging, such as cardiovascular diseases and cancer, but no scientific evidence to date suggests that the rate of aging of any animal has yet been modified. Highly optimistic projections of life expectancy have been supported by evidence of a falling risk of death from major diseases of old age and by the apparent effects of substances like the human growth hormone (GH) on some manifestations of aging. (The latter results have been wrongly interpreted by the proponents of extreme forecasts of life expectancy as a reversal of aging. However, the benefits disappear once GH treatment is stopped; there is even some evidence from animal models to suggest that GH has a life-shortening effect.) In short, there is no theoretical or scientific evidence to support the claims of anticipated dramatic increases in human life expectancy based on existing scientific knowledge.

Conclusion

Questions about the biology of aging and the average longevity of populations have always been of great fascination to scientists and the lay public. The ongoing research of gerontologists from a broad range of scientific disciplines has, in the early twenty-first century, produced a more complete understanding of the underlying biological forces that contribute to aging and the duration of life. Moreover, scientists have succeeded in experimentally extending the lifespan of several non-human organisms, leading some to believe it is only a matter of time before the same will be done for humans.

The significant advances that have been made in understanding the biology of aging are rarely incorporated into the assumptions governing estimates of future longevity. This may have the effect of making contemporary demographic forecasts of human life expectancy overly optimistic—that is, unless advances in the biomedical sciences proceed at a faster pace than in recent decades.

See also: *Biodemography; Biology, Population; Evolutionary Demography; Gompertz, Benjamin; Life Span; Oldest Old.*

BIBLIOGRAPHY

Bourgeois-Pichat, Jean. 1978. "Future Outlook for Mortality Decline in the World." *Population Bulletin of the United Nations* 11: 12–41.

Carnes, Bruce A., and S. Jay Olshansky. 1993. "Evolutionary Perspectives on Human Senescence." *Population and Development Review* 19(4): 793–806.

———. 1997. "A Biologically Motivated Partitioning of Mortality." *Experimental Gerontology* 32: 615–631.

Carnes, Bruce A., S. Jay Olshansky, and D. Grahn. 1996. "Continuing the Search for a Law of Mortality." *Population and Development Review* 22(2): 231–264.

Cassel, Christine K., H. J. Cohen, E. B. Larson, et al., eds. 2002. *Geriatric Medicine.* New York: Springer.

Chopra, Deepak. 2001. *Grow Younger, Live Longer: 10 Steps to Reverse Aging.* New York: Harmony Books.

de Grey A. D. N. J., B. N. Ames, J. K. Andersen, et al. 2002. "Stock G. Time to Talk SENS: Critiquing the Immutability of Human Aging." *Annals New York Academy of Science* No. 959.

Deevey, E. S. Jr. 1947. "Life Tables for Natural Populations of Animals." *Quarterly Review of Biology* 22: 283–314.

Finch, C. E., M. C. Pike, M. Witten, 1990. "Slow Mortality Rate Accelerations During Aging in Some Animals Approximate That of Humans." *Science* 24: 902–905.

Fossel, M. 1997. *Reversing Human Aging.* New York: Quill Publishing.

Gruman, G. J. 1966. "A History of Ideas About the Prolongation of Life." *Transactions of the American Philosophical Society* 56(9): 1–102.

Johnson T. E. 1990. "Increased Life Span of Age-1 Mutants in Caenorhabditis elegans and Lower Gompertz Rate of Aging." *Science.* 249: 908–912.

Kannisto, V., J. Lauritsen, A. R. Thatcher, and James Vaupel. 1994. "Reduction in Mortality at Advanced Ages." *Population and Development Review* 20: 793–810.

Klatz, Ronald. 1998. *Grow Young with HgH: The Amazing Medically Proven Plan to Reverse Aging.* New York: Harper Perennial Library.

Le Bourg, E. 2000. "Gerontologists and the Media in a Time of Gerontology Expansion." *Biogerontology* 1: 89–92.

Medawar, Peter B. 1952. *An Unsolved Problem of Biology.* London: Lewis.

Melov S., J. Ravenscroft, S. Malik, et al. 2000. "Extension of Life-Span with Superoxide Dismutase/Catalase Mimetics." *Science* 289: 1,567–1,569.

Miller, Richard. 2002. "Extending Life: Scientific Prospects and Political Obstacles." *The Milbank Quarterly* 80(1): 155–174.

Oeppen, J., and James W. Vaupel. 2002. "Broken Limits to Life Expectancy." *Science* 296: 1,029–1,030.

Olshansky, S. Jay. 1988. "On Forecasting Mortality." *The Milbank Quarterly* 66(3): 482–530.

Olshansky, S. Jay, and Bruce A. Carnes. 1997. "Ever Since Gompertz." *Demography* 34(1): 1–15.

Olshansky, S. Jay, Bruce A. Carnes, Christine Cassel. 1990. "In Search of Methuselah: Estimating the Upper Limits to Human Longevity." *Science* 250: 634–640.

Olshansky, S. Jay, Bruce A. Carnes, and A. Désesquelles. 2001. "Prospects for Human Longevity." *Science* 291(5508): 1,491–1,492.

Olshansky, S. Jay, Bruce A. Carnes, and R. Butler. 2001. "If Humans Were Built to Last." *Scientific American* (March).

Olshansky, S. Jay, L. Hayflick, and Bruce A. Carnes. 2002. "Position Statement on Human Aging." *Scientific American* (June).

Roizen, Michael F. 1999. *Real Age: Are You As Young As You Can Be?* New York: Cliff Street Books.

Rose, M. R. 1984. "Laboratory Evolution of Postponed Senescence in *Drosophila melanogaster.*" *Evolution* 38: 1,004–1,010.

Vaupel, James W., and A. E. Gowan. 1986. "Passage to Methuselah: Some Demographic Consequences of Continued Progress Against Mortality." *American Journal of Public Health* 76: 430–433.

Wachter, Kenneth W., and C. E. Finch, ed. 1997. *Between Zeus and the Salmon: The Biodemography of Longevity.* Washington, D.C.: National Academy Press.

Williams, George C. 1957. "Pleiotropy, Natural Selection, and the Evolution of Senescence." *Evolution* 11: 298–311.

S. Jay Olshansky
Bruce A. Carnes

AGING OF POPULATION

The aging of population (also known as demographic aging and population aging) is a term that is used to describe shifts in the age distribution (age structure) of a population toward people of older ages. A direct consequence of the ongoing global fertility transition (decline) and of mortality decline among people of older ages, population aging is expected to be among the most prominent global demographic trends of the twenty-first century. Population aging is progressing rapidly in many industrialized countries, but developing countries whose fertility declines began relatively early also are experiencing rapid increases in the proportion of elderly people. This pattern is expected to continue, eventually affecting the entire world.

Population aging has many important socioeconomic and health consequences, including an increase in the old-age dependency ratio. It presents challenges for public health (in particular, the increasing burden of health care costs on national budgets) as well as for economic development (such as the shrinking and aging of the labor force and the nonviability of pay-as-you-go social security systems).

Defining and Measuring

Because the study of population aging often is driven by concern about the burden it imposes on retirement systems, the aging of population often is measured by increases in the percentage of people in the retirement ages. The definition of retirement ages varies, but a typical lower cutoff number is 65 years. A society is considered relatively old when the proportion of the population age 65 and over exceeds 8 to 10 percent. By this standard the proportion of elderly people in the United States was 12.6 percent in 2000, compared with only 4.1 percent in 1900; it is projected to increase to 20 percent by the year 2030.

A related measure of population aging is the elderly dependency ratio (EDR): the number of individuals of retirement age divided by the number of those of working age. For convenience working age may be assumed to start at 15 years, although increasing proportions of individuals pursue their education beyond that age, remaining financially dependent (on the state or, increasingly, their parents) or borrowing against their own future incomes. The ratio of the elderly dependent population to the economically active (working) population also is known as old-age dependency ratio, age-dependency ratio, or elderly dependency burden and is used to assess intergenerational transfers, taxation policies, and saving behavior.

Another indicator of the age structure is the aging index (sometimes referred to as the elder–child ratio), which is defined as the number of people age 65 and over per 100 youths under age 15. In 2000 only a few countries (Germany, Greece, Italy, Bulgaria, and Japan) had more elderly persons than youths (that is, an aging index above 100). By 2030, however, the aging index is projected to exceed 100 in all developed countries, and the indexes for several European countries and Japan are expected to exceed 200. In the United States the index was 57 in 2000; by 2030 it is projected to rise to 109. Aging indexes are much lower in developing countries than in the developed world, but the proportional rise in the aging index in developing countries is expected to be greater than that in developed countries.

These indicators of population aging are head-count ratios (HCRs); that is, they simply indicate the number of individuals in large age categories. These indicators fail to take into account the age distribution within the large categories, in particular among the elderly. When the fertility and mortality trends responsible for population aging have been fairly regular over time, population growth is positively correlated with age: The oldest age groups are growing fastest. This implies that if the proportion of the population over age 65 is increasing, within that 65-and-over population the proportion over age 80, for example, is also increasing. Health, financial situation, and consumption patterns may vary greatly between 65-year-olds and 80-year-olds, but this heterogeneity in the elderly population is concealed in simple ratios.

Increasing attention is paid to the "oldest olds" (typically defined as persons age 80 and over), a category that is expanding rapidly. The number of centenarians, a longtime subject of curiosity, is growing even faster: Estimated at 180,000 worldwide in 2000, it could reach 1 million by 2030.

The second class of indicators of population aging include the standard statistical measures of location: the median, mean, and modal ages of the population. The median age—the age at which exactly half the population is older and half younger—is the most widely used indicator. For the year 2000 the median age in the United States was 36 years, a typical value for most developed countries. The median age for Africa was 18 years. Because it is more sensitive to changes at the right-hand tail of the age distribution (the oldest old ages), the mean age of population may be preferred to the median age in studying the dynamics of population aging.

Because population aging refers to changes in the entire age distribution, any single indicator may be insufficient to measure it. The age distribution of a population is often very irregular, showing scars of past events (wars, depressions, etc.), and cannot be described by only one number without a significant loss of information. Changes in the age distribution also may occur in a very irregular fashion over the age range, hence much information would be lost in a single-index summary.

A more adequate approach to describing population aging is through a set of percentiles. Alternatively, a graphical approach may be used that involves analyzing population pyramids. Demographers commonly use population pyramids to describe both age and sex distributions of populations. Youthful populations are represented by pyramids with a broad base of young children and a narrow apex of older people, and older populations are characterized by more uniform numbers of people in the age categories.

Demographic Determinants

To understand the demographic factors that cause population aging, demographers often refer to the *stable population model*. This model assumes that age-specific fertility and mortality rates remain constant over time, resulting in a population with an age distribution that eventually ceases to change: It becomes "stable." Conversely, the model suggests that in a population closed to migration any change in age structure, population aging in particular, can be caused only by changes in fertility and mortality rates.

The influence of changes in fertility rates on population aging may not be obvious at first sight. With everything else held constant, however, a fertility decline reduces the size of the most recent birth cohorts relative to the previous birth cohorts, reducing the size of the youngest age groups relative to that of the older ones.

The effects of changes in mortality rates on population aging appear more intuitive but are in fact ambiguous. Reductions in mortality rates do not necessarily contribute to population aging. More specifically, declines in the mortality rates of infants, children, and persons younger than the population's mean age tend to lower that mean age. Clearly, a reduction of neonatal mortality—death in the first month of life—adds individuals at age zero and thus should lead to the same alleviation of population aging that an increase in childbearing does.

Population aging thus is related to the demographic transition, the processes that lead a society from a demographic regime characterized by high rates of fertility and mortality to one characterized by lower fertility and mortality rates. In the course of this transition, the age structure is subjected to different influences. In the typical sequence the transition begins with successes in preventing infectious and parasitic diseases that most benefit infants and young children. The result is an improvement in life expectancy at birth. Fertility, however, tends to remain unchanged, thus producing large birth cohorts and an expanding proportion of children relative to adults. Other things being equal, this initial decline in mortality generates a younger population age structure.

After initial and sometimes very rapid gains in infant and child mortality have been achieved, further mortality declines increasingly benefit people of older ages and eventually are accompanied by fertility declines. Both changes contribute to a reversal of the early effect of mortality decline on the age structure, and this synergy is known as the double aging process. Most developed countries today are experiencing such a process, but further analysis suggests that their history of declining mortality is the dominant factor in current aging.

Mortality declines continue in these countries: Indeed, the decrease in mortality rates among those age 85 years and over has accelerated since the 1950s. This latest phase of mortality decline, which is concentrated in the older age groups, is becoming an important determinant of population aging, particularly among women.

The rate of population aging may be modulated by migration. Immigration marginally slows population aging (in Canada and Europe, for example) to the extent that immigrants are younger than the population average and have higher fertility than do the native-born. However, emigration of working-age adults accelerates population aging, a phenomenon that can be observed in some Caribbean countries. Population aging in those countries also is accelerated by the immigration of elderly retirees from other countries and the return migration of former emigrants who are above the average population age.

Dynamics

The current level and pace of population aging vary widely by geographic region and usually within regions as well, but virtually all nations were experiencing growth in the number of elderly residents at the beginning of the twenty-first century (for selected regions and countries, see Table 1). The proportion of the world population age 65 and over increased from 5.2 percent in 1950 to 6.9 percent in 2000. In Europe, however, the proportion was 14.7 percent in 2000. The highest proportions used to be found in Northern Europe (e.g., 10.3 percent in Sweden in 1950), but by 2000 they were in Southern Europe (e.g., 18.1 percent in Italy).

The proportions of elderly people are lower outside of Europe, with the notable exception of Japan, where this figure increased from 4.9 percent in 1950 to 17.2 percent in 2000. The age structure of the United States continues to be influenced by the large birth cohorts of the baby boom (people born from 1946 through 1964) who are not yet age 65. The proportion of the elderly population in the United States, which was 12.3 percent in 2000, remains low compared to the average in other developed countries.

Population aging has the following notable features:

1. The most rapid growth occurs in the oldest age groups: the oldest old (80-plus or 85-plus years) and centenarians (100-plus years) in particular. In other words, population aging is becoming "deeper," with a disproportionately rapid accumulation of particularly old and frail people.

2. Population aging is particularly rapid among

women, resulting in "feminization" of population aging (because of lower mortality rates among women). For example, in the United States in the population 65 years and older in 2000 there were 20.6 million women and 14.4 million men, or a ratio of 143 women for every 100 men. The female-to-male ratio increases with age, reaching 245 for persons 85 and over.

3. Another consequence of lower female mortality is the fact that almost half of older (65-plus years) women (45%) in 2000 were widows, living without spousal support.

4. Population aging also causes changes in living arrangements, resulting in increasing numbers of older people living alone (about 30% of all noninstitutionalized older persons in 2000 lived alone in the United States).

5. Because older persons usually have lower income and a higher proportion of them live below the poverty line, population aging is associated with poverty, particularly in developing countries.

Twenty-First Century Projections

Population aging in the future will depend on demographic trends, but most demographers agree that the fertility and mortality changes that would be required to reverse population aging in the coming decades are very unlikely to occur. According to the 2000 United Nations medium population projections, population aging in the first half of the twenty-first century should exceed that of the second half of the twentieth century. For the world as a whole, the elderly (65-plus) will grow from 6.9 percent of the population in 2000 to a projected 19.3 percent in 2050 (Table 1). In other words, the world average would be higher in 2050 than the current world record.

All regions are expected to see an increase, although it should be milder in some regions, such as Africa, where the projected increase is from 3.3 percent in 2000 to 6.9 percent in 2050. However, in Latin America and the Caribbean the increase is projected to be from 5.4 percent in 2000 to 16.9 percent in 2050, higher than the current European average. The projected increase is even more spectacular in China: from 6.9 percent in 2000 to 22.7 percent in 2050.

Although population aging thus is becoming a worldwide phenomenon, the most developed coun-

TABLE 1

Percentage of Population at Ages 65 and Older

Major Area, Region, and Country	Percent		
	1950	2000	2050
World	5.2	6.9	19.3
Africa	3.2	3.3	6.9
Latin America and the Caribbean	3.7	5.4	16.9
China	4.5	6.9	22.7
India	3.3	5.0	14.8
Japan	4.9	17.2	36.4
Europe	8.2	14.7	29.2
Italy	8.3	18.1	35.9
Germany	9.7	16.4	31.0
Sweden	10.3	17.4	30.4
United States	8.3	12.3	21.1

Note: Estimated and projected percentages of the elderly (65 + years) in selected areas, regions, and countries of the world: 1950, 2000, and 2050. ("Medium projection.")

SOURCE: United Nations (2001).

tries probably will continue to be the forerunners. The United Nations projections for 2050 suggest that there will be 29.2 percent of elderly persons in the European population as a whole but more than 30 percent in a number of individual European countries (such as Italy) and perhaps as much as 36.4 percent in Japan. Again, the projected increase appears less dramatic in the United States: from 12.3 percent in 2000 to 21.1 percent in 2050.

There is uncertainty in any projection, but it is important to note that previous population projections underestimated rather than overstated the current pace of population aging. Before the 1980s the process of population aging was considered to be a consequence of fertility decline alone, and it was predicted that the pace of population aging would decrease after stabilization of fertility rates at a low level. The rapid decline in old-age mortality that was observed in developed countries in the last decades of the twentieth century significantly accelerated population aging. At the beginning of the twenty-first century, old-age mortality trends are becoming the key demographic component in projecting the size and composition of the world's future elderly population.

Current and future uncertainties about changing mortality may produce widely divergent projections of the size of tomorrow's elderly population. For example, the U.S. Census Bureau's middle-mortality series projection suggests that in the United States there will be 14.3 million persons age 85 and over in the year 2040, whereas the low-mortality (high life expectancy) series implies 16.8 million. Alternative projections, using assumptions of lower death rates and higher life expectancies, have produced estimates ranging from 23.5 million to 54 million persons age 85 and over in 2040.

Social and Economic Implications

Although population aging represents a success story for humankind (survival to old ages has become commonplace), it also poses profound challenges to public institutions that must adapt to a changing age structure.

The first challenge is associated with the marked increase in the older retired population relative to the shrinking population of working ages, which creates social and political pressures on social support systems. In most developed countries rapid population aging places strong pressure on social security programs. For example, the U.S. social security system may face a profound crisis if radical modifications are not enacted. Cuts in benefits, tax increases, massive borrowing, lower cost-of-living adjustments, later retirement ages, and combinations of these elements are being discussed as the painful policies that may become necessary to sustain pay-as-you-go public retirement programs such as Medicare and Social Security. Privatization and shift to a funded scheme in retirement programs are also considered as potential options to cope with population aging.

Population aging also presents a great challenge for health care systems. As populations age, the prevalence of disability, frailty, and chronic diseases (Alzheimer's disease, cancer, cardiovascular and cerebrovascular diseases, etc.) is expected to increase dramatically. Some experts are concerned that human society may become a "global nursing home" (Eberstadt 1997).

The aging of the population is a global phenomenon that requires international coordination of national and local actions. The United Nations and other international organizations have developed recommendations that are intended to mitigate the adverse consequences of population aging. These recommendations include reorganization of social security systems; changes in labor, immigration, and family policies; promotion of active and healthy lifestyles; and more cooperation between governments in resolving the socioeconomic and political problems posed by population aging.

On the positive side, the health status of older people within a given age group has been improving over time. More recent generations have a lower disease load. Older people can live vigorous and active lives until a much later age than they could in the past and, if encouraged to be productive, can be economic contributors to society. Moreover, current intensive biomedical anti-aging studies may further extend the healthy and productive period of human life in the future.

See also: *Age Structure and Dependency; Fertility, Below-Replacement; Life Span; Mortality Decline; Oldest Old; Second Demographic Transition.*

BIBLIOGRAPHY

Administration on Aging. 2001. *A Profile of Older Americans: 2001.* Washington, D.C.: U.S. Department of Health and Human Services.

De Grey, Aubrey D. N., Leonid Gavrilov, S. Jay Olshansky, L. Stephen Coles, Richard G. Cutler, Michael Fossel, and S. Mitchell Harman. 2002. "Anti-aging Technology and Pseudoscience." *Science* 296: 656–656.

Eberstadt, Nicholas. 1997. "World Population Implosion?" *Public Interest* 129: 3–22.

Gavrilov, Leonid A., and Natalia S. Gavrilova. 1991. *The Biology of Life Span: A Quantitative Approach.* New York: Harwood Academic.

Kinsella, Kevin, and Victoria A. Velkoff. 2001. *An Aging World: 2001.* U.S. Census Bureau, Series P95/01–1. Washington, D.C.: U.S. Government Printing Office.

Lutz, Wolfgang, Warren Sanderson, and Sergei Scherbow. 2001. "The End of World Population Growth." *Nature* 412: 543–545.

Preston, Samuel H., Christine Himes, and Mitchell Eggers. 1989. "Demographic Conditions Responsible for Population Aging." *Demography* 26: 691–704.

Preston Samuel H., Patrick Heuveline, and Michel Guillot. 2001. *Demography: Measuring and Modeling Population Processes.* Oxford: Blackwell.

United Nations. 2001. *World Population Prospects: The 2000 Revision.* New York: United Nations.

LEONID A. GAVRILOV
PATRICK HEUVELINE

AIDS

Acquired Immune Deficiency Syndrome (AIDS) was first noticed and described in the United States in 1981, initially in homosexual men. Further cases in hemophiliac patients were reported in 1982. The publication of accounts of this new disease in the newsletter *Morbidity and Mortality Weekly Reports* triggered responses from physicians in other developed countries who had recently come across similar constellations of symptoms, which indicated a breakdown of the immune system in individuals who had no known exposure to radiation or immunosuppressant drugs.

Origins of HIV

The Human Immunodeficiency Virus (HIV) that is the cause of AIDS was first isolated by Luc Montagnier at the Pasteur Institute in Paris in 1983. HIV is a retrovirus, which means that it stores its genetic information as RNA, stimulating the production of DNA copies of its genome when it enters a host cell. A systematic testing of stored serological samples carried out in the late 1990s in a search for the origins of this disease revealed the earliest documented occurrence of HIV dating from 1959. This was in a blood sample taken from a male subject "L70," one of a number of hospital patients from Western and Central Congo seen in Leopoldville in that year.

HIV is believed to have arisen as a result of ancestral viruses crossing the species barrier, from chimpanzees and monkeys to man. Such crossovers are believed to have occurred at least twice, with the more virulent strain, HIV-1, originating from a simian immunodeficiency virus (SIV) of chimpanzees, and HIV-2 coming from an SIV usually found in sooty mangabey monkeys. Modeling studies based on the genetic diversity of the HIV viruses, reported by B. Korber and colleagues, estimate that the species crossover occurred between 1920 and 1940. It is

believed that the virus was present in isolated human populations in rural Central Africa from this time, and began to spread more widely in the 1960s and 1970s, as a result of wars, tourism, and social changes linked to modernization, which all contributed to increased population mobility.

In the 1980s and 1990s HIV/AIDS was identified in every region of the world. UNAIDS, the Joint United Nations Programme on HIV/AIDS, has estimated that 42 million adults and children worldwide were infected with HIV by the end of 2002. Of this number 29 million (70%) were living in sub-Saharan Africa. Table 1 shows the estimated numbers of infected persons in each of the world's major regions at the end of 2002.

Etiology and Disease Progression

HIV spreads by direct contact through body fluids. This may occur during sexual intercourse, or as a result of mother-to-child transmission during pregnancy, delivery, or breastfeeding. The virus may also be transferred in blood used for transfusions, or in blood products, such as the clotting factor supplied to hemophiliacs. Finally, it can be spread by unsterilized hypodermic needles and surgical instruments, so outbreaks among injectable drug users (IDU) are common where injecting equipment is shared. In the 1990s it was speculated that the species transfer may have occurred as a result of live polio vaccine being cultivated in infected primate livers, but this theory has been discounted, as no traces of the virus were found in stored vaccine samples. However, mass vaccination campaigns could have helped to spread the virus in the 1960s, if needles were reused during the campaigns, or left behind and subsequently reused in poorly equipped hospitals. The virus is very fragile: it cannot survive outside of the human host cell and cannot be spread by insect bites, by casual touching, or by sharing of food utensils or clothes.

Both HIV-1 and HIV-2 target specific cells of the immune system: the T-cells, which are the human body's main immunological defense against infection. Primary infection with HIV in an adult usually results in rapid multiplication of the virus in the lymph system, and a rapid decline in T-cells. An immune response is usually provoked within four to six weeks, and after this time antibodies to HIV can be detected in the blood. The disease then enters a latent phase, which has a median duration of around

TABLE 1

Selected Characteristics of the HIV/AIDS Epidemic, by World Region, End of 2002

	Epidemic started	Adults & children living with HIV/AIDS	Adults & children newly infected with HIV	Adult prevalence rate*(%)	Percent of HIV positive adults who are women	Main modes of transmission for adults living with HIV/AIDS**
Sub-Saharan Africa	late '70s early '80s	29.4 million	3.5 million	8.8	58	Hetero
North Africa and Middle East	late '80s	550,000	83,000	0.3	55	Hetero, IDU
South and South-East Asia	late '80s	6.0 million	700,000	0.6	36	Hetero, IDU
East Asia and Pacific	late '80s	1.2 million	270,000	0.1	24	IDU, Hetero, MSM
Latin America	late '70s early 80's	1.5 million	150,000	0.6	30	MSM, IDU, Hetero
Caribbean	late '70s early 80's	440,000	60,000	2.4	50	Hetero, MSM
Eastern Europe and Central Asia	early '90s	1.2 million	250,000	0.6	27	IDU
Western Europe	late '70s early '80s	570,000	30,000	0.3	25	MSM, IDU
North America	late '70s early '80s	980,000	45,000	0.6	20	MSM, IDU, Hetero
Australia and New Zealand	late '70s early '80s	15,000	500	0.1	7	MSM
Total		**42 million**	**5 million**	**1.2**	**50**	

*The proportion of adults aged 15 to 49 living with HIV/AIDS
**Hetero - heterosexual transmission; IDU - transmission through injecting drug use; MSM - sexual transmission among men who have sex with men

SOURCE: UNAIDS (2002a).

nine years in the absence of treatment in developing and developed countries alike. During this latent phase the number of T-cells declines steadily. Eventually, the immune system is so compromised that it is no longer able to respond adequately to a range of infections and cancers, such as Kaposi's sarcoma, that usually pose little threat to healthy individuals. Once such clinical manifestations of AIDS occur, death follows rapidly: in the studies reviewed by J. T. Boerma and colleagues, survival times of five to nine months were reported in developing countries, 9 to 26 months in developed countries.

In infants, the disease usually progresses much more rapidly, because the immature immune system cannot respond adequately in the primary infection phase. Median survival time of infected infants in the absence of treatment is around two years.

HIV mutates rapidly both within an infected individual and across individuals as the infection spreads in a population. The resulting diversity of forms makes it difficult to develop an effective vaccine, and ensures the rapid emergence of drug resistant forms.

Epidemiological Evidence

On a national basis, AIDS epidemics are characterized as generalized if HIV prevalence exceeds 1 percent in the adult population aged 15–49. In developing countries, almost all the evidence for HIV prevalence levels in the general population comes from the anonymous screening of blood samples obtained from pregnant women in antenatal clinics. As a consequence there is very little direct evidence on HIV prevalence among men. Subject to the resulting uncertainties in assessing prevalence levels, UNAIDS estimates that only 5 of the 45 countries of sub-Saharan Africa did not have generalized epidemics by 2000. Adult prevalence had already reached over 20 percent in Southern Africa, and lay between 10 percent and 20 percent in most of Eastern and Central Africa. Western African countries, especially those where HIV-2 is the predominant strain, generally had lower rates, between 2 percent and 5 percent. In the first years of the twenty-first century, HIV prevalence was either stagnant or increasing all over Africa, except for Uganda, where the epidemic appeared to have passed a turning point, with a decline in prevalence from 14 percent in the early 1990s to around 8 percent at the end of the decade.

The other region with a generalized epidemic is the Caribbean, where adult prevalence was over 1 percent by 2001 in nine countries. Southeast Asia as a whole had a prevalence of 0.6 percent in 2001, but in three countries, Cambodia, Myanmar, and Thailand, adult prevalence was over 1 percent, though in Thailand a strong downward trend was evident by this time in the general population. The future course of the epidemic in Asia will be largely determined by trends in the most populous countries, India and China, in both of which HIV infection is concentrated in the high-risk groups (sex workers and IDU) and in particular regions. (Six states in India recorded prevalence levels over 1 percent in 2001; Yunan province in China recorded an increase from 6 percent to 10 percent between 2000 and 2001 in prevalence among sex workers.)

The sub-populations most strongly affected by the epidemic vary widely by region, as shown in Table 1. In high-income industrialized countries by 2002, most of the persons living with HIV were men who had sex with men (MSM) or IDU. Eastern Europe and Central Asia have epidemics that are concentrated among IDU—but these are among the fastest growing epidemics in populations that are difficult to monitor.

There is evidence, summarized by M. Caraël and K. Holmes, that male circumcision is an important risk reduction factor. Consistent condom use has been shown to be effective in reducing sexual transmission in MSM epidemics in industrialized countries. Paradoxically, it does not emerge as a protective factor in community studies in Africa since condoms are mainly used by those who are already infected or believe themselves to be at very high risk. Co-infection with other sexually transmitted diseases has been found to significantly enhance the transmission of HIV.

Population mobility is likely to have been an important factor in the initial spread of HIV, and is implicated in the rapid spread of HIV in Southern African countries in the late 1990s. These countries had a tradition of male labor migration to mines and commercial farming estates that encouraged the formation of temporary partnerships and the growth of commercial sex.

Demographic Impacts of AIDS in Africa

In the epidemics driven by MSM or IDU, the number of males infected exceeds that of females by a factor of two to ten. However, in heterosexually spread epidemics, the number of infected females generally exceeds that of infected males. Several factors account for this: males tend to have more sexual partners than females; HIV transmission from male to female is more efficient than from female to male; and most of all, there are more females than males at risk of infection because of the age difference between sexual partners and the steeply tapering youthful age distribution.

In Africa, where generalized epidemics began in the 1980s, strong evidence of an impact on national mortality trends was detected in the 1990s. Almost all African countries lack national vital registration systems, so cause of death data are not available, and most of the evidence for trends in age-specific mortality rates comes from census and survey data, either from direct questions about household deaths in the year preceding the survey, or indirect enquiries about the survival of relatives. Griffith Feeney has used mortality data from a variety of secondary sources to show that adult mortality in Zimbabwe more than doubled between 1982 and 1997, spanning the time when HIV prevalence rose from virtually zero to almost 30 percent.

In the context of the HIV epidemic, the most widely used indirect estimation techniques, such as the child survival and orphanhood methods, yield mortality estimates that are biased downward, because of the high correlation between the survival of parents and children. Reports of household deaths may also be incomplete as households tend to dissolve upon the death of the head. However, using new analytical techniques based on reported survival of siblings, Ian Timaeus has demonstrated significant rises in adult mortality in the most severely affected countries. For example, five Eastern and Southern African countries that included sibling survival questions in Demographic and Health Survey rounds in the late 1990s recorded large increases in the probability of dying between age 15 and age 60: from an average of 28 percent, five years before the survey, to 45 percent in the survey year. Estimated HIV prevalence at the time of the surveys in these countries averaged 24 percent. By contrast, in five West African countries, with an average HIV prevalence of 2 percent, similar analyses of DHS sibling survival data collected in the 1990s indicated a continuing modest improvement in this index of adult mortality, from 26 percent to 22 percent over a similar 5-year period.

The most compelling evidence about the scale of the impact on mortality comes from longitudinal community based studies, in which repeated serological testing is accompanied by demographic surveillance. Studies of this type were established in East African countries in the early 1990s and subsequently in Southern Africa. They have shown that mortality rates among HIV infected adults are 10 to 15 times the rates observed among uninfected individuals. The relative risk of mortality among HIV-positive individuals has been shown to increase with epidemic maturity, as the balance between individuals who were recently infected and those who have been living with the disease for some time shifts in favor of the latter, who are closer to developing full-blown AIDS. Duration of survival post-infection in adults is strongly related to age at infection, with much quicker progression to AIDS among those infected at a later age.

Community-based studies rarely provide direct comparisons of mortality in HIV-infected and uninfected children, because of the problems of ascertaining the HIV status of a newborn infant. Maternal HIV antibodies cross the placental barrier much more readily than the virus itself, and the commonly available, relatively inexpensive serological tests detect the presence of antibodies rather than virus. However, such studies have also shown that the mortality among children of HIV-infected mothers is between 2.5 and 4 times that observed among children of uninfected mothers. Hospital-based studies (reported by L. Kuhn and Z. A. Stein) have shown that in the absence of antiretroviral therapy, mother-to-child transmission of the virus occurs in about 30 percent of cases, suggesting that mortality rates for HIV infected children could be 5 to 10 times the rates observed among uninfected children.

Although there is strong evidence on the scale of excess mortality among HIV infected persons, considerable uncertainty remains concerning the number and distribution of deaths due to HIV. Official estimates of historical and current deaths in the worst affected countries are based on models fitted to incomplete time series of prevalence data from a limited number of sentinel sites that perform anonymous tests on pregnant women. The predominantly urban character of sentinel clinics means that they tend to be based in communities with relatively high HIV prevalence.

HIV also has an impact on fertility, with HIV-positive women experiencing significantly lower fertility rates than uninfected women. Biological explanations for this effect include increased fetal losses and stillbirths, increased menstrual irregularities and decreased spermatogenesis in male partners. Social mechanisms are probably even more important, as women who are suspected of being HIV-positive will find it harder to remarry following widowhood and divorce, both of which occur more frequently among the HIV positive. Community-based studies have shown that the overall reduction in fertility in HIV-positive women can range from 10 percent to 40 percent, with older HIV positive women experiencing proportionately larger reductions. Since HIV lowers fertility, estimates of HIV prevalence based on anonymous surveillance of pregnant women attending prenatal clinics tend to underestimate HIV prevalence among women in the community.

Evidence of an impact of HIV on the population age structure is harder to find, because of countervailing demographic tendencies. The increased mortality due to HIV slows population growth, which would tend to make the population structure older. However, since adults are disproportionately affected compared to children, their early death tends to make the age structure younger. At a subnational level, internal migration, which is very high among young adults, often masks or exacerbates the impact on the age structure.

In the worst-affected countries of Southern Africa, where HIV prevalence was estimated to have passed 20 percent by the year 2000 (Botswana, Lesotho, Malawi, Namibia, South Africa, Swaziland, Zambia, and Zimbabwe), life expectancy is projected to fall below 40 years. These countries may well experience periods of negative population growth in the first few decades of the twenty-first century. This is particularly likely to occur in populations that have already experienced significant fertility declines by the time the HIV epidemic took hold. Estimates and projections of the effect on population size in the worst-affected countries, made by the United Nations Population Division, are shown in Figure 1. South Africa is an example of a country in which AIDS is likely to cause negative population growth—as seen in the projections in Figure 2.

Socioeconomic Consequences

It has been estimated (by Alan Whiteside and Clem Sunter) that AIDS has caused annual per capita economic growth to fall by 0.5 to 1.2 percentage points in about half the countries of sub-Saharan Africa. Absenteeism and illness in the work force mean that employers face increasing costs in recruitment, training, insurance, and sick pay.

A 2001 report from the UN Food and Agriculture Organization estimates that 7 million farm workers have died from AIDS-related causes since 1985, and 16 million more are expected to die by 2020, with a consequent decrease in agricultural production. Children of families in which the adults are too sick to work are often taken out of school to work on family farms and to care for their relatives, and orphans tend to have low school attendance rates because the families who care for them cannot afford an extra set of school fees. Teachers are disproportionately affected by AIDS—in 1999, according to UNAIDS, over 15,000 teachers died in sub-Saharan Africa. Because of the age profile of AIDS deaths, it is the most productive part of the labor force that will be lost, and families will lose parents who have not yet finished bringing up their children.

The health sector has come under severe stress in many African countries. Public expenditure surveys in 1997 showed that in 7 out of 16 countries health spending on AIDS exceeded 2 percent of GDP, and accounted for between 25 percent and 70 percent of the total public health expenditure. This generally represents spending on treatment of opportunistic infections, since most African countries cannot afford antiretroviral therapy, except possibly in the one-off doses that are used at delivery to prevent mother-to-child transmission.

Policy Responses

UNAIDS has estimated that US$10 billion per year will be needed in low- and middle-income countries to combat AIDS in the first decade of the twenty-first century.

Official silence and outright denial have paralyzed efforts to control the epidemic in many countries. Uganda, one of the few countries to admit the problem and encourage public discussion early on, is the only African country in which there is clear evidence of a decline in prevalence. Policy responses that have been advocated include education to raise awareness and promote behavioral change; encour-

FIGURE 1

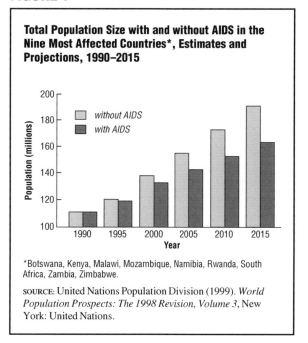

Total Population Size with and without AIDS in the Nine Most Affected Countries*, Estimates and Projections, 1990–2015

*Botswana, Kenya, Malawi, Mozambique, Namibia, Rwanda, South Africa, Zambia, Zimbabwe.

SOURCE: United Nations Population Division (1999). *World Population Prospects: The 1998 Revision, Volume 3*, New York: United Nations.

agement of voluntary counseling and testing; the promotion and social marketing of condoms and the treatment of other STDs to lower transmission probabilities. Thailand is also widely recognized as a success story in the fight against AIDS; there, the key strategy was the 100 percent condom use campaign in brothels. Thailand has also recorded a marked decrease in the proportion of men having sex with commercial sex workers.

Treatment with antiretrovirals is in great demand by people suffering with HIV, but is very expensive and unlikely to do much to stem the spread of the epidemic in the poorest countries of sub-Saharan Africa. Vaccines and microbicides offer more hope as preventive strategies, but major research efforts are still needed in the development of these medical interventions. Antiretroviral drugs, such as nevirapine, have had proven success when administered in single doses to pregnant women and their newborn infants, but since such treatment does not affect disease progression in mothers, they cannot slow the overall development of the epidemic, or the growth in the number of AIDS orphans.

The demographic consequences of the AIDS epidemic are relatively easy to project if age and sex specific infection rates can be accurately forecast. Unfortunately, there is little agreement among epidemiologists on robust and widely applicable meth-

FIGURE 2

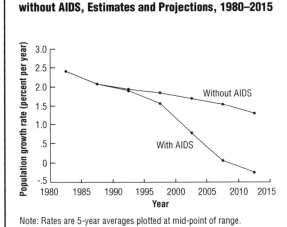

South Africa: Population Growth Rate with and without AIDS, Estimates and Projections, 1980–2015

Note: Rates are 5-year averages plotted at mid-point of range.

SOURCE: United Nations Population Division (2001). *World Population Prospects: The 2000 Revision, Volume 1.* New York: United Nations.

ods for projecting long-term trends in infection, and the data requirements for the more sophisticated projection tools make them unsuitable for most countries in sub-Saharan Africa. Relatively simple models based on fitting parametric curves to observed time series of HIV prevalence in antenatal clinics have been used successfully by UNAIDS for short-term projections. Because these simple models are not structured by sex and age, they are of limited use in making long-term demographic projections. In the absence of effective interventions, most analysts agree that a continuation of the trends observed in the late 1990s could lead to adult prevalence levels of over 25 percent in many African countries in the first decade of the twenty-first century.

See also: *Black Death; Diseases, Infectious; Emerging Infectious Diseases; Epidemics; Mortality Reversals.*

BIBLIOGRAPHY

Boerma, J. T., A. J. Nunn, and J. A. Whitworth. 1998. "Mortality Impact of the AIDS Epidemic: Evidence from Community Studies in Less Developed Countries." In *Demographic Impact of AIDS,* ed. M. Caraël and B. Scwartlander. *AIDS* 12 (Supplement 1): 3–14.

Caraël, M., and K. Holmes, eds. 2001. "The Multicentre Study of Factors Determining the Different Prevalences of HIV in Sub-Saharan Africa." *AIDS* 15 (Supplement 4): 1–132.

Collaborative Group on AIDS Incubation and Survival including the Cascade EU Concerted Action. 2000. "Time from HIV-1 Seroconversion to AIDS and Death before Widespread Use of Highly-active Antiretroviral Therapy: A Collaborative Re-analysis." *Lancet* 355: 1,131–1,137.

Feeney, Griffith. 2001. "The impact of HIV/AIDS on Adult Mortality in Zimbabwe." *Population and Development Review* 27: 771–780.

Food and Agriculture Organization, Committee on World Food Security. 2001. *The Impact of HIV/AIDS on Food Security.* Rome: Food and Agriculture Organization.

Korber, B., B. Gaschen, K. Yusim, R. Thakallapally, C. Kesmir, and V. Deours. 2001. "Evolutionary and Immunological Implications of Contemporary HIV-1 Variation." In *The Changing Face of HIV and AIDS,* special issue of *British Medical Bulletin,* ed. Robin A. Weiss, Michael W. Adler, and Sarah L. Rowland-Jones. Oxford: Oxford University Press.

Kuhn, L., and Z. A. Stein. 1995. "Mother-to-Infant HIV Transmission: Timing, Risk Factors and Prevention." *Paediatric and Perinatal Epidemiology* 9: 1–29.

Marx, P. A., P. G. Alcabes, and E. Drucker. 2001. "Serial Human Passage of Simian Immunodeficiency Virus by Unsterile Injections and the Emergence of Epidemic Human Immunodeficiency Virus in Africa." *Philosophical Transactions of the Royal Society of London, Series B* 356(1410): 911–920.

Morgan D., C. Mahe, B. Mayanja, J. M. Okongo, R. Lubega, and J. A. G. Whitworth. 2002. "HIV-1 Infection in Rural Africa: Is There a Difference in Median Time to AIDS and Survival Compared with that in Industrialized Countries?" *AIDS* 16: 597–603.

Morgan, D., and J. A. G. Whitworth. 2001. "The Natural History of HIV-1 Infection in Africa." *Nature Medicine* 7(2): 143–145.

Timæus, Ian. 1998. "Impact of the HIV Epidemic on Mortality in Sub-Saharan Africa: Evidence from National Surveys and Censuses." In *Demographic Impact of AIDS,* ed. M. Caraël and B. Scwartlander. *AIDS* 12(Supplement 1): 15–27.

UNAIDS. 2002a. *AIDS Epidemic Update—December 2002.* Geneva: UNAIDS.

UNAIDS. 2002b. Report on the Global HIV/AIDS Epidemic 2002. Geneva: UNAIDS.

UNAIDS. 2002c. "Improved Methods and Assumptions for Estimation and Projection of HIV/AIDS Epidemics: Recommendations of the UN-AIDS Reference Group on HIV/AIDS Estimates, Modelling, and Projections." *AIDS* 16(Special Issue): W1–W14.

Whiteside, Alan, and Clem Sunter. 2000. *AIDS, the Challenge to South Africa.* Cape Town, South Africa: Human & Rouseau Tafelberg.

Zaba, Basia, and Simon Gregson. 1998. "Measuring the Impact of HIV on Fertility in Africa." In *Demographic Impact of AIDS*, ed. M. Caraël and B. Scwartlander. *AIDS* 12(Supplement 1): 41–50.

INTERNET RESOURCE.

UNAIDS. 2003. "HIV/AIDS Information and Data." <http://www.unaids.org/hivaidsinfo/>.

Basia Zaba

ALCOHOL, HEALTH EFFECTS OF

In the year 2000, total per capita alcohol consumption was 9.5 liters in the countries in the European Union, 7.7 liters in Australasia, 7.0 liters in Eastern Europe, 6.7 liters in North America, 4.1 liters in Latin America, and 2.3 liters in the rest of the world. Compared with the figures for 1990, consumption decreased in the richer regions and increased in the poorer regions. These estimates are based on 58 countries with reliable data. Alcohol from home production and other non-registered sources is not included, although these can be important sources of alcohol in poor countries. Although wide differences exist, there is a general trend toward homogenization of per capita alcohol consumption and of the relative shares of beer, wine, and spirits worldwide.

Distribution of Alcohol Consumption

The distribution of alcohol consumption in a population is typically skewed, with a minority (e.g., 10%) accounting for the bulk (e.g., 50%) of the total consumption. On average men consume much more alcohol than women do. By age, consumption peaks among young adults and then gradually decreases, except among alcoholics, who usually increase their consumption with age (progressively or with fluctuations). Some manage to become ex-drinkers or moderate drinkers. The proportion of abstainers varies greatly by country, ranging from as low as about 10 percent in countries with high alcohol consumption to practically 100 percent in countries that shun alcohol.

Effects on Health and Mortality

Alcohol intake influences the risk of death, disease, injuries, and mental illness. In general populations the relationship between alcohol intake and total mortality is curvilinear. Abstainers have slightly higher mortality than do moderate drinkers, and heavy drinkers have much higher mortality than do the other two groups. On average mortality among drinkers equals that among abstainers at the level of 40 grams per day of alcohol for men and 20 grams per day for women. (One drink contains approximately 12 grams of alcohol.) The relationship between alcohol intake and the overall occurrence of diseases, hospital admissions, and leaves of absence is also curvilinear.

Mortality among alcoholics after treatment is from two to six times the level of the general population. Such death rates shorten the lifespan of this group by 6 to 18 years. Excess mortality is due partly to tobacco use and unhealthy living habits.

Heavy alcohol intake increases strongly the incidence of liver cirrhosis, respiratory and gastrointestinal tract cancer, hemorrhagic stroke, hypertension, and injuries. Less strong but clear increases can be found for chronic pancreatitis and cancers of the liver, colon, and rectum. Heavy drinking also causes cardiomyopathy, peripheral neuropathy, myopathy, and hepatitis. Alcohol drinking is not related to the incidence of ischemic stroke and peptic or duodenal ulcers.

Alcohol weakens sensorimotor coordination. Thus, alcohol use, especially at levels producing intoxication, increases the risk of accidents, violence, and self-harm. The probability of becoming involved in a serious or fatal traffic accident increases with rising blood alcohol concentration. Some but not all studies show an exponential increase in that risk.

Several studies have found an increased risk of (female) breast cancer among drinkers compared with abstainers, but the low relative risk and the multitude of potential confounding factors make it difficult to draw any firm conclusions about causality.

The risk of spontaneous abortion, intrauterine growth retardation, premature birth, and fetal alcohol syndrome is increased by alcohol intake. The available data are not sufficient to indicate whether there is a safe limit for cognitive developmental deficits. The only absolutely safe course is to abstain during pregnancy.

Research strongly supports the view that moderate alcohol intake decreases the risk of coronary heart disease. Compared with abstainers, the lowest relative risk of coronary heart disease is 22 percent lower at the level of consumption of 29 grams per day, according to high-quality studies. Most of the decrease in coronary heart disease risk is due to an increase in high-density lipoprotein (HDL) cholesterol. A moderate intake of alcohol seems to decrease the risk of dementia, diabetes, and gallstones. Blood pressure is likely to increase with an alcohol intake exceeding 25 grams per day. Heavy drinkers show increased atherosclerosis, an increased risk of tachyarrhythmias, and decreased variability of heart rhythm.

Moderate drinkers have better emotional and social adjustment and fewer psychiatric hospital admissions than abstainers. These differences may, however, be due to the inclusion of people with mental problems in the group of abstainers. Alcohol is likely to be harmful for the mentally ill because it may aggravate their symptoms and interfere with drug treatment.

Some observations suggest that wine may be especially beneficial for health, but others disagree. The differences in health effects between alcohol consumed as beer, wine, and spirits might be explained by varying drinking patterns related to different beverages.

No definite safe or optimal levels of alcohol intake can be ascertained because self-reports of alcohol intake tend to be underestimates. Potential benefits and harm from alcohol intake vary between individuals, depending on their drinking patterns and other risk factors. For a moderate intake level and pattern of use, the evidence suggests that the health benefits outweigh the risks.

See also: *Diseases, Chronic and Degenerative; Tobacco-Related Mortality.*

BIBLIOGRAPHY

Bruun, Kettil, Griffith Edwards, Martti Lumio, Klaus Mäkelä, Lynn Pan, Robert E. Popham, Robin Room, Wolfgang Schmidt, Ole-Jorgen Skog, Pekka Sulkunen, and Esa Österberg. 1975. *Alcohol Control Policies in Public Health Perspective*, Vol. 25. Forssa: Finnish Foundation for Alcohol Studies.

Chick, Jonathan. 1999. "Can Light or Moderate Drinking Benefit Mental Health?" *European Addiction Research* 5(2): 74–81.

Corrao, Giovanni, Vincenzo Bagnardi, Antonella Zambon, and Sarino Arico. 1999. "Exploring the Dose-response Relationship between Alcohol Consumption and the Risk of Several Alcohol-related Conditions: A Meta-analysis." *Addiction* 94(10): 1551–1573.

Corrao, Giovanni, Luca Rubbiati, Vincenzo Bagnardi, Antonella Zambon, and Kari Poikolainen. 2000. "Alcohol and Coronary Heart Disease: A Meta-analysis." *Addiction* 95(10): 1,505–1,523.

Poikolainen, Kari. 1996. "Alcohol and Overall Health Outcomes." *Annals of Medicine* 28(5): 381–384.

Productschap. 2002. *World Drink Trends 2002*. Schiedam, Netherlands: Productschap voor Gedistilleerde Dranken.

Rimm, Eric B., Paige Williams, Kerry Fosher, Michael Criqui, and Meir J. Stampfer. 1999. "Moderate Alcohol Intake and Lower Risk of Coronary Heart Disease: Meta-analysis of Effects on Lipids and Haemostatic Factors." *British Medical Journal* 319(7224): 1,523–1,528.

KARI POIKOLAINEN

ANCIENT WORLD, DEMOGRAPHY OF

The study of classical antiquity traditionally has been concerned with the history of Greek and Roman civilization and its sphere of influence in the Mediterranean and beyond from the early first millennium B.C.E. to the seventh century C.E. and covers sociopolitical formations that range from Greek city-states to the Roman Empire. Owing to the paucity of quantifiable evidence, demographic conditions in the ancient world are at best sporadically documented and can be reconstructed only in the most basic terms. Tombstone inscriptions, skeletal remains, and literary accounts are the most widely available sources of demographic information. In addition several hundred census returns, birth certificates, and death declarations from Greco-Roman Egypt have survived on papyrus scrolls.

Mortality

Ancient populations were characterized by high birth rates and death rates. Mean life expectancy at birth is conventionally put in a range from 20 to 30 years, although these limits may have differed in particularly hazardous (e.g., malarial) or healthy (e.g., high-altitude) environments. Age records from some 300 census returns from Roman Egypt (first to third centuries C.E.) have been used to reconstruct an age distribution that is consistent with model life tables that suggest a mean life expectancy at birth of around 22 to 25 years. Corroborating evidence has been derived from select cemetery populations, a Roman schedule used to calculate annuities known as "Ulpian's Life Table," and tombstones in Roman North Africa. Literary texts suggest comparably low levels of life expectancy even among the Roman elite. However, demographic readings of most of these sources remain controversial: Age records in epitaphs are distorted by age and gender preferences, and skeletal samples may not mirror the age structure of actual past populations. An alternative reading of the Egyptian census data points to significant differences between urban and rural populations, with particularly high attrition rates in large cities.

Local mortality levels were determined largely by the prevalence of endemic diseases. Seasonal mortality patterns that are discernible in large samples of tombstones reveal great regional diversity but hint only vaguely at the nature of the underlying disease environment. Attested seasonal fluctuation in adult death rates is generally more pronounced than is the case in more recent pre-modern Mediterranean populations and suggests unusually high vulnerability to infectious diseases past childhood and correspondingly high levels of overall morbidity and mortality.

The principal causes of death defy quantification but are amply documented in ancient medical literature and other textual sources: Next to ubiquitous gastrointestinal diseases, malaria and tuberculosis played a major role. Malaria in particular gradually expanded in low-lying parts of Greece and Italy. Leprosy began to spread from Egypt during the Roman period, whereas cholera and louse-borne typhus seem to have been unknown. Smallpox first appeared in epidemic form (possibly in Athens in 430 B.C.E. and probably throughout the Roman Empire in the 160s through 180s C.E.) but may have become endemic in late antiquity. Plague, confined to the southeastern hinterlands of the Mediterranean for most of this period, erupted in a massive pandemic in the 540s C.E.

Fertility

Birth rates cannot be directly established on the basis of ancient sources; under prevailing levels of life expectancy, the total fertility rate must have averaged 5 to 6 (that is, five to six live births per woman surviving to menopause). The total marital fertility rate for Roman Egypt has been put at about 8 to 9 and was probably similar in other parts of the ancient world. According to Egyptian census returns, 95 percent of freeborn children were born in wedlock. These documents provide the only quantitative evidence of fertility. The documented maternal age distribution of childbirths implies a natural fertility regime with a peak in the twenties and continuing substantial fertility during the thirties and into the forties and no sign of parity-related birth control. In principle, early and nearly universal marriage for women must have necessitated some degree of fertility control within marriage. Mean birth intervals of three to four years in Roman Egypt corroborate this assumption. Cultural preferences for extended breast-feeding (for up to three years) may have contributed to extended birth spacing. A broad array of putative contraceptives and abortifacients were discussed in ancient literature, and at least some of the recommended chemical agents may have been efficient. In addition postpartum measures such as child exposure and infanticide appear to have been widely (although not universally) condoned and were not curbed until late antiquity. The extent to which families practiced intrusive forms of birth control, exposure, or infanticide remains unknowable and controversial.

In the literary tradition, elite families are most commonly associated with family limitation employed to preserve their socioeconomic standing. Evidence of high (i.e., male-dominated) sex ratios has been taken to indicate a high incidence of sex-specific infanticide but may only reflect biased recording practices. Whereas the best quantitative data, from Roman Egypt, indicate neither deliberate family limitation nor female infanticide, qualitative accounts for Greece and Rome raise the possibility of a more widespread application of postnatal measures in general and discrimination against female offspring in particular.

Marriage

Greeks and Romans of all classes practiced strict serial monogamy. (Although socially and legally condoned forms of concubinage and other sexual relations of married men facilitated a limited degree of de facto polygyny, overt polygamy appears to have been confined to the Macedonian aristocracy.) Child marriage was not common. Anecdotal evidence for the age at first marriage in Greece points to 14 to 15 years for women and perhaps 30 years for men. Tombstone inscriptions for commoners throughout the western half of the Roman Empire suggest a median of about 20 years for women and about 30 years for men, whereas literary texts report earlier marriage among the aristocracy. The census data from Roman Egypt yield medians of 17 to 18 and 25 years for women and men, respectively. Women began marrying around age 12, and almost all had married by the late twenties; among men, two-thirds had married by age 30, and 90 percent by age 50. The documented prevalence of early female and late male marriage foreshadows the Mediterranean marriage pattern observed in recent centuries and reveals broad continuity over time.

Divorce could be initiated by either sex and normally was not stigmatized or constrained by legal or religious injunctions. Remarriage was common for men but rare for women over age 30. In Roman Egypt two-thirds of men but only one-third of women were still married at age 50. Before the rise of Christianity, celibacy did not have favorable connotations.

Marriages were commonly virilocal (residence of a married couple with the husband's family) and often entailed the transfer of bridal dowries, which are best documented for elite circles. Slaves were legally incapable of entering marriages but often formed de facto unions among themselves. The intensity of endogamy varied along a west-east gradient. Although consanguineous unions were rare in Roman culture (with exceptions among the elite), marriage of first cousins is well attested for Greece and the Levant. Occasional half-sibling unions are also known from the Greek world. Roman Egypt in the second and third centuries C.E. stands out for the almost unique and still unexplained practice of full brother-sister marriage that accounts for one-sixth of all unions known from census returns.

Household Structure

There was no term for the nuclear family. In addition to parents and children, the Greek oikos and the Roman familia or domus included other individuals under the control of the head of the household, such as coresident kin and slaves. Although literary and legal texts emphasize the social and legal inclusivity of the Roman family, funerary commemoration in the western half of the Roman Empire tends to focus on the nuclear family. By contrast, evidence from the eastern Mediterranean points to more complex households. The Egyptian census data reveal a split between conjugal and complex households (composed of extended or multiple families) of 51 percent against 26 percent in the cities and 37 percent against 43 percent in the countryside and a greater presence of lodgers and slaves in urban households. High mortality constricted family size. The only known average is 4.3 members in Roman Egypt. Adoption was a well-established practice, but its incidence is unknown except for the fact that it was common among the Roman elite.

Partible inheritance in Greece and Rome encouraged the fragmentation of estates. In Athens daughters would receive dowries in lieu of an inheritance, but under Roman law they could also formally inherit. Women generally could own property but were to varying degrees subject to supervision by their male guardians. However, the patriarchal character of ancient households envisaged in the legal tradition was in practice often qualified by high mortality and other dislocations.

Population Size

The population totals reported in ancient literature are frequently shaped by rhetorical stylization and ignorance. Many are merely symbolic figures, and reliable references are rare. In classical antiquity the Mediterranean and adjacent regions experienced significant population growth, with more rapid expansion in the west than in the more developed Near East. After prolonged growth following an initial slump, by the fourth century B.C.E. the Greek population in the Aegean and in settlements in Sicily, southern Italy, and the Black Sea area may have approximated five million, divided among up to 1,500 separate communities, most of them with no more than a few hundred or thousand citizens. Athens, the largest and best-known Greek city-state, had an adult male citizen population of around 25,000 to 40,000 and a total population of perhaps 150,000 to 250,000 residents, including aliens and slaves. Periodic census counts from the third to the first century B.C.E. provide a rough idea of the demographic development of the Roman citizenry. A dramatic jump from 910,000 adult male citizens in 69 B.C.E. to a total of 4,063,000 in 28 B.C.E. has been interpreted as a sign of improved coverage or of a switch to the recording of all Romans instead of adult men only. Whereas the latter reading suggests an Italian population of 5 million to 6 million, the former implies a total closer to 13 million to 14 million. Although comparative evidence from later periods lends credibility to the lower estimate, which is now favored by most scholars, this issue has not been fully resolved. The gross population of the Roman Empire may have peaked at 60 million to 70 million in the second century C.E., with 50 to 60 percent residing in the European provinces and 20 to 25 percent each in western Asia and North Africa. The empire included perhaps 2,000 cities, headed by the capital city of Rome with about one million residents.

Although from the late second century C.E. onward recurrent epidemics may have depressed population numbers, the eastern part of the empire in particular remained densely populated into late antiquity. Only the disintegration of the western half of the empire in the fifth century and the onset of plague in the sixth century appear to have caused substantial demographic contraction. Roman levels of population density generally were reattained in Europe by the High Middle Ages, but this did not occur until the nineteenth century in Greece and the former Asian and African parts of the empire.

Population Thought

Demographic thought was poorly developed and never formally set out in theoretical terms; stereotypical moralizing and philosophical abstraction dominate the record. In the fourth century B.C.E the Athenian philosopher Plato considered eugenics and a fixed population size essential ingredients of his model of an ideal state. In a strongly pronatalist vein, most other sources stress the desirability of large populations as an index of military strength and general vigor. As a logical corollary, the ancient rhetorical tradition is permeated by concerns about supposedly declining birth rates and the resultant demographic contraction. This anxiety also manifested itself in Roman legislation enacted by the first emperor, Augustus (27 B.C.E–14 C.E.), to encourage nuptiality and reproduction by granting privileges to prolific couples and discriminating against the celibate and the childless, particularly among the elite. Demographic thinking in early modern Europe was profoundly influenced by this pronatalist stance. In late antiquity, Christianity brought a more systematic condemnation of fertility control and novel sympathy for celibacy.

See also: *Disease and History; Historical Demography; Paleodemography.*

BIBLIOGRAPHY

Bagnall, Roger S., and Bruce W. Frier. 1994. *The Demography of Roman Egypt.* Cambridge, Eng.: Cambridge University Press.

Beloch, Julius. 1886. *Die Bevölkerung der Griechisch-Römischen Welt.* Leipzig: Duncker & Humblot.

Brunt, Peter A. 1971. *Italian Manpower 225 B.C.–A.D. 14.* Oxford: Clarendon Press.

Eyben, Emiel. 1980/1981. "Family Planning in Graeco-Roman Antiquity." *Ancient Society* 11/12: 5–82.

Frier, Bruce W. 1994. "Natural Fertility and Family Limitation in Roman Marriage." *Classical Philology* 89: 318–333.

———. 2000. "Demography." In *The Cambridge Ancient History,* 2nd ed., Vol. 11, ed. Alan K. Bowman, Peter Garnsey, and Dominic Rathbone. Cambridge, Eng.: Cambridge University Press.

Hansen, Mogens H. 1985. *Demography and Democracy: The Number of Athenian Citizens in the Fourth Century B.C.* Herning, Denmark: Systime.

Parkin, Tim G. 1992. *Demography and Roman Society.* Baltimore: Johns Hopkins University Press.

Pomeroy, Sarah B. 1997. *Families in Classical and Hellenistic Greece: Representations and Realities.* Oxford: Clarendon Press.

Sallares, Robert. 1991. *The Ecology of the Ancient Greek World.* London: Duckworth.

Saller, Richard P. 1994. *Patriarchy, Property and Death in the Roman Family.* Cambridge, Eng.: Cambridge University Press.

Saller, Richard P., and Brent D. Shaw. 1984. "Tombstones and Roman Family Relations in the Principate: Civilians, Soldiers, and Slaves." *Journal of Roman Studies* 74: 124–156.

Scheidel, Walter. 1996. *Measuring Sex, Age and Death in the Roman Empire: Explorations in Ancient Demography.* Ann Arbor, MI: Journal of Roman Archaeology.

———. 2001. *Death on the Nile: Disease and the Demography of Roman Egypt.* Leiden, Netherlands: Brill.

———. 2001. "Progress and Problems in Roman Demography." In *Debating Roman Demography,* ed. Walter Scheidel. Leiden, Netherlands: Brill.

———. 2001. "Roman Age Structure: Evidence and Models." *Journal of Roman Studies* 91: 1–26.

WALTER SCHEIDEL

ANIMAL ECOLOGY

Animal ecology concerns the relationships of individuals to their environments, including physical factors and other organisms, and the consequences of these relationships for evolution, population growth and regulation, interactions between species, the composition of biological communities, and energy flow and nutrient cycling through the ecosystem. From the standpoint of population, the individual organism is the fundamental unit of ecology. Factors influencing the survival and reproductive success of individuals form the basis for understanding population processes.

Two general principles guide the study of animal ecology. One is the balance of nature, which states that ecological systems are regulated in approximately steady states. When a population becomes large, ecological pressures on population size, including food shortage, predation, and disease, tend to reduce the number of individuals. The second principle is that populations exist in dynamic relationship to their environments and that these relationships may cause ecological systems to vary dramatically over time and space. One of the challenges of animal ecology has been to reconcile these different viewpoints.

Populations depend on resources, including space, food, and opportunities to escape from predators. The amount of a resource potentially available to a population is generally thought of as being a property of the environment. As individuals consume resources they reduce the availability of these resources to others in the population. Thus, individuals are said to compete for resources. Larger populations result in a smaller share of resources per individual, which may lead to reduced survival and fecundity. Dense populations also attract predators and provide conditions for rapid transmission of contagious diseases, which generate pressure to reduce population size.

Changes in population size reflect both extrinsic variation in the environment that affects birth and death rates and intrinsic dynamics that result in oscillations or irregular fluctuations in population size. In some situations, the stable state may be a regular oscillation known as a limit cycle. Ecological systems also may switch between alternative stable states, as in the case of populations that are regulated at a high level by food limitation or at a low level by predators or other enemies. Switching between alternative stable states may be driven by changes in the environment.

Population Increase

In the absence of the effects of crowding, all populations have an immense capacity to increase. This capacity may be expressed as an exponential growth rate, *r*, which describes the growth of a population in terms of its relative, or percentage, rate of increase, like continuously compounded interest on a bank account. The constant r is often referred to as the Malthusian parameter. For a population growing at an exponential rate, the number of individuals (N) in a population at time t is $N(t) = N(0)e^{rt}$ where $N(0)$ is the number of individuals at time 0. Accordingly, the increase in a single time unit is e^r, which is the constant factor by which the population increases during each time period. The rate of increase in the number of individuals is then given by $dN/dt = rN$. The doubling time in years of a population growing exponentially is $t_2 = (ln\ 2)/r$, or roughly $0.69/r$.

Estimated exponential annual growth rates of unrestrained populations range from low values of 0.077 for sheep in Tasmania and 0.091 for Northern elephant seals, to perhaps 1.0 for a pheasant population, 24 for the field vole, 10^{10} for flour beetles in laboratory cultures and 10^{30} for the water flea *Daphnia*. Human populations are at the lower end of this range, but a realistic exponential growth rate of 0.03 (or slightly above 3% per year) for some human populations is equivalent to a doubling time of about 23 years and a roughly thousand-fold increase in 230 years. Clearly, no population can maintain such a growth rate for long. (Expansion at the estimated annualized rates just cited for the field vole, flour beetle, and water flea is necessarily utterly fleeting.)

The exponential growth rate of a population can be calculated from the schedule of fecundity at age x (b_x) and survival to age x (l_x) in a population. These "life table" variables are related to population growth rate by the Euler, or characteristic, equation,

$$1 = \int_{x=0}^{\infty} e^{rx}\, l_x b_x\, dx,$$

whose solution requires matrix methods. When the life table is unchanging for a long period, a population assumes a stable age distribution, which is also an intrinsic property of the life table, and a constant exponential rate of growth. Thus, assuming constant birth and death rates, the growth trajectory of a population may be projected into the future. However, because populations are finite and births and deaths are random events, the expected size of a population in the future has a statistical distribution that may include a finite probability of 0 individuals, that is, extinction. As a general rule, the probability of extinction decreases with increasing population size and increasing excess of births over deaths.

Population Regulation

Balancing the growth potential of all populations are various extrinsic environmental factors that act to slow population growth as the number of individuals increases. High population density depresses the resources of the environment, attracts predators, and, in some cases, results in stress-related reproductive failure or premature death. As population size increases, typically death rates of individuals increase, birth rates decrease, or both. The result is a slower growth rate and a changed, usually older, population. The predominant model used by animal ecologists to describe the relationship of population growth rate to population size (or density) is the logistic equation, in which the exponential growth rate of the population decreases linearly with increasing population size:

$$r = r_0 \left(1 - \frac{N}{K}\right),$$

where r_0 is the exponential growth rate of a population unrestrained by density (i.e., whose size is close to 0) and K represents the number of individuals that the environment can support at an equilibrium level, also referred to as the carrying capacity of the environment. Accordingly, the rate of growth of the population is expressed as

$$\frac{dN}{dt} = r_0 N \left(1 - \frac{N}{K}\right).$$

Notice that when $N < K$, the growth rate is positive and the population grows. When $N > K$, the density-dependent term $(1 - N/K)$ is negative and the population declines. When $N = K$, the growth rate is 0 and a stable, steady-state population size is achieved. This depressing impact of density on the population growth rate is known as negative feedback.

The differential form of the logistic equation may be integrated to provide a function for the trajectory of population size over time,

$$N(t) = \frac{K}{1 + \left[\dfrac{K - N(0)}{N(0)}\right] e^{-rt}} .$$

The curve is sigmoid (S-shaped), with the rate of growth, dN/dt reaching a maximum (the inflection point) at $N = K/2$. Because this is the density at which individuals are added to the population most rapidly, the inflection point also represents the size of the population from which human consumers can remove individuals at the highest rate without causing the population to decline. Thus, the inflection point is also known as the point of maximum sustainable yield.

Density dependence can take on a variety of forms. One of these is a saturation model where the exponential growth rate remains constant and positive until a population completely utilizes a nonrenewable resource such as space, and population growth stops abruptly. The approach of a population to an equilibrium level determined by density-dependent processes can be altered by environmentally induced changes in the intrinsic rate of population growth or in the carrying capacity of the environment.

Difficulties in finding mates and maintaining other social interactions at low densities, including group defense against predators, may also cause the population growth rate to decrease as density declines (the Allee effect), and, below a certain density threshold, may even result in population decline to extinction. This type of response is a *positive* feedback, one that promotes population instability. For example, after commercial hunting had reduced populations of the passenger pigeon to low levels, the decline in social interactions in this communally nesting species is thought to have doomed it to extinction.

Populations have inherent oscillatory properties that can be triggered by time lags in the response to changing density and which cause populations to fluctuate in a perpetual limit cycle, with alternating population highs and lows. In these cases higher values of r can send a population into unpredictable chaotic behavior, increasing the risk of extinction. In a population with continuous reproduction, regular population cycles occur when there is a lag, often equal to the period of development, in the response of a population to its own density effects on the environment. When the time lag is of period τ, limit cycles develop when $r\tau$ exceeds $\pi/2$, and the period of the cycle is 4 to 5 times τ.

Metapopulations

Most natural populations consist of many subpopulations occupying patches of suitable habitat surrounded by unsuitable environments. Oceanic islands and freshwater ponds are obvious examples. But fragmentation of forest and other natural habitats resulting from clearing land for agriculture or urban development is increasingly creating fragmented populations in many other kinds of habitats. These subpopulations are connected by movement of individuals, and the set of subpopulations is referred to as a metapopulation. Metapopulations have their own dynamics determined by the probabilities of colonization and extinction of individual patches. A set of simple metapopulation models describes changes in the proportion of patches occupied (p). When the extinction probability (e) of an individual patch is independent of p, the rate of loss of subpopulations is simply pe. The rate of colonization is proportional to the number of patches that can provide potential colonists and the proportion of empty patches that are available to receive them. Hence, colonization is equal to $cp(1-p)$, where c is the rate of colonization.

The metapopulation achieves a steady state of number of patches occupied when colonization balances extinction, that is $pe = cp(1-p)$, or $\hat{p} = 1-e/c$. In this model, as long as the rate of colonization exceeds that of extinction, the metapopulation will persist. In more complex models, particularly when the probability of population extinction is reduced by continuing migration of individuals between patches (which keeps the sizes of subpopulations from dropping perilously low), the extinction rate and colonization rate both depend on patch occupancy p. In this case, the solution to the metapopulation model has a critical ratio of colonization to extinction, below which patch occupancy declines until the metapopulation disappears. Thus, changes in patch size or migration between patches can cause an abrupt shift in the probability of metapopulation persistence.

Predator-Prey Interactions

The dynamics of populations are influenced by interactions with predator and consumer populations. Because these interactions have built-in lag times in population responses, they often result in complex dynamics. Among the most spectacular fluctuations in size are those in populations of snowshoe hares and the lynx that prey on them. Population highs and lows may differ by a factor of 1,000 over an oscillation period of about ten years. Oscillation periods in other population cycles of mammals and birds in boreal forest and tundra habitats may be either approximately four years or nine to ten years.

The biologists Alfred Lotka and Vito Volterra independently developed models for the cyclic behavior of predator-prey systems in the 1920s. The most basic model expresses the rate of increase in the prey population in terms of the intrinsic growth capacity of the prey population and removal of prey individuals by predators, which is proportional to the product of the predator and prey population sizes. The growth of the predator population is equal to its birth rate, which depends on how many prey are captured, minus a density-independent term for the death of predator individuals. The joint equilibrium of the prey and predator populations is determined by the predation efficiency and the relative rates of birth and death of the prey and predator, respectively. However, the equilibrium is neutral, which means that any perturbation will set the system into a persisting cycle. More complex models of predator-prey interactions include a balance between various stabilizing factors, such as density-dependent control of either population, alternative food resources for predators, and refuges from predators at low prey densities, and destabilizing factors, such as time lags in the response of the predator and prey to each other. For the most part, these models predict stable predator and prey populations under constant conditions.

Both empirical and experimental studies have shown that the rate of predation is nonlinear, violating one of the assumptions of the Lotka-Volterra model. When predation is inefficient at low prey densities and predator populations are limited by density-dependence at high predator densities, there may be two stable points. One of these is at a high prey population level limited by the prey population's own food supply, the other at a low prey population level limited by predators. When a prey population, such as a crop pest, is released from predator control following depression of the predator population by extrinsic factors such as climate, disease, pesticides, and so on, the prey may increase to outbreak levels and become a severe problem. Thus, agricul-

tural practices that incidentally depress the populations of natural control organisms can have unwanted consequences.

A special kind of predator-prey model is required to describe the interactions between parasites, including disease-causing organisms, and their hosts. These models need to take into account the fact that parasites generally do not kill their hosts, that the spread of parasites among hosts may depend on population density and the presence of suitable vectors, and that hosts may raise defensive immune reactions. Immune reactions create a time lag in the responses of parasite and host populations to each other and may result in strong fluctuations in the prevalence of parasitic diseases.

Conclusion

The study of animal populations tells us that for any given set of conditions the size of a population is limited by the resources available to it. The human population is no exception. At high densities, the stresses of poor nutrition and social strife all too often signal a reduced quality of life.

The study of animal populations has provided guidelines for the management of nonhuman populations, including those of domesticated animals, game birds and mammals, fish stocks, species of conservation concern, pests, and disease organisms. In general, fragmentation and simplification of systems lead to exaggerated population fluctuations and the development of alternative stable states, and they may thus increase the probability of epidemics, pest outbreaks, and extinction. Hunting, overfishing, and overgrazing have led to severe reduction in some food sources and deterioration of habitat quality. Controls on populations are so complex that manipulation of environmental factors in complex systems often results in unforeseen consequences. In a classic case, nineteenth-century hunting of sea otters on the Pacific coast of North America resulted in the explosion of populations of their sea urchin prey, which in turn seriously harmed the kelp beds that serve as important nurseries for fish stocks. Many such examples show how difficult it is to replace natural controls with human management, although the need to maintain a high quality of life for the human population in an increasingly stressed environment makes it imperative that we learn to do this wisely.

See also: *Biogeography; Biology, Population.*

BIBLIOGRAPHY

Anderson, Roy M., and Robert M. May. 1991. *Infectious Diseases of Humans. Dynamics and Control.* Oxford: Oxford University Press.

Ballou, Jonathan D., Michael E. Gilpin, and Thomas J. Foose, eds. 1995. *Population Management for Survival and Recovery. Analytical Methods and Strategies in Small Population Conservation.* New York: Columbia University Press.

Begon, Michael, Martin Mortimer, and David J. Thompson. 1996. *Population Ecology: A Unified Study of Animals and Plants,* 3rd edition. Oxford: Blackwell Science.

Caswell, Hal. 2001. *Matrix Population Models: Construction, Analysis, and Interpretation,* 2nd edition. Sunderland, MA: Sinauer Associates.

Gotelli, Nicolas J. 2001. *A Primer of Ecology,* 3rd edition. Sunderland, MA: Sinauer Associates.

Hanski, Ilkka A., and Michael E. Gilpin, eds. 1997. *Metapopulation Biology, Ecology Genetics, and Evolution.* San Diego, CA: Academic Press.

Nisbet, Roger M., and William S. C. Gurney. 1982. *Modelling Fluctuating Populations.* New York: Wiley.

Pielou, Elizabeth C. 1997. *Mathematical Ecology.* New York: John Wiley.

Pimm, Stuart L. 1991. *The Balance of Nature?* Chicago: University of Chicago Press.

Tilman, David. 1982. *Resource Competition and Community Structure.* Princeton, NJ: Princeton University Press.

ROBERT E. RICKLEFS

ANIMAL RIGHTS

The debate over animal rights revolves around a simple question: Do any nonhuman animals have rights? Like many simple questions, this one quickly becomes complex. What are rights? Do human beings have them? If so, what rights do people have, and why do people have them?

These questions have divided theoreticians over the past three centuries and more. Some of these thinkers (for example, the philosophers John Locke and Immanuel Kant) maintain that humans have rights. Others (for example, the philosophers David Hume and Jeremy Bentham) maintain that humans do not. The debate has been as intense as it has been protracted. Not surprisingly, adding animals to the mix only complicates matters.

The Terms of the Debate

Some things are clear. The debate concerns the moral rights of animals, not their legal rights. To ask what legal rights animals have is a straightforward empirical question that can be answered by using standard empirical methods (for example, consulting state and federal legislative databases). In 2002 the German Parliament voted to include respect for animal rights in the Constitution; that same year, the United States Congress passed legislation that explicitly excludes rodents and birds from the protection provided by the animal welfare act.

To ask what moral rights animals have, by contrast, is to ask a normative question that no amount of empirical inquiry can answer. Only normative reasoning can answer normative questions. The answers with the best arguments on their side are the ones that should be accepted; they are the ones that tell people how they should live. Understandably, who has the best arguments is the question that fuels the debate.

Fundamental Rights

The fundamental right in dispute is the right to be treated with respect. To have this right is to occupy a singularly important position, one that limits what other people are morally free to do. Those who have this right (to borrow Kant's terminology) are never to be treated merely as means to other persons' ends.

What Kant's injunction means in practice is that harm done to those who possess this right cannot be justified merely by showing that as a result of that harm someone else is better off. In other words, the obligation to respect the rights of the individual are morally more important than any obligation to benefit others, even society as a whole.

Philosophers have defended a variety of criteria that explain why people have rights, both the right to be treated with respect and other, derivative rights, including the rights to life and bodily integrity. The standard view (the one favored by the majority of thinkers) limits rights to moral agents.

Moral Rights and Moral Agents

Moral agents are rational; they have the capacity to bring reason to bear on their moral decision making. Moral agents also are autonomous; they are free to choose between right and wrong. This is why moral agents are morally responsible for their acts.

According to the standard view, then, there is an elegant symmetry between being morally responsible on the one hand and having moral rights on the other hand. Only those who are morally responsible (that is, only moral agents) have moral rights. Once proponents of the standard view add that, at least among terrestrial beings, only human beings are moral agents, their conclusion follows: Only humans have rights.

There are problems with the standard view, however. At least as far back as the philosopher Porphyry (233–306 C.E.) critics have pointed out that many human beings (all young children and the seriously mentally disadvantaged of any age, for example) are not moral agents. Thus, given the standard view, these humans lack moral rights.

This is no small deficiency. Bereft of rights, these human beings do not occupy the same moral position occupied by moral agents. Since they are bereft of rights, there is nothing about the moral status of these human beings that prevents anyone from taking their lives or injuring their bodies in pursuit of benefits for others, whether the beneficiaries are the few or the many.

It is hard to imagine how any friend of humanity could accept this repugnant conclusion. Certainly serious proponents of children's rights or the rights of the mentally disadvantaged cannot accept it. Their challenge is to find an acceptable alternative to the standard view.

An Alternative View

A plausible alternative begins with a characterization of moral patients. Moral patients are individuals who, though they lack the capacities necessary for moral agency, can be the object of direct moral wrongdoing. Young children who are physically abused by their parents are an example. They cannot do anything wrong, but grievous wrong can be done to them.

Some critics of the standard view use this judgment as a basis for revising that view. Only humans have rights, but human moral agents are not the only humans who have rights; human moral patients have rights too.

The revised standard view, then, is no less humanistic than the standard view (rights are restricted to humans only), but unlike the standard view, it avoids the repugnant conclusion. People are not free to take the life or injure the body of a young child, for example, just to secure benefits for themselves or others.

There is a problem with the revised standard view, however. Few even modestly informed people believe that all nonhuman animals are, as the philosopher René Descartes argued, mindless machines. On the contrary, most people agree with naturalist Charles Darwin: Not only do some nonhuman animals have a mental life, the mental life of some of them (nonhuman mammals, for example) is significantly more developed than what is found in many human beings.

Advocates of the revised standard view therefore face a serious dilemma. If they maintain that human moral patients have rights, it is difficult to see how they can consistently avoid accepting the same conclusion for nonhuman mammals. However, if these advocates insist that those animals lack rights, it is difficult to see how they can consistently maintain that human moral patients have them. Logically, it seems, advocates of the revised standard view cannot have it both ways.

Whether or not advocates can escape this dilemma, the challenge they face captures part, although not the whole, of the spirit of the animal rights debate. It is not difficult to propose a criterion for possessing rights that nonhuman animals cannot satisfy. The standard view does that. What is far more difficult (some would say impossible) is to find a criterion that all human moral patients satisfy but that every nonhuman animal fails.

Unless such a criterion is devised, the possibility that at least some nonhuman animals have rights cannot be summarily dismissed. Instead, the arguments for and against animal rights must be carefully examined with a view to discovering which among them are the best. That discovery would indicate which answers people should accept and how people should live.

The Significance of the Answers

Unlike many questions in philosophy, whose answers have no direct bearing on the "real world," the questions posed in the animal rights debate are fraught with practical significance. The answers people give have implications for what people should eat, wear, and do for entertainment; what careers people should pursue and what values they should teach their children; and what population policies they should favor and what development programs they should support. All this and much more, all of it touching on some of the most important areas of human life, is affected by how people answer that "simple" question: Do any nonhuman animals have rights? Paradoxically, few questions are more directly relevant to how people should live.

See also: *Environmental Ethics.*

BIBLIOGRAPHY

Cohen, Carl, and Tom Regan. 2001. *The Animal Rights Debate.* New York: Rowan and Littlefield.

Frey, R. G. 1980. *Interests and Rights: The Case against Animals.* Oxford, Eng.: Clarendon Press.

Pluhar, Evelyn. 1995. *Beyond Prejudice: The Moral Significance of Human and Nonhuman Animals.* Durham, NC: Duke University Press.

Regan, Tom. 1983. *The Case for Animal Rights.* Berkeley, CA: University of California Press.

———. 2001. *Defending Animal Rights.* Champaign, IL: University of Illinois Press.

Regan, Tom, and Peter Singer, eds. 1976–1989. *Animal Rights and Human Obligations.* Englewood Cliffs, NJ: Prentice-Hall.

Rollin, Bernard. 1981. *Animal Rights and Human Morality.* Buffalo, NY: Prometheus Books.

Sapontzis, Steven. 1987. *Morals, Reason, and Animals.* Philadelphia, PA: Temple University Press.

Singer, Peter. 1975. *Animal Liberation.* New York: Avon Books.

TOM REGAN

ANTHROPOLOGICAL DEMOGRAPHY

Anthropological demography is an intersection of two already heterogeneous disciplines. Each has taken that limited part of the intellectual equipment of the other that seems to serve it best. Paradoxically, the segment of anthropology that is most interested in technical demography (human evolution and ecology) finds among demographers the smallest interest in its own ultimate goals, while many cultural anthropologists whose interpretive skills might benefit demography are least interested in or even hostile to it as an empirical enterprise. Nevertheless, among the like-minded, there has been substantial progress.

Substantive and Theoretical Content

The intersection of anthropology and demography may be thought of in two ways: the first substantive, the second theoretical.

Substantive content. *Substantively,* the intersection has two foci:

1. The investigation of demographic topics and/or the application of demographic methods in traditional anthropological contexts. This intersection is occupied by some archaeologists, biological anthropologists, evolutionary ecologists, and a few ethnographers.

2. The application of anthropological methods or understandings of human behavior to demographic investigations in any investigative context. This intersection is occupied by a growing number of demographers seeking to improve generalizations based on sociological or economic theory, by reference to anthropological or culture theory.

The range of these two substantive foci can be quite broad. The first would certainly include ethnographic, archaeological, or biological anthropological studies of population and resources, fertility, mortality, migration, and nuptiality (marriage practices) in nonliterate societies. Such studies in literate societies would also be included if the investigations were explicitly anthropological in method (for example, using intensive ethnographic techniques such as participant observation). Studies in historical demography that focused on traditional concerns of ethnography, such as kinship, family, and household, would also fall within this category. On the fringes of these studies, however, lies a mass of traditional ethnographies dealing in qualitative detail with topics of salient interest in demography: nuptiality, especially the social relations created or maintained by marriage alliances; the recruitment of individuals into social groups in ways that condition reproductive relationships; the role of fertility in establishing social status, socialization, and the onset of sexual activity; gender relations; migration; care of the aged; and death. To the extent that such studies are rigorous and contribute to an understanding of demographic processes, per se, they belong in the first category. Otherwise, their contribution may be in the second.

Theoretical content. *Theoretically,* there are two interests that tend to differentiate some parts of anthropology from demography and sociology but that in an unexpected way ally it with economics. These interests are:

1. The behavior of *systems* or aggregates versus the behavior of *actors.* Demographers are typically interested in populations, although they are obliged sometimes to consider the constituent actors (as when seeking to change their behavior). Many ethnographers are most interested in individuals, although they are willing sometimes to consider individuals' commonalities (as when generalizing to cultural or institutional patterns).

2. A focus on *central tendency* versus a focus on *variation.* Many demographers are more interested in the former; many ethnographers are most interested in individual or at least subsocietal differences.

These interests are not independent of the subfields or historical practices of anthropology. They differentiate archaeology, biological anthropology, and traditional, structural-functional ("British") social anthropology; they thus differentiate a scientific anthropology on the one hand from more recent trends in interpretivist or activist cultural anthropology on the other. The first set of fields is concerned largely with systemic relationships and may concentrate more on broad averages. The second set is distinguished by its sharp questioning of the validity of systemic characterizations. While sharing with earlier social anthropologists and sociologists a recognition of the importance of institutional structures, many modern ethnographers are more concerned with issues of local knowledge and its exchange between individuals—or "culture"—and especially the agency or individual freedom to exercise choice within institutional and cultural boundaries. While disavowing the economist's assumptions of universal rationality and insisting on the primacy of local culture, the modern ethnographer is also concerned with how choices are made or interpersonally negotiated but in a cultural and moral marketplace. Modern ethnographers would also contest the kind of institutional determinism sometimes found in sociological approaches to social action, insisting on localized actor-driven interpretations of institutions. Thus, like economists, modern ethnographers are interested in how people make choices but according to particularistic rather than universalistic rules. Like sociologists they are interested in how institutions relate to individual behavior, but they are more interested in how individuals bend or break cultural rules than in how they follow them.

Demography in Anthropology

The relationships between archaeology, biological anthropology, and evolutionary ecology on the one hand and demography on the other are straightforward, but in them demography is more important to anthropologists than anthropology is to demographers.

Ideas about the interactions between population and resource base have been fundamental to archaeology, for example in the Marxist-oriented views about technological response to population pressure on resources espoused by V. Gordon Childe, later evident to demographers in the ethnographically motivated analyses of Ester Boserup and in the work of Mark N. Cohen. At the same time, some investigations suggested that plant domestication and population response may have also followed a more Malthusian scenario in which technological innovation is fortuitous, and population increases in response. The findings of archaeological demography are of great importance to demographic theory, especially to questions of population equilibrium. Archaeological attempts to discuss population-resource balance are limited, however, by their lack of technical demographic sophistication and difficulties of demographic measurement in archaeological contexts. Attempts to discern cause and effect between population pressure and technological innovation are limited by the absence of precise, fine-grained chronologies and by problems of potential infinite regress in which population change and technological change alternate over time with no clear causal precedence.

The centrality of these same issues of population and resources to biological anthropology and evolutionary ecology emerges from T. R. Malthus's own anticipation of the concepts of fitness and selection from randomly occurring variability that were later proposed by the nineteenth-century English naturalist Charles Darwin. For Malthus, innovation was fortuitous with respect to the population-resource balance; in the same way, for Darwin, the appearance of variability was fortuitous with respect to selection.

Biological anthropologists have two major demographic interests. The first is to describe the fundamental demographic parameters of the species under conditions unaffected by modern life. Much of this work is paleodemographic, depending on the evaluation of recovered skeletal material. The work may also be conducted through comparison with the primate cousins of humans. The second interest, which is more precisely part of evolutionary ecology, is to explain how the more than 99 percent of human history spent in hunting and gathering has led, by selection, to the underlying physiology and psychology of humans and indeed to the institutional structures and cultural components that are evident in demographic processes today. A major focus is on the evolution of life histories, that is, typical demographic profiles of individuals with their underlying physiological and psychological characteristics; this focus is shared with evolutionary psychology. Much of the demographic work done in modern paleodemography, biological anthropology, and evolutionary ecology is technically sophisticated. The practice of demography in these fields has advanced greatly since the withering critique delivered by William Petersen in 1975.

But it is the relationship between demography and ethnography that is at once the most promising to practicing demographers and the most problematic.

Demography and Ethnography

A focus on demographic issues or data as an integral or even an underlying part of ethnographic investigation is evident in the work of early British struc-

tural-functional scholars and was strongly advocated by Ludwik Krzywicki in 1934. Raymond Firth's work on Tikopia, originally published in 1936, was explicitly demographic, showing the pressure of expanding population on limited resources and its consequences in demographic processes. In the United States, similar concerns were evident in the ecological work of Julian H. Steward and Roy Rappaport and in the cultural materialism of Marvin Harris. Emphasis on the gathering of basic demographic data, even if only in a rudimentary census, was standard practice for most ethnographers until perhaps the 1980s, when the interests of social and cultural anthropology turned from empirical to interpretivist approaches. Paradoxically, it was just then that demographers, dissatisfied with the apparent failure of their own empirical approaches to achieve sustainable generalizations about fertility change, began to appeal to anthropology to provide explanations that would at least work in local contexts, even if they were not always generalizable. A harbinger of this trend was seen in demographic work on "excess" fertility in modern nonindustrial societies that included work by anthropologists and focused on structural-functional relations between social systems and demographic behavior.

Data collection approaches. In part, this appeal was for ethnographers to provide locally gathered and fine-grained data (the first substantive focus, above) or locally significant meanings or behavioral motivations (the second substantive focus). The need for such data and meanings was fueled by the policy-driven emphasis, in demography, on the introduction or implementation of fertility control in nonindustrial societies. In order to introduce such control, policymakers had to change the behavior of actors and needed advice on how to do so. Initially, demographers sought to identify universalistic criteria (in typically economic fashion). But they soon came to appreciate that they had to understand more local motivations for the maintenance of high fertility and to identify those factors that might persuade actors to lower it. This endeavor, however, is problematic. Whereas most demographers use data gathered at a population level, usually by survey or census methods, most ethnographers work at an individual, household, or at most the level of the local group (e.g., village). The outcomes of these different enterprises are often not comparable. The averages obtained from surveys and censuses may be stable, but such sources are limited in their depth. The richness of ethnographic data is unachievable by other methods, but the data are from small samples and can be quite unstable. Much demographic data gathered by ethnography had been unreliable or presented in forms incompatible with accepted demographic analytic techniques (as in the use of nonstandard age ranges).

In response to these challenges, some anthropologists began to do explicit and methodologically informed demographic investigations. Some demographers explicitly invoked and attempted to implement ethnographic techniques or to work with ethnographers. The principal outcome of such endeavors has been the emergence of the subfield of microdemography. In this subfield's simplest applications, ethnographers deliver a new empirical grist for the demographer's mill—"add fieldwork and stir" (Kertzer and Fricke, p. 2). At its best, microdemography seeks to situate and explicate demographic behavior in local terms.

At the same time, placing demographic behavior in social and cultural context continued, for example in "family systems theory," which relates kinship and family structures to demographic decision-making, or in taking account of overarching political-economic structures. Despite the conflict between structural-functional and intepretivist views within cultural anthropology itself, these approaches, taking into account the broad conditions under which most actors in a given social environment may exercise their agency, have been most productive. There is a strong similarity between these efforts and institutionally or value-oriented social demography. In parallel is a continuation of the emphasis on cultural milieu and communication between actors in the network-oriented research of some demographers.

One problem encountered by the joining of ethnography and demography and shared with the survey approach is a lack of temporal depth. Many of the problems that interest demographers are dynamic and occur across generations, often several generations. Only a series of compatibly designed and comparably implemented surveys or censuses can meet the demand for time depth. Even such surveys are usually impoverished for the purposes of institutional contextualization or interpretation, because they focus on the usual limited set of social and economic variables (education, income, etc.), and these usually only as of the date of survey, even when life-

long or cross-generational reproductive histories are recovered. While rich and informative about individuals, ethnographic data cannot go much beyond life histories, so that transgenerational processes are unrecoverable, except by the taking of genealogies, which are notoriously biased and often recounted principally to legitimate current social structures. In consequence, both demographers and anthropologists have turned to history, either by using historical or ethnohistorical sources or by doing long-term revisitation fieldwork involving more than one generation of fieldworkers.

Defining culture. Despite these advances—implementation of technical demographic methods by some ethnographers, entry into fieldwork by some demographers, attempts to recover transgenerational temporal depth by ethnographers and demographers, and the focus on demographic matters by historians—serious problems remain. One of these is the problematic nature of culture as an explicator of behavior. An idea invented by anthropologists, and elaborated especially by the American school—associated with the anthropologist Franz Boas (1858–1942)—culture is a fuzzy concept, more definable as the complement of other things (biology, institutions, environment, etc.) than in its own right. Attempts to define it continue in anthropology. Inquiring and dissatisfied demographers, seizing on culture to extricate themselves from the failures of transition theory in explaining demographic change, have laid hold of a very slippery fish. Their colleagues in sociology and ethnography have not solved the puzzle of how environment, institutions, and values interact to condition individual behavior, and of course it is that individual behavior, aggregated into population statistics, that is the focus of demographic interest. The deficiencies of demographic theory are not ameliorated by the poverty of social theory.

Role of quantification. A third point of difficulty, beyond the limits of what is recoverable by ethnographic fieldwork and what can be utilized from the concept of culture, is the markedly different mindsets of most ethnographers and most demographers. All demographers are comfortable with mathematics and the use of numerical indicators as measures of or at least as proxies for conditioning variables and outcomes. While demographers are intense critics of the quality of their data, so that they constantly doubt particular facts, they believe in the existence of facts and that facts can be known at least approximately. They are also comfortable with statistical notions of indeterminacy and especially with precise descriptions of uncertainty.

By contrast, many ethnographers are uncomfortable with mathematics. They are disinclined to accept or are even hostile to the use of numerical indicators. While earlier ethnographers were uncritically accepting of the truth of informants' statements, modern ethnographers doubt the possibility of determining objective truth at all. Where demographers would rely on probabilities, ethnographers would retreat into literary vagueness. Yet the ethnographers have an important point in their insistence on the interpersonally negotiated nature of social "facts," and the mathematical "hard core" of demographic investigation is softer than the demographers think. Indeed, the shift of some demography from empirical computation to a search for social meanings that inform individual decisions may have exposed an underbelly of unknowability that bedevils all attempts to understand behavior. Petersen's critique of demography in the hands of anthropologists is well matched by Nancy Scheper-Hughes's 1997 attack on studies of the human condition in the hands of demographers.

Prospects

Despite these caveats, both anthropology and demography have benefited from the interaction between the two fields. Many more anthropologists are now sensitive to and often technically equipped to deal with demographic issues. Many more demographers are now alert to the need to define relevant decision-making units and personal goals in terms of local patterns of action, rather than in terms of familiar Western categories. Whether these advances can be sustained depends on the ability of demographers to broaden their theoretical horizons and on the determination of anthropologists to exercise empirical rigor. The alliance between demography and anthropology (aside from modern cultural anthropology) is well-grounded and durable but would be improved if the interests of demographers were more general and less tied to contemporary policy-driven issues. The flirtation between a demography unsatisfied in its own house and looking for some theoretical excitement in cultural anthropology can be rescued from mere flirtation under three conditions:

1. Recognition of the continuing analytical utility of institutional structures, even when they are evaded or modified by actors. Interpretivist ethnographers should recognize such structures, while functionalist ethnographers and social demographers should take them with a grain of salt.

2. A discriminating use of the concept of culture. Demographers must realize that culture may not live up to the allure of a first encounter. Nevertheless, the economists among them would profit by explicitly incorporating local preferences into their formulations. Ethnographers should seek to lay bare how choices are actually made rather than simply enlarge on how informants talk about their feelings.

3. A mutual understanding of goals and limitations. Critical and activist ethnographers must do a better job of the ethnography of demography in order to understand what it is demographers actually do, and why they do it, especially how they are driven to rely on and are then constrained by their data sources. Demographers must understand the intensely local and primarily political-humanistic agenda of interpretivist ethnography.

See also: *Caldwell, John C.; Caste; Culture and Population; Evolutionary Demography; Gender; Hunter-Gatherers; Indigenous Peoples; Nomads; Paleodemography; Prehistoric Populations; Primate Demography.*

BIBLIOGRAPHY

Bongaarts, John, and Susan C. Watkins. 1996. "Social Interactions and Contemporary Fertility Transitions." *Population and Development Review* 22: 639–682.

Boserup, Ester. 1965. *Conditions of Agricultural Growth: The Economics of Agrarian Change under Population Pressure.* Chicago: Aldine.

Caldwell, John C., Bruce Caldwell, and Pat Caldwell. 1987. "Anthropology and Demography: The Mutual Reinforcement of Speculation and Research." *Current Anthropology* 28: 25–34.

Childe, V. Gordon. 1964. *What Happened in History,* revised edition. New York: Penguin.

Clark, Sam, Elizabeth Colson, James Lee, and Thayer Scudder. 1995. "Ten Thousand Tonga: A Longitudinal Anthropological Study from Southern Zambia." *Population Studies* 49: 91–109.

Cohen, Mark N. 1977. *The Food Crisis in Prehistory: Overpopulation and the Origins of Agriculture.* New Haven, CT: Yale University Press.

Das Gupta, Monica. 1997. "Kinship Systems and Demographic Regimes." In *Anthropological Demography: Toward a New Synthesis,* ed. David I. Kertzer and Tom Fricke. Chicago: University of Chicago Press.

Firth, Raymond. 1968. *We, the Tikopia: Kinship in Primitive Polynesia,* 3rd edition. Boston: Beacon Press.

Fricke, Tom. 1997. "Culture Theory and Demographic Process: Toward a Thicker Demography." In *Anthropological Demography: Toward a New Synthesis,* ed. David I. Kertzer and Tom Fricke. Chicago: University of Chicago Press.

Gage, Timothy B. 1998. "The Comparative Demography of Primates: With Some Comments on the Evolution of Life Histories." *Annual Review of Anthropology* 27: 197–221.

Greenhalgh, Susan, ed. 1995. *Situating Fertility: Anthropology and Demographic Inquiry.* Cambridge, Eng.: Cambridge University Press.

Hammel, E. A. 1990. "A Theory of Culture for Demography." *Population and Development Review* 16: 455–485.

Harris, Marvin, and Eric B. Ross. 1987. *Death, Sex, and Fertility.* New York: Columbia University Press.

Hassan, Fekri A. 1981. *Demographic Archaeology.* New York: Academic Press.

Hill, Allan G. 1997. "'Truth Lies in the Eye of the Beholder': The Nature of Evidence in Demography and Anthropology." In *Anthropological Demography: Toward a New Synthesis,* ed. David I. Kertzer and Tom Fricke. Chicago: University of Chicago Press.

Hill, Kim, and Hillard Kaplan. 1999. "Life History Traits in Humans: Theory and Empirical Studies." *Annual Review of Anthropology* 28: 397–430.

Howell, Nancy L. 1986. "Demographic Anthropology." *Annual Review of Anthropology* 15: 219–246.

———. 2000. *Demography of the Dobe !Kung,* 2nd edition. New York: De Gruyter.

Kertzer, David I., and Tom Fricke, eds. 1997. *Anthropological Demography: Toward a New Synthesis.* Chicago: University of Chicago Press.

Krzywicki, Ludwik. 1934. *Primitive Society and Its Vital Statistics.* London: Macmillan.

Lesthaeghe, Ron, and Johan Surkyn. 1988. "Cultural Dynamics and Economic Theories of Fertility Change." *Population and Development Review* 14: 1–45.

Petersen, William. 1975. "A Demographer's View of Prehistoric Demography." *Current Anthropology* 16: 227–245.

Pollak, Robert A., and Susan C. Watkins. 1993. "Cultural and Economic Approaches to Fertility: A Proper Marriage or a Mésalliance?" *Population and Development Review* 19: 467–496.

Rappaport, Roy. 1967. *Pigs for the Ancestors.* New Haven, CT: Yale University Press.

Scheper-Hughes, Nancy. 1997. "Demography without Numbers." In *Anthropological Demography: Toward a New Synthesis,* ed. David I. Kertzer and Tom Fricke. Chicago: University of Chicago Press.

Schofield, Roger, and David Coleman. 1986. "Introduction." In *The State of Population Theory: Forward from Malthus,* ed. Roger Schofield and David Coleman. Oxford: Blackwell.

Skinner, G. William. 1997. "Family Systems and Demographic Processes." In *Anthropological Demography: Toward a New Synthesis,* ed. David I. Kertzer and Tom Fricke. Chicago: University of Chicago Press.

Steward, Julian H. 1936. "The Economic and Social Basis of Primitive Bands." In *Essays in Honor of A. L. Kroeber,* ed. R. H. Lowie. Berkeley: University of California Press.

Swedlund, A. C. 1978. "Historical Demography as Population Ecology." *Annual Review of Anthropology* 7: 137–173.

Wood, James W. 1990. "Fertility in Anthropological Populations." *Annual Review of Anthropology* 19: 211–242.

Zubrow, E. B., ed. 1976. *Demographic Anthropology.* Albuquerque: University of New Mexico Press.

EUGENE A. HAMMEL

ANTHROPOMETRY

Anthropometry is the science of human body measurement. Anthropometric data include measures of length, breadth, and weight of the body, circumferences of body parts, amounts of muscle and fat, the weight and size of body organs, and the size, shape, and density of bones. Many anthropometric measurements can be taken on the living, some may be taken on skeletal samples from historical burials or archaeological contexts, and other measurements are only feasible from autopsy after death. Anthropometric data are used in population research to understand the health, social, economic, and political conditions of groups of people, especially when conventional indicators (e.g., medical records, extent of schooling, gross domestic product, real wages) are not available. Such groups of people include most historical populations, slaves, archaeological populations, and many people alive today living in traditional cultures.

Kinds of Anthropometric Measures

Table 1 lists several kinds of anthropometric measures, their meaning, and methods of assessment. Height is a measure of the total history of growth of the individual. Centimeters of height accumulate over time and are the product of complex biological, behavioral, and ecological interactions. Weight represents total body mass and is a measure of recent events. Weight is more labile than height to short-term influences of diet, activity, and health. Weight may decrease over time, but height does not do so, at least during the first decades of life. The height and weight of any single individual is not of much use in population studies, but the heights and weights of many individuals from a defined group may reveal a great deal of information. Expected amounts and rates of growth in height and weight for healthy individuals at given ages from birth to maturity are well established.

These data may be used as references to compare the growth of members of the particular group under study. Significant deviations from the reference usually indicate some ecological disturbance to growth, such as poor nutrition, disease, abnormal lifestyle, psychosocial problems, and even war. Genetic disturbances to growth are well known, but usually affect individuals and not whole populations. Variations in physical growth and population struc-

ture are sensitive indicators of the quality of the environment and may be used as a mirror, reflecting rather accurately the material and moral conditions of that society.

Interpreting Anthropometric Data

Reference data are also available for virtually all anthropometric measures, and as is the case for height and weight, such references may be used to interpret the determinants of growth and development. The length of body segments (such as sitting height), thickness of skinfolds, and circumferences are used to characterize body proportions and body composition, especially the amount of muscle and fat. These measures provide more detailed evidence of health or disturbances to growth; for example, adults with short legs relative to total stature often experienced malnutrition and disease during infancy and childhood.

Radiographs reveal the degree of formation of the skeleton. The amount of skeletal maturation provides an indication of biological age, which is not identical to chronological age. Early maturers will have more advanced skeletal development than late maturers. Rate of maturation influences many biosocial capacities of the individual, including fertility. Rate of maturation may in turn be influenced by environmental quality. Finally, handgrip strength provides a measure of total physical fitness, especially as it relates to physical work capacity. In populations in which physical labor is important, greater size, skeletal maturity, and strength lead to greater productivity.

Anthropometric measurements can be collected relatively quickly and inexpensively. When properly collected, they are safe, painless, and minimally invasive. Still, taking measurements requires the cooperation, understanding, and informed consent of all participants. As children are often the subjects of growth studies it is necessary that the guardians of these children (parents, school authorities) be fully informed as to the nature of the measurements and the purpose of the research, and provide consent for the measurements. More generally, sensitivity by those conducting the research to the cultural values of the subjects is essential.

Anthropometric Data in Population Studies

An example of the use of anthropometric data in population studies comes from a survey of 8,000 years of human growth in Latin America. The data

TABLE 1

Anthropometric Measurements Commonly Taken in Research Studies

Anthropometric measure	Meaning	Method
Height	Total skeletal growth in length	Maximum length from soles of feet to vertex of head measured in the standing position (infants may be measured lying down)
Weight	Total mass of all body tissues and organs	Value of nude, or minimally clothed, body weight as assessed from a reliable balance or scale
Sitting height	Length of trunk and head. The subtraction of sitting height from stature provides an estimate of leg length	Maximum length from buttocks to vertex of head, measured with subject seated on table or chair
Head circumference	In infancy and early childhood it provides an estimate of brain growth	Maximum perimeter of head measured above the eyebrows
Skinfolds at various body sites (e.g., on the arm, back, abdomen, and leg)	Amount of adipose tissue stored at that site	Thickness of a double fold (a "pinch") of fat and skin at the site of interest
Circumference of arm, leg, abdomen, etc.	Amount of all tissue, especially fat, muscle, and bone, at the site of measurement	Usually the perimeter of relaxed arm, leg, etc. measured at the same place as the skinfold
Hand-wrist x-ray	Used to estimate maturity of the skeleton, a measure of biological age	The size and shape of the bones of the hand, wrist and forearm indicate the amount of progress toward biological maturity of the skeleton
Handgrip strength	Used to estimate overall physiological fitness of the individual	Subject maximally squeezes a dynamometer to assess muscular strength of the hand

Note: This is a partial list of commonly taken measures. Many other measurements can be, and often are, assessed in research and clinical studies. The choice of measurements is determined by the purposes of the study.

SOURCE: Compiled by author.

are for 597 samples of adult height for men and women, representing 32,922 individual measurements of stature on the living or estimates of stature from archaeological and cemetery samples. The people are Native Americans and low socioeconomic status mestizos (people of mixed Spanish and Native American heritage). The data and main trends in height are presented in Figure 1. The data were analyzed by plotting the mean value for each sample and then fitting a distance-weighted least square regression line, a type of average curve.

The oldest data in this set are for skeletal remains of a foraging people living along the coast of Ecuador. These people ate a wide variety of foods, including abundant fish and shellfish, and lived in relatively small social groups, with low population density. Their bones, teeth, and stature all indicate that they were relatively healthy. The next group includes the remains of horticulturists from Peru. They produced a wide variety of garden foods, and also hunted and gathered wild animal and plant foods. The density of the population was low to moderate, and the people seem to have been orga-

nized into tribal-type groups, with minimal social stratification. Their growth shows evidence of increasing adaptation to sedentary life and improvement of nutrition and health.

The data from 1,000 B.C.E. to 1750 C.E. come from people who practiced intensive agriculture. Several lines of evidence indicate that, overall, these people experienced reductions in stature, longevity, and health compared with the earlier periods. Agriculture may have produced a more monotonous and lower quality diet for the majority of people. The people also lived in larger and denser populations with more intensive and invasive social and political control, and strong social stratification. The social differences are expressed in stature, as the political elites were the tallest men and women in the samples. After 1500 C.E., average statures decline rapidly as a consequence of the European conquest and the social and biological insults that were imposed on the native people. During the historic period (after 1873) most Latin Americans lived by means of subsistence agriculture and wage labor. Politically, the general tendency was to have systems of local dicta-

FIGURE 1

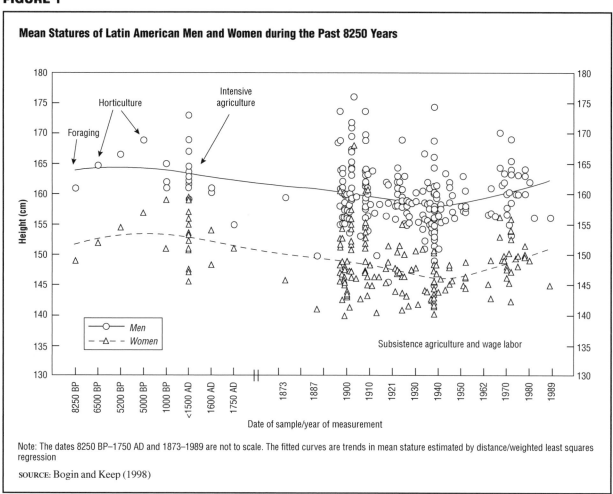

Mean Statures of Latin American Men and Women during the Past 8250 Years

Note: The dates 8250 BP–1750 AD and 1873–1989 are not to scale. The fitted curves are trends in mean stature estimated by distance/weighted least squares regression

SOURCE: Bogin and Keep (1998)

torship, with economic exploitation by European and North American countries. The health and nutrition of Amerindians and rural mestizos suffered under this system. These conditions remained in place up through the first half of the twentieth century in much of Latin America. The worldwide economic depression of the 1930s intensified these already deleterious conditions for the biological, economic, and social well being of Native Latin Americans. The negative trend in stature until 1939 may be a consequence of these environmental conditions.

The positive trend in stature from 1940 to 1989 is associated with the worldwide economic recovery sparked by World War II. Latin America benefited from this recovery and did not suffer the ravages of the war in Europe, Asia, and the Pacific. Postwar economic growth continued, especially with foreign investment. This expanded economies, helped to in-

crease the rate of urbanization, and the redistribution of the population via rural-to-urban migration. The positive trend for stature may be an outcome of these changes in the standard of living and demographic structure.

Conclusion

These brief examples, and many others like them, show how anthropometric data serve population studies as general measures for the quality of life, as quantitative economic indicators of the standard of living, and as summary measures of human welfare.

See also: *Biodemography; Data Collection, Ethical Issues in; Demographic Surveys, History and Methodology of; Nutrition and Calorie Consumption.*

BIBLIOGRAPHY

Bogin, Barry. 1999. *Patterns of Human Growth,* 2nd edition. Cambridge, Eng.: Cambridge University Press.

———. 2001. *The Growth of Humanity.* New York: Wiley-Liss.

Bogin, Barry, and Ryan Keep. 1998. "Eight Thousand Years of Human Growth in Latin America: Economic and Political History Revealed by Anthropometry." In *The Biological Standard of Living and Economic Development: Nutrition, Health, and Well Being in Historical Perspective,* ed. John Komlos and Joerg Baten. Munich: Fritz Steiner.

Tanner, James M. 1986. "Growth as a Mirror for the Conditions of Society: Secular Trends and Class Distinctions." In *Human Growth: A Multidisciplinary Review,* ed. Arto Demirjian. London: Taylor and Francis.

INTERNET RESOURCE.

National Center for Health Statistics. 2000. "CDC Growth Charts: United States." <http://www.cdc.gov/growthcharts/>.

BARRY BOGIN

ARCHAEOGENETICS

Archaeogenetics is the reconstruction of ancient demography from patterns of gene differences in contemporary populations. Population size, population movements, and subdivision into partially-isolated subpopulations leave characteristic signatures in the DNA of contemporary populations. New technologies for cheaply and rapidly examining DNA from human populations along with new theories and methods from population genetics have yielded important insights into human history. The literature in this field is of uneven quality: this article focuses on data and interpretations that are widely replicated and that have statistical support.

History of Human Numbers

Most theory about genetic diversity and population history describes neutral genes (the term "gene" here is used loosely to refer to any arbitrary DNA sequence). Much of the data in the literature derives from non-coding regions of the genome, because these are most likely to have been unaffected by natural selection. Genetic diversity in population studies refers to the average difference between two genes chosen at random: In the simplest case, it is simply heterozygosity, the probability that two random genes are different from each other.

Mutation introduces new diversity in a population, while genetic drift—the process by which each generation is effectively a sample with replacement of the gene pool of the previous generation—causes loss of diversity. The rate of diversity gain is the mutation rate; in humans, in the nuclear genome (that is, the DNA contained in the cell nucleus), the mutation rate is usually taken to be 10^{-9} per nucleotide position per year. The rate of loss of diversity is proportional to the reciprocal of the *effective size, N_e,* of the population. Effective size is the size of an ideal population with statistical properties equivalent to those of a real population. Many people in human populations have not yet reached reproductive age and many others are past the age of reproduction; neither of these groups influences the effective size. For humans, the effective size of a population is usually estimated to be one third of the census size.

Effective size is the inverse of the rate of diversity loss, and since effective size may fluctuate over time, the average rate of diversity loss is the average of the reciprocal of effective size (that is, it is the harmonic mean rather than the ordinary mean). A population that fluctuates in size between 1,000 and 10,000, and thus has a mean size of 5,500, has a long-term effective size of about 1,800. Because of this, genetic diversity in a population is sensitive to long term minima and less sensitive to maxima.

Direct estimates from genes put long-term effective size for the human species in the range 10,000 to 20,000. Since there are approximately 6 billion humans alive today, this small effective size suggests that the number of human ancestors has been drastically smaller, consistent with a recent origin of our species from a small founding population. Fossil and archaeological evidence support such a founding event, and place it about 100,000 to 200,000 years ago.

In order to infer more about demographic history, it is necessary to introduce some results of coalescent theory, the theory of the history of a sample

FIGURE 1

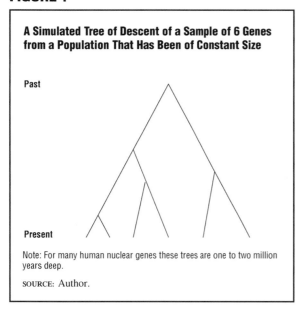

A Simulated Tree of Descent of a Sample of 6 Genes from a Population That Has Been of Constant Size

Past

Present

Note: For many human nuclear genes these trees are one to two million years deep.

SOURCE: Author.

of genes from a population. Consider a sample of n genes drawn from a population. These n genes are tips of a tree of descent, called a *coalescent tree*: if one could follow their history backward in time, one would find that occasionally two of the genes are copies of the same gene in a parent in the previous generation—a *coalescent event*. Coalescent events reduce the number of ancestors of the sample: continuing backward, eventually one arrives at a single ancestor of all n genes—the *most recent common ancestor* (MRCA) of the sample.

A coalescent tree, with the vertical axis proportional to time, might look like Figure 1. There are six genes in the sample depicted, and as one follows them back in time the number of ancestors of the sample is six, then five after the first coalescence, then four, three, two, and finally the single common ancestor of all the genes. A tree like this, descending from a single random mating population of constant size N_e, has the following properties:

(1) The expected time back to coalescence of any pair of genes is $2N_e$ generations.

(2) The expected time to the MRCA is $4N_e$ generations for large sample size n.

(3) The expected total branch length of the tree is $4N_e \Sigma(1/i)$ generations where the index of summation i goes from 1 to $n-1$.

Mutations are rare and occur randomly in time and across sites on a gene. If u is the mutation rate per site per generation, then, corresponding to (1) and (2) above:

(1') The average pairwise difference between sequences is $4N_e u$.

(2') The expected total number of mutations in the set of sequences is $4N_e u\Sigma(1/i)$.

Given knowledge of the mutation rate, either of the above two expressions provides an estimate of the effective size of population, N_e.

As an illustration of property (1'), the Human Genome Project has found that a single nucleotide difference between chromosome pairs occurs on average once every 1,000 bases in the human genome, so the average pairwise difference is 10^{-3}. The mutation rate of 10^{-9} per year corresponds to a rate of 25×10^{-9} per generation, and substituting these figures in the expression (1') yields an estimate of human effective size of 10^4. Thus, the human species has genetic diversity equivalent to that of a species whose effective size has been constant at 10 thousand, corresponding to a census size of 30 to 40 thousand people.

Now consider a coalescent tree from a population that originated from a small number of founders and then grew rapidly to a large size. During the time when it was large, few coalescent events occurred, but before it grew the population was very small and coalescence was rapid. A gene tree from such a population might look like Figure 2, a pattern described as "star-" or "comb-" like. The total branch length of the tree is nearly proportional to the sample size n; the mean pairwise difference between samples is slightly greater than $2Tu$ where T is the time since the population growth occurred; and the top of the tree is only slightly earlier than T generations ago.

Differences among DNA sequences sampled from trees like those in Figure 1 and Figure 2 are the bases for inferences about ancient demography from DNA. First, a mutation that occurs in the tree of Figure 2 is likely to occur in one of the long terminal branches, so that it will be found only once in the sample; a mutation in the tree of Figure 1 is likely to occur near the top and hence would be represented in the sample with many copies. Hence "excess singletons and rare types" is an indicator of population expansion in the past. Second, all the pairwise differences among sequences from Figure 2 will be roughly equal, since the times separating the sequences are similar. Pairwise differences from Figure 1, on the other hand, will be erratic and differ a lot among themselves.

The first genetic marker to be studied intensively with an interest in coalescences was human mitochondrial DNA (mtDNA)—the DNA that is contained in the cell's mitochondria rather than its nucleus. It was found that the human mtDNA tree was like that of Figure 2, with the time of expansion T estimated to be 80,000 years ago. This pattern indicated that the human species had a focal origin, and that the genetic contribution to modern humans of most of the world population of archaic humans, like the Neanderthals of Europe, was either nonexistent or vanishingly small.

Unfortunately, subsequent studies of other genetic systems—using nuclear rather than mitochondrial DNA—have not confirmed this picture. The issue of when and how the human population grew from only a few thousand to 6 billion is the subject of lively current debate. Some nuclear genes show no evidence of population expansion, while others show mild evidence of expansion, consistent with population growth since the end of the last ice age (around 12,000 years ago). The contending hypotheses are:

(A) There was a founding event and subsequent population expansion about 100,000 years ago, as suggested by mtDNA and some other genetic systems, but pervasive natural selection in the nuclear genome has obscured the signature of this event.

(B) A new genotype appeared before 100,000 years ago and spread throughout the species, leading to replacement of some of the genome and incorporation of genes from archaic populations at other parts of the genome. According to this hypothesis, mtDNA, the Y chromosome, and some other parts of the nuclear genome underwent replacement, but much of the nuclear genome did not.

(C) The major numerical expansion of humans has taken place since the last ice age. Many nuclear genes coalesce about 1.8 million years ago, around the time of the expansion of modern human's precursor species, *Homo erectus,* out of Africa. This corresponds to 72,000 generations at 25 years per generation. Under a constant population size model, this would imply an effective population size N_e of

FIGURE 2

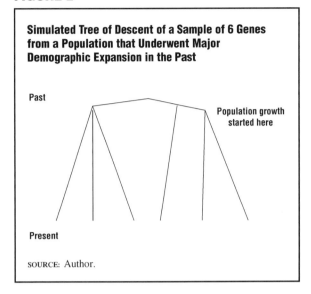

Simulated Tree of Descent of a Sample of 6 Genes from a Population that Underwent Major Demographic Expansion in the Past

Past

Population growth started here

Present

SOURCE: Author.

$(72,000 \div 4) = 18,000$, which lies comfortably within the range of genetic estimates of N_e. In other words, the small human effective size reflects a focal origin 1.8 million years ago. According to this hypothesis, the evidence from human mtDNA of massive expansion over the last 100,000 years is an artifact.

Published estimates of coalescence times of nuclear genes are generally well below 1.8 million years, but the absolute values of these estimates should not be taken seriously. They rely on knowledge of the mutation rate, which is calculated from chimpanzee-human differences and the assumed time since the two species separated. Problems with this calculation may lead to a substantial overestimation of the rate. Taking this into account, almost all of the data on coalescence times of nuclear genes are consistent with hypothesis C, but hypothesis C is inconsistent with the expansion signature in mitochondrial DNA and the evidence of expansion from some other families of markers. Scholars at the beginning of the twenty-first century found some version of hypothesis B to be the most promising.

Human Diversity in Detail

The example given above showing an estimate of human N_e of 10,000 was based on single nucleotide differences along a pair of genes. These differences are called *Single Nucleotide Polymorphisms* (SNPs), and they are one of several important classes of genetic markers. Another class is repeat polymorphisms, genes where there are repetitions of a DNA sequence. Many of these are in non-coding DNA, but they also occur in genes and affect the protein that the gene produces. Generically these are called *Variable Number of Tandem Repeats* (VNTRs). If the repeat motifs are very short—two to four bases— they are called *Short Tandem Repeats* (STRs) or microsatellites. Commonly used STRs for identification and for studies of evolution are tetranucleotide repeats with four base motifs, and dinucleotides with two. Trinucleotide repeats are less likely to be neutral since, with three base motifs, they can affect genes more easily.

The earlier example suggested that SNP density is a natural statistic for describing genetic diversity within a population. The corresponding natural statistic for VNTR loci is the variance of repeat length in a sample of genes. Mutations change repeat length by a small amount, so that the mean squared difference between two chromosomes, as well as the probability they are the same length, should be monotonically related to the time elapsed since the common ancestor of the chromosomes, hence to the effective size of the population.

Human within-population diversity is highest in Africa and declines as one moves away from Africa. This is seen in the scatterplot in Figure 3, taken from Henry C. Harpending and Elise Eller's 1999 work. The horizontal axis of the figure is genetic distance from Africa; the vertical axis is average heterozygosity—the probability that two STR genes are the same length, averaged over 60 short repeat polymorphisms. The plot shows the relationship between how genetically different a population is from the African average and within-population genetic diversity. Populations more different from Africans are less diverse, and the relationship is nearly linear. This pattern is thought to be part of the signature of the African origin of our species and the loss of diversity associated with repeated founder effects during colonization at the edge of the expansion. While Figure 3 only includes Old World populations, other data sources show that the decline continues into the New World: American Indian populations are 15 to 25 percent less diverse than African populations. Direct studies of SNP density are likely to shed further light on this pattern as additional data become available.

Just as within-population diversity describes how different two genes from the same population are on average, between-population diversity de-

FIGURE 3

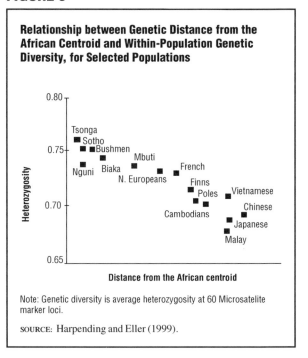

Relationship between Genetic Distance from the African Centroid and Within-Population Genetic Diversity, for Selected Populations

Note: Genetic diversity is average heterozygosity at 60 Microsatelite marker loci.

SOURCE: Harpending and Eller (1999).

scribes how much greater is the average difference between genes from different populations relative to overall average gene differences. In other words, total diversity of a sample of populations can be partitioned into within- and between-population components in a way completely analogous to the analysis of variance in statistics.

The fraction of diversity between populations is conventionally written as F_{st}. Various kinds of genetic data have been used to estimate F_{st}. For large human populations like those in Figure 3, all the estimates are in the range of 10 to 15 percent. One interpretation of this is that if the world's peoples were to mate at random, average within-population diversity would increase by this amount; another interpretation is that F_{st} measures relative within-population similarity or shared genetic material. Thus the excess shared genetic material within human subpopulations relative to the whole world is 10 to 15 percent. In a famous early discussion of this point, Richard Lewontin (1972) emphasized that 10 to 15 percent is a small amount and drew the conclusion that differences among human populations or races are insignificant. On the other hand, the excess shared genetic material within a population between grandparent and grandchild is 12.5 percent (one-eighth), and society does not regard the genetic similarity between grandparent and grandchild as trivial.

See also: *Biology, Population; Evolutionary Demography; Paleodemography; Prehistoric Populations.*

BIBLIOGRAPHY

Di Rienzo, Anna, and Allan C. Wilson. 1991. "Branching Pattern in the Evolutionary Tree for Human Mitochondrial DNA." *Proceedings of the National Academy of Sciences USA* 88: 1,597–1,601.

Harpending, Henry C., and Elise Eller. 1999. "Human Diversity and Its History." *Biodiversity* pp. 301–314.

Harpending, Henry C., and Alan Rogers. 2001. "Genetic Perspectives on Human Origins and Differentiation." *Annual Review of Genomics and Human Genetics* 1: 361–385.

Hudson, Richard R. 1990. "Gene Genealogies and the Coalescent Process." *Oxford Surveys in Evolutionary Biology* 7: 1–44.

Lewontin, Richard C. 1972. *Evolutionary Biology,* Vol. 6: *The Apportionment of Human Diversity,* ed. Theodosius H. Dobzhansky, Max K. Hecht, and William C. Steere. New York: Appleton-Century-Crofts.

Rogers, Alan R., and Lynn B. Jorde. 1995. "Genetic Evidence on the Origin of Modern Humans." *Human Biology* 67: 1–36.

Takahata, Naoyuki, Sang-Hee Lee, et al. 2001. "Testing Multiregionality of Modern Human Origins." *Molecular Biology and Evolution* 18: 172–183.

Henry C. Harpending

ARIÈS, PHILIPPE

(1914–1984)

Philippe Ariès was born in Blois, in the Loire Valley of France, to an old Bordeaux family. He studied history and geography at the Sorbonne but did not graduate. During the pre-war years, Ariès haunted the rightist-monarchist circles of the *Action Française.* In 1941 he became an instructor at the École des Cadres of La Chapelle-Saint-Serval, which had just been created near Paris by the Vichy government, and in 1943 he was appointed head of the Center of Documentation of the Research Institute on Citrus Fruits. His most important book, *Histoire des populations françaises et de leurs attitudes devant la vie,* was published in 1948 (2nd edition, 1971). It did not provoke any reaction from academic historians, but immediately attracted the attention of demographers. From 1950 to 1975, Ariès directed a series at Plon Editions and contributed regularly to the royalist *Nation française* from 1955 to 1966. His second major publication, *L'Enfant et la vie familiale sous l'Ancien Régime* (1960), translated as *Centuries of Childhood,* was a bestseller among scholarly books in the United States. He was invited to lecture in the United States, and he found financial support for his research there. Ariès's other major books, *Essai sur l'histoire de la mort en Occident* (1975) and *L'Homme devant la mort* (1977), earned him recognition at last as a prophet in his own country. He was elected Director at the École des Hautes Études en Sciences Sociales in 1978, and was called to contribute to the official anthology of the "new history." When he died in 1984, shortly after the death of his wife and lifelong collaborator, he was no longer an isolated pioneer, but one of the founders of demographic history and the unquestioned master of the history of mentalities.

Although he characterized himself as a "Sunday" historian, Ariès was by no means an occasional researcher but an authentic "everyday" scholar. Paralleling the triumphant socioeconomic history launched by the *Annales* school, he was the herald of a new cultural history, documenting the attitudes of people in their daily existence toward life, love, and death. Demography was the key that allowed him to unlock the secrets of the private domain, and the family was the privileged axis of his history of mentalities. Ariès showed that childhood, adolescence, and the indissoluble marriage were relatively recent concepts. Following Adolphe Landry (1934), he argued that the pursuit of pleasure and happiness, added to the growing rationalization of behavior, had led to the deliberate strategy of couples to separate sexuality from procreation, opening the way to birth control and to a general liberation of sexual mores. This development coincided, too, with a changing conception of death—for Ariès, the topic where the "collective unconscious" could best manifest itself. To describe how the "tamed Death" of the Middle Ages was transformed into the "forbidden Death" of the present day, Ariès and his wife made extensive and imaginative use of iconography.

Ariès did not escape some critics who reproached this "banana seller" for the lack of representativeness of his assertions, the deficiency of his quantitative measures, and his neglect of the role played by the State. But during the 1970s and 1980s, the "new history"—that is, cultural history—prevailed over the socioeconomic history of the 1950s and 1960s (even if there was, after Ariès, a risk of fragmentation of this learning). As the chronicler of everyday life in that "world we have lost," according to Peter Laslett's book, Ariès had rightly perceived many of the symptoms of future change. But he could hardly have foreseen the scope of the upheaval that the mores in Western societies were experiencing even within one or two decades of his own passing.

See also: *Culture and Population; Family: History; Historical Demography; Second Demographic Transition.*

BIBLIOGRAPHY

SELECTED WORKS BY PHILIPPE ARIÈS

Ariès, Philippe. 1960. *L'Enfant et la vie familiale sous l'Ancien Régime,* Paris: Plon. Translated as *Centuries of Childhood: A Social History of Family Life,* 1962. New York: Vintage Books.

———. 1971. *Histoire des populations françaises et de leurs attitudes devant la vie de depuis le XVIIIe siècle,* 2nd edition. Paris: SELF.

———. 1975. *Essai sur l'histoire de la mort en Occident du Moyen-Age à nos jours.* Paris: Seuil. Translated as *Western Attitudes toward Death: From the Middle Ages to the Present,* 1974. Baltimore: Johns Hopkins University Press.

———. 1977. *L'Homme devant la mort.* Paris: Seuil. Translated as *The Hour of Our Death,* 1981. New York: Knopf.

———. 1980. "Two successive motivations for the declining birth rate in the West." *Population and Development Review* 6(4): 645–650.

———. 1983. *Images de l'homme devant la mort.* Paris: Seuil. Translated as *Images of Man and Death,* 1985. Cambridge, MA: Harvard University Press.

Ariès, Philippe, ed. 1986. *Le Temps de l'histoire* (1954). Paris, Seuil.

———. 1980. *Un Historien du dimanche.* Paris: Seuil.

Ariès, Philippe, and Georges Duby, eds. 1991. *A History of Private Life.* Cambridge, MA: Belknap Press.

SELECTED WORKS ABOUT PHILIPPE ARIÈS

Gros, Guillaume. 2002. *Philippe Ariès (1914–1984). Un traditionaliste non-conformiste: de l'Action Française à l'École des Hautes Études en Sciences Sociales.* Paris: Institut d'Études Politiques.

Hutton, Patrick M. 2002. "Philippe Ariès and the Secrets of the History of Mentalities." *Historical Reflections/Reflexions historiques* 28(1): 1–19.

Landry, Adolphe. 1982 [1934]. *La révolution démographique: Études et essais sur les problèmes de la population.* Paris: Institut national d'études démographiques.

Laslett, Peter. 1984. *The World We Have Lost,* 3rd edition. New York: Scribner.

JACQUELINE HECHT

ARTIFICIAL SOCIAL LIFE

Most demographic research either develops or uses some kind of theory or model: for instance, a theory of fertility or a model of the class system. Generally, such theories are stated in discursive English, although sometimes the theory is represented as an equation (for example, in regression analysis). In the 1990s researchers began to explore the possibilities of expressing theories as computer programs. The advantage is that social processes can then be simulated in the computer and in some circumstances it is even possible to carry out "experiments" on artificial social systems that would otherwise be quite impossible.

Although the simulation of social dynamics has a long history in the social sciences, the advent of much more powerful computers, more powerful computer languages, and the greater availability of data have led to increased interest in simulation as a method for developing and testing social theories.

The logic underlying the methodology of simulation is not very different from the logic underlying statistical modeling. In both cases, a model is constructed (for example, in the form of a computer program or a regression equation) through a process of abstraction from what are theorized to be the actually existing social processes. The model is then used to generate expected values that are compared with empirical data. The main difference between statistical modeling and simulation is that the simulation model can itself be "run" to produce output, while a statistical model requires a statistical analysis program to generate expected values.

Advantages of Simulation

Paradoxically, one of the main advantages of simulation is that it is hard to do. To create a useful simulation model, its theoretical presuppositions need to have been thought through with great clarity. Every relationship to be modeled has to be specified exactly and every parameter has to be given a value, for otherwise it will be impossible to run the simulation. This discipline means that it is impossible to be vague about what is being assumed. It also means that the model is potentially open to inspection by other researchers in all its detail. These benefits of clarity and precision also have disadvantages, however. Simulations of complex social processes involve the estimation of many parameters and adequate data for making the estimates can be difficult to come by.

Another benefit of simulation is that it can, in some circumstances, give insights into the "emergence" of macro level phenomena from micro level action. For example, a simulation of interacting individuals may reveal clear patterns of influence when examined on a societal scale. A simulation by Andrzej Nowak and Bibb Latané (1993), for example, shows how simple rules about the way in which one individual influences another's attitudes can yield results about attitude change at the level of a society, and a simulation by Robert Axelrod (1995) demonstrates how patterns of political domination can arise from a few rules followed by simulated nation-states.

Agent-Based Simulation

The field of social simulation has come to be dominated by an approach called agent-based simulation (alternatively called multi-agent simulation). Although other types of simulation such as those based on system dynamics models (using sets of difference equations) and microsimulation (based on the simulated aging of a survey sample to learn about its characteristics in the future) are still undertaken, most simulation research now uses agents.

Agents are computer programs (or parts of programs) that are designed to act relatively autonomously within a simulated environment. An agent can represent an individual or an organization, according to what is being modeled. Agents are generally programmed to be able to "perceive" and "react" to their situation, to pursue the goals they are given, and to interact with other agents, for example by sending them messages. Agents are generally created using an object-oriented programming language and are constructed using collections of condition–action rules. The agent examines its rules to identify those whose conditions hold true in its current situation and then executes ("fires") the actions determined by just those rules. The effect of firing the rules will normally be to alter the agent's situation, and thus in the next cycle a different set of rules will fire.

Agent-based models have been used to investigate the bases of leadership, the functions of norms, the implications of environmental change on organizations, the effects of land-use planning constraints on populations, the evolution of language, and many other topics. Examples of research can be found in the *Journal of Artificial Societies and Social Simulation.*

While most agent-based simulations have been created to model real social phenomena, it is also possible to model situations that could not exist in our world, in order to understand whether there are universal constraints on the possibility of social life (for example, can societies function if their members are entirely self-interested and rational?). These are at one end of a spectrum of simulations ranging from those of entirely imaginary societies to those that aim to reproduce specific settings in great detail.

An interesting variant on agent-based modeling is to include people in place of some or all of the computational agents. This transforms the model into a type of multiplayer computer game, which can be valuable for allowing the players to learn more about the dynamics of some social setting (for example, business students can be given a game of this type in order to learn about the effects of business strategies). Such games are known as participatory simulations.

The Potential of Simulation

Although computer simulation can be regarded as simply an another method for representing models of social processes, it encourages a theoretical perspective which emphasizes emergence, the search for simple regularities that give rise to complex phenomena, and an evolutionary view of the development of societies. This perspective has connections with complexity theory, an attempt to locate general principles applying to all systems which show autonomous behavior—including not only human societies, but also biological and physical phenomena.

See also: *Simulation Models.*

BIBLIOGRAPHY

Axelrod, Robert. 1995. "A Model of the Emergence of New Political Actors." In *Artificial Societies: The Computer Simulation of Social Life,* ed. Nigel Gilbert and Rosaria Conte. London: UCL.

Carley, Kathleen, and Michael Prietula. 1994. *Computational Organization Theory.* Hillsdale, NJ: Lawrence Erlbaum.

Epstein, Joshua M., and Robert Axtell. 1996. *Growing Artificial Societies: Social Science from the Bottom Up.* Cambridge, MA: MIT Press.

Gilbert, Nigel. 1999. "Computer Simulation in the Social Sciences." Special issue of *American Behavioral Scientist* 42.

Gilbert, Nigel, and Klaus G. Troitzsch. 1999. *Simulation for the Social Scientist.* Milton Keynes, Eng.: Open University Press.

Nowak, Andrzej, and Bibb Latané. 1993. "Simulating the Emergence of Social Order from Individual Behaviour." In *Simulating Societies: The Computer Simulation of Social Phenomena,* ed. Nigel Gilbert and Jim Doran. London: UCL Press.

INTERNET RESOURCE.

Journal of Artificial Societies and Social Simulation. <http://www.soc.surrey.ac.uk/JASSS/>.

NIGEL GILBERT

ASYLUM, RIGHT OF

The Universal Declaration of Human Rights proclaims that:

> 1. Everyone has the right to seek and to enjoy in other countries asylum from persecution. 2. This right may not be invoked in the case of prosecutions genuinely arising from non-political crimes or from acts contrary to the purposes and principles of the United Nations. (Universal Declaration of Human Rights, Article 14)

This does not establish a right to asylum, only a right to seek asylum, and if successful in doing so, to enjoy that asylum. There is no corresponding obligation on the part of states to grant asylum. As the right to asylum has never been codified, its granting is at the discretion of states. Thus, the right to decide whether someone is deserving of asylum lies with the state in which the asylum application is lodged. The 1951 Convention Relating to the Status of Refugees (Geneva Convention) and 1967 Protocol to that Convention (New York Protocol) set some limits on the sovereign right to determine who is a refugee. Two articles are of particular importance: the definition of refugee in Article 1 of the Convention, and the protection of *non-refoulement* (that is, protection against forcible return) under article 33. These articles state respectively that:

> The term "refugee" shall apply to any person who: . . . 2). . . .owing to a well-founded fear of being persecuted for reasons of race, religion, nationality, membership of a particular social group or political opinion, is outside the country of his nationality and is unable or, owing to such fear, is unwilling to avail himself of the protection of that country. . .(Geneva Convention, Article 1)

And,

> No Contracting State shall expel or return ('refouler') a refugee in any manner whatsoever to the frontiers of territories where his life or freedom would be threatened on account of his race, religion, nationality, membership of a particular social group or political opinion. (Geneva Convention, Article 33)

As of February 1, 2002, 140 states were signatories to the Convention; 138 had signed the Protocol; and

135 had signed both. All European Union states are signatories to both documents. Many states in Asia have signed neither instrument. In Africa, the majority of states have not only signed the Convention and Protocol, but also a regional (Organization of African Unity) convention, extending the status of refugee to those fleeing conflicts in the region.

The states that have committed themselves to the laws and principles set out in the Convention and Protocol have divergent means of applying the tools of refugee protection. For example, some states grant refugee status only when persecution at the hands of a state or governmental actor is feared, and not in the case of persecution at the hands of a nonstate militia or other such group. For many states, conferring recognition as a refugee depends on persecution that is objectively demonstrated as targeting the individual in question. Those fleeing war, which targets whole populations, fall outside the definition as thus interpreted.

In a number of developed states, a person who is deemed not to qualify for refugee status (according to the definition cited above) but who cannot be returned to his or her country of origin (pursuant to the *non-refoulement* stipulation) may be granted a form of supplementary or complementary protection. This is the case in most of the European Union (EU) member states and in Canada, but not in the United States. This type of humanitarian status frequently has fewer rights attendant to it: There may be greater restrictions on the possibilities for family reunification, or a time limit may be applied to the length of legal residence before permit renewal. The issue of the length of time for which asylum or protection may be granted has been a contentious one in many states. Although the cessation clauses (1C) of the 1951 Convention mean that refugee status may be withdrawn if circumstances change in the country of origin, Convention status has been viewed by most states as something of permanence, at least in terms of the residence rights they confer with it.

In other situations states have sought to create explicitly temporary forms of protection. The most striking instance applied to people fleeing former Yugoslavia, including Bosnia and Kosovo, to other European states in the 1990s, who were granted temporary protection rather than refugee status. These people were deemed to be fleeing generalized violence rather than individualized persecution. But the move toward temporary forms of protective status was also driven by the administrative difficulty of dealing with a greatly increased number of asylum claims in a short period. Increasingly, time limits are being attached to the status granted to refugees. The Netherlands, for example, enacted a new Aliens Law in 2000, granting only three years residence (in yearly increments) in the first instance to persons deemed to be in need of protection.

Since the mid-1980s European states have adopted policies and practices that limit the rights of those not returned to their countries of origin, whether or not they are granted a Convention refugee status. This is partly a reaction to a real or perceived increase in xenophobia, prompted especially by concerns about asylum-seekers' access to various forms of welfare services, in money or in kind, that is available to the resident population. In part it is also because the key foreign policy support for the asylum system has changed dramatically since the end of the Cold War. The Convention definition of a refugee was written with World War II fresh in the collective memory, and the Cold War as a developing phenomenon. When the Cold War ended, political authorities in the West saw the definition as no longer fully relevant. Moreover, they started to seek partners in the newly democratic states who would take on their share of the refugee protection burden. One means of burden-shifting came with the development of the concept of a "safe third country": If asylum-seekers passed through a country in which they could have sought and enjoyed protection before reaching their desired destination, some states consider that they should be the responsibility of that country and should be returned to it. Burden-shifting trends are apparent within the EU, and between EU member states and their eastern neighbors. They are also influencing asylum policymaking in Southern Africa, Australia, and elsewhere.

As countries have tightened their asylum systems, they have seen a rise in migrant smuggling. In turning to unconventional methods of transportation and assistance in acquiring documentation, refugees become doubly vulnerable: first, as victims of persecution and second, as frequent victims of exploitation.

A further trend, emphasized by reactions to the terrorist attacks of September 11, 2001, is the linking of security and asylum issues, not only at the causal end of refugee movements, but also at the destination of the protection seeker. As states seek greater control over entry to their territories, they increasingly turn to resettlement programs of the kind seen in the U.S., Canada, Australia, and New Zealand. In these programs persons to be resettled are selected in their country of origin or a neighboring state—thereby, it is hoped, taking the initiative away from smugglers as well as permitting earlier screening for criminal background or terrorism threat. This potentially also narrows the opportunities for asylum seeking.

See also: *Ethnic Cleansing; Genocide; Immigration Policies; Refugees, Demography of.*

BIBLIOGRAPHY

Convention Relating to the Status of Refugees. 1951. 189 United Nations Treaty Series (UNTS) 137

Goodwin-Gill, Guy S. 1996. *The Refugee in International Law.* Oxford: Clarendon Press.

Gowlland-Debbas, Vera, ed. 1996. *The Problem of Refugees in the Light of Contemporary International Law Issues.* The Hague, The Netherlands: Martinus Nijhoff.

Hathaway, James C. 1991. *The Law of Refugee Status.* Toronto: Butterworths.

Nicholson, Frances, and Patrick Twomey. 1999. *Refugees Rights and Realities: Evolving International Concepts and Regimes.* Cambridge, Eng.: Cambridge University Press.

OAU Convention Governing Specific Aspects of Refugee Problems in Africa. 1969. 1001 UNTS 45.

United Kingdom Home Office. 2002. *Secure Borders, Safe Haven: Integration with Diversity in Modern Britain.* London: Crown Publishers.

Universal Declaration of Human Rights 1948. *American Journal of International Law* 1949 (Supplement) 43(3).

Vreemdelingen Wet 2000 [Asylum Act 2000]. 2000. The Hague: Staatsblad. 495 December 7, 2000.

INTERNET RESOURCES.

Protocol to the Convention Relating to the Status of Refugees. 1967. 606 UNTS 267. Available at the United Nations High Commissioner for Refugees website. <http://www.unhcr.ch>.

van Selm, Joanne. 2001. "Access to Procedures: Safe Third Countries, *Safe Countries of Origin* and Time Limits." United Nations High Commissioner for Refugees website. <http://www.unhcr.ch/cgi-bin/texis/vtx/home/>.

JOANNE VAN SELM

B

BABY BOOM, POST–WORLD WAR II

No twentieth-century demographic phenomenon in the developed countries has attracted greater attention than the "baby boom"—the sustained post–World War II fertility increases in many developed countries that produced large birth cohorts from the mid-1940s to the mid-1960s. The magnitude of the baby boom, especially in the United States, has made it a demographic event with widespread, long-lasting, and well-chronicled consequences. But demographers have focused their most serious attention on explaining why the baby boom occurred and on forecasting fertility in its aftermath. The baby boom (and the subsequent bust) is widely seen as epitomizing demographic forecasting failure. It remains demography's primary example of the unpredictability of population trends and is frequently cited as evidence that the knowledge base on human fertility is grossly deficient. However, the demographic phenomena that produced the baby boom are well known, and there is a plausible social history of the circumstances that spawned that upsurge of births.

Defining Baby Booms and Echoes

A baby boom, as a generic concept, is a large increase in the number of births relative to some previous year or average (i.e., an increase in birth cohort size). This can result from two factors: a rise in the number of potential childbearers (i.e., women aged 15 to 44, partly a function of past cohort size) and the increased average risk of having a child. When fertility increases result from large cohorts entering the childbearing years (i.e., only the first factor), demog-

raphers call this fertility increase an "echo" of a previous baby boom.

The post–World War II baby boom, however, was not driven by trends in cohort size: Indeed, the boom of the 1950s and early 1960s was produced by the small cohorts born during the 1930s. (Likewise, the American baby bust of the late 1960s and 1970s occurred in the face of the maturing baby boom.) Thus, it is clear that birth rates, not generation size, have been the key factor in the postwar upsurge of births. For this reason, researchers focus attention on changes in fertility rates as the phenomena to be explained. More specifically, there is a focus on the total fertility rate (TFR)—the number of births women would have if they experienced the age-specific fertility rates of a given period.

Fertility Increases During the Baby Boom

Figure 1 shows the U.S. TFR from 1917 to 2001. The baby boom TFR maximum is 3.68, which was reached in 1957. TFR lows preceding and following the baby boom were 2.15 and 1.74 respectively. Also note that the post–World War II baby boom lasted roughly two decades in the United States. The basic features of this TFR increase can be observed in most Western developed countries. In a 1974 study demographer Arthur Campbell analyzed data for 18 Western countries with TFRs that approximated 2 in the 1930s. TFRs for these same countries were 2.7 by the early 1950s and 3.1 by the early 1960s. All of these countries experienced subsequent sharp fertility declines. By the early 1980s all of the countries studied by Campbell had TFR values below 2.1. Table 1 presents some of Campbell's data for individual countries, updated through the 1990s; all show key features visible in the U.S. data.

73

FIGURE 1

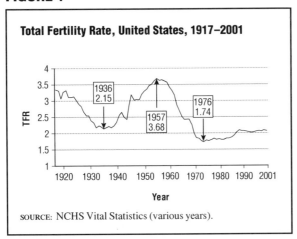

Total Fertility Rate, United States, 1917–2001

SOURCE: NCHS Vital Statistics (various years).

An additional feature of the postwar baby boom was the pervasiveness of the fertility increases and declines among subgroups within countries. For instance, in the United States all major racial and educational groups participated in both the baby boom and the subsequent bust.

In contrast to its pervasiveness across geographic areas and social groups, the baby boom can be traced to a few dynamic, demographic components. TFR changes can reflect changes in the ages that women have births (i.e., the timing or tempo of childbearing) and/or changes in the number (or quantum) of children that women eventually bear. To capture the relative importance of these changes the TFR can be usefully disaggregated into age and parity components. This disaggregation allows measurement of timing (or tempo) and number (or quantum) changes.

Table 2 shows demographer Norman Ryder's classic decomposition of the U.S. baby boom and subsequent baby bust. From a low point in the mid-1930s to its peak in 1957, the TFR increased from 2.15 to 3.68. Column one shows that somewhat less than half (42%) of this birth increase can be attributed to changes in the quantum component; the remainder can be accounted for by timing shifts toward younger ages at childbearing. Further, the quantum increases are almost entirely due to increased first and second births (88%) and the timing shifts are primarily attributed to age at first birth (78%). Such decomposition shows that earlier and pervasive parenthood accounts for the majority of the baby boom increase in the TFR. Likewise, post-1957 TFR declines were driven by timing changes,

in this case toward later ages of childbearing, with rising age at first birth the most important component. Post-1957 quantum changes did include important declines in third or higher order births.

Other decompositional demographic analysis provides important clues regarding whether explanations should center on cohort or period factors. The evidence is unequivocal: Postwar fertility trends in developed countries are largely accounted for by period shifts; in given calendar years, fertility rates show pervasive changes across ages. Stated differently, there is little evidence that birth year strongly conditions responses to current events.

Causes of the Baby Boom and Bust

Economist Richard Easterlin's explanation of the baby boom has spawned a large body of research. While Easterlin's theory yields valuable insights, empirical evidence requires substantial adjustments. In brief, in 1973 Easterlin identified shifts in relative income across generations as the primary cause of the baby boom. Specifically, those who were children during the 1930s were raised in uncertain times and in very modest economic circumstances. They reached adulthood in the economically prosperous postwar years and compared their economic circumstances favorably to those of their families of origin (i.e., they had high relative income). As a result, at young ages, baby boomers felt prepared to marry early and to have children early. Later, in a 1978 study, Easterlin stressed the role of relative cohort size in producing shifts in the economic well-being of successive generations. Those born and raised during the depression were members of small cohorts compared to those born during the baby boom. Small cohorts, in contrast to large ones, experienced relatively favorable conditions in educational and employment settings (had high relative income) and thus married and had children earlier. Easterlin's thesis had substantial intuitive appeal and could account for the earlier and more universal parenthood that characterized the baby boom. In addition, cohort size data accurately predicted the American fertility boom and bust. However, there is little evidence at the micro level that relative income is strongly associated with the timing of family formation or the number of children born. Since relative income is the key causal/behavioral mechanism in Easterlin's theory, this negative evidence is highly problematic. In addition, Easterlin's argument is clearly cohort-based while the empirical demo-

TABLE 1

Total Fertility Rates for Selected Low-Fertility Countries: 1930s–1995

Country	Pre-WW II (1930s)	Post-WW II (Early 1950s)	Baby Boom Peak	Baby Bust (1975)	Contemporary Levels (1985)	(1995)
Australia	2.16 (1933)	3.09 (1950-52)	3.51 (1961)	2.20	1.89	1.83
Austria	1.65 (1933-34)	2.07 (1950-52)	2.81 (1963)	1.83	1.47	1.40
Belgium	1.96 (1933-37)	2.37 (1948-52)	2.69 (1964)	1.74	1.51	1.55
Canada	2.69 (1936-40)	3.53 (1950-52)	3.93 (1959)	1.83	1.64	1.65
Denmark	2.13 (1936)	2.53 (1950-52)	2.63 (1963)	1.92	1.45	1.80
United Kingdom	1.83 (1939)	2.15 (1950-52)	2.88 (1964)	1.81	1.80	1.71
Germany (West)	2.03 (1934)	2.06 (1951-53)	2.54 (1964)	1.45	1.28	1.34
France	2.07 (1934-38)	2.85 (1949-53)	2.86 (1964)	1.93	1.82	1.70
Netherlands	2.63 (1933-37)	3.17 (1948-52)	3.19 (1961)	1.66	1.51	1.53
Norway	1.84 (1932-35)	2.6 (1951-55)	2.96 (1964)	1.98	1.68	1.87
Sweden	1.7 (1933-37)	2.31 (1948-52)	2.49 (1964)	1.78	1.74	1.74
Switzerland	1.75 (1937)	2.34 (1950-52)	2.66 (1964)	1.61	1.52	1.48
United States	2.04 (1934-36)	3.08 (1949-51)	3.76 (1957)	1.78	1.84	2.03

SOURCE: Campbell (1974); OECD publications.

graphic evidence indicates the dominance of period change. Thus, substantial empirical evidence challenges Easterlin's theory and the scientific soundness of generalizing his arguments.

An adequate understanding of the baby boom requires a period orientation—period explanations "emphasize society-wide shifts that appear to affect all groups at the same time, as if there were something in the air that influenced everyone's lives" (Cherlin, p. 31). This *something* is much harder to identify precisely because multiple factors are changing across periods. Sociologist Andrew Cherlin approaches the task of explaining period trends in the United States through contrasting the social history of the 1950s and 1960s to the 1970s and 1980s. For instance, the breadwinner family, traditional gender-role ideology, and a robust economy characterized the 1950s. In this environment, marriage and

childbearing occurred sooner and were within the reach of many. In contrast, the 1970s brought greater participation of women in the labor force, ideologies stressing individualism and self-actualization, and economic stagnation. Individuals responded to these period conditions in ways that suggested a common understanding of their meaning and that were not influenced by cohort-specific socialization experiences. These social histories provide plausible explanations for changes in the dynamic demographic components described above and broadly characterize many Western industrialized countries in these decades. Comparative work across countries might identify the most important period factor or set of factors. However, isolating cause in a continually evolving social system poses difficult challenges; a compelling retrospective social history might be all that can be reasonably attained.

TABLE 2

Decomposition of the Change in the Total Fertility Rate in the American Baby Boom: Quantum and Tempo Components (percentage distributions)

Quantum/Tempo	Baby boom (from start to peak) (1936–1957)			Baby bust (from peak to trough) (1958–1975)		
Quantum effect	42			45		
Parity 0 & 1		37	*88*		17	*38*
Parity 2+		5	*12*		28	*62*
(Total quantum)		(42)	*(100)*		(45)	*(100)*
Tempo effect	58			55		
Age at first birth		45	*78*		31	*56*
Other timing changes		13	*22*		24	*44*
(Total tempo)		(58)	*(100)*		(55)	*(100)*
Total effect	100	(100)		100	(100)	

SOURCE: Ryder (1980).

Underemphasized in Cherlin's U.S. baby boom social history is the importance of new methods of contraception and more widely available abortion. In 1977 demographers Charles Westoff and Norman Ryder characterized the 1965 to 1975 period as a "contraceptive revolution." The import of effective fertility control interacts with changes in the timing of fertility described above. Compared to the baby boom, baby bust women had more effective fertility control, had children later, reached their desired family sizes at later ages, and thus were at lower risk of having unintended births for a fewer number of years. A substantial proportion of births during the baby boom can be classified as unwanted (i.e., women claimed that prior to the relevant pregnancy they preferred to have no more children), a proportion that declined during the baby bust. Thus, the effectiveness and availability of birth control contributed to the pace and magnitude of the baby bust.

Could There Be Another Baby Boom?

In the twenty-first century, economically advanced countries are very unlikely to experience sustained fertility at baby boom levels (i.e., TFR greater than 2.5); in fact, it is generally expected that below-replacement fertility will prevail with occasional periods of very low (TFR less than 1.5) fertility. This forecast rests on the observed secular decline in high parity births. As noted above, high parity births played a very limited role in the baby boom fertility increases of the 1950s and 1960s, and the baby bust included an acceleration of the trend away from large—three or more children—families. The prohibitive costs of large families in developed coun-

tries, and the absence of powerful and persuasive ideologies that encourage having many children, combined with effective means of fertility control make a return to large families extremely unlikely. Instead, any future baby booms will result from the same demographic mechanisms responsible for the post–World War II baby boom: earlier family formation and nearly universal parenthood. Earlier childbearing ages and pervasive two-child families could conceivably produce a future baby boom of substantial size. But nearly universal parenthood does not seem likely in contexts in which women have substantial nonfamilial opportunities. Thus for most developed countries, the more likely future includes few large families and fairly high rates of voluntary childlessness. Baby booms are likely to be modest in size and will result primarily from changes in the timing of fertility.

See also: *Cycles, Population; Fertility, Below-Replacement; Population Decline.*

BIBLIOGRAPHY

Bongaarts, John, and Rodolfo A. Bulatao, eds. 2000. *Beyond Six Billion: Forecasting the World's Population.* Washington, D.C.: National Academy Press.

Bongaarts, John, and Griffith Feeney. 1998. "On the Quantum and Tempo of Fertility." *Population and Development Review* 24: 271–291.

Campbell, Arthur A. 1974. "Beyond the Demographic Transition." *Demography* 11(4): 549–561.

Cherlin, Andrew J. 1992. *Marriage, Divorce, Remarriage,* rev. edition. Cambridge, MA: Harvard University Press.

Easterlin, Richard A. 1973. "Relative Economic Status and the American Fertility Swing." In *Family Economic Behavior,* ed. E. B. Sheldon. Philadelphia: Lippincott.

———. 1978. "What Will 1984 Be Like? Socioeconomic Implications of Recent Twists in Age Structure." *Demography* 15: 397–432.

———. 1987. *Birth and Fortune: The Impact of Numbers on Personal Welfare.* Chicago: University of Chicago Press.

Macunovich, Diane J. 2002. *Birth Quake: The Baby Boom and Its Aftershocks.* Chicago: University of Chicago Press.

Morgan, S. Philip, and Rosalind B. King. 2001. "Why Have Children in the 21st Century? Biological Predisposition, Social Coercion, Rational Choice." *European Journal of Population* 17: 3–20.

Ní Bhrolcháin, Márie. 1992. "Period Paramount? A Critique of the Cohort Approach to Fertility." *Population and Development Review* 18: 599–629.

Pampel, Fred C., and H. Elizabeth Peters. 1995. "The Easterlin Effect." *Annual Review of Sociology* 21: 163–194.

Rindfuss, Ronald R., and James A. Sweet. 1977. *Postwar Fertility Trends and Differentials in the United States.* New York: Academic Press.

Ryder, Norman B. 1980. "Components of Temporal Variations in American Fertility." In *Demographic Patterns in Developed Societies,* ed. R. W. Hiorns. London: Taylor and Francis.

Sweet, James A., and Ronald R. Rindfuss. 1983. "Those Ubiquitous Fertility Trends: United States 1945–79." *Social Biology* 30: 127–139.

United Nations. 2001. *World Population Prospects: The 2000 Revision.* New York: United Nations.

Westoff, Charles F. 1987. "Perspective on Nuptiality and Fertility." In *Below-Replacement Fertility in Industrial Societies,* ed. K. Davis, M. S. Bernstam, and R. Ricardo-Campbell. New York: The Population Council.

Westoff, Charles F., and Norman B. Ryder. 1977. *The Contraceptive Revolution.* Princeton, NJ: Princeton University Press.

S. Philip Morgan

BECKER, GARY S.

(1930–)

Gary S. Becker received his Ph.D. in economics from the University of Chicago in 1955. He taught at Columbia University from 1957 to 1970, after which he returned to the University of Chicago. He was awarded the Nobel Prize for Economics in 1992. His numerous other distinctions include the Irene B. Tauber Award from the Population Association of America in 1997, in recognition of his many contributions to demography and population studies.

Beginning with his 1957 analysis of the economics of discrimination, Becker's work builds on the assumption that rational economic choice governs all spheres of human behavior. His approach of using standard economic models to analyze demographic behavior is demonstrated in his classic 1960 paper on the economics of fertility. Becker drew an analogy between decisions about childbearing and decisions about the purchase of consumer durables. Like consumer durables, Becker argued, children are long-term investments in which decisions about both quantity and quality play an important role. Becker observed that in the case of consumer durables such as automobiles or televisions, increases in income often led to greater increases in the quality of the good rather than in the number of units purchased. According to Becker, this quantity-quality tradeoff plays an important role in explaining why increasing income does not necessarily lead to higher fertility. This analysis of the quantity-quality tradeoff in fertility was further formalized and refined in later work by Becker and other economists, such as Robert Willis.

Becker's other important insight about the economics of fertility also helps explain why there is often a negative association between income and fertility. Building on his 1965 research on the economics of time allocation, Becker emphasized the fact that children are relatively time-intensive compared to other commodities, making children relatively more expensive to high-wage couples than to low-wage couples. This recognition of the relationship between the value of time and the cost of children has had a profound influence on understanding trends in fertility in both high-income and low-income countries.

In a similar use of standard economic tools in the modeling of demographic and social processes, Becker's work on the economics of marriage in 1973 and 1974 formalized the analogy between marriage markets and other markets in which two sides combine to form matches or partnerships. His analysis of assortative mating drew on a long tradition in mathematics and economics of assignment problems. Becker concluded from these models that there would be positive assortative mating in the marriage market when traits are complementary and negative assortative mating when traits are substitutes. Becker also developed models of the economics of divorce, noting that imperfect information and changes in characteristics may eventually cause the gains of marriage to fall below what was expected at the time of marriage.

Another of Becker's important contributions to research on families was his analysis of intra family resource allocation. Beginning with his influential paper on social interactions in 1974, he developed models exploring the importance of altruism in the family. One result was what he called the Rotten Kid Theorem, which argues that even a selfish child will act to maximize overall family well-being, since this will cause the household head (assumed to be an altruist) to increase the child's consumption. This has broad and often surprising implications for government policy. For example, the Rotten Kid Theorem implies that a government program designed to increase food consumption of school children may have little effect, since household heads may simply reduce their own transfers to children to offset the government grant, effectively neutralizing the program. As with many of Becker's results, the Rotten Kid Theorem holds in its strictest form only under particular assumptions. In 1989, economist Theodore Bergstrom provided a useful analysis of the conditions under which the Rotten Kid Theorem does and does not apply. Becker's model of the family has also been criticized from a feminist perspective, for example, by Nancy Folbre in 1997.

Building on his work on quality-quantity trade-offs, intra-family allocations, and human capital,

Becker has made important contributions to research on intergenerational transmission of inequality. A series of papers coauthored with Nigel Tomes developed models exploring issues such as how assortative mating and quality-quantity tradeoffs in fertility affect the distribution of income in a society. Becker subsequently expanded this work into models exploring the role that fertility and child investments play in the long-term dynamics of economic growth.

Becker provides a convenient overview of his approach to economics in his 1993 Nobel Prize lecture. A more comprehensive summary of his contributions to the economics of fertility, marriage, and the family is provided in his book *A Treatise on the Family* (1991).

See also: *Economic-Demographic Models; Family Demography; Microeconomics of Demographic Behavior; Partner Choice.*

BIBLIOGRAPHY

SELECTED WORKS BY GARY S. BECKER.

Becker, Gary S. 1957. *The Economics of Discrimination.* Chicago: University of Chicago Press.

———. 1960. "An Economic Analysis of Fertility." In *Demographic and Economic Change in Developed Countries.* Princeton, NJ: National Bureau of Economic Research.

———. 1964. *Human Capital: A Theoretical and Empirical Analysis, with Special Reference to Education.* New York: Columbia University Press.

———. 1965. "A Theory of the Allocation of Time." *Economic Journal* 75(299): 493–517.

———. 1973–1974a. "A Theory of Marriage," pts I and II. *Journal of Political Economy* 81(4): 813–846; 82(2): S11–S26.

———. 1974b. "A Theory of Social Interactions." *Journal of Political Economy* 82(6): 1,063–1,093.

———. 1991. *A Treatise on the Family,* enlarged edition. Cambridge, MA: Harvard University Press.

———. 1993. "Nobel Lecture: The Economic Way of Looking at Behavior." *Journal of Political Economy* 101(3): 385–409.

Becker, Gary S., and Robert J. Barro. 1988. "A Reformulation of the Economic Theory of Fertility." *Quarterly Journal of Economics* 103(1): 1–25.

Becker, Gary S., Edward L. Glaeser, and Kevin M. Murphy. 1999. "Population and Economic Growth." *American Economic Review* 89(2): 145–149.

Becker, Gary S., Elisabeth M. Landes, and Robert T. Michael. 1977. "An Economic Analysis of Marital Instability." *Journal of Political Economy* 85(6): 1,141–1,188.

Becker, Gary S., and H. Gregg Lewis. 1973. "On the Interaction between the Quantity and Quality of Children." *Journal of Political Economy* 81(2), Part II: S279–S288.

Becker, Gary S., Kevin M. Murphy, and Robert Tamura. 1990. "Human Capital, Fertility, and Economic Growth." *Journal of Political Economy* 98(5), Part II: S12–S37.

Becker, Gary S., and Nigel Tomes. 1979, "An Equilibrium Theory of the Distribution of Income and Intergenerational Mobility." *Journal of Political Economy* 87(6): 1,153–1,189.

SELECTED WORKS ABOUT GARY S. BECKER.

Bergstrom, Theodore. 1989. "A Fresh Look at the Rotten Kid Theorem and Other Household Mysteries." *Journal of Political Economy* 97(5): 1,138–1,159.

Folbre, Nancy. 1997. "The Future of the Elephant-Bird." *Population and Development Review* 23(3): 647–654.

Willis, Robert. 1973. "A New Approach to the Economic Theory of Fertility Behavior." *Journal of Political Economy* March–April: S14–S64.

DAVID LAM

BERELSON, BERNARD

(1912–1979)

Bernard Berelson was an influential thinker and writer on population issues during the 1960s and 1970s, when population growth became a global concern and international assistance to family planning programs in developing countries increased substantially. Berelson's career mixed academic ap-

pointments and administrative and policy positions in international development assistance groups. He was, in Parker Mauldin's phrase, a "practical scholar" whose work contributed to social science and to the improvement of family planning programs (1979, p. 260).

Berelson was graduated from Whitman College in 1934. He received his Ph.D. from the University of Chicago in 1941 and joined the Foreign Broadcast Service of the Federal Communications Commission. He later served as research director of Columbia University's Bureau of Applied Social Research and held appointments as professor at the University of Chicago and as director of the Ford Foundation's Behavioral Science Program. Before becoming involved in the population field, Berelson produced important books on voting, graduate education, and human behavior.

Berelson joined the Population Council in 1962 as director of its communication research program. He became vice president in 1963 and president in 1968. He remained in that position until 1974, when he resigned, in part because of disagreements with John D. Rockefeller 3rd, the Council's founder and chairman of its board of trustees, about new directions in population policy and the importance of family planning for slowing population growth. Berelson continued as a senior fellow at the Council until his death in 1979.

Berelson excelled at summarizing important scientific work, pointing out missing pieces, and spelling out implications. He had a well-developed sense of what research findings would make a practical difference, and his influential syntheses shaped the knowledge-base and the direction of field programs. His contributions in this mode include "Beyond Family Planning" (1969); "The Great Debate on Population Policy: An Instructive Entertainment" (1975); "The Record of Family Planning Programs" (1976); "Paths to Fertility Reduction: The Policy Cube" (1977); and "The Condition of Fertility Decline in Developing Countries, 1965–75" (1978). Some 14 of his articles and essays were posthumously published in a volume edited by John A. Ross and W. Parker Mauldin (1988). That volume also includes Berelson's full bibliography. His writings on population reflect the conviction that population growth was "among the great problems on the world agenda," because "rapid population growth retards social and economic development." From these premises he drew the conclusion that "everything that can properly be done to lower population growth rates should be done" (Ross and Mauldin, 1988, p. 42).

Berelson encouraged collaboration between scientists and family planning providers to develop innovative service delivery programs and to evaluate them carefully. The best-known example was the Taichung experiment in Taiwan, but similar approaches were used in South Korea, Thailand, and Bangladesh to evaluate specific family planning interventions and to reassure government leaders that program interventions would be politically and socially acceptable. Similar work continues in the twenty-first century in Ghana and other places in Africa.

Berelson's impact on the population field is also evident in a number of other ways. He established the journal *Studies in Family Planning,* and in 1965 organized the first international conference on population programs and edited the report of that conference. Together with John D. Rockefeller 3rd, Berelson promoted the World Leaders Declaration on Population, which was released in 1967. He served as a member of the U.S. Commission on Population Growth and the American Future, and provided an array of useful ideas on communicating family planning messages.

See also: *Family Planning Programs; Freedman, Ronald.*

BIBLIOGRAPHY

SELECTED WORK BY BERNARD BERLESON.

Berelson, Bernard, and Gary A. Steiner. 1964. *Human Behavior: An Inventory of Scientific Findings.* New York: Harcourt, Brace and World.

SELECTED WORKS ABOUT BERNARD BERLESON.

Harr, John Ensor, and Peter J. Johnson. 1991. *The Rockefeller Conscience.* New York: Scribners.

Lincoln, Richard. 1989. "Review of *Berelson on Population.*" *Population and Development Review* 15(1): 150–153.

Mauldin, W. Parker. 1979. "Bernard Berelson: A Personal Appreciation." *Studies in Family Planning* 10(10): 259–261.

Ross, John A., and W. Parker Mauldin, eds. 1988. *Berelson on Population.* New York: Springer-Verlag.

PETER J. DONALDSON

BERTILLON, JACQUES

(1851–1922)

Jacques Bertillon was a French physician and statistician, who played a key role in developing the international classification of causes of death and was a leader of France's pronatalist movement. Several members of Bertillon's family were distinguished in the field of demography. His maternal grandfather, Achille Guillard (1799–1876), coined the term *demography* (1855); his father, Louis-Adolphe (1821–1883), taught the first course in demography at the Paris Medical School (1875) and was director of the *Bureau de Statistique Municipale* in Paris—a post also held by Jacques.

Several decades of effort had been devoted to devising a classification for the causes of deaths by the time Bertillon began his research in the area. He used the work he had done on Parisian death data, and drew on the scheme proposed by William Farr (1807–1883), which had been adapted to the new bacteriological knowledge. The resulting classification system, known as the Bertillon classification, was first promulgated at the Chicago conference of the International Statistical Institute in 1893 and was accepted by the American Health Association in 1897. It became the International Classification in 1900 after approval by an international commission in Paris.

Bertillon also wrote demography manuals and a series of studies on fertility characteristics, the latter using the latest statistical techniques, such as parity-specific birth probabilities. But Bertillon is better known in France as the founder, in 1896, of the first pronatalist movement, the *Alliance nationale pour l'accroissement de la population française.* He attempted to explain why couples had small families (adducing reasons such as high taxation and small apartments), proposed new pronatalist measures such as a cash bonus for the fourth child, and conceived the notion of population aging. It was largely at his urging, through the *Conseil Supérieur de la Natalité,* that a law was passed in 1920 forbidding dissemination of birth control information and techniques.

See also: *Causes of Death; Demography, History of; Disease, Concepts and Classification of; Farr, William.*

BIBLIOGRAPHY

SELECTED WORKS BY JACQUES BERTILLON.

Bertillon, Jacques. 1883. *Étude démographique du divorce et de la séparation de corps dans les différents pays de l'Europe.* Paris: G. Masson.

———. 1895. *Cours élémentaire de statistique.* Paris: Société d'études scientifiques.

———. 1911. *La dépopulation de la France, ses conséquences, ses causes, mesures à prendre pour la combattre.* Paris: Alcan.

SELECTED WORKS ABOUT JACQUES BERTILLON.

Bourdelais, Patrice. 1993. *L'âge de la vieillesse. Histoire du vieillissement de la population.* Paris: Odile Jacob.

Dupâquier, Michel. 1983. "La famille Bertillon et la naissance d'une nouvelle science sociale: la démographie." *Annales de démographie historique* 293–311.

Dupâquier, Jacques, and Michel Dupâquier. 1985. *Histoire de la démographie.* Paris: Perrin.

PATRICE BOURDELAIS

BIBLIOGRAPHIC AND ONLINE RESOURCES

For many years, demographers and other social scientists with population interests considered themselves fortunate to have available the annotated bibliographic journal *Population Index,* which was published from 1937 to 2000. With early computerization, *Popline* and *Medline* also provided useful easily searchable bibliographies. As high-speed Internet access became available, researchers could routinely draw on a much wider array of bibliographic resources and other research tools. The power of this technology derives from the speed at which information can be transmitted, the low costs involved for end users, the relative ease with which content can be updated or revised, the seemingly limitless amounts of information that can be carried, the superior graphic possibilities offered by electronic displays as compared to paper, and the scope for interactivity between user and information. Users have masses of information at their fingertips, albeit together with similar masses of dubious or tendentious material that libraries might have screened out. The new ways of accessing, processing, and disseminating information and data that the Internet allows are having a notable effect on the way researchers work and interact—in what is likely to be just the beginning of a long-term, technology-driven process.

Various categories of online resources are relevant to demographic research. Practically every major population training and research center and many statistical offices throughout the world have web sites giving information about their activities and often providing access to their publications. Software for various demographic procedures and computations can be downloaded, often without cost. Vast amounts of demographic data are also obtainable from remote locations. Such data may come in the form of files that can be downloaded and archived in the user's computer for further processing, or in the form of interactive databases presenting data that can be tailored to meet the user's needs. Bibliographic resources are increasingly abundant—from the online catalogs of major libraries around the world to online libraries containing the actual texts of publications, including books. Nearly all demographic journals and newsletters have an Internet presence—a web site that shows at least the table of contents, usually an abstract, and in some cases the full text of articles.

Given the volume of demographic material available, users face an increasing problem of identifying and retrieving data and information in an efficient way. There are essentially two strategies to extract information from the Internet: "searching" and "browsing." Searching works best when what is being sought can be conceptualized with a distinctive keyword. A search engine such as Google can then mine the Internet for occurrences of that keyword. (There are a large number of search engines. A survey of them and discussion of search-engine technology and use can be found at a site called Search Engine Watch, which is maintained by Internet.com.)

A critical factor in the success of any search is the formulation of the query—the key word or phrase should not be conceptually too broad or too narrow. In 2002 the keyword "population" by itself yielded some 15.9 million documents on Google— far too many to be of practical interest. Adding another keyword—say, a country name—in a Boolean search procedure might be needed to trim the total to manageable numbers.

But in many cases, users may be looking for something that cannot be easily indexed in keywords. Like a reader leafing through interesting parts of a book rather than perusing the index, the Internet user may prefer to browse relevant sites and survey what is available before narrowing the search in a particular direction. Some sites that might be used in this fashion are noted below, grouped in three categories: portals, databases, and content-rich sites.

Portals

The pioneer portal in the population field was the Demography and Population Studies section of the World Wide Web Virtual Library, maintained by the Demography Program of the Australian National University. *Popnet*, which describes itself as "the directory for global population information" is another high-quality population portal—comprehensive, well-organized, and attractively presented. It is maintained by the Population Reference Bureau, which has population information as its core mandate. *DemoNetAsia* offers another comprehensive repertory of online resources of particular interest to demographers.

In addition there are a number of more specialized portals. The Population Information Network (POPIN), maintained by the United Nations Population Division, aims to provide access to population information on the web sites of the entire United Nations system. In the area of reproductive health, Johns Hopkins University manages the Reproductive Health Gateway and the United Nations Population Fund sponsors a Population and Reproductive Health portal in the Development Gateway web site. In the area of migration, the Migration Policy Institute runs the Migration Information Source.

Databases

Both bibliographic and statistical databases should be noted. Among the bibliographic databases, *Popline*, which contains several hundred thousand records and is maintained by Johns Hopkins University, provides citations with abstracts of the worldwide literature in the field of population, with an emphasis on family planning and related health issues. *Population Index*, as mentioned, for over six decades was the primary reference tool on the world's population literature. Its database covering the years from 1986 to its demise in 2000, containing almost 50,000 records—many in subject areas not well covered by *Popline*—is available online from Princeton University's Office of Population Research and is a valuable tool for literature searches pertaining to that period.

Online statistical databases present demographic indicators and projections for individual countries or regions, as well as data in the broader field of population and development. The main demographic databases are those of the United Nations Population Division and the U.S. Bureau of the Census. Notable among the numerous databases covering aspects of population and development is the World Bank's World Development Indicators Data Query. The DemoNetAsia web site offers a list of databases and databanks (noninteractive statistical data archives in population and closely related subjects). The Internet Crossroads maintained by the University of Wisconsin and the Virtual Data Library of the University of North Carolina's Carolina Population Center cover a broader range of the social science data resources that are available online.

Content-Rich Sites

The web sites of many population research and teaching institutions are essentially electronic versions of traditional brochures, designed to present information about the institution rather than as a resource to support the work of others. The sites of the various professional associations in the population field are mainly services for their members. There are, however, notable exceptions: institutions whose web sites are rich in documents and other resources, such as software, databases, and repertories of links. These include: INED, France's Institut national d'études démographiques (National Institute of Demographic Research); the Population Research Institute of Pennsylvania State University; the Carolina Population Center of the University of North Carolina; and the Max Planck Institute for Demographic Research. An Internet application of particular interest concerns distance learning. For demography, the Distance Advancement of Population Research project at the Carolina Population Center is a pioneering effort in this area.

Most demographic journals also have web sites. Some, such as *International Family Planning Perspectives* or the Population Reference Bureau's *Population Bulletin*, make their full contents available online, but the majority either limit themselves to tables of contents and abstracts or restrict online access to subscribers. *Demographic Research,* a free, peer-reviewed journal, is published exclusively online. A comprehensive list of population periodicals available online is offered by DemoNetAsia.

A major storehouse of past population research is the contents of the main English-language population journals compiled by the JSTOR (Journal Storage) project. The full text of every issue of nine population journals (*Demography,* 1964–; *Family Planning Perspectives,* 1969–; *International Family Planning Perspectives,* 1979–; *International Migration Review,* 1966–; *Population: An English Selection,* 1989–; *Population and Development Review,* 1975–; *Population Index,* 1937–1985; *Population Studies,* 1947–; and *Studies in Family Planning,* 1963–), from first publication up to the volume several years before the current year, is available online, in searchable form. Hard copies of individual articles can be printed. (Numerous other journals in the social sciences and humanities are also included.) Access to JSTOR is typically through institutional subscription by universities or major libraries.

Conclusion

Many of the advantages of the Internet can turn into problems and sources of inefficiency. The ease with which web sites can be started and revised results in a low degree of stability; in addition, as web sites age and expand, maintenance becomes increasingly time and resource consuming and is often neglected. Quality control is frequently poor. In a number of countries, inadequate telecommunication infrastructures and sometimes explicit policies discourage users and limit the Internet presence of their institutions. As a result, Internet use for research can sometimes be frustrating.

Nevertheless, the Internet has established itself as an essential utility in workplaces and homes throughout most of the world, radically changing expectations about how easy it should be for researchers to gain access to and disseminate information and to interact with other researchers regardless of geographical distance. As its use spreads further, it will revolutionize the way demographers and others work and collaborate—very much as computers did in the 1970s and 1980s.

See also: *Journals, Population.*

BIBLIOGRAPHY

INTERNET RESOURCES.

Australian National University. Demography Program. 2002. "World Wide Web Virtual Library: Demography and Population Studies." <http://demography.anu.edu.au/VirtualLibrary>.

Demographic Research. 2002. <http://www.demographic-research.org>.

DemoNetAsia. 2002. "The DemoNetAsia Links Directory." <http://demonetasia.org/links.htm>.

———. 2002. "DemoNetAsia Links: Databases." <http://demonetasia.org/links/linksdbases.htm>.

———. 2002. "DemoNetAsia Links: Population Journals." <http://demonetasia.org/links/linksjournals.htm>.

Google. 2002. <http://www.google.com>.

Institut national d'études démographiques. 2002. <http://www.ined.fr>.

International Family Planning Perspectives. 2002. <http://www.agi-usa.org/journals/ifpp_archive.html>.

Internet.com. 2002. "Search Engine Watch." <http://www.searchenginewatch.com>.

Johns Hopkins University. 2002. "Popline." <http://www.popline.org>.

———. 2002. "Reproductive Health Gateway." <http://www.rhgateway.org>.

JSTOR (Journal Storage). 2002. <http://www.jstor.org>.

Max Planck Institute for Demographic Research. 2002. <http://www.demogr.mpg.de>.

Migration Policy Institute. 2002. "Migration Information Source." <http://www.migrationinformation.org>.

Pennsylvania State University. Population Research Institute. 2002. <http://www.pop.psu.edu>.

Population Reference Bureau. 2002. "Popnet." <http://www.popnet.org>.

Princeton University. Office of Population Research. 2002. "Population Index." <http://popindex.princeton.edu>.

United Nations. Population Division. 2002. Population Information Network (POPIN). <http://www.un.org/popin>.

———. 2002. "World Population Prospects Population Database." <http://esa.un.org/unpp>.

United Nations Population Fund. 2002. "Population and Reproductive Health." <http://developmentgateway.org/node/146526>.

U.S. Bureau of the Census. 2002. "International Data Base." <http://www.census.gov/ipc/www/idbnew.html>.

University of North Carolina. Carolina Population Center. 2002. <http://www.cpc.unc.edu>.

———. 2002. "Distance Advancement of Population Research." <http://www.cpc.unc.edu/projects/dapr/dl>.

———. 2002. "Virtual Data Library." <http://www.cpc.unc.edu/dataarch>.

University of Wisconsin. 2002. "Internet Crossroads in the Social Sciences." <http://dpls.dacc.wisc.edu/newcrossroads/index.asp>.

World Bank. 2002. "World Development Indicators Data Query." <http://www.worldbank.org/data/dataquery.html>.

ARMINDO MIRANDA

BIODEMOGRAPHY

Biodemography is an omnibus term for the numerous connections between demography and biology.

Demography has multiple points of contact with biology, as well as with mathematics, statistics, the social sciences, and policy analysis. The biology–demography interface was central to the research of two distinguished demographers, Alfred J. Lotka (1880–1949) and Raymond Pearl (1879–1940), in the early decades of the twentieth century. Lotka developed concepts and methods that are still of fundamental importance in biodemography; his two most significant books are *Elements of Physical Biology* (1925) and *Théorie Analytique des Associations Biologiques* (1934–1939). Pearl pioneered biodemographic research on several species, including flatworms, the aquatic plant *Ceratophyllum demersum, Drosophila,* and humans. He founded two major journals, the *Quarterly Journal of Biology* and *Human Biology* and helped found both the International Union for the Scientific Investigation of Population Problems (which later became the International Union for the Scientific Study of Population) and the Population Association of America.

At the beginning of the twenty-first century biodemography is reemerging as a locus of cutting edge demographic research. It is clearly accepted that fertility, mortality, morbidity, and other processes of profound interest to demographers have a basic biological component. Moreover, biology is fundamentally a population science and there is growing recognition that biological studies can benefit greatly from demographic concepts and methods. From a biologist's perspective, biodemography envelops demography because it embraces research pertaining to: any nonhuman species; populations of cells or molecules within an individual; populations of genotypes; and biological measurements related to age, health, physical functioning, and fertility. Within this vast territory, several research foci are noteworthy and are briefly described below.

Evolutionary Demography

Nothing in biology, the eminent biologist Theodosius Dobzhansky (1900–1975) asserted, makes sense except in light of evolution. It is equally valid to say that nothing in evolution can be understood except in light of demography. Evolution is driven by population dynamics governed by age schedules of fertility and survival. Lotka emphasized this. Following his groundbreaking research, models of the evolution of fertility, mortality, and other life-history patterns have been based on stable population theory. Lotka's equation

$$\int_0^\omega e^{-ra}\ell(a)m(a)da = 1$$

specifies the intrinsic growth rate, *r*, of a closed population, typically of females, as a function of the proportion, ℓ(*a*), of newborns surviving to age *a* and the age-specific probability of maternity (or fertility), *m(a)*. If a new subspecies emerges as a result of mutation, the subspecies is assumed to have an evolutionary advantage if its intrinsic growth rate is greater than that of other subspecies.

William D. Hamilton (1936–2000) used this perspective to model the evolution of senescence: In an influential article published in 1966 he argued that evolutionary pressures would inevitably result in a rising trajectory of age-specific death rates. Hamilton was a biologist who studied stable population theory and other aspects of demography at the London School of Economics. Recently the demographer Ronald D. Lee reconsidered the evolution of senescence and concluded that age-specific death rates can increase, decrease, or remain constant over age in various periods of life depending on the nature of intergenerational transfers of resources from parents to children, for example. Other demographers, including Shripad Tuljapurkar and Kenneth W. Wachter, have also explored this issue, from different perspectives.

Comparative Biodemography

Much can be learned by comparing mortality and fertility patterns across species. Relying on Gompertz's Law (developed by English actuary Benjamin Gompertz [1779–1865]), it had been thought that death rates rose exponentially at adult ages for almost all species. A dozen or so species, from yeast, worms, and insects to humans, have now been studied in sufficiently large numbers for the age trajectory of mortality at advanced ages to be reliably understood. For all these species, including humans, death rates either level off or decline at sufficiently advanced ages. Explaining this surprising deceleration of mortality is an active area of research in biodemography. One of the leaders in this field is James R. Carey, who has also done important comparative biodemographic research on the role of the elderly in nature and on the duration of life in thousands of species.

Ecodemography

Lotka was deeply interested in the dynamics of interacting species. This interest is commemorated in the Lotka-Volterra equation (the model was developed independently by Lotka in 1925, and Italian mathe-

matician Vito Volterra in 1926), which describes cycles in the populations of predators and prey. The yet to be solved two-sex problem in demography (i.e., how to satisfactorily incorporate both males and females in models of fertility and population growth) demonstrates how difficult it is to study interacting populations. Research in this area is crucial to understanding environmental stability and population–environment interactions.

Demography of a Species

Humans are but one of millions of species of living organisms. Life tables and many of the other basic concepts and methods of demography can be applied to any species. Life tables, including age-specific maternity rates, have been estimated for hundreds of species. Research has also been done on populations of populations of a species, such as honeybee hives.

Experimental Biodemography

To test demographic hypotheses, experiments can be conducted with nonhuman populations. Pearl pioneered this powerful form of research, focusing on whether population growth followed a logistic pattern. In the 1990s demographers, working with biologists, designed and carried out experiments to test whether there is a genetically determined maximum length of life for individuals in all or most species. No sign of a maximum was found in genetically identical populations of yeast, worms, and insects, casting doubt on whether humans were subject to such a limit. More recently, various biodemographic experiments have been conducted to explore the relationship between fertility and mortality. Among genetically identical individuals in controlled environments, reproduction decreases subsequent probabilities of survival. Other experiments have been conducted to determine the impact of lethal and sub-lethal stress on the subsequent mortality of a cohort. Mortality selection (the death of the frail) and hormesis (the increased resistance of individuals who survive) increase future survival chances whereas debilitation decreases them.

Genetic Demography

Some individuals die young; others live to an advanced age. Some individuals have no children; others have many. The genetic and common environment components of these variations—in lifespans, fertility, and other demographic characteristics—

can be analyzed in humans using data on twins, siblings, cousins, and other relatives of various degree. These data are available in genealogies and in twin, household, parish, and other population registries. In nonhuman species, inbred and crossbred lines can be studied. It is not necessary to have information from DNA about specific genes: it is necessary rather to have information about the proportion of genes shared by two individuals and about shared nongenetic influences. Analysis of variance methods, correlated frailty approaches, and nested event-history models have been applied by demographers. Hans-Peter Kohler has studied how much of the variation in number of children can be attributed to genetic variation in family size preferences among potential parents, and Anatoli Yashin has analyzed genetic variation as it relates to susceptibility to various diseases and to mortality in general.

Another topic in genetic demography concerns the genetic structure and dynamics of a population. Data about population size, migration flows, and inbreeding can lead to insights into the genetic heterogeneity of a population. Information from DNA about genetic polymorphisms (i.e., mutations) can be used to determine the genetic structure of a population and to make inferences about the influence of migration and inbreeding on the population.

Molecular Demography

A central goal of molecular demography is to identify genetic polymorphisms that affect mortality, morbidity, functioning, fecundity, and other sources of demographic change. Some of this research has focused on finding genetic variants that influence longevity. This relationship can be studied by analyzing changes with age in the proportion of survivors who have some specific allele (i.e., version of a gene). If in a given cohort the allele becomes more frequent with age, that allele may be associated with lower mortality.

Some research concerns how differences in the frequency of a particular allele among populations lead to differences in mortality patterns and life expectancy. Douglas Ewbank, for example, has studied the demographic impact of variants of the *ApoE* gene in various population distributions. Other research, by Richard Udry, has focused on how hormone levels influence behavior relevant to fertility and family dynamics, and in particular the differences in behavior between males and females.

Epidemography

Demography and epidemiology intersect and overlap. Demographers frequently focus on how diseases and disabilities influence the structure and dynamics of a population, whereas epidemiologists are more typically concerned with how population patterns of a specific disease can shed light on the etiology, prevention, and cure of the disease. Many demographers, however, have acquired substantial knowledge of the biology of various diseases and disabilities and have developed models of morbidity and mortality. Some of these models relate disease and disability patterns and trends in a population to consequences for health-care systems. Kenneth G. Manton is a leading researcher in this field.

Biometric Demography

Demographers since the last half of the twentieth century have become increasingly involved with the design of surveys and the analysis of survey data, especially that pertaining to fertility or morbidity and mortality. Various kinds of physical measurements (such as height and weight), physiological measurements (for example, of blood pressure and cholesterol levels), nutritional status (as assessed by analysis of blood or urine and other methods), physical performance (for example, hand-grip strength or ability to pick a coin up from the floor), and genetic makeup (as determined by analysis of DNA) have been added to surveys, including those conducted by Kaare Christensen, Noreen Goldman, Maxine Weinstein, and Zeng Yi. These biological measurements (biomarkers) can be used as covariates in demographic analyses in much the same way that social and economic information is used.

Paleodemography

Skeletal remains are the source of information about prehistoric populations regarding sex, age at death, lifetime morbidity and nutrition, as well as, for women, number of children born. Hence, a main focus of paleodemography is determining how to extract more information from bones. This requires a sophisticated understanding of biology as well as facility with methods of using physical indicators to determine sex and to estimate age at death and other variables. A promising recent advance has been the development, by Ursula Wittwer-Backofen and Jutta Gampe, of methods to count annual rings deposited in teeth as a way of determining age at death. (Roughly similar methods can be used to estimate the age of animals in the wild, with teeth used for mammals and otoliths, ear bones, for fish). Lesions in bones and minerals in teeth and bones can shed light on health and nutritional histories. Information about human population development for the long period during which written records were scarce or nonexistent thus hinges on biological information.

See also: *Aging and Longevity, Biology of; Animal Ecology; Archaeogenetics; Biology, Population; Evolutionary Demography; Life Span; Lotka, Alfred; Paleodemography; Sociobiology.*

BIBLIOGRAPHY

Carey, James R. 1993. *Applied Demography for Biologists.* New York: Oxford University Press.

Finch, Caleb E., James W. Vaupel, and Kevin Kinsella, eds. 2001. *Cells and Surveys: Should Biological Measures Be Included in Social Science Research?* Washington, D.C.: National Academy Press.

Hamilton, William D. 1996. *Narrow Roads of Gene Land,* Vol. 1. Oxford: W. H. Freeman.

Hoppa, Robert D., and James W. Vaupel. 2002. *Paleodemography: Age Distributions from Skeletal Samples.* Cambridge, Eng.: Cambridge University Press.

Kingsland, Sharon E. 1995. *Modeling Nature.* Chicago: University of Chicago Press.

Kohler, Hans-Peter, Joseph L. Rodgers, and Kaare Christensen. 1999. "Is Fertility Behavior in Our Genes: Findings from a Danish Twin Study." *Population and Development Review* 25(2): 253–288.

Manton, Kenneth G., and Anatoli Yashin. 1999. *Mechanisms of Aging and Mortality: The Search for New Paradigms.* Odense, Denmark: Odense University Press.

Udry, J. Richard. 1994. "The Nature of Gender." *Demography* 31(4): 561–573.

Vaupel, James W., James R. Carey, Kaare Christensen, Thomas E. Johnson, Anatoli I. Yashin, Niels V. Holm, Ivan A. Iachine, Vaino Kannisto, Aziz A. Khazaeli, Pablo Liedo, Valter D. Longo, Zeng Yi, Kenneth G. Manton, and James W. Curtsinger. 1998. "Biodemographic Trajectories of Longevity." *Science* 280: 855–860.

Wachter, Kenneth W., and Caleb E. Finch, eds. 1997. *Between Zeus and the Salmon: The Biodemography of Longevity.* Washington, D.C.: National Academy Press.

JAMES W. VAUPEL

BIOGEOGRAPHY

The global spread and growth of human populations has had a profound, lasting, and often irreversible impact on the flora and fauna of continents, islands, and oceans. Humans depend on nature's living resources for food, energy, medicine, construction, recreation, and education. Even low human densities may lead to overexploitation and extinction of a plant or animal species, especially if the animals are big and have a restricted diet and distribution like the giant panda (*Ailuropoda melanoleuca*) of China. High human densities inevitably cause the displacement of nonhuman natural habitats, the simplification of ecosystems, and the proliferation of waste products that may act as pollutants of natural systems. Human-caused extinction processes have exceeded the natural extinction rates of flora and fauna for several centuries.

Human Impact on Birds

Birds provide a good example of the human impact on biodiversity. They are the best known group of animals, occur on all continents, and respond quickly to changing environmental factors. Some 12 percent (1,186 bird species) of all birds are globally threatened with extinction; among these, habitat loss, fragmentation, and degradation constitute the major survival threat for 1,008 bird species. Exploitation and the impact of invasive species are the second- and third-most important risk factors.

In prehistoric times, human dispersal across the globe was followed by rapid and major extinction waves of vertebrate animals on several continents as well as on many Pacific islands; scores of flightless island bird species vanished within a few hundred years after the arrival of the Polynesian settlers.

Human Populations and Ecosystems

The domestication of plants and animals was a revolutionary event in human history that stimulated human population growth and changed the face of the earth. The need for cropland and pastures has not abated and massive deforestation, the transformation of natural prairies, and the draining of wetlands continue worldwide. In Europe, only 15.6 percent of the land remains undisturbed as of 2003; equivalent values for North America are 56.3 and for Africa 48.9 percent. Only 22 percent of the earth's original forest remains in large natural blocks.

Habitat Destruction and Alien Species Introduction in the United States

Habitat destruction and degradation have emerged as the most pervasive threat to U.S. biodiversity, endangering 85 percent of imperiled and federally listed species. The historic range and population of the California condor (*Gymnogyps californianus*) collapsed along the Pacific coast of North America when Europeans settled there and began to convert California's Central Valley into rangeland and later into cotton, alfalfa, and rice fields.

Urbanization causes a sometimes drastic reduction in native species. The birds of Honolulu are almost completely non-native, introduced birds from Asia, Europe, and Central America. Other metropolitan regions in India, China, South America, and Africa contain species sets that have adapted and benefited from high human densities. Many weed, pest, and disease species thrive in dense human conglomerations; indeed, some disease organisms can only maintain themselves in urban landscapes. Some predict that this species set will constitute the global flora and fauna of the twenty-first century.

The introduction of alien species has become the second-most important risk factor for threatened U.S. biota. Competition with or predation by alien species affects some 49 percent of the imperiled species. Some of the alien species originate from deliberate introductions (many game fish species) while others are escaped pets or have inadvertently been transported on trucks, planes, and ships into the country. Some lakes and rivers in the United States have more alien than native fish species. Additional survival problems in U.S. waterways arise from chemical and thermal pollution. After flowering plants (1,031 species critically imperiled), native aquatic life is most at risk: freshwater fishes (300), stone flies (260), freshwater mussels (202), and crayfishes (165 species).

The American West still contains large blocks of wildlands that have never been modified; a unique patchwork of urban, rural, and protected open space constitutes the modern bio-landscape. Southern California is a "hotspot" of global biogeographic significance with an unusually high number of endemic species restricted to this region. The development pressure on the remaining open space lands is intense, transportation links have fragmented wildlife habitats, and pollution threatens entire ecosystems. A similar situation exists in Florida where heavy human immigration and rapid urbanization processes threaten the survival of the Everglades and other irreplaceable ecosystems.

Threats to Biodiversity in the Tropics

Many of the biologically richest and most threatened landscapes are in the tropics. After Australia, the four countries richest in endemic higher vertebrates (mammals, birds, reptiles, and amphibians) found nowhere else are Mexico (761), Brazil (725), Indonesia (673), and the Philippines (473 species). These countries face difficult problems in their rural environments due to burgeoning human populations. The management and conservation of their increasingly fragmented forest landscapes constitutes a major national and international challenge. A remarkable conservation endeavor concerns the fate of the remaining five tiger (*Panthera tigris*) subspecies stretching from India to Northeast Siberia; three subspecies are already extinct (Caspian, Bali, and Javan tiger). A powerful coalition of conservation groups with worldwide support has slowed the habitat loss in tiger habitats and hopes to safeguard the remaining wild tiger populations in reserves that often lie adjacent to densely populated agricultural areas.

Threats to the Oceans

In the oceans of the world, fish resources have been overexploited in the Atlantic and Northern Pacific. Large whales were nearly exterminated before a worldwide ban on whaling was agreed upon by most whaling nations. The exceptional richness of coral reef ecosystems in the Pacific and Southeast Asia is also at risk due to high demand for tropical fishes and corals in Europe, North America, and East Asia. The reefs are poisoned and plundered by impoverished fishermen, a classic repetition of the overexploitation of living resources that culminated in the extinction of some 484 animal species since 1600.

Habitat Destruction: Past and Future

In hindsight, the case histories of extinct animals show the human folly of reckless habitat destruction, hunting, and trapping as well as the absence of sustainable use and resource management. The benefits of nature's riches and the unique species diversity of each continent are at greater risk in the early twenty-first century than ever before in human history. Both the developed and the developing countries face challenging land-use decisions for their human and non-human inhabitants.

See also: *Carrying Capacity; Geography, Population; Sustainable Development.*

BIBLIOGRAPHY

BirdLife International. 2000. *Threatened Birds of the World.* Barcelona and Cambridge, Eng.: Lynx Edicions and BirdLife International.

Cox, George W. 1999. *Alien Species in North America and Hawaii: Impacts on Natural Ecosystems.* Washington, D.C.: Island Press.

Flannery, Tim, and Peter Schouten. 2001. *A Gap in Nature: Discovering the World's Extinct Animals.* New York: Atlantic Monthly Press.

Groombridge, Brian, ed. 1992. *Global Biodiversity: Status of the Earth's Living Resources.* London: Chapman and Hall.

Heywood, Vernon H., ed. 1995. *Global Biodiversity Assessment.* New York: Cambridge University Press.

Quinn, John R. 1994. *Wildlife Survivors: The Flora and Fauna of Tomorrow.* Blue Ridge Summit, PA: TAB Books/McGraw-Hill.

Seidensticker, John, Sarah Christie, and Peter Jackson, eds. 1999. *Riding the Tiger: Tiger Conservation in Human-Dominated Landscapes.* Cambridge, Eng.: Cambridge University Press.

Steadman, David W. 1995. "Prehistoric Extinctions of Pacific Island Birds: Biodiversity Meets Zooarchaeology." *Science* 267: 1,123–1,131.

Stein, Bruce A., Lynn S. Kutner, and Jonathan S. Adams. 2000. *Precious Heritage: The Status of Biodiversity in the United States.* New York: Oxford University Press.

HARTMUT S. WALTER

BIOLOGY, POPULATION

Population biology is the study of the ecological and evolutionary aspects of the "distribution and abundance of animals"(Andrewartha and Birch 1954). The ecological aspect focuses on living organisms as individuals, groups, species, and interacting assemblages of species. The evolutionary aspect focuses on genetic and environmental changes that shape observed characteristics—the phenotypes—of organisms past and present. Like demography, population biology is a discipline with fuzzy boundaries that shade into specialized subjects: ecology *per se,* not directly concerned with evolution; population genetics, focused on genetic change and variation, and evolution; epidemiology, concerned with host–parasite associations; paleobiology, focused on the historical record; behavioral ecology; physiological ecology; and many others. This entry is a selective account of population biology at the start of the twenty-first century.

From Individual to Population

A basic unit of analysis in population biology is the individual, with a focus on the individual as *ontogeny*—a process of development and change from birth to death. Demographers and ecologists often use the terms life cycle or life history for this process. The transitions that occur during development can be complex in different species, involving distinct developmental stages that can differ in terms of actual habitat (e.g., water, land, or air), growth and form, feeding, and reproduction. A staggering variety of life cycles is observed in nature, to the delight of natural historians since before Charles Darwin, but this variety challenges scientific analysis. As just one example of the scale of variation, population biologists deal with species whose characteristic life spans range from an hour (or less, for bacterial division) to centuries (long-lived trees such as redwoods).

The study of life cycles in population biology focuses on the qualitative and quantitative analysis of life cycle transitions—their sequencing, rates, interaction, proximate determinants, and evolutionary determinants. An organizing principle here, enunciated by the statistician Ronald Fisher (1890–1962) in the 1930s and implicit even in the work of Darwin, is the allocation of resources—in the course of life, individuals gather resources such as energy and materials that are allocated among processes such as metabolism, growth of reproductive and other body parts, foraging, repair of internal systems, mating, and reproduction. It is commonly accepted that life cycles in nature are adapted to the environments in which they are found—it would be surprising if they were not—and hence that resources must be allocated over the life cycle in an optimal way. The claim of optimality in population biology is loosely supported by the notion that Darwinian natural selection results in life cycles that have a high *fitness* in their environmental context relative to other possible life cycles. It is difficult to say how fitness is to be measured in a given context, or how an optimum is defined, but in practice optimality conditions can be defined by the context and nature of life cycles. Foraging birds or large predators, for example, are likely to be efficient in terms of how they use their time or focus their effort. Many population biologists employ such criteria, plus the tools of optimality theory, to gain useful insight into life cycles.

The environment in which organisms live is critically important, as it is in all demographic studies. A major component of the environment is *biotic:* the set of other individuals with which any given individual interacts. In the simplest case, the density of other individuals in space and time and how this density affects life cycle transitions is of primary importance. Thus, death rates can be regulated by density-dependent interactions between individuals of the same species (such as competition or cannibalism), or interactions between individuals of different species (a familiar example is predation; less familiar may be symbiosis, a mutually beneficial relationship exemplified by rhizobia bacteria that live in structures called nodules on the roots of plants and fix atmospheric nitrogen for the plants in return for energy and a habitat). In a finer-grained view, interactions can depend on the characteristics and behavior of the individuals involved. Competition for food, for example, may depend on body size; success in attracting a mate can depend on phenotypes such as plumage or antler size; and so on. The *abiotic* environment also plays a major role by setting resource levels, environmental conditions (such as light or moisture or temperature), and the predictability or unpredictability of such factors.

The analysis of interactions between individuals requires aggregation from individuals to populations, a process affected by scale in space and time. The simplest case is an isolated population of a single species, such as a bacterial culture in a laboratory Petri dish. Spatially localized populations in nature are often studied as isolated populations if migration is not significant. More generally, populations have patchy distributions over space, and a population may really be an aggregation over many spatial patches connected by migration. Depending on the species, a population may occupy some spatial locations only some of the time, as with migrating birds or butterflies that trace a roughly regular spatial migration route in the course of a year. In other cases, local patches can be ephemeral, supporting a small population of a species for a small part of an occasional year. Spatial distributions may be weakly or strongly determined by underlying physical and biological features in space and time.

For a population of a single species, the key questions concern dynamics: How and why do population numbers and composition change over time and space; what is the short-run and long-run variability in population; what is the viability (i.e., ability to persist at reasonable numbers) of a population? These questions are also central to the sciences of conservation biology and population management. Conservation biologists are typically interested in viability, in the likelihood of extinction, and in spatial distributions; exploited populations (e.g., for fishing, hunting, recreation) are, in a surprising number of cases, actively managed for abundance and persistence.

From Populations to Ecosystems

As noted, interactions between individuals of different species can be important in the life cycles of individuals and in the dynamics of populations. Some interactions between pairs of species are studied using common concepts and methods. Examples include interactions between predator and prey, host and parasite, or species competing for similar resources. Interactions play a central role in population biology, underlying pattern and process in ways that were first highlighted by the British ecologist Charles Elton (1900–1991) and the American ecologist G. Evelyn Hutchinson (1903–1991); current paradigms in the field build on the work of the American ecologists Robert MacArthur and Edward O. Wilson, among others.

Predator–prey interactions are often analyzed in terms of the response of predator behavior to changes in the distribution and abundance of prey—a general theory for this functional response of the predator has been developed and successfully applied in several cases.

Host–parasite interactions are more complex because parasites come in many varieties, from parasitic organisms that spend part or all of their life cycle within one or more hosts, to insect parasitoids that spend their adult lives outside a host but need to find, and lay their eggs inside or on, a host. There are useful general methods for analyzing different classes of host–parasite interaction. A significant part of the science of host–parasite interactions originated in the study of human malaria, with the work of the great British epidemiologist Ronald Ross (1857–1932), and from subsequent epidemiological work on human and non-human disease. Since about 1980 population biologists and epidemiologists have paid increasing attention to the transmission and control of viral infections ranging from influenza to HIV.

Competitive interactions vary depending on what competition exists (for space, food, mates, and so on) and the type of competitive interaction (which may involve quite distinct abilities, e.g., efficiency at finding a resource, or ability to displace other individuals from a resource). Here too, a number of general principles of analysis have been developed and tested. Individual behavior clearly plays a key role in interactions, and behavioral ecology is the study of behaviors and their evolution.

Moving up in scale from pair-wise interactions, there are communities of species that interact in many different ways over some spatial region. The complexity of communities depends on their diversity (measured in terms of the numbers and relative abundance of different species), their trophic structure (if all species in the community are arranged into a who-eats-whom pyramid there is a hierarchy of levels; the subset of species at each level is called a trophic level), and the network of interactions between each species and the rest. Communities range from a few dozen bacterial species in a square foot of soil to assemblages of hundreds of species in a large national preserve or park. Still further up in scale, there are ecosystems that may contain numerous communities that interact weakly with each other, from complete islands to areas of subcontinental scale. As spatial scale changes, so does the time scale over which communities display significant change. For communities and ecosystems, ecologists are concerned with their dynamics, viability, resilience (ability to withstand perturbations such as changing environmental conditions or invasion by new species), biodiversity, and biogeography. A subject of increasing interest is the dynamic interaction between humans and ecosystems.

Evolutionary Ecology

In population biology, evolution can make causality run from individual characteristics to interactions (e.g., the outcome of competition is determined by the characteristics of competing individuals), or from interactions to characteristics (e.g., characteristics such as plumage displays can evolve in response to their impact on relative mating success). Time scale is important in determining which effects are studied: In the conventional paradigm, evolutionary changes are usually much slower than ecological changes. Even so, the evolutionary changes people can observe and document are those that take place over a period shorter than the human life span. The classic example is the change in the moth *Biston betularia* from mostly light to mostly dark individuals in the half-century beginning in about 1848 as the industrial revolution increasingly polluted Britain. Many population biologists are concerned with historical evolutionary processes that generated the behaviors, interactions, and life cycles observable in the present; others, with how evolution is changing the patterns observed in the early twenty-first century.

Much of evolutionary ecology generalizes Darwin's insights: Elton did so in 1930, with an emphasis on the evolution of individual characteristics in ecological contexts. But many new insights have emerged in studying phenomena that Darwin did not consider or found too challenging. The study of social evolution—how collective behavior evolves—was given a solid basis by the British evolutionary biologist William Hamilton (1936–2000) in 1964, by the introduction of the concept of inclusive fitness, which extends fitness to include the effects of an individual's behavior on the fitness of kin. Work on social traits in behavioral ecology and evolution has also provided insights in subjects such as anthropology and human ecology. Evolutionary questions that remain topics of active research include aspects of the evolution of sex and sex ratios, the evolution of senescence (the British biologist J. B. S. Haldane (1892–1964) and the British immunologist Peter Medawar (1915–1987) were pioneers in this area), and the evolution of larger-scale patterns in ecology.

Population Genetics

Evolutionary ecologists tend to think largely in terms of natural selection as the main force for adaptation and evolution. Population genetics takes a more careful look at the evolutionary process. The American population biologist Richard Lewontin (born 1929) emphasized that evolution is a multi-level affair: An individual's genes make up its genotype; genotype plus environment interact to determine the individual's phenotype. The crux is the presence of heritable genetic variation between individuals—variation is modified by differential selection on phenotypes, by random events (especially *drift*, the unavoidable randomness in choosing a finite sample from a finite population), and by the introduction of naturally occurring random mutations into genotypes. Evolution is the consequence of a dynamic process of change in the genetic variation within populations under the forces of selection, drift, and mutation. Many basic features of evolution were worked out by Fisher, Haldane, and the American population geneticist Sewall Wright (1889–1988) in the 1930s and 1940s.

In subsequent decades population geneticists have brought increasing experimental power to bear on the measurement and characterization of genetic and phenotypic variability within populations, from the early studies of the American population geneticist Theodosius Dobzhansky (1900–1975) on chromosome structures in fruit flies (the genus *Drosophila*) to current studies of genetic sequences and gene microarrays. A striking overall finding is that there is a huge amount of genetic variability within populations, and a key question in population genetics is why so much variability exists. In broad terms, there are two answers. One, originating with Dobzhansky, holds that selection is responsible for much of the variation; the other, originating with the Japanese population geneticist Motoo Kimura (born 1925), holds that much variation is simply neutral, a consequence of mutation followed by random drift, and has little selective significance. It is known that each answer applies in some domain of nature, but precise formulation and testing of these and more sophisticated hypotheses remains an important subject for research.

Since about the 1980s, population geneticists have increasingly turned to the analysis of phylogeny, the historical relationships among lineages of organisms or their parts (including their genes). Given a sample of genes from different humans in the year 2000, for example, one can ask whether these genes exist as the result of evolution from a single ancestral population, and estimate the time it took for the current genetic variation to materialize. Phylogenetics also provides powerful insights into the evolutionary *trees* that have resulted in variation between species as found at the beginning of the twenty-first century.

To someone concerned with human demography, population genetics is key to understanding how genetics and evolution have shaped aspects of human traits and behavior. Population genetics has been strikingly effective in the analysis of genetic variants that have major effect on health (such as the *Apo E* locus, implicated in Alzheimer's disease and atherosclerosis). Biodemographers look to population genetics as a way of identifying segments of the genome that have major effects on quantitative traits such as components of mortality. Demographers are becoming interested in the genetic contribution to traits as diverse as fertility and health, partly stimulated by the availability of modern technologies for extracting genetic information from small samples of human cells collected in surveys. However, it is far from obvious that genetic analyses can sensibly inform an understanding of complex traits that have major social and cultural components. As demographers' earlier experience with eugenics demonstrates, there are sound historical reasons to be cautious and precise in such work.

See also: *Aging and Longevity, Biology of; Animal Ecology; Biodemography; Darwin, Charles; Lotka, Alfred; Sociobiology.*

BIBLIOGRAPHY

Andrewartha, Herbert G., and Louis C. Birch. 1954. *The Distribution and Abundance of Animals.* Chicago: University of Chicago Press.

Crow, James F. 1986. *Basic Concepts in Population, Quantitative, and Evolutionary Genetics.* New York: W. H. Freeman.

Elton, Charles S. 2001. *Animal Ecology* (1927), with new introductory material by Mathew A. Leibold and J. Timothy Wootton. Chicago: University of Chicago Press.

Fisher, Ronald Aylmer. 1958. *The Genetical Theory of Natural Selection,* rev. 2nd edition. New York: Dover Publications.

Futuyma, Douglas J. 1998. *Evolutionary Biology,* 3rd edition. Sunderland, MA: Sinauer Associates.

Hutchinson, G. Evelyn. 1965. *The Ecological Theater and the Evolutionary Play.* New Haven, CT: Yale University Press.

Krebs, John R., and Nicholas B. Davies, ed. 1997. *Behavioural Ecology: An Evolutionary Approach.* Cambridge, MA: Blackwell Science.

Lewontin, Richard C. 1974. *The Genetic Basis of Evolutionary Change.* New York: Columbia University Press.

Maynard Smith, John. 1998. *Evolutionary Genetics,* 2nd edition. New York: Oxford University Press.

Ricklefs, Robert E., and Gary L. Miller. 2000. *Ecology,* 4th edition. New York: W. H. Freeman.

SHRIPAD D. TULJAPURKAR

BIRTH CONTROL, HISTORY OF

Evidence of attempts at contraception and induced abortion are found in many societies. Many preliterate societies used a variety of herbal remedies in attempts to suppress fertility or to induce menstruation. Literary evidence of contraception is found in the work of Egyptian, Classical, and Arabic writers, such as the Greek physicians Disocorides and Soranus (first–second centuries C.E.), the Roman historian Pliny the Elder (died 79 C.E.), and the Arabian physician and philosopher Avicenna (died 1037 C.E.). Archaeological evidence of induced abortion has been found in a Romano-Gallic site in the Netherlands where the skeleton of a young a woman was discovered with a bone stylet, which was used to induce abortion, in the pelvis.

In classical times, the principal export of the Mediterranean port of Cyrene was a plant called silphion. Related plants demonstrate oxytocic properties, and sylphion seems to have been such an effective abortifacient that it was harvested to extinction. The oldest pictorial representation of a mechanical abortion is in a bas relief illustrating massage abortion in the great temples of Angkor Wat in Cambodia (1150 C.E.). The image depicts devils in masks pounding the abdomens of women who appear to be about 20 weeks pregnant. An identical procedure continues to be widely used in contemporary Southeast Asia.

The Judeo-Christian Tradition

Induced abortion is mentioned once in the Bible (Exod. 21:22), which categorizes it as a crime, but explicitly not as murder. *Coitus interruptus* is mentioned once in a passage in Genesis (38: 9). The story of Onan, "who spilled it [his seed] on the ground" is well known. Talmudic commentators are divided as whether God slew Onan because he practiced withdrawal, or because he disobeyed his father's command to make Tamar, his dead brother's wife, pregnant.

The New Testament makes no comment on any aspect of fertility regulation, but Saint Paul, in his letters, places women in an inferior position to men. The early fathers of the Church became increasingly conservative in their interpretation of human sexuality. Saint Augustine (died 430) had the same mistress for many years, with whom he had one child, and he may have practiced *coitus interruptus.* He taught that original sin had been passed down the generations in the semen, much like some precursor to the HIV virus, and therefore the unbaptized were condemned to eternal damnation. He argued that nocturnal erections were evidence of human sin because they were not under the control of the human will. Given such interpretations, Saint Augustine was led to conclude that the only justification for sexual intercourse was to perpetuate the human race. In his words, "that which is done for lust must be done in such a way that it is not for lust's sake" (*Contra Julianum,* 5, 9). Other western theologians constructed even more contrived restraints on human sexuality. By the later Middle Ages, intercourse was forbidden on Sundays, Fridays (the day when Christ died), feast days (which were numerous), and throughout the 40 days of Lent. In effect, intercourse was forbidden for approximately half the year. Women were told that if they had a congenitally abnormal baby it was because they had sex during menstruation or during some forbidden time.

Augustine condemned all types of artificial conception, including periodic abstinence. But in the late-nineteenth century, contrived exceptions began to be constructed to permit use of the rhythm method (abstinence limited to what was believed to be the fertile period of the woman's menstrual cycle). In 1920 the Lambeth Conference of Anglican Bishops moved to a cautious recognition of licitness of all artificial contraception. The Second Vatican Council (1962–1965), which marked a watershed in Catholic teaching in a variety of domains, was expected to move the Catholic Church in the same direction. Most people expected that the approval of contraception would be widened, at least to include the then newly available oral contraceptives. Pope Paul VI, who became pope in 1963, set up a commission to review the topic, which eventually included five women. The majority of the commission voted to revise the church teaching of birth control. However, Paul VI rejected these recommendations and published the encyclical *Humanae vitae* in 1968. It condemned any contraception, defined as "action, which is either before, at the moment of, or after sexual intercourse, that is specifically intended to prevent procreation—whether as an end or a means." It was a linear continuation of Augustine's teachings.

Only fragments of written information exist to illuminate the pain these teachings brought to countless women and their families over the centuries. An Inquisitor condemning Albigensian heretics to the stake (circa 1320) in Montaillou, France, interrogated one woman who had had a sexual relationship with a priest. "What shall I do if I become pregnant by you? I shall be ashamed and lost," she said. "I have a certain herb" responded her lover, "the one the cowherds hang over a cauldron of milk in which they have put some rennet to stop the milk curdling" (Le Roy Ladurie). Between 1647 and 1719, in Colyton (in Devon, England), the mean age of marriage for women rose to 29.6 years. In one parish in Somerset only one in 200 pregnancies was to women under age 17. Ecclesiastical court records show that while many women went to the altar pregnant, premarital sex was limited to a very short interval before marriage. Women who did bear a bastard child could be publicly whipped on market day—with extra stripes if they did not breastfeed their baby. In 1671, a French aristocrat, Madame de Sévigné wrote to her daughter, "I beg you, my love, do not trust to two beds; it is a subject of temptation. Have someone sleep in your room."

The Nineteenth Century

With industrialization, urbanization, and some fall in infant mortality, the pressure to control family size grew. The first articulated efforts to disseminate knowledge about family planning technologies date from the early-nineteenth century. They began with English Free Thinkers such as Francis Place (1771–1854) and John Stuart Mill (1806–1873). Place had 15 children and he understood the sufferings of fac-

tory workers and servants in the big cities. He wrote what contemporaries called the *Diabolical Handbills* describing the use of a sponge inserted vaginally. In 1832, the American physician Charles Knowlton (1800–1850) published anonymously *The Fruits of Philosophy,* which described post-coital douching. Several publishers were prosecuted under obscenity laws in the United States and Britain for republishing Knowlton's work.

In 1871, Charles Bradlaugh (1833–1891), a Free Thinker who had been elected to the British Parliament, and Annie Besant (1847–1933), a writer who had rejected the conventions of marriage and joined the Secular movement, deliberately challenged the law by republishing *The Fruits of Philosophy.* Their trial was widely reported in daily papers and sales of the book rose from 1,000 a year to 100,000 in three months. Bradlaugh and Besant were acquitted on a technicality. A substantial and continued decline in the British birth rate began at that time, most likely driven by increasing use of withdrawal and rising abortion rates, along with the commercial availability—albeit under the counter—of condoms and spermicides. Historical demography suggests that withdrawal, along with delayed marriage, was being used to limit family size in Elizabethan England and *coitus interruptus* almost certainly played a major part in the decline in family size in France that began in the eighteenth century. Even in the mid-twentieth century *coitus interruptus* remained one of the most common methods of contraception in Europe.

In nineteenth-century England, abortion up to the time of quickening was legal. But in 1861, the Offenses Against Persons Act not only made abortion at any time during pregnancy a crime, but even the intention to commit an abortion became a felony. During the same period, every state in the United States passed a law against abortion, although women struggled to terminate unintended pregnancies. In 1871, Ely van de Warkle described abortion practices in Boston, Massachusetts. To test their safety, he purchased the many herbal remedies that were available at that time and either ate them, or gave them to his dog. "The luxury of an abortion," he wrote in the *Journal of the Boston Obstetrical Society,* "is now within the reach of the serving girl."

In America, a dry goods salesman named Anthony Comstock began a one-man crusade against obscenity. Amongst other things, the law he successfully lobbied Congress to pass in 1873 defined all types of contraception as pornographic. Comstock also persuaded his wife to visit a well-known New York abortionist who called herself Madame Restell. She begged her for an abortion, which Restell promised to provide. Comstock then had Restell arrested. She cut her throat the night before her trial was to begin. Comstock described this as a "bloody end to a bloody business."

Class differences in both attitudes to and practice of birth control persisted through the nineteenth century. By 1900, in England, clergymen and doctors were having families that were only one quarter the size of those of miners and dock laborers. Yet it was the professional classes that were most opposed to making family planning available to the working classes.

Twentieth Century

It is difficult to reconstruct the sexual conservatism of late-nineteenth century Europe and North America. Marie Stopes (1880–1958) was one of the first women with a Ph.D. in Britain. The daughter of a middle class Edinburgh family, she married a fellow botanist called Ruggles Gates. He proved to be impotent and it is a measure of the ignorance of the time that it seems to have taken some while for his wife to discover that something was missing from her marriage. As a divorced virgin in 1918, she penned a book called *Married Love*. In flowery and convoluted language, and without mention of any of the anatomy of the genitalia, she argued that woman had a right to enjoy sexual pleasure in marriage. This novel view helped make the book widely read—both in Britain and in many other countries.

World War I generated a lively debate between those interested in family planning and a body of militaristic lobbyists who argued that contraception was unacceptable because it interfered with the birth of the next generation of soldiers. In 1920, Russia under the leadership of Lenin became the first country to legalize abortion. Several Scandinavian countries passed tortuous and complicated abortion legislation between the 1930s and the late-1950s. In 1966, Britain struck down Queen Victoria's 1861 Offenses against Persons Act forbidding abortion. This example led to important changes in some of the countries of the British Commonwealth (including India, Singapore, and Zambia). Over the next 30 years, every European country, except Malta and Ireland, had passed legislation making safe abortion widely available. In Italy, the decision was the result of a nationwide referendum in 1974.

The spread of contraception and safe abortion between 1960 and 1990 facilitated—some would say, caused—the marked fall in the total fertility rate that took place in Western countries. Low fertility had been achieved in parts of Europe between World War I and World War II, when abortion—although illegal—became relatively widely available in some places. For example, knowledgeable sources estimated one abortion for every live birth in Hamburg in the 1930s. In Vienna the abortion rate was thought to be 20 for every 1,000 women and the very low total fertility rate of 1.2 was thought to be one-third the result of abortion and two-thirds the result of contraception—probably, mainly *coitus interruptus*. A generalized pattern of low fertility in the West was widely predicted in the 1930s by demographers, anticipating declining populations by the second part of the twentieth century. This was not to be: To demographers' surprise, the postwar decades first brought a baby boom that was followed by rapid decline of fertility to well below replacement levels in many European countries.

In the 1950s and 1960s, the lowest birth rates in the world were in Eastern Europe, again based on widespread use of withdrawal backed up by abortion. In the twenty-first century the total fertility rate of most Western countries is below 2. A similar rapid decline in fertility that has occurred in most other parts of the world also owes much to the improved availability and range of contraceptive choices and access to safe abortion; examples include South Korea, Taiwan, Thailand and Sri Lanka.

Historically, the twentieth century not only saw increasing access to reproductive choices, but also witnessed important reversals of this trend. It is notable that many twentieth-century dictators took steps to restrict reproductive choices. One of the first moves that the Nazis made when Hitler came to power was to close down what had been a promising beginning to family planning services in Germany and Austria. It was in Nazi dominated Vichy France in 1942 that the last execution of an abortionist took place. Stalin in Russia and Nicolae Ceausescu in Romania both reversed previously liberal abortion laws.

The first family planning clinic to be established was in the Netherlands in the 1880s. Birth control leader Margaret Sanger (1883–1966) opened a clinic in Brooklyn, New York in 1917. Immediately, large numbers of women attended, but ten days later the police, enforcing the Comstock laws, closed it down. In Britain, Stopes opened her first family planning clinic in 1921. In the United States, precedents were developed that held that if physicians prescribed contraceptives "for the cure and prevention of disease" then their use was deemed to fall outside the Comstock laws. (*Congressional Globe* 1873: 1436). In 1937, this precedent was reinforced in the case of *United States v. One Package of Japanese Pessaries,* 13 F. Supp. 334 (E.D.N.Y. 1936). These developments brought short-term relief to those trying to provide contraceptive services, but it also contributed to the undue medicalization of contraceptive practice, particularly as at that time the only clinical methods were vaginal barriers. The last of the U.S. Comstock laws were not struck down until the Supreme Court ruling of 1965 in *Griswold v. Connecticut,* 381 U.S. 479 (1965).

In 1966, the British abortion law was reformed to take into account the "woman's total environment" (The Abortion Act, 1967). Framing abortion as a medical problem helped dull political opposition, but the fine print of medical regulation in England delayed for decades the introduction of safe abortion that would require only day care. When Commonwealth countries such as India and Zambia adopted a version of the British Abortion Law, medical restrictions meant that the law had little or no effect on the frequency of unsafe abortions.

Griswold was based on the right to privacy and this also became the foundation of the unexpected decision of the U.S. Supreme Court in 1972 in *Roe v. Wade,* 410 U.S. 113 (1973), to strike down the anti-abortion laws that remained across America. *Roe v. Wade* also framed abortion as a right to privacy and an issue of religious toleration rather than a medical issue. "We need not resolve the difficult question of when life begins," wrote the justices, "when those trained in the respective disciplines of medicine, philosophy and theology are unable to arrive at any conclusion."

Fertility Regulation Methods

All the methods of contraception now in use, except for systemically active oral contraceptives, implants, and injections, were available and documented by the end of the nineteenth century. Condoms made from sheep caeca, which date back to the seven-teenth century, have been discovered by archaeologists. Famed diarist James Boswell describes using a condom with a prostitute in London in 1763. Condoms became widely available with the invention of vulcanization of rubber by Charles Goodyear and Thomas Hancock in 1844. The cervical cap was described in the early nineteenth century in Germany and the diaphragm was available by the turn of the twentieth century. The manufacturing and distribution of contraceptives was poorly regulated until well into the second half of the twentieth century. Sales were illegal in the United States, France, and several other European countries. In Britain sales were "under the counter." Intrauterine Devices (IUDs) began to be used in the late-nineteenth century. In the 1920s Ernst Grafenberg, a German gynecologist, did extensive work on IUDs, but after fleeing Nazi persecution he found that political freedom in America did not entail the freedom to continue his research. IUDs went through a renaissance of interest in the 1960s, when flexible plastic devices, such as the Lippes Loop, replaced the metal rings used previously. In 1971, Hugh Davis launched the Dalkon Shield. He claimed very low pregnancy rates without revealing that he counseled the clinical trialists also to use spermicides with the device. Deaths occurred due to rapidly spreading septicemia in pregnant women with a Dalkon Shield in situ. The legal cases that followed bankrupted the A. H. Robbins Company that had marketed the device, and led to a great reluctance to use any type of IUD in the United States. In Finland, obstetric and gynecological specialist Tapani Lukkenian devised the first hormone-releasing IUDs; in Chile, obstetric and gynecological specialist Jaime Zipper devised the first copper-releasing IUDs.

James Young Simpson, Queen Victoria's gynecologist, describes what twenty-first century society would call manual vacuum aspiration, a method of abortion, but the method was lost. The current method of manual vacuum aspiration, used for abortions up to the tenth week of pregnancy, was described by Harvey Karman in 1972.

In the 1920s, reproductive physiologist Ludwig Hablandt described the physiological basis of oral contraception. But the method made no progress, partly because of the lack of a cheap source of steroid and also because contraceptive research was not academically acceptable. The U.S. National Institutes of Health was forbidden by congressional mandate to support contraceptive research and, until the 1960s, the Vatican blocked any assistance from the World Health Organization in family planning. When Gregory Pincus, John Rock, and M.C. Chang, working in the Worcester Institute outside Boston, finally developed the Pill in the 1950s, contraception was still illegal in Massachusetts. For this reason, the initial large-scale trials were conducted in Puerto Rico. In 1963, American obstetrician and gynecologist John Rock, a devout Catholic, wrote *The Time Has Come: A Catholic Doctor's Proposal to End the Battle over Birth Control.* Rock argued that hormonal contraceptives should be licit because they imitated the natural processes whereby pregnancy and lactation inhibited ovulation. He died an embittered member of his Church. In 1966, obstetrician and gynecologist Elismar Coutino in Brazil demonstrated that an injectable form of progesterone, administered every three months, was a highly effective contraceptive.

One of the few genuine advances in birth control technology in the late-twentieth century was the discovery by reproductive physiologist Étienne-Émile Baulieu in France of the anti-progestigen Mifepristone (RU-486), an abortifacient effective if used during the first 50 days of pregnancy. Although Mifepristone is widely available in Europe, the controversy surrounding its development and use delayed its introduction in the United States.

Conclusion

The history of birth control is one of controversy, of slow progress in technology and scientific analysis, of legal restraints, and of medical conservatism. It is a tale of two steps forward and one step backward.

The twenty-first century has opened with a serious demographic divide. The Western nations and the emerging economies of Latin America and Asia have total fertility rates of 2.5 or less, while much of sub-Saharan Africa, Pakistan, and parts of northern India have total fertility rates of 5 or more. The legal and social attitudes toward family planning and abortion in the remaining high fertility countries has similarities to the situation in Europe and North America in the early twentieth century, in that contraception is not readily accessible to much of the population and abortion is illegal (or legal but difficult to get, as in India). Interestingly, countries furthest removed from the western cultural influence have had the most rapid fertility transitions; one was communist China in the 1970s and 1980s, and the other the Islamic Republic of Iran in the 1980s and 1990s. Undoubtedly, there were sad cases of coercion in China, although a plausible case can be made that if a national program had been started a decade earlier, a purely voluntary decline might have occurred as in South Korea and Taiwan. Iran shows that making family planning choices available leads to rapid fertility decline, even in a conservative religious theocracy.

Much of the proximate cause of the demographic divide within the contemporary world can be traced back to the uneven rate in which fertility regulation technologies have spread around the world. While the British Empire introduced significant public health measures, such as vaccination, clean water, and sewage treatment to many parts of the world, it opposed family planning. Birth control organizations began in the 1930s in India, as did an awareness of rapid population growth, but the country had to wait until independence before it could put in place any birth control policies. Many high fertility nations still have anti-abortion legislation that has existed since colonial times.

See also: *Contraception, Modern Methods of; Family Planning Programs; Induced Abortion: History; Infanticide; Reproductive Rights; Sanger, Margaret.*

BIBLIOGRAPHY

Himes, Norman E. 1963 [1936]. *Medical History of Contraception.* New York: Gamut Press.

Le Roy Ladurie, Emmanuel. 1979. *Montaillou: The Promised Land of Error.* New York: Vintage Books.

Mohr, James C. 1978. *Abortion in America: The Origins and Evolution of National Policy, 1800–1900.* New York: Oxford University Press.

Noonan, John T. 1967. *Contraception. A History of Its Treatment by the Catholic Theologians and Canonists.* Cambridge, MA: Harvard University Press.

Potts, Malcolm, and Thomas Tsang. 1995. "History of Contraception." In *Gynecology and Obstetrics,* pp. 1–23. Philadelphia: Lippincott-Raven.

Ranke-Heinemann, Uta. 1990. *Eunuchs for Heaven: The Catholic Church and Sexuality.* London: Andre Deutsch.

Wrigley, Edward Anthony. 1966. "Family Limitation in Preindustrial England." *Economic History Review* 29: 82.

David Malcolm Potts

BIRTH RATE

See *Fertility Measurement*

BLACK DEATH

In any textbook on infectious diseases the chapter on plague will describe three pandemics of bubonic plague.

The Three Pandemics

The first pandemic—the plague of Justinian—originated in Egypt, erupted in Constantinople in 541 c.e., spread to Ireland by 544, but did not touch England until 120 years later. The second pandemic originated in India, China, or the steppes of Russia. It touched the shores of Western Europe (Messina) in the autumn of 1347, then spread across the continent, striking places as remote as Greenland. The disease recurred periodically through the eighteenth century and possibly into the nineteenth century. Despite claims in some textbooks, the plague of Marseilles in 1720–1721 was not this pandemic's European finale. In 1743 an estimated 48,000 people perished from the plague in Messina, and in 1770–1771, over 100,000 people died in Moscow. The third pandemic began in the mid-nineteenth century, spread slowly through the Chinese province of Yunnan, and did not reach Hong Kong until 1894. From there, steamship commerce aided its transmission across much of the world. However, except for India and a few other subtropical regions, its spread was confined largely to the docks of Sydney, Lisbon, Hamburg, Glasgow, and San Francisco. Instead of millions of deaths as Europeans feared, the death counts in temperate zones rarely surpassed 100.

Were the Three Plagues the Same?

The reason for claiming an identity among these three waves of epidemic rests on the supposedly unmistakable signs of bubonic plague. For the first wave of plague no quantitative records such as burials or last wills and testaments survive, and few narrative sources describe even the signs or symptoms. Paul the Deacon's *Historia Langobardorum*, written around 790 and describing plague in rural northern Italy in the 560s, is the most explicit. It points to "swellings of the glands . . . in the manner of a nut or a date" in the groin "and in other rather delicate places followed by an unbearable fever." The Emperor Justinian was afflicted with a boil in the groin and survived. Abbess Aethelthryth in 680 was less lucky; she died from a large boil under her jaw—a strange site for modern plague.

Differences between Medieval and Modern Plague

Few other examples of individual cases of plague can be gleaned from these sources, but the epidemiological clues point to a disease that was not characteristic of the plague whose agent (*Yersinia pestis*) was discovered in 1894.

The "first pandemic" spread rapidly and caused high mortality, especially among those, such as monks and nuns, who lived under the same roof, suggesting a highly contagious person-to-person airborne disease. In 664 the plague took only 91 days to travel 385 kilometers (239 miles) as the crow flies from Dover to Lastingham, England. By contrast, as the microbiologist Robert Koch commented in 1900, modern bubonic plague is a rat disease in which humans occasionally participate. Because the rat does not travel far, the bubonic plague of the twentieth century moved overland at a rate of about 12 to 15 kilometers (7 to 9 miles) a year. Thus, modern plague, even with the advantage of railways and automobiles, would need 25 years to cover the distance traveled in 3 months by the early medieval plague. Further, no literary or archaeological evidence shows the existence of rats in Anglo-Saxon England and no source mentions any signs or symptoms of this plague in England or Ireland. Despite this lack of evidence, some historians remain convinced that this disease was the bubonic plague discovered at the end of the nineteenth century.

The narrative sources for the "second pandemic" set off by the Black Death of 1347–1352 explode in number and variety. In addition to hundreds of chronicles from abbeys, city-states, and principalities across Europe, the plague tract, written for the most part by university-trained doctors, became one of the earliest forms of "popular literature" by the early fifteenth century. Further, the survival of thousands of last wills and testaments, necrologies, burial records, manorial rolls, and lists of ecclesiastical vacancies allows quantitative analyses of this plague, including its cycles of mortality, its seasonality, and the characteristics of its victims: age, sex, occupation, class, and locality. In addition to these rich sources, citywide burials and "Bills of Mortality" spread from Tuscany to north of the Alps in the late fifteenth century and as early as the 1420s (in Florence) began to indicate causes of death. Yet despite this wealth of information, no evidence links these late medireview and early modern European plagues to any disease carried by rodents and from which rodents were the first to die.

The epidemiological evidence raises further suspicions. First, like the early medieval plague, the second pandemic was a fast mover, spreading in a day as far as modern plague travels in a year. Doctors and chroniclers marveled at the Black Death's lightning-fast transmission and contagion—a word frequently used by doctors and chroniclers, who claimed that the plague spread by breath, touch, and even sight. For later strikes they distinguished plague from other diseases by this epidemiological feature as much as by the bubo. To reconcile the differences between the late medieval and modern plagues, historians and scientists say that the Black Death's speed and contagion relied on its pneumonic form and claim that as with modern plague, once it became airborne, it became "highly contagious" and free from rodents.

However, these claims are mistaken, as Wu Tien Teh discovered with the Manchurian plagues of 1911 and 1922. First, this disease was primarily an infliction of a rodent, *tarabagan*, whose pelt became a highly-prized commodity in the early twentieth century. Secondly, even in tightly packed train cars Wu observed that the infected rarely passed the disease to fellow passengers. As a consequence the worst-known epidemic of pneumonic plague, that of Manchuria in 1911, infected and killed less than 0.3 percent of the population exposed to the disease as opposed to fatality rates that were as high as 40 percent from the Black Death.

Thirdly, the seasonality of the late medieval plagues does not resemble that of modern plague. Modern plague can be sustained only within a narrow temperature band (50 to 78°F) accompanied by high levels of relative humidity because of its dependence on fleas as its vector. By contrast, bouts of late medieval plague could occur at almost any time of year, including January, in places as inhospitable to modern plague as Norway. Further, in the warmer Mediterranean areas the Black Death and its recurrent strikes peaked consistently at the warmest and driest times of the year (June and July), the least likely time for modern plague to peak in light of the rat flea's fertility cycle in those areas.

Fourthly, modern plague has never attained the mortalities seen with major instances of the Black Death or even with those of many of its minor assaults. In the summer months of 1348 Florence may have lost as much as three-quarters of its population. From manorial records, villages in Cambridgeshire and around St.-Flour (Auvergne) lost 76 percent of their populations, and according to chroniclers, places such as Trapani on the western coast of Sicily were totally abandoned. Further, although later strikes of plague in the seventeenth century were not as widespread as the first wave of the Black Death, they could be equally devastating, as they were for Genoa and Naples in 1656–1657, when two-thirds of those populations were destroyed. By contrast, modern plague has never approximated such levels of human carnage—not even in India, where over 95 percent of the modern plague's casualties have occurred. The highest mortality for any city in any plague year was in Bombay City in 1903, when less than 3 percent of its population perished from plague.

Fifthly, the cycles and trends of the second and third pandemics have been entirely different. Because humans have no natural immunity to *Yersinia pestis* and cannot acquire immunity, plague cases and mortality in India increased for a decade or more and then jumped randomly from year to year before declining in the 1920s as a result of rats (not humans) acquiring immunity to the pathogen. Similar patterns occurred in Brazil, Thailand, Vietnam, and other subtropical regions later in the century, even after the introduction of DDT, antibiotics, and modern sanitary measures.

Moreover, the age structure of the victims of modern plague did not change over the twentieth century. As with the first strike on virgin-soil populations, those in the prime of life, between ages 20 and 40, are the plague's principal victims. By contrast, the Black Death over its first 100 years shows a remarkable adaptation between its pathogen and human hosts. By the fourth strike in the 1380s the disease was claiming as little as one-twentieth the toll taken in 1348, and as chroniclers across Europe describe and the rare burial records in Siena confirm, it had become largely a childhood disease.

Misleading Similarities

Why have historians and scientists been so certain that the two pandemics were the same? They point to Boccaccio and occasionally to a handful of chroniclers, insisting that their descriptions of swellings point to the unmistakable signs of *Yersinia pestis*. But first, as health workers in Asia are taught in the early twenty-first century, swellings in the lymph nodes are not unique to plague, hence cultures of the infected regions must be taken. Second, Boccaccio as well as other chroniclers and physicians, from Michele da Piazza in Messina (1347) to doctors of the plague of London (1665), went beyond the bubo to describe various sizes and colors of pustules, rashes, and carbuncles that covered the victims' bodies. Some, such as Geoffrey le Baker in England and Giovanni Morelli in Florence, pointed to these as the more deadly signs, far worse than buboes as large as hens' eggs in the lymph nodes. Moreover, buboes of the late medieval plagues were not confined to the lymph nodes but are described on shins, arms, the face, and under the breasts. By contrast, from over 3,000 clinical reports of plague from hospitals around Bombay City in 1896–1897, only 5 percent of the victims who developed the plague boils had more than one, and in not a single case did those or smaller spots spread over the victims' bodies. Moreover, with modern bubonic plague, from 60 to 75 percent of the plague boils form in the groin because fleas generally bite on or below the shins. However, not a single medieval source points to the groin as the buboes' principal site. Instead, from miracle cures found in saints' lives and doctors' reports, the late medieval boils' usual location was the neck, behind the ears, or on the throat.

Results of the Black Death

Historians have seen the Black Death as responsible for the insurrections of the late fourteenth century, the end of serfdom and feudalism, the rise of vernacular languages, the Reformation, and even modernity at large. Whether the plague can explain such broad and often time-lagged changes is open to debate. Often the immediate and longer-term consequences of the Black Death differed or were the opposite of one another, and its effects varied. For instance, immediately after the Black Death places such as Florence vigorously recouped many of their losses through quick rises in fertility and by drawing migrants from the hinterlands. Curiously this demographic pattern changed in the fifteenth century. Fertility fell perhaps because the disease, although now less lethal, killed greater proportions of those who could replenish population numbers—the young—and cities in northern and central Italy attracted fewer migrants from the countryside. In part this decline stemmed from improved conditions created for peasants by the population losses and the resultant rising demand for agricultural labor.

However, the economic and social consequences of the Black Death and depopulation were not the same across Europe, as worsening conditions for rural labor in Eastern Europe attest. Neither were the Black Death and its successive strikes as "universal" as contemporaries claimed. Plague may not have touched places such as Douai in Flanders until 1400, and population losses in Hainault, Holland, northern Germany, parts of Poland, and Finland were notably lower than they were in many other cities and regions across Europe. Historians have yet to analyze these diverging demographic histories forged by the late medieval plagues or analyze the effects they may have had on economic development and social transitions in the early modern period.

The psychological and cultural consequences of the plague were not uniform over time. In 1348 the clergy, merchants, and physicians evoked God's wrath, looked to the stars, and imagined bizarre happenings in distant lands to explain the Black Death. Except for frenzied acts of expiation—flagellant movements and the burning of Jews—Europeans saw no efficacy in human intervention and looked on doctors' cures as only quickening the pace of death.

However, as early as the second strike of plague in the 1360s, the explanations and immediate reactions to the plague's mass mortalities took an about-face. Instead of referring to floods of frogs, worms that killed by their stench, and black snows that melted mountains, chroniclers and doctors explained the outbreak of new plagues by turning to the human sphere: wars, poverty, and overcrowding. Physicians recommended remedies and procedures they believed had cured them and their patients, and armed with the repeated experiences of plague, they claimed to have surpassed the ancients in the art of healing. No doubt, such success had less to do with their medicine than with their immune systems. Change from utter despondency over the first plague to a new culture of hope and hubris by the end of the fourteenth century rested on the particular character of the Black Death and its recurring bouts—the swiftness with which late medieval Europeans and the new bacillus (whatever it might have been) adapted to each other.

See also: *AIDS; Epidemics; Historical Demography; World Population Growth.*

BIBLIOGRAPHY

Benedict, Carol. 1996. *Bubonic Plague in Nineteenth Century China.* Stanford, CA: Stanford University Press.

Biraben, Jean-Noël. 1975–1976. *Les Hommes et la Peste en France et dans les Pays Européens et Méditerranéens,* 2 vols. Paris: Mouton.

Blockmans, W. P. 1980. "The Social and Economic Effects of Plague in the Low Countries 1349–1500." *Revue Belge de Philologie et d'Histoire* 58: 833–863.

Burnet, Sir Marfarlane. 1962. *Natural History of Infectious Disease,* 3rd edition. Cambridge, Eng.: Cambridge University Press.

Carmichael, Ann G. 1986. *Plague and the Poor in Renaissance Florence.* Cambridge, Eng.: Cambridge University Press.

Catanach, I. J. 1988. "Plague and the Tensions of Empire: India 1896–1918." In *Imperial Medicine and Indigenous Societies,* ed. David Arnold. Manchester, Eng.: Manchester University Press.

Cipolla, Carlo. 1979. *I Pidocchi e il Granduca: Crisi Economica e Problemi Sanitari nella Firenze del '600.* Bologna: Il Mulino.

Cohn, Samuel K. 1992. *The Cult of Remembrance and the Black Death: Six Renaissance Cities in Central Italy.* Baltimore: Johns Hopkins University Press; revised edition: 1997.

——. 1999. *Creating the Florentine State: Peasants and Rebellion, 1348–1434.* Cambridge, Eng.: Cambridge University Press.

——. 2002. *The Black Death Transformed: Disease and Culture in Early Renaissance Europe.* London: Arnold and Oxford University Press.

Cole, Stewart T., and Carmen Buchrieser. 2001. "Baterial Genomics: A Plague o' Both Your Hosts." *Nature* 413: 467–470.

Cook, Gordon, ed. 1996. *Manson's Tropical Diseases,* 20th edition. London: W.B. Saunders.

Dubois, Henri. 1988. "La Dépression: XVIe et XVe Siècles." In *Histoire de la Population Française,* Vol. I, ed. Jacques Dupâquier. Paris: Presses Universitaires de France.

Hatcher, John. 1977. *Plague, Population and the English Economy 1348–1530.* London: Macmillan.

Maddicott, J. R. 1997. "Plague in Seventh-Century England." *Past and Present* 156: 7–54.

Pollitzer, Robert. 1954. *Plague.* Geneva: World Health Organization.

Twigg, Graham. 1984. *The Black Death: A Biological Reappraisal.* New York: Schocken Books.

White, Norman F. 1918. "Twenty Years of Plague in India with Special Reference to the Outbreak of 1917–18." *Indian Journal of Medical Research* VI: 190–236.

SAMUEL COHN, JR.

BLAKE, JUDITH

(1926–1993)

Judith Blake was born in New York City and spent most of the first three decades of her life there. She received her B.S. degree *magna cum laude* from Columbia University in 1951 and her Ph.D. in Sociology, also from Columbia, in 1961. Her first exposure to social demography came through a course co-taught by demographers Hope Eldridge and Kingsley Davis (1908–1997), whom she later married.

Blake moved to Berkeley, California, in 1955 and initially held a series of lectureships, first in the School of Nursing at the University of California, San Francisco, and later in Sociology and then Speech at the University of California, Berkeley. Having completed her dissertation, in 1962 she was appointed Acting Assistant Professor of Demography in the School of Public Health at Berkeley. She quickly advanced to the rank of Professor and along the way established the Graduate Group in Demography (1965), soon to become the Department of Demography (1967), with herself as Chair.

The Department of Demography could not withstand the tumultuous anti-war protest years at Berkeley, and, under a new Chancellor, the department was disbanded in the early 1970s. Nevertheless, Blake, together with her two faculty colleagues in the department (demographers Samuel Preston and Nathan Keyfitz) and Kingsley Davis in the Sociology Department, managed to train an impressively large number of prominent demographers in a relatively short period of time. Following the closing of the department, Blake moved for a short while to the university's School of Public Policy. Then, in 1976, she became the first holder of the Fred N. Bixby Chair in Population Policy at the University of California, Los Angeles (UCLA), with joint appointments in Public Health and Sociology. Blake was the first woman at UCLA to be appointed to an endowed chair.

From the beginning, Blake was intensely interested in the determinants and consequences of fertility-related attitudes and behaviors. Her dissertation, which was published as *Family Structure in Jamaica: The Social Context of Reproduction* in 1961, explored why Jamaica's birth rate was so much lower than Puerto Rico's. One of her most original and influential articles, "Social Structure and Fertility: An Analytic Framework," co-authored with Davis in 1956, identified a set of intermediate variables through which any social factors affecting fertility must operate. This line of research endures in contemporary work on the proximate determinants of fertility.

Blake's research on American fertility was wide ranging. In a 1968 article, she criticized economists for equating children with consumer durables and for ignoring important components of the opportunity cost of childrearing and other non-economic determinants of fertility differentials. She showed that, in their fertility attitudes and practices, American lay Catholics and non-Catholics were actually quite similar and that the Vatican's influence over the use of contraception was minimal. In her influential book *Family Size and Achievement* (1989), Blake demonstrated that single children were not disadvantaged in terms of their sociability and that children with few or no siblings experienced higher levels of material well-being and cognitive development. She showed that earlier studies of attitudes to-

ward abortion were simplistic, and she accurately predicted (to her dismay) the emergence of a backlash against abortion in the United States. She drew forceful attention to the pronatalism inherent in U.S. laws and institutions, including the emerging women's movement, and argued, at a time when U.S. fertility was still near its postwar peak and well above replacement level, that a reduction in fertility could be accomplished by a lifting of these incentives rather than by an introduction of disincentives.

Whether in her teaching, her performance at professional meetings, or in her published work, Judith Blake was invariably intellectually challenging and often provocative. She did not shy away from controversy, and she was a fearless and penetrating critic both of her own work and that of others. Her scientific contributions to social demography were recognized with her election as President of the Population Association of America in 1981, and, at the time of her death, she served as editor of the *Annual Review of Sociology*.

See also: *Davis, Kingsley; Fertility, Proximate Determinants of; Population Thought, Contemporary.*

BIBLIOGRAPHY

SELECTED WORKS BY JUDITH BLAKE.

Blake, Judith. 1961. *Family Structure in Jamaica: The Social Context of Reproduction.* New York: Free Press.

————. 1968. "Are Babies Consumer Durables? A Critique of the Economic Theory of Reproductive Motivation." *Population Studies* 22: 5–25.

————. 1972. "Coercive Pronatalism and American Population Policy." In *Aspects of Population Growth Policy: U.S. Commission on Population Growth and the American Future,* 6: 85–108, ed. Robert Parke Jr. and Charles F. Westoff. Washington, D.C.: Government Printing Office.

————. 1989. *Family Size and Achievement.* Berkeley: University of California Press.

————. 1994 (1972). "Fertility Control and the Problem of Voluntarism." *Population and Development Review* 20: 167–177.

Davis, Kingsley, and Judith Blake. 1956. "Social Structure and Fertility: An Analytic Framework." *Economic Development and Cultural Change* 4: 211–235.

SELECTED WORKS ABOUT JUDITH BLAKE.

Bourque, Linda B., Judith Blake, Jennifer Frost, Thomas Espenshade, Ronald Lee, Valerie Oppenheimer, and Jean van der Tak. 1995. "A Biographical Essay on Judith Blake's Professional Career and Scholarship." *Annual Review of Sociology* 21: 449–477.

THOMAS J. ESPENSHADE

BOSERUP, ESTER

(1910–1999)

Ester Boserup was a Danish economist and internationally renowned writer on population and agrarian development. She graduated from the University of Copenhagen in 1935 and began her career in the Danish civil service, dealing with practical problems related to trade policy and regulatory issues. In 1947 Boserup moved to Geneva, having taken a position with the newly established United Nations Commission for Europe. The move marked the beginning of several decades of work in various international posts, assignments, and consultancies in the field of development economics, entailing long stays in India and Africa and extensive participation in international meetings, conferences, and committees. Living in Brissago, Switzerland, she remained professionally active until the early 1990s and was a productive scholar until her death at the age of 89.

Boserup rose to international prominence as an eminent social scientist and an influential intellectual figure with the publication, in 1965, of her book *The Conditions of Agricultural Growth: The Economics of Agrarian Change under Population Pressure.* In India, she and her husband, the economist Mogens Boserup, had been part of the research team working on the massive study *Asian Drama: An Inquiry into the Poverty of Nations,* under Swedish economist Gunnar Myrdal. As a result of this experience, she became increasingly convinced that the then generally accepted theory of zero marginal productivity and agrarian surplus population in densely-populated developing countries was an unrealistic theoretical construction. She resigned from the Myrdal study and started work on her book on the conditions of agricultural growth, drawing in addition on studies she conducted in Africa. The book challenged the dominant Malthusian paradigm (accepted by the majority of classical economists) on the relationship between population growth and technical progress by arguing that population pressure can lead to agricultural intensification and to the adoption of improved methods of production. Looking back at her career at the end of her life, in a slim autobiographical volume published in 1999, Boserup gave a pithy summary of her 1965 message: "my conclusion was the opposite of the general opinion at that time, when it was believed that the carrying capacity of the globe was nearly exhausted and that the ongoing demographic transition in developing countries would result in soaring food prices and mass starvation" (p. 21). Two other important (and widely translated) books followed; they addressed the two major topics to which she had devoted most of her research and writings in the 1970s and 1980s: *Woman's Role in Economic Development* (1970) and *Population and Technological Change: A Study of Long-Term Trends* (1981). A selection of Boserup's major essays, *Economic and Demographic Relationships in Development,* appeared in 1990. In a review of that volume in *Population and Development Review* (December 1990, p. 775), the agricultural economist Vernon Ruttan commented: "Ester Boserup's writings have had a major impact over the last quarter century on the evolution of thought in anthropology, demography, economics, and sociology about the interrelationships among economic, demographic, and technical change."

BIBLIOGRAPHY

SELECTED WORKS BY ESTER BOSERUP.

Boserup, Ester. 1965. *The Conditions of Agricultural Growth: The Economics of Agrarian Change Under Population Pressure.* Chicago: Aldine.

———. 1970. *Woman's Role in Economic Development.* London: Allen and Unwin.

———. 1981. *Population and Technological Change: A Study of Long-Term Trends.* Chicago: University of Chicago Press.

———. 1985. "Economic and Demographic Interrelationships in Sub-Saharan Africa." *Population and Development Review* 11(3): 383–397.

———. 1987. "Population and Technology in Pre-industrial Europe." *Population and Development Review* 13(4): 691–701.

———. 1990. *Economic and Demographic Relationships in Development.* Baltimore: Johns Hopkins University Press.

———. 1999. *My Professional Life and Publications 1929–1998.* Copenhagen, Denmark: Museum Tusculanum Press.

PAUL DEMENY

BOTERO, GIOVANNI

(1543–1617)

Giovanni Botero was an Italian statesman, political writer, and upholder of the principles of the counter-reformation of the Catholic Church. Botero was a major figure in the early history of the social sciences and was recognized as the originator of modern population theory, in some important respects anticipating English economist T. R. Malthus. He was a member of the Jesuit order and held various diplomatic posts in France and Spain, and later in Rome. His ten-volume work *Della Ragion di Stato* (The Reason of State) (1589) is comparable in interest, if not in length, to Italian political philosopher Niccolò Machiavelli's *The Prince* (1513). Botero's book, like that of his more famous predecessor, is written for the prince who intends to conserve with prudence the domain he won by force. However, Botero's prince must be virtuous, religious, and faithful to the Catholic Church, "the eternal seat of power," and in this he opposed the lay vision of Machiavelli's prince. A later work, *Relazioni Universali* (1593–1596), describes the state of Christianity throughout the world.

In the field of demography, Botero is mainly of interest for the three-volume work *Cause della grandezza e magnificenza delle città* (The Greatness of Cities) (1588). In this work, the subject of population, seen as the wealth of a city or nation, is at the center of a quantitative depiction of human society. Botero had a quantitative vision of overpopulation, anticipating theories that became established much later. He contended that the civil development of populations did not lie in the possession of more riches, but above all in the numerical increase and productive activities of the people themselves. Botero attributed the increase of populations to the *generative virtue* of man and the *nutritional virtue* of the city. When the latter is insufficient, he argued, the solution lies in the creation of colonies, as practiced by the ancient Romans: the export of population as a relief valve for demographic excess. (This idea had already been introduced by Machiavelli in the *Discorsi sopra la prima deca di Tito Livio,* which suggested that when the demographic mass exceeds the productivity of the earth, famine, disease, or floods will take place.) In effect, Botero produced a first doctrinal draft of a theory of population, more than 200 years before Malthus. Despite the distance in time and, in some respects, in philosophy, the similarity between the thinking of the late-eighteenth-century Protestant clergyman Malthus and the late-sixteenth-century writing of the Jesuit Botero goes beyond the basic framework of their analytic approach. For example, Botero's views on the types and *modus operandi* of what came to be known as "positive checks" and "preventive checks" to population growth are a remarkable anticipation of Malthus's familiar treatment, even if the latter is set out in a more rigorous and modern fashion. Like Malthus (who did not know about the work of his Italian predecessor), Botero also sought to ground his reasoning in observable demographic facts, even though that effort was largely frustrated by his lack of access to reliable statistics and by his misconceptions about the demography of both the ancient and the contemporary world.

See also: *Demography: History of; Malthus, Thomas Robert.*

BIBLIOGRAPHY

SELECTED WORKS BY GIOVANNI BOTERO.

Botero, Giovanni. 1583. *De Regia Sapienza.* Milano: Pacifico Ponti.

———. 1591–1596. *Delle Relazioni Universali.* Rome: Giorgio Ferrari.

———. 1956 (1588). *The Greatness of Cities,* trans. Robert Peterson. New Haven: Yale University Press; originally published as *Delle Cause della Grandezza e Magnificenza delle Città.* Rome: Giovanni Martinelli.

———. 1956 (1589–1596). *The Reason of State,* 10 vols., trans. P. J. and D. P. Waley; originally published as *Della Ragion di Stato,* Venice: I

Gioliti; Ferrara: Vittorio Baldini Stampator Ducale; 1596. Torino: Gio. Dominico Tarino.

ITALO SCARDOVI

BRASS, WILLIAM

(1921–1999)

The Scottish demographer and statistician William Brass is best known for his imaginative, elegant, and innovative contributions to methods for demographic estimation. Although always insistent on methodological rigor, Brass was, as he used to say, "a practical man" for whom the ultimate justification of a method was that it helped answer an important question and solve a problem.

After graduating from Edinburgh University in 1947 with a degree in mathematics and natural philosophy, Brass joined the East African Statistical Department as a statistician. While working there he developed a lifelong interest in sub-Saharan Africa and the problems of demographic estimation based on deficient or defective data. In 1955 he joined Aberdeen University to work on the application of mathematical models to medical statistics but maintained his interest in demographic estimation.

A year's leave of absence at Princeton University's Office of Population Research in 1961–1962 to work on the demography of tropical Africa proved to be a turning point in his career. During that period Brass developed several of his signature demographic estimation methods, notably methods for estimating child mortality from women's reports of their children ever born and their children who had died, for evaluating reported fertility rates by comparison with measures of lifetime fertility, and for the use of the logit transformation to fit life tables to fragmentary data. Those methods were applied systematically to the survey data from Africa then available.

In 1965 Brass moved to the London School of Hygiene and Tropical Medicine, first as a reader and then as a professor of the new field of medical demography. He continued to develop new methods as data availability and quality improved, including methods for estimating adult mortality from data on

the survival of parents, the evaluation of data on deaths by age through comparisons with age distributions of the living, the relational Gompertz fertility model, methods to evaluate birth history data, and ways to use truncated data on parity progression for women of reproductive age to study fertility change. He applied those methods, among others, in an authoritative analysis of fertility trends in Kenya that was published as part of a series of reports on the population dynamics of sub-Saharan Africa produced by the U.S. National Academy of Sciences.

Many of the methods originally developed by Brass have been developed further by others. A full bibliography of Brass's writings is included in the commemorative volume *Brass Tacks* (2001).

See also: *Demography, History of; Estimation Methods, Demographic.*

BIBLIOGRAPHY

SELECTED WORKS BY WILLIAM BRASS.

Brass, William. 1975. *Methods for Estimating Fertility and Mortality from Limited and Defective Data.* Chapel Hill: University of North Carolina Press.

———. 1981. "The Use of the Gompertz Relational Model to Estimate Fertility." *International Population Conference, Manila,* 3: 345–362.

Brass, William, John Blacker, and Basia Zaba, eds. 2001. *Brass Tacks: Essays in Medical Demography: A Tribute to the Memory of Professor William Brass.* London: Athlone Press.

Brass, William, and Ansley J. Coale. 1968. "Methods of Analysis and Estimation." In *The Demography of Tropical Africa,* W. Brass, A. J. Coale, P. Demeny, D. F. Heisel, F. Lorimer, A. Romaniuk, and E. van de Walle. Princeton NJ: Princeton University Press.

Brass, William, and Kenneth Hill. 1973. "Estimating Mortality from Orphanhood." *International Population Conference, Liège,* 3: 111–123.

Brass, William, and Carole Jolly, eds. 1993. *The Population Dynamics of Kenya.* Washington, D.C.: National Academy Press.

Brass, William, and Fatima Juarez. 1983. "Censored Cohort Parity Progression Ratios from Birth Histories." *Asian and Pacific Census Forum* 10: 5–13.

Brass, William, and Hoda Rashad. 1992. "Evaluation of the Reliability of Data in Maternity Histories." In *The Analysis of Maternity Histories,* ed. Allan Hill and William Brass. Liège, Belgium: Ordina Editions.

KENNETH H. HILL

BUSINESS DEMOGRAPHY

Business demography entails the application of demographic concepts, data, and techniques to the practical concerns of business decision makers. This loosely organized field includes but is not limited to site selection, sales forecasting, financial planning, market assessment, consumer profiles, target marketing, litigation support, and labor force analysis. Specific applications have evolved over time, reflecting changes in data sources, computer technology, statistical techniques, and the business environment. This entry surveys the major features of this eclectic and rapidly changing field, focusing on the United States.

Evolution of the Field

Businesses have based decisions on demographic data and techniques since the late nineteenth century. The emergence of business demography as a distinct field, however, is quite recent. The release of 1970 census data in machine-readable form gave rise to an electronic data industry that grew from a handful of companies to at least 70 competitors by the mid-1980s. Although the number of data vendors has declined since that time, many new firms focusing on marketing, survey research, trend analysis, mapping, and software development have been established. As the field matured, it became routine for businesses to base decisions on the advice of consultants and employees skilled in collecting, analyzing, and interpreting demographic data.

Responding to these developments, the Population Association of America formed a Committee on Business Demography in 1982, which, together with the Committee on State and Local Demography, launched the publication of the newsletter *Applied Demography* in 1985. During that formative period two commercially oriented magazines (*American Demographics* and *Business Geographics*) were launched, reporting on demographic trends, data

availability, technological advances, and business applications. Business demography thus coalesced into a visible and well-established area of endeavor, although the field remains loosely defined and organized.

The Practitioners

Business demographers fall into three distinct groups. The first group consists of analysts employed by private companies whose work pertains specifically to those companies and their business activities (e.g., market analyses, customer profiles, site selection). The second group consists of analysts with firms that create demographic databases (e.g., population estimates, consumer spending, lifestyle clusters), develop proprietary software applications, and perform customized research (e.g., estimates and projections of the population residing within five miles of a supermarket). These firms serve both government agencies and business enterprises. The third group consists of individual consultants who undertake specific projects for individual clients. For some of these practitioners, consulting is a full-time activity; for most, it is a part-time pursuit outside their regular work activities.

Not all practitioners have formal training in demography. Indeed, the diversity in training, educational background, and current occupation reflects the eclectic nature of business demography as a field. Many practitioners have backgrounds in economics, geography, marketing, statistics, survey research, real estate, or other disciplines. Even those with formal demographic training have acquired many job skills principally through work experience rather than academic training. Few academic programs extend their demographic focus to the field of business, and few business schools offer training in demographic applications.

The Tools

The tools of business demography parallel those that demographers use generally: data from a variety of sources, computer hardware and software, and basic demographic concepts, measures, and techniques. Those tools are set apart by the purposes for which they are used. Business demography is intended to clarify and inform business decisions rather than to advance knowledge. The tools of demography are described elsewhere in this encyclopedia; here the focus is on their business applications.

Data sources include publicly available censuses, surveys, and administrative records (e.g., building permits, registered voters, Medicare enrollees); proprietary surveys (e.g., of new or repeat purchasers); and firm-specific records (e.g., customer files, business transactions). The availability and reliability of such data vary considerably across levels of geography and among countries. Typically, the smaller the area is, the more difficult it is to obtain useful data. Because business decisions often pertain to local markets, there is a premium on assembling reliable data for small areas.

Exponential increases in computing power and data storage capacity have greatly expanded the possibilities for organizing, integrating, and analyzing data. Computer networks enable analysts to share information and transfer data globally over the Internet. Powerful software packages have largely automated statistical analysis and reporting functions. Advances in geocoding and the displaying of spatial information through geographic information systems (GIS) have been especially influential, as many analyses call for data that are grouped into customer service areas, market analysis zones, and other uniquely defined geographic areas. The ability to use these computing tools effectively is crucial for many business demographers.

The concepts and measures of business demography focus primarily on dimensions relevant to commerce and enterprise: population composition (e.g., age, sex, race, income), consumer units (e.g., individuals, families, households), demographic events (e.g., births, deaths, marriage, migration), and the distribution of demographic characteristics and events across geographic areas (e.g., counties, census tracts, postal code areas). Business demographers have extended these measures by using consumer data. For example, geodemographic segmentation systems classify neighborhoods with similar demographic characteristics and consumer preferences into lifestyle clusters. Owing to business demography's emphasis on decision making, techniques that update recent census data and project future values play a particularly important role.

Demographers introduce fresh perspectives to the business world because they can envision business problems differently than business people ordinarily do (for example, distinguishing among age, period, and cohort effects that reshape a market). They inform and advise, broaden perspectives, and serve as catalysts for organizational change. By exposing business people to new perspectives, demographers can elevate management thinking from an operational to a strategic level.

Examples

The business concerns that demographers address are many and varied. Accurate sales forecasts depend on foreseeing changes in population size and composition. Human resource planning requires data on the characteristics of the labor force and the personnel needs of the business enterprise. Site analyses require information on local populations within reach of a particular geographic location. Financial planning requires information on how demographic changes affect cash flows and return on investment. Many projects require population estimates and projections, often with detailed characteristics (e.g., age or income). The following illustrations suggest the range of business applications.

Marketing and retailing. Demographic information and analysis have become essential to identifying, locating, and understanding the diverse consumer groups that form markets for goods and services. For example, newspaper publishers and editors recognize that they must adapt to the powerful demographic and societal changes that are transforming reading habits and readers' interests. Many readers live alone, are divorced or remarried, or are cohabiting. Among married couples, fewer have children at home but more anticipate future elder-care obligations. Accompanying these diverse lifestyles are new interests and obligations. Demographers can identify the changing demographics of newspaper readers, helping publishers cater to collections of small audiences with certain shared interests who constitute an increasingly segmented readership. Demographers also can devise and calibrate specialized tools for segmenting customers.

Human resource planning. The demographics of a corporate work force have important long-term implications for benefits, productivity, and profitability. General Motors, for example, spends more than $3 billion annually on health care for its current and former employees and their dependents. Since health-care expenditures vary greatly by age, information on likely future changes in the age structure is critical. Hallie Kintner and David Swanson (1997) analyzed the expected longevity of General Motors employees, developed a series of projections by age and sex, and made recommendations to the company's senior management that helped the company control health-care costs.

Site selection and evaluation. Geographic proximity to consumer markets is important because most retail transactions are made at specific locations. Productive retail sites generally are situated in the middle of dense consumer populations or are readily accessible to the potential users of a firm's goods and services. Local availability of an appropriately skilled labor force also is critical for many businesses. Evaluating a proposed site or weighing the comparative merits of several competing sites is another way demographers support business decision making.

Tracking emerging markets. As markets have globalized, businesses have increasingly focused on international markets, including the emergence of consumers within the massive populations of developing countries such as India and China. A defining characteristic of emerging economies is rapid economic growth, along with the ripening market potential that accompanies such growth. Anticipating future growth of consumer markets poses distinctive problems that are amenable to demographic analysis. With only a minimum of data, demographic accounting models can capture the upward economic mobility of newly prosperous consumers.

Conclusions

Business demography is a problem-driven field with an emphasis on using rather than advancing knowledge. Its practitioners address problems and inform decision making within a specific business context. Its tools and perspectives are drawn from demography generally but are applied to the practical needs of the business community. It is an eclectic and continually evolving field that is responsive to the opportunities that expanding data sources, statistical techniques, demographic methods, and information technology offer. Although its focus has been primarily on small areas, new applications and trends toward globalization are pushing it increasingly into broader areas with national and international implications. Future opportunities in business demography promise to be diverse.

See also: *Small-Area Analysis; State and Local Government Demography.*

BIBLIOGRAPHY

Kintner, Hallie J., and David A. Swanson. 1997. "Estimating Vital Rates from Corporate Databases: How Long Will GM's Salaried Retirees Live?" In *Demographics: A Casebook for Business and Government,* ed. Hallie J. Kintner, Thomas W. Merrick, Peter A. Morrison, and Paul R. Voss. Santa Monica, CA: RAND.

Lauderdale, Diane S., and Bert Kestenbaum. 2000. "Asian American Ethnic Identification by Surname." *Population Research and Policy Review* 19: 283–300.

Mitchell, Susan. 1995. "Birds of a Feather." *American Demographics* 17(2): 40–48.

Morrison, Peter A., and Allan F. Abrahamse. 1996. "Applying Demographic Analysis to Store Site Selection." *Population Research and Policy Review* 15: 479–489.

Morrison, Peter A., Morlie H. Levin, and Paul M. Seever. 1996. "Tracking Growth of Emerging Consumer Markets Worldwide: Where Demographic Analysis Fits In." Paper presented at the Sixth International Conference on Applied and Business Demography, Bowling Green, OH.

Pol, Louis G., and Richard K. Thomas. 1997. *Demography for Business Decision Making.* Westport, CT: Quorum Books.

Russell, Cheryl. 1984. "The Business of Demographics." *Population Bulletin* 39(3). Washington, D.C.: Population Reference Bureau.

Siegel, Jacob S. 2002. *Applied Demography: Applications to Business, Government, Law and Public Policy.* San Diego, CA: Academic Press.

Voss, Paul R. 1997. "Targeting Wealthy Ex-Wisconsinites in Florida: A Case Study in Applied Demography." In *Demographics: A Casebook for Business and Government,* ed. Hallie J. Kintner, Thomas W. Merrick, Peter A. Morrison, and Paul R. Voss. Santa Monica, CA: RAND.

Weiss, Michael J. 1988. *The Clustering of America.* New York: Harper & Row.

STANLEY K. SMITH
PETER A. MORRISON

C

CALDWELL, JOHN C.

(1928–)

John C. Caldwell began an academic career later than most professional demographers, having spent nearly a decade as a secondary school teacher before starting his Ph.D. studies at the Australian National University (ANU). Since his first academic appointment (at the University of Ghana) in 1962, his research output—much of it in collaboration with his wife, Pat Caldwell—has been prolific, amply compensating for the late start. His early years as a demographer were spent at the Population Council, where he worked in various regions of Africa. Since 1970, his base has been at the ANU, where he is a professor of demography, heading the Department of Demography until 1988 and then serving as associate director of ANU's National Centre for Epidemiology and Population Health. He has engaged in extended periods of fieldwork in Africa and South Asia and has organized numerous multi-country research projects. He has served as the president of the International Union for the Scientific Study of Population (1994–1997).

Caldwell's most notable contributions to population studies have been in the fields of fertility transition and health transition. His works are cited almost *de rigeur* by those in these fields. His wealth flows theory, first set out in a 1976 article, traced the onset of fertility transition to changes in the direction of intergenerational transfers within the family. Although criticized for its lack of testability, it captured the imagination of many researchers—from the fields of anthropology and economics as well as demography—and stimulated greater attention to field-based micro-demographic research. The theory illustrates Caldwell's willingness to theorize provocatively based on less than complete evidence, and thereby inspiring numerous research studies by others intent on testing his propositions.

Caldwell has done much to revive interest in population theory and give it a greater role in promoting research. He has also made original contributions in many areas of demographic theory. These include the focus on family relationships and family economics for explaining demographic change; the identification of education as a major factor in the survival of individuals and their children; and the significance of the position of women in determining demographic change. Since the late 1980s, he has made a major contribution to the study of the AIDS epidemic in developing countries, notably in Africa, in its social and behavioral context, and to health transition research more generally, through his editorship of the journal *Health Transition Review*.

In addition to his contributions to theory, Caldwell has also had an important impact on the methodology of population studies. The emphasis he has placed on anthropological-type field research in demography has been adopted by many other demographers, and has fostered a more symbiotic relationship between anthropologists and demographers in studying matters related to demographic change.

See also: *Anthropological Demography; Demography, History of; Health Transition; Intergenerational Transfers; Population Thought, Contemporary.*

BIBLIOGRAPHY

SELECTED WORKS BY JOHN C. CALDWELL.

Caldwell, John C. 1982. *Theory of Fertility Decline.* London: Academic Press.

———. 1986. "Routes to Low Mortality in Poor Countries." *Population and Development Review* 12(2): 171–220.

———. 2001. "The Globalization of Fertility Behavior." In *Global Fertility Transition,* Supplement to *Population and Development Review* 27: 93–115.

Caldwell, John C., and Pat Caldwell. 1986. *Limiting Population Growth, and the Ford Foundation Contribution.* London: Frances Pinter.

———. 1996. "The African AIDS epidemic." *Scientific American* 174(3): 40–46.

Caldwell, John C., P. H. Reddy, and Pat Caldwell. 1988. *The Causes of Demographic Change: Experimental Research in South India.* Madison: University of Wisconsin Press.

SELECTED WORKS ABOUT JOHN C. CALDWELL.

Schultz, T. Paul. 1983. "John C. Caldwell, Theory of Fertility Decline." *Population and Development Review* 9(1): 161–168.

Willis, Robert J. 1982. "The Direction of Intergenerational Transfers and Demographic Transition: The Caldwell Hypothesis Re-examined." *Population and Development Review* 8(Supp.) (82): 207–234.

GAVIN W. JONES

CANCER

Cancer is the common name for a group of 100 or more chronic, progressive diseases, all characterized by abnormal and continuous multiplication of cells in a particular tissue or organ without reference to the needs of the body. This commonly gives rise to a solid mass or tumor composed of such cells (e.g., in the lung, breast, or brain), but it can also affect almost any tissue or organ, including the blood-forming cells of the bone marrow (leukemias), the immune defense system (lymphomas), and the soft tissues, such as muscles, cartilage, or blood vessels (sarcomas). Invasion of the organ or tissue of origin by a malignant tumor—called a neoplasm, or new growth—can itself be fatal, but cancer mortality arises mainly from the tendency of most cancers to metastasize elsewhere in the body and to disable or destroy vital organs such as the brain, lung, liver, or bone marrow.

Cancer afflicts all animals as well as humans. The ultimate cause of all cancers is failed control of the growth, reproduction, or senescence (aging) of cells. This is due in turn to inherited and/or acquired damage to cellular DNA, giving rise to a malignant clone comprising all the descendant cells of the original cancerous cell. Inherited susceptibility can greatly increase the risk of developing cancer, but it appears to account for only a small proportion of all cancers, and congenital malignancy is extremely rare. Cumulative genetic damage acquired over the course of life accounts for the occurrence of most cancers. Knowledge in this domain is likely to increase rapidly with further progress in cancer genetics following the completion of the Human Genome Project.

Among the known environmental causes of cancer, use of tobacco (smoking, chewing, sucking, or inhaling) is the most important and most widely recognized. Tobacco use probably accounted for up to a third of all cancers in 2000, and a higher proportion of all cancer deaths, since it is a cause of some of the most fatal cancers—lung, larynx, pharynx, esophagus, and pancreas. Other causes include:

- Exposure to certain chemicals and other substances. For example, benzene exposure is a cause of leukemias, and exposure to asbestos produces mesothelioma of the lung lining and abdomen.

- Ionizing radiation. X-rays and γ-radiation cause solid tumors as well as leukemias.

- Solar or artificial ultraviolet radiation. Exposure produces skin cancers including melanoma.

- Obesity. Obesity increases the risk of breast and colon cancers.

- Infection by certain bacteria. For example, *Helicobacter pylori* is a cause of stomach cancer.

- Infection by certain viruses. Certain human papilloma viruses (HPV) cause cervical cancer; some hepatitis viruses cause liver cancer; human immunodeficiency virus (HIV) causes Kaposi sarcoma and other cancers.

- Infection by certain parasites. For example, some liver flukes can cause biliary tract cancers, and schistosomes are a cause of bladder cancer.

Many cancers can be prevented by avoidance of exposure to the underlying cause or risk factor. Thus, 90 percent of lung cancers that are directly attributable to tobacco use would not occur in the absence of exposure; almost all mesotheliomas would be avoided if asbestos exposure were eliminated. Vaccination against hepatitis B can prevent associated liver cancers, and vaccination against HPV will almost certainly prevent cervical cancers. Mass population screening, in which selected groups of the entire population are systematically invited for regular diagnostic tests, has been shown to reduce mortality from some cancers by detecting tumors at an early stage before they are clinically detectable or give rise to symptoms, and when treatment is more effective for most cancers. The cancers most widely screened for are breast cancer in women aged 50 to 69 (using mammography), and cervical cancer in women of reproductive age and up to age 60 (using a cervical smear or direct visualization). Screening for bowel cancer by detection of occult blood in the stool is also likely to reduce mortality. Mortality from cancers that do occur would be greatly reduced if all patients were diagnosed earlier, investigated thoroughly, and treated appropriately.

Around the turn of the twenty-first century, the International Agency for Research on Cancer (part of the World Health Organization) estimated that about 10 million people worldwide developed cancer every year, and that 6.9 million cancer deaths occurred in 2000, or 12.4 percent of the global death toll. Estimates of global mortality from the most common cancers are shown in Table 1. The economic cost of cancer is huge: over $100 billion dollars a year in medical expenditure and lost productivity in the U.S. alone in 2000. The human cost is incalculable.

The total number of cancers arising in a population depends on the size of the population, its age and sex structure, and the age- and sex-specific risks of developing cancer. All three components differ

TABLE 1

Estimates of Worldwide Cancer Mortality (Thousands of Deaths per Year), by Sex, 2000: Selected Cancers and All Cancers Combined

Cancer	Males	Females	Total	Percent of total
Trachea/bronchus/ lung	895	318	1213	17.5
Stomach	464	280	744	10.7
Liver	433	193	626	9.0
Colon/Rectum	303	276	579	8.4
Breast	0	458	459	6.6
Esophagus	274	139	413	6.0
Mouth and oropharynx	242	98	340	4.9
Lymphomas, multiple myeloma	173	118	291	4.2
Cervix uteri	—	288	288	4.2
Leukemia	145	119	265	3.8
Prostate	258	—	258	3.7
All cancers	3918	3011	6930	100.0

SOURCE: World Health Organization (2001). *World Health Report*, Statistical Annex Table 2 (pp. 144–9).

between countries and populations, and over time. Population growth and aging both lead to an increase in the annual number of new cancers. About half of all cancers in 2000 arose in developed countries, with just a quarter of the world's population, but the proportion of cancers arising in developing countries is set to rise substantially as the relatively young populations in those countries increase and become older. About half of all cancers occur over the age of 65 years. Primary prevention to reduce the risk of developing cancer at any given age is, and will remain, the most effective long-term strategy for cancer control.

See also: *Diseases, Chronic and Degenerative; Tobacco-Related Mortality.*

BIBLIOGRAPHY

Coleman, Michel, Jacques Estève, Philippe Damiecki, Annie Arslan, and Hélène Renard. 1993. *Trends in Cancer Incidence and Mortality* (IARC Scientific Publications No. 121). Lyon: International Agency for Research on Cancer.

Miller, Anthony, Jocelyn Chamberlain, Nick Day, Matti Hakama, and Philip Prorok. 1990. "Report on a Workshop of the UICC Project on Evaluation of Screening for Cancer." *International Journal of Cancer* 46: 761–69.

Peckham, Michael, Herbert Pinedo, and Umberto Veronesi, eds. 1995. *Oxford Textbook of Oncology.* Oxford, Eng.: Oxford Medical Publications.

Peto, Julian. 2001. "Cancer Epidemiology in the Last Century and the Next Decade." *Nature* 411: 390–395.

Tomatis, Lorenzo, A. Aitio, Nick Day, Elisabeth Heseltine, John Kaldor, Anthony Miller, et al., eds. 1990. *Cancer: Causes, Occurrence and Control* (IARC Scientific Publications No. 100). Lyon: International Agency for Research on Cancer.

World Health Organization. 2001. *The World Health Report 2001.* Geneva: World Health Organization.

MICHEL P. COLEMAN

CANNAN, EDWIN

(1861–1935)

Edwin Cannan was an English economist whose many publications included some material on population, almost all of which is still considered important. Cannan spent his entire working life at the London School of Economics, joining the teaching staff of that school at its foundation in 1895, becoming a professor of political economy in 1907, and retiring in 1926.

Cannan is credited with developing the notion of an optimum population. He rejected the Malthusian argument that there is an inherent tendency toward overpopulation. In his first book, *Elementary Political Economy* (1888), Cannan wrote: "[P]roductiveness of industry is sometimes promoted by an increase of population, and sometimes by a decrease" (p. 22). He believed that in a specific area of land a definable amount of labor is required for the maximum productiveness that is possible. He subsequently elaborated those ideas, especially in *Wealth* (1914, 3rd ed. 1928), and used the expression *optimum population.* The optimum may rise or fall with changes in knowledge or capital, but in practical and moral terms any resulting policy (which in principle should recognize the interests of future generations) can only specify a direction of movement at any particular time.

The *Economic Journal* for December 1895 included Cannan's "The Probability of a Cessation of the Growth of Population in England and Wales during the Next Century." That article presented the first cohort-component population projection, in which each age group is dealt with separately, and births, deaths, and migration are taken into account separately. His projection assumed the same number of births each ten years as had occurred in the period 1881–1890 (and thus a declining rate of childbearing) and the same proportionate losses at each age as a result of mortality and emigration combined as was observed between the 1881 and 1891 censuses.

Cannan correctly predicted, against contemporary opinion, the continuation of the decline in the birthrate in Britain that had begun recently. This was a remarkable achievement. As John Hajnal commented in a paper presented at the 1954 World Population Conference, Cannan "could publish 36 years later, in 1931, a paper which said in effect 'I told you so'" (p. 46). Even though, as Hajnal noted, "the accuracy of his forecast was not outstanding. . .[and] by 1911, i.e., only 15 years after the forecast was made, the population enumerated at the census exceeded the prediction by 7 per cent and by 1916 the population had increased beyond his estimate of the maximum it would ever reach. . . . Cannan's forecast, though inaccurate, predicted an unexpected development by acute analysis"(pp. 46–47, 48).

Cannan later became aware that the birthrate had declined in other Western countries and in *Economic Scares* (1933), perhaps 40 or 50 years before this became empirically incontrovertible, declared that "the cause of it—birth control—will doubtless in time affect the rest of the world" (p. 92). He foresaw also, though, that for many years non-Western countries would experience considerable and even enhanced population growth "owing to decrease of huge infant mortality."

See also: *Demography, History of; Optimum Population; Projections and Forecasts, Population.*

BIBLIOGRAPHY

SELECTED WORKS BY EDWIN CANNAN.

Cannan, Edwin. 1888. *Elementary Political Economy.* London: H. Frowde.

—. 1895. "The Probability of a Cessation of the Growth of Population in England and Wales during the Next Century." *Economic Journal* 5: 505–515.

—. 1914. *Wealth.* London: P. S. King.

—. 1933. *Economic Scares.* London: P. S. King.

—. 1997. *Collected Works,* 8 vols., ed. Alan Ebenstein. London: Routledge/Thoemmes Press.

SELECTED WORKS ABOUT EDWARD CANNAN.

De Gans, Henk A. 1999. *Population Forecasting 1895–1945.* Dordrecht, the Netherlands: Kluwer Academic Publishers.

Hajnal, John. 1955. "The Prospect for Population Forecasts." *Proceedings of the World Population Conference* 3: 43–53.

Robbins, Lionel. 1927. "The Optimum Theory of Population." In *London Essays in Economics: In Honour of Edwin Cannan,* ed. Theodor E. Gregory and Hugh Dalton. London: Routledge.

C. M. LANGFORD

CANTILLON, RICHARD

(1697–1734)

Born in Ireland, Richard Cantillon made a fortune as a banker through clever speculation in England and on the continent, before being murdered by a disgruntled servant. His only surviving work, entitled *Essay on the Nature of Commerce in General,* may have been written either in English or in French, but only the French version, published in 1755, has survived. The work has been called the first systematic treatise on economics.

Cantillon's view that all value originates in the land influenced the Physiocrats, and his theory of money is deemed especially important. His views of population involve an early discussion of what would later be called the Western European pattern of marriage. Society is divided into three classes: the proprietors who draw their wealth from ownership of the land; the entrepreneurs (Cantillon originated the term's use in economics) who include farmers, traders, craftsmen, and others who live from the uncertain profit of their activities; and hired laborers.

The tastes, fashions, and modes of living of the proprietors determine the use of the land, and hence the number of people in the state; the private property system is the ultimate regulator of population size. If the proprietors choose to use the land or the rent they receive from it for purposes other than the "Maintenance of Man" (such as for the purchase of luxury goods), numbers will diminish. "Men multiply like Mice in a barn if they have unlimited Means of Subsistence," he wrote (Cantillon, 2001, p. 37). Cantillon contended that the size of population is not limited by mortality (as Adam Smith believed), but by marriage, since men of the lower classes fear the prospect of insufficient means to support a family, and men of higher means do not want to lose status. "Most men desire nothing better than to marry if they are set in a position to keep their Families in the same style as they are content to live themselves" (2001, p. 35). That style, in Europe, implied a relatively high level of living.

Cantillon presents China as an alternative demographic model without private property and with universal and early marriage. This results in a large population living at a low material standard, recurrent famines despite a highly productive agriculture, and the practice of infanticide as a check on numbers. In the late eighteenth century political economist T. R. Malthus would echo these ideas, although there is no evidence that he had read Cantillon's *Essay.*

See also: *Population Thought, History of.*

BIBLIOGRAPHY

SELECTED WORKS BY RICHARD CANTILLON.

Cantillon, Richard. 1952 (1755). *Essai sur la nature du commerce en général,* texte de l'édition originale de 1755, avec des études et commentaires par Alfred Sauvy [et al.]. Paris: Institut national d'études démographiques.

—. 2001. *Essay on the Nature of Commerce in General.* Contains background materials, including the 1881 essay by the economist W. Stanley Jevons. New Brunswick, NJ: Transaction Publishers.

SELECTED WORKS ABOUT RICHARD CANTILLON.

Spengler, Joseph J. 1954. "Richard Cantillon: First of the Moderns." *Journal of Political Economy* 62: 281–295, 406–424.

ETIENNE VAN DE WALLE

CARDIOVASCULAR DISEASE

In industrialized countries cardiovascular disease is the leading cause of death. In the United States in 1998, the death rate from heart disease per 100,000 population was 268.2; such deaths numbered 725,000, comprising 31 percent of all deaths. The great majority of coronary heart disease (CHD) occurs among older individuals. In the United States, in 1998, the proportion of CHD deaths occurring to persons 65 years and older was 84 percent—90 percent among women and 77 percent among men. Table 1 shows the steep increase of CHD death rates by age in the United States. Yet coronary heart disease and other cardiovascular diseases such as stroke and peripheral vascular disease are not diseases of aging. There are many populations of older individuals in which the incidence of heart attacks is very low.

Atherosclerosis is the basic pathology that causes heart attacks. The atherosclerotic disease begins early in life and progresses over time. This evolving atherosclerotic disease represents the "silent" or incubation period to the clinical disease, heart attack. The onset of the heart attack can occur rapidly and in about 20 percent of the cases is associated with sudden death. The amount of specific saturated fatty acids, cholesterol, and polyunsaturated fatty acids in the diet, as well as specific genetic susceptibility factors, determine the blood levels of low-density lipoprotein (LDL) cholesterol and the number of LDL particles in the blood that together predict, to a considerable degree, the extent of atherosclerosis.

Consequences of Urbanization and Industrialization

With urbanization and industrialization, and with increasing longevity, populations usually experience a transition from a high prevalence of infectious dis-

TABLE 1

Death Rates per 100,000 Population from Heart Disease by Age and Sex, United States, 1998		
Age	Males	Females
35–44	42	16
45–54	149	52
55–64	405	173
65–74	996	524
75–84	2,382	1,587
85 and older	6,354	5,898

SOURCE: U. S. Bureau of the Census (2001).

eases and nutritional deficiencies to higher caloric intake; decreased physical activity, especially related to work; and higher intakes of both saturated fat and cholesterol in the diet. The rise in the incidence of coronary heart attacks in such populations may not occur until many years after the changes in diet and lifestyle and the rise in LDL cholesterol. The evidence of a rising epidemic of CHD will most likely first be noted among young and middle-aged individuals, signaled by a rise in the LDL cholesterol level. Unfortunately, by the time this occurs, there is extensive atherosclerosis in the population and a likelihood of subsequent higher rates of heart attack.

In developing countries, the rising incidence of CHD initially affects the better educated. There is a major increase in the use of health resources for treating cardiovascular disease in these populations, with a potential drain on resources and technology in other areas of the health system.

These same populations also typically experience an increase in caloric intake and a decrease in work-related energy expenditure. There is an increase in high-fat, calorically dense foods, often resulting in obesity, as well as an increase in processed foods whose salt (sodium chloride) content is undesirably high. These factors lead to elevated blood pressure and hypertension. This pattern is now occurring in Africa, especially in west Africa, as well as in populations of African origin in Caribbean countries.

Obesity, Diabetes, and Other Risk Factors

In many industrialized countries such as the United States, Britain, and Canada, there has been a substantial increase in obesity and diabetes. The risk of diabetes is associated with weight gain and obesity, as well as with specific genetic conditions, i.e., host susceptibility. Populations of southeastern Asian origin, including American Indians and aboriginal populations in Canada, have especially high rates of diabetes—along with the complications of diabetes. The latter include CHD and small-vessel complications of diabetes such as blindness, neurological changes, and kidney failure, and such complications can necessitate amputations. The substantial increases in body weight are due to both an increase in the total caloric intake and a decrease in work-related physical activity without a sufficient compensating increase in leisure-time physical activity.

There are other important lifestyle factors that increase the risk of heart attack among individuals with severe underlying atherosclerosis. These factors act by causing a thrombus or clot in a blood vessel or by changing the characteristics of the atherosclerotic disease.

The increase in cigarette smoking in many countries, in addition to causing major epidemics of smoking-related cancers, leads to increased risk of CHD in populations where dietary changes have increased the prevalence of atherosclerotic disease. Interestingly, in populations where diet has not changed and LDL cholesterol levels have not risen, a high prevalence of cigarette smoking is not associated with a substantial increase of CHD, although it does increase the risk of cancer. This pattern has been found in China and Japan. Unfortunately, in many developing-country populations, the increasing prevalence of cigarette smoking parallels the rise in LDL cholesterol and obesity, creating the potential for severe epidemics of CHD. At the same time, the decline in CHD mortality in many industrialized countries since the 1970s was partly attributable to decreases in cigarette smoking and blood LDL cholesterol levels, along with improved treatment of hypertension.

In all industrialized societies, the number and percent of the population over the age of 65 is increasing. In these older populations, treatment of cardiovascular disease is the leading determinant of health-care costs.

In summary, the extent of cardiovascular disease in a population can be gauged very easily by measurement of a few risk factors, mainly the levels of LDL cholesterol, blood pressure, obesity, cigarette smoking, extent of diabetes, and the age distribution of the population. Cardiovascular diseases are pre-

ventable. In the prevention effort the focus, however, needs to be on the prevention of the evolving silent disease, atherosclerosis. Treatment of individuals who have developed clinical CHD and stroke requires a huge commitment of technical and medical resources.

See also: *Disease, Burden of; Diseases, Chronic and Degenerative; Mortality Decline; Tobacco-Related Mortality.*

BIBLIOGRAPHY

Pearson, T. A., D. T. Jamison, and H. Trejo-Gutierrez. 1993. "Cardiovascular Disease." In *Disease Control Priorities in Developing Countries,* ed. D. T. Jamison. New York: Oxford University Press.

Yusuf, Salim, Srinath Reddy, Stephanie Ounpuu, and Sonia Anand. 2001. "Global Burden of Cardiovascular Diseases. Part I: General Considerations, the Epidemiologic Transition, Risk Factors, and Impact of Urbanization." *Circulation* 104: 2,746–2,753.

———. 2001. "Global Burden of Cardiovascular Diseases. Part II: Variations in Cardiovascular Disease by Specific Ethnic Groups and Geographic Regions and Prevention Strategies." *Circulation* 104: 2,855–2,864.

LEWIS H. KULLER

CARRYING CAPACITY

Carrying capacity is the maximum population size that a species can maintain indefinitely in a given area—that is, without diminishing the capacity of the area to sustain the same population size in the future. Carrying capacity is thus a function of both the resource requirements of the organism and the size and resource richness of the area. The carrying capacity of an area with constant size and richness would be expected to change only as fast as organisms evolve different resource requirements.

Measuring Carrying Capacity

The concept is simple, but it is notoriously difficult to measure. The identity and dynamics of resources critical to a species, and the complex of other factors that regulate its population size, are typically poorly known. Moreover, as usage of the term has spread beyond its original context—to do with sustainable stocking levels of domestic livestock on rangeland—into disciplines such as ecology, carrying capacity has taken on subtle but substantive differences in meaning. For instance, in theoretical population ecology, carrying capacity is defined by the parameter K (the equilibrium density of a species) within the logistic equation of population growth. These variations in meaning make it difficult to apply the term consistently across disciplines. Despite these limitations, most authors consider at least the broad concept (as defined above) to be an important heuristic tool.

Carrying Capacity and Human Beings

Applied to human beings, the carrying capacity concept is further complicated by the unique role that culture, broadly interpreted, plays in our species. Three culturally linked factors stand out as critical: individual differences in types and quantities of resources consumed; rapid evolution in patterns of resource consumption; and technological and other cultural change. To take the case of energy consumption, which can be considered a proxy for overall resource use, in 1990 an average person in a developed nation used about 7.1 kilowatts of energy per year, while the average person in the developing world used just 0.9 kilowatts per year. (These averages of course mask large variation at the individual level.) Moreover, economic, social, and technological development bring vast changes in patterns of energy consumption: Global energy consumption has increased more than 20 fold since 1850, and there have been dramatic changes in the composition of energy sources and technologies.

Carrying capacity for human beings is thus highly variable across space and time, depending on levels and styles of living and their supporting technologies and social systems. Ten thousand years ago, at the dawn of agriculture, the world's human population was somewhere between 2 and 20 million, perhaps an indication of global carrying capacity under those conditions. The cultural (including technological) advances associated with the development of agriculture allowed human populations to expand far beyond the levels possible under the resource demands of a hunter-gatherer lifestyle. A few populations have retained that preagrarian pattern of resource use.

Biophysical and Social Carrying Capacity

Biologists distinguish between *biophysical* carrying capacity—the maximum population size that could be sustained biophysically under given technological capabilities—and *social* carrying capacity—the maximum that could be sustained under a specified social system and its associated pattern of resource consumption.

At any level of technological development, social carrying capacities are necessarily lower than biophysical carrying capacity, because the latter implies a factory-farm lifestyle that would be both universally undesirable and also unobtainable because of inefficiencies inherent in social systems. For example, what is considered to be food by a society is largely culturally determined. A population that eats large quantities of grain-fed meat requires four to five times more grain than a population sustained by a solely vegetarian diet. A vegetarian diet is more efficient from a caloric point of view than a meat-oriented one, but is not widely acceptable in many societies. Further inefficiencies, from a biophysical standpoint, result from unequal resource distribution—at local, national, and international scales. The higher the level of inequality, the smaller the population that can be sustained. Many other aspects of culture play significant roles in determining carrying capacity, ranging from patterns of investment in education and social development to frequency and severity of warfare.

Sustainability

A sustainable condition, process, or activity is one that can be maintained without interruption, weakening, or loss of valued qualities. Sustainability is thus a necessary and sufficient condition for a population to be at or below carrying capacity. The wide appeal of sustainability as a societal condition or goal reflects the moral conviction that the current generation should pass on its inheritance of natural wealth—not unchanged but undiminished in potential—to support future generations.

Are the collective activities of today's human population sustainable? The answer is clearly no. Many essential activities, notably food and energy production, are maintained only through the exhaustion and dispersion of a one-time inheritance of natural capital. Maintenance of the world's present human population, and accommodation of its anticipated growth, requires safeguarding the critical resources and services that are provided by this natural capital. A partial list of these includes: generation and renewal of fertile agricultural soil; provision of fresh water, energy, construction materials, and minerals; purification of air and water; mitigation of flood and drought; waste treatment and nutrient cycling; seed dispersal; generation and maintenance of biodiversity; protection from ultraviolet radiation; stabilization and moderation of climate; and crop pollination. In many parts of the world, the natural capital stocks providing this stream of goods and services are being severely degraded and depleted.

The Ecological Footprint

Ecological footprint analysis is a heuristic tool that turns the carrying capacity issue around, asking what productive land area would be required to sustain a given population's activities. It is calculated that the productive land of about two and a half more planet Earths would be required to support a global population of 6 billion people at a consumption level comparable to that of the present-day inhabitants of Vancouver, Canada, the home base of the originator of the concept.

See also: *Ecological Perspectives on Population; Land Use; Limits to Growth; Sustainable Development; Water and Population.*

BIBLIOGRAPHY

Daily, Gretchen C., and Paul R. Ehrlich. 1992. "Population, Sustainability, and Carrying Capacity." *BioScience* 42: 761–771.

Daily, Gretchen C., Tore Söderqvist, Sara Aniyar, Kenneth Arrow, Partha Dasgupta, Paul R. Ehrlich, Carl Folke, AnnMarie Jansson, Bengt-Owe Jansson, Nils Kautsky, Simon Levin, Jane Lubchenco, Karl-Göran Mäler, David Simpson, David Starrett, David Tilman, and Brian Walker. 2000. "The Value of Nature and the Nature of Value." *Science* 289: 395–396.

Dhondt, André A. 1988. "Carrying Capacity: A Confusing Concept." *Acta œcologica* 9: 337–346.

Hardin, Garrett. 1986. "Cultural Carrying Capacity: A Biological Approach to Human Problems." *BioScience* 36: 599–606.

Holdren, John P. 1991. "Population and the Energy Problem." *Population and Environment* 12: 231–255.

Rees, William, and Mathis Wackernagel. 1994. "Ecological Footprints and Appropriated Carrying Capacity: Measuring the Natural Capital Requirements of the Human Economy." In *Investing in Natural Capital,* eds. AnnMarie Jansson, Monica Hammer, Carl Folke, and Robert Costanza. Washington, D.C.: Island Press.

JAI RANGANATHAN
GRETCHEN C. DAILY

CASTE

The word *caste* probably comes from the Portuguese word *casta*, meaning "species" or "breed" in relation to botany and animal husbandry. It was first applied by the Portuguese to describe the predominant organizing principle of Indian society. The word subsumes two kinds of categorization. One categorization is religious, represented by the word *varna*, which means "color" in Sanskrit. According to the varna principle, Hindus are divided into four caste groups, together with a fifth group, the untouchables, that exists outside the caste system. The other categorization is by what is called *jati*, the endogamous, (that is, in-marrying) birth grouping that determines a person's social position and duties and primary nonfamilial allegiances. There are thousands of jatis, often with highly contested (and changing) rankings by varna—and even within a particular varna.

The origins of caste are debated but probably include a mixture of scriptural injunctions, ancient ideas about racial exclusivity, long-term occupational heredity, and colonial categorizations and impositions that converted local endogamous units into pan-Indian groupings.

Caste-like categorizations also exist in some other societies, although without the fine grades of classification found in India. The best-known example outside South Asia is that of the Burakumin ("village people"—social outcasts, known also by the more pejorative term *Eta*) in Japan, a group of about 2.5 million that has faced persistent barriers to social, economic, and marital integration into mainstream Japanese society based on their ancestry.

Institutionalization of Caste

So tenacious is the hold of caste (and the concepts of social ranking and exclusivity associated with it) that it is a continuing feature of the Indian diaspora even in the developed countries of the West—witness, for example, the caste details specified in the marriage advertisements in Indian publications in the United States. Caste categories are often applied also to non-Hindus of the Indian subcontinent. Sociologists have recorded the caste-consciousness of Muslim and Christian communities in India, the caste referring to that of the Hindu ancestors of these groups before they converted to Islam or Christianity. Such caste-consciousness restricts social intercourse and deters marriages across these ancestral caste lines.

This institutionalization of the social hierarchy implicit in caste rankings in Hinduism is politically important because of the commitment of the post-independence Indian government to a casteless society and to affirmative action to improve the situation of the lowest castes. Pan-Indian and regional caste loyalties have been exploited by both the upper and lower castes to press economic and political demands, increasing intercaste rivalries. In the process, the lower castes have become better able to organize and resist the authority of the upper castes.

Demographic Implications

There are also more direct demographic implications of caste endogamy and caste hierarchy. The widespread acceptance of caste rankings has meant that groups lower down in the hierarchy try to raise their status by adopting the practices of the higher castes—a phenomenon the sociologist M. N. Srinivas termed *Sanskritization*. Sanskritization is not modernization, though the latter usually accompanies the former. Instead, Sanskritization often entails copying the most traditional, oppressive, and insular habits of the upper castes and giving up of many of the social and, especially, gender equalities and freedoms that characterized the lower castes. In many respects caste is little different from class, and in most societies, as observers such as Mary Wollstonecraft, the eighteenth-century English feminist and writer, and others have pointed out, the upper

classes have not been known for greater gender sensitivity.

Caste is an important marker of demographic outcomes. India's censuses and official surveys no longer collect information on caste as such (all censuses from 1872 to 1941 included some question on caste), but they do separate out the Scheduled Castes (SCs) and Scheduled Tribes (STs). The Scheduled Castes are the former untouchables, and the Scheduled Tribes are the non-Hindu tribal groups that have remained outside the Indian cultural mainstream. The numerous jatis that make up these two groups have been listed for the purposes of affirmative action. Many of the affirmative policies also apply to what are called the "Other Backward Castes" (OBCs), a mixture of the lowest castes in the fourfold varna system and those untouchable groups that have converted to other religions. Together, SCs (about 19% of the population), STs (about 9%), and OBCs (about 32%) account for some 60 percent of the total population of India (a share that was probably fairly stable over the twentieth century). It is difficult to be sure, because these categories are more fluid than they appear.

In spite of affirmative action policies, socioeconomic differences by caste continue to be large. Even using the three broad caste-group categories, there are significant differences in fertility, mortality, and health that are not explained by differences in standard socioeconomic factors such as income and education. For example, the 1998–1999 Indian National Family Health Survey (NFHS) found infant mortality rates (per 1,000 births) of 83 for the SCs, 84 for the STs, 76 for the OBCs, and 62 for the other (upper) castes. The corresponding levels of under-five mortality were 119, 127, 103, and 83. The disadvantage of the SC and ST groups is obvious. Fertility differences are less stark: The total fertility rate in 1998–1999 was 3.15 for the SCs, 3.06 for the STs, 2.83 for the OBCs, and 2.66 for the other castes. For fertility, the regional contrasts in India are much larger.

Caste in India also continues to be a determinant of demographic behavior because it is strongly associated with socioeconomic class, and socioeconomic differentials in fertility and mortality are still marked at this stage of the demographic transition. For instance, literacy levels among ever-married female respondents in the NFHS were 27 percent for the SCs, 21 percent for the STs, 39 percent for the

OBCs, and 56 percent for the other castes; corresponding figures for regular exposure to the mass media were 52 percent, 38 percent, 59 percent, and 69 percent. As can be seen in all these indicators, the Scheduled Tribes are the most disadvantaged groups, significantly worse off than even the untouchables. Not only are these tribal groups at the lowest levels of socioeconomic development, they are also the least organized for any kind of concerted political action.

For historical (often to do with the emergence of charismatic leaders), demographic (often to do with their relative numbers), political (often to do with mass mobilization), and cultural (often to do with the position of women) reasons, caste plays more or less salient roles and the relative power of the lower castes differs in different parts of the country. The future of caste as an organizing principle of society is also difficult to predict. With education, urbanization, and all the forces associated with modernization, it could become less relevant in all but the most intimate areas of social relations (that is, marriage) and a less obvious marker of demographic behavior. However, it is also plausible that the upheavals of modernization will mean more caste-based conflict and unrest before this happy homogenization of socioeconomic aspirations and achievements comes about.

See also: *Social Institutions; Social Mobility.*

BIBLIOGRAPHY

Bailey, Frederick George. 1960. *Tribe, Caste, and Nation: A Study of Political Activity and Political Change in Highland Orissa.* Bombay, India: Oxford University Press.

Bayly, Susan. 1999. *Caste, Society and Politics in India from the Eighteenth Century to the Modern Age.* Cambridge, Eng.: Cambridge University Press.

Beteille, Andre. 1969. *Castes, Old and New: Essays in Social Structure and Social Stratification.* Bombay, India: Asia Publishing House.

Dangle, Arjun, ed. 1992. *Poisoned Bread: Translations from Modern Marathi Dalit Literature.* Hyderabad, India: Orient Longman.

Das, Veena. 1977. *Structure and Cognition: Aspects of Hindu Caste and Ritual.* Delhi, India: Oxford University Press.

Dirks, Nicholas B. 2001. *Castes of Mind: Colonialism and the Making of Modern India.* Princeton, NJ: Princeton University Press.

Dumont, Louis. 1970. *Homo Hierarchicus: An Essay on the Caste System.* Chicago: University of Chicago Press.

International Institute for Population Studies. 2000. *India: National Family Health Survey II, 1998–1999.* Mumbai, India: International Institute for Population Studies.

Moon, Vasant. 2001. *Growing Up Untouchable in India: A Dalit Autobiography.* Oxford: Rowman and Littlefield.

Srinivas, M. N. 1962. *Caste in Modern India, and Other Essays.* New York: Asia Publishing House.

ALAKA MALWADE BASU

CAUSES OF DEATH

Information on cause of death is essential for understanding trends and inequalities in mortality. Compiling this information requires a consistent scheme for classifying causes of death and an appropriate system for registration and record-keeping. Both were developed during the nineteenth century and had become systematic in all industrialized countries at the beginning of the twentieth century. In these countries medical certification of the cause of death is routine. This is not the case, however, in most developing countries. "Verbal autopsies"—information about the symptoms and conditions which accompanied the death obtained by questioning close relatives of the deceased—can contribute some knowledge of causes of death, especially for children, but they cannot produce reliable statistics of mortality by cause.

Classification of Causes of Death

After lengthy debate, the first international classification of diseases and causes of death, largely devised by Jacques Bertillon (1851–1922), was adopted in 1893. There have been ten subsequent revisions, none of them radically changing the original structure although producing severe disruptions in time series on causes of death. The *International Statistical*

Classification of Diseases and Related Health Problems—Tenth Revision (*ICD-10*), was adopted by the World Health Organization (WHO) in 1989.

Ten of the *ICD-10*'s 21 chapters refer to a specific bodily system, such as Chapter VI, "Diseases of the nervous system," and Chapter X, "Diseases of the respiratory system." Some other chapters refer to etiological processes, like Chapter I, "Certain infectious and parasitic diseases," and Chapter II, "Neoplasms." Still others are linked to a particular period of life, like Chapter XVI, "Certain conditions originating in the prenatal period," and Chapter XV, "Pregnancy, childbirth and the puerperium."

Such a structure makes it difficult to identify homogeneous pathological processes. Trends in distinct pathologies can depend on common factors and may be influenced through appropriate intervention. To identify these processes, several authors have suggested alternative classifications, drawing on the concept of avoidable mortality. Causes of death can be divided into "avoidable" and "unavoidable." While this may be helpful in designing health policies at a particular time, it is of little value in analyzing trends as medical progress continually shifts diseases into the avoidable category.

Ideally, a useful classification should make it possible to distinguish between different etiologies. Marc d'Espine promoted this idea in the nineteenth century, in the debates surrounding the first version of the *International Classification.* At a time when the nature of the diseases was so little known, such an exercise would have been wholly utopian. With twenty-first-century medical science, an etiological classification could be designed—and in fact has been partially attempted, using French data. In this exercise trends in mortality from different processes (such as infectious, tumoral, or degenerative processes) could be followed more precisely. The exercise was especially useful in tracking infectious disease mortality. Although many infectious diseases are covered in *ICD-10*'s first chapter, "Certain infectious and parasitic diseases," others are scattered through the remaining chapters. For instance, influenza falls in Chapter X, "Diseases of the respiratory system," and appendicitis in Chapter XI, "Diseases of the digestive system." Reclassifying diseases according to etiological criteria as infectious processes permits a better estimate of the weight of infection in total mortality.

Identifying Causes of Death

A death is the result of successive pathological processes that may have appeared or developed because of other preexisting conditions. Most studies on causes of death refer to only one cause. To insure some coherence in identifying this "underlying" cause, WHO recommends a model two-part medical death certificate and rather strict rules for coding. In Part I of the death certificate, the physician reports all the conditions that are directly responsible for the death in the reverse order they appeared. The first line contains the "direct" cause that immediately produced the death, and the last line the "initial" cause that induced the processes which finally led to the death. In Part II, the physician reports all other "contributory" causes that are not directly responsible for the death but which may have contributed to it. Coding rules help the physician to choose from among all these conditions the one which is considered to be the "underlying" cause of death. In most cases, this is the disease reported on the last line of Part I. However, in some specific cases the order of the pathological processes may be reconsidered by the authorities in charge of coding and another condition, reported elsewhere in the certificate, may be chosen as underlying cause of death.

The identification of only one cause of death considerably reduces the amount of information reported in the death certificate. This loss of information becomes increasingly serious under conditions of very low mortality. With very low mortality, most deaths occur at old ages to persons who may be suffering from several chronic diseases, making it difficult to choose the main cause of death. Hence efforts are being made to find ways of taking into account all the information reported in the death certificate, through multiple-cause analysis. Two approaches can be used. In the first, all mentions of a disease are noted, whatever the place they occupy in the death certificate. This approach highlights the part played in mortality by conditions like diabetes or alcoholism, which are seldom reported as the underlying cause of death but often contribute to deteriorating health. In the second approach, the most frequent associations of causes are examined, so as to identify sequences of pathological processes that are more lethal than others. Multiple-cause analysis is an important challenge for future studies of mortality and morbidity.

Problems of Comparability in Time and Space

Although nearly all countries producing regular statistics of deaths by cause use the current *ICD* and WHO's classification rules, comparability among countries is limited because of substantial differences in medical practice and coding habits. One such problem is in use of the category "ill-defined causes." Some countries where diagnoses tend to be imprecise assign many deaths to this category. For instance, for the year 1996, almost 12 percent of deaths in Portugal were classified into Chapter XVIII, "Symptoms, signs and abnormal clinical and laboratory findings, not elsewhere classified," compared to 4.5 percent in Russia, and less than 0.1 percent in Hungary. Consequently, before making international comparisons of specified causes of death, the deaths attributed to ill-defined causes must be redistributed into specified causes. If the probability for a death being recorded as having an ill-defined cause is independent of the actual cause of death, it is possible to proportionally redistribute deaths from ill-defined causes into all the specified categories. More sophisticated methods of redistribution can also be used. Beyond the general problem of ill-defined causes, international comparisons are affected by systematic differences in diagnostic practice. A case in point concerns myocardial infarction and other ischemic heart diseases: some countries, such as France, prefer the first diagnosis; others, such as the United Kingdom, prefer the second. To compare the level of mortality from ischemic heart diseases, it is better to combine the two pathologies (myocardial infarction and other ischemic heart diseases). In the same way, in theory *ICD-10* allows one to distinguish between cancer of the cervix and other cancers of the uterus. In practice the distinction is not made on the same criteria from one country to another and a comparison of deaths classified as "cancer of the cervix uteri" would lead to erroneous conclusions. In general, in any investigation that uses a detailed cause of death, it is necessary to consider at the same time all other causes that may be confused with it.

Problems of comparability are still more serious when dealing with time trends. As with cross-national comparisons, a prior redistribution of deaths from ill-defined causes is necessary. Such categorization of deaths generally decreased as diagnostic precision improved. For instance, in France, use of the category fell from 30 percent in 1925 to 6 percent in 1996. More problematic for comparisons over time are the breaks introduced in the time series by the successive revisions of the *ICD*. As medical knowledge expands, the contents of the *ICD* are revised: new disease designations are added, and others are removed. The number of items in the *ICD* has risen from 203 in the first classification of 1893 to more than 10,000 in *ICD-10*. To observe long-term trends, it is necessary to reclassify deaths using a constant medical definition of the cause. This would be relatively straightforward if registration authorities produced a double classification of deaths under the old and new classifications whenever a revision came into effect, but that is seldom done. Thus, reconstruction of long-term cause-of-death series for any country usually requires long and meticulous work to insure medical and statistical coherence. The few countries for which this has been done include France, the Netherlands, and some countries of the former Soviet Union.

Main Trends in Causes of Death

Until the 1960s in industrialized countries, the principal contribution to rising life expectancy was the reduction of mortality from infectious diseases and the subsequent decrease in infant mortality. Following this fundamental change in the pattern of causes of death, the pace of increasing life expectancy slowed under the double effect of the emergence of man-made diseases (diseases due to tobacco and alcohol, and traffic accidents) and the growing weight of chronic diseases (cardiovascular diseases, cancer). From the 1970s, life expectancies continued increasing because of successes in controlling man-made diseases and in reduction of mortality from cardiovascular diseases, especially among the elderly. However, this resumption of progress was not general. Countries of Eastern Europe (including the former Soviet Union) lagged in the control of the chronic diseases and their life expectancy, especially for males, stagnated or even decreased.

The situation in developing countries shows even greater contrasts. Some countries, such as China, South Korea, Mexico, and Tunisia, have followed the same path as the developed world and, thanks to a rapid decrease in mortality from infectious diseases, have reached high levels of life expectancy. In contrast, countries of sub-Saharan Africa have largely failed to control infectious diseases. The emergence of AIDS and the reemergence of diseases like malaria contribute to the poor health status of these populations.

See also: *Bertillon, Jacques; Disease, Burden of; Disease, Concepts and Classification of; Epidemiological Transition; Farr, William; Mortality, Age Patterns of; Mortality Decline.*

BIBLIOGRAPHY

Bourgeois-Pichat, Jean. 1952. "Essai sur la mortalité biologique de l'homme." *Population* 7(3): 381–394.

Holland, W. W., dir. 1993. *European Community Atlas of Avoidable Death,* 2nd edition, volume 2. Oxford, Eng.: Oxford University Press.

Ledermann, Sully. 1955. "La répartition des décès de cause indéterminée." *Revue de l'Institut international de statistique* 23(1): 3.

Meslé, France. 1996. "Les causes médicales de décès." In *Démographie: analyse et synthèse. Causes et conséquences des évolutions démographiques.* Paris: CEPED/DSD.

———. 1999. "Classifying Causes of Death According to an Aetiological Axis." *Population Studies* 53(1): 97–105.

———. 1996. "Reconstructing Long-Term Series of Causes of Death." *Historical Methods* 29(2): 72–87.

Meslé, France, and Jacques Vallin. 1984. "The Problem of Studying Mortality Patterns By Cause over a Long Period of Time: An Example from France, 1925 to 1978." In *Methodologies for Collection and Analysis of Mortality Data,* ed. Jacques Vallin, John Pollard, and Larry Heligman. Liège: IUSSP, Ordina Éditions.

Omran, Abdel R. 1971. "The Epidemiologic Transition: A Theory of the Epidemiology of Population Change." *Milbank Memorial Fund Quarterly* 49(4): 509–538.

World Health Organization. 1992. *International Statistical Classification of Diseases and Related Health Problems,* 10th revision, volume 1. Geneva: World Health Organization.

Wolleswinkel-van den Bosch, Judith. 1998. *The Epidemiological Transition in the Netherlands.* Rotterdam: Erasmus University.

INTERNET RESOURCES.

Vallin, Jacques and France Meslé. 1998. "Les causes de décès en France depuis 1925." *Institut national d'études démographiques.* <http://matisse.ined.fr/~tania/causfra/data/>.

World Health Organization. 2001. <http://www.who.int/whosis>.

FRANCE MESLÉ

CENSUS

A population census, which usually is just called a census, is a count of the population of a country on a fixed date. National governments conduct censuses to determine population sizes, growth rates, and characteristics (such as sex, age, marital status, and ethnic background) for the country as a whole and for particular regions or localities. Generally governments collect this information by sending a questionnaire in the mail or dispatching an interviewer to every household or residential address in the country. The questionnaire asks the head of the household or a responsible adult living in the household (the respondent) to list all the people who live at the address on a particular date and answer a series of questions about each of them. Over a period of months or years the government census office aggregates and tabulates the answers and reports the results to the public.

Censuses are very expensive and elaborate administrative operations and thus are conducted relatively infrequently, generally at five- or ten-year intervals. Between censuses governments estimate the size and characteristics of the population by extrapolating past trends or drawing on other data sources. Periodic sample surveys are one such source. In the United States, the Current Population Survey of around 50,000 households is conducted monthly. The Census Bureau is planning a new rolling sample survey called the American Community Survey to provide the same level of local area detail available in a decennial census by cumulating and averaging sample estimates over a five-year period.

History

Censuses have been conducted since ancient times. Early censuses were conducted sporadically and generally were used to measure the tax or military capacity of an area. Examples include Roman and Chinese censuses, the Domesday Book, occasional city surveys such as the Florentine *Catasto,* and records of medieval manors. Unlike modern censuses, they tended to count only adult men, men liable for military service, or tithables (people liable to pay taxes) along with landholdings. The results were used for administrative purposes and were not extensively tabulated or regarded as public records. Nevertheless, historical demographers have derived estimates of total populations from them.

Census taking in the modern sense requires the conception of a uniform, countable unit of analysis. Hence, census taking had to await the development of the state and the emergence of the concept of the commensurate household. The latter occurred in the medieval European west: In the ancient world rich households with large slave labor forces could not be considered "commensurate" with the hovels of the poor. In modern censuses the household or family serves as the unit of analysis or the locus for counting the members within it.

The modern periodic census of all persons is an invention of the early modern period in Europe. One of its purposes was to monitor the progress of overseas colonies. Thus, repeated counts were taken of the colonial American population in the seventeenth and eighteenth centuries, starting in the 1620s in Virginia. In Canada, French efforts to count the population began in 1665–1666 in what is now Quebec, and censuses were conducted at irregular intervals after Canada became a British colony in 1763. Sweden began to conduct censuses in the mid-eighteenth century by tallying the records in its vital registration. England and Wales instituted a regular census on a ten-year cycle in 1801. By the early nineteenth century census taking had begun to be a regular function of government in Western Europe and North America, and in the twentieth century it spread throughout the world.

Functions and Techniques

Censuses serve a variety of purposes in different countries. At a minimum a census provides a measure of the size of the population of a country, which can be compared with the population in the past and the populations of other countries and used to make estimates of the likely population in the future. Governments use census information in almost all aspects of public policy, such as determining how many children an educational system must serve, determining where to put new roads, and providing the denominators of other measures (e.g., per capita income, crime rates, and birth rates and death rates). Private businesses use census data for market analysis in deciding where to locate new businesses or where to advertise particular products. Government agencies and private researchers use the census to provide the "sampling frame" for other types of survey research.

In the United States the census is taken during the tenth year of each decade. The resulting population count provides the data for reapportioning seats among the states in the House of Representatives and the Electoral College and for redrawing district boundaries for seats in the House, in state legislatures, and in local legislative districts. In Canada and many European countries a full census is taken during the first year of every decade. Canada also takes an abridged census during the sixth year of the decade. Canadian population data are used to apportion seats among the provinces in the House of Commons and to draw electoral districts.

Most countries create a permanent national statistical agency to take the census, such as the United States Bureau of the Census or Statistics Canada. This agency usually undertakes a public review process to determine the questions that will be asked. Most censuses ask for basic demographic information such as the age, sex, educational background, occupation, and marital status of an individual. Race, ethnic or national origin, and religious affiliation are important questions in some countries. Other questions often include a person's place of birth, relationship to the household head, individual or family income, type of house, citizenship, movement in the last five years, and language spoken at home. Questions that are routine in one nation may be controversial in another. In the United States questions on religious affiliation are not asked in the census because they are seen as an infringement of the First Amendment right to freedom of religion. Other nations, such as India, do collect this kind of information. Questions on the number of children born to a woman were quite controversial in China in the early twenty-first century because of their connection with the government's one-child policy. A question on income was considered controversial in the United States in 1940, when it was first asked; it is no longer considered problematic.

Questions also change in response to public debate about the state of society. For example, Americans wanted to know which households had radios in 1930 and introduced questions on housing quality in 1940. Canada asks census questions on unpaid work done in the home.

Census taking can be divided into several phases. In the first phase the census agency divides the country into geographic divisions, makes maps and address lists, and prepares instructions for the local census takers. To conduct the count, large numbers of temporary workers may be hired or other government employees, such as schoolteachers, may be called on. The census agency prepares, prints, and mails the questionnaires to households or has them delivered by enumerators.

In the second phase a responsible adult or household head in every household, family, or equivalent entity is asked to fill out the form or respond to the enumerator and supply the required information about each member of the household. (In the current U.S. practice a brief set of questions on a "short form" is asked of all people, usually including name, age, sex, race and ethnicity, and relationship to the household head. A sample of households is asked to complete a more complicated "long" form, which can have many detailed questions on work status, income, housing, educational background, citizenship, and recent moves.)

In the third phase the census agency enters the data into a computer and tabulates the responses for the nation, states or provinces, and cities, towns, and other local jurisdictions. The agency also cross-tabulates the answers, for example, reporting not only the number of people in a local area but the number of people in five-year age cohorts, for each sex, and for local areas. The agency publishes only the tabulated results of the count and keeps the individual responses confidential. In the United States the individual census forms are stored in the National Archives and eventually opened to the public. People then may use them to research the history of their families or construct genealogies.

The choice of census technique for a particular country is the result of its social and political traditions and technological capacities. The U.S. Census is highly automated and is conducted primarily by mail. Canada sends enumerators to deliver the census form to each household, to be completed and returned by the household head. Other nations use more labor-intensive techniques for collecting and tabulating the data, sometimes requiring people to stay home to await the census taker on census day.

The U.S. Census

The U.S. Census was mandated in the 1787 Constitution. This census was the first count in the world designed to provide population figures for apportioning the seats in the national legislature. Direct taxes levied on the states were also to be apportioned on the basis of population. At that time almost 20 percent of the American population consisted of enslaved African Americans. The framers debated whether slaves were "persons" or "property" and thus whether states should receive representation for their slave populations. The framers developed what came to be called the Three-Fifths Compromise, which discounted the size of the slave population as the equivalent of 60 percent of the free population when determining the apportionment of the House. (The abolition of slavery also abolished the compromise, but the tradition of counting the different racial groups in the population continued.)

In the first census, taken in 1790, assistant U.S. marshals were instructed to travel the country and ask six questions at each household: the name of the family head and for each household the number of free white males age 16 and over; the number of free white males under 16, the number of white females, the number of other free people (the free colored), and the number of slaves. The marshals recorded and totaled the figures for the local jurisdiction and sent them to the U.S. marshal for the state, who totaled the figures for the state and sent them to the President. The census counted 3.9 million people.

In later years the census became more elaborate, with more questions asked and more data published. In 1850 Congress mandated a census schedule (form) with a line of questions for each person, including name. A temporary Census Office, as it was then called, was set up in Washington to compile the responses and publish the results. By 1880, when the American population topped 50 million, the census was still compiled by hand, using a primitive tally system. In 1890 the Census Office introduced machine tabulation of the responses, and each person's answers were converted to codes punched into Hollerith cards, a precursor to the IBM punch card. The cards then were run through counting machines. This was the beginning of modern data processing and led to further innovations in tabulating large amounts of data. In the 1940s the Census Bureau commissioned the construction of the first nondefense computer, UNIVAC, to tabulate the 1950 census. In the late 1950s the Census Bureau developed an electronic scanning system called FOSDIC (Film Optical Scanning Device for Input to Computers) to transfer the answers on the census form to a computer.

In 1940 the United States began to collect some census information from a sample of the population and thereafter slowly shifted the detailed questions on the census to the long form sent to only about 15 to 25 percent of households. In 1970 the census became primarily a mail enumeration as the Census Bureau developed automated address files for the country. In the year 2000 over 90 percent of the roughly 110 million residential addresses in the United States received the census form by mail. If the Census Bureau does not receive a response, it sends an enumerator to determine whether the address is correct and to get the information from the household at the address.

Availability of Census Data

Until the 1980s statistical agencies published census results in large volumes of numeric tables, sometimes hundreds of those volumes. Since that time census results have become available electronically on disc, magnetic tape, and CD-ROM or the Internet. Retrospective print compilations of census data are available in libraries, and some have begun to be converted to an electronic format and posted on the World Wide Web. For example, basic population tabulations from American censuses from 1790 to 1960 are available from data compiled by the Interuniversity Consortium for Political and Social Research (ICPSR).

Availability of the original census forms varies by country. With the exception of the forms from the 1890 census, the original schedules for the U.S. censuses survive. If a country's forms are available, historical public use samples of population censuses may exist in electronic form. These samples have been compiled online, including the Integrated Public Use Microdata Series (IPUMS) for American data

and planned international compilations that can be viewed on the Internet.

Issues

Censuses can become embroiled in political or social controversy simply by reporting information relevant to ongoing issues in a society. Complaints about the census generally involve concerns about the accuracy of the count, the propriety of particular questions, and the uses to which the data are put.

Censuses require public understanding, support, and cooperation to be successful. Concerns about government interference in private life can prevent people from cooperating with what is an essentially voluntary counting process. People may be wary of giving information to a government agency or may regard particular census questions as invasions of privacy.

When public trust is lacking, people may fail to cooperate. Individuals in illegal housing units, those who are resident in the country illegally, and those who do not wish to reveal their economic or social situation to a government agency are reluctant to respond to a census. In a more serious challenge, some people claim that censuses should not be conducted at all on the grounds that the results will not be held in confidence. In the Netherlands the legacy of the Nazi era, during which census records were used to identify Jews for deportation, was one of the major justifications for ending census taking in 1971.

Some political challenges to the census claim that the census does not count the population well enough. All censuses contain errors of various kinds. People and addresses are missed, and people may misunderstand or fail to answer some questions. Census officials have developed elaborate procedures to catch and correct errors as the data are collected and to impute missing answers from the answers to other questions. Nevertheless, some errors inevitably remain.

Various methods are used to measure the accuracy of censuses. Census results may be compared with population information from other sources, such as the records of births, deaths, and marriages in vital statistics. Commonly, a second, sample count (a postenumeration survey, or PES) is collected shortly after the complete census. Its results are matched against those of the census, allowing estimates to be made of the number of those missed and those who have been counted twice or are in the wrong geographic location. Some nations, such as Canada and Australia, adjust their census results for omissions and other errors.

In the United States, city dwellers, the poor, and minorities tend to be undercounted in the census relative to the rest of the population. Officials representing such undercounted jurisdictions claim that these jurisdictions have suffered loss of political representation and government funding as a result of incorrect data. Litigation seeking to compel adjustment of census results has been unsuccessful in the United States. The question of adjustment has also emerged as a political controversy in Congress: Republicans generally have opposed adjusting for the undercount, and Democrats have supported it. In 2001 the U.S. Census Bureau certified the unadjusted results of the 2000 census as the official results on the grounds that it could not guarantee that the adjusted census results were more accurate than the unadjusted count.

See also: *Databases, Demographic; Data Collection, Ethical Issues in; Demographic Surveys, History and Methodology of; Demography, History of; Population Registers.*

BIBLIOGRAPHY

Anderson, Margo. 1988. *The American Census: A Social History.* New Haven, CT: Yale University Press.

Anderson, Margo, and Stephen E. Fienberg. 2001. *Who Counts? The Politics of Census Taking in Contemporary America.* New York: Russell Sage Foundation.

Cassedy, James. 1969. *Demography in Early America: The Beginnings of the Statistical Mind.* Cambridge, MA: Harvard University Press.

Choldin, Harvey. 1994. *Looking for the Last Percent: The Controversy over Census Undercounts.* New Brunswick, NJ: Rutgers University Press.

Curtis, Bruce. 2001. *The Politics of Population: State Formation, Statistics, and the Census of Canada, 1840–1875.* Toronto: University of Toronto Press.

Eckler, A. Ross. 1972. *The Bureau of the Census.* New York: Praeger.

Glass, David. 1973. *Numbering the People.* Farnborough: Saxon House.

Herlihy, David. 1985. *Medieval Households.* Cambridge, MA: Harvard University Press.

Seltzer, William. 1998. "Population Statistics, the Holocaust, and the Nuremberg Trials." *Population and Development Review* 24: 511–552.

Wells, Robert. 1975. *The Population of the British Colonies in America before 1776: A Survey of Census Data.* Princeton, NJ: Princeton University Press.

Worton, David A. 1997. *The Dominion Bureau of Statistics: A History of Canada's Central Statistics Office and Its Antecedents: 1841–1972.* Kingston, Ontario: McGill-Queens University Press.

INTERNET RESOURCES.

Integrated Public Use Microdata Series (IPUMS). 2002. <http://www.ipums.org>.

Interuniversity Consortium for Political and Social Research (ICPSR). 2002. <http://www.icpar.umich.edu>.

Statistics Canada. 2002. <http://www.statcan.ca>.

U.S. Department of Commerce, U.S. Census Bureau. 2002. <http://www.census.gov>.

U. S. Historical Census Data Browser. 2002. <http://fisher.lib.virginia.edu/census/>.

MARGO ANDERSON

CENTRAL PLACE THEORY

Central place theory is a conceptual statement about the relative locations, numbers, and economic functions of the different-sized urban places in a region. Within a framework of several assumptions concerning the character of the region (for example, that it is a uniform physical plain, evenly settled and over which movement is possible in all directions) and the rational economic behavior of both the region's farm population as consumers and of the producers of goods and services in the urban centers, the theory allows for predictions to be made about the hierarchical ordering of the urban places and the spatial patterning of their market areas within the region. The most widely reported of these results is the urban pattern that has the regular hexagonal market areas of the more numerous smaller urban places nested within those of the fewer larger centers, as is shown in Figure 1.

The term "central place" was coined by the geographer Mark Jefferson in 1931 to refer to the fact that, "cities do not grow up of themselves; countrysides set them up to do tasks that must be performed in central places." Jefferson's reference to the functional complementarity that exists between urban places and the surrounding rural regions was not a new idea; indeed, it had been the subject of numerous empirical studies by European geographers and American rural sociologists earlier in the same century. The later emphasis upon theorizing about these urban–rural relations flowed mainly from the work of two German scholars, Walter Christaller (1893–1969) and August Lösch (1906–1945).

In 1933 Christaller, a geographer, published his dissertation on the central places of southern Germany, in which he inductively derived laws about the "size, number and distribution of central places." It was he who first proposed the hypothetical pattern shown in Figure 1. In his schema, each center within a hierarchy of urban places offers a set of economic goods and services for the surrounding farm population. The range of these goods and services—the average distance that people from the rural area will travel to obtain them—defines the extent of the center's tributary or market area. The smaller the settlement, the fewer the functions offered and the smaller its market area. Larger places offer everything that the smaller places do along with some higher order functions. For example, in the smallest hamlet there may be only a gas station and a general store, while in the slightly larger village these same functions may be supplemented by a post office and a bank. The ideal market area of each place would be circular and overlap with those of neighboring places of the same size. The hexagonal set of market areas eliminates these overlapping zones of competition and allows for the market areas of the smaller centers to be nested within those of the larger ones.

The system shown in Figure 1, with six centers located at the vertices of the hexagonal market area of the next larger urban place, conformed to what Christaller called the "marketing principle," and he elaborated upon the variations of this pattern that would result from distortions of the transportation

FIGURE 1

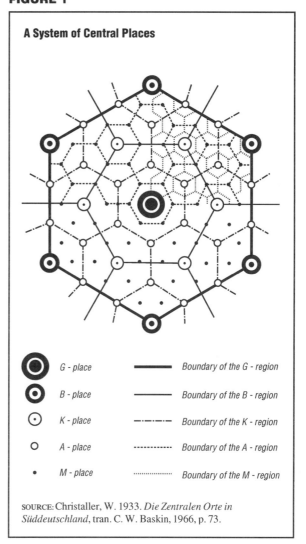

A System of Central Places

◉ G - place   —————— Boundary of the G - region

◉ B - place   —————— Boundary of the B - region

⊙ K - place   —·—·—·— Boundary of the K - region

○ A - place   ------------ Boundary of the A - region

· M - place   ··············· Boundary of the M - region

SOURCE: Christaller, W. 1933. *Die Zentralen Orte in Süddeutschland*, tran. C. W. Baskin, 1966, p. 73.

network and the nature of the administrative districts within the region. A more formal generalization of such a system is found in the work of Lösch, an economist. His book, *The Economics of Location,* published in German in 1939, presented a deductive schema for the emergence of systems of urban places and market areas within what he called an "economic landscape." In his formulation, the spatial arrangement of urban places and their market areas shown in Figure 1 is but one of a number of possible results.

English translations of these works of Christaller and Lösch first appeared in the 1950s. Geographers, especially in North America, quickly seized upon them as they were seeking to move their discipline in the direction of more quantitative and theoretical work. Those social scientists engaged in the development of the newly emergent field of "regional science" also took an interest. Central place theory subsequently fostered many lines of scholarly activity. On the empirical level, it has provided the framework for numerous studies of urban hierarchies and market area systems in different parts of the world. Those studies of the central United States completed by the geographer Brian Berry and of northern China by the anthropologist G. W. Skinner are among the most widely cited. Berry showed also how the theory could be used to analyze the hierarchy of retail centers within a large metropolitan area such as Chicago. On the theoretical front, many have sought to outline mathematical statements of the theory, to elaborate upon and extend the economic arguments that underpin it, and to demonstrate how it can be integrated with other forms of theoretical spatial analysis. The contributions, among many, of Hendricus Bos, Andrew Krmenec, and Adrian Esparza, Michael Kuby, Gordon Mulligan, and John Parr illustrate these continuing lines of investigation. Central place theory also has provided the underpinnings for regional planning schemes in different countries around the world. Notable among these efforts were those of Swedish geographers who in the 1950s and 1960s helped shape national planning policies for the locations of schools, hospitals, and regional centers. Alan Pred has suggested that "this redrawing of the map of Sweden unquestionably represents the most significant contribution of central place research to that country's planning" (1973).

See also: *Cities, Systems of; Density and Distribution of Population; Geography, Population; Lösch, August.*

BIBLIOGRAPHY

Berry, Brian J. L. 1967. *Geography of Market Centers and Retail Distribution.* Englewood Cliffs, NJ: Prentice-Hall.

Bos, Hendricus C. 1965. *Spatial Dispersion of Economic Activity.* Rotterdam: University Press.

Christaller, Walter. 1966 (1933). *Die zentralen Orte in Süddeutschland,* trans. Carlisle W. Baskin. Englewood Cliffs, NJ: Prentice-Hall.

Jefferson, Mark. 1931. "Distribution of the World's City Folks." *The Geographical Review* 21: 446–465.

King, Leslie J. 1984. *Central Place Theory.* Beverly Hills, CA: Sage.

Kolb, J. H. 1923. "Service Relations of Town and Country." *University of Wisconsin Agricultural Experiment Station Bulletin* No. 58.

Krmenec, Andrew J., and Adrian Esparza. 1993. "Modeling Interaction in a System of Markets."*Geographical Analysis* 25(4): 354–368.

Kuby, Michael. 1989. "A Location-Allocation Model of Lösch's Central Place Theory: Testing on a Uniform Lattice Network." *Geographical Analysis* 21(4): 316–337.

Lösch, August. 1954 (1939). *Die räumliche Ordnung der Wirtschaft,* trans. W. H. Woglom and W. F. Stolper. New Haven, CT: Yale University Press.

Mulligan, Gordon. 1982. "Tinbergen-type Central Place Systems." *International Regional Science Review* 7(1): 83–91.

Parr, John B. 1978. "Models of the Central Place System: A More General Approach." *Urban Studies* 15(1): 35–49.

Pred, Alan R. 1973. "Urbanization, Domestic Planning Problems and Swedish Geographic Research." *Progress in Geography* 5: 1–76.

Skinner, G. William. 1964–65. "Marketing and Social Structure in Rural China, Parts I and II." *Journal of Asian Studies* 24: 32–43, 195–228.

LESLIE J. KING

CHILDLESSNESS

Childlessness, according to the International Union for the Scientific Study of Populations (IUSSP) demographic dictionary, "refers to the state of a woman, man or couple who have been so far infertile." It should be distinguished from sterility or infecundity, terms which describe impairment of the capacity to conceive or the capacity to produce a live child. Childlessness can be measured for any person or couple in position to have (or to have had) a child, whatever the reason they did not do so. Definitive childlessness, measured at the end of reproductive life, will be treated here. As with other demographic phenomena, proportions childless can be measured in a population at a given time or for a particular cohort (set of individuals with a certain statistical characteristic in common). This entry will focus on the latter.

Causes of childlessness belong to two main categories:

- Involuntary childlessness—the consequence of sterility or infecundity, which may be congenital or caused by malnutrition or disease, especially sexually transmitted disease.
- Voluntary childlessness—the outcome of a deliberate choice, resulting from sexual abstinence, contraception, or abortion, or a consequence of social circumstances such as the absence of an available partner, or inability to provide for a family.

Involuntary childlessness is more frequent in less developed countries but is decreasing with their development; voluntary childlessness is the dominant form in most developed countries and is increasing.

Sources of Data and Measurement

Information on childlessness can be drawn from censuses and surveys or from vital registration. Most censuses and many specialized surveys have questions about the number of children ever born to women or couples, allowing calculation of the proportions childless for a cross-section of the population by various criteria, such as age or duration of marriage at the time of the census or survey. If they contain questions on the reproductive histories of women or couples, or if consecutive censuses are close enough, it is possible to study trends of childlessness by such criteria over time and for birth or marriage cohorts. These trends can also be observed from vital registration data on annual numbers of live births by birth order. In this case, the study of childlessness is the complement of the study of first birth order fertility. Both data sources have measurement problems. In censuses and surveys, the quality of responses, especially on retrospective questions, diminishes with age, especially for older respondents as a result of memory alteration and selection effects. With vital statistics, difficulties come from the multiplicity of definitions used to classify births according to birth order. Births may refer only to those within the current marriage or to all births of the mother. Birth order classification can refer to live births only or to all births (live births and stillbirths), in the latter case underestimating the level of childlessness; in the same manner, to define the order of a live birth, only live births or all births can be taken into account, the latter overestimating childlessness.

The most serious measurement difficulty comes from the definition of birth order used by some countries, especially some in Western Europe, such as France (until recently), Germany, or the United Kingdom: birth order among all the live births of the current marriage. This definition made sense when births outside marriage, and divorces and remarriages, were rare; the increase of births to unmarried women, the high proportion of marriages ended by divorce, and the frequency of remarriages, lead to a larger and larger gap between measurements based on each definition. The very high proportion of first births born out of wedlock, and the frequency of marriages entered into after the beginning of family formation, lead to overestimation of the rate of first births and consequently an underestimation of permanent childlessness. Another group of countries, including Bulgaria, Croatia, Slovenia, Yugoslavia, Portugal, and Romania, use the concept of biological birth order. In these countries, childlessness proportions based on annual data from civil registration and annual population estimates typically yield values well below 5 percent—the level which would be considered the absolute minimum for the incidence of sterility in a population. These very low estimates may reflect not only the questionable quality of data collected, but also the effect of selection through migration. The latter leads to overestimating the first-birth fertility rate if childless women leave the country or if nonresident women come to the country to give birth.

Trends and Levels

Differences in data availability between developed and developing countries mean that trends and levels of childlessness are much better known in low-fertility societies than under high-fertility conditions. In the developed countries childlessness, defined as the proportion of women who had had no live birth by the end of their reproductive life, was at a low level among cohorts experiencing the baby boom years of the 1950s and 1960s. For women born in the early 1940s childlessness was around 10 percent. It rose rapidly for successive later cohorts. The 1960s birth cohorts exceed 20 percent childlessness in a number of European countries, including England and Wales, Austria, Italy, Finland, and Ireland, and in the western part of Germany. This level, however, is still lower than that of cohorts born in the early twentieth century. In Central and Eastern Europe, childlessness has been at a much lower level

(5–10 percent) until recent years when it has been converging to Western European patterns. This is indicated by the proportions childless in cohorts that are approaching the end of reproductive life. Thus, for example, the proportions were as high as 20 percent for the early 1970s cohorts in Poland and Slovakia. (The rise is much smaller in Russia.) At least some of the increase in childlessness is probably due to reduced marriage frequency not offset by a corresponding rise in the frequency of consensual unions and extra-marital births.

The United States experienced an upward trend in childlessness similar to Western Europe's and preceding it by about ten years. It reached 17 percent among women born in 1953, only to level off and even decrease slightly thereafter (15.5 percent among the 1965 cohort).

In some countries, especially those with substantial emigration, the level of childlessness, measured from vital statistics, may have been somewhat underestimated. This may be the case for Portugal, the former Yugoslavia, Bulgaria, and Romania.

The postponement of motherhood in all European countries increases the risk of childlessness because of decreasing fecundability after age 30. The rising infecundity caused by postponed motherhood cannot be fully compensated by medical techniques, as shown by surveys such as the 1998 Netherlands Fertility and Family Survey. The development of in vitro fertilization and similar medical procedures have allowed some women to have children that they would not have had otherwise, but many women who postponed childbearing will never have a birth even with the help of the new techniques.

Social Implications of Childlessness

High rates of childlessness in developed countries create the potential for social conflict. The state (and parents) on the one hand and the childless on the other have differing interests on matters such as the financing of social welfare, pensions, aged care institutions, and education. If children are consumer goods for their parents they are also investments in the future for society. The developed world might encounter a situation familiar in developing countries, where women are often blamed for childlessness regardless of the cause of their infertility. Alternatively, there is the possibility of further institutionalization of a childless lifestyle, entrenching high levels of childlessness.

See also: *Adoption; Family Size Intentions; Fecundity; Fertility, Below-Replacement; Infertility.*

BIBLIOGRAPHY

Frinking, Gerald. 1988. "Childlessness in Europe: Trends and Implications." In *Lifestyles, Contraception and Parenthood: Proceedings of a Workshop,* eds. Hein Moors and Jeannette Schoorl. The Hague: Netherlands Interdisciplinary Demographic Institute.

Poston, Dudley L. 1982. "International Variability in Childlessness: A Descriptive and Analytical Study." *Journal of Family Issues* 3 (4): 473–491.

Poston, Dudley L., and Baochang Gu. 1983. "Measurement of Childlessness with World Fertility and National Census Data." In *American Statistical Association, Proceeding of the Social Statistics Section* 401–406.

Prioux, France. 1993. "L'infécondité en Europe." In *European Population,* Vol. 2: *Demographic Dynamics,* ed. Alain Blum and Jean-Louis Rallu. Paris: INED; John Libbey Eurotext.

Rowland, Donald T. 1998. "Cross-National Trends in Childlessness." Working paper in demography 73; Australian National University, Canberra.

Steehof, Liesbeth, and Andries De Jong. 2001. "Infecundity: A Result of Postponed Childbearing." European Population Conference 2001, June 7–9. Theme A, Session A3, Helsinki.

JEAN-PAUL SARDON

CHILD MORTALITY

See *Infant and Child Mortality*

CHINESE, OVERSEAS

Over the five thousand years of Chinese civilization, Chinese people have migrated to virtually all the areas in the world. Ethnic Chinese living outside mainland China (including Hong Kong and Macao) and Taiwan, usually referred to as the overseas Chinese, reside in almost every country. Their total number, according to the estimate cited below, exceeds 30 million. A famous Chinese poem notes that, "wherever the ocean waves touch, there are overseas Chinese."

Who Are the Overseas Chinese?

Definitions of the overseas Chinese vary from country to country and from scholar to scholar. Decisions on who is overseas Chinese are made by governments, both Chinese and foreign, by the individual persons concerned, by the larger societies alongside and within which the Chinese settlers live, and by individual scholars.

The scholar Lynn Pan represents the Chinese people in a series of four concentric circles. The innermost circle refers to Chinese living permanently in the People's Republic of China (PRC). The next circle consists of Chinese living in Taiwan, Hong Kong, and Macao, as well as Chinese citizens living or studying outside China. The third circle includes those "unequivocally identified as overseas Chinese"; these are what she calls the hyphenated Chinese (e.g., Chinese-Americans or Sino-Thais) (Pan, 1999). They are people who are "Chinese by descent but whose non-Chinese citizenship and political allegiance collapse ancestral loyalties." The last circle contains persons of "Chinese ancestry who have, through intermarriage or other means of assimilation, melted into another people and ceased calling themselves Chinese."

The term *hua ren* is commonly used to refer to overseas Chinese who have been naturalized by their host countries, and the term *hua qiao* to overseas Chinese who have retained their Chinese nationality and would likely consider themselves as sojourners. The 30 million-plus estimate of overseas Chinese is based on a broad definition that includes all persons with Chinese ancestry living outside the mainland and Taiwan, including *hua ren*, *hua qiao*, and *hua yi* (the descendants of Chinese parents).

Patterns of Chinese Emigration

According to scholars such as Gungwu Wang and Wen Zhen Ye, there have been four major patterns of Chinese migration during the past two centuries. The first is the *Huashang* (Chinese trader) pattern, which is characterized by merchants and artisans—often with their colleagues and members of their extended families—going abroad and eventually set-

ting up businesses. The migrants are usually males, and over one or two generations many of them settled down and brought up local families (Wang, 1991, p. 5). *Huashang* migration has been the dominant pattern of Chinese emigration to other Asian countries, particularly to Southeast Asia before 1850. It is likely that the earliest Chinese emigration, which was to Japan or the Philippines during the Qin Dynasty (221–207 B.C.E.), was of the *Huashang* type. And whereas the other three patterns have definite temporal periods associated with them, *Huashang* has always been important.

The second is the *Huagong* (Chinese coolie) pattern, which existed from about the 1850s through the 1920s. This migration involved the "coolie trade," supplying labor for gold mining and railway building in North America and Australia. Chinese emigrants under the *Huagong* pattern were often men of peasant origin, and the migrations were usually non-permanent in that a "large proportion of the contract laborers returned to China after their contract came to an end" (Wang, 1991, p. 6).

The third is the *Huaqiao* (Chinese sojourner) pattern. Sojourners included migrants of all social levels, but most were well-educated professionals. This pattern emerged after the downfall of Imperial China in 1911 and was strongly tied to feelings of nationalism. Beginning in the 1920s many teachers left China for Southeast Asia to instruct the children of earlier Chinese immigrants in these countries. The pattern continued until the 1950s.

The fourth is the *Huayi* (Chinese descent) pattern, a more recent phenomenon that has been prevalent since the 1950s. It involves persons of Chinese descent, *Huayi*, in one foreign country migrating or re-migrating to another foreign country.

Most of the global migration of Chinese in the early twenty-first century is of the *Huashang* type, and it will likely continue to be so in the future.

Size and Distribution of the Overseas Chinese Population

Data on the numbers of overseas Chinese are assembled from several sources, mainly issues of the *Overseas Chinese Economy Year Book* and the *Encyclopedia of Overseas Chinese*. The estimated total number of overseas Chinese at the end of the twentieth century was about 32 million, living in 130 countries. Their distribution around the world is uneven, with more than 98 percent of overseas Chinese living in

76 countries. About 24 million (85% of the total) are found in 21 Asian countries, three-quarters of whom are in just three countries: Indonesia (7 million), Thailand (6 million), and Malaysia (over 5 million). Nearly 4 million Chinese live in the Americas, almost 2.5 million of whom are in the United States.

Origins of the Overseas Chinese

The largest numbers of Chinese emigrants have historically been from the Guangdong and Fujian provinces, with fewer from the Zhejiang province, Shanghai, and other parts of southeastern China. Since the closing decades of the twentieth century, however, the origins of the emigrants have differed depending on whether their migration is legal or illegal. Legal migrants mainly hail from the large urban areas such as Beijing, Shanghai, Guangzhou, and Tianjin. The illegal migrants are mainly from Fujian and Zhejiang provinces. Currently, most of the migration from China is illegal. In several years of the 1990s, there were as many as 180,000 persons leaving China each year, most of them illegal. As of 2002, there are an estimated 250,000 illegal Chinese immigrants in the U.S. The illegal migrants are assisted by human smugglers, known as snakeheads (*shetou*). Although cargo ship, or container truck, smuggling has been the dominant image of human smuggling from China to the United States and Europe, increasing numbers of illegal migrants leave China by air. The smuggling industry is made up of international networks, many based in Taiwan, that are deeply entrenched in the infrastructure of the sending communities in China and in many transit countries. The fees paid the shetou and their associates ranged from $18,000 per person in the 1980s, up to $35,000 to $40,000 per person in the 1990s, to $60,000 or more around 2000. The smuggling business is a very lucrative enterprise. One snakehead in the U.S. began her business in the 1980s and twenty years later had netted in excess of $40 million.

The Future

The future growth of the overseas Chinese population will be affected more by trends in international migration than by natural increase. Controls on immigration in the major host countries restrict the scale of legal migration from China, but there is a sizable flow of unauthorized migrants, especially to the United States. There is a possibility of rapid increase in those numbers: The migration expert Douglas Massey has written that "China's movement towards markets and rapid economic growth may contain the seeds of an enormous migration . . . that would produce a flow of immigrants [to the United States and other countries] that would dwarf levels of migration now observed from Mexico" (p. 649). The political sociologist Jack Goldstone calls the potential for international migration from China a "tsunami on the horizon" (1997). But even conservative forecasts see the numbers of overseas Chinese becoming steadily larger in future decades.

See also: *Ethnic and National Groups.*

BIBLIOGRAPHY

Campbell, Persia Crawford. 1923. *Chinese Coolie Emigration to Countries Within the British Empire.* London: P.S. King and Son.

Fitzgerald, Charles P. 1965. *The Third China: The Chinese Communities in South-East Asia.* London: Angus and Robertson.

———. 1972. *The Southern Expansion of the Chinese People.* New York: Praeger.

Goldstone, Jack A. 1997. "A Tsunami on the Horizon? The Potential for International Migration from the People's Republic of China." In *Human Smuggling: Chinese Migrant Trafficking and the Challenge to America's Immigration Tradition,* ed. Peter J. Smith. Washington, D.C.: The Center for Strategic and International Studies.

Guillon, Michelle, and Emmanuel Ma Mung, eds. 1992. "The Chinese Diaspora in Western Countries." *Revue européenne des migrations internationales* 8(3).

Kung, Shien Woo. 1962. *Chinese in American Life.* Seattle: University of Washington Press.

Kwong, Peter. 1987. *The New Chinatown.* New York: Hill and Wang.

Legge, James. 1886. *A Record of Buddhist Kingdoms: Being an Account by the Chinese Monk Fa-hein of His Travels in India and Ceylon (a.d. 399–414) in Search of the Buddhist Books of Discipline.* Oxford: Clarendon Press.

Massey, Douglas S. 1995. "The New Immigration and Ethnicity in the United States." *Population and Development Review* 21: 631–652.

McKenzie, Roderick D. 1925. "The Oriental Invasion." *Journal of Applied Sociology* 10: 120–130.

Mei, June. 1979. "Socioeconomic Origins of Emigration: Guangdong to California, 1850–1882." *Modern China* 5: 463–501.

Overseas Chinese Economy Year Book Editorial Committee. 1996 and 2000. *Overseas Chinese Economy Year Book 1995 and 1999.* Taipei: Overseas Chinese Affairs Commission.

Pan, Lynn. 1989. "Fewer but Richer." *Far Eastern Economic Review* 143: 44.

———. 1999. *The Encyclopedia of the Chinese Overseas.* Cambridge, MA: Harvard University Press.

Poston, Dudley L., Jr., and Mei-Yu Yu. 1992. "The Distribution of the Overseas Chinese." In *The Population of Modern China,* ed. Dudley L. Poston, Jr. and David Yaukey. New York: Plenum Press.

Poston, Dudley L., Jr., Michael Xinxiang Mao, and Mei-Yu Yu. 1994. "The Global Distribution of the Overseas Chinese Around 1990." *Population and Development Review* 20: 631–645.

Purcell, Victor. 1965. *The Chinese in Southeast Asia.* London: Oxford University Press.

Renmin, Ribao (overseas edition). 1985. "Why Are There So Many Overseas Chinese?" (In Chinese) August 29: 8.

Shen, Yiyao 1970. *A Century of Chinese Exclusion Abroad.* Hong Kong: You Lian Printing House.

So, Alvin Y., Nan Lin, and Dudley L. Poston, Jr., eds. 2001. *The Chinese Triangle of Mainland China, Taiwan and Hong Kong.* Westport, CT: Greenwood Press.

Stewart, Watt. 1951. *Chinese Bondage in Peru: A History of the Chinese Coolie in Peru, 1849–1874.* Durham, NC: Duke University Press.

Uchida, Naosaku. 1960. *The Overseas Chinese: A Bibliographical Essay Based on the Resources of the Hoover Institution.* Stanford, CA: Stanford University Press.

Wang, Gungwu. 1991. *China and the Chinese Overseas.* Singapore: Times Academic Press.

Williams, Lea E. 1960. *Overseas Chinese Nationalism: The Genesis of the Pan-Chinese Movement in Indonesia, 1900–1916.* Glencoe, NY: The Free Press.

Ye, Wen Zhen. 2000. "International Migration Patterns." In *The Changing Population of China,* ed. Xi Zhe Peng and Zhi Gang Guo. Malden, MA: Blackwell Publishers.

DUDLEY L. POSTON, JR.

CITIES, DEMOGRAPHIC HISTORY OF

Before the twentieth century, the populations of urban places, and especially the great cities, faced at least one important problem: how to replace themselves. Conventional wisdom has it that ancient, medieval, early-modern, and early-industrial cities were incapable of growing naturally, that mortality was normally in excess of fertility, and that a net balance of in-migrants was necessary to keep the population at even a stationary level, let alone allow its numbers to grow. This has been called the "urban graveyard effect." Eighteenth-century English economist T. R. Malthus, in the second edition of his *Essay on the Principle of Population* (1803) provides the following description:

> There certainly seems to be something in great towns, and even in moderate towns, peculiarly unfavourable to the early stages of life: and the part of the community upon which the mortality principally falls, seems to indicate that it arises more from the closeness and foulness of the air, which may be supposed to be unfavourable to the tender lungs of children, and the greater from the superior degree of luxury and debauchery usually and justly attributed to towns. (Malthus, pp. 256–257)

And,

> To fill up the void occasioned by the mortality in towns, and to answer all further demands for population, it is evident that a constant supply of recruits from the country is necessary; and the supply in fact always flowing in from the redundant births of the country. Even in those towns where the births exceeded the deaths, this effect is produced by the marriages of persons not born in the place. (Malthus, p. 257)

These brief passages also reflect a vocabulary about cities and the countryside that was commonly used. While towns display "luxury" and "debauchery," there are "redundant births" in the country ready and willing to fill up the urban void. And in towns, those who suffer most from excess mortality are the children with their "tender lungs." And how else can urban growth be supported but by the offspring of those not born in the towns, that is, the children of migrants?

Such observations required an empirical foundation. Among European populations, it became possible to examine the balance of births and deaths in some detail only after an effective system of parish registers had been established. In England, this means after 1538, and in France, after 1685. Parish registers provide demographers with the number of baptisms, burials, and marriages that can be used to approximate the numbers of births and deaths, and to estimate the general size of the population responsible for those vital events. From such data it is possible to judge the potential for natural population growth in urban compared with rural parishes and thereby to establish the extent to which there is likely to have been excess mortality in the towns.

Many studies exist on seventeenth-, eighteenth-, and nineteenth-century European towns (including those in the Americas, southern Africa, and Australia and New Zealand) based on parish registers, or complemented by Bills of Mortality, which illustrate Malthus's observations. Broadly speaking, urban mortality was higher and fertility lower than in rural areas. In the centuries before the introduction of such registration, however, it is very difficult to discern demographic trends in any detail and it is particularly difficult to identify differences between urban and rural places. In medieval and ancient cities, the assumption that mortality was very high was based on literary references to plagues, invasions, and natural disasters, but it has proved difficult to quantify these events, just as it has been difficult to assess the population sizes of towns in this period. However, there is ample evidence, for fifteenth- and sixteenth-century Italy, to show that its towns were severely affected by outbreaks of bubonic plague; they were far more vulnerable to repeated and severe demographic crises than the countryside. This is true of early modern towns in general.

The development of family reconstitution, a form of nominal record linkage, in the 1950s and 1960s revolutionized historical demographic studies. Estimates of age-specific mortality and fertility rates

from parish register data became possible and a far more detailed picture was drawn, especially of the demography of rural parishes. Family reconstitution techniques work to greatest advantage where there is low population turnover so that individuals named in baptism, marriage, and burial registers may be linked within the same parish. If migration is at a high level, individuals will disappear since they may move among parishes between vital events. In these circumstances, the ideal outcome is that baptism and burial registers can be linked to establish estimates of early childhood mortality, especially infant mortality rates.

Researchers' current understanding of urban historical demography rests, therefore, on the following: a long-standing assumption regarding the existence of an urban graveyard effect; many examples of negative natural growth in individual early modern and late medieval towns; and detailed evidence of excess early childhood mortality in urban places.

There are also several points of continuing disagreement. In 1978 historian Allan Sharlin challenged the view that early modern cities were bound to have had natural population decline, and instead focused attention on migration. He argued that while the permanent residents of a city may have been capable of replacing themselves, thereby generating natural growth, the temporary migrants attracted to the city as unmarried workers were likely to add substantially to the number of prematurely deceased, since they confronted, for the first time, the high-risk urban disease environment. In this model, the natural decrease of populations in early modern towns is associated with the mortality of migrants rather than that of the city-born. Many urban historians believe the model overstates the reality, although they accept that attempts to test Sharlin's hypothesis have added considerably to an appreciation of the role of migrants and their potentially distinct demography. The debate on the hypothesis has also encouraged some demographers to challenge the graveyard assumption. They ask:

1. Were the largest cities at all times subject to natural decline and dependent for their growth on in-migrants from the countryside?;

2. At what level in the urban hierarchy were the effects of size or population density so substantial that natural decline was likely to

be experienced? (In other words, did small towns often escape this problem?);

3. What particular diseases were involved and which sections of the population were most affected?; and

4. What was the role of marriage, new household formation, and fertility among migrants and permanent residents?

None of the questions raised are easy to answer. Studies of eighteenth-century London and Paris demonstrate clearly that both cities had birth deficits: They depended on rural migrants to sustain themselves and to grow. In Paris, population increased from 510,000 to 581,000 in the century between 1700 and 1800, and in London, from 575,000 to 865,000 during the same period. But for a town like York (with a population of 12,000 in 1600), there is evidence, for a period in the second half of the sixteenth century during which slow natural growth did occur, that the total number of baptisms exceeded that of burials. This effect may have been repeated in other smaller towns. It is not possible to describe accurately the demographic characteristics of places at different levels in the urban hierarchy until the nineteenth century when many states developed their own civil systems of vital registration. For Victorian England and Wales, there was, in general, an inverse association between life expectancy at birth and both population size and density of the town in which a person lived. Life expectancy was from five to ten years lower in the large towns than in the small towns, and the latter had life expectancies, in turn, a further five to ten years lower than the rural districts. There was a clear urban-rural mortality gradient.

The nineteenth century was also the period in which efforts were first made to record cause of death in a systematic fashion, data which show the effect of water- and air-borne infectious diseases, especially in creating excess early childhood mortality in urban places. For example, measles was an epidemic disease with a particular sensitivity to variations in population density. Children aged from six months up to ten years that lived in towns were especially vulnerable. Measles alone would have made a considerable contribution to the urban-rural mortality gradient, but its effect was accentuated by scarlet fever and whooping cough among children, and diarrhea among infants. Similar patterns may have existed in earlier centuries when smallpox, for exam-

ple, would have added to the childhood mortality rate.

Apart from the methodological revolutions brought about by family reconstitution and computer-based analysis of large and complex data sets, urban historical demography has also been influenced by the shift in research emphasis away from work on demographic crises and mortality toward nuptuality and fertility. Age at marriage, proportions marrying and re-marrying, marital and non-marital fertility, and the practices of breastfeeding or using wet nurses are factors drawn on in explaining long-term changes in the population growth rates of cities, as well as differences among urban environments.

Cities as Parasites or Growth Engines?

Economic historians have long debated whether cities should be regarded as parasites or engines of economic growth. This debate reflects a sense of ambivalence in Western culture toward the city. While the city states of ancient Greece and Rome, and renaissance Italy, represented the pinnacle of civilization—indeed they were its defining expressions—the merchant and industrial cities of more recent centuries generated strong and mixed emotions. Malthus regarded Georgian London as rich yet debauched, while to lexicographer and author Samuel Johnson (1709–1784) it exemplified the very vitality of life. Demographers have also expressed mixed feelings. In 1987 economic historian E. A. Wrigley, for example, depicted seventeenth and eighteenth century London as a "death trap," but he also demonstrated its importance for economic and social change in preindustrial England. London absorbed England's surplus rural population; it acted as a single, integrated market for food products and consumer goods as well as finance; it stimulated agricultural production especially in its region; and it set the social fashions and was the center of political power. Until the rise of the industrial cities of the English midlands, London had no rivals, and even afterward the competition was relatively short lived. Florence in the fifteenth century, on the other hand, has been likened to a shining sun in a countryside drained of wealth and enterprise.

Urbanization

Urbanization depends on the ability of the urban population of a country or region to grow at a faster rate than its non-urban population. Usually this implies that the urban sector is experiencing natural growth and net in-migration from the rural sector, although it may also involve reclassification of places from rural to urban as they acquire larger populations or non-agricultural functions. In principle, it is possible for urbanization to progress while the graveyard effect persists, but rapid urbanization requires rapid urban growth and that demands both net transfers from the rural to the urban population and the capacity of city dwellers to more than replace themselves. In the past, rates of urbanization have been slow, although with considerable variations between regions. Western Europe was perhaps 8 to 10 percent urban by 1800 and 30 to 35 percent urban by 1900, whereas China only reached 36 percent urbanization in 2000. These varying historical levels of urbanization are difficult to interpret. Apart from the problem of different definitions of "urban," they probably reflect both variations in the progress of economic development and culturally based attitudes to the urban way of life: tolerated in Europe, restricted in China.

See also: *Family Reconstitution; Historical Demography; Urbanization; World Population Growth.*

BIBLIOGRAPHY

de Vries, Jan. 1984. *European Urbanization, 1500–1800.* London: Methuen.

Galley, Chris. 1998. *The Demography of Early Modern Towns: York in the Sixteenth and Seventeenth Centuries.* Liverpool: Liverpool UniversityPress

Malthus, Thomas Robert. 1989 (1803). *An Essay on the Principle of Population.* Cambridge, Eng.: Cambridge University Press.

Sharlin, Allan. 1978. "Natural Decrease in Early Modern Cities: A Reconsideration." *Past and Present* 79: 126–138, and 92: 175–80.

van der Woude, Ad, Jan de Vries, and Akira Hayami, eds. 1990.*Urbanization in History.* Oxford: Clarendon Press.

Woods, Robert. 2000. *The Demography of Victorian England and Wales.* Cambridge, Eng.: Cambridge University Press.

Wrigley, E. A. 1987. *People, Cities and Wealth.* Oxford: Blackwell.

ROBERT WOODS

CITIES, FUTURE OF

The twenty-first century will be the first urban century, as the world largely completes its "urban transition." With the proportion of the world's population living in urban areas projected to pass the 50 percent mark in 2007, cities are increasingly the arena for the most important developments affecting people's lives, such as globalization, economic transformation, cultural diversification, ecological change, political movements, and even warfare. As the rural-to-urban shift continues, attention has been switching from simple measures of urbanization toward the redistribution of population among different sizes and types of urban settlement, the physical and social restructuring of individual cities and their wider urban regions, the quality of life offered by these places, and the governance issues raised by these changes, not least the challenge of ensuring their sustainability and reducing their vulnerability.

Distribution of Urban Population by City Size

According to the United Nations, 39.5 percent of the world's urban population were living in agglomerations of at least 1 million residents in the year 2000. According to projections, this proportion is expected to grow, at least in the first fifteen years of the twenty-first century, reaching 43 percent by 2015. The share of the urban population accounted for by "megacities" of at least 10 million residents more than doubled between 1975 and 2000, but even then stood at less than 1 in 10 and is projected to increase only marginally by 2015. At the other end of the scale, urban settlements with under 500,000 inhabitants were home to half of the world's urban people in 2000, indicating that the median city size of urban areas stood at 500,000. Further details are provided in Table 1.

The distribution of urban populations by city size varies among world regions. The share accounted for by cities of at least 10 million residents in the Less Developed Regions (LDRs) had already overtaken that in the More Developed Regions (MDRs) by 2000 (Table 1). At 15.1 percent, it was then highest in Latin America and the Caribbean, but through to 2015 it is expected to fall in all major regions except Asia. Meanwhile, Europe is distinctive in its large share of urban residents living in agglomerations of under 500,000 inhabitants, but is similar to

North America in that the share is expected to grow. Great care, however, is needed in interpreting these figures, especially where planning controls have restricted the continuous built-up area of a settlement but not its functional reach.

The Largest Urban Agglomerations

The rise in the number of agglomerations with at least 5 million inhabitants was one of the major demographic trends of the late twentieth century and is continuing in the twenty-first. Rising from a mere eight in 1950 to 22 in 1975, the number reached 41 in 2000 and is expected to grow to 59 by 2015, according to the United Nations. Moreover, this growth has become almost entirely a phenomenon of the LDRs. In 1950 LDRs accounted for only two of the eight, but by 2015 their tally will have risen to 48, including all but one of the extra 18 expected to be added to this roster between 2000 and 2015.

Many of these large agglomerations are growing rapidly, but the population of some has stabilized, at least within their defined boundaries (Table 2). Bombay (Mumbai), Lagos, and Dhaka are expected to experience spectacular growth, putting them in a position to pass Tokyo in size soon after 2015. On current trends Tokyo is expected to have the same number of residents in 2015 as in 2000, while New York, fifth in 2000, is expected to slip to eighth in the list by 2015. Even some LDR agglomerations that previously grew rapidly are now gaining at more modest rates, including São Paulo, Mexico City, and Buenos Aires. The numbers living in agglomerations of 5 million people or over are expected to increase by 205 million between 2000 and 2015, but little more than half of this increase is due to population growth in the cities in this category in 2000; the rest will be due to additional cities entering the category.

Counterurbanization and Reurbanization

The slowing growth rate of some of the largest urban agglomerations, along with the expected decrease in the share of the urban populations living in megacities, can be related to the phenomenon of counterurbanization. The term itself is normally restricted to the shift in population distribution down the city-size hierarchy, though it can also refer to above-average population growth in rural, or non-metropolitan, areas. Population deconcentration away from large-city regions to smaller ones, or at least a slowing of the rate of metropolitan concentration, was observed quite widely across the developed

TABLE 1

Distribution of Urban Population by Size of Urban Settlement for Selected Areas of the World, Estimates and Projections, 1975–2015

Area	Population Size Class (millions)	1975	2000	2015
		(percent of urban population)		
World	10.0 or more	4.4	9.2	9.8
	5.0-10.0	8.2	5.4	6.5
	1.0-5.0	21.2	24.7	26.3
	0.5-1.0	11.4	10.5	9.8
	Under 0.5	54.8	50.0	47.6
More developed regions	10.0 or more	4.9	7.4	7.1
	Under 0.5	57.4	53.2	51.9
Less developed regions	10.0 or more	4.0	10.1	10.7
	Under 0.5	52.5	48.6	46.1
Africa	10.0 or more	0.0	8.1	7.4
	Under 0.5	68.0	56.9	53.2
Asia	10.0 or more	5.3	11.1	12.4
	Under 0.5	49.1	46.1	43.2
Europe	10.0 or more	0.0	0.0	0.0
	Under 0.5	63.6	63.0	63.3
Latin America & Caribbean	10.0 or more	10.8	15.1	13.0
	Under 0.5	55.9	47.7	45.4
North America	10.0 or more	8.8	12.5	11.4
	Under 0.5	44.1	38.7	40.7
Oceania	10.0 or more	0.0	0.0	0.0
	Under 0.5	42.6	44.1	42.5

Note: Size class is based on millions of inhabitants. Urban settlements are classified according to size in the year shown (i.e. a floating definition). Except for the world, only the top and bottom of the five size classes are shown.

SOURCE: United Nations (2000).

world in the 1970s. This led to suggestions that a new postindustrial pattern of human settlement was emerging, based principally on more footloose forms of economic activity and aided by improvements in transportation and communications.

A subsequent slowdown in population deconcentration, allied with signs of renewed large-city growth in some MDR countries, has prompted a lively debate about the validity of this interpretation. One suggestion is that all cities go through cycles of development that progress from strong core growth through internal decentralization to a stage when the city as a whole loses out to newer settlements before undergoing a period of reurbanization, as its obsolescent economy and infrastructure are rejuvenated in a new wave of investment. Most cases of renewed large-city growth in the MDRs can be linked to economic restructuring, especially employment increases in service sector activities such as finance, media, government, research, and higher education,

TABLE 2

Population of the World's Twelve Largest Urban Agglomerations in 2000 and Projected to 2015

	2000		2015	
Rank	Name	Population (millions)	Name	Population (millions)
1	Tokyo	26.4	Tokyo	26.4
2	Mexico City	18.1	Bombay/Mumbai	26.1
3	Bombay/Mumbai	18.1	Lagos	23.2
4	Sao Paulo	17.8	Dhaka	21.1
5	New York	16.6	Sao Paulo	20.4
6	Lagos	13.4	Karachi	19.2
7	Los Angeles	13.1	Mexico City	19.2
8	Calcutta	12.9	New York	17.4
9	Shanghai	12.9	Jakarta	17.3
10	Buenos Aires	12.6	Calcutta	17.3
11	Dhaka	12.3	Delhi	16.8
12	Karachi	11.8	Metro Manila	14.8

SOURCE: United Nations (2000).

and, often, to acceleration in international immigration. Sociodemographic factors have also played a part. A period of high fertility and family building occurring between the 1950s and the 1970s was followed by one with lower fertility, greater frequency of divorce and separation, and the rapid growth of non-family households with a decreased preference for suburban and small-town lifestyles.

The Changing Internal Form of Cities

The traditional, preindustrial form of an urban settlement is one with a central meeting place for transactional activities such as commerce, government, and worship, surrounded by housing, workshops, and neighborhood services and with the wealthiest, most influential inhabitants living closest to the center. Industrial cities also tended to grow around a single center, though in this case the focus was the zone of factories that were the reason for their growth, and it was the low-paid, including recent immigrants, that lived closest to the center amid the factory-generated pollution and squalor. Better-off people, with more secure jobs, higher incomes, and shorter working hours, tended to move to lower-density areas toward the edge of these cities—a process that accelerated with improvements in passenger transport, especially the development of the automobile. Suburbs—so named because these areas were situated beyond the main urban core and lacked employment opportunities and urban facilities such as high-level services—dominated the

physical growth of cities through most of the twentieth century.

The twenty-first-century city looks as if it will be very different from the inherited monocentric city with its surrounding suburbs. Suburbs have altered in character as manufacturing has been relocated there to take advantage of larger sites and better access to intercity highways and as shopping and office centers have grown up close to the wealthier residents and to mothers wanting to work while raising their families. Cities that are essentially products of the automobile age, of which Los Angeles remains the classic example, developed a more polycentric urban form from the outset. Similarly, older established cities have seen the emergence of "edge cities" and similar out-of-town retail/office complexes that have drawn trade and jobs from their main cores and in some cases threatened to eclipse them. At the same time, the industrial city's distinction between wealthier suburbs and poorer central city has been breaking down as lower-income families have found homes in more peripheral locations through government-subsidized housing schemes and illegal squatter settlements. Low-income migrants arriving in cities are less likely than in the past to settle in their core, now tending to be spread more evenly across the whole metropolitan area.

There remains, however, intense speculation over the future form of cities. At one extreme is the possibility of a return to the form of the preindustrial city, with an acceleration of the back-to-the-city movement of younger professional people and also perhaps of the wealthier elderly wishing to participate in a resurgence of cultural activities there. In direct contrast is the idea that, with further improvements in transport and telecommunications, exurban development will become the norm, incorporating the further growth of edge cities but leading on to an even more dispersed pattern of settlement than traditional urban sprawl. Melvin Webber's "nonplace urban realm" or what Edward Soja calls the "exopolis" would be characterized by lack of structure and absence of cores, where the only type of center that individuals would be able to experience is their own home. Possibly both these patterns will be represented in some parts of some countries, but the norm is more likely to be some amalgam comprising an extensive urban field with a set of interlinked components that vary in terms of their functional specialization and population characteristics—like the Megalopolis as originally articulated by Jean Gottmann.

Quality of Life in Cities

The stereotypical image of cities includes congestion, high costs, worn-out infrastructure, and a generally poor quality of life, to be contrasted with notions of a "rural idyll." The large city, even before the nineteenth century, was a place to be avoided on account of its problems in dealing with human and animal waste and the attendant problems of disease, which gave rise to sudden demographic crises as well as underlying high mortality. The suburban marrying of the urban and the rural, most consciously articulated in the notion of the "garden city," has traditionally been seen to offer the best of both worlds. Moreover, by primarily involving the middle class, the middle-aged, and the dominant ethnic group, the suburban movement has reinforced the negative image of the "inner city," leaving behind those with fewer resources to support both their own households and communal services. The resultant higher levels of deprivation, morbidity, and ethnic tension, and also crime, violence, and other antisocial behavior, have only served to fuel the urban exodus.

This picture of the "urban penalty" has, however, been challenged, not just by the changing form of the city but most notably by the experience of LDRs. The introduction of modern medicine and the basic public-health infrastructure to LDRs, proceeding faster in larger urban areas than in more remote rural regions, has given rise to an "urban advantage." This has been most marked in terms of health and longevity, but has affected the quality of life more generally, aided by the availability there of greater opportunities for work and education. Urban areas have also been associated with fuller emancipation of women and declining fertility. On the other hand, the urban advantage in the LDRs is now seen as being under threat from several quarters, including the deterioration of economic conditions, reductions in government spending on urban health infrastructure, the rise of virulent communicable diseases including HIV/AIDS, and not least the continuing urban population explosion. The general vulnerability of the least developed countries to problems that include economic uncompetitiveness, social inequalities, environmental pressures, internal ethnic tension, terrorism, and international political conflict, are increasingly being focused on their cit-

ies, raising questions about the long-term sustainability of their recent gains in living standards.

Governance Issues

Political and administrative factors have always had a major influence on the growth and nature of cities and on the living standards enjoyed by their residents, even if more immediate events led to the wholesale collapse of cities in earlier civilizations. Even without the military operations that have engulfed cities in such troubled parts of the globe as the Balkans, the Middle East, the former Soviet Union, and Afghanistan, the quality of governance can make a huge difference. Notable examples in the past include Singapore's drive toward "world city" status under the leadership of Prime Minister Lee Kwan Yew and the salvaging of New York City's reputation and pride by Mayor Rudolph Giuliani, helping it to withstand the trauma of the terrorist attack on September 11, 2001.

Even in MDRs, the future pattern of urban governance is by no means clear. Probably the most contentious issue is whether the larger urban agglomerations should be administered by a single elected body, albeit with a lower tier of local government. Where central cities are administered separately from their suburbs, it appears that greater social inequalities develop and overall metropolitan performance can suffer. Except perhaps in the smallest or most centralized countries, neither national governments nor provincial authorities, where they exist, have proven adequate to secure the required extent of internal redistribution of resources or to achieve the needed degree of inter-agency coordination for these complex urban regions. Throughout the urban system, however, issues arise concerning the level to which government should be decentralized, whether single authorities should control all aspects of governance or if tasks should be split between separate boards, and the manner in which the executive powers should be subject to democratic accountability.

Given the fragile state of affairs prevailing in many LDRs, these issues would seem to be even more crucial for their cities; and they are probably more intractable. A key problem is the sheer pace of urbanization, which renders obsolete the forms of governance that for generations had generally served well for what were largely rural territories, and makes it difficult for city boundaries to keep up with the mushrooming reality on the ground. One challenge is the unifying of urban and rural jurisdictions in order to take account of the increasingly close interaction between city cores and their hinterlands. Since these evolving metropolitan regions tend to be central to national economic prosperity, there is a strong argument that if they are to reach their full potential they should not remain under the restrictive control of local government. And the hierarchical nature of traditional governance does not fit well with the emerging structures based on networks and horizontal relationships.

See also: *Residential Segregation; Suburbanization; Urbanization; World Population Growth.*

BIBLIOGRAPHY

Batten, David F. 1995. "Network Cities: Creative Urban Agglomerations for the 21st Century." *Urban Studies* 32 (7): 313–327.

Brockerhof, Martin. 2000. "An Urbanizing World." *Population Bulletin* 55 (3): 1–44.

Castells, Manuel. 1997. *The Rise of the Network Society.* Oxford: Blackwell.

Champion, Tony. 2001. "Urbanization, Suburbanization, Counterurbanization and Reurbanization." In *Handbook of Urban Studies,* ed. Ronan Paddison. London: Sage.

Garreau, Joel. 1991. *Edge City: Life on the New Frontier.* New York: Doubleday.

Gottmann, Jean. 1961. *Megalopolis: The Urbanized Northeast Seaboard of the United States.* New York: Twentieth Century Fund.

National Academy of Science Panel. 2002. *Report of the NAS Panel on Urban Population Dynamics.* Washington, D.C.: National Academy of Sciences.

National Research Council. 2002. *Cities Transformed: The Dynamics of Urban Demographic Change in Developing Countries.* Panel on Urban Population Dynamics, Mark Montgomery and Richard Stren, ed. Washington D.C.: National Academy Press.

Pacione, Michael. 2001. *Urban Geography: A Global Perspective.* London and New York: Routledge.

Soja, Edward. 1992. "Inside Exopolis." In *Variations on a Theme Park: The New American City and the End of Public Space,* ed. Michael Sorkin. New York: Hill and Wang.

United Nations. 2000. *World Urbanization Prospects: The 1999 Revision.* New York: United Nations.

United Nations Centre for Human Settlements. 1996. *An Urbanizing World: Global Report on Human Settlements, 1996.* Oxford: Oxford University Press for United Nations Centre for Human Settlements (Habitat).

———. 2001. *Cities in a Globalizing World: Global Report on Human Settlements, 2001.* London and Sterling, VA: Earthscan Publications Ltd. for United Nations Centre for Human Settlements (Habitat).

Webber, Melvin M. 1964. "The Urban Place and the Nonplace Urban Realm." In *Explorations into the Urban Structure,* eds. Melvin. M. Webber et al. Philadelphia: University of Pennsylvania Press.

TONY CHAMPION

CITIES, SYSTEMS OF

Systems of cities are human interaction networks and their connections with the built and natural environments. The study of city systems is a subcategory of the more general topic of settlement systems. Once humans began living in fairly permanent hamlets and villages, it became possible to study the interactions of these settlements with one another. It is rarely possible to understand such settlements without knowing their relationships with the rural and nomadic populations that interact with them. Archaeologists and ethnographers map out the ways in which human habitations are spread across space, providing a fundamental window on the lives of the people in all social systems. The spatial aspect of population density is perhaps the most fundamental variable for understanding the constraints and possibilities of human social organization. The settlement size distribution—the relative population sizes of the settlements within a region—is an important and easily ascertained aspect of all sedentary social systems. The functional differences among settlements are a fundamental aspect of the division of labor that links households and communities into larger polities and systems of polities. The emergence of social hierarchies is often related to size hierarchies of settlements; the monumental architecture of large settlements is related to the emergence of more hierarchical social structures, such as complex chiefdoms and early states.

The Growth of City Systems

Uruk, built in Mesopotamia on the floodplain between the Tigris and Euphrates Rivers about 5,000 years ago, was the first large settlement that we call a city. Other cities soon emerged on the floodplain, and this first system of cities materialized in a region that had already developed hierarchical settlement systems based on complex chiefdoms. For seven centuries after the emergence of Uruk, the Mesopotamian world-system was an interactive network of city-states competing with one another for glory and for control of the complicated transportation routes that linked the floodplain with the natural resources of adjacent regions. The relationship between cities and states is a fundamental aspect of all complex social systems. The political boundaries of states are rarely coterminous with the interaction networks in which settlements are embedded, and so settlement systems must be studied internationally.

Both cities and states got larger with the development of social complexity, but they did not grow smoothly. Cycles of growth and decline and sequences of uneven development are observed in all the regions of the world in which cities and states emerged. The invention of new techniques of power and production made possible more complex and hierarchical societies. The processes of uneven development by which smaller and newer settlements overcame and transformed larger and older ones has been a fundamental aspect of social evolution since the invention of sedentary life.

The role of city systems in the reproduction and transformation of human social institutions has been altered by the emergence and eventual dominance of capitalist accumulation. Whereas the most important cities of agrarian tributary states were primarily centers of control and coordination for the extraction of labor and resources from vast empires by means of institutionalized coercion, the most important cities in the modern world have increasingly supplemented the coordination of force with the manipulations of money and the production of commodities.

The long rise of capitalism was promoted by semiperipheral capitalist city-states, usually maritime coordinators of trade protected by naval power. The fourteenth century Italian city-states of Venice and Genoa are perhaps the most famous of these, but the Phoenician city-states of the Mediterranean exploited a similar interstitial niche within a larger system dominated by tributary empires. The niche pioneered by capitalist city-states expanded and became more dominant through a series of transformations from Venice and Genoa to the Dutch Republic (led by seventeenth-century Amsterdam) and eventually the nineteenth-century *Pax Britannica*, coordinated by Victorian London, the great world city of the nineteenth century. Within London the functions mentioned above were spatially separated: empire in Westminster and money in the City. In the twentieth-century hegemony of the United States these global functions became located in separate cities (Washington, DC and New York City).

Global Cities

The great wave of globalization in the second half of the twentieth century has been heralded (and protested) by the public as well as by social scientists as a new stage of global capitalism with allegedly unique qualities based on new technologies of communication and information processing. Some students of globalization claim that they do not need to know anything about what happened before 1960 because so much has changed that the past is not comparable with the present. Most of the burgeoning literature on global cities and the world-city system joins this breathless present-ism. But claims about the uniqueness of contemporary globalization can only be empirically evaluated by studying change over time, and by comparing the post–World War II wave of globalization with the great wave of international trade and investment that occurred in the last decades of the nineteenth century. All social systems have exhibited waves of spatial expansion and intensification of large interaction networks followed by contractions. Researchers should investigate which aspects of the current wave are unique and which are repetitions of earlier pulsations. Historical comparison is essential for understanding the most recent incarnation of the system of world cities.

According to theorists of global capitalism, during the 1960s the organization of economic activity entered a new period expressed by the altered structure of the world economy: the dismantling of industrial centers in the United States, Europe, and Japan; accelerated industrialization of several Third

FIGURE 1

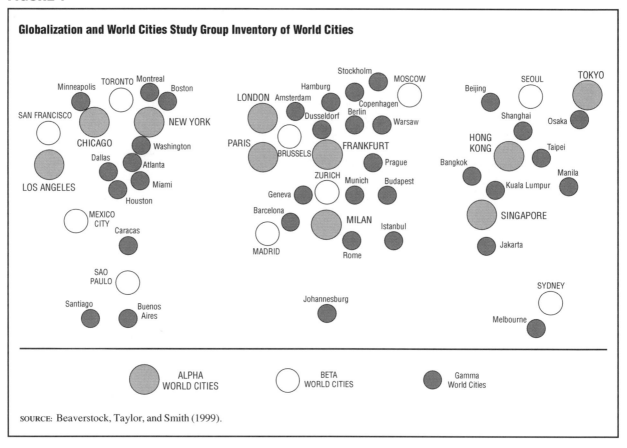

Globalization and World Cities Study Group Inventory of World Cities

ALPHA WORLD CITIES

BETA WORLD CITIES

Gamma World Cities

SOURCE: Beaverstock, Taylor, and Smith (1999).

World nations; and increased internationalization of the financial industry into a global network of transactions. With the emerging spatial organization of the "new international division of labor," John Friedmann identified a set of theses known as the "world city hypotheses" concerning the contradictory relations between production in the era of global management and political determination of territorial interests. Saskia Sassen and others have further elaborated the "global city hypotheses." Global cities, it is argued, have acquired new functions beyond acting as centers of international trade and banking. They have become: concentrated command points in the organization of the world-economy that use advanced telecommunication facilities, important centers for finance and specialized producer service firms, coordinators of state power, sites of innovative post-Fordist forms of industrialization and production, and markets for the products and innovations produced. During the 1990s New York City specialized in equity trading, London in currency trading, and Tokyo in large bank deposits. Jon Beaverstock, Peter Taylor, and Richard Smith use

Sassen's focus on producer services to classify 55 cities as alpha, beta, or gamma world cities based on the presence of accountancy, advertising, banking/finance, and law firms (see Figure 1). The website of the Globalization and World Cities Study Group and Network at Loughborough University is a valuable resource for the study of systems of world cities.

The most important assertion in the global cities literature is the idea that global cities are cooperating with each other more than world cities did in earlier periods. The most relevant earlier period is that of the *Pax Britannica,* especially the last decades of the nineteenth century. If this hypothesis is correct, the division of labor and institutionalized cooperative linkages between contemporary New York City, London, and Tokyo should be greater than were similar linkages between London, Paris, Berlin, and New York City in the nineteenth century. Obviously communications technologies were not as developed in the nineteenth century, though intercontinental telegraph cables had already been laid, and Japan was not yet a core power in the world-system. But support for the hypothesis would require fuller investigation of the nature and strength of coordination among nineteenth-century world cities.

Another important hypothesis of the global cities literature is based on Sassen's (1991) observations about class polarization and the part-time and temporary employment within globalizing cities. The research of Gareth Stedman Jones on Irish immigration into London's East End in the nineteenth century shows that a somewhat similar process of peripheralization of the core was occurring during the *Pax Britannica.*

Analyzing Global Cities

Much of the research on the global city system is based on case studies of particular cities that seek to identify the processes leading to their emergence and positioning within the larger system. Janet Abu-Lughod traces the developmental histories of New York City, Chicago, and Los Angeles through their upward mobility in the world city system. While these U.S. metropolises share similar characteristics with other world cities, they have substantial differences in geography, original economic functions, transportation, and political history and serve as fascinating cases for comparative analyses of globalization.

With appropriate data, social network analysis can be a valuable tool for studying the webs of flows and connections among cities, including flows of capital, commodities, information, and people. Network analysis produces quantitative indicators of structural characteristics of networks and of nodes (cities) within networks. For example, measures of network centrality are useful for examining the hierarchical aspects of the world city system. Quantitative measurement of the structures of connections and dominance relations among cities—whether these are based on links to global commodity chains, international business, financial and monetary transactions, or critical flows of information, can provide an important window on change over time in the global urban hierarchy.

The data necessary for analyzing the structure of the world city system are difficult to obtain because most statistical information is aggregated at the national level rather than at the city level. But researchers are making heroic efforts to locate data on characteristics of and interactions among cities. For example, using airline passenger flows between the world's leading cities for 1977 through 1997, David Smith and Michael Timberlake offer evidence of change in the structure of the world city system. These data estimate the frequency of face-to-face contacts among corporate executives, government officials, international financiers, and entrepreneurs that grease the wheels of global production, finance, and commerce. Among other findings, their results place London, New York City, and Tokyo at the top of the global city hierarchy, supporting Sassen's views. Further, while many core cities continue to occupy central positions in the global hierarchy, network roles of other cities have shifted during this time. Latin American world cities have declined in their central positioning and strength in network linkages, while Asian cities and secondary cities on the West Coast of the United States (the Pacific Rim) have moved into more central positions within the world city system.

Settlement systems continue to be a fundamental framework for the analysis of social change. The megacities in powerful and more minor countries, and the high density of cities on most continents that is revealed by satellite photos of city lights at night would seem to portend Isaac Asimov's *Trantor,* a planet entirely encased by a single steel-covered city. But if the reaction against twentieth-century globalization resembles the reaction against nineteenth-century globalization, the Earth's settlement system may be soon facing difficulties that even Asimov did not envision. The global village needs to invent mechanisms of integration that can transcend the centrifugal forces that have so often beset the modern system of cities in recent centuries.

See also: *Central Place Theory; Cities: Future; Density and Distribution of Population; Geography, Population; Geopolitics; Urbanization.*

BIBLIOGRAPHY

Abu-Lughod, Janet L. 1999. *New York, Chicago, Los Angeles: America's Global Cities.* Minneapolis: University of Minnesota Press.

Baum, Scott. 1997. "Sydney, Australia: A Global City? Testing the Social Polarization Thesis." *Urban Studies* 34(11): 1881–1901.

Beaverstock, Jon V., Peter J. Taylor, and Richard G. Smith. 1999. "A Roster of World Cities." *Cities* 16: 445–458.

Brenner, Neil. 1998. "Global Cities, Global States: Global City Formation and State Territorial Restructuring in Contemporary Europe." *Review of International Political Economy* 5: 1–37.

Chase-Dunn, Christopher. 1992. "The Changing Role of Cities in World-Systems." In *World Society Studies,* ed. Volker Bornschier and Peter Lengyel. Frankfurt and New York: Campus Verlag.

Friedmann, John. 1986. "The World City Hypothesis." *Development and Change* 17: 69–84.

———. 1995. "Where We Stand: A Decade of World City Research." In *World Cities in a World-System,* ed. Paul Knox and Peter Taylor. New York: Cambridge University Press.

Grosfoguel, Ramon. 1994. "World Cities in the Caribbean: the Rise of Miami and San Juan." *Review* 17: 351–381.

Hall, Peter. 1996. "The Global City." *International Social Science Journal* 48: 15–23.

Jones, Gareth Stedman. *A Study in the Relationship Between Classes in Victorian Society. Part 1: The London Labour Market and the Causal Labour Problem.* London: Penguin.

Kowarick, L., and M. Campanario. 1986. "San Paulo: the Price of World City Status." *Development and Change* 17: 159–174.

Machimura, Takashi. 1992. "The Urban Restructuring Process in the 1980s: Transforming Tokyo into a World City." *International Journal of Urban and Regional Research* 16: 114–128.

Sassen, Saskia. 1991 and 2001. *The Global City: New York, London, Tokyo.* 2nd edition Princeton, NJ: Princeton University Press.

———. 2000. *Cities in a World Economy.* Thousand Oaks, CA: Pine Forge Press.

Slater, Eric. 2000. "The Return of the Capitalist City: Global Urbanism in Historical Perspective." Ph.D. diss., State University New York, Binghamton.

Smith, David A. 2000. "Urbanization in the World-System: A Retrospective and Prospective." In *A World-Systems Reader: New Perspectives On Gender, Urbanism, Cultures, Indigenous Peoples, And Ecology,* ed. Thomas D. Hall. Boulder, CO: Rowman and Littlefield.

Smith, David A., and Michael Timberlake. 1995. "Cities in Global Matrices: Toward Mapping the World-System's City System." In *World Cities in a World-System,* ed. Paul L. Knox and Peter J. Taylor. New York: Cambridge University Press.

———. 1998. "Cities and the Spatial Articulation of the World Economy through Air Travel." In *Space and Transport in the World-System,* ed. Paul Ciccantell and Stephen G. Bunker. Westport, CT: Greenwood Press.

———. 2001. "World City Networks and Hierarchies, 1977–1997: An Empirical Analysis of Global Air Travel Links." *American Behavioral Scientist* 44: 1,656–1,678.

Todd, Graham. 1995. "Going Global in the Semi-periphery: World Cities as Political Projects, the Case of Toronto." In *World Cities in a World-System,* ed. Paul L. Knox and Peter J. Taylor. New York: Cambridge University Press.

Yeoh, Brenda. 1999. "Global/Globalizing Cities." *Progress In Human Geography* 23: 607–616.

INTERNET RESOURCE.

Globalization and World Cities Study Group and Network, Loughborough University. 2002. <http://www.lboro.ac.uk/gawc/>.

CHRISTOPHER CHASE-DUNN
ANDREW JORGENSON

CLIMATE CHANGE AND POPULATION

| HISTORY | Roderick J. McIntosh |
| FUTURE | Brian C. O'Neill |

HISTORY

Climate change results from alterations (sometimes quite subtle) to the heat and mass exchange between land, ocean, atmosphere, ice sheets, and space. The major driving forces of climate change are those generated by plate tectonics (the distribution of mass around the world) and variation in incoming solar radiation (*insolation*).

Relatively small changes in plate tectonics can have large and geographically distant consequences.

The beginning of the northern hemisphere ice ages, for example, can be linked to uplift between 4 and 5 million years ago (abbreviated Ma) that shut off the Isthmus of Panama and altered flow of the seas around Indonesia and Iceland. Around 5.9 Ma, the shift and crunch of the African land mass moving against Europe produced the Messinian Salinity Crisis. The Mediterranean Sea dried out to a stark salt desert, then refilled with water and redried multiple times. The familiar Mediterranean climate ended, disrupting eastern African forests and, apparently, changing the trajectory of primate evolution—these climate changes yielded the divergence of the evolutionary lines, leading to chimpanzees and humans.

Seemingly small deviations in the amount of incoming solar radiation can have enormous and sometimes abrupt effects on climate. Overlapping solar cycles of different periods produce a complex rhythm of solar radiation reaching the earth. Terrestrial cycles in turn influence how much of that insolation strikes different latitudes. Further complicating matters, heat is transported along the ever-changing land-ocean-atmospheric system, and water vapor and other gasses keep some fraction of heat from reradiating out into space.

There are solar production cycles with periods of 11.2, 22, 66, 80, 150, and 405 years. Total insolation passed to the Earth is also affected by a 2,400-year cycle in the Earth's magnetic field and (perhaps) by a return, about every 100,000 years, of intergalactic dust clouds. However, the climate effects are often unpredictable. For example, the well-attested 11.2 year sun-spot cycle is correlated with an approximately 11 year cycle of oscillations in the global monsoonal system, upon which a majority of the world's populace depends for its rains. While the Indian Ocean and Asian monsoons generally correlate well with the West African monsoons, sometimes the latter can be out of phase with the sun-spot cycle. This happened in 1985, frustrating predictions of an early end to the Sahelian Drought.

Three other driving mechanisms of climate change, all well-researched, are the variations in insolation controlled by the so-called Milankovitch or orbital-beat cycles. These are:

1. Eccentricity (changes in the shape of Earth's orbit), cycling at 100,000 years, overlain by an important 413,000 year "complementary eccentricity" cycle;

2. Obliquity (changes to the tilt of the Earth's axis), cycling at 41,000 years; and

3. Precession (shifting schedule of the equinoxes), with a paired cyclicity of 23,000 and 19,000 years.

The overlay of these cycles produces a complex rhythm. For example, new dating for the majority of ice ages blanketing the high latitudes over the last several million years reveals a remarkably regular orbit-beat. If continued, this pattern would suggest that the Earth is nearing an end to the current Holocene (interglacial) warm conditions, which have lasted 10,000 years. However, the last time these cycles aligned as they do today (around 420,000 years ago, abbreviated 420 Ka), there was a 30,000-year super-Holocene—more than double the usual duration, very much hotter, and with sea level 15 meters above today's. Whatever the extent of future global warming based on human activities, it is possible that there will be a natural warming trend for another 20,000 years.

Measuring Climate Change

Advances in observation methods, modeling, and research methods, particularly deep-sea drilling and ice-cap or glacial coring, have made the measurement of climate change possible. No less important are advances in absolute dating. Scientists are able to date variability resolvable at the annual and decadal time-scales by dendrochronology, counting the yearly growth of tree rings. Tree-ring growth can also be used to reconstruct annual precipitation—a process called dendroclimatology. Coral, ice cores, and laminated marine drift also allow year-by-year dating in addition to bearing evidence of climate effects. At the century time-scale, climatologists can count the layers in deep-sea cores and begin to explore the record of global temperature change by measuring relative proportions of oxygen isotopes ^{18}O and ^{16}O in the annual strata of ice cores or in shells of marine organisms. For dating at the millennial time-scale, investigators rely upon radiocarbon (^{14}C). At the 100,000 year time-scale, dates can be derived from thermoluminescence, amino acid racemization, and uranium series.

In most parts of the world, precise instrument-measured data on precipitation, temperature, sea surface temperature (SST), and other climate indicators do not extend far back in time. With rare exceptions, such as some Chinese compilations, even the best long-term historical records tend to be anecdotal or refer only to extreme events. However, the combination of these fragmentary records with the accumulating information from ice and coral cores, dendroclimatology, and other seasonal to centennial measures such as oxygen isotope proportions, have revolutionized the study of normal climate variability over the last 10,000 years. These are the foundational data for the global warming debates.

While climatologists cannot directly measure the timing and severity of the hundreds of ice ages that have occurred during the past several million years, they can measure proxies, such as isotopes of oxygen in the ocean waters. Higher levels of ^{18}O oxygen isotopes in the oceans correlate with larger ^{16}O oxygen isotope-enriched ice sheets. The shells or skeletons of phytoplankton or zooplankton that fall to the sea bottom form layers of stratified ooze, identifiable in ocean-bottom cores. Figure 1, based on a 20,000 year long core lifted from the northwest coast of Africa, illustrates the temperature reconstruction of the sea surface as it recovered from its −8.5°C minimum at the Last Glacial Maximum. The same core yields indirect measures of intensified monsoon rains, inferred from decreases in wind-blown dust, and of disintegrating ice, inferred from debris—called *lithics*—carried long distances on ice floes and eventually dropped to the ocean floor as the floes melt. These jagged variations in rainfall and sea surface temperature contrast with the smooth and gradual changes in the Milankovitch values for solar radiation, underscoring the complexity of the Earth's climate systems.

Climate Change in History

Environmental determinism, popular in the 1920s and 1930s, sought to find climatic and environmental causes for broad historical trends such as the rise or fall of civilizations. Historians and archaeologists now totally reject such efforts. Even at a much more modest level, attempts to correlate climate or habitat variability with societal characteristics (such as ethnic diversity) must be hedged with numerous qualifications. The case for *Homo climaticus* founders on the complexities of culture. Nevertheless, some observations on how humans respond to climate-induced stress and risk are broadly applicable over time and space. The growing field of historical ecology investigates how communities adapt to *normal* conditions, even though these conditions may be characterized by large interannual or interdecadal unpredictability.

The most consequential demographic event in human history occurred during the last glaciation, maybe as recently as 30 Ka Cold-adapted *Homo neanderthalensis* became extinct, perhaps at the hands of his close cousins—*Homo sapiens sapiens,* or modern humans—recently arrived from Africa. Hominids became a mono-species for the first time in over 6 million years. The demographic consequences of this extinction, in terms of territorial and resource competition, are incalculable.

The monumental changes occurring not long after the Late Glacial Maximum of 18 to 16 Ka are apparent in Figure 1. The abrupt and global climate change episodes, called Heinrich Events, would have had devastating effects on non-adaptive communities. Greenland coring shows a severe warming spike at around 15,000 years before the present (abbreviated B.P.), followed by almost 4,000 years of alternating, rapid-onset warm and cold phases, each lasting at least several hundred years. The coldest such phase was the Younger Dryas, which lasted over 1,000 years, beginning c. 13 Ka. At around 11,650 B.P., the Earth warmed five to ten degrees Celsius within perhaps 20 years, an astonishingly sudden increase. A steady rise in sea level—from a low of 121 meters below modern levels around 18 Ka—accompanied this change in global climate at the end of the last glaciation. Archaeology records population dislocations throughout this period, including the movement of Siberian peoples over the Bering Strait land bridge to North America. Archaeology also suggests that c. 15,000 B.P. was a beginning, in the Near East and elsewhere, of radical new dietary and resource habits. Humans showed a new interest in previously ignored plants and animals, matched by migratory ferment as people searched out these new resources—the so-called Broad Spectrum Exploitation. These new habits, the new tools invented for the new foods, and attendant "folk genetic" observations (experience-based knowledge about the effects of purposeful manipulation on future generations of various species) anticipate the first experiments in plant and animal domestication that occur over wide arcs of the Far East, Mesopotamia, Mesoamerica, and savanna Africa at c. 10,000 B.P. With food production came village life, slowly increasing population densities, poor early city sanitation and other public health conditions, and epidemic-scale

FIGURE 1

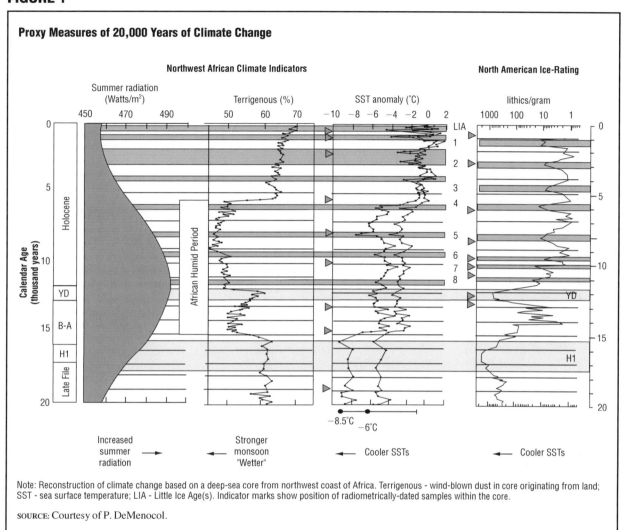

Proxy Measures of 20,000 Years of Climate Change

Note: Reconstruction of climate change based on a deep-sea core from northwest coast of Africa. Terrigenous - wind-blown dust in core originating from land; SST - sea surface temperature; LIA - Little Ice Age(s). Indicator marks show position of radiometrically-dated samples within the core.

SOURCE: Courtesy of P. DeMenocol.

evolutionary epidemiology, arising from the new intimacy of humans and their animal partners.

While it is not possible to say that these early Heinrich Events *caused* agriculture and pastoralism, the intensified adjustments humans made to climate change clearly included experiments in food production. Globally, the oceanic conveyor system had stabilized in the warm Holocene mode after around 10,000 B.P.; however, there were hiccups in the system at 7,500 B.P. (warm Hypsithermal), at 4,500 to 4,000 B.P. (cold sub-Boreal), at 2,760 to 2,510 B.P. (sub-Atlantic), and at 950 to 1100 C.E. (Medieval Warm Epoch). Some dramatic regional excursions, such as the European Little Ice Ages of the late 1500s to early 1800s C.E., were not global in reach, however profound their effect upon the economies, political life, and social world of the affected communities.

While historians cannot say that the Roman Empire collapsed because of the end of the Mediterranean climatic optimum at around 450 C.E., imperial industrial farming in what is now the North African Sahara was effectively shut down by this global change. That change had its contrasting counterpart south of the Sahara in growing populations and trade, including a thriving urban civilization along the Middle Niger.

Beyond these abrupt shifts of global or subglobal climate, populations throughout history have had to adjust to shorter-duration, but equally abrupt stress conditions. Peter DeMenocol (2001) documents the massive collapse of long-established complex state systems associated with drought or instability at around 2200 B.C.E. (Akkadian, Mesopotamia), 600 C.E. (Mochica, Peruvian coast), and 800 to

1000 C.E. (Classic Maya, Yucatan). Although these appear to be climate-caused collapses, other high-density, centralized states safely pass through analogous stresses. The thirteenth century collapse of the pueblo societies of the American Southwest, with precipitous population declines from warfare and out-migration, was plausibly a consequence not of a single event—the Great Drought of 1276 to 1299 C.E.—but of longer episodes of climate unpredictability and environmental degradation at 1130 to 1180 C.E. and 1270 to 1450 C.E. These were communities that had endured severe droughts before, but they lacked the economic and political resilience to counter multi-decade periods of unpredictability.

Even more recently at a still shorter time-scale, but reaching far back in prehistory, populations in large regions of the globe have had to deal with another unpredictable system, made familiar through contemporary weather forecasting: El Niños (in full, El Niño Southern Oscillations, or ENSO) and La Niñas. These are just the most notorious of several global barimetric pressure oscillation systems. ENSO have an apparent period of 3.5 to 4.0 years, but regularly skip a beat. Moreover, they appear to fall into clusters of high or low intensity. In spite of great advances in understanding, ENSO are not entirely predictable. The maize farmer in Zimbabwe may have sufficient advance warning after the onset of an ENSO year, but the anchovy fisherman in Peru may not. The fates of Peru's pre-Columbian civilizations have turned on the interacting quasi-periodicity of the ENSO, as have those of millions of South Asians, the victims of monsoonal-driven periods of drought and plenty.

There is, fortunately, a realistic hope that recognition of the rhythms and causes of climate change can be linked to knowledge of natural and human ecology, alleviating a great deal of suffering. Much is already known about regional modes of rainfall variability: The infamous Sahelian Drought is now known to be one of six recurrent African modes. Twenty-first century research is investigating what causes the abrupt shifts from one mode to another, with the aim of finding means of predicting the next mode shift. Such indicators may one day allow governments and international agencies to devise early warning mechanisms that are not only predictive, but preemptive.

See also: *Paleodemography; Peopling of the Continents; Prehistoric Populations; World Population Growth.*

BIBLIOGRAPHY

Bradley, Raymond S. 1999. *Paleoclimatology. Reconstructing Climates of the Quaternary,* 2nd edition. San Diego: Harcourt.

Cashdan, Elizabeth. 2001. "Ethnic Diversity and Its Environmental Determinants: Effects of Climate, Pathogens, and Habitat Diversity." *American Anthropologist* 103(4): 968–991.

Crumley, Carole L. 1994. *Historical Ecology: Cultural Knowledge and Changing Landscapes.* Santa Fe, NM: School of American Research Press.

Dean, Jeffrey S. 2000. "Complexity Theory and Sociocultural Change in the American Southwest." In *The Way the Wind Blows: Climate, History and Human Action,* ed. Roderick J. McIntosh, Joseph A. Tainter, and Susan Keech McIntosh. New York: Columbia University Press.

DeMenocol, Peter B., Joseph Ortiz, Tom Guilderson, Jess Adkins, Michael Sarnthein, Linda Baker, and Martha Yarusinsky. 2000. "Abrupt Onset and Termination of the African Humid Period: Rapid Climate Response to Gradual Insolation Forcing." *Quaternary Science Reviews* 19: 347–361.

DeMenocol, Peter B. 2001. "Cultural Responses Top Climate Change during the Late Holocene." *Science* 292(5517): 667–673.

Dunbar, Robert B. 2000. "Climate Variability During the Holocene: An Update." In *The Way the Wind Blows: Climate, History and Human Action,* ed. Roderick J. McIntosh, Joseph A. Tainter, and Susan Keech McIntosh. New York: Columbia University Press.

Droxler, Andre, and J. Farrell. 2000. "Marine Isotope Stage 11 (MIS 11): New Insights for a Warm Future." *Global and Planetary Change* 24: 1–5.

Fagan, Brian M. 1999. *Floods, Famines, and Emperors: El Niño and the Fate of Civilizations.* New York: Basic Books.

———. 2000. *The Little Ice Age, How Climate Made History, 1300–1850.* New York: Basic Books.

Hsu, Cho-yun. 2000. "Chinese Attitudes Towards Climate." In *The Way the Wind Blows: Climate, History and Human Action,* ed. Roderick J. McIntosh, Joseph A. Tainter, and Susan Keech McIntosh. New York: Columbia University Press.

Krijgsman, W., F. J. Hilgen, I. Raffi, F. J. Sierro, and D. S. Wilson. 1999. "Chronology, Causes and Progression of the Messinian Salinity Crisis." *Nature* 40: 652–655.

McIntosh, Roderick J., Joseph A. Tainter, and Susan Keech McIntosh, eds. 2000. *The Way the Wind Blows: Climate, History and Human Action.* New York: Columbia University Press.

National Research Council. 1999. *Global Environmental Change: Research Pathways for the Next Decade.* Washington, D.C.: National Academy Press.

Nicholson, Sharon E. 2000. "The Nature of Rainfall Variability over Africa on Time Scales of Decades to Millennia." *Global and Planetary Change* 26: 137–158.

Taylor, Kendrick. 1999. "Rapid Climate Change." *American Scientist* 87(4): 320–327.

RODERICK J. MCINTOSH

FUTURE

The threat of human-induced climate change, popularly known as global warming, presents a difficult challenge to society. The production of so-called greenhouse gases. (GHG), as a result of human activity, mainly due to the burning of fossil fuels such as coal, oil, and natural gas, is expected to lead to a generalized warming of the Earth's surface, rising sea levels, and changes in precipitation patterns. The potential effects of these changes are many and varied—more frequent and intense heat waves, changes in the frequency of droughts and floods, increased coastal flooding, and more damaging storm surges—all with attendant consequences for human health, agriculture, economic activity, biodiversity, and ecosystem functioning. Some of these consequences could be positive—for example, increased agricultural productivity in some areas—but most are expected to be negative. Responding to this challenge is complicated by the considerable uncertainty that remains in projections of how much climate will change, how severe, on balance, the effects will be, how they will be distributed geographically, and how costly it would be to reduce greenhouse gas emissions. In addition, the long-term nature of the effects of climate change means that if emissions are reduced now, the costs will be borne in the near term

while the (uncertain) benefits will be realized largely in the long term—decades and even centuries into the future. Moreover, because sources of emissions are widely dispersed among nations, no single country can significantly reduce future global climate change just by reducing its own emissions. Any solution to the problem must eventually be global. Demographic factors are important to all of the key aspects of the climate change issue: they play important roles as drivers of greenhouse gas emissions, as determinants of the effects of climate change on society and ecosystems, and in considerations of climate change policy.

Population and Greenhouse Gas Emissions

Most studies of the influence of population on energy use and greenhouse gas emissions focus on population size and fall into one of two categories: decomposition analyses and sensitivity analyses. A smaller number consider additional compositional variables such as age structure and household type. Limited attention has been given to the potential role of urbanization.

Decompositions of emissions rates into components attributable to each of several driving forces have been performed on national and regional data on historical emissions, on scenarios of future emissions, and on cross-sectional data. All such decompositions begin with a multiplicative identity, a variation of the well-known *I-PAT* equation as applied to greenhouse gas emissions. *I-PAT* describes the environmental impact (I) of human activities as the product of three factors: population size (P), affluence (A), and technology (T). The goal in such exercises is to quantify the importance of the P, A, and T variables in producing environmental impacts, usually in order to prioritize policy recommendations for reducing them. However, such exercises suffer from a long list of ambiguities inherent in decomposing index numbers (such as the I in *I-PAT*) that make results difficult, if not impossible, to compare.

There are a number of ways to perform the decomposition, and each method leads to a different result. In addition, the choice of variables to include in the decomposition, differences in the level of disaggregation, the need to consider interactions between the variables on the right-hand side of the equation, and the inertia built into trends in individual variables all affect the results and complicate interpretation. These ambiguities have been the basis of attacks on methods of quantitative analysis and have generated heated scientific debates about the relative importance of various factors without, however, resulting in any clear resolutions.

An alternative approach to analyzing the role of population in energy use and carbon dioxide emissions has been sensitivity analysis—that is, comparing scenarios from an energy-emissions model in which various assumptions about driving forces are tested in a systematic way. Models used in such studies have ranged from simple *I-PAT*-type formulations to more complex energy-economy models. Most work to date has focused on the influence of population size: On balance, the results indicate that although population momentum limits the plausible range of population sizes over the next several decades, in the longer term alternative patterns of population growth could exert a substantial influence on projected emissions. Incorporating relationships between population growth and income growth can substantially change the emissions expected from particular demographic and economic scenarios, but does not significantly change the sensitivity of results to alternative population growth assumptions.

Work focused on both direct energy use by households and indirect use (energy used in the production and transport of other goods consumed by the household) has identified household characteristics as key determinants of residential energy requirements. Household size appears to have an important effect (independently from income), most likely due to the existence of substantial economies of scale in energy use at the household level. Age is also important: Other things equal, households headed by the middle-aged tend to have higher consumption and energy requirements than those headed by the young or the old. These patterns, when combined with projected changes in the composition of populations by age and living arrangements, imply that compositional change may have an important effect on aggregate energy use and emissions above and beyond the scale effect of population size.

There have been few studies of the potential for urbanization (and spatial patterns of settlement in general) to affect future greenhouse gas emissions. Generally, this factor is considered only implicitly in emissions scenarios by assuming it to be essentially an income effect. However, analysis of cross-national variation in energy use and emissions suggests that urbanization leads to greater emissions above and beyond the influence of per capita income.

Population and the Effects of Climate Change

Demographic factors will strongly influence the effects that climate change may have on society, as well as influencing the ways that societies respond to those effects. Perhaps most directly, the expected increase in the population of low-lying coastal areas as urbanization (and urban deconcentration) proceeds is likely to exacerbate the effects of future sea level rise associated with global warming, including increased damage from extreme weather events. In addition, there are potential impacts—some of which might be positive—on agricultural production, one of the most intensively studied areas of climate change consequences; at the same time, population growth will raise the demand for food and fiber. The potential for climate change to expand the numbers of environmental refugees has also attracted wide interest. While global climate change may not presage a century of massive refugee movement, stresses associated with global change may intensify the pressures that already drive internal, regional, and intercontinental migration.

Future levels of fertility, population growth, and age structure will each play a role in societal responses to the effects of climate change. For the remaining high-fertility countries, a case can be made that lower fertility at the household level and slower population growth at the regional and national levels would ease the challenges faced by countries in the areas of health, migration, and food production. A qualification specific to health is that lower fertility accentuates population aging and thus puts pressure on health resources. Another, general, qualification is that policies affecting fertility are unlikely to be key strategies, since more direct means of improving social resilience under conditions of stress are available. Among these are better management of agricultural resource systems, more vigorous development and equitable distribution of health resources, and elimination of institutional rigidities that trap impoverished populations in environmentally unstable environments.

Population and Climate Change Policy

Many population-related policies—such as voluntary family planning and reproductive health programs, and investments in education and primary health care—improve individual welfare among the least well-off members of the current population. They also tend to lower fertility and slow population growth, reducing GHG emissions in the long run and improving the resilience of populations vulnerable to climate change. Therefore, they qualify as win-win policies of the sort identified for priority action in analyses of the potential effects of climate change. The existence of a climate-related external cost to fertility decisions lends support to such programs, not only because they assist couples in having the number of children they want, but also because they tend to lower desired fertility. Several studies have estimated the magnitude of these external factors to be on the order of hundreds to thousands of dollars per birth. These estimates depend on a number of factors, including geographical location (on average, births in developing countries where consumption is lower have a smaller external effect than births in industrialized countries), the magnitude of assumed future greenhouse gas emissions reductions, the costs of emissions reductions, and the discount rate. Nonetheless, the conclusion that the external costs are substantial appears to be robust, partly because meeting long-term climate change limitation goals will eventually require steep emissions reductions, and a smaller population inevitably reduces the need for the most expensive emissions reductions at the margin.

These conclusions do not imply that population policies are the most effective or equitable policies for addressing potential problems of climate change. More direct means of reducing GHG emissions and enhancing the functioning of institutions are available. Arguably, however, policies related to population should be part of a broad range of policies to reduce greenhouse gas emissions and to improve social resilience to the expected effects of climate change, and of global environmental change in general. Population-related policies have not yet entered explicitly into serious discussions of climate change policy. Little consideration has been given even to differential population growth among industrialized countries when negotiating country-specific emissions reduction targets. This is likely due to the sensitivity of the issue, given the long-running debate over the relative importance of population size and growth, as compared to high levels of per capita consumption, in affecting the environment in a deleterious fashion.

See also: *Ecological Perspectives on Population; Energy and Population; Natural Resources and Population.*

BIBLIOGRAPHY

Bongaarts, John., Brian C. O'Neill, and Stuart R. Gaffin. 1997. "Global Warming Policy: Population Left Out in the Cold." *Environment* 39(9): 40–41.

Dietz, Thomas, and Eugene A. Rosa. 1997. "Effects of Population and Affluence on CO2 Emissions." *Proceedings of the National Academy of Sciences USA* 94, pp. 175–179.

Ehrlich, Paul R., and John Holdren. 1971. "Impact of Population Growth." *Science* 171: 1212–1217.

MacKellar, F. Landis, Wolfgang Lutz, Christopher Prinz, and Anne Goujon. 1995. "Population, Households, and CO2 Emissions." *Population and Development Review* 21(4): 849–865.

MacKellar, F. Landis, Wolfgang Lutz, Anthony J. McMichael, and Astri Suhrke. 1998. "Population and Climate Change." In *Human Choice and Climate Change*, Vol. 1: *The Societal Framework*, ed. Steve Rayner and Elizabeth L. Malone. Columbus, OH: Battelle Press.

O'Neill, Brian C., F. Landis MacKellar, and Wolfgang Lutz. 2001. *Population and Climate Change*. Cambridge, Eng. Cambridge University Press.

O'Neill, Brian C., and Lee Wexler. 2000. "The Greenhouse Externality to Childbearing: A Sensitivity Analysis." *Climatic Change* 47: 283–324.

O'Neill, Brian C., and Belinda Chen. 2002. "Demographic Determinants of Household Energy Use in the United States." In *Methods of Population-Environment Analysis, A Supplement to Population and Development Review* 28: 53–88.

Parikh, Jyoti, and Vibhooti Shukla. 1995. "Urbanization, Energy Use and Greenhouse Effects in Economic Development." *Global Environmental Change* 5(2): 87–103.

Schipper, Lee. 1996. "Lifestyles and the Environment: The Case of Energy." *Daedalus* 125: 113–138.

Yang, Christopher, and Stephen Schneider. 1998. "Global Carbon Dioxide Emissions Scenarios: Sensitivity to Social and Technological Factors in Three Regions." *Mitigation and Adaptation Strategies for Global Change* 2: 373–404.

BRIAN C. O'NEILL

COALE, ANSLEY JOHNSON

(1917–2002)

American demographer Ansley Johnson Coale was educated entirely at Princeton University (where he earned a B.A., M.A., and Ph.D.) and spent his entire academic career at its Office of Population Research, serving as director from 1959 to 1975. He served as president of the Population Association of America from 1967 to 1968 and as president of the International Union for the Scientific Study of Population from 1977 to 1981.

He was remarkably prolific, publishing more than 125 books and articles on a wide variety of demographic topics. He also trained and served as mentor to many students who later became leaders in the field.

His first influential work was *Population Growth and Economic Development in Low-Income Countries* (1958), coauthored with the economist Edgar Hoover. The results, which showed that slowing population growth could enhance economic development, had a major impact on public policy and set the research agenda in this field. This was followed by *Regional Model Life Tables and Stable Populations* (1966), coauthored with Paul Demeny. These model life tables established new empirical regularities and proved invaluable in the development of later techniques for estimating mortality and fertility in populations with inaccurate or incomplete data. Coale, along with demographer William Brass (1921–1999), pioneered the development and use of these techniques, first explicated in the United Nations manual *Methods of Estimating Basic Demographic Measures from Incomplete Data* (Coale and Demeny, 1967), and in *The Demography of Tropical Africa* (1968).

Coale was an accomplished mathematician (he taught radar at the Massachusetts Institute of Technology during World War II), and his *The Growth and Structure of Human Populations* (1972) is an es-

sential textbook in formal demography. The publication of this book was more remarkable in view of the circumstance that the original source materials (notes, hand-drawn figures, tables), carefully collected over the course of many years, were accidentally discarded by a new custodian who did not recognize their significance; everything had to be reconstructed from scratch.

Perhaps Coale's major scientific contribution was to the understanding of the demographic transition. He was the intellectual architect of the European Fertility Project, which examined the historical decline of marital fertility in Europe. Initiated in 1963, the Project eventually resulted in the publication of eight major country monographs and a concluding volume, *The Decline of Fertility in Europe* (1986), edited by Coale and Susan Watkins, summarizing the change in childbearing over a century in 700 provinces in Europe.

See also: *Demographic Transition; Demography, History of; Fertility Transition, Socioeconomic Determinants of; Renewal Theory and the Stable Population Model.*

BIBLIOGRAPHY

SELECTED WORKS BY ANSLEY J. COALE.

Brass, William, Ansley J. Coale, Paul Demeny, Don Heisel, Frank Lorimer, Anatole Romaniuk, and Etienne van de Walle. 1968. *The Demography of Tropical Africa.* Princeton, NJ: Princeton University Press.

Coale, Ansley J. 1965. "Factors Associated with the Development of Low Fertility: An Historic Summary." In *Proceedings of the World Population Conference, Belgrade, 1965,* Vol. 2. New York: United Nations. 205–209.

———. 1970. "Man and His Environment." *Science* 170 (October 9): 132–136.

———. 1972. *The Growth and Structure of Human Populations: A Mathematical Investigation.* Princeton, NJ: Princeton University Press.

———. 1973. "The Demographic Transition Reconsidered." In *International Population Conference, Liège,* Vol. 1, pp 53–72. Liège: IUSSP.

———. 1974. "The History of the Human Population." *Scientific American* 231(3): 41–51.

Coale, Ansley J., and Paul Demeny. 1966. *Regional Model Life Tables and Stable Populations.* Princeton, NJ: Princeton University Press. (2nd edition, New York: Academic Press, 1983.)

———. 1967. *Methods of Estimating Basic Demographic Measures from Incomplete Data.* New York: United Nations.

Coale, Ansley J., and Edgar M. Hoover. 1958. *Population Growth and Economic Development in Low-Income Countries.* Princeton, NJ: Princeton University Press.

Coale, Ansley J., and Susan Cotts Watkins, eds. 1986. *The Decline of Fertility in Europe.* Princeton, NJ: Princeton University Press.

JAMES TRUSSELL

COHABITATION

Cohabitation can be defined as a nonmarital coresidential union—that is, the relationship of a couple who live together in the same dwelling but who are not married to each other. Such relationships can also be called informal unions, since, unlike marriages, they are normally not regulated by law, nor is the occurrence of a cohabiting relationship officially registered. Cohabitation seems to be increasing in prevalence all over the Western world. The trend is regarded as an inherent part of the transformation of Western family patterns that has been called the second demographic transition. Less is known about cohabitation than about most other demographic phenomena. Detailed information about it, typically focusing on or limited to women only, comes mainly from surveys.

Levels and Trends

The Scandinavian countries have the highest levels of cohabitation in Europe. At the other extreme are the Southern European countries, together with Ireland. The rest of Europe falls in between. In the mid-1990s 32 percent of Swedish women 20 to 39 years old were cohabiting, and 27 percent of Danish women. In southern Europe less than 10 percent of women in this age group were cohabiting—in Italy, only two percent. Countries in the intermediate category show figures in the range 8 to 18 percent, with France, the Netherlands, Austria, and Switzerland at

the high end, and Belgium, Great Britain, and Germany at the low end. Where cohabitation is well established, the first union is almost always a cohabiting union. (In Sweden, less than five percent of young women start their partnered life by getting married.)

Cohabitation in the United States has been increasing, both within cohorts and over time. By 1995 about a quarter of unmarried women between the ages 25 and 39 were living with an unmarried partner. This would place the United States near the lower end of the intermediate European group. Australia and Canada (with the exception of the province of Quebec, where cohabitation occurs more frequently than in the rest of the country) are similarly positioned, while New Zealand is at the upper end of that group.

Trends over time are difficult to assess. It seems likely that cohabitation started to become common in Sweden in the 1960s, followed by Denmark, and somewhat later by Norway. According to Ron Lesthaeghe, there was a second phase, roughly between 1970 and 1985, when premarital cohabitation spread from the Nordic countries to other parts of the developed world. Children born within cohabiting unions also first became a significant share within all births in the Nordic countries. There, by the 1990s, roughly half of all births were nonmarital. (Among first births in Sweden, two-thirds are nonmarital; 84 percent of those are born to cohabiting parents.) Outside Scandinavia, except for a few countries (France, Austria, and New Zealand), cohabiting unions are typically childless. In both Sweden and Austria, the median age at first birth is lower than the median age at first marriage.

Cohabitation everywhere is most common among young people, primarily those in their twenties, but there is also a noticeable trend in many countries for older women increasingly to choose to cohabit instead of marrying after the dissolution of a marriage (postmarital cohabitation).

Cofactors and Explanations

In contemporary Western countries, many choices that were largely socially prescribed in the past have become options. This creates a new set of risks and a higher degree of uncertainty for individuals. New stages in the life course have emerged, resulting in a "destandardization" of family formation patterns. Cohabitation and living independently without a partner before moving into a couple relationship are such stages. Cohabitation can thus be seen as one component in a process in which individual behavior is becoming less determined by tradition and institutional arrangements and more open to individual choice.

It has been argued that those who cohabit desire something fundamentally different from a marital union. Cohabitors may demand more personal autonomy, gender equity, and flexibility; they may have chosen cohabitation in order to avoid binding commitments. However, these desires are likely to change over the life course. Cohabiting couples in Sweden tend to marry at a stage in their life course connected with a preference for union stability. This stage is usually reached after less than five years spent cohabiting and becoming a parent. Attitude surveys confirm that despite the existence of widespread and widely accepted nonmarital cohabitation (even when children are born into those unions), marriage remains a positive option among young adults in Sweden.

Demographers disagree on whether country differences in the prevalence of cohabitation are likely to disappear over time, or if they represent fundamental structural and cultural differences between societies that will persist. Within a society, diffusion theory can describe the spread of the practice. In a first phase, unmarried cohabitation is a distinct deviation from norms, practiced only by those who oppose the institution of marriage or have insufficient means for marriage. In a second phase cohabitation becomes a short-lived (and childless) introduction to marriage. Finally, when social acceptance for cohabitation has become established, cohabiting relationships of long duration become common, as well as childbearing within these unions.

Cohabitation, Union Dissolution, and Fertility

It is well known that cohabiting unions are more fragile than marriages. Differences seem to be most marked at short durations. It has also been shown that married couples who began their relationship by cohabiting face an increased risk of marital dissolution. It is likely that this is due to self-selection of more dissolution-prone individuals into cohabitation before marriage.

With the exception of Sweden, levels of cohabitational childbearing are low in most countries even when cohabitation is common. Within the foreseeable future it does not seem likely that marriage will be replaced by cohabitation as the preferred type of union for procreation. Antonella Pinelli and co-authors have found that cohabitation favors childlessness and postpones the arrival of the first child. Thereby it contributes to lower overall fertility. However, many cohabiting unions are transformed into marriages, and this favors fertility. These complex interrelationships make definite conclusions difficult. On the one hand, the weakening of the norms upholding marriage is likely to have some negative effects on fertility. On the other hand, in egalitarian countries with extensive institutional supports for parenthood, "modern" patterns of behavior, such as cohabitation, may be more compatible with fertility.

Legal Status

As of 2000 France and the Netherlands were the only countries to have instituted formal registration of partnerships for both heterosexual and homosexual couples, making registered cohabitation functionally and legally equivalent to marriage in most respects. Sweden, Denmark, and Finland have taken a more pragmatic approach to cohabiting couples. Over time family law has come to be applied to married and cohabiting couples in much the same way, without completely erasing the differences. For example, cohabiting couples do not automatically acquire inheritance rights on a partner's property, nor do they have the legal responsibility to provide for each other. However, the relationship between parents and their children is regulated in the same way for cohabiting couples as for married couples.

See also: *Family: Future; Fertility, Nonmarital; Marriage; Second Demographic Transition.*

BIBLIOGRAPHY

Bernhardt, Eva. 2002. "Cohabitation and Marriage among Young Adults in Sweden: Attitudes, Expectations and Plans." In *Scandinavian Population Studies*, Volume 13: *Nordic Demography: Trends and Differentials.* Oslo, Norway: Unipub Forlag.

Bumpass, Larry, and Hsien-Hen Lu. 2000. "Trends in Cohabitation and Implications for Children's Family Contexts in the United States." *Population Studies* 54(1): 29–41.

Duvander, Ann-Zofie. 1999. "The Transition from Cohabitation to Marriage: A Longitudinal Study of the Propensity to Marry in Sweden in the Early 1990s." *Journal of Family Issues* 20(5): 698–717.

Kiernan, Kathleen. 2002. "The State of European Unions: An Analysis of FFS Data on Partnership Formation and Dissolution." In *Partnership and Fertility: Unity and Diversity,* ed. Miroslav Macura and Gijs Beets. New York and Geneva: United Nations.

Klijzing, Eric, and Miroslav Macura. 1997. "Cohabitation and Extra-Marital Childbearing: Early FFS Evidence." In *Proceedings of the IUSSP General Conference, Beijing.* Liège: International Union for the Scientific Study of Population.

Lesthaeghe, Ron. 1995. "The Second Demographic Transition in Western Countries: An Interpretation." In *Gender and Family Change in Industrialized Countries,* ed. Karen O. Mason and Ann-Magritt Jensen. New York: Oxford University Press.

Lillard, Lee A. et al. 1995. "Premarital Cohabitation and Subsequent Marital Dissolution: A Matter of Self-Selection?" *Demography* 32: 437–497.

Mills, Melinda. 2000. *The Transformation of Partnerships: Canada, the Netherlands and the Russian Federation in the Age of Modernity.* Amsterdam: Thela Thesis Population Studies Series.

Noack, Turid. 2001. "Cohabitation in Norway: An Accepted and Gradually More Regulated Way of Living." *International Journal of Law, Policy and the Family* 15: 102–117.

Pinelli, Antonella, Alessandra DeRose, Paola Di Guilio, and Alessandra Rosina. 2002. "Interrelations Between Partnership and Fertility Behaviours." In *Partnership and Fertility: Unity and Diversity,* ed. Miroslav Macura and Gijs Beets. New York and Geneva: United Nations.

EVA BERNHARDT

COHORT ANALYSIS

A cohort is a set of individual items (usually persons) that have in common the fact that they all ex-perienced a given event during a given time interval. For example, the "U.S. marriage cohort 1995–1999" consists of all persons who got married in the United States in the period from 1995 to 1999. In demography birth cohorts are of particular importance and frequently are referred to simply as cohorts (e.g., "the 1960 cohort" or "cohort 1960," indicating all persons born in 1960).

Cohort analysis is the study of dated events as they occur from the time of the event that initiated the cohort. For example, one can analyze the first births of marriage cohort 1995–1999 or the mortality of birth cohort 1960 (and compare this with the mortality of, say, birth cohort 1930). Cohort analysis often is contrasted with *period analysis,* the study of events occurring in multiple cohorts at a particular historical time, such as during a specified calendar year.

Applications

There are two main applications of cohort analysis. The first could be termed cohort analysis in its own right: the study of how behavior develops over the life course, with the initiating event (e.g., marriage) serving as a key explanatory factor, marking the start of the exposure to risk of the dependent event of interest (e.g., marital fertility). Since the 1980s powerful statistical techniques have been available that allow, using micro-level data, a much more detailed study of how behavior develops over the life course: Besides the event initiating the cohort, a wide range of additional explanatory variables (including time-varying ones) can easily be included.

The second main application is to study temporal variation at the level of the aggregate population through changes in life course behavior over successive cohorts. For example, research seeking to explain the baby boom of the 1960s may focus on the fertility level of the cohorts that were of reproductive age during the 1960s. The underlying idea is that aggregate demographic events cannot be properly understood without paying attention to the conditioning life course situation of the individual members of the population. It is in this sense that the term *cohort analysis* is especially well known in demography, in particular because of the pioneering work of the demographer Norman B. Ryder in the 1950s and 1960s.

Ryder stressed the crucial importance of the flow of successive cohorts into the population (which he termed demographic metabolism) for adapting modern society to changed external conditions. Cohorts differ because they have experienced certain key historical events (e.g., economic conditions, the introduction of the contraceptive pill) at different and sometimes critical ages. History determines a cohort's destiny. Because of this, it is important to differentiate by cohort when one is studying aggregate behavior. An example in demography is the presence of cohort effects in mortality (e.g., Barker 1994): Experiencing a famine or war at younger ages has a permanent impact on survival for the cohorts that are involved.

Demographic Translation

Ryder was also concerned with the relationship between time series of fertility measures on a period basis and those on a cohort basis. Fertility is most commonly measured by demographers in terms of the schedule of age-specific fertility rates (ASFRs) and derived summary statistics, notably the total fertility rate (TFR)—the sum of the ASFRs—and the mean age at childbearing (MAC). ASFRs can be arranged in a Lexis surface, with the period (calendar year) on the horizontal axis and age on the vertical axis. Each ASFR belongs to a period (vertical section) and a cohort (diagonal section). As a consequence, summary statistics such as the TFR can be calculated in two ways: on a period basis, summing ASFRs vertically, and on a cohort basis, summing ASFRs diagonally. If the level (quantum) and timing (tempo) of fertility are constant over time, period and cohort indicators are exactly equal. However, if level and/or timing are not constant, period and cohort indicators are not identical. For example, if subsequent cohorts have their children at increasingly higher ages (fertility postponement; that is, MAC rises over time), the annual number of births is depressed and the period TFR becomes smaller than the cohort TFR for all the cohorts involved.

Ryder investigated the mathematical relationships between such period and cohort time series of fertility indicators, establishing what is now known as demographic translation theory. A famous translation formula is $TFR_{period} = TFR_{cohort} /(1 + annual$ $change\ in\ MAC_{cohort})$, linking period and cohort TFRs under the conditions of a constant quantum of cohort fertility but with the cohort tempo shifting linearly over time. Using this formula, one can calculate the drop in period fertility that results from a postponement of childbearing that does not alter ultimate family size.

Some researchers believe that such translation formulas can be used to estimate cohort fertility from period fertility. The inherent problem in calculating cohort fertility indicators is that one has to wait until the cohort has finished childbearing: For cohorts still of reproductive age, one observes only part of their fertility career (i.e., up until now). It is tempting to try to use the full period information to make statements about these cohorts' future fertility. Unfortunately, such attempts are hazardous. Any procedure used in an attempt to estimate cohort quantum from period quantum is based on simplifying assumptions, the justifiability of which can only be verified empirically: by comparing the estimated cohort fertility with the actual cohort fertility. But if actual cohort fertility is known, the translation procedure is no longer needed.

Hypothetical Cohort

Age-specific indicators of demographic behavior, such as fertility rates and mortality rates, that are all measured during a single period refer to different cohorts. Nevertheless, one can ask what would happen to a cohort if over its lifetime it were to behave according to the age-specific indicators observed during this particular period. For example, it is possible to calculate the average life span of a fictitious group of persons surviving according to the age-specific mortality rates observed in the United States during the year 2002. Such calculations on period data are then interpreted as if they applied to a cohort. Such a cohort is known as a hypothetical cohort or synthetic cohort. Hypothetical cohorts can be very useful analytically but should never be confused with true cohorts, which experience age-specific rates that are typically not independent from one year to the next.

Period versus Cohort?

The work of Ryder and others has initiated a heated and unresolved debate between followers of the cohort approach and adherents of the period approach. In their extreme forms these two approaches as they are applied to fertility can be described as follows:

> *Cohort approach:* Each cohort, shaped by the historical conditions under which it reaches reproductive age, follows its own fertility

career. Year-by-year changes in fertility are caused by new cohorts replacing old cohorts in the reproductive age span. Period fertility measures are just the average of the underlying cohort fertility measures.

Period approach: Aggregate fertility is driven by current conditions. If conditions change, period fertility changes also. Cohorts shape their fertility career as they go through time. Cohort fertility measures are just the average of the underlying period fertility measures.

As is always the case with extreme positions, the truth lies in between. The extreme cohort position ignores the fact that cohorts (in fact, individual persons) do not start their reproductive career with cast-iron fertility targets but instead modify their fertility behavior as period conditions change. The extreme period position ignores the fact that family formation is a lifetime enterprise, and as a consequence, period effects affect cohorts differently, depending on the life course position the cohorts currently hold and the fertility choices they have made. For example, a period effect such as the introduction of reliable contraceptives will have a much larger effect on the fertility of cohorts currently 20 years old than on the fertility of cohorts currently 40 years old.

Indeed, a birth cohort is not only a set of individuals born during the same period in the past but also a set of individuals each of whom experiences a period effect at the same stage of the life course (current year = birth year + age). This double significance of the cohort concept alone should make it clear that both the period perspective and the cohort perspective are needed to understand aggregate fertility or any other type of demographic behavior.

Period measures of fertility indicate how many children are born each year and, consequently, how the age structure of the population changes over time. Cohort measures of fertility indicate the extent to which individual members of the population reproduce themselves. Although both sets of measures are taken from the same Lexis surface and therefore refer to the same babies and mothers, the exact relationship between period and cohort measures depends on so many factors (notably, shifts over time in the age pattern of fertility) that it is sensible to treat them as two fundamentally different concepts of the quantum of fertility.

See also: *Baby Boom; Easterlin, Richard A.; Event-History Analysis; Henry, Louis; Lexis Diagram; Life Course Analysis; Ryder, Norman B.*

BIBLIOGRAPHY

Barker, David. 1994. *Mothers, Babies, and Disease in Later Life.* London: British Medical Journal Publishing Group.

Elo, Irma, and Samuel H. Preston. 1992. "Effects of Early-Life Conditions on Adult Mortality: A Review." *Population Index* 58: 186–212.

Hobcraft, John, Jane Menken, and Samuel H. Preston. 1982. "Age, Period and Cohort Effects in Demography: A Review." *Population Index* 48: 4–43.

Ní Bhrolcháin, Maire. 1992. "Period Paramount? A Critique of the Cohort Approach to Fertility." *Population and Development Review* 18: 599–629.

Pressat, Roland. 1972. *Demographic Analysis.* Chicago: Aldine.

Ryder, Norman B. 1964. "The Process of Demographic Translation." *Demography* 1: 74–82.

———. 1965. "The Cohort as a Concept in the Study of Social Change." *American Sociological Review* 30: 843–861.

———. 1968. "Cohort Analysis." In *International Encyclopedia of the Social Sciences,* ed. D. L. Sills. New York: Macmillan and Free Press.

van Imhoff, Evert. 2001. "On the Impossibility of Inferring Cohort Fertility Measures from Period Fertility Measures." *Demographic Research* 5: 23–64.

Wunsch, Guillaume J., and Marc G. Termote. 1978. *Introduction to Demographic Analysis: Principles and Methods.* New York: Plenum.

EVERT VAN IMHOFF

COMMON PROPERTY RESOURCES

Throughout the world there are assets that are neither private nor state property, but common proper-

---

ty. The term denotes a class of institutions that govern the ownership and rights-of-access to assets. Common property assets are to be distinguished from "public goods," in that, unlike the latter, use by someone of a unit of a common property asset typically reduces the amount available to others by one unit (in economic terminology, such an asset is rivalrous in use). The institution of common property creates and harbors reciprocal externalities. As some of the most interesting examples of common property assets are natural resources, this entry is restricted to them.

Global and Local Commons

Broadly speaking, there are two types of common property resources. Assets that are mobile and have a global reach are subject to "open access," in that everyone in principle has access to them. Earth's atmosphere, as both a source of human well-being and a sink for depositing effluents, is the classic example: For physical reasons, the atmosphere cannot be privatized, nor can it be expropriated by any state. In a pioneering article published in 1954, H. Scott Gordon argued that an asset that is everyone's property is in fact no one's property. He showed that resources under open access are overused, in that it is in the public interest to restrict their use. His reasoning was simple—given that resource bases are finite in size, they have positive social worth. But an open access resource is free to all who use it. So, the cost that each user incurs is less than what it ought ideally to be. Under open access the rents attributable to the resource base are dissipated; there is excessive use. A user tax (or, alternatively, a quota) suggests itself as public policy.

It will be noticed that the production of public goods and the use of open access resources reflect features that are mirror opposites of one another: In the absence of collective action, there is an undersupply of public goods and an overuse of open access resources. Garrett Hardin's admirable metaphor, "the tragedy of the commons" (Hardin, 1968, pp. 1,243–1,248), is applicable to open access resources. Climate change owing to anthropogenic causes is a an example of such a "tragedy." In earlier millennia demand would have been small, and such resource bases as the atmosphere and the open seas would legitimately have been free goods. But in the twenty-first century the matter is different.

However, there are geographically localized resources that are common property to well-defined groups of people, but to which people not belonging to the groups do not have a right of access. It has now become customary to refer to such assets as "common-property resources," or CPRs, which is an unfortunate usage, since open access resources are common property too. In what follows, CPRs are refered to as "local commons."

The theory characterizing the use of local commons was developed by Partha Dasgupta and G. M. Heal (1979, pp. 55–78) as a timeless, noncooperative game involving N players (N>1). Their model took the form of a modified version of the Prisoners' Dilemma game. They showed that if N is smaller than the number who would have exploited the resource had it been open access, rents do decrease to some extent, but not entirely. The authors noted however, that, as the local commons are spatially confined, monitoring one another's use of the resource is possible. The authors thereby argued that communities should in principle be able not only to reach agreement on the use of the local commons, they should also be able to implement the agreement. Dasgupta and Heal explored both taxes and quotas as possible regulatory mechanisms. A large and rich empirical literature on the local commons in poor countries has grown since then, confirming those predictions of the theory (Murphy and Murphy, 1985; Wade, 1988; Ostrom, 1990, 1996; Feeny et al., 1990; Baland and Platteau, 1996; among many others).

Examples of Local Commons

The local commons include grazing lands, threshing grounds, lands temporarily taken out of cultivation, inland and coastal fisheries, irrigation systems, woodlands, forests, tanks, ponds, and recreation grounds. In poor countries property rights to the local commons have been found most often to be based on custom and tradition; they are usually not backed by the kind of deeds that would pass scrutiny in courts of law. Therefore, tenure is not always secure—a vital problem.

Are the local commons extensive? As a proportion of total assets, their presence ranges widely across ecological zones. There is a rationale for this, based on the human desire to reduce risk. Communal property rights enable members of a group to reduce individual risks by pooling their risks. An almost immediate empirical corollary is that the local commons are most prominent in arid regions, mountain regions, and unirrigated areas, and least prominent in humid regions and river valleys. Another corollary is that income inequalities are less in those locations where the local commons are more prominent. Aggregate income is a different matter, though; it is the arid and mountain regions and unirrigated areas that are the poorest.

Studies in a number of dry rural districts in India by N. S. Jodha, published in 1986, have revealed that the proportion of household income based directly on the local commons is in the range 15 to 25 percent. W. Cavendish has arrived at even larger estimates from a study of villages in Zimbabwe published in 2000. The proportion of household income based directly on local commons is 35 percent, the figure for the poorest quintile being 40 percent. Such evidence as Jodha and Cavendish have unearthed does not, of course, prove that the local commons in their samples were well managed, but it does show that rural households would have strong incentives to devise arrangements whereby they *would* be managed.

Are the local commons managed communally? Not invariably, but in many cases they are, or have been in the past. The local commons are typically open only to those having historical rights, through kinship ties or community membership. Their management is mediated by social norms of behavior that arose in long-term relationships among members of the community. An empirical corollary is that, unless the local commons assume a legal status, in the contemporary sense, their management would be expected to break down if members become separately mobile during the process of economic development. Theories of social capital, much discussed in recent years, have found an apt testing ground in the local commons. The management structures of local commons have been found to be shaped by the character of the natural resource under their jurisdiction. For example, communitarian institutions governing coastal fisheries have been discovered to be different in design from those governing local irrigation systems.

That the local commons have often been managed is the good news. There are, however, two unfortunate facts. First, a general finding is that entitlements to products of the local commons is, and was, frequently based on private holdings: richer households enjoy a greater proportion of the benefits from the commons, a finding that is consonant with cooperative game theory. In extreme cases access is restricted to the privileged in the community (for example, caste Hindus in India as shown by Beteille in 1983).

The second unfortunate fact is that the local commons have degraded in recent years in many poorer parts of the world. One reason for this was previously noted: growing mobility among members of rural communities. Another reason has been population pressure, making opportunistic behavior among both locals and outsiders the inevitable response of economic desperation. Yet another reason has had to do with the state establishing its authority by weakening communitarian institutions, but unable or unwilling to replace them with an adequate structure of governance; this situation is observed especially in the Sahel region of Africa.

Fertility Response

Theoretical considerations suggest that there is a connection between common property management and household size. The point is that part of the cost of having children is passed on to others whenever a household's access to common property resources is independent of its size. Moreover, if social norms bearing on the use of the local commons degrade, parents pass some of the costs of children on to the community by overexploiting the commons. This is an instance of a demographic free-rider problem— an externality.

The poorest countries are in great part agriculture-based subsistence economies. Much labor is needed there even for simple tasks. Moreover, households lack access to the sources of energy available to households in advanced industrial countries. In semi-arid and arid regions water supply is often not even close at hand, nor is fuelwood nearby when the forests recede. From age six or so, children in poor households in the poorest countries must help care for their siblings and domestic animals; soon afterwards, they are required to fetch water and collect fuelwood, dung (in the Indian subcontinent), and fodder. Very often, they do not go to school. Children of age from 10 to 15 years old have been routinely observed to work at least as many hours as adult males (Bledsoe 1994; Filmer and Pritchett 2002).

When poor households are further impoverished owing to the deterioration of the commons, the cost of having children increases even though the benefit increases too. D. Loughran and L. Pritchett in their work published in 1998, for example, found in Nepal that households believed that resource scarcity raised the net cost of children. Apparently, increasing firewood and water scarcity in the villages did not have a strong enough effect on the relative productivity of child labor to induce higher demand for children, given the effects that worked in the opposite direction. Degradation of the local commons acted as a check on population growth.

However, theoretical considerations suggest that in certain circumstances, increased resource scarcity (brought about, perhaps, by institutional deterioration) induces population growth. Households find themselves needing more "hands" when the local commons begin to be depleted. No doubt additional hands could be obtained if the adults worked even harder, but in many cultures customary roles do not permit men to gather fuelwood and fetch water for household use. No doubt, too, additional hands could be obtained if children at school were withdrawn and put to work, but in the poorest countries many children do not go to school anyway. When all other sources of additional labor become too costly, more children would be expected to be produced, thus further damaging the local commons and, in turn, providing the household with an incentive to enlarge yet more. Of course, this does not necessarily mean that the fertility rate will increase; if the infant mortality rate were to decline, there would be no need for more births in order for a household to acquire more hands. However, along this pathway poverty, household size, and degradation of the local commons could reinforce one another in an escalating spiral. By the time some countervailing set of factors diminished the benefits of having further children and stopped the spiral, many lives could have been damaged by worsening poverty.

Kevin Cleaver and Götz Schreiber, in a study published in 1994, have provided rough, aggregative evidence of a positive link between population increase and degradation of the local commons in the context of rural sub-Saharan Africa, and N. Heyser (1996) for Sarawak, Malaysia. In a statistical analysis of evidence from villages in South Africa, R. Aggarwal, S. Netanyahu, and C. Romano (2001) have found a positive link between fertility increase and environmental degradation; while D. Filmer and Pritchett (2002) have reported a weak positive link in the Sindh region in Pakistan. Such studies are suggestive of the ways reproductive behavior in poor countries is related to the performance of institutions that govern the local commons.

See also: *Externalities of Population Change; Hardin, Garrett; Natural Resources and Population; Water and Population.*

BIBLIOGRAPHY

Agarwal, Anil, and Sunita Narain. 1989. *Towards Green Villages: A Strategy for Environmentally Sound and Participatory Rural Development.* New Delhi: Centre for Science and Environment.

Agarwal, Bina. 1986. *Cold Hearths and Barren Slopes: The Woodfuel Crisis in the Third World.* New Delhi: Allied Publishers.

Aggarwal, R., S. Netanyahu, and C. Romano. 2001. "Access to Natural Resources and the Fertility Decision of Women: The Case of South Africa." *Environment and Development Economics* 6(2): 209–36.

Baland, Jean-Marie, and Jean-Philippe Platteau. 1996. *Halting Degradation of Natural Resources: Is There a Role for Rural Communities?* Oxford: Clarendon Press.

Béteille, André, ed. 1983. *Equality and Inequality: Theory and Practice.* Delhi: Oxford University Press.

Bledsoe, C. 1994. "'Children Are Like Young Bamboo Trees': Potentiality and Reproduction in Sub-Saharan Africa." In *Population, Economic Development and the Environment,* eds. K. Lindahl-Kiessling and H. Landberg. Oxford: Oxford University Press.

Cavendish, W. 2000. "Empirical Regularities in the Poverty-Environment Relationships of Rural Households: Evidence from Zimbabwe." *World Development* 28: 1979–2003.

Chopra, Kanchan, Gopal K. Kadekodi, and M. N. Murty. 1990. *Participatory Development: People and Common Property Resources.* New Delhi: Sage.

Cleaver, Kevin M., and Götz A. Schreiber. 1994. *Reversing the Spiral: The Population, Agriculture, and Environment Nexus in Sub-Saharan Africa.* Washington, D.C.: World Bank.

Dasgupta, Partha. 1999. "Social Capital and Economic Progress." In *Social Capital: A Multifacet-*

ed Perspective, ed. P. Dasgupta and I. Serageldin. Washington, D.C.: World Bank.

———. 2000. "Population and Resources: An Exploration of Reproductive and Environmental Externalities." *Population and Development Review* 26(4): 643–689.

Dasgupta, Partha, and G. M. Heal. 1979. *Economic Theory and Exhaustible Resources.* Cambridge: Cambridge University Press.

Dasgupta, P., and K.-G. Mäler. 1991. "The Environment and Emerging Development Issues." *Proceedings of the Annual World Bank Conference on Development Economics 1990* (Supplement to the *World Bank Economic Review*) 101–132.

Feeny, D., F. Berkes, B. J. McKay, and J. M. Acheson. 1990. "The Tragedy of the Commons: Twenty-two Years Later." *Human Ecology* 18(1): 1–19.

Filmer, D., and L. Pritchett. 2002. "Environmental Degradation and the Demand for Children: Searching for the Vicious Circle in Pakistan." *Environment and Development Economics* 7(1): 123–146.

Gordon, H. Scott. 1954. "The Economic Theory of Common-Property Resources." *Journal of Political Economy* 62: 124–142.

Hardin, G. 1968. "The Tragedy of the Commons." *Science* 162: 1,243–1,248.

Heyser, N. 1996. *Gender, Population and Environment in the Context of Deforestation: A Malaysian Case Study.* Geneva: United Nations Research Institute for Social Development.

Jodha, N. S. 1986. "Common Property Resources and the Rural Poor." *Economic and Political Weekly* 21: 1,169–1,181.

Lopez, R. 1998. "The Tragedy of the Commons in Côte d'Ivoire Agriculture: Empirical Evidence and Implications for Evaluating Trade Policies." *World Bank Economic Review* 12: 105–132.

Loughran, D., and L. Pritchett. 1998. "Environmental Scarcity, Resource Collection, and the Demand for Children in Nepal." Poverty, Environment and Growth Working Paper Series 19. Washington, D.C.: World Bank.

McKean, M. 1992. "Success on the Commons: A Comparative Examination of Institutions for Common Property Resource Management." *Journal of Theoretical Politics* 4: 256–268.

Murphy, Yolanda, and Robert Murphy. 1985. *Women of the Forest.* New York: Columbia University Press.

Nerlove, M. 1991. "Population and the Environment: A Parable of Firewood and Other Tales." *American Journal of Agricultural Economics* 75(1): 59–71.

Ostrom, Elinor. 1990. *Governing the Commons: The Evolution of Institutions for Collective Action.* Cambridge: Cambridge University Press.

———. 1996. "Incentives, Rules of the Game, and Development." *Proceedings of the Annual World Bank Conference on Development Economics, 1995* (Supplement to the *World Bank Economic Review* and the *World Bank Research Observer*).

———. 1999. "Social Capital: A Fad or a Fundamental Concept?" In *Social Capital: A Multifaceted Perspective*, ed. P. Dasgupta and I. Serageldin. Washington, D.C.: World Bank.

Ostrom, Elinor, and R. Gardner. 1993. "Coping with Asymmetries in the Commons: Self-Governing Irrigations Can Work." *Journal of Economic Perspectives* 7: 93–112.

Wade, Robert. 1988. *Village Republics: Economic Conditions for Collective Action in South India.* Cambridge: Cambridge University Press.

PARTHA DASGUPTA

COMMUNISM, POPULATION ASPECTS OF

Communist rule was the twentieth century's most dramatic, distinctive, and fateful political innovation. Armed with a utopian but atheist ideology and with powerful, far-reaching state apparatuses built to actualize their official ideals, Communist governments were expressly committed to upending existing earthly economic and political arrangements and constructing in their stead a socialized paradise—that is, "communism"—free from the injustice, alienation, and exploitation that humanity had heretofore suffered under "capitalism" and all other previous historical orders.

Communist governance was distinguished by the absolute and unchallenged primacy of a ruling

Marxist-Leninist party, state ownership of major national industries and other critical "means of production," and a command-style system of "central economic planning" through which political decisions (rather than market forces) allocated goods and services within the national economy. Communist power was initially established over the Russian Empire (renamed the Union of Soviet Socialist Republics [USSR], also known as the "Soviet Union") through the Bolshevik Revolution of 1917; over the following seven decades, war and revolution brought many more populations under Communist sway.

At its zenith—a decade or so before the 1989–1991 collapse of Eastern European socialism and of the Soviet Union—the reach of Communist-style governments stretched across Eurasia from Berlin and Prague to Vladivostok and Shanghai, and from the frozen Siberian tundra down to Indochina; additional Communist outposts could be found in the New World (Cuba) and in sub-Saharan Africa (Ethiopia). In 1980, the world's 17 established Marxist-Leninist states presided over roughly 1.5 billion persons (out of a total world population of approximately 4.4 billion). At that apogee, over a third of humanity lived under regimes that professed the "communist" intent. The encompassed populations represented a remarkable variety of cultures, ethnicities, levels of material attainment, and demographic structures.

Communist Ideology and Its Bearing on Population Policy

Despite their prolixity, the founding theoreticians of Communism offered little concrete guidance to their adherents regarding population affairs. The German political philosopher Karl Marx (1818–1883) railed against the English economist T. R. Malthus (1766–1834) and his demographic theories, calling him "a shameless sycophant of the ruling classes" (Marx 1953, p. 123). However, Marx was completely Delphic about the purported "special laws of population" that he foresaw for socialist and communist society. The German socialist Friedrich Engels (1820–1895) was only slightly more forthcoming. According to his vague assurance, "if . . . communist society finds itself obligated to regulate the production of human beings, just as it does the production of things, it will be precisely this society and this society alone which can carry this out without difficulty" (Engels 1881, p. 109). (Perhaps Marx's and Engels's most important contribution to demographic

discourse lay in popularizing the term *proletariat;* interestingly enough, their chosen designation for what they saw as history's destined "class" drew on the Latin word for the lowest rung of classical Rome's citizenry—those viewed as contributing to the state only through having children.)

V. I. Lenin (1870–1924), leader of the Bolshevik Revolution and draftsman of the Soviet state, had almost nothing to say about demographic questions in his small library of writings (apart from a passing observation that the weight of sheer human numbers could bear on the international class struggle). He did, however, famously pronounce that "we [Communists] recognize nothing private" (Schapiro 1972, p. 34)—and that declaration of principle, more than anything else, prefigured the Communist approach to population issues.

For in country after country, Communist regimes eager to reconstitute society through their own variants of "scientific socialism" avowed that there were no legitimate limits on their authority. Given the awesomely ambitious mandate it conferred upon itself, and the essentially unrestricted means it granted itself for accomplishing its own objectives, Communist rule naturally had far-reaching demographic repercussions—though these repercussions were often entirely inadvert and quite unanticipated by the states that set them in motion.

Mortality

"It is time to realize that of all the valuable capital the world possesses, the most valuable and most decisive is people," the Soviet ruler Joseph Stalin (1879–1953) once declared (Stalin 1945, p. 773). In the spirit of this dictum, Communist governments, after securing power, typically attempted to augment the welfare and productivity of the more disadvantaged classes from the old order through such measures as land redistribution, mass primary schooling and literacy campaigns, and expansion of medical access through an extensive system of state health workers (e.g., *feld'sher* in the Soviet Union, "barefoot doctors" in the People's Republic of China). Under these and allied interventions, local mortality levels usually declined—often at a rapid pace.

Within eight years of China's 1949 Communist victory, for example, reliable estimates suggest the country's life expectancy may have soared by as much as 20 years, while its infant mortality rate may have dropped by half or more. Dramatic progress against disease and mortality was likewise registered in many other, disparate regions under Communist rule. In the late 1950s and early 1960s, for example, estimated life expectancy at birth was 10 to 25 years higher in the Soviet Union's five Central Asian republics than in nearby Afghanistan, Pakistan, or India. In the 1970s, Cuba enjoyed one of the very lowest official infant mortality rates, and one of the very highest expectations of life at birth, of any Caribbean or Latin American country. Perhaps most interesting, independent estimates indicate that the Soviet Union's pace of postwar health progress was so robust that, by the early 1960s, life expectancy in the USSR was almost equal to that in the United States—and Soviet life expectancy was poised to surpass America's if trends continued just a few more years.

But any appreciation of Communism's genuine achievements in improving public health and lowering general mortality also requires an appreciation of the powerful, independent historical factors at play in these outcomes. In both the postwar Soviet Union and early postliberation China, for example, life expectancy was clearly buoyed by the restoration of civil order after prolonged and devastating periods of war and upheaval; mortality levels, in other words, almost certainly would have fallen during those very years, regardless of the particular health policies the governments implemented. Cuba, for its part, could indeed claim to be one of the healthiest Latin countries in the 1970s, but before the 1959 revolution, by the criteria of life expectancy and infant mortality, Cuba had been the *healthiest* country in the tropical Americas. In Eastern Europe, infant mortality rates did decline swiftly in the 1950s under new Communist regimes, but infant mortality rates had also been dropping rapidly beforehand, in the 1920s and 1930s, under the region's previous and now officially reviled ancien régimes. In the Korean peninsula, partitioned after World War II between a Communist North and non-Communist South, something approaching a controlled experiment on the independent contribution to health progress of Communist policies had accidentally been framed; demographic reconstructions suggest the level and pace of improvement in life expectancy in the two Koreas over the quarter century following the 1953 Korean War armistice were virtually identical.

Under the best of circumstances, Communist claims to a superior systemic competence in ministering to the health of the masses were thus some-

what debatable. And the best of circumstances did not always obtain, because under Communist rulers, the radical reconstitution of "feudal" or "capitalist" society very often involved the embrace of ruthless measures that doomed their citizens to death en masse. A precise tally of the human cost of these deadly interventions will probably never be possible, but demographic reconstructions and historical records provide approximate magnitudes.

The collectivization of agriculture in the Soviet Union in 1932–1933 (which resulted in estimated excess mortality of perhaps 4 million in the Ukraine and an additional 2 million elsewhere in the USSR) was but one of numerous deliberate Communist economic campaigns that resulted in massive loss of life for Communist citizens. Virtually every Communist state in Asia suffered famine when its rulers collectivized agriculture. In the case of China, the death toll in the wake of the 1958–1959 "Great Leap Forward" is estimated to be in the range of 30 million. (North Korea's famine, which struck in the mid-1990s, was caused by catastrophic economic mismanagement rather than collectivization. Tentative estimates of its toll range between 600,000 and 1 million or more.) Ethiopia's 1984–1985 food disaster, which may have killed 700,000 people, should also be included in the tally of Communist famines. It can be safely stated that if someone died of famine in the course of the twentieth century, that person probably lived under a Communist government.

State-made famine was not the only form of mortality crisis visited upon the populations of Communist states. State-sponsored violence was also pervasive in Communist regimes and was often meted out to the disfavored and suspect strata of the new society with particular enthusiasm. Under Stalin's absolute rule (1929–1953), millions of Soviet citizens were executed during successive terror campaigns or perished as prisoners under the murderous conditions of the "Chief Administration of Corrective Labor Camps" (better known as the Gulag). In Yugoslavia, Marshal Tito's regime may have killed as many as a million of its ostensible citizens in the 1940s—as many as half a million of them after World War II was over. In China, at least several million landlords and other "bad elements" were slaughtered during the land reform of the early 1950s. Many sources guess that a million or more victims were later claimed by Red Guard terror during Mao Zedong's "Cultural Revolution" that commenced in 1966, with some respectable guesses placing the death toll from the Cultural Revolution as high as 7 million. In Cambodia, the Khmer Rouge's 1975–1979 reign may have consigned a fifth or even more of the country's 7 million people to death by starvation or execution. In theory human beings may indeed be the most valuable capital in the world, as Stalin averred, but in practice under Communist governments many human lives were evidently assigned an official value of zero.

A final noteworthy characteristic of Communist mortality patterns were the long-term increases in death rates that beset the Soviet Bloc in the decades immediately preceding the collapse of the Soviet Union. After rapid and pronounced general mortality declines in the 1950s and early 1960s, age-specific mortality rates for various Soviet age groups began to rise: first middle-aged men, then almost all adult male age groups, then many adult female age groups. In the early 1970s, the official Soviet infant mortality rate recorded significant increases—after which point Moscow forbade release of this bell-weather statistic, and increasingly restricted publication of other mortality data. When Soviet leader Mikhail Gorbachev's glasnost campaign in the late 1980s unveiled, among other things, the previously suppressed mortality figures, it became apparent that Soviet male life expectancy was actually lower, and Soviet female life expectancy only barely higher, than they had been in the early 1960s—an extraordinary outcome for a literate, urbanized, and industrial society during peacetime.

Anomalous though it may have been, the Soviet Union's mortality experience was not unique. By the late 1980s prolonged stagnation or even retrogression in health and mortality levels were being reported in every other Warsaw Pact state in Eastern Europe—and in Communist Yugoslavia as well. (In the decade following the collapse of the Soviet Union, life expectancy in the Soviet Union's former Eastern European satellite states seemed to return to the familiar industrial-society pattern of steady, secular improvements; in every one of the 15 former Soviet republics, however, overall life expectancy was estimated by the U.S. Bureau of the Census to have been lower in 2001 than it was in 1991, the final year of Soviet rule.)

Fertility

Fertility levels under Communism spanned a wide range. At one extreme were populations with ex-

traordinarily high fertility rates, such as Mongolia in the late 1960s and early 1970s, with an estimated total fertility rate of 7.3; at the other extreme were societies where sub-replacement fertility prevailed, such as Hungary from the late 1950s onward. At particular times in given countries, Communist governments have attempted to elicit increases, or alternatively decreases, in national fertility levels, and at still other junctures or in other locales have indicated no particular preference for the course that fertility trends and childbearing patterns should take.

Among the instruments that Communist governments used in pronatal policy (especially in postwar Eastern Europe, with its relatively low levels of fertility) were child bonuses and allowances, increased maternity benefits, and preferential housing allocations. As best as can be determined, however, these incentives provided only a modest stimulus to childbearing, a result quite in keeping with the limited success of pronatal policies attempted in non-Communist countries. On the other hand, Communist governments typically relaxed restrictions on divorce, liberalized access to abortion, and encouraged the use of birth control and family planning techniques. All of these policies might be expected to constrain or perhaps reduce fertility levels to some degree, although again, the demographic impact of such essentially "voluntary" policies was probably modest in most cases.

The swiftest and surest means of altering a population's fertility levels, of course, is *involuntary* family planning. In principle, Communist governments had no objections to such measures, and when specific Communist regimes chose to engineer major and rapid changes in local childbearing patterns, they grasped for precisely these sorts of options.

In Communist Romania, the government of Nicolae Ceausescu limited parental volition over childbearing in an attempt to raise the birth rate. In late 1966, abortion, which had been the primary means of national birth control, was suddenly and unexpectedly proscribed. The following year, Romania's birth rate nearly doubled, though only temporarily; infant and maternal mortality also surged as a result of the surprise decree.

Elsewhere—most notoriously, in China—Communist rulers used coercion to press the birth rate down. In 1979, after a decade of strong antinatal pressure that saw fertility nearly halved, Beijing unveiled the so-called One Child Policy, under which parents had to receive the permission of the state before bringing a pregnancy to term, facing legal, financial, and physical punishments if they failed to comply. Under the One Child Policy, China's fertility level is believed to have fallen below the replacement level (a by-product of the policy was increased underreporting of births)—a result pleasing to China's birth planners, but one purchased through widespread human rights abuses, including involuntary abortions and delivery-room destruction of unapproved newborns. In effect for over two decades (although enforced with varying severity), the One Child Policy received a formal legal basis, as well as reaffirmation, with the adoption of a national law on population and birth planning in December 2001.

Migration

Communist governance came to some societies, such as the German Democratic Republic (East Germany), that were already largely urbanized and industrialized, and to others—Cambodia, Ethiopia, and Mongolia among them—in which urban and industrial transitions had barely begun. Because Communist regimes favored forced-pace modernization—and evidenced a particular fondness for the augmentation of heavy industry—their economic plans correspondingly sought to engineer the movement of people from country to city and from farm to factory. In a very real sense, massive internal migration was indispensable for the success of the Communist planned economy.

What was most distinctive about migration patterns under Communist governance, however, was not the scope of planned migration per se, but rather the scale of *involuntary* migration. In every new Communist regime, a network of political prison camps was established for the newly designated "enemies of the people." Archival documents suggest that in 1953, the year of Stalin's death, the Soviet Gulag and its annexes may have contained over 5 million of the Soviet Union's 190 million people; China's *laogai* likewise processed many millions of political convicts. In Vietnam and elsewhere, distrusted elements of the population were detained for indefinite durations in "reeducation camps." Unlike other Marxist-Leninist governments, the Khmer Rouge in Cambodia forcibly de-urbanized the nation (Cambodia's cities had been temporarily swollen by a wartime exodus from the countryside) and relocated the country's population into a system of makeshift communes and prison camps.

Communist governance also generated large streams of refugees—escapees fleeing from the new order or driven out by some particular policy or practice promoted by the regime. In the wake of the Russian Revolution, for example, out-migration from the Soviet Union is thought to have totaled about 2 million; roughly 2 million Chinese likewise relocated from Mainland China to the island of Taiwan with the Communist victory over the Nationalists in 1949. Between 1945 and 1950, approximately 12 million ethnic Germans (known as *die Vertriebene*, or "the expellees") relocated to West Germany and Austria from regions to the east that had fallen under Communist power. Between 1949 and 1961—when the East German government built the Berlin Wall to stanch its demographic hemorrhage—over 3.5 million citizens of the German Democratic Republic, nearly a fifth of its original population, walked over to West Germany. A roughly similar fraction of the local population fled from North Korea to South Korea after the peninsula's 1945 partition and before the 1953 Korean War ceasefire. It is thought that in the late 1970s about 2 million of Ethiopia's 33 million people fled the incoming *Dergue* (the revolutionary junta that took power in 1974), and that in the decade after Saigon's surrender to Hanoi in 1975, a million or more South Vietnamese left their newly Communized homeland, many as desperate "boat people." And over a million Cubans have emigrated or fled from Cuba since Fidel Castro's seizure of power—a figure that compares with a total Cuban population of about 7 million at the time of the 1959 revolution. Apart from annexation of nearby territories, not a single Marxist-Leninist state experienced any appreciable inmigration of outsiders during its tenure in power.

Population Structure

Given the great variety of mortality schedules and childbearing patterns observed under Communist governments in the twentieth century, it follows that there was no "typical" population structure for a Communist society. But the population structures of Communist societies did nevertheless tend to bear one distinguishing feature: an unusual degree of irregularity. Due in large part to demographic perturbations caused or encouraged by the leadership—many of these perturbations having already been noted above—the age-sex pyramids of Communist countries were typically disfigured by unexpected deficits in particular birth cohorts or by peculiar and biologically aberrant imbalances in the sex ratio. Russia and China offer contrasting examples of the latter phenomenon.

In the Soviet Union's January 1989 census, the sex ratio in the Russian Soviet Federated Socialist Republic (predecessor to the Russian Federation) was just over 88 males per 100 females. That compared with the U.S. sex ratio of about 97. Although part of the difference can, of course, be attributed to Russia's catastrophic losses in World War II, not all of the difference can be so explained: Poland also suffered grievously in World War II, but its 1990 sex ratio was about 95. The Russian Republic's deficit of men spoke not only to World War II (and Stalin's rule) but also to extreme excess male mortality during the peacetime years of the 1960s, 1970s, and 1980s.

In China, on the other hand, the November 2000 census reported a countrywide sex ratio of nearly 107—almost 10 percentage points higher than that of the contemporary United States. Historically, China's population, like that of some other Asian societies, has been marked by a curious deficit of "missing females," due to unusually high differential mortality. Yet in large measure, the current discrepancy is due to an "excess" of males— especially younger males. According to official Chinese reports, China's sex ratio at birth in 2000 was nearly 117; this figure compares with a ratio of 104 to 107 in most other historical human populations. This biologically extraordinary disproportion was an unexpected by-product of the One Child Policy—or more specifically, the conjuncture of extreme pressure for small families, a continuing cultural preference for sons, and the availability of sex-selective abortion. As a result of China's past and continuing population plans, China's future leaders will have to cope with an enormous army of unmarriageable young men.

See also: *Famine in China; Famine in the Soviet Union; Forced Migration; Marx, Karl; Mortality Reversals; One-Child Policy; Optimum Population; Population Policy.*

BIBLIOGRAPHY

Ashton, Basil, Kenneth Hill, Alan Piazza, and Robin Zeitz. 1984. "Famine in China, 1958–61." *Population and Development Review* 10: 613–645.

Banister, Judith. 1987. *China's Changing Population.* Palo Alto, CA: Stanford University Press.

Courtois, Stéphane, Nicolas Werth, Jean-Louis Panne, Andrzej Paczkowski, Karel Bartosek, and Jean-Louis Margolin. 1999. *The Black Book of Communism: Crimes, Terror, Repression.* Cambridge, MA: Harvard University Press.

Eberstadt, Nicholas. 1988. *The Poverty of Communism.* New Brunswick, NJ: Transaction Publishers.

———. 2000. *Prosperous Paupers and Other Population Problems.* New Brunswick, NJ: Transaction Publishers.

Engels, Friedrich. 1953 (1881). "Letter to Kautsky, February 1, 1881," In *Marx and Engels on Malthus,* ed. Ronald L. Meek. New York: International Publishers.

Goodkind, Daniel M., and Loraine A. West. 2001. "The North Korean Famine and Its Demographic Impact." *Population and Development Review* 27: 219–238.

Heuveline, Patrick. 1998. "'Between One and Three Million': Towards the Demographic Reconstruction of a Decade of Cambodian History (1970–79)." *Population Studies* 52(1): 49–65.

Lutz, Wolfgang, Sergei Scherbov, and Andrei Volkov, eds. 1994. *Demographic Trends and Patterns in the Soviet Union before 1991.* New York: Routledge.

Marx, Karl. 1954 (1863). *Theories of Surplus Value,* Vol. II. In *Marx and Engels on Malthus,* ed. Ronald L. Meek. New York: International Publishers.

Meek, Ronald L., ed. 1954. *Marx and Engels on Malthus: Selections from the Writings of Marx and Engels Dealing with the Theories of Thomas Robert Malthus.* New York: International Publishers.

Nydon, Judith A. 1984. "Public Policy and Private Fertility Behavior: The Case of Pronatalist Policy in Socialist Romania." Ph.D. diss., University of Massachusetts.

Petersen, William. 1975. *Population.* New York: Macmillan.

Rummel, R. J. 1998. *Statistics of Democide: Genocide and Mass Murder since 1900.* New Brunswick, NJ: Transaction Publishers.

Schapiro, Leonard B., ed. 1972. *Totalitarianism.* New York: Praeger.

Stalin, J. V. 1945. *Problems of Leninism.* Moscow: Foreign Languages Publishing House.

NICHOLAS EBERSTADT

CONDORCET, MARQUIS DE

(1743–1794)

Marie Jean Antoine Nicolas de Caritat, marquis de Condorcet, was a mathematician, politician, educational reformer, and utopian philosopher in the period leading up to and during the French Revolution. His works in mathematics include a recasting of the mathematical portion of Denis Diderot's *Encyclopédie* in a supplement, *Encyclopédie méthodique* (1784–1785). In the most memorable of his mathematical books, *Essai sur l'application de l'analyse à la probabilité des décisions rendues à la pluralité des voix méthodique* (1785), he argued that in moral sciences the mathematical base of all analysis has to be probability.

While thousands were being conscripted and there were food riots in Paris, Condorcet wrote pamphlets on public education, the rights of women, and other hotly debated issues of the time. In his view inequality in learning fostered tyranny, and it was education that had engendered the Enlightenment. He was a member of the governing group of the Girondins, a party, as Thomas Carlyle put it, of "the respectable washed Middle Classes." A Girondin constitution that Condorcet wrote was rejected in favor of the Jacobin alternative.

In October 1793 the Committee of Public Safety under Maximilien Robespierre (1758–1794) executed the Girondin leaders; Condorcet was tried in absentia and sentenced to death. While in hiding, with revolutionary soldiers and loaded tumbrels passing under his window, he wrote his most famous work, *Esquisse d'un tableau historique des progrès de l'esprit humain,* a history of human progress from its outset to its imminent culmination in human perfection. Soon the human race would attain universal truth, virtue, and happiness. All inequalities of wealth, education, opportunity, and sex would disappear. The earth would provide sustenance without limit, and all diseases would be conquered. "Man will not become immortal," he stated, but "we do not know what the limit is [or even] whether the general laws of nature have determined such a limit."

This book, published posthumously in 1795, is remembered largely because along with the works of William Godwin, it was a target of Thomas Robert Malthus's *Essay on the Principle of Population* (1798). The *Equisse* was, in Malthus's words, "a singular instance of the attachment of a man to principles, which every day's experience was so fatally for himself contradicting." In particular, Malthus objected to Condorcet's belief that the shortage of subsistence brought about by population growth would be automatically canceled. In Malthus's mature theory he also offered a similarly optimistic future, but he believed that the lower classes would adopt the small family typical of the middle class, thus elimination any population crisis.

Condorcet was arrested, reportedly because although he was disguised as a commoner, he ordered an omelet with "an aristocratic number of eggs," and died in prison, possibly by suicide.

See also: *Malthus, Thomas Robert; Population Thought, History of.*

BIBLIOGRAPHY

SELECTED WORKS BY CONDORCET.

Condorcet, Marie Jean Antoine Nicolas de Caritat, marquis de. 1767–1789/1994. *Arithmétique politique: textes rares ou inédits.* Paris: Institut National d'études démographiques and Presses Universitaires de France.

————. 1795. *Esquisse d'un tableau historique des progrès de l'esprit humain.* [Paris: Agasse]. Paris: Dubuisson et Cie., 1864. Translated as *Sketch for a Historical Picture of the Progress of the Human Mind.* Westport, CT: Hyperion Press, 1955.

————. 1846–1849. *Oeuvres,* 12 vols., ed. A. Condorcet O'Connor and M. F. Arago. Paris: Firmin-Didot.

————. 1976. *Condorcet: Selected Writings,* ed. Keith Michael Baker. Indianapolis: Bobbs-Merrill Co.

SELECTED WORKS ABOUT CONDORCET.

Baczko, Bronislaw, ed. 1982. *Une èducation pour la démocratie: Textes et projets de l'époque révolutionnaire.* Paris: Èditions Garnier Fréres.

Dumazedier, Joffre, ed. 1994. *La Leçon de Condorcet: Une conception oubliée pour tous nécessaire à une république.* Paris: Éditions l'Harmattan.

Frazer, James George. 1933. *Condorcet on the Progress of the Human Mind.* Oxford: Clarendon Press.

Goodell, Edward. 1994. *The Noble Philosopher: Condorcet and the Enlightenment.* Buffalo, NY: Prometheus.

Palmer, R. R. 1985. *The Improvement of Humanity: Education and the French Revolution.* Princeton, NJ: Princeton University Press.

Rothschild, Emma. 2001. *Economic Sentiments: Adam Smith, Condorcet, and the Enlightenment.* Cambridge, MA: Harvard University Press.

Schapiro, J. Salwyn. 1978. *Condorcet and the Rise of Liberalism.* New York: Octagon.

WILLIAM PETERSEN

CONFERENCES, INTERNATIONAL POPULATION

International conferences have a long history in the affairs of nations, but it was not until a quarter-century after the birth of the United Nations that international conferences began to assume a central role in formulating social policies on a global scale. Since the environmental conference held in Stockholm in 1972, a meeting regarded as highly successful, thematic conferences have become an established mechanism to guide the United Nations and member states in addressing a diverse array of social problems. Participation in these conferences, initially confined to government representatives and technical experts, has increasingly become more open to a broad spectrum of nongovernmental organizations (NGOs).

The Early Years

In the period between World Wars I and II, participants at numerous scientific meetings discussed the perceived dangers inherent in the uneven distribution of world population, and canvassed the possible role for organized migration as a safety valve. The World Population Conference held in Geneva in 1927, though not a League of Nations (predecessor to the United Nations) meeting, was pivotal in moving the League toward engaging with population questions. The conference was organized by Margaret Sanger, who recognized that scientific attention and the mantle of the League of Nations could legitimize "overpopulation" as a subject for discussion in international forums. Sanger invited eminent scientists, but found that their acceptance was conditional on there being no propagandizing for Malthusian ideas or birth control; indeed, she was led to remove her name from the official documentation.

The League was officially unable to accept Sanger's invitation to be represented as an institution, but interested staff were permitted to attend in their personal capacities and the International Labour Office displayed keen interest. An outcome of the meeting was the creation of the International Union for the Scientific Investigation of Population Problems (IUSIPP), a non-governmental organization comprised mainly of demographers and others with a strong interest in population issues. IUSIPP convened three meetings in Europe prior to the outbreak of World War II, meetings marred by Franco-German rivalry and the efforts of Nazi Germany to legitimize its anti-Semitism and demands for lebensraum.

The Scientific Conferences

Birth control remained a sensitive topic in the early years of the United Nations, although there was some support from influential actors and agencies within the U.N. system to move the issue cautiously forward. The United Nations Population Commission sponsored two world population conferences—in Rome in 1954 and Belgrade in 1965—devoted to scientific and technical subjects and structured around research on demographic trends and methods. They were jointly convened with the International Union for the Scientific Study of Population (IUSSP, the successor to IUSIPP) and interested U.N. Specialized Agencies. The conference participants were invited as individual experts rather than as representatives of governments, and the meetings were not authorized to approve resolutions or make recommendations to governments. Nevertheless, while focusing on research aspects of population issues, the meetings allowed some discussion of family planning programs to take place without arousing controversy.

The Inter-Governmental Conferences

The United Nations, with strong support from the United States as well as from some western European and Asian nations, convened the first of three decennial intergovernmental population conferences at Bucharest in 1974. In this conference, and in its successors in Mexico City (1984) and Cairo (1994), representatives of governments replaced the individual experts of earlier years, a change appropriate for discussion of population policy. The context had changed markedly between 1965 and 1974. A number of countries were now feeling the pressures of rapid population growth, and several Asian countries had long since implemented family planning programs. As early as 1961, the UN Economic Commission for Asia and the Far East (ECAFE, later ESCAP) had convened an intergovernmental meeting in New Delhi that had productively discussed population policy. And in 1969, the United Nations Population Fund (UNFPA) had been established with the expectation that it would encourage the United Nations and its agencies to become more active in confronting problems of rapid population growth. Significantly, initial support for the creation of UNFPA came from a voluntary contribution from the United States.

The Bucharest and Mexico City conferences provided the occasion for governments to advance their own political and ideological agendas, often at variance from the organizers' plans and expectations. At Bucharest, a large group of Third World states presented a quasi-Marxist analysis: they argued that population problems were really symptoms of imbalances in the world economic system, and strenuously urged the establishment of a more equitable New International Economic Order responsive to the needs of developing nations. They were also distrustful of the Draft Plan of Action that was submitted for the conference's approval as undermining national sovereignty by laying down a global policy to which all countries would be expected to adhere.

Ten years later at Mexico City, the United States government unexpectedly departed from its earlier stance by rejecting the premise that rapid population growth hindered development. In the midst of President Ronald Reagan's campaign for reelection, in what was widely interpreted as a move to solidify the support of the Republican right wing, the head of the American delegation at Mexico City declared that "population growth is, in itself, a neutral phenomenon" and advocated the adoption of market economies as the answer to rapid population growth (United States 1984). Less government interference in the economy, according to this line of reasoning, would foster economic growth and thereby lower fertility. Additionally, in what turned out to be the most contentious part of the Reagan administration's statement at the Conference, the United States articulated its Mexico City Policy—to withhold U.S. government funds from organizations that performed or promoted abortion in foreign countries using money from non-U.S. sources, extending the prohibition on using U.S. funds for abortion that was already in effect.

Despite the political and ideological differences aired on the floor, both the Bucharest and Mexico City conferences concluded by approving, by a near-consensus, documents that were supportive of family planning programs. Characteristic of recommendations emanating from UN conferences, these action programs failed to elicit a greater commitment to broad population policies, and donor contributions ceased to grow in real terms.

Responding to a general dissatisfaction with developing-country governance, the United Nations and its more influential member states sought to engage more fully with non-government organizations as providers of services and watchdogs of government programs. This was a role that NGOs themselves increasingly were demanding, and for which they were already organizing.

Consistent with this perspective, the secretariat for the International Conference on Population and Development (ICPD)—held in Cairo in September 1994—accredited a total of 1,254 NGOs, the largest number being American. Building on the experience of other UN conferences, especially the Conference on the Human Environment in Rio de Janeiro in 1992, the Cairo secretariat gave NGOs unprecedented access to the conference preparations and proceedings. Already highly organized and supported by several western governments and foundations, the NGOs redefined "population policy," shunning demographic objectives and replacing them with a very broad agenda of women's issues, including women's reproductive and sexual health, gender equality, and women's rights and empowerment. For the first time, the Cairo Programme of Action also included chapters on funding, follow-up activities, and the monitoring of implementation—and allowed for the continued involvement of NGOs. Once the conference was over, the Women's Caucus (organized by NGOs prior to the ICPD) pursued a strategy aimed at ensuring that the Cairo agenda would be endorsed by subsequent UN conferences—notably the Social Summit, the Conference on Human Rights, and the Beijing Conference on Women.

A Retrospective View

With hindsight, the most significant effect of the Cairo conference was the renewed vigor it brought to a somewhat weary field in need of new allies and supporters. While the conference reinvigorated population policy and engendered a high degree of support, especially among women's health groups and feminists, the new dynamism came at a certain cost. At Bucharest and Mexico City, both the ability of individual women to regulate their own fertility and the needs of society to limit population growth were central to the discourse and disagreements. The Cairo process, by contrast, was less concerned with the problems associated with population size and growth. In their place, the Cairo Programme of Action recommended a wide range of reproductive and sexual health services, as well as education, primarily for women and girls. Thus, the turn of the twenty-first century saw two of the great social revolutions of modernity—birth control and women's emancipation—part ways in important respects. It is likely that future international population conferences will recognize these differences and may, of necessity, attempt to bridge them.

See also: *Population Organizations: United Nations System; Population Policy; Population Thought, Contemporary; Sanger, Margaret.*

BIBLIOGRAPHY

Finkle, Jason L., and Barbara B. Crane. 1975. "The Politics of Bucharest: Population, Development and the New International Economic Order." *Population and Development Review* 1(1): 87–114.

———. 1985. "Ideology and Politics at Mexico City: The United States at the 1984 International Conference on Population." *Population and Development Review* 11(1): 1–28.

McIntosh, C. Alison, and Jason L. Finkle. 1995. "The Cairo Conference on Population and Development: A New Paradigm?" *Population and Development Review* 21(2): 223–260.

Notestein, Frank W. 1954. "World Population Conference, Rome, August 31–September 10." *Population Index* 20(4): 241–249.

Singh, Jyoti Shankar. 1998. *Creating a New Consensus on Population.* London: Earthscan Publications.

Symonds, Richard, and Michael Carder. 1973. *The United Nations and the Population Question, 1945–1970.* New York: McGraw Hill.

United Nations. 1995. *Report of the International Conference on Population and Development: Cairo, 5–13 September 1994.* New York: United Nations.

United States. 1984. "Policy Statement of the United States of America at the International Conference on Population." In *Population and Development Review* 10(3): 574–579.

C. ALISON MCINTOSH
JASON L. FINKLE

CONTRACEPTION, MODERN METHODS OF

Human reproduction is regulated by a synchronized series of events that result in the production of mature sperm and eggs and the preparation of the woman's reproductive tract to establish and maintain a pregnancy. With a growing understanding of the links in the chain of reproductive events, opportunities to advance contraceptive technology have also increased.

Throughout human history, most societies and cultures have understood that sexual intercourse introduces the male factor responsible for fertilization. Consequently, for centuries people attempted to prevent pregnancy by the simple and direct procedure of withdrawing the penis prior to ejaculation. This practice, termed withdrawal or *coitus interruptus,* has a slang name in virtually every language. In relatively recent times, mechanical barriers or chemicals introduced into the vagina in various formulations have been employed to thwart the sperm. Sperm have been confronted with vulcanized roadblocks or been plunged into creams, ointments, gels, foams, or effervescent fluids containing mercurial compounds, weak acids, soaps, or biological detergents. Strange concoctions used or recommended have ranged from crocodile dung in antiquity to Coca Cola in the twentieth century. Post-coital douching also became popular early in history.

Contraceptive technology finally caught up with modernity when hormones were discovered and scientists turned their attention to the woman's ovulatory cycle. The principle of periodic abstinence timed to avoid coitus near the day of ovulation was the first method of fertility regulation that relied on this new knowledge. This contraceptive method was developed in the 1920 when, independently, two scientists, a Japanese, Kyusaka Ogino, and an Austrian, Herman Knaus, in 1925 recognized that a woman should avoid sex around the middle of a menstrual month if she did not intend to become pregnant.

The Ogino-Knaus method was based on emerging understanding about the endocrinology of the ovarian cycle in women, establishing that ovulation occurs about fourteen days before the first day of the next expected menstrual flow. These pioneer endocrinologists understood when the egg would be released although they did not know how long it remained fertilizable, or how long sperm survive in the fallopian tube. Scientists now estimate that the egg remains viable for one day after its release from the ovary and that the sperm retains its viability in the female tract for six or seven days.

Hormonal Contraceptives for Women

It was several decades before the necessary knowledge was marshaled to develop effective means to prevent ovulation medically and launch the era of hormonal contraception.

The pill. Gregory Pincus, Director of the Worcester Foundation for Experimental Biology in Massachusetts, led the scientific effort that resulted in the first oral contraceptive, recognized around the world simply as *the pill.* Before the pill, twentieth

century couples had a limited choice of contraceptive methods, largely ineffective unless used with great diligence. A 1935 survey revealed that contraceptive use in the United States was evenly divided among the condom, douche, rhythm, and withdrawal. Failure rates must have been high, forcing many women to choose between high fertility or illegal and unsafe abortions. Since 1960, when the U.S. Food and Drug Administration (FDA) first approved the pill, more than 130 million women have used the method, avoiding multitudes of unwanted pregnancies and abortions.

Oral contraceptives suppress ovulation using a combination of estrogen and progestin. By 2000, over 50 products with different progestins, lower doses, and various schedules of administration had supplanted the original pill. Some products offer a change in dose over the month, attempting to mimic the hormonal levels of the ovarian cycle. The main modification has been a significant lowering of the amounts of both hormones delivered. Modern oral contraceptives contain less than one-twentieth of the dose of the original pill, which results in a lower incidence of side effects.

The pill has been the subject of greater post-marketing surveillance for safety than any other pharmaceutical product. A study published in 1999 reported on 25 years of follow-up of over 45,000 women. Countless other studies have documented not only the safety but also the non-contraceptive health benefits of oral contraceptives: decreased risk of endometrial and ovarian cancer; decreased risk of colon cancer; decreased anemia; decreased dysmenorrhea; and maintenance of bone density. Oral contraception use also reduces the incidence of benign breast disease (cysts) and does not increase the overall risk of breast cancer, but there are uncertainties regarding long-term use for those who start using the method when they are teenagers. If there is an added health risk, it appears to be small and may be offset by careful surveillance.

Since it was first introduced, the pill has been marketed as a three-week-on and one-week-off method, thus creating a monthly pseudo-menstruation. Over the years, some doctors have counseled women to take the pill continuously to avoid menstruation, both for convenience and for medical reasons. Seasonale®, the first product designed for longer uninterrupted use (for three months at a time) was undergoing final testing for FDA approval in 2003.

Beyond the pill, hormonal contraception has evolved to include the continuous use of a progestin alone by oral administration (the minipill), by injection, or by sub-dermal implants. New delivery systems for estrogen/progestin contraception have created a birth control skin patch and a vaginal ring contraceptive.

Contraceptive injections. Elsimar Coutinho, a Brazilian gynecologist, was the first to demonstrate that injections of 150 mg of the synthetic progestin medroxyprogesterone acetate (Depo-Provera®) can inhibit ovulation for three-month durations. After several decades of use for other gynecological purposes, Depo-Provera® was approved as a contraceptive in the United States in 1993. It offers a high level of effectiveness in preventing pregnancy (99.7%) and the ability to suppress menstruation. An injection every three months replaces the need to remember to take a pill every day. By not having a monthly period, women can avoid monthly cramps, and reduce their risk for endometriosis and uterine fibroids. Although it is as effective as surgical sterilization, the method is reversible; women who wish to become pregnant after stopping the drug usually do so within a year. Because it has no estrogen, this method does not maintain normal bone density, hence it could lead to the development of osteoporosis. An alternative system that addresses this problem combines Depo-Provera® with ethinylestradiol, the estrogen found in many oral contraceptives, taken as a monthly injection. With this system, a woman has a monthly menstruation, and maintains bone density.

Contraceptive implant. Another drug delivery system that provides a continuous dose of progestin is the sub-dermal implant. The first contraceptive implant was NORPLANT®, developed by scientists at the Population Council in New York. It consists of six flexible tubes of Silastic® containing the progestin levonorgestrel. The contraceptive steroid is released at a slow and relatively constant rate for 5 years. This long-acting characteristic is the main advantage of this and other implant systems. In the case of NORPLANT®, one visit to a clinic for the simple insertion procedure replaces taking a pill daily for five years. Ovulation-suppression is the main mechanism of action. During the first two years of use 80 percent to 90 percent of cycles are clearly anovulatory (no eggs are released). By the fifth year about 50 percent of cycles are ovulatory. The high level of contraceptive protection (99.8%)

covering the entire five-year span depends on an additional mechanism of action: the prevention of sperm from ascending into the female reproductive tract, so that fertilization cannot occur. This is achieved through an effect on the woman's cervical mucus. In a normal cycle, the mucus becomes less viscous and more abundant at about mid-cycle, facilitating sperm transport when ovulation is about to occur. In Norplant® users, the mucus remains scanty, thick, and impenetrable to sperm.

Other implant systems have been developed that last for one year or three years, and have the advantage of reducing the number of implants, thus simplifying the insertion and removal procedure. The first single implant method, a three-year system, is IMPLANON®, which contains the progestin etonorgestrel, a so-called third-generation progestin. Another three-year system, JADELLE®, contains the contraceptive hormone levonorgestrel. By 2002, JADELLE® had received FDA approval; IMPLANON® is used in many European countries.

Vaginal ring contraceptive. NuvaRing® is the first monthly vaginal ring for contraception. A woman using the vaginal ring inserts and removes it herself so that it is not a clinic-dependent method. This novel contraceptive was approved for marketing in the United States in 2001. It is based on the combined release of a low dose of progestin and estrogen over a 21-day period of use. The steady flow of hormones (etonorgestrel and ethinyl estradiol) prevents ovulation as its main mechanism of action. Women begin using NuvaRing® around the fifth day of their menstrual period, and leave it in place for three weeks. The ring is removed for a week so that a menstrual flow can occur, and a new ring in placed in the vagina for the next cycle. Since it is not a barrier method, the exact positioning of the ring is not important for its effectiveness (about 99%).

Birth control patch. The ORTHO EVRA™ birth control patch was approved by the FDA in 2001. This transdermal system delivers the combination of a progestin and estrogen (norelgestromin/ethinyl estradiol) in a one-time weekly dose. The system is 99 percent effective. The thin, beige patch delivers continuous levels of the two hormones through the skin into the bloodstream. A new patch is used weekly for three consecutive weeks. The fourth week is patch-free so that a menstrual-like bleeding can occur. Like other hormonal contraceptives, the primary mechanism of action is ovulation suppression. Other contraceptive patches are being developed. One of these employs a transparent material to make the patch less evident, particularly for women with darker skin.

Progestin-releasing intrauterine system. Late in 2000, the FDA approved a levonorgestrel-releasing intrauterine system that had been available in Europe for 10 years. Developed by Population Council scientists, MIRENA® is a long-acting contraceptive that lasts for five years, and is more than 99 percent effective. In addition to its ease of use for women, it has the advantage that menstrual periods tend to become shorter and lighter. Some women experience an absence of menstrual bleeding after one year. Studies suggest several mechanisms that prevent pregnancy: thickening of cervical mucus, which prevents the passage of sperm, inhibition of sperm motility, and suppression of endometrial growth. Approximately eight out of every ten women who want to become pregnant will establish a pregnancy in the first year after MIRENA® is removed. Insertion and removal of MIRENA® is a short procedure done by a trained health care professional.

Emergency Contraception

Post-coital contraception that could prevent a pregnancy from becoming established has been possible for several decades. During the 1960s, orally active estrogenic products were shown to initiate menstrual-like bleeding when taken within a few days of unprotected intercourse. Bleeding and sloughing of the uterine lining means that pregnancy cannot take place even if a fertilized egg is present. In the 1960s, the product used most frequently to cause this was diethylstilbestrol (DES). Subsequently, it was demonstrated that a high dose of the conventional pill, a combination of estrogen and progestin, when taken up to 72 hours after intercourse can prevent pregnancy from becoming established. Now referred to as "emergency contraception," several products have been sold in European countries for many years and two were introduced in the United States in 1999. Prevens® consists of four high-dose oral contraceptive pills all to be taken within 48 hours. A second product, marketed initially in Hungary, is a progestin-only product that causes far fewer of the transient side effects of the combination pill. It is distributed in the United States under the name Plan B®.

Emergency contraception does not work by terminating an early pregnancy. Its action is prior to implantation.

Nonhormonal Intrauterine Devices (IUDs)

Modern inert IUDs. The most widely used reversible contraceptive by global count in 2001 is not any of the hormonal methods but the intrauterine device. The IUD is little used in the United States, but has 120 million users in the developing countries. (It accounts for more than half of all couples using reversible contraception in China, Cuba, Turkey, and Vietnam.) The IUD is also commonly used in Europe: For example, it is used by 30 percent of contracepting women in Sweden and Norway. Its appeal lies in simplicity of use, ease of reversibility, absence of medical side effects, low cost, and high effectiveness.

Modern IUD research began at about the same time that the final stages of research on oral contraceptives were in progress. Despite intensive research, scientists do not fully understand why the presence of a foreign body in the uterus prevents pregnancy. The evidence clearly indicates that the IUD is a pre-fertilization method: The presence of fertilized eggs in IUD users cannot be demonstrated.

Copper-releasing IUDs. The Lippes loop and other plastic IUDs of the 1960s were highly effective compared to other contraceptive methods, but the real breakthrough in effectiveness occurred when copper-releasing IUDs were developed. This started as a small laboratory research project by Jaime Zipper in Santiago, Chile. It is not known why the release of copper in the uterus is so effective in preventing pregnancy. There is evidence from animal studies that the copper ions released from the copper wire attached to the plastic IUD act to stop most sperm before they reach the fallopian tube, but there are probably other mechanisms of action, as well, that account for the high level of effectiveness in preventing pregnancy. In a seven-year study, the World Health Organization found that the contraceptive effectiveness of the Copper T-380A is equal to that of surgical sterilization. The device maintains its effectiveness for 10 to 12 years. It can be realistically described as reversible sterilization.

Table 1 compares the contraceptive effectiveness of the major modern contraceptive methods in use in 2002, and updated from Hatcher (1998), for which there are adequate data based on a variety of studies.

TABLE 1

Pregnancy Rates Associated with Use of Birth Control Methods

Method	Rate of pregnancy with typical use (%)	Lowest expected rate of pregnancy (%)
Sterilization		
Male Sterilization	0.15	0.1
Female Sterilization	0.5	0.5
Hormonal Methods		
Implant (Norplant™)	0.05	0.05
Hormone Injection		
(Depo-Provera®)	0.3	0.3
Combined Pill		
(Estrogen/Progestin)	5	0.1
Minipill (Progestin only)	5	0.5
Interuterine Devices (IUDs)		
Copper T	0.8	0.6
Mirena®	0.1	0.1
Barrier Methods		
Male Latex Condom	14	3
Diaphragm	20	6
Vaginal Sponge		
(no previous births)	20	9
Cervical Cap		
(no previous births)	20	9
Female Condom	21	5
Spermicide (gel, foam,		
suppository, film)	26	6
Natural Methods		
Withdrawal	19	4
Natural Family Planning		
(calendar, temperature,		
cervical mucus)	25	1-9
No Method	85	85

Note: Estimates of the percent of women likely to become pregnant while using a particular contraceptive method for one year. "Typical Use" rates assume that the method either was not always used correctly or was not used with every act of sexual intercourse. "Lowest Expected" rates assume that the method was always used correctly with every act of sexual intercourse.

SOURCE: Hatcher, Robert A., et al., eds. (1998).

The fertility transition in less developed countries will have to be accomplished essentially using the present armamentarium of contraceptive devices in combination with other methods of birth control. New contraceptives will need to offer broader product profiles. Couples will be looking for non-contraceptive health benefits, particularly for the prevention of sexually transmitted diseases. High priority is being given to developing a vaginal gel that is microbicidal and spermicidal so that women, on their own initiative, can use a contraceptive that will protect them from sexually transmitted disease including HIV/AIDS. New products have been designed that emphasize menstruation suppression. This option provides health benefits and gives women control not only of when they will have a pregnancy, but if and when they will menstruate.

Contraceptives Used by Men

The development of methods of contraception that would be used by men is promising. The condom and the vasectomy operation are effective because they prevent sperm from entering the female without interfering with the male libido or potency. The development of a medical method that would stop sperm production would be easy; however, most approaches either inhibit the man's production of testosterone or elevate levels to an unsafe height. This problem can be overcome by the use of a testosterone-like compound, MENT®, that acts as a substitute for testosterone in many beneficial ways while suppressing sperm production and protecting the prostate gland against hyper-stimulation. MENT® is being studied in Europe for possible use as hormone replacement therapy in aging men but once on the market for that purpose, possibly in 2003, its use as a male contraceptive would be evident. There is also considerable basic research on approaches that would not inhibit sperm production but would interfere with the final maturation processes of the sperm once they leave the testis. This would make the sperm unable to fertilize eggs.

See also: *Birth Control, History of; Family Planning Programs; Reproductive Technologies.*

BIBLIOGRAPHY

Connell, Elizabeth B. 2002. *The Contraception Sourcebook.* New York: Contemporary Books.

Hatcher, R. A., et al. 1998. *Contraceptive Technology.* 17th edition. New York: Ardent Media.

United States Census Bureau. 1999. *World Population: 1998.* Appendix X. Washington, D.C.: Government Printing Office.

SHELDON J. SEGAL

CONTRACEPTIVE PREVALENCE

Contraceptive prevalence measures the extent to which contraception is being used in a population, in particular among women of reproductive age (conventionally, between 15 and 50). Prevalence is the proportion, expressed as a percentage, of women of reproductive age currently using a method of contraception.

This definition, however, presents several ambiguities regarding the base population, the reference period, and what constitutes a method of contraception, lending itself to variations in measurement. As to the base population, ideally prevalence should cover all sexually active partners—men and women—of reproductive age. In practice, however, information on contraceptive use is most often sought only from women, often only married women. (The "married" group usually includes those in consensual unions in countries where such unions are common.) In most countries, the vast majority of women of reproductive age is married or in an informal consensual union, so this restriction does not greatly affect estimates of contraceptive prevalence. However, in countries where large proportions of unmarried women are sexually active, prevalence estimates based solely on currently married women may not reflect the true level of overall contraceptive use. For example, in the developed countries around 1990, contraceptive prevalence among unmarried women ranged from 47 percent in the United States to 75 percent in Belgium.

Another problem in defining the base population concerns the extent to which all women of reproductive age are exposed to the risk of conception at a particular time, given that some women may be infecund or may not be sexually active while others may be seeking to become pregnant. It is for this reason that, in practice, contraceptive prevalence does not attain the theoretical maximum value of 100 percent.

The definition of contraceptive prevalence centers on current use, and the distinction between past and current contraceptive use can be problematic. Most surveys that have asked about the current use of a method of contraception have asked about use "now" or "within the last month"; sometimes other reference periods are specified. Moreover, there is usually no information collected about the regularity with which the method is employed or about the respondent's understanding of correct use. The fuzziness in the timeframe for measuring use and the difficulty of identifying exactly the women who are exposed to the risk of conception during the

specified period undermine the status of prevalence as a *rate*. It can be recorded, rather, as a simple percentage.

What is considered as contraceptive use is also somewhat subjective, given the differing effectiveness of different methods and the varying motives for use. Contraceptive methods are usually grouped into two broad categories, modern and traditional. Modern methods are those that require clinical services or regular supply: they include female and male surgical contraception (sterilization), oral contraceptive pills, intrauterine devices (IUDs), condoms, injectible hormones, vaginal barrier methods (including diaphragms, cervical caps, and spermicidal foams, jellies, creams, and sponges), and, more recently, subdermal contraceptive implants. The traditional methods—also known as non-supply methods to distinguish them from modern supply methods—include the rhythm method, withdrawal (coitus interruptus), abstinence, douching, prolonged breastfeeding, and a variety of folk methods. Nonetheless, the labels "modern" or "traditional" are inexact: for example, both the condom and the rhythm method have a long history of use, yet the condom is considered modern and the rhythm method traditional.

Almost all surveys about contraceptive use have asked about rhythm and withdrawal, but there has been less consistency regarding other traditional methods. A particular difficulty arises with practices whose main motivation may not have been to prevent pregnancy but which may do so in fact—notably, abstinence and breastfeeding. Some surveys have explicitly excluded such practices from the definition of contraception.

In some African countries, there is a tradition of lengthy abstinence from sexual relations following a birth, but surveys often report prolonged abstinence as the method currently used by a substantial proportion of women. The distinction between contraceptive and noncontraceptive motives for this traditional practice is not clear-cut, and many women who practice lengthy postnatal abstinence evidently do not regard it as contraception. Most surveys do not include abstinence, or postnatal abstinence specifically, in the definition of contraception—including surveys conducted in sub-Saharan Africa. When women spontaneously report that they were practicing prolonged abstinence for contraceptive reasons, they may be recorded under the category of "other" methods.

Breastfeeding has fertility-inhibiting effects and in societies that practice prolonged breastfeeding, fertility is depressed. As in the case of abstinence, most surveys have not included breastfeeding in the list of contraceptive methods. In cases where it has been included, the number of women that identify breastfeeding as their contraceptive method is typically a small fraction of the number that are currently breastfeeding.

Depending on the society, folk methods of contraception may include a large number of herbal preparations, manipulation of the uterus, vigorous exercise, adoption of particular postures during or after intercourse, incantations, and the wearing of charms. The effectiveness of these methods has never been scientifically evaluated: some are wholly fanciful, others may be highly unreliable, and still others probably act as abortifacients rather than as contraceptives. Women often do not mention folk methods unless the survey inquires about them specifically, and most surveys do not include probing questions dealing with specific folk methods.

Sources of Information on Contraceptive Prevalence

Surveys are considered the best source of data on contraceptive practice, since they can record the prevalence of all methods, including those that require no supplies or medical services. Most surveys ask respondents broadly similar questions to measure contraceptive use. Women are first asked what methods they know about, and the interviewer then names or describes methods that were not mentioned by the respondent. Respondents are then asked about use of each method that was recognized. This procedure helps make clear to the respondent what methods are to be counted as contraceptive. When methods are not named by the interviewer, the level of use tends to be underreported. In particular, it does not occur to many persons to mention methods such as withdrawal and rhythm, which require no supplies or medical services.

Organized family planning programs keep records on their clients who come for contraceptive supplies or services. These records are another main source of information about contraceptive prevalence. However, data from this source have the serious drawback of excluding use of contraception obtained outside the program, including modern methods supplied through nonprogram sources as well as methods that do not require supplies or medical services. In addition, the process of deriving reasonably accurate prevalence estimates from the information in family planning program records is much less straightforward than the direct questions posed in representative sample surveys.

Contraceptive Prevalence

Prevalence levels range from 4 to 10 percent in pretransitional societies, where fertility is typically high, to 70 to 80 percent in posttransition, low-fertility countries. (As mentioned above, in practice, contraceptive prevalence never attains the maximum value of 100 percent.) In 1997 contraceptive prevalence for the world as a whole was estimated to be 62 percent—that is, 62 percent of currently married women between ages 15 and 50 were using a method of contraception. Regional average levels of prevalence range from 25 percent in Africa to over 65 percent in Asia and Latin America and the Caribbean. The average prevalence for developed countries was 70 percent.

The reported level of contraceptive use in pretransitional societies is very low for both modern methods and traditional methods. For example, contraceptive prevalence in Chad in 1996 was 4 percent (Chad's total fertility rate exceeded 6); in Uganda in 1995 it was 15 percent. The prevalence of modern method use was 1 percent in Chad and 8 percent in Uganda. A large proportion of married contraceptive users in Chad reported the use of traditional methods of contraception: rhythm and withdrawal. It is likely that many women in pretransitional societies use traditional methods that are not captured in the standard surveys.

In the low-fertility countries, the great majority of women not using contraception are pregnant, seeking to become pregnant, infecund, or sexually inactive. Because of the relatively high levels of prevalence already reached in these countries, there is little room for further increase. In developed countries, certain traditional methods—including withdrawal and various forms of the calendar rhythm method—are commonly used: together they account for 26 percent of total contraceptive use in the low-fertility developed countries, compared with just 8 percent in the less developed regions. However, recent trends indicate that the prevalence of modern methods is increasing at the expense of traditional methods. In France, for example, between

1978 and 1994 the use of modern methods increased from 48 to 69 percent, even as the use of all methods decreased by 4 percent. Contraceptive prevalence in the United States in 1995 was estimated to be 76 percent of women who were married or in a union. Female sterilization was the most popular method, with a prevalence of 24 percent, followed by the pill, at 16 percent.

Empirical Relationship between Prevalence and Fertility

There is a strong relationship between contraceptive prevalence and the overall level of childbearing as measured by the total fertility rate. (The total fertility rate indicates the average number of children that would be born per woman according to childbearing rates of the current period.) Cross-national data show that the total fertility rate decreases, on average, by 0.7 children for every 10 percentage-point rise in contraceptive prevalence. This translates into 1 child fewer for every 15 percentage-point increase in contraceptive prevalence. Contraception is the most important of the proximate determinants of cross-national differences in fertility. (Other major proximate determinants of these differences are patterns of marriage and sexual activity outside of marriage, the duration of breastfeeding, and the practice of induced abortion—none of them as strongly associated with fertility as contraceptive use.)

See also: *Family Planning Programs; Fecundity; Fertility, Proximate Determinants of.*

BIBLIOGRAPHY

Abma, Joyce, et al. 1997. "Fertility, Family Planning, and Women's Health: New Data from the 1995 National Survey of Family Growth." *Vital and Health Statistics* 23(19): 61.

United Nations. 2002. "Family Planning." In *World Population Monitoring 2002 Reproductive Rights and Reproductive Health: Selected Aspects.* New York: United Nations.

United Nations. 2000. *Levels and Trends of Contraceptive Use as Assessed in 1998.* New York: United Nations.

VASANTHA KANDIAH

COST OF CHILDREN

At least since 1800 there has been a growing awareness that children are a cost factor for the household. To raise children, parents, or the household at large, must undertake a variety of direct expenditures. Children also require a time investment by their parents, some of which might otherwise be used in gainful economic activity. The latter costs, measured not as money spent on children but in lost earnings, are termed the parents' opportunity costs of children.

Examining parents' decisions about having children in sheer economic terms is often undertaken only with reluctance. The rewards of having children tend to be primarily emotional, associated with a mixture of altruistic and self-serving impulses: to nurture, to continue the bloodline, to balance family life, to satisfy curiosity about one's offspring, and to create relationships based on love. At the same time, and most evident in traditional agricultural societies, children yield economic rewards (1) by supplying labor resources to the family enterprise, often from an early age; and (2) when grown, by providing a measure of physical and economic security to parents, especially in the latter's old age, for which no equivalent institutional means may be readily available. If only implicitly, parents are likely to balance the costs of raising children against expectations of children's material and immaterial utility. An example of the cost of child-rearing becoming the object of a cold economic calculus can be seen in the decisions made by slave-owners as described by the economic historians Robert Fogel and Stanley Engerman. For slave-owners, the cost of raising slaves was in economic terms analogous to cattle-breeding.

In the nineteenth century the cost of children became a prominent consideration in policies addressing poverty. In order to ensure welfare equality among poor families irrespective of their number of children, families with many children would have to be supported by a cost-of-children subsidy. Later on, assessment of child costs also became pertinent in establishing the levels of family allowances and tax rates.

The first and classical study bearing on the cost of children is by the statistician Ernst Engel, who in 1895 published a study for the Prussian government. His name is still known through Engel's Law, which states that the food share in the household budget falls with rising income. There was considerable interest in the cost of children through most of the twentieth century, but some waning of interest in the later years. The main reason seems to be that there is no generally accepted scientific solution to the problem of what the costs of children are and that it seems impossible that one will be found.

Socializing the Costs of Children

Nevertheless most modern societies accept the idea that families and especially poor families should be partly subsidised in order to mitigate the welfare differences that may be caused by differences in the number of children. There are two questions. (1) What subsidies would be needed to neutralize the differences in family size? (2) If those amounts can be identified, should the state's subsidy be set at the level needed for complete neutralization, or at a lower or even a higher level? (A subsidy higher than needed for neutralization might be adopted as a means to raise the birth rate.) The second question is clearly a political issue, which is not the subject of this article. The first question is the relevant one.

It was noted that there is no generally accepted scientific solution to the problem. The practical solution chosen is just to let politicians and/or civil servants make decisions on the basis of intuition and compromises among interest groups such as the parents of large families. This is the route taken in most countries and explains the diversity in child-friendly regulations among countries.

A distinction may be drawn between household subsidies delivered in kind and those provided as income supplements. In-kind subsidies are in the form of state provision of below-cost education, health facilities, childcare, and even school meals. The objective is not only welfare equalization. For instance, education and the removal of illiteracy not only benefits the child who gets the education but also has a large positive external effect for others. But even if those policies are in force, the household itself still incurs substantial child-related expenses for food, clothing, shelter, insurance, etc. These can be offset by family allowances or family-size-dependent tax deductions. Benchmark estimates are needed in order to establish welfare-neutral compensations. Whether the actual subsidies provided are under-, over-, or just compensating is a matter of political choice.

Methods of Estimating the Cost of Children

A naive, but still popular, approach is to determine expenditures for children by bookkeeping and budget surveys. However, this approach raises two problems.

(1) What expenditures are necessary and thus may be called costs and what expenditures should not be seen as necessary costs? This depends very much on the cultural environment (establishing expenditure norms) and on the level of wealth of the household (wealthier families spend more on their offspring than poorer families [can] do). If the normative cost of children that is to be established is to be used for taxation and social security purposes, it is felt by many that it is unacceptable to assign to richer families a higher cost of children and as a consequence a higher per-child tax deduction. This leads to the ethical presumption that the cost of children is to be set equal to the cost incurred by a normative household, which is typically chosen at the minimum income level.

(2) The second problem in the bookkeeping solution is that of joint costs. There are many items in household expenditures that cannot be assigned exclusively as benefiting one particular member. Examples are expenditures on housing, health, insurance, television, etc. Decisions on how to assign such expenditures between parents and children are partly arbitrary. Recognition of economies-of-scale effects (cheaper by the dozen) introduces further complexities. The best-known household expenditure scale is probably the so-called Oxford scale, which is adopted more or less as the official scale by the OECD and the EU. It sets the first adult at 1.0, other adults at 0.7, and children (below 16 years) at 0.5. This scale, although not based on firm research results, is frequently used in official statistics to compare household welfare.

More sophisticated methods of estimating costs of children are the so-called 'adult good' method and the 'food-share' method. The adult good method (developed by E. Rothbarth and Angus Deaton and John Muellbauer) is based on the idea that one may identify a specific part of expenditures in the household budget, e.g. cigarettes, alcohol, etc., as *adult* expenditures. Let the monthly household expenditures be $2000. Assume that the adult's expenditures amount to $800 before the birth of the first child and $400 after the child has been born. Then the cost of the first child would be $800 to $400. This method also involves arbitrary elements. What are 'adult goods' and is the consumption of adult goods representative for 'adult welfare'? It may be assumed that if the birth of a child is the result of a voluntary choice by the parents, parental well being is increased by having that child—that is, increased by more than the loss in adult welfare caused by the resulting reduction in adult expenditures.

The 'food-share' method, which is influential in social security policy in the United States, is based on seminal research by economist Mollie Orshansky. She assumed that the share of food in family expenditures is an index of the family's welfare. For example, suppose food makes up 33 percent of total family expenditures before the first child's birth in a household with a $2000 per month income, and increases to 40 percent after the child is born. Assume further that the one-child household would again spend 33 percent on food if its income increased to $2500. Then the cost of the child is considered to be $500. Notice that the food share in accord with Engel's Law falls with increasing income. The method assumes that food-share represents household's welfare, which is dubious, and that the cost of children varies with income level.

A third approach to estimating the cost of children is subjective. Individuals are asked how satisfied they are with their income. It is found that respondents are less satisfied with the same income, the more children they have to support from it. This method was proposed by Bernard van Praag and Arie Kapteyn, who worked at the time at Leyden University in the Netherlands and is known in the literature as the Leyden method. On the basis of these satisfaction surveys it can be estimated how much has to be given to a household to keep it at the same financial satisfaction level after the birth of an additional child.

Although this method is less arbitrary than the methods previously described, it too has problems. First, the cost of children thus defined again increases with income. Second, it is unclear whether financial satisfaction is a good proxy for the metaphysical concept of household well-being. It is quite probable that non-financial satisfaction with life increases with the birth of a child. Third, the cost of the child will differ between one- and two-earner families. However, it may be argued that the additional money spent on external childcare will be roughly equivalent to the income forgone by the mother, if she would stay at home to care for her own children.

Although there is no generally accepted definition of the cost of children or accepted method of assessment, the various methods have some common features. Generally each shows an economies-of-scale pattern. For the objective methods, costs per additional child seem to diminish with rising family size at an exponential power of about 0.50. For subjective methods, the corresponding profile is consistently flatter, at about 0.30. Subjective estimates, however, implicitly take existing family allowance systems and the price of education into account. So the estimated costs of children are in a sense complementary to the family allowance system. In countries with liberal family allowance systems, and education and health care costs covered by the state, the estimated subjective costs will be smaller than in countries where parents receive fewer or no such benefits. For instance, significant differences in estimated child costs have been found between the Netherlands and Germany on one hand and the United Kingdom and Russia on the other.

In most countries even at the minimum income family income levels there is not a complete state compensation for the costs of children. For higher income levels, this holds a fortiori. If the financial consequences are among the determining factors in a couple's decisions concerning numbers of children, then most countries have a system that is discouraging childbearing. A few countries—for example, France and Canada—have a much more liberal system with the explicit purpose of increasing numbers of births. However, the effects are modest.

A final question that should be asked is whether children not only impose costs but also offer benefits in terms of an addition to general well-being. It might be argued that parents decide on having a child by comparing the expected benefits and costs to their well-being. For the first child the benefit will be evaluated as being larger than the cost. As the marginal benefit falls with each new child, at some specific family size the additional cost will be assessed to be larger than the additional benefit. Then the optimum family size is reached. If this theory were true the cost of a child is still more difficult to define. An attempt in this direction has been made by van Praag and Erik Plug, who found that the optimum number of children increases with income. Hence children are a luxury good.

Almost all states utilize some cost-of-child concept for minimum income families but the operationalization is mainly based on political decisions, sometimes enriched by the ideas of experts and social workers. If most of the population supports that practice, it is clearly acceptable, although not founded on widely accepted economic science. For an extensive survey, refer to the article by van Praag and Marcel Warnaars in the *Handbook of Population and Family Economics*.

See also: *Family Allowances; Family Policy; Microeconomics of Demographic Behavior.*

BIBLIOGRAPHY

Deaton, Angus S., and John Muellbauer. 1986. "On Measuring Child Costs: With Applications to Poor Countries." *Journal of Political Economy* 94: 720–744.

Engel, Ernst. 1895. "Die Lebenskosten Belgischer Arbeiterfamilien früher und jetzt—ermittelt aus Familienhaushaltrechnungen." *Bulletin de l'Institut International de Statistique* 9:1–149.

Fogel, Robert W., and Stanley L. Engerman. 1974. *Time on the Cross: The Economics of American Negro Slavery.* Boston: Little Brown.

Orshansky, Mollie. 1965. "Counting the Poor: Another Look at the Poverty Profile." *Social Security Bulletin* 28: 3–29.

Rothbarth, E. 1943. "Note on a Method of Determining Equivalent Income for Families of Different Composition." In *War-time Patterns of Saving and Spending,* ed. Charles Madge. Cambridge, MA: Cambridge University Press.

van Praag, Bernard M. S., and Arie Kapteyn. 1973. "Further Evidence on the Individual Welfare Function of Income: An Empirical Investigation in the Netherlands." *European Economic Review* 4: 33–62.

van Praag, Bernard M. S, and Erik J. S. Plug. 1999. "The Cost and Benefits of Children." In *Fighting Poverty: Caring for Children, Parents, the Elderly and Health,* ed. Stein Ringen and Philip R. deJong. Aldershot: Ashgate.

van Praag, Bernard M. S., and Marcel F. Warnaar. 1997. "The Cost of Children and the Use of Demographic Variables in Consumer Demand." In *Handbook of Population and Family Economics,* Vol. 1A, ed. Mark R. Rosenzweig and Oded Stark. Amsterdam: Elsevier.

BERNARD M.S. VAN PRAAG

CRIME, DEMOGRAPHY OF

Crime is an act that violates criminal law and is punishable by the state. Such an act is considered juvenile delinquency if the person who commits it is not legally an adult in the jurisdiction where he or she engaged in the offense. Juvenile delinquency also includes status offenses such as underage drinking or truancy, which are only offenses because the perpetrator is under a legal adult age. Because of lack of uniformity in definitions and differences in accuracy and completeness of reporting, international comparisons of crime rates are exceedingly difficult and error-prone. This entry focuses on demographic aspects of crime in the United States.

Crime Data and Trends

There are three major sources of data on crime and delinquency in the United States. First is the Federal Bureau of Investigation's (FBI) Uniform Crime Reports (UCR). These data provide summary counts of crimes reported to police agencies. The UCR presents detailed data on seven categories of crime, called the index offenses (or Part I crimes). These include four violent offenses—murder and nonnegligent manslaughter, forcible rape, robbery, and aggravated assault—and three crimes against property—burglary, larceny-theft, and motor vehicle theft. Reported crime counts are also provided in the UCR for a set of twenty-one additional (Part II) crimes. The second major source of crime data is the National Crime Victimization Survey (NCVS), which collects information on crime victimization from household interviews. Because many crimes are not reported to the police, NCVS data show much higher rates of victimization than the UCR. However, both UCR and NCVS data tend to exhibit quite similar long-term crime trends. The third data source, collected through self-report surveys of youth (e.g., the National Youth Survey) or the general population, reflects crime and delinquency offending.

FIGURE 1

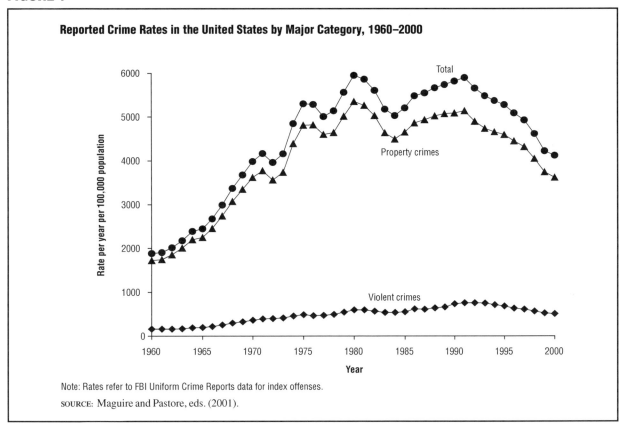

Reported Crime Rates in the United States by Major Category, 1960–2000

Note: Rates refer to FBI Uniform Crime Reports data for index offenses.

SOURCE: Maguire and Pastore, eds. (2001).

The most extensive time series of crime rates in the United States are available for the UCR index offenses. Annual rates for the years 1960 to 2000 of total, property, and violent index crimes per 100,000 population are presented in Figure 1. The United States experienced dramatic increases in rates of reported index crimes in the three decades following 1960, but these rates then dropped every year from 1991 to 2000. The rate of violent crime more than quadrupled between 1960 and 1991—from 161 to 758 per 100,000 population annually. By 2000 the violent crime rate had fallen to about 500 per 100,000, a rate not seen since the late 1970s. Within the category of violent crime, the number of murders (including non-negligent manslaughter) in the United States was 23,000 in 1980 and 15,500 in 2000; the corresponding rates per 100,000 population were 10.2 in 1980 and 5.5 in 2000. The rate of reported property crime has been somewhat more volatile over time, but still tripled between 1960 and 1991; its subsequent steady decline resulted in a 2000 rate similar to that experienced in the early 1970s. Figure 1 also clearly shows that property crimes comprise the vast majority of all index offenses. In 2000, for

example, the four violent index crimes constituted just 12.3 percent of all index offenses.

Demographic Predictors of Crime

Demographic factors such as age, sex, and race play an important role in understanding variation in crime rates across time and place. Demographic features of the population effect crime rates in two distinct ways. First, characteristics of population structure have *compositional* effects: crime rates are higher when demographic groups that have greater levels of involvement in crime constitute a larger share of the population. Second, aspects of population structure may have *contextual* effects on crime when they exert causal influences on criminal motivations and opportunities for crime independent of individual level for criminal tendencies.

The incidence of crime by age group exhibits a consistent pattern: it increases sharply between early and late adolescence (around age 17), and then declines. The late-adolescent peak in offending rates—the "age-crime curve"—is one of the few established empirical regularities in the demography of crime, although debate over the nature of this relationship continues. Scholars such as Michael Gottfredson and Travis Hirschi argue that the age-crime curve is essentially invariant across subpopulations based on sex, race, income, and other characteristics, and cannot be explained by social processes that vary across age. Others argue that the relationship between age and crime varies by offense type and historical period. Contextual hypotheses regarding the effects of age structure have emphasized the negative impact of disproportionately youthful populations on the capacity for social control by societies and other collectivities.

The relationship between sex and crime is also well-established, with men exhibiting consistently higher rates of criminal activity, particularly for serious crimes such as the violent index offenses. The explanation for sex differences in criminal activity is also the subject of continued debate. The widespread view presented by John Hagan, John Gillis, and A. R. Simpson links gender inequality with variation in criminal activity. In this view, sex differences in crime rates should narrow as women achieve greater social equality with men. In contrast, other scholars such as Darrell J. Steffensmeier and Emilie Anderson Allan suggest that criminal activity by women is likely to be higher in contexts where gender inequality—and the corresponding level of crime-inducing disadvantage among women—is most pronounced. Contextual hypotheses regarding the effect of the population sex ratio (the ratio of the number of men to women) have drawn attention to the potential role of high sex ratios on the social valuation of women. Contexts in which there are relatively few women may result in greater protection of women from victimization.

Official statistics on reported crimes and arrests show that African Americans are over-represented as both offenders and victims in most types of serious crimes in the United States. The causes of the large black–white difference in criminal involvement are controversial. Some researchers have contended that distinct cultural orientations toward violence produce the racial differences in the crime rates. However, most recent research attributes the largest part of the race gap in violent crime to differences in the structural circumstances of African Americans and whites. African Americans have higher levels of disadvantages such as poverty than whites, and these disadvantages are associated with greater violent criminal offending and victimization. In addition,

African Americans tend to live in more highly disadvantaged communities that produce social conditions that are more conducive to crime. When African Americans and whites live in comparable community settings, rates of violence are quite similar.

See also: *Homicide and Suicide.*

BIBLIOGRAPHY

Easterlin, Richard A. 1987. *Birth and Fortune: The Impact of Numbers on Personal Welfare.* Chicago: University of Chicago Press.

Gottfredson, Michael, and Travis Hirschi. 1990. *A General Theory of Crime.* Stanford, CA: Stanford University Press.

Hagan, John, John Simpson, and A. R. Gillis. 1987. "Class in the Household: A Power-Control Theory of Gender and Delinquency." *American Journal of Sociology* 92: 788–816.

Krivo, Lauren J., and Ruth D. Peterson. 1996. "Extremely Disadvantaged Neighborhoods and Urban Crime." *Social Forces* 75: 619–650.

———. 2000. "The Structural Context of Homicide: Accounting for Racial Differences in Process." *American Sociological Review* 65: 547–559.

Sampson, Robert J., and William Julius Wilson. 1995. "Toward a Theory of Race, Crime, and Urban Inequality." In *Crime and Inequality*, ed. John Hagan and Ruth D. Peterson. Stanford, CA: Stanford University Press.

South, Scott J., and Steven F. Messner. 1987. "The Sex Ratio and Women's Involvement in Crime: A Cross-National Analysis." *Sociological Quarterly* 28: 171–188.

Steffensmeier, Darrell J., and Emilie Andersen Allan. 1996. "Gender and Crime: Toward a Gendered Theory of Female Offending." *Annual Review of Sociology* 22: 45–87.

Steffensmeier, Darrell J., Emilie Andersen Allan, Miles David Harer, and Cathy Streifel. 1989. "Age and the Distribution of Crime." *American Journal of Sociology* 94: 803–831.

U.S. Department of Justice, Federal Bureau of Investigation, *Crime in the United States, 2000.*

INTERNET RESOURCE.

Maguire, Kathleen, and Ann L. Pastore, eds. 2001. *Sourcebook of Criminal Justice Statistics,* Table 3.120. <http://www.albany.edu/sourcebook/>.

LAUREN J. KRIVO
CHRISTOPHER R. BROWNING

CULTURE AND POPULATION

Demographers have long suspected that understanding population processes requires an understanding of culture. The need to take account of culture is an empirical issue, growing from the recognition of otherwise unexplainable differences in such demographically relevant areas as fertility, marriage practices, and kinship systems.

Acknowledgment of a cultural dimension in population studies has an intellectual genealogy that includes those nineteenth- and early-twentieth-century British bureaucrats who administered an empire by pivoting their data collection strategies along observed markers of ethnic and other identities. It took a more sustained scholarly turn from this administrative past with the post–World War II debates over development programs and the rationality of widely differing fertility regimes across societies. Later developments—such as the inability of simple demographic transition theories to account for variations in the pattern of fertility change across Europe's cultural regions—clinched the importance of cultural factors beyond changing patterns of urbanization, literacy, infant and child mortality, and industrialization. Finally, John C. Caldwell's movement into micro-demography in the 1970s and 1980s encouraged highly localized studies of population processes involving intimate, long-term contact between researchers and the people being studied. These studies opened population research to its most recent engagement with cultural explanation.

This engagement has brought a usable theory of culture for demographic analysis within the reach of population researchers. A theory of culture for demography must necessarily enhance, rather than do away with, existing analytic approaches based on the social survey and multivariate models. Incorporating culture into demography may nevertheless demand revision of the longstanding assumptions underlying some population research. This demographically viable theory of culture emphasizes understanding concrete and highly local situations. For demography, a working theory of culture would lead to better-specified models through the definition of novel independent variables, a refined interpretation of existing standard variables, and the greater understanding of actor motivations.

A Theory of Culture

Contemporary cultural analysis allows researchers to incorporate local systems of meaning and motivation into demographic explanations while accounting for a dynamic relationship between individual actors and their institutional contexts. Earlier definitions of culture emphasized normative institutions and betrayed a legalistic concern with rules for social organization. Contemporary culture theorists have increasingly moved toward definitions that emphasize shared systems of symbolic meaning that both construct and are constructed by the active participation of their members. As scholar David Kertzer writes, from being the "cultural dopes" of earlier theories, people are recognized to actively negotiate and manipulate the cultural symbols available to them and, in so doing, create the possibilities for culture change. This trend toward emphasizing systems of meaning, along with the understanding that discrete cultural systems are themselves embedded within larger political worlds, challenges some of the assumptions in older demographic analyses. At the same time, these developments offer workable solutions that enhance the specificity and explanatory power of population research. They also offer more empirically satisfying understandings of how the shared and intersubjective nature of culture can be linked to variable individual experience and action.

Examples of cultural approaches, spawned in part by a welcoming openness among demographers themselves, abound in recent collections of demographic research by anthropologists. Although differing in emphasis, these approaches use definitions that share important characteristics for understanding meaning in cultural terms. In Clifford Geertz's classic phrasing, which captures the sense of meaning and motivation, cultural patterns may be taken as both models *of* and models *for* reality.

As models *of* reality, cultural patterns constitute the perceived worlds of human actors and define how behaviors receive their symbolic meaning within a field of relationships. The same behaviors may hold entirely different meanings across settings. Beginning with cultural models of reality allows demographers to discover what is significant from the point of view of the actors themselves. Both demographers like Caldwell and anthropologists like Eugene Hammel recommend attention to cultural models of reality as a starting place for analysis.

As a model *for* reality, culture offers a partial resolution to the problem of establishing motivation for actors operating within a common cultural context—the cultural logic of why people do what they do. Although the cultural emphasis on the localized nature of motivations requires a change from the assumptions of some approaches (specifically, that people act rationally to achieve universal goals), it does not by itself do away with the assumption of rational actors altogether.

While these two features of culture, as models of and for reality, promise enhanced demographic analyses, other characteristics make it difficult to use the culture concept in demography. Culture, whether as model of or model for reality, exists in the background understanding of its members. Cultural models are not necessarily consciously held, so that the actors themselves are unlikely to be able to provide a coherent account of their own key frames of meaning and motivation. The discovery of these models requires analysis beyond the face-value responses to questions posed by researchers in focus groups or surveys, and may require attention to domains that appear superficially remote from the proximate determinants of demographic phenomena.

Contemporary cultural theorists assert that a concern for meaning need not preclude using empirical data, although it may require quantitative analysts to broaden the criteria for what counts as a valid argument and to be more open to reformulation and reinterpretation. A truism for culture theory is that cultural systems are at some level coherently integrated. Those themes that have key cultural salience are likely to echo across markedly different domains such as oral traditions, ritual, and everyday practices. From this perspective, symbolic constructions, recurrent themes present in myths and legends, and even the layout of physical space may all be used as empirical indicators to support an interpretation of key cultural elements that have demographic significance.

Applications to Population Research

The most immediate outcome of demographic attention to culture may be the reinterpretation of existing standard variables. For cultural theorists, no behavior is devoid of cultural meaning. Kertzer argues that cultural explanations, coupled with attention to political economy, reintroduce the emotional and symbolic sides of human beings into demographic models, and thereby link apparently discrete behaviors to a whole system of meanings. Even the more proximate determinants of demographic events, such as the role of education in age at marriage, can be significantly reinterpreted through cultural understanding.

Few relationships, for example, are more consistent than the positive association between schooling and age at marriage: the higher the schooling level, the older the age at marriage. Demographic Transition Theory in its earlier, classic form took education at face value to be an indicator of modernization and argued that it correlated with secularization, increased rationality, and heightened individual autonomy. Such understandings ignore both the possibility that marriage may have implications for relationships involving family groups larger than the two individuals united by it, and the potential for symbolic, in addition to utilitarian, meanings for education.

An analysis from rural Pakistan by Tom Fricke and colleagues confirmed the positive association but included the puzzling finding that a substantial fraction of women who attended school only briefly, without completing a full year, also married at later ages than those who never attended school at all. Using local understandings and practices for reinterpreting the meaning of this variable, the authors suggested that education was part of a larger world of symbolic status indicators. The new cultural reading of education as a marker of family status placed the experience of schooling within a wider array of prestige markers that are at play in marriage negotiation in this specific context. In a setting where no woman chose her own husband, actual educational attainment and its implications for autonomy were secondary.

By attending to local systems of meaning and practice, researchers introduce novel variables beyond the immediately demographic into analysis. Thus, by noting the culture of sin, the institutional role of the Catholic Church, and changes in family and work within an existing kinship system, Kertzer integrates cultural and economic explanations in his study of the rising practice of infant abandonment in eighteenth- and nineteenth-century European societies. Susan Greenhalgh's reinterpretation of Chinese fertility transitions extends the focus on individual families to larger institutional contexts, such as the demise of pre-existing state systems of mobility. In his analyses of marriage change, Fricke introduces individual variations in culture-specific elements of the marriage process to show how symbols are redeployed by active agents who pursue their options within a common framework of meanings. All three of these studies suggest that these novel variables must be arrived at through an understanding of concrete empirical situations.

The use of cultural models also complicates the understanding of motivations. Even if general motivations such as improved social, economic, and political status may be said to characterize all people, the understanding of avenues for achieving these general goals is always conditioned by concrete local histories and circumstances. Moreover, the content and demographic implications of these general categories can vary considerably depending on the larger system of which they are a part. Examples of the value of considering the cultural aspects of motivation are found in the contrast between how patrilineal families influence fertility in Greenhalgh's studies of China and in Fricke's studies of Nepal. Where cultural models stress the autonomous responsibility of the patrilineal family for its own well being, security and mobility goals may encourage high fertility. Where cultural models stress cooperation between patrilineal units, high fertility may be a secondary consideration (since the responsibility for well being includes multiple lineages united by marriage). Similarly, Tim Dyson and Mick Moore's contrast of demographic regimes in north and south India turns on this difference and demonstrates how women's symbolic roles within two pre-transition settings can differ because of their different relationships to larger organizational features.

Implications for Population Research

In spite of increased academic interest, incorporating culture into demographic analysis remains problematic. Anthropology, the discipline of culture's greatest theoretical elaboration, has a different research orientation and style from demography. These differences are compounded by the difficulty

of translating the new understandings of culture into terms that present population specialists with a demographically usable model. While population researchers have themselves recognized the need to include culture in their research, the apparent difficulties in using it, the need to rethink fundamentals, and demography's disciplinary orientation toward multivariate analyses of individual-level variations raise the constant temptation to ignore culture in favor of more easily gathered and analyzed measures.

Anthropologists point to two strains of demographic explanation that fail to make use of these revised theories. The first tends to leave out culture altogether by positing universally applicable goals to rational actors whatever the context. At the level of aggregate analysis, the inattention to cultural context replicates the failure of classic Demographic Transition Theory. At the level of individual analysis, the inattention leaves out the highly localized meanings of standard variables in favor of more universal and decontextualized interpretations. Even when these analyses incorporate subjective states through the measurement of values and attitudes, they are unlikely to achieve a fully realized cultural view of meaning because they undervalue its shared patterns in favor of individual variation.

The second strain in demographic explanation tends to focus on institutional contexts, but falls prey to the static treatment of culture widely adhered to within anthropology itself a half century ago. Individual actors are not acknowledged as thinking and emotion-laden participants and strategists in this approach. Here, culture exists in the form of ironclad rules followed by its unquestioning members. While these group measures have the advantage of easy use as independent variables in multivariate models, they have encouraged the use of such ill-considered cultural categories as "Muslim cultures" or "Confucian cultures" and the like. These categories leave out local histories and contexts, along with the possibility of demonstrating the mechanisms by which cultural variables may influence demographically relevant behaviors.

Although the precise mechanisms that connect culture and population processes may best be investigated through the kinds of long-term and intensive studies characteristic of micro-demography and anthropological fieldwork, the sensitive use of cultural understandings in demographic analysis is far less demanding. Cultural demography does not require that every researcher learn a field language and spend months in a single community. Many of the individual studies and collections cited here are, in fact, reliant on secondary data sets or involve historical materials. Culturally sensitive population studies require an assumption that people engage their worlds in terms of highly various and local systems of meaning, and a willingness to explore existing sources with an eye to relating those meanings to demographic outcomes.

See also: *Anthropological Demography; Caldwell, John C.; Mass Media and Demographic Behavior; Religions, Population Doctrines of; Values and Demographic Behavior.*

BIBLIOGRAPHY

Caldwell, John C. 1982. *Theory of Fertility Decline.* New York: Academic Press.

Coale, Ansley J., and Susan Cotts Watkins, eds. 1986. *The Decline of Fertility in Europe.* Princeton, NJ: Princeton University Press.

D'Andrade, Roy G., and Claudia Strauss, eds. 1992. *Human Motives and Cultural Models.* New York: Cambridge University Press.

Dyson, Tim, and Mick Moore. 1983. "On Kinship Structure, Female Autonomy, and Demographic Behavior in India." *Population and Development Review* 9: 35–60.

Fricke, Tom. 1997. "Marriage Change as Moral Change: Culture, Virtue, and Demographic Transition." In *The Continuing Demographic Transition,* ed. G. W. Jones, R. M. Douglas, J. C. Caldwell, and R. M. D'Souza. New York: Oxford University Press.

Fricke, Tom, Sabiha H. Syed, and Peter C. Smith. 1986. "Rural Punjabi Social Organization and Marriage Timing Strategies in Pakistan." *Demography* 23: 489–508.

Geertz, Clifford. 1973. *The Interpretation of Cultures.* New York: Basic Books.

Greenhalgh, Susan. 1988. "Fertility as Mobility: Sinic Transitions." *Population and Development Review* 14: 629–674.

———, ed. 1995. *Situating Fertility: Anthropology and Demographic Inquiry.* New York: Cambridge University Press.

Hammel, Eugene A. 1990. "A Theory of Culture for Demography." *Population and Development Review* 16: 455–485.

Kertzer, David I. 1997. "The Role of Culture in Demography." In *The Continuing Demographic Transition,* ed. G. W. Jones, R. M. Douglas, J. C. Caldwell, and R. M. D'Souza. New York: Oxford University Press.

Kertzer, David I., and Tom Fricke, eds. 1997. *Anthropological Demography: Toward a New Synthesis.* Chicago: University of Chicago Press.

Lorimer, Frank, ed. 1954. *Culture and Human Fertility.* Paris: UNESCO.

Wuthnow, Robert. 1987. *Meaning and Moral Order: Explorations in Cultural Analysis.* Berkeley: University of California Press.

TOM FRICKE

CYCLES, POPULATION

A population cycle occurs when the growth rate of population varies over time in some fairly recognizable fashion. This might be due to changes in patterns of migration, or fluctuations in birth and death rates. Although it is generally accepted that there are cycles of varying length in economic activity, there is less agreement on the topic of population cycles.

T. R. Malthus was the first to posit the existence of population cycles, which he argued were the result of a pattern of economic and demographic feedback. An abundant harvest might temporarily raise wages, but the higher wages would cause an increase in birth rates, leading in turn to an increase in the number of laborers and hence to a decline in real wages. This decline in real wages would be met either by reduced birth rates (the "preventive check") or by an increase in mortality rates (the "positive check"). In either event, Malthus suggested that these fluctuations would cause population growth rates—and real wages—to cycle about some fairly constant level.

Later theorists thought that Malthus's theory was rendered obsolete by technological innovation, as the industrial revolution produced steady increases in both population and real wages. But the theory of population cycles was revived by the economist Simon Kuznets (1901–1985), who studied patterns of growth in the nineteenth and early twentieth centuries in the United States and identified what have come to be known as "Kuznets cycles": pronounced fluctuations of 15 to 25 years' duration in the growth of population, labor force, households, output, and capital stock. He suggested that an increase in the demand for labor, spurred perhaps by technological innovation, might generate increased immigration rates, and the new immigrants would further increase the demand for labor because of increased demand for housing and other goods and services. This feedback effect would gradually die away, returning population growth to its pre-immigration level. Such cycles were not thought to be self-generating, but rather were the result of an exogenous change in the demand for labor.

Richard Easterlin suggested that these Kuznets cycles changed significantly in the second half of the twentieth century because of changes in immigration policy. With tighter restrictions on immigration, any exogenous growth in the demand for labor could not be met through increased immigration, and would instead produce higher wages for the indigenous labor force, especially for younger workers. These improved wages would then result in an earlier age at marriage and higher birth rates, generating an urban economic boom and thus further increasing the demand for labor.

Easterlin's emphasis on younger workers, and on their wages relative to those of older workers, was a significant extension of Kuznets's original theory, since it introduced for the first time a credible mechanism for creating self-generating population (and economic) cycles. Easterlin developed this concept more fully in his later work, where he hypothesized that the small Depression-era birth cohorts of the 1930s had experienced a significant increase in their relative wages because of imperfect substitutability between older and younger workers: the younger workers were in short supply relative to older workers, and thus benefited most from the post–World War II economic boom. They married earlier and at higher rates, and exhibited a sharp increase in fertility rates that produced the 1946–1964 baby boom. When the large baby-boom birth cohort entered the labor market in the 1970s, however, they had the opposite experience: they were in excess supply relative to older workers. Their reduced relative wages

caused them to postpone or forgo marriage and childbearing, producing the low birth rates of the post-1960s "baby bust."

Easterlin's model failed to predict actual events in the 1980s, however, when it was expected that smaller birth cohorts would begin to experience improved labor market conditions. Diane Macunovich (1999) has suggested that the effects of birth cohort size may produce asymmetric population cycles. When the size of birth cohorts entering the labor market is increasing, young workers not only supply labor for the economy, they also add to demand for goods and services as they set up their own households—an effect similar to that observed by Kuznets. Thus, when the size of the cohort entering the labor market is increasing, the negative effect of their oversupply of labor is offset to some extent by a stimulative effect on the economy, as producers expand production capacity to meet demand. The opposite would occur when the size of entry-level cohorts begins to decline and producers find themselves with excess production capacity. This latter effect would have been masked for the small birth cohorts entering the labor market in the 1950s because of the pent-up demand from the war years, but it was experienced fully by the cohorts entering the labor market in the 1980s. This suggests that if self-generating population cycles do occur, they cannot be expected to have a regular period or amplitude.

Several researchers have focused on determining whether population cycles are theoretically possible—that is, whether they can be represented by a formal mathematical model—and whether the observed U.S. cycles conform to an acceptable theoretical model. Ronald Lee (1974) defined a family of models that might encompass an Easterlinian feedback mechanism, identifying two types of cycle that could be generated: short-term or transient cycles, and longer-term sustained cycles. Lee concluded that parameter values for what he termed a cohort model estimated from the U.S. experience between 1917 and 1982 could not sustain longer-term cycles. However, he suggested that longer term cycles could be generated by what he called a period model, in which period fertility depends on total labor force size.

In parallel with this work, Paul Samuelson (1976) developed what he termed "an oversimplified version of the Easterlin theory" using a two-generation overlapping generations model—a model that Gustav Feichtinger and Gerhard Sorger (1989) later extended to a continuous-time model. Using nonlinear differential equations, Feichtinger and Sorger were able to generate an Easterlin cycle with a period of about 43 years. They pointed out that a discrete-time framework, although more appropriate for describing population dynamics, does not yield the period length of the Easterlin cycle.

Frank Denton and Byron Spencer (1975) and Joseph Anderson (1982) presented simulation models examining the cyclical implications of an Easterlinian model, demonstrating that demoeconomic behavior is predominantly nonperiodic, hence essentially unpredictable.

Kenneth Wachter attempted to determine the characteristics of a "viable feedback model" for sustained fertility cycles, and concluded that "there *are* viable feedback models for U.S. births, but very few, and they are very special." He demonstrated that an Easterlin type of relative cohort size model can be one of these "special" cases—especially if the timing as well as the level of the younger cohort's fertility is affected by relative cohort size. Alternatively, the Easterlin model can produce sustained cycles if a "bandwagon" effect causes the fertility of other age groups to follow that of the younger cohorts. However, Wachter emphasized that institutional factors and period effects make it very difficult to test for population cycles given the relatively short time period of available data (p. 124).

C. T. Cyrus Chu and Huei-Chung Lu (1995) again took up the models specified by Lee and Wachter. They tested a version that incorporated both Lee's period and cohort models, and found that "there indeed exists a limit cycle solution for the U.S. fertility data; however, this limit cycle solution is not stable, and therefore the population trajectory will not converge to that limit cycle" (p. 54). However, their model made no allowance for specific period effects that might have influenced the observed pattern of fertility in the second half of the twentieth century. Thus, as Chu and Lu emphasize the existence and nature of population cycles remains an area for further research.

See also: *Baby Boom; Easterlin, Richard A.; Economic-Demographic Models; Kuznets, Simon.*

BIBLIOGRAPHY

Anderson, Joseph M. 1982. "An Economic-Demographic Model of the U.S. Labor Market." In *Research in Population Economics,* Vol. 4, ed. J. Simon and P. Lindert. Greenwich, CT: JAI Press.

Chu, C.T. Cyrus, and Huei-Chung Lu. 1995. "Toward a General Analysis of Endogenous Easterlin Cycles." *Journal of Population Economics* 8: 35–57.

Denton, Frank T., and Byron G. Spencer. 1975. *Population and the Economy.* Lexington, MA: Lexington Books.

Easterlin, Richard A. 1968. *Population, Labor Force, and Long Swings in Economic Growth: The American Experience.* New York: National Bureau of Economic Research.

Feichtinger, Gustav, and Gerhard Sorger. 1989. "Self-Generated Fertility Waves in a Non-Linear Continuous Overlapping Generations Model." *Journal of Population Economics* 2: 267–280.

Lee, Ronald Demos. 1974. "The Formal Dynamics of Controlled Populations and the Echo, the Boom and the Bust." *Demography* 11: 563–585.

———. 1976. "Demographic Forecasting and the Easterlin Hypothesis." *Population and Development Review* 2: 459–72.

Macunovich, Diane J. 1999. "The Fortunes of One's Birth: Relative Cohort Size and the Youth Labor Market in the U.S." *Journal of Population Economics* 12: 215–272.

Samuelson, Paul A. 1976. "An Economist's Non-Linear Model of Self-Generated Fertility Waves." *Population Studies* 30: 243–248.

Wachter, Kenneth W. 1991. "Elusive Cycles: Are There Dynamically Possible Lee-Easterlin Models for U.S. Births?" *Population Studies* 45: 109–135.

Wachter, Kenneth W., and Ronald Demos Lee. 1989. "U.S. Births and Limit Cycle Models." *Demography* 26(1): 99–115.

DIANE J. MACUNOVICH

D

DARWIN, CHARLES

(1809–1882)

The naturalist Charles Robert Darwin expounded the first successful theory of evolution based on the processes of natural selection in botanical and animal populations. The son of a physician and the grandson of a well-known polymath, Erasmus Darwin, Charles Darwin drifted from medicine at Edinburgh to preparation for a career in the Church of England at Cambridge while enjoying country pursuits such as hunting, shooting, and specimen collection throughout his young adulthood. Recognition of his skills as a naturalist first came in the form of an offer to undertake the geological, zoological, and botanical side of the official naval survey of the South American coast carried out by the HMS *Beagle* from 1831 to 1836. Upon his return, private wealth enabled Darwin to remain an independent scientist for the rest of his life.

In the course of trying to make sense of his observations, Darwin hit upon the main ideas that were later to constitute the theory of natural selection. Reading the economist T. R. Malthus's *Essay on Population* in 1838 provided an essential step in that process. Darwin was familiar with competition for survival in the animal kingdom, but the quasi-mathematical form of Malthus's theory of the potential force exerted by population growth on resources in unchecked populations proved fruitful. It revealed that there was a persistent process at work by which individual members of any species that possessed slight advantages in the struggle for survival would succeed while others either failed to breed or went extinct. Lack of room and nourishment sets up a competition in which the better adapted have a greater chance of breeding and thus of passing on the original variation. Publication of Darwin's findings was much delayed: *The Origin of Species by Means of Natural Selection, or the Preservation of Favoured Races in the Struggle for Life* was not published until 1859 after Darwin learned that the scientist Alfred Russel Wallace (1823–1913), who had also been influenced by reading Malthus, was about to publish a similar theory.

The study of animal populations in terms of why they fail to show the exponential properties suggested by Malthus's geometric ratio, the interaction between birth rates and death rates, and the effect of density and territoriality in constraining fluctuations in population size followed in the wake of the interest shown in human populations. For Darwin and Wallace that interest centered on positive checks and their implications for natural selection.

Detailed studies of the principles of population interaction and competition were delayed until the twentieth century. David Lack, for example, showed that birds exercise reproductive control through natural selection. Clutch size converges on the "efficient" solution: It corresponds to the largest number of young for which the parents can on average find sufficient food.

Malthus, who was attacked for stressing the aspects of behavior that humankind shares with animals, became important to biology precisely because of this fact. Malthus's habits as an observer, balancing speculation with detailed observation, are similar to those involved in natural history. Any reader with the experience of Darwin and Wallace would recognize the same mentality, procedures, and need to fill the gaps in knowledge created by the absence of scope for controlled experimentation with natural populations. Ultimate and proximate causes need to be separated, but that can be done only with great difficulty. Migration to other regions also causes similar problems when one tries to draw inferences. This led to Darwin's problem in proving that what could be observed as a result of artificial selection was also true of natural selection. Because of the current availability of accurate human population statistics, Darwin's observations continue to offer a benchmark for noting differences in animal population behavior.

Darwin's theory, having acknowledged its debts to the human or social sciences, exerted a reciprocal influence on the study of human populations. It did this not so much through questions involving quantities, Malthus's sole concern, but through questions affecting qualitative changes in human populations as judged by intelligence or other properties deemed to be heritable. This question was first addressed by Darwin's cousin, Francis Galton (1822–1911), whose studies of the inheritance of intelligence, though first undertaken without a knowledge of genetic transmission mechanisms, launched the field known as eugenics. Darwin appropriated Galton's ideas on the effect of inheritance in his *Descent of Man* (1871), giving his personal blessing to one version of a doctrine already in circulation, social Darwinism, or what would later be called sociobiology.

See also: *Animal Ecology; Biology, Population; Eugenics; Evolutionary Demography; Galton, Francis; Malthus, Thomas Robert; Sociobiology.*

BIBLIOGRAPHY

Barlow, Nora, ed. 1969. *The Autobiography of Charles Darwin, 1809–1882.* New York: Norton Library.

Bowler, Peter J. 1976. "Malthus, Darwin, and the Concept of Struggle." *Journal of the History of Ideas* 37: 631–650.

Browne, Janet. 1995. *Charles Darwin; Voyaging.* London: Jonathan Cape.

Darwin, Charles. 1985 (1859). *The Origin of Species by Means of Natural Selection, or the Preservation of Favoured Races in the Struggle for Life.* London: Penguin.

———. 1998 (1871). *The Descent of Man and Selection in Relation to Sex.* Great Minds Series. Amherst, NY: Prometheus Books.

Galton, Francis. 1972 (1869). *Hereditary Genius; An Inquiry into its Laws and Consequences.* Gloucester, MA: Peter Smith.

Lack, David. 1952. *The Natural Regulation of Animal Numbers.* Oxford: Oxford University Press.

DONALD WINCH

DATA ASSESSMENT

In a perfect world, data would always be complete, accurate, current, pertinent, and unambiguous. In the real world, data is generally flawed on some or all of these dimensions. Data assessment in practice has tended to focus on completeness and accuracy, and that is the focus of these notes. Currency, pertinence and clarity deserve more attention than they receive, perhaps, but their assessment requires very different methods.

Assessment is sometimes thought of as a preliminary to analysis proper. This is a useful distinction in some circumstances, but in general the assessment of error and the drawing of substantive conclusions are two sides of the same coin. This is suggested by the symbolic equation "Data = Reality + Error", in which "Reality" represents conclusions drawn from the data that are valid despite the error and "Error" represents spurious conclusions suggested by the data as a result of error. Since all conclusions fall into one or the other of these two categories, conclusions about error are at the same time conclusions about reality, and conversely.

Data may be defined as systematic information about the members of some statistical aggregate. *Systematic* means that the same information is available for every entity, with exceptions only for missing values and inapplicable cases (e.g., age at first marriage for a never married woman). *Statistical aggregate* refers to a collection of entities (e.g., persons, births, deaths, households) defined by explicitly stated rules for inclusion. Data consist concretely of (1) a collection of *records,* one for each entity in the statistical aggregate, each record containing information about the entity it represents, and (2) one or more texts describing the statistical aggregate and the content of the records. The records and associated documentation are often referred to as a *data set. Statistics* are indicators, usually but not necessarily numerical, derived from one or more data sets.

The term *data* in common usage may refer either to data or to statistics. Census data, for example, may refer either to census information on individual persons and households or to the tabular data contained in census publications, such as total population size and the distribution of population by age and sex.

Direct Assessment

There are two general approaches to the assessment of data, direct and indirect. Direct assessment consists of evaluating the coverage and content of a data set. *Coverage* refers to the faithfulness of the correspondence between the records that constitute the data set and the statistical aggregate the data set represents. Data sets may omit records for some entities that should be represented and include records that should not be included. Improper inclusions occur when a data set includes more than one record for the same entity, includes records for entities not in the statistical aggregate, or includes fictitious records. *Content* refers to the completeness and accuracy of the information contained on the records in the data set.

Direct assessment requires a record-matching study, in which two data sets are compared. The records in each data set are divided into two groups: matched records, which represent entities represented by records in the other data set, and unmatched records, the remainder. Numbers of matched and unmatched records provide a basis for assessing coverage. Comparison of corresponding values on matched records provides a basis for assessing content.

The value of information on coverage provided by a record-matching study is limited by *response correlation bias,* which exists whenever the inclusion of an entity in one data set is not independent of its inclusion in the other data set. In the extreme case of perfect correlation, both data sets would consist entirely of records representing the same entities, and matching would provide no information on coverage. Strict independence is unattainable in practice, but a modicum of independence is necessary for a record-matching study to yield useful information on coverage.

In a 1974 publication, Eli S. Marks, William Seltzer, and Karol J. Krotki provided a useful general discussion of record-matching studies. John G. C. Blacker wrote a 1977 article containing a critical assessment of record-matching studies in demography.

Record-matching studies for population censuses require a post-enumeration survey, a survey taken after the census for the purpose of evaluating its quality. Matching studies for civil registration data may involve special surveys or draw on other sources of data, such as newspaper reports of births and deaths.

Record-matching studies may be used to assess content error in population surveys. Coverage is less important for survey data than for population census or civil registration data because information is obtained only for a sample. Assessment of coverage for survey data generally focuses on the percentage of households or persons in the sample for whom it was possible to obtain data and on any selection biases that might arise from the exclusions.

Indirect Assessment

Direct assessment of data sets is expensive, both because a second data set is required for comparison and because matching is often a complex and difficult process. The results of direct assessment are, moreover, limited by response correlation bias and by the tendency of data sets collected at the same or nearly the same time to have similar content error. The indirect approach, by which data sets are assessed by analyzing the accuracy of statistics derived from them, is generally far less expensive and will often give results as good as or better than direct assessment.

Assessment of a statistic is concerned with its accuracy, that is, with how close it is to the true value it represents. The principle means for assessing the accuracy of a statistic is comparison with other statistics. Comparison may take many forms. In some cases it may rely on general knowledge rather than on specific comparison statistics. Sex ratios at birth in national populations, for example, tend to be about 105 male births per 100 female births. Should survey data indicate a much higher value, it might be concluded that the completeness of reporting of female births was deficient. Such conclusions must always take due account of context, however. A sex ratio at birth of 130, for example, might indicate sex-selective abortion rather than defective data.

FIGURE 1

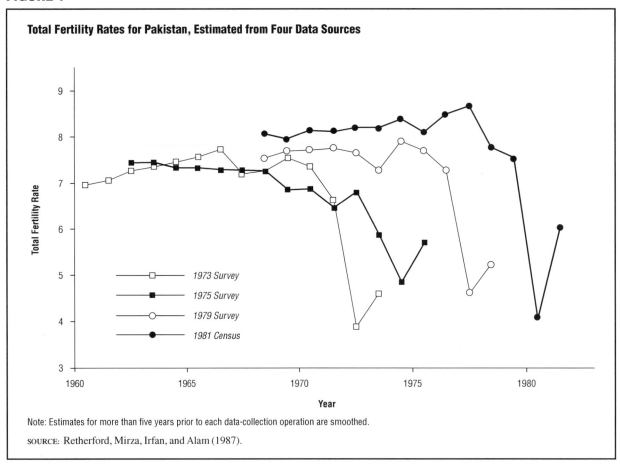

Total Fertility Rates for Pakistan, Estimated from Four Data Sources

Note: Estimates for more than five years prior to each data-collection operation are smoothed.

SOURCE: Retherford, Mirza, Irfan, and Alam (1987).

Direct comparisons with other statistics generally provide the strongest conclusions about data quality. Consider for example Figure 1, which shows retrospective estimates of total fertility rates for Pakistan from four successive data sets. Taken in isolation, each retrospective series of estimates shows a sharp decline in fertility followed by a rise at the end of the series. Comparison of the four series, however, shows that these declines are spurious, for none of the declines indicated by the first three data sets is confirmed by any of the following data sets. The four series taken together suggest not only that there was no fertility decline but that fertility rose slightly between 1960 and the late 1970s.

This example illustrates how error patterns in statistics derived from data sets can be used to draw conclusions about data quality. In each of the four data sets there is a tendency for too few births to be reported during the second and third years prior to the year of data collection. Direct assessment is unlikely to reveal these errors because they tend to af-

fect all data collection operations. The errors are revealed by the comparison of retrospective series of estimates derived from data sets collected in different years. Because many demographic estimation procedures provide such retrospective series of estimates, such comparisons are often possible.

Statistics derived from higher quality data sets will generally be more accurate than statistics derived from lower quality data sets, but there is no simple, general relation between the quality of a data set and the accuracy of statistics derived from it. A population census with perfect coverage would yield a perfectly accurate total population, for example, but a census that omitted some persons who should have been included and included the same number of persons who should have been omitted would also yield a perfectly accurate total. The latter scenario is unlikely, as omissions nearly always exceed improper inclusions, but the example illustrates the indeterminacy of the relation between data quality and the accuracy of statistics.

See also: *Age Measurement; Census; Estimation Methods, Demographic.*

BIBLIOGRAPHY

Blacker, John G. C. 1977. "Dual Record Demographic Surveys: A Re-assessment." *Population Studies* 31: 585–597.

Marks, Eli S., William Seltzer, and Karol J. Krotki. 1974. *Population Growth Estimation: A Handbook of Vital Statistics Estimation.* New York: Population Council.

Retherford, Robert D., G. Mujtaba Mirza, Mohammad Irfan, and Iqbal Alam. 1987. "Fertility Trends in Pakistan: The Decline That Wasn't." *Asian and Pacific Population Forum* 1(2): 1, 3–10.

GRIFFITH FEENEY

DATABASES, DEMOGRAPHIC

Demographic databases are systematic listings or files of statistical information on the characteristics of the members of a population, typically at the level of individuals, families, or households. A database of the population of the United States has been compiled every ten years since the first census was conducted in 1790. This was initially limited to such basic demographic information as age, sex, and race. It has grown to include much fuller demographic profiles of people, including education, employment and occupation, marital status, and income, along with characteristics of both the household and the housing unit.

Early Uses of Demographic Databases

Demographic databases, first as paper reports and then, with the advent of the computer, as electronic files, have become widely used in both the public and private sectors. In the case of the decennial U.S. census, before 1970 very little demographic information in the form of cross-tabulations was available in any format other than paper volumes. Demographic and social statistics for geographic areas ranging from states to cities to neighborhoods had to be sought in hundreds of separate volumes. Any attempt to aggregate this information required transforming it into a machine-readable form. Maps associated with the data were supplied separately; no geographic information systems were available.

Since 1970 the Census Bureau has increased the amount of information available in machine-readable form and at the same time has reduced the amount available on paper. For example, about 450,000 pages were published from the 1990 census; the total from the 2000 census is expected to be about 100,000 pages.

Problems and Opportunities Associated with Electronic Files

The shift to electronic files poses some potential problems. There is the risk that computers of the future will not be capable of reading information produced in the recent past. Moreover, federal statistical agencies in the United States, to save funds and speed delivery, have used the Internet both as an archive and as a means of data retrieval; there is no assurance that future users of the data will have easy access.

As a result of the use of computers, data users are no longer limited to data aggregated into geographic areas. Databases composed of information on individuals, commonly known as public use microdata samples, are also commonly available in machine-readable form. (They are carefully screened to ensure that information about specific individuals cannot be determined.) For the U.S. census, these samples, extracted from the full set of census returns, enable researchers to develop cross-tabulations not found in the summary files produced by the Census Bureau. Another enhancement to basic demographic databases is the ability to map aggregate information by using geographic line files that can be interpreted by computer mapping software.

The Internet and Electronic Linkage

The Internet, along with high-speed computers, has enabled researchers to move beyond the analysis of just a single database. Linkage of demographic information from disparate sources is readily attainable. For example, health records from hospitals can be linked with social security information and further linked to educational attainment data. This ability to link files, even with personal identifiers eliminated from the records, raises the possibility that individuals could be identified and their demographic and socioeconomic information disclosed. This potential for disclosure is an issue for both governmental statistical agencies and the private sector.

The Private Sector

Demographic databases are important tools in the private sector. Deciding where to build a plant or open a store and gauging whether a sufficient market exists for a proposed product require the use of demographic databases, if necessary created by the private sector. The first major private sector database, the "Survey of Buying Power," was published in 1929. It consisted of demographic and socioeconomic data for all counties and cities in the United States. Like the census, the survey eventually was produced in machine-readable form.

Private sector producers of demographic databases have moved beyond basic demographic and geographic tabulations. Through the use of statistical techniques such as factor analysis and cluster analysis, techniques that enable researchers to combine demographic variables into clusters composed of similar lifestyle characteristics, specialized databases have been generated for geographies such as postal codes and company trading areas. Information from warranty cards submitted by purchasers of products, subscription lists, telephone directories, and other sources is linked to create databases that can be used for direct marketing purposes. Although these linked files are nongovernmental, questions of privacy and confidentiality are still relevant.

A Public Good

In the United States demographic databases compiled by the federal statistical agencies are considered a public good. These agencies have no copyright protection and are permitted to charge for their data only to the extent that the charges cover the cost of dissemination. It is assumed that the cost of collection has already been paid by the taxpayers, and the agencies are supported through the federal budget. The United States is nearly alone in following this policy. In most other countries national statistical offices are expected to pay their own way, charging users for their data. At the same time these offices are pressured to make their information available electronically on the Internet or through other means so that as many people as possible have access to it.

Databases in the Future

The integration of demographic databases through the use of advanced computer capabilities may eventually give researchers the capability of one-stop shopping, with databases linked not only nationally but internationally. The United Nations and other international organizations, through their publications and the Internet, already produce and publish some databases of international demographic statistics. In the future researchers may be able to retrieve data on characteristics such as race, education, and income, taking account of all the different definitions, based on comprehensive metadata, in the form of one international file.

See also: *Bibliographic and Online Resources; Business Demography; Census; Data Collection, Ethical Issues in; Demographic Surveys, History and Methodology of; Longitudinal Demographic Surveys; State and Local Government Demography.*

BIBLIOGRAPHY

Anderson, Margo J. 1988. *The American Census: A Social History.* New Haven, CT: Yale University Press.

Doyle, Lane, and Zayatz Theeuwes. 2001. *Confidentiality, Disclosure, and Data Access.* Washington, D.C.: Elsevier.

Russell, Cheryl. 1984. *The Business of Demographics.* Washington, D.C.: Population Reference Bureau, *Population Bulletin,* Vol. 39.

Spar, Edward J. 2000. "The Private Sector." In *Encyclopedia of the U.S. Census.* Washington, D.C.: CQ Press.

"Survey of Buying Power." *Sales and Marketing Management,* annual publication. New York: Sales and Marketing Management Magazine.

United Nations. *Statistical Yearbook,* annual publication. New York: United Nations.

U.S. Department of Commerce, U.S. Census Bureau. 2001. *Introduction to Census 2000 Data Products.* Washington, D.C.: U.S. Government Printing Office.

U.S. Office of Management and Budget. 2002. *Statistical Programs of the United States Government.* Washington, D.C.: U.S. Government Printing Office.

Weiss, Michael. 1988. *The Clustering of America.* New York: Harper & Row.

EDWARD J. SPAR

DATA COLLECTION, ETHICAL ISSUES IN

Ethics in demographic data collection, or in demographic research more generally, has received little explicit attention in the population field and no formal guidance from the principal professional associations. This is in contrast with the treatment of ethics in anthropology, sociology, statistics, and medical research. Ethical discussions in the population field have focused almost exclusively on the ethical dimensions of population policies and programs.

As a result, available ethical guidance comes primarily from national and international professional associations in allied fields. The major concerns of professional associations are proper behavior among members of the profession and by members of the profession toward others—students, employers and donors of research funds, research subjects or respondents, and the general public or society at large.

Applied to demographic data collection, the most relevant topics are (1) promoting the neutrality and objectivity of the data collection operations and outputs, including issues of professional competence and integrity, and (2) safeguarding the autonomy of research subjects or respondents, including the protection of respondents and the entire study population from potential harm.

Since the official statistics generated by governmental sources, such as population censuses or birth and death registration systems, are a major source of demographic data, national and international norms relating to official statistics are also a relevant source of ethical guidance. However, these norms are primarily directed toward the behavior of governments and institutions rather than the actions of individual practitioners.

Professional and Scientific Integrity

The code of ethics of the American Sociological Association advises sociologists to "adhere to the high-est possible technical standards that are reasonable and responsible in their research. . .act with honesty and integrity; and avoid untrue, deceptive, or undocumented statements. . .and avoid conflicts of interest and the appearance of conflict." The United Nations Fundamental Principles of Official Statistics, the International Statistical Institute's Declaration on Professional Ethics, and the American Statistical Association's Ethical Guidelines for Statistical Practice provide similar guidance.

Protecting Respondents and Other Research Subjects

Norms relating to confidentiality and the protection of human research subjects include the succinct statement in the Fundamental Principles of Official Statistics: "individual data collected by statistical agencies for statistical compilation. . .are to be strictly confidential and used exclusively for statistical purposes." The Code of Ethics of the American Sociological Association states that sociologists "have an obligation to ensure that confidential information is protected" so as to shield sensitive information obtained in research. Sociologists are also to "inform themselves fully about all laws and rules which may limit or alter guarantees of confidentiality. They determine their ability to guarantee absolute confidentiality and, as appropriate, inform research participants. . . of any limitations to this guarantee at the outset." The International Statistical Institute's Declaration on Professional Ethics and the American Statistical Association's Ethical Guidelines for Statistical Practice set out similar ethical obligations.

Also of relevance are the requirements that governments and other funding agencies impose on their grantees. Laws and other regulatory efforts are often designed to achieve many of the same ends as ethical norms; however, they are distinct approaches to misconduct and, in specific instances, they may be at variance with one another. Accordingly, researchers need to be aware of both the ethical and legal constraints relevant to their planned research and data collection efforts.

Current norms and regulations designed to protect human research subjects were initially developed as a reaction to the Nazi medical experiments carried out on concentration camp inmates during World War II. Over the years, by simple extension, the area of concern has broadened to include both

TABLE 1

Factors Contributing to Higher-Risk Demographic Data Collection and Research Based on Potential for Respondent or Group Harm

A. Critical factors
1. Population studied is weak or otherwise vulnerable.
2. Data gathering or research involves variables that are on "sensitive" topics, typically topics that are or can be used to identify or stigmatize one or more vulnerable groups, or use classifications that permit the identification or stigmatization of such groups.

B. Aggravating factors
1. All or substantially all of population is covered (i.e., sampling is not used).
2. Longitudinal data gathering is involved, or the activity can be linked to a longitudinal system.
3. Participation is mandatory or is effectively coerced.
4. Little or no input from the subject population in planning the data gathering or research activities. (The risk potential is further enhanced if there are substantial inputs in terms of expertise, staff, or funds from foreign persons or institutions.)
5. The data gathering or research is carried out in a war, a period of civil disruption, or during or shortly after a similar emergency.
6. Little or no attention given to organizational, operational, methodological, and technological safeguards against the misuse of information obtained for non-statistical purposes.
7. Confidentiality assurances provided to respondents have limited or no legal basis.
8. Ethical reviews are not carried out, are perfunctory, or are heavily influenced by utilitarian consideration.

Note: The presence of either or both critical factors gives rise to a presumption of risk and each additional aggravating factor present further augments such risk. On the other hand, it should be emphasized that the presence of crititcal and aggravating factors does not mean that actual harm has occurred.

SOURCE: Compiled by author.

---

experimental and non-experimental threats and has been adopted, without substantial modification, by social science researchers more generally. Thus, the related protections focus on safeguarding against invasive acts on the body or mind of the research subject, particularly through biomedical and psychological experiments, that threaten the physical or mental well-being of that subject. A key element of such protections is the general requirement that the voluntary, informed consent of each individual research subject must be obtained before any research is begun.

Besides the areas of experimental psychology and the work of some cultural anthropologists, virtually all demographic and related social science research and data gathering is minimally intrusive in terms of the original biomedical model and its extensions. Certainly the primary purpose and mode of the bulk of such data collection is simply the gathering of minimally sensitive information with the intent of characterizing populations rather than any individual respondent. Indeed, under the traditional informed consent paradigm many demographic data collection activities would be categorized as "minimally invasive." However, the need to protect respondents from harm arising from the information they provide imposes a responsibility on researchers to keep such information confidential. The inclusion of more sensitive health information and various biomarkers and anthropometric data (such as HIV status) in some demographic surveys calls for a higher level of respondent protection.

Under certain circumstances, information itself may pose real risks to human research subjects and their families, or to other members of the group to which these respondents belong. For example, as William Seltzer and Margo Anderson demonstrated, information on individuals and their group membership obtained through population registration and other routine data collection activities has been associated with major human rights abuses including genocide, forced migration, and internment. Historically, the risks have had particularly serious consequences for those in small, politically weak groups or in groups that were otherwise the object of attack. In the case of DNA testing, the risks lie primarily in the sensitivity of information obtained rather than in the degree of invasiveness of the procedure, and that those potentially at risk are not only the individual research subjects but also others with similar genetic characteristics.

The degree of risk associated with any demographic data collection effort or program is a function of many factors, including: the method of data collection, study design, the population being studied, the variables employed, and the level and methods of analysis. Table 1 summarizes those factors that seem to have contributed to elevated risks of misuse in the past.

As important as ethical considerations may be in promoting responsible demographic data collection, other kinds of safeguards can also play a role in protecting against possible misuse. These include substantive safeguards, methodological and technological safeguards, organizational and operational safeguards, and legal safeguards. Indeed, the use of multiple safeguards is perhaps the best defense against the misuse of demographic data and population data systems, and one goal of ethical awareness is to ensure that adequate attention has been devoted to these other safeguards.

Ethical norms also help temper the zeal of those promoting and implementing action and research programs and related demographic data gathering activities. These advocates or researchers are often so convinced of the importance and beneficence of research and data gathering that the resulting risks to others are minimized or ignored. Indeed, some of the most serious ethical lapses in research can be attributed to a lack of awareness that the particular activity presented any ethical issue at all.

See also: *Anthropometry; Census; Population Registers.*

BIBLIOGRAPHY

Annas, George J., and Grodin, Michael eds. (1992) *The Nazi Doctors and the Nuremberg Code: Human Rights in Human Experimentation.* New York: Oxford University Press.

Kultgen, John. 1988. *Ethics and Professionalism.* Philadelphia: University of Pennsylvania Press.

Murphy, Timothy F. and Marc A. Lappe, eds. 1994. *Justice and the Human Genome Project.* Berkeley: University of California Press.

Reich, Warren T., ed. 1995. *Encyclopedia of Bioethics,* revised edition. New York: Macmillan-Simon.

Seltzer, William and Margo Anderson. 2001. "The Dark Side of Numbers: The Role of Population Data Systems in Human Rights Abuses." *Social Research* 68: 2 (Summer): 481–513.

Vanderpool, Harold Y., ed. 1996. *The Ethics of Research Involving Human Subjects: Facing the 21st Century.* Frederick, MD: University Publishing Group.

INTERNET RESOURCES.

American Sociological Association. 1997. "Code of Ethics." <http://www.asanet.org/members/ecoderev.html>.

American Statistical Association. 1999. "Ethical Guidelines for Statistical Practice." <http://www.amstat.org/profession/ethicalstatistics.html>.

International Statistical Institute. 1986. "Declaration of Professional Ethics for Statisticians." <http://www.cbs.nl/isi/ethics.htm>.

WILLIAM SELTZER

DAVIS, KINGSLEY

(1908–1997)

One of the foremost demographers of his time and one of the most eminent and influential figures in twentieth-century American social science, Kingsley Davis made major contributions to demographic theory, the sociology of the family, and especially the understanding of the world demographic transition.

In 1930 Davis received a bachelor's degree in English from the University of Texas, where he was editor of the literary magazine. In 1932 he enrolled as a graduate student in Harvard's sociology department, receiving a doctorate in 1936. At Harvard he studied under Talcott Parsons, Pitrim Sorokin, W. Lloyd Warner, and Carle Zimmerman but did not take the one course in population offered by E. B. Wilson. He received no training in formal demography until 1940–1941, when as a postdoctoral fellow at the Social Science Research Council he studied under Samuel Stouffer at the University of Chicago and at the U.S. Bureau of the Census.

Davis held academic appointments at Clark University (1936–1937), Pennsylvania State University (1937–1944), Princeton University (1942–1948), Columbia University (1948–1955), the University of California at Berkeley (1955–1977), the University of Southern California (1977–1990), and the Hoover Institution (1981–1992). He was president of the American Sociological Association in 1959 and president of the Population Association of America in 1962–1963 and received the Population Association of America's Irene B. Taueber Award for Outstanding Research in Demography in 1978. In 1965 he was the first sociologist to be elected to the U.S. National Academy of Sciences.

Davis first achieved a considerable reputation for his research on the family, but his interest in population dynamics and related policy matters was evident in his earliest writings. An article, "Reproductive Institutions and the Pressure for Population," published when Davis was 28, offered an incisive analysis of the decline of the birthrate in modern industrial societies, locating the cause in the "ripening incongruity between our reproductive system (the family) and the rest of modern social organization" (1937, p. 290; 1997, p. 612). Davis rounded out the analysis with an original and provocative discussion of the policies, actual and potential, that can be used in an attempt to resolve that incongruity. The article foreshadowed not only the main topics Davis pursued throughout his long scientific career but also the distinctive and often combative style with which he explored important social phenomena.

Davis's preoccupation with demographic research proper began, however, with his appointment at Princeton University in 1942. At that university he wrote an influential article, "The World Demographic Transition" (1945), and did the major work on his opus, *The Population of India and Pakistan* (1951). In 1956, with Judith Blake, then his wife, he coauthored a path-breaking article on social structure and fertility, identifying the variables through which social factors can affect human reproduction. His 1963 presidential address to the Population Association of America, "The Theory of Change and Response in Modern Demographic History," was an important contribution to demographic transition theory. Influential works on world urbanization and international migration followed.

Davis was an engaged scholar, often writing on demographic topics and policy issues for a wide audience. His arresting and forceful critique of the inability of family planning programs to achieve population stabilization that appeared in *Science* in 1967 spawned many heated debates in academia and in Washington policy circles. Davis contended that in implying that the only requirement for fertility reduction was a perfect contraceptive device, family planners avoided discussion of the possibility that fundamental changes in social organization were necessary prerequisites.

In the last stage of his scientific career Davis continued to explore changes in the family and in sex roles and their effect on fertility. He also organized influential conferences that focused attention on the causes and consequences of below-replacement fertility levels and the relationship between resources, the environment, and population change.

Davis was a compelling teacher, and many prominent demographers trained under his stewardship. He wrote with exceptional clarity. His linguistic innovations include the terms *population explosion* and *zero population growth*. Moreover, along with his colleague Frank Notestein, he was the first to popularize the term *demographic transition*.

See also: *Blake, Judith; Demographic Transition; Demography, History of; Fertility, Proximate Determinants of; Population Thought, Contemporary.*

BIBLIOGRAPHY

SELECTED WORKS BY KINGSLEY DAVIS.

Davis, Kingsley. 1937. "Reproductive Institutions and the Pressure for Population." *Sociological Review,* July, pp. 289–366. Reprinted in *Population and Development Review* 23: 611–624 (1997).

———. 1945. "The World Demographic Transition." *Annals of the American Academy of Political and Social Science* 237: 1–11.

———. 1949. *Human Society.* New York: Macmillan.

———. 1951. *The Population of India and Pakistan.* Princeton, NJ: Princeton University Press.

———. 1963. "The Theory of Change and Response in Modern Demographic History." *Population Index* 29: 345–366.

———. 1967. "Population Policy: Will Current Programs Succeed?" *Science* 158: 730–739.

———. 1969/1972. *World Urbanization 1950–1970.* Berkeley, CA: Institute of International Studies.

———. 1973. *Cities: Their Origin, Growth and Human Impact.* San Francisco: W. H. Freeman.

———. 1984. "Wives and Work: The Sex Role Revolution and Its Consequences." *Population and Development Review* 10(3): 397–417.

Davis, Kingsley, and Judith Blake. 1956. "Social Structure and Fertility: An Analytic Framework." *Economic Development and Cultural Change* 4: 211–235.

Davis, Kingsley, ed., with M. S. Bernstam. 1991. *Resources, Environment, and Population: Present Knowledge, Future Options.* New York: Oxford University Press. Supplement to Vol. 16 of *Population and Development Review.*

Davis, Kingsley, ed., with M. S. Bernstam and R. R. Campbell. 1987. *Below-Replacement Fertility in Industrial Societies: Causes, Consequences, Policies.* New York: Cambridge University Press. Supplement to Vol. 12 of *Population and Development Review.*

SELECTED WORKS ABOUT KINGSLEY DAVIS.

Petersen, William. 1979. "Davis, Kingsley." In *International Encyclopedia of the Social Sciences,* ed. David L. Sills. Vol. 18: *Biographical Supplement.* New York: Free Press.

DAVID M. HEER

DEATH RATE

See *Mortality Measurement*

DEFORESTATION

Unlike the mere harvesting of trees for timber, deforestation changes a forest of growing trees into a different type of land cover. In France from 800 to 1300 C.E., the forests shrank by half, and in the United States from 1800 to 1920, the forests shrank by fully one-third. The replacement of forests, which ancient people might have seen as removing the lair of bandits and supernatural evil, in the twenty-first century seems a major transformation of the earth for the worse and hence an environmental threat.

Current Deforestation

During the 1990s the Food and Agriculture Organization (FAO) of the United Nations mounted a global survey to monitor changing forest areas. For the period from 1990 to 2000 FAO estimated that global deforestation was occurring at the average rate of 0.22 percent per year. Global forests shrank about 9 million hectares (ha) during the decade, an area roughly the size of Portugal or Hungary, or the state of Indiana. The global rates, however, cloak large regional differences, from 0.78 percent per year for deforestation in Africa, to its opposite, 0.08 percent per year afforestation in Europe. Among nations with more than one million ha of forest, the rates ranged widely—from deforestation at 3 percent or more per year in Niger, Ivory Coast, and Nicaragua to afforestation at 1 percent or more per year in seven nations as diverse as Belarus, China, Cuba, and Portugal.

Changes in land cover, including deforestation, are dynamic. The shrinkage of the earth's tropical forests from 1980 to 1990 was studied in a 1997 FAO survey of 3 billion ha of land (an area the size of Africa, or more than three times the land area of the United States) with several types of land cover. The forest with closed canopy in 1980 covered roughly half the surveyed area and is represented in Figure 1 as 100 percent. A decade later 93.3 percent of the 1980 forest was still closed; two percent of the 1980 forest had become open (i.e., open and fragmented forest plus long fallow); 1.8 percent had become shrub and short fallow; and 0.3 percent had been converted to plantations of trees. The largest conversion, 2.7 percent, was to other land cover, a category that includes permanent agriculture, cattle ranching, and water reservoirs, among others. Small conversions from open-canopied forest, and even smaller ones from the other classes of cover, to closed-canopy forest added a fraction of one percent to the 1990 closed forest. The small conversions to closed forest leave the impression that deforestation tends to be permanent.

Figure 2 describes forest change over almost the same decade (1982 to 1992) for a developed nation (the United States) that had earlier lost one-third of its forest. Fully 96.4 percent of non-federally-owned forest remained and conversions from other covers to forest slightly more than offset the lost 3.6 percent, expanding forest cover a little during the decade. Figures 1 and 2 exemplify the dynamic nature of changing land use, regional differences, and, instead of only deforestation, the possibility of afforestation.

The complexity of land cover change and differences in the definition of what a forest is make for uncertain estimates of the rate of deforestation. For example, the 0.5 percent change of forest to federal ownership shown in Figure 2 does not necessarily entail deforestation. Nor does the change from closed to plantation forest seen in Figure 1. FAO is attempting to generate consistent estimates of change using a uniform definition of forest area and applying remote-sensing techniques. In the end, while there is no doubt that deforestation is proceed-

FIGURE 1

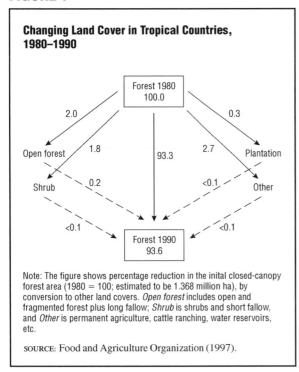

Changing Land Cover in Tropical Countries, 1980–1990

Note: The figure shows percentage reduction in the inital closed-canopy forest area (1980 = 100; estimated to be 1.368 million ha), by conversion to other land covers. *Open forest* includes open and fragmented forest plus long fallow; *Shrub* is shrubs and short fallow, and *Other* is permanent agriculture, cattle ranching, water reservoirs, etc.

SOURCE: Food and Agriculture Organization (1997).

ing in the tropics and afforestation is occurring in developed nations, some arbitrariness in estimated rates is inevitable.

Causes

Harvesting trees for lumber and pulp, even clear cutting the forest and allowing it to grow anew, does not qualify as deforestation. In developed nations, exemplified by the United States, lumber and pulp products have a declining role in the economy, so the overall impact of harvesting is diminishing over time. Authentic changes from forest to other cover occur when all the forest is removed for its products or the land is put to other use. Continually removing fuel wood can denude the land. In southern Africa, fuel wood accounts for about three-quarters of all energy use, and about 95 percent of all wood products were consumed for fuel. In the three rapidly deforesting countries cited above, Niger, Ivory Coast, and Nicaragua, two-thirds or more of the energy in each country came from wood in 1995. In the four countries that were mentioned above as having afforestation—Belarus, China, Cuba, and Portugal—wood represented less than one-twentieth of the energy source. In the first three countries population was rising faster than 2.4 percent per year during the

period, while in the latter four the rate rose at less than 1 percent per year.

In 1803 economist T. R. Malthus wrote, "When acre has been added to acre till all the fertile land is occupied, the yearly increase of food must depend upon the amelioration of the land already in possession. This is a stream which, from the nature of all soils, instead of increasing, must be gradually diminishing" (Malthus 1992, p.17). Since Malthus wrote, the shrinkage of forests has often been attributed to expansion of cropland to supply an inexorably multiplying population. As countries have developed, however, they modified the connection between population size and cropland. Wealth increases expenditure on food but not in proportion to rising income. Eating more animal products can increase the need for feed, but the rise in protein intake per person tapers off in wealthy nations. Increasing yields per ha lower the need for cropland. In many countries, the events of the twentieth century produced an outcome that Malthus could not have envisioned: More and richer people were able to eat better while cropland scarcely changed or even shrank. In the 1990s in developed nations, the per capita supply of calories and protein and the total cropland declined by a fraction of 1 percent per year; in the developing world, calorie consumption rose by 0.7 percent per year and protein consumption by 1.2 percent, while cropland rose only by 0.3 percent per year.

Worldwide during the 1990s, a period during which the population was increasing by 80 million per year, forests shrank by nearly 1 million ha per year. But over the same period, cropland shrank—by 100,000 ha per year. Maintaining the Malthusian view that an increasing population requires more cropland, causing deforestation, thus becomes difficult. The role of grazing in deforestation is less clear because of the blurred distinction between pasture and woodland. (For this reason FAO abandoned reporting pasture area, although it did report that cattle numbers fell 2 percent per year in developed countries and rose 1.3 percent in developing countries during the period from 1990 to 1999.)

Geographers Alexander Mather and Coby L. Needle reasonably concluded from these estimates: "Outright rejection of the notion that forest trends are related to population trends is no more justifiable than an unqualified assertion that population growth is *the* driver of deforestation" (p.10).

Why Deforestation Matters

Why do some people see deforestation as an evil? An immediate reason is that eliminating forests may lead to a timber shortage. Traveling through New York and New England two centuries ago, President Timothy Dwight of Yale University worried that the voracious demand for fuel would deforest that region; yet at the beginning of the twenty-first century those areas again grow wide forests. The fear of timber shortage, of course, may be well justified in nations that continue to depend on fuel wood and are suffering deforestation.

Environmental consequences are another reason for concern about deforestation. Denuding land decreases evaporation from foliage and encourages rapid runoff and erosion. The loss of forest habitat can lead to the extinction of certain species. And, through diminished absorption of carbon dioxide in forest biomass, deforestation adds perhaps 20 percent to the carbon dioxide released from other anthropogenic sources, contributing to possible global warming.

Finally, the esthetic and emotional effects of deforestation, even if unmeasurable, cannot be ignored. Supported by myth, art, and literature, a veneration for forests persists.

Transition

An era of rising population and deforestation that has evolved into an era of afforestation in some nations despite rising population has been labeled the forest transition by Mather and Needle. If deforestation is feared and since the global population is certain to grow in the first part of the twenty-first century, this transition must continue to be the goal.

Planting trees directly expands forests. By the end of the twentieth century, forest plantations comprised 5 percent of global forest cover and were expanding at 2.4 percent per year. Plantations, which can sometimes produce timber faster than natural forests, can spare natural ones from harvest. Maintaining existing cropland in usable condition and raising crop yields spare forests from agricultural encroachment. Developing other types of fuel lessens the need to cut forests for fuel wood. These processes are contributing to the forest transition that is evident in an increasing number of countries in the first years of the twenty-first century.

See also: *Land Use; Natural Resources and Population; Sustainable Development.*

FIGURE 2

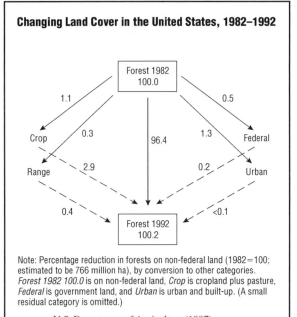

Changing Land Cover in the United States, 1982–1992

Note: Percentage reduction in forests on non-federal land (1982=100; estimated to be 766 million ha), by conversion to other categories. *Forest 1982 100.0* is on non-federal land, *Crop* is cropland plus pasture, *Federal* is government land, and *Urban* is urban and built-up. (A small residual category is omitted.)

SOURCE: U.S. Department of Agriculture (1997).

BIBLIOGRAPHY

Clawson, Marion. 1979. "Forests in the Long Sweep of American History." *Science* 204: 1168–1174.

Dwight, Timothy. 1969. *Travels in New England and New York,* Volume 4. Cambridge, MA: Belknap Press of Harvard University Press.

Food and Agriculture Organization. 1997. *State of the World's Forests.* Rome: Food and Agriculture Organization.

Food and Agriculture Organization. 2001. *FRA 2000 Global Tables.* Rome: Food and Agriculture Organization.

Malthus, T. R. 1992 (1803). *An Essay on the Principle of Population.* Cambridge, Eng.: Cambridge University Press.

Mather, Alexander S., and Coby L. Needle. 2000. "The Relationship of Population and Forest Trends." *The Geographical Journal* 166: 2–13.

Palo, Matti, and Jussi Uusivuori. 1999. *World Forests, Society and Environment.* Dordrecht, the Netherlands: Kluwer Academic Publishers.

Schama, Simon. 1995. *Landscape and Memory.* New York: Knopf.

U.S. Department of Agriculture. 1997. "Agricultural Resources and Environmental Indicators, 1996–

97." *Agricultural Handbook,* No. 712. Washington, D.C.: U.S. Department of Agriculture.

Waggoner, Paul E., and Jesse H. Ausubel. 2001. "How Much Will Feeding More and Wealthier People Encroach on Forests?" *Population and Development Review* 27: 239–257.

Wernick, Iddo K., Paul E. Waggoner, and Jesse H. Ausubel. 1998. "Searching for Leverage to Conserve Forests." *Journal of Industrial Ecology* 1: 125–145.

INTERNET RESOURCES.

Food and Agriculture Organization. <http://www.fao.org/>.

U.S. Energy Information Agency.<http://www.eia.doe.gov/>.

PAUL E. WAGGONER

DEMOGRAPHIC AND HEALTH SURVEYS

The Demographic and Health Surveys (DHS) project is designed to produce accurate and timely information on population, health, and nutrition in developing countries. DHS surveys are national sample surveys that provide key data for planning, monitoring, and evaluating programs in these areas. DHS data also play a major role in furthering international understanding of global population and health trends. The surveys provide an unparalleled body of comparable data on demographic, health, and nutrition indicators and are a primary source of reproductive and health information for Africa, Asia, Latin America, and the Caribbean.

Program Inception

The DHS program started in 1984 as a follow-up to the World Fertility Survey and the earlier Contraceptive Prevalence Surveys. Through the end of 2002, 145 DHS surveys of reproductive-age women had been conducted in 68 countries. In addition, 74 surveys of men had been conducted in 44 countries. Most DHS surveys have a sample size of 4,000 to 8,000 women, but several have had substantially larger samples. The 1998–1999 National Family Health Survey in India included interviews with 90,303 ever-married women.

Funding

The DHS program is funded by the United States Agency for International Development as part of the MEASURE Program, which is comprised of five related projects focusing on data collection, analysis, and dissemination. Additional funding for surveys in individual countries often is obtained from the United Nations Children's Fund (UNICEF), the United Nations Population Fund, the World Bank, the United Kingdom's Department for International Development, and other organizations. ORC Macro, based in Calverton, Maryland, provides technical and administrative support for the DHS program. Surveys are implemented by agencies in participating countries, under contract with ORC Macro.

The principal objectives of the DHS program are as follows:

• To improve the information base for policy development, economic and social planning, and the management of population and health programs;

• To promote the widespread dissemination and use of DHS data by policymakers and planners;

• To expand institutional capabilities in participating countries to collect and analyze survey data;

• To improve methodologies and procedures for conducting and analyzing demographic and health surveys.

The content of the surveys has varied over time, depending on emerging problems and the needs of data users, including participating governments, nongovernmental organizations, international agencies, and funding agencies. The surveys are based on a standard set of core questionnaires. Additional questionnaire modules on topics of interest, as well as country-specific questions, may be added to the core questionnaires in each country. This ensures that the questionnaires will be most relevant to the needs of each country while allowing for cross-country comparisons of findings on the core topics.

The current content of the core questionnaires covers topics such as fertility, fertility preferences, family planning, marriage, women's empowerment, sexual activity, reproductive health, child health, environmental health, nutrition, AIDS and other sexually transmitted diseases, and socioeconomic conditions. The questionnaire modules on HIV/AIDS, maternal mortality, and female genital mutilation have been used the most frequently. In addition, some recent surveys include biomarker tests for anemia, HIV, syphilis, lead levels, cholesterol, vitamin A, and hepatitis B.

Findings

The vast array of findings from the DHS surveys have been detailed in hundreds of reports and research papers. Among their findings, DHS surveys have documented a decline in fertility in most parts of the developing world, high discontinuation rates for specific contraceptive methods in many countries, relatively high percentages of female-headed households in sub-Saharan Africa and the Caribbean, a strong preference for sons in many countries, the adverse effect of short intervals between births on the survival prospects of infants, and a substantial level of unmet need for family planning in most countries.

DHS surveys have also found high levels of anemia among children and women in India and the Central Asian republics, a high prevalence of chronic energy deficiency among women in sub-Saharan Africa, relatively high levels of obesity among women in the Middle East and North Africa, and a strong effect of poor feeding practices on the nutritional status of young children. Additional findings include substantial advances in public knowledge about AIDS and an increase in condom use during high-risk sexual encounters in AIDS-affected countries, the importance of the empowerment of women in promoting improvements in the health of both women and children, and inadequate vaccination coverage for vaccine-preventable diseases among young children in almost all the developing countries covered.

Advantages and Disadvantages

No single type of survey or data collection instrument can provide all the information necessary to inform policymaking decisions and monitor and evaluate population, health, and nutrition programs. However, the DHS surveys provide a rich and varied base of information in these areas. Some of the specific advantages of the DHS surveys are the following:

- Data are collected in a standard fashion to facilitate comparisons across countries and over time;
- DHS surveys produce generalizable data from nationally representative samples;
- The DHS program produces detailed manuals for interviewers, supervisors, household listers, and sampling statisticians to promote uniformity in procedures;
- DHS surveys incorporate extensive quality controls, including the production of field quality tables throughout the fieldwork and multiple levels of supervision and monitoring to detect and correct errors at an early stage;
- DHS data sets are made widely available over the Internet at no cost to the user;
- The collection of information on a wide variety of topics in a single survey allows in-depth study of the relationships among population, health, and nutrition variables;
- DHS surveys provide an important vehicle for the collection of biological specimens and the measurement of biological markers of health status in a cost-effective manner;
- Recent DHS data sets are geo-coded to allow linking of DHS data and other data in geographic information systems.

Among the limitations are the following:

- DHS samples are generally not large enough to provide estimates for small geographic areas, which often are needed for monitoring and evaluating decentralized programs;
- DHS surveys in a specific country are typically conducted every three to six years so that annual estimates of key indicators are not available from the surveys;
- Like any large-scale national sample survey, DHS surveys are fairly costly;
- DHS samples are not large enough to produce reliable estimates of the levels or trends of some relatively rare phenomena, such as maternal mortality.

More details about the Demographic and Health Surveys are available on the DHS website, which includes information about all DHS surveys, directions for obtaining data sets, and instructions for ordering or downloading DHS publications. In addition, the website contains an online database tool, the STATcompiler, that allows users to build customized tables for hundreds of indicators based on DHS surveys in more than 60 countries.

See also: *Anthropometry; Data Assessment; Demographic Surveys, History and Methodology of; World Fertility Survey.*

INTERNET RESOURCE

Demographic and Health Surveys. 2003. <http://www.measuredhs.com>.

FRED ARNOLD

DEMOGRAPHIC SURVEILLANCE SYSTEMS

Collecting information on population dynamics in a defined geographic area is a practice that is as old as demography itself. Parish records and civil registers provided information that was used in the earliest attempts to characterize mortality and population dynamics. The earliest known calculations of mortality rates were based on civil registers for a segment of London.

Fertility models have been based on archival registers that are similar to contemporary surveillance systems. The first model life tables were based on population register mortality regimes.

In the twentieth century the role of population observatories expanded from description to investigation. Early studies focused on epidemiological questions (e.g., Goldberger et al. 1920). After World War II, controlled trials were used for the demographic evaluation of health experiments (e.g., Ferebee and Mount 1962) and research stations were created where vital registration in defined geographic areas was applied to estimate demographic characteristics and carry out an expanding range of epidemiological, social policy, and demographic studies. By the 1960s the health and population research role of those research stations and population laboratories was recognized as an area of scientific specialization within the field of demography. The term *demographic surveillance system* (DSS) came to be used to

connote the technologies associated with the continuous monitoring of births, deaths, and migration in a defined population over time.

Descriptive Demography and Health Interventions

At the beginning of the twenty-first century approximately 50 DSS health and population research centers were in operation around the world. Although some surveillance systems were established for the purpose of descriptive demography, the aim of most contemporary applications is to evaluate the impact of health interventions. Well-established demographic surveillance systems can provide concomitant support for multiple social, demographic, and economic investigations. Some are sites for pharmaceutical trials. In the year 2002, 28 DSS research centers were participants in the INDEPTH Network, an international organization that disseminates DSS information.

Survey Designs

The early era of population registration occurred in settings that were closed to migration. Such settings no longer exist. Surveillance systems in modern populations have to deal with migration. Establishing surveillance requires a baseline census to describe the initial population of a site by age and sex and selected other characteristics. Two contrasting strategies then are employed to update the baseline census data:

1. The *individual observation approach* records the timing and incidence of all births, deaths, and migration in and out of study areas so that the risk of events at the individual level can be defined precisely at any point in time. Migration is defined in terms of an individual's arrival at or departure from a surveillance observation unit such as the extended family, a nuclear household, or a dwelling unit over a specified period of time. Definitions of migration specify the length of time that must elapse before migration is registered as an event. Recording and managing such information represent most of the task load of individual observation systems. Most continuous demographic surveillance systems incorporate procedures for recording marital events, causes of death, and status in a household structure defined by headship or

by spousal, parental, and familial relationships.

2. The *population observation model* registers births and deaths and employs repeat censuses to estimate populations at risk of these events over time. Studies conducted by the British Medical Research Council in Gambia and in eastern and southern Africa used this approach (e.g., Greenwood et al. 1990). Dual registration systems were used to adjust coverage errors in population laboratories. This approach has been useful in descriptive demography and studies that employ area units of analysis. Health interventions consigned to clusters of households, for example, can be evaluated by monitoring births and deaths over time, enumerating cluster populations at the baseline and at the end of the project period, and estimating cluster populations over the study period. This approach obviates the need to monitor individual migration continuously or to link event data with individual census registers, thus simplifying data management processes and reducing the complexity of field operations in comparison to individual surveillance approaches.

Despite the advantages of the aggregate population observation approach, most demographic surveillance systems that have been established since the 1990s have utilized continuous individual registration designs. This practice can be explained in part by the advent of low-cost computer technologies that overcome many of the limitations of the individual surveillance approach (e.g., MacLeod et al. 1996) and the emergence of health technologies that require individual-level trials.

Individual observation expands the range of social, demographic, and health research that can be conducted in conjunction with surveillance. In the individual continuous observation approach, any cross-sectional study that records demographic surveillance identification numbers eventually permits a longitudinal study of demographic processes. A few well-designed surveillance sites have produced several thousand scientific publications (e.g., Behar et al. 1968; Scrimshaw et al. 1968; D'Sousa 1984; Menken and Phillips 1990). The longest-running and best-known DSS is Matlab, in Bangladesh.

Cohort and Panel Studies

Cohort and panel studies are alternatives to the DSS approach for longitudinal health research. Cohort studies observe a specified subgroup in a population over time and are closed to the addition of study individuals as time progresses. Panel research involves interviewing an open cohort of individuals over time. Cohort and panel designs are appropriate when a single longitudinal study is designed to answer a specific research question about a segment of a population. However, launching a succession of cohort and panel studies in a specific population is more costly than DSS approaches because each new panel or cohort study requires a new enumeration, new field procedures, and the repeated development of specialized computer systems.

Limitations

The comprehensiveness of a DSS's demographic coverage represents the principal limitation. The required scale of the data collection imposes limits on the range of information that can be compiled about other topics. Sample cohort and survey studies sometimes are conducted in conjunction with DSS operations to expand the range of information available for longitudinal research. Cluster-sampling techniques are sometimes used to reduce the quantity of data collected and lower the costs. Surveillance is costly if field management and computing procedures are not well developed because errors can multiply over time and constrain analyses. The representativeness of DSS data sometimes is questioned both because the localities chosen for surveillance operations are likely to be unrepresentative of wider populations and because the presence of researchers and associated program activities may influence the behaviors that are observed.

See also: *Demographic Surveys, History and Methodology of; Longitudinal Demographic Surveys; Population Registers.*

BIBLIOGRAPHY

Behar, M., Nevin S. Scrimshaw, Miguel A. Guzman, and John E. Gordon. 1968. "Nutrition and Infection Field Study in Guatemalan Villages, 1959–1964. VIII: An Epidemiological Appraisal of Its Wisdom and Errors." *Archives of Environmental Health* 17: 814–827.

D'Souza, S. 1984. "Population Laboratories for Studying Disease Processes and Mortality: The

Demographic Surveillance System, Matlab." In *Methodologies for the Collection and Analysis of Mortality Data,* ed. Jacques Vallin, John H. Pollard, and Larry Heligman. Proceedings of a Seminar at Dakar, Senegal, July 17–10. Liège, Belgium: Ordina Editions.

Ferebee, S. H., and F. W. Mount. 1962. "Tuberculosis Morbidity in a Controlled Trial of the Prophylactic Use of Isoniazid among Household Contacts." *American Review of Respiratory Diseases* 85: 495–521.

Goldberger, Joseph, G. A. Wheeler, and E. Sydenstricker. 1920. "A Study of the Relation of Diet to Pellagra Incidence in Seven Textile Mill Communities of South Carolina in 1916." *Public Health Reports* 35: 648–713.

Greenwood, B. M., et al. 1990. "Evaluation of a Primary Health Care Programme in the Gambia and Its Impact on Mortality and Morbidity in Young Children." *Journal of Tropical Medicine and Hygiene* 93: 87–97.

INDEPTH Network. 2002. *Population, Health, and Survival at INDEPTH Sites.* Ottawa, Canada: International Development Research Centre.

Kasprzyk, Daniel, et al. 1989. *Panel Surveys.* New York: Wiley.

Linder, F. E. 1971. "The Concept and the Program of the Laboratories for Population Statistics." Laboratories for Population Statistics Scientific Series No. 1, March.

MacLeod, B. B., J. Phillips, and F. Binka. 1996. "Sustainable Software Technology Transfer: The Household Registration System." In *Encyclopedia of Library and Information Science,* Vol. 58, Supplement 21, ed. K. Allen. New York: Marcel Dekker.

Menken, J., and J. F. Phillips. 1990. "Population Change in a Rural Area of Bangladesh: 1967–1987." *Annals of the American Academy of Political and Social Science* 510: 87–101.

Mozumder, K. A., et al. 1990. "The Sample Registration System: An Innovative System for Monitoring Demographic Dynamics." *Asia-Pacific Journal* 5: 63–72.

Scrimshaw, N. S., et al. 1968. "Nutrition and Infection Field Study in Guatemalan Villages, 1959–1964. V: Disease Incidence among Preschool Children under Natural Village Conditions with Improved Diet and with Medical and Public Health Services." *Archives of Environmental Health* 16: 233–234.

JAMES F. PHILLIPS

DEMOGRAPHIC SURVEYS, HISTORY AND METHODOLOGY OF

Demographic surveys are surveys that wholly or primarily collect information on population characteristics and on the causes and consequences of population change. In addition, demographic surveys can be a name given to surveys that contain mostly demographic information although they also contain information of a non-demographic nature.

Historical Overview of Population Surveys

Population censuses attempt to measure characteristics of the total population of a country or territory through the *full* enumeration of all persons and relevant events. Surveys have emerged as alternatives to census taking with the development of statistical sampling techniques that permit interviewing only a part of the population of interest to obtain estimates that are valid for the population as a whole.

Population surveys have a long history, including the 1086 Domesday survey in England. This survey, as well as most other early surveys, was a social survey dealing with living conditions and poverty. Many of these studies were carried out in the eighteenth and nineteenth centuries, but none was based on true probability sampling methods. The first study that employed probabilistic sampling was a 1913 study by A. L. Bowley on the living conditions of the working classes in five English cities. Survey research in the demographic field only came into wide usage in the mid-1900s.

Demographic surveys are often taken in conjunction with a census. This was done for the first time in 1940, in the United States. The items covered in the census were significantly increased for 5 percent of the census population, making it possible to collect extensive additional information without increasing the burden on all census respondents and at relatively small additional cost.

One of the first demographic surveys was conducted by Raymond Pearl in 1939, covering 31,000 women in American hospitals. Other early U.S. demographic surveys include the Current Population Survey (CPS) carried out monthly by the Bureau of the Census since 1940; the 1941 Indianapolis study by Pascal Whelpton and Clyde Kiser; the 1960 Growth of American Families Study by Whelpton, Arthur Campbell, and John Patterson; and the 1965 and 1970 National Fertility Surveys carried out by Charles F. Westoff and Norman B. Ryder of Princeton University. The National Center for Health Statistics (NCHS) carried out six rounds of the National Survey of Family Growth (NSFG) between 1973 and 2002.

The CPS is focused on employment and unemployment and economic activity but additional questions are added from time to time to obtain information on other population characteristics. One of its advantages is its large sample size: 50,000 households. The data from the CPS serve to update information on the U.S. population between the decennial censuses. Annual demographic data files are available from this source. The other early surveys mentioned above were designed to provide information specifically related to fertility, family planning, and family formation. They sampled women in the fertile age group, with sample sizes below 10,000.

The NCHS undertakes a number of health related survey activities that provide significant demographic information, such as the National Health and Nutrition Examination Survey, which has been carried out eight times since 1960. The round that began in 1999 has been converted into a continuous survey in which 5000 people are surveyed annually in 15 locations in the United States.

Most developed countries have survey activities similar to those in the United States. Periodic labor force surveys are a major source for demographic information. Special demographic surveys have been more rare. The 1946 survey on fertility in Britain by David Glass and Eugene Grebenik was a forerunner for fertility surveys that were carried out in the 1960s in Belgium, Canada, Greece, Hungary, The Netherlands, the United Kingdom, and the Soviet Union. In the 1970s similar surveys were conducted in 15 European countries as an offshoot of the World Fertility Survey (WFS) program, which operated from 1973 to 1984 but was mainly focused on developing countries. A further round of fertility surveys, the Fertility and Family Surveys in Countries of the Economic Commission for Europe Region, was carried out in the 1990s in about twenty countries under the sponsorship of the United Nations Population Fund (UNFPA).

In developing countries, the main sources of demographic information, aside from population censuses, are labor force and economic surveys, and surveys on population and health. Among the latter, the Puerto Rico studies on family planning by Paul K. Hatt in 1947 and Reuben J. Hill, Mayone Stycos, and Kurt W. Back in 1959 were some of the earliest. In India, the 1952 Mysore study was groundbreaking. In the 1960s more than 125 fertility and related surveys were carried out in the developing world, a majority in Africa. Special demographic surveys have most often been achieved through participation in international survey programs like the WFS. The ongoing Demographic and Health Surveys (DHS) program funded by the United States Agency for International Development (USAID) has sponsored over 150 surveys in the period from 1984 to 2001. Among other international programs that have contributed significantly to the availability of demographic survey data in developing countries are the World Bank–sponsored Living Standards Measurement Surveys (LSMS) program, which has carried out over 30 complex surveys since 1985; the UNICEF sponsored Multiple Indicator Cluster Survey (MICS) program, with over 120 surveys since 1995; the Centers for Disease Control and Prevention (CDC) USAID-sponsored surveys, in operation since 1985, with over 40 surveys; the Contraceptive Prevalence Surveys (CPS), also sponsored by USAID, which carried out 39 surveys over 1976–1984; and numerous smaller survey efforts.

Longitudinal Surveys

There is a basic distinction between surveys that are planned to provide a snapshot of the population under study at the time of the survey and those planned to provide repeated information on the same sample populations. The former are usually called single-round surveys, the latter are called panel or longitudinal surveys. A longitudinal survey can measure changes in the population with greater precision than could be achieved by drawing on retrospective information collected in single-round surveys (given the likelihood of recall error by respondents) or by comparing the results from two surveys that are based on independent samples. The effect of programmatic interventions in the period between surveys can also be measured more easily.

These advantages of the longitudinal design are balanced by a number of important disadvantages. Longitudinal surveys are generally more costly; the sample population is affected by death and migration; and the respondents may suffer respondent's fatigue if interviewed on too regular a basis. In developing countries an added problem is locating the exact households to be revisited, given the absence of good addresses and the inaccessibility of some sample areas. A particular example of longitudinal surveys are demographic surveillance systems (DSS) These systems reinterview the residents of a small and specific geographic area on a regular schedule. Interviews can happen as often as once every two weeks, as in the Matlab area of Bangladesh. The DSS design is ideal for studying change in a population. The major drawback is that the survey area is typically not representative of the population in the country.

Some of the problems of longitudinal surveys can be overcome in a hybrid design that combines a single round and a longitudinal survey. In this design the sample clusters are the same in each successive survey, but the individual respondents need not be the same. The characteristics of people in a specific sample cluster are more homogeneous than the characteristics of people in different clusters, thus making the samples more similar than if the samples had been totally independent. This provides greater precision in the estimates of change.

Sampling Strategies

Sampling is a difficult task even when the necessary baseline data about the population to be sampled are readily available. In the United States, most research institutions obtain their basic data from the U.S. Bureau of the Census and other government agencies that collect basic statistical information or from commercial firms that sell samples and sampling frames. Most developing countries lack updated census and other information that can serve as secure sampling frames. More often than not, special field operations are necessary to develop an appropriate sample frame by creating up-to-date listings of households or dwellings.

Probability sampling consists of randomly selecting the desired number of subjects from a complete list of all similar subjects in the sample universe. It depends on mechanical random selection and ensures that every element in the population of interest has a known, positive probability of selection. The way samples are actually drawn will depend on what the samples are expected to represent. For instance, if a sample is expected to provide information for a country as a whole and also for each of four of its provinces, each of those provinces needs to be allocated a large enough sample to permit calculation of the required indicators with the desired level of precision.

One factor that helps determine the type of sample to be drawn is whether the sampled individuals will be interviewed through a personal or a phone interview. For personal interview samples, it is typically too costly to interview people who are chosen individually from a list of all individuals in the sample universe. Kish calls this element sampling. For this and other reasons, most personal interview samples are drawn under cluster sampling. Cluster sampling selects groups of elements, with each group or cluster containing contiguous sampling elements (e.g., an urban block). Using cluster sampling implies that all the elements of the population are represented and identifiable in one of the clusters. The size of the clusters and the number of elements to be selected in each selected cluster will be determined by the objectives of the study and the field costs of the survey. The major advantage of cluster sampling is cost savings in the fieldwork; the major drawback is that the homogeneity of elements within each cluster means that the variance *between* elements is greater.

Developments in Data Processing

Some of the main bottlenecks in getting survey data published shortly after data collection have traditionally been the hardware, software, and manpower available for processing the information collected. In the 1960s and early 1970s most surveys were still processed by coding the information on special coding sheets and entering that information on punch cards that were then used in computer analysis of the data. Survey researchers typically had to operate through intermediaries at computer centers to have the data tabulated. With the advent of microcomputers in the late 1970s and the creation of appropriate software, it became possible to do most data processing in-house. Until the mid-1980s, the speed of the available processors and software limitations still made the processing of large surveys a difficult enterprise.

Large data collection efforts such as censuses were most often processed using optical readers. This avoided the onerous task of entering the data by hand and speeded up their availability for analysis. Due to special requirements of page layout and the necessarily limited length of the questionnaires, few comprehensive surveys were processed through the optical reader process.

One of the major problems in survey data processing is how to create a file that is free of structural or consistency errors in the variables. Such a file is created through detailed editing of the data and, where possible, imputation of missing data. This editing eliminates the errors introduced during the interview, in the coding process, and in data entry. The availability of microcomputers for data entry made it possible to build structural, range, and some consistency checks into the data entry program and resulted in fewer errors in initial data files. Further consistency checking can eliminate these types of errors altogether. The development of appropriate software for these stages of processing has been a major factor in the earlier availability of survey data. The Demographic and Health Surveys program developed its Integrated System for Survey Analysis (ISSA), which can handle all data entry, editing, and tabulation. The Netherlands' Institute of Statistics developed a similar program called BLAISE, while the CDC developed the widely used program called EPI-info. Statistical analysis packages such as SPSS and SAS also contributed much to the speedier publication of survey data.

The continued development of personal computers and the availability of laptops and handheld computers are further facilitating survey processing. Frequently, data are entered on a handheld computer or laptop during the interview, thus obviating the need for further data entry. In addition, checks incorporated during the interview can ensure that the resulting files are largely free of error, which minimizes the need for extensive cleaning of the data. There are already instances where survey data are instantly transmitted from the interviewer's computer to a central computer for tabulations.

The proliferation of software and equipment has also had its drawbacks, especially in developing countries. Too many different systems are in use, making it more difficult to build the capacity of organizations to process their own surveys.

Telephone Surveys

Telephone surveys are the most common and cheapest way to collect information for marketing and other purposes. For obtaining demographic survey data, they can only be used where all the sample population is reachable by phone. This excludes developing countries. In the United States, the proportion of households with a phone rose above 90 percent in the 1970s, making it possible to sample nearly as well in a telephone survey as through personal interviews. This has generated a fast-growing telephone interviewing industry.

A major advantage of telephone surveys is that the sample design has no impact on the speed of data collection. Distance between sample subjects is not a problem. Another major advantage is quality control, particularly where the telephone interviews are conducted by means of a Computer Assisted Telephone Interviewing (CATI) system. This system can control the sample selection, the flow of the interview, and the quality of data entry. A further advantage is that the use of a CATI system ensures instant availability of the data. Telephone surveys are generally considered to be unsuitable for interviews of longer than 20 minutes, particularly if the subject matter of the interview requires a high degree of cooperation. Due to their cost-effectiveness, telephone surveys are also used in combination with other methods of data collection. Short screening interviews are often done by phone to determine which respondents should receive a more comprehensive personal interview. Sampling for telephone interviews poses its own challenges, however, due to the existence of unlisted phone numbers. A technique called "list assisted random digit dial" is used to decide how many telephone numbers to select from telephone lists with different occurrences of unlisted numbers.

See also: *Census; Demographic and Health Surveys; Longitudinal Demographic Surveys; World Fertility Survey.*

BIBLIOGRAPHY

Adlakah, Arjun, Jeremiah M. Sullivan, and James R. Abernathy. 1980. "Recent Trends in the Methodology of Demographic Surveys in Developing Countries." *Scientific Report Series,* No. 33.

Baum, Samuel, Kathleen Dopkowski, William G. Duncan, and Peter Gardiner. 1974. "The World Fertility Survey Inventory." *World Fertility Survey Occasional Papers,* nos. 3–6.

Cleland, John, and Christopher Scott. 1987. *The World Fertility Survey: An Assessment.* Oxford: Oxford University Press.

Dekker, Arie. 1997. "Data Processing for Demographic Censuses and Surveys with Special Emphasis on Methods Applicable to Developing Country Environments." *Netherlands Interdisciplinary Demographic Institute (NIDI) Report No. 51.* The Hague, Netherlands: NIDI.

Hatt, Paul K. 1952. *Backgrounds of Human Fertility in Puerto Rico: A Sociological Survey.* Princeton, NJ: Princeton University Press.

Hill, Reuben, J. Mayone Stycos, and Kurt W. Back. 1959. *The Family and Population Control: A Puerto Rican Experiment in Social Change.* Chapel Hill: University of North Carolina Press.

International Development Research Center. 2002. *Population and Health in Developing Countries, Vol. 1, Population, Health and Survival at IN-DEPTH Sites.* Ottawa, Canada: International Development Research Center.

Kalton, Graham. 1983. *Introduction to Survey Sampling.* Beverly Hills, CA: Sage.

Lavrakas, Paul J. 1993. *Telephone Survey Methods, Sampling, Selection and Supervision.* Applied Social Research Methods Series, Vol. 7. London: Sage.

Lloyd, Cynthia B., and Catherine M. Marquette. 1992. *Directory of Surveys in Developing Countries: Data on Families and Households, 1975–92.* New York: Population Council.

Macro International Inc. 1996. *Sampling Manual.* DHS-III Basic Documentation Number 6. Calverton, MD: Macro International.

Moser, Claus A., and Graham Kalton. 1972. *Survey Methods in Social Investigation.* 2nd edition. London: Heinemann, 1971. New York: Basic Books.

Pearl, Raymond. 1939. *The Natural History of Population.* London. Oxford University Press.

Population Council. 1970. *A Manual for Surveys of Fertility and Family Planning; Knowledge, Attitudes, and Practice.* Population Council: New York.

Ryder, Norman B., and Charles F. Westoff. 1971. *Reproduction in the United States, 1965.* Princeton, NJ: Princeton University Press.

Shyrock, Henry S. Jr., Jacob S. Siegel, et al. 1971 (3rd rev. printing, 1975). *The Methods and Materials of Demography.* 2 vols. Prepared for the U.S. Bureau of the Census. Washington D.C.: U.S. Government Printing Office.

Tablin, Delphine. 1984. "Comparison of Single and Multi-round Surveys for Measuring Mortality in Developing Countries." In *Methodologies for the Collection and Analysis of Mortality Data,* eds. Jacques Vallin, John Pollard, Larry Heligman. Liège, Belgium: International Union for the Scientific Study of Population, Ordina Editions.

United Nations. 1961. *The Mysore Population Study.* (ST/SOA/Series A/34). New York, NY: United Nations.

United Nations. 1984. *Handbook of Household Surveys.* (ST/ESA/STA/SER.F/31). New York: United Nations.

Whelpton, Pascal K., and Clyde V. Kiser, eds. 1946 (rev. 1950, 1952, 1954, 1958). *Social and Psychological Factors Affecting Fertility,* 5 vols. New York: Milbank Memorial Fund.

Martin Vaessen

DEMOGRAPHIC TRANSITION

The term *demographic transition* refers to the decline in mortality and fertility from the high rates characteristic of premodern and low-income societies to the low rates characteristic of modern and high-income societies. Demographic transition is a central concept in demography, and there is a large literature examining the nature and the causes of the phenomenon. On the face of it, demographic transition is simply a description of a pattern of historical trends in vital rates. The influential discussions of demographic transition, however, interweave description with explanation of mortality and fertility declines, and this has made it difficult to separate the descriptive concept from the far more controversial "theory" of demographic transition.

History of the Concept

Although the term demographic transition originated with Frank W. Notestein in the mid-twentieth century, the first systematic effort to describe distinctive demographic regimes that represented historical stages linked to broader societal changes is credited to the work of the French demographer Adolphe Landry dating back to the first decade of the twentieth century. In Landry's formulation, elaborated in greater detail in a book published in 1934, demographic regimes are a function of the material aspirations of individuals and the productive potential of the economic system. In the "primitive" regime characteristic of subsistence economies, mortality but not fertility is constrained by economic factors, and population size tends to the maximum that economic resources can support. In the "intermediate" regime, in an effort to preserve family wealth, fertility is depressed by late marriage and celibacy, and population size falls below the maximum that the economy can support. The "modern" regime emerges when economic productivity reaches high levels and individuals have well-formulated aspirations for a high standard of living. To facilitate the achievement of those material aspirations, fertility becomes an object of conscious limitation, chiefly through various techniques of birth control but also through late marriage and celibacy. Population size is far smaller than the economy could support were individuals willing to accept lower standards of living—indeed negative population growth rates are a distinct possibility.

An alternative three-stage formulation of demographic transition was offered by the American demographer Warren Thompson in 1929. Thompson classified the countries of the world into three groups: (1) countries with high birth rates and high but declining death rates, facing the prospect of rapid population growth; (2) countries with declining birth and death rates in certain socioeconomic strata, with the rate of decline in death rates outstripping the rate of decline in birthrates; and (3) countries with rapidly declining birth and death rates, with fertility declining more rapidly than mortality, resulting in a declining population growth rate. Thompson assumed that these three groups were representative of historical stages. But by limiting his purview to contemporary demographic regimes, Thompson offered a truncated evolutionary scheme—he described neither a full-fledged pretransition regime nor a posttransition regime. In ad-

dition, Thompson had less to say about the causes of demographic change than his predecessor Landry and his successors Notestein and Kingsley Davis.

Notestein's formulation has probably been the most influential, appearing just at the onset of a five-decade period of widespread concern about the development-retarding effects of rapid population growth in Africa, Asia, and Latin America. Notestein held that the lessons he had distilled from the European historical experience were applicable to other regions and could inform public policies. Like Thompson, Notestein focused on the societal variation he observed at the time and therefore devoted limited attention to pretransitional regimes. He was aware that mortality decline was well underway in Africa, Asia, and Latin America yet fertility was essentially unchanged; these societies with high-population-growth potential constituted his first type of demographic regime. A second were those countries where fertility decline was well established but incomplete (Japan, the Soviet Union, and the southern cone of South America), and the third type were the low mortality and fertility populations of Europe, North America, and Australia. What gave Notestein's piece special power was his succinct yet compelling explanation for the declines in mortality and fertility (discussed below). One crucial element in Notestein's argument was that mortality is likely to respond more quickly than fertility to the forces of change, and therefore it is all but inevitable that societies experience a transitional period during which birth rates exceed death rates by a substantial margin, generating rapid population growth.

The Demography of Demographic Transition

Since the 1950s the standard formulation of demographic transition comprises three stages: pretransition regimes, characterized by high (and fluctuating) mortality and high fertility; transitional regimes, characterized by declining mortality and declining fertility, with mortality decline typically running ahead of fertility decline, resulting in population growth; and posttransitional regimes, with low mortality and low (and possibly fluctuating) fertility. The pretransition and posttransition regimes are assumed to be essentially in long-term equilibrium, with transitional regimes acting as a bridge between the two. In pretransition regimes, life expectancy at birth is less than 40 years and women bear on average between five and eight births over their reproductive lifespan, whereas in posttransition regimes, life expectancy at birth exceeds 65 years and women bear on average 2.5 or fewer births.

As empirical studies have accumulated, it has become apparent that pretransition and posttransition regimes are far from uniform in their vital rates. In general, pretransition mortality was lower in Europe than in Africa and Asia—life expectancy closer to 40 years in the former and 30 years in the latter. Even within Europe there was great variability in mortality rates, with the percentage of children dying in infancy ranging from over 30 percent in parts of Bavaria to 10 percent in southern England at the onset of demographic transition. Mortality was also characterized by substantial variation over time, reflecting nutritional adversity and epidemics of infectious disease. Nonmarriage and late marriage significantly reduced fertility rates in pretransition Europe, whereas marriage of women was close to universal in most African and Asian societies and generally occurred soon after menarche (the first menstrual period). As a result, in African and Asian societies fertility levels were higher, even though postpartum sexual abstinence and extended breastfeeding had a moderating effect on fertility rates. There is evidence, still subject to some dispute, that deliberate and conscious regulation of childbearing—the spacing of births—and perhaps of family size as well was common in pretransition African and Asian societies. Fertility within marriage appears to have been subject to far less control in pretransition Europe, although withdrawal was a widely known method of contraception that later was extensively practiced to control fertility in many parts of Europe.

Posttransition populations also show considerable variability in their demographic rates. Continuing declines in mortality at older ages have led to life expectancies at birth approaching 80 years in some European, North American, and East Asian countries, whereas life expectancy has slid below 70 years in eastern Europe because of deteriorating health conditions. The AIDS pandemic, affecting transitional societies especially in eastern and southern Africa, is further demonstration that improvements in health are not necessarily permanent, indeed that reductions in life expectancy on the order of 15 to 20 years can occur over a period as short as two decades. Such nonuniform trends in mortality in transitional and posttransition populations were not foreseen in the original formulations of the demographic

transition. Furthermore, fertility in posttransition countries has in general failed to settle on the replacement level of an average of just over two births per woman over the reproductive lifespan. For decades, births per woman remained substantially above that level, ranging between 2.5 and 3 in the southern cone of South America (Argentina, Chile, and Uruguay) in what seemed a relatively stable posttransition regime. In contrast, in the decades since 1970, fertility has fallen below replacement in most European countries, and even below 1.5 births per woman in some countries of southern and eastern Europe.

The combinations of death rates and birth rates observed in pretransition and posttransition populations allow for modest demographic growth and decline, although over long stretches of time growth rates in pretransition societies were close to zero (typically less than 0.5 percent per year). The rate of population growth in pretransition and posttransition societies is dwarfed by the rate of growth in transitional societies—a result of the time lag between the mortality and fertility declines during the process of transition and, additionally but not universally, a temporary fertility increase early in the transitional stage. Such temporary fertility increases are in all likelihood a physiological response to improved maternal and child health and changes in postpartum practices. The "transition multiplier"—the ratio of the posttransition population size to the pretransition population size—is determined by the extent to which birth rates exceed death rates and the length of time during which that condition prevails. Transition multipliers are high when fertility decline begins from a high initial level and occurs substantially later than mortality decline and proceeds slowly.

An important aspect of the dynamics of transition is that population growth does not immediately subside once fertility falls to replacement level. The high fertility and low childhood mortality of the transitional demographic regime further accentuates the young age-structure that characterizes pretransition populations. This means that for several decades relatively large cohorts pass through the childbearing years. The additional population growth that occurs while the age-structure shifts to its posttransition shape is called population momentum. Population momentum is a substantial component of population growth over the course of demographic transition, typically contributing 30 to 40 percent of the total growth. Formal demographic analysis and simulation exercises demonstrate that population momentum is inversely related to the level of posttransition fertility and to the pace of fertility decline.

The demographic transitions in European populations differed substantially from the transitions in non-European populations in the magnitude of the rate of transitional population growth. In Europe, where the decline in fertility followed close on the heels of the decline in mortality, both starting from relatively low pretransition levels, the rate of natural increase (birth rates minus death rates) during the transitional period from 1800 to 1950 ranged between 0.5 and 1 percent per year, and the transition multiplier was roughly four (a ratio moderated somewhat by overseas emigration). In most non-European populations, mortality declines began during the first decades of the twentieth century and became steep in the decades after World War II, whereas fertility declines (from relatively high initial levels) began in earnest only after 1960 or later. As a result, many non-European countries experienced population growth rates of 2 to 3.5 percent per year for four decades or longer, and the transition multipliers (calculated using projected population numbers) range from 8 to 20. The highest multipliers are found in those countries with slow fertility declines, for example the Philippines, where the pretransition population size was about 8 million, the 2002 population was 79 million, and the posttransition population size is projected to be as high as 150 million, according to the United Nations, and Guatemala (pretransition population of 1.4 million, 2002 population of 12 million, and posttransition population projected as high as 30 million). In no European country did demographic transition produce population growth on this proportionate scale. Population multipliers of this magnitude, often combined with a pretransition population size that was large in absolute terms, are bound to have many and varied repercussions for social, economic, political, and cultural systems—some positive but no doubt also some deleterious.

Explanations for Demographic Transition

The many efforts, from Landry to the present, seeking to identify the forces generating demographic transition fall into two major sets. One regards fertility decline as an inevitable response to the population growth induced by mortality decline, which is therefore all that requires explanation. The second views fertility decline as a response to a richer and more diverse set of social, economic, political, and cultural forces.

While mortality decline has presented less of an explanatory challenge than fertility decline, there has been ample debate about its causes. Economic transformations that improved standards of living—food, clothing, sanitation, housing—appears to account for much of the decline of mortality in Europe. Samuel Preston argued in 1975, however, that economic change, as captured by growth in income per capita, accounts for only a small fraction of mortality decline in non-European populations in the twentieth century. Political stability and the emergence of effective nation-states complement the effects of economic change by leading to more reliable access to food and improved public sanitation. New medical technologies made a minor contribution to the decline of mortality in Europe in the eighteenth and nineteenth centuries but were a major factor in the sharp reduction in mortality from infectious diseases in the developing countries in the twentieth century. A final factor is improved personal hygiene (hand washing, preparation of food, and so forth), with new habits adopted in response to formal school instruction, public-health education campaigns, and word-of-mouth information.

Some scholars have argued that mortality decline is a sufficient cause of fertility decline and hence accounts for the demographic transitions of the past two centuries. Strictly speaking, the explanatory factor is not mortality decline but population growth. In 1963 Davis described household-level strain created by significantly larger younger generations vying for valued economic and social resources. Successively larger cohorts (in particular, the increase in the ratio of sons to fathers) disrupt the equilibrium of the traditional family. Other scholars have noted that mortality decline, normally accompanied by improved health of the population, should increase economic productivity and through that channel exercise a positive indirect effect on fertility. Finally, mortality decline encourages a change in personal psychologies away from fatalism toward a greater sense of self-control over one's destiny, and this facilitates the exercise of deliberate fertility regulation.

Fertility declines have occurred under widely varying social and economic circumstances but virtually never in the absence of mortality decline, and this can be taken as strong evidence that mortality decline is the primary cause of fertility decline. Theories of demographic *homeostasis* posit that human societies gravitate toward demographic regimes with growth rates near zero; multiple and diverse societal institutions act as governors on population growth and enforce the tendency to oscillate near zero growth. Marked departures meet with the appropriate demographic response—increases in fertility to make up for mortality crises, decreases in fertility in response to mortality decline, or migration that offsets increases or decreases in rates of natural increase (a key element in Davis's theory of "multiphasic response"). While appealing as a general theory of population dynamics, homeostatic theory is not very informative about the demographic transitions that occurred during the nineteenth and twentieth centuries. The end results of these transitions, as noted earlier, were multifold increases in population size. It is not clear how homeostatic theory accommodates this failure of fertility or migration to compensate for the impact of mortality declines. Moreover, the diversity of the pretransition equilibrium levels of fertility and mortality and of the lags between mortality and fertility declines, as reflected in the large variation in transition multipliers, is a major empirical fact that demands explanation. Surely the explanation lies in the conditioning influence of social, economic, and cultural forces.

In the second set of explanations for fertility decline, mortality decline is not the sole causal agent. Indeed, Notestein, in his seminal 1945 work, hardly mentioned mortality decline as a motivation for fertility decline. Instead he argued that both mortality and fertility decline in response to urbanization and changes in the economy (which changed the costs and benefits of children and led to rising standards of living and increased material aspirations) and to growth in individualism and secularism. Notestein's argument has been elaborated in a large subsequent literature on the causes of fertility decline that has featured economic forces, cultural changes, and changes in birth control costs.

Economic theories of fertility decline focus on the causal impact of changes in the costs and benefits of children and childrearing. The fundamental cause of fertility decline is the (perceived) decreasing affordability of large numbers of children. Demographers have resisted giving pride of place to microeconomic changes in models of fertility decline, perhaps be-

cause of disciplinary biases but more importantly because of weak empirical associations between macroeconomic changes and fertility decline. The Princeton European Fertility Project, for example, uncovered no systematic relationship at the provincial level between the onset of fertility decline and socioeconomic variables such as levels of urbanization and nonagricultural employment. But other empirical research that has had access to a larger number of economic variables that provide a more complete portrait of the economic system, as well as studies conducted at lower levels of aggregation (the local community or the household), attribute much greater causal impact to economic change. This includes studies on fertility declines in England, Italy, Bavaria, and Prussia. Moreover, it seems likely that cognitive dimensions—in particular, economic aspirations and expectations—mediate the relationship between economic change and fertility. The causal force may not be economic circumstances per se but rather the relationship between economic aspirations and expectations (that is, what individuals want as opposed to what they expect). This can explain why fertility declines have occurred in the presence of both improving and deteriorating economic conditions.

Mortality decline and economic change are the core elements of a model for fertility decline. High fertility is compatible neither with low mortality nor with high-income, modern economies. Both mortality regimes and economic systems have been transformed during the past two centuries, to an extent and at a rate that are extraordinary by any measure. If one wishes to go back further in the causal chain and ask why this has occurred, inevitably one is led to the scientific and technological revolutions of the past four centuries. Ultimately it is these revolutions that lengthened life expectancy and made bearing large numbers of children inconsistent with modernity.

Another stream in the literature on the causes of fertility decline emphasizes the determining role of attitudes about and values related to family life. Ron Lesthaeghe has proposed that the decline of fertility in Europe was caused by the synergistic effects of economic changes and changes in the moral and ethical domain. Lesthaeghe stresses the emergence of secularism, materialism, individualism, and self-fulfillment as dominant values that in combination undermine the satisfactions derived from having children. John C. Caldwell argued in 1982 that a shift in the morality governing family life—in particular, a higher valuation of the conjugal relationship and of investments in children—leads to a dismantling of high-fertility reproductive regimes. Fertility decline is triggered by emotional nucleation of the family, itself a response to broader economic and cultural changes. For both scholars, the critical cultural change has less to do with the value of children narrowly defined and more to do with the nature of intergenerational relations and the perceived contribution of childbearing to the achievement of a desired standard and style of living. But whether changing mentalities and moralities about family life are themselves a sufficient cause of sustained and substantial fertility decline is doubtful, absent the precondition of mortality decline. Certain cultural changes, of course, might provoke both mortality and fertility declines, for example an increase in the value placed on investments in children, per child.

A final cluster of determinants of the timing and pace of fertility decline can be gathered under the heading "costs of birth control." The argument is that various economic, social, psychic, and health factors can make birth control practices prohibitively costly, and hence the reduction or elimination of such costs is a prerequisite for fertility decline. Ansley Coale and Richard Easterlin both highlighted the potentially important causal role of the costs of birth control, and the empirical record now contains numerous studies that demonstrate that reduction in birth control costs can accelerate fertility decline. In the period since 1960, the most prominent strategy for reducing birth control costs has been the provision of contraceptives free of charge or at nominal price through public and private family planning programs. But limited access to contraception is by no means the only obstacle to use, and some scholars have argued that personal knowledge and social legitimacy of contraception are perhaps more critical than the mere provision of contraceptive technology.

Conclusion

The debate that began in the 1950s and is still continuing about the aims of population policy and the nature and scope of interventions can be viewed as a debate about how to weight the various determinants of demographic transition. If one follows Notestein's reading of the European historical experience, then the decisive factors are social and economic change, and the availability of contracep-

tive technology is of little importance. Davis as well leaves one less than sanguine about the likely contribution of programs that make family planning and reproductive health services more accessible and less expensive. Coale and Easterlin provide a stronger rationale for investment in such programs. Rapid population growth—a function of the gap between mortality and fertility declines—has been a primary public policy concern. But the demography of pretransition and posttransition populations differ in many other respects—posttransition, the age-structure of the population is older, individuals' lives are far lengthier, and childrearing occupies a much smaller portion of those lives. These outcomes of demographic transition increasingly are the focus of public policy debates about population dynamics.

See also: *Davis, Kingsley; Development, Population and; Epidemiological Transition; Fertility Transition, Socioeconomic Determinants of; Health Transition; Homeostasis; Landry, Adolphe; Notestein, Frank W.; Mortality Decline; Second Demographic Transition; Thompson, Warren S.*

BIBLIOGRAPHY

Caldwell, John C. 1982. *Theory of Fertility Decline.* London: Academic Press.

Chesnais, Jean-Claude. 1992. *The Demographic Transition.* Oxford: Oxford University Press.

Cleland, John. 2001. "The Effects of Improved Survival on Fertility: A Reassessment." In *Global Fertility Transition,* Supplement to Volume 27 of *Population and Development Review,* ed. Rodolfo A. Bulatao and John B. Casterline. New York: Population Council.

Coale, Ansley. 1973. "The Demographic Transition Reconsidered." In *International Population Conference,* Vol. 1. Liège, Belgium: International Union for the Scientific Study of Population.

Coale, Ansley J., and Susan Cotts Watkins, eds. 1986. *The Decline of Fertility in Europe.* Princeton, NJ: Princeton University Press.

Davis, Kingsley. 1963. "The Theory of Change and Response in Modern Demographic History." *Population Index* 29: 345–366.

Easterlin, Richard. 1975. "An Economic Framework for Fertility Analysis." *Studies in Family Planning* 6: 54–63.

Goldstein, Joshua. 2002. "Population Momentum for Gradual Demographic Transition." *Demography* 39: 65–74.

Hirschman, Charles. 1994. "Why Fertility Changes." *Annual Review of Sociology* 20: 203–233.

Landry, Adolphe. 1934. *La revolution démographique*. Paris: Sirey.

Lloyd, Cynthia, and Serguey Ivanov. 1988. "The Effects of Improved Child Survival on Family Planning Practices and Fertility." *Studies in Family Planning* 19: 141–161.

Mason, Karen Oppenheim. 1997. "Explaining Fertility Transitions." *Demography* 34: 443–454.

Montgomery, Mark, and Barney Cohen, eds. 1998. *From Death to Birth: Mortality Decline and Reproductive Change*. Washington, D.C.: National Academy Press.

Notestein, Frank W. 1945. "Population: The Long View." In *Food for the World*, ed. Theodore W. Schultz. Chicago: University of Chicago Press.

Preston, Samuel. 1975. "The Changing Relation between Mortality and Level of Economic Development." *Population Studies* 29: 231–248.

Wilson, Chris, and Pauline Airey. 1999. "How Can a Homeostatic Perspective Enhance Demographic Transition Theory?" *Population Studies* 53: 117–128.

JOHN B. CASTERLINE

DEMOGRAPHICS

See *Business Demography; State and Local Government Demography*

DEMOGRAPHY, HISTORY OF

Demography is the study of a human population, a definable group of people, and of additions to and subtractions from its number. A population is increased by births and immigration and decreased by deaths and emigration. In a "closed population," there is no migration and attention is paid only to reproduction and mortality. Demographers prefer to study populations that are sufficiently large to be unaffected by the idiosyncratic behavior of individuals. Nevertheless, most would argue that their findings are the best description of the behavior of the typical individual. Demographers, especially when studying recent times, are almost always interested in change; consequently, the time dimension is stronger in their work than it is in most social sciences.

Demography is not easy to practice. Its practitioners need to know the numbers and vital rates of large human aggregations and require some comprehension of mathematics and scientific concepts to do their analyses. Adequate measurements of large populations require wealth and a centralized administration and have developed slowly. Historically, such measurements were not carried out for demographic purposes but to assess military strength or the tax base. Frequently, the data were not centralized, making analysis difficult. The registration of births and deaths usually was done for legal purposes such as establishing inheritance rights and was not equally relevant to all parts of society.

The Materials of Demography

Censuses, although usually not including all individuals, were carried out in the ancient world in powerful states such as Egypt, Babylon, Persia, India, and China as well as in some Greek city-states. Republican Rome took a census every five years. More recently, the Domesday Book in eleventh-century England listed landowners, listed undertenants by a single name, and did not list other family members and non-tenants. By the fourteenth and fifteenth centuries there were tax registers in England, France, and the Netherlands and various kinds of counts in German and Italian cities as well as in Spain and Portugal.

The rise of the powerful nation-state made full censuses inevitable. William Petty (1623–1687) campaigned for them in Restoration England. Quebec held a complete census of its very small population in 1665, and at the end of the seventeenth century England, France, and Iceland took censuses that were neither aggregated nor published, while Prussia followed in 1748 and Sweden in 1749. Population registers spread in Scandinavia, starting with Sweden in 1686.

Censuses proliferated in the late eighteenth century: Switzerland in 1798, the United States (mandated by its constitution) in 1800, England and France in 1801, Ireland in 1813, and over 20 more countries by the 1860s. These were not modern censuses initially. Detailed age data and separate lines for each individual were not instituted until the middle of the nineteenth century, and training courses for enumerators came later. Norway undertook the first census sampling in 1900. Censuses in most of the developing world did not occur until the second half of the twentieth century (India, where census taking began in the 1870s, is the most important exception), and not all populations have yet been subjected to a census.

Vital registration still does not characterize much of Asia and nearly all of Africa. Christendom had an advantage in this regard because of the sacramental nature of baptisms, marriages, and funerals and an increasing tendency to record those events. Toledo in Spain made parish registration compulsory in 1497, and the Council of Trent in 1563 did the same for baptisms and marriages in the whole Catholic world. In England in 1538 Thomas Cromwell ordered the church to register all baptisms, marriages, and burials; in the following year France did the same thing for baptisms and burials. In 1635 Buddhist temple registration began in Japan.

With the decline of national churches as Protestant sects and freethinking emerged, it was inevitable in the West that church registration would be succeeded by secular state registration and that births and deaths would replace baptisms and funerals, respectively. This was already the case in the Scandinavian population registers, which were followed by civil registration in France in 1804 under the Napoleonic Code and in England and Wales in 1837. Nevertheless, death registration was not backed up by death certification, with its greater likelihood of correctly stating a cause, until 1855 in Scotland, 1865 in the Netherlands, and 1874 in England and Wales. In the United States vital registration, in contrast to the census, was a state, not a federal, responsibility. As a result, although vital registration began early in Massachusetts, the official registration area, where registration was largely complete, expanded only slowly from the late nineteenth century until its completion in 1933. The first birth statistics for the area were not published until 1915, and in spite of efforts by the American census, much less is known about nineteenth-century American demography than is known about that of Europe or Australia.

The situation in the developing world was partly rectified by the development in the last few decades of the twentieth century of national sample surveys (usually concentrated on women of reproductive age and including only 5,000 to 10,000 respondents). Successively, there were the so-called KAP surveys (on knowledge, attitudes, and practices with regard to fertility) in 1962–1973, the World Fertility Survey (WFS) from 1973 through 1984, and the Demographic and Health Surveys (DHS), begun in 1984 and still continuing. The WFS covered 61 countries; DHS surveys had been held in 69 countries by 2001, and repeated at least twice in 45 of them. All these surveys collected fertility data; the DHS and WFS collected mortality data as well, although these data usually were regarded as sufficient to provide reliable estimates only for infants and young children.

Other sources included specialized surveys, such as the Indianapolis Study of 1941; efforts by the census bureau or department to collect vital data, especially in the United States during the second half of the nineteenth century; and special demographic surveys, particularly in Francophone Africa in the 1950s. Later in the twentieth century huge demographic surveys were carried out in China (starting with the 1981 one-in-a-thousand sample survey) and India. The computer has allowed demographers to undertake their own analyses of surveys and census samples, thus lessening their dependence on statistical offices and profoundly changing the nature of the discipline.

The Analysts

The Italian Renaissance and the era of European voyages and religious missions to distant continents first stirred interest in estimating population size. The Counter-Reformation and the rise of the Jesuits also came into the picture. Estimates of urban, national, and global populations are associated with Giovanni Botero (1544–1617), Marino Marini (1614–1661), and Giovanni Riccioli (1598–1671). Botero in his 1588 publication *Cause della Grandezza. . .delle Città* analyzed the factors determining the growth and prosperity of cities and in his 1596 *Relazioni Universali* anticipated the economist T. R. Malthus's argument about the relationship between growth in population and pressure on resources.

Little demographic analysis occurred before about 1660. The exception was a continuing interest in mortality rates for the purpose of calculating annuities and tontines. There is a surviving rough life table from third-century Rome that was used for this purpose. Mortality was to continue to dominate demographic interest until the late nineteenth century, partly because it varied more than did fertility as epidemics or famines struck.

Modern demography had to wait for large-scale datasets, scientific interest in their analysis, and sufficient development in mathematics to allow that analysis. Francis Bacon (1561–1626), whom all the early English demographers credited with showing them the way, had, especially in *Novum Organum,* published in 1620, developed the inductive method and had stressed the need in science to collect facts and search for form in them to identify the underlying natural laws. The early English demographers knew and worked beside Isaac Newton (1643–1727), who was discovering the laws of physics. However, most sixteenth- and seventeenth-century demographers were, like Newton, also searching for a divine pattern and, like him, were Protestants. There are later parallels with the economist Adam Smith's "hidden hand" and Malthus's emphasis on divine underpinnings. The necessary mathematical knowledge was not intuitive, and it is no accident that demographic analysis often was advanced by astronomers such as Edmond Halley (1656–1743) and Pierre Simon La Place (1749–1827) and mathematicians such as Leonhard Euler (1707–1783).

The development of the discipline of demography is usually traced to seventeenth-century England, especially among the founders of the Royal Society. John Graunt (1620–1674), a London merchant often described as the father of demography, employed Bacon's approach and his own experience with merchant bookkeeping to analyze the London Bills of Mortality, or death records, which had been kept since 1532. His major work, published in 1662, established such canons of demography as checking and correcting the data and then searching for regularities. Graunt showed that in sufficiently large populations there was an excess of male births, higher mortality in infancy than at any other age except extreme old age, and a longer female than male lifespan and constructed a prototype of the life table that later would be made rigorous by Halley. Graunt's friend William Petty (1623–1687) applied quantitative methods to the social sciences; pioneered household enumeration, especially for studying the population of cities; and published in 1683

Political Arithmetic, whose title encapsulates the nature of demography. In 1696 Gregory King (1648–1712) drew upon the scattered returns of England's first census and other sources to prepare a manuscript (not published until 1801) calculating the population of England (and estimating continental and global numbers) and computing for 1695 birth, death, and marriage rates as well as age structure.

A notable eighteenth-century advance was Richard Price's (1723–1791) work on actuarial science, which laid the foundations for the British insurance industry. Price argued that knowledge in the natural sciences entails an understanding of probabilities, a view descending from the philosophers René Descartes (1596–1650), John Locke (1632–1704), and David Hume (1711–1776). But in the eighteenth century demography was no longer an exclusively English pursuit. There was a major Swiss contribution from Jean Louis Muret (1715–1796), a mathematician who first devised birth, death, and marriage rates. His contemporary Leonhard Euler (1707–1783), working mostly in Russia and Prussia, created the mathematical theory of both life tables and stable populations, the foundations of modern formal demography. In Sweden, Per Wargentin (1717–1783) employed the first Swedish census and the population registration system to publish in 1766 the first national life table. The commanding figure in eighteenth-century empirical demography was a German, Johann Peter Süssmilch (1707–1767), who published in 1741 and 1761–1762 *Die Göttliche Ordnung (The Divine Order with regard to the Human Species, as demonstrated by birth, death and reproduction),* an influential treatise (never translated into English). In search for proof of a divine order in the regularity of demographic events he amassed data from a huge number of sources and provided material for succeeding demographers, including T. R. Malthus (1766–1834). Malthus, in his *First Essay* (1798), with its postulate of population growth being restricted by the slow increase in resources, made a major contribution to population theory. In the succeeding editions of that work over the next three decades he assembled a mass of supporting empirical materials. Pierre Simon Laplace (1749–1827), a French astronomer and mathematician, continued the work on probability, which he applied to mortality, life expectancy, and the length of marriages.

In the eighteenth century empirical demography did not develop as rapidly as might have been anticipated, mainly because issues of cost and popular resistance delayed the advent of national censuses and vital registration systems. The situation changed rapidly in the nineteenth century. From 1855 the term *demography* came into use and from 1882 the International Conferences on Hygiene and Demography were held. A second cause for the development of the discipline was a downward movement in mortality rates in most Western countries and, toward the end of the century, the beginning of a fertility decline. The focus of the discipline shifted from analyzing stasis to analyzing change. Statisticians such as the Belgian Adolphe Quetelet (1796–1874) and the German Wilhelm Lexis (1837–1914) turned their attention to the movement over time in social measures, especially demographic ones. The analysis of geographic and social differentials in mortality, as well as its changes over time, provided guidance in the battle against disease.

The dominant figure in this effort was William Farr (1807–1883), who analyzed the causes and levels of deaths in England in the *Annual Report of the Registrar General* from 1839 to 1880, meeting a need arising partly from the problems of the new industrial cities. The analysis of fertility assumed importance once widespread fertility decline began in Western countries in the last third of the nineteenth century. Questions about live births to women appeared in the U.S. census starting in 1900 and in those in Britain and other countries in its empire starting in 1911. Methods for measuring fertility, which eventually yielded such commonly used measures as the gross and net reproduction rates, evolved in the strong demographic group in the Prussian/German Statistical Office in Berlin in the second half of the nineteenth century with the work of Richard Bockhe, leading in the twentieth century to further development by R. R. Kuczynski (1876–1947) in England and Alfred Lotka (1880–1949) in the United States. Interest in changing fertility levels emerged in various countries. In France the focus was on the low level of natural increase following the defeat in the Franco-Prussian War in 1870; in England, led by Francis Galton (1822–1911), the founder of the eugenics movement, it was on differential fertility by social class, with the supposed tendency of the less intelligent to outbreed the bright; and in the United States it was on the higher birthrate among immigrants than among the native-born. Such ideas, together with the older Malthusian concern with the pressure of population on food and other resources,

would foster the development of demography in the twentieth century and often make the subject politically sensitive.

The twentieth century witnessed further development of demography's analytic techniques as the number of professionals working in the field greatly increased. Population growth models drew together mortality and fertility approaches. Stable population analysis that had originated in the work of Euler and was developed further by Laplace, Lotka, Ansley Coale (born 1917), and Álvaro López Toro (1926–1972); it was modified for quasi-stable populations by Coale, Paul Demeny (born 1932), and Samuel Preston (born 1943). Mathematical analysis by Nathan Keyfitz (born 1913) and others explored further demographic interrelations. Reacting to swings in the rate of population growth, population projection methodology developed component methods (based on separate age and sex components) stemming from work in 1895 by Edwin Cannan (1861–1935), logistic curve approaches from a 1920 paper by Raymond Pearl (1875–1940) and Lowell Reed (1886–1966), and cohort analysis from a 1936 paper by Pascal Whelpton (1893–1964). Post–World War II interest in the developing world led William Brass (1921–1999) to develop "indirect" methods for estimating vital rates and trends from limited census and survey data. This advance allowed fertility and mortality to be estimated not only for contemporary countries without vital registration but also for many historical populations.

Institutionalization

Until the twentieth century the only sense in which demography was a discipline was that there was a growing body of knowledge, both theoretical and empirical, and some teaching of that knowledge in university courses such as statistics and economics. Beginning in the 1920s that situation changed as the West become wealthier, university education expanded in volume and diversity, and interest in population phenomena was stimulated first by the eugenics movement and then by low birth rates in the West during the economic depression of the 1930s.

In the United States foundations played an initial role in the establishment of a population research center led by Warren Thompson (1887–1973) and Whelpton in Ohio in 1922 and the Office of Population Research (OPR) directed by Frank Notestein (1902–1983) at Princeton University in 1936.

The Milbank Memorial Fund in New York established its own Population Research Office in 1928 and funded population survey research in China in the following year. In 1936 the Population Investigation Committee was formed in Britain. Population courses had been given at the London School of Economics from the 1930s in the Social Biology Department and from 1936 in Princeton's OPR. A graduate department of demography was established at the Australian National University in 1952.

Demography has struggled to be accepted as a full and continuing university discipline, and its existence has depended to a considerable degree on professional associations, specialized journals, and conferences. The International Union for the Scientific Investigation of Population Problems was founded in 1928 and was reconstituted as the International Union for the Scientific Study of Population (IUSSP) in 1947. The emphasis on the term *scientific,* which is not common in other disciplines, was intended to suggest that members' research and teaching were not biased by attitudes toward birth control or eugenics. In 1931 the Population Association of America (PAA) was formed. Both the International Union and the PAA had periodic journals that provided limited outlets for publication, but in the 1930s and early 1940s more demographic articles appeared in the *Milbank Memorial Fund Quarterly.* Specialized journals appeared later: *Population* in France in 1946, *Population Studies* in Britain in 1947, and *Demography* in 1963 and *Population and Development Review* in 1975 in the United States. From its inception the International Union held periodic conferences with published proceedings.

The remarkable expansion of demography in the second half of the twentieth century was largely the product of concern about "population explosion" in the developing world during a period of unprecedented international technical assistance. The United Nations set up a Population Division in 1946, the Population Council was founded in 1952, and the Ford Foundation brought considerable funding to the field starting in 1959. Later, governments were to become even greater sources of support, with the U.S. Agency for International Development (USAID) moving toward massive financial inputs to population programs starting in the early 1960s. By the end of the 1960s the United Nations Fund for Population Activities (UNFPA, now the United Nations Population Fund) had been established. Population research centers with associated teaching programs were set up in many universities in the United States and other Western countries. They tended to focus on fertility, with a strong emphasis on developing countries. The United Nations helped establish demographic research and training centers in Asia, Latin America, and Africa. Scholarships provided by foundations, governments, and international agencies permitted many students in developing countries to take graduate degrees in the population field in Western universities. The funding also permitted the IUSSP and the United Nations to hold large international conferences.

Demography remained unsure about its disciplinary boundaries, especially in the sense of whether it was defined by its empirical studies and their analysis or could be equated with a larger area of intellectual inquiry—population studies—which includes the cause and impact of demographic change. If the latter was the case, it had a claim to be a social science and a need to draw on such fields as economics, sociology, and anthropology for methodology and explanations.

The Recent Past and the Future

By 1970 it was known that fertility decline had begun in much of the developing world except for sub-Saharan Africa. In the early 1980s the Ford Foundation ceased funding the population field, and the population centers it supported foresaw difficulties. Since that time government and international support has tended to move from demographic teaching and research to family planning programs in the developing world. Population centers had to adjust to the new conditions. Some of them developed a greater interest in public health issues in developed countries. Keyfitz wrote that further concentration on methodology would not be rewarding and that the existing methodology should be applied to the great global problems. A few demography programs disappeared, but most moved toward greater integration within universities. Research on developing countries declined. Demography had for over a century been focused on population change, and that change appeared to be coming to a halt as the demographic transition neared an end with low and nearly equal birth rates and death rates.

That halt has not occurred, with the result that demography in its organized institutional condition seems to have an assured future. The reason for this is that the demographic transition does not necessarily produce equal fertility and mortality levels but instead may lead to very low fertility and declining population numbers. By the beginning of the twenty-first century, 44 percent of the world's population lived in countries with fertility at or below the long-term replacement level and much of Europe exhibited fertility well below that level. The first demand on demographers was to investigate the resulting changes in the age structure, with the realization that the old-age pensionable population appeared to be moving in many developed countries from 10 percent in 1950 to 15 to 20 percent in 2000 and ultimately might reach levels beyond 30 percent. In the longer run, and probably first in Europe, the interest of demographers probably will focus on the nature of population decline and the efficacy of interventions to counter it.

See also: *Botero, Giovanni; Brass, William; Cannan, Edwin; Coale, Ansley Johnson; Demographic and Health Surveys; Euler, Leonhard; Farr, William; Galton, Francis; Graunt, John; Journals, Population; Keyfitz, Nathan; King, Gregory; Kuczynski, R. R.; Lotka, Alfred; Malthus, Thomas Robert; Notestein, Frank W.; Pearl, Raymond; Petty, William; Population Organizations; Population Thought: History of; Quetelet, Adolphe; Süssmilch, Johann; Thompson, Warren S.; Whelpton, P. K.; World Fertility Survey.*

BIBLIOGRAPHY

Bulatao, Rodolfo A., and Ronald D. Lee, eds. 1983. *Determinants of Fertility in Developing Countries: A Summary of Knowledge.* New York: Academic Press.

Caldwell, John, and Pat Caldwell. 1986. *Limiting Population Growth, and the Ford Foundation Contribution.* London: Frances Pinter.

Demography, 30 (4) (thirtieth anniversary issue), November 1993.

Hauser, Philip M., and Otis Dudley Duncan, eds. 1959. *The Study of Population: An Inventory and Appraisal.* Chicago: University of Chicago Press.

Hodgson, Dennis. 1983. "Demography as a Social Science and a Policy Science." *Population and Development Review* 9 (1): 1–34.

Kreager, Philip. 1991. "Early Modern Population Theory." *Population and Development Review* 17 (2): 207–227.

Lorimer, Frank. 1959. "The Development of Demography." In *The Study of Population: An Inventory and Appraisal,* ed. Philip M. Hauser and Otis Dudley Duncan. Chicago: University of Chicago Press.

McNicoll, Geoffrey. 1992. "The Agenda of Population Studies: A Commentary and Complaint." *Population and Development Review* 18 (1): 399–420.

Petersen, William, and Renee Petersen. 1985. *Dictionary of Demography: Biographies.* Westport, CT: Greenwood Press.

Population. 1995. Fiftieth anniversary volume.

Population Studies, 50 (3) (fifty-year retrospective), November 1996.

JOHN C. CALDWELL

DENSITY AND DISTRIBUTION OF POPULATION

Population distribution refers to the way in which the members of a population or of a specified subgroup of a population (for example, defined by age, sex, or ethnic status) are dispersed physically in a specific area. Population density provides a comparative measure of distribution with respect to a geographic area that usually is expressed as persons per square kilometer (or per square mile) of land. More specialized density measures also may be defined, such as population per unit of cultivatable land.

The Distribution of the World's Population

Population distribution on a global scale is highly uneven, with the greater part of the world's population living in the northern hemisphere and in countries in the less developed world. Less than 10 percent of the world's population lives in the southern hemisphere, and 80 percent lives between 20 degrees and 60 degrees north latitude. Table 1 shows the growth of the world population since 1950 and its changing distribution projected to 2050. By the year 2000 approximately 74 percent of the world's population lived in Africa and Asia (excluding the Russian Federation) on only 40 percent of the world's land area. Europe accounted for 12 percent of global population, with a further 8.6 percent in Latin America and the Caribbean, 5.2 percent in North America

TABLE 1

	Population (millions)			Population change (percent)	
Region	1950	2000	2050	1950–2000	2000–2050
United States and Canada	172	314	438	83	39
Latin America and the Caribbean	167	519	806	211	55
Europe (including Russia)	548	727	603	33	-17
Africa	221	794	2,000	259	152
Asia (excluding Russia)	1,399	3,672	5,428	162	48
Oceania	13	31	47	138	52
World	2,520	6,057	9,322	140	54

Size and Population Change by Major World Region, Estimates and Projections, 1950 and 2050

SOURCE: United Nations Population Division (2000). (2050 figures are those of the U.N.'s 2000 revision "medium" projection.)

(the United States and Canada), and 0.5 percent in Oceania.

The increased population concentration in the less developed world reflects the exceptionally rapid growth of population in those areas since the middle of the twentieth century and lower growth and in some cases stability, and more recently even decline, in the more developed countries. Table 2 shows the ten most populous countries in the year 2000. The stylized maps presented in Figure 1 show how population is distributed by country and region and the broad changes in relative sizes over time.

The Environment, Society, and the Economy

Population density per square kilometer on a global scale is related to a number of factors both in the physical environment and in society and the economy. Although the physical environment does not play a straightforward deterministic role, extremes tend to discourage human settlement. Climate is a major factor. In very cold and very hot environments the range of crops that can be grown, if any, is limited, and this inhibits human survival. Accordingly, large areas of the globe are empty. Thus, in Lapland there is only 1 person per square kilometer, and in the Gobi Desert only 1.4.

Altitude is also significant. Mountain soils are usually thin, and at high altitudes temperatures and the oxygen content of the air decrease rapidly. This makes agriculture less productive, with additional problems created by difficulty of access and transport. Lowland areas tend to attract settlement more readily, with more intensive farming and industrial and commercial development. Coastal areas are often more attractive to settlement: Around two-

thirds of the world's population lives within 500 kilometers of the sea. Natural vegetation also may be a deterrent to human settlement, with, for example, the great rain forests such as the Amazon being poorly suited for high population densities. Negative factors in the environment do not always discourage settlement: For example Bangladesh, prone to major environmental hazards such as flooding, sustains a very high population density. A hot and humid environment near the equator permits cultivation to take place year-round.

Population distribution within continents and countries is also highly variable and is apt to change significantly over time. Within the countries of Western Europe, for example, population densities range from very high concentrations in the Netherlands to much lower densities in much of France and Spain. Within the United Kingdom, which is an area with overall high density, regional densities vary from over 600 persons per square kilometer in the urban counties of the southeast and northern England to well under 100 in large tracts of Wales and Scotland. Figure 2 illustrates the wide disparities in population density in the United States.

Population redistribution through migration, as well as population growth or decline, takes on increasing significance at smaller geographic scales. On a global scale migration has been of great importance historically in determining distributions of population, especially in relation to the great transatlantic migrations of the nineteenth and early-twentieth centuries. Redistribution of population also rewrote the world cultural map. Within countries industrialization and migration have gone hand in hand, entailing major redistribution from rural to

FIGURE 1

Size and Distribution of World Population by Countries, 1950, 2000, and 2050

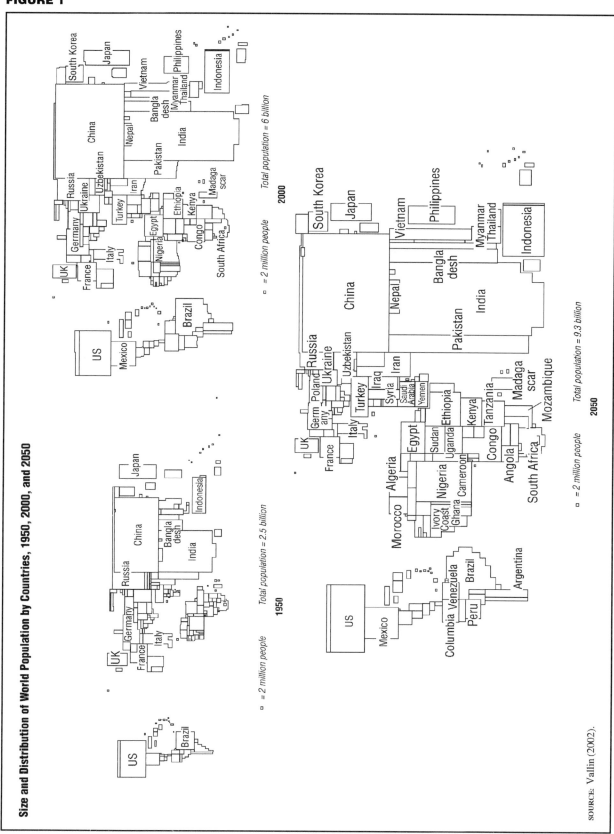

SOURCE: Vallin (2002).

FIGURE 2

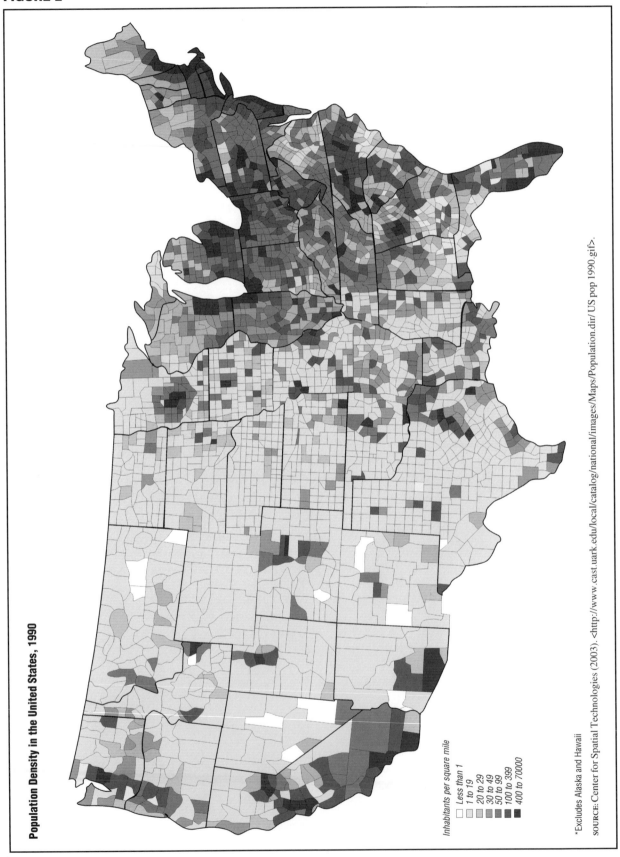

Population Density in the United States, 1990

Inhabitants per square mile
- Less than 1
- 1 to 19
- 20 to 29
- 30 to 49
- 50 to 99
- 100 to 399
- 400 to 70000

*Excludes Alaska and Hawaii

SOURCE: Center for Spatial Technologies (2003). <http://www.cast.uark.edu/local/catalog/national/images/Maps/Population.dir/ US pop 1990.gif>.

TABLE 2

Ten Most Populous Countries in 2000

Rank	Country	Population (millions)	Percent of world population	Cumulative percentage
1	China	1,275	21.1	21.1
2	India	1,009	16.7	37.8
3	United States	283	4.7	42.5
4	Indonesia	212	3.5	46.0
5	Brazil	170	2.8	48.8
6	Russian Federation	145	2.4	51.2
7	Pakistan	141	2.3	53.5
8	Bangladesh	137	2.3	55.8
9	Japan	127	2.1	57.9
10	Nigeria	114	1.9	59.8

SOURCE: United Nations, Population Division (2002).

urban areas. In the countries of the more developed world, for example, in much of Western Europe, rural depopulation and urban growth have been a salient feature since 1850. In the less developed world rapid urbanization since 1945, compounded by high levels of overall population increase, has redrawn the map of population distribution in many countries. Distribution also can be affected directly by government policy, for example, by the encouragement or discouragement of international migration.

Mapping Population Density

Attempts to map population distribution and density date back to the early-nineteenth century. Graduated shading was used in a map of Prussian population densities in 1828, dots were used to represent population in France in 1830 and in New Zealand in 1863, and a variety of methods were employed to map population by the Irish railway commissioners in 1837. The later part of the nineteenth century saw the use of cartograms, in which regions are depicted as proportional to their population size rather than their geographic area. (See Figure 1.)

A simple and frequently used representation of population distribution that complements mapping is the Lorenz curve. A straight diagonal line represents an even distribution of population over the areas selected, and the larger the gap between the curve and the diagonal line, the greater the degree of concentration of population. Figure 3 illustrates both the method and the distribution of subgroups within a population compared to the population as

a whole, in this case the distribution of two ethnic minority populations in Great Britain in 1991: persons of Irish and Bangladeshi origin. The horizontal axis indicates the cumulative percentage of these two groups, and the vertical axis indicates the cumulative percentage of the total population over the districts (in this case census wards) into which the country has been divided. Note the highly concentrated population of Bangladeshi origin compared to the more evenly spread Irish population.

Problems with Measures of Density

There are a number of general problems with measures of density. Population data are collected for highly variable geographic units that are rarely homogeneous in terms of economic and environmental characteristics. A density figure is simply an average with all the limitations that that implies, and care needs to be taken both in the definition of the population and in the areal or other units being used, particularly when comparisons are made at different geographic scales. Measures of population density extend beyond the crude density of population, the number of people per unit area. Useful national comparisons may be based on density defined in relation to cultivatable or cultivated land. For example, in Egypt overall population density is low in relation to the total national territory but high if population numbers are related to cultivated land, which is dependent on irrigation from the Nile.

Other calculations have been made to relate population numbers to levels of national income and standards of living. At the city level, measures such as the density of population per household or housing unit and the average number of persons per room provide a useful way of describing patterns of settlement. Thus, in the Paris agglomeration at the time of the 1999 census of population, for example, the number of persons per household varied from 2.82 in the outer suburbs to 1.87 in the inner city. The mean number of persons per room in the central area declined from 1.02 in 1962 to 0.74 in 1999.

See also: *Carrying Capacity; Central Place Theory; Geography, Population; Land Use; Peopling of the Continents.*

BIBLIOGRAPHY

Chrispin, Jane, and Francis Jegede. 2000. *Population, Resources and Development,* 2nd edition. London: HarperCollins.

FIGURE 3

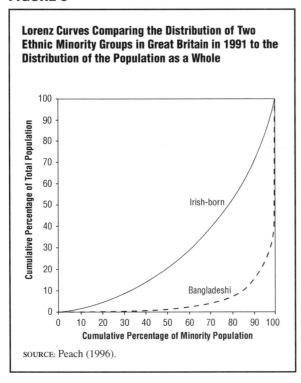

Lorenz Curves Comparing the Distribution of Two Ethnic Minority Groups in Great Britain in 1991 to the Distribution of the Population as a Whole

SOURCE: Peach (1996).

Clarke, John I. 1972. *Population Geography*, 2nd edition. Oxford: Pergamon.

Peach, Ceri. 1996. "Does Britain Have Ghettos?" *Transactions of the Institute of British Geographers*, new series 21: 216–235.

Plane, David A., and Peter A. Rogerson. 1994. *The Geographical Analysis of Population, with Applications to Planning and Business*. New York: Wiley.

Vallin, Jacques. 2002. "The End of the Demographic Transition: Relief or Concern?" *Population and Development Review* 28(1) 108–109.

PHILIP E. OGDEN

DEVELOPMENT, POPULATION AND

Economic development refers to the structural transformation of human society from subsistence economy to urban-industrialism, and to the sus-tained rise in productivity and income that results. The transformation is seen in the structure of production, consumption, investment, and trade; in financial and other economic institutions; in occupations, educational levels, health conditions, and rural-urban residence; and in people's perceptions of the natural and social worlds and of their own agency. Political development is in some respects an overlapping process, yielding the values and institutions of the democratic state. *Development*, however, is commonly taken to mean economic development, with political development taken for granted.

Development is linked in various ways to population change. The transformation in demographic regimes from high to low birth and death rates—the demographic transition—can be added to the list of structural changes constituting development: Indeed, in terms of its direct effect on human well-being and its social and economic implications, it is arguably the most important of those changes. Population growth, unleashed by sustained mortality decline or by migration, is a force of its own in the development process, sometimes seeming to promote development, more often impeding it, and always diluting its achievements. While countries are the principal level at which such relationships have their effect, the influence of population change can extend to broader regional development and even to the global economy, with implications too for geopolitics and major environmental systems. Breaking down population growth by age group, source of growth (natural increase versus migration), and other characteristics reveals further links. The subject of population and development is concerned broadly with all such interactions: with how populations and economies impinge on each other and with the consequences that ensue.

Scale and Pace of Development

In the early 1800s, with industrialization barely underway, the world population stood at one billion; as late as 1930 it had reached just 2 billion; by the end of the twentieth century it had passed 6 billion. While dramatic enough to be described as an "explosion," this growth in population seems almost modest in comparison to the expansion of the global economy in the same period. Angus Maddison's index of gross world product (at constant prices, though the calculations required are complicated and inherently somewhat dubious over these time intervals) set at 1 in 1820, reaches 5 in 1929, 40 in 1990. It had probably exceeded 50 by 2000.

Along both dimensions this growth was extraordinarily uneven. The populations of Europe and North America expanded markedly over the nineteenth century as mortality yielded to improved living standards, the spread of education, and early public health measures. The region's share of the world population rose from about one-fifth to about one-third. Subsequently, mortality declines spread to Latin America, Asia, and Africa, creating a dramatic surge in population growth rates—and shifts in the global demographic balance that are relegating Europe and North America to the world's demographic margins (a 17% population share in 2000, a projected 12% share by 2050). The large reductions in mortality have been perhaps the most remarkable achievement of the post-World War II world. Life expectancy in the developing countries rose from about 40 years in 1950 to an estimated 64 years at the beginning of the twenty-first century.

Fertility levels followed, or seem to be following, the same regional course. In the West, aside from some forerunners (France and the United States), the decline got broadly underway in the late nineteenth and early twentieth century, spreading to the non-industrialized world after World War II but becoming widespread only in the 1960s or later. (Some regions, notably much of sub-Saharan Africa, had shown scant decline by the end of the twentieth century.)

The picture of regionally staggered onsets of demographic transition around the world, eventually (if only after a tenfold or more rise in population size) leading to conditions of low, zero, or perhaps negative population growth at low mortality levels, suggests a large measure of commonality in demographic experience. In cross-section, however, it is the diversity of demographic situations that is most striking. In the early decades after World War II arraying countries by mortality or fertility levels showed strongly bimodal distributions; in 2000, the bimodality had largely disappeared but the variance—reflecting the distance between leaders and laggards in the transition—remained high.

Economic growth used to seem well depicted by a similar kind of staged process, with poor countries successively reaching "take off" speed and embarking on rapid and sustained economic development. That expectation has only partially been borne out.

In the worldwide emphasis on development that emerged with the ending of colonial rule after World War II, many countries experienced economic growth spurts, sometimes for long enough to be proclaimed *miracles,* but few by the end of the twentieth century had attained income levels comparable to those of the early industrializers. Many countries, and some whole regions (sub-Saharan Africa in the 1980s and 1990s), experienced periods of economic stagnation or retrogression. Using a standard measure of absolute poverty—expenditure averaging less than a dollar per day at 1990 purchasing power—the world's poor numbered around 1.2 billion persons (20% of the world's population) in the late 1990s.

The variegated global experience of growth in populations and incomes since the industrial revolution is depicted in summary fashion in Figure 1, based on the estimates of Maddison. (The years identified are those selected by Maddison as reflecting significant junctures in global development, but the smooth trajectories drawn in the figure skirt over intervening fluctuations.) The chart reveals the contrasts among major countries along both axes; the impressive steepening of the trajectories for China and to a lesser degree India; and the bleak performance of the African region (a doubling of population in the last quarter of the twentieth century with no overall gain in real per capita income).

Population Size and Development

Under the mercantilist doctrine that prevailed in early modern Europe, a larger population was valued as a source of a nation's wealth. Malthusianism punctured that belief. From Malthus onward, both popular and official opinion has tended to see population growth as a threat to development. Increases in production could only too easily be dissipated in additions to population rather than invested in capital accumulation. Resource scarcities—in arable land, later also in other natural resources—were seen as always looming on the horizon and were brought nearer by demographic expansion. Malthusian views lay behind India's concerns about its population growth both prior to and after independence. They were the basis of China's sudden conversion in the 1970s to a policy of hard-nosed birth control. They attained wide prominence in the West in the same decade through the *Limits to Growth* thesis propounded by environmentalists.

Malthusian thinking had a more checkered history in economics. Resource-dependence has been

FIGURE 1

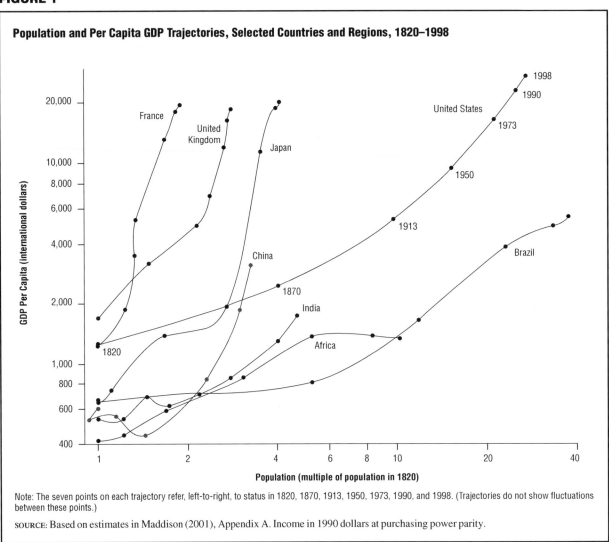

Population and Per Capita GDP Trajectories, Selected Countries and Regions, 1820–1998

Note: The seven points on each trajectory refer, left-to-right, to status in 1820, 1870, 1913, 1950, 1973, 1990, and 1998. (Trajectories do not show fluctuations between these points.)

SOURCE: Based on estimates in Maddison (2001), Appendix A. Income in 1990 dollars at purchasing power parity.

steadily reduced as technology has advanced and human capital has grown. Non-renewable resources have found vastly expanded supplies in some cases and ready substitutes in others, banishing fears of an era of diminishing returns and rendering earlier worries about the imminent exhaustion of particular resources (coal in England, for instance) almost quaint. As Harold J. Barnett and Chandler Morse wrote: "the social heritage consists far more of knowledge, equipment, institutions, and far less of natural resources, than it once did" (1963: 11–12).

Resource constraints cannot be wholly assumed away, especially if development is equated with human well-being. Fresh water is often mentioned as a potentially limiting factor; so-called positional goods, such as unique environments, are by defini-

tion scarce. Standard measures of economic performance mask the effects of changes in the natural environment. "Environmental services"—for example, pollination of crops—may be a significant ingredient of human welfare, but yet remain statistically invisible. Aesthetic criteria generally, and hence a whole range of quality distinctions—in production and consumption as well as in environmental conditions—tend to be neglected when it comes to measurement.

Population-resource interactions are mediated by human institutions: markets or management regimes that serve to ration access to the resource by potential users. In some circumstances, these arrangements break down, or possibly they never emerged in the first place, leading to depletion or degradation as the demands on the resource increase. A classic stylized account of this, intended to model possible external effects (externalities) of population growth, is Garrett Hardin's "tragedy of the commons." The tragedy is the decline through overuse—and through institutional incapacity—of an open-access, common-property resource. Analogues of these local-level externality problems exist at higher levels of social organization, even internationally.

Population Growth and Development

Twentieth-century theorizing about development was influenced by neoclassical growth models that, in contrast to the "classical" model, allowed steady expansion of both economies and populations, with technological progress given a central role in outcomes. Any adverse effects of the overall scale of the economy in relation to its resources were assumed negligible—or outweighed by positive effects. Some economists saw population growth actually boosting technological change—a case supported by the work of Danish economist Ester Boserup (1910–1999) on long-run agrarian change. Many others saw population growth as a fairly neutral factor in development performance. The range of viewpoints is captured by two major reports on the subject from the U.S. National Academy of Sciences, from 1971 and 1986: The first found a strong case for limiting population growth, the second at most a very weak one. Whatever the theoretical arguments, in the post-World War II decades, at least until the 1980s, aggregate income data did not show a significant negative effect of population growth on development: At the country level the years of fastest economic and demographic growth often coincided.

If researchers ask not about the effects of rapid population growth on development but about those of reduced mortality and fertility, the consensus is clear. As well as its obvious and immediate meaning for a society's welfare and for what is sometimes termed its human development, high mortality has various adverse effects on economic development. There is the evident waste of human resources, often embodying substantial public and private investments in education and skills. The AIDS epidemic has been particularly damaging in this respect: In many of the worst affected countries the disease cuts a swath through the educated strata of the society. High mortality is also associated with heavy morbidity, and sometimes with impaired physical and cog-

nitive development, with detrimental economic consequences. Within families, the death of a parent may harm the educational opportunities and broader life-prospects of the children: Again, AIDS mortality is the most prominent case in point, leading to a drastic rise in orphanhood and child destitution in a number of African countries. The benefits for development of improvements in health conditions and lower levels of mortality are thus clearly apparent.

The benefits of a fertility decline are somewhat less obvious—again, aside from the immediate welfare gain if it lessens "unwanted" births or improves reproductive health. Research suggests that lower fertility may improve access to health services and education, and more generally expand opportunities to escape poverty. One important route for such benefits is through a lowering of the child dependency rate: For a period of some two decades after a fertility decline there are fewer dependent children but no fewer workers, freeing up resources for investment. This straightforward proposition, advanced in a classic study by Ansley J. Coale and Edgar M. Hoover in the 1950s, was the main economic case for the worldwide expansion of family planning programs in the 1960s. Later it lost favor, along with many other arguments specific to developing economies, in the general disdain for development economics as a distinct branch of economics. It experienced a revival in the 1990s, coming to be seen by some as an important element in explaining the "Asian miracle"—the remarkable economic performance of East and Southeast Asian countries from the 1970s to the 1990s. The dramatic falls in birth rates in this region, beginning in the 1960s, are held to have yielded a "demographic bonus" of investment that boosted the development effort—not least, through improvements in human capital. However, the conditions under which any such bonus can be put to good use may be quite exceptional, lessening the value of the Asian miracle as a general policy lesson.

Promoting Demographic Transition

As discussed above, both mortality and fertility declines are favorable for development. The rapid population growth that is their usual accompaniment (since mortality typically falls first) is an offsetting factor, but moderates as the transition proceeds. These relationships can be viewed as positive feedbacks in the development process, forming a virtuous circle by which success breeds success: Sustained economic growth on the one hand and attainment of a modern demographic regime on the other. The components of population change are ingredients in the overall pattern of development, but for the most part they have the nature of dependent variables. Demographic transition is welcomed for the immediate welfare gains that low mortality and low fertility bring, but the proper policy focus to achieve those gains is on the broad development effort.

Many researchers and development planners, however, would adopt a much less passive stance on population policy. If there are proven means of intervention that can speed the mortality and fertility declines, then the gains both for immediate welfare and for the development effort can be reaped much earlier than would otherwise happen.

Mortality. For mortality, the appropriate means of intervention were evident. The long-running debate over the relative significance of the factors bringing about mortality improvement—transference of medical knowledge from the developed countries, expansion of public health facilities, and improved social and economic conditions—have been largely resolved, particularly through the pioneering work in the 1970s of demographer Samuel H. Preston.

Preston showed that there was a fairly tight but nonlinear relationship between life expectancy and per capita income among countries at a given time, and second that this relationship has shifted systematically over time. The relationship around 1990 is shown as a scatter plot (and fitted curve) in Figure 2, based on World Bank estimates: It is steep at low income levels, but flattens out at higher levels. Figure 2 also indicates the shifts in the relationship over time, drawing on sparser historical estimates. The major shifts have been twofold: (1) a decline in the per capita income level (in purchasing-power terms) at which this flattening takes place—that is, in the income level above which further income increases can be expected to make only slight contributions to improve mortality; and (2) an overall upward shift of the life expectancy-income relationship—a country with a given real per capita income in the early twenty-first century is likely to have considerably lower overall mortality than a country reaching the same income level some decades earlier would have had.

Cross-sectional analysis of this kind indicates that the effect of development on mortality is largest for countries at the lowest income levels. At the upper income ranges mortality is increasingly dissociated from economic change, reflecting both an educated demand for health services and the affluence to afford them. In the lower- and middle-income ranges, however, at any given income level there is a diversity of mortality outcomes across countries. Differences in income distribution, levels of education, public health expenditures, and the design and reach of the health system—all of them factors influenced by development policy—are the main contributors to that diversity.

Fertility. The degree to which fertility can be lowered by policy interventions has been a highly controversial issue in population and development studies, despite the casual assumption of many that the standard interventions—family planning programs—are of proven efficacy. But effective interventions of some sort are needed: The demographic bonus or any other economic advantages accruing from fertility decline are of interest because of the presumption that there are policy measures that can lower fertility other than through the normal course of development itself. Otherwise those advantages are reduced to the status of some helpful positive feedback generated by successful development.

At a broad level the factors behind fertility transition are not mysterious. Principally, there is a falling "demand" for children, traceable to a host of actual and anticipated changes in families' circumstances—in survivorship rates, in the family economy, in educational and labor market opportunities, and in related normative images of family and society. Also contributing to fertility decline are greater knowledge and availability of modern contraceptive methods and, in some situations, strong government efforts to promote smaller families. Development affects fertility mainly through alterations in the setting within which fertility decisions (and other decisions that incidentally bear on fertility) are taken. Three routes can be distinguished: (1) through alterations in the array of economic benefits and costs associated with marriage and childraising; (2) through shifts in social and administrative pressures on individuals and couples bearing on fertility-related decisions or their outcomes; and (3) through changes in internalized values concerning marriage and fertility instilled by education, socialization, and acculturation. The three routes are not wholly distinct, making for possibilities of double-counting.

(1) *Economic benefits and costs.* Fertility, like other kinds of behavior subject to individual choice, responds to changes in expected net economic benefits attaching to it. The increasing monetization of exchange relations that comes with economic development gives greater salience to this calculus. (Of course, no careful or even conscious calculation of benefits and cost need be assumed.) The economic shifts that take place are mostly in the direction of reducing the net benefits of high fertility.

The time entailed in childraising may be seen as more costly—for the poor, competing with opportunities to increase their earnings; for the better off, competing also with newfound forms of consumption.

Education beyond primary level becomes increasingly necessary for labor market success and its cost is often onerous even when supposedly publicly financed. This cost, together with other direct costs of children and the physical demands of their upbringing, is more likely to be borne fully by parents rather than shared among kin.

Social changes make any anticipated economic returns from children less assured. The insurance value of children is lessened as modern financial institutions emerge.

Improvements in health conditions presumably also affect the economics of fertility, altering individual planning horizons and parents' expectations of death or debility both for themselves and for their children.

Finally, government-supported family planning programs may lower the economic costs of birth control. How important those costs are, is disputed. Economist Lant Pritchett (1994, p. 25) points out that, under any reasonable assumption about the economics of children, those costs can be no more than a very small fraction of the (capitalized) net return—or net cost—anticipated from having a child.

(2) *Social and administrative pressures.* Social pressures from kin or community are probably felt less on the direct question of family size (except regarding childlessness and very small families) than on related matters such as age at marriage, approval or disapproval of particular practices of birth control, and restrictions on sex roles. Social influence entails scope for *contagion* and *bandwagon* effects. These effects are of course not confined to societies

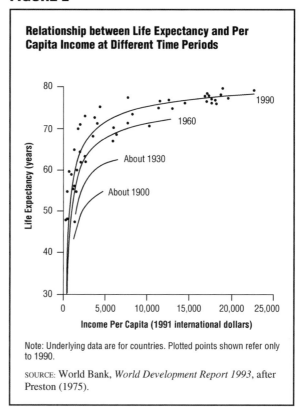

FIGURE 2

Relationship between Life Expectancy and Per Capita Income at Different Time Periods

Note: Underlying data are for countries. Plotted points shown refer only to 1990.

SOURCE: World Bank, *World Development Report 1993*, after Preston (1975).

experiencing demographic transition: It is likely that social pressures in contemporary low-fertility societies reinforce economic rationales for one- or two-child families by implicitly censuring family sizes above three.

In some countries in particular periods there have also been administrative pressures that bear directly on fertility. Such pressures peaked in the 1970s in Asia, principally in China and (more briefly) India, but also, less rigorously, in Indonesia and some other countries. Except for China, the pressures ebbed with the decline of fertility.

(3) *Internalized values.* The effects of values on fertility are not well understood or agreed upon. Some researchers believe them to have an independent effect on fertility, others as being rationalizations of behavior. They may be enduring realities—so that, for example, fertility decline could be a way of maintaining traditional family values in a changed economic setting. Or they may be altered by contact with new conditions. Some amount of value change is undeniable. For members of subsistence societies, almost osmotically but with many plausible transmission routes, perceptions of the family, of authori-

FIGURE 3

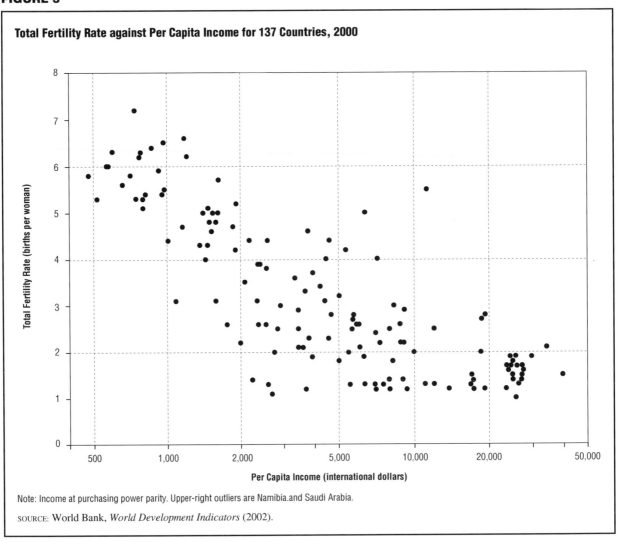

Total Fertility Rate against Per Capita Income for 137 Countries, 2000

Note: Income at purchasing power parity. Upper-right outliers are Namibia.and Saudi Arabia.

SOURCE: World Bank, *World Development Indicators* (2002).

ty, of the future, even of time, gradually come into alignment with those to be found in the modern industrialized world.

The combined net effect of these various changes has been strongly antinatalist, promoting the shift from quantity to "quality" of children. Disentangling the contributing factors to the fertility transition, however, has been a perennial source of argument, particularly over the putative roles of *development* (often narrowly construed as income growth) and *ideational change* (often construed as acceptability of family planning). The income-fertility relationship, shown as a scatter plot in Figure 3, makes clear both that a broad negative relationship exists and that there is a lot of variance remaining to be attributed to other factors. But such factors would necessarily include also the many as-

pects of development poorly captured by measures of income.

Population and Development Futures

In broad outline, the global economic and demographic trends observed over the second half of the twentieth century would support an expectation over the first half of the twenty-first century of continued, if uneven, improvement in economic conditions and, partly in consequence, an approaching end of the demographic transition. That demographic outcome, indeed, is the future built into the medium-variant population projections of the United Nations, which (in the 2000 revision) portray the world's fertility dropping from 2.8 children per woman in the 1990s to 2.1 (replacement level) by around 2050, and life expectancy increasing in the same period from 65 years to 74 years. The world population, under this scenario, would rise from 6 billion in 2000 to 9 billion in 2050, but by then the annual increment would have dropped from 80 million people to around 40 million—and zero (and perhaps negative) population growth would be in sight. Closely tied to these trends would be a substantial aging of population, continued rapid urbanization in the less developed regions, and continuation of the major shift in the balance of world population toward the South.

Both in evaluating this scenario and in probing its ingredients, consensus quickly wanes. The range of interpretations of past experience is magnified in looking ahead. The most sanguine outlook is sketched in economist Richard A. Easterlin's *Growth Triumphant,* in which the population explosion is a passing phenomenon, ushering in a future of sustained economic growth led by ever-higher material aspirations. Erstwhile poor countries successively build the complex economies and settlement densities already found in the rich countries. Economic globalization is frequently depicted as a route to such affluence, open to all, although bringing with it not just new opportunities but also new systemic fragilities.

More cautious or circumspect assessments of the future extrapolate emerging problems as well as favorable trends. Such problems include: supporting the necessary scale of transfer payments to the aged as their numbers multiply; avoiding fertility collapse to levels far below replacement, with its eventual implication of radical population decline; maintaining the quality of socialization and education of children in the face of crumbling families and weakened local communities; lessening the ecological damage associated with rising average consumption levels; and coping not only with the large remaining public health agenda in poor regions but also with new or reemerging infectious disease threats. The future food situation, though in the aggregate far from dire by many informed accounts, is increasingly technology-dependent and regionally disparate. The greenhouse effect, the atmospheric warming caused by increased amounts of carbon dioxide and other gases, has the potential to create ramifying changes in the environment, affecting crop production (perhaps positively), disease vectors, natural ecosystems, sea levels, and weather patterns. Greenhouse gas emissions are linked to population growth as well as to industrialization.

Population change will also have political consequences, and political developments, in turn, clearly have the capacity to modify future economic and demographic trends. "Failed states," according to Robert D. Kaplan, owe their ungovernability partly to population growth and the ecological degradation and poverty tied to it. Environmentally-related political instability, some have argued, will become common in many regions. But while examples of economic retrogression and associated political turbulence will surely continue to be found in the future, so too will cases of recovery and eventual return to paths of stable positive growth.

At the international level, the changes in relative population sizes and in age distributions among countries that are occurring will have major political implications. Combined with persisting economic differences they identify potential faultlines of international conflict. Large-scale migration from poor to prosperous countries is another politically sensitive issue that will not lessen in importance—filling some part of the demographic deficits created by very low fertility, and in doing so creating the increasingly ethnically-diverse societies of the Western world.

See also: *Demographic Transition; Economic-Demographic Models; Fertility Transition, Socioeconomic Determinants of; Mortality Decline; National Security and Population.*

BIBLIOGRAPHY

Ahlburg, Dennis A., Allen C. Kelley, and Karen Oppenheim Mason, eds. 1996. *The Impact of Population Growth and Well-Being in Developing Countries.* Berlin: Springer-Verlag.

Barnett, Harold J., and Chandler Morse. 1963. *Scarcity and Growth: The Economics of Natural Resource Availability.* Baltimore: Johns Hopkins Press.

Birdsall, Nancy, Allen C. Kelley, and Steven W. Sinding, eds. 2001. *Population Matters: Demographic Change, Economic Growth, and Poverty in the Developing World.* Oxford: Oxford University Press.

Boserup, Ester. 1981. *Population and Technological Change: A Study of Long-Term Trends.* Chicago: University of Chicago Press.

Coale, Ansley J., and Edgar M. Hoover. 1958. *Population Growth and Economic Development in*

Low-Income Countries. Princeton: Princeton University Press.

Demeny, Paul, and Geoffrey McNicoll, eds. 1998. *The Earthscan Reader in Population and Development.* London: Earthscan Publications.

Easterlin, Richard A. 1996. *Growth Triumphant: The Twenty-first Century in Historical Perspective.* Ann Arbor: University of Michigan Press.

Furedi, Frank. 1997. *Population and Development: A Critical Introduction.* New York: St Martin's Press.

Hirsch, Fred. 1976. *Social Limits to Growth.* Cambridge, MA: Harvard University Press.

Kaplan, Robert D. 1996. *The Ends of the Earth: A Journey at the Dawn of the Twenty-first Century.* New York: Random House.

Kuznets, Simon. 1979. *Growth, Population, and Income Distribution.* New York: Norton.

Maddison, Angus. 2001. *The World Economy: A Millennial Perspective.* Paris: Organisation for Economic Co-operation and Development.

Population and Development Review. 1975–. New York: Population Council, quarterly.

Preston, Samuel H. 1975. "The Changing Relation Between Mortality and Level of Economic Development." *Population Studies* 29: 231–248.

Pritchett, Lant H. 1994. "Desired Fertility and the Impact of Population Policies." *Population and Development Review* 20: 1–55.

United Nations Department of Economic and Social Affairs. 1973. *Determinants and Consequences of Population Trends,* rev. edition, Vol. 1: *New Summary of Findings on Interaction of Demographic, Economic, and Social Factors.* New York: United Nations.

U.S. National Academy of Sciences. 1971. *Rapid Population Growth: Consequences and Policy Implications,* Report of the Study Committee of the Foreign Secretary, National Academy of Sciences. Baltimore: Johns Hopkins Press.

U.S. National Academy of Sciences. 1986. *Population Growth and Economic Development: Policy Questions.* Report of the Working Group on Population Growth and Economic Development, National Research Council. Washington, D.C.: National Academy Press.

World Bank. 2001. *World Development Report 2000/2001: Attacking Poverty.* New York: Oxford University Press.

GEOFFREY McNICOLL

DIETARY REGIMES

Dominant patterns of food consumption have changed substantially as human societies evolved during tens of thousands of years of gathering and hunting, millennia of traditional pastoralism and settled farming, and a century of modern intensive agriculture. As a result, nearly 90 percent of humanity now enjoys at least an adequate food supply, and an increasing share of the world's population now worries about excess, rather than about shortages, of food.

Diets of Foraging Societies

The enormous diversity of foraging societies—ranging from maritime hunters with relatively easy access to highly nutritious aquatic animals to foragers in arid environments where tubers and seeds provided the bulk of food energy—means that there has never been a single typical gatherer-hunter diet. Societies exploiting the constant presence or regular migrations of mollusks, fatty fish (cod, salmon), and marine mammals (seals, whales) had by far the highest intake of both animal protein and lipids. These maritime foragers could have derived 30 to 50 percent of their food energy from animal protein. The only land foragers who could have approached that pattern, at least seasonally, were the cooperative hunters of megaherbivores; the best example of this strategy is mass killings of North American bisons by driving them over precipices. Given the typically low success rates in hunting the fast-running mid-size and small herbivores living on grasslands and in forests, most foragers had only a limited supply of animal foods. And, as nearly all small and most mid-size animals are very lean, their diets were particularly short of fat.

Archaeologists have used remains and nutrient analyses of wild plant and animal foods consumed by foragers that survived into the twentieth century to estimate the dominant composition of prevailing pre-agricultural diets. These reconstructions conclude that plant foods, generally consumed within hours after being gathered, supplied 65 to 70 percent of all food energy. Proteins made up about a third of food energy (a share nearly three times as high as that recommended at the end of the twentieth century), and lipids about 20 percent. Average intakes of vitamins and minerals were generally well above the modern recommended daily allowances (RDA). These conclusions may not be representative of all foraging societies, because of the limited number of examined archaeological sites and because the foraging societies that survived into the twentieth century did so in mostly marginal environments. These marginal environments include, counterintuitively, tropical rain forests where hunting success is low, as most animals are arboreal, and hence relatively small and inaccessible in high canopies.

Pre-Industrial Diets

Archaeological findings and written documents offer a wealth of information about the composition of diets in antiquity, but translating these accounts into quantitative summaries of average or typical intakes is very difficult. Information about crop yields and animal productivity cannot be converted into average supply rates because of large, and highly variable, post-harvest food losses. Perhaps the only permissible generalization in accord with documentary and anthropometric evidence is the absence of any clear upward trend in per capita food supply during the millennia of traditional pre-industrial farming. In fact, stagnation or deterioration of food supply had not been uncommon. A reconstruction of ancient Mesopotamian ration lists indicates that daily energy supplies between 3000 and 2400 B.C.E. were about 20 percent above the early-twentieth-century mean for the same region. Similarly, the Han dynasty records show that during the fourth century B.C.E. a peasant was expected to provide each of his five family members with nearly half kilogram of grain a day, the rate equal to the North Chinese mean during the 1950s.

As the following examples illustrate, better information available for the last four centuries of the second millennium does not show any substantial nutritional improvements until the latter half of the nineteenth century. Annual per capita grain and meat supply in Rome fell by 25 to 30 percent during the seventeenth century. At the end of the eighteenth century, Sir Frederic Morton Eden found that the poorest English peasants consumed little or no milk

or potatoes, no oatmeal, and seldom any butter, but occasionally a little cheese; he noted that even bread, their chief staple, was in short supply. Similarly, a third of the rural population in Eastern Prussia could not afford enough bread as late as 1847.

Diets of most pre-industrial populations were thus highly monotonous, not very palatable, and barely adequate in terms of basic nutrients. In most of Europe pre-industrial diets were dominated by bread (mostly dark, often with little or no wheat flour), and included coarse grains (oats, barley, buckwheat), turnips, cabbage, and, after 1570, potatoes. These ingredients were served in thin soups and stews, with evening meals indistinguishable from breakfasts and midday food. Similarly, in Asian peasant diets cereals—millet, wheat, rice, and after 1530, corn—supplied more than four-fifths of all food energy. Major sources of protein included soybeans in East Asia and lentils and chickpeas in the South. Millet, tubers such as cassava and yams, and legumes like peanuts were the staples of sub-Saharan Africa, and corn and beans were dominant throughout pre-Colombian America. Quinoa and a huge variety of potatoes were essential for survival in the Andean environment.

Vegetables and fruits enlivened the monotony of cereal and legume staples, but, unless preserved by pickling or drying, they were only seasonally abundant in temperate climates. Common European vegetables included turnips, cabbages, onions and carrots, while apples, pears, plums, and grapes brought the largest fruit harvests. Cabbages, radishes, onions, garlic, and ginger were the main vegetables consumed in China, and pears, peaches, and oranges were favorite fruits. Two quintessential Mesoamerican vegetables, tomatoes and peppers, became cultivated worldwide after 1600.

Typical pre-industrial meat consumption was very low, averaging no more than 5 to 10 kilograms per year, and roasts and stews were usually eaten only during festive occasions. Consequently, animal foods provided less than 15 percent of all dietary protein, and saturated animal fats supplied only around 10 percent of all food energy. Low meat consumption persisted not only during the early phases of European modernization in the nineteenth century, but into the twentieth century as well. Median annual meat intake in France was only about 20 kilograms per capita during the 1860s, and it was barely above 10 kilograms per capita in England. Monotonous diets, major consumption inequalities in both regional and socioeconomic terms, and recurrent food shortages and even famines persisted until the nineteenth century in Europe and well into the twentieth century in Asia and Africa, leaving the majority of peasants in all traditional farming societies with food supplies below optimal levels necessary for healthy and vigorous life.

Diets in the Age of Mechanized Agriculture

Major dietary change got under way in Europe only in the mid-nineteenth century and its scope ranged from eliminating any threat of famine to the founding of restaurants and emergence of the *grande cuisine*. Slow decline in the average consumption of staples was accompanied by growing intakes of animal foods and sugar. Cheaper imports of cane sugar and the introduction of the diffusion process to produce sugar from beets after 1860 in Europe and North America made refined sucrose easily obtainable for the first time in human history. This period of rapid dietary change led Ernst Engel (1821–1896), a German statistician, to formulate the eponymous law stating that the poorer a family, the higher its share of total expenditure spent on food. The law remains valid today—for nations as well as families: While an average American family spends only about one-seventh of its disposable income on food, the percentage is still more than 40 in China's cities.

The pace of Western dietary change accelerated after World War II as increasingly mechanized agriculture, supported by high energy subsidies and relying on new high-yielding crops, began producing surpluses of food. Mechanized agriculture improved the quality and variety of food, and supplied both staples and fancy foodstuffs at relatively decreasing prices. Foodstuffs that were previously too expensive or simply inaccessible began appearing in everyday diets. Chilled shipments of out-of-season fruits and vegetables and a growing trade in ocean fish and specialty foodstuffs eventually erased the seasonal availability of all but a few perishable plant species and diffused food items whose consumption was previously confined to specific areas (such as cactus pears, litchi, salmon, and sea bass).

Diets in the Twenty-First Century

Average per capita food supply at the beginning of the twenty-first century is in excess of 3,000 kilocalories per day in all Western nations and very close to 3,000 kilocalories per day in Japan. More than 30 percent, and in some circumstances even more than 40 percent, of all food energy comes from lipids, annual meat consumption is in excess of 70 or even 100 kilograms per capita, and in comparison to all pre-industrial diets, the modern Western diet is too high in sodium and too low in indigestible fiber. Incredibly, in spite of the surfeit of food and the common fortification of such staples as flour, many people in Western societies have micronutrient deficiencies, and several million people in North America go hungry.

The actual food energy requirement in modern, largely sedentary societies is only about 2,000 kilocalories per day, and the huge gap between the supply and the need explains both a great deal of food waste and the unprecedented extent of obesity that is being incessantly, and not very successfully, combated by ubiquitous dieting. Western diets in general, and obesity in particular, have been associated with the rise of such widespread "civilizational" diseases as cardiovascular illnesses and diabetes. The Mediterranean diet has been advocated as a healthy alternative, but the average intakes of Mediterranean populations have been shifting in the direction of less healthful Northern diets with declining consumption of bread, fruit, potatoes, and olive oil.

An excessive quantity of inexpensive food is accompanied by a still-increasing diversity of food supply brought by extensive intra- and intercontinental trade (including perishable foodstuffs ranging from tuna fish to grapes), by the commingling of food traditions in nations with large immigrant populations, and by the globalization of many previously spatially restricted food and beverage items such as leavened breads, pizza, sushi, beer, and wine. At the same time, more single-person households, high rates of female employment, and reduced willingness to cook have brought an astonishing rise in the consumption of fast foods whose dominant ingredients are saturated fat (in hamburger, pizza, and taco empires) and refined sugar (in doughnut and coffee shops). The picture of modern food customs would not be complete without noting extensive food faddism, cultism, and quackery, practices ranging from megavitamin regimens to pseudo-scientific diets (from vegan to macrobiotic), and consumption of both natural and synthetic food supplements (from echinacea extracts to zinc lozenges). A new concept, made possible by genetic engineering, is the use of food as medicine (called "nutraceuticals").

In contrast to the rich world's food surpluses, average daily food supplies below 2,000 kilocalories per capita are still common in the world's most impoverished countries where some 95 percent of the world's more than 800 million malnourished people can be found (about 200 million in India, 140 million in China). Dietary transitions that took more than a century in the West are being compressed into just a few decades in many rapidly modernizing Asian countries. They are marked, on one hand, by declining consumption of cereal grains and even more rapid reduction in the consumption of legumes and, on the other hand, by rising intakes of plant oils, animal foods (meat as well as aquacultured fish and crustaceans), fruits, and sugar. Post-1980 China is the best example of this process as it has moved from a barely adequate diet dominated by staple grains and basic vegetables to a total per capita supply nearly equaling the Japanese mean (about 2800 kilocalories per day in 2000).

In spite of the indisputable globalization of tastes, national and regional food preferences are evident around the world and food taboos, only weakly held in the West in the early twenty-first century, remain strong among nearly two billion Muslims and Hindus. Further homogenization of tastes will be accompanied by further diffusion of "exotic" foodstuffs and by the development of hybrid cuisines and new eating habits. Regardless of the unpredictable specifics of future dietary changes, there is no doubt that these new global trends will demand more resources for production of higher-quality and specialty foods—more fertilizers and pesticides for perfect fruit, high-protein feed for aqua-cultured carnivorous fish—and for their worldwide distribution. Manipulating these trends through pricing is hardly an option in a world where commodity prices have been in a prolonged and nearly universal decline. Public education about healthy nutrition is imperative, but it is an uphill task in societies suffused with gluttony-promoting advertisement and hedonist values, and lacking dietary discipline.

See also: *Food Supply and Population; Nutrition and Calorie Consumption.*

BIBLIOGRAPHY

Flandrin, Jean-Louis, and Massimo Montanari, eds. 1999. *Food: A Culinary History from Antiquity to the Present.* New York: Penguin Books.

Kiple, Kenneth F., and Kriemhild Coneè Ornelas, eds. 2000. *The Cambridge World History of Food.* Cambridge, Eng.: Cambridge University Press.

Smil, Vaclav. 2000. *Feeding the World.* Cambridge, MA: MIT Press.

VACLAV SMIL

DIFFUSION IN POPULATION THEORY

Theorizing about the forces driving the transition from high to low fertility has been dominated by opposition between *structural explanations* and those referred to as *diffusion-based explanations*. The same opposition is ubiquitous, if less obvious, in the literature on health and mortality, international migration, and spatial and residential patterns. This contrast is not unique to population theory: A similar division is widely seen in the literature on the emergence of nation-states in political sociology, within the theory of social organizations, and in the study of the economic behavior of individuals and firms.

An important illustration of this opposition and one that has long been a problem in population theory relates to the explanation of the secular fertility decline in Western Europe that began around 1850. The phenomenon was initially thought to be a result of economic, social, and political transformations that altered the social context within which childbearing took place. These transformations are seen as *structural* changes, that is, changes emerging from larger societal transformations that alter the economics of fertility (for example, changes that affect the conditions of individuals' decision-making about childbearing). Some of these transformations are directly related to industrialization and the shifting division of labor and occupational structure. Others, such as the transition to a regime of low infant and child mortality, are thought to be secondary products of these large-scale transformations (and perhaps only loosely connected to them) but with a direct effect on fertility.

The empirical evidence from historical and contemporary societies stubbornly refuses to fit neatly into the patterns of conventional interpretations.

Fertility declined in Western Europe in areas where such structural changes both did and did not occur. Onset was remarkably concentrated in time, much more so than the timing of onset of structural changes. In addition, the attainment of low fertility regimes follows a geographic contour that is more consistent with ethnic, cultural, linguistic, and political cleavages than anticipated by the structural explanation.

Similarly, what explanation exists for the more recent sharp fertility decline in Bangladesh, where economic development and large-scale industrialization are still elusive goals but where the total fertility rate dropped from 7 children per woman to nearly 3.5 children per woman in thirty years? Or for the statistics in Brazil where the total fertility rate is 2.8 children per woman at the outset of the twenty-first century after topping 6.5 children per woman just forty years before? According to classic indicators of economic development and industrialization, even though Brazil has experienced deeper economic transformations than Bangladesh, its fertility levels are still not commensurate with the relatively limited influence of these changes. Further, the internal regional disparities in economic development are overshadowed by a remarkable homogeneity of fertility regimes.

The inconsistencies between fertility patterns predicted by structural explanations and those actually observed has led many researchers to abandon the structural perspective in favor of one that emphasizes the importance of dissemination of new ideas and the diffusion of modern fertility behaviors.

An analogous, and even older, controversy between structuralist and diffusionist theories exists over explanations of changes in mortality and health regimes. On one side are explanations that interpret the secular mortality decline as a result of economic transformations and improvements in standards of living. On the other side, mortality decline is seen as a result of the spread of medical technology and of the dissemination of advances in public health and individual hygiene that reduce exposure to infectious diseases.

Anatomy of the Theoretical Divide

What is the main distinction between a structuralist explanation and one based on diffusion? Structural explanations of behavioral changes seek the cause in the alteration of preferences and opportunities that result from either changes in the positions that individuals occupy (individual social mobility) or from the reshuffling of resources associated with a given social position (e.g., structural social mobility or redistribution of wealth). In contrast, diffusion explanations attempt to identify a mechanism that leads to cumulative adoption of behaviors by some individuals, even when their social position, or the resources associated with them, change only minimally or remain unaltered. In diffusion models, the behavior *spreads* and is adopted by individuals irrespective of their socioeconomic positions, including among those whose social or economic positions are such that a hypothetical cost–benefit calculation would not necessarily favor the new behavior. An individual adopts the new behavior as a result of a re-evaluation of choices in light of the behavior of other people, not as a strategic response or accommodation to a realignment of resources associated with the individual's position in the social system. Diffusion models are built on the central idea that individuals transfer partial or total control of their own behavior to others. The implied decision process is at least as complicated as those normally associated with structural explanations.

Diffusion processes do not always involve adoption of new behaviors. In fact, they may include abandonment of a recently adopted behavior or resistance to change. The course of fertility decline in Europe revealed a marked tendency to proceed along, or be halted by, ethnic, linguistic, and religious boundaries. The resulting geographic clustering of fertility levels and patterns has been construed as evidence for the hypothesis that fertility changes were strongly driven by ideational or cultural changes, transmitted by diffusion mechanisms, rather than as supporting a structural explanation of fertility decline. The existence of a clustering of fertility changes along cultural lines could be evidence of diffusion of either a new behavior (such as adoption of contraception along with acceptance of a low-fertility norm) in areas were fertility declined below what would be expected based on existing levels of industrialization and urbanization (structural changes), or of resistance to the new behavior (rejection of birth control and adherence to a high-fertility norm) in areas where fertility remained higher than expected.

Thus there is a contrast between an explanation that infers an expected behavior from a reading of individual socioeconomic positions (the structuralist explanation), and an alternative explanation that infers a pattern of expected behavior from the likely adherence of actors to ethnic, religious, or cultural prescriptions or beliefs shared by others in the same community, including individuals belonging to different social classes or occupying different socioeconomic positions. In the latter case, the likelihood of adherence to prescriptions increases as a function of others' adherence to them (or others' resistance to the novel behavior). Who is included in the group referred to as "others" is a key ingredient of the theory, as is the identification of the exact mechanisms that secure adherence to prescriptions and beliefs.

Both the structuralist and the diffusionist explanations rest on the idea that individuals are decision makers, acting in uncertain environments, sorting through limited information on prices, utilities, constraints, and potential outcomes of alternative behaviors, elucidating their own preferences, and ultimately taking some course of action. Whereas investigators are normally careful to produce a thorough definition of the decision-making process associated with the structuralist explanation, they all too often fail to specify the decision-making process associated with diffusion—to the point that the process appears, in many instances, to consist of passive contagion and the irrational or *arational* adoption of a behavior. Lack of theoretical specificity leads to accepting diffusion explanations as concession to failure, a fall-back position taken when one cannot confirm a structuralist explanation.

In both sociology and demography, most of the evidence adduced to distinguish between the two contending explanations of behavioral change is derived from aggregate, not individual, data. Since the individual adoption process is not well specified, it is unclear what type of aggregate evidence would be determinative. This leads to the common but methodologically flawed practice of inferring the validity of a diffusion explanation from the failure to support the validity of a structural one. A central problem in sociology and demography, and in economics as well, is the inability to identify key processes from observables.

The Identification Problem or How to Falsify Diffusion Theories with Observables

The only way to convincingly choose between a diffusionist or a structuralist theory is by observing patterns of behavior under conditions that hold the dis-

tribution of individuals by social positions and the distribution of resources associated with those positions constant, while allowing variations in conditions that trigger the spread of the behavior (participation in social networks, etc.). If the prevalence of the behavior grows, it cannot possibly be due to structural factors (they are constant) but to diffusion. The difficulty, however, is that at least one of the three mechanisms of diffusion identified above mimics the effects of structural changes: namely, when social positions or resources associated with them change as a result of the process of diffusion itself. Put another way, if we are to identify diffusion effects, the ideal experiment cannot allow the diffusion feedback mechanism to operate and simultaneously maintain invariance in individual characteristics. Thus, even under ideal conditions, it is difficult to sort out precisely how much of the ultimate change in behavior is due to all diffusion mechanisms, and how much to secondary changes in the social structure induced by diffusion itself. In the cases of interest here, including the study of fertility, the conditions are far from ideal; hence it is virtually impossible to make the necessary distinctions. This limitation is irrelevant when the feedback mechanism is weak or if its operation requires long time lags.

Needless to say, there are few ideal experiments. With few exceptions, the evidence marshaled in favor or against diffusion either coarsely identifies the processes of diffusion that the theorist postulates as empirically relevant or, worse, is unspecific, simply referring to *what is left over* after accounting for measurable conditions associated with individual positions and resources.

A behavior model must be a representation of individuals choosing among a set of alternatives, under a set of constraints. The model must seek to account for the persistence (or abandonment) of a behavior over time. This can be done most efficiently by imagining that individuals may occupy two states, one representing adoption of the target behavior and the other adoption of a different behavior (or refusal to adopt the behavior). Transitions between these two states are a function of the individuals' characteristics associated with social and economic conditions (costs and utilities), external characteristics acting as constraints or facilitators, the influence of external sources of ideas, and the influence of each individual's linkages to social networks. To the extent that individuals' transition rates are dependent on factors affecting the stock of external sources of ideas or their interaction with social networks, a diffusion explanation acquires greater credibility.

Advances in the empirical identification of diffusion as a feasible mechanism that triggers large-scale behavioral transformations depends on the ability of the scientific community (a) to precisely define the empirical processes through which external sources of influence and those associated with social networks alter the willingness, the ability, and/or the readiness of individuals to adopt or resist behavioral change, and (b) to gather empirical information on the mechanisms through which external sources and social networks operate to produce change.

Conclusions: Where Do We Go From Here?

The theoretical divide described above is still a reality in various areas of demography and continues to be a subject of theoretical debate in sociology and economics. Its nature, however, has been redefined and enriched. Testing theories that pose diffusion as a plausible phenomenon no longer rests on dubious arguments about residual explanations without identifying the precise mechanisms involved. Instead, there have been significant theoretical improvements, drawing elements from social network and social learning theories and applying ideas from economics on relations between individual behavior and aggregate properties of a system. These developments offer the prospect of progress toward the objective described in (a) above.

In addition to advances in theory and modeling, there is a need for more and richer information on aggregate and individual patterns of change. Efforts to identify social networks through both large-scale longitudinal surveys and ethnographically based research are promising developments addressing the issue raised in (b) above.

See also: *Action Theory in Population Research; Culture and Population; Demographic Transition; Fertility Transition, Socioeconomic Determinants of; Mass Media and Demographic Behavior; Social Networks; Values and Demographic Behavior.*

BIBLIOGRAPHY

Carlsson, Gosta. 1966. "The Decline of Fertility: Innovation or Adjustment Process?" *Population Studies* 20: 149–174.

Cavalli-Sforza, Luca L., and Marcus W. Feldman. 1981. "Cultural Transmission and Evolution: A Quantitative Approach." *Monographs in Population Biology,* No 16.

Cleland, John, and C. Wilson. 1987. "Demand Theories of the Fertility Transition: An Iconoclastic View." *Population Studies* 41: 5–30.

Coleman, J. S. 1990. *Foundations of Social Theory.* Cambridge, MA: Harvard University Press.

Lesthaeghe, Ron, and C. Vanderhoeft. 2001. "Ready, Willing, and Able: A Conceptualization of Transitions to New Behavioral Forms" In *Social Processes Underlying Fertility Changes in Developing Countries,* ed. John Casterline and B. Cohen. Washington D.C.: National Research Council Press.

Montgomery, Mark, and John Casterline. 1993. "The Diffusion of Fertility Control in Taiwan: Evidence from Pooled Cross-Section, Time Series Models." *Population Studies* 47(3): 457–479.

Palloni, Alberto. 2001. "Diffusion in Sociological Analysis: How Useful Is It for the Study of Fertility and Mortality?" In *Social Processes Underlying Fertility Changes in Developing Countries,* ed. John Casterline and B. Cohen. Washington, D.C.: National Academy Press.

Rogers, Everett M. 1995. *The Diffusion of Innovations,* 4th edition. New York: The Free Press.

Rosero-Bixby, Luis, and John B. Casterline. 1993. "Interaction Diffusion and Fertility Transition in Costa Rica." *Social Forces* 73(2): 435–462.

———. 1993. "Modelling Diffusion Effects in Fertility Transition."*Population Studies* 47(1):147–167.

Strang, David. 1991. "Adding Social Structure to Diffusion Models: An Event History Framework." *Sociological Methods and Research* 19: 324–353.

Valente, Thomas W. 1995. *Network Models of the Diffusion of Innovations.* Cresskill, NJ: Hampton Press.

ALBERTO PALLONI

DISABILITY, DEMOGRAPHY OF

Disability is one dimension of morbidity, or ill health. In the United States disability is defined as the inability because of poor health to perform tasks or social roles that are considered normal for one's age. Disability is the end of a process of health change that begins with the onset of diseases and conditions that may lead to the impairment or loss of function—the loss of the physical ability to perform certain tasks or motions—and then to disability. The process is termed the "disability process" by Lois Verbrugge and Alan Jette and is shown in Figure 1.

Definitions

The distinction between disability and impairment and loss of function is that disability can be affected by the circumstances of a person's environment or the demands of social roles, whereas loss of function is internal to the person. Loss of function occurs "within the skin"; disability results from a combination of factors "within" and "outside the skin." A complication of cross-national research on disability is that countries that employ the World Health Organization's International Classification of Impairment, Disability, and Handicap (ICIDH) define disability the way researchers in the United States define impairment and use the word *handicap* to define what is known as disability in the United States.

Disability thus often is defined in terms of the normal tasks in various age groups. For young people school disability is the inability to attend a mainstream school. For those in the working ages work disability is the inability to perform the tasks required at work. For older persons disability often is defined in terms of the inability to live independently and provide self-care. Operationally, this often is measured as the ability to perform what are called "activities of daily living" and "instrumental activities of daily living."

As these definitions make clear, changes in the environment without changes in innate ability can affect the level of disability. This fact underlies the Americans with Disabilities Act of 1990. Schools that provide services for children with functioning problems can reduce school-age disability; workplace adaptations can reduce work disability; and the development of technology and assistive devices as well as changes in housing design can reduce old-age disability.

FIGURE 1

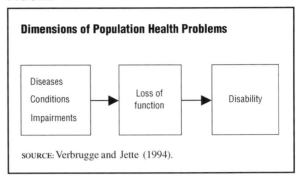

Dimensions of Population Health Problems

Diseases / Conditions / Impairments → Loss of function → Disability

SOURCE: Verbrugge and Jette (1994).

Levels of Disability

The level of disability is related to both age and sex. Generally, as a person's age increases, the level of disability increases because of the greater incidence of specific diseases and conditions, both physical and mental, and loss of function. For instance, among non-institutionalized American males in 1997 the proportion with disability or some limitation in activity ranged from 7 percent at age 18 to 36 percent at age 65 and over. Women generally report higher levels of disability in the older ages; the proportion with limitations in activity among women 65 and over was 42 percent in 1997. This is related to women's higher levels of morbid diseases such as arthritis.

Persons of lower socioeconomic status have higher levels of disability than do those of higher status. In the United States in 1997, 25 percent of persons with family incomes less than $20,000 were limited in activity; this was true of only 6 percent of persons from households with incomes of $75,000 and over. The relationship between socioeconomic status and disability is caused by numerous risk factors and life circumstances related to lower status and the earlier onset of all dimensions of morbidity.

Unlike mortality, disability is not an "absorbing" state. It is a state of impaired health from which a person can recover and that a person then can re-enter. People may experience a number of periods of significant disability in their lives or may never be disabled. Although many people experience significant disability in the last year of life, some individuals die without experiencing loss of function or disability.

The level of disability has declined since the early 1980s among some segments of the American population. This is generally true for the older population, but the decline appears to be concentrated among those with higher socioeconomic status.

The level of disability in a population results from a combination of the rate of incidence of disability and the rates of survival among those with and without disability. It is possible for mortality decline to result in a longer-lived disabled population and increases in age-specific levels of disability. Researchers in a number of countries have found evidence that would support this set of circumstances for the period of the 1970s. Many countries, however, have experienced reductions in disability along with reductions in mortality that began by the 1980s.

The Decline in Disability

The decline in disability in the United States appears to be related to the increase in education among the older population. It is possible that this trend reflects current educational shifts and may not continue with increases in education at higher levels. In addition, the pattern of change for some younger cohorts is not promising. Middle-aged cohorts born in the baby-boom years report higher levels of disability at these ages than earlier cohorts did. In the past age-specific disability increased regularly as a cohort aged, implying that the baby boom cohort may have higher levels of disability in old age than current cohorts of older persons.

See also: *Accidents; Aging of Population; Disease, Burden of.*

BIBLIOGRAPHY

Blackwell, Debra L., and Luong Tonthat. 2002. "Summary Health Statistics for the U.S. Population: National Health Interview Survey, 1997." *Vital and Health Statistics* 10: 204.

Crimmins, Eileen M., and Yasuhiko Saito. 2001. "Trends in Disability-Free Life Expectancy in the United States, 1970–1990: Gender, Racial, and Educational Differences." *Social Science and Medicine* 52: 1629–1641.

Freedman, Vicki A., and Linda G. Martin. 1998. "Understanding Trends in Functional Limitations among Older Americans." *American Journal of Public Health* 88: 1457–1462.

Manton, Kenneth G., and XiLiang Gu. 2001. "Changes in the Prevalence of Chronic Disability in the United States Black and Nonblack Population above Age 65 from 1982 to 1999." *Proceedings of the National Academy of Sciences* 98: 6354–6359.

Reynolds, Sandra, Eileen M. Crimmins, and Yasuhiko Saito. 1998. "Cohort Differences in Disability and Disease Presence." *The Gerontologist* 38: 578–590.

Verbrugge, Lois M., and Alan M. Jette. 1994. "The Disablement Process." *Social Science and Medicine* 38: 1–14.

EILEEN M. CRIMMINS

DISASTERS

Disasters are sudden, large-scale events that result in substantial numbers of deaths and injuries or severe economic losses. Natural disasters, the subject of this article, are disasters that are not precipitated by human agency. A disaster occurs when vulnerable people are severely impacted by a hazard in a way that recovery is unlikely without external aid. Vulnerability is a function of a group's socioeconomic condition; the poor are more vulnerable than the rich.

Deaths and Injuries

According to the International Federation of Red Cross and Red Crescent Societies (IFRC), a total of 39,073 people were reported killed by disasters in 2001. This figure is lower than the decade's annual average of around 62,000. Earthquakes proved to be the world's deadliest disasters, accounting for over half the year's toll. Over the decade, however, hydrometeorological hazards have claimed 71 percent of all lives lost to disasters.

From 1992–2001, countries of Low Human Development (LHD) have accounted for just one-fifth of the total number of disasters, but over half of all disaster fatalities. On average 13 times more people die per reported disaster in LHD countries than in countries of high human development. In 2001, a total of 170 million people were reported affected by disasters (IFRC 2002).

Economic Losses

In the 10 years ending in 2001, economic losses from natural disasters averaged nearly $580 billion a year. In real terms, this is a 7.7 fold increase in losses from the decade of the 1960s. Because of the relative size of developed- and developing-world incomes, the per capita impact of the economic losses was 20 times greater in the developing countries. According to a 2000 study by the World Bank, between 1990 and 1998, 94 percent of the world's major natural disasters and 97 percent of all natural disaster-related deaths occurred in developing countries.

The staggering total of losses in the developing world is a consequence of the vulnerability of low income countries to natural hazards. The cost of disasters to developing countries extends beyond the immediate impact on the poor. Studies indicate that natural disaster losses can eliminate economic growth. "The escalation of severe disaster events triggered by natural hazards and related technological and environmental disasters are increasingly posing a substantive threat to both sustainable development and poverty-reduction initiatives" (UN, ISDR, p. 3).

Future Trends

Natural disaster losses are forecast to increase dramatically during the first 50 years of the twenty-first century. The global cost of natural disasters is anticipated to exceed $300 billion annually (in 2000 dollars) by the year 2050—a five-fold increase over the 1990s. Two broad demographic trends directly contribute to the increasing losses from natural hazards in the developing world: the increase in population and the concentration of population in large cities. World population will likely increase by 2 billion persons between 2000 and 2025, and by a further billion by 2050, almost all of it in the developing world. The urban concentration is also rising. In developing countries, more than 40 percent of the population now live in urban areas, a percentage that is projected to reach 57 percent by 2030 (and up to 75 percent in Latin America and the Caribbean). Urbanization increases risk by concentrating people and investments in limited geographic zones. As a result, natural hazards can inflict substantial damage in a very short time. Hurricane Andrew, for example, inflicted $20 billion in damages in a few hours when it struck the Miami, Florida area in 1992.

Large cities are highly vulnerable to natural disasters, more so since substantial proportions of their populations are often poorly housed in fringe settlements. Nearly half the world's largest cities are situated in major earthquake zones or tropical cyclone tracks. Substantial increases in economic losses from disasters are highly probable.

See also: *Accidents.*

BIBLIOGRAPHY

Blakie, Piers, Terry Cannon, Ian Davis, and Ben Wisner. 1994. *At Risk: Natural Hazards, People's Vulnerability, and Disasters.* Routledge: New York.

Charveriat, Celine. 2000. *Natural Disasters in Latin America and the Caribbean: An Overview of Risk.* Washington, D.C.: Inter-American Development Bank.

Freeman, Paul K., Leslie A. Martin, Reinhard Mechler, Koko Warner, and Peter Hausmann. 2001. *Catastrophes and Development: Integrating Natural Catastrophes into Development Planning,* Disaster Risk Management Working Papers Series No. 4. Washington, D.C.: The World Bank.

International Federation of Red Cross and Red Crescent Societies (IFRC). 2002. *World Disaster Report 2001: Focus on Recovery.* Bloomfield, CT: Kumarian Press Inc.

Mitchell, James K., ed. 1999. *Crucibles of Hazard: Mega-Cities and Disasters in Transition* New York: United Nations University Press.

Munich Reinsurance Company (Munich Re). 2002. *Topics: Annual Review: Natural Catastrophes 2001* Munich, Germany: Munich Reinsurance Company.

United Nations Population Fund (UNFPA). 1999. *The State of the World Population 1999.* New York: United Nations Population Fund.

World Bank. 2001. *World Development Report 2000/2001: Attacking Poverty.* New York: Oxford University Press.

INTERNET RESOURCES.

Bendimerad, Fouad. 2000. *Megacities, Megarisk.* Disaster Management Facility, World Bank <http://www.worldbank.org/dmf/knowledge/megacities.html>

United Nations International Strategy for Disaster Reduction (ISDR). 2002. *Natural Disasters and Sustainable Development: Understanding the Links Between Development, Environment and Natural Disasters,* Working Paper No. 5 [Revised Edition]. <http://www.unisdr.org>.

United States Bureau of the Census (Census Bureau). 1999. *World Population Profile: 1998.*<http://www.census.gov/ipc/www/wp98001.html/>

Paul K. Freeman

DISEASE, BURDEN OF

Statistics on the health status of populations have been collected for centuries but typically have been collected for specific purposes. Vital registration systems have been in existence since the seventeenth century in some European countries and provide valuable information on numbers of dead by age and sex, and, in combination with census counts, on the overall level of mortality and its changes. Where all or most deaths are certified as to the underlying cause by a qualified medical practitioner—a much later development, even in Europe—these systems are a useful source of data on leading health problems. In countries where vital registration is still deficient, estimates of death rates by cause of death for the population classified by age and sex can be built up from data on mortality collected in surveys or through demographic surveillance systems, supplemented by a "verbal autopsy" (questioning relatives of the deceased) to arrive at the cause of death based on reported symptoms at or around the time of death.

Data on the incidence or prevalence of specific diseases and injuries have been collected in many countries for decades to serve as the basis for determining epidemiological priorities and for the evaluation of specific disease control programs. However, these data are often fragmentary or limited to a specific sub-population and are of limited value for assessing overall population health levels.

To give guidance in setting global priorities for the health sector, the causes and extent of ill-health and premature mortality in populations around the world need to be assessed. To be truly useful, such assessments must take into account not only the conditions leading to premature death, defined with reference to some standard survival curve, but also the prevalence, severity, and duration of the non-fatal consequences, or sequelae, of diseases and injuries. The Global Burden of Disease Study was initiated in the early 1990s to assess the contribution of over 100 diseases and injuries to premature death and ill-health in 1990, using a single metric. The study was subsequently expanded to include the estimated impact of ten major risk factors on disease and injury burden worldwide, also as of 1990. A revision of the study, under preparation, provides similar information for the year 2000.

Measuring the Disease Burden

The concept of capturing both the fatal and non-fatal effects of a specific disease or injury in a single metric is attractive for policy formulation since it permits a more complete assessment of the benefits of specific interventions. Clearly, an event-count framework, such as the number of deaths and the number of incident cases, is inappropriate as a guide for health policy since that framework does not take into account the public health implications of preventing deaths at younger versus older ages, nor does it capture variations in the duration and severity of non-fatal incident cases. In order to overcome these limitations, a time-based metric was constructed to gauge the total loss from disability and premature death—namely, Disability-Adjusted Life Years (DALYs). DALYs combine the number of years of life lost (YLLs) due to death prior to the normal life span and the number of years lived with a disability, weighted by the severity of the disability (YLDs). Hence for any disease, DALYs = YLLs + YLDs.

To estimate YLLs, a standard life expectancy of 82.5 years for females and 80.0 years for males was used to yield age-specific life expectancy targets or *norms* for the assessment of years of life lost at each age. For the calculation, the world was divided into eight regions and the same life expectancy target was assumed to apply to each region. To calculate YLDs, all major sequelae were identified for each disease or injury (e.g., measles, ischaemic heart disease, or motor vehicle accidents). A total of 107 diseases and injuries were considered, yielding a set of 483 disabling sequelae. For each of these sequelae and for each age and sex group, the incidence and average duration of the disability were estimated, and the resulting estimate of total person-years of disabled life were weighted by an assessment of the severity of the disability (see below). The results for each disability were applied to the total of incident cases in 1990 to calculate YLDs for the cause.

The disability weights were arrived at in the following manner. A representative sample of 22 *indicator conditions* was taken from the full set of 483 sequelae, spanning the range of severity from very mild (e.g., vitiglio on the face) to very severe (e.g., quadriplegia). Based on the opinions of public health experts familiar with the characteristics of each condition, the person trade-off technique and other health-state valuation methods were used to assign each indicator condition a disability weight in the range from 0 (perfect health) to 1 (death). The resulting weights were then grouped into seven broad severity classes and each class given the average weight of the conditions in it. All remaining 461 conditions were then assigned to one of the seven classes based on their characteristics.

Finally, an age-weighting function was introduced to assign greater weight to years lived (or lost) at younger ages, its shape reflecting empirical evidence about societal values. Thus, for example, several studies have shown that individuals prefer to save the lives of young adults over young children, if forced to choose. A 3 percent discount rate was also applied to both YLLs and YLDs to bring future years back to present-value terms. Thus, for example, a year of life lived at age 40 sometime in the future has a different, less certain value for society than a year of life lived by a 40 year old today.

Data Sources

Vital registration data on causes of death were used, with adjustments for miscoding and underreporting, for about 80 countries. For India and China, sample registration systems and disease surveillance points yielded reliable data on mortality conditions for representative samples of the population. Other available sources such as demographic and epidemiological surveillance sites and community-based research studies were used to estimate disease patterns in some regions, particularly in sub-Saharan Africa and parts of Asia. For each disease, experts provided estimates of incidence, duration, and case-fatality rates, by age, sex, and region, which were modeled via the disease modeling software DISMOD to ensure inter-

nal consistency of all epidemiological parameters. Projections to 2020 were also made on the basis of a broad deterministic model relating levels of income, education, and smoking to observed mortality rates over the period from 1950 to 1990.

Findings

Each disease or injury was classified into one of three broad groups:

- Group I, communicable, maternal, perinatal, and nutritional conditions;
- Group II, non-communicable diseases;
- Group III, injuries.

Worldwide, one death in every three is from a Group I cause. Virtually all of these deaths are in developing regions. One death in ten is from Group III causes (injuries), and just over half of all deaths worldwide in 1990 were from Group II causes (non-communicable diseases). In most developing regions, Group II causes of death already exceeded Group I causes in 1990, indicating that the epidemiological transition was well advanced. In these regions, the ratio of Group II to Group I deaths in 1990 was 4.5 in China and 2 in Latin America. The transition was less advanced in India, where the ratio was 0.8, and least advanced in sub-Saharan Africa, with a ratio of 0.4.

Just over 50 million people died worldwide in 1990, the leading causes of death being ischaemic heart disease (6.3 million deaths); stroke (4.4 million); lower respiratory diseases (primarily pneumonia, 4.3 million; diarrheal diseases (2.9 million); perinatal conditions, (2.4 million); and chronic obstructive pulmonary disease (primarily chronic bronchitis and emphysema, 2.2 million). Looking at years of life lost, however, yields a different ranking because the various causes of death have different average age patterns. The leading causes of YLLs were lower respiratory infections (11.7% of global YLLs for 1990), diarrheal diseases (10.2%), and perinatal conditions (8.9%)—followed at some distance by ischaemic heart disease (4.5%), measles (3.9%), and tuberculosis and stroke (3.5%). Arguably, this ranking is much more relevant for prioritization of programs to prevent premature mortality than the ranking by numbers of deaths.

When disease burden is assessed on the basis of DALYs, rather than deaths, conditions that are not leading causes of death but are nonetheless prevalent

TABLE 1

Leading Causes of Loss of Disability-Adjusted Life Years (DALYs), 1990

	World	DALYs (million)	% total	Developed Regions	DALYs (million)	% total	Developing Regions	DALYs (million)	% total
1.	Lower respiratory infections	112.9	8.2	Ischaemic heart disease	16.0	9.9	Lower respiratory infections	110.5	9.1
2.	Diarrheal diseases	99.6	7.2	Unipolar major depression	9.8	6.1	Diarrheal diseases	99.2	8.1
3.	Perinatal conditions	92.3	6.7	Cerebrovascular disease	9.4	5.9	Perinatal conditions	89.2	7.3
4.	Unipolar major depression	50.8	3.7	Road traffic accidents	7.1	4.4	Unipolar major depression	41.0	3.4
5.	Ischaemic heart disease	46.7	3.4	Alcohol use	6.4	4.0	Tuberculosis	37.9	3.1
6.	Cerebrovascular disease	38.5	2.8	Osteoarthritis	4.7	2.9	Measles	36.5	3.0
7.	Tuberculosis	38.4	2.8	Trachea/Bronchus/Lung cancers	4.6	2.8	Malaria	31.7	2.6
8.	Measles	36.5	2.6	Dementias	3.8	2.4	Ischaemic heart disease	30.7	2.5
9.	Road traffic accidents	34.3	2.5	Self-inflicted injuries	3.8	2.3	Congenital abnormalities	29.4	2.4
10.	Congenital abnormalities	32.9	2.4	Congenital abnormalities	3.5	2.2	Cerebrovascular disease	29.1	2.4
	Top 10 causes	583.1	42.3	Top 10 causes	69.0	42.9	Top 10 causes	535.3	43.9

SOURCE: World Health Organization (Murray and Lopez, 1996a, Table 5.2).

and disabling are given increased prominence. Worldwide, about 1.38 billion DALYs were lost as a result of premature deaths and new incident cases of disease and injury in 1990. The leading causes of DALYs in developed and developing regions are shown in Table 1. The global pattern more or less mirrors that suggested by YLLs, with the notable exception of depression, which ranks as the fourth leading cause of DALYs lost worldwide and the second leading cause in developed countries. As might be expected, more than half of the top ten leading causes of DALYs lost in developing regions are Group I causes, reinforcing the need for strengthened disease control measures for communicable diseases in poorer populations. Preliminary results for 2000 suggest a similar pattern, with the exception of HIV/AIDS, which was estimated to have caused 6.1 percent of the global DALYs lost in 2000, making it the third leading cause of DALYs lost in that year.

In terms of underlying causes of the burden of disease and injury, by far the most significant of those quantified was protein-energy malnutrition, which alone was estimated to have caused 16 percent of DALYs lost in 1990, followed by unsafe water and sanitation (6.8%). Unsafe sex, tobacco, alcohol, and occupational risks each causes about 2.5 percent to 3.5 percent of the disease and injury burden, about the same as measles and malaria. Quantifying disease burden both in terms of disease outcomes (e.g., lung cancer, ischaemic heart disease) and underlying attributable causes (e.g., tobacco, high blood pressure)

provides critical input for allocative decisions in health sector programs.

Conclusion

The burden of disease approach has stimulated wide interest and debate about the construction of summary measures of population health, such as DALYs, and on the applicability of these methods in various countries. The data requirements for estimating mortality, incidence, prevalence, and duration of disease and injury in an internally consistent fashion has stimulated a reevaluation of the utility of traditional data collection in the health sector and has identified key gaps in knowledge about the causes and levels of major health problems. In developed countries, this has led to greater efforts to improve the cross-population comparability of survey data on the prevalence of disabling conditions; in developing countries, it has demonstrated the urgency of improving knowledge about the levels, patterns, and causes of adult mortality. As more children survive to adulthood, reliable data on their survival and trends in leading causes of death and disability will become increasingly important.

See also: *Disability, Demography of; Epidemiological Transition; Health Transition; Mortality Decline.*

BIBLIOGRAPHY

Murray, Christopher J. L., and Alan D. Lopez. 1996a. *The Global Burden of Disease: a Comprehensive Assessment of Mortality and Disability from Dis-*

eases, Injuries and Risk Factors in 1990 and Projected to 2020. Cambridge, MA: Harvard School of Public Health on behalf of the World Health Organization and the World Bank.

———. 1996b. "Evidence-based Health Policy: Lessons from the Global Burden of Disease Study." *Science* 274: 740–743.

———. 1997a. "Mortality by Cause for Eight Regions of the World: Global Burden of Disease Study." *Lancet* 349: 1,269–1,276.

———. 1997b. "Alternative Projections of Mortality and Disability by Cause, 1990–2020: Global Burden of Disease Study." *Lancet* 349: 1,498–1,504.

ALAN D. LOPEZ

DISEASE, CONCEPTS AND CLASSIFICATION OF

The classification of diseases is the subject of the branch of medicine called nosology. Contemporary classification efforts range from those primarily intended to clarify and standardize the nomenclature of diseases, such as the College of American Pathologists' Systematized Nomenclature of Medicine (SNOWMED) and the National Institute of Health's Unified Medical Language System (UMLS), to taxonomies focused on diagnostic terminology that emphasize an ordered hierarchical system reflecting natural relationships between diseases, such as the World Health Organization's International Statistical Classification of Diseases and Related Health Problems (ICD).

The Early History of Disease Classification

The classificatory approach to disease is ancient, but the classification of diseases in a modern sense dates roughly from the fifteenth and sixteenth centuries. The concept that diseases are directly identifiable through their symptomatology is most evident in the revolutionary work of Paracelsus (born Theophrastus von Hohenheim, 1493–1541). Paracelsus's suggestion that natural symptoms may provide direct evidence leading to a probable diagnosis or classification of a disease despite a potentially unobservable

cause of the illness was evident in practice by the seventeenth century, when nosology took form.

Throughout the eighteenth century the pathological view was guided by the concept that a specific cause could be identified for all episodes of ill health, and physicians concentrated on the observation of symptoms and the categorization of disease. Even the inevitability of death from natural causes and the presumption of a biologically acceptable risk of infant death gave way to perceptions that a cause for all illnesses could be diagnosed and that these causes of disease constituted social problems that could be resolved.

Swedish naturalist Carolus Linnaeus (1707–1778), best known for his botanical classifications, attempted to provide a systematic classification of diseases during that period. His classification is notable for including a broad range of morbidity conditions, including functional health limitations (loss of movement, impeded motion, etc.) and mental health conditions as they were understood at the time (delirium, melancholia, bulimia, etc.). In a fashion similar to his botanical classification, Linnaeus designated genera, species, and subspecies of disease. Not surprisingly, his classification is not predicated on a single classificatory principle. Linnaeus did emphasize symptomatology. However, his classification reflects elements of alchemy, astrology, and the prevailing miasmatic environmental view of disease. Other, similar classification attempts by individual physicians of that time (e.g., Francois Bossier de Lacroix's *Nosologia Methodica* and William Cullen's *Classification*) were not theoretically grounded and did not embody a clear notion of symptoms derived from causal agents. Arguably, the effect was to produce complex nosologies, competing classifications, and confusion.

The Nineteenth Century and the Advent of Germ Theory

Competing conceptions of disease were and still are also rooted in strongly held social hypotheses and are debated in the context of political, economic, and religious interests. The establishment over the course of the early nineteenth century of various "centres of calculation" in England, including the General Register Office (GRO), the Alkali Inspectorate, and the inspectors of the Passenger Acts and Factory Acts, provided a governmental context for often lively debates about the development of morbidity and mortality measurement (Bartley et al. 1997). Social Darwinists, using the concepts developed by the scientist Francis Galton, even challenged the wisdom of efforts directed at reporting and eradicating all diseases, especially the apparently "selective" preponderance of infant deaths among the poor. The rising influence of insurance companies and the actuarial trades generated corporate and economic interest in accurate statistics. However, related implications for the payment of benefits probably added to local and familial pressures to record and report information selectively. Religious institutions, including both the Anglican Church and non-Anglican denominations, had a vested interest in the registration of vital events and in conceptions of disease that included moralistic and attributional causation. Even in the present time diseases are often considered to be caused by moral failings on the part of those who suffer their effects.

The early foundations of disease classification reflected both the sociopolitical context of the nineteenth century and the contest between highly moralistic conceptions of the underlying cause of disease and principles of scientific reporting and classification. Popular conceptions of disease in turn influenced many public health initiatives, which frequently were directed toward improving the moral behaviors (idleness, drunkenness, etc.) of the lower classes that were considered the cause of their suffering.

Despite an early understanding of the infectious nature of many diseases, through most of the nineteenth century classifications of disease were not informed by the concepts of germ theory. Instead, the major prevailing concepts of disease were grounded in the remnants of a miasmatic view of disease. For many diseases the idea of disease vectors and infectious transmission came slowly. Poisonous vapors, atmospheres, environments, and toxins were conceived to be responsible for even infectious diseases. Edwin Chadwick's etiological hypothesis, which stated that poverty and environmental conditions including sanitation were primarily responsible for harmful disease environments, refined the miasmatic view and shaped the sanitary movement in England.

In midcentury, the prevailing nosological classification treatise in America was Daniel Drake's *Systematic Treatise,* which arranged diseases into five large classes (autumnal fevers, yellow fever, typhus fevers, eruptive fevers, and phlogistic fevers) and was strongly influenced by a miasmatic or environmental conception of disease. Drake's *Treatise* differed, however, from the work of many of his predecessors in visualizing at least some diseases (e.g., cholera and malaria) as being due to minute animalcules or germs that typified various environments. In fact, germ theory represented a rapid but not unanticipated transformation. Many physicians and scientists were rethinking the pathology of diseases over the last half of the nineteenth century. The two names that are most commonly associated with the new germ theory are those of Robert Koch and Louis Pasteur. Koch's bacterial swab test for the tuberculin bacillus and Pasteur's work on surgical septicemia and rabies were among the major medical developments that quickly altered both clinical practice and the widespread conceptions of disease among practitioners. The bacterial age of medicine, perhaps more than any subsequent medical development, altered fundamental conceptions of disease. The external miasmatic locus of disease became internal, the moral became the biological, the natural became seemingly preventable, and a new medical science was enshrined in both concepts and regulatory institutions.

Regulation of Statistical Reporting and the Evolving Quality of Classifications

The later nineteenth century was also a period of dramatic change in the statistical reporting of diseases. After the British adoption of civil registration (1837) and the formation of the American Statistical Association in Boston (1839), Massachusetts in 1842 became the first state to implement a modern record-keeping system for deaths and cause of death information in the United States. Over the next half century changes in both reporting institutions and classifications of disease were dramatic. For example, the nomenclature for tuberculosis, the leading nineteenth-century killer throughout much of the Western world, evolved in regard to recorded deaths, as shown in Table 1 for two Massachusetts mill towns, Northampton and Holyoke. In 1850 all these deaths were recorded as being due to consumption. By 1880 the vast majority were labeled phthisis, a term that had long been in use. Eventually, after the advent of Koch's bacterial test and an international classification of diseases (1900), virtually all such deaths were labeled using the still-current nomenclature of pulmonary tuberculosis.

Despite the evolving nomenclature, the recorded causes of death also demonstrate continuing social biases. Gender, ethnicity, occupation, and wealth and other social distinctions were associated with both the likelihood of attributing specific diagnoses to individuals and the quality of reported diagnoses as modern classification systems evolved. Three-quarters of the reports of deaths from unintentional injuries to men, for example, gave informational circumstances of the accident, while only a third of those for women included such qualifying information. Even for infectious diseases within similar age ranges, such as tuberculosis deaths in persons age 15 to 64, men were significantly more likely to have more detailed diagnoses recorded. Riess (1997) identifies the major changes in recording the causes of death over the nineteenth century as being due to (1) the shifting ecology of disease, (2) shifting definitions of health and disease, (3) shifting definitions of death and causes of death, (4) the changing construction of death records, and (5) changes in the use of medical statistics. To these factors should be added the dramatic changes in population composition such as those resulting from the aging, urbanization, immigration, and industrialization of the Western world.

The ICD Family of Disease Classifications and Professional Nosology

As medical science and reporting systems advanced, so did demands for a standardized classification of diseases for both clinical and statistical purposes. A number of medical statisticians, including William Farr (1807–1883), the Register General of the GRO, and French physician Jacques Bertillon (1851–1922), attempted to provide more refined classifications of disease and establish the principles on which classifications were based. The notable efforts of Bertillon to refine a classification of diseases using principles informed by germ theory were dramatically advanced when the French government convened in 1900 the first international conference to revise and promote the Bertillon International Classification of Causes of Death (ICD). Successive conferences were held by the French government in 1909, 1920, 1929, and 1938. The continued standardization and development of a central family of classifications was ensured in 1946 when the International Health Conference entrusted the World Health Organization (WHO) with the responsibility for the sixth revision of the International Lists of Diseases and Causes of

TABLE 1

Percentage of Deaths in Northampton and Holyoke, Massachusetts, for Selected Literal Causes, 1850–1912

Years	Consumption	Phthisis	Tuberculosis
1850–1852	22.44	0.00	0.00
1860–1862	18.69	3.16	0.00
1870–1872	13.40	1.26	0.00
1880–1882	4.88	9.90	0.46
1900–1902	1.51	3.02	4.75
1910–1912	0.11	0.88	6.57

SOURCE: Compiled by author.

Death and expanded the classification to include nonfatal diseases.

The WHO has maintained responsibility for the ICD family of disease classifications, the most widely used system for nosology. The ICD (current version in use in 2003 is 10) is a generic disease classification used for most cause of death nosology (list of diseases). However, clinical modifications (currently ICD 9cm) and special-purpose nosologies (e.g., ICD-0 for oncology and ICF for functioning, disability, and health), modeled after the ICD, are also widely used. As demands for contextual and qualifying information have increased in the last several decades, the basic ICD codes for diseases have been extended with additional qualifying codes. For example, V codes were added to record reasons for encounter or factors related to health status, E codes to record external causes of injury and ill health, M codes for the morphology of neoplasms, and so on. This entire ICD family of classifications is maintained by the WHO in cooperation with collaborating centers throughout the world that sometimes offer their own embellishments.

Although disease classification systems have a long history, professional nosology involving the coding of diseases from literal diagnoses expanded dramatically in the last half of the twentieth century. Many hospitals began experimenting with clinical use of the 1948 ICD. In 1962 the U.S. Public Health Service produced an adaptation (ICDA) for use in hospital records. This was followed by ICD8 and ICD9cm for clinical use. However, nosologists were often considered clerical workers who performed a necessary but only tolerated task. The profession achieved stature in the late twentieth century as the critical importance of the efforts of its practitioners to medical research became clear. However, nosology has begun to decline once again in the face of an increasing use of electronic records and the growing promise of automated nosology.

The Predictability of Change in Concepts and Classifications

The evolving history of disease and the growth in knowledge of diseases guarantee continual change in both concepts and classifications of diseases. Those conceptions and classifications have experienced and reflected radical changes in underlying etiologies, shifting sociopolitical environments, the changing composition of host populations, and the growing social organization of medicine. Just as the advent of germ theory had a strong influence on conceptions and classifications of diseases in the nineteenth century, advancing knowledge of diseases will continue to change conceptions and classifications in the twenty-first century.

The genomic revolution, bringing profound advances in understanding the genetic foundations of disease, is one likely source of such change (Cantor and Smith 1999). Another source is the still-controversial advances in evolutionary biology, which threaten to erode entrenched boundaries between infectious and noninfectious, or chronic and acute, diseases (e.g., Ewald 2000). A third source of change will be trends in the incidence and nature of diseases themselves and in their host populations. The growing impact of poorly defined chronic conditions that are relegated to residual, symptomatic diagnoses, such as Alzheimer's disease, fibromyalgia, Gulf War syndrome, and chronic fatigue, challenges existing concepts and classifications. The increasing age, growing urbanism, declining fertility, and changing socioeconomic and occupational composition of the world's population will alter the emphases placed on different groups of diagnoses. Even among conditions that once were assumed to be well understood, such as childhood asthma, trends in disease challenge existing etiologies. Indeed, an overly rigid adherence to diagnostic classifications inherited from the nineteenth century may occasionally be an obstacle to future growth in the understanding of disease, just as heavily moral and religious conceptions of disease retarded the advancement of germ theory and the development of current concepts and classifications.

See also: *Bertillon, Jacques; Causes of Death; Disease, Burden of; Farr, William.*

BIBLIOGRAPHY

Armstrong, David. 1986. "The Invention of Infant Mortality." *Sociology of Health and Illness* 8(3): 211–232.

Bartley, George, Davey Smith, and David Blane. 1997. "Vital Comparisons: The Social Construction of Mortality Measurement." In *The Sociology of Medical Science and Technology*, ed. M. A. Elston. Oxford, Eng.: Blackwell.

Cantor, Charles R., and Cassandra L. Smith. 1999. *Genomics: The Science and Technology behind the Human Genome Project.* New York: Wiley.

Cassedy, James H. 1986. *Medicine and American Growth 1800–1860.* Madison: University of Wisconsin Press.

Commission Internationale Chargée de Reviser les Nomenclatures Nosologiques. 1903. *Nomenclatures des Maladies (Statistique de Morbidité—Statistique des Causes de Décès) avec Notices et Annexes par Jacques Bertillon.* Mountévrain: Impr. Typographique de l'Ecole d'Alembert.

Ewald, Paul. 2000. *Plague Time: The New Germ Theory of Disease.* New York: Anchor Books.

Foucault, Michel. 1963. *The Birth of the Clinic: An Archeology of Medical Perception.* London: Tavistock.

Hacking, Ian. 1975. *The Emergence of Probability.* Cambridge, Eng.: Cambridge University Press.

Hess, Volker. 1993. *Von der Semiotischen Zur Diagnostischen Medizin: Die Entstehung der Klinischen Methode zwishen 1750 und 1850. Aghandlungen zur Geschichte der Midizin und der Naturwissenshaften, No. 66.* Husum, Germany: Matthiesen Verlag.

Riess, Günter B. 1997. "Cause of Death as a Historical Problem." *Continuity and Change* 12: 175–188.

Starr, Paul. 1982. *The Social Transformation of American Medicine.* New York: Basic Books.

DOUGLAS L. ANDERTON

DISEASE AND HISTORY

Like climate and geography, disease belongs to a category of influences whose importance is easy to acknowledge but difficult to specify. It is indisputable that disease is an important human experience that occupies time; causes discomfort, pain, and death; diverts resources from other uses; and may kill individuals or groups of people at critical moments. However, it is difficult to decide how much weight to assign to the disease experience, show that resources diverted to coping with disease would otherwise have been deployed in a particular way, or prove that a death or many deaths altered the course of events. The historical challenge that disease poses is evident in the two levels on which historians discuss the issue.

Two Views of Disease

On one level, disease has monumental significance. According to Roy Anderson and Robert May, infectious diseases have been "the most significant agents of natural selection acting on human populations since the. . .agricultural revolution." Because Europeans, Asians, and Africans shared a particularly competitive disease pool, they carried with them to the Americas, Australia and New Zealand, and the Pacific islands an advantage of prior exposure to many diseases as well as diseases new to those territories that caused sickness and death in virgin-soil populations. Andrew Nikiforuk claims that "an alarming tide" of new and resurgent diseases threatens in the twenty-first century to undo human gains in material comfort, population size, and longevity. Disease plays the role of a Greek god, powerful but unpredictable. For Nikiforuk, the presence of malaria accounts for the decline of the civilization of classical Greece and its absence accounts for rapid population growth and civil war in modern Sri Lanka. The fourteenth-century Black Death made English the language of intellectual discussion and created the commercial revolution. The main actors in this drama are dread diseases—leprosy, plague, smallpox, and syphilis—that kill and maim and diseases known for the vast range of their effects, such as malaria, tuberculosis, and influenza. On this level disease is given an implausible degree of credit, and the cause-and-effect relationships remain indecipherable and murky.

On the other level, disease appears as a background force with profound but unspecifiable importance and is given implausibly little credit as a historical force. Nevertheless, it is on this level that the most useful insights have been acquired. Three approaches merit discussion here. First, there is the history of attempts to explain disease, all of which have proved unsatisfactory or incomplete. Second, there is the increasingly rich history of diseases: the profile of maladies that cause sickness and death. Third, there is the deployment of information about disease as a cause of sickness and death in an attempt to diminish morbidity and mortality.

Explaining Disease

In written history attempts to explain disease date from classical antiquity. Hippocrates, in a summary of older traditions, incriminated airs, waters, and places: the complex of environmental circumstances in which people live. The Ayurvedic tradition in India and the Greek physician Galen, working in the second century C.E., pointed instead to imbalances in the body among entities called humors. Hippocratic ideas emphasized the usefulness of avoiding certain things, such as swamps, whereas Ayurvedic-Galenic ideas pointed to medical treatment and to behaviors designed to conserve health. In the West the Galenic tradition carried more weight until the late seventeenth century, when the physician Thomas Sydenham and others revived Hippocratic ideas. From the claim that environmental forces, perhaps especially the decomposition of organic matter, give rise to disease and from the allied idea that diseases are transmitted through the air arose the notion of controlling disease by cleansing the environment. That laid the foundations of public health, which initially, after 1840, was directed less often at disease matter carried in the air than at such matter carried in water, especially water contaminated with human waste.

Two contrary explanations for disease and its transmission arose in the nineteenth century. First, after noticing the disease-ridden life of impoverished urban residents, protomedical sociologists incriminated crowding, bad housing, a lack of air and sunlight, and other circumstances of the urban environment as disease enablers or provocateurs, although not agents. Asiatic cholera and tuberculosis, the first a fearsome epidemic disease and the second the leading cause of death in Western Europe in the nineteenth century, fit this conception of disease causation and transmission. Second, evidence began to accumulate in mid-century that specific disease agents could be identified, and not just for a few diseases. By the 1890s the scientists Louis Pasteur and Robert Koch had identified enough germs to give precedence to the idea that specific diseases are caused by specific pathogens. Germ theory temporarily displaced the conditions of poverty as the leading explanation for disease, even though the germ theorists initially claimed far too much, associating germs with all diseases and failing to clarify the process of causation.

None of these ideas has maintained its dominance. Germ theory reigned from about 1890 to about 1970 before giving way to a revival of modernized humoral ideas that stress the individual's responsibility to conserve health. It encountered difficulty in explaining why lower socioeconomic groups so often die earlier and suffer more sickness than do elites, even in social democracies. At the end of the twentieth century these three traditions—humoral, sociological, and biomedical—all played important roles in explaining disease.

Profiling and Theorizing about Disease

More and more research attention was directed toward discovering the major diseases of the past. Scientists learned how to detect specific diseases from skeletal remains, complementing the insights of morbid pathology into the postmortem signs of disease first acquired in the early nineteenth century. Researchers also learned how to decode some of the diseases mentioned vaguely in historical texts, recognizing tuberculosis, typhus, bubonic plague, dysentery, and some forms of heart disease. They learned how to construct profiles of the major diseases and injuries causing sickness and death for a few areas in the seventeenth and eighteenth centuries and for many more areas of the world in the nineteenth century.

This research, which remains in progress, has produced a general description of evolution in the leading causes of death in recent times, a description that has some theoretical elements and is associated with the name of the demographer Abdel Omran and the idea of epidemiologic transition. Omran's original formulation identified three disease eras: one of pandemic infections, another of receding pandemics, and a third dominated by chronic diseases of the body organs. Death rates declined in the second and third stages, giving rise to population growth and increased longevity.

More recently the term *health transition* has been used to describe these phenomena. Under that term scholars have tried to add to the theoretical understanding of change over time in the identity of diseases causing sickness and death and to learn more about how to control and manage disease. Health transition theory also corrects some of the misleading elements of older ideas: Pandemics did occur in the distant past, but they were not the major killers, which instead were commonplace diseases that are mostly familiar in the early twenty-first century. This new approach also has been able to assimilate many important distinctions in regard to disease and its avoidance, such as exposure and resistance, nutritional status while sick, and immune status. However, there is still nothing available to formulate a general theory of disease in the past.

Collecting Information about Disease

Whereas informed eighteenth-century medical commentators in the West preferred the idea that diseases are inconstant, capable of changing in the same person from one day to the next, and nonspecific in their origins, the idea arose in the nineteenth century that diseases are specific, having particular causes, pathways, periods of incubation, durations, lethalities, biases by sex and age, and other distinctive characteristics. One effect of this idea was the promotion of efforts to create disease taxonomies, which led to the development at the century's end under French guidance of an international scheme of disease classification. By the end of the twentieth century that scheme had evolved through ten editions into a classification of diseases and injuries under 26 headings, each with many subdivisions.

Progress in identifying diseases; uncovering the postmortem signs of disease as well as the signs, symptoms, and chemistry of disease among the living; and classifying diseases increased the importance of knowing the diseases that were said to cause sickness and death. Some countries and cities had long tried to collect information about diseases causing death; that effort gained momentum in the nineteenth and early twentieth centuries, at least among rich countries that could afford the required investment of expertise and money. However, most of the world's population remained undiagnosed in regard to the causes of death. Even in rich countries the causes of most sickness episodes were not recorded. Some diseases were "notifiable," especially communicable diseases about which early warning was wanted. However, the sicknesses of everyday life and many noncommunicable diseases and injuries were poorly counted and recorded. Nevertheless, this idea led to an effort to produce a schedule of all the diseases in the world causing sickness and death, rank them by their scale and effect and perhaps also by their preventability or treatability, and then try to reduce the number of unnecessary deaths from about 54 million persons a year across the globe around 2000 to the 30 million or fewer that would take place if all the world were as well served by disease prevention as the rich countries are.

Disease remains a threat in the present and the future. Too many people, especially infants and children, die each year in light of the degree of human understanding of disease and the potential to control it. There is also too much sickness, much of which could be avoided through less poverty, the application of public health measures and medical knowledge and by a global population better informed about germ theory and risk factor theory. Moreover, there remains the threat of new or resurgent diseases that could defy the means of control currently available. Nevertheless, what is most remarkable about disease and history is the marked retreat of disease since about 1800. It is principally the waning of communicable diseases, especially diseases of childhood, that accounts for the rising life expectancy of the last 200 years, arguably the most important achievement of humankind during that period.

See also: *Black Death; Epidemiological Transition; Health Transition; Mortality Decline; Tuberculosis.*

BIBLIOGRAPHY

Anderson, Roy, and Robert May. 1991. *Infectious Diseases of Humans: Dynamics and Control.* Oxford: Oxford University Press.

Bobadilla, José Luis, Julio Frenk, Rafael Lozano, et al. 1993. "The Epidemiologic Transition and Health Priorities." In *Disease Control Priorities in Developing Countries,* ed. Dean T. Jamison, W. Henry Mosley, Anthony R. Measham, José Luis Bobadilla, et al. Oxford: Oxford University Press.

Crosby, Alfred. 1972. *Columbian Exchange: Biological and Cultural Consequences of 1492.* Westport, CT: Greenwood.

Hays, J. N. 1998. *The Burdens of Disease: Epidemics and Human Response in Western History.* New Brunswick, NJ: Rutgers University Press.

Johansson, S. Ryan, and Carl Mosk. 1987. "Exposure, Resistance, and Life Expectancy: Disease and Death during the Economic Development of Japan, 1900–1960." *Population Studies* 41: 207–235.

Karlen, Arno. 1996. *Man and Microbes: Disease and Plagues in History and Modern Times.* New York: Putnam.

Kiple, Kenneth F., ed. 1993. *The Cambridge World History of Human Disease.* Cambridge, Eng.: Cambridge University Press.

———. 1997. *Plague, Pox, and Pestilence.* New York: Barnes & Noble.

McNeill, William. 1977. *Plagues and Peoples.* Garden City, NY: Anchor.

Murray, Christopher J. L., and Alan D. Lopez, eds. 1996. *The Global Burden of Disease: A Comprehensive Assessment of Mortality and Disability from Diseases, Injuries, and Risk Factors in 1990 and Projected to 2020.* Cambridge, MA: Harvard University Press.

Nikiforuk, Andrew. 1992. *The Fourth Horseman: A Short History of Epidemics, Plagues and Other Scourges.* London: Fourth Estate.

Omran, Abdel. 1971. "The Epidemiologic Transition: A Theory of the Epidemiology of Population Change." *Milbank Memorial Fund Quarterly* 49: 509–538.

Riley, James C. 2001. *Rising Life Expectancy: A Global History.* Cambridge, Eng.: Cambridge University Press.

JAMES C. RILEY

DISEASES, CHRONIC AND DEGENERATIVE

Chronic and degenerative diseases (CDDs) are morbid pathological processes characterized by slow development, long duration, and gradual deterioration in the functioning of the affected tissue, organ, or

TABLE 1

Revision Dates for the International Classification of Diseases (ICD)

Period in Use	ICD Revision	U.S. Adaptation for Morbidity
1949–1957	ICD-6	
1958–1967	ICD-7	
1968–1978	ICD-8	ICDA-8
1979–1998	ICD-9	ICD-9-CM
1999 and after	ICD-10	ICD-9-CM

SOURCE: NCHS (2001).

organ system. These diseases generally involve asymptomatic preclinical stages, gradual progression to manifest symptoms, and terminal stages ranging from mild discomfort to lethality. Their incidence is correlated with age and in many cases is approximately proportional to the fifth, sixth, or seventh power of age. Their durations typically extend from the time of the initial symptoms to the time of death. Their prevalence reflects the cumulative effects of incidence and duration. They can kill afflicted individuals in a variety of ways. For example, persistent high blood pressure (hypertension, a chronic condition) is a risk factor for stroke (an acute manifestation of cerebrovascular disease), which may be lethal if it is not treated immediately.

CDDs are generally noncommunicable (noninfectious). There are numerous exceptions, however, including AIDS, which is caused by human immunodeficiency virus types 1 and 2 (HIV-1 and HIV-2); stomach ulcers/cancers caused by the bacterium *Helicobacter pylori*; liver cancers caused by hepatitis B virus; and cervical cancers caused by human papillomaviruses. Other significant pathogens include herpes simplex virus types 1 and 2 (possibly linked to Alzheimer's disease and schizophrenia), human herpes virus 6 (possibly linked to multiple sclerosis), and *Chlamydia pneumoniae* (possibly linked to Alzheimer's disease and heart disease).

Classification of Diseases

The International Classification of Diseases (ICD) is a statistical classification system for mortality and morbidity that is maintained and updated every one or two decades by the World Health Organization (WHO). The periods covered by the last five revisions and their adaptations for use in the United States are listed in Table 1.

The ICD-9-CM (clinical modification) adapts the ICD for hospital indexing and other clinical uses, adding codes for factors that influence health status and contact with health services. The alphabetical indexes of the ICD-9 and ICD-9-CM contain approximately 60,000 and 75,000 distinct diagnostic entries, respectively. In practice, however, 1998 U.S mortality files indicate that the ICD-9 describes approximately 5,600 causes of death.

Causes of Death

Estimates of the incidence and prevalence of major CDDs are limited by the progressive nature of those diseases and the lack of disease registries covering the population. Consequently, substantial use is made of cause of death data from national vital statistics files. These data are coded according to WHO protocols embodied in the ICD's underlying cause selection rules, where the underlying cause of death is defined as "(a) The disease or injury which initiated the train of events leading directly to death, or (b) the circumstances of the accident or violence which produced the fatal injury" (WHO 1975).

An important limitation is that each tabulated underlying cause of death is an aggregation of etiologically distinct diseases. For example, the top 15 underlying causes of death at age 65 and older in the United States in 1998, with the range of ICD-9 codes indicated in parentheses, were:

1. Heart diseases (390–398, 402, 404–429)
2. Malignant neoplasms (140–208)
3. Cerebrovascular diseases (430–438)
4. Chronic obstructive pulmonary diseases (490–496)
5. Pneumonia and influenza (480–487)
6. Diabetes mellitus (250)
7. Accidents and adverse effects (E800–E949)
8. Nephritis, nephrotic syndrome, and nephrosis (580–589)
9. Alzheimer's disease (331.0)
10. Septicemia (038)
11. Aortic aneurysm (441)
12. Atherosclerosis (440)
13. Hypertension (with or without renal disease) (401 and 403)
14. Chronic liver disease and cirrhosis (571)
15. Suicide (E950–E959)

These 15 causes accounted for 87 percent of deaths among the elderly in 1998. Only pneumonia/influenza and septicemia (numbers 5 and 10) are clearly infectious in nature, accidents and adverse effects (number 7) may involve chronic debilitation and treatment (e.g., hip fracture), and suicide (number 15) is associated with depression and chronic mental illness. The remaining 11 causes represent predominantly noninfectious CDDs, accounting for 79 percent of deaths. All 15 "causes" are aggregations of distinct elementary disease/injury components.

Another limitation is that each death can have only one tabulated underlying cause—the one cause that supposedly initiated the train of events leading directly to death. To the extent that there are other, nonunderlying ("contributory") causes indicated on the medical condition field of the death certificate, there is additional information on the impact of CDDs over time and across populations. For example, the top five nonunderlying causes of death at age 65 and older in the United States in 1998 were heart diseases (number 1 above), hypertension (number 13), chronic obstructive pulmonary diseases (number 4), diabetes mellitus (number 5), and cerebrovascular diseases (number 3). Malignant neoplasms (number 2) were ranked ninth. Furthermore, the joint three-way occurrence of heart diseases, hypertension, and diabetes mellitus on the death certificates was 3.3 times higher than expected, assuming independent causes. Combined with cerebrovascular diseases, the joint four-way occurrence was 11.8 times higher than expected under conditions of independence. Similar results for other cause combinations demonstrate that nonunderlying causes reflect complex processes and distinctive patterns of joint dependence. Conversely, these results indicate that analytic models based on independent causes (e.g., multiple decrement life tables) may be substantially biased.

A third limitation relates to the accuracy of reported causes of death. Autopsy and medical record studies show that accuracy decreases across the categories of malignant neoplasms, heart diseases, and cerebrovascular diseases, with substantial variation within each category. Most errors are due to incorrect diagnoses and incorrect sequencing of the underlying cause when multiple and possibly interacting diseases are operating at the time of death.

TABLE 2

Life Expectancy at Age 65 in the United States and Japan, Selected Years 1950–1998

Year	Males		Females	
	U.S.	Japan	U.S.	Japan
1950–1951	12.8	11.3	15.1	13.3
1970	13.1	12.5	17.0	15.3
1980	14.0	14.6	18.3	17.7
1998	16.0	17.1	19.2	22.0

SOURCE: Preston et al. (1972); Kinsella and Velkoff (2001).

Mortality Statistics

Seventy-five percent of deaths in the United States in 1998 occurred at age 65 and older, and this rate is gradually increasing. Most deaths involved CDDs as underlying or contributory causes. The average reported number of causes was 2.0 per 1998 U.S. death at ages 65 to 94, 1.9 at ages 95 to 99, and 1.8 at ages 100 and older. When stratified by underlying cause, the averages ranged from 1.8 for malignant neoplasms to 2.9 for diabetes mellitus. Different causes exhibited different patterns of change over age and time and unique multiway associations consistent with their nature as distinct, related physiological processes.

Quantification of temporal changes in CDDs presents major challenges because of the lack of comprehensive models. Summary measures based on total and cause-specific life tables generally are used for public policy planning. For example, recorded life expectancies at age 65 in the United States and in Japan since the middle of the twentieth century for selected years are shown in Table 2.

Life expectancy at age 65 increased significantly after 1950 in both countries, but the relative increases in Japan were more than double those in the United States, with the largest differences being for females in the period 1980–1998. Comparisons of age and cause patterns of mortality in the United States, Japan, and Sweden have shown that the U.S. cause, but not age, pattern was similar to Sweden's. In a 1988 study Machiko Yanagishita and Jack Guralnik identified declines in cerebrovascular and heart diseases as the primary reasons for Japan's surpassing Sweden in the mid-1970s as the top-ranked country in life expectancy. The top three causes of death in Japan during 1965–1980 were cerebrovascular diseases, malignant neoplasms, and

TABLE 3

Age-Standardized Death Rates in the United States: Top Four Underlying Causes, Selected Years 1950–1998

Underlying Cause	1950	1970	1980	1998
Heart diseases	586.6	492.7	412.1	272.4
Malignant neoplasms	193.9	198.6	207.9	202.4
Cerebrovascular diseases	180.7	147.7	96.4	59.6
Chronic obstructive pulmonary diseases	N/A	28.3	37.2	42.0

SOURCE: NCHS (2001).

heart diseases. Japanese statistics through 1999 show that malignant neoplasms have replaced cerebrovascular diseases as the top-ranked cause of death and that heart diseases have replaced cerebrovascular diseases in the second-place ranking.

Comparisons of mortality patterns within and between countries must consider changes in incidence, prevalence, duration, severity, and treatment of the various CDDs. Each one exhibits unique patterns consistent with the complex and heterogeneous nature of the underlying disease processes. For example, the temporal changes in age-standardized underlying cause death rates (per 100,000 population) for the top four causes identified above for the U.S. are shown in Table 3.

The table clearly shows that the patterns of change differ significantly by cause, with large relative declines for cerebrovascular and heart diseases, a trend reversal for malignant neoplasms, and large relative increases for chronic obstructive pulmonary diseases.

Morbidity Measures

Recognition of the complex nature of CDDs has led to the development of procedures for summarizing the population health impact of these diseases in ways that do not require full specification of the relevant physiological processes. These procedures generally employ age-specific prevalence estimates from national health surveys and epidemiological studies that are combined with life-table statistics, using the method developed by Daniel Sullivan in 1971. For example, Diane Wagener and her colleagues used this method in a 2001 study to estimate that 17 percent of male life expectancy and 19 percent of female

life expectancy at birth in the United States in 1995 was lived with some degree of activity limitation as a result of chronic health conditions.

In a 1996 study Christopher Murray and Alan Lopez presented comprehensive analyses of the morbidity and mortality burden of lethal and nonlethal diseases for developed and developing countries worldwide. Those authors extended Sullivan's method to measure disease burden two ways: (1) using *disability-adjusted life expectancy* (DALE), which is the expected number of years of life lived in full health, and (2) using *disability-adjusted life years* (DALYs), which are additive, time-weighted measures of the severities of specific diseases, including years of life lost to premature deaths from lethal diseases.

Murray and Lopez reported that 86 percent of deaths in developed countries in 1990 were due to noncommunicable diseases (i.e., noninfectious CDDs), with 22 to 25 percent of remaining life expectancy at age 60 spent disabled. Corresponding results for developing countries indicated that 47 percent of deaths were due to noncommunicable diseases, with 31 to 48 percent of remaining life expectancy at age 60 spent disabled. Murray and Lopez projected that the global fraction of deaths from noncommunicable diseases would rise from 55 percent in 1990 to 73 percent in 2020 (from 86 percent to 89 percent in developed and from 47 percent to 70 percent in developing countries). They provided quantitative estimates of the impact on DALYs of a range of disease risk factors, including alcohol, tobacco, illicit drugs, air pollution, inadequate sanitation, physical inactivity, and malnutrition.

In a 2000 study Colin Mathers and his colleagues estimated DALEs for 191 countries: Japanese females and males were both top ranked within the respective sex, followed by French females and Swedish males, respectively.

Morbidity/Mortality Pathways

Studies of monozygotic and dizygotic twins indicate that 25 to 30 percent of variability in the length of life is heritable. Heritable single-gene defects produce 1,500 distinct, rare diseases, 98 percent of which emerge by age 50. Natural selection accounts for their rarity; existing equilibriums may be altered by effective medical treatments.

Factors contributing to the nonheritable 70 to 75 percent of length of life variability include environmental, nutritional, behavioral, and lifestyle influences beginning with fetal, postnatal, and childhood development; socioeconomic and demographic factors such as race/ethnicity, gender, education, income, occupation, stress, social support, and other social conditions; and epidemiologic risk factors such as diet, exercise, weight, tobacco, alcohol, cholesterol, and blood pressure.

Continued progress against major CDDs can be expected to result from improved understanding of the pathways through which CDDs develop, innovative forms of primary prevention, and medical diagnostic and pharmaceutical treatment protocols that permit disease detection and treatment at successively earlier stages in the morbid process.

See also: *Cancer; Cardiovascular Disease; Disease, Burden of; Epidemiological Transition; Mortality Decline.*

BIBLIOGRAPHY

Fogel, Robert W., and Dora L. Costa. 1997. "A Theory of Technophysio Evolution, with Some Implications for Forecasting Population, Health Care Costs, and Pension Costs." *Demography* 34: 49–66.

Himes, Christine L. 1994. "Age Patterns of Mortality and Cause-of-Death Structures in Sweden, Japan, and the United States." *Demography* 31: 633–650.

Japan Statistical Yearbook. 2002. Tokyo: Statistics Bureau and Statistics Center, Ministry of Public Management, Home Affairs, Posts and Telecommunications.

Jimenez-Sanchez, Gerardo, Barton Childs, and David Valle. 2001. "Human Disease Genes." *Nature* 409: 853–855.

Kinsella, Kevin, and Victoria A. Velkoff. 2001. *An Aging World: 2001.* Washington, D.C.: U.S. Census Bureau, Series P95/01-1, U.S. Government Printing Office.

Mathers, Colin D., Ritu Sadana, Joshua A. Salomon, Christopher J. L. Murray, and Alan D. Lopez. 2000. "Estimates of DALE for 191 Countries: Methods and Results." *Global Programme on Evidence for Health Policy Working Paper No. 16.* Geneva: World Health Organization.

McKusick, Victor A. 2000. "Online Mendelian Inheritance in Man, OMIM (TM)." Bethesda, MD: McKusick-Nathans Institute for Genetic Medicine, Johns Hopkins University, and National Center for Biotechnology Information, National Library of Medicine.

Murray, Christopher J. L., and Alan D. Lopez. 1996. *The Global Burden of Disease,* Volume 1. Cambridge, MA: Harvard University Press.

National Center for Health Statistics (NCHS). 2001. *Health, United States, 2001: With Urban and Rural Health Chartbook.* Hyattsville, MD: National Center for Health Statistics.

Pennisi, Elizabeth. 2001. "Behind the Scenes of Gene Expression." *Science* 293: 1064–1067.

Preston, Samuel H., Nathan Keyfitz, and Robert Schoen. 1972. *Causes of Death: Life Tables for National Populations.* New York: Seminar Press.

Stallard, Eric. 2002 (in press). "Underlying and Multiple Cause Mortality at Advanced Ages: United States 1980–1998." *North American Actuarial Journal* 6(3).

Strohman, Richard. 2002. "Maneuvering in the Complex Path from Genotype to Phenotype." *Science* 296: 701–703.

Sullivan, Daniel F. 1971. "A Single Index of Mortality and Morbidity." *HSMHA Health Reports* 86: 347–354.

Thompson, Craig B. 1995. "Apoptosis in the Pathogenesis and Treatment of Disease." *Science* 267: 1456–1462.

Wagener, Diane K., Michael T. Molla, Eileen M. Crimmins, Elsie Pamuk, and Jennifer H. Madans. 2001. "Summary Measures of Population Health: Addressing the First Goal of Healthy People 2010, Improving Health Expectancy." *Statistical Notes,* No. 22. Hyattsville, MD: National Center for Health Statistics.

World Health Organization (WHO). 1975. *Manual of the International Statistical Classification of Diseases, Injuries, and Causes of Death, Based on the Recommendations of the Ninth Revision Conference, 1975.* Geneva: World Health Organization.

Yanagishita, Machiko, and Jack M. Guralnik. 1988. "Changing Mortality Patterns That Led Life Expectancy in Japan to Surpass Sweden's: 1972–1982." *Demography* 25: 611–624.

Zimmer, Carl. 2001. "Do Chronic Diseases Have an Infectious Root?" *Science* 293: 1974–1977.

ERIC STALLARD

DISEASES, INFECTIOUS

Infectious diseases are caused by microbial agents (e.g., bacteria, fungi, parasites, prions, and viruses) or by their toxic by-products. Infectious diseases have been an inevitable and ubiquitous part of life since humans evolved. Although the contagious nature of many diseases had been observed since early in recorded history, the microbial origin of infectious diseases was not scientifically established until the late nineteenth century, when Robert Koch (1843–1910) demonstrated that the bacterium Bacillus anthracis is the causative agent of anthrax infection. Koch set forth four postulates that must be fulfilled to establish the microbial cause of an infectious disease:

1. Identify a specific organism from a patient with the disease;

2. Obtain a pure culture of that organism;

3. Reproduce the disease in experimental animals using the pure culture; and

4. Recover the organism from the infected animals.

Since Koch's time, causative agents and routes of infection have been described for thousands of infectious diseases of humans and animals. The impact of an infectious disease on an individual or animal can range from trivial to fatal. The impact of an infectious outbreak on a society can range from negligible to devastating.

Infectious diseases are undoubtedly among the most powerful factors that influence human demographics. In some cases, the impact of disease has been widespread, direct, and dramatic, as when epidemics and pandemics of plague, syphilis, cholera, and influenza caused substantial and concentrated morbidity and mortality in the fourteenth to twentieth centuries. At other times, the influences have been less direct, as in the late-nineteenth century when trypanosomiasis (African sleeping sickness) rendered large tracts of Africa uninhabitable until its insect vector, the tsetse fly, was controlled.

Classification Systems of Infectious Diseases

Several unofficial classification systems exist for infectious diseases. Some are based on causative agent and others on route of transmission. The following broad categories by causative agent are generally utilized in academic and microbiologic research institutions:

Bacterial diseases (e.g., salmonellosis, tuberculosis, syphilis);

Viral infections (e.g., West Nile encephalitis, measles, chickenpox, poliomyelitis, HIV);

Fungal infections (e.g., yeast infections, histoplasmosis);

Parasitic protozoan (e.g, cryptosporidiosis, malaria) and metazoan infections (e.g., hookworm, onchocerciasis);

Prion diseases (infectious proteins that are the agents of bovine spongiform encephalopathy or "mad cow disease" and Creutzfeldt-Jacob disease in humans); and

Rickettsial diseases (e.g., typhus and Rocky Mountain spotted fever).

Classification of diseases by route of transmission is typically used in public health and prevention-oriented disease control programs. Categories include:

Diseases transmitted from person-to-person, including respiratory illnesses transmitted by coughing (e.g., influenza and tuberculosis) and systemic diseases transmitted via sexual contact (e.g, HIV, syphilis, and gonorrhea);

Food-borne and waterborne diseases, including illnesses transmitted via the fecal-oral route (e.g., typhoid and hepatitis A) or via contaminated water (e.g., cryptosporidiosis and giardiasis);

Bloodborne infections (e.g., hepatitis B and C);

Healthcare-acquired (nosocomial) infections, including surgical wound infections (e.g., staphylococcal infections);

Diseases transmitted by animals or insects, including zoonotic infections (e.g., Escherichia coli H7:O157 and rabies) and vectorborne infections (Lyme disease and yellow fever);

Infections acquired from the environment (Legionnaires' disease, inhaled in water droplets, and coccidioidomycosis, acquired from dust or soil).

Sometimes, vaccine-preventable diseases (such as rubella, mumps, and pertussis—whooping cough), infections of travelers (many diarrheal diseases), and antibiotic-resistant bacterial infections (such as methicillin-resistant Staphylococcus aureus) are regarded as unique categories, as are opportunistic infections (such as Pneumocystis pneumonia and cytomegalovirus retinitis), that are generally restricted to persons with immunodeficiencies. A sad commentary on contemporary society is represented by the category of infectious agents that may be used as biological weapons (including smallpox virus, anthrax spores, and botulinum toxin).

The International Statistical Classification of Diseases and Related Health Problems, issued by the World Health Organization (WHO), is the major official codification of all diseases, conditions, and injuries. The tenth revision (ICD-10) is the latest in a series that began in 1893 as the Bertillon Classification or International List of Causes of Death. The ICD is continually being revised as new conditions, including emerging infections, are described. Every infectious and non-infectious disease of humans is assigned a unique 3-digit number (plus multiple decimal places) in the ICD system. These numbers are used in many medical and public health records, including hospital discharge reports, billing records, and death certificates. The Control of Communicable Diseases Manual, the widely available and standard American Public Health Association handbook of infectious diseases, lists ICD codes for each of the several hundred infectious diseases it describes in its alphabetically arranged entries.

Control of Infectious Diseases in Developed Nations

Rapid progress in control of infectious diseases characterized the late nineteenth and early-twentieth centuries. Deaths from infectious disease declined markedly in the United States during the first half of the twentieth century (see Figure 1). This major demographic change both contributed to, and is reflected in, the sharp drop in infant and child mortality and the more than 30-year average increase in life expectancy at birth achieved over the ensuing years.

In 1900, the three leading causes of death were pneumonia, tuberculosis (TB), and diarrhea and enteritis, which (together with diphtheria) were responsible for one-third of all deaths (see Figure 2).

About 40 percent of these deaths were deaths of children below the age of five. Cancer accounted for only 3.7 percent of deaths, because few people lived long enough for it to develop. Coming into the twenty-first century, heart disease and cancers account for almost three-quarters of deaths, with 5 percent due to pneumonia, influenza, and human immunodeficiency virus (HIV), the cause of acquired immunodeficiency syndrome (AIDS).

In 1900, 30.4 percent of children in the United States died before their fifth birthdays; in 1997, the figure was 1.4 percent. Despite this overall progress in the developed world, the twentieth century also witnessed two of the most devastating epidemics in human history. The 1918 influenza pandemic killed more than 20 million people, including 500,000 Americans, in less than a year—more deaths in a comparable time period than in virtually any war or famine. The last decades of the century were marked by the recognition and pandemic spread of HIV, resulting in an estimated 22 million deaths by the year 2000. UNAIDS (the Joint United Nations Programme on HIV/AIDS) projects another 65 million deaths by 2020. These episodes illustrate the volatility of infectious disease death rates and the unpredictability of disease emergence.

Twentieth century landmarks in disease control in the United States included major improvements in sanitation and hygiene, the implementation of universal childhood vaccination programs, control of food-borne diseases, and the introduction of antibiotics.

Sanitation and hygiene. The nineteenth century shift in U.S. population from country to city that accompanied industrialization, along with successive waves of immigration, led to overcrowding and poor housing. The municipal water supplies and rudimentary waste disposal systems that existed at the time were quickly overwhelmed. These conditions favored the emergence and spread of infectious illnesses, including repeated outbreaks of cholera, TB, typhoid fever, influenza, yellow fever, and food-borne illnesses such as shigellosis.

By 1900, however, the incidence of many of these diseases had begun to decline, due to the implementation of public health improvements that continued into the twentieth century. Sanitation departments were established for garbage removal, and outhouses were gradually replaced by indoor plumbing, sewer systems, and public systems for

FIGURE 1

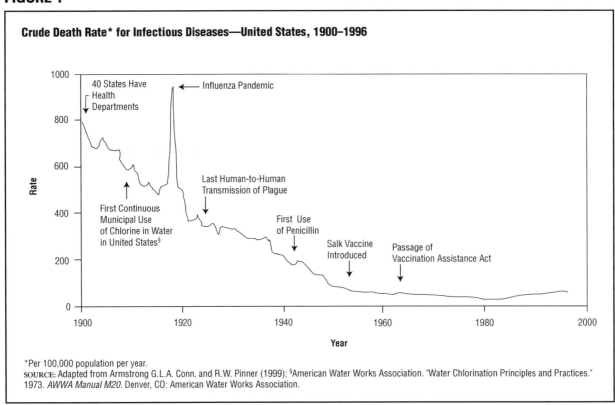

Crude Death Rate* for Infectious Diseases—United States, 1900–1996

*Per 100,000 population per year.
SOURCE: Adapted from Armstrong G.L.A. Conn, and R.W. Pinner (1999); §American Water Works Association. "Water Chlorination Principles and Practices." 1973. *AWWA Manual M20.* Denver, CO: American Water Works Association.

solid waste disposal. The incidence of cholera, which reached its peak between 1830 and 1896, a period during which Eurasia and North America experienced four pandemics, began to fall, as water supplies were insulated from human waste by sanitary disposal systems. Chlorination and other treatments of drinking water began in the early 1900s and became widespread by mid-century, sharply decreasing the incidence of cholera, as well as typhoid fever and other waterborne diseases. The incidence of TB declined, as improvements in housing reduced crowding and TB control programs were put in place. In 1900, TB killed 200 out of every 100,000 Americans, most of them city residents. In 1940 (before the introduction of antibiotic therapy), TB remained a leading killer, but its mortality rate had decreased to 60 per 100,000 persons.

Vaccination programs. The advent of immunization also contributed greatly to the prevention of infectious diseases. Strategic vaccination campaigns virtually eliminated diseases that were common in the United States during the beginning and middle decades of the century—including diphtheria, tetanus, pertussis, polio, smallpox, measles, mumps, rubella, and Haemophilus influenzae type b meningi-

tis. Starting with the licensing of the combined diphtheria-pertussis-tetanus (DPT) vaccine in 1949, state and local health departments began providing childhood vaccinations on a regular basis, primarily to poor children. In 1955, the introduction of the Salk polio vaccine led to the federal appropriation of funds to support childhood vaccination programs initiated by states and local communities. In 1962, a federally coordinated vaccination program was established through the passage of the Vaccination Assistance Act—a landmark piece of legislation that has been continuously renewed and in the early twenty-first century supports the purchase and administration of a full range of childhood vaccines. WHO's Expanded Program on Immunization seeks to extend these benefits globally.

The success of vaccination programs in the United States and Europe gave rise to the twentieth-century concept of *disease eradication*—the idea that a selected disease could be eliminated from all human populations through global cooperation. In 1980, after an 11-year campaign (1967–1977) involving 33 nations, WHO declared that smallpox had been eradicated worldwide—about a decade after it had been eliminated from the United States

FIGURE 2

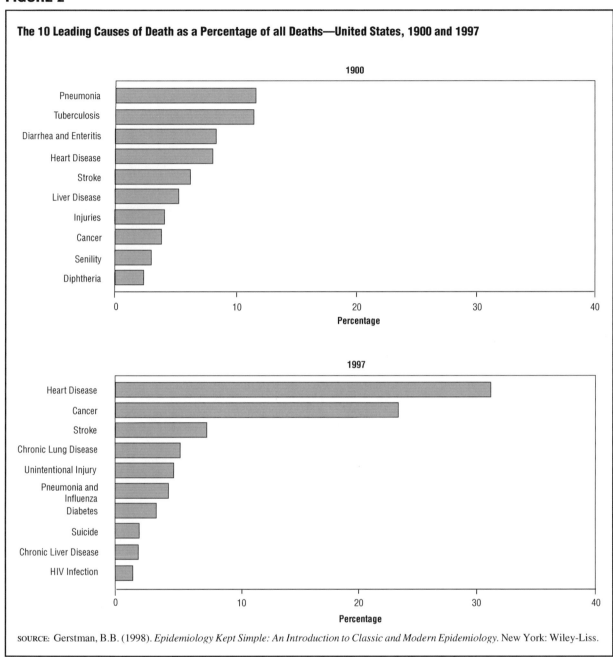

The 10 Leading Causes of Death as a Percentage of all Deaths—United States, 1900 and 1997

SOURCE: Gerstman, B.B. (1998). *Epidemiology Kept Simple: An Introduction to Classic and Modern Epidemiology.* New York: Wiley-Liss.

and the rest of the Western Hemisphere. Polio and dracunculiasis (also called guinea worm disease, a waterborne, parasitic non-vaccine-preventable illness) were targeted for global eradication in the early twenty-first century, and many other infectious diseases may be targeted in the future, including measles, Haemophilus influenzae type b infections, filariasis, onchocerciasis, rubella, and hepatitis B.

Control of food-borne diseases. One of the disease control duties assumed by state and local health departments in the twentieth century was the regulation of food handling practices at food processing plants, restaurants, and retail food stores. The need for such regulation is illustrated by the famous story of Typhoid Mary, an Irish immigrant cook and typhoid carrier who worked at a number of New York restaurants in the 1920s and infected more than a hundred people before the New York City health department placed her under house arrest. The story of Typhoid Mary (who was treated very harshly) illustrates not only the growing expectation among Americans that government should promote public health, but also a tendency (which continues to this day) to associate infectious disease problems with immigrants or minority populations, rather than with specific risk factors or behaviors. During the 1980s, for example, the gay community was unjustly blamed for the AIDS epidemic, and in the early 1990s, the Navajo Nation was stigmatized when an outbreak of hantavirus pulmonary syndrome occurred in their community.

The second half of the twentieth century saw a notable rise in illness caused by nontyphoidal Salmonella species, and an explosion of knowledge made possible by modern molecular techniques resulted in identification of a growing list of previously unrecognized, and in some cases, new food-borne and waterborne agents. These include Escherichia coli O157:H7, Campylobacter spp., Cryptosporidium parvum, Listeria monocytogenes, Legionella spp., and caliciviruses. A 1999 report estimated an annual incidence of 76 million food-borne illnesses in the United States, with 325,000 hospitalizations and 5,000 fatalities. In 1993, the largest outbreak of waterborne illness in U.S. history occurred when an estimated 400,000 persons in Milwaukee, Wisconsin were infected with the parasite Cryptosporidium.

Factors linked to the continued challenges of food-borne and waterborne illnesses include (1) changing dietary habits that favor foods more likely to transmit infection (e.g., raw seafood, sprouts, unpasteurized milk and juice, and fresh fruits and vegetables that may be inadequately washed); (2) globalization of the food supply; (3) mass production practices; and (4) aging and inadequately maintained water supply systems. Mass food production and distribution, while resulting in an abundant and usually safe food supply, has also increased the potential for large and geographically dispersed outbreaks of illness.

Antibiotics. The discovery of the antibiotic penicillin—and its development into a widely available medical treatment—was a major landmark in the control of infectious diseases. Penicillin and other antibiotics that were subsequently developed allowed quick and complete treatment of previously incurable bacterial illnesses. Discovered fortuitously in 1928, penicillin was not developed for medical use until the 1940s, when it was produced in significant quantities and used by the Allied military in World War II to treat sick or wounded soldiers.

Antibiotics have been in civilian use since the end of World War II, and have saved the lives and health of millions of persons with typhoid fever, diphtheria, bacterial pneumonia, bacterial meningitis, syphilis, gonorrhea, plague, tuberculosis, and streptococcal and staphylococcal infections. Drugs have also been developed to treat viral diseases (e.g., amantadine, ribavirin, zidovudine, and acyclovir); fungal diseases (e.g., nystatin, ketoconazole, and amphotericin B); and parasitic diseases (e.g., chloroquine, mebendazole, and metronidazole).

Unfortunately, these therapeutic advances have been tempered by the emergence of drug resistance in bacteria, parasites, viruses, and fungi. Diseases that have been significantly affected by antibiotic resistance include staphylococcal infections, gonorrhea, tuberculosis, pneumococcal infections, typhoid fever, bacterial dysentery, malaria, and HIV/AIDS. Reasons for the swift development of antimicrobial resistance include the natural tendency of organisms to mutate and share genetic material. However, this process has been facilitated by the following factors: (1) injudicious prescribing of antibiotics by the medical, veterinary, and agricultural industries; (2) unrealistic patient expectations resulting in requests for antibiotic treatment of nonbacterial infections; (3) the economics of pharmaceutical sales; and (4) the growing sophistication of medical interventions, such as transplant surgery and chemotherapy, that require the administration of large quantities of antibiotics. Growing antibiotic resistance poses a substantial threat to the gains in infectious disease control and warrants fresh approaches to promoting wise antibiotic stewardship by prescribers, patients, and industry so that the efficacy of these drugs can be sustained for future generations.

Animal and insect control. The twentieth century witnessed major advances in the control of disease transmission by animal and insect pests. In the United States, nationally sponsored, state-coordinated vaccination and animal control programs eliminated dog-to-dog transmission of rabies. Malaria, which had been endemic throughout the Southeast, was reduced to negligible levels by the late 1940s, through regional mosquito control programs that drained swamps and killed mosquito larvae in bodies of water.

The threat of plague epidemics in the United State was also greatly diminished. During the early

1900s, infected rats and fleas were introduced via shipping into port cities along the Pacific and Gulf coasts (e.g., San Francisco, Seattle, New Orleans, Galveston, and Pensacola), as well as into Hawaii, Cuba, and Puerto Rico. The most serious outbreaks occurred in San Francisco from 1900 to 1904 (121 cases/118 deaths) and 1907–1908 (167 cases/89 deaths). The last major rat-associated outbreak of plague in the United States occurred in 1924 and 1925 in Los Angeles. This outbreak, which was characterized by a high percentage of pneumonic plague cases, included the last identified instance in the United States of human-to-human transmission of plague (via inhalation of infectious respiratory droplets from coughing patients).

The introduction of West Nile virus, transmitted from birds to humans via mosquitoes, into North America in 1999 underlined the importance of maintaining insect control programs. In the four years after West Nile virus was first reported in New York City, it had spread to 43 states. Moreover, during the summer of 2002, West Nile virus infections were reported in patients who received organ transplants or blood from infected persons.

Opportunities and Challenges for the Twenty-first Century

Future advances in molecular biology, bioinformatics, and other areas are likely to revolutionize the detection, treatment, control, and prevention of infectious diseases during the twenty-first century. Advances in microbial genomics will enable epidemiologists to identify any microbial species, subtype, or strain within hours or minutes. A detailed understanding of human genetics will help physicians target vaccines and prophylactic drugs to the most susceptible individuals, while improved knowledge of human immunology will stimulate the development of vaccines that not only prevent disease but also boost the immunity of people who are already infected with HIV or other pathogens. Moreover, in-depth knowledge of climatic and environmental factors that influence the emergence of animal- and insect-borne diseases (facilitated by the availability of remote sensing technologies) will inform public health policy and allow public health authorities to predict outbreaks and institute preventive measures months in advance.

Although the impact of technology on the control of infectious diseases has been overwhelmingly

positive, certain twentieth-century technological advances have created new niches and modes of transmission for particular pathogens; for example: (1) The bacteria that cause Legionnaire's disease have been spread through modern ventilation systems; (2) HIV and hepatitis B and C viruses have been spread through unscreened blood donations; (3) Food-borne diseases like Salmonellosis and E. coli O157 infections have been spread through centrally processed food products that are distributed simultaneously to many states or countries; and (4) Airplanes have replaced ships as major vehicles of international disease spread. More people are traveling to tropical rain forests and other wilderness habitats that are reservoirs for insects and animals that harbor unknown infectious agents. This incursion is due not only to economic development (e.g., mining, forestry, and agriculture), but also to missionary or other volunteer work and an expanded tourist trade that caters to individuals who wish to visit undeveloped areas.

In the United States, increasing suburbanization, coupled with the reversion of agricultural land to secondary growth forest, has brought people into contact with deer that carry ticks infected with Borrelia burgdorferi, the causative agent of Lyme disease, and has brought household pets into contact with rabies-infected raccoons.

A development with potentially profound implication for disease prevention and treatment is the blurring of the distinction between infectious and chronic diseases. Infectious causes may be found for many chronic cardiovascular, intestinal, and pulmonary diseases. Current research suggests that some chronic diseases formerly attributed to lifestyle or environmental factors are actually caused by or intensified by infectious agents. For example, most peptic ulcers—long thought to be due to stress and diet—are now known to be caused by the bacterium Helicobacter pylori. Several types of cancers, including some liver and cervical cancers, are linked to infectious agents. Chlamydia pneumoniae infection has been proposed as a contributor to coronary artery disease, and enteroviruses appear to be associated with type 1 diabetes mellitus in some children. Thus, in the future it is possible that some forms of cancer, heart disease, and diabetes, may be treated with antimicrobial drugs or prevented by vaccines.

The general success in reducing morbidity and mortality from infectious diseases during the first three-quarters of the twentieth century led many medical and public health experts to become complacent about the need for continued research into treatment and control of infectious microbes. However, subsequent developments—including the appearance of AIDS, the reemergence of tuberculosis (including multidrug-resistant strains), and an overall increase in U.S. infectious disease mortality between 1980 and 1998 (see Figure 1)—have reinforced the realization that as long as microbes can evolve and societies change, new diseases will inevitably arise. Furthermore, infectious diseases continue to be responsible for almost half of mortality in developing countries, where they occur primarily among the poorest people. About half of infectious disease deaths in these countries can be attributed to just three diseases—HIV/AIDS, TB, and malaria. WHO estimates that these three diseases cause over 300 million illnesses and more than 5 million deaths each year.

See also: *AIDS; Black Death; Emerging Infectious Disease; Epidemics; Influenza; Tuberculosis.*

BIBLIOGRAPHY

Armstrong, Gregory L., Laura A. Conn, and, Robert W. Pinner. 1999. "Trends in Infectious Disease Mortality in the United States during the 20th Century." *Journal of the American Medical Association* 281: 61–66.

Center for Disease Control. 1998. "Ten Great Public Health Achievements—United States, 1900–1999." *Morbidity and Mortality Weekly Report* 48: 241–243.

———. 1998. "Achievements in Public Health, 1900–1999: Impact of Vaccines Universally Recommended for Children—United States, 1990–1998." *Morbidity and Mortality Weekly Report* 48: 243–248.

———. 1997. "Status Report on the Childhood Immunization Initiative: Reported Cases of Selected Vaccine-preventable Diseases—United States, 1996." *Morbidity and Mortality Weekly Report* 46: 665–671.

Chin, James, ed. 2000. *Control of Communicable Diseases Manual,* 17th edition. Washington, D.C.: American Public Health Association.

Crosby, Alfred W., Jr. 1976. *Epidemic and Peace, 1918.* Westport, CT: Greenwood Press.

Estes, J. Worth, and Billy G. Smith, eds. 1997. *A Melancholy Scene of Devastation: The Public Response to the 1793 Philadelphia Yellow Fever Epidemic.* Canton, MA: Watson Publishing International.

Etheridge, Elizabeth W. 1992. *Sentinel for Health: A History of the Centers for Disease Control.* Berkeley: University of California Press.

Fleming, William L. "The Sexually Transmitted Diseases." In *Maxcy-Rosenau Public Health and Preventive Medicine,* 11th edition, ed. John M. Last. New York: Appleton-Century-Crofts.

Garrett, Laurie. 1994. *The Coming Plague: Newly Emerging Diseases in a World Out of Balance.* New York: Farrar, Straus and Giroux.

Hinman, Alan. 1990. "1889 to 1989: A Century of Health and Disease." *Public Health Rep* 105: 374–380.

Khan Ali S., Alexandra M. Levitt, and Michael J. Sage. 2000. "Biological and Chemical Terrorism: Strategic Plan for Preparedness and Response: Recommendations of the CDC Strategic Planning Workgroup." *Morbidity and Mortality Weekly Report* 44(RR04): 1–14.

Kortepeter, Mark G., and Gerald W. Parker. 1999. "Potential Biological Weapons Threats." *Emerging Infectious Diseases.* 5: 523–527.

Lederberg, Joshua, and Robert Shope, eds. *Emerging Infections: Microbial Threats to Health in the United States.* Washington D.C.: National Academy Press.

Mead, Paul S., Laurence Slutsker, Vance Dietz, Linda F. McCaig, Joseph S. Bresee, Craig Shapiro, Patricia M. Griffin, Robert V. Tauxe. 1999. "Food-related Illness and Death in the United States." *Emerging Infectious Diseases* 5: 607–625.

Mullan, Fitzhugh. 1989. *Plagues and Politics: The Story of the United States Public Health Service.* New York: Basic Books.

Selvin, Molly. 1984. "Changing Medical and Societal Attitudes Toward Sexually Transmitted Diseases: A Historical Overview." In *Sexually Transmitted Diseases.* ed. King K. Holmes, Per-Anders Mardh, P. Frederick Sparling, and Paul J. Wiesner. New York: McGraw-Hill.

D. Peter Drotman
Alexandra M. Levitt

FIGURE 1

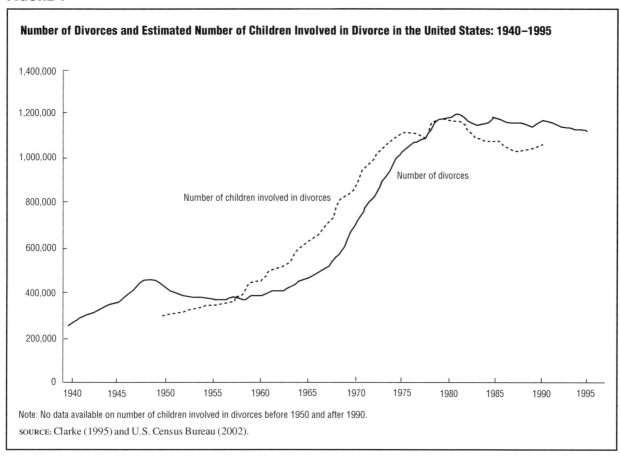

Number of Divorces and Estimated Number of Children Involved in Divorce in the United States: 1940–1995

Note: No data available on number of children involved in divorces before 1950 and after 1990.

SOURCE: Clarke (1995) and U.S. Census Bureau (2002).

DIVORCE

The legal dissolution of marriage has reached historically high levels in most industrial societies. In the United States, divorce rates have been increasing for more than a century. They increased steeply in the 1960s and 1970s and subsequently leveled off, as shown in Figure 1. Slightly less than half of all first marriages in the United States in the early twenty-first century end in divorce. This proportion is roughly the same in Sweden. The figures are somewhat lower (around 40% per marriage) for other Nordic countries, the United Kingdom, Belgium, and most countries of the former Soviet Union. In most other industrial societies, divorce rates are rising, although they are still considerably lower than in the United States.

With the exception of parts of Asia and Latin America, dissolution of marriage is also common, although statistically less well documented, in the developing world. The proportion of women separated or divorced between the ages of 45 and 59 in-creased on average from 7 percent in the 1980s to 10 percent in the 1990s in Latin America and the Caribbean (the corresponding figures are 5 percent and 9 percent in Europe as a whole and 9 percent and 14 percent in other developed regions). As a combined effect of death, separation, and divorce, in many countries in sub-Saharan Africa, more than one-third of women experience dissolution of marriage before reaching the end of childbearing years.

The rise in divorce in the industrialized countries has been attributed to (1) smaller gains from marriage than in the past; (2) the declining social stigma of divorce; and (3) a relaxation of divorce laws, as represented by the introduction of no-fault divorce. These factors are thought to mutually reinforce each other. For example, increases in divorce reduce social stigma and foster the liberalization of divorce law. Higher expectations of divorce may encourage precautionary behavior (for example, waiting to have children) that itself may reduce the benefits of staying married. In turn, expectation of ease of divorce may encourage less careful deliberation before entering into marriage, which in itself could increase the likelihood of divorce. The plateau in divorce rates in the United States since about 1980 remains largely unexplained.

Although divorce ends individual marriages, most often the individuals who divorce remarry, often to partners who are themselves divorced. Current U.S. remarriage rates imply that about three-quarters of divorced men and two-thirds of divorced women eventually remarry. Divorce and remarriage have, in concert, changed family structure, increasing the number of single-parent headed households and of marriages in which one or both of the spouses was formerly divorced, and increasing the prevalence of step-relationships within families.

The principal impact of divorce that concerns social scientists is its effect on children. Social scientists working with observational data are not able to determine directly whether children of divorce are worse off than those of parents who remain married. Studies that have tried to control for factors other than divorce have yielded mixed results, but some have found that children of divorce do fare worse in various ways in comparison to children brought up in intact marriages. Another consequence of divorce is the economic hardship associated with the dissolution of households, which often falls disproportionately on women.

Higher rates of divorce might be expected to increase the quality of marriage in a society by allowing those in unsatisfactory marriages to choose new partners. On the other hand, it can also be argued that higher divorce rates may have negative consequences for all marriages because couples will be reluctant to make marriage-specific investments, like having children, which might enhance the advantages of marriage. The validity of either of these theories remains unproven.

Marriages most at risk of divorce include those entered into at an early age. There is also a socioeconomic gradient to divorce, such that those with more education and higher income face slightly lower risks of divorce. Part of the effect of socioeconomic status is mediated through age at marriage (those who attend college are less likely to marry young), but multivariate analysis reveals that, even after controlling for age at marriage, those couples who are poor and less educated face slightly higher risks of divorce.

The age pattern of divorce, or more accurately the duration pattern, is such that following the first year, divorce rates decline consistently as the length of the marriage increases. Contrary to popular belief, there is no increase in divorce after seven years of marriage (the *seven year itch*) apparent in the U.S. pattern. Part of the declining risks of divorce related to duration may be due to the winnowing out of marriages with high risks of divorce. But the advantages of marriage (and associated disadvantages of divorce) are themselves also thought to increase with time. There are more likely to be children, the division of household labor becomes more established, and the amount of other forms of so-called marriage-specific capital increases.

The economic theory of marriage and divorce, pioneered by the economist Gary Becker emphasizes—by analogy with the theory of comparative advantage in international trade—the benefits of marriage that come from the sexual division of labor. According to this theory, the advantages have declined over time as women have entered the labor market and thereby reduced men's comparative advantage as income earners. At the same time, the theory argues that technological advances in the home have reduced women's comparative advantage in housework. In contrast, sociological theories of divorce emphasize the increasingly individualistic and hedonistic orientation of modern societies, and the decline in normative expectations that marriage should be a life-long commitment.

Measures

Divorce, like other demographic rates, can be measured cross-sectionally at a given time (period measure) or along the lifecycle (cohort measure), and at the aggregate or individual level.

The most commonly used aggregate measures are annual rates of divorce. The simplest measure, called the *crude divorce rate,* is estimated by dividing the total number of divorces in a year by the total mid-year population. The crude divorce rate can be influenced by changes in the population at risk. For example, if age-at-marriage is delayed, the proportion of married people will decrease and the rate will decline even if the risks of divorce to married people remain the same.

A more refined measure, that takes into account the number of marriages at risk, is the *general divorce rate,* which divides the total number of divorces by the number of married women (a proxy for the number of marriages). The general divorce rate can be thought of as the chance that a randomly chosen couple will divorce in a given year. It is less influenced by changing population composition although it can be influenced by changes in the distribution of marriages by duration. For example, a population with many recent marriages may have a higher general divorce rate because divorce rates are higher for new marriages. The general divorce rate is less often reported than the crude divorce rate because it requires estimation of the number of married women in the population.

In the United States, the crude divorce rate in 1998 was 4.2 per 1000, down from a peak of 5.2 per 1000 in 1980 but nearly double the rate observed in the 1950s. The general divorce rate was 19.5 per 1000 in 1996, slightly more than double the rate observed in the 1950s.

Age- and duration-specific measures of divorce can be used to estimate individual probabilities of divorce. For example, the above-cited estimate that 1 of every 2 first marriages in the United States ends in divorce is calculated by constructing a nuptiality table (analogous to a life table) from marital-duration-specific divorce rates. Estimation of duration-specific rates can be difficult to because it requires counts of marital duration not only for couples that divorce, but also those that remain intact. To calculate such refined rates, data from sample surveys, rather than data from censuses or national registration systems, are often used.

In Europe, a period measure called the total divorce rate, applying to a synthetic (cross-sectional) lifetime, is sometimes reported. This rate, in the same manner as the total fertility rate or the total first marriage rate, sums the age-specific divorce rates (divorces per woman, either married or unmarried) at a given time. This measure is informative but, like the general divorce rate, can be influenced by variations in the population at risk.

In the United States the collection of detailed divorce certificate data was discontinued by the federal government as a cost-savings measure and because the information provided by reporting states was incomplete. Thus, apart from the aggregate rates, most of what is known about divorce differentials and trends is inferred from sample surveys with retrospective marital histories, like the Census Bureau's Current Population Survey or the Survey of Income Program Participation.

As long-term cohabitation increases, which is the case especially in Western Europe, divorce rates alone give an increasingly incomplete picture of actual separation levels.

See also: *Cohabitation; Family: Future; Family Demography; Marriage.*

BIBLIOGRAPHY

Becker, Gary. 1991. *A Treatise on the Family,* enlarged edition. Cambridge, MA: Harvard University Press.

Cherlin, Andrew J. 1992. *Marriage, Divorce, Remarriage,* 2nd edition. Cambridge, MA: Harvard University Press.

Clarke, Sally C. 1995. "Advance Report of Final Divorce Statistics, 1989 and 1990." *Monthly Vital Statistics Report* 43(9).

Goldstein, Joshua R. 1999. "The Leveling of Divorce in the United States." *Demography* 36(3): 409–414.

McLanahan, Sarah, and Gary Sandefur. 1994. *Growing Up with a Single Parent.* Cambridge, MA: Harvard University Press.

Preston, Samuel H., and John McDonald. 1979. "The Incidence of Divorce within Cohorts of American Marriages Contracted since the Civil War." *Demography* 16: 1–25.

Schoen, Robert, and Nicola Standish. 2001. "The Retrenchment of Marriage: Results from Marital Status Life Tables for the United States, 1995." *Population and Development Review* 27(3): 553–563.

United States Census Bureau. 2001. *Statistical Abstract of the United States: 2001.* Washington, D.C.: US Government Printing Office.

JOSHUA R. GOLDSTEIN

DUMONT, ARSÈNE

(1849–1902)

Arsène Dumont studied law and, after reading the results of the 1880 French census, resolved to devote his life to the study of the causes of low fertility, or, in his preferred formulation, depopulation. Dumont never married or held an official position and supported his research with personal resources in the forlorn hope of obtaining a university position. His closest professional affiliation was with the French anthropological society. When his wealth was exhausted, he committed suicide.

Although Dumont resorted to official statistics to describe fertility and mortality as immediate causes of low population growth, his originality consisted in using an ethnographic approach to probe for its psychological and social causes. His method involved evaluating the moral climate of village communities in various regions of France rather than looking at individual behavior. He would describe features of the environment, local production and occupations, and the appearance and lifestyle of the inhabitants and use that information to interpret their reproductive behavior and test various theories. The village ethnologies thus assembled served as raw material for three books in which Dumont presented his theory on the causes of fertility decline. The best known of these works was *Dépopulation et Civilisation* (1890).

Dumont rejected the eugenic theories of his day, which attributed low fertility to biological mechanisms. The pursuit of "individual idealism" in democratic societies, in which men could climb the social ladder and improve their standard of living, was the mechanism leading to fertility decline. Dumont used the arresting metaphor of "social capillarity" to describe that phenomenon. In the same way that oil ascends the wick of a lamp, molecule by molecule, to burn and produce light, the social matter climbs, individual by individual, toward the higher life of art, politics, and science, and in this process children represent an impediment. If democratic societies wanted to survive, they had to control this socially destructive process.

Dumont was visualizing a balance between the benefits of modern life and their deleterious effects on reproduction. An objective of policy would be a birthrate of twenty-five per thousand and three births per marriage, close to replacement-level fertility in the prevailing mortality conditions. Local economic development would stimulate fertility and discourage migration to the cities.

Although his views were not popular in his time, Dumont influenced subsequent demographers, including the British social historian Joseph A. Banks, who applied the notion of social capillarity to the tendency of the middle classes in Britain to reduce the size of their families so that their children could rise on the social scale.

See also: *Population Thought, History of; Social Mobility.*

BIBLIOGRAPHY

Banks, Joseph A. 1954. *Prosperity and Parenthood: A Study of Family Planning among the Victorian Middle Classes.* London: Routledge & Kegan Paul.

Dumont, Arsène. 1890. *Dépopulation et Civilisation: Étude Démographique.* Paris: Lecrosnier et Babé. Reissued, with a biographical and critical introduction by André Béjin. Paris: Economica, 1990.

———. 1898. *Natalité et Démocratie: Conférences Faites à l'École d'Anthropologie de Paris.* Paris: Schleicher.

———. 1901. *La Morale Basée sur la Démographie.* Paris: Schleicher Fréres.

ETIENNE VAN DE WALLE

E

EASTERLIN, RICHARD A.

(1926–)

Born in Ridgefield Park, New Jersey, American economist, demographer, and economic historian Richard A Easterlin received a degree in mechanical engineering from the Stevens Institute of Technology in 1945, and a Ph.D. in economics from the University of Pennsylvania in 1953. He was drawn into demography through participation in a project conducted from 1953 to 1956 on population redistribution and economic growth with economist Simon Kuznets and demographer Dorothy Thomas. Easterlin's association with Kuznets was also the impetus for his interest in empirical research, and his concern with understanding real world situations, both of which are evident in all of his work.

Easterlin spent nearly 30 years as a faculty member at the University of Pennsylvania, where he was William R. Kenan Jr. Professor of Economics from 1978 to 1982, before moving to the University of Southern California to become University Professor in the department of economics. He is a Fellow of the American Academy of Arts and Sciences, and a member of the National Academy of Sciences. He has been president of the Population Association of America (PAA) (1978) and of the Economic History Association (1979–1980).

Easterlin's 1978 presidential address to the PAA, which was titled "What Will 1984 Be Like? Socioeconomic Implications of Recent Twists in Age Structure," was the first comprehensive presentation of what came to be known as the *Easterlin Hypothesis*—the proposition that the relative size of a birth cohort determines the labor market outcome of its members, which in turn has repercussions on a host of other socioeconomic characteristics including fertility, creating the potential for continuing fluctuations in the relative size of birth cohorts. The hypothesis has stimulated a large amount of empirical research both in the United States and Europe, in efforts to confirm or refute it. The results appear to provide some support for his hypothesis, but suggest that institutional factors and period effects might ameliorate the impact of changing relative cohort size, reducing the likelihood of continuing regular fluctuations. In addition, some work suggests that the mediating link between relative cohort size and income might be more complex than that envisioned in the original Easterlin hypothesis. In an extension of this work, Easterlin has made significant contributions to research on preference formation, suggesting that the life cycle trend in average happiness is flat because aspirations vary with level of income.

The possibility of fertility cycles deriving from the relative economic status of successive cohorts is of major interest to demographers. Easterlin is also well known in demography for developing, in collaboration with his wife, demographer Eileen Crimmins, a comprehensive framework for analyzing social and economic aspects of fertility transition in terms of the demand for children, the "supply" of children, and the cost of fertility control. This supply/demand or synthesis framework, often referred to as the Easterlin-Crimmins model, has become for many researchers an accepted way of categorizing fertility variables.

See also: *Cycles, Population; Economic-Demographic Models; Kuznets, Simon; Population Thought, Contemporary.*

BIBLIOGRAPHY

SELECTED WORKS BY RICHARD A. EASTERLIN.

Easterlin, Richard A. 1968. *Population, Labor Force, and Long Swings in Economic Growth.* New York: Columbia University Press.

———. 1978."What Will 1984 Be Like? Socioeconomic Implications of Recent Twists in Age Structure." *Demography* 15: 397–432.

———. 1987. *Birth and Fortune: The Impact of Numbers on Personal Welfare,* 2nd edition. Chicago: University of Chicago Press.

———. 1987. "Easterlin Hypothesis." In *The New Palgrave: A Dictionary of Economics,* ed. John Eatwell, Murray Milgate, and Peter Newman. New York: The Stockton Press.

———. 1987. "Fertility." In *The New Palgrave: A Dictionary of Economics,* ed. John Eatwell, Murray Milgate, and Peter Newman. New York: The Stockton Press.

———. 1996. *Growth Triumphant: The Twentieth Century in Historical Perspective.* Ann Arbor, MI: University of Michigan Press.

———. 1999. "How Beneficent is the Market? A Look at the Modern History of Mortality." *European Review of Economic History* 3(3): 257–294.

———. 2001. "Income and Happiness: Towards a Unified Theory." *Economic Journal* 111(473): 465–484.

Easterlin, Richard A., and Eileen M. Crimmins. 1985. *The Fertility Revolution: A Supply-Demand Analysis.* Chicago: University of Chicago Press.

SELECTED WORKS ABOUT RICHARD A. EASTERLIN.

Blaug, Mark, ed. 1986. *Who's Who in Economics: A Biographical Dictionary of Major Economists 1700–1986,* 2nd edition. Cambridge, MA: MIT Press.

DIANE J. MACUNOVICH

ECOLOGICAL PERSPECTIVES ON POPULATION

Human population size profoundly influences the state of the environment, which in turn has sweeping effects on human vital rates, as well as on the health, standards of living, and personal satisfaction of individual human beings. For most of the approximately five million years of human history, populations exerted mostly local and reversible influence on the environment. But beginning with the agricultural revolution some 10,000 years ago, that changed dramatically.

Human Domination of the Biosphere

From about 1850 to 2002, the human population increased some five-fold and consumption per person about four-fold. The scale of the human enterprise, then, has expanded roughly twenty-fold; as a result, *Homo sapiens* has become a truly global ecological force.

There is no significant area of the biosphere that has not been altered by human activities. Synthetic pesticides and radioactive materials from nuclear weapons tests have been dispersed globally, and humans have dramatically altered the distribution of key elements such as carbon and nitrogen throughout the land, atmosphere, and oceans. Only a few extremely deep parts of the ocean may still be relatively pristine. More obviously, humans have cut down forests, plowed plains, exterminated many species and populations, paved over large areas, and otherwise transformed most of the land surface. People have released a great variety of novel poisons into the environment, and have degraded oceans and most freshwater bodies by overfishing and pollution.

Ecosystems, Ecosystem Services, and Natural Capital

An ecosystem is defined simply as the community of organisms (plants, animals, microbes) that reside in a given area and the physical environment with which they interact. Human beings are always elements of the ecosystems in which they live, be it the ecosystem of a village, a city, a watershed, a region, a country, or the entire planet. Ecosystems supply human beings with the material basis of life, including food, water, oxygen, wood, energy sources, and metal ores. They also supply an array of indispensable "ecosystem services." These services include climate stabilization; provision of fresh water; control of floods; generation and replenishment of soils essential to agriculture and forestry; detoxification and disposal of wastes; recycling of nutrients; control of the majority of potential crop pests; pollination of crops; provision of forest products and seafoods; and maintenance of a vast genetic library from which humanity has already drawn its crop plants, domestic animals, and a critical portion of its medicines. In extracting benefits from ecosystems, humans also inevitably modify those ecosystems.

The organisms, soils, aquifers, ores, and other features of ecosystems can be thought of as "natural capital": a more fundamental ingredient of economic well-being than the human-made physical and human capital that modern economies so carefully evaluate and husband. The loss of natural capital is all too often irreversible on a time scale relevant to human societies.

Human Impacts on Ecosystem Services

Humans alter ecosystems not only by extracting materials and services from them but also by returning materials and energy (e.g., carbon dioxide, heat, other wastes, synthetic chemicals) to them. In the course of becoming the dominant animal on Earth, human beings also have destroyed outright many natural components of ecosystems through habitat destruction, overexploitation, and depletion, reducing the ability of many natural systems to supply goods and services in the future. On the positive side, the goods and services that are being extracted sustain, at least for the present, a population of more than 6 billion individuals.

A trade-off that is often ignored is the cost in ecosystem degradation that is often a counterpart to the benefits people derive from ecosystem services. Locally, destruction of a wetland may damage its waste disposal service to the degree that artificial treatment is required to protect people from polluted water. Paving over recharge areas may disrupt the flow of clean water into local wells, and overexploiting a local fishery may drive the resource to economic extinction—that is, to the level where harvesting is no longer worth the effort.

Regionally, deforestation of a watershed that formerly discharged a relatively constant surface flow of water may lead to a series of alternating droughts and floods. In Honduras, a combination of population growth and inequitable land tenure ar-rangements led to forest loss and numerous people living in areas lacking natural protection from floods. In 1998 Hurricane Mitch, an unusually severe storm, killed thousands of people and left hundreds of thousands more homeless in Honduras—illustrating the ecological principle that high population density can produce disproportionate per-capita impacts of climatic and other factors that on the surface might seem independent of demography.

There is a small but growing trend toward investing in the restoration of ecosystem assets. In another regional example, New York City's population growth required it to seek more and more distant water sources, and the city eventually developed the Catskill/Delaware Watershed as its main source. The watershed is 100 miles to the north of the city, and it originally supplied water of fabled purity. By the late 1980s, though, water quality had declined to the point where it no longer met Environmental Protection Agency (EPA) standards. The cause was itself indirectly connected with the growth and affluence of New York's population: Suburban sprawl and rising demands for recreation and second homes placed higher demands on the watershed. The city was faced with the choice of building costly new treatment facilities or controlling development in the watershed ecosystem. Economic analyses showed that controlling development for improving water quality would cost far less, even without taking into account the other benefits of preserving the watershed, and that was the solution chosen.

Globally, climate change—traceable primarily to the anthropogenic injection of greenhouse gases into the atmosphere, itself strongly correlated with both human population size and consumption of fossil fuels for energy—threatens to damage agricultural production in many areas, inundate low-lying coastal areas, and spread tropical diseases into temperate regions. Population-related global warming also endangers coral reefs through bleaching, and threatens the persistence of ecologically and economically important tropical reef fisheries.

Loss of biodiversity—the plants, animals, and microorganisms with which humanity shares Earth—is an important element in the degradation of ecosystems related to increasing human numbers. It is especially critical because losses of species diversity, including genetically diverse populations of those species, are irreversible. In addition, it is often very difficult to find substitutes that can play the same roles as the organisms that are gone, so that restoration of certain ecological services may be difficult or impossible. Areas of high biodiversity and high human population density frequently coincide, which puts the living parts of local ecosystems at risk.

Overexploitation and resulting degradation reduce the productivity of ecosystems. Major fisheries such as cod and Atlantic swordfish are threatened with economic extinction by overharvesting in response to growing demand, especially from increasingly affluent consumers. In poor countries, tropical forests and their precious stores of biodiversity are threatened with destruction by overexploitation for timber, combined with the need for farmland to feed growing populations.

Generally, the more people there are the more they extract from, emit pollutants into, and disrupt ecosystems. But numbers of people alone do not tell the whole story; how they behave also contributes to the resultant loss of ecosystem products and services. Environmental scientists generally divide that behavior into two factors: affluence (how much each person consumes on average) and technology, a complex factor that includes both the technologies of production and the sociopolitical and economic arrangements necessary for production and distribution to take place. This is the basis of the $I = PAT$ equation: **I**mpact on life-support systems is the product of **P**opulation size, **A**ffluence, and **T**echnology. The equation suggests that, from an ecological viewpoint, the worst problems of overpopulation are likely to be found not in populous poor nations like India and China, but in populous rich ones like the United States because of the latter's high levels of per-capita consumption.

It is important to note that, although population growth is an important driver of environmental deterioration, in some cases it is possible to ameliorate its impact. For instance, growing populations contributed to an increasing flow of chlorofluorocarbons (CFCs) into the atmosphere, threatening the destruction of the important ozone layer. But technological changes, entailing substituting less destructive chemicals for CFCs, largely removed the threat. However, in many other areas such as the provision of water to homes, industry, and agriculture, opportunities for substitution are more limited and often involve high costs. Locally, environmental outcomes are complicated by the existence of positive feedback involving population growth. As a favorable example, additional people moving into a forested area may supply capital to provide jobs that do not depend on logging, to install sewage treatment plants, and to take other measures that help protect the environment. The better conditions that result in turn attract more people, who (up to a point) may further improve conditions.

The Epidemiological Environment

The human epidemiological environment determines susceptibility to disease. It is shaped by a complex of biophysical, economic, sociocultural, and political factors in which the size and structure of the population are key variables. Demographic factors have been important in increasing susceptibility to epidemic disease. Many diseases require a certain host population size in order to maintain themselves; for instance, measles requires agglomerations of 200,000 to 500,000 in order to persist. The growing world population brings ever larger groups into contact with the animal reservoirs of pathogens potentially able to colonize *Homo sapiens*. This increases the probability that more HIV-like or "killer flu"-type epidemics will occur in the future.

Factors contributing to higher risks to public health include greater geographic mobility, urbanization (especially the growth of urban fringe settlements), large numbers of malnourished (and thus immune-compromised) people, declining water quality, misuse of antibiotics (leading to increasing problems with resistant pathogens), widespread distribution of recreational intravenous drugs with sharing of needles, and bioterrorism. While these risks are relatively well understood and advances in molecular biology should strengthen the human drug and vaccine armamentarium, and there is little question that the present perilous state of the epidemiological environment could be substantially improved despite the opposing effects of demographic pressures and mobility. Substantial advances, however, will require intensification of medical effort, especially better provision of public health services in developing nations.

Defining Overpopulation

Overpopulation (or population overshoot) is much discussed but rarely defined. From an ecological standpoint, the biophysical carrying capacity—that is, the maximum population size that can be long sustained under given technological capabilities—

has no direct connection to population density. Overpopulation may best be defined as occurring when the number of people is larger than can be supported over the long term by the flow of income from natural capital, since depletion of that capital will constrain future generations. There are complexities in this definition, such as accounting for depletion of nonrenewable resources (economists generally do this by considering possibilities for substitution) or gauging overpopulation for countries heavily involved in international trade, but more precision is rarely required. The basic point is that remaining somewhat below carrying capacity is essential in order to avoid excessive damage to ecosystems and thus reduce negative feedbacks from ecosystems to human populations. Where no such margin for error exists, the result too often is a "natural disaster" as exemplified by Hurricane Mitch's devastation in Honduras.

Population Structure

Population growth is not the only demographic factor important in the human impact on ecosystems. The age structure of the population and its spatial distribution can also be important. With population aging, for example, there is often a rising proportion of single-person households, with greater per capita demands on fuel. In southwestern China, for instance, the aging population requires more home heating than was required when the average age was lower, increasing the consumption of fuel-wood from disappearing forests. In many countries there is steady migration into coastal areas with damaging consequences for the marshes and mangroves that serve as nursery areas for many marine fishes, and, in the longer run, where people are increasingly vulnerable to sea-level rise. Urbanization and international migration also have ecosystem effects, which can be very complex.

Ecological Sustainability and Environmental Ethics

An important ecological issue is that of sustainability: whether supporting the human population today might limit the ability of future generations to sustain themselves. This raises complex questions. Some are technical: How much reliance can be placed on technological progress to find substitutes for the natural capital now being depleted? Other, more contentious questions are ethical: What are a population's obligations to future generations, given

that their reproductive decisions also influence the size of those generations? What duties of stewardship does the human population owe to other species and to the natural environment? Such questions are too rarely systematically explored.

The Scientific Consensus

The consensus of the scientific community on the interrelationship of demographics and the environment was well expressed in a 1993 statement by the world's scientific academies. This said, among many things:

> Throughout history and especially during the twentieth century, environmental degradation has primarily been a product of our efforts to secure improved standards of food, clothing, shelter, comfort, and recreation for growing numbers of people. The magnitude of the threat to the ecosystem is linked to human population size and resource use per person. Resource use, waste production and environmental degradation are accelerated by population growth. . . . As human numbers further increase, the potential for irreversible changes of far-reaching magnitude also increases. Indicators of severe environmental stress include the growing loss of biodiversity, increasing greenhouse gas emissions, increasing deforestation worldwide, stratospheric ozone depletion, acid rain, loss of topsoil, and shortages of water, food, and fuel-wood in many parts of the world. (National Academy of Sciences)

See also: *Carrying Capacity; Environmental Ethics; Environmental Impact, Human; Natural Resources and Population; Sustainable Development.*

BIBLIOGRAPHY

Daily, Gretchen C., ed. 1997. *Nature's Services: Societal Dependence on Natural Ecosystems.* Washington, D.C.: Island Press.

Daily, Gretchen C., and Paul. R. Ehrlich. 1996. "Global Change and Human Susceptibility to Disease." *Annual Review of Energy and the Environment* 21: 125–144.

Dasgupta, Partha. 2001. *Human Well-being and the Natural Environment.* Oxford, Eng.: Oxford University Press.

Ehrlich, Paul R., Anne H. Ehrlich, and John P. Holdren. 1977. *Ecoscience: Population, Resources, Environment.* San Francisco: W.H. Freeman and Co.

Ehrlich, Paul R., and John Holdren. 1971. "Impact of Population Growth." *Science* 171: 1212–1217.

Gleick, Peter H., ed. 1993. *Water in Crisis: A Guide to the World's Fresh Water Resources.* New York: Oxford University Press.

Heywood, Vernon H., ed. 1995. *Global Biodiversity Assessment.* Cambridge, Eng.: Cambridge University Press.

Holdren, John. 1991. "Population and the Energy Problem." *Population and Environment* 12: 231–255.

Holdren, John P., and Paul R. Ehrlich. 1974. "Human Population and the Global Environment." *American Scientist* 62: 282–292.

Jansson, AnnMari, Monica Hammer, Carl Folke, and Robert Costanza, eds. 1994. *Investing in Natural Capital: The Ecological Economics Approach to Sustainability.* Washington, D.C.: Island Press.

Liu, Jianguo, et al. 2001. "Ecological Degradation in Protected Areas: The Case of Wolong Nature Reserve for Giant Pandas." *Science* 292: 98–101.

McMichael, Anthony J. 2001. *Human Frontiers, Environments and Disease: Past Patterns, Uncertain Futures.* Cambridge, Eng.: Cambridge University Press.

Myers, Norman. 1991. *Population, Resources and the Environment: The Critical Challenges.* London: United Nations Population Fund.

National Academy of Sciences, USA. 1993. *A Joint Statement by Fifty-eight of the World's Scientific Academies. Population Summit of the World's Scientific Academies.* New Delhi, India: National Academy Press.

Pimm, Stuart L. 2001. *The World According to Pimm.* New York: McGraw-Hill.

Postel, Sandra L., Gretchen C. Daily, and Paul R. Ehrlich. 1996. "Human Appropriation of Renewable Fresh Water." *Science* 271: 785–788.

Vitousek, Peter M., Paul R. Ehrlich, Anne H. Ehrlich, and Pamela A. Matson. 1986. "Human Appropriation of the Products of Photosynthesis." *BioScience* 36: 368–373.

Vitousek, Peter M., Harold A. Mooney, Jane Lubchenco, and Jerome M. Melillo. 1997. "Human Domination of Earth's Ecosystems." *Science* 277: 494–499.

PAUL R. EHRLICH
ANNE H. EHRLICH

ECONOMIC-DEMOGRAPHIC MODELS

Economic-demographic models are designed to describe in formal terms the main effects of demographic change on economic activity and those of economic activity on demographic change. The goal of these models is to forecast how the linked population-economy system will evolve over time, provide insights into the effects of policy change, or both.

The attempt to understand how population processes interact with the economy was at the center of interest in the work of the classical economists, most notably T. R. Malthus (1766–1834), as well as Adam Smith (1723–1790), David Ricardo (1772–1823), and John Stuart Mill (1806–1873), although their theories seldom were expressed in terms of mathematical formulas. In the development of neoclassical economics through the first half of the twentieth century, consideration of such interactions was largely neglected. Subsequently, formal modeling of the mutual impact of demographic and economic variables received a strong impetus. This was in part the logical outcome of the novel ambition to construct comprehensive multivariate models of the workings of the economy and partly a result of the renewed post–World War II interest in the role of rapid population growth in the economic development of low-income countries. This entry discusses salient aspects of economic-demographic modeling efforts during the last few decades of the twentieth century.

Models of Developed Economies

Until the mid-1960s economic models were constructed principally to yield short-run forecasts. Because it was commonly believed that demographic effects were relatively unimportant in explaining variations in short-run economic activity, the models ignored demographic change, treating population as an exogenous variable. Similarly, economic effects were absent from demographic models because those models were concerned with long-run forecasts, time periods over which economic effects were considered unpredictable.

The first economic model to incorporate demography other than as an exogenous variable was the Brookings model of the U.S. economy, which was built in the 1960s. In this model population affected the labor market, which affected marriage and household formation, which in turn affected the economy through the nonbusiness construction sector. Population also affected government revenues and expenditures.

As described by Dennis Ahlburg, the next generation of models—mostly known by their abbreviated titles or institutional provenance, such as the Wharton, DRI, Chase, and Hickman-Coen models in the United States; the RDX and CANDIDE models in Canada; and the BACHUROO model in Australia—introduced fine-gauge age disaggregation in the production and consumption sectors. The DRI model introduced a highly elaborate demographic-economic system that forecast the size of consumer populations and the income available to those groups. The models also linked changes in age structure to changes in labor supply, unemployment, and wages.

In the late 1970s the Wharton model added an endogenous demographic sector that included births, marriage, divorce, work, and education as variables that affected and were affected by economic variables. The main linkages between the demographic sector and the economic model were income and labor force participation and household formation. Subsequently, the Wharton model introduced an endogenous demographic projection methodology so that it expressed the total fertility rate, migration rate, and life expectancy as functions of economic and demographic variables. These demographic variables in turn had effects throughout the economic model.

The main purpose of these models was short-run forecasting, but they also could give policymakers insights into the effects of policy changes without the need to carry out those changes. The usefulness of those simulations depended on the accuracy with which a model captured the economic and demographic structure of a country. Generally,

demographic change in these models had only a relatively modest effect on the aggregate rate of economic growth.

Economic-demographic models of this type continue to be refined and applied widely. For example, the San Diego Association of Governments employs a simultaneous nonlinear model to produce medium- to long-term (20-year) forecasts of 700 economic and demographic variables. The Netherlands Interdisciplinary Demographic Institute is modeling economic-demographic scenarios for Europe at the national and regional levels. The International Institute for Applied Systems Analysis has developed a multiregional economic-demographic model to simulate various long-run economic growth scenarios for Europe and assess the economic impacts of population aging.

Models of Developing Countries

Formal economic-demographic models for developing countries were designed to illuminate the interaction between population and other variables in the development process and evaluate the consequences of various policies on economic and demographic variables. The best known of these models is the pioneering model by Ansley Coale and Edgar Hoover of the Indian economy, whose findings were cited widely to justify government interventions to limit fertility. In this model economic growth essentially depends on the resources devoted to productive investments. Population growth has a negative impact on economic growth because it increases current consumption and welfare-type outlays at the expense of savings and productive investments. Two shortcomings of the model are that it assumes costless fertility and mortality reduction and omits labor from the production function. This means that population growth adds consumers but does not add producers. Omitting labor is defensible only for medium-term calculations, the period of 15 to 20 years during which a decline in the birthrate leaves the size of the population of labor force age unaffected.

Almost all the other early economic-demographic models of low-income countries agreed with the Coale-Hoover conclusion that rapid population growth slowed the pace of economic growth, although the mechanisms yielding that outcome varied. An exception was the model proposed by Julian Simon. Simon's model assumed that relatively rapid population growth produces strong economic growth, at least in the long run. Output in the model is a positive function of "social overhead capital" (better roads and communication, economies of scale in production, improved government and organization, and better health services). Social overhead capital in turn is a costless function of population growth; this is an important and questionable assumption. The significance of Simon's model is that it suggests that although the short-term impact of population growth may be negative, there may be more than compensating positive effects in the future. Thus, the net impact of population growth for various specified time horizons is an open empirical question.

Later models became larger and more complex. As discussed by Dennis Ahlburg, the Bachue series of models developed by the International Labour Organization contained multisectoral input-output submodels and treated population in a highly disaggregated way (by age, sex, location, and education). Those models endogenized the components of population change and determined both the level of employment and the size distribution of incomes across households. The Bachue models are intended to be long-term policy-oriented simulation models rather than short-term forecasting models.

Models of this type have had only a limited impact on policy analysis and planning because of their complexity, the often conflicting specifications of key economic-demographic relationships, very different empirical estimates of those relationships, and the fact that a single equation (the production function) often has a dominant impact on the properties of the model regardless of the specification of the rest of the model. (The strengths and weaknesses of these models are discussed in Brian Arthur and Geoffrey McNicoll's, Warren Sanderson's, and Ahlburg's works.)

In the 1990s a series of country-specific models was constructed that added environmental interactions to the economic-demographic system to produce population-development-environment (PDE) dynamic simulations. Only sectors considered important to a particular country are modeled in detail, and simplicity of specification is emphasized to aid comprehension of the user. Wolfgang Lutz, Alexia Prskawetz, and Sanderson discuss examples of these models.

Economic Growth Models

Interest in the determinants of economic growth, which was the motivation for some of the earliest neoclassical growth theories, resurfaced in the late 1980s with simple single-equation models that tried to explain relative rates of economic growth across countries. Economic growth was expressed as a function of economic, demographic, institutional, and other variables.

The dominant model in this so-called new growth theory comes from the work of Robert Barro and is derived from an extended version of the neoclassical growth model. It embodies the idea of conditional convergence: The lower the starting level of real per capita gross domestic product in relation to its long-term or steady-state level, the higher the predicted growth rate. The significance for demography is that the long-term growth rate can be affected by the growth rate of population and by other factors, such as the savings rate, that may be affected by demographic change.

Capital had always played a critical role in models of economic growth, and the new growth models broadened the concept of capital to include education and health. Economic growth depended on the relationship between the initial and target levels of output. The target level of output depended on government policies (including not only spending and tax rates but also the rule of law, the protection of property rights, and political freedom) and household behavior (savings, labor supply effort, fertility, and health). Geographic endowments such as a temperate climate and ecological conditions that impede the spread of diseases or favor cash crops also can affect economic growth directly or through their impact on institutions.

Barro estimated the basic model with data on a panel of about 100 countries from 1960 to 1990. He found that economic growth was higher the lower the fertility rate, the longer the life expectancy, and the higher the level of education. These arguments are similar to those of Coale and Hoover. Other determinants of growth were the maintenance of the rule of law, lower levels of government consumption, lower inflation, and improved terms of trade.

Allen Kelley and Robert Schmidt and others have extended the demographic specification of the basic growth model and explored the adjustment or transition to the long-run equilibrium. Those researchers argued that the impact of demography on economic growth was a function of the levels of fertility and mortality rates, the timing of changes in fertility and mortality, and the sensitivity of the economy to those changes. Differences in levels and timing can create significant shifts in the age structure of the population that can affect economic growth in addition to the direct effect of births and deaths. Disaggregating population change into its components and more fully specifying the dynamics allow the effect on economic growth to be positive, negative, or zero. Many earlier models did not allow such flexibility. Population size and density also appear in some of those models. A larger population can lead to economies of scale in the provision of roads, communication systems, research and development, and markets and institutions. Higher population densities can lead to lower per-unit costs and increased efficiency of investments, particularly in agriculture. The effects of population size and density have been found to vary considerably across countries.

Kelley and Schmidt developed several extended growth models with data from a panel of 86 countries for the period 1960–1995. (A single model could not suffice because of disagreement among economists on structural details.) They reached the qualified conclusion that declining fertility and mortality reinforce each other in encouraging economic growth. Because fertility and mortality declines necessarily offset each other in their effect on population growth, this finding underscores the importance of distinguishing the components of population change rather than using population growth as a single variable. It also illustrates the importance of specifying the dynamics of the effect of demography on economic growth (current high fertility decreases growth, but fertility lagged by a generation increases growth). Kelley and Schmidt also found small positive effects of population size and density.

The "Demographic Gift"

The effect of changes in age structure on economic growth, a relationship treated in the Coale-Hoover model, was investigated further by researchers in the 1990s. Coale and Hoover had argued that high fertility resulted in a high youth dependency rate that depressed aggregate savings rates and thus economic growth. However, this is just the initial phase of the changes in age structure that accompany the demographic transition. The ratio of the population of labor force age to total population is low when fertility is high, rises as declining fertility lowers child dependency, and eventually falls as population aging sets in. The second phase of this shift is a period in which the demands the population makes on resources are relatively low but the economic contributions (through work, savings, and investments) are potentially great. The resulting (potential) impetus on economic growth has been referred to as the "demographic gift" or "demographic bonus."

David Bloom and Jeffrey Williamson found that the rate of economic growth rose faster as the ratio of the working-age population to the total population rose. Although the exact mechanisms by which this effect occurs are unclear, it seems that changes in the age structure are associated with shifts from unpaid work to paid work, increased health and education of workers, and increases in savings and capital accumulation.

Ronald Lee, Andrew Mason, and Tim Miller showed that during the demographic gift period savings and wealth can increase faster, spurring economic growth because of favorable shifts in the age structure and changes in life expectancy and total fertility. In a case study of Taiwan they found that as much as one-half of the increase in savings rates was due to demographic factors. Other studies investigated the influence of demographic change on the "economic miracle" of East Asia in the 1980s and early 1990s and concluded that the demographic gift caused one-quarter to one-third of the rapid economic growth that took place.

The conclusion that can be drawn from this event is that under the right conditions it is possible for a rapid demographic transition to generate large increases in savings and wealth that can stimulate economic growth. It appears that the "demographic gift" of rapidly falling fertility and mortality can translate into higher economic growth if there are supportive policies, markets, and institutions. The practical challenge indicated by the modeling is to bring about conditions that will convert the "gift" into the reality of economic growth.

See also: *Development, Population and; Intergenerational Transfers; Microeconomics of Demographic Behavior; Migration Models; Simon, Julian L.; Simulation Models.*

BIBLIOGRAPHY

Acemoglu, Daron, Simon Johnson, and James Robinson. 2001. "The Colonial Origins of Comparative Development." *American Economic Review* 91: 1369–1401.

Ahlburg, Dennis A. 1987a. "The Impact of Population Growth on Economic Growth in Developing Nations: The Evidence from Macroeconomic-Demographic Models." In *Population Growth and Economic Development: Issues and Evidence,* ed. D. Gale Johnson and Ronald D. Lee. Madison: University of Wisconsin Press.

———. 1987b. "Modeling Economic-Demographic Linkages: A Study of National and Regional Models." In *Forecasting in the Social and Natural Sciences,* ed. Kenneth C. Land and Stephen H. Schneider. Dortrecht, the Netherlands: D. Reidel.

Arthur, W. Brian, and Geoffrey McNicoll. 1975. "Large-Scale Simulation Models in Population and Development: What Use to Planners?" *Population and Development Review* 1: 251–265.

Barro, Robert J. 1997. *Determinants of Economic Growth.* Cambridge, MA: MIT Press.

Bloom, David, and Jeffrey G. Williamson. 1998. "Demographic Transitions and Economic Miracles in Emerging Asia." *World Bank Economic Review* 12: 419–455.

Coale, Ansley J., and Edgar M. Hoover. 1958. *Population Growth and Economic Development in Low-Income Countries.* Princeton, NJ: Princeton University Press.

Kelley, Allen C., and Robert M. Schmidt. 2001. "Economic and Demographic Change: A Synthesis of Models, Findings, and Perspectives." In *Population Matters: Demographic Change, Economic Growth, and Poverty in the Developing World,* ed. Nancy Birdsall, Allen C. Kelley, and Steven W. Sinding. Oxford: Oxford University Press.

Lee, Ronald D., Andrew Mason, and Tim Miller. 2001. "Saving, Wealth, and Population." In *Population Matters: Demographic Change, Economic Growth, and Poverty in the Developing World,* ed. Nancy Birdsall, Allen C. Kelley, and Steven W. Sinding. Oxford: Oxford University Press.

Lutz, Wolfgang, ed. 1994. *Population-Development-Environment: Understanding Their Interactions in Mauritius.* Berlin: Springer-Verlag.

Lutz, Wolfgang, Alexia Prskawetz, and Warren C. Sanderson, eds. 2002. *Population and Environment: Methods of Analysis.* Supplement to *Population and Development Review,* Vol. 28.

MacKellar, Landis, and Tatiana Ermolieva. 1999. "The IIASA Social Security Reform Project Multiregional Economic-Demographic Growth Model: Policy Background and Algebraic Structure." Interim Report IR-99-007. Laxenburg, Austria: International Institute for Applied Systems Analysis.

Sanderson, Warren C. 1980. *Economic-Demographic Simulation Models: A Review of the Usefulness for Policy Analysis.* Laxenburg, Austria: International Institute for Applied Systems Analysis.

San Diego Association of Governments. 1993. *DEFM Forecast 1993 to 2015.* Volume 1: *Model Overview.* San Diego, CA: San Diego Association of Governments.

Simon, Julian L. 1977. *The Economics of Population Growth.* Princeton, NJ: Princeton University Press.

DENNIS AHLBURG

ECONOMICS OF POPULATION

See *Cost of Children; Development, Population and; Economic-Demographic Models; Family Allowances; Family Bargaining; Immigration, Benefits and Costs of; Microeconomics of Demographic Behavior.*

EDUCATION

In the last part of the nineteenth century, the enforcement of compulsory schooling laws in most countries of Europe and in North America made school participation universal for all children. Starting in the early twentieth century, the United States led the way towards mass schooling at the secondary level with roughly 50 percent of young people earning high school diplomas by the 1940s. Susan Cotts Watkins, an American sociologist, in her study of the demographic integration of Europe from 1870 to 1960, identifies schooling as the most important aspect of nation building, particularly because of the enforcement of a national language. Since the end of World War II and the subsequent transition to nationhood of many former colonies, the spread of mass formal schooling has become a global phenomenon.

Progress towards mass formal schooling can be measured by examining changes in the educational distribution of the adult population or by looking at trends in the enrollment and attainment of the current school-age population. Figure 1 depicts trends from 1960 to 2000 in the percent of the adult population completing at least primary school, and in the percent of the adult population completing at least some secondary education, by region, as calculated by Robert J. Barro and Jong-Wha Lee in 2000, using data from censuses with intercensal adjustments based on net enrollment data. Dramatic progress has been recorded in all regions from a very low base in most of the developing world. As of 2000, while only 43 percent of the population in developing countries had completed at least a primary education, over 70 percent of these go on to attain some secondary education, which represents roughly one-third of the adult population. By contrast roughly 85 percent of adults living in advanced or transitional economies have completed primary school and the vast majority of these go on to at least some secondary education. Accompanying this growth in educational attainment has been a narrowing of the gender gap.

Despite progress, large gaps remain in primary and secondary enrollment rates both between regions and within regions of the developing world. In some cases past rates of growth have declined or been reversed in recent years. Sub-Saharan Africa remains a conspicuous laggard. Despite impressive growth in the early post-colonial period, as of 2000, no more than a quarter of the adult population in sub-Saharan Africa had completed primary school. Economic slowdowns in many countries of that region in the 1980s and 1990s have been linked with a stalling of past economic growth and in some cases actual declines in enrollments among the current school age population. Boys have been particularly affected.

Trends in the enrollment among school age populations are more difficult to measure and compare because of the well known inaccuracies of United Nations Educational, Scientific and Cultural Organization enrollment data that are based on Ministry of Education reports that are often exaggerated. Figure 2, which is based on 1990s household survey data from 41 developing countries participating in the Demographic and Health Surveys, the majority in Sub-Saharan Africa, shows the range of primary completion rates currently prevalent within each of the developing regions for young people aged 20 to 24. In all regions, there are some countries that have achieved close to universal primary completion rates. However the ranges are wide in each region and especially so in Africa. Among the 24 sub-Saharan African countries with data for the 1990's, the median value for primary completion rates is no more than one-third of the population aged 20 to 24.

The Consequences of Education for Demographic Outcomes

A great amount of empirical evidence, reviewed by Shireen Jejeebhoy in 1999, has documented the strong statistical association at the individual level between the number of grades (or levels) of schooling attained (particularly for women) and various subsequent demographic outcomes including the age of marriage, the number of births, child health and mortality, and children's educational attainment. There are various hypotheses as to the causal forces underlying this relationship but no definitive findings. The relationship could be explained by the following:

1. The increased knowledge and skills acquired in school;

2. The status it confers on those who receive it;

3. Its effect on participation and on potential earnings in the labor market (and by extension the opportunity costs associated with high fertility); and/or

4. By its effects on personal autonomy and agency, particularly in the case of girls and young women.

A 1999 U.S. National Research Council report, *Critical Perspectives on Schooling and Fertility in the Developing World*, found no clear answers. Indeed, with reference to hypothesis 4 above, other research points to the conservative nature of schooling as a socializing agent, particularly for girls, suggesting the possibility that schooling could reinforce existing

FIGURE 1

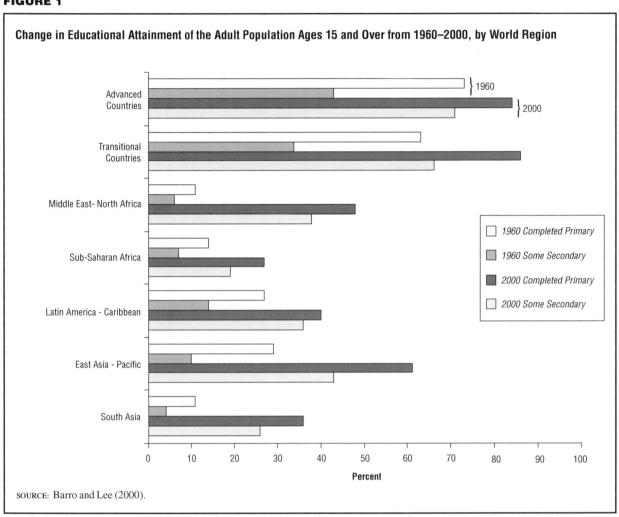

Change in Educational Attainment of the Adult Population Ages 15 and Over from 1960–2000, by World Region

SOURCE: Barro and Lee (2000).

gender hierarchies rather than enhancing gender equity. Nonetheless, policy makers have concluded from the empirical evidence that investments in girls' schooling have high social and economic returns.

A different interpretation of the relationships between schooling and demographic outcomes is based on exploring the societal forces that trigger the fertility transition, or what some economists call the *quantity-quality transition* during which families decrease fertility and increase their investments in children. There is clear historical evidence that the enforcement of compulsory schooling laws and the spread of state power through national schooling systems using a common language and curriculum were key forces in reducing the demographic diversity prevalent in Europe in the mid-nineteenth century and in triggering the onset of European fertility

transitions. In 1980, Australian demographer John C. Caldwell theorized that the arrival of mass formal schooling in developing countries would also serve as a trigger for the demographic transition, particularly if it involved both boys and girls and particularly if it involved socialization in Western middle class values. A recent review of the evidence in Africa by Lloyd, Kaufman and Hewett (2000) provides strong empirical support for this relationship. Further evidence at the country level comes from in-depth case studies in Nepal and Pakistan in which data collected at the community level show the positive effect of school availability on contraceptive use, even when the parents themselves have no formal education.

Once begun, the quantity-quality transition can be self-propelling. Although there is a natural tendency for rates of return to education to decline as

FIGURE 2

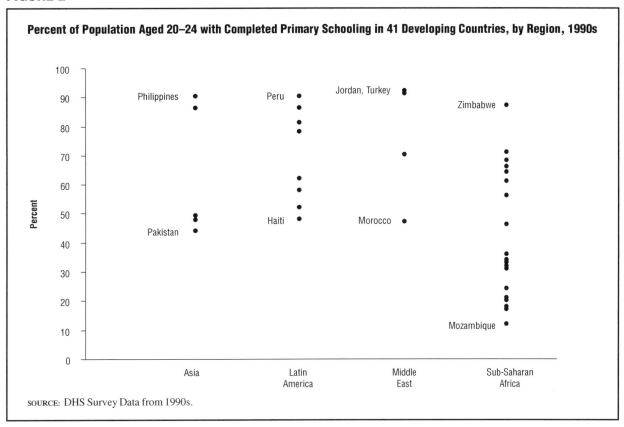

Percent of Population Aged 20–24 with Completed Primary Schooling in 41 Developing Countries, by Region, 1990s

SOURCE: DHS Survey Data from 1990s.

more children are educated, evidence from many Asian countries examined by Mark R. Montgomery, Mary Arends-Kuenning and Cem Mete in 2000 shows that this effect can be counteracted by beneficial macroeconomic changes resulting from increases in trade, physical capital, and technology, thus sustaining the quantity-quality transition.

Policy Implications

Educational opportunities of children are harmed by having many siblings in the home. The evidence for this, reviewed by economist Cynthia B. Lloyd in 1994, shows the disadvantage to children from large families to be greater in contexts where schooling is available but not fully subsidized by the state and where family support networks are confined to biological parents and their children. Furthermore, the negative consequences are particularly felt by girls, leading to intra-familial inequality in schooling levels among children in the same family.

Further research has explored the effects of unwanted fertility on investments in children's schooling in a range of developing country settings and has found that in the "middle to latter phases of a fertility transition, the positive effects of mother's education on children's education are likely to be reinforced by reductions in the incidence in unintended or excess fertility" (Montgomery and Lloyd, p. 249). Thus differences between families in their ability to achieve their fertility preferences will lead to intra-familial as well inter-familial inequalities in schooling outcomes.

Evidence of significant differences in enrollment rates across income or socioeconomic groups in a variety of different settings lends support to a variety of anti-poverty policy interventions in developing countries to reduce the costs to parents of sending their children to school as a means of increasing enrollments and achievement. Preliminary evidence suggests very positive short-term effects of such interventions.

While much has been learned about the familial determinants of enrollment and attainment, much less is known about the school factors—quality and content of instruction, degree of crowding, character of physical plant—that may also play a role. In 1996,

David Card and Alan Krueger suggested this as a promising avenue for future research. They contend that it is "unclear whether this relationship [between school quality and educational attainment] results because students respond to the economic incentives created by a rise in the return to schooling [because of better quality] or because they find it more enjoyable to attend schools with smaller classes or better-paid teachers" (Card and Krueger, p. 123). Thus, they hint at the possibility that attitudes towards school and schooling may be another pathway of influence between school quality and grades attained besides cognitive competencies—a pathway that has been shown in numerous studies on school effectiveness to be positively affected by certain school quality factors such as time to learn, material resources, and the quality of teaching.

In less-developed countries where enrollment even at the primary level is far from universal, the potential implications of school quality for educational attainment are profound. Indeed, a major vehicle through which school quality may affect cognitive competencies, earnings and subsequent demographic outcomes is through its impact on retention and educational attainment. Only a few studies in Ghana, Kenya, and Egypt have explored this relationship. There is some intriguing evidence that parents may be highly sensitive to visible changes in school quality in choosing between schools when school choice is available.

A review of the large and growing body of literature indicates various gaps in data and research: (1) comparable population-based data on enrollment, progression, and grade attainment by age and sex for all countries in the world; (2) longitudinal studies of the pathways through which educational attainment affects subsequent adult decisions relating to the timing of marriage, the size of the family, and investments in children as well as child rearing practices that affect children's health and mortality and their subsequent progress in school; and (3) longitudinal studies of the effect of specific elements of school quality on progression to higher levels of schooling, transitions into the labor market and into marriage, and subsequent parental decision-making about fertility, childrearing, and investments in children's education.

Study of the education-demographic nexus is also becoming of increasing relevance in the high-income countries. Rising rates of return in the labor market to higher education (not only in absolute terms but also differentially) for both men and women have resulted in a steady rise in the proportion of the population with post-secondary schooling. For example, the 2000 U.S. census results show that the percentage of people 25 to 29 years old completing college has risen to 29 percent—its highest level ever—with the completion rates of young women now slightly exceeding those of young men. The resulting increases in labor force participation of women even after marriage and childbearing in response to rising rates of return in the labor market have led to dramatic changes in the family, including delayed child bearing, increasing rates of childlessness, higher divorce rates, greater rates of female hardship, and larger proportions of dual career couples observed in most industrialized countries.

See also: *Adolescent Fertility; Fertility, Below-Replacement; Fertility Transition, Socioeconomic Determinants of; Literacy.*

BIBLIOGRAPHY

Barro, Robert J., and Jong-Wha Lee. 2000. "International Data on Educational Attainment: Updates and Implications," CID Working Paper No 42. Cambridge, MA: Center for International Development, Harvard University.

Bledsoe, Caroline H., John B. Casterline, Jennifer A. Johnson-Kuhn, and John G. Haaga, eds. 1999. *Critical Perspectives on Schooling and Fertility in the Developing World.* Washington, D.C.: National Academy Press.

Caldwell, John C. 1980. "Mass Education as a Determinant of the Timing of Fertility Decline." *Population and Development Review* 6(2): 225–255.

Card, David, and Alan Krueger. 1996. "Labor Market Effect of School Quality: Theory and Evidence." In *Does Money Matter? The Effect of School Resources on Student Achievement and Adult Success,* ed. G. Burtless. Washington, D.C.: Brookings Institution.

Filmer, Deon, and Lant Pritchett. 1999. "The Effect of Household Wealth on Educational Attainment: Evidence from 35 Countries." *Population and Development Review* 25(1): 85–110.

Jejeebhoy, Shireen J. 1995. *Women's Education, Autonomy and Reproductive Behaviour; Experience from Developing Countries.* Oxford, Eng.: Clarendon Press.

Kremer, Michael, Sylvie Moulin, David Myatt, and Robert Namunyu. 1997. "Textbooks, Class Size and Test Scores: Evidence from a Prospective evaluation in Kenya," IPR Working Paper Series.

Lloyd, Cynthia B. 1994. "Investing in the Next Generation: The Implications of High Fertility at the Level of the Family." In *Population and Development: Old Debates, New Conclusions,* ed. Robert Cassen. Washington D.C.: Overseas Development Council.

Lloyd, Cynthia B., Carol E. Kaufman, and Paul Hewett. 2000. "The Spread of Primary Schooling in Sub-Saharan Africa: Implications of Fertility Change." *Population and Development Review* 26(3): 483–515.

Meyer, John W., Francisco O. Ramirez, and Yasemin N. Soysal. 1992. "World Expansion of Mass Education, 1987–1980." *Sociology of Education* 65(2): 128–149.

Montgomery, Mark R., Mary Arends-Kuenning, and Cem Mete. 2000. "The Quantity-quality Transition in Asia." *Population and Economic Change in East Asia,* ed. C.Y. Cyrus Chu and Ronald Lee, Supp. to *Population and Development Review* 26: 223–256.

Montgomery, Mark R., and Cynthia B. Lloyd. 1999. "High Fertility, Unwanted Fertility, and Children's Schooling." In *Critical Perspectives on Schooling and Fertility in the Developing World,* ed. Caroline Bledsoe, John B. Casterline, Jennifer A. Johnson-Kuhn, and John G. Haaga. Washington, D.C.: National Academy Press.

Summers, Lawrence H. 1994. "Investing in All the People; Educating Women in Developing Countries." EDI Seminar Paper No 45.

Watkins, Susan Cotts. 1991. *From Provinces into Nations: Demographic Integration in Western Europe, 1970–1960.* Princeton, NJ: Princeton University Press.

Cynthia B. Lloyd

EMERGING INFECTIOUS DISEASES

Emerging infectious diseases are those that have newly appeared in the human population or are rapidly increasing in incidence (number of cases) or geographic range. As with the periodically reported outbreaks of Ebola (a viral hemorrhagic fever with high mortality) in Africa, emerging infectious diseases may seem mysterious and dramatic, but in fact specific factors responsible for their emergence can be identified (Table 1). The emergence of an infectious disease can be seen as a two step process—introduction and establishment/dissemination—that these factors precipitate or promote in one, or both, phases. HIV/AIDS, Ebola, and hemolytic uremic syndrome (caused by certain strains of the bacterium *Escherichia coli* in food or water) are among the notable infectious diseases that were first identified in the latter decades of the twentieth century. Others, such as influenza, reappear periodically causing major epidemics or even pandemics (epidemics that affect the entire world). With increasing globalization and geographic mobility of populations, each part of the world is now vulnerable to infections that might first arise in any other part.

Introduction of Infectious Disease

In analyzing infections that have emerged, it is apparent that many diseases existed in nature before gaining access to the human population, often as a result of changed ecological or environmental conditions that placed humans in contact with previously inaccessible pathogens or the natural hosts that carry them. The term *viral traffic* (or, more generally, microbial traffic) was coined to represent processes involving the access, introduction, or dissemination of existing pathogens to new host populations. Ecological changes and major demographic changes (such as population migrations) often precipitate emergence. Many of these changes are anthropogenic. Infections transmitted by mosquitoes, which include malaria, dengue, yellow fever, West Nile fever, Rift Valley fever, and many others, are often stimulated by the presence of dams, irrigation projects, or open water storage since mosquitoes breed in water.

In terms of the introduction phase, examples of infections originating as zoonoses (infections transmissible from animals to humans) suggest that the *zoonotic pool*—introductions of pathogens from

TABLE 1

Factors in the Emergence of Infectious Diseases

Factor	Examples of specific factors	Examples of diseases
Ecological changes (including those due to economic development and land use)	Agriculture; dams, changes in water ecosystems; deforestation/reforestation; flood/drought; famine; climate changes	Schistosomiasis (dams); Rift Valley fever (dams, irrigation); Argentine hemorrhagic fever (agriculture); Hantaan (Korean hemorrhagic fever) (agriculture); Hantavirus pulmonary syndrome, southwestern US, 1993 (weather anomalies)
Human demographics, behavior	Societal events: Population growth and migration (movement from rural areas to cities); war or civil conflict; economic impoverishment; urban decay; factors in human behavior such as: sexual behavior (including urban prostitution and "sex-for-drugs"); intravenous drug use; diet; outdoor recreation; use of child care facilities (high-density settings)	Introduction of HIV; spread of dengue; spread of HIV and other sexually transmitted diseases
International travel and commerce	Worldwide movement of goods and people; air travel	Dissemination of HIV; dissemination of mosquito vectors such as Aedes albopictus (Asian tiger mosquito); ratborne hantaviruses, intoduction of cholera into South America, dissemination of 0139 (non-O1) cholera organism (ships)
Technology and Industry	Food production: Globalization of food supplies; changes in food processing and packaging; Health care: New medical devices; organ or tissue transplantation; drugs causing immunosuppression; widespread use of antibiotics	Food processing: Hemolytic uremic syndrome (E. coli contamination of hamburger meat), bovine spongiform encephalopathy; Health care: Contaminated injection equipment (Ebola, HIV); Transfusion associated hepatitis (hepatitis B, C); opportunistic infections in immunosuppressed patients; Creutzfeldt-Jakob disease from contaminated batches of human growth hormone (medical technology)
Microbial adaptation and change	Microbial evolution, response to selection in environment	Changes in virulence and toxin production; development of drug resistance (antimicrobial resistant bacteria, chloroquine resistant malaria); "antigenic drift" in influenza virus
Breakdown in public health measures	Curtailment or reduction in prevention programs; lack of, or inadequate, sanitation and vector control measures	Resurgence of tuberculosis in United States; cholera in refugee camps in Africa; resurgence of diphtheria in former Soviet republics

Note: Categories are not mutually exclusive; several factors may contribute to emergence of a disease.

SOURCE: Morse, S.S. (1995).

other species—is an important and potentially rich source of emerging pathogens or their precursors, some of which might become successful under conditions that favor transfer to human hosts. HIV is a possible case of such transfer. Although the original ancestors of HIV-1 are not known with certainty, the best current evidence suggests that HIV-1 originated as a zoonotic introduction, possibly from chimpanzees; this may have occurred several times. There is somewhat better evidence for a probable zoonotic origin as regards HIV-2 (another lentivirus that causes AIDS), with the sooty mangabey monkey the likely source. As an illustrative example, an infected man, identified in rural Liberia, had a strain of HIV-2 that closely resembled viruses taken from the sooty mangabey monkey, the presumed reservoir of

a virus with a close ancestral connection to HIV-2. That such individuals can be identified suggests that zoonotic introductions of viruses such as HIV may well occur from time to time in isolated populations, and probably often escape notice. In the case of HIV-1, key factors in its success after introduction were the social and demographic changes in the last half of the twentieth century (such as migration to cities) that gave the virus access to a larger population, and other social changes (e.g., drug-related use of contaminated injection equipment, growth of the commercial sex trade) that allowed more facile transmission of the virus to new individuals despite its relatively low natural transmissibility.

Although it is common to think of infectious diseases as causing acute outbreaks, at the beginning of the twenty-first century there is increasing recognition that infections can also be the cause of chronic diseases. Hepatitis B is responsible for many cases of liver cancer worldwide. Recent pioneering work by gastroenterologist Barry Marshall implicated the bacterium *Helicobacter pylori* in gastric ulcers and cancer. Molecular biologists Yuan Chang and Patrick S. Moore, of Columbia University, identified a novel herpesvirus (now known as human herpesvirus 8) as the likely cause of Kaposi's sarcoma.

Establishment and Dissemination

Once introduced, the success of the pathogen in a new population depends on its establishing itself and then disseminating within the population. Many zoonotic introductions are highly virulent but not readily transmissible from person to person, thus preventing their establishment. Both chance and the evolutionary potential of the pathogen play a role in determining whether the infection will establish itself.

Human intervention and social change, in addition to providing opportunities for the introduction of pathogens, also provide increasing opportunities for dissemination. Ebola in Africa is usually introduced into humans by contact with its still unknown natural host in the forest, but most of the subsequent cases of the disease occur in hospitals through use of contaminated injection equipment. A number of factors have led to the resurgence in tuberculosis worldwide: HIV infection increases susceptibility to tuberculosis, while high density settings such as day care centers, homeless shelters, and prisons enhance the probability of transmission. Human migration from rural areas to cities, especially in areas with a high degree of biodiversity, can introduce remote pathogens to a larger population. HIV is the best known beneficiary of introduction by migration, but many other diseases may proliferate in this way. After its likely first move from a rural area into a city, HIV-1 spread via highways to other regional cities. Later, by long distance routes including air travel, it progressed to places even further away than the initial site of the infection. The increasing volume of air travel affords pathogens vast opportunities for globalization.

The globalization and industrialization of the food supply and other goods also offer pathways for microbial traffic. The strains of *Escherichia coli* that cause hemolytic uremic syndrome were probably once limited to a few relatively isolated populations of cattle, but have spread as cattle are collected into large central processing facilities. Bovine spongiform encephalopathy (BSE, so-called mad cow disease), which has been identified in Britain since the 1980s, may have been an interspecies transfer of scrapie from sheep to cattle. Widespread use of animal byproducts as feed supplements, in combination with changes in rendering processes that allowed the scrapie agent in sheep byproducts to contaminate the feed, may have been responsible for its introduction and spread in cattle and eventually, in a variant form, to the human population.

Basic public health measures, including clean water and immunization, and improving nutrition have made major contributions to the relative decline of infectious diseases, and remain essential. Re-emerging diseases are those that were previously decreasing in the human population but are again on the upswing. Usually the diseases are those that were once controlled but are staging a comeback due to breakdowns in public health or control measures. The resurgence of diphtheria in the former Soviet Union in the 1990s (as immunization programs lapsed due to lack of resources) is an example. Re-emerging diseases should be a reminder that complacency can lead to the resurgence of many infectious diseases that were once thought to be vanquished.

Infectious diseases have a long history, and are likely to remain significant causes of illness and death in the foreseeable future. Some emerging diseases, like HIV/AIDS, have become worldwide public health crises (there were an estimated 40 million HIV infected individuals at the end of 2001, and according to the World Health Organization, an annual death toll of about 3 million.) Other diseases, such as Ebola, are dramatic but fortunately have remained localized, with limited public health impact.

Biowarfare and Bioterrorism

At the beginning of the twenty-first century, biowarfare and bioterrorism have emerged as related concerns. While nature has been the main source of emerging infections, humans have also on occasion attempted to introduce or disseminate disease intentionally. Historians have suggested that the Tatars catapulted dead bodies into the Crimean city of Kaffa (present day Feodossiya in Ukraine) during a siege in 1346, possibly starting the Black Death (bubonic plague). Smallpox, a dreaded natural scourge since ancient times, was declared conquered in 1980 after a major, and successful, eradication campaign. As a result, control measures were ended, and most of world population is now vulnerable to reintroduction, raising concerns in the event that terrorists succeed in obtaining samples of the virus. In autumn 2001, anthrax letters—envelopes containing a powder of highly concentrated anthrax spores enclosed in a letter—were sent to media and Senate offices in the United States. By the end of the outbreak in late November, there had been 23 cases of anthrax, with 5 deaths; none of the victims were themselves the actual addressees of the letters. Both emerging infectious diseases and bioterrorist attacks can be viewed as involving unexpected outbreaks of infectious disease (although, in the case of biowarfare or bioterrorism, introduced through direct human intervention rather than by the other, usually incidental, means described for natural outbreaks). Conceptually, many of the steps that need to be taken to avoid both types of introduction are similar, beginning with effective public health surveillance to detect and respond to unexpected infectious disease outbreaks.

Detection and Prevention

Fortunately, since most new natural infections have limited ability to establish themselves or disseminate, public health catastrophes like the AIDS pandemic are rare. But which infection will be the next smallpox or AIDS, or even the next pandemic influenza, and how can one prevent it? Global events such as AIDS will occur from time to time, and the risk may well be increasing as factors favoring emergence increase worldwide. Many, although not all, of the facilitating factors for infectious disease emergence are anthropogenic. And though early warning and detection are prerequisite to an effective response, public health infectious disease surveillance remains fragmented and incomplete. An enhanced global system, with the capability to recognize both common and novel infectious diseases, is both possible and necessary.

See also: *AIDS; Disease and History; Diseases, Infectious; Mortality Reversals; Tuberculosis.*

BIBLIOGRAPHY

Haggett, Peter. 2000. *The Geographical Structure of Epidemics.* Oxford: Oxford University Press/ Clarendon Press.

Hahn, Beatrice H., George M. Shaw, Kevin M. De Cock, and Paul M. Sharp. 2000. "AIDS as a Zoonosis: Scientific and Public Health Implications." *Science* 287: 607–614.

Lederberg, Joshua, Robert E. Shope and Stanley C. Oaks, Jr. eds. 1992. *Emerging Infections: Microbial Threats to Health in the United States.* Washington, D.C.: National Academy Press.

Morse, Stephen S. 1990. "Regulating Viral Traffic." *Issues in Science and Technology* 7: 81–84.

———. 1991. "Emerging Viruses: Defining the Rules for Viral Traffic." *Perspectives in Biology and Medicine* 34: 387–409.

———. ed. 1993. *Emerging Viruses.* New York and Oxford: Oxford University Press.

———. 1995. "Factors in the Emergence of Infectious Diseases." *Emerging Infectious Diseases* 1: 7–15.

———. 2002. "The Vigilance Defense." *Scientific American* 28 (No. 4, October): 88–89.

Morse, Stephen S., Barbara Hatch Rosenberg, and John P. Woodall.1996. "Global Monitoring of Emerging Diseases: Design for a Demonstration Program." *Health Policy* 38: 135–153.

Webster, Robert G. 1998. "Influenza: An Emerging Microbial Pathogen." In *Emerging Infections,* ed. Richard M. Krause. San Diego, CA: Academic Press.

INTERNET RESOURCES.

Centers for Disease Control and Prevention. "Emerging Infectious Diseases." <http://www.cdc.gov/ncidod/eid/>.

———. "CDC Bioterrorism Preparedness and Response." <http://www.bt.cdc.gov/>.

International Society for Infectious Diseases. "ProMED-mail." <http://www.promedmail.org/>.

STEPHEN S. MORSE

EMPLOYMENT

See *Labor Force*

ENERGY AND POPULATION

How significantly does the size and growth of world population affect the demand for energy? The short answer: possibly less than one might expect. Whatever the extent of the population-energy connection, the concern that growing energy use threatens the sustainability of the underlying energy resource base is understandable, but perhaps unwarranted.

To address the issue of the effect of population size and growth on energy demand, the fact that the link between population and energy involves two intermediate connecting elements must be recognized. The first link relates to levels and changes in economic development, approximated by income or gross domestic product (GDP) per capita. (The two terms are used interchangeably throughout this article.) Typically, the greater a region's per capita income, the greater its per capita consumption of energy: The average per capita GDP and energy consumption of the world's developing countries are, respectively, only about one-seventh and one-eighth those of industrial areas. Notwithstanding this marked per capita disparity, given the sheer population size of developing regions—over three-quarters of the world total—the absolute amount of energy consumption and of GDP are relatively large: one-third of world energy use and about two-fifths of world GDP.

What is true of prevailing levels in the relationship between per capita income and energy is also true of rates of change over time since as income per capita rises, so does per capita energy use. The reason is evident. Energy—electricity to run motors, fuels for transport, and hundreds of other applications—is a vital complement to other investments for boosting productivity and stimulating economic growth. In turn, that very growth gives rise to acquisition of household necessities and creature comforts associated with increased energy usage.

Even though income and energy use are conspicuously correlated, the degree of the relationship is by no means perfect and unvarying, which raises the second point to consider in linking population and energy. Even at comparable levels of per capita GDP, the volume of energy use will differ among countries and regions, depending on structural characteristics of the economy, spatial features, climate, fuel and power prices, government conservation policies, and other factors. Similarly, changes in per capita income need not signify commensurate rates of energy use; for example, shrinkage of energy-intensive manufacturing and expansion of lower energy-use service activities can contribute to de-coupling growth of GDP and energy use.

Such de-coupling has manifested itself in a number of advanced countries, and may, in time, manifest itself in the world's poorer countries as they continue to develop. In the United States, a plot of energy use per unit of GDP from the third quarter of the nineteenth century and well into the greater part of the twentieth century shows what is basically a bell-shaped curve, in that there was a rise in energy intensity peaking in the 1920s and falling steadily thereafter. In the first half of this period, greater energy use per unit of GDP was associated with the growth of large-scale manufacturing and energy-associated infrastructure. As that process of heavy industrialization began to taper off towards the last several decades of the twentieth century, a growing relative role of non-manufacturing activity meant a commensurate slowdown in the growth rate of energy consumption, although continuing, of course, its steady growth in absolute terms. That slowdown, it should be added, benefited as well from certain non-structural factors, such as energy and economic efficiency improvements in electricity generation and other sectors.

Quantifying the Linkage

With this background, consider Table 1 as a way of highlighting, for recent years and the projected near term, the complex interrelationships among changes in population, economic development, and energy consumption. Its aggregated and simplified layout notwithstanding, the table is instructive in identifying the three broad factors that go into the determination of changes in total energy use. (Strictly speaking, the change in energy use is the *multiplicative product* of the three factors; but, when relatively small numbers are involved, as here, it is effectively the *sum of additive* items.) The items in this decomposition, expressed in terms of percentage changes, are:

$$\textit{Population} + \textit{GDP per capita} + \textit{Energy per unit of GDP} = \textit{Energy}$$

The decade of the 1990s saw economic growth (i.e., GDP per capita) dominating population growth as a factor in energy consumption growth in

TABLE 1

Decomposing the Population-Energy Link: Major World Regions

(AVERAGE ANNUAL PERCENTAGE RATES OF CHANGE)

	1990-1999 (actual)	1999-2020 (projected)
Population		
Industrial	0.6	0.4
EE/FSU	0.0	0.0
DC	1.7	1.3
World	1.4	1.1
GDP per capita		
Industrial	1.6	2.2
EE/FSU	-3.4	4.3
EE/DC	3.2	3.9
World	1.3	2.8
Energy per unit of GDP		
Industrial	-0.6	-1.4
EE/FSU	-1.1	-2.5
DC	-1.1	-1.4
World	-1.7	-1.6
Energy consumption		
Industrial	1.6	1.2
EE/FSU	-4.5	1.7
DC	3.8	3.8
World	1.1	2.2

Note: EE/FSU=Eastern Europe and the former Soviet Union; DC=developing countries. "Energy" refers to the sum of the different energy sources, aggregated according to their respective calorific properties.

SOURCE: Historic population and energy data and all projections from U.S. Department of Energy, Energy Information Administration, *International Energy Outlook 2001* (March 2001), Tables A2, A3, and A16. Historic GDP data from United Nations Development Programme, *Human Development Report 2001* (New York/Oxford: Oxford University Press for UNDP, 2001), p. 181.

both industrialized and developing regions. (Worldwide rates were strongly influenced by developments in the former Soviet Union/Eastern Europe, here included for completeness; but their erratic record for the greater part of the decade hampers meaningful analysis.) Even if population growth had been less than estimated, it is conceivable—though by no means assured—that offsetting economic performance would have accelerated the growth in energy use above that shown in the table.

An important step in this de-composition exercise is to flag the contribution of the changing relationship between energy and GDP, often referred to as changing "energy intensity." Interestingly, in both industrial and developing regions, its (negative) role in dampening the growth in energy use was vastly greater than the growth of population in stimulating it.

The framework employed in Table 1 is easily augmented to indicate the extent to which energy growth compounded or attenuated certain environmental problems. For example, with respect to the problem of greenhouse warming, a worldwide degree of *de-carbonization*—through, among other ways, limited substitution of (carbon-lean) natural gas for (carbon-rich) coal—which allowed carbon dioxide emissions to rise considerably less than energy consumption, can be demonstrated. In the future, that process of de-carbonization—aided by gradual introduction of (zero-carbon) renewable resources—is likely to endure, though not sufficiently to preclude an absolute, and perhaps dangerous, rise in carbon dioxide emissions.

Table 1 includes the U.S. Department of Energy's 20-year "business as usual" projections, showing a doubling in the annual rate of worldwide energy consumption growth, and reflecting—at least over that time span—the credible assumption of ample supply and relatively level prices into the future. For developing regions, the effect of an 0.4 percentage point reduction in the population growth rate is more than offset by a 0.7 percentage point increase in per capita economic growth. That observation is not meant to assert a demonstrated inverse trade-off between population growth and per capita income growth—a matter that remains elusive after many years of study and, in any case, demands a more in-depth analysis than that provided by the macro indicators employed here. Thus, a 1994 World Bank assessment—in line with other expert studies—notes that "[a]ttempts to demonstrate consistent cross-national macroeconomic effects of high rates of population growth have, for the most part, been inconclusive" although suggesting "that rapid growth (above 2 percent a year) inhibits efforts to raise incomes in poor countries with high fertility and youthful age distributions" (World Bank, pp. 36–37).

The Longer-Term Picture

The 20-year time horizon sketched out above provides no reassurance that demographic-economic pressures building in the coming decades of the twenty-first century might not begin to put pressure on availability of the energy resources to which successful development prospects around the world are importantly tied. However, before turning to the question of the longer-term adequacy of exploitable energy resources, researchers should consider the plausible longer-term evolution of the demographic and economic factors underlying changes in energy use. To a degree greater than the 1990 to 2020 trend depicted in the table, growing energy requirements over the longer-term future will almost surely reflect the consequence of rising income to a significantly greater degree than the effect of population growth. The 2000 United Nations projections attest dramatically to decelerating population growth: The *medium* projections show world population rising from 6.06 billion in 2000 to 9.32 in 2050—a number that is 1.5 billion less than that projected just four years earlier. Looked at in another way, the *low* projection for 2050, issued in 2000, approximates the medium projection issued in 1996. Successive reductions like these are due in large part to strikingly lower fertility experience in a number of major developing countries. As a result, population growth between 2000 and 2050 is currently projected to grow at an average annual rate of 0.86 percent, in contrast to the 1.77 percent rate between 1950 and 2000.

Although long-term GDP per capita growth involves its own degree of uncertainty and conjecture, the range of possibilities considered in numerous analyses cluster around a mid-point of around 1.6 percent per year in the period 2000 to 2050. Coupling 0.86 percent population growth with 1.6 percent GDP/capita growth signifies total GDP growth of around 2.5 percent. There will, of course, be wide regional and national disparities around these worldwide averages. The implication for developing countries—with a prevailing per capita GDP of roughly $3500 (1999 price level) becomes especially important. A rough breakdown of the 1.6 percent per capita growth rate worldwide could mean a rate of around 2.2 percent for developing countries, which would yield per capita GDP of approximately $10,600 in 2050. This would represent a solid gain in living standards, although that income level is still well below the per capita GDP in industrial countries of about $22,000 in 2002. Nevertheless, compared with the prevailing disparity in per capita GDP (the one-seventh ratio mentioned above), the gap by 2050, implied by the assumption as stated, would narrow to a ratio of around one-fourth.

If worldwide GDP growth can reasonably be projected at a yearly rate of 2.5 percent, it also seems reasonable, in turn, to view 2.5 percent as the *upper* bound to long-term energy growth because, particularly in an era focused on technologies and practices that promote economically more efficient energy

usage, a time trend of declining energy intensity can be taken as virtually certain. (To cite just one of many examples of such technological changes: A newly commissioned power plant can generate a kilowatt hour of electricity at less cost and using half the raw energy input than a plant built a mere dozen years ago.) These considerations and a review of various studies support the position that, with worldwide GDP growth over the next 50 years proceeding at an average annual rate of around 2.5 percent (that is, somewhat below the long-term historical trend), a *best guess* for the concomitant increase in energy use is an annual rate of approximately 1.3 percent, the difference reflecting an assumed annual energy intensity improvement factor of around 1.2 percent, is about as large a reduction as can be defended on the basis of historical and empirical grounds.

If a yearly energy consumption growth rate of 1.3 percent seems strikingly below historical experience, it still implies that, compared to the year 2000, by the year 2050 the world will see a near-doubling in its annual level of energy consumption. It is widely expected that a disproportionately large share of the 2000 to 2050 increment will originate in developing countries, with China and India leading the demand. Figure 1 shows long-term historic trends and plausible projections in world population, per capita GDP, energy intensity, and energy use, using the de-composition elements introduced earlier. A conspicuous difference between the long-term past and long-term future clearly relates to the changing relative importance of population growth and per capita income growth combined with decreasing energy intensity in driving energy demand. The last two factors seem certain to be much more decisive in the decades ahead than population growth—a trend already foreshadowed in the near-term forecast shown in the table.

The Energy Resource Base

The extent to which the rate of energy growth falls below the rate of economic growth will remain a matter of unusually spirited debate. One important reason for the debate is that as the fall in energy intensity continues, the threat from climate change and other sorts of environmental deterioration, particularly if declining energy intensity is also accompanied by a shift toward non-fossil energy sources, will become more attenuated. On the other hand, as long as fossil fuel combustion remains a major part

FIGURE 1

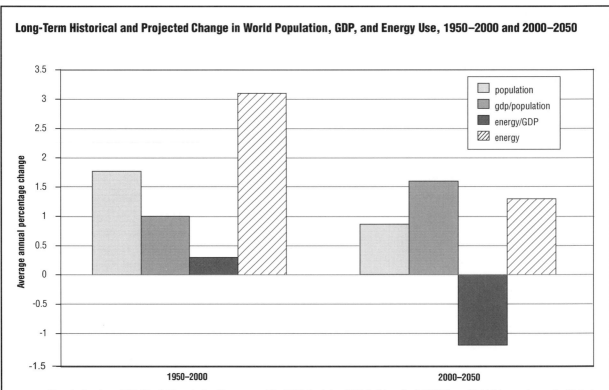

Long-Term Historical and Projected Change in World Population, GDP, and Energy Use, 1950–2000 and 2000–2050

SOURCE: Population from UN, *World Population Prospects–The 2000 Revision* (2001); historical GDP from N. Nakicenovic *et.al., Global Energy Perspectives,* Cambridge Press, 1998, p. 30, updated on the basis of information from US DOE, Energy Information Administation; historical energy estimate based on UN World Bank and DOE/EIA data and checked against chart in Nakicenovic, p. 66. GDP and energy projections are discussed in accompanying text.

of the energy system, the challenge of mitigating climate consequences remains less tractable.

The last discussion leads to the *running out* question: Whatever the way population growth interacts with economic development to spur increased demand for energy, will the identified and likely discoverable resources of fossil energy be adequate to accommodate such future demands? There is no certain answer to that question. However, the fact that fossil fuel resources are finite in the earth's crust has little practical bearing on the answer since, over many decades, new discoveries and innovations in exploration and extraction technology have more than offset rising consumption, with the result that the long-term trend in the real price of energy—the most critical measure of scarcity—has barely changed.

Those facts, although they are often overlooked, deserve brief amplification. Consider, for example, that in 1967, the world's proven oil reserves were estimated at around 418 billion barrels. At then pre-

vailing levels of consumption, projections were that that supply would last some 31 years. By the year 2000, notwithstanding a vast amount of cumulative consumption in the interim, proven oil reserves had risen to 1.05 trillion barrels, equivalent to approximately 40 years of reserves at current consumption levels. Aided by such exploratory breakthroughs as *3-D seismic* and enhanced production capabilities through deep-sea and horizontal drilling, the inflation-adjusted price of crude oil has, notwithstanding periodic volatility, remained virtually stable over the long run. In fact, between the 1950s and the 1990s, the price recorded an inconsequential increase, averaging around 0.3 percent yearly. Similar technological advances can be noted regarding natural gas deposits. Moreover, since natural gas is a geologically young resource, worldwide exploration has yielded many successful discoveries. Exploitable coal deposits exist in such vast abundance that declining use, when it occurs, is much more likely to be due to environmental considerations rather than scarcity factors. In short, while history is an imperfect guide to the future, it seems highly probable that energy scarcity will not manifest itself for decades to come.

One caveat deserves to be added to this somewhat optimistic assessment. It has to do with energy security concerns arising from the concentration of petroleum resources in limited parts of the world. Their abundance notwithstanding, access to these resources could be jeopardized by political turmoil or the exercise of market power. That possibility could reinforce the impetus for a more broad-based energy portfolio, including a progressive shift to renewables, and, conceivably, a revived interest in nuclear power to smooth the longer-term energy transition, which both environmental concerns—especially global warming—and rising prices for conventional energy may in time dictate.

Beyond an Aggregative Perspective

Much of the preceding exposition has been framed in highly aggregated or stylized terms. Even if valid for the world as a whole or for broad regions, such generalized treatment says little about the subtleties, exceptions, and counterfactual experience of individual countries. Forming deeper insights on energy use therefore depends on what can be learned from conditions—not merely economic, but institutional and structural—characterizing populations in different countries.

A few examples suggest the type of considerations involved. People in rural areas of many developing countries gather and use energy, often inefficiently, in the form of firewood or dung for meeting basic needs of cooking and heating. Inevitably, this contributes to erosion and loss of soil fertility and, due to poor combustion, to a widespread incidence of indoor air pollution. While poverty is the primary cause of this practice, limited access to information and the absence, or lax enforcement, of property rights—which might limit such exploitation of the commons—are factors as well. Thus, an early-twenty-first century visitor to Bhutan—an extremely low income country by World Bank standards—will note that the country's farmers receive permanent property rights to small woodlots as a source of firewood and to meet other basic needs. This policy provides farmers with both the responsibility and incentive for adopting and maintaining sustainable forest practices. In particular circumstances, therefore, income is not the sole mediator connecting population and energy.

Energy use in densely-populated urban areas, both in developed and developing societies, exhibits its own unique characteristics. Greater density improves the economics of public transport systems, thereby achieving lower energy use per passenger-kilometer of travel in such places. Multi-family housing, another attribute of high population density, allows for more efficient energy use than single-family homes. It is not surprising that, relative to income, energy use in places like New York City or Philadelphia is significantly less than that in Dallas or Phoenix, which have dispersed settlement patterns.

These findings do not imply that crowding is good, for many things enter into decisions about where to live. Indeed, depending on local conditions, including deficient regulatory policies, higher population density can aggravate energy-producing pollution. Mexico City, for example, illustrates how a crowded metropolitan area, traffic congestion, and a substantial volume of industrial activity lacking effective pollution controls all combine with weather inversions to pose serious environmental and public health problems. And, as in numerous other developing-country cities, significant continuation of urban in-migration, coupled with natural population growth, make the search for solutions more challenging. Even in very large cities that have achieved, or are approaching, middle-income rank—for example, Bangkok or Sao Paulo—it is not clear that political processes and governance are as yet up to the task of managing the intertwined challenges of pollution, congestion, and the provision of adequate municipal services. Specifically with respect to energy use, these qualitative dimensions of rising demand, as much as any demographic pressures on resource availability, will require the prime attention of both researchers and policy-makers in the years ahead.

See also: *Climate Change and Population: Future; Disease and History; National Security and Population; Natural Resources and Population.*

BIBLIOGRAPHY

Birdsall, Nancy. 1992. *Another Look at Population and Global Warming,* Working Paper WPS 1020. Washington D.C.: World Bank.

Darmstadter, Joel. 2001. "The Energy-CO_2 Connection: A Review of Trends and Challenges." In

Climate Change Economics and Policy, ed. Michael A. Toman. Washington, Resources for the Future.

———. 2001. "On Population and Resources," An Exchange Between D. Gale Johnson and Partha Dasgupta. *Population and Development Review.* 27(4): 739–754.

United Nations. 2001. *Population, Environment and Development.* New York: Department of Economic and Social Affairs, Population Division.

World Bank. 1994. *Population and Development: Implications for the World Bank.* Washington D.C.: World Bank.

JOEL DARMSTADTER

ENVIRONMENTAL ETHICS

Unqualified references to "population" typically refer to the human population. This is no doubt true of the vast majority of entries in this encyclopedia, which thus might more accurately be titled *The Encyclopedia of Human Population.* As things stand, however, species-specific references to the particular kind of "population" under discussion typically occur only in the context of specialized discussions in biology and ecology, especially the field of population biology.

These observations indicate a morally relevant point: The implicit understanding that the term *population* typically refers, unless otherwise specified, to the human population both reflects and reinforces the implicit assumption that human populations are the ones that really matter, the ones that, morally speaking, really count. There is of course a legitimate place for the widespread discussion of issues relating to human population, but why are these discussions not explicitly referred to as discussions relating to the human population so as to acknowledge the basic fact that humans live on this planet alongside a great many other, nonhuman kinds of populations to which humans are evolutionarily related?

Anthropocentrism

Acknowledging the ongoing human-centered (anthropocentric) nature of people's thinking, including the empirical and moral distortions that this introduces, has been a central motivating factor in the development of the field of inquiry that has become known as environmental ethics or, more generally, environmental philosophy. These empirical and moral distortions have included claims (in the Western tradition at least) along the lines that "we" (meaning the human population) dwell at the center of the universe; that humans and humans alone possess a soul and are created in the image of God, to whom they have a privileged personal relationship; that humans occupy the highest (and therefore most perfect) position in a scale of nature (Aristotle's influential *scala naturae*); that humans occupy the highest earthly position in a great chain of being that stretches all the way up to God (a view that permeated medieval thinking); and that humans are essentially and uniquely rational (a view that runs from the early Greek philosophers through the greatest thinkers up to the present yet is called into question by what has been learned from Sigmund Freud and the developments in clinical psychiatry and psychology since Freud as well as from human cognitive psychology, comparative psychology, and cognitive ethology).

As John Passmore argues, the history of ideas reveals that these kinds of anthropocentric views have been employed in varying forms to underpin the morally charged conclusion that humans are either exclusively or overwhelmingly valuable relative to all other earthly kinds and that these other earthly kinds are therefore people's to do with as they will. Indeed, as Passmore notes, throughout the history of Western philosophical thinking, "It is constantly assumed that whatever else exists does so *only for the sake of the rational*"(p. 15) (emphasis added). This sort of thinking has patently obnoxious upshots.

To take just one kind of example, Passmore states: "In so far as cruelty to animals was wrong, this was only because, so it was argued by [Thomas] Aquinas, by [Immanuel] Kant, and by a multitude of lesser thinkers, it might induce a callousness towards *human* suffering. There was nothing wrong with cruelty to animals *in itself*" (p. 113). It seems almost inconceivable today that highly intelligent thinkers of any period could maintain that nonhuman animals were not capable of suffering (a view to which René Descartes, the father of modern philosophy, was committed) or that they could suffer but that their suffering was of no direct moral consequence. However, up until at least Kant's time the most influential thinkers in the Western tradition believed precisely this.

The Argument against Anthropocentrism

Correcting anthropocentrically fueled intellectual distortions—or undermining them by showing their irrelevance to defensible moral conclusions—has been one of the central theoretical motivating factors for environmental ethicists. The central practical motivating factor has been the increasing sense, especially since the 1960s and the birth of the modern environmental movement, of a number of gathering ecological crises. It is the conviction of environmental ethicists that these theoretical and practical factors are directly related: that how people think about—or fail to think about—the value of the world around them has a direct connection with the ecological crises that people are experiencing today. Things might have turned out otherwise: People might have had a set of views that resulted in a far more ecologically respectful approach to the world around them yet still suffer from a range of ecological crises resulting from, say, an asteroid impact. However, it seems that the current ecological crises are largely anthropogenic, that is, of human origin. If it is true that there is a direct connection between these anthropogenic crises and the ways in which people think about and value the world, then environmental ethics must be thought of as a discipline that carries profound significance for the future of habitable life on Earth. Thus, Edward O. Wilson concluded a 1989 paper with the reflection that

> Environmental ethics, still a small and neglected branch of intellectual activity, deserves to become a major branch of the humanities during the next hundred years. In the end, when all the accounting is done, conservation will boil down to a decision of ethics based on empirical knowledge: how we value the natural world in which we evolved and now, increasingly, how we regard our status as individuals. (p. 7)

Environmental ethics did not arise as a formal field of inquiry until the 1970s. Its official birth—after a period of gestation during the 1970s that saw the publication of a number of influential papers and books—perhaps can be dated to 1979 with the publication of *Environmental Ethics*, the first refereed journal in the field. Echoing the point made at the beginning of this entry about the term *popula-*

tion, environmental ethicists have been unrelenting in pointing out that the discipline of ethics, and of philosophy generally, has been directly responsible for introducing and defending profoundly anthropocentric biases into Western thought.

A significant upshot of these biases is that the subject area known as ethics (or moral philosophy) has been focused almost exclusively on humans for the 2,500 years from the time of the Greek founders of this area of inquiry until at least the 1970s. Yet when people today hear the term environmental ethics, they think of it as a minor, specialized offshoot of a "main game" that is known purely and simply as ethics, when in fact environmental ethics represents a vast enlargement of the traditional boundaries of that main game. This is the case because it is the environmental ethicists who have deliberately and systematically criticized the traditional restriction of moral status to human beings on scientific, pragmatic, logical, moral, and even experiential grounds and at the same time have opened up the issue of moral status in order to address the question of what kinds of entities ought to be granted moral status and why. This means that it would be more logical, informative, and intellectually honest to change the name of what traditionally has been referred to as *ethics* to *human ethics* and to change the name of *environmental ethics,* which can mistakenly suggest a more specialized area of inquiry, to *general ethics.*

Ethical arguments that extend moral status beyond the human sphere typically begin by making two critically damaging points against the restriction of moral status to humans. The first is the logical point that it is not possible to identify a single morally relevant characteristic that distinguishes all humans from all nonhumans. For example, even if one accepted the idea that rationality (or the abilities that follow in its wake, such as the capacity to act as a moral agent) should be the criterion for moral status, one would find that there is a now standard objection to this view: the argument from marginal cases. This is the objection that such a view would not even include all humans, since some humans have not yet developed this capacity (infants), some have lost it and will never regain it (e.g., the senile, people in a persistent vegetative state), and some will never develop it (e.g., people who are profoundly retarded or brain damaged). Should it be permissible to do anything to these people, for example, experiment on them, as can be done to other animals, including other primates, humankind's closest evolutionary cousins, who can often lay more claim to rationality than can these "marginal cases"? However, if one tries to come up with a morally relevant characteristic that will include all humans, including these marginal cases, one will find that one is employing a criterion of moral status that also includes a great many nonhuman beings.

The second argument against the restriction of moral status to humans is the moral point that the traditional criteria that have been advanced for moral status—such as those of rationality or actual or potential moral agency and those that rest on highly contested religious assumptions—are irrelevant to the basic reason why most people think it is categorically wrong, say, to torture a baby. The basic reason most people think that this is categorically wrong is not because the baby is actually or even potentially rational, capable of moral agency, or endowed with a soul but simply that the baby will suffer if this is done and that there is no justification for inflicting that suffering. However, if this is the basic reason, consistency of reasoning—or what might simply be called intellectual honesty—demands that one should not inflict unnecessary suffering on any being that is capable of suffering (i.e., any sentient being).

This essentially is the argument that was advanced by the philosopher Jeremy Bentham (1748–1832), the founding father of utilitarianism, and later was taken up and elaborated by Peter Singer. For Singer and other animal liberationists, consistency requires that equal consideration be given to equal degrees of pain no matter who the bearer of that pain is; to say that one should be concerned about pain only when it occurs in humans and not when it occurs in other primates, cats, birds, or fish is akin to saying that one should be concerned about pain only when it is experienced by men or whites. It amounts, in other words, to a morally indefensible form of discrimination, which Singer refers to as speciesism.

Nonanthropocentric Arguments

Other thinkers have developed different arguments for attributing moral status to nonhuman animals. These arguments range from Tom Regan's "subject-of-a-life" approach to animal rights, which would attribute the same degree of moral status to many nonhuman animals that is attributed to humans, to

Richard Ryder's "painism" approach, which Ryder argues combines the best of Singer's and Regan's approaches, to R. G. Frey's "unequal value thesis" and Charles Birch and John Cobb's "richness of experience" approach, both of which only go halfway toward accepting Singer's argument in that they accept the moral significance of sentience but attribute different degrees of moral status to nonhuman animals—and people—on the basis of their overall capacity for richness of experience.

If one accepts any of these arguments even partially, one has attributed at least some degree of moral status to the members of a great many kinds of populations other than human populations. The implications of this for human action, including the incursion of human populations on nonhuman populations, are potentially immense.

However, that is just the beginning of the nonanthropocentric argument. Other thinkers go even further and argue that living things per se (such as plants) embody certain kinds of interests (such as the need for light and water) whether these living things are sentient or not. For example, physician Albert Schweitzer advanced a "reverence for life" ethic that has found more contemporary and perhaps more philosophically rigorous statement in the work of both Kenneth Goodpaster and Paul Taylor. Other environmental ethicists have noted that all the approaches discussed so far—anthropocentric, zoocentric, and biocentric—focus on individual entities: humans, nonhuman animals (or at least some nonhuman animals), and living things (including plants), respectively.

For these thinkers, there is something that is even more radically different about environmental ethical thought than its rejection of anthropocentrism: its questioning of any ethic, no matter how nonanthropocentric, that confines itself to an individualistic moral focus. In their view, what is profoundly revolutionary about environmental ethical questions is that they force people to take seriously the idea that certain kinds of complex wholes—paradigmatically, ecosystems and the ecosphere itself—may be proper foci of moral concern in their own right.

This idea was first seriously advanced in an ecological context by the American forester and conservationist Aldo Leopold in the culminating section ("The Land Ethic") of *A Sand County Almanac*, originally published in 1949. Contemporary environmental ethicists such as J. Baird Callicott and James Heffernan have drawn different kinds of inspiration from Leopold's pioneering Land Ethic in elaborating more philosophically rigorous versions of ecological holism. Other environmental philosophers, such as the advocates of "deep ecology" and "ecofeminism," are impatient with formal philosophical arguments about moral status per se and want instead to construct a type of ecological virtue ethics in which the point of the ethical enterprise would be to cultivate a wider and deeper sense of identification with the world around humankind in the case of deep ecology or a more caring attitude toward that world in the case of ecofeminism. Again, the implications of these nonanthropocentric views —biocentric, ecocentric, deep ecological, and ecofeminist—for the scale and rate of human impact on the natural world are potentially immense. This realization raises significant ethical questions about the built environment—both how people build and how people live in built environments—that are just beginning to be explored from an environmental ethical perspective.

However, lest these approaches (or at least those which are explicitly concerned with questions of moral status) sound like a simple continuum—a kind of linear bus ride in which different people who consider these issues get off at stops labeled anthropocentrism, zoocentrism, biocentrism, and ecocentrism (or ecological holism), depending on how far they feel the arguments oblige them to go—it must be pointed out that there are some very sharp turns and even disjunctions along this path.

To start with, nonanthropocentric environmental ethicists in general have an argument with the whole Western ethical tradition, which has systematically excluded and even denigrated the moral status of all members and aspects of the nonhuman world. However, even within the nonanthropocentric environmental ethical fold there are major divisions and disagreements. One of the most theoretically difficult and practically urgent is the argument between those who adopt an individualistic focus and those who adopt a holistic focus. Recent research suggests that the second leading cause of loss of biodiversity in the world today is introduced species that have become invasive and outcompeted indigenous species. What to do? In the case of invasive (nonhuman) animals such as feral cats and foxes in Australia, the animal liberationist—and certainly the animal rights advocate—is committed to saying in effect, "Leave

the invasive animals alone; they have as much right to live as any other animals," whereas the ecocentrist is committed to saying, "Do whatever is necessary to get rid of the invasive animals; we have a duty to preserve the characteristic diversity of this region." There are real-world examples of precisely this sort of confrontation. Thus, Callicott once characterized the argument about animal liberation as a "triangular affair," a three-way argument between anthropocentric ethicists, animal welfare advocates, and ecocentrists.

The Future of Environmental Ethics

These kinds of debates are both important and overdue. Environmental ethics or, more logically, general ethics is overturning the Western ethical tradition, is still in its infancy, and both promises and needs to become, as Wilson said, a major branch of intellectual inquiry in the next hundred years.

See also: *Animal Rights; Ecological Perspectives on Population; Future Generations, Obligations to; Sustainable Development.*

BIBLIOGRAPHY

Birch, Charles, and John Cobb. 1981. *The Liberation of Life.* Cambridge, Eng.: Cambridge University Press.

Callicott, J. Baird. 1980. "Animal Liberation: A Triangular Affair." *Environmental Ethics* 2: 311–338.

———, ed. 1987. *Companion to a Sand County Almanac: Interpretive and Critical Essays.* Madison: University of Wisconsin Press.

Cohen, Carl, and Tom Regan. 2001. *The Animal Rights Debate.* Lanham, MD: Rowman and Littlefield.

Fox, Warwick. 1995a. *Toward a Transpersonal Ecology: Developing New Foundations for Environmentalism.* Albany: State University of New York Press, and Totnes, Devon, Eng.: Green Books.

——— 1995b. "Anthropocentrism." In *Conservation and Environmentalism: An Encyclopedia*, ed. Robert Paehlke. New York and London: Garland Publishing.

———, ed. 2000. *Ethics and the Built Environment.* London: Routledge.

Heffernan, James. 1982. "The Land Ethic: A Critical Appraisal" *Environmental Ethics* 4: 235–247.

Johnson, Lawrence. 1991. *A Morally Deep World: An Essay on Moral Significance and Environmental Ethics.* Cambridge, Eng.: Cambridge University Press.

LaFollette, Hugh. 1997. *Ethics in Practice: An Anthology.* Malden, MA, and Oxford: Blackwell.

Passmore, John. 1980. *Man's Responsibility for Nature: Ecological Problems and Western Traditions.* 2nd edition. London: Duckworth & Co.

Ryder, Richard. 2001. *Painism: A Modern Morality.* London: Centaur Press.

Singer, Peter. 1990 (1975). *Animal Liberation,* 2nd edition. London: Jonathan Cape.

Warren, Mary Anne. 1997. *Moral Status: Obligations to Persons and Other Living Things.* Oxford: Oxford University Press.

Wilson, Edward O. 1989. "Conservation: The Next Hundred Years." In *Conservation for the Twenty-First Century,* ed. David Western and Mary Pearl. New York and Oxford: Oxford University Press.

Zimmerman, Michael, general ed. 2001. *Environmental Philosophy: From Animal Rights to Radical Ecology.* Upper Saddle River, NJ: Prentice Hall.

WARWICK FOX

ENVIRONMENTAL HEALTH

The word environment as applied to health is elastic in use. Conventionally it refers to the external factors—physical, chemical, and microbiological—that impinge on human health, usually through shared exposures among members of communities or whole populations, and that therefore are not under the control of individuals. A broader definition embraces the social environment, including the aspects of social capital that influence health within the community at large. Indeed, in the early twenty-first century about half of all people live in urban environments as *Homo sapiens* becomes an urbanized

species. The urban environment is essentially a habitat: a system of interacting physical, demographic, social, and cultural environments. These wider dimensions of the environment necessitate a more ecological, systems-based approach.

External environmental exposures can be either natural or human-made and have a local, regional, or global scale. The modern preoccupation is with human-made environmental hazards. Historically, however, concerns focused on aspects of the natural environment, including weather extremes, infectious agents, physical disasters, and local micronutrient deficiencies. For example, one-fifth of the world population lives on ancient, leached, and often mountainous iodine-deficient soils. This puts many populations at risk of iodine deficiency disorders, including goiter, reproductive impairment, and congenital disorders, including cretinism (Hetzel and Pandav 1994).

The environmental health agenda also must encompass the risks to population health that result from humankind's larger-scale disruption of the planet's ecological and geophysical systems. These are the systems that provide nature's "goods and services": climatic stability, food yields, the supply of clean fresh water, and the healthy functioning of biotically diverse natural ecosystems that recycle nutrients, cleanse the air and water, and produce useful materials. This disruption or depletion of the biosphere's life support systems can affect health through pathways that are less direct and sometimes less immediate than the effects of specific traditional hazards.

In industrialized countries attention has been directed predominantly to the plethora of chemical contaminants entering air, water, soil, and food, along with physical hazards such as ionizing radiation, nonionizing radiation, urban noise, and road trauma. In the popular understanding prototypical environmental health events include the disasters of Chernobyl, Bhopal, Seveso, Minamata Bay, and the Great London Smog of 1952. As technologies evolve and as levels of consumption rise, the list of candidate hazards lengthens: In the late 1990s questions arose about the cancer hazard of electromagnetic radiation from mobile phones, the risk to a fetus from chlorinated organic chemicals in chlorine-treated water supplies, and the possible toxicity and allergenic and other consequences of genetically modified foods. In low-income countries the major environmental concerns continue to be the microbiological quality of drinking water and food, the physical safety of housing and work sites, indoor air pollution, and traffic hazards.

The relative importance of environmental exposures as a cause of human disease and premature death remains a matter of contention. Depending on definitions and assumptions, estimates of the environmental contribution to the global burden of disease and premature death vary. The World Health Organization has estimated that about 25 percent of the global burden, as measured in disability-adjusted life years (DALYs), is caused by environmental hazards, along with around one-sixth of the total burden in children. Kirk Smith and colleagues (1999), in an analysis that encompassed disease initiation, progression, and case outcome, estimated that 25 to33 percent of the global burden of disease and premature death is attributable to direct environmental risk factors.

Relationships between Environment, Population, Poverty, and Health

The relationships among ambient environmental conditions, socioeconomic circumstances, demographic change, and human health are complex and multidirectional. Some of the relationships are immediate; for example, poverty today causes malnutrition today. Other relationships involve long time lags; for example, current poverty contributes to the need to clear local forests for fuel and to farm marginal lands, inducing ecological attrition and hunger in the future. Time lags aside, there is not a simple linear causal chain connecting these variables. Population pressure and poverty in rural populations often lead to land degradation, with consequences for supplies of food and materials. Meanwhile, poverty influences fertility rates, and vice versa. Environmental degradation often causes further impoverishment and also may impair health through increases in infectious disease, nutritional deficiencies, and toxic environmental exposures.

In many African, Asian, and Latin American countries life expectancy is 20 to 30 years less than it is in rich Western countries. Infectious diseases remain the main killer, particularly of children below five years of age. Much of this health deficit reflects the widespread poverty, adverse social consequences of export-oriented economic development, and environmental adversity caused by the exploitation of natural resources.

Some larger-scale environmental stresses may heighten social tensions, leading to conflict and adverse health consequences. For example, Ethiopia and the Sudan, upstream of Egypt, increasingly need the Nile's water for their crops. Worldwide, approximately 40 percent of the world's population, living in 80 countries, now faces some degree of water shortage. The prospect of international conflict caused by environmental decline, dwindling resources, and ecological disruption enlarges the shadow over the prospects for human health.

It is difficult to confirm or refute the widely assumed linkage between poverty, environment, and health. Both poverty and environmental degradation, through independent pathways, increase risks to health. There is also a strong but complex relationship between income level and environmental quality. For many important environmental pollutants, as average incomes rise, the effect on environmental quality can be represented by an inverted U-shaped curve. Initially the pollutant loads increase; then, as wealth, literacy, and political liberalism increase, negative feedback processes emerge and societies act to reduce those pollutants. However, the indexes of several larger-scale sources of environmental degradation, such as emissions of the greenhouse gas carbon dioxide, display a continuing increase. These are "global commons" problems for which there is not yet sufficiently clear evidence of adverse social, economic, or health consequences to generate negative feedback responses through the policy process. Humankind has not yet learned how to mitigate, with international cooperation, these large-scale threats.

Conclusion

Throughout history human communities have depleted natural resources and degraded local ecosystems. Often the consequences have been a recession in local human numbers and impairment of nutrition, health, and social viability. Demographers have long debated the classic Malthusian problem in which local population needs exceed the local environmental carrying capacity. In the early twenty-first century that postulated process of ecological deficit budgeting has become global, an unprecedented development for humankind with significant implications for human population health.

For the last two centuries environmental health concerns in the industrializing world have focused mainly on toxicological or, less often, microbiological risks to health from specific agents in the local environment. In low-income countries the traditional hazards from infectious agents in air, food, and water, along with malnutrition and the physical hazards of living environments, have predominated. The escalating impact of human numbers and economic activity has begun to alter some of the major global biophysical systems that underpin the health of humans and all other species. Humankind is at risk of incurring global ecological deficits as, increasingly, people live beyond the planet's overall environmental carrying capacity.

See also: *Climate Change and Population: Future; Disease and History.*

BIBLIOGRAPHY

Diamond, Jared. 1998. *Guns, Germs and Steel. The Fate of Human Civilizations.* London: Jonathan Cape.

Gleick, Peter H. 2001. *The World's Water 2000–2001.* Washington, D.C.: Island Press.

Grossman, G. 1995. "Pollution and Growth: What Do We Know?" In *The Economics of Sustainable Development,* eds. I. Goldin, and L. A. Winters. Cambridge, Eng.: Cambridge University Press.

Hetzel, Basil S., and C. S. Pandav. 1994. *SOS for a Billion: The Conquest of Iodine Deficiency Disorders.* Bombay, India: Oxford University Press.

Homer-Dixon, T. F. 1994. "Environmental Scarcities and Violent Conflict: Evidence from Cases." *International Security* 19: 5–40.

Logie, Dorothy E., and Solomon R. Benatar. 1997. "Africa in the 21st Century: Can Despair Be Turned to Hope?" *British Medical Journal* 315: 1444–1446.

McMichael, Anthony J. 2001. *Human Frontiers, Environments and Disease: Past Patterns, Uncertain Futures.* Cambridge, Eng.: Cambridge University Press.

McMichael, Anthony J., and John W. Powles. 1999. "Human Numbers, Environment, Sustainability and Health." *British Medical Journal* 319: 977–980.

Smith, Kirk, Carlos Corvalan, and Tord Kjellstrom. 1999. "How Much Global Ill Health Is Attributable to Environmental Factors?" *Epidemiology* 10: 573–584.

World Health Organization. 1997. *Health and Environment in Sustainable Development: Five Years after the Earth Summit.* Geneva: World Health Organization.

A. J. McMichael

ENVIRONMENTAL IMPACT, HUMAN

Since the late nineteenth century, changes to the global environment have been profound—and mostly in the direction of degradation. Such changes include ozone destruction, widespread smog, devastating erosion, river blockages and channelization altering water flow and preventing nutrients from reaching deltas and seas, the frenzied clearing of tropical forest for timber and arable land, the collapse of ocean fisheries and other common-access resources, and heightened extinction rates. As the historian John McNeill chronicles, humans, propelled by population growth, migration, and urbanization, and by the worldwide drive for development with its penchant for the industrial "Motown cluster" of automobiles, oil, chemicals, and plastics, have powerfully transformed the planet.

But as the cultural geographer David Lowenthal once astutely pointed out, "the acceleration of environmental transformations blinds us to their antiquity." Antiquity is the focus here: Did human hands aggressively shape the environment prior to the modern or industrial era? Did indigenous people walk lightly on the land? People in preindustrial times surely possessed comprehensive environmental knowledge and were ecologists in the sense of thinking about the environment and its components in interrelating, systemic (but always culturally specific) fashion; some were environmentalists in their expressed concern for the state of the environment. But what counts when considering the human impact on the environment is how people behaved. Did they conserve resources—that is, intentionally use them wisely to maintain their future availability, and avoid waste, despoliation, and the like—or did they take quite different action with other ends in mind, leading rapidly or ultimately to depleted resources and unsustainable futures?

Despite widespread infatuation with the late-twentieth-century image of indigenous people living lives consistently in balance and harmony with nature, the answers to these questions are complex. They can be sought in the scientific, archaeological, and historical record, as well as in ethnographies of nineteenth- to twentieth-century indigenous people living traditional lives. The latter offer useful ways to imagine preindustrial times with respect to the use of fire, animal extinctions, food production and village life, and extirpations linked to the emergence of market economies. Special attention is given here to the North American case.

Fire

Human-induced fire is as old as our species, Homo sapiens, and might have evolved as long as one-half to one million years ago as one of the earliest hominid tools. The evidence of fire is in the archaeological and historical record on all continents and innumerable islands. Because fire has transformative effects on ecosystems, landscape—that is, culturally modified environment—is as ancient as humankind. Wilderness, defined as territory untrammeled by humankind, became increasingly uncommon after humans began using fire.

North America, for example, was far from the pristine, primeval land the Europeans imagined it to be when they arrived. Instead the continent, as noted by an early-seventeenth-century Dutch mariner off the East Coast, was "smelt before it is seen." Everywhere, the Native American Indians torched the land. They burned to improve subsistence, to create favorable ecological niches, to drive animals from one place to another, to increase production of crops or berries and other gathered foods, to set the stage for new plant growth that would attract herbivores and, in turn, carnivores in another season. They knew what would happen to the land and to plants and animals as a result of their burns. Their use of fire revealed keen awareness of the systemic interrelationships that are at the core of the conception of an ecosystem. Indians possessed their own theories of animal behavior (ethnoethology) and gave ecosystems cultural definition with spaces and links that would not necessarily appear in a Western conservation biologist's depiction of the ecosystem. They were ecologists, if ecology also can be ethnoecology. But these first North Americans did not always burn with ecological consequences in mind. Some often used fire as an offensive or defensive weapon, to

drive enemies before them or to cover their own escape. Many lit fires to send signals to each other, communicating a variety of desires and plans. Others who lived in forests set them ablaze to ease travel. Many of these fires, as well as others, raged beyond control, deeply scorching the land beyond short-term utility, killing animals, and burning until extinguished by rain or halted by rivers.

Determining the precise ecological consequences of long-past fires can be daunting because archaeologists cannot always know whether fires were natural (caused by lightning) or anthropogenic. Yet in North America certain ecosystems are fire-succession ecosystems in which human hands were present in their maintenance if not at their inception. For example, widespread ponderosa pine forest requires periodic fire to eliminate competing understory, and in the absence of fire these pines grow so densely that the forest stagnates or changes to one dominated by shade-tolerant species. Chaparral, a scrub community in the North American West, is fire-induced and will endure as a robust ecological community only if managed by fire (which many Indians did, to the benefit of useful plants and the animals attracted to them). Longleaf pine forests in the Southeast require regular fires to remove competing plants and destructive fungus. Longleaf pines are fire-adapted in growth and in fire's absence fail to reproduce or survive, and the forest changes to one dominated by other pines and deciduous trees. Finally, the eastern sections of the vast North American plains and prairies, where moisture allowed natural succession by oaks, aspens, and willows, were maintained and quite possibly induced by human-originated fires.

In short, when Europeans gazed upon North America for the first time and many imagined an untouched Edenic wilderness, they actually were looking in large part upon a cultural, anthropogenic landscape produced and maintained by fire. Many landscapes in other regions of the world had similar pyrogenic histories.

Animal Extinctions

Humans are implicated in animal extinctions long before the highly publicized ones of the modern period. One episode occurred at the end of the era known as the Pleistocene in North America, where the destruction of numerous species of animals followed closely on the heels of the initial arrival of hunting-gathering Paleoindians some 13,000 to 14,000 years ago (Australia has a similar history at an earlier time). The Pleistocene extinctions were remarkable. At least 35 mammalian genera disappeared, many in the millennium beginning 11,000 years ago. Animals familiar and unfamiliar, widespread and local, and large and small vanished. Many were large animals, the so-called megafauna: hulking, tusked mammoths and mastodons; slow-moving giant ground sloths; the armored 2,000-pound, six-foot long glyptodonts, a kind of giant armadillo; single-hump camels; 300-pound giant beavers; hyena-like dire wolves; short-faced bears; scimitar-toothed and great saber-toothed cats, and others.

Debate is sharp over why these animals became extinct. Some researchers point to climate, which can be linked to six other extinction episodes in the last ten million years in North America. The climate was in the throes of significant change at the end of the Pleistocene, when temperatures warmed markedly, and winters became colder and summers hotter. Entire habitats changed overnight. Grasses, plants, and invertebrate and vertebrate organisms flourished or died. Were the consequences dire for key herbivores with the potential to transform the environment, and therefore for species linked to them? There are more questions than answers about the consequences of climatic and vegetational changes on specific species, and about the precise mechanisms involved in the impact of climate on particular species.

Moreover, unlike earlier extinctions in North America, during the Pleistocene extinctions there existed men and women with a distinctive hunting technology and definite taste for species now extinct. Humans' likely role in the extinctions is argued by the other protagonists in the debate. Perhaps climate change left certain animals susceptible to a Paleoindian *coup de grace*.

One way to think about what happened in North America is to consider the large island of Madagascar, where, in the wake of human arrival some 1,500 years ago, large flightless birds, giant tortoises, hippos, more than 15 species of lemurs, and other animals became extinct. They vanished after people appeared during a long dry spell in an oscillating (wet to dry) climate. This coincidence doomed more species than either humans, desiccation, or vegetation changes alone could have.

Yet even in the absence of such coincidence, preindustrial humans were highly efficient predators who, under the right conditions, were fully capable of depleting faunal resources. For example, as people colonized the Pacific (1600 B.C.E. to 1000 C.E.), they induced widespread environmental change and exterminated thousands of species of birds. In Hawaii, colonizers cleared land with fire, diverted streams for irrigation, transformed forested coastal areas into farms and grasslands, changed mudflats into fishponds, and introduced animals. Birds vanished with their habitats or were overwhelmed by their utility as food or commodities (for example, feathers to ornament clothing); over one-half of endemic avian species were extinct when Europeans arrived. This pattern was repeated on other islands. Birds and some other animals almost completely disappeared from small islands like Easter Island, Mangaia, and Tikopia. Even on the large island of New Zealand, Polynesian colonizers deforested vast sections of the land and hunted 13 species of moas—ostrich-like flightless birds, one of which towered over men and women—to extinction before turning their attention to the small birds, shellfish, fish, and seals that remained.

Food Production, Population Size and Density, and Village Life

The extinction of birds in the Pacific is just one example of environmental change caused by food producers. From 8500 to 2500 B.C.E., a potent combination of forces for change emerged independently in Southwest Asia, China, Mesoamerica, the Andes, and what is now the eastern United States: permanent villages occupied by more people living more densely than before, with economies based on domesticated plants and animals. This way of life, anchored in food production, spread to other parts of the globe. It supported population densities 10 to 100 times as great as in most foraging societies (even as such crowding left people susceptible to diseases originating in domesticated animals and unsanitary conditions). Demography was not the only important determinant in this changing relationship between humans and the land—acquisitive intentions, resource abundance, impact of technology, and precise environmental understandings played important roles—but it was nevertheless significant. Everywhere it was practiced, this new way of life contained potential for significant environmental change—in villages and especially in the most densely settled areas where urbanism emerged.

In America north of the Rio Grande, where there were probably no more than 4 to 7 million people on the eve of European arrival (equal to the 2000 population of Colorado or Virginia), the pressures could be sensed in the Southwest and along the Mississippi, where densely-settled societies emerged, flourished, and (from the eleventh through fourteenth centuries c.e.) disappeared. These changes happened because the settlers' demand for wood for fuel, construction, and other purposes overtaxed forests; because they did not foresee the long-term consequences of delivering, through irrigation canals, saline waters to salt-sensitive crops planted in salty fields where the water table was high; or for other reasons. Farther south and centuries earlier, the Maya had degraded and deforested their own terrain, which with other factors set the stage for the abandonment of their striking ceremonial centers by 900 c.e..

These events repeat the pattern established earlier in the Old World. Canal siltation, waterlogging, and salinization doomed urban life in Mesopotamia, despite the shift from wheat to salt-resistant barley. People in the Near East denuded forests to satisfy the demand for wood, especially for use as household fuel and to prepare lime plaster. Domesticated animals (not an environmental problem in the Americas) were an important part of the production mix and were clearly linked, through heavy grazing, to defoliation and erosion. In ancient Greece and Rome, deforestation and erosion, which were prominent environmental problems, were caused by clearing lands for cultivation; grazing by cattle, sheep, goats, and pigs; and the demand for charcoal for domestic fuel and lumber for building construction and shipbuilding. Deforestation was extensive in many parts of the classical Mediterranean world. Permanently eroded and degraded, these lands were subject to flooding, siltation, desiccation, and disease—all clearly worrisome to some contemporaries who remarked upon man's effects on nature. As the archaeologist Charles Redman suggests, productive strategies often seem to have undermined whatever balance might fortuitously or deliberately have existed in cycles of decline and recovery, and to have left societies vulnerable to the unexpected—like adverse climate change.

On the eve of the transformations leading to the modern era, fifteenth-, sixteenth-, and seventeenth-century Europeans profoundly altered entire portions of their continent. Woodcutters in search of fuel, iron and other mineral smelters on the make for charcoal, and farmers seeking new arable land all assaulted forests on a broad front. Naval and merchant interests could never get enough timber for ships. Hunters systematically killed wolves and other predators. In England, marshes were drained for conversion to arable land. People engaged in brewing, brick making, dyeing, and other industries oblivious to the environmental consequences. Urban skies were darkened by the pollution from burning sulfur-laden coal. Some fled to the countryside as an escape from modern ills, but many went about their lives seemingly without regard for the wastes that fouled water and air.

Commodity-Linked Extirpations

From ancient times, as production rose above subsistence levels, the development of trade and markets increased the pace of environmental exploitation. In ancient Greece and Rome, for example, the demand for wildlife products in household and military subsistence, the commercial marketplace, private sport, and the arena led to the widespread decline of animal stocks and extirpations both on islands and the mainland. The need to protect domesticated crops from competing grazers and domesticated animals from predators also contributed to extirpations.

Environmental destruction reached a new level with the rise of capitalism in seventeenth-century Western Europe. The subsequent global spread of Europeans affected the environmental history of all continents. In North America, Europeans arrived along with microbes that were harmless to them, inadvertently unleashing horrific epidemic diseases among the Indians. These diseases killed great numbers of indigenous people and in the short run lessened pressures on ecosystems. But the Europeans also came with an unrelenting and expansive belief that environmental goods were commodities for exploitation. This commodification of the environment, together with increasingly capital-intensive industrial designs, ultimately proved profoundly transformative. Indigenous people responded by becoming primary suppliers of environmental goods such as animal pelts and skins in exchange for a variety of desired, highly valued consumer goods. The two most famous commodities from the sixteenth through the nineteenth centuries were deerskins and beaver pelts, willingly supplied by indigenous people to the point of extirpation of white-tailed deer and beaver populations.

It is often assumed that indigenous people like the Native Americans possessed a primordial conservation ethic that they abandoned as they participated in Western systems of commodification. If the global ethnography of hunting and foraging people in modern times is any guide, this assumption is erroneous. Restraint in harvesting wildlife is rare among such people, who instead make choices that maximize efficiency or promise high yields. Moreover, in the case of the North American Indians, the hunt was ruled by culturally defined respect for prey species which, properly approached in thought and deed, gave themselves up for sustenance and use and thereby gained the opportunity to be reborn to be killed another day. For restraint to be practiced, this indigenous belief in reincarnation had to be reconciled with Western-style conservation.

Conclusion

Neither the antiquity of environmental change nor the enormous scale of transformation in the modern global environment should be in dispute. In some cases, ancient and modern behavior produces similar results: Extinction of a species is forever, whether at the end of the Pleistocene, on a Polynesian island 500 years ago, or in twentieth-century North America. Moreover, some small-scale modern environmental changes at least superficially mimic ancient ones associated with the emergence of densely settled village life based on domestication. The major difference is one of scale, linked to population size and technology: In the past, the changes were local or regional; in the early twenty-first century they have global potential. The tempo of change has also risen markedly. Yet one should be humbled by the fact that the consequences of ancient destructive practices are often visible today—although noting the irony that, in places like Greece, the long history of environmental degradation produced the aestheticized landscapes that many now admire, in ignorance of their origin.

See also: *Biogeography; Carrying Capacity; Ecological Perspectives on Population; Hunter-Gatherers; Prehistoric Populations; Sustainable Development.*

BIBLIOGRAPHY

Diamond, Jared. 1997. *Guns, Germs, and Steel: The Fates of Human Societies.* New York: W. W. Norton.

Goudie, Andrew. 1990. *The Human Impact on the Natural Environment,* 3rd edition. Cambridge, MA: MIT Press.

Hughes, J. Donald. 1994. *Pan's Travail: Environmental Problems of the Ancient Greeks and Romans.* Baltimore, MD: Johns Hopkins University Press.

Kirch, Patrick V. 1997. "Microcosmic Histories: Island Perspectives on 'Global' Change." *American Anthropologist* 99(1): 30–42.

Krech, Shepard, III. 1999. *The Ecological Indian: Myth and History.* New York: W. W. Norton.

Krech, Shepard, III; Carolyn Merchant; and J. R. McNeill, eds. 2003. *Encyclopedia of World Environmental History.* New York: Routledge.

Lowenthal, David. 1990. "Awareness of Human Impacts." In *The Earth as Transformed by Human Action: Global and Regional Changes in the Biosphere over the Past 300 Years,* ed. B. L. Turner II, W. C. Clark, R. W. Kates, J. F. Richards, J. T. Matthews, and W. B. Meyer. Cambridge, Eng.: Cambridge University Press.

McNeill, John R. 2000. *Something New Under the Sun: Environmental History of the Twentieth Century.* New York: W.W. Norton.

Redman, Charles L. 1999. *Human Impact on Ancient Environments.* Tucson: University of Arizona Press.

SHEPARD KRECH III

EPIDEMICS

Epidemic diseases break out, reach a peak, and subside; endemic diseases cause a relatively constant amount of illness and death over time (see Figure 1). Epidemic diseases can be new or normally endemic to a community. They break out on a local level and remain localized, or spread out in diffusion waves to surrounding communities. Very large-scale epidemics that strike several continents or the entire globe are called pandemics. Although relatively infrequent, pandemics are exceptionally disruptive; the economic, social, and demographic damage they do insures that they receive the lion's share of attention from both contemporaries and historians.

Defining Epidemics

The most familiar epidemic diseases are propagated by direct contact between infected and uninfected persons, as is the case with tuberculosis, smallpox, measles, polio, syphilis, and AIDS, among others. But some of the most devastating epidemic diseases were and are transmitted to human beings by insect vectors, such as bubonic plague, malaria, typhus, and yellow fever. Among the epidemic diseases spread by water-borne pathogens are cholera, typhoid, and dysentery. Some epidemic outbreaks do not involve microorganisms at all; these common vehicle epidemics can be caused by food-borne or other toxins (e.g., ergotism). Under certain circumstances, even vitamin deficiency diseases like scurvy (Vitamin C) or night blindness (Vitamin A) can break out suddenly in certain populations. Every epidemic disease has its own distinctive etiology, and its own complex relationship with both natural and social environments.

Epidemiologists identify epidemic outbreaks by observing the statistical behavior of a specific disease over time, based on the number of reported cases and/or deaths the disease causes. In theory, if zero cases of a specific disease are expected in a normal year, then even one observed case can signal an epidemic and call for a public health response. This reasoning was used in 1976 to declare a national public health emergency in the United States, based on a single unexpected death from a type of influenza that seemed similar to the 1918 outbreak.

By using statistical criteria alone, more and more diseases have been perceived as taking epidemic form. Around 1950, several chronic diseases were classified as epidemics, including lung and breast cancer and ischemic heart disease. Some slowly-developing "social" diseases—like alcoholism and drug addiction—and a few mental diseases like depression have also been described as epidemics. But instead of erupting and subsiding in a year or less, chronic-, social-, or mental-disease epidemics rise and fall over several decades. As a consequence, they can only be observed by experts with access to high quality morbidity and/or mortality data.

History of Epidemics

The existence of epidemics has been recorded since the beginning of written history, and in all probability they predate it. Just as epizootics (epidemic animal diseases) have always been part of the demogra-

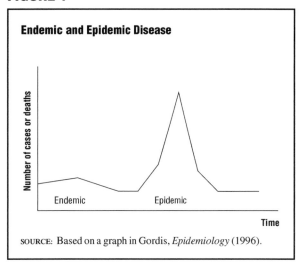

FIGURE 1

Endemic and Epidemic Disease

Number of cases or deaths

Endemic   Epidemic

Time

SOURCE: Based on a graph in Gordis, *Epidemiology* (1996).

phy of animal populations, epidemics were part of the evolution of human populations. It is widely supposed that during the transition from hunting and gathering to agriculture, when human beings began to live in larger groups and at higher densities, the frequency—and possibly the severity—of epidemics increased. Subsequently, the development of cities made epidemic disease an even greater threat to human life.

But knowledge about epidemics and mortality in history is necessarily limited by the relative absence of reliable quantitative data. Although the Black Death is one of history's most famous and well-researched epidemics, data problems have kept everything about the epidemic controversial, except for the fact that it arrived in Southern Europe in 1347 and spread to Northern Europe by 1352. Historians continue to disagree on whether or not the "plague" was one disease or several. (Before the seventeenth century, plague was still a generic concept used in connection with any sudden outbreak of disease.) Accounts from the time often describe the plague as killing the majority of the living. Most historians, however, believe that about one third of Europeans died in the first outbreak, although estimates range from less than a fifth to more than two thirds. Subsequently, major epidemics seem to have erupted with sufficient frequency and intensity in Europe that the continent's population was cut in half. Demographic recovery took two centuries or more.

It was the continuing social and economic disruption caused by recurrent outbreaks of plague that led city officials in Europe, particularly in Renaissance Italy, to develop novel measures of disease management, including the formal surveillance of mortality. By 1500, several cities in Italy were tracking deaths on a week-by-week basis, and trying to distinguish between those that were and were not caused by plague. These data have been used to estimate that, on average, plague outbreaks in the 1400s and 1500s multiplied the normal number of urban deaths by a factor of four to seven (Del Panta and Livi Bacci 1979, p. 72). In Sienna, when the normal death rate was about 35 per 1,000 per year, mortality increased by a factor of five to ten during a plague year (Livi-Bacci 2001, p. 39). In Florence, it has been estimated that epidemic disease caused 38 percent of the total number of deaths among girls under age 15 in the two centuries after the first outbreak of bubonic plague (Morrison, Kirshner and Molho 1985, p. 531).

The ancient Greek concept of *epidemic* was revived in connection with increasingly sophisticated disease surveillance systems, and was used by leading physicians to speculate on the natural causes of any sudden outbreak of disease. (Outbreaks of "influenza" received that name because university-educated physicians once thought they were caused by astral influences). Eventually all the other diseases thought to be causes of death were tracked as well.

London followed the example of cities in Italy, and by the early 1600s its officials had institutionalized the continuous surveillance of death and its causes. Thus, when John Graunt (1620–1674) published demography's founding text in 1662 (*Natural and Political Observations Made Upon the Bills of Mortality*), he could draw on more than a half-century of annual data on about 70 diseases that were thought to be causes of death. The data made it very clear that, while bubonic plague remained the most lethal epidemic disease, smallpox epidemics seemed to be getting worse. In 1665, London, with a population of about 500,000, could still lose some 80,000 lives to plague, while Copenhagen lost 20,000 people out of its total population of 60,000 in 1711.

There were no more major outbreaks of bubonic plague in Europe after the 1720s. Historians still disagree about the relative importance of human agency (particularly in the form of public health measures) versus exogenous natural causes in its disappearance. The evidence is inconclusive for Europe, but it is worth noting that outside Western Europe, in countries such as Russia, Turkey, Egypt, China, and India, bubonic plague continued to erupt on a large scale long after 1720. It ceased to do so only after European-style public health measures were adopted and enforced.

When T. R. Malthus published the first edition of his essay on population in 1798, there was enough mortality data—both urban and rural—to hypothesize about the role played by more ordinary epidemics in the regulation of population growth. To Malthus, sudden outbreaks of disease were just one of a set of four mortality-related positive checks on growth, the others being poverty, war, and famine (which he regarded as the last and most deadly positive check). Subsequent historical research suggests that before the twentieth century most deaths that occurred during wars and famines were caused by epidemic disease, not by battle casualties or starvation. Since the poor are often (but not always) hardest hit by epidemic disease, there seems limited value in distinguishing between poverty, war, famine, and epidemic disease as separate checks on population growth, at least before 1900.

Modern Study of Epidemics

Modern demographic historians tend to study epidemic disease as part of "crisis mortality," those sudden increases in deaths or death rates that were a general feature of pre-modern mortality patterns. In theory, mortality crises can be caused by natural disasters as well as by wars, persecution, genocide, and famine; but in practice most crises were caused by epidemics, at least before the early twentieth century. Using historical data, demographers have attempted to gauge how much death rates must rise above some "normal" or background level of mortality in order to constitute a mortality crisis. No agreement has been reached on how to measure either "normal" or "crisis" mortality—especially in cities, where death rates were exceptionally volatile. Thus the relative importance of crisis mortality, and by implication, epidemic disease, in keeping life expectancy levels low (below 40 years) before the modern era remains a matter of controversy.

In theory, the extent to which epidemics as mortality crises can regulate population growth depends on their frequency, amplitude, and duration. But with respect to amplitude, using a high threshold to identify a mortality crisis (for example, requiring that the crisis death rate must be at least five times the "normal" level) would mean that mortality crises (and, by implication, major epidemics) were too infrequent to check population growth in most places and times. In contrast, if death rates must only exceed normal levels by 10 percent, then frequent mortality crises (caused mostly by epidemics) would clearly have been the major brake on population growth in the past. In general, the importance of mortality crises, or epidemics, cannot be assessed independently of the demographic criteria used to identify them.

The uncertainties connected with crisis mortality stimulated demographic research on all short-term fluctuations in pre-modern populations, including marriages and births as well as deaths. In some localities, harvest failures could cause grain shortages, rising prices, and (with a lag) rising death rates, mostly in connection with epidemic disease. But in other cases, a steep rise of grain prices has been observed to lag behind the sharp rise in death rates associated with an outbreak of epidemic disease. Historical research suggests that up to half of all epidemics in early modern Europe broke out and caused mortality crises for reasons unconnected to harvest failures, high prices, or food shortages. The implication is that some epidemics were Malthusian—meaning that they were related to increasing poverty and malnutrition—while others were not.

From a biological standpoint, this conclusion is not surprising, since those diseases that take epidemic form are differentially, not equally, sensitive to the nutritional status of the individuals exposed. This observation is relevant to the study of economic development, where it is still widely but mistakenly assumed that whenever per capita incomes rise, nutrition will improve and death rates will fall automatically without public health reforms. This overlooks the extent to which economic development stimulated urbanization, and thus the frequency with which density-dependent, air- and water-borne diseases broke out. The empirical evidence is that death rates rose during Europe's development, despite rising income levels, until effective measures were taken to control infectious diseases that often took epidemic form.

During the twentieth century, the same story can be told on a global scale: it is primarily the decline of the infectious and parasitic diseases as leading causes of death that produced the global rise of life expectancy. These diseases were first targeted for control through public health measures because of their close connection to epidemic outbreaks of disease and death. Wherever common epidemics were prevented by effective measures of disease control, death rates declined and remained relatively flat from year to year.

The last traditional mortality crisis in the developed countries occurred in 1918 as part of a worldwide pandemic of influenza. This one outbreak was estimated to have caused more deaths in one year than World War I did in several years. (Estimates range from 20 to 40 million deaths caused by influenza, versus 15 million for war-related losses). Nevertheless, in America and Europe influenza was not particularly lethal; many more people were infected than died. In the United States, although one-third of the population is estimated to have developed the symptoms of influenza, at most less than 3 percent of the infected died (Davies 1999, p. 219). Even so, the influenza epidemic produced at least 500,000 excess deaths; as many as 650,000 if pneumonia cases are included. Had death rates prevailing during the epidemic continued, life expectancy levels in the United States would have dropped by 12 years (Noymer and Garenne 2000, p. 568). Instead, death rates quickly returned to normal levels, and subsequently resumed their decline.

Despite the relative absence of mortality crises in the last half of the twentieth century, new pathogenic diseases (newly discovered, newly reportable, or newly resurgent) have continued to turn up at the rate of six to seven per decade (Karlen 1996, p. 6). Most of these new epidemics caused few cases and fewer deaths. Indeed, in most modern epidemics, even those producing hundreds of thousands of cases, so few die that life expectancy levels are not affected. For example, an epidemic of dengue fever broke out in Brazil in 2002. In the Rio de Janeiro area alone, over 400,000 cases were reported. There were fewer than 20 deaths.

While the twentieth century saw undeniable progress in disease control, the twenty-first century began in the shadow of an unusually deadly epidemic disease. HIV-AIDS was discovered in the United States; based on 31 suspicious deaths, it was declared a new epidemic in 1981. Subsequently hundreds, then thousands, of Americans began to die from the disease. But unlike a classic epidemic disease, AIDS fatalities in the United States took more than a decade to reach their peak. By 1995 AIDS was causing

50,000 deaths a year, but even this carnage was insufficient to appreciably increase the death rate at the national level. With respect to the developed countries (and many developing ones), AIDS has not been sufficiently deadly to prevent the continued rise in life expectancy at birth.

In Sub-Saharan Africa, however, the scale of HIV-AIDS deaths has been compared to that of the bubonic plague. Because the data are often defective or incomplete, it is hard to estimate the impact. Nevertheless demographers have made valuable contributions to the estimation of the impact of AIDS on Africa's future population growth, age-structure, and fertility, as well as on mortality. United Nations estimates for 1995 through 2000 indicate that in 35 highly-affected African countries, life expectancy at birth is about 6.5 years lower than it would have been in the absence of AIDS. In the 11 worst-affected countries, life expectancy at birth may drop to 44 years by 2005–2010, instead of reaching 61 years.

As the tragic social and economic implications of the HIV-AIDS epidemic unfold in the twenty-first century, demographers reflect that epidemic disease has long been a major force in human demographic history. It is possible that research on earlier epidemics may offer valuable insights into the continuing threat posed by both epidemic disease and mortality crises to human welfare.

Further Reading

Epidemics in Europe have received the most historical attention. L. Del Panta (1980) has reconstructed major epidemics in various Italian cities over five centuries. J. Biraben (1975) studied epidemics in early modern France. English epidemics are the subject of C. A. Creighton's classic, mostly descriptive, two volume history (1891). E. A Wrigley and R. Schofield's *Population History of England* (1981: Part 2, Sections 8 and 9) takes a more quantitative approach, and focuses on smaller-scale outbreaks in England, as do S. Scott and C. Duncan (1998). Recently, more research has been done on epidemics outside Europe: China (C. Benedict, 1996); Japan (A. Janetta, 1987), India and the Near East (S. Watts, 1997). For China, traditional sources have been used to compile a list of hundreds of major epidemics occurring between 243 B.C.E. and 1911 C.E. (W. Mc-Neil, 1976). But the data available are not sufficiently accurate or detailed to permit detailed comparative work until the late nineteenth and early twentieth centuries (P. Cliff, P. Haggett, and M. Smallman-Raynor, 1998).

See also: *AIDS; Black Death; Disease and History; Epidemiological Transition; Famine, Concepts and Causes of; Health Transition; Influenza; Mortality Decline.*

BIBLIOGRAPHY

Benedict, C. 1996. *Bubonic Plague in Nineteenth Century China.* Stanford, CA: Stanford University Press.

Biraben, J. 1975. *Les hommes et la peste.* The Hague: Mouton.

Charbonneau, H., and A. Larose, eds. 1979. *The Great Mortalities: Methodological Studies of Demographic Crises in the Past.* Liège: Ordina Editions.

Cliff, P., P. Haggett, and M. Smallman-Raynor. 1998. *Deciphering Global Epidemics.* Cambridge, Eng.: Cambridge University Press.

Creighton, C. 1891. *A History of Epidemics in Britain from AD 664 to the Extinction of the Plague,* 2 vols. Cambridge, Eng.: Cambridge University Press.

Del Panta, L. 1980. *Le epidemie nella storia demografica Italiana (secoli XIV-XIX)* Turin.

Easterlin, R. 1999. "How Beneficent is the Market? A Look at the Modern History of Mortality." *European Review of Economic History* 3: 257–294.

Flinn, M. 1981. *The European Demographic System 1500–1820.* Baltimore: Johns Hopkins University Press.

Haggett, P. 2000. *The Geographical Structure of Epidemics.* Oxford, Eng.: Oxford University Press.

Jannetta, A. 1987. *Epidemics and Mortality in Early Modern Japan.* Princeton, NJ: Princeton University Press.

Johansson, S., and C. Mosk. 1987. "Exposure Resistance and Life Expectancy: Disease and Death during the Economic Development of Japan, 1900–1960." *Population Studies* 41: 207–235.

Karlen, A. 1996. *Plague's Progress: A Social History of Disease.* London: Indigo Edition.

Kiple, K. 1993. "The Ecology of Disease." In *Companion Encyclopedia of the History of Medicine,* Vol. 1. London: Routledge.

Lee, J., and Wang Feng. 1999. *One Quarter of Humanity: Malthusian Mythology and Chinese Realities, 1700–2000.* Cambridge, Eng.: Harvard University Press.

Livi Bacci, M. 2001. *The Population of Europe: A History,* 3rd edition. Oxford, Eng.: Blackwell Publishers.

McNeil, W. 1976. *Plagues and Peoples.* Garden City, NY: Anchor Press.

Mosk, C., and S. Johansson. 1986. "Income and Mortality: Evidence from Modern Japan." *Population and Development Review* 12: 415–440.

Noymer, A., and M. Garenne. 2000. "The 1918 Influenza Epidemic's Effects on Sex Differentials in Mortality in the United States." *Population and Development Review* 26: 565–581.

Omran, A. 1971. "The Epidemiologic Transition: A Theory of the Epidemiology of Population Change." *Milbank Memorial Fund Quarterly* 49: 509–538.

Palloni, A. 1988. "On the Role of Crises in Historical Perspective: An Exchange." *Population and Development Review* 14: 145–158.

Preston, S. 1976. *Mortality Patterns in National Populations.* New York: Academic Press.

Preston, S., N. Keyfitz, and R. Schoen. 1972. *Causes of Death: Life Tables for National Populations.* New York: Seminar Press.

Riley, J. 2001. *Rising Life Expectancy: A Global History.* Cambridge, Eng.: University of Cambridge Press.

Scott, S., and C. Duncan. 1998. *Human Demography and Disease.* Cambridge, Eng.: Cambridge University Press.

Spielman, A., and M. D'Antonio. 2000. *A Natural History of Our Most Persistent and Deadly Foe.* London: Hyperion.

Timæus, I. 1997. "Mortality in Sub-Saharan Africa." In *United Nations Symposium on Health and Mortality.* Brussels: United Nations.

United Nations (UNAIDS and WHO). 1998. *Report on the Global HIV/AIDS Epidemic.* Geneva: United Nations.

Watts, S. 1997. *Epidemics and History: Disease, Power, and Imperialism.* New Haven, CT: Yale University Press.

Wrigley, E. A., and R. Schofield. 1981. *The Population History of England 1541–1871: A Reconstruction.* Cambridge, MA: Harvard University Press.

S. RYAN JOHANSSON

EPIDEMIOLOGICAL TRANSITION

The term *epidemiological transition* refers to the shift in cause-of-death patterns that comes with the overall decline of death rates. In European countries the fall in death rates, which began after the middle of the eighteenth century, came about because of a decline in infectious disease mortality (chiefly from cholera and tuberculosis). The victory over infectious diseases allowed people to live longer and hence to develop the chronic degenerative diseases that became the main causes of death during the twentieth century: heart disease, cardiovascular disease, and malignant tumors.

Before the eighteenth century the epidemiological pattern was far from stable but the shifts that occurred had no significant effect on the level of mortality: Some infectious diseases diminished in lethality, but other diseases replaced them. In the 1960s it was thought that increases in life expectancy in the most advanced countries were nearing completion, but from the 1970s a major decline in cardiovascular disease allowed new progress. (The fall of cardiovascular mortality began earlier in a number of countries—dating back to at least 1925 in France.) Under the double effect of the continuation of the decline in infectious disease mortality, now largely eliminated, and the decline in cardiovascular mortality, it is the weight of mortality due to cancers that has been increasing.

The epidemiological transition is one component of a series of concurrent changes in population health. Running parallel to it is a functional component, referring to change in functional health status of the population (that is, abilities and disabilities), and a gerontological component, referring to the increasing proportion of the old and very old age groups in the population, with their distinctive health problems. The term *health transition* is used to describe these various components in combination.

A Theory of Epidemiology of Population Change

The characterization of long-run changes in cause of death as an epidemiological transition was first made by the public-health physician Abdel R. Omran in 1971 in a paper that became a classic in the literature of public health. "During the transition," Omran wrote, "a long shift occurs in mortality and disease patterns whereby pandemics of infection are gradually displaced by degenerative and man-made diseases as the chief form of morbidity and primary cause of death" (Omran, p. 516). He distinguished three stages:

1. The stage before the transition, "*The Age of Pestilence and Famine* when mortality is high and fluctuating, thus precluding sustained population growth" (Omran, p. 516). Average life expectancy at birth is low and variable, in the range of 20 to 40 years.

2. The transitional stage, "*The Age of Receding Pandemics* when mortality declines progressively and the rate of decline accelerates as epidemic peaks become less frequent or disappear. The average life expectancy at birth increases steadily from about 30 to 50 years. Population growth is sustained and begins to describe an exponential curve" (Omran, p. 517).

3. The stage after the transition, "*The Age of Degenerative and Man-Made Diseases* when mortality continues to decline and eventually approaches stability at a relatively low level. The average life expectancy at birth rises gradually until it exceeds 50 years. It is during that stage that fertility becomes the crucial factor in population growth" (Omran, p. 517).

Omran proposed three basic patterns of epidemiological transition: the classical (Western) pattern, the accelerated pattern (represented by Japan), and the contemporary or delayed pattern followed by most developing countries in Latin America, Africa, and Asia. He argued that the reduction of mortality during the nineteenth century in Western countries was determined primarily by ecobiologic and socioeconomic factors, the influence of medical factors being largely inadvertent until the twentieth century.

What should be retained from this schematic picture formulated in the early 1970s? Not a lot, according to the demographer John C. Caldwell. In 2001 Caldwell wrote, "What happened in the mortality transition was the conquest of infectious disease, not a mysterious displacement of infection by degeneration as the cause of death. The resulting demographic transition with its changing age of death and the existence of large numbers of people afflicted with chronic degenerative disease (rather than life-threatening infectious disease) is important for planning health services and medical training, which is the current focus of the burden of disease approach" (p. 159). Other criticisms of Omran's account are that he suggested that the mortality decline would stop during the Age of Degenerative and Man-Made Diseases and that the epidemiological transition is universal, even if delayed for less-developed countries.

A Fourth Stage of the Transition

In a later contribution to the subject, S. Jay Olshansky and A. Brian Ault described the third stage of the transition as a plateau in epidemiological history where mortality once again attains an equilibrium, with a life expectancy at birth reaching into the 70s. This value was believed in the 1970s to be close to the biological limit to the average length of human life. As Olshansky and Ault noted, however, a few years prior to the publication of Omran's theory, the United States and other Western nations began to experience a rapid decline in death rates, mainly due to a decline in mortality from cardiovascular disease. To take into account this unexpected change, Olshansky and Ault proposed adding a fourth stage to the transition, the Age of Delayed Degenerative Diseases. During this stage the ages at death increase because the decline in mortality is concentrated at advanced ages. The age pattern of mortality by cause of death remains largely the same as in the third stage, but the age distribution of deaths from degenerative causes shifts progressively toward older ages. Such a transition is likely to have a significant effect on the size of the population at advanced ages and on the health and the vitality of the elderly. All sections of the elderly population grow markedly, particularly the numbers of the oldest old. (A critical question raised by such a development is whether declining mortality at advanced ages will result in additional years of health or additional years of senility.)

How long can this fourth stage of the epidemiological transition last? Olshansky and Ault inquired whether more debilitating conditions would replace heart disease and cancer as the main killers or whether people would die a non-disease-related "natural death" as James Fries suggested in 1980. But Olshansky and Ault contended that the shift to the fourth stage is the last of the transitions, given the likelihood that the human lifespan is finite.

The Cardiovascular Revolution

During the fourth stage proposed by Olshansky and Ault, the cause-of-death pattern continues to be modified because deaths are postponed toward older ages and the relative incidence of degenerative causes of death, cardiovascular diseases, and cancers varies by age. Thus the concept of a distinct fourth stage being added to Omran's three stages is debatable. An alternative description would show a lengthened third stage characterized by shifting proportions of degenerative and human-made diseases, thus preserving a pattern of epidemiological transition with three "ages." According to France Meslé and Jacques Vallin, however, this would not take into account the major epidemiological change represented by the "cardiovascular revolution." These authors divide the transitional stage into a first phase characterized by the decline in the infectious diseases and a second phase led by the decline in cardiovascular diseases, with possible additional phases to come. The study of mortality levels and cause-of-death patterns are of little practical help in assessing exact dates for the change from Omran's second stage to his third stage (around the 1960s) and even less for dating the change from Omran's third stage to the Olshansky and Ault's fourth stage (around the 1970s). The number of years separating the second and the fourth stages appears to vary across countries. But in reality the cause-of-death pattern exhibits a more or less smooth modification over time rather than discontinuous change.

The Dispersion of Individual Lifespans

According to Jean-Marie Robine, the study of the dispersion of individual lifespans provides support for the existence of only three stages:

1. The reference stage that precedes the fall in mortality—Omran's Age of Pestilence and Famine—which came to an end during the eighteenth or nineteenth centuries, depending on the country.

2. A first stage of transition, when the level of mortality fell and tended to stabilize as a consequence of the decline in infectious diseases affecting mainly children, resulting in a very large reduction in the disparities of individual lifespans around the mode. This Age of Receding Pandemics came to an end in the 1950s in the countries that had gone furthest in the transition, such as northern and western Europe, North America, and Japan.

3. A new stage of transition (represented by these same regions) in which the mortality decline at adult ages, including the very old, becomes relatively larger than at younger ages and where the increase in life expectancy is no longer associated with a significant reduction in the dispersion of individual lifespans.

This new stage corresponds less to Omran's third stage—which in the early twenty-first century appears to have a weak empirical foundation—and more to the fourth stage proposed by Olshansky and Ault. It could be labeled the Age of the Conquest of the Extent of Life. This is the age when humans, having finally been liberated from the great epidemics, are increasingly able to experience the full extent of the potential duration of life. This stage too may eventually come to an end, perhaps to be succeeded by a further stage. Whether this will be the Age of Limits or something else is not known. But at present, in exploring their potential longevity, humans are making unexpected discoveries—such as finding that it is possible to live well beyond 100 years.

Deviations from the Epidemiological Transition

For a period after World War II, all developing countries seemed to be moving through an epidemiological transition; since the 1960s, that was no longer the case. Some countries, most notably those of eastern Europe, failed to experience the cardiovascular revolution, thus deviating from the pattern described above. And a number of African countries, such as Nigeria, Zambia, and Zimbabwe, were struck by AIDS epidemics or by the resurgence of earlier diseases, without having completed the second stage of the transition. In the middle of the 1960s, life expectancies in the countries of eastern Europe and the Soviet Union entered a period of stagnation or regression resulting from the combined effects of increased cardiovascular mortality, violence, and alcoholism.

See also: *Disease, Burden of; Diseases, Chronic and Degenerative; Diseases, Infectious; Health Transition; Mortality Decline; Mortality Reversals; Oldest Old.*

BIBLIOGRAPHY

Caldwell, John C. 2001. "Population Heath Transition." *Bulletin of the World Heath Organization* 79: 159–160.

Caselli, Graziella, France Meslé, and Jacques Vallin. 2001. "Les entorses au schéma de la transition épidémiologique." Paper presented to the general conference of the International Union for the Scientific Study of Population, Salvador, Brazil, August 2001.

Frenk, Julio, José Luis Bobadilla, Claudio Stern, Tomas Frejka, and Rafael Lozano. 1991. "Elements for a Theory of the Health Transition." *Health Transition Review* 1: 21–38.

Meslé, France, and Jacques Vallin. 2000. "Transition sanitaire: Tendances et perspectives." *Médecine/science* 16: 1,161–1,171.

Meslé, France, and Vladimir M. Shkolnikov. 2000. "Russie: Une crise sanitaire sans précédents." *Espace, populations, sociétés* 2: 253–272.

Myers, Georges, Vicki Lamb, and Emily Agree. 2002. "Patterns of Disability Change Associated with the Epidemiologic Transition." In *Determining Health Expectancies*. Chichester: John Wiley & Sons, Ltd.

Olshansky, S. Jay, and A. Brian Ault. 1986. "The Fourth Stage of the Epidemiologic Transition: The Age of Delayed Degenerative Diseases." *Milbank Quarterly* 64: 355–391.

Omran, Abdel R. 1971. "The Epidemiologic Transition: A Theory of the Epidemiology of Population Change." *Milbank Memorial Fund Quarterly* 29: 509–538.

Robine, Jean-Marie. 2001. "Redefining the Stages of the Epidemiological Transition by a Study of the Dispersion of Life Spans: The Case of France." *Population: An English Selection* 13(1): 173–194.

JEAN-MARIE ROBINE

ESTIMATION METHODS, DEMOGRAPHIC

Demographic estimation methods have been developed to cope with inadequacies frequently found in standard demographic data. In settings where population statistics are of good quality, key descriptive demographic measures are calculated as occurrence/exposure rates, with occurrences recorded by a vital statistics system and exposure time obtained from population estimates, the latter typically census-based. In many developing countries, data from these sources may simply not be available, or may be affected by systematic errors that bias the resulting measures.

An Overview of Estimation

Improvements in demographic data have reduced the need for demographic estimation. For example, the birth histories widely collected in sample surveys in developing countries provide adequate measures of fertility and child mortality from occurrence/exposure data. However, measures for small areas and of other population parameters, such as adult mortality and migration, still often require estimation. Even when population statistics are generally adequate, estimation methods have proved useful for tracing historical trends in demographic parameters, and are also helpful for estimating some parameters of current population dynamics that are particularly hard to measure, such as migration.

Demographic estimation methods can be broadly categorized into three groups: those that estimate rates from *changes in stocks,* those that are based on *consistency checks,* and those that are based on *indirect estimation.* The ideas underlying the three groups are illustrated below with examples.

Changes in Stocks

Stocks, such as the number of people in a population over age 50 or the number of children ever born to a cohort of women, change as a result of demographic events. Changes in stocks can therefore be used to draw inferences about underlying demographic rates. In situations where demographic events are not directly recorded, or are recorded with unacceptable levels of error, changes in population aggregates between two observations can be used as a basis to estimate the number of events between the two observations. Estimation methods based on changes in stocks are all residual methods, so results are sensitive to even quite small errors in the components.

The estimation of mortality through intercensal survival provides a simple example. Suppose that population censuses have been held in 1990 and 2000 in a population that has experienced negligible migration. The population aged 30–34 in 2000 represents the survivors of the population aged 20–24 in 1990. If the data are accurate, the survivorship ratio approximates a standard life table function:

$$\frac{{}_5L_{30}}{{}_5L_{20}} \approx \frac{{}_5P_{30}^{2000}}{{}_5P_{20}^{1990}}$$

where ${}_5L_x$ is the life table person-years lived between ages x and $x+5$, and ${}_5P_x^y$ is the population aged x to $x+5$ in year y. Thus, in principle, a life table after early childhood can be derived for any population with two census age distributions that has experienced little migration, though in practice, the method is adversely affected by age misreporting errors, particularly at older ages, and possibly by age-differential under- or over-count.

Fertility can be estimated from changes in the average parity (or average number of children ever borne) of a cohort of women between two observations. The change in average parity measures their cumulative fertility between the two observations, if selection effects through attrition—by death or migration—are negligible. A cumulative fertility distribution for a hypothetical cohort experiencing the fertility rates of the period between the two observations can then be obtained by summing the cohort changes. Period age-specific rates can be estimated from the hypothetical cohort parities in a number of ways, perhaps the simplest of which is fitting of the relational Gompertz fertility model proposed by British demographer William Brass in 1981.

If accurate population estimates—such as from successive census counts—are available for two points in time, net migration can be estimated as a residual from the Demographic Balancing Equation, which expresses the identity that population change during the time interval between the two population counts must be equal to the difference between the additions to the population (births and in-migrants) and the losses (deaths and out-migrants). Thus

$$NM^{t_1-t_2} = P^{t_2} - P^{t_1} - B^{t_1-t_2} + D^{t_1-t_2}$$

where NM is the number of net migrants between t_1 and t_2, P is the population at time t_1 or t_2, and B and D are the numbers of births and deaths respectively between t_1 and t_2. Applying this method to the United States, with a 1990 population count of 248.710 million, a 2000 population count of 281.421 million, and 39.837 million and 22.775 million intercensal births and deaths, net migration between the two censuses is estimated as 15.649 million.

Consistency Checks

Consistency checks seek to compare two or more measures of the same demographic parameter. Consistency between two measures is a necessary, but not sufficient, condition of their validity. If they are found to differ, assumptions about patterns of error can under certain circumstances provide a basis for adjustment, to obtain unbiased measures of the parameter in question even if both data sources are themselves biased. Brass proposed two consistency checks that have been widely used in demographic estimation.

The P/F Ratio Method (Brass 1964) compares current and lifetime measures of fertility. Current fertility estimates for developing countries with weak statistical systems may be in error for a number of reasons: births may not all be registered, and responses to survey questions on both recent births and birth histories may suffer from omission or misreporting of date of occurrence. Brass suggested a simple consistency check for situations in which fertility is not changing rapidly and additional information is available on each woman's lifetime fertility. Age-specific fertility rates can be cumulated from the start of childbearing to obtain measures equivalent to lifetime fertility (for a hypothetical cohort) at exact ages. Measures F comparable to average parities P for five year age groups can then be obtained by interpolating between the point values using standard fertility models (for instance, the relational Gompertz fertility model mentioned above). Consistency is assessed by calculating ratios of average parity P to interpolated, cumulated age-specific fertility F' for each age group.

Brass then goes further to argue that typical errors in the age-specific fertility rates, for example omission of births from registration, may not vary by age, therefore all the F' values will be incorrect by a constant factor, whereas the reporting of children ever born, the basis of the P's, may be most accurate for younger women. Thus, when the P/F ratios indicate inconsistency, the ratios for younger women may provide appropriate adjustment factors for the age-specific fertility rates at all ages. A simple assumption about error patterns turns a consistency check into an adjustment method.

In practice the simple assumptions just stated may be incorrect: current and lifetime fertility may be inconsistent because fertility is changing, rather than because of data errors. Changing fertility can be accommodated if information on lifetime fertility is available for two time periods, allowing the calculation of lifetime fertility for a hypothetical cohort.

Brass (1975) proposed a way to use the Demographic Balancing Equation to evaluate information on deaths by age. The equation can be written in terms of rates, and also for age groups. In a population experiencing negligible migration, the open-ended age group x and over $(x+)$ experiences exits only through deaths at ages x and over, and entries only through birthdays at age x. Thus

$$b(x+) = r(x+) + d(x+)$$

where $b(x+)$, $r(x+)$, and $d(x+)$ are the entry (birthday), growth, and death rates for the age segment $x+$. $b(x+)$ can be estimated from an age distribution as $N(x)/N(x+)$, where $N(x)$ is an estimate of the population passing through age x in a year and $N(x+)$ is the population aged $x+$. Similarly, $d(x+)$ can be estimated as $D(x+)/N(x+)$, where $D(x+)$ is deaths in a year at ages x and over. If deaths are reported with completeness c, constant at all ages relative to the population numbers, then $d(x+) = (1/c)D^o(x+)/N(x+)$, where $D^o(x+)$ is observed deaths x and over. If the population is then assumed to be demographically stable, the growth rate $r(x+)$ is constant for all x. Thus

$$N(x)/N(x+) = r + (1/c)D^o(x+)/N(x+)$$

If the assumptions are correct, the birthday rates and the observed death rates over a range of ages x should be linearly related; the intercept estimates r, the stable growth rate, and the slope estimates $(1/c)$, the reciprocal of the completeness of death registration. Once again, by making simplifying assumptions, the consistency check (of death rates based on recorded deaths against death rates computed from the difference between entry rates and growth rates) provides a basis for adjustment.

If information is available about the population age distribution at two points in time, the assumption of stability can be relaxed, and the last expression can be written as

$$b(x+) - r^o(x+) = k + (1/c)d^o(x+)$$

where $r^o(x+)$ is the observed growth rate of the population $x+$, and k can be interpreted as the error in the growth rate due to change in enumeration completeness.

Indirect Estimation

Indirect estimation seeks to estimate a demographic parameter that is difficult to measure directly from some indicator that can be accurately recorded and is largely, but not exclusively, determined by the parameter of interest. The effects of confounding variables on the indicator are then allowed for, so that the parameter of interest can be estimated.

The most widely used example, due to Brass, estimates infant and child mortality from the proportion dead among children ever borne by women classified by age. Prior to the widespread use of birth histories in countries with deficient demographic statistics, infant and child mortality were especially hard to measure because of omission of early infant deaths from registers or retrospective reports. Brass realized that the proportion dead among children ever born was largely determined by the level of child mortality, but was also affected by the time location of the women's births prior to the survey and by the age pattern of mortality risk in childhood. The older the women, the longer on average their children would have been exposed to mortality risk and hence the higher, other things being equal, would be the proportion dead. However, controlling for women's ages, exposure would also be longer in a population of early childbearers than a population of late childbearers, and hence the former would have a higher proportion dead than the latter. Brass used simple fertility and child mortality models to simulate proportions dead for different fertility patterns to develop conversion factors to adjust an observed proportion dead for the effects of the age patterns of childbearing. His initial method has been extended by several authors, increasing the range of model patterns, extending the technique to data classifying women by duration of marriage, and placing reference dates on the estimates in order to estimate trends.

The Brass method and its successors greatly increased knowledge of levels and trends in childhood mortality in the developing world. Although the widespread use of birth histories in surveys has reduced the need to apply the method for national level estimates, the simplicity of the questions needed, and hence the ability to include them in population censuses, makes the method ideal for small area estimates of levels and trends of child mortality.

Indirect methods have also been developed to estimate demographic parameters from population age distributions assuming stability, to estimate adult mortality from proportions of respondents with surviving mother or surviving father and from proportions of brothers and sisters surviving. A method based on survival of sisters has been developed to measure maternal mortality, which is difficult to measure because the events are relatively rare and cause of death is often misclassified. Wendy Graham and colleagues suggest asking female respondents about the survival of their ever-married sisters, and identifying presumed maternal deaths by whether a dead sister was pregnant, delivering, or within two months of delivery at the time of death. Arguing that maternal deaths would follow approximately the pattern of overall fertility, except for rather higher numbers at young and old ages to reflect higher risks, the authors developed a method for estimating the lifetime risk of maternal death by extrapolating from the partial experience of each age cohort. An estimate of total fertility was then used to convert the measure of lifetime risk into the more widely used indicator, the Maternal Mortality Ratio. The indirect estimate obtained from this method refers to a time point at least 12 years before the survey, and the indirect approach has been largely superseded by the use of direct measurement based on a complete sibling history.

See also: *Actuarial Analysis; Brass, William; Data Assessment; Fertility Measurement; Life Tables; Mortality Measurement; Population Dynamics.*

BIBLIOGRAPHY

Arretx, Carmen. 1973. "Fertility Estimates Derived from Information on Children Ever Born Using Data from Censuses." International Population Conference, Liège 1973, Vol. 2: 247–261.

Brass, William. 1964. "Uses of Census or Survey Data for the Estimation of Vital Rates." Paper presented to the African Seminar on Vital Statistics, Addis Ababa, December 1964.

———. 1975. *Methods for Estimating Fertility and Mortality from Limited and Defective Data.* Chapel Hill, NC: University of North Carolina.

———. 1981. "The Use of the Gompertz Relational Model to Estimate Fertility." *International Population Conference, Manila 1981,* Vol. 3. Liège: International Union for the Scientific Study of Population.

Brass, William, and Kenneth Hill. 1973. "Estimating Mortality from Orphanhood." *International Population Conference, Liège 1973,* Vol. 3. Liège: International Union for the Scientific Study of Population.

Coale, Ansley, and Paul Demeny. 1968. *Methods for Evaluating Basic Demographic Measures from Limited and Defective Data.* New York: United Nations.

Feeney, Griffith. 1980. "Estimating Infant Mortality Trends from Child Survivorship Data." *Population Studies* 34: 109–128.

Graham, Wendy, William Brass, and R. W. Snow. 1989. "Estimating Maternal Mortality: The Sisterhood Method." *Studies in Family Planning* 20: 125–135.

Hill, Kenneth. 1987. "Estimating Census and Death Registration Completeness." *Asian and Pacific Population Forum* 1: 8–24.

Hill, Kenneth, and James Trussell. 1977. "Further Developments in Indirect Mortality Estimation." *Population Studies* 31: 313–334.

Sullivan, Jeremiah. 1972. "Models for the Estimation of the Probability of Dying Between Birth and Exact Ages of Early Childhood." *Population Studies* 26: 79–97.

Timæus, Ian. 1992. "Estimation of Adult Mortality from Paternal Orphanhood: A Reassessment and a New Approach." *Population Bulletin of the United Nations* 33: 47–63.

Timæus, Ian, Basia Zaba, and Mohamed Ali. 2001. "Estimation of Adult Mortality from Data on Adult Siblings." In *Brass Tacks: Essays in Medical Demography,* eds. Basia Zaba and John Blacker. London: The Athlone Press.

Trussell, James. 1975. "A Re-estimation of the Multiplying Factors for the Brass Technique for Determining Childhood Survivorship Rates." *Population Studies* 33: 97–107.

United Nations. 1983. *Manual X: Indirect Techniques for Demographic Estimation.* New York: United Nations.

KENNETH HILL

ETHICS, POPULATION

See *Animal Rights; Asylum, Right of; Data Collection, Ethical Issues in; Environmental Ethics; Euthanasia; Future Generations, Obligations to; Genetic Testing; Reproductive Technologies: Ethical Issues*

ETHNIC AND NATIONAL GROUPS

The term *ethnic group* has no single agreed-on definition in English. Its Greek origins refer to a nation or a people, but by the fifteenth century the word "ethnic" had a connotation of "heathen." A typical modern American definition (Merriam-Webster's Collegiate Dictionary) is "a: of or relating to large groups of people classed according to common racial, national, tribal, religious, linguistic, or cultural origin or background; b: being a member of an ethnic group; c: of, relating to, or characteristic of ethnics." However, if "religious," "racial," and "national" groups are included under the general rubric of "ethnic," what explains the common usages "ethnic and national groups," "ethnic and religious groups," and "racial and ethnic groups"? Such linguistic ambiguities cannot be resolved easily; therefore, the use of the term in this article is broad and inclusive.

The Use of Classifications

Governments around the world routinely collect demographic data classified according to ethnic, na-

tional, tribal, racial, linguistic, cultural, and other categories. The categorizations are typically country-specific—deemed to be suitable to their particular circumstances—thus, cross-country comparisons are difficult and can be misleading. As an example, although some states collect detailed data on the national origins or religions of their residents, others consider these categories improper in official statistics.

Classifications of ethnic and national groups within a country often are linked to sensitive political issues of power, control, and contested territorial boundaries. Therefore, they typically are determined by political rather than scientific or technical decisions.

Overall, the distinguishing quality of data on ethnic and national groups is variability. Even states with otherwise similar recent histories, cultures, political structures, and economic systems (e.g., the liberal democracies of Europe, North America, Asia, and Oceania) demonstrate marked differences in the manner in which they collect, classify, and report data on ethnic and national groups. Moreover, even within a state attitudes toward parallel categories of data are often inconsistent, applied differentially depending on the degree of historical and political sensitivity.

For example, in the U. S. censuses conducted from 1790 through 2000 more or less detailed data have been collected on race, national origin, ethnic origin, and ancestry. However, over the same period of more than two centuries essentially no official U.S. data have been collected on religion.

Changes in the U.S. Census

Early U.S. racial categories were simple—white, Negro, and Indian—but there have been numerous subsequent revisions, mostly in the direction of greater complexity. Until 1960 a respondent's "race" was determined by census interviewers; since that time it has been based on self-identification on a mailed questionnaire. As a result of pressure from a few influential members of Congress, the 2000 U.S. Census "race" classifications had no fewer than sixteen categories, with most of the new categories identifying a substantial number of distinct "races" in the Asian and Pacific regions. Many of these categories (e.g. "Samoan," "Guamanian or Chamorro," "Asian Indian," "Filipino," "Korean," and "Vietnamese") would more commonly be treated as national rather than racial categories.

After a political debate involving vociferous lobbying by interest groups for and against the change, the U.S. Census Bureau decided that a respondent should be allowed to select more than a single race.

In addition to race, the 2000 U.S. Census contained additional and often overlapping questions on "Hispanic origin" and "ancestry." These questions produced many statistical anomalies. Although the Census Bureau considers that any person self-identified as Hispanic to also have a race, about 40 percent of Hispanic respondents in both the 1980 and 1990 censuses reported no racial or other ethnic identity. Furthermore, in studies in which Hispanic respondents were re-interviewed, about 10 percent of the respondents did *not* identify themselves as Hispanic in the second interview.

The "ancestry" question that was sent to a 17 percent sample of households also produced responses generally considered highly subjective and variable. Changes in a "for example" list intended solely to illustrate by example what is meant by "ancestry" produced dramatic numerical changes in responses. Apparently, the mere mention or lack of mention of "German" or "Cajun" as examples of "ancestry" leads to dramatic changes in the numbers reporting such an ancestry, making tabulations of U.S. data by ancestry highly unreliable.

Despite the enormous effort by the U.S. government to collect detailed (if sometimes noncredible) data on race, Hispanic origin, and ancestry, essentially no data have been collected on one of the other main cultural markers of societies: religion.

Censuses Elsewhere

Other countries have different sensitivities about ethnic groups and different data-collecting strategies. In France there have been passionate debates about the acceptability of collecting any official data on "race," "ethnic origin," "national origin," or "ancestry." The French republican concept of the *citoyen* is seen by some as forbidding the government from collecting any information on such matters, and under the *jus soli* principle the national origin of any child born within French borders is "French." Others argue (on much the same grounds as do civil rights groups in the United States) that it is essential to have such data to determine the extent of, and correct problems caused by, discrimination against racial, ethnic, national, linguistic, and religious minorities.

In the neighboring country Germany, which together with France forms the fulcrum of the European Union, wholly different concepts prevail. The German state has long followed the opposing nationality principle of *jus sanguinis,* that is, nationality by "blood" rather than by place of birth. Thus, in Germany there are large numbers of persons classified as "foreigners" ("non-Germans") who were born and have lived the whole of their lives in Germany. Meanwhile, hundreds of thousands of *aussiedler*—populations of German ethnic extraction that have lived for generations in Russia and the former Soviet republics—have been preferentially admitted to Germany for permanent residence and upon admission are automatically classified as "Germans." Current legislation has somewhat modified these traditional concepts of German nationality.

Similar policies are in place elsewhere. The term *patrial* is used in some countries to describe persons who were born and raised elsewhere and have the nationality of other countries but who by dint of cultural and historical family ties (often limited to the origins of grandparents) are granted special access and residence permits and frequently expedited paths to citizenship in the "home country." Such practices are followed in a diverse range of countries in addition to Germany, including Italy, Spain, Israel, Japan, and the United Kingdom.

Categories Created by Governments

Official categories play a role in creating or solidifying ethnic categories and in eliminating or submerging categories that are considered politically problematic. The statistical and now ethnic concept of "Hispanic" was a creation of the U.S. Census Bureau. As was noted above, pressure from influential members of Congress led the Census Bureau to add numerous race categories, most of which involved people from Asia and the Pacific region. The Soviet Union under Stalin established over 100 "nationalities" for citizens of that country, with those designations taken as permanent and recorded prominently both in official statistics and in each individual's internal identification documents. Decisions by government political and statistical organs may have the effect of minimizing the importance of social-cultural-linguistic differences, as in the French government's position that the collection of data on national origins is inconsistent with French concepts of nationality.

Changes and Variations in Ethnic Identity

Ethnic and national groups may experience reduction or blurring of their distinct identities over time as they become integrated into the majority population. The most powerful source of such blurring is intermarriage because the ethnic and/or national identities perceived by the children of those marriages are commonly quite different from those of their parents. Intermarriage among established racial, ethnic, and linguistic groups has been rising in many settings, resulting in far more complex categories of identity in the succeeding generations.

Differing political traditions are also important in the emergence of ethnic categories. Four stylized types can be identified. The first are traditions in which ethnic commonalities are seen as defining the boundaries of the nation, as expressed in the German concept of the *Volk* (the people) and the Mexican concept of *la Raza.* (The term *raza*—literally "race" and colloquially "the people"—refers to the *mestizaje,* or mixed racial and ethnic identity of indigenous, European, and African heritage found in the former Spanish colonies of the Americas.) The second is the political tradition that defines national membership by religion, as in Israel's openness to Jews from all over the world (although native-born adherents of other religions also are defined by law as citizens of Israel). The third is the tradition in which persons from any national or linguistic background can become citizens if they assimilate culturally and linguistically, as in the French openness to naturalizing all types of foreign-born persons as long as they become fluent in French. The fourth is the tradition that defines membership in solely political terms, in which a foreign-born person may be naturalized with only minimal knowledge of the local language and culture, as in the United States, Canada, and Australia (what the French call, with a far-from-correct ethnic referent, the "Anglo-Saxon" notion of multiculturalism).

There are many circumstances in which ethnic bonds unite groups that straddle national boundaries but do not control their own national state. Several of these cases have presented long-standing problems of national and ethnic identity, resulting in persistent tensions and in some cases separatist or even violent movements. Examples include the cases of the Basque, Kurdish, and Roma groups. Less common are transborder ethnic groups that also identify with a state, (e.g., Hungarians in Romania and Slovakia and Russians in the former republics of the Soviet Union, such as Estonia, Latvia, Lithuania, and Kazakhstan).

See also: *Chinese, Overseas; Languages and Speech Communities; Racial and Ethnic Composition; Religious Affiliation; States System, Demographic History of.*

BIBLIOGRAPHY

Anderson, Benedict. 1984. *Imagined Communities.* London and New York: Verso.

Bissoondath, Neil. 1994. *Selling Illusions: The Cult of Multiculturalism in Canada.* Toronto: Penguin Books.

Brubaker, Rogers. 1992. *Citizenship and Nationhood in France and Germany.* Cambridge, MA: Harvard University Press.

Fuchs, Lawrence H. 1990. *The American Kaleidoscope: Race, Ethnicity, and the Civic Culture.* Hanover and London: Wesleyan University Press.

Glazer, Nathan. 1975. *Affirmative Discrimination: Ethnic Inequality and Public Policy.* New York: Basic Books.

Schuck, Peter H., and Roger M. Smith. 1985. *Citizenship Without Consent: Illegal Aliens in the American Polity.* New Haven: Yale University Press.

Skerry, Peter. 1993. *Mexican Americans: The Ambivalent Minority.* New York: Free Press.

Teitelbaum, Michael S., and Jay M. Winter. 1998. *A Question of Numbers: High Migration, Low Fertility, and the Politics of National Identity.* New York: Hill and Wang.

Thernstrom, Stephan, ed. 1980. *Harvard Encyclopedia of American Ethnic Groups.* Cambridge, MA: Harvard University Press.

U.S. Commission on Immigration Reform. 1997. *Becoming An American: Immigration and Immigrant Policy.* Washington, D.C.: Government Printing Office.

MICHAEL S. TEITELBAUM

ETHNIC CLEANSING

Ethnic cleansing, once a term of perpetrators, has become a term of art in the study of population movements. The term spread to English and other languages from Serbian in 1992, as the mass media broadcast a label that was borrowed from the lexicon of Serbian perpetrators. Although ethnic cleansing may be a new coinage, variants involving *cleansing* as the purification of the nation are not. In fact, similar language was used throughout the twentieth century, by Czechs, Poles, Ukrainians, and others. Indeed, Stalin's purges (*chystki*) could easily be translated as *cleansing*, as could Hitler's racial hygiene (*Säuberung*).

Although use of the term in scholarly discourse remains controversial, its function is fairly clear. The term is most often used to mean something like "coercive actions justified in national terms designed to clear territories of putatively undesirable populations without aspiring to their total physical extermination." It thus occupies some of the broad middle ground between voluntary migration and genocide. Part of the analytical value of the term is precisely that it captures a willingness to use force that need not include the willingness to exterminate the entire population.

Ethnic Cleansing and National Politics

Implicit in the idea of ethnic cleansing is a certain modern nationalist view of history and politics. In most, if not all, versions of modern nationalism, legitimate political power in a given territory is believed to be vouchsafed in a mass nation. According to certain important variants of modern nationalism, national identity is determined by ethnicity, which is connected to language and family origin. Ethnic cleansing connects these two ideas. Political legitimacy over territory rests with the nation; the nation is an ethnic group; therefore it is reasonable to expel other ethnic groups from desired territory. Since the political execution of ethnic cleansing involves the realization of a certain idea, the analytic use of the term ethnic cleansing involves a judgment about motives.

Such ideas are only one of a set of necessary conditions for the actual event. Most cases of ethnic cleansing involve the following conditions:

1. The prior collapse of state authority;
2. The cover of a larger war;
3. The practical anticipation of future states to be created;
4. Dedicated cleansers, with military or police training, at work far from home;
5. Historical propaganda that both requires cleansing to be plausible and justifies cleansing already underway;
6. A conscious escalatory push by dedicated elites and propagandists, allowing individual experiences to be understood as a national war; and
7. A motive for seizing property that implicates society after the cleansing has begun.

Ethnic cleansing has nothing to do with ancient hatreds. The idea that ethnic groups exist and are constitutive of national identity is modern. In recorded cases of ethnic cleansing, hostility did not simply express itself in violence. Rather, international and domestic political factors created a propitious moment for the expression of ethnic nationalism. Ethnic nationalists then seek to use existing institutions, such as armies, police forces, or partisans, for new purposes. The cover of war and the habit of military discipline often facilitates the commencement of ethnic cleansing.

Ethnic cleansing, once begun, tends to self-perpetuate. Some perpetrators acquire the habits of murder and rape, and many construe the reaction of victims as a reason to continue. While political circumstances create the opportunity for ethnic cleansers to begin their work, the social world they create then allows ethnic cleansing to continue. The initiation of ethnic cleansing usually requires the breakdown of international order and the rule of law; its progress usually brings the destruction of local norms and customs.

By murdering individuals in the name of the nation, ethnic cleansers in effect target their own group for revenge. Once vengeance is taken, survivors on both sides will see the other as the aggressor, and propagandists can present both sides as nations. What began as an attack by a small number of people against certain localities becomes a battle of nation upon nation. With time, the property motive tends to become increasingly important. Leaders are ideologically motivated; their first followers often seek revenge; but others soon realize that coveted property is there for the taking. These dynamics are most important in cases where there are, or come to be, two national sides. In some cases of ethnic cleansing, the state or another actor enjoys a monopoly or near-monopoly on force. Nazi and Soviet ethnic cleansing are the most important examples.

Ethnic Cleansing and International Politics

In many cases, ethnic cleansing is regulated by treaty, and comes to be seen as a matter of regulated population movements. Yet accords such as Lausanne (1923) and Potsdam (1945) serve to legitimize an ongoing practice. The first regulated the mutual expulsions of Greeks and Turks; the second the flight of Germans from Eastern Europe. Much the same can be said of the agreements between Turkey and Bulgaria (1913) and between the Soviet Union and communist Poland (1944). Although such agreements preserved the semblance of international order, they organized and legitimated ethnic cleansing that was already underway.

Because ethnic cleansing is associated with modern nationalism, it is a phenomenon of the twentieth century. Because it usually requires demanding permissive conditions, its main instances are associated with war, and especially world war. Major examples of ethnic cleansing include:

1. the Bulgarian-Greco-Turkish "exchanges" of 1913–1922;

2. the massacre of Armenians in Turkey in 1915–1922;

3. the deportation of "enemy nations" in Stalin's Soviet Union in 1935–1938;

4. the ethnic cleansing of Jews and Poles from Nazi Germany and occupied Poland in 1939–1941;

5. the mass murder of Poles by Ukrainian insurgents in 1943–1944 and the Polish response;

6. the forced mutual repatriations of Ukrainians from Poland and Poles from the Soviet Union in 1944–1946;

7. the expulsion of the Germans and Hungarians from Czechoslovakia in 1945–1946;

8. the expulsion of Germans from eastern Europe in 1945–1947; and

9. the murder of Bosnians, Kosovars, and others in the Yugoslav wars of 1992–1999.

It is impossible to rigidly separate ethnic cleansing from migration, on the one side, and genocide, on the other. Ethnic cleansing works in part by creating conditions in which people choose to leave a given territory. People need not have been coerced themselves to make such a decision. Ethnic cleansing in practice almost always involves acts of genocide, even if it falls short of the total destruction of a group. Ethnic cleansers may be indifferent to the survival of individuals; they may even wish to exploit them in some other locations, as with the resettlement of Ukrainians from Poland in 1947 or Stalin's pre-World War II cleansings. Yet ethnic cleansing may also provide a transition to full-scale genocide. In Hitler's Final Solution, policies of ethnic cleansing preceded a policy of total physical annihilation of Jews in Germany and the occupied territories. As the term ethnic cleansing has entered historical discussions, it has helped to shed light on the stages of Hitler's policy immediately antecedent to the Jewish Holocaust.

Soviet ethnic cleansing may be divided into two phases, before and after direct contact with German practices. Before and during World War II, Stalin deported all or part of nine "enemy nations" to the Soviet east. After World War II, Stalin deported all Poles west, across the newly expanded borders of the Soviet Union. In both cases, the motivation was the preservation of communist power and the creation of political calm, but the second involved accepting the need to remove groups not only from their homes but from the Soviet Union itself. The Soviet Union was not a national state, and neither were its constituent republics, but its leaders were aware of national questions, and sought to exploit or, at a minimum, defuse national questions. This new ethnic quality in postwar Soviet policy was part of a general trend, as the connection of homogeneity and stability came to be widely accepted.

After World War II, not only the Soviet Union but the United States and Britain accepted that ethnic homogeneity was needed for European peace. After the end of the Cold War, these perspectives changed. The United States, Britain, and their NATO allies prosecuted a war in Yugoslavia in 1999 with the express aim of bringing ethnic cleansing to a halt. Ethnic cleansing came to function as a term of both perpetrators and human rights activists, as a term of moral endorsement and moral opprobrium. The shock of the Yugoslav wars and the fact of a Western military response forced a reconsideration of the history of the twentieth century, in which ethnic cleansing as a social fact took a prominent place.

See also: *Communism, Population Aspects of; Forced Migration; Genocide; Refugees, Demography of.*

BIBLIOGRAPHY

Browning, Christopher. 2000. *Nazi Policy, Jewish Workers, German Killers.* Cambridge, Eng: Cambridge University Press.

DeZayas, Alfred M. 1977. *Nemesis at Potsdam: The Anglo-Americans and the Expulsion of the Germans: Background, Execution, Consequences.* London; Boston: Routledge & Kegan Paul.

Ladas, Stephen. 1932. *The Exchange of Minorities: Bulgaria, Greece, and Turkey.* New York: Macmillan.

Martin, Terry. 2001. *The Affirmative Action Empire: Nations and Nationalism in the Soviet Union.* Ithaca, NY: Cornell University Press.

Naimark, Norman. 2001. *Fires of Hatred: Ethnic Cleansing in Twentieth-Century Europe.* Cambridge, MA: Harvard University Press.

Renan, Ernest. 1996 (1882). "What is a Nation?". In *Becoming National.* trans. and ed. Geoff Eley and Ronald Grigor Suny. New York: Oxford University Press.

Snyder, Timothy. 2002. *The Reconstruction of Nations: Poland, Ukraine, Lithuania, Belarus, 1569–1999.* New Haven, CT: Yale University Press.

Ther, Philipp, and Ana Siljak. 2001. *Redrawing Nations: Ethnic Cleansing in East-Central Europe, 1944–1948.* Lanham: Rowman and Littlefield.

Weber, Max. 1996 (1914). "The Origins of Ethnic Groups" from *Economy and Society.* In *Ethnicity* trans. and ed. John Hutchinson and Anthony Smith. Oxford: Oxford University Press.

TIMOTHY SNYDER

EUGENICS

Eugenics, a term derived from the Greek for well-born, is the science of improved breeding applied to humans. The eugenics movement was one of several initiatives that originated in the late nineteenth century, and which focused on the problem of the urban poor. The new Darwinian biology with its emphasis on evolutionary success and survival of the fittest was seen as providing an alternative ameliorative route to the efforts of the environmentalists, the sanitarians, and the public health movement. Fear of urban degeneration coincided with the beginning of the demographic transition with its sharply lowered fertility, especially marked in the upper socioeconomic classes.

The Early Movement

The eugenics movement began in Britain, but its appeal and its organization was international. It was particularly important in the United States and Germany. Francis Galton (1822–1911), explorer and amateur scientist, and cousin of English naturalist Charles Darwin, produced the founding documents, his *Hereditary Genius* of 1869 and *Natural Inheritance* of 1889. It was nature, not nurture, he claimed, that determined that eminent men were usually the sons of eminent fathers. The statistical methods he suggested—the normal curve, correlation, and regression—were developed by his admirer, the statistician Karl Pearson (1857–1936), working at University College, London, to measure the effect of heredity. Their work lent scientific support to the idea that class differentials represented levels of inherited natural ability and of civic worth. In this intellectual climate, the so-called professional model of class structure based on the occupation of male breadwinners, proposed by statistician William Farr (1807–1883) in 1851, reached its fully developed form in the British Census of 1911. It put the professional and intellectual groups in Class I, skilled labor in Class III, and unskilled and casual labor in Class V, with fill-in classes between. This classification scheme encouraged a linear view of society with the professional class as the most highly evolved. If indeed ability was inherited, and if classes corresponded to biological subtypes as Galton supposed, the differential decline in fertility in Class I was a national catastrophe. It was a catastrophe that the eugenists sought to publicize and to remedy.

As primary education became compulsory and the poorest and most deprived began to enter the new elementary schools in the last quarter of the century, children who could not keep up academically came to be seen as a compelling problem. Mary Dendy, secretary of the Lancashire and Cheshire Association for the Permanent Care of the Feebleminded, and Ellen Pinsent, chair of the Special Schools Subcommittee of the Birmingham Education Committee, founded the National Association for Promoting the Welfare of the Feebleminded in 1896. Their "welfare" entailed segregation and control of the children they selected as feebleminded for the rest of their lives starting in 1902 on a farm at Sandlebridge in Cheshire. Seen in Galtonian terms, feeblemindedness was inherited: Segregation would prevent its propagation.

The eugenics movement began in earnest after the turn of the twentieth century, taking additional impetus from the diffusion of Mendelian theory (named after Austrian botanist Gregor Mendel) after 1901. The Eugenics Education Society's (1907) founding drive was started by Sybil Gotto, another Galton admirer, then a young widow interested in social problems. The society took the now elderly Galton as its figurehead. It was mainly a propaganda group rather than a scientific society, but its projects included teaching the science of heredity and research on the inherited nature and relationships of the urban poor—what it called its Pauper Pedigree Project, a pauper being the term for someone receiving relief under the poor law. Its methodology was typically that of the pedigree, an easily understood and convincing demonstration of heredity. It focused on the elevated fecundity of the pauper class, in which, it alleged, every family, in their terms, was studded with paupers, the impoverished, inebriates, criminals, and the feebleminded. The Royal Commission on the Care and Control of the Feeble Minded of 1909, strongly supported by the Society, led to the segregationist Mental Deficiency Act (1914). Eugenists pointed to this Act as their proudest success.

Eugenics in the United States

In the United States, eugenics was first fostered by the American Breeders' Association (founded in 1903, renamed the American Genetic Association in 1914), in which a subcommittee concerned itself with human heredity, supporting itself scientifically on Mendelism and on the collection of pedigrees. Interestingly, the stockbreeders generally were uninterested in Mendelism; it was impossible to use it in pursuing practical, quantitative objectives, such as enhanced egg production and milk yield, or even improving the racing performance of thoroughbreds. Charles B. Davenport (1866–1944), Harvard Professor of Zoology and Director of the Eugenics

Record Office at Cold Spring Harbor, New York, preached Galton and eugenics to his Harvard students. In *Heredity in Relation to Eugenics* (1911), he applied Mendelism to the inheritance of psychological traits such as memory, temperament, general bodily energy, and criminality as well as intelligence. Many of his exemplary pedigrees came from psychologist Henry H. Goddard, superintendent of the Training School for Defectives, Vineland, New Jersey. Low mental acumen was a unit character determined by Davenport to be a recessive condition due to the absence of a factor for intelligence. If the factor was absent in both parents, it would be absent in the children. Davenport's nominee as superintendent of the Eugenics Record Office was Harry H. Laughlin, an agriculturalist from Iowa who trained as a biologist specializing in heredity under Davenport at Cold Spring Harbor. As superintendent, he organized a collection of pedigrees mainly of poor families showing what he claimed to be inherited mental and social problems, and supported the campaign for eugenic sterilization. The first state sterilization law was passed in Indiana in 1907, and by 1917, 15 other states had legalized the sterilization of a number of different types of people deemed to be "defective." In 1923, an American Eugenics Society was formed, led by the Yale economist Irving Fisher; it soon had 28 state committees. But after World War I, the "vulgar Mendelism" of the early pedigrees was increasingly rejected by scientists. In the 1930s, the Eugenics Record Office began to lose its funding and eventually closed in 1939. Sterilization on eugenic grounds, however, continued. The numbers picked up after 1930 and the practice continued into the 1970s in the United States and Canada, until the laws permitting it were repealed one by one. Approximately 60,000 sterilizations took place under this system, usually of the poor, and often of "wayward girls," deemed "moral imbeciles" because they had given birth to a child out of wedlock. Science, in fact, mainly supplied only the rhetoric for eugenics. It was as much a political as a scientific movement, and its greatest success in the United States had been in persuading Congress in 1924 to limit immigration from the supposedly inferior populations of southern and eastern Europe.

Eugenics in Europe

In Britain, the Eugenics Society, as it was now called, led a campaign to legalize eugenic sterilization, from about 1930. But sterilization, even voluntary sterilization, was never legalized there. The Society's focus on controlling the "disturbing" fertility of the urban poor led to support for birth control clinics, though not for their rather quarrelsome advocate, Marie Stopes, even though she was an enthusiastic eugenist herself. It was also involved in setting up the International Union for the Scientific Investigation of Population Problems (IUSIPP), following a congress organized in Geneva in 1927 by Stopes's American counterpart, birth control leader Margaret Sanger (1879–1966). The congress was attended by leading eugenists from every country in which there was an organized movement. The first president of IUSIPP was American population ecologist and geneticist Raymond Pearl (1879–1940) of Johns Hopkins University, with Sir Bernard Mallet (1859–1932), retired Registrar-General of Britain, of the British Eugenics Society, as vice-president and treasurer. Its British component was the British Population Society, the members of which were all active in the Eugenics Society; IUSIPP's announcements and proceedings appeared in the Society's publication, the *Eugenics Review*. In 1936, another organization, the Population Investigation Committee was set up by the Eugenics Society as an autonomous joint committee, with the stated intention of developing a questionnaire on fertility. The project was interrupted by the outbreak of World War II, but the Committee survived, initially kept going by a series of grants from the Society. Its activities increasingly defined mainstream demography.

The country in which eugenics was both the most highly developed, and the most destructive, was Germany. Its earliest advocate was Wilhelm Schallmeyer (1857–1919), Darwinist, psychiatrist, and author of a thesis on the *Pressing Problem of the Physical Degeneration of Civilised Man* (1891). Like the British and American eugenists, he pointed to the burden on the state of caring for the "pauper idiot" who could produce nothing for society. Alfred Ploetz (1860–1940), a German physician, started the world's first eugenic society in 1905. Its focus was on what he termed the damage to the Caucasian race done by the protection of its weakest members. From the start it was envisaged as part of an international movement, and in 1912, the first Eugenics Congress met in London to hear papers by a mix of scientists, statisticians, social reformers and political activists. The Permanent International Eugenics Committee was an outcome of the Congress. Interrupted by World War I, there were two further inter-

national congresses, both held in United States, in 1921 and 1932.

German eugenicists soon left behind the simplistic pedigree methods of the British and the Americans. The Stuttgart statistician Wilhelm Weinberg took the lead in mathematizing Mendelism, a complex system of calculations taken up first by eugenists such as Fritz Lenz, a geneticist, and by the Munich psychiatrist Ernst Rüdin who applied it to the inheritance of schizophrenia. But, from the early 1920s, Mendelism was abandoned for Rüdin's more politically persuasive method, which he called empirical prognosis. A collection of data on the prevalence of a spectrum of different abnormalities in the families of schizophrenics could be used to point to the need for a sterilization program. The Nazi government in 1933 enacted the sterilization law, planned by Rüdin and modeled on laws in the United States, as soon as it came to power. Sterilization became compulsory for patients and families with several types of mental diseases and disabilities. Roughly 600,000 sterilizations took place. Racism was not at first a necessary part of this hereditarian program, but with state support, it expanded into systematic euthanasia, first for the inhabitants of mental hospitals, then for people with other chronic diseases, and finally for Jews, Gypsies, homosexuals, Communists, and Slavs. The Nazis thus managed to justify the extermination of several million of their own citizens. After World War II ended, the Nuremberg tribunal was unable to indict anyone for forced sterilization. The German law, it was pointed out, derived from American laws and the practice of forced sterilization was still legal in the United States.

Post-World War II Eugenics

In the 1930s, the British Eugenics Society endured attacks on its science and its ideology by left-wing geneticists. The attackers, Lancelot Hogben (1895–1975) of the London School of Economics, and J. B. S. Haldane (1892–1964) of University College, London, were offended by the eugenists' conflation of social class and social worth, and their rejection of the influence of environment. Hogben placed his hopes on genetic linkage and on blood groups as a genetic marker: If a trait is linked to a blood group, he felt, it must be truly biological, and not environmentally determined. The psychiatrist Lionel Penrose (1898–1972) attacked the association of feeblemindedness with an inherited pauper class.

After World War II, political changes in Britain eroded the class system. Its links to differential fertility and pauperism became less acceptable with the end of the poor law and the coming of the welfare state. The image of eugenics also suffered from its association with Naziism. Under Penrose, *Annals of Eugenics* became *Annals of Human Genetics* in 1954. In 1968, the *Eugenics Review* closed, and the Society turned to third world overpopulation and fertility in the *Journal of Biosocial Science.* In the United States, the Population Council, founded in 1952, also focused on the third world and its problems. The Council's first executive officer was the Wall Street banker Frederick Osborn (1889–1981), who had been president of the American Eugenics Society from 1946 to 1952; the offices of the Population Council and the Eugenics Society were initially at the same address. During the 1970s, eugenic sterilization of poor young women tailed off. More modern genetic counseling focused not on poverty and fertility, but on genetic disease. Amniocentesis was not expected to identify the social problem group, as the erstwhile pauper class was now called.

In 1989 the British Eugenics Society became the Galton Institute. The Institute has recently been interested in exploring its own past, a history of serious importance since the eugenic problematic has molded present day human genetics and population studies.

See also: *Demography, History of; Galton, Francis; Pearl, Raymond; Quality of Population; Reproductive Technologies: Ethical Issues; Sanger, Margaret.*

BIBLIOGRAPHY

Broberg, Gunner, and Nils Roll-Hansen. 1996. *Eugenics and the Welfare State: Sterilization Policy in Denmark, Sweden, Norway and Finland.* East Lansing: Michigan University Press.

Burleigh, Michael. 1994. *Death and Deliverance: Euthanasia in Germany 1900–1945.* Cambridge, Eng.: Cambridge University Press.

Kevles, Daniel J. 1985. *In the Name of Eugenics: Genetics and the Uses of Human Heredity.* Cambridge, MA: Harvard University Press.

Mazumdar, Pauline M.H. 1992. *Eugenics, Human Genetics and Human Failings: the Eugenics Society, its Sources and its Critics in Britain.* London: Routledge.

Reilly, Philip R. 1991. *The Surgical Solution: A History of Involuntary Sterilization in the United States.* Baltimore, MD: Johns Hopkins University Press.

Schneider, William H. 1990. *Quality and Quantity: The Quest for Biological Regeneration in Twentieth Century France.* Cambridge, Eng.: Cambridge University Press.

Soloway, Richard A. 1990. *Demography and Degeneration: Eugenics and the Declining Birthrate in Twentieth Century Britain.* University of North Carolina Press.

Stepan, Nancy Leys. 1991. *The Hour of Eugenics: Race, Gender and Nation in Latin America.* Ithaca, NY: Cornell University Press.

Thomson, Mathew. 1998. *The Problem of Mental Deficiency: Eugenics, Demography and Social Policy in Britain, c. 1870–1959.* Oxford: Clarendon Press.

Pauline M. H. Mazumdar

EULER, LEONHARD

(1707–1783)

Arguably the greatest mathematician of the eighteenth century, Leonhard Euler, a Swiss, made basic contributions to every branch of mathematics then being studied. His enduring place in the history of demographic analysis is assured due to his 1760 formula for a stable population.

An analysis of the formula begins by considering a population with fixed and known death rates at each age and a constant number of births per unit time in all generations. From the death rates, it is possible to create a life table giving the probability of survival to age x, denoted $l(x)$. If the number of births is $b(0)$, the population in the age group from x to $x + dx$, where dx is small, is $b(0)l(x)dx$, a constant over time. If the number of births is increasing at an exponential rate, r, t years into the future the number of births would be $b(0)e^{rt}$. Similarly, t years in the past, the number of births would have been $b(0)e^{-rt}$. Thus, taking the formula for births t years ago, and multiplying by $l(x)$, the proportion of births surviving to age x, gives a stable population with the age distribution $b(0)l(x)dx = b(0)l(x)e^{-rx}dx$. Euler was the first to develop this formula, which is the starting point for much subsequent population modeling.

If survivorship remains fixed and $r(x)$ varies, then the formula remains the same, but has a different interpretation; and more generally, allows for survivorship to vary as well. Then, given birth and death rates as they vary with time, researchers have the usual formula for population at the end of any time interval. At first this was called forecasting, but the unreliability of the process led to the more modest term *projection*, meaning simply the working out of the consequences of the assumed regime of birth and death rates.

The theory above stated has been reformulated as a set of partial differential equations more applicable to numerical work. Neither of these continuous models, developed as theory, is convenient for calculation with real data.

While Euler never went beyond fixed rates, he can reasonably be described as the originator of the field of projection and prediction that preoccupies demographers, and even more so, the public at the beginning of the twenty-first century.

Well over a century after Euler, demographer Alfred Lotka (1880–1949), with much wider demographic (and additional environmental) interests, published, in 1907, the renewal equation, the fundamental relationship in population dynamics, that permitted calculation of the rate of increase implied by a regime of birth and death rates.

Euler, called by his contemporaries the Prince of Mathematicians, commanded the respect of kings and the public, and above all of mathematicians. He was a lifelong friend of the brothers Daniel and Nicholas Bernoulli. He held an appointment at the University of Basel. He was invited to Russia by Catherine the Great, and to Berlin by Frederick the Great, both powerful patrons of the arts and sciences during the eighteenth-century Enlightenment. Euler's private life, however, was far from happy. He was blind for almost twenty years before his death. In 1768, he lost many of his unpublished papers when his house was destroyed in a fire. He died of apoplexy.

See also: *Demography, History of; Lotha, Alfred J.; Renewal Theory and the Stable Population Model.*

BIBLIOGRAPHY

SELECTED WORKS BY LEONHARD EULER.

Euler, Leonhard. 1977 (1760). ''A General Investigation into the Mortality and Multiplication of the Human Species,'' trans. Nathan and Beatrice Keyfitz. In *Mathematical Demography: Selected Papers,* ed. David Smith and Nathan Keyfitz. New York: Springer-Verlag.

SELECTED WORKS ABOUT LEONHARD EULER.

Lotka, Alfred J. 1907. ''Relation Between Birth Rates and Death Rates.'' *Science N.S.* 26: 21–22.

NATHAN KEYFITZ

EUTHANASIA

Euthanasia is the intentional taking of a person's life from a beneficent or kind motive—typically in a case of grave and terminal illness. Increasingly, however, the term is also used of cases in which a person, though gravely ill, is not immediately threatened with death. She simply does not want to live out the life to which illness has condemned her.

Three distinctions figure prominently in discussions of euthanasia: the distinction between active and passive euthanasia; the distinction among voluntary, involuntary, and non-voluntary forms; and the distinction between physician-assisted suicide and euthanasia.

Active and Passive Euthanasia

Active euthanasia involves taking steps to terminate a life. Passive euthanasia involves omitting steps to save a life or withdrawing treatment. At present, active euthanasia is frowned upon by law and the medical profession, whereas passive euthanasia—for example, withdrawing a ventilator that keeps alive a patient whose further care is deemed futile—is not.

The question of whether one can sustain a distinction between active and passive euthanasia is hotly debated. A person will die if injected with a large enough dose of morphine, which may be given in the guise of pain relief, but he will also die if feeding tubes are removed. In a patient whose further care is deemed futile, what is the moral difference between these two ways of producing death?

Voluntary, Involuntary, and Non-Voluntary Euthanasia

A distinction may be drawn among voluntary, involuntary, and non-voluntary euthanasia. In voluntary euthanasia, the steps taken to end life are taken with the patient's consent, and often at her instruction.

In involuntary euthanasia, the steps taken are without the consent of the patient, and without his request; in fact, euthanasia may be something to which he explicitly would not consent.

Non-voluntary euthanasia typically refers to taking steps to end the life of someone deemed incompetent by medical and legal authorities. The steps are taken at the consent of a trustee whom the person has designated to represent her interests. This can prove problematic if the patient has no designated trustee empowered to consent. It is possible that, if a trustee is then appointed to represent a patient's interests and consents to euthanasia on her behalf, the case has been transformed into one of involuntary euthanasia.

Physician-Assisted Suicide and Euthanasia

A distinction is usually drawn today between physician-assisted suicide and euthanasia. One useful way of marking this distinction is to say that, in the former, the last causal actor is the patient, whereas in the latter it is the doctor.

A doctor supplies a terminally ill patient who is competent, who is not suffering unduly from depression, and who voluntarily requests assistance in dying with a pill that will prove lethal. If the patient takes the pill and swallows it, the doctor does not produce the patient's death; the patient does so through accepting the pill and deciding to swallow it. The pill produces death only if it is swallowed, and the doctor does not force it down the patient's throat; rather, the patient voluntarily swallows it.

Euthanasia, Quality of Life, and Aging

The morality of so-called "mercy killing" has had a long history. This is inevitable, for there are two central facts about the human condition that dominate moral consideration of the topic.

First, the quality of human life can deteriorate massively, so that someone may remain alive, but in effect can come to have "no life." The objection is sometimes made that no one is entitled to say that someone else's life is not a life worth living; but it is possible to say this of those in permanently vegetative states or of anencephalic infants, who live lives that no one would wish for anyone. Indeed, the whole topic of physician-assisted suicide has arisen precisely because many of those condemned to live out lives blighted by amyotrophic lateral sclerosis and the like state that they do not wish to do so. If they are regarded as having a right to refuse treatment, then they do not have to live out their lives. But if they are not so regarded, or if they are no longer competent to insist upon this right, or if they have no advanced directive that is honored by authorities, then they are forced to continue to live.

Second, improved living conditions, increased prosperity, better health care, and technological innovation have increased human longevity dramatically. A larger elderly population has made nursing homes more important, has made geriatrics into a major medical science, and has focused attention upon the lives—and deaths—of elderly men and women. As they come to face death, especially as they come to face death in the context of lives plagued by illness and degenerative disease, the moral and social aspects of suicide, assisted death, and euthanasia inevitably become topics of debate. This is particularly true of moral implications as societies come to give greater weight to individual autonomy and to permit individuals a say in their own treatment and the ending of their lives.

Euthanasia and the Law

Relaxation of prohibitions against physician-assisted suicide and active voluntary euthanasia were frequently urged at the turn of the twenty-first century, and Oregon, the Netherlands, and the Northern Territory of Australia took some steps toward relaxation (since put on hold in the Australian case in the late 1990s). Preliminary data from both Oregon and the Netherlands suggest that neither physician-assisted suicide nor active voluntary euthanasia is yet used by a significant part of the elderly as a preferred option of ending lives. In 1998 in Oregon only 15 deaths were reported under the new law there, and the update of data in the Netherlands in 1995 found that vastly more patients chose to forego treatment than to take advantage of the suicide law. The option continues to exist, however.

The Morality of Euthanasia

Whatever the specific objections to relaxation of prohibitions on physician-assisted suicide and active voluntary euthanasia may be, opponents have fostered fear of a "slippery slope" as one of the lurking dangers of such a course. This means a fear that voluntary euthanasia shall soon pass to involuntary euthanasia; that competent patients requesting death shall soon pass to incompetent persons who have no idea what they are requesting (or for whom euthanasia is requested by someone else); that letting physicians prescribe pills for competent patients who voluntarily request assistance in dying shall soon pass to physicians killing off patients in all kinds of situation, for all sorts of nefarious reasons; that assisted death and euthanasia as socially approved options shall soon pass to circumstances in which patients feel pressured for various reasons to choose one of these options, even when they would otherwise want to prolong their lives.

Opponents of change almost always urge slippery-slope objections not only against social changes but against even thinking about changes, and this has long been the case with active voluntary euthanasia. In fact, good evidence is needed to believe such claims. However, for many opponents of active voluntary euthanasia, slippery-slope concerns are at bottom not the main argument. In circumstances where it was clear that slippery-slope effects were exceedingly unlikely to arise, few opponents to active voluntary euthanasia would remove their objections.

Most religions continue to insist that life is a gift from God that can only be justly taken by God. To many adherents it follows that quality of life concerns are not centrally germane to the whole issue of the prolongation of life. Advocates believe the fact that physician-assisted suicide and active voluntary euthanasia give voice to the value of autonomy, to the demands of patients to have a say in their own treatment, and to the wish of many to be able to decide not only how they will live but also how they will die, is unlikely to carry the day as a moral argument.

See also: *Religions, Population Doctrines of; Reproductive Technologies: Ethical Issues.*

BIBLIOGRAPHY

Beauchamp, Tom. L., ed. 1996. *Intending Death: The Ethics of Assisted Suicide and Euthanasia.* Englewood Cliffs, NJ: Prentice-Hall.

Brock, Dan. 1993. *Life and Death: Philosophical Essays in Biomedical Ethics.* Cambridge, Eng.: Cambridge University Press.

Callahan, Daniel. 1993. *The Troubled Dream of Life: Living with Mortality.*New York: Simon and Schuster.

Dworkin, Gerald., R. G. Frey, and Sissela Bok. 1998. *Euthanasia and Physician-Assisted Suicide.* Cambridge, Eng.: Cambridge University Press.

Rachels, James. 1986. *The End of Life: Euthanasia and Morality.* Oxford, Eng.: Oxford University Press.

VanDerMass, P. J., G. van der Wal, I. Haverkate, et al. 1996. "Euthanasia, Physician-Assisted Suicide, and Other Medical Practices Involving the End of Life in The Netherlands." *New England Journal of Medicine* 335: 1699–1705.

Verhovek, S. H. 1999. "Oregon Reporting 15 Deaths in 1998 Under Suicide Law." *New York Times,* February 18, 1998, A1.

R. G. FREY

EVENT-HISTORY ANALYSIS

Event-history analysis is a set of statistical methods designed to analyze categorical or discrete data on processes or events that are time-dependent (i.e., for which the timing of occurrence is as meaningful as whether they occurred or not). One example of such time-dependent processes is mortality: variation across individuals is not captured by the lifetime probability of dying (which is one for every individual), but by differences in the age at which death occurs. Another example is marriage: here, variation across individuals is captured by both the lifetime probability of getting married and differences in age at marriage.

Event-history analysis, sometimes called survival analysis, has applications in many fields, including sociology, economics, biology, medicine, and engineering. Applications in demography are particularly numerous, given demography's focus on age and cohorts. In addition to mortality, demographic events that can be investigated with event-history analysis include marriage, divorce, birth, migration, and household formation.

Comparison to Life Table Analysis

Event-history analysis has its roots in classical life table analysis. In fact, life table analysis is one of the methods covered by event-history analysis, and many of the concepts of event-history analysis, such as survival curves and hazard rates, have equivalents in a conventional life table. One difference from life table analysis is that event-history analysis is based on data at the individual level and aims at describing processes operating at that level. Also, whereas conventional life table analysis is deterministic, event-history analysis is probabilistic. Hence, many event-history analysis outcomes will have confidence intervals attached to them. Another feature of event-history analysis relative to conventional life table analysis is the use of covariates. Event-history analysis makes it possible to identify factors associated with timing of events. These factors can be fixed through time (such as ethnicity or parents' education), or vary with time (such as income and marital status).

Whereas conventional life table analysis can be applied to both longitudinal and cross-sectional data, event-history analysis requires longitudinal data. Longitudinal data can be collected either in a prospective fashion by following individuals through time, or retrospectively by asking individuals about past events.

Censored Data and Time-Varying Covariates

Because of its longitudinal nature, event history data have some features which make traditional statistical techniques inadequate. One such feature is *censoring,* which means that information on events and exposure to the risk of experiencing them is incomplete. *Right censoring,* the most common type of censoring in event-history analysis, occurs when recording of events is discontinued before the process is completed. For example, in longitudinal data collection, individuals previously included in a sample may stop contributing information, either because the study is discontinued before they experience the

event of interest, or because they discontinue their participation in the study before they experience the event. Another, less common, type of censoring is *left censoring,* which occurs when recording is initiated after the process has started. In the remainder of this article, censoring will refer to right censoring.

It is important to include censored individuals in event-history analysis, because the fact that they did not experience the event of interest in spite of their exposure is in itself meaningful. Censoring can be handled adequately as long as it is independent—that is, as long as the risk of being censored is not related to the risk of experiencing the event, or, equivalently, provided that individuals censored at any given time are representative of all other individuals. If the two risks are related, however, the estimates obtained can be seriously biased.

Another particular feature of survival data is the potential presence of time-varying covariates. For example, an individual's income may vary over time, and these variations may have an effect on the risk of experiencing events. If this is the case, it is important to include information on these variations in the analysis.

Unlike traditional statistical techniques such as ordinary least squares (OLS), event-history analysis can handle both censoring and time-varying covariates, using the method of maximum likelihood estimation. With the maximum likelihood approach, the estimated regression coefficients are the ones that maximize the likelihood of the observations being what they are. That is, the set of estimated coefficients are more likely than any other coefficient values to have given rise to the observed set of events and censored cases.

Hazard Rates

An important concept in event-history analysis is the hazard rate, $h(t)$. The hazard rate is the risk or hazard that an event will occur during a small time interval, $(t, t+dt)$. It corresponds to the rate of occurrence of an event (number of occurrences/amount of exposure to the risk of occurrence) during an infinitesimal time or age interval. If the event under study is death, then the hazard rate is called the force of mortality, $\mu(x)$, where x is age. Event-history analysis can be used to explore how hazard rates vary with time, or how certain covariates affect the level of the hazard rate.

Types of Analysis

Methods of event-history analysis fall into three categories:

1. Nonparametric, in which no assumption is made about the shape of the hazard function;

2. Parametric, requiring an assumption about how the hazard rate varies with time; and

3. Semiparametric, requiring an assumption about how the hazard rate varies across individuals but no assumption about its overall shape.

Nonparametric Models

The life table approach to analyzing event history data is a nonparametric method. It is very similar to traditional life table construction in demography, although it is based on cohort rather than period data. The logic behind the life table approach is to calculate $Q(t_i)$, the probability of "failing" (for instance, dying) in the interval $[t_i, t_i+n]$, from data on $N(t_i)$, the number of individuals at risk of failing at time t_i, and $D(t_i)$, the number of failures between t_i and t_i+n. The number of individuals at risk needs to be adjusted for the fact that some individuals, $C(t_i)$, will be censored—that is, removed from the risk of experiencing the event during the interval. Hence $Q(t_i)$ can be expressed as:

$$Q(t_i) = \frac{D(t_i)}{N(t_i) - 0.5 \cdot C(t_i)}$$

The proportion of persons surviving at time t_i, $S(t_i)$, is then obtained as the product of the probabilities of surviving over all earlier time intervals as shown below.

$$\hat{S}(t_i) = \prod_{j=0}^{i-1} \left[1 - Q(t_j)\right]$$

Another output of the life table method is the hazard rate, $h(t_i)$, which is simply calculated by dividing the number of events experienced during the interval t_i by the number of person-years lived during the interval. The number of person-years is estimated by assuming that both failures and censored cases occur uniformly through the interval. Hence $h(t_i)$ is given by:

$$h(t_i) = \frac{D(t_i)}{n \cdot \left(N(t_i) - 0.5 \cdot D(t_i) - 0.5 \cdot C(t_i)\right)}$$

The above equations can produce biased results when time intervals are large relative to the rate at which events occur. If failures and censored cases are recorded with exact time, it is possible to correct for these biases by use of what is known as the Kaplan-Meier method. Suppose that d_j is the number of deaths at exact time t_j, and that N_j is the number of persons at risk at time t_j. The Kaplan-Meier estimator of the survival curve $S(t)$ is defined as:

$$\hat{S}(t) = \prod_{j:t_j \leq t} \left[1 - (d_j / N_j)\right]$$

where N_j is obtained by subtracting all failures and censored cases that occurred before t_j from the initial size of the cohort. Compared to the life table method, the Kaplan-Meier method produces a more detailed contour of the survival curve. It is more appropriate than the life table approach when the recording of events is precise. The Kaplan-Meier method permits calculation of confidence intervals around the survival curve and the hazard rate. It also makes it possible to calculate survival curves for two or more groups with different characteristics, and to test the null hypothesis that survival functions are identical for these groups.

Parametric and Semiparametric Models

Although nonparametric life table approaches can perform some tests across groups, they do not permit direct estimation of the effect of specific variables on the timing of events or on the hazard rate. In order to estimate such effects, one needs to use regression models that fall into the category of fully parametric or semiparametric methods.

Accelerated failure-time models. The most common fully parametric models are called accelerated failure-time models. They postulate that covariates have multiplicative effects both on the hazard rate and on timing of events. They commonly take T_i, the time at which the event occurs, as a dependent variable. A general representation of accelerated failure-time models is:

$$\log T_i = \beta_0 + \beta_1 x_{i1} + \ldots + \beta_k x_{ik} + \sigma \varepsilon_i$$

where T_i is the time at which the event of interest occurs for individual i, and $x_{i1}, \ldots, x_{ik}$ is a set of k explanatory variables with coefficients β, ε_i is an error term, and σ is a scale parameter. (Taking the logarithm of T_i ensures that the timing of events will be positive whatever the values of the covariates for a specific individual.)

This model can be adapted to various situations by choosing a specific distribution for the error term ε_i. Common distributions chosen include normal (when the distribution of T_i is log-normal), extreme value (when the distribution of T_i is Weibull), logistic (when the distribution of T_i is log-logistic), and log-gamma (when the distribution of T_i is gamma). Accelerated failure-time models are fully parametric precisely because they require the choice of a model distribution of failure times. Although the above equation resembles that of an OLS regression, the estimation must be performed using the maximum likelihood procedure in order to accommodate the presence of censored cases. Regression coefficients in accelerated failure time models can be interpreted by calculating $100(e^\beta - 1)$, which is an estimate of the percentage change in the time at which the event occurs for a one-unit increase in a particular independent variable.

Proportional hazard models. Another type of regression model in event-history analysis is the proportional hazard model. Such models postulate that the set of covariates acts in a multiplicative way on the hazard rate. A general formulation of proportional hazard models is:

$$\log h_i(t) = \log h_0(t) + \beta_1 x_{i1} + \ldots + \beta_k x_{ik}$$

where $h_0(t)$ is the baseline hazard that is increased or decreased by the effects of the covariates.

This model is called proportional hazard because for any two individuals the ratio of the risk of the hazard is constant over time. If the form for $h_0(t)$ is specified, the result is a fully parametric model. The most common specifications for $h_0(t)$ are the exponential, Weibull, and Gompertz models. Like accelerated failure time models, fully-parametric proportional hazard models are estimated using the maximum likelihood procedure.

Proportional hazard models can also be estimated without specifying the shape of $h_0(t)$. In an influ-

ential paper, D.R. Cox (1972) showed that if one assumes that the ratio of the hazards for any two individuals is constant over time, one can estimate the effect of covariates on hazard rates with no assumption regarding the shape of $h_0(t)$, using a "partial likelihood" approach. These models, commonly called Cox regression models, are semiparametric because of the absence of any assumption regarding the time structure of the baseline hazard rate. In order to interpret the coefficients (β_i) of such regressions, one can calculate the percent change in the hazard rate for a one-unit increase in the variable, using again the transformation $100(e^\beta - 1)$. Cox regression models, which also can be easily adapted to accommodate time-varying covariates, are probably the most popular of available event history models.

Generalizations

In some cases it is important to distinguish among different kinds of events. For example, in demography it is sometimes necessary to focus on deaths from particular causes rather than on deaths from all causes. In such situations, individuals are being exposed to "competing risks," which means that at any time they face the risk of experiencing two or more alternative events. All the methods described above can be adapted to handle multiple events by estimating separate models for each alternative event, treating other events as censored cases. As in the case of censoring, the assumption is that risks of experiencing alternative events are independent of one another; violation of this assumption leads to biased estimates.

There are cases where the event of interest occurs in discrete time intervals. This can happen because of the nature of the event, or because the timing of events is not exactly recorded. Event-history analysis includes methods that are specifically designed for dealing with discrete time. The basic principle behind these models is to use discrete time units rather than individuals as the unit of observation. By breaking down each individual's survival history into discrete time units and pooling these observations, it is possible to estimate a model predicting the probability that the event occurs during a time interval, given that it has not occurred before. Such models are easy to implement and are computationally efficient. Also, since the unit of observation is a time interval, it is easy to include covariates taking different values for different time intervals.

All the models presented here assume that two individuals with identical values of covariates have identical risks of experiencing the event of interest. If there are no covariates in the model, the assumption is that risks are identical for all individuals. Such assumptions can be problematic in survival analysis. In fact, if some important characteristics are not accounted for, the aggregate risk may appear to decrease with time because the proportion of individuals with lower risks increases as time passes. Thus, in the presence of unobserved heterogeneity, it may be erroneous to use survival analysis to make inferences about individuals' risks. Although there are solutions to handle this potential bias, options for dealing with unobserved heterogeneity are limited and are highly sensitive to the underlying assumptions of the models.

Another implicit assumption in all the models discussed above is that events can be experienced only once, which implies that individuals are removed from the population "at risk" after they experience the event. There are many situations, however, in which events are repeatable. For example, a person who had a child or changed jobs can experience those events again. Under these circumstances, it is still possible to use single-event methods by analyzing each successive event separately, or by using a discrete-time analysis where the unit of observation is a time interval and where all time intervals, assumed to be independent for a single individual, are pooled together. However, these strategies are unsatisfactory for many reasons, and specific methods exist to deal with repeatable events. As in the case of unobserved heterogeneity, options for dealing with repeatable events are still limited.

See also: *Cohort Analysis; Estimation Methods, Demographic; Life Tables; Multistate Demography; Stochastic Population Theory.*

BIBLIOGRAPHY

Allison, Paul D. 1995. *Survival Analysis Using the SAS System: A Practical Guide.* Cary, NC: SAS Institute.

Cleves, Mario, William W. Gould, and Roberto Gutierrez. 2002. *An Introduction to Survival Analysis Using Stata.* College Station, TX: Stata Corporation.

Collett, David. 1994. *Modelling Survival Data in Medical Research.* London: Chapman and Hill.

Courgeau, Daniel, and Eva Lelièvre. 1992. *Event History Analysis in Demography.* Oxford, Eng.: Clarendon Press.

Cox, David R. 1972. "Regression Models and Life Tables." *Journal of the Royal Statistical Society* B(34): 187–220.

Manton, Kenneth, Eric Stallard, and James W. Vaupel. 1986. "Alternative Models for the Heterogeneity of Mortality Risks among the Aged." *Journal of the American Statistical Association* 81: 635–44.

Palloni, Alberto, and Aage B. Sorensen. 1990. "Methods for the Analysis of Event History Data: A Didactic Overview." In *Life Span Development and Behavior,* ed. Paul B. Baltes, David L. Featherman, and Richard M. Lerner. Hillsdale, NJ: Erlbaum.

Trussell, James, Richard K. B. Hankinson, and Judith Tilton. 1992. *Demographic Applications of Event History Analysis.* Oxford, Eng.: Clarendon Press.

Wu, Lawrence L. 2003. "Event History Models for Life Course Analysis." In *Handbook of the Life Course,* ed. Jeylan Mortimer and Michael Shanahan. New York: Plenum.

Michel Guillot

EVOLUTIONARY DEMOGRAPHY

The fields of human demography and population biology share intellectual roots and a common set of methodological tools for describing and analyzing population processes. The two disciplines, however, have developed independently with very little cross-fertilization. They developed independently probably because human populations experienced very rapid changes in patterns of mortality and fertility from the mid-nineteenth century to the early twenty-first century, suggesting to demographers that explanations of human population processes must be inherently social rather than biological.

Evolutionary demography analyzes population processes as reflecting the optimizing force of natural selection, the process by which alternative genotypes change in frequency due to differential reproduction of the phenotypes with which they are associated in given environments. Thus, gene coding for physiological and psychological mechanisms regulating fertility, mortality, and investment in offspring are seen to evolve under the influence of natural selection. Even though gene frequencies in populations are expected to change rather slowly over generational time, this does not imply similarly slow rates of change in demographic outcomes. Both plants and animals are capable of very rapid and *adaptive* (i.e, fitness-enhancing) adjustments in vital rates. Thus, rapid changes in human fertility and mortality per se do not imply a major discontinuity between humans and other organisms that would require a completely independent explanatory framework.

This article presents a broad overview of evolutionary demography, with a specific focus on humans. It considers three themes: (1) the timing of life events, including development, reproduction, aging, and risks of mortality; (2) the regulation of reproductive rates and parental investment in offspring; and (3) sexual dimorphism and its relationship to mating and marriage patterns.

Human Life History Adaptation in Comparative Perspective

Humans lived as hunter-gatherers for the vast majority of their evolutionary history (the genus *Homo* has existed for about 2 million years). Some life history features can be determined from the fossil record, but it is not yet possible to estimate many vital statistics from paleontological and archaeological remains. Modern hunter-gatherers are not living replicas of humans's Stone Age past because global socioeconomic forces affect them all. Yet, in spite of the variable historical, ecological, and political conditions affecting them, there is remarkable similarity among foraging peoples, and even the variation often makes adaptive sense. Comparisons between foraging peoples and other modern primates are an important source of information about the life histories of human ancestors and the selection pressures acting upon them.

Relative to other mammalian orders, the primate order is slow-growing, slow-reproducing, long-lived, and large-brained. Humans are at the extreme of the primate continuum. Figure 1 illustrates the differences between human foragers and wild-

living chimpanzees. The age-specific mortality profile among chimpanzees is relatively V-shaped, decreasing rapidly after infancy to its lowest point (about 3% per year) at about 13, the age of first reproduction for females, increasing sharply thereafter. In contrast, mortality among human foragers decreases to a much lower point (about 0.5% per year) and remains low with no increase between about 15 and 40 years of age. Mortality then increases slowly, until there is a very rapid rise beginning around age 70. The pattern is much more "block U-shaped." The strong similarities in the mortality profiles of the foraging populations suggest that this pattern is an evolved life history characteristic of the human species.

As a result of these differences in mortality patterns, hunter-gatherer children experience higher survival rates than chimpanzees to age of first reproduction: about 60 percent to age 19 versus 35 percent to age 13. Chimpanzees also have a much shorter adult lifespan than humans. At first reproduction, chimpanzee life expectancy is an additional 15 years, compared to 38 more years among human foragers. Importantly, women spend more than a third of their adult lives in a postreproductive phase, whereas very few chimpanzee females survive to reach this phase. Fewer than 10 percent of chimpanzees survive to age 40, but some 15 percent of hunter-gatherers survive to age 70.

Age profiles of net food production (food produced minus food consumed) also differ sharply (see Figure 1). Among chimpanzees, net production before age five is negative, representing complete, then partial, dependence upon mother's milk. The second phase is independent juvenile growth, lasting until adulthood, during which net production is zero. The third phase is reproductive, during which females, but not males, produce a surplus of calories that they allocate to nursing. Humans, in contrast, produce less than they consume for some 15 to 22 years, depending on the group. Net production becomes increasingly negative until about age 14 and then begins to climb. Net production of adult humans is much higher than in chimpanzees and peaks at about 35 to 45 years of age. This peak is about five times as high as the chimpanzee peak. The human age profile of production could not exist if humans had the same mortality profile as chimpanzees. Only 30 percent of chimpanzees reach the age when humans produce what they consume on average, and

FIGURE 1

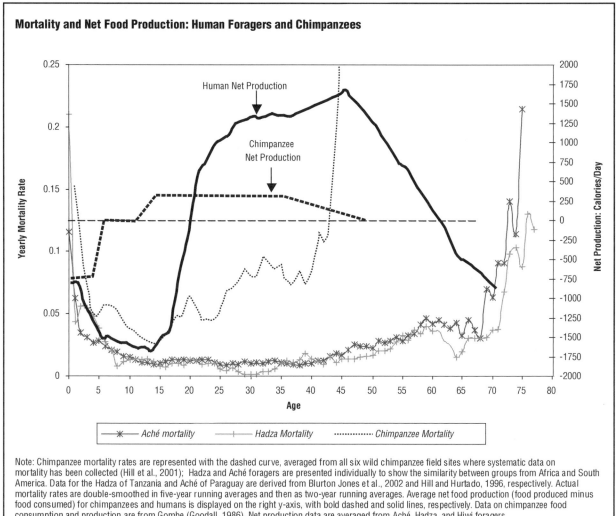

Mortality and Net Food Production: Human Foragers and Chimpanzees

Note: Chimpanzee mortality rates are represented with the dashed curve, averaged from all six wild chimpanzee field sites where systematic data on mortality has been collected (Hill et al., 2001); Hadza and Aché foragers are presented individually to show the similarity between groups from Africa and South America. Data for the Hadza of Tanzania and Aché of Paraguay are derived from Blurton Jones et al., 2002 and Hill and Hurtado, 1996, respectively. Actual mortality rates are double-smoothed in five-year running averages and then as two-year running averages. Average net food production (food produced minus food consumed) for chimpanzees and humans is displayed on the right y-axis, with bold dashed and solid lines, respectively. Data on chimpanzee food consumption and production are from Gombe (Goodall, 1986). Net production data are averaged from Aché, Hadza, and Hiwi foragers.

SOURCE: Kaplan and Robson (2002).

fewer than 10 percent reach the age when human production peaks.

High levels of knowledge and skill are needed to acquire the variety of high-quality resources humans consume. These abilities require a large brain and a long time commitment to physical and psychological development. This extended learning phase during which productivity is low is compensated for by higher productivity during the adult period. Because productivity increases with age, and therefore the return on the investment in the development of offspring occurs at an older age, the time investment in skill acquisition and knowledge leads to selection for lowered mortality rates and greater longevity. Thus, it is likely that the long human lifespan co-evolved

with the lengthening of the juvenile period, increased brain capacities for information processing and storage, and intergenerational resource flows.

Regulation of Reproduction under Natural Fertility Regimes

Traditionally, demographers have attempted to understand the onset and termination of reproduction and birth intervals in natural fertility regimes in terms of proximate determinants (i.e, those that have direct mechanistic impacts on fertility, such as coital and breast-feeding frequencies). For the most part, these determinants are treated as givens and there has been little consideration of the causal processes shaping them. In contrast, evolutionary demographers approach these determinants in terms of design and ask *why* the physiological, psychological, and cultural processes that regulate fertility take the forms that they do.

There is mounting evidence that human reproductive physiology is particularly specialized toward the production of high-quality, large-brained offspring. Two implications of this specialization are rigid control over embryo quality and a series of adaptations on the part of both mother and offspring designed to ensure an adequate energy supply for the nutrient-hungry, fast-growing brain. Given the massive investment in human offspring, this system ensures that investment is quickly terminated in an offspring of poor genetic quality. Fetal growth is more rapid in humans than in gorillas and chimpanzees, and both mother and offspring store exceptional amounts of fat, probably to support an equally exceptional rate of expensive brain growth during the first five years of life.

The physiological regulation of ovulation, fertilization, implantation, and maintenance of a pregnancy is highly responsive to energy stores in the form of fat, energy balance (calories consumed minus calories expended), and energy flux (rate of energy turnover per unit time). Low body fat, weight loss due to negative energy balance, and extreme energy flux (either very low intake and very low expenditure, or very high intake and very high expenditure) each lower monthly probabilities of conceiving a child that will survive to birth. Seasonal variation in workloads and diet has been shown to affect female fertility. Variation across groups in both age of menarche (first menstrual period) and fertility has been linked to differences in food intake and workload.

Behavior and the underlying psychological processes that govern parental investment in offspring affect fertility indirectly via maternal physiology. One route is through breast-feeding. Patterns of breast-feeding and solid food supplementation vary both cross-culturally and among mother–infant pairs. Unlike the growing body of knowledge about the physiological pathways mediating the effects of nursing, much less is known about the cultural, psychological, and physiological determinants of the duration and intensity of nursing, and the respective roles of the mother and infant in the process.

The second route relates to the additional energetic constraints involved in provisioning children.

The age/sex profile of work and productivity, along with a system of food distribution, determine the net energy available for reproduction among women. People in foraging societies are sensitive to ecological variability in the trade-offs regarding children's work effort and their provisioning. Thus, natural selection appears to have acted upon both the psychology of parental investment and maternal physiology to produce a flexible system of fertility regulation. The key to this system is that maximizing lifetime-expected resource production through the optimal allocation of activities and food flows will tend also to maximize fitness when all wealth is in the form of food and when extra food translates into higher fertility. Nevertheless, empirical applications of optimality models, designed to determine whether the onset and termination of reproduction and the size of interbirth intervals actually maximize fitness, have produced mixed results.

Role of Men in Human Reproduction

Unlike most other male mammals, men in foraging societies provide the majority of the energy necessary to support reproduction. Among the ten foraging societies for which quantitative data on adult food production are available, men on average contributed 68 percent of the calories and almost 88 percent of the protein; women acquired the remaining 32 percent of calories and 12 percent of protein. Given that, on average, 31 percent of these calories are apportioned to support adult female consumption, 39 percent to adult male consumption, and 31 percent to consumption of offspring, women supply 3 percent of the calories to offspring and men provide the remaining 97 percent.

Complementarity between the investments of each sex in reproduction appears to be the principal force favoring decreased sexual dimorphism (i.e., differential expression of traits by males and females, respectively) and increased male parental investment. This kind of complementarity can occur when both direct care and resources are important to offspring viability, but they conflict with one another. For example, among many flying bird species, protection and feeding of nestlings are incompatible, leading to biparental investment and turn-taking in feeding and nest protection by males and females.

Hunting, as practiced by humans, is largely incompatible with the evolved commitment among primate females toward intensive mothering, carrying of infants, and lactation-on-demand in service of high infant survival rates. First, it often involves rapid travel and encounters with dangerous prey. Second, it is often most efficiently practiced over relatively long periods of time rather than in short stretches, because of search and travel costs. Third, it is highly skill-intensive, with improvements in return rate occurring over two decades of daily hunting. The first two qualities make hunting a high-cost activity for pregnant and lactating females. The third quality, in interaction with the first and second, generates life course effects such that gathering is a better option for females, even when they are not lactating, and hunting is a better option for males. Because women spend about 75 percent of their time either nursing or more than three months pregnant during their reproductive lives, they never get enough practice to make it worth while to hunt, even when they are not nursing or pregnant, or are postreproductive.

Human females evidence physiological and behavioral adaptations that are consistent with an evolutionary history involving extensive male parental investment. They decrease metabolic rates and store fat during pregnancy, suggesting that they lower work effort and are being provisioned. Women in foraging societies decrease work effort during lactation and focus on high-quality care. In contrast, nonhuman primate females do not store appreciable fat, increase work effort during lactation, and as a result, have increased risk of mortality. The human specialization could not have evolved if women did not depend on men for most of their food provisioning throughout human history.

Extensive cooperation among men and women would make sense only if the reproductive performance of spouses were linked. When women reach menopause in their late forties, men have the option to continue reproducing with younger women but they do not generally do so. Among the Aché, for example, 83 percent of all last births for women also represent a last child for the fathers.

Because men support reproduction only indirectly by affecting the energy intake rates of women and children, it is not surprising that spermatogenesis (the formation of sperm) is buffered from variations in food intake. Natural selection on male physiology and behavior appears to reflect the trade-off between mating investment and survival. Androgens, most notably testosterone, affect muscularity, competitiveness, and high-risk behavior, but they reduce immune function and fat storage, which, in turn, affect survival. Future research on the male endocrine system is likely to elucidate how natural selection has operated to produce both individual variation and age-related changes in male physiology and behavior.

Extra-Somatic Wealth and Its Implications for Human Demography

With the advent of agriculture and pastoralism (livestock raising), wealth storage in the form of land, livestock, luxury goods, and, eventually, money became commonplace practices. Around the globe, responses to these new economic practices were highly patterned and exhibited remarkable uniformity in response to similar ecological conditions. First, men became actively involved in competition for access to resources, which, in turn, were used for access to women. Second, parental investment extended beyond food and care, and well-defined inheritance practices emerged.

Among pastoralists, the male warfare complex, where livestock are stolen and brides are captured, became common. Patrilineal inheritance (through the male line) of livestock also became the norm, and men gained access to women through the transfer of bride wealth to the women's families. Polygyny (the taking of more than one wife), practiced to a much lesser degree among foragers, resulted from differences in wealth, and the number of wives increased in relation to wealth.

In the case of agriculture, social stratification of wealth increased in relation to the patchiness of arable land, with highly fertile river valleys generating the most intensive competition and the greatest wealth differentials. In a 1993 study of six despotic empires (Mesopotamia, Egypt, Aztec Mexico, Inca Peru, and imperial India and China), Laura Betzig detailed the impressive convergence of cultural evolution. Powerful men sequestered large harems of women (several thousand in the case of rulers) and enforced their exclusive sexual access. Nevertheless, legal marriage—being highly restricted and often monogamous, and controlling inheritance—was differentiated from concubinage. Marriages were often strategic, between families of similar social class, or involving dowries that were exchanged for the upward mobility of women. Inheritance often was distributed differentially with sibships, with the most common pattern being primogeniture. Because the complex societies of North and South America developed in the absence of contact with the Old World, cultural convergences between the New and Old Worlds are likely the result of an evolved human psychology interacting with new technologies of production (which themselves were most likely reactions to demographic pressures and reduced returns from foraging).

Such responses are largely consistent with evolutionary logic and are analogous to the behavior of other organisms, although there is some evidence that human responses to extra-somatic wealth may not be fitness-maximizing. It is possible that the psychology of social status striving, which was perhaps adaptive in foraging societies, is no longer adaptive in the context of extra-somatic wealth.

Demographic Transition

It is almost certainly the case that reproductive behavior in post–demographic transition societies (that is, those in which small families are the norm and mortality rates are low) is not fitness-maximizing. Even taking into account the effects of low fertility on increased parental investment and subsequent adult income of offspring, fertility is much lower than the predicted level for maximizing descendants. For example, a study of men's reproductive behavior in Albuquerque, New Mexico, found that the number of grandchildren was maximized by men with 12 or more children (the highest number reported), even though mean fertility was just over two children.

Nevertheless, just as increased payoffs to skill and mortality reduction may underlie the original evolution of long-term child dependence and human longevity, similar changes may explain the dramatic lowering of fertility accompanying modernization. Education is the best and most consistent predictor of fertility variation, both within and among nations. The payoffs to education have changed for two reasons. Changes in the technology of production within education-based labor markets have led to very high returns on parental investments in children's education. Changing medical technology and improved public health have greatly reduced mortality rates for all age groups. Increased survival rates during the period of parental investment increase the expected costs per child born, favoring further increases in offspring quality. In-

creased survival during the adult period increases the expected years of return on educational investments, further increasing the incentive to invest in children's education.

In response to the increased payoffs on investments in education and the expected costs of those investments, parents determine the number of children they can afford to rear, given their wealth. These factors result in fertility being regulated by a consciously determined fertility plan realized through birth-control technology and/or controlled exposure to sex. The low mortality rates also allow parents to plan reproduction at the outset, because the number of children born accurately predicts the number of children that will reach adulthood.

A great deal of further research is necessary, however, before there is a full understanding of why these changes in socioecology (i.e., the physical, biotic and social conditions characterizing the environment) have resulted in such low levels of fertility and high levels of parental investment and wealth consumption. People are not simply maximizing family wealth because net wealth of families would be maximized by higher fertility than is currently observed. Nor are they maximizing personal consumption; in that case, they would have no children. One possible hypothesis is that social dynamics of small groups in hunting and gathering economies resulted in greater fitness for those of higher social standing and selected for a psychology in which relative social position of self and offspring is valued highly. This psychology may have been fitness-maximizing under traditional conditions. If relative, as opposed to absolute, wealth and social standing guide human decisions regarding parental investment and fertility, it is possible that "runaway" consumption and investment in children's education result from the interaction of this psychology with modern education-based labor markets and consumption possibilities.

Conclusions

Evolutionary demography is best viewed not as an alternative to traditional approaches but rather as a general theoretical framework that existing models will contribute to and enhance. Economic modeling is fundamental to evolutionary analysis. Economists are primarily concerned with conscious, rational decision processes, but these are only a subset of the regulatory mechanisms of controlling fertility. Feminist demography details the conflicts of interest between men and women, and how they vary with social context. A more basic evolutionary understanding of why men and women differ and how socioecology affects the extent to which the behavior and goals of the two sexes converge and diverge will enrich such insights. Because information about the costs and benefits of alternative behavioral options is often socially acquired, the understanding of cultural diffusion is critical. Evolutionary logic provides a framework for the analysis of the active role that people play in determining which ideas they chose to adopt.

The application of evolutionary theory to humans is complicated by technological and social change. Given that evolution is a historical process, organized, flexible responses to environmental variation evolve when populations are exposed to fluctuations that are patterned and, to some extent, regular. When organisms are exposed to new, and radically different, environments, however, it is possible that their responses may be nonadaptive, reflecting physiological and psychological traits that evolved in the context of more ancient environments. The response of drastically reduced fertility may be a case in point. The analysis of a species in a novel, rapidly changing environment poses special challenges, but an understanding of the evolutionary past of humans should assist in explaining the present and predicting the future.

See also: *Animal Ecology; Archaeogenetics; Biodemography; Biology, Population; Darwin, Charles; Hunter-Gatherers; Paleodemography; Primate Demography; Sociobiology.*

BIBLIOGRAPHY

Bailey, Robert C., Mark R. Jenike, Peter T. Ellison, Gillian R. Bentley, Alica M. Harrigan, and Nadine R. Peacock. 1992. "The Ecology of Birth Seasonality among Agriculturalists in Central Africa." *Journal of Biosocial Science* 24: 393–412.

Betzig, Laura. 1993. "Sex, Succession, and Stratification in the First Six Civilizations: How Powerful Men Reproduced, Passed Power on to Their Sons, and Used Their Power to Defend Their Wealth, Women, and Children." In *Social Stratification and Socioeconomic Inequality,* ed. Lee Ellis. New York: Praeger.

Blurton Jones, Nicholas G. 1986. "Bushman Birth Spacing: A Test for Optimal Interbirth Intervals." *Ethology and Sociobiology* 4: 145–147.

Blurton Jones, Nicholas G., Kristen Hawkes, and Patricia Draper. 1994. "Differences between Hadza and !Kung Children's Work: Original Affluence or Practical Reason?" In *Key Issues in Hunter-Gatherer Research,* ed. Ernest S. Burch and Linda J. Ellana. Oxford: Berg.

Blurton Jones, Nicholas G., Kristen Hawkes, and James O'Connell. 2002. "The Antiquity of Post-reproductive Life: Are There Modern Impacts on Hunter-Gatherer Post-reproductive Lifespans?" *Human Biology* 14: 184–205.

Bock, John. 2002. "Learning, Life History, and Productivity: Children's Lives in the Okavango Delta, Botswana." *Human Nature* 13: 161–197.

Bongaarts, John, and Robert G. Porter. 1983. *Fertility, Biology, and Behavior: An Analysis of Proximate Determinants.* New York: Academic Press.

Boone, James. 1986. "Parental Investment and Elite Family Structure in Preindustrial States: A Case Study of Late Medieval–Early Modern Portuguese Genealogies." *American Anthropologist* 88: 859–878.

Borgerhoff Mulder, Monique. 1988. "Reproductive Success in Three Kipsigi Cohorts." In *Reproductive Decisions,* ed. Timothy Clutton Brock. Cambridge, Eng.: Cambridge University Press.

Bribiescas, Richard G. 2001. "Reproductive Ecology and Life History of the Human Male." *Yearbook of Physical Anthropology* 44: 148–176.

Dickemann, Mildred. 1979. "The Ecology of Mating Systems in Hypergynous Dowry Societies." *Social Science Information* 18: 163–195.

Ellison, Peter T. 2001. *On Fertile Ground: A Natural History of Human Reproduction.* Cambridge, MA: Harvard University Press.

Goodall, Jane. 1986. *The Chimpanzees of the Gombe: Patterns of Behavior.* Cambridge, Eng.: Cambridge University Press.

Hill, Kim, and A. Magdalena Hurtado. 1996. *Aché Life History: The Ecology and Demography of a Foraging People.* Hawthorne, NY: Aldine de Gruyter.

Hill, Kim, Christophe Boesch, Jane Goodall, Anne Pusey, Jennifer Williams, and Richard

Wrangham. 2001. "Mortality Rates among Wild Chimpanzees." *Journal of Human Evolution* 40(5): 437–450.

Hurtado, A. Magdalena, Kristen Hawkes, Kim Hill, and Hillard Kaplan. 1985. "Female Subsistence Strategies among Aché Hunter-Gatherers of Eastern Paraguay." *Human Ecology* 13: 29–47.

Hurtado, A. Magdalena, and Kim Hill. 1990. "Seasonality in a Foraging Society: Variation in Diet, Work Effort, Fertility, and the Sexual Division of Labor among the Hiwi of Venezuela." *Journal of Anthropological Research* 46: 293–345.

Irons, William 1979. "Cultural and Biological Success." In *Natural Selection and Social Behavior*, ed. Napoleon A. Chagnon and William Irons. North Scituate, MA: Duxbury Press.

Kaplan, Hillard S. 1996. "A Theory of Fertility and Parental Investment in Traditional and Modern Human Societies." *Yearbook of Physical Anthropology* 39: 91–135.

Kaplan, Hillard S., Jane Lancaster, John Bock, and Sara Johnson. 1995. "Does Observed Fertility Maximize Fitness among New Mexican Men? A Test of an Optimality Model and a New Theory of Parental Investment in the Embodied Capital of Offspring." *Human Nature* 6: 325–360.

Kaplan, Hillard S., Kim Hill, Jane B. Lancaster, and A. Magdalena Hurtado. 2000. "A Theory of Human Life History Evolution: Diet, Intelligence, and Longevity." *Evolutionary Anthropology* 9: 156–185.

Kaplan, Hillard S., Kim Hill, A. Magdalena Hurtado, and Jane B. Lancaster. 2001. "The Embodied Capital Theory of Human Evolution." In *Reproductive Ecology and Human Evolution,* ed. Peter T. Ellison. Hawthorne, NY: Aldine de Gruyter.

Kaplan, Hillard S., and Arthur Robson. 2002. "The Emergence of Humans: The Coevolution of Intelligence and Longevity with Intergenerational Transfers." *Proceedings of the National Academy of Sciences* 99: 10,221–10,226.

Lancaster, Jane, Hillard S. Kaplan, Kim Hill, and A. Magdalena Hurtado. 2000. "The Evolution of Life History, Intelligence, and Diet among Chimpanzees and Human Foragers." In *Perspectives in Ethology: Evolution, Culture, and Behavior,* ed. Françios Tonneau and Nicholas S. Thompson. New York: Plenum.

Mueller, Ulrich. 2001. "Is There a Stabilizing Selection around Average Fertility in Modern Human Populations?" *Population and Development Review* 27: 469–498.

Pennington, Renee. 2001. "Hunter-Gatherer Demography." In *Hunter-Gatherers: An Interdisciplinary Perspective,* ed. Catherine Panter-Brick, Robert H. Layton, and Peter Rowley-Conwy. Cambridge, Eng.: Cambridge University Press.

Pike, Ivy L. 1999. "Age, Reproductive History, Seasonality, and Maternal Body Composition during Pregnancy for Nomadic Turkana of Kenya." *American Journal of Human Biology* 11: 658–672.

Poppitt, Sally D., Andrew M. Prentice, Eric Jequier, Yves Schutz, and Roger G. Whitehead. 1993. "Evidence of Energy Sparing in Gambian Women during Pregnancy: A Longitudinal Study Using Whole-Body Calorimetry." *American Journal of Clinical Nutrition* 57: 353–364.

Wood, James W. 1994. *Dynamics of Human Reproduction: Biology, Biometry, and Demography.* New York: Aldine de Gruyter.

HILLARD KAPLAN

EXTERNALITIES OF POPULATION CHANGE

By externalities researchers mean those effects of human activities that occur without the agreement of the people who are affected. Logging in the upland forests of watersheds can cause water runoff and inflict damage on farmers and fishermen in the lowlands. The damage is an externality if those who suffer damage are not compensated by mutual agreement. Free-riding on the common property resources is another example of an activity that gives rise to externalities. The former example involves a "unidirectional" externality, while the latter reflects "reciprocal" externalities.

The above are examples of "external disbenefits." In contrast, when someone becomes literate at his own cost, he benefits not only himself, but also those others who are now able to correspond with him. This is an example of an "external benefit." More generally, the private production of public goods involves (reciprocal) external benefits.

The Theory of Externalities

The theory of externalities was discussed first by the economists A.C. Pigou (1920) and Erik Lindahl (1928). They noted that there is an over-supply of activities inflicting external disbenefits and an under-supply of activities conferring external benefits. Pigou in particular noted that externalities reflect a wedge between the (net) private and social benefits of human activities, the wedge being symptomatic of economic inefficiency. As remedy, Pigou suggested government intervention in the form of taxes and subsidies on the production of external disbenefits and benefits, respectively. Lindahl in contrast provided an outline of markets for externalities, assuming that such markets could be established. Lindahl noted that if the markets were efficient, they would eliminate the externalities. Ronald Coase (1960) generalized Lindahl's idea and stressed that even the direction of an externality (who affects whom) is a reflection of the structure of property rights. He argued, for example, that if the law recognizes polluters' rights, a negotiated settlement would have the lowland farmers and fishermen pay the upland firms to reduce logging. On the other hand, if the law recognizes pollutees' rights, a negotiated settlement would have the logging firm pay the farmers and fishermen for the right to engage in logging. Coase argued that in the absence of transaction costs there *could* be no externalities, because the parties would negotiate their way to an efficient allocation of resources (Coase's claim, even though seemingly tautological, is questionable, as shown by Kenneth Arrow [1971] and David Starrett [1973]). However, the externality would prevail if the costs of negotiation were prohibitive and the state remained aloof from the problem. In short, Coase argued that externalities are symptomatic of institutional failure.

Until recently economists did not take externalities seriously. Economics textbooks relegated the subject to later chapters. In the twenty-first century, however, studies on externalities abound, in large measure owing to a recognition that they are a key ingredient of environmental problems.

Reproductive and Environmental Externalities

The theory of externalities can be employed to explain the high fertility prevailing in many of the poorest regions of the contemporary world. This is done in a series of publications by Partha Dasgupta (1993, 1995, 2000), using the working hypothesis that people's reproductive decisions are based on their own interest but that the outcomes are inefficient because of reproductive or environmental externalities.

What could cause the private and social costs and benefits of reproduction to differ? Large-scale migrations of populations occasioned by crop failure, war, or other disturbances are an obvious form of externality. But by their very nature they are not persistent. Of those that are persistent, four deserve special mention: crowding, cost-sharing, interactions among institutions, and contagion.

Crowding. One likely source of externality is the finiteness of space. Increased population size implies greater crowding. Space being a common property, households acting on their own would not be expected to take into account the crowding externalities they inflict on others. The local commons in rural areas of poor countries offer an illustration. The private costs of having children are less than the social costs if the extent to which households have access to the commons is independent of household size. Crowding externalities favor high fertility.

Cost-sharing. Fertility behavior is influenced by the structure of property rights (e.g., rules of inheritance). In his analysis of fertility differences between preindustrial seventeenth- and eighteenth-century Northwest Europe, on the one hand, and Asiatic preindustrial societies on the other, the statistician John Hajnal (1982) distinguished between "nuclear" and "joint" household systems. He observed that in Northwest Europe marriage normally meant establishing a new household, which implied that the couple had to have, by saving or transfer, sufficient resources to establish and equip the new residence. This requirement in turn led to late ages at marriages. It also meant that parents bore the cost of rearing their children. Indeed, fertility rates in England averaged around the relatively low level of four children per woman in the years between 1650 and 1710, long before modern family planning techniques became available and long before women became widely literate (Coale, 1969; Wrigley and Schofield, 1981). Hajnal contrasted this with the Asiatic pattern of household formation, which he saw as joint units consisting of more than one couple and their children.

Parental costs of procreation are also lower when the cost of rearing the child is shared among the kinship. In sub-Saharan Africa fosterage within the kinship group is commonplace: children are not raised solely by their parents. The shared childrearing responsibility creates a free-rider problem if the parents' share of the benefits from having children exceeds their share of the costs. From the point of view of parents collectively, too many children are produced in these circumstances. In sub-Saharan Africa, communal land tenure within the lineage social structure has in the past offered further inducement for men to procreate. Moreover, conjugal bonds are frequently weak, so fathers often do not bear the costs of siring children. Weak conjugal bonds, communal land tenure, and a strong kinship support system of children, taken together, result in high fertility.

Interactions among institutions. Externalities are prevalent when market and nonmarket institutions co-exist. How and why might such externalities affect fertility behavior? A number of pathways suggest themselves.

When established long-term relationships break down, people look for alternatives to further their economic opportunities. The growth of markets in towns and cities, by making children less reliable as an investment for old age, can lead to a reduction in fertility. On the other hand, those who face particularly stressful circumstances may resort to draconian measures to build new economic channels. The anthropologist Jane Guyer (1994) has observed that in the face of deteriorating economic circumstances, some women in a Yoruba area of Nigeria have borne children by different men so as to create immediate lateral links with them. Polyandrous motherhood enables women to have access to more than one resource network.

Mead Cain (1981, 1983) showed that where capital markets are nonexistent and public or community support for the elderly are weak, children provide security in old age. The converse is that if communitarian support systems decline, children become more valuable. But communitarian support systems in rural areas may degrade with the growth of markets in cities and towns. So there is a curious

causal chain here: growth of markets in towns and cities can lead to an increase in fertility in poor villages, other things being the same. There is scattered evidence of this. N. Heyzer (1996) has observed that one half of the total forest area in Sarawak, Malaysia, has now been lost, disrupting the lives of indigenous people in different ways. Communities that lived in the heart of the forest were most severely affected, while others, living near towns, were able to turn from swidden agriculture to wage labor. This transformation, however, involved male migration, leaving women behind to cope with a decreasing resource base. As subsistence alternatives declined, children became one of the few remaining resources that women could control. There was thus a new motivation for having children: to help their mothers with an increased workload.

Conformity and "contagion." That children are seen as an end in themselves provides another mechanism by which reasoned fertility decisions at the household can lead to an unsatisfactory outcome for the collectivity of all households. The mechanism arises when traditional practice is perpetuated by conformity. Procreation in closely-knit communities is not only a private matter, it is also a social activity, influenced by both family experiences and the cultural milieu. Behavior is conformist if, other things being equal, each household's most desired family size is the greater, the larger is the average family size in the community. So, conformism is the source of an externality (one person's behavior influences another's desires).

There can be many reasons for conformist behavior. Whatever the reason, there would be practices encouraging high fertility rates that no household would unilaterally desire to break. Thus, so long as all others follow the practice and aim at large family size, no household on its own would wish to deviate from the practice. However, if all other households were to restrict their fertility rates, each would desire to restrict its fertility rate as well. In short, conformism can be a reason for the existence of multiple reproductive equilibria. Moreover, a community could get stuck at one mode of behavior even though another (equilibrium) mode of behavior would be better for all. Social systems involving conformist behavior are called "coordination games." The reference group that influences individual behavior expands as newspapers, radio, television, and the Internet transmit information about other lifestyles.

Dasgupta (2000) has shown that such pathways can give rise to demographic transitions: fertility rates display little to no trend over extended periods, only to cascade downward over a relatively short interval of time, giving rise to the classic logistic curve of diffusion processes.

Demographers have made few attempts to discover evidence of behavior that is guided in part by an attention to others. In an exception to this neglect, Richard Easterlin, R. Pollak and M. Wachter (1980) studied intergenerational influence in a sample of families in the United States, reporting a positive link between the number of children with whom someone had been raised and the number of children they themselves had. Another exception is the study by Susan Cotts Watkins (1990) of demographic change in Western Europe over the period from 1870 to 1960. Watkins showed that in 1870, before the large-scale declines in marital fertility had begun, demographic behavior differed greatly among provinces (e.g., counties and cantons) but differences within provinces were low—suggesting an influence of local communities on behavior. By 1960 interprovincial differences had narrowed, a convergence she explains in terms of increases in the geographical reach of national governments and the spread of national languages.

A study in Bangladesh could also point to contagious behavior. An experimental birth control program in Matlab Thana, Bangladesh, showed both a substantial rise in contraceptive use in villages offered intensive services and a modest rise in its use in the set of "control" villages that were offered no such special services. The uptake was reflected in the fertility rates, which declined in both sets of villages but faster in the treatment area. The new fertility behavior spread to the control villages, but the contagion was less than complete.

See also: *Common Property Resources; Cost of Children; Intergenerational Transfers; Population Policy.*

BIBLIOGRAPHY

Arrow, K. J. 1971. "Political and Economic Evaluation of Social Effects of Externalities." In *Frontiers of Quantitative Economics,* ed. M. Intriligator. Amsterdam: North Holland

Baumol, W. M., and W. Oates 1975. *The Theory of Environmental Policy.* Englewood Cliffs, NJ: Prentice-Hall.

Bongaarts, J., and S. C. Watkins. 1996. "Social Interactions and Contemporary Fertility Transitions." *Population and Development Review* 22(4): 639–682.

Cain, M. 1981. "Risk and Insurance: Perspectives on Fertility and Agrarian Change in India and Bangladesh." *Population and Development Review* 7(3): 435–474.

Cain, M. 1983. "Fertility as an Adjustment to Risk." *Population and Development Review* 9(4): 688–702.

Caldwell, J. C., and P. Caldwell. 1990. "High Fertility in Sub-Saharan Africa." *Scientific American* 262(5): 82–89.

Coale, A. J. 1969. "The Decline of Fertility in Europe from the French Revolution to World War II." In *Fertility and Family Planning: A World View,* ed. S. J. Behrman, L. Corsa, and R. Freedman. Ann Arbor: University of Michigan Press.

Coase, R. 1960. "The Problem of Social Cost." *Journal of Law and Economics* 3.

Dasgupta, P. 1993. *An Inquiry into Well-Being and Destitution.* Oxford: Clarendon Press.

———. 1995. "The Population Problem: Theory and Evidence." *Journal of Economic Literature* 33(4): 1,879–1,902.

———. 2000. "Population and Resources: An Exploration of Reproductive and Environmental Externalities." *Population and Development Review* 26(4): 643–689.

Easterlin, R., R. Pollak, and M. Wachter. 1980. "Toward a More General Model of Fertility Determination: Endogenous Preferences and Natural Fertility." In *Population and Economic Change in Developing Countries,* ed. R. Easterlin. Chicago: University of Chicago Press.

Guyer, J. L. 1994. "Lineal Identities and Lateral Networks: The Logic of Polyandrous Motherhood." In *Nupitality in Sub-Saharan Africa: Contemporary Anthropological and Demographic Perspectives,* eds. C. Bledsoe and G. Pison. Oxford: Clarendon Press.

Hajnal, J. 1982. "Two Kinds of Preindustrial Household Formation Systems." *Population and Development Review* 8(3): 449–494.

Heyser, N. 1996. *Gender, Population and Environment in the Context of Deforestation: A Malay-*

sian Case Study. Geneva: United Nations Research Institute for Social Development.

Hill, K. 1992. "Fertility and Mortality Trends in the Developing World." *Ambio* 21(1): 79–83.

Lindahl, E. 1958. "Some Controversial Questions in the Theory of Taxation." In *Classics in the Theory of Public Finance,* ed. R. A. Musgrave and A. T. Peacock. London: Macmillan.

Mäler, K.-G. 1974. *Environmental Economics: A Theoretical Enquiry.* Baltimore: Johns Hopkins University Press.

Meade, J. E. 1973. *The Theory of Externalities.* Geneva: Institute Universitaire de Hautes Etudes Internationales.

Pigou, A. C. 1920. *The Economics of Welfare.* London: Macmillan.

Starrett, D. 1972. "Fundamental Non-Convexities in the Theory of Externalities." *Journal of Economic Theory* 4(1): 180–199.

Starrett, D. A. 1973. "A Note on Externalities and the Core." *Econometrica* 41(1): 179–183.

Watkins, S. C. 1990. "From Local to National Communities: The Transformation of Demographic Regions in Western Europe 1870–1960." *Population and Development Review* 16(2): 241–72.

Wrigley, E. A., and R. S. Schofield. 1981. *The Population History of England 1541–1871: A Reconstruction.* Cambridge, Eng.: Edward Arnold.

PARTHA DASGUPTA

EXTINCTION, HUMAN

Even a small risk of near-term human extinction (within one century, for example) should be taken seriously, considering the stake. It is therefore remarkable that there has been so little systematic study of this topic—less than on the life habits of the dung fly. Some particular threats have been studied, however, and some thinkers have made attempts to synthesize what is known about the risks of human extinction. Because many of the dangers are hard to quantify, it is often necessary to fall back on informed subjective risk estimates.

Threats to near-term human survival include:

- *Nanotechnology disaster.* Advanced molecular manufacturing will make it possible to construct bacterium-scale self-replicating mechanical robots that can feed on dirt or other organic matter, and that could be programmed to destroy the biosphere by eating, poisoning, or burning it, or by blocking out sunlight. This capability could be extremely dangerous, and countermeasures could take a long time to develop. While the possibility of global-scale nanotech accidents shouldn't be ignored, deliberate misuse poses the gravest risk.

- *Nuclear holocaust.* Current arsenals are probably insufficient to obliterate all human life, although it is hard to be certain of this because science has a poor understanding of secondary effects (such as impact on global climate—"nuclear winter"). Much larger arsenals may be created in future arms races.

- *Superbugs.* Advanced biotechnology will almost certainly lead to better medicine, but it could also be used to create a super-pathogen. Increased urbanization and travel could also increase the risk posed by natural pandemics.

- *Evolution or re-engineering of the human species.* While natural biological human evolution takes place on time-scales much longer than a hundred years, one can imagine that scientists will develop technologies, such as nanomedicine (medical interventions based on mature nanotechnology) or very advanced genetic engineering, that will enable them to re-design the human organism to such a degree that these new humans become what could arguably be classified as a different species. Alternatively, humans might be able to "upload" their minds into computers. Evolution in a population of "uploads" could happen on much shorter time-scales than biological evolution. (Whether human extinction in this sense would be a bad thing presumably depends on what humans become instead.) Further, some have suggested the possibility that humans are currently living in a simulated world within computers built by some super-advanced civilization. If so, then one possible risk is that these simulators will decide to terminate the simulation.

- *Artificial intelligence takeover.* In this scenario, a badly programmed superhuman artificial intelligence is created and proceeds to destroy humanity.

- *Something unforeseen.* Certainly scientists cannot anticipate all future risks; none of the risks listed here were known to people a hundred years ago.

Additionally, a number of lesser risks deserve mention: *physics disasters*—there have been speculations that high-energy physics experiments could knock the space nearest Earth out of a metastable vacuum state, and future developments in theoretical physics may reveal other disturbing possibilities; *asteroid or comet impact*—this is a small but real threat; *runaway global warming*—the warming effect would have to be very large to kill all humans; and *annihilation in encounter with an extraterrestrial civilization.*

To directly estimate the probability of human existence a century into the future, statisticians would analyze the various specific failure-modes, assign them probabilities, and then subtract the sum of these disaster probabilities from one to determine the success probability. A complementary, indirect way of estimating this success probability is by studying relevant theoretical constraints. One such constraint is based on the Fermi paradox: Could the absence of any signs of extraterrestrial civilizations be due to the fact that that nearly all civilizations reaching a sufficiently advanced stage develop some technology that causes their own destruction? Another is the highly controversial Doomsday argument. The Doomsday argument purports to show that there is now indexical information about current humanity's position in the human species that lends support to the hypothesis that there will not be a significantly larger number of people living after us than have lived before us. Others include the simulation argument mentioned above and studies of risk estimation biases. It is possible that there is a "good story" bias shaping perceptions of risk; scenarios in which humankind suddenly and uncinematically becomes extinct may rarely be explored because they are boring, not because they are improbable.

The gravest near-term risks to human existence are of humanity's own making and involve present or anticipated technologies. Of course, it does not follow that trying to stop technological progress would make the world safer—it could well have the opposite effect. A sensible approach to risk reduc-tion would involve increasing awareness and funding more research on "existential risks;" fostering peace and democracy to reduce the risks of future war; promoting development of protective technologies such as vaccines, anti-viral drugs, detectors, nanotech defense systems, and surveillance technologies; creating a comprehensive catalogue of threatening meteors and asteroids; and retarding the development and proliferation of dangerous applications and weapons of mass destruction. Another possible longer-term approach to risk-reduction involves colonizing space. Proactive approaches must emphasize foresight: In managing existential risks, there is no opportunity to learn from mistakes.

Prospects for long-term human survival remain unclear. If humans begin to colonize other planets, it may be much harder to cause the extinction of the widely-scattered species. Whether the physical laws of the universe will permit intelligent information processing to continue expanding forever is an open question. Scientists' current best understanding of the relevant physics seems to rule this out, but cosmology and quantum gravity still hold many mysteries. If humans survive another hundred years, the species and their intelligent machine descendents may well have a *very* long time to look for possible loopholes.

See also: *Disasters; Future Generations, Obligations to; Outer Space, Colonization of.*

BIBLIOGRAPHY

Bostrom, Nick. 2002. *Anthropic Bias: Observation Selection Effects in Science and Philosophy.* New York: Routledge.

Drexler, K. Eric. 1985. *Engines of Creation: The Coming Era of Nanotechnology.* London: Fourth Estate.

Jaffe, Robert L., et al. 2000. "Review of speculative 'disaster scenarios' as RHIC." *Review of Modern Physics* 72: 1125–40.

Leslie, John. 1996. *The End of the World: The Science and Ethics of Human Extinction.* London: Routledge.

Morrison, David, et al. 1994. "The Impact Hazard." In *Hazards Due to Comets and Asteroids.* T. Gehrels. Tucson: The University of Arizona Press.

INTERNET RESOURCES.

Bostrom, Nick. 2002. "Existential Risks: Analyzing Human Extinction Scenarios and Related Hazards." *Journal of Evolution and Technology* 9. <http://www.transhumanist.com/volume9/risks.html>.

Freitas, Robert A., Jr. 2000. "Some Limits to Global Ecophagy by Biovorous Nanoreplicators, with Public Policy Recommendations." *Foresight Institute.* Richardson, TX: Zyvex Preprint. <http://www.foresight.org/NanoRev/Ecophagy.html>.

Gubrud, Mark. 2000. "Nanotechnology and International Security." *Foresight Institute, Fifth Foresight Conference on Molecular Nanotechnology.* <http://www.foresight.org/Conferences/MNT05/Papers/Gubrud/index.html>

NICK BOSTROM

F

FAMILY

HISTORY	Andrejs Plakans
FUTURE	Frank F. Furstenberg

HISTORY

Historical research on individual families in the Western world was carried out by genealogists long before the field was systematized in the 1960s and 1970s. In those two decades, however, as a result of the confluence of new initiatives and organizational developments in several disciplines, family history established itself as a specialized endeavor with strong links to cognate disciplines such as demography, sociology, and anthropology. The "new social history," proceeding from the influence of the French *Annales* school, pursued the history of "structures of long duration," including microstructures such as families, households, and kin groups.

The pioneering essays in *Population in History* (Glass and Eversley 1965) demonstrated the potential of the historical study of populations, and John Hajnal's essay on European marriage patterns in that volume put forth a seminal hypothesis about an important aspect of the long-term evolution of European family life. The formation of the Cambridge Group for the History of Population and Social Structure in 1967 resulted in an inclusive program for both historical demography and family/household structural analysis on the basis of historical sources such as parish registers and household listings. Independently of these initiatives, Philippe Ariès's *Centuries of Childhood* (1962) pointed to im-

portant historical shifts in the manner in which children were socialized.

By the early 1970s these initiatives had coalesced into a research agenda that dealt with the family, broadly defined, in both the distant and the recent past and used a wide variety of analytical concepts and approaches. Over the next 30 years the agenda widened to include questions not dealt with by the "founding generation."

Family Households and Historical Demography

In the decades between 1970 and 2000 historical demography and family history developed simultaneously, with findings on historical patterns of mortality, fertility, marriage, and migration creating in any historical period the context in which the family as a social structure had to be understood and with the historical sources used in family history (household listings, parish registers) providing much of the raw data for historical-demographic generalizations. It was clear that decisions about marriage, childbearing, and geographical movement always involved the family in some fashion; death, by contrast, was not a result of personal decisions but did have wide ramifications for family structure and life.

Changes in marital, childbearing, and migration behaviors were shown to be interrelated with changes in family size and structure over time. In pre-modern, pre-contraceptive societies, in which births outside wedlock brought stigma for both the mother and the child, most births took place after marriage. Consequently, the age at first marriage was identified as an important variable influencing the ultimate size of the nuclear family group. Normally, women bore children every two years; hence, marriage in the late teens, in contrast to the late twenties, could result in a size difference in offspring groups of four or five, assuming the same levels of infant and child mortality.

Hajnal's (1965) hypothesis of "western" and "eastern" marriage patterns on the European continent proposed that in the western half of the continent marriages on average took place when both partners were in their late twenties, whereas in the eastern half women tended to marry in the late teens. The larger number of ever-born children per couple in the east, however, was offset by higher levels of infant and child mortality. In the east both long- and short-distance movement was restricted by institutions such as serfdom so that localities retained more of the human material out of which cultural choices often fashioned families that were more complicated than those in the west. The survival into later life of the initially somewhat larger sibling groups and the reduced pace of dispersion of those groups meant that there were more related adults in a given locality who could live together if they chose to do so. Mean family household size in Western Europe averaged four to five persons, whereas in the east it was closer to eight to nine. In the west the proportion of family households with more than two generations and with complex structures was low; in the east, by contrast that proportion tended to be high.

These pre-modern interrelationships between demographic patterns and family structures were dissolved during the "demographic transition," when mortality, and later fertility, started to decline. The timing of the onset of the transition and its duration were the subject of the Princeton Fertility Project that was initiated in the 1970s. Although the project failed to show convincingly the precise relationship between demographic, cultural, and socioeconomic change, it did demonstrate that the timing of the beginning of the decline varied substantially across the continent. The transition started first in Western Europe, notably in France, in the early nineteenth century. Central Europe experienced it in the middle decades of the century, and it did not take hold in the eastern part of the continent until the late nineteenth and early twentieth centuries. The project also noted the presence of "pioneering" localities where fertility decline began earlier than in the surrounding areas in all of Europe's regions.

At the family level, the transition meant that couples could count on more of their children surviving past the childhood years, increasing pressure on family resources. One response to this pressure was to begin to limit childbirth, initially by spacing births and then with the aid of artificial means of birth control. This had the effect of delinking age at first marriage from the start of childbearing: the end of a historical pattern. The increased probability of survival of each individual child, entailing educational expenses first for boys and later for girls as well, meant that the ideal number of children per couple fell steadily.

Coinciding with the demographic transition were political reforms that lifted restrictions on movement, especially in Eastern Europe. As the industrial and service sectors grew and as urban areas became more capable of absorbing in-migrants, the dispersion of sibling groups became a more common occurrence, diminishing the scope for complex families. Large multi-generational complex family groups remained important only in those areas, such as Serbia, where cultural imperatives for their creation were particularly strong. These shifts were not as meaningful in Western countries where even in earlier times family complexity had for the most part manifested itself in elderly parents coresiding with married children rather than as the coresidence of married siblings.

Relationships between demographic patterns and family structures still existed in the twentieth century but the connection was weakening. By the end of the century, in the domains of marriage, family formation, and childbearing, cultural imperatives and personal choice seemed to have moved into positions of dominance in all the regions of Europe. Marriage was no longer a prerequisite to sexual gratification, as the stigma of premarital sex had nearly vanished and cohabitation of unmarried persons had become widely accepted. The timing of marriage became increasingly disconnected from the question of offspring, which was determined more by the economic and professional readiness of couples to "begin having children." Divorce had lost it stigma as well. Net reproduction fell below one (the replacement level) first in Western and then in Eastern European countries. Low fertility, together with increased life expectancy, meant that most European populations were aging, with steadily increasing proportions of elderly persons and falling proportions of children.

Historical Changes in Family Structure

Although it was possible to trace from historical-demographic trends the different consequences for different aspects of family life, changes in the structure of family groups *as groups* required different kinds of evidence. The systematic study of family household structure over time began in the late 1960s with the work of the Cambridge Group, particularly the investigations by Peter Laslett of the "listing of inhabitants." Thousands of those listings were uncovered throughout the Continent and were mined for their content. In some localities, nominal listings were randomly spaced over time; in others, they were made at systematic intervals.

In these listings it was possible to research family structure at moments in past time or in a series of moments. Occasionally communities recorded information about family groupings continuously, permitting the tracking of changes in family groups over long stretches of generations. Some listings carefully recorded the relationship between each member and the group head, whereas others left it unspecified. Some lists distinguished between groups, whereas in others such boundaries had to be interpreted. Successful record linkage involving household listings and parish registers sometimes could be used to enrich both kinds of evidence.

Research on these sources demonstrated the flaws in various earlier claims about structural changes, expanded geographical coverage of family research, and showed that the boundaries of the family in the past were much more porous than had been thought. Geographically, Europe and North America rapidly became the best-researched parts of the world, but historical sources revealed significant historical information about China and Japan as well. Within Europe the western countries and Scandinavia became the most thoroughly researched regions, with southeastern Europe, Italy, and Iberia in second place and Eastern Europe not yet explored fully. Several typologies of European patterns, an east-west division, and a four-part division, served as useful guides to research but were questioned with regard to oversimplification. Chronologically, research was most thorough for the centuries between the seventeenth and nineteenth, with the classical world remaining to be described fully. For the twentieth century, questions of family dynamics largely supplanted questions of structural change.

Broadly speaking, research on Europe since the early 1970s has shown that although nineteenth-century sociological theories of familial evolution describing a trajectory from simple to complex structures held in some regions, they misrepresented the history of other regions. The simply structured two-generational family (father, mother, children) everywhere and always accounted for a significant proportion of all family groupings, and in the European west this structure was predominant ever since the availability of historical records. Elsewhere in Europe the story was more complicated. In the European east (including Russia), under conditions of serfdom that limited movement, and in some regions of the Balkans where local traditions celebrated joint ownership of land and property, complex family structures (coresidence of married siblings and of parental couples with married children) historically represented a significant proportion of any community's total family households. Similar statistical importance of complex groups was found in localities of such widely dispersed countries as Finland, France, and Italy, where these patterns usually were associated with labor needs and inheritance patterns. Wealthier family households were generally more complex than poorer ones, though there are many exceptions to this generalization. The growing size of the "middle class" during the nineteenth century introduced value-based preferences that favored the small nuclear unit.

In most localities a family household almost always contained various nonrelated members: farmhands, apprentices, lodgers, and paupers. Family structure varied with the age of the household head, exhibiting the "family developmental cycle" (from simple to complex to simple as the head aged). Over time until the twentieth century, complicated groups tended to change the nature of their complexity from horizontal to vertical: married siblings earlier in the developmental cycle and aging parents coresident with a married child later. A unilinear evolutionary pattern (from wholly complex to wholly simple) at the local level, however, could not be found anywhere, as family groups responded to crises by expanding their ranks, becoming simple again when times turned less threatening. The association of particular familial structures with particular ethnic or nationality groups was shown to be irrelevant, and so claims about the "typical French family" or the "typical German family" fell by the wayside. From the functional viewpoint, familial units everywhere reacted to plenty and to adversity generally in the same fashion.

During the twentieth century, however, there was a convergence of structural patterns throughout Europe, though this question has yet to receive a conclusive answer. Also, since the mid-twentieth century new forms of cohabitation have emerged that have required redefinition of what a "family" and a "household" are. The definitions that served to keep research comparable for the pre-twentieth century period have been revealed to be increasingly time-specific.

The early programs of the Cambridge Group to systematize historical family research and make it comparative eventually were criticized as researchers turned increasingly to the study of family dynamics in the past. It was suggested that the constant changes in family life made talk of "structures" irrelevant because any family could experience numerous structural changes in the course of its existence. Some researchers shifted the focus from the family group to individuals within the family group, underlining the interconnectedness between the group's evolution and the individual lives of the persons within the group. Indeed, in the course of time research on the history of the family tended to leave the question of "structure" behind, preferring to look instead at the intergenerational transmission of property (inheritance) within the family group, the distribution of power (patriarchal authority) within it, the effects on it of state policy (public welfare institutions), the experience of crises within the group (widowhood and widowerhood), and the play of emotions within it (parent–child relationships). Some researchers have begun to investigate other social groups of a quasi-familial nature, such as guilds and brotherhoods. The study the of history of the family presents a clear example of a field developing new research directions before early questions were fully answered.

Household, Family, and Kin Group

Successful studies of kinship within the family coresidential group in the European past showed that when kin beyond the head's immediate family were present, they tended to be kin of a certain kind, for the most part patrilineal. Thus, in the European context there was a higher probability that the coresident parental couple would be the husband's parents, that the coresident siblings of the head would be the husband's brothers, and that the coresident married offspring would be the sons rather than the daughters. These configurations were all predictable from knowledge of the way patrilineal societies worked at any time and in any place. What was always of interest in the European past was who was excluded from the domestic group and on what basis. From the very beginning this question hovered just offstage: If kinship within the domestic group was important, what was the significance of kin ties that crossed household boundaries?

The strongest argument for looking beyond the family household for important family connections lay in already documented behaviors. Aristocracies of various kinds as well as wealthy urban patriciates had always had a keen interest in their lineages, and a similar preoccupation existed in some peasantries, in France for example. In some areas of Europe such as Albania, clan-like organizations were said to have continued to exist well into the twentieth century. Unfortunately, the functioning of larger kin groups is poorly documented in the European past. Whether the influence of the larger kin group on families was peripheral and weak or strong but subtle was an empirical question and could not be answered with any certainty unless such larger kin ties were mapped and the dynamics of domestic units within them were explored.

Several hypotheses about these matters emerged in the course of research. Laslett (1988) contended that people who lived in nuclear families encountered difficulties when faced with crises such as widowhood, unemployment, sickness, and senility. Accordingly, they sought support from their kin or, in the absence of kin, from friends, neighbors, or institutions in the community at large. Yet in the European historical record kin groups were not simply exemplars of the "ethic of amity" (Fortes 1969); they involved antagonisms and divisions as well, especially when disputes involved property, position, or other forms of wealth. Moreover, large kin-linked formations could experience internal shifts. In his explorations of kinship formations in the German village of Neckarhausen in the period from 1600 to 1900, David Sabean (1990, 1998) showed that large kin configurations could undergo transformations of emphasis even while retaining general characteristics such as "patrilineality." Marriage choices within large configurations changed, as did the persons whose job it was to cultivate and maintain kin relations. Sabean's larger point is that the characterization of a kinship system as bilateral or patrilineal was only the first step because historians confronted historical kinship not as a full-blown "system" but as a collection of concrete acts and transactions, each of which had to be understood and interpreted. The temporal changes that are worth knowing about could occur without changing the general "tilt" of the entire system. However, in order to understand the meaning of the change-producing decisions, those decisions have to be laid against a reconstructed network showing how the makers of everyday decisions, within the domestic group context and outside it, were related to each other. A full understanding of the growing autonomy of the domestic group and its growing tendency to make collective decisions without reference to any outside persons required knowledge of the larger group from which autonomy was sought. If the modern state gradually assumed many of the functions that supportive kin networks may have served in earlier times, this transfer of obligations did not cancel, even as it may have weakened, kin ties, and such ties continued to stand ready to be reactivated when the state failed in its duties. Important questions of this kind remain largely unanswered for most of the European continent.

See also: *Family Reconstitution; Henry, Louis; Historical Demography; Household Composition; Laslett, Peter.*

BIBLIOGRAPHY

Anderson, Michael. 1980. *Approaches to the History of the Western Family 1500–1914.* London: Macmillan.

Ariès, Philippe. 1962. *Centuries of Childhood: A Social History of Family Life,* trans. Robert Baldick. New York: Knopf.

Coale, Ansley J., and Susan Cotts Watkins, eds. 1986. *The Decline of Fertility in Europe.* Princeton, NJ: Princeton University Press.

Fortes, Mayer. 1969. *Kinship and the Social Order: The Legacy of Lewis Henry Morgan.* Chicago: Aldine.

Glass, David, and D. E. C. Eversley, eds. 1965. *Population in History.* Chicago: Aldine.

Hajnal, John. 1965. "European Marriage Patterns in Historical Perspective." In *Population in History,* ed. David Glass and D. E. C. Eversley. Chicago: Aldine.

Hareven, Tamara K. 1996. *Aging and Generational Relations over the Life Course.* Berlin: De Gruyter.

Kaser, Karl. 1995. *Familie und Verwandschaft auf dem Balkan: Analyse einer Untergehenden Kultur.* Vienna: Suhrkampf.

Kertzer, David. 1991. "Household History and Sociological Theory." *Annual Review of Sociology* 17: 155–179.

Laslett, Peter. 1966. "The Study of Social Structure from Listings of Inhabitants." In *An Introduction to English Historical Demography.* New York: Basic Books.

———. 1983. "Family and Household as Work Group and Kin Group: Areas of Traditional Europe Compared." In *Family Forms in Historic Europe,* ed. Richard Wall, J. Robin, and Peter Laslett. Cambridge, Eng.: Cambridge University Press.

———. 1988. "Family, Kinship, and Collectivity as Systems of Support in Pre-Industrial Europe: A Consideration of the 'Nuclear-Hardship' Hypothesis." *Continuity and Change* 3: 153–175.

Laslett, Peter, and Richard Wall, eds. 1972. *Household and Family in Past Time.* Cambridge, Eng.: Cambridge University Press.

Plakans, Andrejs. 1984. *Kinship in the Past: An Anthropology of European Family Life 1500–1900.* Oxford: Blackwell.

Ruggles, Steven. 1990. "Family Demography and Family History: Problems and Prospects." *Historical Methods* 23: 22–33.

Sabean, David. 1990. *Property, Production, and Family in Neckarhausen, 1700–1870.* Cambridge, Eng.: Cambridge University Press.

———. 1998. *Kinship in Neckarhausen 1700–1870.* Cambridge, Eng.: Cambridge University Press.

Segalen, Martine. 1985. *Fifteen Generations of Bretons: Kinship and Society in Lower Brittany 1720–1980.* Cambridge, Eng.: Cambridge University Press.

Smith, Daniel Scott. 1993. "The Curious History of Theorizing about the History of the Western Nuclear Family." *Social Science History* 17: 325–353.

Wall, Richard, J. Robin, and Peter Laslett, eds. 1983. *Family Forms in Historic Europe.* Cambridge, Eng.: Cambridge University Press.

Wetherell, Charles. 1998. "Historical Social Network Analysis." *International Review of Social History* 43, Supplement: 125–144.

Wrigley, E. A., ed. 1966. *An Introduction to English Historical Demography*. New York: Basic Books.

———. 1969. *Population and History*. New York: McGraw-Hill.

ANDREJS PLAKANS

FUTURE

Changes in the institution of the family probably occur more rapidly in modern and modernizing societies than in the past, but historians and anthropologists have long been aware that shifts in kinship and marriage practices take place even in traditional societies, albeit at a slower pace. What is also true in the early twenty-first century, far more than in the past, is that through social science research, government reports, and stories in the mass media, people are acutely conscious of the changes that are taking place in family norms and behaviors. It is known that the family is changing, but it is nonetheless difficult to project the course of that change beyond a decade or two. Charting the future of the family, then, is an exercise in imagination or science fiction.

Having conceded an inability to read the future, there are certain straws in the wind that can provide some clues of what might be in store for the Western family. Also, it may be worth revisiting ideas about convergence in family forms that were popular in the middle decades of the twentieth century.

Future of Marriage in the West

The widespread practice of cohabitation, the rising age of marriage, and high levels of marital instability have lead some observers to question the viability of the institution of marriage. Certainly, the practice of lifelong monogamy, which became the cornerstone of the Western family with the spread of Christianity, has given way to more varied arrangements: consensual unions not sanctioned by state or church; single-parenthood; homosexual unions; and conjugal succession or "serial marriage." Such arrangements have always existed in many societies, but without the legitimacy that they are accorded today.

The conditions that have given rise to greater variation in family forms in which childbearing or,

at least, childrearing occurs can be traced to many different factors. The decline of church and state authority to shape public morality is one important source of family change. The breakdown of strict gender roles that once created a high degree of interdependence between spouses is another powerful impetus for revising matrimonial arrangements. The spread of education and of the ideology of choice is a third reason for increasing variability in family forms and in the roles of family members.

It appears unlikely that any of these conditions that have undercut the hegemony of the nuclear family are going to recede. Yet it is entirely possible that customs and fashions, economic forces, or the growth of state authority may influence the distribution of family types within and between Western nations. In the United States, for example, politicians are mounting strenuous efforts to promote marriage. Whether public policies or official rhetoric are likely to have any effect on marriage practices is at best dubious.

According to David Ellwood and Christopher Jencks (2001), variation in family forms in the United States is much more conspicuous as one goes down the socioeconomic ladder. Over the past several decades, family behavior among the privileged has changed little, while in other social strata rates of marital instability and single-parenthood have increased, especially among the poor. This observation suggests that the flux in marriage may be partly produced by economic strains or, perhaps, by gender discord resulting from changing expectations of men and women. The exploration of class differences in family forms is an intriguing area for further investigation.

Future of Fertility in the West

If the fate of marriage is unpredictable, low fertility within marriage appears to have a more secure future. Technological developments in fertility control have increased the ability of couples to manage fertility effectively. Given the high cost of children and low levels of mortality during childhood, large family size is becoming a relic of the past. It is difficult to imagine conditions that will produce, once again, a demand for large families.

The challenge of raising fertility to replacement levels has become an urgent issue of public policy in many Western nations. More than any other, this policy problem is likely to have important effects on the family. The difficulty of combining work and family roles and the high costs involved in rearing children are leading many parents to severely restrict childbearing. It seems likely that societies will experiment with arrangements that alleviate the private costs of rearing children and with building institutions that enable parents to combine work and family roles more easily. Innovations in these areas are already evident, but there is likely to be a good deal more institutional invention as technology allows parents of children to work in the home, or as day-care arrangements permit parental monitoring of children's safety and comfort.

Techniques of Reproduction

Nowhere has reality come closer to science fiction, if not actually surpassing it, than in the area of reproductive technology. Fertility has become ever-more controllable through new medical and biological procedures. The capacity of parents to predetermine at least some of their children's physical characteristics is just around the corner; however, it is not at all clear how different societies will handle the potential benefits and abuses of new reproductive technologies. It seems likely that legal prescriptions will be developed to impose rules on the use of new reproductive technologies, and equally likely that such regulations will create a black market in the use of proscribed practices.

Future of Kinship in the West

High rates of divorce and remarriage reshaped kinship arrangements in last half of the twentieth century. Rising levels of cohabitation and nonmarital childbearing have added complexity to the family as broadly defined. The links across households produced by nonresidential parents and their partners, not to mention their siblings, parents, and children, have created wider but shallower family bonds. Moreover, gay couples and their families have established new kinship arrangements not formed by blood or marriage—the traditional ways of constructing a family. Western societies allow greater latitude in defining family but, in doing so, may be attaching lower levels of obligation to kinship.

Kinship has always been socially constructed, even if members of a society come to think of these ties as "natural." Parent and child relationships based on biological and genetic ties tended to be seen as fundamental, while in-law relations created by legal arrangements were accepted as socially binding.

By the beginning of the twenty-first century, both of these axes of kinship had become more questionable in law and practice. The father who sires a child but never lives with him or her has less relevance than the sociological parent (man or woman) who is the mother's partner and helps in raising the child. Moreover, this partner's family becomes part of the child's family, with views of rights and obligations to the child that may be highly variable. Relatively little research exists on new family forms, especially on the way that these forms affect family members' relations with each other in every day practice.

The charting of kinship bonds over time within nontraditional families is an attractive way of understanding how such bonds are created and maintained, and illustrates the strength of relationships in families that are not established by blood or marriage. Students of the family should examine the transfer of property, the keeping of family albums, the frequency of family reunions, and many other everyday aspects of behavior as ways of establishing the meaning of kinship in alternative and traditional families. As yet, virtually no literature exists on this topic.

Convergence of Western and Non-Western Families

In the 1960s some social scientists argued that family systems were converging across the world, gradually moving toward a Western model. The sociologist William J. Goode argued that the fit between the nuclear family and the needs of a modern economy would ultimately force different kinship systems to take on the Western form. Although there is abundant evidence of change in kinship systems worldwide, the evidence suggesting convergence to a Western model of the family is equivocal at best.

It may be still too soon to detect the movement away from complex to simpler forms of the family. However, the thesis put forth by family sociologists in the mid-twentieth-century seems naive in light of what has occurred in the West. In the first place, the assumption of a uniquely appropriate fit seems doubtful in view of the vast changes that have taken place in the Western form of the family and the continuing stresses that are evident between work and family. Moreover, it is clear that traditional forms of the family persist even as economic change takes place.

Will plural marriage—polygamy—where it still exists survive economic development and the spread of Western corporate institutions? Can multi-generational households co-exist with modern economic markets that promote the interests of individuals over aggregates? It seems likely that some accommodations will occur as economic development advances and the market economy spreads to non-Western nations. Clearly, fertility has declined and may continue to drop, forcing changes in household structure and living arrangements. It remains to be seen, however, whether the kinship arrangements that result will have a Western look.

Variations in family forms worldwide have been more resilient than many observers predicted. Goode's thesis that the Western, nuclear family would be imported to nations of varied kinship arrangements has not yet come true, even though changes in marriage and divorce practices and fertility are evident in many developing nations. The hegemony of the nuclear family is less evident and variety is more apparent. In this respect, kinship is proving to be a more durable feature of culture than was thought by those who predicted the demise of the family or the convergence of family forms to a single model.

See also: *Childlessness; Cohabitation; Divorce; Fertility, Below-Replacement; Fertility, Nonmarital; Marriage; Parenthood; Partner Choice.*

BIBLIOGRAPHY

Ellwood, David T., and Christopher Jencks. 2001. "The Growing Differences in Family Structure: What Do We Know? Where Do We Look for Answers?" Paper prepared for the New Inequality Program. New York: Russell Sage Foundation.

Goode, William J. 1963. *World Revolution and Family Patterns.* New York: Free Press of Glencoe.

Johnson, Coleen. 1988. *Ex Familia: Grandparents, Parents, and Children Adjust to Divorce.* New Brunswick, NJ: Rutgers University Press.

Popenoe, David. 1996. *Life without Father.* New York: Free Press.

Waite, Linda, and Maggie Gallagher. 2000. *The Case for Marriage: Why Married People Are Happier, Healthier, and Better off Financially.* New York: Doubleday.

Weston, Kath. 1991. *Families We Choose: Lesbians, Gays, Kinship.* New York: Columbia University Press.

Wilson, James Q. 2002. *The Marriage Problem.* New York: HarperCollins.

FRANK F. FURSTENBERG

FAMILY ALLOWANCES

Family allowances (also known as child allowances or child benefits) are cash transfers made by governments to families with children. The allowances usually are paid monthly to parents. In 2001 family allowances were provided to families in most industrialized countries and some developing countries. Family allowance schemes vary greatly across countries, especially in terms of their amounts, eligibility criteria, and mode of financing. Furthermore, these schemes have been the subject of significant reforms during the preceding few decades.

History of Family Allowances

Family allowances have a history that goes back to the late nineteenth century. Their origin can be traced to France, where several private and public family allowance schemes were introduced in the 1890s. Under these schemes, allowances were paid to wage earners as a supplement to their wages to help families meet their needs. In the following decades private family allowance schemes gained popularity among employers. To administer these schemes, equalization funds (*caisses de compensation*) were set up throughout France, each of them grouping a number of employers. By 1923 there were an estimated 120 funds in operation, covering 7,600 firms and distributing family allowances to 880,000 wage earners, or about 20 percent of all wage earners.

These schemes were the object of numerous criticisms. Workers' organizations were critical of the fact that only workers at selected firms benefited from the allowances, that different rates of family allowances were in force in the different equalization funds, and that, since the funds were under employers' control, the allowances could be terminated at any time. Instead, they called for family allowance schemes to be administered by the state. Their call

FIGURE 1

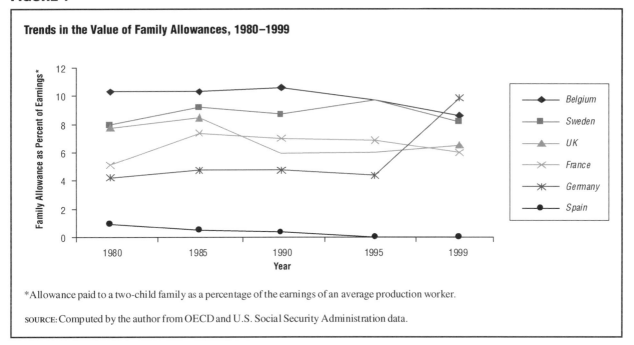

Trends in the Value of Family Allowances, 1980–1999

*Allowance paid to a two-child family as a percentage of the earnings of an average production worker.

SOURCE: Computed by the author from OECD and U.S. Social Security Administration data.

was answered in 1932 with the adoption of a state-administered family allowance scheme that extended allowances to all wage earners with children. In 1939 the minimum family allowance rates were made uniform across regions (*départements*).

In the other industrialized countries, the adoption of state-administered universal family allowance schemes was preceded by various other schemes, including widows' and orphans' pensions (introduced in the 1910s and 1920s in several countries), family cost-of-living bonuses, and assistance schemes for large families. Aimed at helping families financially, several of these earlier schemes were targeted at low-income families and/or were restricted to large families. By 1949 universal family allowance schemes were in place in 15 industrialized countries.

During subsequent decades, family allowance schemes were adopted in most other industrialized countries, with the notable exception of the United States. In the 1950s and 1960s these schemes underwent various changes, such as the harmonization of rates across different categories of workers, the elimination of means tests, and the increase in coverage to include all children. (Previously, allowances were often provided beginning only with a family's third child.) Additional programs were introduced to provide further assistance to low-income families and single-parent families.

This historical expansion of state support for families ended in the 1980s. Restricted budgets and growing levels of unemployment led governments in Australia, Canada, Italy, New Zealand, Portugal, and Spain in the 1980s and 1990s to impose means tests on previously universal family allowances or to replace them by other means-tested schemes.

Trends in the Value of Allowances in Selected Countries

The size of the allowances received by families varies substantially across countries. In Western Europe in 1999 the highest allowances for a two-child family were found in Luxembourg, Germany, and Belgium. In Luxembourg the amount exceeded $300 (U.S.) per month, more than 14 percent of the average monthly earnings of a production worker.

Figure 1 shows the trends in the value of allowances for a two-child family in selected countries, expressed as a percentage of the average monthly earnings of a production worker. Between 1980 and 1999 the value decreased in Belgium, the United Kingdom, and Spain. In Germany it strongly increased after a major reform in 1996. It should, however, be noted that family allowances represent only one form of public financial support for families. Tax relief for children also is provided in several countries, along with other means-tested benefits. The country rankings therefore vary depending on the type of cash support considered. They also vary by the age and number of children, household income, and family type.

Effects of Family Allowances on Welfare and Fertility

Although mainly intended as a welfare benefit for families with children, family allowances have also been seen by some governments as a way to encourage parents to have more children. Such pronatalist attitudes prevailed in France, Germany, Italy, and Spain during World War II and have since been observed (in some periods) in various other countries, such as Singapore and Israel. In countries where pronatalist objectives have dominated, allowances have tended to be larger for children of higher birth order and to be supplemented by generous birth grants.

The effect of such allowances and grants on fertility is questionable. Blanchet and Ekert-Jaffé (1994) have estimated that family allowances like those provided in France have resulted in a fertility rate about 0.2 child higher. On the basis of cross-national data from 22 countries and a time series spanning the period 1970–1990, Gauthier and Hatzius (1997) have estimated that a 25 percent increase in family allowances would result in an increase in the total period fertility rate of 0.07 children per woman. Cash support for families may encourage parents on average to have more children, but the effect is very small.

It sometimes is argued, especially in the United States, that means-tested cash benefits may have the unintended consequence of encouraging low-income families, single mothers, and teenage girls to have children. The empirical evidence, however, suggests that this is not the case, or that any such effect is very small. Similarly, family allowances and other types of cash benefits for families with children have been found to have no effect or a limited effect on women's likelihood of marrying or divorcing, their use of welfare, and their labor force participation. The same is true of the provision of maternity and childcare benefits and child care facilities. The decision to have a child or to withdraw from the labor market has undeniable economic consequences. Family allowances and other types of support for families, however, appear to have limited effects on these decisions.

See also: *Cost of Children; Family Policy.*

BIBLIOGRAPHY

Blanchet, Didier, and Olivia Ekert-Jaffé. 1994. "The Demographic Impact of Family Benefits: Evidence from Micro-Model and from Macro-Data." In *The Family, the Market and the State in Ageing Societies,* ed. J. Ermisch and N. Ogawa. Oxford, Eng.: Clarendon Press.

Bradshaw, Jonathan, John Ditch, Hilary Holmes, and Peter Whiteford. 1993. "A Comparative Study of Child Support in Fifteen Countries." *Journal of European Social Policy* 3(4): 255–271.

Gauthier, Anne H. 1996. *The State and the Family: A Comparative Analysis of Family Policies in Industrialized Countries.* Oxford, Eng.: Clarendon Press.

Gauthier, Anne H., and Jan Hatzius. 1997. "Family Benefits and Fertility: An Econometric Analysis." *Population Studies* 51: 295–306.

Glass, David. 1940. *Population Policies and Movements in Europe.* Oxford, Eng.: Clarendon Press.

King, Leslie. 2002. "Demographic Trends, Pronatalism, and Nationalist Ideologies in the Late Twentieth Century," *Ethnic and Racial Studies* 25(3): 367–389.

MacNicol, John. 1992. "Welfare, Wages, and the Family: Child Endowment in Comparative Perspective, 1900–50." In *In the Name of the Child: Health and Welfare, 1880–1940,* R. Cooter, ed. London: Routledge.

Moffitt, Robert. 1992. "Incentive Effects of the U.S. Welfare System: A Review." *Journal of Economic Literature* 30(1): 5–62.

ANNE H. GAUTHIER

FAMILY BARGAINING

Bargaining approaches to family decision-making developed in the last two decades of the twentieth century. Because interactions between spouses are simpler than most other family interactions, bargaining approaches have been most fully articulated in the context of marriage. This entry begins by describing pre-bargaining approaches to interactions between spouses and then surveys bargaining approaches. It concludes by discussing briefly the application of bargaining approaches to other interactions within families—between parents and children and between elderly parents and adult children.

Bargaining Approaches and Game Theory

Bargaining approaches are based on game theory and this entry uses the terms bargaining approaches and game-theoretic approaches interchangeably. Within game theory, the threshold distinction is between noncooperative and cooperative games. Cooperative game theory analyzes outcomes or solutions under the assumption that the players can communicate freely and make costlessly-enforceable agreements. Thus, cooperative game theory treats all feasible outcomes as potential equilibria. In contrast, noncooperative game theory treats as potential equilibria only those outcomes that correspond to self-enforcing agreements in the sense that each player's strategy is a best response to the strategies of the others.

Economists say that an equilibrium is "efficient" (or "Pareto efficient" or "Pareto optimal") if no individual can be made better off without someone else being made worse off. Efficiency implies that any division of a cake is efficient provided it leaves none on the plate and none on the floor—thus, a division may be efficient without being fair or equitable. The efficiency of social arrangements and practices is a central concern of economics, yet pre-bargaining models of the family and cooperative bargaining models simply assumed that families are efficient. A major advantage of approaches based on noncooperative game theory is that they do not assume efficiency and thus allow us to investigate the conditions that enable families to achieve and sustain efficient outcomes.

Becker's Altruist Model

Gary Becker, in his work of 1974 and 1981, proposed the first model of family decision-making or household collective choice, his "altruist" model. Three implications of Becker's altruist model deserve attention. First, it implies that family decisions are Pareto efficient. Second, it implies a distribution of the benefits and burdens of family life in which the head of the family—Becker's altruist—attains his most preferred point in the feasible set. Third, it implies that family members pool their resources.

The altruist model is rigged to produce these results, but none of these results—efficiency, the lopsided distribution of benefits and burdens, or pooling of family resources—is an essential feature of bargaining models of family decision-making. Robert A. Pollak in 1985 interprets Becker's altruist model as an "ultimatum game" in which one family member can confront the others with take-it-or-leave-it offers. Without the ultimatum game interpretation, the conclusions of the altruist model and of Becker's so-called Rotten Kid Theorem hold only in a narrow range of environments. This is discussed in Theodore Bergstrom's 1989 article, the introduction to the enlarged edition of Gary Becker's *Treatise of the Family* published in 1991, and in Robert Pollack's 2003 paper.

Bargaining Models

Cooperative bargaining models of marriage were introduced by Marilyn Manser and Murry Brown in 1980 and Marjorie B. McElroy and Mary J. Horney in 1981 as an alternative to Becker's altruist model. A typical cooperative bargaining model of marriage assumes that if the spouses fail to reach agreement, both husband and wife receive the utilities associated with a default outcome. The utilities associated with the default outcome are usually described as the "threat point." In Manser and Brown and in McElroy and Horney the threat point is interpreted as divorce, while in the "separate spheres" model of Shelley Lundberg and Robert A. Pollak, introduced in their 1993 article, the threat point is interpreted as a noncooperative equilibrium within the marriage.

The Nash bargaining model, developed by John Nash in 1950, provides the leading solution concept in cooperative bargaining models of marriage. The utility received by husband or wife in the Nash bargaining solution depends on the threat point; the higher a spouse's utility at the threat point, the higher the utility that spouse will receive in the Nash bargaining solution. This dependence is the critical empirical implication of Nash bargaining models: the couple's expenditure pattern depends not only on prices and the couple's total income, but also on the threat point.

The income-pooling hypothesis. As the divorce-threat and separate spheres models show, cooperative bargaining does not imply income pooling. If the fraction of the couple's income controlled by each spouse individually affects the threat point, then it will affect the couple's expenditure pattern and the relative well-being of husbands and wives. This dependence implies that public policy, for example, tax and welfare policy, may affect distribution within marriage.

Empirical rejections of family income pooling have been the most influential in weakening economists' attachment to the altruist model. Income pooling implies a restriction on family demand functions that appears simple to test: If family members pool their incomes and allocate the total, then only total income will affect demands. The fraction of family income received or controlled by one family member should not influence those demands. A large number of later empirical studies have rejected pooling, finding instead that earned or unearned income received by the husband or wife significantly affects demand patterns when total income or expenditure is held constant.

For technical reasons discussed in Shelly Lundberg and Robert Pollak's 1996 work, the pooling hypothesis is not simple to test. The ideal test would be based on an experiment in which some husbands and some wives were randomly selected to receive income transfers. A less-than-ideal test could be based on a natural experiment in which some husbands or some wives received an exogenous income change. Lundberg, Pollak, and Terence J. Wales in 1997 examine the effects of such a natural experiment—the policy change in the United Kingdom that transferred substantial resources from husbands to wives in the late 1970s. The policy change involved child allowances, a program of government transfer payments to parents. The child allowance payments were conditioned on the number of children in the family, but not on family income, so that, in welfare-program terminology, the program is not "means tested." Lundberg, Pollak, and Wales find strong evidence that a shift toward relatively greater expenditures on women's goods and children's goods coincided with this income redistribution, and they interpret this finding as a rejection of the pooling hypothesis.

Because efficiency is much more difficult to test than pooling, the discussion of efficiency has focused on theoretical issues. The most convincing rationale for the usual assumption that bargaining in marriage leads to efficient outcomes is the belief that efficiency is likely to emerge from repeated interactions in environments that remain stable or change slowly over time. Most, but not all, marital bargaining involves repeated interactions in stable environments. Lundberg and Pollak in 2001 argue that when a decision affects future bargaining power, inefficient outcomes are plausible. If the spouses could make binding commitments—in effect, commitments to refrain from exploiting future bargaining advantages—then this source of inefficiency would disappear. But spouses seldom can make binding commitments regarding future allocations within marriage. As an example, Lundberg and Pollak consider the location problem of a two-earner couple, where the husband would be advantaged in future bargaining by one location and the wife by the other. Location decisions provide transparent and analytically tractable examples of choices likely to affect future bargaining power, but the logic of the analysis applies to many other decisions. For example, decisions about education, fertility, and labor force participation are also potential sources of inefficiency.

The possibility of divorce (perhaps followed by remarriage) limits the scope for bargaining within marriage by placing bounds on the distributions that can emerge as equilibria. The assumption that individuals are rational implies that no one would accept less than he or she would receive outside the marriage. "Divorce bounds" apply to all bargaining models, cooperative and noncooperative. The divorce bounds depend upon the costs of divorce, including psychic costs, the resources available to divorced individuals, and conditions in the remarriage market. When the divorce bounds are tight, there is little scope for bargaining within marriage. Bargaining models of marriage are motivated by the assumption that, in at least some marriages, the divorce bounds are loose enough that the allocation of the surplus is worth modeling.

Extensions

Bargaining approaches based on game theory provide a framework for analyzing not only interactions between spouses but all strategic interactions involving family members. Yoram Weiss and Robert J. Willis, in their 1985 and 1993 articles, show how the analytical tools of game theory can be used to investigate the distribution of child support responsibilities between ex-spouses. Because bargaining models are most tractable in simple strategic situations—two-person games in relatively stable environments—it is not surprising that bargaining models of marriage are better developed than bargaining models of interactions between parents and children. Nor is it surprising that models of interactions between parents and children are better developed than bargaining models of interactions in blended families or in families that span three or more generations. Nevertheless, bargaining models of marriage are not simple and, in the interest of tractability, analysis usually focuses on relatively stable environments and avoids dynamic ones in which decisions in one period affect bargaining power in the future.

Despite the differences among bargaining models and despite their complexity, bargaining models offer the most promising analytic approach to understanding the formation, dissolution, and functioning of households and families. Although bargaining models are unlikely to lead directly to equations that can be estimated, they are a fruitful source of hypotheses about regularities that may be found in data and of interpretations of such empirical regularities.

See also: *Becker, Gary S.; Microeconomics of Demographic Behavior; Partner Choice.*

BIBLIOGRAPHY

Becker, Gary S. 1974. "A Theory of Social Interactions." *Journal of Political Economy* 82(6): 1063–1094.

———. 1981; enlarged edition, 1991. *A Treatise on the Family.* Cambridge, MA: Harvard University Press.

Bergstrom, Theodore C. 1989. "A Fresh Look at the Rotten Kid Theorem—and Other Household Mysteries." *Journal of Political Economy* 97(5): 1138–1159.

Lundberg, Shelly, and Robert A. Pollak. 1993. "Separate Spheres Bargaining and the Marriage Market." *Journal of Political Economy* 101(6): 988–1010.

———. 1996. "Bargaining and Distribution in Marriage." *Journal of Economic Perspectives* 10(4): 139–158.

Lundberg, Shelly, Robert A. Pollak, and Terence J. Wales. 1997. "Do Husbands and Wives Pool Their Resources? Evidence from the U.K. Child Benefit." *Journal of Human Resources* 32(3): 463–480.

Manser, Marilyn, and Murray Brown. 1980. "Marriage and Household Decision-Making: A Bargaining Analysis." *International Economic Review.* 21(1): 31–44.

McElroy, Marjorie B., and Mary J. Horney. 1981. "Nash-Bargained Household Decisions: Toward a Generalization of the Theory of Demand." *International Economic Review.* 22(2): 333–349.

Pollak, Robert A. 1985. "A Transaction Cost Approach to Families and Households." *Journal of Economic Literature* 23(2): 581–608.

———. 2003. "Gary Becker's Contribution to Household and Family Economics." *Review of Economics of the Household* 1.

Weiss, Yoram, and Robert J. Willis. 1985. "Children as Collective Goods in Divorce Settlements." *Journal of Labor Economics* 3(3): 268–292.

———. 1993. "Transfers among Divorced Couples: Evidence and Interpretation." *Journal of Labor Economics* 11(4): 629–679.

ROBERT A. POLLAK

FAMILY DEMOGRAPHY

Family demography is the study of the composition of families and of the transitions individuals make into and out of various types of families. Family composition includes factors such as the number of family members, their ages, marital and cohabitation status, and relationship to other family members. Transitions include life-course characteristics such as the timing and duration of cohabitation, marriage, separation, divorce, and remarriage.

Demographers developed the field of family demography during the mid-twentieth century as a means of better understanding the number and timing of births. In the 1950s and 1960s, when most births in Western countries occurred within marriages, family demographers mainly studied the nuclear family of husband, wife, and children. But as the family changed in similar ways throughout most Western countries, family demographers broadened their focus to include adults living independently, single-parent families, cohabiting couples (unmarried couples living together), and rates of divorce and remarriage. As birth rates declined during the second half of the twentieth century, family demographers began to study these family forms independent of their impact on fertility.

In 1940 the U.S. Bureau of the Census published its first report classifying families into different types; categories included normal (meaning a married couple), other male headed, and all female headed. Labeling families with a married husband and wife "normal" reflects the dominance of the nuclear family in the mid-twentieth century. As that dominance faded, the bureau changed its terminology, broadened its categories, and began to collect more information in its monthly *Current Population Survey.* In the 1970s surveys conducted for other purposes, such as the Panel Study of Income Dynamics, provided useful information, and in the 1980s and 1990s specialized surveys such as the National Survey of Families and Households provided the first detailed information about cohabitation. In the United Kingdom one of the first sets of papers on family demography was presented at a 1983 meeting of the British Society for Population Studies. Family demographers in Western Europe, including Louis Roussel and Ron Lesthaeghe, published influential books and articles during the 1980s and 1990s about the enormous changes in European families.

At about the middle of the twentieth century, demographers noted a demographic transition involving a long-term decline in fertility and mortality rates. After 1965, as the post–World War II baby boom faded, family demographers began to write of a "second demographic transition." This transition refers to the set of changes in family formation and childbearing including increases in independent living among young adults, extensive premarital cohabitation, older ages at marriage, high levels of divorce, fertility at or below the population replacement levels, and increased childbearing outside of marriage. Economists such as Gary Becker theorized that changes in family formation occurred because the economic gains of the traditional breadwinner–homemaker marriage decreased: As women's employment opportunities rose, so did the cost in lost wages of remaining a full-time housewife. Ideational theorists such as Lesthaeghe and Johan Surkyn asserted that the second demographic transition reflected a long-term shift in societal values toward greater individual autonomy and self-fulfillment, and away from moral obligations to

family and society. Just as the economic changes were said to reduce the gains in efficiency that being married provides, the ideational changes were said to reduce the satisfaction and fulfillment that people gained from being married and raising children.

Independent Living

At the beginning of the twentieth century, most young adults lived at home until marriage. The prevailing values of the time discouraged independent living, many families relied on young adults' contributions to household income, and a shortage of housing for single people limited opportunities for leaving the family home. All of these factors changed after mid-century, and the typical age at marriage rose. As a result of these changes, the percentage of young adults living by themselves or with roommates increased during the last half of the twentieth century. The rise in divorce rates through the 1960s and 1970s also resulted in a greater number of formerly married adults living on their own.

At the turn of the twentieth century, a majority of the elderly lived in their children's homes. This, too, changed during the twentieth century, as increased life expectancies and greater affluence among the elderly led to a substantial increase in the number of older people living alone. Yet even though most of the elderly lived apart from their children by the year 2000, they tended to see them regularly and to provide assistance to them.

Marriage

Through the 1950s age at marriage was the most important determinant of fertility in the Western countries because sexual intercourse was mostly limited to married couples. In Western countries marriage typically occurs well after young women become fertile. This delay is an important contributing factor to the relatively small family size in Western countries, even before industrialization.

Figure 1 illustrates the change in percentage of 20- to 24-year-old women and men in the United States who had ever been married, from 1890 to 1998. At the beginning of the twentieth century, marriages occurred at relatively older ages, so that fewer 20- to 24-year-olds had married. During the baby boom years of 1945 to 1965, the typical age at marriage dropped sharply, so that the proportion of young adults who had ever been married increased. After the baby boom, ages at marriage rose back to

FIGURE 1

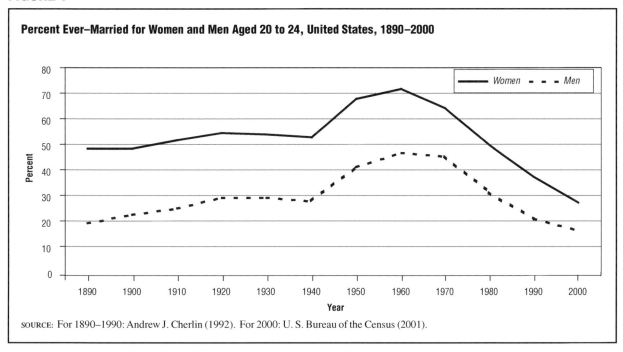

Percent Ever–Married for Women and Men Aged 20 to 24, United States, 1890–2000

SOURCE: For 1890–1990: Andrew J. Cherlin (1992). For 2000: U. S. Bureau of the Census (2001).

the pre–baby boom levels for men and rose even further for women. At the end of the twentieth century, the mean age at first marriage in the United States was approximately 25 for women and 27 for men, and the percentage of ever-married young adults was at or near an historic low. Young adults in the 1990s were marrying later because higher education and early investment in a career were considered extremely important, the labor market opportunities for men without college educations had diminished, and sexual relations outside of marriage were more culturally acceptable and carried less risk of an unwanted pregnancy due to improved contraceptive technology such as the birth control pill.

Although rates decreased from the 1960s through the 1990s, marriage remained an important part of the Western family system. Throughout most of the twentieth century, at least 90 percent of all individuals eventually married in the United States, and nearly as many married in most other Western nations. Marriage rates were lowest for adults who came of age during the Great Depression of the 1930s, and highest for those who came of age during the baby boom. Joshua Goldstein and Catherine Kenney projected in 2001 that about 90 percent of white young adults in the United States would eventually marry, but that only about two-thirds of African-American young adults would. According to the

U. S. Bureau of the Census, 64 percent of children in the United States lived with both biological or adoptive parents in 1996, but marriage was not as dominant a family form as it was a half-century before. More and more individuals were living in unmarried couples, single-parent families, and stepfamilies.

Cohabitation

Prior to the last few decades of the twentieth century, cohabitation, a living arrangement in which an unmarried couple share a household, was uncommon in most Western countries except among the poor. Beginning in the 1960s, cohabitation increased among all social classes, but remained more prevalent among the less affluent and less educated. At the end of the twentieth century, a majority of young adults in the United States lived in a cohabiting relationship prior to marrying. Premarital cohabitation was even more common in many Scandinavian and Northern European countries. Cohabitation after the disruption of a marriage was also widespread. In fact, about a third of cohabiting couples in the United States in 2000 had a child from a partner's previous marriage or relationship. Cohabitation increased because of improvements in birth control, such as the introduction of the birth control pill in 1960 and the legalization of abortion in 1973; the stagnant earning prospects of young men in the 1970s and 1980s, which discouraged marriage; and the greater societal acceptance of sex outside of marriage.

The meaning of cohabitation seems to vary from couple to couple. For some, cohabitation is similar to a trial marriage. An American survey from the 1990s indicates that young adults were most likely to choose "couples can be sure they are compatible before marriage" as the primary reason a couple would decide to cohabit. Consistent with this view, most cohabiting couples in the United States in the 1990s either broke up or married within a few years. Half remained living together outside of marriage for one year or less, and only one out of ten cohabiting couples lasted as long as five years. Studies from the 1990s also show that a majority of cohabiting white couples marry before the birth of a child. For others, however, cohabitation may be a substitute for marriage: cohabiting African-American couples are less likely to marry before a child's birth than are whites. For some others, cohabitation may be merely a continuation of the single life—a living arrangement that does not require but does not preclude commitment.

Marital Dissolution

Until the mid-nineteenth century formal divorce was rare in Western nations, although informal separations undoubtedly occurred. Prior to 1858 divorces could only be granted in England by acts of Parliament and most petitioners were men who claimed their wives were adulterous. In the latter part of the nineteenth century, it became easier to gain a divorce, as the legislatures of Western countries added grounds such as habitual drunkenness or mental cruelty. Figure 2 shows the annual divorce rate in the United States from 1860 to 1998. The figure illustrates that divorce rates rose steadily but gradually until the 1960s, with the exception of a temporary surge after World War II. Between 1960 and 1980 the divorce rate virtually doubled in the United States, and similar increases occurred in other Western countries. Between 1980 and 2000 divorce rates settled on a high plateau, with perhaps a slight decline toward the end of the century. Demographers for the U.S. National Center for Health Statistics have developed projections of lifetime levels of divorce that young adults are likely to experience. These projections assume that the duration-

specific rates of the early twenty-first century will continue to hold, and will therefore overestimate lifetime divorce if duration-specific rates fall in the future, and provide underestimates if these rates rise. The projections suggest that about half of all first marriages in the United States would end in divorce or permanent separation. The projections for many other Western nations are nearly as high. Divorces tend to occur early in marriages—about half occurring within the first seven years in the United States—and are more common among families with lower income, African Americans, and persons who cohabited prior to marrying, married as teenagers, or whose parents divorced.

Several social trends contributed to the rise in divorce over the second half of the twentieth century. One cultural trend was a greater emphasis on personal fulfillment, which made divorce a more acceptable option for people who felt unfulfilled by their marriages. Economic trends also affected divorce rates: Increased employment opportunities for women led to a rise in the number of wives working outside the home. Employment gave wives greater economic independence, which made divorce a feasible option for those who were unhappy in their marriages. In the 1970s and 1980s in the United States, decreasing economic opportunities for men without a college education may have reduced their earning potential and also increased the stresses on some marriages.

Remarriage

Before the twentieth century, most remarriages followed widowhood. But the decline in mortality rates and the rise in divorce rates during the twentieth century changed remarriage, so that by the end of the century more than nine in ten remarriages in the United States followed a divorce. According to the U.S. National Center for Health Statistics, at 2001 rates 75 percent of divorced women in the United States would remarry within 10 years. At the beginning of the twenty-first century, remarriage was more likely among non-Hispanic whites than among African Americans or Hispanic Americans. The latter two groups generally had lower income levels and therefore benefited less from the legal protections marriage provides. In addition, the lesser centrality of marriage in African-American kinship and the Catholic Church's opposition to remarriage may influence these racial and ethnic differences.

FIGURE 2

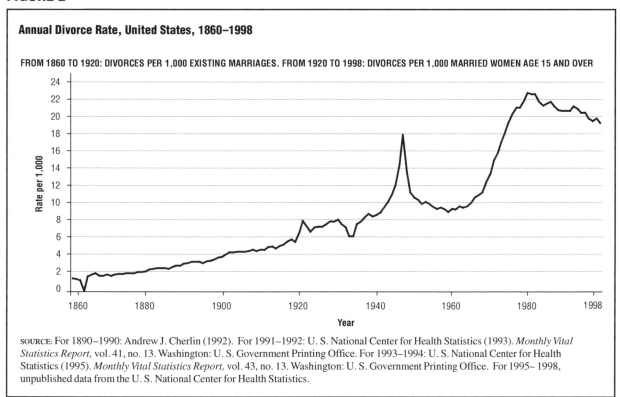

Annual Divorce Rate, United States, 1860–1998

FROM 1860 TO 1920: DIVORCES PER 1,000 EXISTING MARRIAGES. FROM 1920 TO 1998: DIVORCES PER 1,000 MARRIED WOMEN AGE 15 AND OVER

SOURCE: For 1890–1990: Andrew J. Cherlin (1992). For 1991–1992: U. S. National Center for Health Statistics (1993). *Monthly Vital Statistics Report,* vol. 41, no. 13. Washington: U. S. Government Printing Office. For 1993–1994: U. S. National Center for Health Statistics (1995). *Monthly Vital Statistics Report,* vol. 43, no. 13. Washington: U. S. Government Printing Office. For 1995–1998, unpublished data from the U. S. National Center for Health Statistics.

Studies at the end of the twentieth century indicate that remarriages are somewhat more likely to end in divorce than first marriages. The higher risk of divorce may result from the lack of culturally agreed upon norms for how remarried persons should interact with partners and children. In addition, people who divorce and remarry may be more likely, because of their experiences or their personalities, to end a marriage if they are having difficulties. Remarriages after divorce often create complex stepfamilies that extend across more than one household. For example, children from previous marriages may live with or be in contact with parents in other households. Remarriages are even more likely to be preceded by a period of cohabitation than are first marriages. During the 1980s and 1990s cohabiting unions were more common and remarriages were delayed among individuals divorced five years or less.

Childbearing Outside of Marriage

In the 1950s more than 90 percent of children were born to married mothers in most Western countries. Beginning in the 1960s the percentage of children born outside of marriage began to rise. By the end of the twentieth century, one-third of all births in the United States were to unmarried mothers. In Great Britain this figure was slightly more than one-third, and in Sweden, slightly more than one-half of births were to unmarried mothers. In the United States, strong racial and ethnic differences exist in the rates of births outside of marriage; 22 percent of births to non-Hispanic whites, 42 percent to Hispanics, and 69 percent to African Americans were to unmarried mothers in 1999. A majority of these unmarried mothers in the United States formed single-parent families, but about four in ten were cohabiting with men at the time of their child's birth. Cohabitation rates for parents were even higher in Western Europe, with at least six in ten unmarried mothers cohabiting in Great Britain, and more than nine in ten in Sweden. Unmarried teenagers who give birth tend to have lower completed education, lower incomes, and less stable marriages than women who do not give birth until their twenties. Having a child as an unmarried teenager may make it difficult to complete one's education or to gain labor market experience, or teenagers who are likely to give birth may already be from disadvantaged backgrounds.

Family and Household Composition

All of the developments discussed above have greatly changed the typical household composition of families in the Western nations. In the first half of the twentieth century, the percentage of families headed by two parents increased because mortality rates fell and divorce rates were still relatively low. But in the second half of the twentieth century, the percentage of families headed by two parents decreased due to the rise in divorce, cohabitation, and childbearing outside of marriage. For example, in the United States in 1950, single parents headed only 7 percent of all families with children under 18; the corresponding figure in 2000 was 27 percent. Even the simple one- versus two-parent distinction is increasingly inadequate as an indicator of diverse household composition, because some single parents are cohabiting and some two-parent households are stepfamilies.

The living arrangements of children have changed dramatically over the course of the twentieth century. In the mid-twentieth century, about half of all children in the United States were living with a father who worked outside the home and a mother who was a full-time homemaker. By the 1990s only about one-fourth of children were living in these so-called breadwinner–homemaker families. The great increase in married women working outside the home, as well as trends in marriage, cohabitation, and divorce rates, had produced more families with two earners as well as more single-parent families. Children at the end of the twentieth century were also more likely to live in a series of different family arrangements as their parents moved into and out of marital and cohabiting unions. At 2000 rates, for example, about 40 percent of children in the United States would witness the breakup of their parents' marriages, and about 10 percent would witness the breakup of two marriages. Moreover, about 40 percent of children would spend some time living with a parent and her or his cohabiting partner.

Children's Well-Being

The great changes in the demography of families over the course of the twentieth century affected children's well-being. In general, children living in single-parent families in 2000 had levels of well-being that were lower than children in two-parent families. Studies of divorce, for instance, suggest that it raises the risks of undesirable outcomes in the lives of children, such as dropping out of school, having a child before marrying, or having mental health problems. Some of these difficulties, however, may have preceded the divorce and may reflect other underlying problems (such as poverty or parental depression) rather than the number of parents in the home. Other studies suggest that a majority of children whose parents divorce will not experience serious long-term problems. Children who were living with a biological parent and a stepparent in 2000 had levels of well-being that were no better, on average, than children in single-parent households. Some studies suggest that the more transitions in family structure that a child experiences (as when parents divorce or remarry), the more difficult his or her adjustment becomes.

Research generally indicates that the increases in childbearing outside of marriage, divorce rates, and remarriage have been detrimental to children's well-being, although the long-term effects are not yet known. There is little evidence, however, that having both parents work outside the home is detrimental to children, except perhaps for infants. Other demographic trends may have been positive for children: lower fertility means that they have fewer brothers and sisters and should therefore receive more parental time and resources; rising levels of parental education may help parents ready children for school and assist them in learning.

Diversity or Decline?

There is no question that the place of marriage in the family systems of the Western nations has declined over the past half-century. Once the near universal setting for bearing and raising children, marriage rates during the twentieth century decreased as single-parenthood and cohabitation increased. Marriage is still highly valued, but it is not as necessary to be married as it used to be: In Western society in the twenty-first century, it is possible to have a long-term sexual relationship without marrying, it is possible to support oneself economically without marrying, and it is possible to shun marriage and still be respected by family and community. Marriage, then, has declined as an institution. The more difficult question is whether, more broadly, the family has declined as an institution, and on this point there is continuing debate. According to some, the family has declined because the living arrangements that have become more common are not as good for children, and possibly adults, as marriage. According to others, the family has always been changing and has weathered that change much better than its critics have feared. The growing diversity of family life, some assert, has some positive effects, such as providing greater opportunities for women who want to combine a career with raising a family.

See also: *Divorce; Fertility, Nonmarital; Household Composition; Life Course Analysis; Marriage.*

BIBLIOGRAPHY

Becker, Gary S. 1991. *A Treatise on the Family,* enlarged edition. Cambridge, MA: Harvard University Press.

British Society for Population Studies. 1983. "The Family." *Occasional Paper* 31.

Bumpass, Larry L., James A. Sweet, and Andrew Cherlin. 1991. "The Role of Cohabitation in Declining Rates of Marriage," *Journal of Marriage and the Family* 53: 913–27.

Bumpass, Larry L., and Hsien-hen Lu. 2000. "Trends in Cohabitation and Implications for Children's Family Contexts in the United States." *Population Studies* 54: 19–41.

Cherlin, Andrew J. 1992. *Marriage, Divorce, Remarriage,* revised and enlarged edition. Cambridge, MA: Harvard University Press.

Cherlin, Andrew J. 1999. "Going to Extremes: Family Structure, Children's Well-Being, and Social Science." *Demography* 36: 421–428.

Cherlin, Andrew J., and Frank F. Furstenberg, Jr. 1992. *The New American Grandparent: A Place in the Family, A Life Apart.* Cambridge, MA: Harvard University Press.

Goldscheider, Frances K., and Calvin Goldscheider. 1993. *Leaving Home Before Marriage: Ethnicity, Familism, and Generational Relationships.* Madison: University of Wisconsin Press.

Goldstein, Joshua R., and Catherine T. Kenney. 2001. "Marriage Delayed or Marriage Forgone? New Cohort Forecasts of First Marriage for U.S. Women." *American Sociological Review* 6(4): 506–519.

Hernandez, Donald J. 1993. *America's Children: Resources from Family, Government, and the Economy.* New York: Russell Sage Foundation.

Kiernan, Kathleen E. 2001. "European Perspectives on Nonmarital Childbearing." In *Out of Wedlock: Causes and Consequences of Nonmarital Fertility,* ed. Lawrence L. Wu and Barbara Wolfe. New York: Russell Sage Foundation.

Lesthaeghe, Ron. 1995. "The Second Demographic Transition: An Interpretation." In *Gender and Family Change in Industrialized Countries,* ed. Karen O. Mason and Ann-Marie Jensen. Oxford: Clarendon Press.

Lesthaeghe, Ron, and Johan Surkyn. 1988. "Cultural Dynamics and Economic Theories of Fertility Change." *Population and Development Review* 14: 1–45.

Roussel, Louis. 1989. *La Famille Incertaine.* Paris: Editions Odile Jacob.

Smock, Pamela J. 2000. "Cohabitation in the United States: An Appraisal of Research Themes, Findings, and Implications." *Annual Review of Sociology* 26: 1–20.

U.S. Bureau of the Census. 2001. "Living Arrangements of Children: 1996." *Current Population Reports,* 70–74.

U.S. National Center for Health Statistics. 2000. "Nonmarital Childbearing in the United States, 1940–99." *National Vital Statistics Reports,* 48: 16.

U.S. National Center for Health Statistics. 2001. "First Marriage Dissolution, Divorce, and Remarriage: United States." *Advance Data from Vital and Health Statistics,* 323.

ANDREW J. CHERLIN

FAMILY LIFE CYCLE

The concept of the life cycle was originally developed for individuals and was then extended to an aggregate, the family, in influential articles published in the 1930s. The life cycle for a family includes three major phases. The first, family formation, extends from marriage to the birth of the first child. The second phase, family development, consists of extension as children are born and contraction as they leave home. The third phase, family dissolution, extends from the death of the first spouse to the death of the second spouse.

As originally formulated, the concept of a family life cycle was crucially linked to the nuclear family, the events of marriage and childbearing, and a presumed continuity of membership. Later social scientists broadened the definitions of the family and its phases and avoided restrictive or normative definitions that require formal marriage or childbearing. Many individuals never marry, many couples never have children, and many couples divorce and remarry with or without children. It is common to encompass these broad variations under the rubric of the life course, rather than the life cycle, for families as well as for individuals.

Analytical Approaches

Many of the attributes of a family are simply the attributes of the members of that family and can be studied with individuals as units of analysis. The concept of the family life course has value to the degree that the lives of family members are interdependent, with a collective identity and continuity over time.

Because the family is a social unit, usually consisting at least of two adults or one adult and at least one child, it inherently has less continuity than an individual person. An individual has dates of birth and death, but there is much less precision about the dates when a family begins or ends. There may be a typical or modal life course for a family and typical amounts of time spent in different phases, but the sequences and durations can vary greatly.

Much research has tried to articulate the links between individuals and families. For example, most individuals make a transition from being a child in one family—the family of socialization—to being an adult in another family. Life table methods have been devised to produce synthetic measures, such as the expected number of years that an individual would spend as a child in a two-parent household, as a married adult with children living in the household, as a widowed person, and so on. Another strategy is to follow a family over time by linking it to a particular member, termed an index person, such as the senior female. When the family status of such a woman determines the family unit, it is possible to describe transitions in the woman's life course as transitions in the family's life course. There is less concern than in the past over identifying a single individual as the head of the family. For example, the U.S. Census Bureau last used this concept in the 1970 census.

Family Formation and Development

A family generally begins with a union between a man and a woman. (In some countries, same-sex unions are also accorded a legal status equivalent to that of the family.) High levels of education and legal protections have led to greater economic independence for women, and their status is less tied to being married and to the status of their spouse than in the past. Thus, age at marriage has risen for couples in Europe and the United States; couples may cohabit for years before marrying, and some couples never marry. Many women work after marriage, sometimes because of a need for two incomes and sometimes because of the importance of work itself for the woman's identity.

The traditional link between marriage and childbearing has been weakened in several respects. Many married couples never have children, and many children are raised by a single parent, either never-married or divorced. Increased education and labor force participation of women has had substantial effects on the pattern of childbearing. Children tend to be born later and closer together.

In virtually all developed countries, fertility is below replacement level, and in most developing countries it has fallen dramatically since the 1960s. In general, parents provide far more support for their children than they expect ever to receive in return. A large share of family resources is dedicated to the education and socialization of children, although children tend not to regard their behavior as a reflection on their family. In low-fertility countries, it is increasingly common to have no children at all, either by choice or because extensive delay impaired the ability to conceive. Most people would prefer to have two children, ideally a boy and a girl. A substantial proportion of births beyond two are motivated by a desire to have a child of each sex.

Young adults often have an extended period of financial and emotional dependence upon their parents, even if they no longer live with them. Nevertheless, in developed countries the support of elderly parents is not generally seen as the responsibility of their adult children.

Family Dissolution and Reconstitution

Divorce and widowhood are approximately equally common endings for a marriage. Divorce tends to occur at a much earlier stage, often while children are present. Thus many children are likely to spend several years with a single parent, more often the mother than the father. Alternatively, because most divorces are followed by a remarriage, various kinds of blended households can arise. Children who are biological half siblings or stepsiblings may be raised, and may self-identify, as full siblings.

The generalizations in this article have been biased toward the situation in the United States, Europe, and other developed countries. Beyond these generalizations, there is considerable diversity across racial and ethnic groups, educational levels, and some religions. Probably the most important contemporary issue is the compatibility, or lack thereof, between women's labor force participation and their role in a family.

See also: *Household Composition; Intergenerational Transfers; Life Course Analysis.*

BIBLIOGRAPHY

Bongaarts, John, Thomas K. Burch, and Kenneth W. Wachter, eds. 1987. *Family Demography: Methods and Their Application.* Oxford: Oxford University Press.

Mason, Karen Oppenheim, and An-Magritt Jensen. 1995. *Gender and Family Change in Industrialized Countries.* Oxford: Oxford University Press.

Mason, Karen Oppenheim, Noriko O. Tsuya, and Minja Kim Choe, eds. 1998. *The Changing Family in Comparative Perspective: Asia and the United States.* Honolulu, HI: East-West Center.

Oppenheimer, Valerie Kincade. 1982. *Work and the Family: A Study in Social Demography.* New York: Academic Press.

Waite, Linda J., ed. 2000. *The Ties That Bind: Perspectives on Marriage and Cohabitation.* New York: Aldine de Gruyter.

Yi, Zeng. 1991. *Family Dynamics in China: A Life Table Analysis.* Madison: University of Wisconsin Press.

THOMAS W. PULLUM

FAMILY PLANNING PROGRAMS

Family planning programs are organized outreach activities, often under government auspices, that distribute information, services, and supplies for modern means of fertility regulation. While they vary greatly, the following are regarded as the principal ingredients of an acceptable program:

- A delivery system that includes, at a minimum, community clinics and referrals to secondary and tertiary health centers for complications, side-effects, sterilizations, and, where legal, abortion services. In many cases, the delivery system includes community-based household distribution systems.

- A range of contraceptive methods, including both temporary and permanent methods of contraception. Often this range includes "traditional" or "natural" methods.

- Good counseling services and fully-informed consent and choice in the decision to use a method, and which method to use.

- Accurate information about contraception and its side-effects, and appropriate referrals for alternative methods.

Origins

The birth control movement had its roots in Europe, principally Great Britain, and the United States in the nineteenth century, but it began to grow rapidly during the two decades before World War II. It was a movement closely allied with feminism and was led by Marie Stopes (1880–1958) in Britain and Margaret Sanger (1883–1966) in the United States. Its principal aim was to grant to individuals, but especially women, control over their own reproduction.

The global family planning movement in a sense began in 1952. In that year, a group of birth control activists, the heads of the family planning associations in eight western and Asian countries (the Federal Republic of Germany, Hong Kong, India, the Netherlands, Singapore, Sweden, the United Kingdom, and the United States) met in Bombay for the purpose of forming an international organization to spread birth control information and technology. The result was the International Planned Parenthood Federation.

Among the western countries, the family planning movement was at the outset strictly a private and philanthropic enterprise, and its leaders were not necessarily guided by identical motivations. Some, often called "neo-Malthusians" after the English economist and population theorist T. R. Malthus (1766–1834), were primarily driven by concerns about rapid population growth and its implications for social, economic, and political well-being. Eugenicists, active prior to World War II, were concerned with perceived dysgenic effects of fertility differentials that they traced to low contraceptive use among the lower classes. Still others, the "family planners," were motivated by a desire to bring modern contraception and its benefits to the largest possible number of people and to liberate them from the burden of unwanted pregnancies and childbearing. Some of the early leaders, like Sanger, had roots in each of these three camps.

Also in 1952, the Indian government identified uncontrolled fertility and the high rate of population growth as a national problem and promulgated the first national population policy. During the decade that followed, Taiwan, South Korea, Hong Kong, Pakistan, and Singapore initiated family planning activities. By the mid-1960s most of the countries of South and East Asia had established nationwide government programs.

Debate about "Supply" and "Demand"

Both the neo-Malthusians and the family planners believed that national family planning programs were urgently needed. For the planned parenthood movement, family planning programs were the goal. For demographers and population control advocates, family planning was a means to an end. But not all neo-Malthusians saw family planning programs as necessarily an effective means. Many scholars and intellectuals viewed family planning programs as perhaps a necessary but hardly a sufficient means to bring down high birth rates in poor countries. This skepticism about the ability of family planning programs to reduce fertility, particularly programs in which individuals and couples participate on a purely voluntary basis, resulted in a deep and sometimes bitter debate about what constituted appropriate population policy.

At the heart of the debate were these questions:

- Were people sufficiently motivated to limit their childbearing that voluntary family planning programs could bring about substantial fertility declines?

- If sufficient motivation existed, would organized programs be needed to spread birth control practice?

- Were additional measures ("beyond family planning") required to change childbearing behavior, either through inducement or coercion?

- Would people respond to direct appeals to bear fewer children?

- What priority should family planning programs command in comparison to other health programs and among government social expenditures in general?

One approach to seeking answers to these questions was through a series of surveys of knowledge, attitudes and practice (KAP) regarding fertility and birth control. These surveys were conducted in a number of countries from the late 1950s through the 1960s. They asked mostly women, but sometimes also husbands, how many children they wanted, whether they knew about and/or approved of family planning, whether they had ever used a family planning method, and so on. The surveys demonstrated a much higher than expected level of what was called "latent demand" for family planning: women knew about it, generally approved of it, and in many cases wanted fewer children than they actually had, or wanted to postpone or avoid the next birth, but were nonetheless not practicing a method. This information was used to try to persuade governments in developing countries to adopt population policies, with voluntary family planning programs as a central element.

Early Program Efforts and International Assistance

By the early 1960s the invention of both the birth control pill—the oral contraceptive—and the intrauterine contraceptive device (IUD) revolutionized family planning. Now, for the first time, easy-to-use, unobtrusive and easily distributed contraceptives could be made available at relatively low cost to entire populations.

The new technologies permitted large-scale family planning programs to be established or greatly expanded. With modern contraceptives, it became much easier to mount experimental service delivery systems and to test, in practice, how people would respond to the availability of family planning services. A number of field experiments were set up

FIGURE 1

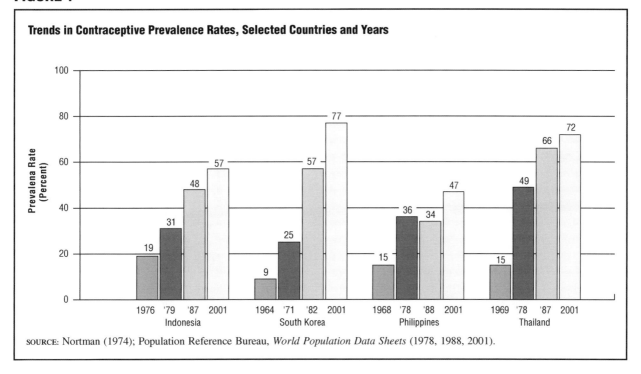

Trends in Contraceptive Prevalence Rates, Selected Countries and Years

SOURCE: Nortman (1974); Population Reference Bureau, *World Population Data Sheets* (1978, 1988, 2001).

around the world. One of the earliest and most successful was the Taichung experiment in Taiwan. A carefully designed experiment, with both treatment and control areas and excellent data collection and monitoring, the Taichung project demonstrated that there could be a strong and lasting effect from a voluntary family planning program.

International assistance for population programs began in the late 1950s and grew in the early and mid-1960s. In 1958 Sweden became the first western country to provide assistance for family planning with grant aid to Sri Lanka. Projects quickly followed in India, Pakistan, and other countries. Other western donors followed suit, providing grants to the International Planned Parenthood Federation and in a few cases directly to governments in developing countries. But the big breakthrough in public support for international family planning came in the late 1960s, first in 1966 and 1967 when the United States officially began to provide population assistance through the Agency for International Development (USAID), and a year later when the United Nations Fund for Population Activities (UNFPA—today called the United Nations Population Fund) was established and began to operate as a mechanism for channeling donor funds to developing countries.

Disappointing Results in South Asia

While the Taichung experiment and early program efforts in East Asia looked promising, the results of large-scale family planning program efforts in South Asia were quite discouraging. India and Pakistan both decided in the early 1960s to mount major national family planning programs based primarily on the IUD. While the programs were voluntary, women were strongly encouraged to accept IUD insertions, often in camp-like settings or on special days at clinics and dispensaries. In addition, the providers of the services, especially doctors trained to insert IUDs, received payments on a per-case basis.

Evaluations carried out a few years after these programs were initiated revealed widespread discontinuation of use, rampant rumors (often false) about side-effects, many cases of fraudulently reported insertions, and virtually no effect on birth rates. These results were disheartening to the two governments and to family planning advocates outside South Asia. Moreover, they seemed to confirm the skepticism of many demographers toward the family planning approach to fertility decline.

The failures of the IUD programs in India and Pakistan severely diminished support for the family planning approach and reinforced the view that a

FIGURE 2

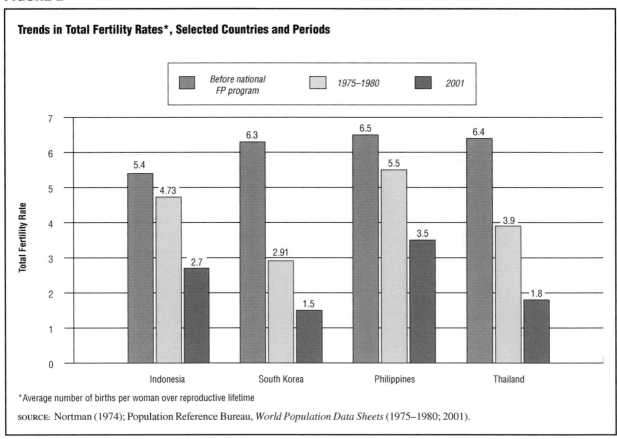

Trends in Total Fertility Rates*, Selected Countries and Periods

[Legend: Before national FP program | 1975–1980 | 2001]

Indonesia: 5.4, 4.73, 2.7
South Korea: 6.3, 2.91, 1.5
Philippines: 6.5, 5.5, 3.5
Thailand: 6.4, 3.9, 1.8

Y-axis: Total Fertility Rate (0 to 7)

*Average number of births per woman over reproductive lifetime

SOURCE: Nortman (1974); Population Reference Bureau, *World Population Data Sheets* (1975–1980; 2001).

broader "developmental" approach to population policy was required—an approach that, in programmatic terms, emphasized raising literacy levels, especially for girls; reducing infant and young child mortality; improving employment opportunities for women; establishing mechanisms to provide old-age social and economic security; and generally reducing the conditions of poverty and underdevelopment that give rise to a high demand for children.

Many economists, arguing that high fertility was a rational response to poverty and high child loss due to mortality, began to gain influence among development planners and policymakers. In South Asia there were calls for approaches beyond family planning, including cash incentives, "no-birth" bonus schemes, and even outright coercion on couples to limit their childbearing.

USAID's "Supply-Side" Approach

Notwithstanding such disappointing early results in South Asia, USAID, by then the largest donor of international population assistance, adopted an almost pure family planning approach as it rapidly expanded its population operations in the late 1960s and early 1970s. USAID's population program director, R. T. Ravenholt, believed firmly that there were millions of women throughout the world who, if given access to safe and effective methods of contraception, would use them. He often stated that true demand could only be measured in the context of actual availability of services. He was determined that USAID would do everything it could to ensure that such services would be available in as many countries as possible.

East Asian countries other than China, Vietnam, and North Korea (which in their family planning programs mixed the provision of services with application of strong administrative pressures to ensure that the services had clients) turned out to be the ideal testing ground for USAID's "supply-side" approach. Governments there, increasingly worried about rapid population growth and encouraged by the success of the Taichung experiment and Taiwan's subsequently successful family planning program, were now ready to move ahead with family planning programs (see Figure 1). A key figure in promoting this evolution of thinking and policy in the region was Spurgeon "Sam" Keeny of the Population Council.

Following the early efforts of planned parenthood pioneers and of organizations such as the Population Council, USAID moved quickly to establish major assistance programs in Korea, the Philippines, Indonesia and Thailand—and all of them thrived. The adoption of contraception grew rapidly in the early 1970s and fertility soon fell, in some cases more dramatically than ever before seen (see Figure 2). These were among the earliest major family planning success stories at a national level and they helped to restore confidence in the family planning approach.

Bucharest—the 1974 World Population Conference

The continuing uncertainty about the effectiveness of the family planning approach set the stage for the debate that ensued at the first intergovernmental World Population Conference, held in Bucharest under United Nations auspices in August 1974. Western delegations, led by the United States, hoped that the Bucharest Conference would adopt a global demographic goal, and that individual countries could be persuaded to set demographic targets for themselves—expressed either in terms of the rate of population growth or declines in birth rates. But this aspiration faced fierce opposition, both to demographic targets and to Western neo-Malthusianism. Many developing countries, supported by the Soviet bloc, China, and other non-aligned and socialist states, denied that rapid population growth was the serious problem alleged by the West and attacked efforts to push them toward adopting anti-natalist policies and programs as "neo-colonialist" or "imperialist." In addition, countries with large Roman Catholic populations and strong Vatican influence opposed efforts to spread modern birth control technologies—an opposition that has remained a constant at international conferences on population ever since.

This opposing coalition successfully blocked the United States and its Western allies in their efforts to press a strong demographic agenda. On the other hand, the vast majority of countries agreed on language that established access to family planning information and services as a basic right. In the words

of the World Population Plan of Action adopted at Bucharest in 1974, it is "the basic human right of all couples and individuals to decide freely and responsibly the number and spacing of their children and . . . to have access to the necessary education, information and means to do so."

It is important to note that many of the countries of East and Southeast Asia that had already adopted anti-natalist population policies and strong family planning programs remained relatively quiet during the debate, refusing to join the more vocal opponents of the neo-Malthusian approach in Latin America, the Middle East, and Africa. India, the population policy and family planning pioneer, was among the most vocal countries in its opposition to Western-imposed population policies and family planning programs and was the strongest advocate of the alternative "developmental" approach. The head of the Indian delegation, Minister of Health Karan Singh, uttered perhaps the most famous quote at the Bucharest conference: "Development is the best contraceptive."

Progress after Bucharest

The debate about family planning reached a peak of intensity at Bucharest, largely owing to the absence of solid empirical evidence regarding the effect of family planning programs on fertility. Apart from scattered evidence from a few experimental projects and some highly suspect statistics generated by family planning programs themselves, there was little information from which persuasive conclusions could be drawn.

Fortunately, in the early 1970s USAID and UNFPA had agreed to launch the World Fertility Survey (WFS). The WFS was to collect information from women (and later their partners) in as many developing countries as possible on fertility aspirations, actual fertility experience, knowledge about and attitudes toward contraception, use of contraception, and many other variables, including socioeconomic background factors such as education, religion, income, and occupation. The purpose of the survey was to help developing countries, as well as donor nations and international organizations, to measure both what was happening to fertility and the reasons behind whatever changes were discovered.

The WFS was a great success. In its first five years, it conducted surveys in more than 40 coun-

FIGURE 3

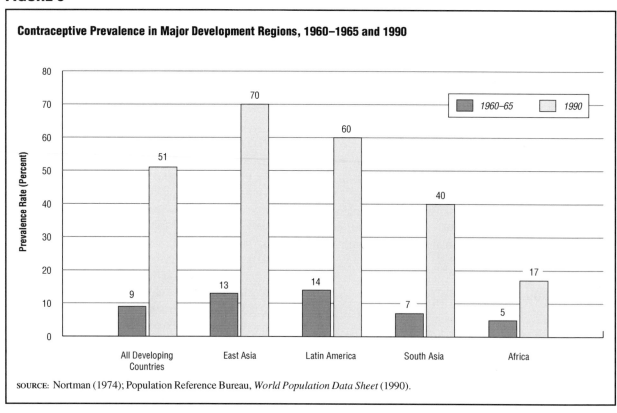

Contraceptive Prevalence in Major Development Regions, 1960–1965 and 1990

SOURCE: Nortman (1974); Population Reference Bureau, *World Population Data Sheet* (1990).

tries, including many of the largest. By the late 1970s analysis of these surveys and comparisons among them indicated that social and economic development variables, were, indeed, powerful determinants of fertility but that family planning programs in many countries were accelerating the rate of fertility change and, in some cases, apparently having an independent effect on it.

Another scientific enterprise that helped to resolve the debate was a family planning experiment in the Matlab area of Bangladesh. There, the International Centre for Diarrhoeal Disease Research maintained a detailed demographic and health surveillance system that permitted measurement of the effects of a variety of health interventions. Taking family planning as one of these, scientists succeeded in demonstrating that even in a highly impoverished, resource-constrained setting, the provision of a reasonably high quality family planning program could bring about significant and lasting effects on fertility. The Matlab Project seemed to disprove the assertion that fertility could not decline except in the context of broadly and substantially improved living standards.

The decade between the Bucharest Conference and its successor, the International Conference on Population (ICP) in Mexico City, held in 1984, was a period of consolidation and expansion of family planning programs. Nearly all countries, whatever their position had been at Bucharest, either developed or permitted the development of family planning service delivery programs during this decade. This was true whether countries had explicit anti-natalist population policies or not. Indeed, many countries in Latin America, for example, encouraged the expansion of voluntary family planning programs on the grounds that they were shown to improve both maternal and child health. The Mexico City conference, which was intended as a review of the World Population Plan of Action adopted at Bucharest, strongly reaffirmed the idea that family planning should be a basic right that governments should ensure for their people.

In the mid and late 1980s family planning programs flourished. Impressive gains in contraceptive use were recorded in nearly all parts of the world, and there were corresponding declines in fertility (Figure 3). By the end of the decade, contraceptive

FIGURE 4

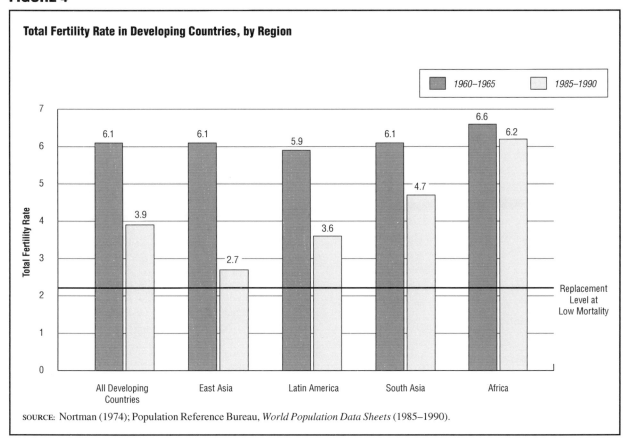

Total Fertility Rate in Developing Countries, by Region

SOURCE: Nortman (1974); Population Reference Bureau, *World Population Data Sheets* (1985–1990).

use globally was estimated to be over 50 percent among women of reproductive age, and the total fertility rate had fallen from its mid-1960s peak of around six children per woman to less than four (Figure 4). A significant majority of women in the developing world were getting contraceptive supplies and services from publicly-supported family planning programs.

New Challenges

But there had been clouds building on the family planning horizon for a number of years. Critics of the family planning movement began to call for reforms over concerns that some countries, including such large countries as India, China, Bangladesh, and Indonesia, were employing coercive or semi-coercive measures to induce people to limit their fertility. Feminist groups in several countries began calling quite vocally and insistently for a broader, more inclusive approach to women's health needs. They called this new approach "reproductive health."

Some in the reproductive health movement blamed the demographic goals of many family planning programs for creating a narrow perspective that often ignored women's health. They insisted that programs should no longer provide just contraceptives and family planning information, but should also attend to other women's health problems such as unsafe abortion, sexually transmitted diseases and reproductive tract infections (including HIV/AIDS), and emergency obstetrical care. Furthermore, they argued, the family planning approach ignored such other important aspects of population policy as girls' education, women's employment, the empowerment of women in matters of inheritance and political participation, and reducing infant and child mortality. These feminists called for comprehensive population policies that replaced demographic targets with holistic concern about women's well being, most especially their health.

By the early 1990s these calls for reform and for the reproductive health approach had penetrated the thinking of many international organizations and donor agencies. Governments in the developing world were somewhat slower to respond, but the issue exploded onto the world political stage at the International Conference on Population and Development (ICPD) at Cairo in 1994, the third decennial intergovernmental population conference.

It is probably fair to say that the family planning approach to population policy ended at Cairo, to be replaced, in the ICPD Programme of Action, by what was now being called the reproductive and sexual health and rights approach. To be sure, family planning remained a significant, even a central, part of reproductive health, but the 180 or so governments that gathered at Cairo clearly rejected demographic and family planning targets in favor of the more comprehensive approach. While Bucharest and Mexico City had certainly mentioned these other measures, it was not until Cairo that the international women's movement had acquired sufficient strength to place the empowerment of women at the forefront of population policy.

In the years since Cairo, most governments around the world have modified their population and health policies to conform with the Cairo Programme of Action. Governments vary widely, though, in the extent to which they have really made the transition from family planning to a more comprehensive approach. For many governments the rhetoric of Cairo has not been translated into real program reforms.

See also: *Birth Control, History of; Contraception, Modern Methods of; Contraceptive Prevalence; Induced Abortion: Prevalence; Population Policy; Reproductive Rights; Sanger, Margaret; Unwanted Fertility*

BIBLIOGRAPHY

Berelson, Bernard. 1969. "Beyond Family Planning." *Science* 163: 533–543.

Berelson, Bernard, and W. Parker Mauldin. 1978. "Conditions of Fertility Decline in Developing Countries, 1965–1975." *Population and Development Review* 9 (5): 84–148.

Bongaarts, John. 1991. "The KAP-Gap and the Unmet Need for Contraception." *Population and Development Review* 17 (2): 293–313.

———. 1994. "Population Policy Options in the Developing World." *Science* 263 (5148): 771–776.

Bongaarts, John, W. Parker Mauldin, and James F. Phillips. 1990. "The Demographic Impact of Family Planning Programs." *Studies in Family Planning* 21 (6): 299–310.

Bruce, Judith. 1990. "Fundamental Elements of the Quality of Care: A Simple Framework." *Studies in Family Planning* 21 (2): 61–91.

Cleland, John, and Christopher Wilson. 1987. "Demand Theories of the Fertility Transition: An Iconoclastic View." *Population Studies* 41 (1): 5–30.

Critchlow, Donald T. 1999. *Intended Consequences: Birth Control, Abortion, and the Federal Government in Modern America.* New York: Oxford University Press.

Davis, Kingsley. 1967. "Population Policies: Will Current Programs Succeed?" *Science* 158: 730–735 (10 November).

Dixon-Mueller, Ruth. 1993. *Population Policy and Women's Rights: Transforming Reproductive Choice.* New York: Praeger Publishers.

Donaldson, Peter. J. 1990. *Nature Against Us: The U.S. and the World Population Crisis, 1965–1980.* Chapel Hill: University of North Carolina Press.

Freedman, Ronald. 1979. "Theories of Fertility Decline: A Reappraisal." *Social Forces* 58 (1): 1–16.

Freedman, Ronald, and John Y. Takeshita. 1969. *Family Planning in Taiwan: An Experiment in Social Change.* Princeton, NJ: Princeton University Press.

Harkavy, Oscar. 1995. *Curbing Population Growth: An Insider's Perspective on the Population Movement.* New York: Plenum Press.

McIntosh, C. Alison, and Jason. L. Finkle. 1995. "The Cairo Conference on Population and Development: A New Paradigm?" *Population and Development Review* 21 (2): 223–260.

Nortman, Dorothy L. 1974. "Population and Family Planning Programs: A Factbook." *Reports on Population/Family Planning,* No. 2.

Piotrow, Phillis T. 1973. *World Population Crisis: The United States Response.* New York: Praeger Publishers.

Population Reference Bureau. Annual. *World Population Data Sheet.* Washington, D.C.: Population Reference Bureas.

Pritchett, Lant H. 1994. "Desired Fertility and the Impact of Population Policies." *Population and Development Review* 20 (1): 1–55.

Ravenholt, R. T. 1969. "AID's Family Planning Strategy." *Science* 163: 124 and 127 (10 January).

Robey, Bryant, Shea O. Rutstein, Leo Morris, and Richard Blackburn. 1992. "The Contraceptive Revolution: New Survey Findings." *Population Reports* Series M, No. 11. Baltimore, MD: Johns Hopkins University.

Sinding, Steven W. 2000. "The Great Population Debates: How Relevant Are They for the 21st Century?" *American Journal of Public Health* 90 (12): 1841–1846.

Sinding, Steven W., John A. Ross, and Allan G. Rosenfield. 1994. "Seeking Common Ground: Demographic Goals and Individual Choice." *International Family Planning Perspectives* 20 (1): 23–27, 32.

United Nations. 1994. *Program of Action of the International Conference on Population and Development.* New York.

Watkins, Susan C. 1987. "The Fertility Transition: Europe and the Third World Compared." *Sociological Forum* 2 (4): 645–673.

Women's Declaration on Population Policies. 1993. International Women's Health Coalition. New York.

STEVEN W. SINDING

FAMILY POLICY

Family policies are a subset of government social policies that have as their object the well-being or the behavior of families, particularly families with children.

Conflicts of Principle in Family Policy

To what extent and in what circumstances should a government policy be directed at the family rather than at the individual person on the one hand or at larger social units such as communities on the other? The answer to the question is not straightforward because policies at different levels, particularly at the family and individual levels, often have outcomes that conflict. A policy that has benefits at the family level may have negative effects on individuals within the family. For example, a cash benefit provided to low-income families that is means-tested by family income may be a work disincentive to individuals within low-income families because the cash benefit would be withdrawn as the family income rose. Here a family policy designed to promote family stability by providing an income supplement to low-income families may conflict with a policy to promote self-reliance of individuals through employment. Family policy, policy designed to produce family-level outcomes, is rife with such conflicts.

One response to this conflict would be to assert that there should be no family-level policy, with the contention being that policies directed at individuals will flow through to families without distorting the behavior of individuals in unintended ways. The problem with this approach is that, without family-related incentives, individuals may be better off remaining as individuals and not forming themselves into families. The most obvious example relates to children. If a society provides no recognition of the costs of raising children and the loss of income and career potential related to having children, this may discourage individuals from having children. Yet very low fertility has obvious deleterious outcomes for the society as a whole. Where people already have children, the negative outcome of not providing support to those with children is the possibility that, through poverty or neglect, poor development outcomes for children will flow on to negative social outcomes.

The other central conflict in the design of family policy is the extent to which one family form is favored by policy over other forms. In most advanced industrialized countries, at least in the first half of the twentieth century, family support policy favored the family in which the father was in paid employment and the mother stayed at home to care for the children. This "male breadwinner model" of the family was backed by the social values of the time. Family policies of this era were founded on the assumption that mothers were not in paid employment. No supports were provided to working mothers, even to those who were single parents, because such supports were seen as providing the wrong incentives. The marriage bond was seen as weakened if women were able to support themselves, and children were seen as vulnerable if their mothers were in paid employment. Subsequently, with the advance of the women's movement, policies based on the assumption of the male breadwinner model of the family have come under intense criticism, the result of which is reflected in the evolution of contemporary family policies.

In the conflicts between individual and family approaches and between support of one family form over another, resolution must rely upon a determination of social values. The more that values are in flux and the more pluralistic is the society, the harder it is to resolve these conflicts. Ideally, a social consensus would be built around a chosen policy direction, but where a small number of votes can make a difference, governments are often reluctant to address these fundamental issues. This description encapsulates the state of family policy at the beginning of the twenty-first century. Governments, fiscally unable to satisfy all preferences in a pluralistic society, may satisfy none adequately.

Objectives of Family Policy

Family policy has three broad objectives:

- Family foundation: to support and strengthen family relationships;
- Nurture: to support families to care for their dependent members;
- Reproduction: to support the production of the next generation of productive adults.

Forms of Family Policy

Family policy takes four main forms:

- Legal: laws designed to promote family policy objectives;
- Financial: tax or transfer policies that favor family policy objectives;
- Industrial: policies related to wages or working conditions that favor family policy objectives;
- Services: provision, subsidization, or promotion of services that support family policy objectives.

Types of Family Policy According to Form

Family policies often have overlapping objectives. Thus, it is convenient to talk about particular family policies in terms of their four main forms.

Legal. Marriage laws define who is able to marry (in terms of kin relationship, minimum age, sex of partner, whether already married, and so on) and whether or not people getting married are able to make their own free choice about marrying. Marriage laws also conventionally define the rights and responsibilities of the partners to the marriage and may also define the legal status of children born to the marriage. These laws are designed to meet the family-foundation and nurture objectives and generally reflect social or religious values surrounding the institution of marriage. Divorce laws specify the circumstances under which divorce is permitted, how matrimonial property is to be distributed, and the care and financial support of any children of the marriage. Here again it is family-foundation and nurture aims that are paramount. Over time, divorce laws in most countries have been liberalized, reflecting the enhanced value attached by societies to individual rights in comparison to family rights.

There may also be laws that relate to the care, protection, and financial support of children, satisfying the nurture and reproduction aims. Many countries also have laws that define the responsibilities of adult children for their aged parents. These laws are often not effective in practice because they require parents to instigate a legal action against their children.

Finally, industrial legislation may prohibit discrimination in employment on the grounds of pregnancy status, gender, or family status.

Financial. Governments may favor families through the tax or cash transfer systems. Such policies take three main forms: periodic cash payments, lump-sum payments or low-interest loans, and tax rebates, credits, or deductions.

Periodic cash payments generally take the form of payments made to parents in respect of each child. The payments might vary according to the age of the child. For example, it could be considered that a higher payment should be made when a child is very young to compensate for the expected loss of income of parents at that stage. Alternatively, payments may be higher when children are older and more expensive. The payment may also vary by birth order. If the third child is considered to be particularly important as far as reproduction policy is concerned (on the assumption that many parents would anyway wish to have two children), then a much larger payment could apply to this child (and subsequent children). Essentially, these payments are a form of horizontal equity—that is, a recognition through the tax-transfer system of the additional costs of raising children. Some vertical equity (equalization of incomes across households) might be applied if the payments are income-tested, that is, if they are reduced or eliminated as income rises. As already noted, however, income-tested payments can be inefficient if they create work disincentives for second earners.

Lump-sum payments or loans include payments at the time of birth of a baby (e.g., baby bonus, maternity benefit), at the time a child starts school, or at some other age. An establishment loan (or family founding loan) may be provided at the start of a marriage or relationship with segments of the loan being written off as the couple has each child. There could be endowment schemes contributed to by the government and the family to spread the costs of children across the lifetime. Repayments of loans might be tied to a small percentage of earned income, that is, child costs might be paid off as income rises. Births might be deemed to be equivalent to (large) lump-sum contributions to social insurance or retirement pension schemes. As reproduction policy instruments, however, immediate benefits are more likely to be successful than deferred benefits. That is, assistance with immediate housing costs is probably more likely to affect fertility decision-making than the promise of future assistance with university education or a higher old-age pension.

Tax rebates, credits, or deductions (collectively called tax expenditures) may include tax reductions or credits based on the presence of a child or a spouse. Again, these measures can be targeted to children of different ages or different birth orders. Rebates and credits allow for social equity; deductions are generally socially inequitable with the rich benefiting most. While cash payments may be more closely targeted to the need (that is, more likely to be spent on the child) than benefits delivered through the tax system, tax expenditures are less visible to those concerned with fiscal restraint than are cash expenditures. Tax approaches may thus be more politically sustainable in certain contexts than cash approaches.

Tax may be applied on the separate incomes of the two members of a couple (individual taxation) or on their joint incomes (couple taxation). The use of couple taxation is sometimes described as inefficient because it can affect the level of involvement in the labor force of the second earner—that is, it operates as a work disincentive. As women's work force participation rates have increased, countries have moved in the direction of individual taxation.

Industrial. There are a range of potential policy measures that are designed to assist parents to combine work and family responsibilities. These policies may have the aim of supporting reproduction, but they can also arise as a means of protecting individual and family rights in relation to work. Parental leave (maternity or paternity leave) provides the right of return to a position following leave related to the birth of a child. Leave policy has many nuances such as its duration, whether the leave is paid and at what level, eligibility criteria, how much of the leave is available to mothers or to fathers, and whether there is a right of return to part-time work.

If the leave is paid, should the payment be made by the employer, by social or private insurance, or directly by the government? Payment by employers presents a major burden on small businesses. As having a pregnant worker is a high-cost but low-risk situation, insurance is the obvious approach to paid maternal leave. There is some evidence that leave entitlements of up to three years have a more significant impact on childbearing than one-year leave entitlements.

Flexible working hours, part-time work, and short-term leave for family-related purposes assist families to combine work and family. If the nature of the occupation allows work to be done at home, appropriate provision might be made for this option from time to time but especially when the child is an infant. Overlap of standard work hours and school hours is a work-family benefit.

Services. Education and information services can be directed at enhancing the quality of family relationships, aiding persons in coping with and managing the needs of dependent or disabled family members, family planning and health care, or the management of family finances.

There is a wide range of direct family services that can assist families to deal with children and other dependent family members. Beyond services that are universally required, such as education and health, the most general of these is child care, but the list also includes services that are related to a particular illness or disability, services that assist family members to care for aged persons, respite care services, and sporting and recreational services.

A fundamental policy in this area is the provision of free or subsidized child care of high quality to support the work and family aspirations of parents and to assist in the child's development. It can be argued that child care should be equally available to those who are not employed as this may allow them opportunities for training or for job-seeking as well as providing socially beneficial development opportunities for their children. Besides free provision, the main forms of public support include capital grants to child-care centers and subsidized child-care fees. As an alternative, some countries provide tax breaks for child-care expenses. Child-care expenses might also be exempted from consumption or value-added taxes or, if paid by the employer, treated as a business expense. Arrangements might be made to facilitate the care of children by their grandparents. Child-care eligibility is often tied to the age of the child, especially where there is an emphasis upon parental leave in the child's earliest years. Policy needs to address the balance between parental leave and child-care provision according to community standards. Child care includes the need for "out-of-school-hours" care. This can be provided at a neighborhood center or at the child's school.

See also: *Cohabitation; Family Allowances; Intergenerational Transfers; Marriage; Population Policy.*

BIBLIOGRAPHY

Ditch, John, Helen Barnes, and Jonathan Bradshaw, eds. 1998. *Developments in National Family Policies in 1996.* Brussels: Commission of the European Communities, D.G.V.

Gauthier, Anne. 2002. "Family Policies in Industrialized Countries: Is There Convergence?" *Population*–English Edition 57(3): 447–474.

Kamerman, Sheila B. 2001. *Early Childhood Education and Care: International Perspectives.* New York: Columbia University, Institute for Child and Family Policy.

Kamerman, Sheila B., and Alfred J. Kahn, eds. 1997. *Family Change and Family Policies in Great Britain, Canada, New Zealand, and the United States.* Oxford, Eng.: Clarendon Press, Oxford.

McDonald, Peter. 2002. "Sustaining Fertility through Public Policy; the Range of Options." *Population*–English Edition 57(3): 417-446.

Millar, Jane, and Andrea Warman. 1996. *Family Obligations in Europe.* London: Family Policy Studies Centre.

Organisation for Economic Co-operation and Development. 1997. "Family, Market, and Community: Equity and Efficiency in Social Policy." *OECD Social Policy Studies 21* Paris.

INTERNET RESOURCE.

The Clearing House on International Developments in Child, Youth and Family Policies at Columbia University. <http://www.childpolicyintl.org>.

PETER MCDONALD

FAMILY RECONSTITUTION

Family reconstitution is the process of reconstructing historical data on family membership, the relationships among family members, and family change over time from often incomplete registers of vital events and similar sources. The techniques of family reconstitution are an important part of the tool kit of historical demographers.

Historical Development of the Practice

The genealogical renaissance of the late-nineteenth century provided the modern starting point for reconstituting families. Of course, the practice has had a much longer lineage: In the Old Testament there are long lists of family trees and lines of descent. And in later periods, whenever the issues of descent and origins were considered to be of particular importance, genealogies were traced back through the family archives. Much of this early study was one-sided: It usually considered only the male line of descent through first-born heirs (only for royalty and princely houses was a much wider root system considered to be of interest). The late nineteenth century saw the democratization of this practice when it was realized that the vital registers of Renaissance and Reformation states provided a way to study the origins of whole populations. Much of the early effort in this field went to the preservation of records that could be analyzed in a more individualized fashion by private researchers. Any large university library is likely to hold proceedings of nineteenth-century local record societies, along with privately published books detailing the archival rescue work of concerned social investigators from that time.

Before World War II the demographic analysis of these records was a very marginal pursuit. To be sure there was a small controversial literature among economic historians of early industrial England, who argued about whether the population rise of the period from 1750 to 1850 was the result of rising birthrates or falling death rates. But this research was based on aggregative analysis, not the reconstitution of families. The flourishing *Ortssippenbücher* (local kinship books) studies in Nazi Germany, which were concerned to glorify *Blut und Boden* (blood and soil) and thereby enhance the vanishing ties of an increasingly urban society with its landed past, are something of an exception to such a generalization, although the rationale of this first-stage effort of family reconstitution was the concern with racial purity rather than insight into demographic change.

Louis Henry's Pioneering Work

The major breakthrough in the study of historical vital records came in France and can be linked directly to the pioneering work of Louis Henry (1911–1991). In his capacity as director of research at the Institute national d'études démographiques (INED), Henry was asked by French President Charles de Gaulle to determine why Frenchmen (and women) were raising so few children. (This *faiblesse de berceau* [failure of the cradle] had long been an issue in French military thinking.) Henry realized that at least part of the answer to de Gaulle's question called for an understanding of pre-Revolutionary (that is, prior to 1789) demographic dynamics—about which the parish registers of the ancien régime (the pre-Revolutionary political order) provided a unique source of information. Henry set out to exploit these registers, with an eye to demographic issues rather than genealogical ones. He devised a method to rework these primary data by reallocating the vital events recorded by the church into what might be termed demographic units of reproduction.

The first family reconstitution studies were labor intensive. Every baptism (birth), burial (death), and marriage was encoded on a separate piece of colored paper. Henry had chosen the Norman village of Crulai, near the cheese-making town of Camembert, to be his test case. It was a fortuitous choice, because Crulai's vital records ran in an unbroken series from the middle of the seventeenth century until the Revolution. Crulai's vital records were also kept in an exacting manner. For each birth

event, for example, not only was the child's name and date of baptism recorded but the village clerk also noted the father's name and occupation and place of residence as well as the mother's father's name, occupation, and place of residence. Even if there were two or three young women called Jeanne Mance living in Crulai at the same time, the chance that they shared all these other individualizing characteristics was virtually nil. Ambiguities of individual identification were all but nonexistent.

The many thousands of color-coded pieces of paper were sorted according to family name, event, date, and so on. Henry (and his research associate, Étienne Gautier) then laboriously assembled these data into family units of reproduction. Each family was assigned its own starting date—the date of a couple's marriage. (Those married outside the village were discarded, wastage that was seen as a necessary cost in establishing a reliable core sample.) Subsequent events were added to the family record until the stacks of color-coded pieces of paper had been reassigned into new units of analysis—units that could answer demographic questions.

Crulai was a propitious choice for substantive reasons, too. Surprisingly, the average age at first marriage for both men and women was the mid-twenties; only 10 percent of all brides were teenagers—the same as the percentage of women who married for the first time after their thirtieth birthday. Henry also discovered that for the cohorts marrying before 1740 there was no discernible difference in age-specific fertility rates between those marrying earlier than average and those marrying later than average, but for the post-1740 cohorts the later-marrying women had higher fertility in their thirties than did their sisters, cousins, and neighbors who differed from them only in marrying earlier than average.

Using the labor of INED students, a national sample of reconstituted village populations was soon created. But if it was thus a fairly straightforward matter to establish the quantitative parameters of ancien régime demography, explaining the results proved to be a far more complicated matter. Indeed, the history of family reconstitution studies in most European countries has followed a similar course: first the establishment of quantitative parameters, then arguments about the meaning of the results.

The statistics derived from family reconstitution studies have provided a veritable mountain of facts.

The interpretation of these facts, however, has not—and indeed cannot—be addressed within a purely demographic form of analysis. In parish register demography of the early modern period the time has clearly come to acknowledge the truth of the twentieth-century English poet Stephen Spender's point:

> Of course, the entire effort is to put oneself
>
> Outside the ordinary range
>
> Of what are called statistics.

See also: *Family: History; Hayami, Akira; Henry, Louis; Historical Demography; Laslett, Peter.*

BIBLIOGRAPHY

Dupâquier, Jacques. 1988. *Histoire de la population française*, Vol. 2: *De la Renaissance à 1789*. Paris: Presses universitaires de France.

Gautier, Étienne, and Louis Henry. 1958. *La population de Crulai: Paroisse normande*. Paris: Presses universitaires de France.

Henry, Louis. 1967. *Manuel de démographie historique*. Paris: Presses universitaires de France.

Laslett, Peter. 1965. *The World We Have Lost*. London: Methuen.

Levine, David. 1977. *Family Formation in an Age of Nascent Capitalism*. New York: Academic Press.

———. 1998. "Sampling History." *Journal of Interdisciplinary History* 28: 605–632.

Wrigley, E. A., and R. S. Schofield. 1997. *English Population History from Family Reconstitution, 1580–1837*. Cambridge, Eng.: Cambridge University Press.

DAVID LEVINE

FAMILY SIZE DISTRIBUTION

A family is often defined as a group of people who are related through marriage, blood, or adoption. The size of this unit depends on the criteria used for establishing membership. One common application of the term *family size* refers to women alone and counts only the number of children born to them. That is the usage that will be employed here.

Suppose that a person asked a woman how many children she had borne and that she replied, "three." Suppose that the person also asked each of those three children how many children his or her mother had borne. The answer should also be "three." For an individual family, there should be no difference between the "family size" of the mother and the "family size" of a child (that is, the number of children borne to the mother of a particular child).

When measurement is extended to a population, on the other hand, these two measures need not and typically will not have the same value. Consider a population in which one-half of the women have one child and the other half have seven. The mean family size among the women is four. But the mean family size among their children will not be four but some larger number. The reason for the discrepancy is that each woman with seven children leaves seven times as many children to testify about her family size as a woman with one child. In this particular example, the mean family size among the children will be $[7(7) + 1(1)]/8 = 6.25$.

It is clear that the relation between the family size of women and the family size of children depends on how much variability exists in the fertility performance of women. If all women had three children, then all children would derive from three-child families and the mean family size of women, three, would be the same as the mean family size of children. But if there is any spread at all in the distribution of women's family sizes, then women with higher fertility will be overrepresented in reports by children about their mother's childbearing.

The formula that relates the mean family size of children, C^*, to the mean family size of women, W^*, is:

$$C^* = W^* + V/W^*,$$

where V is the variance in family sizes among women. If there is no variance in childbearing among women, then C^* will equal W^*. Any variance whatsoever will increase C^* above W^*.

This relationship would be a mere statistical oddity were it not for the huge variability in childbearing among women in most populations. Among women in the United States who had completed childbearing between 1890 and 1970, the mean family size of their children exceeded the mean family size of women by 1.8 to 3.1 children. The mean family size of children was never less than 4.4 during this period. The variance of family size among women often grows in the course of a fertility transition as subgroups of the population develop small family norms while others retain their previous behaviors. When this happens, family sizes among children decline more slowly than family sizes of women or may even rise.

One striking disparity between the two measures of family size occurred in the United States when the low fertility rates of the Great Depression were replaced by the high fertility rates of the baby boom. Women who bore the bulk of their children during the 1930s wound up with about 2.3 children, whereas those at the peak of their childbearing years in the 1950s bore an average of about 2.7. But the mean family size of the Depression-era children, 4.9, was actually higher than that of the baby boomers, 4.5. The reason for the discrepant trends is that the baby boom was accompanied by much lower variability in family sizes among women. Facile attributions of baby boomers' characteristics to their unusually large families were clearly based on a false premise.

There are several other useful implications of the disparity between the two measures. First, one should not try to infer directly the aggregate fertility levels of women in the past from the accounts of their children. Such histories provide a very biased view of fertility in the past unless they are corrected for variability in the distribution of family sizes. Such corrections are rarely undertaken, and the result is that people often gain an inflated impression of the past volume of childbearing from personal testimonials about the fertility of ancestors.

A second implication is that there must be a "revolt against childbearing" each generation simply to keep a population's fertility rate constant. Women must bear, on average, fewer children than their mothers, or a population's level of fertility would rise sharply every generation.

The relation between family sizes of women and family sizes of children is analogous to several other relations in demography. For example, the mean size of a household when households are the unit of analysis is always less than the mean size of households when individuals are the unit of analysis. The schemes employed for calculating mean household size by most statistical offices, which treat each household as one unit, underestimate the size of household as experienced by members of the population. This distortion extends to the classification of households by other criteria as well. For example, only 38 percent of households in the United States in 1980 contained a child under age 17, but 59 percent of the U.S. population lived in a household containing a child. The reason for the discrepancy is that households containing children were, on average, 52 percent larger than the mean for all household types.

See also: *Childlessness; Fertility, Below-Replacement.*

BIBLIOGRAPHY

Bongaarts, John. 2001. "Household Size and Composition in the Developing World in the 1990s." *Population Studies* 55: 263–279.

Burch, Thomas K. 1972. "Some Demographic Determinants of Average Household Size: An Analytic Approach." In *Household and Family in Past Time,* ed. Peter Laslett. New York: Cambridge University Press.

King, Miriam, and Samuel H. Preston. 1990. "Who Lives with Whom? Individual versus Household Measures." *Journal of Family History* 15: 117–132.

Preston, Samuel H. 1976. "Family Sizes of Children and Family Sizes of Women." *Demography* 13: 105–114.

SAMUEL H. PRESTON

FAMILY SIZE INTENTIONS

There have been survey respondents—women or couples—perhaps predominant in some populations, that were unable or unwilling to report family size preferences. However, virtually all contemporary populations, and very likely all future ones, will consist primarily of persons or couples who strategize about family size. Clearly, declining family size preferences constitute a primary cause of fertility transition and will influence post-transition fertility levels. In societies undergoing fertility transition, observed fertility frequently exceeds stated preferences; in post-transition countries of the 1990s the opposite was true. The study of emerging and changing family size preferences and their relation to behavior provides clues to the nature of fertility decision-making and to the causes of fertility trends and differentials.

Conceptualization and Measurement

An initial distinction should be made between *one's own* family size preferences or goals and those deemed appropriate for the *average* or *typical* family. The latter concept, usually referred to as "ideal family size," assumes a set of time/place-specific norms or expectations regarding appropriate family size. A common survey item of the 1960s in the United States asked: What number of children do you consider ideal for the typical (American) family? Samples of U.S. women in the 1960s produced modal responses of "two" but substantial proportions chose "three" or "four" children.

The collection and use of data on the ideal family size item has diminished over time. Several reasons account for this waning interest. By the 1980s "two children" had become the predominant ideal family size response, but part of this convergence could be attributed to the widespread public perception that population growth could not continue and that an average of two children per woman was required for population stabilization. Also, the declining prevalence of two-parent families in the period from 1960 to 1990 (along with reduced agreement regarding what constituted "the typical family") exposed the contingent nature of family size norms. If appropriate family size depends on individual and couple characteristics (e.g., marital status, economic status), then useful survey questions need to make explicit the situational context. Finally, some have argued that family size norms would be better represented by questions that asked about a range of acceptable family sizes (e.g., what family size is too small? too large?).

One's own family size preferences are anchored in the life course, represented by upward sloping 45° life lines in Figure 1. Person *A* was age 15 in 1965 and was age 50 in 2000. Person *B* was born 25 years later than *A*, reached age 15 in 1990 and 25 in 2000. Let it be assumed that both women were interviewed in January 2000 (represented by a vertical line) and were asked about their past or "retrospective" fertili-

ty behavior (solid part of life line) and their future or "prospective" behavior (dashed part of line). Family size preferences are embedded in both retrospective and prospective life line segments.

Prospective Intent

Commonly used prospective questions ask the respondent (for example, respondent *B* at age 25): Do you intend to have a (or another) child? (And if yes) "How many more children do you intend to have?" These questions raise two fundamental issues. The first is whether fertility intentions—or fertility expectations or fertility desires—should be of paramount, substantive interest. Intentions reflect the respondent's goals (what the respondent plans to do) and, as such, should be strongly linked to subsequent behavior in environments where fertility is controlled. In contrast, expectations invite (sometimes explicitly, but often implicitly) a consideration of impediments that might interfere with one's intentions (such as contraceptive failure or subfecundity) and produce an under-estimate or over-estimate of future fertility. Fertility desires require an even more hypothetical exercise that is linked closely to the concept of "demand for children" (the number of children one would intend if there were no subjective or economic costs to fertility control) and might be seen as a determinant (along with constraints and contingencies) of fertility intentions.

Empirical evidence indicates that many respondents do not detect the differences between these terms or are unable or unwilling to perform the implied conceptual tasks that distinguish them. Further, the demographic literature frequently refers to these questions as family size preferences and ignores the distinctions noted above. Nevertheless, following the admonition that one should ask respondents straightforward questions, intentions seem preferable. Intentions are knowable to the respondent, and thus measurable from respondent reports, and are conceptually important. Intentions are likely to be the stable and dominant component of responses to intended/expected/desired fertility questions. If one wants respondents to consider the additional contingencies implied by expectations or desires, then specific additional questions should be devised to supplement intention questions.

The second issue raised by this pair of questions (i.e., Do you intend a [or another] child? How many more?) is whether prospective intentions are best

FIGURE 1

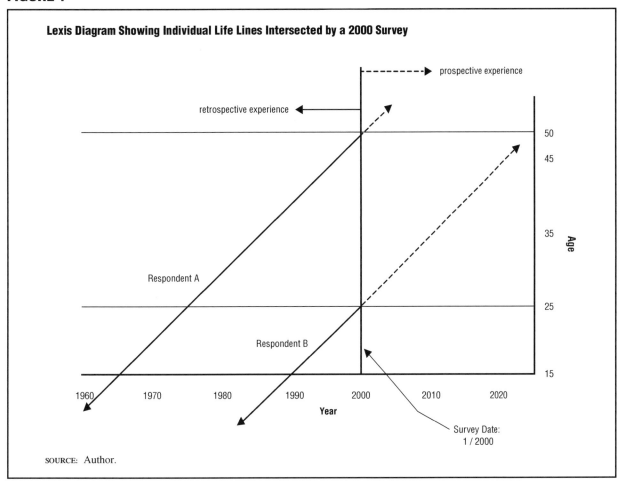

Lexis Diagram Showing Individual Life Lines Intersected by a 2000 Survey

SOURCE: Author.

represented as a *fixed target* or as a *set of sequential decisions*. Prior to the 1960s, inquiries concerning fertility intentions were linked closely to a *fixed target* model (individuals or couples "formulate a desired completed family size and pursued this relative constant target throughout their reproductive life" [Lee, p. 205]). The fixed target model combined with reports of children already born allowed operationalization of *intended parity*. For example, person *B* in Figure 1 is 25 years of age at the time of the survey. Her intended parity is the sum of births to date and her reported intended additional births. Mean intended parity for cohorts has frequently been used to anticipate future fertility trends. The accuracy of forecasts based on intended parity depends on the predictive validity of reproductive intentions as explained below.

Fertility researchers have raised serious concerns about the fixed target model. Specifically, strong substantive arguments and substantial empir-

ical work suggest that fertility decisions are better represented as a series of sequential decisions. Children are generally born one at a time, thereby imposing a set of birth intervals. These intervals allow for a set of sequential decisions or at least for reassessments of earlier decisions. Empirical evidence shows that respondents frequently do revise their intentions/behavior based on changed circumstances. Key to this sequential perspective are the claims that: some births may be normative (first and second) and others less so (third births); experience with prior births may affect the decision to have subsequent births; and some relevant factors change in unanticipated ways, and unanticipated factors can affect decisions. The distinction between fixed target and sequential models is important because it challenges whether a numerical intention (for example, two versus three additional children) has any behavioral consequence in abstraction from the current sequential decision (that is, to have another child).

Retrospective Intent

Turning to retrospective experience (i.e., solid lines in Figure 1), demographers have developed a standard procedure and terminology for identifying "wanted" and "unwanted births." Specifically, respondents are asked to recollect their fertility intention at the time of each pregnancy: "At the time you became pregnant did you: want to become pregnant at that time; want to have children in the future, but not now; or not want any additional children?" The first two responses are coded as wanted (although the second is termed a timing failure) and the third category as unwanted. For women who have completed childbearing (e.g., woman A in Figure 1), wanted fertility reflects women's family size preferences and unwanted fertility a component that could have been avoided by effective birth control. The unwanted component of fertility declines as effective contraception and abortion become widely available.

Additional Measures Derived from Birth Intentions

Prior discussion has focused on an individual life line or (its aggregate equivalent) a cohort. However, much fertility estimation is period-based—it answers the question: What is the level of fertility in a given year? The most commonly used/reported measure of period fertility is the total fertility rate, TFR (the number of births a woman would have if she experienced a given set of period age-specific fertility rates). A related concept is the "wanted total fertility rate": What would the TFR be if unwanted births were identified (as described above) and excluded? John Bongaarts in his work of 1990 proposes an alternative measurement based on more limited data. Specifically, using only prospective fertility intentions (asked in a 2000 survey) births in the previous year (1999 to 2000) are divided into wanted and unwanted. The key assumption is that, for each woman, all births to point t on a life line are wanted and all subsequent births are unwanted. Thus, if a woman wants more children in 2000, then a birth last year must have been wanted. In addition, each woman must have one "last wanted birth." Together these observations/assumptions allow calculation of the wanted total fertility rate (or its complement, the unwanted TFR, given by unwanted TFR = TFR − wanted TFR).

Fertility intentions also allow measurement of the "unmet need for contraception." If a sexually ac-

tive woman intends no more children but is not using contraception, then she is at risk of an unwanted pregnancy (she has an unmet need for contraception). Important programmatic efforts aim to make contraception available to those in need. If large proportions of women have an unmet need for contraceptives, then unwanted conceptions will be common. Programmatic success could be measured by declines in unmet need (and fewer unwanted conceptions).

The Predictive Validity of Reproductive Intentions

Suppose that social, economic, and psychological variables are linked to fertility only through fertility intentions. In other words, all relevant factors affect intentions directly and intentions mediate these more distal effects. Indeed, numerous studies show that fertility intentions predict the subsequent behavior of individuals far better than do demographic and social indicators. However, evidence also clearly indicates a more complex process that produces patterned inconsistency between intentions and behavior. Specifically, some groups are better than others at predicting their future behavior; that is, there is an *interaction* of intent with covariates (e.g., O'Connell and Rogers 1983; Van de Giessen 1992). In addition, some subgroups/periods have higher fertility than others net of intentions, that is, there is a direct effect of group membership/period that bypasses the proximate intention variable (e.g., Thomson 1997; Schoen, Astone et al. 1999). The fact that fertility differences or changes are not always foreshadowed by different or changed intentions challenges the usefulness of intention data for fertility forecasts. In explaining the failure of 1970 intentions data to anticipate the fertility decline between 1970 and 1975, Charles F. Westoff and Norman B. Ryder reasoned that "respondents failed to anticipate the extent to which the times would be unpropitious for childbearing. . .the same kind of forecasting error that demographers have often made" (p. 449). Thus, intentions and other preference measures can provide clues to future trends and differences, but they should not be expected consistently to perform as reliable indicators of future individual or aggregate behavior.

Variation in the predictive validity of fertility intentions provides clues to the fertility decision-making processes. For instance, predictive validity increases if the time frame for the expected behavior is explicit. Consider a pair of twenty-five-year old U.S. women. Both intend to have a first child. But one intends a child soon (within two years) and the other intends to postpone the first birth for at least five years. Research shows that such women behave very differently in the short run (e.g., Rindfuss, Morgan, Swicegood 1988: Chapter 9). Thus, in addition to affirmative and negative responses (to "Do you intend another child?"), a viable strategy—and response—is "wait and see" or "not right now." A question asking if a child is intended in the next few years mimics the operative decision that women or couples make. Cross-national empirical evidence indicates that many women want to postpone the next birth (Lightbourne 1987). Postponement leaves open the possibility that births delayed may be foregone. For instance, substantial research indicates that most U.S. childlessness results from a series of decisions to postpone childbearing—rather than from stable childless intentions from a young age.

Despite credible arguments to the contrary, evidence indicates that aggregate preferences of women and men are quite similar (Mason and Taj 1987) and that couples frequently agree on fertility goals (Mason and Smith 2000; Morgan 1985). Nevertheless, consistency between intention and behavior is greater when partners agree (Thomson 1997; Schoen, Astone et al. 1999). Finally, predictive validity increases if one considers the respondents' level of certainty about their stated intention. Some respondents freely admit that they may change their mind or are uncertain whether they will have another child.

See also: *Childlessness; Family Planning Programs; Fertility, Below-Replacement; Sex Selection; Unwanted Fertility.*

BIBLIOGRAPHY

Bongaarts, John. 1990. "The Measurement of Wanted Fertility." *Population and Development Review* 16: 487–506.

———. 2001. "Fertility and Reproductive Preferences in Post-Transitional Societies." *Global Fertility Transition,* eds. Rodolfo. A. Bulatao and John. B. Casterline. New York: Population Council.

Lee, Ronald D. 1980. "Aiming at a Moving Target: Period Fertility and Changing Reproductive Goals." *Population Studies* 34: 205–226.

Lightbourne, Robert E. 1987. "Reproductive Preferences and Behavior." *The World Fertility Survey: An Assessment,* ed. J. Cleland and S. Chris. Oxford: Oxford University Press.

Mason, Karen. O., and Herbert L. Smith. 2000. "Husbands' Versus Wives' Fertility Goals and Use of Contraception: The Influence of Gender Context in Five Asian Countries." *Demography* 37(3): 299–311.

Mason, Karen. O., and Anju M. Taj. 1987. "Differences Between Women's and Men's Reproductive Goals in Developing Countries." *Population and Development Review* 13: 611–638.

Morgan, S. Philip 1985. "Individual and Couple Intentions for More Children: A Research Note." *Demography* 22: 125–132.

O'Connell, Martin., and Carolyn C. Rogers. 1983. "Assessing Cohort Birth Expectations Data from the Current Population Survey, 1971–1981." *Demography* 20: 369–384.

Rindfuss, Ronald R., S. Philip Morgan, et al. 1988. *First Births in America.* Berkeley, CA: University of California Press.

Ryder, N. B., and C. F. Westoff. 1971. *Reproduction in the United States.* Princeton, NJ: Princeton University Press.

Schaeffer, N. C., and E. Thomson. 1992. "The Discovery of Grounded Uncertainty: Developing Standardized Questions about Strength of Fertility Motivation." *Sociological Methodology* 22: 37–82.

Schoen, R., N. M. Astone, et al. 1999. "Do Fertility Intentions Affect Fertility Behavior?" *Journal of Marriage and the Family* 61: 790–799.

Thomson, E. 1997. "Couple Childbearing Desires, Intentions and Births." *Demography* 34: 343–354.

van de Giessen, H. 1992. *Using Birth Expectation Information in National Population Forecasts. National Population Forecasting in Industrialized Countries.* N. a. H. C. Keilman. Amsterdam: Swets and Zeitlinger.

van de Walle, E. 1992. "Fertility Transition, Conscious Choice and Numeracy." *Demography* 29: 487–502.

Westoff, C. F., and N. B. Ryder. 1977. "The Predictive Validity of Reproductive Intentions." *Demography* 14: 431–453.

S. PHILIP MORGAN

FAMINE, CONCEPTS AND CAUSES OF

Famines usually have demographic causes as well as consequences, and the deaths that result from famines offer a ready means of ranking them. However, defining famine remains a controversial issue. Traditionally famines entailed both a decline in the food supply and excess mortality, but in the twenty-first century a looser definition encompassing periods of chronic hunger in which neither food availability decline (FAD) nor excess mortality is present holds sway. Even confining attention to "famines that kill" leaves room for ambiguity. On the one hand, famines that produce excess mortality usually only represent peaks in chronic or endemic malnutrition that renders "normal" mortality high. On the other hand, famine deaths are often difficult to distinguish from deaths caused by infectious diseases such as malaria and cholera. It follows that the dividing line between crises that reduce the resistance of the poor to disease and harvest shortfalls that result in literal starvation is not always clear-cut.

Why Famines?

Throughout history poor harvests resulting from ecological shocks often have been the proximate cause of famines. Well-known examples include the eruptions of the volcanoes Laki (Iceland in the 1780s) and Tambora (Indonesia in the 1810s); Phytophthora infestans, or potato blight (Europe in the 1840s); and the El Niño drought (Asia in the late 1870s). However, such exogenous shocks were neither a necessary nor a sufficient cause of famine. In sufficiently poor economies the yield variation of the staple crop or crops was enough to produce a famine every decade or two. Back-to-back or repeated harvest shortfalls such as those that occurred in Ireland in the 1840s, India in the 1890s, and China in 1958–1960 have tended to produce the worst famines. Major famines have rarely been the product of live-

stock deaths alone. The severity of such crises also depended on other factors, such as the effectiveness of relief, the quality of the bureaucracy, the size of the voluntary sector, and the threat or presence of warfare in the affected area.

However, for the economist T. R. Malthus overpopulation, which may be defined as a state in which a significant proportion of the population is close to the margin of subsistence, was the fundamental reason for famines. When in 1798 he described "gigantic inevitable famine" as nature's response of last resort, Malthus would influence both the policy and the analytical response to famines for a long time to come.

The connection between famine and overpopulation may be looser than Malthus asserted, but there can be little doubt that throughout history overpopulation has increased vulnerability to famine. The reason is obvious: Historically, those close to subsistence were in no position to save, trade down to more economical foods, or guard against attendant infectious diseases.

Amartya Sen (1981) and others claim that this Malthusian interpretation is less relevant to twentieth-century famines. Though not denying a role for harvest-induced reductions in food availability, Sen emphasizes the impact of market-induced shifts on the purchasing power, or "entitlements," of certain sectors of the population. Sen first applied this entitlements approach to the Great Bengal Famine of 1942–1943, arguing that hoarding and speculation on the part of producers and merchants at the expense of the landless poor, rather than a significant harvest shortfall *per se*, were responsible for the crisis. In this case misjudgments by producers forced prices higher than were justified by food availability and beyond the reach of the poor. Other studies point to the role of market failure in exacerbating famines in Bangladesh in 1974 and in Sudan and Ethiopia in the 1980s. Research on how markets function during famines remains thin, however. Meanwhile Sen's focus on shifting entitlements in the absence of FAD points to the difficulty of imagining *any* famine in which bigger transfers of purchasing power from the rich to the poor would not reduce mortality.

The Demographic Impact

Because famines have nearly always affected backward economies, their human toll is often difficult to measure. In the absence of civil registration, as in Ireland in the nineteenth century and in the Ukraine and China in the twentieth, the highest and lowest estimates of mortality sometimes are set by ideologues. Estimates of excess mortality in the Ukraine in the 1931–1932 famine range from 2 million to 8 million, whereas those of deaths from the Chinese Great Leap Forward famine range from 15 million to 43 million. Claims that the Great Leap famine was the largest in history gloss over uncertainties about its true toll and ignore estimates of 20 million to 30 million deaths from famine in China between 1876 and 1900 and a further 12 million to 20 million in India in the same period.

Although as many as 70 million people died of famine during the twentieth century, in relative terms famine-related mortality was lower than it had been in previous centuries. In Europe the retreat of famine has been a long process. Famine has not been a significant factor demographically in England since the sixteenth century or in France since the early eighteenth century, but much of Europe was subjected to famine in 1740–1741 and 1817–1819. In Ireland the famine of 1740–1741 killed proportionately more people than did the more famous potato famine of the 1840s. Europe's last major subsistence crisis was the Finnish famine of 1868.

In the twenty-first century, for the first time in history, only pockets of the globe, such as parts of Africa, Afghanistan, and North Korea, remain truly vulnerable to the threat of famine. For all the publicity attending modern famines (useful from a humanitarian aid standpoint), their demographic impact is minor. Although it would be naive to rule out more "political" famines in the future, there is little likelihood of population outstripping global food-producing capacity in the next generation or two.

Famines that kill more than a few percent of a country's population are unusual. Exceptions include the "haze famine" that killed one-fourth of Iceland's population in the wake of the eruption of Laki in June 1783 and the famine that killed the same proportion of the population of Cape Verde in the mid-1850s. However, those famines occurred in very small places. The Chinese famine of 1958–1960, so atrocious in absolute terms, killed at most 2 to 3 percent of the total population of China.

Throughout history most famine victims succumbed not to literal starvation but to infectious diseases. In Ireland in the 1840s, for example, only

about one victim in ten died of starvation, broadly defined. Suppression of the immune system from malnutrition increased vulnerability to infectious diseases such as typhoid fever, cholera, and dysentery/diarrhea. Other deaths were attributable to a wide range of partially hunger-sensitive diseases. Famines kill the very young and the very old disproportionately, but those groups are also the most vulnerable in normal times. Women tend to be better at resisting malnutrition, mainly for physiological reasons. Births decline as a result of reductions in sexual activity and in women's capacity to bear children. When the worst of the crisis is over, deaths typically fall below trend for a year or two and births rise above it. This raises the conundrum of whether estimates of the demographic toll of famines that include averted births during famines should also include deaths averted and births induced in its wake. Migration may exacerbate famine by spreading infection (as in Finland in 1868); alternatively, it may act as a form of disaster relief by reducing the pressure on resources, as occurred in Ireland in the 1840s.

The changing role of medical science in reducing mortality from infectious diseases is an interesting issue. Long before the discoveries of the scientists Robert Koch and Louis Pasteur the risks associated with being near fever victims were well understood, though the mechanisms of contamination were not. Moreover, there was a long lag between scientific diagnosis and remedies such as penicillin and electrolytes. In the twentieth century there have been famines in which infectious diseases were the main killers (e.g., Bengal in the 1940s and Ethiopia in the 1970s) and famines in which they killed few people (e.g., Mykonos in 1942–1943 and the western Netherlands during the *Hongerwinter* of 1944–1945). The key seems to be whether infectious diseases are endemic in normal times: If they are, they bulk large when famine strikes.

Public Action

When threatened with famine, in the past the poor relied on compassion on the part of the ruling class and the fear of infection and social unrest. Rarely have such sentiments been enough. In the ancient world capital cities tended to be the best organized for famine relief. Christian ideology may have helped marginally because it called for the rich to be charitable. Although Malthus denied the right of the hungry citizen to subsistence, rulers have long implicitly acknowledged a responsibility to help. They employed a variety of strategies: the maintenance of public granaries, institutionalized care through poor laws, workfare, improvised soup kitchens, and migration schemes. Private charity has rarely been enough in times of severe harvest failure. The record suggests that particularly when a crisis persists, compassion fatigue sets in. In the twenty-first century international relief, both governmental and nongovernmental, supplements local efforts, but with the attendant danger that it shifts responsibility from local elites and oligarchs.

For those early disciples of Malthus who regarded famines as a providential response to overpopulation, public intervention risked leading to even worse famines later. In Ireland and in the Netherlands in the 1840s as in India in the late 1870s there was thus a tension between Malthusian ideology and measures that would minimize mortality. In practice public action was, and still is, often complicated by the problem of agency. Antisocial behavior is an inevitable concomitant of famine: Theft increases, and hospitality diminishes.

Informal systems of mutual help may work at first, but their effectiveness does not last. Concern with cheating is a prominent aspect of controversies about relief policy. The Irish experience in the 1840s is illustrative in this respect. Relief through a system of workfare was initially seen as the best way around such problems, but this was ill geared to help the physically weak and exacerbated the spread of infectious diseases. When it was replaced by food aid, the food was distributed in a non-resalable form in order to minimize abuse. Once the authorities deemed the crisis over, the onus shifted back to reliance on the workhouses established under the Irish poor law of 1838. In Ireland as elsewhere, worries about free riders ended up hurting the vulnerable. The choice between public works schemes and soup kitchens is still a matter of debate.

Post-Famine Adjustment

Malthus saw famine as a harsh remedy that "with one mighty blow level[ed] the population with the food of the world." There is no doubt that in the short run at least famines result in higher living standards for the majority of survivors. To the extent that famines reduce the population but leave largely intact the land endowment and physical capital, famines improve the lot of surviving workers relative to farmers and landowners. The impact on landowners may be intensified by the burden of relief spending. However, if the chaotic conditions that often precede famines prevent landowners from enforcing their property rights, they too may find their incomes rising once normality has been restored.

But are these "benefits" lasting? One consideration is that the gains in terms of higher wages and a higher land–labor ratio may be offset by the long-run impact of famine on the health of affected survivors. Another consideration is whether population growth tends to fill the demographic vacuum left by famine. Good examples are Finland in 1868 and France in the 1690s and 1700s, where the demographic dents made by major famines were repaired within a few years. The evidence is not unanimous, though: In pre–Black Death England in the wake of the agrarian crisis of the 1310s, in post-famine Ireland, and in Tokugawa Japan the demographic damage done by famine persisted. In Ireland the lack of a demographic "rebound" was due at least in part to an increasing resort to the preventive check through later and fewer marriages.

See also: *Food Supply and Population; Nutrition and Calorie Consumption.*

BIBLIOGRAPHY

Bowbrick, Peter. 1986. "A Refutation of Sen's Theory of Famine." *Food Policy* 11(2): 105–124.

Davis, Mike. 2000. *Late Victorian Holocausts: El Niño Famines and the Making of the Third World.* London: Verso.

Devereux, Stephen. 2000. "Famine in the Twentieth Century." Institute of Development Studies Working Paper No. 105, Brighton, Eng.: IDS.

Drèze, Jean, and Amartya K. Sen. 1989. *Hunger and Public Action.* Oxford: Oxford University Press.

Dyson, Tim. 1991. "The Demography of South Asian Famines." *Population Studies* 45(1): 5–25 and 45(2): 279–297.

Dyson, Tim, and Cormac Ó Gráda, eds. 2002. *Famine Demography: Perspectives from the Past and Present.* Oxford: Oxford University Press.

Garnsey, Peter. 1988. *Famine and Food Supply in the Graeco-Roman World.* Cambridge, Eng.: Cambridge University Press.

Hionidou, Violetta. 2002. "'Send Us Either Food or Coffins': The 1941–2 Famine on the Aegaean Island of Syros." In *Famine Demography: Perspectives from the Past and Present,* ed. Tim Dyson and Cormac Ó Gráda, eds. Oxford: Oxford University Press.

Lachiver, Marcel. 1991. *Les Années de Misère: La Famine au Temps du Grand Roi.* Paris: Fayard.

Lomborg, Bjørn. 2001. *The Skeptical Environmentalist: Measuring the Real State of the World.* Cambridge, Eng.: Cambridge University Press.

Lumey, L. H. 1998. "Reproductive Outcomes in Women Prenatally Exposed to Undernutrition from the Dutch Famine Birth Cohort." *Proceedings of the Nutrition Society* 57: 129–135.

Mokyr, Joel, and Cormac Ó Gráda. 2002. "Famine Disease and Famine Mortality: Lessons from the Irish Experience, 1845–1850." In *Famine Demography: Perspectives from the Past and Present,* ed. Tim Dyson and Cormac Ó Gráda. Oxford: Oxford University Press.

Ó Gráda, Cormac. 1999. *Black '47 and Beyond: The Great Irish Famine in History, Economy and Memory.*, Princeton, NJ: Princeton University Press.

———. 2001. "Markets and Famines: Evidence from Nineteenth Century Finland." *Economic Development and Cultural Change* 49(3): 575–590.

Pitkänen, Kari J. 1993. *Deprivation and Disease: Mortality during the Great Finnish Famine of the 1860s.* Helsinki: Finnish Demographic Society.

Ravallion, Martin. 1987. *Markets and Famines.* Oxford: Clarendon Press.

Riskin, Carl. 1998. "Seven Lessons about the Chinese Famine of 1959–61." *China Economic Review* 9(2): 111–124.

Sen, Amartya. 1981. *Poverty and Famines.* Oxford: Oxford University Press.

von Braun, Joachim, Tesfaye Teklu, and Patrick Webb. 1998. *Famine in Africa: Causes, Responses, and Prevention.* Baltimore: Johns Hopkins Press.

Watkins, S. C., and J. Menken. 1985. "Famines in Historical Perspective." *Population and Development Review* 11(4): 647–675.

CORMAC Ó GRÁDA

FAMINE IN AFRICA

In the second half of the twentieth century, sub-Saharan Africa stood out as the region of the world with the slowest growth in agricultural production and the highest rate of population growth. Its population also suffers from the highest rates of undernutrition worldwide. The combination of a poorly nourished but rapidly growing population increases the region's vulnerability to food crises, both natural and man-made. Other factors, however, are needed to explain why periodic famines have struck Africa south of the Sahara in the twentieth century more frequently than other regions. Table 1 summarizes the recent African experience.

Context

Famines figure prominently in African history. John Iliffe has described famine conditions during the colonial period in eastern and southern Africa and Michael Watts has discussed the complex relationships between colonial policies and household production that produced food crises in northern Nigeria continuing into the 1970s. Many food crises in the past were unlikely to have been noticed by outsiders. An exception may have been the francophone countries of the Sahel, where routine reporting of food prices and epidemics were part of the centralized administrative system of the colonial period. In the twenty-first century, the chances of food shortages being noticed are much greater thanks to networks such as the Famine Early Warning System (FEWS) organized by the U.S. Agency for International Development (USAID). Many recent famines in Africa, as Joachim von Braun and others have documented, stem from wars that disrupted food production, distribution, and consumption systems. The food crises of the early 1970s that affected the whole Sahel region, however, seem to have been triggered by a series of exceptionally dry years in a period of longer-term reduction in annual rainfall amounts. Inter-annual rainfall variability increases as total amounts decline. Additional physical challenges to African food producers include tropical soils that are not conducive to high levels of perennial productivity. In the Sahel, cereals such as sorghum and millet contain much lower energy per unit of weight than maize, wheat, and other temperate climate cereals.

The challenges of the physical environment are compounded by under-capitalization of the agricultural sector and by institutional barriers such as land

TABLE 1

Major African Famines in the Later Twentieth Century	
Region	**Years**
Nigeria (Biafra)	1968–1969
Sahel region	1969–1974
Ethiopia	1972–1974
Angola	1974–1976
Zaire (Bas Fleuve)	1977–1978
Uganda	1980
Mozambique	1982–1983
Sahel region	1982–1985
Sudan	1984–1985
Horn of Africa	1983–1985
Mozambique	1985–1986
Sudan	1988
Somalia	1988
Ethiopia/Horn of Africa	1989–1990
Liberia	1992–1993
Somalia	1992–1993
Sudan	1993
Angola	1993–1994
Liberia/Sierra Leone	1995–1996
Zaire/Congo	1997
Sudan	1998

SOURCE: von Braun, Teklu and Webb (1999), Table 1.1.

tenure and sharecropping arrangements that do not compensate individual farmers for productive improvements. Most Sahelian farmers rely heavily on manual labor and have very limited access to machinery even for plowing, seeding, or harvesting. In West Africa much of the cereal cultivation, especially rice, is in the hands of women, whose access to capital and loans is limited. Further, land is generally owned communally and variants of the open-field system still operate. Where available, land that is not in communal cultivation may be allocated to enterprising individuals by local leaders, but only for the time those individuals cultivate the field. In some communities, ethnicity and class restrict access to land, water, and the labor needed to farm. Probably most significant is the low level of development of commercial agriculture except in a few more favored areas. The small external market for millet and sorghum, and for the roots and tuber crops common in the forest belt, discourages the development of capital investments, ports, and communications to the interior.

Causes

The most common explanation of the causes of famine used to be ecological: The consumption needs of a growing population outstrip the capacity of local

farming systems to produce food. The famine of the western Sahel in the early 1970s is a clear example of famine initiated by drought. The scholars von Braun, Tesfaye Teklu, and Patrick Webb have proposed a more complex model in which population growth and environmental changes contribute only to a small extent to food shortages. An important if understudied factor is the growth of the population of animals, particularly sheep and goats instead of cattle, that has contributed to rangeland deterioration and the relocation of pastoralists to increasingly marginal areas. In more recent case studies, including work by Alexander de Waal in Sudan, more emphasis is laid on institutional, organizational, and policy failures. Other precipitating causes of famine include civil wars and ethnic disputes. The low investment in roads and railways, which has been shown to prevent famine by allowing the speedy movement of food between markets, increases poor families' vulnerability to famine. Trade barriers (the constraints on some agricultural imports by the European Union, for example) and the penetration of North American agricultural exporters into African grain markets are additional factors contributing to inadequacies of domestic food production.

The economist Amartya Sen has mounted a strong challenge to the notion that famines are the result of absolute shortages of food. He argued that in most famines there is generally sufficient food, but some people lose the capacity to acquire food due to the collapse of the demand for their labor or the goods and services they produce. They thus lose their "entitlements" to purchase food, while others manage to retain control over dwindling food stocks. The people who are most affected are not the food producers themselves but those in the service trades in towns and cities whose customers, when times are hard, manage without the personal and professional services they offer.

Policy Responses

Sen's work has greatly influenced policies on food aid generally and on famine relief in particular. Although food is still sent to relieve famine in Africa, many donors now focus on restoring people's entitlements through food-for-work schemes or other forms of public works support. This response is based on the successful famine relief measures adopted in the Indian subcontinent, where massive government intervention has prevented a major famine since the Bangladesh famine of 1973. Jean

FIGURE 1

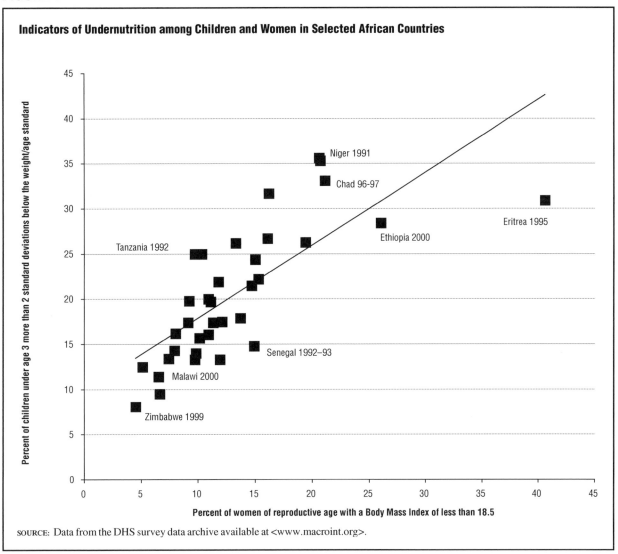

Indicators of Undernutrition among Children and Women in Selected African Countries

SOURCE: Data from the DHS survey data archive available at <www.macroint.org>.

Drèze and Sen have written extensively on the differing origins and policy responses in the Indian subcontinent and in Africa. The notion of food security is now well established and a variety of policies have been implemented to ensure that food is accessible to the poor and to vulnerable subpopulations through micro-credit enterprises and local food reserves. But many of the underlying causes of famine, including poor transport facilities and the undercapitalization of agriculture, have yet to be addressed. Bodies such as the International Livestock Research Institute in Kenya and Ethiopia, the West African Rice Development Association, and the International Institute for Tropical Agriculture as well as other members of the Consultative Group on International Agricultural Research (CGIAR) have made significant contributions to increasing the productivity of some important tropical food crops.

Effects

Disastrous mortality is the effect popularly associated with famine. Detailed studies such as Sen's work on the Bengal famine of 1943, however, show that most of the excess deaths attributable to famine occur not at the time of most acute food shortage but in the ensuing period. The general conclusion, stemming from work by de Waal on Darfur, Sudan from 1984 and 1985, is that famine is just one among many symptoms of social and economic disruption. The excess death rates are then seen largely as the result of a subsequent "health crisis" in which infectious and parasitic diseases cause the excess deaths.

This and the entitlements idea has led to extensive criticism of the food aid "industry" as an inappropriate means to relieve both short- and long-term hunger in poor countries. Rather than focusing on inadequacies of food availability, public attention is now directed more to the distributional effects of economic crises and their consequences—including famine.

Famines have periodically driven people off the land or have forced some reorganization of agriculture, generally away from pastoralism and into both subsistence and commercial agriculture. The urban bias in development has worked against attracting well-educated people and their capital into the agriculture sector. Westernization of the urban diet has reduced the demand for locally produced foodstuffs among those people able to pay the highest prices for food. Sub-Saharan Africa is thus now highly dependent on imported food.

The full implications of widespread undernutrition in Africa are impossible to gauge, but the effects of undernutrition in pregnancy are well known and contribute to the generally low birth weights and poor growth curves of African children. Large proportions of both women and their children are seriously undernourished in the Sahelian countries, Ethiopia, and Eritrea, and indicators of undernutrition also signal serious deficiencies in other African countries, as shown in Figure 1. Undernutrition and periodic starvation adversely affect both the physical and the mental development of children. Fecundity is not affected: even among poorly nourished women, total fertility rates as high as eight children have been recorded.

See also: *Food Supply and Population; Nomads; Nutrition and Calorie Consumption.*

BIBLIOGRAPHY

De Waal, Alexander. 1989. *Famine that Kills: Darfur, Sudan 1984–1985.* Oxford: Clarendon Press.

Drèze, Jean, and Amartya Sen. 1989. *Hunger and Public Action.* Oxford: Clarendon Press.

Iliffe, John. 1990. *Famine in Zimbabwe, 1890–1960.* Gweru, Zimbabwe: Mambo Press.

Mortimore, Michael. 1989. *Adapting to Drought: Farmers, Famines and Desertification in West Africa.* Cambridge, Eng.: Cambridge University Press.

Sen, Amartya. 1981. *Poverty and Famines: An Essay on Entitlement and Deprivation.* Oxford: Clarendon Press.

von Braun, Joachim, Tesfaye Teklu, and Patrick Webb. 1999. *Famine in Africa: Causes, Responses and Prevention.* Baltimore, MD: Johns Hopkins University Press for the International Food Policy Research Institute.

Watts, Michael. 1983. *Silent Violence: Food, Famine and Peasantry in Northern Nigeria.* Berkeley and Los Angeles: University of California Press.

ALLAN G. HILL

FAMINE IN CHINA

There is no complete record of periods of famine in China, but there is no dispute that there were many—although few that were countrywide. From early in China's history the development of physical and social infrastructure would have helped to minimize the effects of famine: irrigation canals and dikes were built to counteract the vagaries of the weather, and administrative measures were adopted to ensure reserve supplies of essential food items and to establish systems of food and seed rationing and distribution. Nevertheless, famine was plausibly one of the factors slowing the long-run increase of China's population to barely perceptible levels until the seventeenth century.

The faster rate of population growth observed over the subsequent two centuries occurred despite the destruction wrought by rebellions, banditry, invasion, and civil war. These events ended with the establishment of the People's Republic in 1949, and the pace of growth rose markedly: China's population doubled in the following half-century. Yet it is during this period that the most destructive famine of China's history occurred, the famine of 1958–1961, associated with the policy known as the Great Leap Forward.

Scale of the 1958–1961 Famine

One of the key programs of the new Communist regime was a far-reaching and comprehensive land reform. Peasants were organized in mutual aid teams,

FIGURE 1

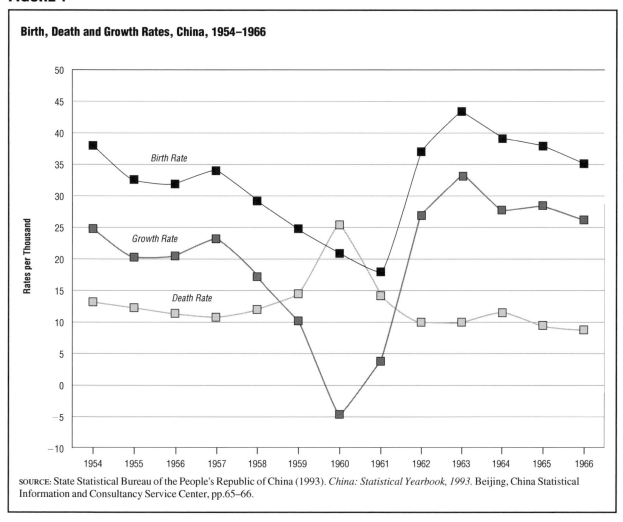

Birth, Death and Growth Rates, China, 1954–1966

Birth Rate

Growth Rate

Death Rate

Rates per Thousand

50
45
40
35
30
25
20
15
10
5
0
–5
–10

1954 1955 1956 1957 1958 1959 1960 1961 1962 1963 1964 1965 1966

SOURCE: State Statistical Bureau of the People's Republic of China (1993). *China: Statistical Yearbook, 1993.* Beijing, China Statistical Information and Consultancy Service Center, pp.65–66.

and teams in turn were grouped into production co-operatives. In 1957, Mao Zedong embarked on the Great Leap, a radical industrialization program with the declared objective to overtake Great Britain in industrial production in 15 years. Labor-intensive development activities would make up for the lack of capital. Heavy industry would be given priority over the agricultural sector, and the agricultural production system would be transformed with modern technology. The peasant cooperatives were grouped into still larger collective units, termed People's Communes.

The results were catastrophic. Both industrial and grain production fell for three consecutive years, 1959–1961, and the standard of living dropped sharply. There were widespread food shortages and then famine. The crisis affected the whole country, but with varying severity across different regions.

The demographic consequences were increased mortality, reduced fertility, a halting of population growth, and a surge in rural-to-urban migration.

China's death rate increased from 10.8 per thousand in 1957 to 25.4 in 1960, a rise of about 130 percent, then fell back to its pre-crisis level by 1962. In total, an estimated 29 million persons died as a direct result of the famine during the period 1958–1961. Twelve million of these (40%) were under the age of 10 years.

The birth rate decreased from 34.0 per thousand in 1957 to 18.0 in 1961, a drop of nearly 50 percent, then rebounded to 37.0 per thousand in 1962. The drop in births was the result of factors such as postponement of marriage, spousal separation, reduced fecundity, and increased spontaneous abortions and stillbirths. During the crisis period, there were about

33 million fewer births than there would have been under non-crisis conditions.

The combined effect of the increased death rate and the reduced birth rate was that the population growth rate during the crisis period decreased from 23.2 per thousand in 1957 to 4.6 in 1960. It rose again to 27.0 per thousand in 1962. (See Figure 1) Rural areas suffered most from the famine. There was considerable migration from affected rural areas to less affected areas, and particularly to the cities.

Causes of the 1958–1961 Famine

The main cause of the famine was an ill-conceived, over-ambitious development program that was carried out with insufficient means. Local cadres were not properly trained and lacked the experience to manage large agricultural production units. Collectivization of farming had weakened private incentives and sapped initiative, cutting the link between effort and reward. Cumbersome target-setting procedures and a four-tier administration (state, province, district, and commune), led to unrealistically high targets. To comply with the pressure to perform, cadres at various levels greatly overestimated or falsified output figures, for a time hiding the magnitude of the production failure from higher levels of the administration. Grain procurement by the government for export and to create reserve stocks thus continued and further aggravated the shortfall of grain supply at the local level. The crisis was deepened by natural disasters: drought, flood, excessive precipitation, plant diseases, and insect infestations affected many parts of the country, although some of these too were the consequence of faulty policies. Once the leadership became aware of the crisis, the Great Leap was swiftly abandoned. Subsequent changes in China's economic and administrative policies, notably the effective re-privatization of agriculture initiated by Deng Xiaoping in the 1970s, make repetition of a human-caused famine in China highly unlikely.

See also: *Communism, Population Aspects of; Food Supply and Population.*

BIBLIOGRAPHY

Ashton, Basil, et al. 1984. "Famine in China, 1958–61." *Population and Development Review* 10: 613–645.

Banister, Judith. 1984. "An Analysis of Recent Data on the Population of China." *Population and Development Review* 10: 241–271.

Calot, Gérard. 1984. "Données nouvelles sur l'évolution démographique Chinoise." *Population* 39: 807–835, 1,045–1,062.

Fairbank, John King. 1992. *China: A New History.* Cambridge, MA: Belknap Press.

Gernet, Jacques. 1996. *A History of Chinese Civilization,* 2nd edition. Cambridge, MA: Cambridge University Press.

Heilig, Gerhard K. 1999. *Can China Feed Itself? A System for Evaluation of Policy Options,* CD-ROM Vers. 1.1. Laxenburg: International Institute for Applied Systems Analyis.

Kane, Penny. 1988. *Famine in China, 1959–61: Demographic and Social Implications.* New York: St. Martin's Press.

Peng, Xizhe. 1987. "Demographic Consequences of the Great Leap Forward in China's Provinces." *Population and Development Review* 13: 639–670.

State Statistical Bureau of the People's Republic of China. 1993. *China: Statistical Yearbook, 1993.* Beijing: China Statistical Information and Consultancy Service Center.

ALPHONSE L. MacDONALD

FAMINE IN IRELAND

The proximate cause of the Great Irish Famine (1846–1852) was the fungus *Phythophtera infestans* (potato blight), which reached Ireland in the fall of 1845. It destroyed about one-third of that year's crop and nearly all of the crop of 1846. After a season's remission it also ruined the harvest of 1848. These repeated shortfalls made the Irish famine more protracted than most. Partial failures of the potato crop were nothing new in Ireland before 1845, but damage on the scale wrought by the blight was utterly unprecedented. However, the famine would not have been so lethal if the population had been less dependent on the potato. Poverty had reduced one-third of the population to almost exclusive dependence on the potato for food. That, coupled with an inadequate response from the authorities, made the consequences of repeated failures devastating.

The Government's Response

The debate about relief measures in the press and in Parliament in the 1840s has a modern resonance. At first the government opted for reliance on the provision of employment through public works schemes. At their height in the spring of 1847 the public works employed 700,000 people, or one-twelfth of the entire population. These measures did not contain the famine, partly because they did not target some of the most needy, partly because the average wage was too low, and partly because they entailed exposing malnourished people (mostly men) to the elements during the worst months of the year. At their peak in early July 1847 the publicly financed soup kitchens that succeeded the public works program reached 3 million people daily. Mortality seemed to fall while they operated, though doubts remain about the effect of a diet of meal-based gruel on weakened stomachs.

The drop in food prices during the summer of 1847 prompted the authorities to treat the famine as a manageable local problem. The main burden of relieving the poor was placed on the workhouses established under the Irish poor law of 1838. Most of the workhouses were ill equipped to meet the demands placed on them, and about one-quarter of all famine mortalities occurred in them. Local histories highlight mismanagement and the impossible burden placed on local taxpayers, and the high overall proportion of workhouse deaths caused by contagious disease is an indictment of this form of relief. The very high mortality in some workhouses in 1850 and even 1851 provides evidence of the long-lasting character of the famine in some western areas. The aggregate sum spent on relief (about £9 million) was too small to make a significant dent in mortality.

Traditional accounts of the famine pit the more humane policies of Sir Robert Peel's Tories against the dogmatic stance of Sir John Russell's Whig administration, which took office in July 1846. That contrast is oversimplified. Although Peel was more familiar with Ireland's problems than were Whig ideologues such as Charles Wood, the crisis confronting him in 1845–1846 was mild compared to what was to follow. Moreover, Peel broadly supported the Whig line in opposition.

At the height of the crisis the policy adopted by the Whigs was influenced by Malthusian providentialism, the conviction that the potato blight was a divinely ordained remedy for Irish overpopulation. The fear that too much kindness would entail a Malthusian lesson not learned also conditioned both the nature and the extent of intervention.

The Effects of the Famine

The Irish famine killed about one million people, making it a major famine by world-historical standards. The death toll is approximate, since in the absence of civil registration excess mortality cannot be calculated directly. This estimate does not include averted births or allow for famine-related deaths in Britain and farther afield. Mortality was regionally very uneven. No part of Ireland escaped entirely, but the toll ranged from one-quarter of the population of some western counties to negligible fractions in Down and Wexford on the east coast. The timing of mortality varied too, even in some of the worst hit areas. In western Cork the worst was over by late 1847, but the effects of the famine raged in Clare until 1850 or even 1851. Infectious diseases rather than literal starvation were responsible for the largest proportion of the mortality. As in most famines, the elderly and the young were the most likely to die, but women proved marginally more resilient than men.

Like all famines, the Irish famine produced a hierarchy of suffering. The rural poor, landless or nearly landless, were the most likely to perish. Farmers faced an effective land endowment reduced by the potato blight and increased labor costs, forcing them to reduce their concentration on tillage. Landlords' rental income plummeted by as much as a third. Many medical practitioners and clergymen died of infectious diseases. Pawnbrokers found their pledges being unredeemed as the crisis worsened. Least affected were those firms and their workforces that relied on foreign markets for raw materials and sales. It is difficult to identify any significant class of "winners": except perhaps those grain merchants who grasped the opportunities offered by the trade in Indian meal when prices were still rising in the autumn of 1846 and in early 1847, lawyers who benefited from the deregulation of land transfers, and pastorally oriented farmers.

The Great Irish Famine was not just a watershed in Irish history but also a major event in global history, with far-reaching and enduring economic and political consequences. In Ireland it brought the era of famines to a brutal end. Serious failures of the potato crop in the early 1860s and late 1870s brought privation but no significant excess mortality. The famine also resulted in a higher living standard for survivors. Higher emigration was another by-product as the huge outflow of the crisis years generated its own "friends and neighbors" dynamic. Only in a few remote and tiny pockets in the west did population fill the vacuum left by the "Great Hunger," and then only very briefly. Whether by reducing the domestic market the famine led to the decline of certain industries remains to be established. Finally, although the introduction of new potato varieties offered some protection against *Phythophtera infestans* thereafter, no reliable defense would be found against it until the 1890s.

See also: *Trans-Atlantic Migration.*

BIBLIOGRAPHY

Bourke, Austin. 1993. *The Visitation of God? The Potato and the Great Irish Famine.* Dublin: Lilliput Press.

Donnelly, James S. 2000. *The Irish Potato Famine.* London: Sutton Publishing.

Gray, Peter. 1999. *Famine, Land and Politics: British Government and Irish Society 1843–50.* Dublin: Irish Academic Press.

Mokyr, Joel. 1985. *Why Ireland Starved: An Analytical and Quantitative History of the Irish Economy 1800–1850.* London: Allen & Unwin.

Ó Gráda, Cormac. 1999. *Black '47 and Beyond: The Great Irish Famine in History, Economy, and Memory.* Princeton, NJ: Princeton University Press.

———. 2001. "Famine, Trauma, and Memory." *Béaloideas* 69: 121–143.

Solar, Peter M. 1989. "The Great Famine Was No Ordinary Subsistence Crisis." In *Famine: The Irish Experience, 900–1900,* ed. E. M. Crawford. Edinburgh: John Donald.

Cormac Ó Gráda

FAMINE IN SOUTH ASIA

Famines have been a recurrent feature in the history of South Asia since the earliest recorded times. For example, the Mughal Empire experienced many such events in the sixteenth and seventeenth centuries, and famines may have occurred even more frequently after the empire's disintegration in the eighteenth century. A particularly severe famine occurred during the rule of the English East India Company in Bengal in 1770, when it was claimed that perhaps 10 million of Bengal's 30 million people died. Such figures must be regarded with great caution, but one can say that famines were common before the nineteenth century, were often severe, usually were precipitated by a failure of the monsoon rains, and together with endemic and epidemic diseases had a significant impact on the overall level of mortality.

The Response to Famine

Major famines continued to occur under East India Company rule in the first seven decades of the nineteenth century. Influenced by the writings of classical economists such as Adam Smith and David Ricardo, company administrators were often unsure how much they should intervene in food markets during times of famine. In addition, their opinions sometimes were influenced by Malthusian beliefs that spending resources on famine relief, and thus saving lives, might only exacerbate the region's population problem over the longer run. Consequently, the responsibility for famine relief during this period was often left to Indian princes, although limited relief measures and related efforts to improve and extend canal irrigation were increasingly undertaken by the British as the nineteenth century progressed.

In the period from 1876 to 1878 huge areas, particularly in southern India, were afflicted by monsoon failure and massive famine. The availability of early census and vital registration data has led to several estimates of excess mortality for this time, varying between 5 million and 8 million in a total population of perhaps 210 million. Such an enormous catastrophe attracted worldwide concern, was embarrassing to the British imperial authorities, and led to the establishment and recommendations of the Famine Commission of 1880. That commission's proposals included the formulation of "Famine Codes" to help local administrators deal with the threat of famine, the provision of guaranteed work at a subsistence wage for people affected by famine distress, and the provision of free famine relief for those deemed too feeble to work.

However, those proposals were not always implemented, and their existence failed to avert two more massive disasters in the 1890s. Estimates of excess mortality in British India from the famine of 1896–1897 vary between 2.5 million and 5 million, and the crisis of 1899–1900 may have led to between 2 million and 4.5 million deaths. In each of these major disasters of the late nineteenth century, epidemics of cholera, diarrheal diseases, and above all malaria broke out during the famines and caused the deaths of millions of starving people. The three famines were the reason that the size of South Asia's population remained fairly static during the 1870s and the 1890s.

Famine in the Twentieth Century

Partly because of the Famine Commission's recommendations, the first four decades of the twentieth century were comparatively free of major food crises. In 1943–1944, however, there was a serious famine in Bengal—then still under colonial rule—in which it is now known that there were about 2.1 million excess deaths in a total population of about 60 million. The immediate triggers of this event were complex, but as with many other food crises around the world during the early 1940s the occurrence of this famine cannot be viewed in isolation from the fact of world war. This was also the last famine in South Asia in which epidemic malaria played a major role in contributing to famine deaths.

After India and Pakistan gained independence in 1947, both the frequency and the severity of famines were greatly reduced. In no small part this has occurred because the region's countries have assumed responsibility for their own food security and health conditions. Also relevant has been the existence to varying extents of comparative press freedom and democratic government. However, in 1965–1966 there was a severe food crisis in the Indian state of Bihar in which there may have been considerable excess mortality, and in the early 1970s in the state of Maharashtra alone there were at least 70,000 excess deaths after the occurrence of severe and widespread drought. Other parts of the region, such as areas of Sri Lanka, were also affected by drought and food scarcity in the early 1970s.

However, probably the most serious famine to affect South Asia since 1947 was that in Bangladesh in the period 1974–1975. The extent of excess mortality resulting from this crisis is hard to gauge, but it seems likely to have been several hundred thousand. The occurrence of this famine cannot be viewed apart from the Bangladesh war of independence in 1971. Indeed, both in its causation and in its demographic consequences there are significant parallels between the 1943–1944 crisis in Bengal and that which hit much of the same region (i.e., Bangladesh) in 1974–1975.

The Twenty-First Century

At the beginning of the twenty-first century, provided that there continues to be relative sociopolitical stability and peace in the region, it is hard to see a major famine affecting the countries of South Asia in the foreseeable future. This is the case mainly because recent decades have seen economic diversification and growth, plus major infrastructural, epidemiological, and health improvements. Also, India, Bangladesh, Pakistan, and Sri Lanka all either hold relatively large stocks of food or have the capacity to purchase emergency supplies if the need arises. This conclusion should not obscure the fact that droughts and harvest failures still occur in the region and have the potential to cause some excess deaths, particularly among the poorest sectors of society. However, famines that cause large-scale devastation and mortality in South Asia appear to be things of the past.

See also: *Food Supply and Population.*

BIBLIOGRAPHY

Ambirajan, S. 1976. "Malthusian Population Theory and Indian Famine Policy in the Nineteenth Century." *Population Studies* 30(1): 5–14.

Dyson, Tim. 1991. "The Demography of South Asian Famines." *Population Studies* 45(1 and 2): 5–25 and 279–297.

Dyson, Tim, and Arup Maharatna. 1991. "Excess Mortality during the Bengal Famine: A Re-Evaluation." *Indian Economic and Social History Review* 28(3): 281–297.

———. 1992. "The Demographic Consequences of the Bihar Famine of 1966–67 and the Maharashtra Drought of 1970–73." *Economic and Political Weekly* 27(26): 1325–1332.

Maharatna, Arup. 1996. *The Demography of Famines—An Indian Historical Perspective.* Delhi: Oxford University Press.

TIM DYSON

FAMINE IN THE SOVIET UNION

This article discusses the three major famines that the Soviet Union experienced. It does not treat regionally-delimited food shortages and famines, which were numerous between 1917 and 1940, or the famine conditions that occurred during World War II, for example in the Leningrad blockade. Famines, of course, were also fairly frequent occurrences in the Tsarist Russian empire, especially in rural areas. The last important one took place in 1891–1892. However this was dwarfed by the famines of the Soviet era.

The first of the major Soviet famines struck between 1918 and 1921, following World War I and the civil war. By 1921 it covered all of Russia. It resulted from severe disorganization of the food supply combined with the consequences of compulsory requisitioning of harvests, a practice that began before the Revolution but continued and was enlarged after it, especially during the civil war. The Bolsheviks sought to ensure food supplies for the towns, where their strongest base of support lay, and for the army. The famine is estimated to have caused about 5 million deaths, either directly from starvation or in the epidemics that followed.

After some hesitation, at the end of June 1921 the Soviet authorities began a large famine relief campaign, helped by some international support from organizations such as the American Relief Administration and the International Committee of the Red Cross. By the end of 1922, although many regions were still suffering from malnutrition, the situation was returning to normal—aided by Lenin's decision to permit small-scale private commercial activity and by an easing of grain requisitions. The Bolsheviks used the famine as a pretext to confiscate church property.

The 1933 famine, the second of the three, was more catastrophic yet than the famine of 1918–1921

and differed in its origins and geographical concentration (Figure 1). It led to more than 6 million deaths, largely in Ukraine, the Lower Volga region, and in the North Caucasus, the main grain producing regions, and also in Kazakhstan, then with a large nomadic population. Its determinants were clearly political: it was the outcome of the forced collectivization of peasant farms, the harsh Stalinist policy of 1928–1929 that followed the less stringent years (1921–1927) of the New Economic Policy. Under the name of dekulakization, millions of peasants, both rich and less rich, were deported; many of them to remote frontier regions, and new collective farms (*kolkhoz*) were established. Many peasants destroyed their livestock rather than giving it to the collectives. Agricultural marketing systems broke down. The situation was worsened by Stalin's decision to continue and even expand the export of grain in order to finance the rapid industrialization envisaged in the second Five Year Plan. The level of forced grain requisitions took no account of the realities of production. The hostility of Stalin, Molotov, Kaganovich, and other Soviet leaders toward the peasants, suspected of hiding their harvest, led in 1931 to measures such as NKVD detachments or groups of workers from the towns being used to confiscate grain—even seed grain.

The pace of grain requisitions did not lessen even when the first signs of famine began to appear, during 1931 and in the summer of 1932. Ukrainian authorities, on the basis of Ukrainian NKVD or Communist party reports, attempted to alert Moscow officials to the looming catastrophe, but Stalin, after initially seeming to be concerned, chose instead to begin a violent attack against "peasant wreckers" and even "Communist staff wreckers." Other regions that traditionally produced a grain surplus—notably North Caucasus and Lower Volga—were similarly subjected to mass-collectivization, dekulakization, and requisitions.

In Kazakhstan, collectivization took the form of forced sedentarization of the nomadic people. This led to a large exodus to other countries, especially to the western regions of China where the population was ethnically similar, and to complete social disorganization among those who remained.

The peak of the famine was in March and April of 1933, when the number of deaths in some regions of Ukraine, Russia, and Kazakhstan were more than ten times normal levels. To avoid massive flows of

FIGURE 1

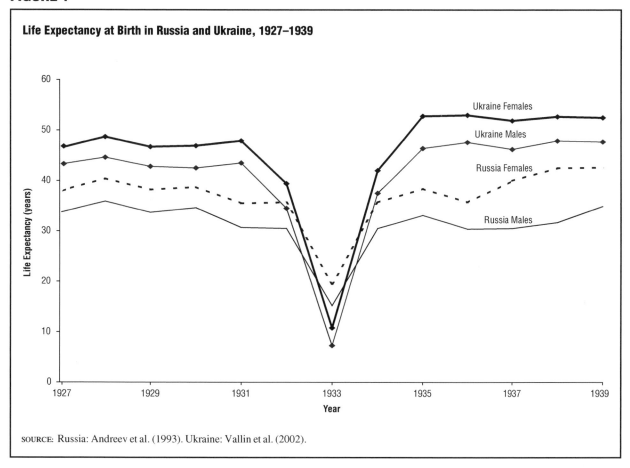

Life Expectancy at Birth in Russia and Ukraine, 1927–1939

SOURCE: Russia: Andreev et al. (1993). Ukraine: Vallin et al. (2002).

migrants, Stalin forbade people to move, a measure enforced by the NKVD. Cases of cannibalism were recorded.

The official Soviet position denied the existence of this famine. It was forbidden to write about it. The only response of the Soviet authorities was to supply seeds for the summer 1933 crop in Ukraine and other areas, thereby helping to end the calamitous consequences of the Stalinist approach to governing the country.

The third and last major Soviet famine followed World War II. Its immediate cause was failure of the 1946 harvest, the result of a drought affecting the western regions of the country. But the deeper origins were in part the same as those of the 1933 famine. After the privations of the war, people were very weak and sensitive to any new shortages. But Stalin wanted to continue to export grain, as well as supplying towns and the army. Compulsory procurements of grain and other foodstuffs from the collective farms were raised beyond the limits of

feasibility. The result was about 1 to 1.5 million deaths from starvation or disease.

See also: *Communism, Population Aspects of; Ethnic Cleansing; Forced Migration.*

BIBLIOGRAPHY

Adamets, Serge. 2003. *Guerre civile et famine en Russie: le pouvoir bolchévique et la population face à la catastrophe démographique, 1917–1923.* Paris: Institut d'Études Slaves.

Andreev, Evgenij, Darskij, Leonid, and Khar'kova, Tatiana. 1998. *Demograficheskaya istoriya Rossii: 1927–1959.* [The Demographic History of Russia: 1927–1959]. Moscow: Informatika.

Blum, Alain. 1994. *Naître, vivre et mourir en URSS, 1917–1991.* Paris: Plon.

Vallin, Jacques, Meslé, France, Adamets, Serguei and Pyrozhkov Serhii. 2003. "A New Estimation of

Ukrainian Losses during the 30's and 40's Crises." *Population Studies* Vol. 3.

Wheatcroft, Stephen. 2001. "O demograficheskikh svidetel'stvakh tragedii sovetskoi derevni v 1931–1933gg." ["About demographic evidence of the tragedy of the soviet villages in 1931–1933"], In *Tragediya Sovetskoi Derevni: Kollektivizatsiya i raskulachivanie, Dokumenty i Materialy,* Vol. 3: *Konets 1930–1933,* ed. I. Zelenin, V. Danilov, L. Viola, R. Manning, R.W. Davies, S. G. Wheatcroft, et al. Rosspen: Moscow. pp. 866–887.

Wheatcroft, Stephen, and Robert Davies. 2002. "Soviet Famine of 1932–33 and the Crisis in Agriculture" In *Challenging Traditional Views of Russian History,* ed. Stephen Wheatcroft. Palgrave: Macmillan. pp. 69–91.

ALAIN BLUM

FARR, WILLIAM

(1807–1883)

William Farr, a physician by training, was the most prominent expert in vital statistics in Great Britain in the nineteenth century. After completing his medical studies in London and in Paris, where he became a disciple of Dr. Pierre-Charles-Alexandre Louis and his *méthode numérique,* Farr set up a practice as a pharmacist in 1833. He contributed a chapter to John Ramsey McCulloch's *A Statistical Account of the British Empire* (1837), showing his skill in presenting and interpreting vital statistics but arguing that the government still had too little knowledge about diseases to be successful in reducing mortality. This was the origin of one of his lifelong concerns: improving data on the cause of death.

Farr joined Britain's General Register Office (GRO) in 1839 as Compiler of Abstracts and became Statistical Superintendant some years later. From 1840 to 1880 he seems to have been the key person behind all the reports issued by the GRO, including the *Annual Reports* to Parliament. As early as 1839 he proposed a classification of causes of death on the basis of illness location in the body. At the first international conference on statistics (1855), he presented a new proposed classification in competition with the Swiss physician and medical statistician Marc-Jacob d'Espine. Great Britain used the first of Farr's schemes for its statistics until 1860 and the second until 1880.

Farr constructed life tables for England and Wales for 1841, 1838–1844, and 1851. The technical innovations he introduced included a formula to derive life-table survival rates from mortality rates and the use of standardized mortality rates. In 1880 he published a sort of reproduction table but did not arrive at the notion of the reproduction rate. For Britain's censuses he added new categories of occupations and disabilities.

Farr participated in many commissions dealing with sanitary reforms, notably for the armies affected by diseases in the Crimea and India. He was a Fellow of the Royal Society, president (1871–1873) of the Statistical Society of London, and the recipient of other forms of academic recognition but never became, as he had hoped, Registrar General.

See also: *Bertillon, Jacques; Causes of Death; Demography, History of; Disease, Concepts and Classification of; Life Tables.*

BIBLIOGRAPHY

Hamlin, Christopher. 1998. *Public Health and Social Justice in the Age of Chadwick. Britain, 1800–1854.* Cambridge, Eng.: Cambridge University Press.

Humphrey, Noel, ed. 1885/1975. *Vital Statistics: A Memorial Volume of Selections from the Reports and Writings of William Farr,* ed. Sanitary Institute of Great Britain. London: Scarecrow.

Stone, Richard. 1997. *Some British Empiricists in the Social Sciences 1650–1900.* Cambridge, Eng.: Cambridge University Press.

Wall, Richard. 1974. *Mortality in Mid 19th Century Britain.* Heppenheim/Bergstrasse, Germany: Gregg International, D.C. Heath.

Woods, Robert, and Nicola Shelton. 1997. *An Atlas of Victorian Mortality.* Liverpool, Eng.: Liverpool University Press.

Wrigley, E. Antony, and Roger Schofield. 1981. *The Population History of England, 1541–1871: A Re-*

construction. Cambridge, Eng.: Cambridge University Press.

PATRICE BOURDELAIS

FECUNDITY

Fecundity is the physiological capability of a woman, man, or couple to reproduce, that is, to produce a live birth. Unless both partners are fecund, no birth can occur. In contrast, *fertility* is the actual reproductive output of an individual, couple, or group. Considerable confusion results from the fact that in French and other Romance languages, the meanings of fecundity and fertility are reversed; for example, the French *fécondité* is equivalent to the English fertility and the French *fertilité* is equivalent to the English fecundity. English-speaking physicians also use fertility to mean fecundity. Confusion also exists because demographers have defined fecundity as the capacity to reproduce but have defined *fecundable* as the capacity to conceive, and *fecundability* as the per-cycle probability of conception, regardless of whether that pregnancy results in a live birth.

Whereas fertility can be directly observed and measured, fecundity cannot. Demographers, statisticians, and epidemiologists have developed techniques for indirectly estimating the incidence of sterility (the inability to produce a live birth), for directly estimating the incidence of fetal loss, and for estimating conception probabilities by cycle day of intercourse. The measures of sterility, fecundability, and conception probabilities necessarily pertain to a couple and not to an individual.

Logically, fecundity depends on a sequence of events. The female must produce an egg capable of being fertilized, the male must produce sperm that can fertilize the egg, fertilization must occur, the fertilized egg must survive to implant in the uterus, and—once implantation has occurred—the pregnancy must result in a live birth. Successful progression along this sequence can be influenced by many factors.

Age

Fecundity varies among individuals and couples of a given age. The fecundity of groups declines with

FIGURE 1

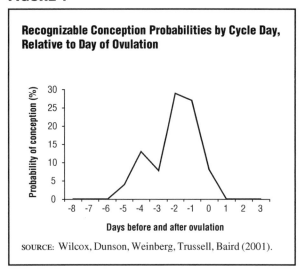

Recognizable Conception Probabilities by Cycle Day, Relative to Day of Ovulation

SOURCE: Wilcox, Dunson, Weinberg, Trussell, Baird (2001).

the aging of women as increasing percentages of women become sterile because they are unable to become pregnant and due to fetal loss. This increase is modest through the 30s and rises sharply thereafter until virtually all women are sterile at about age 50. It is plausible that the fecundity of individual women also declines with age, although that decline is likely to be less pronounced before a rather rapid loss in reproductive capacity is experienced. In contrast, fecundity of males does not appear to decline until well after age 50. The risk of fetal loss rises with age only from the mid-30s or early 40s. There is considerable heterogeneity in the risk of fetal loss— some women are highly prone whereas others are not—thereby creating heterogeneity in fecundity.

Intercourse and Pregnancy-Related Factors

Among ovulating women having intercourse, whether a particular cycle will result in pregnancy depends on the frequency and timing of intercourse. If intercourse does not occur in a fairly narrow time segment extending from five days before ovulation to the day of ovulation, then the risk of pregnancy is exceedingly low (Figure 1).

The more often intercourse occurs within this time segment, the more likely it is that pregnancy will occur; however, the maximum probability is surprisingly small, only about 40 percent. (The maximum probability of conception from a single intercourse optimally timed within a cycle is about 30 percent.) This per-cycle probability of conception, technically known as fecundability (introduced by the Italian demographer and statistician Corrado

Gini in 1924), can be directly estimated without reference to conception probabilities by cycle day among regularly menstruating women not using contraception; a typical value would be about 20 percent among young women. Even when the timing and frequency of intercourse are held constant, fecundability can be reduced by both involuntary and voluntary factors. It is reduced by irregular ovulation around menarche and menopause, lactation (both because ovulation is suppressed and—when ovulation is resumed—because of a decreased likelihood of successful implantation), by smoking, by the sexually transmitted infections chlamydia and gonorrhea (due to tubal scarring), by strenuous physical activity among women, by extreme malnutrition, probably as women get older (at least above age 40), and by use of contraception. Worldwide, the most important of these would be contraception in countries in which deliberate birth control is widespread. When this is not the case, lactation can be an important factor reducing fecundability. Elective abortion reduces fecundity worldwide to a far greater extent than fetal loss.

Sexually Transmitted Diseases

Sexually transmitted infections have major effects on fecundity (and fertility) in certain populations. Syphilis is an important cause of fetal loss among women with primary or secondary infections and may be an important factor contributing to low fertility among certain tribal groups in Burkina Faso and the Central African Republic. Untreated pelvic inflammatory disease caused by chlamydia and gonorrhea is a major cause of tubal scarring and sterility. The low fertility characteristic of Central Africa (a belt extending from the west coast of Cameroon and Gabon through northern Congo into southwest Sudan) in the 1950s and 1960s was attributed to a high prevalence of gonorrhea, long before the additional role of chlamydia was recognized. In sub-Saharan Africa, gonorrhea and chlamydia are still common infections. Widespread in equatorial regions, yaws and pinta, while not sexually transmitted, are closely related to syphilis and are also treatable with penicillin. Mass penicillin campaigns against gonorrhea (New Guinea), yaws (Martinique), and yaws and pinta (Cameroon, Burkina Faso, Congo, and Zambia) were followed by substantial increases in fertility. It is possible that improved diagnosis and treatment of sexually transmitted infections in sub-Saharan Africa as a component of AIDS prevention programs will also result in increased fecundity.

Nutrition

A link between nutrition and fertility has been postulated as a relatively simple explanation for variations in marital fertility in populations that do not use contraception. It is suggested that the lower the nutritional status of a population, the lower the fecundity and hence fertility. Chronic malnutrition probably does result in a delay in menarche, but the reduction in fecundity among adolescents resulting from that delay is unlikely to have an important effect on fertility. When food supplies are so short that there is outright famine and starvation, fecundity and hence fertility are sharply reduced. But when malnourishment is chronic and food intake is above starvation levels, there does not appear to be an important nutrition–fertility link.

The Future

In the not so distant future, the use of current and new technologies in reproductive biology and genetics could greatly modify the situations described above, rendering the infecund fecund.

See also: *Fertility, Age Patterns of; Fertility, Proximate Determinants of; Infertility; Natural Fertility; Spontaneous Abortion.*

BIBLIOGRAPHY

Bongaarts, John, and Robert G. Potter. 1983. *Fertility, Biology, and Behavior.* New York: Academic Press.

Leridon, Henri. 1977. *Human Fertility: The Basic Components.* Chicago: The University of Chicago Press.

Menken, Jane, James Trussell, and Ulla Larsen. 1986. "Age and Infertility." *Science* 233(4771): 1389–1394.

Pressat, Roland. 1985. *The Dictionary of Demography,* ed. Christopher Wilson. Oxford: Basil Blackwell.

Silver, Lee M. 1998. *Remaking Eden: How Genetic Engineering and Cloning Will Transform the American Family.* New York: Avon Books.

Trussell, James, and Chris Wilson. 1985. "Sterility in a Population with Natural Fertility." *Population Studies* 39: 269–286.

Weinberg, Clarise R., Beth C. Gladden, and Allen J. Wilcox. 1994. "Models Relating the Timing of Intercourse to the Probability of Conception and the Sex of the Baby." *Biometrics* 50: 358–367.

Wilcox, Allen J., David B. Dunson, Clarise R. Weinberg, James Trussell, and Donna Day Baird. 2001. "On the Assessment of Post-Coital Contraceptives." *Contraception* 63(4): 211–215.

JAMES TRUSSELL

FEMINIST PERSPECTIVES ON POPULATION ISSUES

Although feminists differ among themselves on many issues, most feminist activists share a commitment to equal rights and resources for women and men. Scholars of gender study the social forces that affect gender inequality. Many of them have pointed out that traditional scholarship in the social sciences, including demography, often ignores gender inequalities or assumes that they are "natural." Because of their critical attention to gender inequality, gender scholars are often referred to as feminist. Both groups of feminists—scholars and activists—have influenced policy debates, moving the issues of women's reproductive health and empowerment closer to the center of development and population policies.

Feminist Activists and Population Policy

Policy debates about population and related debates about economic development, environmental degradation, and inequalities of class, race, nation, and gender raise the issue of women's empowerment. Population policy raises the specific issue of reproductive rights. Feminist activists have made strenuous efforts to ensure that women's empowerment and reproductive rights have a central place in these policy discussions.

Feminists have always been divided on the importance of birth control to women's liberation. Early feminists such as Annie Besant (1847–1933) in England and Emma Goldman (1869–1940) and Margaret Sanger (1883–1966) in the United States were pioneers in the birth control movement. However, most U.S. suffragists at the start of the twentieth century dissociated themselves from birth control, believing that its advocacy was too controversial and might hurt their principal goal of gaining women the right to vote. In later years feminist activists in affluent nations supported access to contraception to allow women and couples to limit fertility, believing that this would improve women's lives and status.

The time and energy women spend in child rearing is a major factor limiting women's participation in employment, politics, and other public roles, and one way to reduce this burden is to have fewer children. (Another way is to increase men's participation in child rearing, but changing men's roles has proved difficult.) In recent decades women's access to legal abortion has been a key feminist issue in the United States.

Some feminists in industrialized countries (the North) have aligned themselves with activists in the population control and environmental movements who see population growth as an important world problem in its own right, threatening the environment and prospects for economic development in the South. These positions sometimes have caused disagreements between Northern and Southern feminists. Feminist activists in the South are often unconvinced that population growth is a high-priority problem. Like many others in their countries, they emphasize the role of poverty, underdevelopment, and unequal distribution of resources between the North and the South as key causes of high fertility rather than seeing high fertility as a major cause of poverty and economic backwardness. This difference of emphasis parallels a debate in the North's environmental movement about whether excessive resource consumption in the North or overpopulation in the South is the more significant problem.

Southern feminists also have been critical of the implementation of population policies, arguing that programs in many countries distributed contraceptive supplies and services with little regard for the health of the women who used them and were evaluated by the number of users or the reduction in fertility rather than by the health and satisfaction of program clients. They are particularly critical of any pressure on women to use birth control. Some regard the affluent northern emphasis on curbing southern fertility as racist or, at best, an excuse not to alter the distribution of resources between the North and the South.

This difference between northern and southern feminists mirrors the interaction of gender with other axes of privilege that arise in within-nation debates on population issues. For example, African-American, Native American, and Puerto Rican women in the United States, though favoring women's access to birth control, have deemphasized high nonmarital birth rates as a critical problem, preferring a policy emphasis on decreasing racism in health systems and employment, improvement of the social safety net, and state provision of universal access to health services. They are more troubled by women being unable to find the resources to raise children decently than by the prospect of women having too many children.

Feminists and the Cairo Agenda

Despite these differences in emphasis, most feminists are united in wanting reproductive freedom and reproductive health services, broadly defined, available to women as a basic human right even when this is resisted by men in their families or by political and religious leaders. The United Nations International Conference on Population and Development in Cairo in 1994 saw the formation of an important coalition between southern and northern feminists. This world forum was a high point of feminist influence on international population policy. Many governments, international agencies, and influential nongovernmental bodies were persuaded of the instrumental value of women's empowerment (in the form of access to education and jobs and more control over all aspects of their lives) in decreasing fertility and promoting sustainable economic development. Beyond this instrumental approach, northern and southern feminists together were influential in winning support for language declaring women's rights and empowerment to be goals in their own right, not only means to stabilize population size. The conference document, known as the Cairo Agenda, supports family planning programs but denounces coercion or numerical targets for contraceptive practice or number of births. Moreover, Principle 4 of the Program of Action states:

> Advancing gender equality and equity and the empowerment of women, and the elimination of all kinds of violence against women, and ensuring women's ability to control their own fertility, are cornerstones of population and development-related programmes.

Southern feminists concerned with reproductive health seek to improve maternal and child health programs, including family planning; offer treatment for reproductive tract infections, sexually transmitted diseases, HIV, and breast cancer; make abortion available; discourage female genital mutilation; and provide sex education that contributes to a satisfying sex life for women that is free from coercion by men. The Cairo document, with its broad language, may make it more likely that some of the resources already committed to population programs will be used to achieve these goals.

Feminist Critiques of the New Home Economics

Feminist scholarship has been strongly critical of much of the "new home economics," the application of microeconomic theory to household behavior that is associated particularly with the work of the economist Gary Becker. Models in this tradition typically ignore issues of distribution within the family, assuming that the family "head" acts altruistically toward other family members and that each family acts to maximize a single utility function. They interpret marriage as an institution that allows men and women to capitalize on the efficiencies of specialization, with husbands engaging in market production for earnings while wives engage in child rearing and other production in the household.

As wage levels rise for both men and women, so does the opportunity cost of having a child and having a woman stay home to rear it. Neoclassical economists believe that higher wage levels lead families to shift to lower fertility, higher female employment, and more purchased child-care services. In Becker's view this also lowers the gains from specialization, which are a major motivation for marriage; therefore, increases in women's wages will lower marriage rates.

How have feminists responded to the new home economics? On the positive side they see it as an advance to recognize household production as real work, unlike the viewpoint of traditional labor economics. Indeed, they would want to follow this recognition to its logical consequence: adding household production to national accounts so that nations keep records on the total product of both their market and household economies rather than including only production involving cash exchange.

However, in many other respects feminists have been critical of the new home economics, particularly in its ignoring of male power over women in the family and society. Some men beat and rape their wives, laws are made and enforced by largely male bodies, major religions teach that women should "submit" to their husbands, a double standard of sexuality is common, and in some poor nations women and girls eat less and receive less schooling and health care than do men and boys, to the detriment of their health and longevity. The image of an altruistic male head who takes all family members' preferences into account disguises the realities of male dominance.

Gender scholars argue that men's greater access to money gives husbands power over their wives. They point out that women can ill afford to argue with their husbands when the husband controls resources in the family and when their economic alternatives if they leave a marriage are grim. In this view the specialization that economists might characterize as "efficient" and productive of "joint gains" disadvantages women relative to men in terms of how material well-being and decision-making power are distributed within families. Some economists are incorporating this perspective in formulating bargaining models of the household, drawing on game theory. Gender scholars argue that men's higher earnings result in part from sex discrimination in labor markets.

Men's power in the family is determined not only by access to money but by a combination of social, cultural, and political forces, including social norms that mandate that women should defer to men's authority, peer group norms among men that valorize sexual conquest and harass women who try to enter "men's" jobs, preferential investment in boys' education, employers' discrimination against women, and low funding of public support for single mothers. These broad social factors constitute and perpetuate gender inequality in the family and other arenas of life.

Many gender scholars agree with Becker that rising wage opportunities for women generally increase women's employment and reduce fertility. However, they point out another consequence ignored in Becker's perspective: When women have more con-

trol over a family's money, more is spent on children. Hence, empowering women may contribute to economic development through improvements in the health and capabilities of the next generation. Conversely, in settings where men receive more of the benefits and women pay more of the costs of rearing children, men may push their wives to have more children and there may be more gender specialization than women would prefer.

Feminist Perspectives on Low Fertility

Although patriarchy may encourage high fertility in poor countries, some gender scholars argue that in affluent nations aspects of the remaining gender inequality now have the opposite effect, contributing to continued fertility decline below the replacement level. Two types of gender role change would diminish gender inequality: Women could increase their participation in traditionally male activities (e.g., wage labor), and men could increase their participation in traditionally female activities. In fact, change in gender roles is highly asymmetric: Both material incentives and social norms encourage women to take on traditionally male pursuits much more than they encourage men to do more housework and care for young children. Women continue to bear more of the costs of raising children. Without changes in men's participation in child rearing, women may continue to reduce the number of children they have or raise children on their own.

Most child-care work—both the unpaid care of children at home and paid jobs such as child-care worker, teacher, nurse, and counselor—is done by women. The time women spend at home reduces their future earnings and pension entitlements as well as lowering their power within a marriage. When done in the market, child-care work has low pay relative to its educational requirements. The usual neoclassical economic explanation of wage differentials net of human capital is that at the margin the intrinsic satisfaction of helping people must compensate for the lack of pay for the worker. Gender scholars believe that this is only part of the explanation. They suggest that gender bias may pervade the labor market at many levels: Care work pays less because of crowding (women are kept out of "male" occupations) and because employers have a blind spot when it comes to the value of work done by women. Those who most need care (children, the sick, and the elderly) are often not able to pay much for this service. However, its social importance is undeniable: It increases the capabilities of recipients (their physical, mental, and emotional health and skills), benefiting both their own well-being and that of many of the people the recipients interact with, making them better parents, workers, and neighbors.

Because markets will not compensate caregivers for these diffuse public goods, feminist scholars have argued that there is a similar rationale for supporting all caregiving work as there is for state support of education. However, such additional claims on state budgets conflict with demands for limiting the size of the public sector. In nations in both the North and the South state payment of the salaries of care workers such as teachers and health workers, as well as the public safety net that provides a minimum income for those doing care work at home, has been challenged by politicians who believe the public sector should be downsized and markets should be expanded. In the South service cuts made under neoliberal structural adjustment policies have often fallen hardest on women. In the North state provision of income to single mothers is under challenge, although income and medical support for the elderly remains uncontroversial and takes up a large share of nonmilitary spending. The affluent countries have collectivized a major traditional benefit of having children while keeping the major cost of children— the opportunity cost of time—private. The extent to which the state collectivizes the costs (including opportunity costs) of rearing children may well affect both women's well-being and their fertility. A feminist perspective offers important insights into these and similar demographic dimensions of public policy.

See also: *Evolutionary Demography; Family Bargaining; Gender; Reproductive Rights; Sanger, Margaret; Women's Status and Demographic Behavior.*

BIBLIOGRAPHY

Agarwal, Bina. 1995. *A Field of Her Own: Gender and Land Rights in South Asia.* Cambridge, Eng.: Cambridge University Press.

Becker, Gary. 1991. *A Treatise on the Family.* Cambridge, MA: Harvard University Press.

Bergmann, Barbara. 1986. *The Economic Emergence of Women.* New York: Basic Books.

Dixon-Mueller, Ruth. 1993. *Population Policy and Women's Rights: Transforming Reproductive Choice.* Westport, CT: Praeger.

Dwyer, Daisy H., and Judith Bruce. 1988. *A Home Divided: Women and Income in the Third World.* Stanford, CA: Stanford University Press.

England, Paula. 1992. *Comparable Worth: Theories and Evidence.* New York: Aldine de Gruyter.

England, Paula, and Michelle Budig. 1998. "Gary Becker on the Family: His Genius, Impact, and Blind Spots." In *Required Reading: Sociology's Most Influential Books,* ed. Dan Clawson. Amherst: University of Massachusetts Press.

England, Paula, and George Farkas. 1986. *Households, Employment, and Gender: A Social, Economic, and Demographic View.* New York: Aldine de Gruyter.

England, Paula, and Nancy Folbre. 1999. "The Cost of Caring." *Annals of the American Academy of Political and Social Sciences* 561: 39–51.

Ferber, Marianne, and Julie Nelson, eds. 1993. *Beyond Economic Man: Feminist Theory and Economics.* Chicago: University of Chicago Press.

Folbre, Nancy. 1994. *Who Pays for the Kids? Gender and the Structures of Constraint.* London: Routledge.

Grown, Caren, Diane Elson, and Nilüfer Çagatay, eds. 2000. *Growth, Trade, Finance and Gender Inequality.* Special Issue of *World Development.*

Hartmann, Betsy. 1995. *Reproductive Rights and Wrongs: The Global Politics of Population Control and Contraceptive Choice,* revised edition. Boston: South End Press.

Hodgson, Dennis, and Susan Cotts Watkins. 1997. "Feminists and Neo-Malthusians: Past and Present Alliances." *Population and Development Review* 23: 469–523.

Ironmonger, Duncan S. 1996. "Counting Outputs, Capital Inputs, and Caring Labor: Estimating Gross Household Product." *Feminist Economics* 2: 37–64.

Kabeer, Naila. 2001. "Family Bargaining." *International Encyclopedia of the Social and Behavioral Sciences* 8: 5314–5319. London: Elsevier.

Lundberg, Shelly, and Robert Pollak. 1996. "Bargaining and Distribution in Marriage." *Journal of Economic Perspectives* 10: 139–158.

O'Connor, Julia S., Ann Shola Orloff, and Sheila Shaver. 1999. *States, Markets, Families: Gender, Liberalism and Social Policy in Australia, Canada, Great Britain and the United States.* Cambridge, Eng.: Cambridge University Press.

Presser, Harriet B., and Gita Sen, eds. 2000. *Women's Empowerment and Demographic Processes.* Oxford: Oxford University Press.

Riley, Nancy E. 1997. "Gender, Power, and Population Change." *Population Bulletin* 52: 1–48.

Sen, Amartya. 1990. "More Than 100 Million Women Are Missing." *New York Review of Books* December 20, pp. 61–66.

Sen, Gita, Adrienne Germain, and Lincoln C. Chen, eds. 1994. *Population Policies Reconsidered: Health, Empowerment, and Rights.* Boston: Harvard University Press.

United Nations. 1994. "Programme of Action" of the 1994 International Conference on Population and Development, Cairo, Egypt, October 18. A/CONF.171/13. New York: United Nations.

Paula England

FERTILITY, AGE PATTERNS OF

For biological and social reasons, the probability of a woman's having a child in a given time interval is strongly influenced by her age. The age pattern of fertility of a woman's cohort (that is, the group of women born at the same time) represents the sequence of births and inter-birth intervals over that cohort's reproductive life span. However, the data needed to calculate cohort age patterns of fertility may be obtained only from special sample surveys or population registers. Period age-specific fertility rates, which are derived from data that are more widely available, relate the annual number of births to women of a particular age group (usually one-year or five-year age groups) within the reproductive age range (15 to 49) to the mid-year population size of that age group. (Age-specific fertility rates may also be computed for men, although that is infrequently done.) The set of such period rates for a

given time necessarily refers to many different cohorts. The sum of those rates is the (period) total fertility rate. The percentage contributions of age-specific fertility rates to the total fertility rate describe the age pattern of fertility. Because the age-specific fertility rates are not affected by the age composition of the population, they are suitable for comparing age patterns of fertility between populations and over time. Monitoring the age patterns of fertility is important for understanding fertility levels and trends.

Fertility Age Patterns

High fertility is associated with childbearing starting early and continuing until the late reproductive years. However, since women in high-fertility populations typically keep bearing children as long as they remain fecund, the age pattern of fertility is relatively flat. Fertility transition occurs through decreases of fertility at both ends of the reproductive life span, resulting in a more convex age pattern. The decrease of fertility at younger ages is often the result of rising ages at marriage, whereas fertility declines at the older ages primarily because of an increasing propensity to limit family size. The balance of these two trends is context-specific and leads either to "aging" or to "rejuvenation" of the age pattern of fertility.

Age Patterns and the Fertility Transition

Different age patterns of fertility are illustrated in Figure 1 for three groups of countries that in the late 1990s were at different stages of the fertility transition. In the pre-transitional least-developed countries (most of them in sub-Saharan Africa) the total fertility rate averages 5.5 children per woman, 40 percent of which is contributed, on average, by women of age 30 and older. For other developing countries that are progressing through the fertility transition, with total fertility rates averaging 2.8 children per woman, this share drops to 30 percent. In the developed countries, where the demographic transition has been concluded and average total fertility rates are 1.6 births per woman, the share has risen again, to 35 percent.

Fertility often decreases more at older ages than at younger ages during the early stages of the fertility transition, thus resulting in a lowering of the mean age at childbearing and rejuvenation of the fertility pattern. This happened in most developed countries from the late nineteenth century until the 1970s. At the early stages of the fertility transition, a similar

FIGURE 1

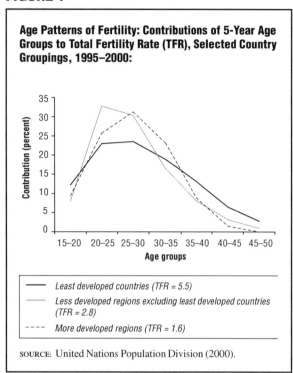

Age Patterns of Fertility: Contributions of 5-Year Age Groups to Total Fertility Rate (TFR), Selected Country Groupings, 1995–2000:

Least developed countries (TFR = 5.5)

Less developed regions excluding least developed countries (TFR = 2.8)

More developed regions (TFR = 1.6)

SOURCE: United Nations Population Division (2000).

FIGURE 2

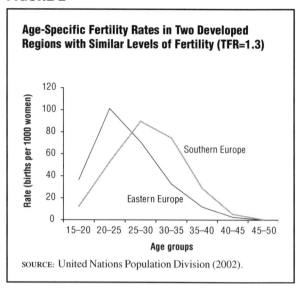

Age-Specific Fertility Rates in Two Developed Regions with Similar Levels of Fertility (TFR=1.3)

SOURCE: United Nations Population Division (2002).

pattern of change was typical for many developing countries of south central and Southeast Asia and Latin America and the Caribbean. Declines in fertility at young ages due to increasing age at marriage initially had a smaller impact on total fertility in comparison to the effects of stopping behavior among older women.

At the later stages of the fertility transition, the balance of these two influences typically shifts, resulting in an increase in the average age of childbearing. In northern Africa and several western Asian countries, the greater part of the fertility decline from the high levels of the 1970s or 1980s to the intermediate or low levels of the 1990s was caused primarily by rising age at marriage, which in the absence of extramarital fertility led to later childbearing.

In the developed countries, fertility decline to replacement level was achieved mostly through a decreasing incidence of high-parity births to relatively older women. Faster decreases of fertility at older ages outweighed the effect on the average age of childbearing of the increasing age at first birth. As a result, the age pattern of childbearing rejuvenated. But the trends toward a younger age pattern of fertility reversed in most developed countries since the

1980s. The aging of age patterns of fertility was especially pronounced in the 1990s. Below-replacement age patterns of fertility are characterized by low levels of fertility among young women (women in their twenties) because of postponement of childbearing until the early and even late thirties and by the fact that large proportions of women stop having additional children after one or two. The shift toward such a pattern has caused the average age at childbearing to rise: Data for around the year 2000 show fertility typically peaking in the age interval from 25 to 29 years; in some countries the peak is in the age group from 30 to 34. In Eastern Europe, however, the age at first birth traditionally was and has remained lower than in other developed regions; consequently, the age pattern of fertility there is young, with the highest fertility in the age group 20 to 24, as shown in Figure 2.

Significance of Age Patterns

Aging of childbearing has an important impact on fertility levels and trends. When childbearing starts before age 20, as is typical in developing countries, the period available for childbearing lasts for approximately 24 years and the period of high fecundity (lasting until around age 35) is 17 to 18 years long. Shortening of the childbearing period in women's lives is an important determinant of persistent below-replacement fertility in many developed and an increasing number of developing countries. In fact, although earlier menarche lengthens the fecund life span, postponement of first births until around age 30 shortens the effectively used fecund period to 12 years and the effectively used period of high fecundability to just 5 to 6 years. When young women postpone births and subsequently try to make up these postponed births in their late 30s or beyond, they are often confronted with increasing likelihood of failure to conceive. Thus, shifts in the schedule of childbearing toward older age depress fertility levels.

See also: *Adolescent Fertility; Mortality, Age Patterns of; Natural Fertility.*

BIBLIOGRAPHY

Hinde, Andrew. 1998. *Demographic Analysis.* New York: Oxford University Press.

Lesthaeghe, Ron, and Paul Willems. 1999. "Is Low Fertility a Temporary Phenomenon in the European Union?" *Population and Development Review* 25(2): 211–228.

Rallu, Jean-Louis, and Laurent Toulemon. 1994. "Period Fertility Measures: The Construction of Different Indices and their Application to France, 1946–89." *Population: English Edition* 6: 59–96.

United Nations Population Division. 2000. "Fertility Trends Among Low Fertility Countries." *Population Bulletin of the United Nations* 40/41: 35–125.

———. 2000. *World Population Prospects: The 2000 Revision.* CD-ROM Sales No. E.01.XII.3. New York: United Nations.

Serguey Ivanov
Vasantha Kandiah

FERTILITY, BELOW-REPLACEMENT

Below-replacement fertility is defined as a combination of fertility and mortality levels that leads to a negative population growth rate, hence a declining population size, in a closed stable population. Equivalent definitions of the term, still with reference to a closed stable population, include: the number of deaths exceeds the number of births; the absolute number of births declines over time; the life-expectancy is below the inverse of the crude birth rate; and the net reproduction rate (NRR) is below one. As the reference to the NRR indicates, *replacement* is most conveniently interpreted for a single-sex (female) population: replacement then means that one female generation replaces itself in the next generation. This condition is satisfied if 1,000 newborn female babies—that is to say, their survivors—give birth to 1,000 female babies over their lifetime; or, equivalently, if 1,000 women at age 15 have female births over their lifetime in numbers that yield 1,000 women survivors at age 15 in the next generation.

The most common measure of fertility, the period total fertility rate (TFR), refers, however, to a two-sex population: it includes both male and female births. TFR indicates the number of births women would have, on average, if during their reproductive lifetime they experienced the age-specific fertility rates observed in a given period (such as a year) in the absence of mortality. It is evident from the definitions above that the TFR, by itself, does not provide an unambiguous definition of below-replacement fertility. Yet a TFR of 2.1 is often referred to as the replacement level fertility. It is in fact a good approximation to replacement level under conditions of very low mortality. The value 2.1 reflects the fact that the sex ratio at birth (the ratio of male births to female births) is about 1.05 in most human populations. Thus replacement of the population would require that, in the complete absence of mortality, women on average have 2.05 children (i.e., 1,000 women would have to have 1,000 female births and 1,050 male births). The small difference between 2.1 and 2.05 allows for the effect of mortality—a good enough approximation, as noted above, in very low mortality populations. In such populations, then, a TFR below 2.1 is below-replacement fertility. But when mortality is higher, below-replacement fertility may be present even though TFR are levels considerably higher than 2.1. How much higher will depend primarily on the overall level of mortality and, to a lesser but not negligible extent, also on the precise age pattern of mortality and fertility. The following are the replacement levels for TFRs associated with various levels of $\mathring{e}_0$ (life expectancy at birth)—a good summary index of the overall level of mortality—and an average age of maternity of 29 years. Each of these combinations yields

TABLE 1

Replacement-Level Total Fertility Rates at Various Levels of Mortality

$\overset{\circ}{e}_0$ (years)	TFR
25	5.21
35	3.83
45	3.08
55	2.61
65	2.30
75	2.11
80	2.06

SOURCE: Coale and Demeny (1983).

stable populations with a zero rate of population growth (see Table 1).

TFR values lower than those indicated imply stable populations with negative growth rates. If the shortfall is substantial, the rate of population decline in the stable state will be rapid. For instance, a TFR of 1.3 implies an annual decline of the population size by approximately 1.5 percent in a stable population with very low mortality levels. Such a decline implies a reduction of the birth cohort by 50 percent and a halving of the population size every 45 years. Small TFR differences become increasingly important when fertility is lower: a difference of 0.3 between a total fertility rate of 1.0 and 1.3 is approximately equivalent, in terms of stable population growth rates, to the more than threefold greater difference between a total fertility rate of 3.2 and 4.2 in high fertility contexts (assuming low mortality in both instances).

If a population is not stable but has an age distribution shaped by fluctuating past fertility and/or mortality levels, the above definitions of below-replacement fertility are no longer equivalent. Replacement in the period sense—that is, a zero difference between births and deaths occurring in a given calendar year—depends strongly on the prevailing age structure of the population. A period TFR of 2.1 (assuming low mortality) may then be associated with a surplus of births over deaths if women of childbearing age represent an unusually high share of the population (compared to the share in the stable population implied by the prevailing fertility and mortality) and a surplus of deaths over births if women of childbearing age are underrepresented. Similarly, replacement in a cohort sense depends on the long-term trend in TFR levels. Thus, temporary

shortfalls of period fertility from replacement level can be consistent with full cohort replacement if there is sufficient subsequent recovery in period fertility. The common, if casual, use of TFR interprets the eventual average fertility a cohort would experience if subject to the current period fertility pattern during its life-course as not just an indicator of the current level of fertility but as implying also its long-term continuation. Hence familiar statements are often used such as "Italian women in the late 1990s have 1.2 children." Such interpretations of the period TFR may, however, be misleading as the ultimate cohort experiences could turn out to be substantially different. In particular, the characteristic postponement of childbearing in many low fertility countries leads to tempo effects that reduce measures of period fertility below the level that would have been observed in the absence of timing changes. In addition, rapid fertility declines and/or delays imply that the period parity distribution is out of equilibrium, with an over-representation of women at higher parities; this condition further depresses period measures such as the TFR due to compositional effects.

Patterns of Below-Replacement Fertility

Fertility at or above replacement levels has prevailed for most of human history: by definition, it was necessary for human survival. As a long-term average, fertility must have been slightly above replacement. Above, since human numbers were growing; slightly, because average long-term growth was very slow. Nevertheless, below-replacement fertility is not a new phenomenon. Many human populations did become extinct in the remote and not so remote past. In almost every such case the main driving force was a high mortality rate that raised the level of fertility that would have been required for population replacement much above the actually prevailing fertility level. However, as mortality (up to the end of the childbearing years) increasingly came under control, fertility behavior became the key determinant of population growth. Low fertility strategies were initially adopted by some subpopulations, such as the bourgeoisie in nineteenth-century Europe, but the practice gradually spread also to other social classes. Despite this spread, overall fertility levels, reflecting still high mortality risks, remained relatively high. For instance, the lowest national fertility level at the beginning of the twentieth century was in France, which had a TFR of 2.79.

Total fertility levels below two, unambiguously below replacement, became common in many countries of the West in the period between World War I and II. This raised considerable concern about depopulation, even though population growth still continued, as the age distribution, reflecting past demographic conditions, temporarily delayed the onset of a decline in population numbers. After World War II, fertility levels rose significantly, creating the unexpected baby boom. But by the late 1950s in the United States and in the early 1960s in much of Europe, the trend reversed and fertility fell rapidly. By the end of the twentieth century, virtually all developed countries and a few developing countries exhibited below-replacement fertility and fertility levels in an increasing number of other developing countries were approaching a TFR of 2.1. The formerly quite distinct fertility regimes of the developed and the developing worlds have become increasingly similar.

Several features of this situation are particularly striking. First, the spread of below-replacement fertility to formerly high-fertility countries occurred at a remarkably rapid pace: The global convergence of fertility indicators has been quicker than the convergence of many other socioeconomic characteristics. Second, earlier notions that fertility levels may naturally stabilize close to replacement level have proven incorrect. In the early 1990s, for instance, fertility levels in Italy and Spain sank below a TFR of 1.3—an unprecedentedly low level for a national population. At the end of the 1990s there were 14 countries in Southern, Central, and Eastern Europe with TFRs of 1.3 or less. Several other countries, such as Germany, Japan, and South Korea, had TFRs not much above 1.3. Third, there has been a remarkable divergence in the fertility levels of developed countries. For instance, the TFR in the United States rose from a trough of 1.74 in 1976 to levels slightly above 2.05 in the late 1990s. Similarly, TFR levels in the Netherlands, Denmark, France, and several other countries have recovered and stabilized at between 1.7 and 1.9. This divergence of fertility levels in developed countries has been accompanied by a shift or even a reversal of many formerly observed associations between fertility and other demographic and social behaviors. For instance, the cross-sectional correlations in OECD countries (member countries of the Organisation for Economic Co-operation and Development) of fertility levels with the first marriage rate, the proportion of births outside marriage, and

the female labor force participation rate have reversed during the period from 1975 to 1999. At the end of the 1990s, divorce levels seemed no longer to be negatively associated with fertility levels in Europe. Hence, there have been crucial changes in the relationships of fertility to its traditional determinants—such as marriage, divorce, leaving home, and female labor force participation. A high prevalence of marriage and long-term partnerships is no longer associated with higher fertility in cross-sectional comparisons among European countries.

This reversal in cross-sectional associations between fertility and related behaviors is in part due to the different demographic factors driving fertility change. Initially, the decline toward low fertility has been strongly related to stopping behavior—that is, to a reduction in higher parity births. More recently, the postponement of fertility—particularly the postponement of first births—has emerged as a crucial determinant of differences in fertility levels among developed countries. For instance, during the period 1980 to 1999 the period mean age at first birth increased from 25.0 to 29.0 years in Spain and from 25.7 to 28.7 years in the Netherlands; in the United States it has increased from 22.0 years in 1972 to 24.9 in 2000. This postponement affects fertility levels through two distinct mechanisms. First, the tempo-distortions described earlier contribute to reduced period fertility levels. (These reductions may be absent or substantially muted in cohort fertility.) Second, delays in childbearing also affect parity progression probabilities because women start being at risk of higher parity births only at later ages.

Determinants of Below-Replacement Fertility

In light of these demographic factors leading to low fertility, explanations must differentiate between contexts where the primary response of individuals to changing socioeconomic circumstances is stopping behavior and contexts in which the primary response is postponement of births. In the former case, the key issue is what determines the demand for children and hence the quantum of fertility (the lifetime number of births per woman or its period equivalent calculated for synthetic cohorts). The frameworks used for explaining fertility decline during the demographic transitions are largely applicable in answering that question. For instance, theories of fertility variously relate reductions in the quantum of fertility to increased child costs, a reversal of intergenerational wealth flows, increased levels of education (especially for females), higher opportunity costs of time due to increased opportunities of female labor force participation, fertility-friendly population policies, and other factors affecting incentives for women or couples to have children. In general, it can be said that countries with below-replacement fertility share an institutional and socioeconomic context that favors an overall low quantum of fertility. In addition, there is evidence that the emergence and persistence of low fertility is also due to the diffusion of low fertility norms and value orientations. This explanation has been particularly emphasized in theorizing about the so-called second demographic transition, in which demographic change in developed countries since the 1970s has been closely linked to ideational shifts toward more postmodern, individualistic, and postmaterialistic value orientations. As a consequence, both acceptability and practice of cohabitation, out-of-wedlock childbearing, and divorce have increasingly spread through young cohorts along with desires for low fertility; these desires were achieved by the availability of effective contraception.

The factors explaining the emergence of below-replacement fertility over time can differ significantly from country to country. For example, as shown by Kohler and his colleagues in 2002, a rise in childlessness (as calculated in period terms) is not a primary driving force leading to very low fertility levels in Southern, Central, and Eastern European countries. Childlessness, however, does constitute an important factor in Germany and Austria. This suggests that even in situations characterized by fertility well below replacement level, biological, social, and economic incentives are generally strong enough to make most women (or couples) want at least one child, and that high levels of childlessness in some countries are likely due to special institutional factors that favor a polarization of fertility behavior toward either childlessness or relatively high fertility.

The reasons for the postponement of childbearing in many developed countries seem to be twofold. First, several factors make late childbearing a rational response to socioeconomic changes. These factors include increased incentives to invest in higher education and labor market experience, and economic uncertainty that may be particularly acute in early adulthood. Second, social interaction effects are likely to reinforce individuals' desire to delay childbearing in response to socioeconomic changes. These interaction effects are a result of social learning and social influence in the decision processes about the timing of fertility, and can also be caused by feedback in the labor and marriage market that make late fertility individually more rational the later the population age-pattern of fertility is. As a consequence of these interaction effects, a delay of childbearing follows what may be called a postponement transition. This is a behavioral shift that shares many characteristics with the earlier fertility transition in Europe and contemporary developing countries: It occurs across a wide range of socioeconomic conditions; once initiated, it results in a rapid and persistent delay in the timing of childbearing; and it is likely to continue even if the socioeconomic changes that initiated the transition are reversed.

In summary, therefore, the emergence and persistence of below-replacement fertility is related to three distinct transition processes: The (first) demographic transition leading to parity-specific stopping behavior within marriage; the second demographic transition resulting in ideational changes and in the rise of non-marital family forms; and, most recently, the postponement transition toward late childbearing regimes. As a consequence of the still ongoing postponement transition, the extent to which specific socioeconomic and institutional contexts accommodate late childbearing has emerged as an essential determinant of cross-country variation in fertility levels. In particular, the delay of childbearing is usually associated with substantially increased investments in female education and labor market experience prior to parenthood—investments that increase the opportunity costs of childbearing in terms of wages foregone. The extent to which these increased opportunity costs affect the quantum of fertility appears to be strongly influenced by the degree of compatibility between childbearing and female labor force participation. Countries with below replacement fertility show marked differences in this regard and these differences are reflected in the degree to which fertility falls short of replacement level. Countries with low compatibility between female labor force participation and childbearing, such as Italy and Spain, exhibit substantially delayed childbearing and especially large reductions in completed fertility.

The Future of Below-Replacement Fertility

Given the socioeconomic and institutional conditions that favor generally low fertility, it is difficult to foresee any widespread tendency for fertility levels in Europe or other developed countries to return to levels persistently above a TFR of 2.1. Many additional countries are likely to experience below-replacement fertility in the near future, and a TFR of 2.1 does not constitute a natural endpoint to the fertility decline. The feasibility of widespread, safe, and reliable childbearing above age 35 that could counteract some of the effects of late-starting motherhood on total fertility, is at best weakly supported by the medical literature, and there are no signs that the process of postponement of childbearing to later ages will come to a halt in the near future.

There are some mechanisms that could potentially lead to a reversal of below-replacement fertility. The quantum and desired level of fertility could be increased by improvements in the economic situation, especially for young adults, and by social policies that provide increased incentives for having children—for example, improved child-care provision, better access to labor markets for women with children, and increased income transfers to families with children. Homeostatic forces may emerge that increase the quantum of fertility as rapid fertility declines lead to substantially reduced relative cohort sizes. When these small cohorts begin higher education, or begin to enter the labor and housing markets, they are likely to encounter substantially more favorable conditions than their older predecessors in large cohorts experienced, and this could lead to an earlier onset and higher level of fertility. This fertility-enhancing effect of small cohort sizes, first proposed by American economist and demographer Richard Easterlin in the context of the U.S. baby boom may be particularly potent in countries in which fertility has fallen far below replacement level.

See also: *Childlessness; Family: Future; Family Policy; Population Decline; Population Policy; Second Demographic Transition.*

BIBLIOGRAPHY

Bongaarts, John, and Griffith Feeney. 1998. "On the Quantum and Tempo of Fertility." *Population and Development Review* 24(2): 271–291.

Brewster, Karin L., and Ronald R. Rindfuss. 2000. "Fertility and Women's Employment in Indus-trialized Nations." *Annual Review of Sociology* 26: 271–296.

Caldwell, John C. 1982. *Theory of Fertility Decline.* New York: Academic Press.

Coale, Ansley J., and Paul Demeny. 1983. *Regional Model Life Tables and Stable Populations*, 2nd ed. New York: Academic Press.

Easterlin, Richard A. 1980. *Birth and Fortune: The Impact of Numbers on Personal Welfare.* Chicago: University of Chicago Press.

Foster, Caroline. 2000. "The Limits to Low Fertility: A Biosocial Approach." *Population and Development Review* 26(2): 209–234.

Gauthier, Anne H. 1996. *The State and the Family: A Comparative Analysis of Family Policies in Industrialized Countries.* New York: Oxford University Press.

Kohler, Hans-Peter, Francesco C. Billari, and José Antonio Ortega. 2002. "The Emergence of Lowest-low Fertility in Europe during the 1990s." *Population and Development Review.* 28(4): 641–680.

Morgan, Philip S., and Rosalind B. King. 2001. "Why Have Children in the 21st Century? Biological Predispositions, Social Coercion, Rational Choice." *European Journal of Population* 17(1): 3–20.

Teitelbaum, Michael S., and Jay Winter. 1985. *The Fear of Population Decline.* London: Academic Press.

Vallin, Jacques, and Graziella Caselli. 2001. "Le remplacement de la population." In *Démographie: Analyse et synthèse,* ed. G. Caselli, J. Vallin and G. Wunsch, pp. 403–420. Paris: PUF–INED.

van de Kaa, Dirk J. 1987. "Europe's Second Demographic Transition." *Population Bulletin* 42(1): 1–59.

Wilson, Chris. 2001. "On the Scale of Global Demographic Convergence 1950–2000." *Population and Development Review* 27(1): 155–172.

HANS-PETER KOHLER
JOSÉ ANTONIO ORTEGA

FERTILITY, NONMARITAL

In nearly all developed countries the proportion of infants that are born to women who are not married increased dramatically in the last decades of the twentieth century. In most cases this is true across all age groups of childbearing women. Behind these trends, however, there are substantial differences in patterns of nonmarital fertility and in the implications for children born to these women. Some of the important dimensions of interest include whether or not the parents of the child are cohabiting at the time of the birth and whether nonmarital childbearing is concentrated among teenagers or those with less education or particular ethnic or other groups in the population.

National Patterns of Nonmarital Fertility

As of 1998 the Scandinavian countries had the highest proportion of births to nonmarried mothers—over half of all births in Sweden and more than 60 percent in Iceland (see Figure 1). The proportion in the United States was approximately one-third, just below the United Kingdom and just above Canada. Southern European countries tend to have low rates: in Italy and Greece, for example, less than 10 percent of births were nonmarital. Japan stands out with its nearly zero rate.

The large majority of nonmarital births in Scandinavian countries are to cohabiting couples. Cohabitation and nonmarital rates generally go hand in hand. However there are exceptions such as Britain, with higher levels of nonmarital childbearing than cohabitation, and the Netherlands and Germany, with high levels of cohabitation and low rates of nonmarital births. In the United States less than half the births to unwed mothers are to cohabiting couples, but this proportion has been increasing.

Nonmarital Fertility in the United States

In the early 1970s about one-half of nonmarital births in the United States were to teenagers but by the mid-1990s, more than two-thirds were to women aged 20 and older. Figure 2 shows the trends in rates over time. The big increase from 1970 onward is in the rates for women 20 to 24; the rates for women 25 to 29 (not shown) have also risen but not by as much. Accompanying this trend has been a rise in the proportion of nonmarital births that are second or higher-order births. By the end of the period these made up one-half of all nonmarital births; in-

deed about one-quarter of all nonmarital births were third or higher-order births.

In the United States, patterns of nonmarital fertility differ by race. In the mid-1990s about one-third of first births were outside marriage; among blacks this proportion was more than 80 percent. The nonmarital birth rates for Hispanics are even higher than those for blacks. The biggest increases in rates since the mid-1970s have been among white women and this has narrowed the differences between blacks and whites. Since 1995 the rates for non-Hispanic white women have been stable while the rates for black women have continued to decrease.

In the late 1990s, the mean age at first nonmarital birth was approximately 21 for both black and white women. The probability of having a second nonmarital birth varies by race. Among black women who had a first nonmarital birth, more than 60 percent have a second nonmarital birth; among white women the corresponding percentage is 35 to 38 percent. Altogether, in 1999, for white women nonmarital births accounted for 27 percent of all their births; for black women, 69 percent; and for Hispanic women, 42 percent.

Rates differ across states or districts and cities within the United States: as of 1999, Washington, DC, had the highest proportion of nonmarital births, at 62 percent. Mississippi, Louisiana, and New Mexico also have rates far above the national average which, as is shown in Figure 1, was 33 percent. Utah has the lowest rate, 17 percent. Most of these differences are thought to reflect the racial/ethnic composition of the populations of these areas.

Economic and Demographic Causes of Nonmarital Childbearing

Various explanations for these patterns have been proposed, some emphasized by demographers, others by economists. According to demographers (see Ventura and Bachrach 2000), the factors underlying the U.S. trends, for example, are an increase in age at marriage, which increases the pool of women able to have nonmarital births; a decline in the birth rate among married women; and an increase in the rate of births among unmarried women of all ages. The fact that nonmarital birth rates and the proportion of births that are nonmarital have increased in most developed countries has led demographers such as Larry Bumpass to argue that these trends reflect so-

FIGURE 1

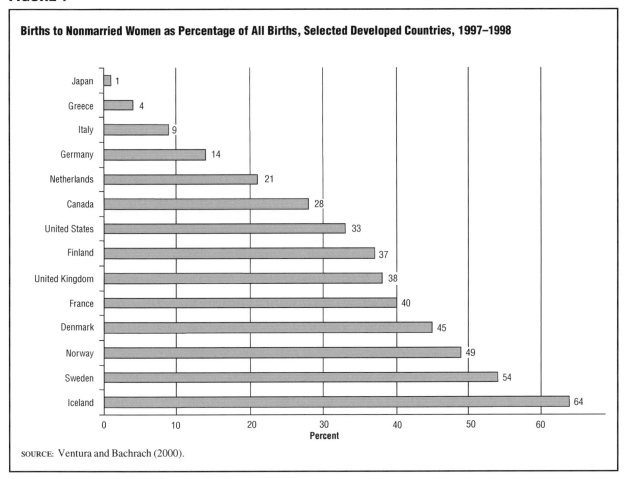

Births to Nonmarried Women as Percentage of All Births, Selected Developed Countries, 1997–1998

SOURCE: Ventura and Bachrach (2000).

cial forces such as increased rates of labor force participation of women, high levels of sex outside of marriage, and high rates of divorce. According to economists, on the other hand, factors that lead a woman to have a child out of wedlock include a low probability of finding an attractive partner (that is, eligible men with good earnings prospects are scarce); the ability to provide for oneself or draw on support from social service programs; the minimal stigma attaching to such behavior—for example, if the woman's mother had had a nonmarital birth or if the behavior was prevalent in the community; high rates of divorce; and the high costs of contraception or avoiding a pregnancy. These factors are linked to characteristics, such as individual schooling, that increase the ability to provide for oneself. Upchurch, Lillard, and Panis, in their work of 2002, go beyond these models and focus on the effects of life course events such as education, marriage, divorce, and childbearing within marriage. They find, for example, that school attendance itself is likely to reduce

nonmarital childbearing, perhaps because it raises the value of time, or perhaps because those in school have better access to contraceptives.

Trends in Nonmarital Childbearing

It is clear that the general trend over recent decades has been toward an increasing proportion of nonmarital births in nearly all developed countries. A far greater proportion of nonmarital births take place in cohabiting unions. A far greater proportion are to women in the working and middle classes. Nonmarital childbearing is clearly much more mainstream than a few decades ago.

See also: *Cohabitation; Family: Future; Marriage.*

BIBLIOGRAPHY

Upchurch, Dawn, Lee Lillard, and Constantijn Panis. "Nonmarital Childbearing: Influences of

FIGURE 2

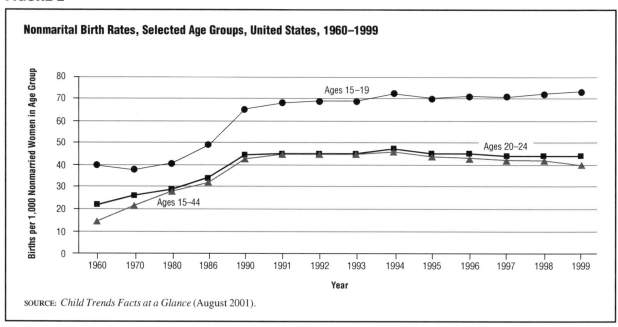

Nonmarital Birth Rates, Selected Age Groups, United States, 1960–1999

SOURCE: *Child Trends Facts at a Glance* (August 2001).

Education, Marriage and Fertility." *Demography* 39(2): 311–329.

Ventura, Stephanie J., and Christine A. Bachrach. 2000. "Nonmarital Childbearing in the United States, 1940–99." *National Vital Statistics Reports* 48(16).

Wu, Larry, Larry Bumpass, and Kelly Musick. 2001. "Historical and Life Course Trajectories of Nonmarital Childbearing." In *Out of Wedlock: Causes and Consequences of Nonmarital Fertility,* ed. Larry Wu and Barbara L. Wolfe. New York: Russell Sage Foundation.

INTERNET RESOURCE.

Child Trends Facts at a Glance. August 2001. <http://www.childtrends.org/PDF/FAAG2001.pdf>.

BARBARA L. WOLFE

FERTILITY, PROXIMATE DETERMINANTS OF

The proximate determinants of fertility are the biological and behavioral factors through which the indirect determinants—social, economic, psychological, and environmental variables—affect fertility. The distinguishing feature of a proximate determinant is its direct connection with fertility. If a proximate determinant, such as contraceptive use, changes, then fertility necessarily changes also (assuming the other proximate determinants remain constant), while this is not necessarily true for an indirect determinant of fertility such as income or education. Consequently, fertility differences among populations and trends in fertility over time can always be traced to variations in one or more of the proximate determinants. The following simple sequence summarizes the relationships among the determinants of fertility.

Social, economic, psychological, environmental variables $\rightarrow$ Proximate determinants $\rightarrow$ Fertility

These relationships were first recognized in the mid-1950s when Kingsley Davis and Judith Blake defined a set of proximate determinants that they called the "intermediate fertility variables." John Bongaarts and Robert C. Potter defined a somewhat different set of proximate determinates in the late 1970s and early 1980s, greatly simplifying the task of construct-

FIGURE 1

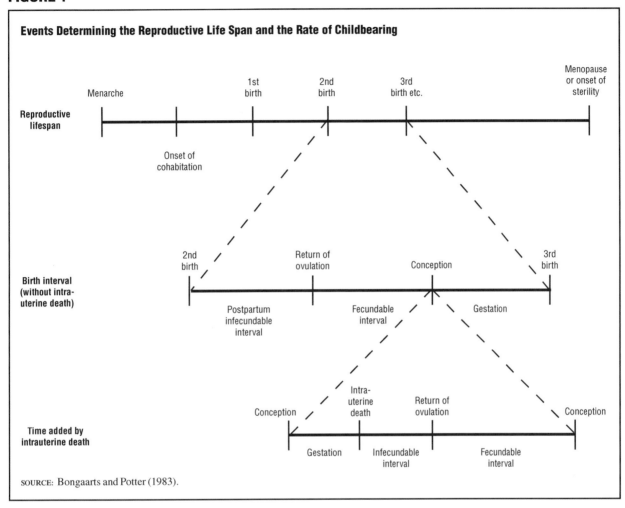

Events Determining the Reproductive Life Span and the Rate of Childbearing

SOURCE: Bongaarts and Potter (1983).

ing models of human reproduction. This set will be presented here.

Proximate determinants are easily identified by examining the events that most immediately affect the duration of the reproductive period and the rate of childbearing during that period (see Figure 1). The potential reproductive years start at menarche, a woman's first menstruation. Actual childbearing in virtually all societies, however, is largely limited to women in socially-accepted sexual unions such as marriage. Since, with few exceptions, first cohabitation takes place some time after menarche, this delay reduces the number of years available for reproduction. If exposure to the possibility of conception is maintained, childbearing can continue until the onset of permanent sterility, which takes place at or before menopause.

While in a sexual union and fecund, women reproduce at a rate inversely related to the duration of

the birth interval: short birth intervals are associated with a high birth rate and vice versa. In the absence of intrauterine mortality, the duration of a birth interval is determined by three time components. The first is the postpartum infecundable interval from birth to the first postpartum ovulation. During this period women are unable to conceive. The second is the fecundable interval (also called the ovulatory interval, or the waiting time to conception) from the first ovulation to conception. During this period women are able to conceive if they have sexual intercourse. The duration of this interval is determined by the monthly probability of conception, which is in turn determined by the level of *fecundability* (the monthly conception probability in the absence of contraception) and by the effectiveness of any contraception practiced. The third time component is a full-term pregnancy interval of nine months. In the event that an intrauterine death occurs, whether spontaneous or induced, the birth interval is lengthened by additional components: the shortened pregnancy is followed by a very brief infecundable period and an additional fecundable period (Figure 1).

This overview of the reproductive process identifies the following proximate determinants:

onset of cohabitation and union disruption;

onset of permanent sterility;

the duration of postpartum infecundability;

fecundability;

use and effectiveness of contraception;

spontaneous intrauterine mortality; and

induced abortion.

The first two of these factors determine the duration of the reproductive period, and the latter five determine the rate of childbearing.

Onset of Cohabitation and Union Disruption

In recent decades cohabitation before marriage or without marriage has become increasingly common, but in most societies marriage remains the main form of socially-sanctioned cohabitation. The mean age for women at first marriage varies widely among populations. In traditional societies in Asia and Africa, first marriage often takes place relatively soon after menarche. In contrast, the mean age at first marriage or cohabitation in a number of European populations is near 25 years. The timing of first marriage is correlated with the prevalence of permanent celibacy; populations with a high age at marriage tend to have high proportions of women who never enter a union and vice versa.

Patterns of union disruption have changed considerably over time. While divorce was historically uncommon worldwide until recent decades, it has increased rapidly in developed countries. In the developed world, a relatively large proportion (in a few cases more than one-third) of all marriages end in divorce. The fertility impact of divorce is minimized by the rapid remarriage of the majority of divorced women of reproductive age. Widowhood was historically an important cause of union disruption in all countries, but its prevalence has declined with the level of mortality. For example, in India in 1901, 46 percent of women had been widowed by age 45. In contrast, in the twenty-first century only a few percent of women in the developed world experience widowhood during their reproductive years.

The mean age at onset of cohabitation, the prevalence of permanent celibacy, and the rate of union disruption are the main determinants of the average proportion of reproductive years women are exposed to the possibility of childbearing. In populations with early and universal cohabitation, the proportion of the potential reproductive years lost is typically one-fifth or less, but this proportion can approach one-half in populations with late onset of cohabitation and a high incidence of permanent celibacy.

Onset of Sterility

Menopause, the complete cessation of menstruation, marks the end of the potential childbearing years. In the United States and western Europe, an individual woman's age at menopause can range from less than 40 to near 60, with averages around 50. Only a few studies have been made in developing countries, and because of various methodological problems including recall errors and age misreporting, it is not clear whether a substantial difference in mean age of menopause exists between the populations of developing and developed countries.

Postmenopausal women are definitely sterile, but the onset of sterility can occur several years before menopause. Menstrual cycles become increasingly irregular in the years before menopause, presumably reflecting a rising incidence of anovulatory cycles. A high risk of spontaneous intrauterine mortality also contributes to reduced fecundity among women over age 40. In addition to these sterility factors for women, there is some sterility (but of lower frequency) among their male partners. The resulting couple sterility is estimated to reach 50 percent when women are in their early forties. This early age of onset of sterility is consistent with observations of a mean age at last birth of around 40 years in many populations that do not practice contraception.

Postpartum Infecundability

The duration of the anovulatory interval after a birth is usually estimated from the delay in the return of menstruation—the interval of postpartum infecundability is assumed to equal the duration of postpartum amenorrhea. This assumption is apparently quite accurate when applied to the average interval in a population, although in some women the first ovulation precedes the first menstruation. It is now well established that the duration and pattern of breastfeeding are the principal determinants of the duration of postpartum amenorrhea. In the absence of breastfeeding the menses return shortly after birth, with average amenorrhea durations of 1.5 to 2 months. As the duration of breastfeeding increases, so does the amenorrhea interval. A woman experiences approximately one additional month of amenorrhea for each two-month increment in breastfeeding duration. With long lactation, mean amenorrhea intervals from one to two years are observed in developed as well as in developing countries. Several studies, comparing entire populations or subpopulations between countries, have documented high levels of correlation between breastfeeding and amenorrhea durations. On the individual level the correlation between lactation and amenorrhea intervals, while still highly significant, is somewhat lower. The most plausible explanation for this, aside from measurement error, is that women differ not only with respect to the duration of breastfeeding, but also with respect to the type and pattern of breastfeeding. Women who fully breastfeed have a lower probability of resumption of menses than women whose infants receive supplemental food such as fluids by bottle or solids. The inhibiting effect of breastfeeding on ovulation and menstruation, as well as the differential impact according to the type and pattern of breastfeeding, are believed to be the result of a neurally-mediated, hormonal reflex system stimulated by the child's sucking the breast nipple.

Fecundability

Fecundability equals the monthly probability of conceiving among women who menstruate regularly but do not practice contraception. Typical average fecundability levels among young cohabiting partners range from 0.15 to 0.25, depending primarily on frequency of intercourse. Lower values are found at higher ages and longer durations of cohabitation. This monthly conception probability is substantially less than 1.0 because fertilization can only take place during a short period—approximately two days—around the time of ovulation in the middle of a menstrual cycle. In addition, some cycles are anovulatory and a substantial proportion (perhaps a third) of fertilized ova fail to implant, or are spontaneously aborted in the first two weeks after fertilization. These aborted fertilizations are usually not counted as conceptions in the demographic literature because they cause little or no disruption in the menstrual cycles and women are often unaware of such brief pregnancies. Levels of fecundability around 0.2

imply that many women do not conceive for a number of months even if they have regular intercourse. Typical average delays to conception range from five to ten months.

Contraception

The prevalence of contraception varies widely among populations. The percent of cohabiting women of reproductive age currently using contraception ranges from near zero in a number of developing countries with high fertility, to above 75 in a number of developed countries. The use of contraception affects fertility because it decreases the risk of conception. The effectiveness of contraception is measured as the percent of reduction in fecundability. For example, a contraceptive with an effectiveness of 90 percent used by a group of women with a fecundability of 0.2 will yield an actual monthly probability of conception of 0.02. Contraceptive effectiveness depends on the method as well as on the motivation and knowledge of the user. In developed countries, the effectiveness of modern methods such as the birth control pill and the intrauterine device (IUD) is more than 95 percent, and the effectiveness of conventional methods such as the condom, diaphragm, or spermicides is around 90 percent. Those levels are believed to be lower in developing countries, but reliable information about effectiveness in these populations is virtually nonexistent.

Spontaneous Intrauterine Mortality

It has proven difficult to make estimates of the risk of intrauterine mortality. Retrospective reports of pregnancy histories of individuals are known to be deficient because of recall errors, but estimates based on prospective studies also vary. This is in large part due to the difficulty in obtaining accurate reporting of intrauterine deaths in the early months of pregnancy, when it may not be easy to distinguish between a delayed menstruation and an early spontaneous abortion. The most carefully designed studies estimate that about 20 percent of conceptions will not end in a live birth (not including embryonic deaths occurring before the first missed menstruation). Nearly half of these spontaneous abortions occur before the third month of pregnancy. This estimate of 20 percent is an average for women of all ages. The risk of intrauterine mortality is lowest in the mid-reproductive period and much higher than average for women in their late thirties and forties. The available evidence does not suggest large differ-

TABLE 1

Rating of Proximate Determinants, with Respect to Sensitivity of Fertility and Variability among Populations

Proximate Determinants	Sensitivity of Fertility to the Determinant	Variability among Populations	Overall Rating
1. Onset of cohabitation and union disruption	+ + +	+ + +	+ + +
2. Onset of permanent sterility	+ +	+	+
3. Postpartum infecundability	+ +	+ + +	+ + +
4. Fecundability	+ +	+ +	+ +
5. Contraception	+ + +	+ + +	+ + +
6. Spontaneous intrauterine mortality	+	+	+
7. Induced abortion	+ +	+ + +	+ + +

+ + + = High; + + = Medium; + = Low or absent.

SOURCE: Adapted from *Studies in Family Planning* 13 (1982).

ences in the risk among societies. However, the probability of a stillbirth (an intrauterine death after the 28th week of gestation) is around 4 percent of conceptions in some poor countries, while it is only about 1 percent in the most developed countries. The reasons for this difference have not been determined conclusively, but health and environmental factors presumably play an important role.

Induced Abortion

Deliberate interventions to terminate pregnancies have been practiced throughout recorded history. In the mid-1990s, the proportion of pregnancies ended by induced abortion ranged from near zero in some countries to more than one-half in some parts of Eastern Europe. The availability of simpler medical techniques, assurance of personal safety, and ease of access have recently increased in many countries. Even where these conditions are not present, as in much of the developing world, the determination to avoid childbirth may lead women to resort to induced abortion.

Analyzing Fertility Levels

Each of these seven proximate determinants directly influences fertility, and together they determine the level of fertility. In studies of fertility levels or differentials it is generally not necessary to devote the same effort to analyzing and measuring each of the proximate determinants because they are not of equal interest. Two criteria can be applied to select the proximate determinants that deserve most attention. The first is the sensitivity of the fertility rate to variation in a determinant; it is relatively uninteresting if large variation produces only a minor change

in fertility. The second criterion is the extent of a determinant's variability among populations or over time. A relatively stable determinant can contribute little to explaining either trends or differentials.

In Table 1, the seven proximate determinants are given an approximate rating for these two criteria. Studies with reproductive models (such as the 1983 study by Bongaarts and Potter) show that fertility is least sensitive to variations in the risk of spontaneous intrauterine mortality, and most sensitive to changes in the proportions of women in union and the prevalence of contraception. Variability is lowest for onset of sterility and risk of spontaneous intrauterine mortality. The overall rating, based on both criteria, indicates that four proximate determinants—onset of cohabitation, postpartum infecundability, contraception, and induced abortion—are the most important for the analysis of fertility levels and trends.

See also: *Blake, Judith; Contraception, Modern Methods of; Contraceptive Prevalence; Davis, Kingsley; Fecundity; Induced Abortion: Prevalence; Infertility; Spontaneous Abortion.*

BIBLIOGRAPHY

Bongaarts, John. 1978. "A Framework for Analyzing the Proximate Determinants of Fertility." *Population and Development Review* 4(1): 105–132.

Bongaarts, John, and Robert C. Potter. 1983. *Fertility, Biology, and Behavior: An Analysis of the Proximate Determinants.* New York: Academic Press.

Davis, Kingsley, and Judith Blake. 1956. "Social Structure and Fertility: An Analytic Framework." *Economic Development and Cultural Change* 4(3): 211–235.

Stover, John. 1998. "Revising the Proximate Determinants of Fertility Framework: What Have We Learned in the Past 20 Years?" *Studies in Family Planning* 29(3): 255–267.

Wood, James W. 1994. *Dynamics of Human Reproduction: Biology, Biometry, Demography.* New York: Aldine de Gruyter.

JOHN BONGAARTS

FERTILITY CONTROL, INDIRECT MEASUREMENT OF

Knowledge of the extent and effectiveness of intentional control of fertility is important in understanding population trends and in theorizing about fertility transitions. Evidence regarding fertility control has played an important role in a long-running debate about contemporary family planning programs.

On one side of the debate, the "continuity" school stresses that intentional fertility control has been known and practiced much earlier than the onset of the demographic transition and certainly well before the initiation of any family planning program. The "discontinuity" school argues that even in the nineteenth century, many populations existed in a pre-rational mode with respect to fertility behavior.

According to the "continuity" school the fertility transition was dominantly triggered by a change in mortality rates and external socio-economic conditions, which lowered the number of births couples wanted. According to the "discontinuity" school, the fertility transition was initiated by the diffusion of the idea that fertility behavior should be brought into the realm of conscious choice.

Members of the "continuity" school were skeptical about the effectiveness of family planning programs in the absence of changes in mortality rates and socio-economic circumstances. Members of the "discontinuity" school were skeptical about any approach that did not directly address people's mindsets. The debate between the two schools was quickly translated into questions about the extent of fertility control and whether or not it was mainly characterized by stopping or spacing.

Information about fertility control practices in contemporary populations is routinely collected by surveys that ask individuals to report on their current and past personal experience. Where it is infeasible to conduct such surveys, it is nevertheless possible to employ indirect methods to obtain some information regarding the extent and nature of deliberate fertility regulation. These are statistical techniques that yield population-level measurements concerning "control," essentially by comparing the pattern of fertility observed in the population of interest with the pattern of a "natural-fertility" population, i.e. one in which fertility control was not practiced. (The population of interest is referred to as the "target" population; the natural-fertility population is termed the "model" population.) This article describes the principal indirect methods of estimating the extent and character of fertility limitation.

Two polar types of fertility limitation are termed *perfect stopping* and *pure spacing*. In the case of perfect stopping, all couples have no more children after they initiate fertility control. Pure spacing behavior occurs when all couples who are ever going to limit their fertility begin control before the birth of their first child. In real populations, neither of these extremes ever occurs. Perfect stopping does not happen because of contraceptive failure. Pure spacing is not observed because some couples desire a first birth as soon as possible after marriage.

Early Approaches

David V. Glass and Eugene Grebenik, in a British census report, developed a "statistical model for the study of desired and achieved family size" (Glass and Grebenik, p. 270), a by-product of which was estimates of the extent of use of fertility control. Their estimator derived from the comparison of two tabulations of women by the number of children they had borne (called parity distributions). Each pair of distributions compared women who had married in a specified age range and were observed (still married) at or beyond the end of the childbearing age-span. Glass and Grebnick's target populations were the married women observed by the 1946 family census of Great Britain, and their chosen (non-controlling) models were the corresponding current- and marriage-age groups recorded by the 1911 census of Ireland as residing in rural areas—specifically, outside the highly urbanized county boroughs.

Glass and Grebenik's approach assumed that couples practice stopping behavior—that is, they begin to control their fertility after reaching a certain number of children ever born, or parity, presumed to be their desired family size. Before that point, couples proceeded from parity to parity according to the parity progression rates of the model population. When they initiate control, their parity progression rates become the rates of the model population multiplied by the fraction $(1-p)$, where p is the probability of having an additional birth at each parity once "family limitation" has begun. Their procedure produced the first indirect measures of the extent of fertility control as a step in the estimation of "desired and achieved family size."

Coale's *M* and *m* and Extensions

Ansley J. Coale, like Glass and Grebenik, apparently came to his indirect measure on his way to another goal. In a 1971 article entitled "Age Patterns of Marriage," Coale devoted little more than a page to his key equation:

$$m(a) = M \cdot n(a) \cdot e^{m \cdot v(a)}$$

where $m(a)$ is age-specific marital fertility at age a, $n(a)$ is the age-specific marital fertility of Hutterites during the period from 1921 to 1930, and M, m, and $v(a)$ are parameters. (The Hutterites, a small religious community located in border regions of midwestern Canada and the United States, are frequently taken by demographers to illustrate a natural fertility population.) The parameter M is the ratio of marital fertility at ages 20 to 24 to Hutterite marital fertility at that age, and m measures "the extent to which control of fertility causes a systematic deviation from the age pattern of natural fertility" (Coale, p. 207).

When $m = 1$, the marital fertility schedule diverges from the Hutterite pattern by roughly the average proportional deviation observed in the 43 age-specific marital fertility schedules reported by the United Nations in its *Demographic Yearbook* for

1965. This implicitly defines the age-specific parameter, $v(a)$. Coale and T. James Trussell made statistical refinements in the method of obtaining these parameters in 1974 and 1978. Coale's approach yields a measure that may be interpreted as reflection of the effects of fertility control, but it provides no estimate of the extent to which the target population engaged in family limitation.

In 1979 Warren C. Sanderson used both parity distributions and the Coale specification for the marital fertility schedule to investigate the evolution of fertility control in the native born white population of the United States from the beginning of the nineteenth century onwards. The parity distributions are those for all women who had ever been married, and were observed at or after the end of the childbearing age-span.

Sanderson denoted $F(q)$ to be the mean fertility of the fraction q of the population with the highest number of children ever born, with $F(1)$ being the mean fertility of the entire cohort. Sanderson then defined a particular value of q, q^*, implicitly from the equation:

$$F(q^*) = B_n/\phi,$$

where B_n is the mean fertility of the population in the absence of fertility limitation, and ϕ is the proportion of couples who are physiologically capable of bearing a child. B_n depends on Coale's M and m parameters and on the age distribution of marriage. Under plausible conditions, $(1 - q^*)$ is a measure of the extent of fertility control.

Cohort Parity Analysis

Cohort parity analysis (CPA) is the name given to an analytic approach to measuring the extent and character of fertility regulation from marriage-age and marriage-duration specific parity distribution data. Paul A. David, Sanderson, and their coauthors developed the methodology, describing it in a series of articles in the 1980s.

Like the Glass and Grebenik procedure, CPA is based on a comparison of parity distributions and treats couples who have ever initiated family limiting behavior as "controllers." CPA also allows for the possibility that couples could initiate fertility reducing behaviors prior to the parity at which they ultimately stop. Unlike Glass and Grebenik, CPA does not assume that people only begin practicing fertility control when they attain their desired family size.

In the CPA framework, couples who do not initiate control proceed upward through the parity distribution according to the model (natural-fertility) parity progression rates. Once controlling behavior has started, all that is known is that parity progression rates must be below those of the model population. CPA does not assume that control is maintained continuously after it is initiated; for example, it allows for the possibility that a couple may use contraception after marriage for three years, again for two years following the birth of their first child, and then continuously after the birth of their second child.

A lower bound on the proportion of cohorts who are practicing birth control is calculated from the target and model populations, and is compared with the level that would result in the population from perfect stopping behavior. A corresponding upper bound on the extent of fertility limitation, similarly calculated, is that which would result were those who controlled to have engaged in pure spacing behaviors. The upper and lower bound estimates are efficient in the sense that, within the CPA framework, there can be no lower upper bound and no higher lower bound.

Because CPA can be applied to cohorts who have not yet completed their childbearing, it is especially useful for studying family limiting behavior among younger couples. David and Sanderson made use of this advantageous property of CPA in a study of fertility control among the married women residing in Ireland's urban areas in 1911. This revealed that not only that there had been a significant amount of family limitation during the preceding decades, but that the extent of control among cohorts of younger women at lower durations of marriage exceeded that among the older women who had reached the end of their childbearing span.

Assessment of the Main Approaches

The two main approaches to estimating the extent of birth control are Coale's *M* and *m* method and cohort parity analysis. Each has its critics and its defenders.

A drawback in Coale's methodology is that it rests solely on the shape of the target age-specific fertility schedule, so that decreases in the level of age-specific marital fertility at young ages (resulting

from "spacing") must show up as reductions in the level of *M*, not increases in the index of the intensity of control, *m*. Yet there is ample evidence of the occurrence of such decreases in *M* in populations undergoing the fertility transition, implying that measured changes in *m* alone understate gains in the extent of control.

Barbara S. Okun, who appraised both methods in a 1994 article, reported that Coale's *m* remained close to zero even in populations where 40 percent of married couples were exercising effective fertility control. Further, *m* was insensitive to changes in the extent of control when such control was low, and large changes in control often registered only as small changes in *m*.

Okun's main criticism of CPA is that the bounds found on the extent of control are highly sensitive to the choice of model distribution. Hence, errors in estimated proportions of controllers would arise when an inappropriate model distribution was used. An inappropriate model distribution is one that is derived from a population that differs from the target population in dimensions that are not considered to be fertility control, but which nevertheless affect fertility. The duration of breastfeeding is often thought to be one such factor. Similarly, in a 1996 article, Okun, Trussell, and Barbara Vaughan criticized CPA on the grounds that the method overstates the gain in the extent of control when the population on which the model parity distribution is based (improperly) contains some controllers. Sanderson subsequently addressed these criticisms by providing a test that helps avoid the use of inappropriate model parity distributions. He also demonstrated formally that CPA lower bounds remain lower bounds, even when the model distribution (inappropriately) includes some controllers.

See also: *Estimation Methods, Demographic; Fertility, Age Patterns of; Natural Fertility.*

BIBLIOGRAPHY

Coale, Ansley J. 1971. "Age Patterns of Marriage." *Population Studies* 25: 193–214.

Coale, Ansley J., and T. James Trussell. 1974. "Model Fertility Schedules: Variations in the Age Structure of Childbearing in Human Populations." *Population Index* 40: 185–258 (Erratum, *Population Index* 41: 572).

David, Paul A., et al. 1988. "Cohort Parity Analysis: Statistical Estimates of the Extent of Fertility Control." *Demography* 25: 163–188.

David, Paul A., and Warren C. Sanderson. 1987. "The Emergence of a Two-Child Norm among American Birth Controllers." *Population and Development Review* 13: 1–41.

———. 1988. "Measuring Marital Fertility Control with CPA." *Population Index* 54: 691–713.

———. 1990. "Cohort Parity Analysis and Fertility Transition Dynamics: Reconstructing Historical Trends in Fertility Control from a Single Census." *Population Studies* 44: 421–455.

Glass, David V., and Eugene Grebenik. 1954. "A Statistical Model for the Study of Desired and Achieved Family Size." In *The Trend and Pattern of Fertility in Great Britain: A Report on the Family Census of 1946.* London: H. M. Stationery Office.

Okun, Barbara S. 1994. "Evaluating Methods for Detecting Fertility Control: Coale and Trussell's Model and Cohort Parity Analysis." *Population Studies* 48: 193–222.

Okun, Barbara S., James Trussell, and Barbara Vaughan. 1996. "Using Fertility Surveys to Evaluate an Indirect Method for Detecting Fertility Control: A Study of Cohort Parity Analysis." *Population Studies* 50: 161–171.

Sanderson, Warren C. 1979. "Quantitative Aspects of Marriage, Fertility, and Family Limitation in Nineteenth Century America: Another Application of the Coale Specifications." *Demography* 16: 339–358.

INTERNET RESOURCE.

Sanderson, Warren C. 2000. "A Users' Guide to the Joys and Pitfalls of Cohort Parity Analysis," Presented to the Stanford Institute for Economic Policy Research Conference, *History Matters: Technology, Population and Institutions,* June 3–5, at Stanford University. <http://www.siepr.stanford.edu>.

PAUL A. DAVID
WARREN C. SANDERSON

FERTILITY MEASUREMENT

This article provides a nontechnical account of the principal indexes used by demographers to gauge the level of fertility of a population. For each measure the main advantages and disadvantages are also noted.

Crude Birth Rate

The simplest indicator of the fertility of a population in a given year is the number of births that year divided by the average size of the population during the year. There is nothing special about the one-year period, but if births are measured over a different period (still in units of years), consistency in comparisons requires that the denominator be the average population over the period times the length of the period—more strictly, the number of "person-years" lived by the population during the period. By convention, the resulting fraction is applied to a standard-sized population of 1,000. The result is the crude birth rate: the number of births per 1,000 population per year. The adjective *crude* is used because none of the structural characteristics of the population that might affect the number of births that occur in the time period, such as the age distribution or the composition by sex, is taken into account, only the total population size. The rate can be simply calculated as a fraction in which the numerator is the number of live births in the population in a year—say, beginning January 1—and the denominator is the midyear (July 1) population, approximating the "average" size of the population over the year.

Thus, from the Institut de la Statistique et des Études Économiques, for France in 2000, see Item 1 from the Formula Table.

The crude birth rate is most often calculated for a single year, although in order to smooth out year-to-year fluctuations published estimates often give an average rate over several years—typically a five-year period. Crude birth rates below about 15 per 1,000 are usually regarded as low; those above about 35 are high. Examples of extreme values are 9 for Spain in 2000 and 52 for Kenya in the 1970s.

Pros. The crude birth rate requires less detailed data than other fertility measures and data that are more likely to be available for a very recent period. It is needed for the calculation of the rate of natural increase (the crude birth rate minus the crude death rate) and the population growth rate (the rate of natural increase plus the net migration rate).

FORMULA TABLE

Examples of Calculation of Birth and Fertility Rates

ITEM 1: BIRTH RATE FRANCE, 2000

$$\text{Crude Birth Rate} = \frac{\text{Births in 2000}}{\text{Total Population, July 1, 2000}} = \frac{778,900}{58,891,913} = 0.0132 = 13.2 \text{ per } 1,000$$

ITEM 2: GENERAL FERTILITY RATE, TURKEY, 1998

$$\text{General Fertility Rate} = \frac{\text{Births in 1998}}{\text{Midyear female population, aged 15–49}} \times 1000 = \frac{1,338,800}{17,184,000} \times 1000 = 77.9$$

ITEM 3: AGE-SPECIFIC FERTILITY RATE, FRANCE, 1998

Age-Specific Fertility Rate for Age Group 20–24

$$= \frac{\text{Births in 1998 to women, aged 20–24}}{\text{Number of women aged 20–24 at midyear}} = \frac{113,895}{1,923,902} = 0.0592 = 59.2 \text{ per } 1,000$$

ITEM 4: MARTIAL FERTILITY RATE, UNITED STATES, 2000

$$\text{Marital Fertility Rate} = \frac{\text{Births to married women, aged 15–49}}{\text{Number of married women, aged 15–49}} = \frac{2,711,771}{35,968,000} = 0.0756 = 75.4 \text{ per } 1,000$$

SOURCE OF DATA: Institut de la Statistique et des Études Économiques; Council of Europe (2000); National Center for Health Statistics and U.S. Census Bureau (2002).

Cons. The crude birth rate is affected by vagaries in the age and sex distribution and by other structural characteristics of the population, such as those resulting from a past baby boom or particularly heavy immigration. An example of such a country would be a Gulf state of the Middle East that has experienced significant immigration of males of working age. In such a case the crude birth rate may be artificially low because the total population contains an unusually high number of males. In addition, the crude birth rate does not provide any insight into individual-level childbearing behavior.

General Fertility Rate

The general fertility rate is similar to the crude birth rate except that it uses a more restricted denominator, the female population of childbearing age, ages 15 to 49. For Turkey in 1998, see Item 2 in the Formula Table.

Pros. The general fertility rate provides a somewhat more refined measure of fertility than the crude birth rate and requires knowledge of only the total number of births and the total female population, ages 15 to 49. In most countries, the female population of childbearing age is about one-fourth of the country's total population, so that the advantage over the crude birth rate is not a great one. When the age-sex structure of the population has been skewed in some way, such as by migration, however, the general fertility rate is often preferable.

Cons. This rate will be skewed somewhat by the distribution of women *within* the childbearing ages, affecting country-to-country comparisons slightly. As with the crude birth rate, it provides no insight into childbearing behavior. The general fertility rate is not as widely used as other measures.

Age-Specific Fertility Rates

Age-specific fertility rates (also called age-specific birth rates) are similar to the crude birth rate but are calculated for specific age groups of women of childbearing age. The range of childbearing ages is conventionally considered to be ages 15 to 49 (sometimes 15 to 44 is used), and a full set of age-specific fertility rates would span this interval—usually either in single-year age groups or, more commonly, in five-year groups: 15 to 19, 20 to 24, . . . , 45 to 49. (Rarely, age-specific fertility rates are also calculated for men.) The numerator of the rate is the number of live births to women in the specific age or age group during a given period and the denominator is the average population of women in that age or age group during the same period. For convenience, age-specific fertility rates are usually presented as rates per 1,000. See Item 3 in the Formula Table for an explanation of the calculations.

Pros. Age-specific fertility rates enable analysis of the pattern of fertility by age of women and analysis of changes in the timing of childbearing. Comparisons between consecutive years may, for example, indicate that women are delaying childbearing and the onset of family formation. Age-specific fertility rates are required for calculation of fertility measures such as the total, gross, and net reproduction rates. They are also required as an input in cohort-component population projections.

Cons. Age-specific fertility rates require detailed data on the number of births by age or age group of mother and data on the number of women of childbearing age by age or age group, data that are seldom available in developing countries. Age-specific fertility rates cannot be directly used to calculate population growth rates or natural increase rates.

Marital Fertility Rates

Marital fertility rates can be calculated either for the full range of reproductive ages (15 to 49 or 15 to 44) or as age-specific rates. The numerator is usually taken as the total number of births to women in the specified age range, regardless of the marital status of the mother; the denominator is the number of currently married women in the specified age range. With the large increase in fertility outside of legal marriage that has occurred in many industrialized countries (with many births occurring in consensual unions or to cohabiting couples), the usefulness of marital fertility rates may be seriously compromised. For that reason, it may be desirable to restrict the numerator to births that occur within legal marriage and to also calculate complementary nonmarital fertility rates. The calculated example is, in fact, based on marital births only. See Item 4 in the Formula Table, using data for the United States in 2000.

Pros. Marital fertility rates enable analysis of marital fertility and the pace and timing of childbearing that occurs within formal marriage, analysis that cannot be performed with other fertility measures.

TABLE 1

Example of Calculation of the Total Fertility Rate, Ethiopia, 2000

Age	Births by age of mother	Number of women	Age-specific fertility rate ×1,000
	(1)	(2)	(1)/(2) × 1,000
15–19	357,390	3,249,000	110
20–24	673,684	2,761,000	244
25–29	601,128	2,277,000	264
30–34	468,472	1,889,000	248
35–39	292,983	1,601,000	183
40–44	132,500	1,325,000	100
45–49	26,784	1,116,000	24
Sum of 5-year age-specific rates (× 1,000)			1,173
Sum of single-year age-specific rates (× 1,000)			5,865

$$Total\ Fertility\ Rate = \sum_{15}^{49} Single\text{-}year\ age\text{-}specific\ fertility\ rates$$

$$= 5 \times \sum_{15-19}^{45-49} Five\text{-}year\ average\ age\text{-}specific\ fertility\ rates$$

$$= 5 \times 1,173\ per\ 1,000 = 5,865\ per\ 1,000 = 5.87$$

SOURCE: Author's example calculated from figures in: Central Statistical Authority [Ethiopia] and Orc Macro; *Ethiopia Demographic and Health Survey 2000* (2001). Addis Ababa, Ethiopia and Calverton, MD: Central Statistical Authority and Orc Macro.

Cons. Marital fertility rates require detailed data on births by age group of mother and possibly by marital status of mother, and on women by age and marital status, data that are seldom available in developing countries. While this rate provides the ability to analyze marital fertility, increases in nonmarital fertility result in only a partial picture of childbearing trends.

Total Fertility Rate

The total fertility rate (TFR) at a given time (technically referred to as the period total fertility rate) is the average number of children a woman would bear in her life if she experienced the age-specific fertility rates prevailing at that time. A closely related measure is the cohort total fertility rate—the average number of children borne by women in an actual birth cohort over their reproductive lives. The period total fertility rate is used much more frequently than the cohort total fertility rate and is always meant when the abbreviation TFR is used without further specification.

Period total fertility rate. The TFR for a given year is calculated by summing the age-specific fertility rates for that year over the range of reproductive ages. Each single-year age-specific fertility rate measures the "risk" that a woman of that age would have a child during the year in question; the sum of those risks equals the number of children a hypothetical woman experiencing those risks would have at the end of her reproductive life. If the age-specific rates are averages for five-year age groups of women, the sum of the age-specific rates must be multiplied by five, as in the example, for Ethiopia in 2000, in Table 1.

The TFR is often discussed in terms of "replacement-level" fertility, or the number of children that women, on average, must produce in order for a population to ultimately reach a stationary state ("zero population growth" position)—neither growing nor declining in size. A value of 2.1 is often cited as replacement-level fertility. The ".1" is required because there are approximately 5 percent more boys born than girls and because not all women survive throughout their childbearing years. The value of 2.1, however, is valid only for countries with low mortality (high life expectancy). In countries with high mortality, that is, when survival rates from birth to maturity are low, a replacement-level TFR is much higher; it can be as high as 3.0.

Pros. The TFR has the immediate intuitive interpretation as the number of children that the average woman will bear in her lifetime. That number can be gleaned only very roughly from other measures. (For example, a crude birthrate of 50 per 1,000 in a country with a normal age-sex distribution means that women on average bear about seven children each; a crude birthrate of 15 would mean about two children.)

Cons. The TFR for a given year does not indicate how many additional children an average woman of any selected age will actually have over her remaining reproductive lifetime. It would do so only if the age-specific fertility rates of that year remained constant over the woman's lifetime. When age-specific fertility rates are changing, such as when women are delaying births from their 20s to their 30s, age-specific fertility rates—and thus the TFR—would be depressed for a time and then rise again when women begin to have children at the older age. Hence the TFR may be a poor measure of the completed fertility of women at or near the end of their

TABLE 2

Example of Calculation of the Gross Reproduction Rate, Ethiopia, 2000

Age	Female births by age of mother	Number of women	Age-specific fertility rate (female births)
	(1)	(2)	(1)/(2) × 1,000
15–19	174,337	3,249,000	54
20–24	328,626	2,761,000	119
25–29	293,233	2,277,000	129
30–34	228,523	1,889,000	121
35–39	142,919	1,601,000	89
40–44	64,634	1,325,000	49
45–49	13,065	1,116,000	12
Sum of 5-year age-specific rates for female births (× 1,000)			572

$$\text{Gross Reproduction Rate} = 5 \times \sum_{15-19}^{45-49} \text{Five-year-average age-specific fertility rates for female births}$$

$$= 5 \times 572 \text{ per } 1,000 = 2,860 \text{ per } 1,000 = 2.86$$

SOURCE: Author's example calculated from figures in: Central Statistical Authority [Ethiopia] and Orc Macro; *Ethiopia Demographic and Health Survey 2000* 2001. Addis Ababa, Ethiopia and Calverton, MD: Central Statistical Authority and Orc Macro.

childbearing years and also a poor predictor of the completed fertility of women at early phases of their reproductive career.

Cohort total fertility rate. The cohort total fertility rate can be calculated in a manner similar to the period total fertility rate, but the calculation can be completed only for women who have already passed through their childbearing years. This rate is based on the actual fertility of an age cohort of women—that is, a group of woman born in the same period, usually a five-year period. (For example, women who were born from 1975 to 1980 are the 1975–1980 cohort.) Cohort fertility rates can be calculated for each five-year period as women pass through their childbearing years and summed to give their completed cohort fertility up to particular ages, such as 20, 25, 30, and so on. For the 1975–1980 birth cohort, the cohort total fertility rate could be calculated only when the youngest of the group pass 50, in the year 2030.

Pros. The cohort total fertility rate allows a precise description of the actual childbearing experience of specific birth cohorts of women. As a measure of reproduction it is superior to estimates made from questions on "children ever born" in censuses and

TABLE 3

Example of Calculation of the Net Reproduction Rate, Ethiopia, 2000

Age	Age-specific fertility rate (female births)	Average person-years lived in age interval ($_5L_x/l_0$)	Effective age-specific fertility rate (net of mortality loss)
	(1)	(2)	(1) × (2)
15–19	54	3.94514	211.7
20–24	119	3.85859	459.3
25–29	129	3.75919	484.1
30–34	121	3.64764	441.3
35–39	89	3.52358	314.5
40–44	49	3.38643	165.2
45–49	12	3.23766	37.9
			Sum 2,114.0
	Net Reproduction Rate (NRR)	=	2.11

SOURCE: Author's example calculated from figures in: Central Statistical Authority [Ethiopia] and Orc Macro; *Ethiopia Demographic and Health Survey 2000* 2001. Addis Ababa, Ethiopia and Calverton, MD: Central Statistical Authority and Orc Macro.

surveys because it does not omit the childbearing experience of women who died before the time of the census or survey.

Cons. This measure requires detailed data on births by age of mother and data on women by birth cohort over a long period, data not often readily available for developing countries. Total cohort fertility can be calculated, by definition, only at the conclusion of a cohort's childbearing years.

Gross Reproduction Rate

The gross reproduction rate (GRR) for a particular year is the average number of daughters that a woman would have if she experienced over her lifetime the age-specific fertility rates of that year. In that it refers only to the number of daughters born to women, not the total number of children, it is a special case of the (period) total fertility rate; in most circumstances (unless the sex ratio at birth is highly unequal) the GRR equals roughly half the TFR.

An example—for Ethiopia in 2000—is given in Table 2.

Pros. The gross reproduction rate, like the total fertility rate, translates other measures of fertility into a clear result: in this case, the number of daughters that a cohort of women is likely to produce in their lifetimes.

Cons. This rate adds little information to the TFR, which is a more widely used measure. The GRR, like the TFR, may be affected by changes in the timing of births even when the total number of lifetime births per woman is not changing.

Net Reproduction Rate

The net reproduction rate (NRR) measures the *effective* fertility in a population, taking account not only of births but also of the fact that not all women born will survive to their own reproductive years. The NRR is the average number of daughters of reproductive age that a woman would have if she experienced over her lifetime the prevailing age-specific rates of fertility and if her daughters experienced the prevailing rates of mortality. If the age schedules of both fertility and mortality for a population remained constant, the net reproduction rate would be a measure of generational replacement. For example, if NRR = 1.5, the next generation would be 50 percent larger than the present generation; if NRR = 0.8, it would be 20 percent smaller. For any population, therefore, the NRR can be taken to indicate the underlying tendency of the population to increase or decrease based on its current fertility and mortality patterns, abstracting from the effects of its current age structure.

An NRR = 1.0 means that each woman in a population will, on average, replace herself exactly in the next generation. For the existing level of mortality, fertility would be precisely at replacement level.

Calculation of the net reproduction rate requires estimates of the female survival rate from birth to each reproductive age or age group, values that would be given in the appropriate female life table. In life-table notation, the average survival rate from birth to age x is L_x / l_0 or, for survival to a five-year age group, $_5L_x / 5 l_0$. An example for Ethiopia is given in Table 3.

Pros. The NRR precisely measures the reproductivity of a population by taking into account the level of fertility and the likelihood that women will survive from birth to each childbearing age.

Cons. The NRR requires detailed data on fertility and female life-table values up to age 50.

Parity Progression Ratios

A parity progression ratio is the proportion of women of a given "parity" (i.e., who have had that

TABLE 4

Example of Calculation of Parity Progression Ratios for Women Born from 1896 to 1900, France

Number of births *(i)*	Number of married women who have had at least *i* births *(N$_i$)*	Parity Progression Ratio *(P$_i$ = N$_{i+1}$ / N$_i$)*
0	1,094,785	0.824
1	901,785	0.690
2	622,447	0.590
3	367,129	0.588
4	216,047	0.605
5	130,802	0.628
6	82,185	0.625
7	51,391	0.635
8	32,645	0.628
9 or more	20,500	

Note: Data are from 1946 Census.

SOURCE: Pressat, Roland (1972).

particular number of live births) who go on to have at least one *additional* child during the course of their remaining childbearing years. This measure is often calculated for married women only.

In the example shown in Table 4, the first parity progression ratio, P_1 (indicating the probability of progressing from parity 0 to parity 1) is calculated by dividing the total number of married women who had at least one child (901,785) by the total number of married women (1,094,294).

Pros. The parity progression ratio allows detailed analysis of family formation and childbearing patterns for a given cohort of women. It is useful for comparisons with other birth cohorts or between the same birth cohorts in different countries.

Cons. The parity progression ratio can be used only to study childbearing patterns among women who have completed their childbearing years and requires detailed data on children ever born from a census or survey.

See also: *Mortality Measurement; Population Dynamics.*

BIBLIOGRAPHY

Bogue, Donald J., Eduardo E. Arriaga, and Douglas L. Anderton, eds. 1993. *Readings in Population Research Methodology, Volume 3. Fertility Research.* Chicago: United Nations Population Fund and Social Development Center.

Coale, Ansley J., and Paul Demeny. 1983. *Regional Model Life Tables and Stable Populations,* 2nd edition. New York: Academic Press.

Council of Europe. 2000. *Recent Demographic Developments in Europe 2000.* Strasbourg: Council of Europe.

National Center for Health Statistics and U.S. Census Bureau. 2002. *Births: Final Data for 2000.* Hyattsville, MD: National Center for Health Statistics and U.S. Census Bureau.

Pressat, Roland. 1972. *Demographic Analysis: Methods, Results, Applications.* Chicago: Aldine Atherton, Inc.

Shryock, Henry S., Jacob S. Siegel, et al.. 1976. *The Methods and Materials of Demography,* Condensed Edition. New York: Academic Press.

Weeks, John R. 2002. *Population, an Introduction to Concepts and Issues.* Belmont, CA: Wadsworth Publishing Company.

CARL HAUB

FERTILITY TRANSITION, SOCIOECONOMIC DETERMINANTS OF

To understand the amazing decline in fertility—the average number of births per woman—in modern times, it is necessary to begin with an examination of high fertility in traditional societies. Fundamentally, fertility was high, typically around five to seven births per woman, because of high death rates. Without high fertility, most societies would have experienced population decline and eventual disappearance. The necessity of high fertility for the survival of the community does not imply that most persons had a conscious awareness of the relationship. Rather, the desire for high levels of childbearing was woven into the cultural fabric and the social institutions of traditional societies.

In addition to strong cultural inducements for marriage and childbearing, the well-being of the family in traditional societies was dependent on having several children who survived to adulthood. Families were the primary economic units as well as reproductive unions. Children were a valued source of household labor and were also the preferred means to guarantee the old-age security of parents. In societies without formal schools, mass media, and modern transportation, family relationships and interactions were the center of social and cultural life. Larger extended families provided more companionship, a wider circle of trust, more protection in times of trouble, and a higher status for patriarchs and matriarchs than did smaller families.

The population problem in traditional societies was maintaining some sort of rough balance between births and deaths. If population decline could threaten community survival, a long period of increasing population numbers would likely outpace the expansion of food and other resources. Although population growth averaged close to zero over long stretches of human history, there were periods during which population size increased across generations. In many cases, out-migration to frontier regions reduced population pressure, but all too frequently it was crisis mortality that brought population numbers back in line with subsistence levels.

These episodes of famine, plague, and war were labeled by the English economist T. R. Malthus (1766–1834) as positive checks, which he thought were inevitable, given the tendency for populations to grow faster than the means of subsistence. The only way to avoid these dismal cycles of demographic growth and implosion, Malthus argued, was through preventive checks, of which the only acceptable variants were moral restraint that encouraged celibacy and the postponement of marriage. Malthus was pessimistic, however, that moral restraint would be sufficient to avert positive checks because of the underlying "passion between the sexes." Malthus was partially right. His pessimistic scenario of expansion and decline did characterize the population dynamics of many premodern societies, although periods of growth could be accommodated for decades or even centuries, depending on the technology of production, the possibilities for long-distance trade, and the size of the frontier. Moreover, plagues, famines, and wars often followed their own dynamics, independent of population size and growth.

The major failing of Malthus's argument, however, was to not notice that even high fertility of five to seven births per woman was well below the maximum number of births (some 15 or 16) that might occur if there were no restraints on childbearing. In all societies, fertility (or infant survival) is held in check in varying combinations by delayed age at marriage, by some proportion of the population never marrying, by long periods of breast-feeding (which suppresses ovulation), and by cultural proscriptions that affect the frequency and timing of sexual intercourse. Folk methods of birth control together with abortion and infanticide would often have also played a role. Such practices, especially delayed age at marriage, reduced fertility in many traditional western European societies by the eighteenth and nineteenth centuries to levels of only four to five births per woman—in circumstances in which the probability of survival to adulthood may have averaged only around 50 percent. The variations in "high fertility" across societies and over time suggest that fertility was regulated in response to socioeconomic conditions and ecological constraints, although most couples may not have been consciously controlling family size.

The major turning point in world demographic history, and the conclusive break from Malthus's predicted cycle, was the sustained declines in fertility that began in France and North America early in the nineteenth century and elsewhere in western European countries around 1880 and that led to small families that averaged about two births per couple by the third decade of the twentieth century. Demographers label a fertility rate of about two births per woman as replacement-level fertility because two children, in the contemporary context of low mortality, are sufficient to replace their parents in the next generation. The transition from high to low fertility was not only an unprecedented demographic revolution but also a cultural revolution with profound implications for the definition of the family and the adult roles of women and men. Modern societies are still in the process of adapting old (and creating new) institutions and gender roles in the wake of the relatively recent transition to low fertility.

About a hundred years after the beginnings of fertility declines in western Europe—declines that with varying delays soon also spread to the rest of that continent—a similar process began in the developing countries of Asia, Latin America, and Africa. This second wave of fertility transitions began soon after the end of World War II in Japan and in the late 1960s and early 1970s in a few other East Asian countries and small island societies. By the 1990s, fertility declines had begun in almost every part of the globe, including areas of persistently high fertility in South Asia and sub-Saharan Africa. Although most of these fertility transitions were still in process and some had far to go by the early twenty-first century, a generalized low-fertility world was in sight. Replacement-level fertility was achieved in some East and Southeast Asian countries in the 1980s and 1990s, and the United Nations assumed (in its medium variant projection series) that almost all developing countries would have below-replacement-level fertility or below replacement fertility by the middle of the twenty-first century.

Demographic Transition Theory

The theoretical task of explaining modern fertility transitions as a consequence (or a delayed consequence) of declines in mortality and of the socioeconomic changes that have transformed rural agrarian societies into modern industrial societies has been the central question of the scientific field of demography. Although some of the basic ideas can be traced back to the first half of the twentieth century and the works of Warren Thompson (1887–1973), Adolphe Landry (1874–1956), and Kingsley Davis (1908–1997), Frank W. Notestein (1902–1983) wrote the classic statement of demographic transition theory in 1953. The central thesis of the theory was generally presented as a three-stage model: the first stage consisting of pretransition societies characterized by high fertility and mortality; a second transitional stage, consisting of societies with declining mortality and, after a lag, declining fertility; and a third and final stage, consisting of posttransitional societies, which lave low mortality and fertility. Although sometimes framed as more of a descriptive account of what has happened, demographic transition theory, as presented by Notestein, was a sophisticated interpretation of how fertility declined in response to declining mortality, the reduced role of the family in economic organization, the growing independence of women from traditional roles, and the shift from customary behavior to calculative rationality spurred by popular education.

Until the 1970s, the theory of the demographic transition was almost universally accepted by demographers and was widely disseminated in introductory textbooks through stylized graphs and an interpretation of declining fertility in response to the modern forces of industrialization, urbanization, and literacy. These processes had occurred in many Western countries during the nineteenth and twentieth centuries and were presumed to be on the near-term horizon of many developing countries. Relative to other theories in the social sciences, demographic transition theory represented one of the most ambitious and convincing interpretations of the momentous social changes of modern times.

The general formulation of demographic transition theory, sometimes summarized as a list of independent variables associated with urbanization, industrialization, and modernity, was often an inadequate guide to cumulative empirical research. Because the many indicators representing the key causal forces were considered interchangeable (and because the unit of analysis was at best vaguely defined), many of the specific hypotheses of the theory, such as the changing cost of children in rural and urban environments, were rarely differentiated from the broader story about industrialization and urbanization. The net result was that in spite of a proliferation of empirical studies, often with contradictory results, relatively few refinements were made to demographic transition theory.

There were, however, two major essays, published by Davis in 1963 and by Ansley Coale (1917–2002) in 1974, that marked major advances from the standard formulation of demographic transition theory. Davis's "theory of change and response in modern demographic history" aimed to broaden the scope of the theory to include, in addition to declines in marital fertility (the standard empirical focus), the variety of ways that populations respond to population pressure (because of declining mortality) in a context of possibilities for socioeconomic mobility. Although declines in mortality and progress toward modernization typically reduce marital fertility (through increasing use of contraception and higher rates of abortion), Davis noted that postponement of marriage, increasing rates of celibacy, and out-migration were also part of the demographic repertoire of adaptation to population pressure. Davis suggested that the timing of the onset and the pace of fertility declines vary across societies (and regions in a society) depending on the relative weights of these responses. Although there have been a few empirical tests of Davis's hypotheses, his "systems approach" to demographic theory is more admired than empirically addressed.

Based on his observations of the varied patterns of fertility decline in late-nineteenth- and early-twentieth-century Europe, Coale suggested that fertility declines were affected not only by socioeco-nomic change but also by the cultural context of the society. In an influential formulation he specified three preconditions for fertility decline (summarized by others as "ready, willing, and able"): (1) "fertility must be within the calculus of conscious choice," (2) "reduced fertility must be advantageous," and (3) "effective techniques of fertility reduction must be available" (Coale 1973, p. 65). Demographic transi-tion theory had primarily focused on the second pre-condition, namely that there must be a perceived so-cioeconomic gain to motivate couples (women) to want fewer children. Presumably, changes in repro-ductive motivations would follow from industrial-ization, urbanization, and other changes in social in-stitutions that lower the economic advantages (or increase the costs) of children.

The first and third preconditions noted by Coale point to factors that had been largely taken for grant-ed by demographers—factors that are irrelevant if the second condition is not satisfied and readily forthcoming if it is. By fertility being within the cal-culus of conscious choice, Coale meant there must be social legitimation for the idea of fertility regula-tion before most couples will act in ways that chal-lenge traditional values of having a large family. This assumption is supported by the 1986 finding of Ron Lesthaeghe and Chris Wilson that secularization (measured by voting for nonreligious political par-ties) was a very important determinant of the timing of fertility decline, net of economic factors, across provinces in Europe. In deeply traditional societies with few external influences beyond the family and religious authorities, couples may not think there are any choices to be made. The third precondition is that couples know how to regulate fertility. The presence of knowledge of fertility limitation in a so-ciety does not mean that all (or even most) couples actually knew how to practice fertility control. With the massive diffusion of information about birth control and the contraceptive supplies and services distributed through family planning organizations and private channels in most contemporary socie-ties, Coale's first and third preconditions are proba-bly less consequential for the modern wave of fer-tility transitions than they were for the earlier transi-tions.

Alternative Theories of Fertility Decline

In the 1970s and 1980s, two streams of demographic research directly challenged the hegemony of demo-

graphic transition theory. The first was the surpris-ing findings from the Princeton European Fertility Project, initially noted in a 1979 article by John Kno-del and Etienne van de Walle and later discussed in detail in the project's 1986 summary volume by Coale and Susan Cotts Watkins. Although the Euro-pean Fertility Project was envisaged as an empirical test of transition theory on its original home ground, the results showed that the pace of fertility decline across provinces and regions of Europe was only modestly correlated with the socioeconomic vari-ables that figured so prominently in the standard theory. Instead, the patterns and pace of fertility decline appeared to be more associated with re-gions that shared common languages and culture than with regions sharing common socioeconomic features.

The second challenge to demographic transition theory came from the results of comparative analy-ses of data from the World Fertility Survey (WFS) project. The WFS project consisted of cross-sectional studies of individual-level correlates of fer-tility behaviors, attitudes, and contraceptive practice in dozens of developing countries around the globe. Although these studies showed that, in general, fer-tility was correlated in the expected direction with female education, urban residence, and other socio-economic variables, the relationships were often modest and many exceptions could be found. Fol-lowing on these findings and the research of Lesthaeghe, John Cleland and Chris Wilson wrote a bold essay, published in 1987, that questioned the empirical validity of demographic transition theory and suggested that an alternative model of culture and fertility, labeled ideational theory, would be a more appropriate theoretical framework. Ideational theory holds that cultural values are the primary in-fluence on fertility. In some cases, cultural values supporting high fertility may be only slowly (and partially) eroded by socioeconomic changes. In other situations, cultural values that shape fertility behavior can change rapidly with the diffusion of ideas independently of socioeconomic change.

There has also been a proliferation of other new theories and accounts of modern fertility transitions. One of these is John C. Caldwell's theory of inter-generational wealth flows. Caldwell posits that mass education and Westernization (values communicat-ed through the mass media and cinema) have popu-larized the idea of "child-centered" families that re-duce the flow of wealth, services, and other valued resources up the generational ladder. Because these changes have made children less valuable, there are fewer incentives to have large families. Another, very influential, theoretical direction was suggested by the application of microeconomic theory to household decision-making regarding choices to have children. And Richard Easterlin has attempted to integrate the economic and sociological approaches to fertility change in a model that takes account of the demand for children, the "supply" of children, and the cost of fertility regulation.

Although there are many insightful ideas and considerable intellectual excitement in the new theoretical literature on fertility transitions, it is sometimes hard to tell what is fundamentally new and what is merely the repackaging of earlier ideas. Karen Oppenheim Mason cogently argued in 1997 that much of the debate on the causes of fertility transitions is in fact concerned with variations in the proximate conditions that influence the timing of fertility declines, and that there is broad agreement over the long-term historical factors, especially mortality decline, that have led to fertility transitions. The portrayal of demographic transition theory as a universal model of modernization and fertility decline is probably too general and vague, but there is a considerable body of evidence that socioeconomic development has been more influential in shaping historical and contemporary fertility declines than many critics have acknowledged.

There are, of course, considerable variations in the timing of the onset and the pace of fertility declines across populations, and across groups and regions within populations, and these variations are often associated with cultural and linguistic factors. The influences of socioeconomic and ideational factors need not, however, be considered as opposing hypotheses, but rather as complementary elements of an integrated theory of fertility change. Fertility, and population growth more generally, clearly respond to societal pressures that threaten the survival and well-being of human communities. Although there is much evidence that socioeconomic development is associated with fertility change in many (but perhaps not all) societies, there is ample room to consider additional hypotheses for other social and cultural factors that influence demographic change in varied circumstances. Observing the rapid spread of fertility transition to almost every region and country, at highly varied levels of socioeconomic de-

velopment, Cleland concluded in 2001 that declines in mortality are the most likely common cause.

The impact of public intervention, particularly family planning programs, on fertility trends continues to be debated. The conventional wisdom, initially proposed in the classic 1976 study by Ronald Freedman and Bernard Berelson, is that the combination of vigorous family planning efforts and a favorable socioeconomic setting produce conditions most likely to lead to lowered fertility. Nevertheless, the task of sorting out the independent and joint effects of setting and policy has been remarkably elusive. The initiation of family planning programs tends to be an inherent part of the process of development itself, and it is difficult to obtain independent empirical assessments of each. Successful governments tend to have effective public programs, including well-managed family planning programs. Within countries, family planning clinics are not distributed randomly but are typically placed in areas of high fertility. Thus, the bivariate (two-variable) association between proximity to family planning services and level of fertility is usually positive. The results of more complex multivariable models are heavily dependent on initial assumptions and the analytical formulations: Several studies show only modest effects of family planning programs; others have reported more positive assessments.

The end of fertility transition was never defined beyond the general expectation that low fertility would approach the replacement level (around two children per couple) within some modest range of fluctuation. This has generally been the case in the United States: The total fertility rate (births per woman) dropped slightly below two births per woman in the mid-1970s, and then rose slightly to around two in the 1990s. In Europe, however, fertility continued its downward descent and by the late 1990s was well below the replacement level and showing no sign of rising. In some eastern and southern European countries in the early twenty-first century, average fertility, as measured by the period total fertility rate (the number of children a woman would eventually bear if current fertility rates persisted) appeared to be approaching one child per couple. One school of thought holds that this is a temporary phenomenon, driven primarily by poor economic conditions and a temporary rise in the average age of childbearing. If fertility is merely being postponed and most couples will eventually have two births, then in the early twenty-first century period measures of fertility are not an accurate prediction of the future. Indeed, survey data on fertility expectations show that most women in industrial societies still want to have two children. But other observers believe that the costs of childbearing (socially and economically) are so high in modern industrial societies that below-replacement fertility is likely to continue indefinitely, with the prospect of declining population size.

Conclusions

The first fertility transitions began in the nineteenth century, and average fertility levels reached about two births per woman in a few western European countries in the early decades of the twentieth century. At the dawn of the twenty-first century, the dominant trend is of a global fertility transition throughout the developing world and a sudden drop to below-replacement-level fertility in many European countries. At first glance, these trends suggest the conclusion that modern fertility transitions are among the most dramatic social changes in human history, yielding a new demographic metabolism that is remolding the character of the family and gender roles.

On the other hand, it is possible to interpret modern fertility transitions as corrective adjustments that are returning the human population to a stationary state where, over the long term, the number of births is approximately equal to the number of deaths. Even with high fertility, most families in premodern societies were of modest size because of high mortality. According to this perspective, the dominant demographic change of the last century is not the decline of fertility, but the rapid increase in population during the transition from the general stability of high morality and fertility to the emerging balance of low mortality and fertility. After several centuries of rapid social change and accelerating demographic growth, the world population reached approximately 1.6 billion in 1900. During the fateful twentieth century, the population of the world grew fourfold to the once barely plausible number of 6 billion in the year 2000. Even with continued slowing, the momentum of population growth is likely to add an additional 2 or 3 billion to the global total by the middle of the twenty-first century. The implications of this era of growth on the human condition and Earth's resources are only slowly being understood.

Both of these apparently different perspectives are valid, and together they suggest why it is so difficult to explain modern fertility transitions. There is no single path that has been common to all the societies that have experienced (or are currently experiencing) declines in fertility. Although population pressure from declining mortality may be the most common factor across societies, there are wide societal variations in the pace of socioeconomic development, the relative role of government and private markets, cultural traditions and gender stratification, and the strength of family planning programs. As Freedman suggested in 1979, there is likely to be a variety of conditions that are "sufficient" to lead to lowered fertility. With further study of these variant conditions and their fertility outcomes, past and future, there is the prospect of creating a simpler, but more comprehensive theory of fertility transition as the central element in understanding world demographic history.

See also: *Coale, Ansley Johnson; Culture and Population; Davis, Kingsley; Demographic Transition; Development, Population and; Freedman, Ronald; Homeostasis; Landry, Adolphe; Mortality-Fertility of Relationships; Notestein, Frank W.; Thompson, Warren S.*

BIBLIOGRAPHY

Bongaarts, John, and Susan C. Watkins. 1996. "Social Interactions and Contemporary Fertility Transitions." *Population and Development Review* 22: 639–682.

Bulatao, Rodolfo A., and John B. Casterline, eds. 2001. *Global Fertility Transition,* Supplement to Volume 27 of *Population and Development Review.* New York: Population Council.

Caldwell, John C. 1982. *Theory of Fertility Decline.* London: Academic Press.

Cleland, John, and Chris Wilson. 1987. "Demand Theories of the Fertility Transition: An Iconoclastic View." *Population Studies* 41: 5–30.

Coale, Ansley J. 1973. "The Demographic Transition Reconsidered." In *International Population Conference,* Vol. 1. Liège, Belgium: International Union for the Scientific Study of Population.

———. 1974. "The History of the Human Population." In *The Human Population: A Scientific American Book.* San Francisco: Freeman.

Coale, Ansley J., and Susan Cotts Watkins, eds. 1986. *The Decline of Fertility in Europe.* Princeton, NJ: Princeton University Press.

Davis, Kingsley. 1945. "The World Demographic Transition." *Annals of the American Academy of Political and Social Science* 237: 1–11.

———. 1963. "The Theory of Change and Response in Modern Demographic History." *Population Index* 29: 345–366.

Easterlin, Richard A. 1978. "The Economics and Sociology of Fertility: A Synthesis." In *Historical Studies of Changing Fertility,* ed. Charles Tilly. Princeton, NJ: Princeton University Press.

Freedman, Ronald. 1979. "Theories of Fertility Decline: A Reappraisal." *Social Forces* 58: 1–17.

Freedman, Ronald, and Bernard Berelson. 1976. "The Record of Family Planning Programs." *Studies in Family Planning* 7: 1–40.

Hirschman, Charles. 1994. "Why Fertility Changes." *Annual Review of Sociology* 20: 203–233.

Knodel, John, and Etienne van de Walle. 1979. "Lessons from the Past: Policy Implications of Historical Population Studies." *Population and Development Review* 5: 217–246.

Lesthaeghe, Ron, and Chris Wilson. 1986. "Modes of Production, Secularization, and the Pace of Fertility Decline in Western Europe, 1870–1930." In *The Decline of Fertility in Europe,* ed. Ansley J. Coale and Susan Cotts Watkins. Princeton, NJ: Princeton University Press.

Lesthaeghe, Ron, and Johan Surkyn. 1988. "Cultural Dynamics and Economic Theories of Fertility Change." *Population and Development Review* 14: 1–45.

Mason, Karen Oppenheim. 1997. "Explaining Fertility Transitions." *Demography* 34: 443–454.

Notestein, Frank W. 1953. "Economic Problems of Population Change." In *Proceedings of the Eighth International Conference of Agricultural Economists.* New York: Oxford University Press.

Thompson, Warren S. 1929. "Population." *American Journal of Sociology* 34: 959–975.

United Nations. 2001. *World Population Prospects: The 2000 Revision.* 2 vols. New York: United Nations.

Wrigley, E. A. 1969. *Population and History.* New York: McGraw-Hill.

CHARLES HIRSCHMAN

FOOD SUPPLY AND POPULATION

The relationship between a population and its food supply is a matter of prime importance. Awareness of this is reflected, for example, in the Chinese characters corresponding to the English word *population*: 人口. In these characters, a human figure appears on the left; an open mouth—requiring food—is on the right. However, it was economist T. R. Malthus's so-called "First Essay" of 1798 that famously portrayed the relationship in its starkest form. If unchecked, wrote Malthus, a population could grow geometrically, but given a limited area of cropland its food supply could grow only arithmetically, at best. These arguments raised the specter of "gigantic inevitable famine," which by raising the death rate would be the ultimate factor in restoring a rough balance between the population's size and its food supply.

Population and Food Supply—Recent History

Concern that population growth might outstrip the capacity to raise food production has been expressed many times since Malthus—particularly during the period from 1950 to 2000, when the world's population increased from about 2.5 billion to 6 billion. Writers like Paul Ehrlich and Lester Brown doubt whether food output can be raised to match this demographic growth. They see a future of mounting food supply difficulties, increasing hunger, and famines. However, the global death toll from famines has fallen very considerably since the mid-twentieth century. And while acknowledging that the world food situation and outlook have many problems, most analysts, including Nikos Alexandratos in 1995; Tim Dyson in 1996; Donald Mitchell, Merlinda Ingco and Ronald Duncan in 1997; and Alex McCalla and Cesar Revoredo in 2001, take a significantly more positive view.

The relationship between food supply and population is complex. There is no doubt that *average* levels of per capita food availability for the world as a whole have increased appreciably during recent decades. Thus the United Nations Food and Agricultural Organization (FAO) estimates that between the period from 1969 to 1971 and the period from 1997 to 1999 the average daily global level of per capita calorie (i.e. food energy) supply rose from 2,413 to 2,802 calories, and the daily availability of protein increased from about 65 to 75 grams per person (calorie and protein figures cited are from FAO, 2002). However, most of the world's population growth during this period happened in poor regions, like South Asia and sub-Saharan Africa, where it is estimated that sizeable fractions of the populations are undernourished (i.e. having levels of food consumption below those required to maintain body weight and support light activity). Consequently, FAO estimates that the total number of undernourished people in the world declined only modestly in the same period: from around 941 million to about 826 million, according to Alexandratos in 1995 and FAO in 2000.

East Asia—Positive Developments

At a broad regional level progress has been very variable. The most positive developments have occurred in East Asia. In China the period since 1980 has seen major gains in average per capita calorie supplies and protein intake, and the diet has generally become better and more diverse. Per capita incomes have risen, and with increased incentives to invest and increase their production, farmers have sharply increased their output of most foodstuffs—notably rice, wheat, fruits, vegetables, and pork. However, because there is little new land that can be brought into cultivation, almost all of this increase in food production has come about through processes of agricultural intensification: the improvements in food supply that China's growing population have enjoyed have occurred mostly through increasing food crop *yields* (i.e. output per unit of harvested area). China has invested heavily in crop research—especially in developing higher yielding varieties of rice—and Chinese farmers have also sharply raised their use of chemical fertilizers.

Southeast Asia, the Middle East, and Latin America—Mixed Results

In Southeast Asia, the Middle East, and Latin America there have also been significant gains in average levels of per capita food availability during recent decades—despite the occurrence of considerable population growth. Diets have generally become more varied, and the populations of these regions have experienced marked rises in their average supplies of calories and protein—again, mainly due to increased food crop yields. The technological developments arising from the so-called *Green Revolution* starting in the late 1960s—especially the introduction of higher-yielding varieties of rice and wheat, combined with greater applications of nitrogenous fertilizers on irrigated land—have benefited most countries.

However, in the Middle East, where water for agriculture is often in short supply, many countries have also turned to purchasing sizeable quantities of cereals on the international market—much of which is then used as livestock feed in order to produce meat. Indeed, some Middle Eastern countries rely upon cereal imports for as much as half of all the grain they use. This is a notable case in which increased trade has augmented food supplies in the face of a significant environmental constraint (i.e. water scarcity) and substantial demographic growth.

Conditions for food production are generally favorable in Latin America, where some countries, notably Brazil and Argentina, are major exporters of products like fruits, vegetables, wheat, and meat. Of course, the positive food situation in these three regions should not obscure the fact of considerable inter-country variation. Cambodia, Peru, and Sudan, for example, have populations with very low per capita supplies of calories and protein. And, as in East Asia, there are significant numbers of poor, undernourished people in each of these regions.

South Asia—Significant Problems

The food situation in South Asia is significantly worse than in the regions discussed above. The FAO estimates that India alone contains about one quarter of all the world's undernourished people; in the years 1996 to 1998 its average calorie supply was estimated at only 2,434 per person per day. A particular problem of the South Asian diet is its lack of high quality protein due, in part, to widespread vegetarianism. It is uncertain whether the nutritional content of the Indian diet has improved much during recent decades, despite significant increases in average incomes and little change in the real price of food. What has happened is that people have diversified the foods they consume, purchasing more fruits, vegetables, and milk, but reducing their consumption of legumes, which are nutritionally rather valuable. Food production in South Asia has benefited from high-yielding varieties of wheat and rice, but there has been little change in the cultivation of traditional coarse cereals. Consequently, the per capita availability of these latter food crops, which tend to be more nutritious, has fallen.

The nutritional status of South Asia's population is generally dismal. In India, for example, nearly half of all children under age three are estimated to be underweight, and a similar proportion of adult women are anemic. However, such health and nutritional problems are often not seen as problematic by the people themselves: Virtually all Indian households report that they have "two square meals a day." With an increasing variety of non-food items available for purchase in local markets, increased per capita incomes have often not been spent on food.

South Asia's population could well increase by 600 million in the first half of the twenty-first century. Average levels of food consumption may well rise, but this demographic growth, and recent trends in food demand and production, do not augur well for a major decrease in the total number of undernourished people.

Sub-Saharan Africa—Widespread Undernourishment, Grim Prognosis

In major world regions the food situation is probably grimmest in sub-Saharan Africa, where FAO (2000) estimates that in the period from 1996 to 1998 about one-third of the total population was undernourished. The region's estimated per capita daily calorie supply for the years 1997 to 1999 suggests scant improvement compared to the 1969 to 1971 period. This is the world's poorest region and it has experienced the fastest demographic growth, with populations often doubling in less than 25 years.

African farmers have been unable to raise their food crop yields at similar rates. In fact, average cereal yields rose very little in the decades around the turn of the century. Consequently, total food output has been increased largely through processes of extensification—increasing the harvested area. Traditional fallow periods have been reduced (often leading to losses in soil fertility) and the area of cropland has been increased by converting tracts of bushland and forest to cultivation. These developments have

sometimes occurred in conditions of sociopolitical instability, and where governments have neglected the agricultural sector. Moreover, until the early 1990s global agricultural research tended to be focused on crops like rice and wheat, which are not widely grown in sub-Saharan Africa. There is no doubt that given appropriate levels of investment this region's agricultural potential is considerable. But most analysts envisage that in the first decades of the twenty-first century average levels of per capita food production and consumption will not rise by much. With the likelihood of considerable future population growth the total number of undernourished people may well increase. Adding to this bleak outlook, the region may continue to experience food crises and famines—often with warfare acting as an important contributory cause.

The Developed World—Obesity, Overproduction, Farm Subsidies

In considering the world's more developed regions, the situation is clearly very different. In most developed countries the number of people who are undernourished is tiny (although the economic disruption following the collapse of communism in Eastern Europe and the former Soviet Union in the 1990s caused real hunger at times). However, in the developed world obesity—linked to overeating and sedentary lifestyles—is often a serious and growing problem (one, it must be said, which is also increasing in many urban areas of the developing world).

Recent decades have seen considerable competition in the agricultural sector, particularly between the United States and the European Union. Both these major food-producing blocs have experienced difficulties in trying to reduce the subsidies they pay their farmers, yet at the same time agricultural yields have continued to rise, often at a brisk pace. Consequently, the overproduction of food in relation to the volume of *effective demand* (the ability of people or nations to pay for it) has been, and continues to be, a serious problem. A consequence is that the prices of many foods, including important cereal crops like wheat and maize (i.e. corn), on the international market remain low. This benefits the developing countries that import these crops—for example, those in the Middle East. But these same low prices are harmful to agricultural producers and exporters in other countries, including some of the poorest developing countries. These problems of international political economy are the subject of ne-

FIGURE 1

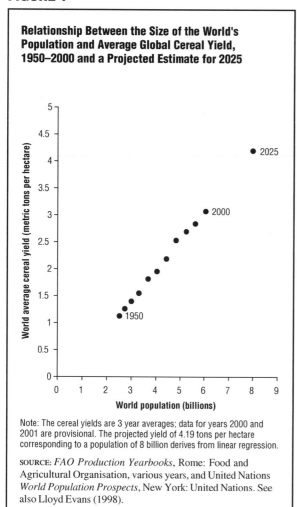

Relationship Between the Size of the World's Population and Average Global Cereal Yield, 1950–2000 and a Projected Estimate for 2025

Note: The cereal yields are 3 year averages; data for years 2000 and 2001 are provisional. The projected yield of 4.19 tons per hectare corresponding to a population of 8 billion derives from linear regression.

SOURCE: *FAO Production Yearbooks*, Rome: Food and Agricultural Organisation, various years, and United Nations *World Population Prospects*, New York: United Nations. See also Lloyd Evans (1998).

gotiations in the World Trade Organization, but they are unlikely to go away.

Summary—Progress and Problems

In summary, progress in feeding the growing world population has been mixed. For most regions the situation has improved; although even in China, where progress has been marked, there remain tens of millions of people who lack the purchasing power to buy sufficient quantities of food. The record of South Asia, however, is best described as patchy; and for sub-Saharan Africa it is bad. There is no doubt that the knowledge, crop varieties, and technologies to significantly raise per capita food supplies in these two regions exist. But the socioeconomic and political conditions for their successful utilization have often been lacking. Moreover, population growth in both regions has probably made the task of raising average levels of food availability per person harder than it would otherwise have been. This situation appears likely to continue into the early decades of the twenty-first century. There will be significant progress in raising average levels of food consumption in most regions, but with South Asia and, still more, sub-Saharan Africa lagging behind. In general, population growth in the developing world will continue to be the main factor contributing to the growth of world cereal demand; and some of this growth in demand will be met by increased production from farmers in more developed regions, especially in North America.

Cereals—Indicator of Diet Quality

This brief account of food and population can appropriately conclude with a comment on cereals, the most important component of the human diet. Cereals make up about half of all direct human caloric intake (as bread or cooked rice, for example), and perhaps two-thirds if account is taken of the large quantities of cereals that are fed to animals to produce meat, milk, and eggs. Cereal data can be used to exemplify the same basic element of identity between a population and its food supply that was illustrated by the Chinese characters for population described above. Figure 1 plots the relationship between the size of the world's population since the early 1950s and the average level of the world cereal yield. It reflects the fact that to a considerable extent the huge growth of the global population during recent decades has both contributed to, and been supported by, the rise in the average world cereal yield. Demographic growth has meant that yields have had to be increased, while at the same time the attainment of higher yields has supported the increasing population. Note that the relationship is fairly tight—sufficiently so to make a reasonably firm prediction that when the world's population reaches 8 billion, which it is projected to do around the year 2025, the world cereal yield will be slightly above four metric tons per hectare. Such a yield will be required to supply food for a world of 8 billion.

See also: *Land Use; Natural Resources and Population; Nitrogen Cycle.*

BIBLIOGRAPHY

Alexandratos, Nikos, ed. 1995. *World Agriculture Towards 2010, An FAO Study.* Chichester, Eng.: John Wiley.

Bansil, P. C. 1999. *Demand for Foodgrains by 2020 AD.* New Delhi: Observer Research Foundation.

Brown, Lester R., Gary Gardner, and Brian Halweil. 1999. *Beyond Malthus: Nineteen Dimensions of the Population Challenge.* New York: W. W. Norton.

Cohen, Joel E., and Nina V. Federoff, eds. 1999. *Colloquium on Plants and Population: Is There Time?* Washington, D.C.: National Academy of Sciences.

Devereux, Stephen. 2000. *Famine in the Twentieth Century.* Working Paper 105. Sussex, Eng.: Institute of Development Studies.

Dyson, Tim. 1996. *Population and Food: Global Trends and Future Prospects.* London and New York: Routledge.

———. 2001. "World Food Trends: A Neo-Malthusian Prospect?" *Proceedings of the American Philosophical Society,* 145(4): 438–455.

Ehrlich, Paul E. 1968. *The Population Bomb.* New York: Ballantine Books.

Evans, Lloyd T. 1998. "Greater Crop Production." In *Feeding a World Population of More Than Eight Billion: A Challenge to Science.* eds. J. C. Waterlow, D. G. Armstrong, Leslie Fowden, and Ralph Riley. New York and Oxford: Oxford University Press and the Rank Prize Funds.

Food and Agricultural Organization (FAO). 2000. *The State of Food Insecurity in the World 2000.* Rome: Food and Agricultural Organization.

IIPS and ORC Macro. 2001. *National Family Health Survey (NFHS-2), 1998–99: India.* Mumbai: International Institute for Population Sciences.

McCalla, Alex F., and Cesar L. Revoredo. 2001. *Prospects for Global Food Security: A Critical Appraisal of Past Projections and Predictions.* Washington, D.C.: International Food Policy Research Institute.

Mitchell, Donald O., Merlinda D. Ingco, and Ronald C. Duncan. 1997. *The World Food Outlook.* Cambridge, Eng.: Cambridge University Press.

INTERNET RESOURCE.

Food and Agricultural Organization (FAO). 2002. *FAOSTAT.* <http://www.apps.fao.org>.

TIM DYSON

FORCED MIGRATION

Prior to the 1920s, international migration was largely unrestricted, and little was done to legally categorize immigrants according to the reason for their movement. Previous centuries had seen large forced population displacements (the Huguenots from France in the seventeenth century being just one example). However, the twentieth century saw massive, forced population movements across international borders, and these gave rise to legal distinctions that have affected all those seeking refuge outside their country of origin.

It is essential to make a distinction between *forced migration* (the subject of this article), which involves the movement imposed on large populations (groups of persons counted in the thousands), on the one hand, and individual migrants, who may or may not be part of a larger group but are persecuted in their country and seek asylum and the legal status of refugee as individuals in another country. The need for distinguishing between the two categories became clear as a result of post-World War II developments when political, religious, or ethnic persecution forced large numbers of people to leave their home countries, making the established procedures for individual consideration of applications for refugee status unworkable. The terms *forced migration* and *forced displacement* are used interchangeably in this article. Deportations within states, such as those in the Soviet Union during the 1940s, in which more than 3 million people were deported within the state, are not dealt with here.

Six specific large forced population displacements are briefly referred to below. These are the displacements of Russians, Armenians, German and Austrian Jews, Hungarians, the Indo-Chinese, and the victims of ethnic cleansing in the former Yugoslavia in the 1990s. These cases are chronologically handled: the League of Nations period, the Cold War period, and the post-Cold War period provide a useful categorization. Worldwide, a great many more people have been forced to flee their homes and cross international borders, as they became the targets of group persecution. However, the six cases highlighted here paint a historical picture of forced migration in the twentieth century.

The League of Nations

The first two cases of forced migration, those of the Russians and the Armenians, can be described as being part of the aftershocks of World War I. The Russian Revolution and the civil war that followed it led to a Bolshevik regime, self-described as a dictatorship of the proletariat, which placed large population groups, declared to be class enemies, in physical jeopardy. Economic collapse, culminating in a massive famine, exacerbated the fears of persecution on political-ideological grounds. By 1921, it is estimated that some 800,000 to 1.5 million Russians fled the country to seek safety and a better future in other European countries. In February 1921, the League of Nations passed its first resolution on refugees and, later that year, held a conference on the question of Russian refugees and appointed a prominent Norwegian, Fritjof Nansen, as High Commissioner for Refugees. Special arrangements included the creation of the Nansen Passport, a travel document for those deprived of the protections normally granted by a state of citizenship to the bearer of a passport.

The disintegration of the Ottoman Empire had disastrous consequences for Armenians, a Christian minority with an ancient and distinct culture living within a Muslim population. Decades of repression in the dying phase of Ottoman rule generated substantial Armenian refugee movements, notably at the end of the Greco-Turkish War (1897). By World War I, the Armenians were essentially a stateless victim group, in the precarious position of being relatively prosperous, middle-class, and urban. In 1915, the Turks had begun what Claudena Skran describes as "a radical method of dealing with the unwanted Armenian minority: genocide" (Skran 1995, p. 44). In addition to massive loss of life, the fledgling Armenian state was besieged by its neighbors, with the Russians and Turkey carving up the territory of the new republic between them. By 1924, more than 200,000 Armenian refugees were spread through Europe, the Balkans, and the Middle East. Many of these eventually settled in the United States. The tragedy of the Armenians was not only that so many fled, but also that so many perished because they did not become refugees.

In Germany, the Nazis's rise to power in early 1933 raised the prospect that a similar situation would eventually develop as to that country's Jewish population: Under Nazi laws, Jews were officially discriminated against on the basis of racial criteria. By October of 1933, the League of Nations had decided that the persecution and exodus of German Jews posed such a problem to other states that a new High Commissioner was appointed specifically for

refugees coming out of Germany. By 1938, 150,000 people, mostly Jews, had fled Germany, and 126,000 fled Austria following the Anschluss in that year. (As it later transpired, these numbers represented a small fraction of the persecuted population that eventually perished in concentration camps and forced labor camps during World War II.) To deal with this migrant flow, two new definitions were created—for those fleeing Germany and for those fleeing Austria, as a result of Nazi persecution. Both the new High Commissioner post, and the new definitions, highlighted a difficult international political problem. Creating specific measures for specific groups of refugees and naming the state from which they fled was tantamount to an explicit international legal and political accusation that a state was engaged in persecuting a minority. Such an accusation, it was argued, did not help in finding a diplomatic solution to the problem. The decision was therefore made to work toward a universal definition of a refugee—making asylum, the granting of refuge, a less overtly political act.

The Cold War

In the immediate aftermath of World War II, there were large numbers of displaced persons—persons outside of their country of origin seeking protection from the war's effects, or deportees or former prisoners of war unwilling to return home fearing persecution. An even larger group consisted of German refugees—citizens of Germany and persons of German ethnicity who formerly resided either in territories now outside the redrawn German borders or who formerly resided as members of the German minority in countries East of Germany. They either fled to the West in anticipation of expulsion or were forcibly expelled. The German refugees were given citizenship rights in either West or East Germany and were readily absorbed into the population within Germany's new borders. (Many residents of East Germany in subsequent years fled to West Germany and settled there.) The non-German displaced persons were eventually also resettled, either in various Western European countries (including Germany) or overseas, mostly in North America and Australia. The difficulties experienced in that process led to the adoption, in 1951, of the Convention Relating to the Status of Refugees. It defined an individual refugee as someone who is outside his or her country of origin and is unwilling or unable to avail himself or herself of the protection of that country due to a well-founded fear of persecution on the grounds of that person's religion, nationality, race, or social group. The definition was in principle universal, in that it did not mention any specific group or state(s), but the Convention did allow for reference to specific acts of persecution occurring in Europe.

The 1951 Convention was aimed both at dealing with the remaining numbers of displaced persons as a result of World War II, and with the new Cold War problem of targeted persecution. The first major challenge to the Convention, as a tool for determining the status of individuals, came in 1956. The anti-Soviet and anti-communist Hungarian uprising of 1956 led to some 200,000 persons fleeing to Austria and Yugoslavia. The Convention was not applied to all Hungarians: Most were protected temporarily in Austria and Yugoslavia, on an ad hoc basis, for up to a year, but virtually all of them were soon resettled throughout Western Europe, the United States, Canada, Australia, and New Zealand. Most of them were simply given legal immigration status in the receiving countries, with employment opportunities readily available in the reconstructing post-World War II economies.

While other forced displacements took place in most world regions in the Cold War years, the next major challenge to the universal system established by the signing of the 1951 Convention and the creation of the office of the United Nations High Commissioner for Refugees originated in Indo-China. As a result of the war in Vietnam and the related political-ideological conflict and severe economic hardship, large numbers of people fled or were, by their own estimation, forcibly expelled from Vietnam, Laos, and Cambodia. From 1975 to mid-1979, some 245,000 Vietnamese, Laotians and Cambodians arrived in Thailand alone. Large numbers of refugees also entered other states neighboring Indo-China, notably Malaysia and Hong Kong: Between 1979 and 1988, some 500,000 Vietnamese "boat people" landed in these countries of presumed first asylum. Thailand and Malaysia called for solidarity from more distant states, in particular for resettlement of the refugees. In these Asian states in which initial protection was sought, the refugees were routinely denied asylum, reflecting the expectation of the receiving states that permanent solutions for these displaced persons would be found in other countries. Large numbers were indeed permanently resettled in developed countries, notably in the United States. As the Vietnamese conflict was settled, the impetus to resettle diminished and the eventual fate of large remaining numbers of displaced persons was to return, often under duress, to their country of origin. No specific status definitions were made for Indo-Chinese refugees, although principles of first asylum followed by resettlement as a permanent solution, and of global solidarity, were developed as a result of two international conferences held in 1979 and 1989 that were devoted to the problem.

Post-Cold War

As the Cold War drew to an end, the states of Western Europe anticipated, and feared, a massive exodus from Eastern Europe: not a forced migration, but one of people who a short time before would indeed have been considered to be refugees. This exodus did not occur on anything like the anticipated scale. However, as war, sparked by long-standing ethnic and religious conflict, broke out in the Balkans, from 1992 to 1995 an estimated 3.5 to 5 million people fled Bosnia Herzegovina, Croatia, and Serbia. Forced migration of whole populations on this scale and within so short a time had not been seen in Europe since World War II. The exodus found the countries of Western Europe both unprepared and with a sharply diminished desire to grant protective status to persons from former communist states. Refusing to grant most of these people the status of refugee, on the ground that they fled generalized violence rather than individually-targeted persecution, European states began to develop a doctrine of temporary protection, based not on the principle of a durable solution ultimately being found in integration, or resettlement, but on voluntary return, or mandatory repatriation as the only acceptable final arrangement. Each state developed its own definition of temporary protection—notwithstanding that this situation arose during a time when the member states of the European Union were seeking harmonization of their asylum policies. In some definitions, the former Yugoslavia was mentioned specifically in new laws and policy documents. The world's management of massive forced displacements seemed to be coming full circle to nationality-based definitions of those who would receive, or be denied as the case might be, protection.

The Kosovo crisis of 1999 evoked a similar response. About half the population of Kosovo, almost a million persons, fled to neighboring Albania and Macedonia. Like Thailand and Malaysia in the 1970s, Macedonia reinforced its appeal to other states for assistance by temporarily closing its border with Kosovo, preventing people from becoming refugees. An evacuation program removed some 90,000 people from Macedonia to Western European states, Turkey, Australia, and the United States during a three-month period, and many more were transferred to Albania. In the summer of 1999, rapid repatriation occurred. As NATO forces and then a United Nations mission took control of the province, the vast majority of the 1 million people who had fled returned, initially from Macedonia and Albania, and over the following months from further afield.

Conclusion

By 2000, virtually all countries of the world had strict control over immigrant entries to their territories, and many were imposing high barriers to entry even for those persons forced to flee their country of origin, whether individually or en masse as described above. Though the moral duty to protect human rights was professed and the legal tools to enact refugee protection worldwide were in place, the actual willingness to grant refuge was clearly absent in most countries—perhaps most obviously in those parts of the world most capable of protecting significant numbers of forced migrants and those farthest away from the countries those migrants would be forced to leave.

See also: *Asylum, Right of; Communism, Population Aspects of; Ethnic Cleansing; Refugees, Demography of; Resettlement; War, Demographic Consequences of.*

BIBLIOGRAPHY

Cohen, Roberta, and Francis M. Deng. 1998. *Masses in Flight: The Global Crisis of Internal Displacement.* Washington, D.C.: Brookings Institution Press.

Indra, Doreen, ed. 1999. *Engendering Forced Migration: Theory and Practice.* New York: Berghahn Books.

Jackson, Ivor C. 1999. *The Refugee Concept in Group Situations.* Dordrecht, Netherlands: Martinus Nijhoff Publishers.

Loescher, Gil. 2001. *The UNHCR and World Politics: A Perilous Path.* Oxford: Oxford University Press.

Skran, Claudena. 1995. *Refugees in Inter-war Europe: The Emergence of a Regime.* Oxford: Oxford University Press.

United Nations High Commissioner for Refugees. 2000. *The State of the World's Refugees 2000.* Oxford: Oxford University Press.

van Selm-Thorburn, Joanne. 1998. *Refugee Protection in Europe: Lessons of the Yugoslav Crisis.* Dordrecht, Netherlands: Martinus Nijhoff Publishers.

Viviani, Nancy. 1996. *The Indochinese in Australia 1975–1995: From Burnt Boats to Barbecues.* Melbourne, Australia: Oxford University Press.

Zolberg, Aristide, Astri Suhrke, and Sergion Aguayo. 1989. *Escape from Violence: Conflict and the Refugee Crisis in the Developing World.* Oxford: Clarendon Press.

JOANNE VAN SELM

FORECASTS, POPULATION

See *Projections and Forecasts, Population*

FREEDMAN, RONALD

(1918–)

Ronald Freedman is a social demographer who has devoted most of his career to the study of fertility and was instrumental in the development of the sample survey as a means of investigating levels, trends, and determinants of fertility. Freedman completed his Ph.D. at the University of Chicago in 1947, writing a dissertation on population distribution in the United States, having already taken up a teaching position in the Department of Sociology at the University of Michigan in 1946. He quickly shifted his attention to fertility and, with a pioneering younger generation of social scientists at Michigan with whom he had formed the Institute of Social Research, began to explore how the sample survey might advance fertility research. Freedman recognized that the sample survey naturally lent itself to the measurement of knowledge and attitudes, an attractive feature given Freedman's deeply sociological approach to fertility that placed considerable emphasis on values and norms.

In 1955, Freedman directed the first national fertility survey in the United States, the Growth of American Families, with Pascal Whelpton. Many had questioned whether intimate matters such as contraceptive behavior could be measured in survey interviews. The results of the 1955 survey largely allayed those concerns, as can be seen in the 1959 book written by Whelpton, Freedman, and Arthur Campbell as a result of this work. The sample survey has subsequently become the primary source of data on reproductive attitudes and behaviors in all regions of the world.

Freedman turned his attention to fertility in developing countries, and, in the early 1960s, forged a relationship with researchers in Taiwan that has been remarkably productive for him and his associates at Michigan since that time. During the 1960s, many national governments (including Taiwan's) and private agencies were considering launching family planning programs in order to accelerate fertility decline, but the likely impact of such programs was the subject of much dispute. Freedman and his Taiwanese collaborators conducted an experiment in the city of Taichung, with new services randomly assigned to a sub-set of neighborhoods. The results, published in 1969 as *Family Planning in Taiwan: An Experiment in Social Change,* demonstrated convincingly that the new family planning services facilitated adoption of modern contraception and, interestingly, that the effects spilled over to adjacent neighborhoods. The Taichung study was a landmark in demographic research and remains one of the few rigorous applications in demography of classic experimental design. Through a succession of island-wide fertility surveys, Freedman and his collaborators charted the course of fertility transition in Taiwan; few transitions are better understood from the standpoint of both causes and consequences.

Freedman became a leading figure in research on fertility in developing countries, authoring many influential papers and serving in numerous advisory capacities. He steadfastly maintained a theoretical perspective strongly grounded in the social sciences, in which socioeconomic conditions, cultural systems, and targeted programs each have causal roles. Freedman was a gifted institution-builder, notably of the Population Studies Center at the University of Michigan, which he directed from its establishment in 1962 through 1971. He had a remarkable ability to spot talent and to bring out the best in those with whom he worked. Freedman was also a dedicated

teacher, serving on the faculty of the University of Michigan for 41 years. Freedman was elected to the U.S. National Academy of Sciences in 1974, and was awarded the IUSSP (International Union for the Scientific Study of Population) Laureate in 2002.

See also: *Demographic Surveys, History and Methodology of; Demography, History of; Family Planning Programs; Fertility Transition, Socioeconomic Determinants of; Whelpton, P. K.*

BIBLIOGRAPHY

SELECTED WORKS BY RONALD FREEDMAN.

Freedman, Ronald. 1961–1962. "The Sociology of Human Fertility." *Current Sociology* 10/11: 35–121.

———. 1979. "Theories of Fertility Decline: A Reappraisal." *Social Forces* 58: 1–17.

———. 1987. "The Contribution of Social Science Research to Population Policy and Family Planning Program Effectiveness." *Studies in Family Planning* 18: 57–82.

Freedman, Ronald, and John Y. Takeshita. 1969. *Family Planning in Taiwan: An Experiment in Social Change.* Princeton: Princeton University Press.

Freedman, Ronald, Ming-Cheng Chang, and Te-Hsiung Sun. 1994. "Taiwan's Transition from High Fertility to Below-Replacement Levels." *Studies in Family Planning* 25: 317–331.

Whelpton, Pascal K., Ronald Freedman, and Arthur Campbell. 1959. *Family Planning, Sterility, and Population Growth.* New York: McGraw-Hill.

JOHN B. CASTERLINE

FUTURE GENERATIONS, OBLIGATIONS TO

Unless something goes drastically wrong in the next few centuries, future people will greatly outnumber those currently alive. The actions of present generations have potentially enormous impact on those who will live in the future. Perhaps the most significant impact is that society's decisions affect who those future people will be—and even if there will be any future people at all.

Despite its obvious importance, intergenerational ethics has not loomed large in traditional moral philosophy. Only since the 1960s have philosophers really begun to grapple with the complexities involved. Much of the discussion has been highly technical, focusing on logical puzzles regarding the value of existence and on the possibility of comparing the lives of different possible individuals. But underlying these difficult-to-understand technicalities are some of the deepest moral questions. What makes life worth living? What do we owe to our descendants? How do we balance their needs against our own?

The Non-Identity Problem

In his classic discussion of the present generation's obligations to future generations, Derek Parfit distinguished two kinds of moral choice. In a *Same People Choice,* society's actions affect what will happen to people in the future, but not which people will come to exist. If an individual's actions does affect who will exist in the future, then one is making a *Different People Choice.* Parfit claimed that Different People Choices are much more frequent than one might expect and that many traditional moral theories cope much better with Same People Choices than with Different People Choices. Taken together, these two claims constitute Parfit's *Non-Identity Problem,* so called because in a Different People Choice, those who would come to exist in one possible outcome are not (numerically) identical to those who would come to exist in an alternative possible outcome.

Suppose the cheapest way to meet the energy needs of the present generation is to build a power plant in a presently unoccupied desert. Experts know that the plant will be safe for several generations but will then leak radiation, harming those living nearby. The choice is made to build this plant, rather than to build a safer, more expensive one somewhere else. To many this behavior seems outrageous. Several common moral principles, however, imply that there is nothing wrong with the decision. Suppose one thinks that an act is wrong only if it wrongs some particular person, that people are wronged only if they are harmed, and people are harmed only if they end up worse off than they would otherwise

have been. Now apply these principles to the choice of energy policy. Suppose the lives of those who suffer from radiation poisoning are worth living overall. If the safer plant was chosen, those future people would never have existed, because their great-grandparents, who moved to the desert to build the plant, would never have met. So the future people have no complaint, because the choice has not harmed them.

Philosophers have responded to the Non-Identity Problem in three distinct ways: (1) Some deny that present-day society has any obligations to future people. For instance, David Heyd is a defender of a "generocentric" position, where the behavior of the present generation is constrained only by obligations to contemporaries and to themselves. (2) "Person-affecting theorists" argue that society does have obligations to particular future people, even if our actions create those people and their lives are worth living. One common approach appeals to rights. If future people have a right to an unpolluted atmosphere, then our current practices might violate that right, even though the resulting people have lives worth living. (3) Utilitarians argue that society should make future humans as happy as possible, regardless of their identity.

The Repugnant Conclusion

Utilitarianism avoids the Non-Identity Problem by treating Different People Choices and Same People Choices analogously. In either case, individuals seek to maximize the happiness of whoever exists. Unfortunately, utilitarianism faces other problems, especially in *Different Number Choices,* where society decides how many people there will be.

In describing Different Number Choices, Parfit imagined a choice between two possible futures, A and Z. In A, there are 10 billion people, all of whom have wonderful lives. In Z, there is a much larger number of people, all of whom have lives that are "barely worth living." Parfit argued that if the second population is sufficiently large, then traditional utilitarianism must prefer Z, because it contains more happiness.

This "Repugnant Conclusion" is the organizing problem of contemporary utilitarian value theory. Some utilitarians reply that the value of a possible outcome should be a function of the average happiness, as well as total happiness. Others embrace the Repugnant Conclusion but argue that the Z future cannot be as bad as Parfit suggested. Debate often focuses on the precise specification of the "zero level"—the point below which a life ceases to be worth living. By definition, the people in Z live just above that zero level. If the zero level is set at a comparatively high level, then life in the Z world might be reasonably worthwhile. Some philosophers argue that, in this case, it would not be repugnant to prefer Z to A.

The Unequal Circumstances Problem

The quality of life of future generations is largely dependent on society's decisions. By contrast, the quality of life for present generations is not affected at all by decisions of future generations. Present generations can do a great deal to posterity, but posterity cannot do anything to them. Western political philosophy has often discussed justice in terms of mutually advantageous reciprocal interaction, either in the actual world or in some hypothetical choice situation. Traditional political theories thus find it hard to generate *any* obligations to future generations.

Some theorists expand the traditional social contract, imagining a contract between different generations, perhaps built on a series of contracts between overlapping generations. Others reject the individualism of much contemporary political philosophy, arguing that only a holistic approach can provide an adequate framework for thinking about our obligations to future generations. If members of the present generation view their own lives as bound together with those of their ancestors and descendants in an intertemporal community, then it is easier to see how they might have obligations to future people.

See also: *Environmental Ethics; Generational Accounting; Intergenerational Transfers.*

BIBLIOGRAPHY

Barry, Brian. 1977. "Justice between Generations." In *Law, Morality, and Society: Essays in Honour of H. L. A. Hart,* ed. P. M. S. Hacker and J. Raz. Oxford: Clarendon Press.

———. 1978. "Circumstances of Justice and Future Generations." In *Obligations to Future Generations,* ed. Richard Sikora and Brian Barry. Philadelphia: Temple University Press.

Heyd, David. 1992. *Genethics: Moral Issues in the Creation of People.* Berkeley: University of California Press.

Kim, Tae-Chang, and Ross Harrison, eds. 1999. *Self and Future Generations: An Intercultural Conversation.* Cambridge, Eng.: White Horse Press.

Mulgan, Tim. 1999. "Teaching Future Generations." *Teaching Philosophy* 22: 259–273.

Parfit, Derek. 1984. *Reasons and Persons.* Oxford: Oxford University Press.

TIM MULGAN

G

GALTON, FRANCIS

(1822–1911)

Sir Francis Galton, scientific polymath, eugenicist, hereditarian and pioneer of statistical methodology, was born in Birmingham, England, the third son of the wealthy banker Samuel Tertius Galton, and the grandson of doctor and poet Erasmus Darwin. Galton began his scientific career, at the age of 16, as a medical student at the Birmingham Free Hospital. From there he moved to King's College London to study medicine, and to Trinity College Cambridge in 1840 to read mathematics. Achieving only a pass degree at Cambridge, due to the first of several mental breakdowns, Galton reluctantly persisted with his medical training. But, coming into a fortune on his father's death in 1844, he abandoned medicine. In 1850, after several idle years, Galton financed and led an exploratory expedition to Southwest Africa, returning in 1852. Lionized by the scientific community, he gradually established himself as one of Victorian Britain's most respected scientists.

Galton's professional energies were mostly devoted to exploring human heredity and developing means by which to study it. And, as heredity could only systematically be investigated at the population level, he made many practical contributions to population studies. Having read, and been profoundly influenced by, English naturalist Charles Darwin's (his half-cousin) *The Origin of Species* (1859), a decade later Galton published *Hereditary Genius* (1869). In this unequivocally Darwinist work, Galton collated hundreds of eminent pedigrees in an attempt to prove that high intellectual ability is largely a function of hereditary endowment. On this basis, he proposed measures to ensure that the more intel-

ligent members of society achieved the highest rates of fertility. (Galton's own marriage, however, was childless.) Galton coined the term *eugenics* in 1883, in his *Inquiries into Human Faculty,* derived from the Greek *eugenes* meaning "good in stock."

Galton was among the first scientists to apply mathematical tools to the study of the inheritance of human mental and bodily traits. He began with rather rudimentary methods. However, it was his consistent fascination with variation around the population mean that later enabled him to develop the fundamental statistical techniques of both correlation and regression—procedures later systematized and more fully explicated by Galton's admirer and first biographer, the statistician Karl Pearson (1857–1936). From 1904, Galton privately financed research fellowships in statistics and eugenics at University College London, and he left money for their continuation in his will.

Galton's interest in heredity was practical as well as numerical. Collaborating with Darwin, he tested the theory of the inheritance of acquired characteristics by transfusing blood among different breeds of rabbit. Galton then bred several generations of sweet-pea plants in an attempt to establish the mechanics of heredity; from his results he formulated the ancestral law of heredity, a model of inheritance later superceded by Mendelian genetics. The same fascination about heredity also stimulated his research on fingerprints (and their use in criminology), unconscious mental phenomena, variation in stature and strength, and the supposed physical indices of criminality. In addition, symptomatic of his polymathic interests, Galton made significant contributions to geography and meteorology; in 1862, he named and described the "anti-cyclone."

Galton was honored with numerous prestigious awards and was knighted in 1909. As a scientist he was idiosyncratic, utterly dedicated and, though frequently naive, often strikingly effective. His maxim was "Whenever you can, count," and his research suggests a man with an almost obsessive compulsion to do so. At the personal level, Galton suffered from an unusually low self-esteem and recurrent mental health problems. Yet, he also displayed a willingness to scandalize popular opinion, and he pushed the materialism of his fellow protagonists of Darwinism further than most would have dared.

Galton's eugenic ideas stimulated demographic research in both Europe and America. But it was his contributions to statistical methodology, made in the context of his hereditarian pursuits, that make Galton such an important figure in the history of population studies.

See also: *Darwin, Charles; Eugenics; Population Thought, History of.*

BIBLIOGRAPHY

SELECTED WORKS BY FRANCIS GALTON.

Galton, Francis. 1869. *Hereditary Genius.* London: Macmillan.

———. 1883. *Inquiries into Human Faculty.* London: Macmillan.

———. 1889. *Natural Inheritance.* London: Macmillan.

SELECTED WORKS ABOUT FRANCIS GALTON.

Gillham, Nicholas W. 2001. *A Life of Sir Francis Galton: From African Exploration to the Birth of Eugenics.* New York: Oxford University Press.

Pearson, Karl. 1914–1930. *The Life, Letters and Labours of Francis Galton,* 3 vols. Cambridge, Eng.: Cambridge University Press.

JOHN WALLER

GENDER

Gender refers not just to differences between women and men but to the socially constructed norms, expectations, patterns of behavior, and ideology surrounding those differences. Gender is an organizing principle in all known societies, shaping individual lives and social institutions. The resulting social organizational patterns and dynamics are known as a gender system.

A distinction is often drawn between "sex" and "gender," with sex referring to the biological differences between women and men (such as in chromosomes, hormones, or secondary sex characteristics) and gender to the social differences between women and men. Gender, according to the scholar Joan Wallach Scott, is thus "a social category imposed on a sexed body" (1986, p. 1056). But this seemingly simple division—sex denoting biology, gender denoting social manifestation—is now understood to be more complicated, because definitions and understandings of sex and biology may themselves be socially constructed. Moreover, it is often difficult to separate biological and social aspects of human behavior, or to point to distinct biological and social influences on the differences between women and men. Real and perceived physical differences between women and men are often part of the meaning and organization of gender. Nonmaterial elements of society are also involved: images, symbols, and language are likewise gendered and underscore and contribute to gender differences.

The conceptualization of gender varies from society to society. Most societies recognize only two genders, male and female, but some societies recognize more than two. The *hijras* of India and the *berdache* in some North American Indian tribes are examples of recognized third genders, with their own expectations and norms.

Gender as a Social Institution

Besides the immediate differences between the societal positions of women and men—for example, that men are more likely than women to engage in warfare or that women are more likely than men to face discrimination in the labor market—gender plays a role as a social institution: it is a set of social and cultural practices that influences the lives of all women and men, and that interacts with other social institutions.

Schooling presents an example of this interaction. Because of differential access to schooling, women in most societies are more likely to be illiterate than men. For instance, women are less likely to be able to read newspapers or directions on medicine bottles. But the implications of differential access to schooling extend beyond the individual level: women are less likely to participate in higher education, less likely to be trained for high-level positions, and thus less likely to influence policy decisions that affect the society. In societies where girls are excluded from education, schools will be geared to boys who make up the majority of the students; employers will also expect to hire males since there will be fewer well-trained females applying for jobs. This pattern may have further ramifications in the economy: If men are not expected to participate equally in family life and make up most of the workers, then employers may structure the workforce using the standard of these male workers and expect workers to work longer hours or be away from home more regularly. Such actions make it even more difficult for women—with their family responsibilities—to break into the ranks of laborers. The gendered nature of illiteracy thus affects the shape of the workforce.

Gender interacts with many other features of society such as class, ethnicity, nationality, and sexuality. Historically in the United States, race interacted with gender in clear and pervasive ways: Evelyn Higginbotham noted in her 1992 work that the term "lady" was applied only to white women; African-American women were never considered "women" in the way that white women were. In contemporary Egypt, class position is an important influence on Muslim women's decisions about whether or not to wear the veil. Many upper-class women in Cairo reject the veil as confining and inappropriate to modern Egyptian life. But Arlene MacLeod pointed out in 1991 that some working class women have taken to wearing the veil because it provides them a freedom of movement outside of the house, and allows them to take jobs and to mix with males in ways that would not otherwise be socially acceptable.

Family and marriage practices are also central components of the gender system. In places where women marry early, where marriage is patrilocal (the bride moves to live with her husband's family), and where lineage is traced through the paternal line, women seem to fare less well than in other family systems. For example, in northern India, women usually marry outside their village, move to their husbands' house and village, and have fewer ties with their natal families after marriage; in southern India, in contrast, women are more likely to marry later, more likely to retain ties to their natal families, and less likely to spend as long living with their husbands' parents. These different patterns of marriage and family are related to the significant disadvantages faced by females in the north compared to those in the south—including lower food consumption, higher child death rates and maternal mortality, and shorter life expectancy.

Gender and Power

Power lies at the heart of any gender system. Gender orders social relationships in such a way that some individuals have greater power than others. "Power to" allows individuals access to material goods, opportunities, and events. Compared to men, women often have less power to go to school, get training, or move freely in public areas. Another kind of power might be described as "power over"—the ability to influence other people in particular ways. In most societies, men occupy positions of power and decision in the government, in religious organizations, and in the economic structure. That positioning gives men more power than women to direct courses of action, policies, and individual lives. Women have nevertheless found numerous ways to resist the gender system and their role in it. This resistance has taken many shapes, from strikes over wages and treatment of women workers in the *maquiladoras* on the U.S.–Mexican border to the way that "office ladies" in Tokyo companies refuse to do work for some bosses. However, such resistance has not overturned the gender system—indeed, in some instances resistance may reinforce underlying beliefs about women, men, and gender.

Persistence of Gender Inequality

Gender systems result from and contribute to "persistent inequalities" between women and men (Tinker, 1990). But like other social institutions, gender is not static. It is created and recreated with every social interaction. While one cannot point to a single cause of gender inequality or fully specify the conditions for change, there are indications that some conditions may lead to a more equitable system. The status of women in some societies seems to be higher where their traditional spheres of work are valued, even though those may be different from men's. Other research has suggested that women's access to the valued resources of the society is the key to greater gender equality. In societies where women enjoy equal access to formal education and education is the main pathway to visible roles in the public sphere, or where women have more control over the money they earn or the land that they farm, women are likely to have roles, voices, and rights that resemble or are equal to those of men. However, increased education and more prominent public and economic roles do not automatically translate into a leveling of gender inequality. With the shift from household to market economy, women may lose their earlier status as household workers but find that in the formal labor market their value is tied to their level of income. Their low wages relative to those of men may translate into decreased power and status.

For decades, scholars have debated the reasons for the existence of gender inequalities in most societies. Some argue that women's different biology and physiology, particularly their smaller size and reproductive capacity, are at the root of gender systems and inequalities. Social scientists, focusing on social and cultural explanations, have more often pointed to the ways that society organizes such activities as reproduction and warfare and attributes different meaning and values to these and other related activities. Early feminist anthropologists argued that women's lower social position is related to women being associated with nature and men with culture in most societies. Other theories have pointed to the ways that women's connection to the private sphere and men's to the public have been at the root of gender hierarchy. These and other theories have been crucial in the development of understandings of gender inequalities, even as they have also been subject to criticism and revision. The connections between gender systems and other social processes, structures, institutions, and ideologies are the focus of much attention from social scientists seeking to understand the continuing pervasiveness and influence of gender systems across the world.

See also: *Feminist Perspectives on Population Issues; Reproductive Rights; Women's Status and Demographic Behavior.*

BIBLIOGRAPHY

Collier, Jane, and Sylvia Yanagisako, eds. 1987. *Gender and Kinship: Essays Toward a Unified Analysis.* Stanford, CA: Stanford University Press.

di Leonardo, Micaela, ed. 1991. *Gender at the Crossroads of Knowledge: Feminist Anthropology in the Postmodern Era.* Berkeley: University of California Press.

Fausto-Sterling, Anne. 1992. *Myths of Gender: Biological Theories about Women and Men.* New York: Basic Books.

Ferree, Myra Marx, Judith Lorber, and Beth Hess. 1999. *Revisioning Gender.* Thousand Oaks, CA: Sage Publications.

Higginbotham, Evelyn. 1992. "African-American Women's History and the Metalanguage of Race." *Signs* 1: 137–69.

MacLeod, Arlene. 1991. *Accommodating Protest: Working Women, the New Veiling, and Change in Cairo.* New York: Columbia University Press.

Marshall, Barbara. 2000. *Configuring Gender: Explorations in Theory and Politics.* Toronto: Broadview Press.

Ogasawara, Yuko. 1998. *Office Ladies and Salaried Men: Power, Gender, and Work in Japanese Companies.* Berkeley: University of California Press.

Risman, Barbara. 1998. *Gender Vertigo.* New Haven, CT: Yale University Press.

Scott, Joan Wallach. 1986. "Gender: A Useful Category for Historical Analysis." *American Historical Review* 91: 1053–1075.

Tiano, Susan. 1994. *Patriarchy on the Line: Labor, Gender and Ideology in the Mexican Maquila Industry.* Philadelphia: Temple University Press.

Tinker, Irene, ed. 1990. *Persistent Inequalities: Women and World Development.* New York: Oxford University Press.

Vogel, Lise. 1993. *Mothers on the Job: Maternity Policy in the U.S. Workplace.* New Brunswick, NJ: Rutgers University Press.

NANCY E. RILEY

GENDER PREFERENCES FOR CHILDREN

Parents and prospective parents, separately or as couples, often have preferences concerning the gender of their children. This article discusses patterns of gender preference in various countries and regions of the world, the different value of sons and daughters, the effect of gender preferences, and the differential treatment of girls and boys.

Patterns of Gender Preference

Gender preferences exhibit a variety of patterns. Most common are a preference for sons and a preference for a balance of daughters and sons (often expressed as a desire to have at least one child of each sex). Son preference is particularly strong in a band of countries from North Africa through the Middle East and South Asia to East Asia. The strongest preference for sons has been found in India, Nepal, Bangladesh, Egypt, South Korea, and China. The diversity of these countries indicates that son preference does not emerge from a single set of cultural or historical experiences. Even in countries with a strong son preference, many parents want to have one daughter among their children. An overall preference for daughters over sons is rare but has been found to exist to a small extent in a few countries in Latin America and the Caribbean.

Widespread preference either for sons or for daughters is not common in developed countries or in most countries in Latin America, sub-Saharan Africa, and Southeast Asia. In these areas, the most common survey responses to questions on the topic indicate a preference for an equal number of daughters and sons, at least one daughter and one son, or no preference at all. Where a preference for a gender balance is paramount, however, some parents prefer to have a son for their first child.

Value of Sons and Daughters

Gender preferences for children can be based on community norms or personal desires. Children of a particular sex are usually desired because they provide certain utilities (that is, satisfactions or tangible returns, primarily in the economic, social, psychological, or religious domains) or they entail smaller costs. Economic considerations often favor sons for their ability to help on the family farm or in the family business, to earn wages from work outside the home, and to provide support for parents when they get old. Sons may also be valued for their ability to help out the family in emergencies and help younger siblings through school. Daughters are more likely to be valued for providing assistance with household chores and caring for younger siblings. Daughters are sometimes seen as a more reliable source of emotional support and even economic assistance to elderly parents, although in many cultures their services are lost to their parents on marriage. Marriage patterns often provide a strong (even an overriding) incentive for preferring sons in countries where large dowry payments are the norm and for preferring daughters where a substantial bride-price is required as is the case in some countries in Africa.

In the social sphere, sons may be seen as useful for enhancing the power and prestige of the family and for carrying on the family line and the family name, and daughters may be wanted to "balance the family." Both daughters and sons may provide companionship and psychological satisfaction for parents, but women often express a particular desire for a daughter for companionship. Although both daughters and sons may be called on for the performance of religious rituals, many religions favor sons for performing religious functions at the time of a parent's death (e.g., burial rites or lighting of the funeral pyre).

Effect of Gender Preferences

One of the most contentious issues regarding gender preferences is the effect of gender preferences on demographic behavior and the extent to which preferences and their impact are likely to change over time. On the one hand, it is argued that couples who have reached their desired family size may nevertheless continue having children if they have not yet achieved their preferred sex composition of children, thereby delaying the transition to low fertility. On the other hand, there are several examples of countries (such as Korea and China) that have achieved very low levels of fertility in a short span of time despite a continuing strong preference for sons. In 1997 Monica Das Gupta and P. N. Mari Bhat posited that gender preference is likely to intensify over time as fertility falls, but the evidence for this effect is not consistent across countries.

There is no doubt that strong gender preferences may have an effect on such demographic outcomes as contraceptive use, fertility behavior, birth spacing, and the incidence of induced abortions, but the magnitude of these effects is uncertain. Fred Arnold has developed a measure to quantify the impact of gender preferences on demographic behavior. This measure is designed to assess what would happen if gender preferences were to suddenly disappear in a country. Application of the measure in a number of countries with a strong preference for sons demonstrates that gender preferences can reduce levels of contraceptive use and increase fertility, but that gender preferences are not likely to be a major obstacle to fertility decline.

One other consequence of gender preferences is the increasing use of sex-selective abortions (and, more recently, chromosome separation techniques applied to the sperm prior to artificial insemination) to achieve the desired number of daughters and sons. In China, Korea, and India, selective use of abortion for female fetuses has resulted in more masculine sex ratios at birth, leading to skewed sex ratios for children (particularly for younger children born into families that already have many children). Such a pattern may have various unfavorable social consequences in the future—not least, a "marriage squeeze" due to a shortage of marriageable women relative to men.

Differential Treatment of Girls and Boys

If parents prefer children of a particular sex (usually sons), they might give favored treatment to those children in health care, nutrition, educational opportunities, or other areas. In most countries, children receive approximately equal treatment regardless of their sex and the nature of gender preferences in the society. There is ample evidence, however, that in some countries with a strong son preference, boys are often given preferential treatment with respect to medical care, educational opportunities, and (less often) food allocation.

In serious cases, discrimination against girls may result in an increased risk of infant and child mortality. In most countries, male mortality is higher than female mortality at almost every age, but Dominique Tabutin and Michel Willems in 1995 showed that in high-mortality countries, females often have an appreciably reduced advantage or even a higher mortality than males during childhood. This pattern is particularly pronounced in South Asia and Egypt. The precise reason for higher than normal mortality among young girls relative to boys in these countries is not certain, but discrimination against girls, particularly in health care, must be considered the most likely cause.

See also: *Family Size Intentions; Sex Ratio; Sex Selection; Women's Status and Demographic Behavior.*

BIBLIOGRAPHY

Arnold, Fred. 1985. "Measuring the Effect of Sex Preference on Fertility: The Case of Korea." *Demography* 22: 280–288.

———. 1997. *Gender Preferences for Children.* Calverton, MD: Macro International.

Basu, Alaka Malwade. 1989. "Is Discrimination in Food Really Necessary for Explaining Sex Differentials in Childhood Mortality?" *Population Studies* 43: 193–210.

Das Gupta, Monica, and P. N. Mari Bhat. 1997. "Fertility Decline and Increased Manifestation of Sex Bias in India." *Population Studies* 51: 307–315.

Gu, Baochang, and Krishna Roy. 1995. "Sex Ratio at Birth in China, with Reference to Other Areas in East Asia: What We Know." *Asia-Pacific Population Journal* 10(3): 17–42.

Hill, Kenneth, and Dawn M. Upchurch. 1995. "Gender Differences in Child Health: Evidence from the Demographic and Health Surveys." *Population and Development Review* 21: 127–151.

Klasen, Stephan, and Claudia Wink. 2002. "A Turning Point in Gender Bias in Mortality? An Update on the Number of Missing Women." *Population and Development Review* 28: 285–312.

Marcoux, Alain. 2002. "Sex Differentials in Undernutrition: A Look at Survey Evidence." *Population and Development Review* 28: 275–284.

Sommerfelt, A. Elisabeth, and Fred Arnold. 1998. "Sex Differentials in the Nutritional Status of Young Children." In *Too Young to Die: Genes or Gender?* New York: United Nations.

Tabutin, Dominique, and Michel Willems. 1995. "Excess Female Mortality in the Developing World during the 1970s and 1980s." *Population Bulletin of the United Nations* 39: 45–78.

Fred Arnold

GENEALOGICAL RECORDS

A genealogy provides an account of the ancestors and descendants of a person or family. It describes the relationships among a group of individuals descended from common ancestors or a founding couple. The primary pieces of information contained within genealogies are individual-level demographic events, including the dates (and often places) of birth, marriage(s), and death. Each of these events links an individual to other persons: A birth ties an individual to parents and siblings; a marriage, to a spouse, in-laws, and children; and a death, to surviving family members. Other information may also be available in a genealogy, although the quality, coverage, and type of information vary.

The descendants of a founding couple are all related, and this web of kinship is generally referred to as a pedigree. The genetic connection between an ancestor and a descendant is often termed a lineage; tracing ancestors through the maternal side of the family is matrilineal, and similarly, through the paternal side, patrilineal. While genealogies contain information about the nature of the blood relationship between any two individuals, they may also contain information on persons and families living in the same place during the same historical period but who are unrelated.

Because the same data are recorded for each individual, genealogies can be used to answer questions related to entire kinship networks, including questions about demographic conditions and change. Topics examined using genealogical data include temporal patterns in fertility, widow and widower survival, longevity, consanguinity, and genetic variation.

Historical and Family Data

Some genealogies span many generations. This historical depth provides opportunities to examine how broader social changes affect family-level patterns in fertility, migration, and mortality. For some historical periods, genealogies are the principal source of data about the prevailing demographic conditions, although the information they provide is unlikely to be representative of the population at large. In other cases, genealogies provide an important supplement to official records of births, marriages, and deaths. Unlike those records, which are collected and maintained at the individual level, genealogical data are organized around nuclear families and extended pedigrees. Such data may allow analysts to estimate patterns of fertility (e.g., age at first birth, parity, birth intervals, age at last birth), marriage (e.g., number and outcome of marriages, polygamy, consanguineous marriages), and mortality (e.g., infant mortality, maternal mortality, widowhood and surviving spouse mortality, longevity). Genealogies also hold data on predictors of these outcomes, such as gender, age, and places and dates of important demographic transitions. In some genealogies, information on religion and social standing are also available. Standard demographic analysis can then be substantially improved and expanded to incorporate explanatory variables associated with characteristics of offspring, siblings and parents.

Kinship

Genealogies offer major opportunities for the study of kinship and its changes over time. Genealogies contain a record of the life course of an individual and the additions and losses to his or her kinship network. From a genealogy, it is possible to discern the family circumstances into which a person is born, the survival of siblings, the timing of the person's marriage and subsequent fertility patterns, the presence and location of in-laws, and the survival of his or her parents. Rather than relying on a static view of family life and structure at an arbitrary age or point in history, genealogical data allow the study of these transitions, their causes and consequences, and their patterning over large stretches of individual and historical time. Assembled as a linked set of life histories, the resulting data can be analyzed using statistical techniques that allow for changes both in outcomes and explanatory factors (e.g., time series analysis, survival models with time-dependent covariates).

Assessing Demographic Behavior within Families and Pedigrees

Genealogies do not generally contain the extensive number of covariates often found in large national demographic surveys. However, they do permit examination of the effects of observable predictors on key demographic outcomes while controlling for a wide range of family characteristics that are unobservable. For example, in a study of infant mortality, it might be of interest to know whether a child's birth order affects its chances of surviving the first year of life. Given that the mortality risks for one child are related to the mortality risks of its siblings (for reasons that are not observable to the demographer), one can exploit the fact that siblings share similar environmental and genetic characteristics. Analytical techniques that take this statistical dependency into account include the estimation of robust standard errors and fixed- and random-effects models.

Genealogies and Studies of Communities

Some genealogies are geographically based so that demographic events affecting a set of pedigrees occur in a defined place. This strategy has been used in places where parish registers and reconstructed family histories of entire villages make it possible to develop a genealogical database. Genealogies constrained by geography, while more limited in their scope, provide an opportunity to study a complete (and often relatively closed) social system. Focusing on a particular region or community during key historical periods can provide insights into the demography of families that would not otherwise be possible.

Non-Random Selection

Demographers are often faced with data that are subject to various forms of non-random selection and the biases that they engender. For example, a study of maternal mortality requires that a woman live to reproductive age, have a partner or be married, and bear children before maternal mortality can be examined. Because many genealogies are a record of extinct cohorts where a person's life and its events are depicted from birth to death, it is possible to observe and understand who has been selected out of the sub-population of interest and to make assessments of any selection biases that omissions may present.

Example: Utah Population Database

A summary account of the large number of genealogies that may be of interest to demographers was given by Natalia Gavrilova and Leonid Gavrilov (specialists in the biodemography of aging) in their 1997 study. What follows is a brief description of one of the world's largest and most comprehensive computerized genealogies: that contained within the Utah Population Database (UPDB). In the 1970s, approximately 170,000 Utah nuclear families were selected from the archives held in the Utah Family History Library, each with at least one member having had a vital event (birth, marriage, death) on the Mormon Pioneer Trail or in Utah. These families have been linked across generations; in some instances, the records span seven generations. The UPDB holds data on migrants to Utah and their Utah descendants (not only Mormons, that is, members of the Church of Jesus Christ of Latter-day Saints) that number more than 1.3 million individuals born from the early 1800s to the mid-1900s and that are linked into multi-generation pedigrees. The UPDB is an active genealogy: New families and their members are continually being added as the UPDB

is linked to other sources of data, including birth and death certificates. Additional information on these families comes from sources such as drivers' license records and the Utah Cancer Registry. With these additions, the database represents over 6 million individuals. Studies using the UPDB can examine the availability of kin, intergenerational transmission of demographic outcomes (e.g., age at first birth, children born), and familial clustering of specific conditions (e.g., extreme longevity, cancer mortality). These latter lines of inquiry are also of interest to anthropologists, biologists, and geneticists.

See also: *Family Reconstitution; Historical Demography.*

BIBLIOGRAPHY

Adams, Julian. 1990. *Convergent Issues in Genetics and Demography.* New York: Oxford University Press.

Bean, Lee L., Geraldine P. Mineau, and Douglas Anderton. 1990. *Fertility Change on the American Frontier: Adaptation and Innovation.* Berkeley: University of California Press.

Bean, Lee L., Geraldine P. Mineau, and Ken R. Smith. 1999. "The Longevity of Married Couples." In *Nearly Everything Imaginable: The Everyday Life of Utah's Mormon Pioneers,* ed. Ronald W. Walker and Doris R. Dant. Provo, UT: Brigham Young University Press.

Dyke, Bennett, and Warren T. Morrill ed. 1980. *Genealogical Demography.* New York: Academic Press.

Jorde, Lynn B. 2001. "Consanguinity and Prereproductive Mortality in the Utah Mormon Population." *Human Heredity* 52: 61–5.

Kerber, Richard A., Elizabeth O'Brien, Ken R. Smith, and Richard M. Cawthon. 2001. "Familial Excess Longevity in Utah Genealogies." *Journal of Gerontology: Biological Sciences* 56: B130–9.

Knodel, John. 1970. "Two and a Half Centuries of Demographic History in a Bavarian Village." *Population Studies* 24: 353–376.

Mineau, Geraldine P., Ken R. Smith, and Lee L. Bean. 2002. "Historical Trends of Survival among Widows and Widowers." *Social Science and Medicine* 54: 245–254.

Willigan, Dennis J., and Katherine A Lynch. 1982. *Sources and Methods of Historical Demography.* New York: Academic Press.

INTERNET RESOURCES.

Gavrilova, Natalia, and Leonid Gavrilov. 1999. "Data Resources for Biodemographic Studies on Familial Clustering of Human Longevity." *Demographic Research.* <http://www.demographic-research.org/Volumes/Vol1/4>.

Utah Population Database. 2003. <http://www.hci.utah.edu/groups/ppr>.

KEN R. SMITH
GERALDINE P. MINEAU

GENERATIONAL ACCOUNTING

Most fiscal analysts realize that official government debts do not include implicit liabilities. But most analysts do not realize that the division of government liabilities between implicit and explicit (official) is arbitrary. The same holds for assessing the share of any particular program that is financed by general revenue. Two observers of the same fiscal reality can use different, but equally valid, fiscal labels, report entirely different levels of implicit and explicit debts, and reach entirely different conclusions about the fiscal condition of particular programs. This is one of several lessons to be learned from examining fiscal policy by means of *generational accounting,* a relatively new method of long-term fiscal analysis that has found increasing application around the world.

Definition of Generational Accounts

Generational accounts represent the sum of the present values of the future net taxes (taxes paid minus transfer payments received) that members of a birth cohort can expect to pay over their remaining lifetimes if current policy is continued. The sum of the generational accounts of all members of all living generations indicates how much people who are now alive will pay toward the government's bills. The government's bills are the sum expressed as a present value of all the government's future purchases of goods and services plus its official net debt (its official financial liabilities minus its official financial assets, including the value of its public-sector enterprises). Bills not paid by current generations must be paid by future generations. This is the zero-sum nature of the *government's intertemporal budget constraint:* the basic building block of modern dynamic analyses of fiscal policy.

This budget constraint can be written as $A + B = C + D$, where D is the government's official net debt, C is the sum of future government purchases valued to the present, B is the sum of the generational accounts of those now alive, and A is the sum of the generational accounts of future generations valued to the present. Given $C + D$, the smaller B (the net payments of those now alive) is, the larger A (the net payments of those yet to be born) must be.

The Fiscal Burden of Future Generations

A critical feature of generational accounting is that the size of the fiscal burden confronting future generations (A) is invariant to the government's fiscal labeling, that is, how the government describes its receipts and payments. Unfortunately, this is not true of the government's reported size of its official debt. In terms of the equation $A + B = C + D$, different choices of fiscal labels alter B and D by equal absolute amounts, leaving C and A unchanged; that is, the values of B and D depend on language and are not economically well defined. However, the value of A and the difference $D - B$ are independent of language and are economically well defined. Since the terms A, B, and C are all present values, they all depend on assumed discount rates, productivity growth rates, and population growth rates. Higher population and productivity growth rates can be expected to raise all three terms. Higher discount rates lower all three terms.

The difference between the lifetime net tax rate of current newborns (the generational account of current newborns divided by their lifetime earnings) and the projected net tax rate on future newborns (the collective net tax burden on future newborns, the term A, divided by the projected present value of their future earnings) measures the imbalance in generational policy. The lifetime net tax rates of current and future newborns are directly comparable because both involve net taxes over entire lifetimes. If the lifetime net tax rate facing future generations is higher than the lifetime net tax rate facing current newborns, current policy not only is generationally imbalanced, it also is unsustainable. In other words, the government cannot continue over time to collect the same net taxes measured as a share of lifetime income from future generations that it would collect under current policy from current newborns without violating the intertemporal budget constraint.

Achieving Generational Balance

The calculation of generational imbalance is an informative counterfactual, not an indication of a likely policy scenario, because it imposes the entire fiscal adjustment needed to satisfy the government's intertemporal budget constraint on those born in the future. Although unrealistic, this counterfactual delivers a clear message about the need for policy adjustments. Once that need is established, interest turns to alternative means of achieving generational balance that do not involve foisting the entire adjustment on future generations.

As an example, one can determine the percentage reduction in C that would lower the size of A (i.e., the size of C + D − B) enough to achieve generational balance. Regardless of the size of that percentage reduction in the present value of government purchases, the policy could be implemented by means of an immediate and permanent cut in the annual flow of those purchases by that percentage. Another example is an immediate and permanent percentage increase in annual income tax revenues. This would raise B—the collective generational accounts of those now alive—and thus reduce A. The precise size of the percentage income tax hike needed to achieve generational balance is found when the growth-adjusted generational accounts of future generations equal those of newborns.

Applications of Generational Accounting

Although it was developed only recently, generational accounting has been applied to more than thirty countries around the world. The generational accounts for the United States that were prepared in June 2001 can be taken as an example. For newborns, who are assumed to pay taxes and receive benefits over their lifetimes in accordance with current (2001) U.S. policy, the lifetime net tax rate was 17.7 percent. For future generations the tax rate required to meet the intertemporal budget constraint was over twice as large: 35.8 percent. Stated differently, future generations, according to the policies in place in 2001, would have to be asked to pay 18.1

cents more per dollar earned than current newborns will pay.

To understand the gravity of the long-term U.S. generational imbalance, suppose the government tried to eliminate the generational imbalance by immediately and permanently raising the federal corporate and personal income tax by a given percentage. How large would the tax hike have to be? The answer as of 2001 was 68.2 percent. An alternative to raising federal income taxes alone is to raise all federal, state, and local taxes. In that case an across-the-board tax hike of 25.7 percent could achieve generational balance. Of course, cutting transfer payments and decreasing government purchases are alternatives to raising taxes. Cutting all Social Security, Medicare, Medicaid, food stamps, unemployment insurance benefits, welfare benefits, housing support, and other transfer payments by 43.5 percent would be another way to eliminate the generational imbalance. Two final options one can consider are immediately and permanently cutting all government purchases by 38.9 percent or totally cutting all federal purchases (the latter course would still not achieve a generational balance: to do so the cut that would be needed is calculated to be 116.9 percent). The U.S. generational imbalance is, as these numbers indicate, of grave national concern. Remarkably, this imbalance is smaller than those of many European countries and of Japan.

While economic growth would mitigate the generational imbalances in the United States and other countries, it represents no panacea. The reason is that in the U.S. and many other countries, government spending is fairly closely tied to the general level of a country's per capita income. Indeed, in the U.S. programs like Social Security are explicitly indexed to the level of real wages earned by workers. Hence, as the economy grows, so do the government's bills.

Immigration is also generally viewed as a cure for generational imbalances. In the United States, simply increasing the number of immigrants, while maintaining their composition, would do little to reduce the size of the intergenerational imbalance. In contrast, allowing only highly skilled and highly educated individuals to immigrate would provide some fiscal relief because these immigrants would pay more in taxes than they receive in benefits. Unfortunately, the source of such immigrants would be Japan and the European Union, which will seek, for the same reasons, to reduce out-migration of skilled workers to the extent possible.

See also: *Future Generations, Obligations to; Intergenerational Transfers.*

BIBLIOGRAPHY

Auerbach, Alan J., Laurence J. Kotlikoff, and Willi Leibfritz, eds. 1999. *Generational Accounting around the World.* Chicago: University of Chicago Press.

Kotlikoff, Lawrence J. 2002. "Generational Policy." In *Handbook of Public Economics,* 2nd edition, ed. Alan J. Auerbach and Martin S. Feldstein. Amsterdam: North Holland.

LAURENCE J. KOTLIKOFF

GENETIC TESTING

Genetic testing has been evolving for many years. The first genetic tests were offered clinically in the late 1950s and early 1960s when disorders associated with missing or extra chromosomes (e.g., Down's syndrome, Klinefelter's syndrome) were identified. During this same period, the first biochemical tests for genetic conditions referred to as inborn errors of metabolism were being identified. There are now thousands of genetic tests available. They are used in virtually all areas of medicine, from primary care to medical specialties.

Types of Genetic Tests

There are three main categories of genetic testing. *Cytogenetic* tests involve the analysis of human chromosomes to identify structural or numerical changes in the chromosomes of an individual's cells. The uniqueness of each chromosome's size and staining features allow them to be individually distinguished and organized into a karyotype. These tests allow a complete analysis of the human genome, though at low resolution—capable of identifying changes that are the size of about 5 million base pairs of DNA. *Biochemical* genetic tests are tests that identify the presence of a genetic condition by the analysis of metabolites, including amino acids, organic acids, and sugar compounds, present in body tissues or fluids or by the analysis of enzymatic activity that reflects an underlying genetic disorder. These tests commonly identify the biochemical abnormality that results from the genetic abnormality and are therefore highly focused. *Molecular* genetic tests involve the analysis of DNA and RNA but also may overlap with any of the other types of testing when protein analysis is part of a molecular test or when a molecular test uses the chromosome as the target for the test (molecular cytogenetics). Molecular genetic tests are usually highly focused and identify DNA changes ranging in size from one base pair to millions of base pairs. Molecular cytogenetic methods bridge the gap between the two technologies.

Uses of Genetic Tests

There are many uses for genetic tests. They can detect genetic changes that are acquired over the lifetime of an individual—for example, those that may reflect the development of cancer and leukemia. These tests can diagnose the condition, gauge the aggressiveness of the disease, guide therapy, and suggest prognoses. However, this group of tests is targeted at changes in specific tissues or organs. Genetic tests can also be directed at the germ line that is characteristic of all cells in an individual and that could be inherited. Such tests can be used to diagnose particular conditions in an individual and can identify other members of his or her family that may be carriers of the condition, and who are at risk of having similarly affected children. Genetic tests can be performed prenatally, at birth, or later in life and can be used to diagnose an individual with late-onset genetic conditions such as Huntington's disease even before the onset of symptoms (presymptomatic testing). Genetic testing can also determine whether someone is likely to respond to a particular drug treatment. When a genetic change is not one that will invariably lead to a particular disease, the identification of a change may indicate susceptibility to a disease. The disease could manifest itself if the appropriate environmental or other nongenetic factors were present. An example of this use of genetic testing is in the determination of predisposition to breast cancer.

The most frequently used genetic tests at the beginning of the twenty-first century are those performed to diagnose newborns with treatable conditions. In the United States, over 4 million newborns are tested each year in public health-mandated screening programs to identify those most likely to have a particular treatable genetic condition. The classic example of this is testing for phenylketonuria (PKU) in newborn infants. Infants with this condition are unable to metabolize a particular amino acid, resulting in the accumulation of a product that leads to mental retardation. Treatment entails removing that amino acid from the infant's diet. Most states currently screen for three to eight genetic conditions but new tests are being introduced that can identify as many as 20 to 30 conditions.

Ethical, Legal, and Social Considerations in Genetic Testing

The power of genetic tests to assess an individual's genetic predispositions raises many concerns. At present comparatively few people outside of the newborn period are being tested for heritable traits and only certain unfavorable genetic traits can be determined, although identification of these may expose the persons affected to unfair discrimination. However, it is estimated that each person has 8 to 20 such genetic changes that could increase risks to them, or to their children. Efforts to protect individual genetic privacy will be increasingly important. As more tests are developed, it will be critical that their scientific and clinical validity be well understood so that people can make informed decisions about testing in the light of the potential benefits and risks.

New Technologies and Applications

New technologies being introduced into genetic testing are distinguished by their ability to test many samples at once for multiple genetic markers at a low cost. Tandem mass spectrometry is capable of testing for many rare biochemical genetic diseases involving amino acids, organic acids, or fatty acids in a single assay. The development of molecular microarrays and DNA and RNA chips allows for a rapid determination of the presence, absence, or expression of many DNA sequences in a single test. Arrays may replace cytogenetic testing that identifys gains or losses of genetic material, although the test results may not provide the underlying reason for that gain or loss. Arrays are also capable of determining whether or not and to what extent a particular gene is being expressed. This capability has permitted the identification of important differences between cancer cells and normal cells, which in turn has led to the development of a new generation of diagnostic tests.

The mapping of the human genome and eventual identification of all genes, combined with powerful analytical and computer technologies, will have a significant impact on the types of genetic tests that are available. Most tests are currently done to detect very rare diseases affecting a small percentage of the population. In the years to come, genetic tests will be developed for more common conditions such as breast cancer or Alzheimer's disease and will identify genetic factors that increase the risk of developing the condition that may often be amenable to change.

See also: *Eugenics; Reproductive Rights; Reproductive Technologies.*

BIBLIOGRAPHY

Bartlett, Kim, Simon J. Eaton, and Morteza Pourfarzam. 1998. "New Developments in Neonatal Screening." *Archives of Diseases in Childhood* 79: 116–119.

Carpenter, Nancy J. 2001. "Molecular Cytogenetics." *Seminars in Pediatric Neurology* 8: 135–146.

Grody, Wayne W. 1999. "Cystic Fibrosis: Molecular Diagnosis, Population Screening and Public Policy." *Archives of Pathology and Laboratory Medicine* 123: 1041–1046.

Lee C., E. Lemyre, P. M. Miron, and C. C. Morton. 2001. "Multicolor Fluorescence In Situ Hybridization in Clinical Cytogenetics." *Current Opinion in Pediatrics* 13: 550–555.

McGlennen, Ronald C. 2001. "Miniaturization Technologies for Molecular Diagnostics." *Clinical Chemistry* 47: 393–402.

MICHAEL S. WATSON

GENETICS, POPULATION

See *Archeogenetics; Biology, Population; Evolutionary Demography*

GENOCIDE

One of the few things undisputed about the term genocide is its origin. It was introduced and discussed at some length in a 1944 book, *Axis Occupation of Europe,* by Raphael Lemkin, a Polish-Jewish jurist writing in the United States. Lemkin defined genocide broadly in terms of

> the destruction of a nation or of an ethnic group. . . . Genocide does not necessarily mean the immediate destruction of a nation, except when accomplished by mass killings. . . . It is intended rather to signify a coordinated plan of different actions aiming at the destruction of essential foundations of the life of a national group, with the aim of annihilating the groups themselves . . . . Genocide is directed against the national group as an entity, and the actions involved are directed against individuals, not in their individual capacity, but as members of the national group.

The attacks on nationhood could be political, social, cultural, economic, biological, religious, moral, or physical. Physical attacks were further subdivided into racial discrimination in feeding, endangering of health, and mass killings. Although he never used the term "cultural genocide," Lemkin seems to have included the cultural destruction of a people within the scope of genocide.

The term was referred to several times during the 1945–1946 Trial of the Major War Criminals at Nuremberg. The indictment, for example, alleged that the defendants "conducted deliberate and systematic genocide, viz., the extermination of racial and national groups, against the civilian populations of certain occupied territories in order to destroy particular races and classes of people and national, racial, or religious groups, particularly Jews, Poles, and Gypsies and others." Since genocide was not at that point recognized as separate crime under international law, at Nuremberg these allegations were included among the "war crimes." Shortly thereafter, the United Nations General Assembly adopted a resolution declaring genocide to be a crime under international law. This resolution both broadened Lemkin's concept of genocide, by adding "political and other groups" to the list of potential victims, and narrowed it, by giving only passing attention to the cultural aspect of Lemkin's concept.

By 1948, when the United Nations Convention on the Prevention and Punishment of the Crime of Genocide was adopted, both the cultural and the political components of the term were ignored, and genocide was defined as:

> any of the following acts committed with intent to destroy, in whole or in part, a national, ethnical, racial or religious group, as such: (a) killing members of the group; (b) causing serious bodily or mental harm to members of the group; (c) deliberately inflicting on the group conditions of life calculated to bring about its physical destruction in whole or in part; (d) imposing measures intended to prevent births within the group; (e) forcibly transferring children of the group to another group.

An important distinguishing feature of the new crime of genocide was that it was not necessarily linked to an overt war, unlike the related concepts of "crimes against humanity" and "war crimes" used at Nuremberg. The same definition of genocide was used, unchanged, in the statutes for the International Criminal Tribunal for the Former Yugoslavia and the International Criminal Tribunal for Rwanda, established in 1993 and 1994, respectively, and in those for the International Criminal Court created in 1998.

Subsequent scholars have varied the definition, particularly to overcome perceived short-comings in the concept of genocide under international criminal law. For example, Irving Lewis Horowitz defined genocide as "a structural and systematic destruction of innocent people by a state bureaucratic apparatus" (1997). Frank Chalk and Kurt Jonassohn defined the term as "a form of one-sided mass killing in which a state or other authority intends to destroy a group, as that group and membership in it are defined by the perpetrator" (1990). And Helen Fein defined it as the "sustained purposeful action by the perpetrator to physically destroy a collectivity directly or indirectly, [the latter] through interdiction of the biological and social reproduction of group members, sustained regardless of the surrender or lack of threat offered by the victim" (1990).

Related terms sometimes associated with or distinguished from genocide include *politicide,* where the victims are defined primarily in political terms; *democide,* encompassing genocide, politicide, massacres, extrajudicial executions, and other forms of mass murder; and *ethnocide,* the destruction of the culture of a population, particularly an indigenous population.

Data and Estimation Issues

Even with agreement on definition, quantifying a genocide is difficult. Limits on geographical scope and time period must be set. But how can the destruction of a people's culture, language, or socioeconomic accomplishments be measured? By default, the focus is usually on the number of deaths, occasionally supplemented with the number of forced migrants or with the monetary value of confiscated property and personal injuries.

Even considering deaths alone, estimates can rarely be made with any degree of precision. For example, there is the question of which deaths to count: (1) only those deaths directly attributable to genocidal killing operations (i.e., mass executions and the like), (2) such direct deaths plus those attributable to malnutrition and ill-health associated with populations confined or dislocated due to other genocidal operations, or (3) any elevated mortality in a target population during a defined period. Genocide mortality, as with mortality generally, may be measured directly as an estimated number of deaths over a period of time or indirectly as the difference in population size before and after, adjusted for fertility, non-genocidal mortality, and net migration. The two approaches are often used together. In countries with reasonably well-developed statistical systems, data from population censuses or population registration systems are often available for the initial population. Indeed, in some of these countries, the perpetrators have used such information to identify and target genocidal victims or as a baseline against which to assess the outcome of a genocide.

Other approaches to estimating genocide mortality do not depend on a preexisting statistical infrastructure. The bureaucratic organization of many large genocides may offer various direct or proxy indicators of scale. Mortality counts can also be derived from mass graves or from retrospective surveys. This last approach, like any survey-based retrospective reporting of deaths, is often subject to substantial response errors. In the 1990s dual and multiple system estimation techniques began to be used to control for these response errors so as to obtain improved estimates of genocide mortality from such retrospective reporting.

The interpretation and analysis of mortality estimates also pose challenges. Estimates presented simply as the number of persons killed, while an excellent indicator of the scale of genocidal operations, often obscure the impact of genocide on the victim population. A better measure of this impact is the proportion of the population killed. For example, in Cambodia from the 1975 to 1979, the Pol Pot regime is estimated to have killed over 1.3 million Khmers (the majority group) and less than 350,000 persons belonging to various ethnic minorities. However, while the Khmer victims made up an estimated 11 percent of the 1975 Khmer population, the minorities taken as a group lost 44 percent of their 1975 population.

An Inventory of Selected Modern Genocides and Genocide-like Events

Table 1, adapted primarily from information in the sources cited in the bibliography, is a tentative and incomplete listing of major genocides in modern times. It indicates the widespread incidence of genocide and its complex and varied character. Many of the assessments and estimates given are disputable: It is the nature of the field that no such inventory would be universally accepted. The table's omissions may be its greatest shortcoming. For example, no mention is made of the African slave trade or the suppression of minorities in the USSR and China. Information about these and many other genocides and similar human rights tragedies can be found in the works cited in the bibliography.

Population Issues

From the perspective of population studies, three aspects of modern genocides are particularly relevant. First, the crime of genocide under international law is defined largely in demographic terms. Three of the five elements of the crime—killings, coercive birth prevention, and the forcible transfer of children—are demographic in nature. On the other hand, forced migration, a frequent precursor to the mass killings of genocide and a major source of "conditions of life calculated to bring about . . . physical destruction" of a group, is not included in the legal definition. Second, the measurement of genocide mortality and survivorship will continue to present major challenges. As with any human rights tragedy, the emotional and political after-effects make objective assessment difficult for both scholars and advocates. In these circumstances, estimates of losses gain credibility by the qualifications that accompany them rather than by the number of significant digits in which they are expressed. Third, from a strictly long-term demographic viewpoint, genocide and re-

TABLE 1

Selected List of Genocides and Genocide-like Events: Perpetrators, Victims, Definitional Issues, and Estimated Mortality

Perpetrator and Time Period	Victims	Covered by UN Genocide Convention	Indigenous Population Involved	Role of Forced Migration	Estimated Mortality (thousands)
Cambodia, 1975-1979	Ethnic minorities	Yes (1)	Some	Varied	about 350
	Khmers	Not clear	No	Major	about 1,300
Europe under Nazis, 1933–1945					
	Jews	Yes (2)	No	Varied	about 6,000
	Roma/Sinti (Gypsies)	Yes (2)	No	Major	230–680
	Others	Varied	No	Varied	7,700 (4)
Guatemala, 1960–1996	Indians and others	Not clear	Yes	Minor	134
Rwanda, April–July 1994	Tutsis	Yes (3)	No	Minor	} over 500
	moderate Hutus	Not clear	No	Minor	
Ottoman Empire, 1915–1922	Armenians	Yes (1)	No	Major	600–2,000
Yugoslavia 1991–1992	Croats and non-Serbs	Yes (3)	No	Important	over 0.2
Bosnia-Herzegovina, 1992–1995	Muslims and Croats	Yes (3)	No	Major	over 9
Kosovo, 1999	ethnic Albanians	Not clear	No	Major	7–14
USSR, 1932–1933	Ukranian population	Not clear	No	Major	3,000–5,000
United States, 1800–1900	Native Americans	Not clear	Yes	Major	200–800

(1) Presumably yes, using the standards now applied in International Criminal Tribunal proceedings.
(2) Reference to term during an International Criminal proceeding.
(3) Indictment or conviction at an UN Tribunal.
(4) Includes an estimated 150,000 handicapped, 3,000,000 Soviet prisoners of war, 4,500,000 Soviet civilians, and a comparatively small number of others.

SOURCE: Adapted by author mainly from material presented in the sources included in the bibliography.

lated state efforts directed toward the destruction of specific populations often fail. For example, those who identify themselves as Armenian, Jewish, or Native American are more numerous or nearly as numerous now than most creditable estimates of their size when genocidal or related activities began. This is not to minimize the terrible short-run impact of genocides in the lives lost, pain to individuals, families, and societies, and the damage to culture. Rather it is a simple testament to the transitory impact of a period of even greatly elevated mortality in the face of the recuperative powers of human populations.

See also: *Forced Migration; Holocaust; Indigenous Peoples; War, Demographic Consequences of.*

BIBLIOGRAPHY

Alvarez, Alex. 2001. *Governments, Citizens, and Genocide: A Comparative and Interdisciplinary Approach.* Bloomington: Indiana University Press.

Andreopoulos, George J., ed. 1994. *Genocide: Conceptual and Historical Dimensions.* Philadelphia: University of Pennsylvania Press.

Ball, Patrick, Wendy Betts, Fritz Scheuren, Jan Dudukovich, and Jana Asher. 2002. *Killings and Refugee Flow in Kosovo, March–June 1999: A Report to the International Criminal Tribunal for the Former Yugoslavia.* Washington, D.C.: American Association for the Advancement of Science and American Bar Association Central and Eastern European Law Initiative.

Chalk, Frank, and Kurt Jonassohn. 1990. *The History and Sociology of Genocide: Analyses and Case Studies.* New Haven, CT: Yale University Press.

Fein, Helen. 1990. "Genocide: A Sociological Perspective." *Current Sociology* 38 (1): 1–126.

———, ed. 1992. *Genocide Watch.* New Haven, CT: Yale University Press.

Horowitz, Irving Lewis. 1997. *Taking Lives: Genocide and State Power,* 4th edition. New Brunswick, NJ: Transaction Publishers.

Jonassohn, Kurt, and Karin Solveig Björnson. 1998. *Genocide and Gross Human Rights Violations in Comparative Perspective.* New Brunswick, NJ: Transaction Publishers.

Kuper, Leo. 1982. *Genocide: Its Political Use in the Twentieth Century.* New Haven, CT: Yale University Press.

Lemkin, Raphael. 1944. *Axis Rule in Occupied Europe: Laws of Occupation, Analysis of Government, Proposals for Redress.* Washington, D.C.: Carnegie Endowment.

United Nations General Assembly. 1946. *Resoultion 96* (I), 11 December 1946. Reprinted in Kuper, 1982.

United Nations. 1948. "Convention on the Prevention and Punishment of the Crime of Genocide." Paris, 9 December 1948. Reprinted in Andreopoulous, 1994 and in Chalk and Jonassohn, 1990.

United States Office of Chief Counsel for the Prosecution of Axis Criminality. 1946. "Nazi Conspiracy and Aggression, Volume I." Chapter III, *International Military Tribunal Indictment No.1, Count 3—War Crimes.* Washington, D.C.: U.S. Government Printing Office.

WILLIAM SELTZER

GEOGRAPHIC INFORMATION SYSTEMS

Geographical Information Systems (GIS) are a rapidly developing branch of information technology that promises to greatly improve the treatment of locational and other spatial variables in population research, policy making, and program development and execution.

GIS Hardware and Software

A GIS comprises sets of computer hardware and software that facilitate the storage, interrogation, manipulation, analysis, modeling, visualization, and interpretation of multiple sets of spatially referenced information. "Spatially referenced" (or "georeferenced") means that each data element in the system has associated with it a specific location on the earth's surface, identified within a common coordinate system—usually latitude and longitude. This additional information about the unit under study (such as person, family, household, farm, factory, health service, or store) allows the analyst to consider (1) the specific characteristics of the unit's location and the immediate vicinity; (2) its location in relation to other units, such as distance of a household from the nearest medical facility; and (3) information about the unit from other data sources.

Geographical Information Systems

A Geographical Information System can be conceptualized as a series of layers of information with each observation in each layer tied to specific points and areas on the earth's surface via a specific latitude and longitude. The layers refer to different characteristics at that place, such as population numbers, educational characteristics, fertility levels, mortality levels, accessibility to health services, and income levels. The data in the layers may be quantitative or qualitative in nature and presented in point, linear, or area format. GIS software allows us to cut vertically through the layers of data and analyze the relationship between the various layers. Provided the data are georeferenced or relate to a specific areal unit, they can be included in the analysis.

A Simplified Model of a Geographical Information System

Georeferencing can be achieved by use of a global positioning system (GPS) to compile the latitude and longitude of each location in question—such as the locations of respondents, sample clusters of villages, buildings, and neighborhoods. Increasingly, countries have developed national systems, which not only provide georeferencing for standard spatial units like census districts, local government areas, electoral districts, and postal codes, but also allow individual addresses to be electronically assigned georeferences. This means that analysis of individual and household data does not have to be constrained by the need to use standard divisions like census blocks or counties; they can be readily assigned to spatial units more relevant to the particular investigation, whether labor market areas, cultural zones, health care catchment areas, or river basins.

For population studies, GIS allows population-related information to be combined with other information on the basis of common geographical locations. Thus, information on fertility or mortality can be linked to data on climate and other dimensions of the physical environment, service provision records, road and transport routes, or cultural variables. At the simplest level, GIS enhances our ability to visualize population information, not only as traditional maps but also in new ways: using animation to depict processes of change, or through use of three-dimensional and virtual-reality type representations. Such visualization can be a powerful way of presenting population information to policy makers and planners.

The 2000-round of global censuses collected a wealth of small-area population data that would be amenable to GIS analysis. Indeed, several countries are geocoding their census results. Most of the surveys conducted under the Demographic and Health Surveys (DHS) program are now georeferenced and allow detailed spatial analysis.

Uses of GIS and SIS

Wider use of GIS could potentially increase the power of many population analyses. The incorporation of GIS into multi-regional modeling, for example, opens new analytical directions in what is already an important and well-developed area of population geography. GIS makes possible the use of larger and more complex data sets and allows ready incorporation of important geographical variables such as accessibility, proximity, and relative location. It also assists in the development of spatially referenced composite variables such as socioeconomic status, locational disadvantage, well-being, and social capital.

What are the major ways in which GIS can be useful in population related analysis? Firstly, demographers have tended to neglect context and place as a causal variable in examining fertility, mortality, migration and other demographic processes. Use of GIS allows the characteristics of where people live and their location relative to large cities, services or other things, which can exert an important influence on people's lives. Demographers have simply differentiated urban and rural areas but the dimension of place is more complex and GIS allows this to be captured and operationalized in analysis. GIS also greatly facilitates the detection of spatial variation in demographic characteristics over space and time. This can be helpful in the identification of causal processes.

The United Nations (1997, pp. 16–17) has identified the following as being important uses of GIS for population related statistics:

- Data management: GIS aids in inventory and database management for censuses and large scale surveys.
- Health issues: GIS allows spatial patterning of the distribution and spread of disease and relates it to environmental, community, accessibility, socioeconomic and demographic characteristics.
- Service provision: GIS allows services to be optimally located where they are most accessible to the largest number of people in need.
- Family planning: Adoption of family planning can be readily related to a range of accessibility, socioeconomic, cultural, community, and service provision characteristics.
- Demographic-environmental relationships: This remains one of demography's most underdeveloped areas and GIS provides a methodology that allows demographic and environmental information (e.g. satellite imagery on forest covers, salinity, soil erosion, deforestation etc.) to be analyzed together.
- Disaster relief planning: GIS allows resources to be deployed in the most cost-effective, timely, and equitable way.

For all its potential advantages for population studies, GIS is not a "silver bullet." Problems still need to be identified, clarified, and articulated. Appropriate information relating to these problems needs to be collected. Appropriate techniques have to be selected and applied to particular problems and the results of SIS analysis need to be carefully interpreted. The technology and methodology is more sophisticated and powerful than anything available in the past, allowing larger, more varied, and more complex data sets to be analyzed, and in a much shorter time. But GIS does not replace the expertise, experience, and judgement of the individual analyst.

See also: *Geography, Population; Remote Sensing.*

BIBLIOGRAPHY

Demographic and Health Surveys. 2000. "New Directions: DHS Surveys Incorporate Geographic Data." *DHS Dimensions* 2(1): 1–2.

Entwisle, B., R. R. Rindfuss, S. J. Walsh, and T. P. Evans. 1998. "Satellite Data and Social Demographic Research." Paper presented at annual meeting of the Population Association of America, March 23rd.

Hugo, G. J. 2001. "Addressing Social and Community Planning Issues with Spatial Information." *Australian Geographer* 32(3) November: 269–293.

Liverman, D., E. Moran, R. Rindfus, and P. Stern, eds. 1998. *People and Pixels: Linking Remote Sensing and Social Science.* Washington D.C.: National Academy Press.

Longley, P., and G. Clarke, eds. 1995. *GIS for Business and Service Planning.* Cambridge: Geoinformation International.

Martin, D. 1996. *Geographic Information Systems and Their Socioeconomic Applications.* London: Routledge.

Rosero-Bixby, L. 1997. "Spatial Dimensions of Family Planning in Costa Rica: The Value of Geocoding Demographic Surveys." In *Demographic Diversity and Change in the Central American Isthmus,* ed. A. Pebley and L. Rosero-Bixby. Santa Monica, CA: Rand.

United Nations. 1997. *Geographical Information Systems for Population Statistics.* Department of Economic and Social Information Statistics Division Studies in Methods. New York: United Nations.

GRAEME HUGO

GEOGRAPHY, POPULATION

Population geography, with intellectual roots that go back to the mid-nineteenth century, studies the way in which spatial variations in the distribution, composition, migration, and growth of population are related to the nature of places. A concern with spatial variation has been the geographer's distinctive contribution to population studies, in comparison to the demographer, who is much more interested in patterns of birth, marriage, and death, and less interested in the influence of migration and spatial variations in general.

Within the discipline of geography, population study has long been important, and increasingly the boundaries between geography and other disciplines interested in population matters—economics, sociology, history, psychology, and biology, as well as demography—are blurred. Population geography is not concerned exclusively with spatial distribution, or with description over theory: it can encompass, for example, the explanation of regional and national levels of fertility, detailed patterns of disease diffusion, and advanced modeling of interregional population growth. Population variables also form a key component in Geographical Information Systems, which allow the processing of large amounts of data for discrete geographical units. Nevertheless, population geographers are more concerned with migration and spatial variation than with other matters. The *International Journal of Population Geography,* founded in 1995, is a useful indicator of the scope of the field.

Development of Population Geography

Lesek Kosinskî traces the origins of population geography back to the German and French schools of human geography of the second half of the nineteenth century and early twentieth century. These schools had a particular concern with population mapping and with the relationship between population and the environment. It was only after World War II, however, that the sub-discipline began to take its modern shape, following the publications of Pierre George (1951) in France (reflecting that country's particular interest in demographic issues), and Glenn T. Trewartha (1953) in the United States. Germany, where demography had been discredited by its association with Nazi policy, and some other countries were slower to follow, although there was significant progress in the Soviet Union, Japan, and India. For Trewartha, "population is the point of reference from which all other elements are observed and from which they all, singly and collectively, derive significance and meaning. It is population which furnishes the focus" (1953, pp. 6 and 14). His "tentative system of content and organisation" for population geography defined the field broadly, including historical population geography, the dynamics of population growth, distribution, migration, population structure, and socioeconomic characteristics. At the core of population geography was a fascination with the global pattern of population distribution and the way it reflected both demographic processes and the wider human and physical environment.

The postwar growth in the field was facilitated by the increased availability of demographic data and impelled by the very obvious relevance of population issues in both the developed and developing countries. Publication of a number of influential textbooks—such as those by John Clarke (1965) and George Demko, Harold Rose, and George Schnell (1970)—gave population geography a firm place in the geography curriculum in many countries. The field was strengthened by an improved institutional environment, marked by the activities sponsored by the Commission on Population Geography of the International Geographical Union (especially from the late 1950s), the Population Specialty Group of the Association of American Geographers (from 1980), and the Population Geography Study Group of the Institute of British Geographers (from 1963). Population geographers have had some, though more limited, involvement with multidisciplinary groups such as the International Union for the Scientific Study of Population.

These early foundations of population geography were quite different from (and indeed had relatively little effect on) demography, but from the 1970s it was increasingly argued that geographers needed to focus more clearly on demographic methods. Thus, texts such as Robert Woods (1979) gave greater emphasis to the central demographic phenomena of fertility and mortality and rather less to migration. The idea was to merge population geography and spatial demography around a core of theory derived from demography. This coincided with the greater use of quantitative methods in geography generally, with texts such as Philip Rees and Alan Wilson's (1977) focusing on the use of population accounts and models for spatial demographic analysis, and Peter Congdon and Peter Batey's (1989) bringing an interdisciplinary view of "regional demography."

Contemporary Population Geography

Although standard texts such as Huw Jones (1981) still took a broadly based view, for some geographers this attachment to the methods of demography signaled an unwelcome narrowing of population geography, distancing it from the rest of geography just at the time when debates about critical social theory in geography were intense. Some population geographers called for a greater awareness of social theory in population geography, for a more critical view of established data sources and theories, and for a move to qualitative as well as quantitative methods. Interestingly, though their impetus came largely from the discipline of geography, their concerns mirrored ones expressed within demography. These critical geographers would agree with the demographer-anthropologist Susan Greenhalgh's view that "reflexivity about the politics of demographic praxis is notably lacking in the field. . . . Neither the global political economies of the 1970s, nor the postmodernisms and postcolonialities of the 1980s and 1990s, nor the feminisms of any decade have had much perceptible impact" (1996, p. 27).

However geographers choose to define their field at a particular moment, their abiding interest is in spatial variations at different scales. Patterns of population growth through time and space, and particularly the demographic transition, have been considered fundamental to the understanding of wider geographical processes of urbanization, industrialization, and the use of resources. There has been a continuing interest in the links between the physical and human environments, for example in the impact of natural disasters.

Attention to fertility and mortality has been directed in particular to highlighting the spatial dimension of patterns and their links with environmental or social conditions—for example the spatial incidence of mortality and disease or fertility. Others have combined demography and geography to produce persuasive portraits of countries or continents. Demographers such as Ansley J. Coale and Susan Cotts Watkins have themselves taken an interest in international and national patterns of demographic change that have clear geographical dimensions. Geographers have also shared with historians an interest in historical geographies of population, reconstructing patterns of fertility and mortality as well as household and family formation through techniques such as family reconstitution and the detailed manipulation of past census, registration, and ecclesiastical records.

Yet population geographers have given most attention to migration, estimating gross and net flows at various scales; building models of interregional flows; and analyzing economic and social causes and consequences. Studies of migration have included international movements, rural-urban, urban-

urban, and intra-urban flows, as well as seasonal and diurnal movements. Geographers like Russell King, Paul White, and John Connell have also looked at the subjective experience of migration, drawing on in-depth surveys and creative literature.

Population geography, through its content and approaches, serves to remind both demographers and practitioners with population interests in other disciplines that demographic changes have spatial as well as temporal dimensions. At the same time it reminds geographers that population characteristics are a key ingredient in the character of places.

See also: *Central Place Theory; Density and Distribution of Population; Geographic Information Systems; Geopolitics.*

BIBLIOGRAPHY

Clarke, John I. 1972. *Population Geography,* 2nd edition. Oxford: Pergamon.

Clarke, John I., ed. 1984. *Geography and Population: Approaches and Applications.* Oxford: Pergamon.

Cliff, Andrew, and Peter Haggett. 1992. *Atlas of Disease Distributions.* Oxford: Blackwell.

Coale, Ansley J., and Susan Cotts Watkins, eds. 1986. *The Decline of Fertility in Europe.* Princeton, NJ: Princeton University Press.

Coleman, David, and John Salt. 1992. *The British Population: Patterns, Trends and Processes.* Oxford: Oxford University Press.

Congdon, Peter, and Peter Batey. 1989. *Advances in Regional Demography: Information, Forecasts, Models.* London: Belhaven.

Demko, George J., Harold M. Rose, and George A. Schnell, 1970. *Population Geography: A Reader.* New York: McGraw-Hill.

George, Pierre. 1951. *Introduction à l'Etude Géographique de la Population du Monde.* Paris: Institut National d'Etudes Démographiques.

Gould, William T. S., and M. Brown. 1996. "Research Review 2: Fertility in Sub-Saharan Africa." *International Journal of Population Geography* 2: 1–22.

Greenhalgh, Susan. 1996. "The Social Construction of Population Science: An Intellectual, Institu-tional and Political History of Twentieth-Century Demography." *Comparative Studies in Society and History* 38: 26–66.

Jones, Huw. 1990. *Population Geography,* 2nd edition. London: Paul Chapman.

King, Russell, Paul White, and John Connell, eds. 1995. *Writing Across Worlds: Literature and Migration.* London: Routledge.

Kosinskî, Lesek. 1984. "The Roots of Population Geography." In *Geography and Population: Approaches and Applications,* ed. John I. Clarke. Oxford: Pergamon.

Noin, Daniel, and Robert Woods, eds. 1993. *The Changing Population of Europe.* Oxford: Blackwell.

Ogden, Philip E. 2000. "Population Geography." In *The Dictionary of Human Geography,* 4th edition, ed. R. J. Johnston, Derek Gregory, Geraldine Pratt, and Michael Watts. Oxford: Blackwell.

Rees, Philip, and Alan Wilson. 1977. *Spatial Population Analysis.* London: Edward Arnold.

Trewartha, Glenn T. 1970. "A Case for Population Geography" (1953). In *Population Geography: A Reader,* ed. George Demko, Harold Rose, and George Schnell. New York: McGraw-Hill.

Woods, Robert I. 1979. *Population Analysis in Geography.* London: Longman.

PHILIP E. OGDEN

GEOPOLITICS

At one time the term *geopolitics* referred almost exclusively to the determining effects of global location and environmental characteristics (climate, soils, topography, etc.) on conflict between powerful states and empires. In popular usage this remains the dominant definition. Since the 1970s the meaning has shifted among scholars toward a more critical appreciation of how interpretations of geographical divisions, conditions, and designations enter into the foreign policies and military strategies of the great powers and their adversaries.

As a result, for example, in the twenty-first century it is how the Middle East is constructed as a region in American foreign policy (including the role of the Israel–Palestine conflict, the rise of militant Islam, and the region's oil in world trade) rather than the environmental characteristics of the region (deserts, relative location between Europe and South Asia, limited resource base beyond oil, etc.) that constitutes the dominant understanding of how geography affects the making of world politics.

Population and Geopolitics

Population characteristics and processes are among the most important elements that enter into geopolitical interpretations. In the classical deterministic geopolitics that prevailed from the 1890s until 1945 population was introduced in terms of a series of differences between dominant states with respect to their need for territorial expansion (known in German as *Lebensraum*): racial hierarchies, comparative fecundity, population vitality (a euphemism linking population growth with the need for territorial expansion), and population degeneration (associated with population decline and/or miscegenation). Writers such as the German Friedrich Ratzel and the Englishman Halford Mackinder preached an organic conservatism in which human history was seen in terms of a struggle between geographically concentrated groups (typically the state or empire of the writer in question) and threatening outsiders, such as other states with burgeoning populations or nomadic invaders sweeping across the land to transform history. In an attenuated form this type of thinking maintains a hold on those who see states as the sole containers of economic activity and as being the exclusive source of political identity. Population size and growth thus are seen as significant indicators of political strength and actual or potential great-power status.

Whether this way of thinking continues to make sense in a world in which national economies are subject to global competitive pressures rather than existing as isolated entities building purely on their internal assets is open to question. Tremendous increases in the mobility of capital, technology, and people suggest that the relationship between population and geopolitics is quite different from the relationship problematically mapped by classical geopolitics. Avant-garde thinking about geopolitics tends to see states as historically contingent actors with powers within their territories and beyond them that wax and wane in capacity and scope rather than as transcendental entities with permanent drives and needs.

How Population Enters into Contemporary Geopolitics

Eschewing the determinism that afflicted and, after the Nazi period, discredited classical geopolitics does not mean abandoning attention to material factors (such as population characteristics and processes) that potentially impinge on the geographical conditioning of world politics. However, it does require seeing those factors as they are refracted through the discourse and practice of politics. In the end it is whether population issues are seen as important by political leaders and mass publics and enter into the calculus of public decision making that matters, not whether there really is a specific population problem per se.

Debates in the most widely circulated foreign policy magazines (such as *Foreign Affairs* and *Foreign Policy*) and in the professional literature on international relations and world politics suggest that a number of population-related issues are of vital importance to contemporary geopolitics. Of course, this assumes that these debates reflect the sensibilities and concerns of many contemporary "intellectuals of statecraft," a term coined by Gearoid Ó Tuathail and John Agnew (1992) to cover the array of policy professionals, military strategists, and politicians involved in shaping foreign policies in the United States and other countries.

European states and states established by European settlers (such as the United States) have long dominated world politics. Japan's status as the sole representative of the rest of the world in the ranks of the great powers is the exception that proves the rule. Though never numerically as prevalent as their global power status would suggest if there was a one-to-one relationship between population size and global political significance, Europeans today constitute a shrinking portion of the world's total population. As the first part of the world to experience the demographic transition, Europe has since been joined by much of the rest. Its loss of demographic singularity can be seen in prophetic terms. In many recent commentaries, the rise of India and China to global political prominence is predicated on the potential linkage between their massive populations and economic growth. As a result, the Eurocentric world of the past four centuries is seen as facing eclipse with the emergence of a world in which the distribution of global power finally catches up with the relative distribution of population.

This logic is based in part on historical analogy with cases such as France in the mid-twentieth century, when population decline seems to have been correlated highly with political immobilism and defeat. However, it also reflects the sense of threat that countries with large and growing populations pose to countries that have passed their demographic peak. In this understanding population growth is taken as a surrogate for a vast array of national characteristics, particularly the idea of national vitality as indicated by population growth and the association of population decrease with national decline (and fewer bodies to throw into battle).

These "classic" ideas persist despite all manner of counterfactual information. For example, countries with smaller populations tend to have higher standards of living and lower levels of inequality in incomes and wealth than do larger countries, and, not unlike smaller families everywhere, countries with smaller populations invest more per capita in their children. At the same time countries with relatively small populations at the time of their initial territorial expansion and relatively few resources, such as Britain and Japan, have been major world powers. There is also tremendous inertia in world politics, giving established powers numerous advantages over rising ones, not the least of which is access to financial and military information that others do not have the resources to acquire. Whether Europe and its overseas offshoots are ripe for eclipse, therefore, is open to doubt.

Less problematic is the view that the global dominance of the rich few over the poor many is politically and environmentally unsustainable over the long term. If anything, the absolute gap between global haves and have-nots has grown since 1980. In this perspective the development gradients between rich countries such as the United States and poorer ones such as Mexico could produce increasing conflict.

The logic here is that of relative deprivation combined with rising expectations. On the one hand, high average affluence exists alongside high average penury. On the other hand, there is increased information about what is possible on the other side of the border and resentment that prospects are so poor on this side. What seems more likely than open conflict—and is already under way—is that people who are able to will try to move from the poor area to the rich one in the hope of bettering their and their children's life chances. This accounts for one of the major intersections between population and geopolitics in the late twentieth century: the massive increase in migration from poor countries to rich ones. This is stimulated in part by the large economic differentials (employment, income, welfare, etc.) between countries but also by the so-called gray dawn in many industrialized countries as the population ages and many economic sectors can continue to function and prosper only if they are staffed by immigrants. Some of these immigrants carry out low-paid labor, but a considerable proportion is involved in highly skilled activities (medicine, software engineering, etc.), thus draining their home countries of many of their most talented and ambitious people.

The vast heterogeneity of the underdeveloped world makes the employment of terms such as the "Third World" and "global South" potentially misleading, however. Such terminology characterizes the world in geopolitical abstractions that disguise the fact that some countries and regions, such as Southeast Asia and coastal China, have made major strides in economic development, whereas others, such as much of Africa, have become less rather then more important to world economics and politics. Of course, growth in incomes and exports is not always synonymous with development, particularly in regard to improvement in the living prospects for the very poor. However, those prospects are definitely not the same everywhere within the erstwhile Third World (a term that is the fruit of the cold war opposition between an American-allied First World and a Soviet-organized Second World), suggesting the limits of the global-rich-versus-global-poor geopolitical scenario.

A more apocalyptic scenario, named "the coming anarchy" by the journalist Robert Kaplan (2000), sees the global development gap as increasingly likely to impose costs on the rich and powerful because of the spread of diseases and famine and the subsequent spilling over of pestilence and political instability into the world at large. This logic is one of contagion from threatening places that cannot be contained by conventional military or economic means.

In this perspective the world is headed for a Malthusian crisis based on a world divided into two halves. According to Kaplan, the danger lies in the spread of diseases (beginning with AIDS) for which there are no cures; the collapse of states whose territories then provide refuge for terrorists, criminals, and drug traffickers; and the specter of perpetual low-intensity conflict involving ethnic cleansing and local warlordism. A world divided between an affluent global North and a penurious global South therefore threatens the long-term prospects of the North as much as those of the South.

This portrayal of geopolitics after the cold war, however, obscures the more specific causes of environmental degradation and disease propagation. In particular, it ignores the dispossession of people to permit resource extraction, the immense increase in the number of refugees because of civil wars, the global debt crisis, the decline of traditional social mores that govern sexual behavior, and the corrupt behavior of local political elites, often supported by foreign sponsors. More generally, it colors a more complex geography in black and white terms, with countries allocated neatly into North and South. Not only are countries internally differentiated in complex ways with respect to the incidence of disease, famine, and instability, the North–South division obscures the degree to which each geopolitical division contains islands and archipelagoes of the other (Garrett 2001). The threat is at home as much as abroad, suggesting that home is where solutions are to be sought, wherever home might be. The geopolitical framing misconstrues more than clarifies the nature of the problems that must be addressed.

The Threat of Terrorism

One population issue relating to the North–South tension that does seem to have had an impact on American geopolitical thinking has taken on special importance since 2001. In the aftermath of the terrorist attacks on New York's World Trade Center and the Pentagon near Washington, DC, on September 11, 2001, much attention has been given to the fact that the Arab world in particular and the Islamic world more generally have a huge number of alienated young men with poor job prospects who are possible recruits into terror networks, such as Osama bin Laden's al-Qaeda, for suicidal terrorist missions. The mismatch between population growth and economic development, the identification of repressive governments with developmental failure, the attraction of a religious utopia based on a return to the caliphate of early Islam, and the role of the United

States in backing repressive and non-Islamist governments are connected by Islamic militants to create a geopolitical worldview counter to the discourses of positive globalization and modernization emanating from Washington and other Western capitals. More specific concerns about the failure of local states to address inequalities and the festering conflict between Israel and Palestine probably have as much to do with recruitment into terror networks as do perceptions of the role of the United States. However, the relative youthfulness of the population in Middle Eastern cities and the well-known disposition of young men to risk life and limb for a cause probably play a contributory role in creating the terrorist threat that has become the main leitmotif of post–cold war global geopolitics.

Conclusion

Contemporary geopolitics therefore is marked by a number of important population-related themes. From the aging of populations and mass immigration to the increasing global divide between haves and have-nots, the possible spread of disease and instability from South to North, and the availability of youthful zealots for terror networks, politicians and commentators are not short of population-related threats against which to organize their countries.

See also: *Geography, Population; Lebensraum; States System, Demographic History of; War, Demographic Consequences of.*

BIBLIOGRAPHY

Agnew, John A. 2001. "Disputing the Nature of the International in Political Geography." *Geographische Zeitschrift* 89: 1–16.

———. 2002. *Making Political Geography.* London: Edward Arnold.

Corbridge, Stuart. 1988. "The Debt Crisis and the Crisis of Global Regulation." *Geoforum* 19: 109–130.

Dalby, Simon. 2001. "Geopolitics and Ecology: Rethinking the Contexts of Environmental Security." In *Environment and Security: Discourses and Practices,* ed. Miriam R. Lowi and Brian R. Shaw. London: Macmillan.

Flinn, Michael W. 1981. *The European Demographic System, 1500–1820.* Baltimore: Johns Hopkins University Press.

Garrett, Laurie. 2001. *Betrayal of Trust: The Collapse of Global Public Health.* New York: Hyperion.

Grigg, David. 1993. *The World Food Problem,* 2nd edition. Oxford: Blackwell.

Harding, Jeremy. 2000. "The Uninvited." *London Review of Books* February 3, pp. 3–25.

Hewitt, Paul. 2002. "Managing the Global Aging Transition." *Brown Journal of World Affairs* 8: 241–249.

Kaplan, Robert. 2000. *The Coming Anarchy: Shattering the Dreams of the Post Cold War World.* New York: Random House.

Kennedy, Paul. 1986. *The Rise and Fall of the Great Powers: Economic Change and Military Conflict from 1500 to 2000.* New York: Random House.

Knox, Paul, and John Agnew. 1998. *The Geography of the World Economy,* 3rd edition. London: Edward Arnold.

Loup, Jacques. 1983. *Can the Third World Survive?* Baltimore: Johns Hopkins University Press.

ÓTuathail, Gearoid, and John A. Agnew. 1992. "Geopolitics and Discourse: Practical Geopolitical Reasoning in American Foreign Policy." *Political Geography* 11: 190–204.

Peterson, Peter G. 1999. *Gray Dawn: How the Coming Age Wave Will Transform America and the World.* New York: Times Books.

Posth, Martin. 2001. "China's Economic Powerhouse." *Internationale Politik,* transatlantic edition 3: 47–54.

Scott, Bruce R. 2001. "The Great Divide in the Global Village." *Foreign Affairs* 80(1): 160–177.

World Bank. 2000/2001. *World Development Report: Attacking Poverty.* New York: Oxford University Press.

JOHN A. AGNEW

GINI, CORRADO

(1884–1965)

Italian statistician Corrado Gini wrote widely on statistical methodology and applied statistics, although he is perhaps best known as the originator of Gini coefficients, characterizing levels of inequality in a distribution. His bibliography includes 87 books and more than 800 papers. Some 200 titles among these are concerned with demographic topics; the areas most frequently discussed by Gini are the sex-ratio at birth, fertility and its measurement, and migratory movements.

Gini's multidisciplinary approach to the study of populations was the starting point for several important scientific initiatives. In 1931 he established the Italian Commission for the Study of Populations (CISP). Made up of eight sections from the natural sciences to the human sciences, CISP was open to those intending to work "without racial prejudice." CISP activities included publication of numerous monographs on anthropological and demographic expeditions and the journals *Metron* and *Genus,* founded by Gini in 1920 and in 1934, respectively. Gini also established the Faculty of Demographic, Statistical, and Actuarial Sciences within the University of Rome in 1936.

French demographer Alfred Sauvy (1898–1990) recognized Gini as one of the few scholars who had contributed to the development of a "general theory" of population (in his article "Démographie" in *Histoire de la Science,* 1957). Gini's contribution was the "cyclical theory," in which the growth of populations is based on a model of the biological cycle of human beings. Gini assumed that the reproductive capacity of populations follows a cyclical trend, and that human societies are renewed by the effect of an intrinsic differential biodemographic factor imparted by the inequality in reproduction rates among social classes (the less-fertile upper classes are replaced in the course of time by elements of the more-fertile lower classes). In the book *Esquémas téoricos y problémas concretos de la poblacion* (1963), published when he was Chairman of the International Institute of Sociology, Gini devoted more than 100 pages in the chapter on demographic theories dealing with the evolution of societies.

Frank W. Notestein (1902–1983), demographer at Princeton University, characterized Gini's theory as "biological" and considered it, together with that of Raymond Pearl (1879–1940), among the outdated concepts in the population field. A broader characterization of Gini's work is given in the biographical entry by Camilo Dagum, statistician and economist, in *The New Palgrave Dictionary of Economics* (1987), where he is described as "An extraordinary prolific writer and thinker, endowed with powerful new ideas . . . a true Renaissance man."

See also: *Population Thought, Contemporary*

BIBLIOGRAPHY

SELECTED WORKS BY CORRADO GINI.

Gini, Corrado. 1908. *Il sesso dal punto di vista statistico.* Milano-Palermo-Napoli: Remo Sandron.

———. 1912. *I fattori demografici dell'evoluzione delle nazioni.* Torino-Roma-Milano: Fratelli Bocca.

———. 1930. "The Cyclical Rise and Fall of Populations." *Population:* 3–139.

———. 1934. *Research on Population.* Cleveland, OH: University of Cleveland.

———. 1934. *Saggi di demografia.* Roma: Cisp, V, Istituto Poligrafico dello Stato.

———. 1945. *Teorie della popolazione.* Roma: Casa Editrice Castellani.

———. 1957. "The Physical Assimilation of the Descendents of Immigrants." *Proceedings of the First International Congress of Human Genetics.* Copenhagen; S. Karger, Basel & New York.

———. 1961. "Some Statistical Research Connected with Sex-ratio." *Bulletin of the International Statistical Institute* 38 (Part III).

ITALO SCARDOVI

GLASS, DAVID

(1911–1978)

David Victor Glass was an English demographer, a sociologist, and the founding editor of *Population Studies.* From 1928, when he became an undergraduate, most of Glass's intellectual life was spent at the London School of Economics (LSE). In 1936, he became Research Secretary of the newly formed Population Investigation Committee (PIC), a full-time research post. In 1946, Glass was appointed Reader in Demography at the LSE; he was appointed Professor of Sociology in 1948.

In 1936 Glass published *The Struggle for Population,* presenting research undertaken for the Eugenics Society. The Society was concerned about Britain's low birth rate and wanted evidence on the pronatalist measures taken in some European countries. A revised and enlarged version appeared in 1940 as *Population Policies and Movements in Europe.*

In 1946, in work for the Royal Commission on Population, Glass (assisted by Eugene Grebenik) conducted a Family Census, based on a ten percent sample of ever-married women in Great Britain. Dates of birth of the respondents' live-born children were recorded, enabling a detailed examination of family building. In their report, Glass and Grebenik presented what may well be the earliest attempt to model fertility. Comparing childbearing in contemporary Britain with the (presumed uncontrolled) childbearing of late-nineteenth-century rural Irish women, and making assumptions about contraceptive effectiveness, they estimated proportions of women attempting to limit their family and desired family sizes.

Glass was influential in bringing about Britain's first national survey of birth control practice (1946–1947), a study sponsored by the Royal Commission. He was a major voice in determining the approach adopted (as he was with later such surveys carried out by the PIC in 1959–1960 and 1967–1968).

In 1947, the PIC established the journal *Population Studies* with Glass as editor. He continued in that position for the rest of his life (from 1954 with Grebenik as co-editor), and made the journal one of the most important in the field.

In 1949, the LSE and Ministry of Labour conducted a large-scale survey focusing on social mobility, exploring the difference between the social class of parents and that of their children. Glass was editor of, and a major contributor to, the project report, published as *Social Mobility in Britain* in 1954.

Glass was a prolific writer on a wide range of demographic topics. An obituary bibliography listed 104 items, published between 1934 and 1976. His interests included both demographic history and the history of demographic ideas and methods. In 1953, Glass edited *Introduction to Malthus: Population in History,* with David Eversley, which appeared in 1965.

See also: *Demography, History of; Population Policy; Population Thought, Contemporary.*

BIBLIOGRAPHY

SELECTED WORKS BY DAVID GLASS.

Glass, David V. 1936. *The Struggle for Population.* Oxford: Clarendon Press.

———. 1940. *Population Policies and Movements in Europe.* Oxford: Clarendon Press. Reprint: 1967. New York: A. M. Kelley.

———. 1973. *Numbering the People: The Eighteenth-Century Population Controversy and the Development of Census and Vital Statistics in Britain.* London: Gordon & Cremonesi.

Glass, David, ed. 1953. *Introduction to Malthus.* New York: Wiley.

———, ed. 1954. *Social Mobility in Britain.* London: Routledge & Paul.

———, ed. 1957. *The University Teaching of Social Sciences: Demography: A Survey Prepared under the Auspices of the International Union for the Scientific Study of Population.* Paris: UNESCO.

Glass, David V., and David E. C. Eversley, eds. 1965. *Population in History; Essays in Historical Demography.* London: Edward E. Arnold.

Glass, David V., and Eugene Grebenik. 1954. *Great Britain Royal Commission on Population Papers,* Vol. 6: *The Trend and Pattern of Fertility in Great Britain; A Report on the Family Census of 1946.* 2 vols. London: H. M. Stationery Office.

SELECTED WORKS ABOUT DAVID GLASS.

Grebenik, Eugene. 1979. "David Victor Glass (1911–1978)." *Population Studies* 33: 5–17.

Langford, Christopher M. 1988. *The Population Investigation Committee: A Concise History to Mark Its Fiftieth Anniversary.* London: Population Investigation Committee.

C. M. LANGFORD

GODWIN, WILLIAM

(1756–1836)

William Godwin was an English Dissenting preacher, a utopian philosopher, a novelist, a man of letters, the founder of philosophical anarchism. He married Mary Wollstonecraft, famous as the author of *Vindication of the Rights of Women* (1792), who died after the birth of their daughter, Mary. Later, Mary married Percy Bysshe Shelley. As the father-in-law of so famous a poet, Godwin was an influential member of a literary circle that included also William Wordsworth, Samuel Taylor Coleridge, and Lord George Gordon Byron. Among Godwin's works of fiction, *Adventures of Caleb Williams* (1794) is an extraordinary combination of a mystery story and an epic of conflict between social classes.

The work for which Godwin is best remembered is *An Enquiry Concerning the Principles of Political Justice* (1793), which denounced all political and social regimes as obstacles to human development. The good life is based entirely on reason, Godwin argued, which is a quality only of discrete individuals; government, law, wealth, marriage, and all other man-made institutions should be abolished. "Everything that is usually understood by the term cooperation is, in some degree, an evil." Since every principle incorporated in a person's mind affects his conduct, "the perfection of man [is] impossible [only because] the idea of absolute perfection is scarcely within the grasp of human understanding." Godwin held that a cultivated person is less eager to gratify his senses, and when sustenance is no longer available, humans will "probably cease to propagate. The whole will be a people of men and not of children." Concurrently, "the term of human life may be prolonged by the immediate operation of the intellect beyond any limits which we are able to assign."

Godwin's prolonged interaction with T. R. Malthus began with the first edition of *Essay on the Principle of Population* (1798), which judged Godwin's portrait of the future as no more than "a beautiful phantom of the imagination." Within days Godwin wrote Malthus, and they met to discuss their differences. Godwin agreed to drop the word "perfectibility," and Malthus conceded that, unlike other species, humans can apply their reason and avoid the dire effects of a limited food supply; the second and subsequent editions of Malthus's book in effect acknowledged that Godwin's criticism was well based. Following this amicable exchange, Godwin wrote a small book, *Parr's Spital Sermon* (1801), in which he expressed his "unfeigned approbation and respect" for Malthus, who had made "as unquestionable an addition to the theory of political economy as any writer for a century past."

This favorable judgment was reversed in a subsequent work, *Of Population* (1820). It is a prolix book and difficult to summarize, with four principal points: Malthus had changed his position from the first edition of the *Essay* (indeed, partly at Godwin's instigation); the world is not full (repeated a dozen times); the two ratios, arithmetic and geometric, misrepresent the potential increase of mankind and its subsistence; the population data cited in the *Essay* did not support its argument. He upbraided Malthus for failing to mention the Bible, not even Adam and Eve as the progenitors of all humanity. China and India, he asserted, "carry back their chronology through millions of years." The enumerated populations of England and Wales in 1801 and 1811 showed a growth of 1.3 million; Godwin announced a possibility that "there was not one human creature more." In an anonymous review of the book in *Edinburgh Review* (June 1821), probably written by Malthus himself, *Of Population* was characterized as "the poorest and most old-womanish performance that had fallen from the pen of any writer" over the past several decades, the product of an "enfeebled judgment." The principal modern edition of *Political Justice*, published by the University of Toronto Press, omits the section on population, ostensibly because its substance is available in *Of Population*.

See also: *Malthus, Thomas Robert; Population Thought, History of.*

BIBLIOGRAPHY

SELECTED WORKS BY WILLIAM GODWIN.

Godwin, William. 1793 (1946). 1946. *Enquiry Concerning Political Justice and Its Influence on General Virtue and Happiness.* Dublin (Toronto: University of Toronto Press).

———. 1797. *The Enquirer: Reflections on Education, Manners, and Literature.* London: G. G. and J. Robinson.

———. 1801 (1968). *Thoughts Occasioned by the Perusal of Dr. Parr's Spital Sermon* (1801). In *Uncollected Writings . . . by William Godwin* (in facsimile), ed. Jack W. Marken and Burton Pollin. Gainesville, FL: Scholars' Facsimiles & Reprints.

———. 1820. *Of Population: An Enquiry Concerning the Power of Increase in the Numbers of Mankind, Being an Answer to Mr. Malthus's Essay on That Subject.* London: Longman, Hurst, Rees, Orme, and Brown.

———. 1831. *Thoughts on Man, His Nature, Productions and Discoveries, Interspersed with Some Particulars Respecting the Author.* London: Effingham Wilson.

SELECTED WORKS ABOUT WILLIAM GODWIN.

Albrecht, William P. 1955. "Godwin and Malthus." *Proceedings of the Modern Language Association* 70: 552–555.

Everett, Alexander H. 1826. *New Ideas on Population: With Remarks on the Theories of Malthus and Godwin,* 2nd edition. Boston: Cummings, Hilliard.

Paul, C. Kegan. 1876. *William Godwin: His Friends and Contemporaries.* 2 vols. London: King.

Petersen, William. 1971. "The Malthus-Godwin Debate, Then and Now." *Demography* 8: 13–26.

Stephen, Leslie. 1963. "Godwin, William." *Dictionary of National Biography*: 64–68.

WILLIAM PETERSEN

GOMPERTZ, BENJAMIN

(1779–1865)

Benjamin Gompertz lived his entire life in London. He came from a prominent Jewish family: His father and grandfather were diamond merchants in London; his youngest brother, Lewis, founded the Society for the Prevention of Cruelty to Animals. In 1810, he married Abigail Montefiore, whose brother, Sir Moses Montefiore, helped found the Alliance Assurance Company in 1824. Gompertz served the company as actuary and chief officer from 1824 until his retirement in 1847. In 1819, he was elected a Fellow of the Royal Society of London. He published four major papers in the *Philosophical Transactions of the Society*, in 1806, 1820, 1825, and 1862. He also wrote 18 other pieces, including nine on astronomical instruments.

On June 10, 1825, Gompertz's most enduring and influential research contribution was read before the Royal Society. The 72-page work, "On the nature of the function expressive of the law of human mortality, and on a new mode of determining the value of Life Contingencies," was largely devoted to calculations and detailed tables. He considered and emphatically rejected the notion of a maximum lifespan. The centerpiece of his work, however, is the formula later known as Gompertz's Law, which Gompertz presented as follows: "the number of persons living at the age of x = $d \cdot g q^x$," where d, g, and q are parameters with g, as Gompertz emphasizes, raised to the power q^x. Many demographers in the twenty-first century are more familiar with this formula in a different guise, namely that the force of mortality is an exponential function of age: $\mu(x) = ae^{bx}$, where Gompertz's q equals e^b, a is the force of mortality at the initial age of 10, 30, or 50 and x is the number of years since the initial age.

Gompertz argued that "death may be the consequence of two generally co-existing causes; the one, chance . . . ; the other, a deterioration, or an increased inability to withstand destruction." He seems to have associated *chance* with the parameter *a* and *deterioration* with the parameter *b*. He stressed that his formula "is deserving of attention because it appears corroborated during a long portion of life by . . . various published tables of mortality." Although in articles published in 1860 and 1862 he applied his formula to ages as young as 10 and as old as 100, he recognized that his law was an approximation and that different values of *a* and *b* were required for different age ranges. In 1860, the British actuary William M. Makeham suggested a simple modification of Gompertz's law, $\mu(x) = ae^{bx} + c$, that provided a much better fit to nineteenth-century European mortality. In developed countries of the twenty-first century, Gompertz's law captures the general pattern of the rise of mortality from about age 30 to about age 95.

See also: *Aging and Longevity, Biology of; Demography, History of; Mortality, Age Patterns of.*

BIBLIOGRAPHY

SELECTED WORKS BY BENJAMIN GOMPERTZ.

Gompertz, Benjamin. 1825. "On the Nature of the Function Expressive of the Law of Human Mortality, and on a New Mode of Determining the Value of Life Contingencies." *Philosophical Transactions of the Royal Society* 115: 513–585.

SELECTED WORKS ABOUT BENJAMIN GOMPERTZ.

Heligman, Larry, and J. H. Pollard. 1980. "The Age Pattern of Mortality." *Journal of the Institute of Actuaries* 107: 49–75.

Makeham, William M. 1860 "On the Law of Mortality, and the Construction of Annuity Tables." *The Assurance Magazine and Journal of the Institute of Actuaries* 8: 301–310.

Thatcher, A. R., V. Kannisto, and James W. Vaupel. 1998. *The Force of Mortality at Ages 80 to 120.* Denmark: Odense University Press.

JAMES W. VAUPEL

GRANDPARENTHOOD

Shifts to low or very low fertility in many developed countries have had, and will continue to have, the effect of making lateral kinship links—such as those with siblings, cousins, aunts and uncles, and nieces and nephews—less available than in the past. However, falls in mortality have increased the "vertical" extension of kinship networks, including grandparent–grandchild. A 1999 British survey, designed by Emily Grundy and Mike Murphy, found that over 75 percent of adults were members of families including at least three living generations. Half of all adults were a grandparent by the age of 50, and 80 percent of 20-year-olds had at least one grandparent alive. This implies that most children in low mortality populations now have the grandparent relationship potentially available to them throughout childhood. In countries with higher mortality and fertility, grandparenthood is also important. Even though higher mortality implies a lower probability of an individual of a given age having a grandparent available, this may be partly offset by earlier childbearing and shorter intergenerational age gaps. The scholars Albert Hermalin, Carol Roan, and Aurora Perez, for example, found that in Thailand in 1995, over 70 percent of people aged 50 to 54 were grandparents, higher than the equivalent proportion in Britain. Moreover, the high prevalence of intergenerational coresidence in many less developed countries implies high levels of interaction between grandparents and at least some of their grandchildren.

From a biological perspective, grandparenthood can be defined as the relationship with the children of one's children. Family dissolution and reformation may also produce social or "step-" grandparent relationships. Older people may become step-grandparents through their own repartnering with a person who has grandchildren or through a child's partnership with someone who has children from a previous relationship.

Family Change and the Role of Grandparents

The increasing complexity of family relationships in many societies has prompted greater policy interest in the role of grandparents as potential "stress-buffers" in times of crisis and as a back-up for grandchildren faced with family disruption. Policy attention has also focused on the rights of grandparents in cases where their relationship with grandchildren is threatened by divorce. In the United States, a recent increase in custodial grandparenthood has led to the development of policies designed to support such families. The role of grandparents is also recognized to have become more important in populations seriously affected by the HIV/AIDS epidemic. One survey conducted in Zaire in the early 1990s found that 34 percent of HIV/AIDS orphans were being cared for by a grandparent.

Even in less extreme circumstances, grandparents may make substantial contributions to the welfare of their children's families. Many grandparents babysit or provide childcare while parents work. Surveys in Thailand, Taiwan, and the Philippines have shown that some 40 percent of people aged 50 and over live in households including minor grandchildren, and about half of those with a coresident grandchild under ten provide child care. In the United States in the mid 1990s, over a quarter of young children with working parents were looked after by a grandparent; studies in European countries have found similarly high, or higher, levels of grandparent involvement in child care. Such support can be particularly important for single parents.

In addition to the practical help that grandparents provide, they may also perform a number of important symbolic functions and undertake the role of "family watchdogs," as well as provide emotional support and advice to their children and grandchildren.

Contact between Grandparents and Grandchildren

Studies in both Western and other populations have found high levels of contact between grandparents and grandchildren. In Britain around half of grandparents see their eldest grandchild at least weekly. Research on variations in the strength of grandparent/grandchild relationships, the extent of contact, and the provision of help by grandparents has identified several consistent themes. There is a strong gender dimension to such relationships, with grandmothers seeing grandchildren more frequently than grandfathers do and providing more help. In the 1999 British survey, for example, two-thirds of grandmothers aged 50 to 59 saw their eldest grandchild at least once a week compared with only 52 percent of grandfathers of the same age. As might be expected, physical proximity has been identified as one of the most important factors affecting intergenerational contact. Grandparents see more of grandchildren when they live close to each other, and of course most of all when they are coresident. In the 1999 British survey referred to above, over half of grandparents aged 50 to 59 lived within 30 minutes journey time of their eldest grandchild, but among grandmothers in their seventies this proportion was only 30 percent, presumably because the older grandparents' eldest grandchild is more likely to have moved away from the childhood home. Level of education (itself associated with proximity) has been found to be negatively associated with the provision of grandchild care, at least in Britain and the United States.

In the early twenty-first century, grandparenthood is attracting growing attention in both popular culture and research. Possibly this reflects a perceived greater need for grandparent involvement because of the increase in family disruption in some societies, including disruption due to parental death in populations with a high HIV/AIDS prevalence. More positive images of older people, or at least of the so-called "young old," and increases in the disposable incomes and health status of significant segments of the older population may also be important. As has been pointed out in several commentaries, though, these changes and the associated greater opportunities for travel and leisure, and in some societies opportunities or pressures to postpone retirement, may mean that at least some grandparents will be less available to maintain intensive contacts with and to help take care of grandchildren.

However, the changing ratio of grandchildren to grandparents implied by population aging suggests that younger generations will increasingly benefit from the wisdom, stability, and resources provided by their grandparents.

See also: *Family Life Cycle; Parenthood.*

BIBLIOGRAPHY

Cherlin, Andrew J., and Frank F. Furstenberg. 1986. *The New American Grandparent: A Place in the Family, A Place Apart.* New York: Basic Books.

Clarke, Lynda, and Helen Cairns. 2001. "Grandparents and the Care of Grandchildren: The Research Evidence." In *Kinship Care,* ed. B. Broad. Dorset, Eng.: Russell House Publishing.

Grundy, Emily, Mike Murphy, and Nicola Shelton. 1999. "Looking Beyond the Household: Intergenerational Perspectives on Living Kin and Contacts with Kin in Great Britain." *Population Trends* 97: 33–41.

Hermalin, Albert, Carol Roan, and Aurora Perez. 1998. "The Emerging Role of Grandparents in Asia." *Research Report No. 98–52.* Ann Arbor: Population Studies Center, University of Michigan.

Kornhaber, Arthur. 1996. *Contemporary Grandparenting.* Beverly Hills, CA: Sage Publications.

Uhlenberg, Peter. 1996. "Mortality Decline in the Twentieth Century and Supply of Kin over the Life Course." *The Gerontologist* 36: 681–685.

LYNDA CLARKE
EMILY GRUNDY

GRAUNT, JOHN

(1620–1674)

John Graunt was the author of the first quantitative analysis of human populations, *Natural and Political Observations* (1662). Widely acclaimed in Graunt's time, the *Observations* charted the course of vital and social measurement for the next century and a half, laying the basis for the emergence of demography and statistics in the nineteenth century.

Graunt cut an unusual figure among the scientific *literati* of his time. A London merchant who lacked higher education and was not versed in the natural sciences and algebra, he became a charter member of the Royal Society. His analyses relied on simple ratios, proportions, and odds and adhered closely to religious and political conventions in which a population's size and strength were considered to reflect a king's ability to govern in accordance with natural and God-given symmetries. However, Graunt's work also showed a keen awareness and originality with respect to contemporary scientific and rhetorical method and made implicit use of probabilistic concepts that were familiar at that time only to a small mathematical elite.

Graunt interpreted the old symmetries of the macrocosm and the microcosm in a new way: If human society has an inherent order of the kind that is supposed to characterize all natural or God-given phenomena, it should be possible to observe quantitative regularities in society that are similar to those a natural historian measures. The bills of mortality kept by London parish clerks provided Graunt with an extensive enumeration with which to explore this idea.

His search for quantitative regularities in a body of social data was without precedent and, as David Glass (1963) remarked, is characteristically statistical. Graunt, of course, knew nothing about those later developments. His method was a synthesis of three sources. The first was the philosopher Francis Bacon's (1561–1626) procedure for compiling natural histories: Graunt first ascertained that the bills were reasonably accurate compilations based on direct observation; he then compiled tables, grouping his observations to allow readers to check his logic and make their own observations. In cases where the bills appeared irregular, he examined and if necessary reclassified them to ensure consistency.

Graunt went beyond Bacon in employing his second methodological source—the arithmetic checks and balances of merchant bookkeeping—as a system to specify inherent natural regularities. Many of the measures he devised on this basis became fundamental to demography (e.g., rates of infant and child mortality, the imbalance of sex ratios at birth, crude vital rates presented as time series). The conception of population Graunt employed, however, remained basically a merchant's pragmatic notion of an *accompt*: Flows of births, deaths, and migrations are dealt with in an *ad hoc* manner rather than being related to a total population in a mathematically consistent way.

Graunt's third methodological source reflects the dual purpose of his observations as both natural *and* political: Each problem he addresses is treated as an exercise in political language as well as in what his contemporary, the economic writer William Petty (1623–1687), called "political arithmetic." A succession of proportions is built up persuasively in his text that demonstrate the capacities of the body politic; Graunt's book is a veritable compendium of *exempla* that show how to construct arithmetic arguments according to the methods used in influential rhetoric textbooks of the early seventeenth century.

Graunt's impressive arguments gave his work two enduring paths of influence. His ratios became the subject of political arithmetic as it was pursued by Petty and other economic writers like Gregory King (1648–1712) as well as many political, medical, and religious writers of the eighteenth century. This tradition, although unable to introduce major technical advances beyond Graunt's arithmetic and much less attentive to or effective in its powers of persuasion, increased awareness of the usefulness of enumerations in an era when such methods were subjects of popular suspicion.

Analytic development followed from one of Graunt's inventions that proved to be of deeper significance than he realized. Graunt's estimate of the number of "fighting men" (i.e., for London's defense) relied on a hypothetical table of mortality by age. Mathematicians interested in the nascent calculus of probabilities, such as mathematician Christian Huygens, astronomer Edmund Halley, and philosopher and mathematician Gottfried Leibnitz (1646–1716), quickly recognized in his reasoning a more general logic for calculating life expectancy. Although Graunt had not employed his table for that purpose, their analyses gave rise to the first abstract model of population: the life table.

The approach to longevity that Graunt inspired remained the only data-based social phenomenon that mathematicians could use to explore probability for over a century. By the early nineteenth century life tables had become the first formal models guiding state finance and corporate practice (in life insurance); this success shaped the data requirements of the newly established national statistical offices, enabling the ratios Graunt pioneered to be developed systematically.

See also: *Demography, History of; King, Gregory; Petty, William; Population Thought, History of.*

BIBLIOGRAPHY

SELECTED WORKS BY JOHN GRAUNT.

Graunt, John. 1662. *Natural and Political Observations Made upon the Bills of Mortality.* London. Reprinted 1973 in *The Earliest Classics: Pioneers of Demography*, ed. P. Laslett. Farnborough, Hants, Eng.: Gregg International.

SELECTED WORKS ABOUT JOHN GRAUNT.

Glass, David V. 1963. "John Graunt and His Natural and Political Observations." *Proceedings of the Royal Society*, Series B, 159: 2–37.

Kreager, Philip. 1988. "New Light on Graunt." *Population Studies* 42: 129–140.

———. 1993. "Histories of Demography." *Population Studies* 47: 519–539.

———. 2002. "Death and Method: The Rhetorical Space of 17th-Century Vital Measurement." In *The Road to Medical Statistics*, ed. Eileen Magnello and Anne Hardy. Amsterdam: Rodopi.

Sutherland, Ian. 1963. "John Graunt: A Tercentenary Tribute." *Journal of the Royal Statistical Society*, Series A, 126: 537–556.

PHILIP KREAGER

H

HARDIN, GARRETT

(1915–)

American biologist and writer on ecology and human population, Garrett Hardin has degrees from the University of Chicago and Stanford, with a specialization in genetics. Hardin's writings about demographic topics reflect broader interests in public policy, both with respect to domestic U.S. issues, such as abortion and immigration, and concerning international affairs, such as foreign assistance. A lucid and engaging writer, he has published widely on these issues, reaching a broad and devoted popular audience and generating controversy with messages that have often been in conflict with prevailing opinions.

In reviewing one of his collections of articles (*Naked Emperors: Essays of a Taboo-Stalker*), the economist Kenneth Boulding commented: "In a day of endangered species, it is good to be able to report that a fine old literary species, the essay, is still alive and flourishing in the habitat of a remarkable mind, that of Garrett Hardin." Some of the felicitous flair of Hardin's prose no doubt derived from an asset thinly possessed by most demographers: extensive reading in and familiarity with the history of ideas about population matters. His book *Population, Evolution, and Birth Control: A Collage of Controversial Readings* appeared in several editions and perhaps helped many readers understand and draw illumination from past intellectual engagements with population issues.

Hardin also lectured extensively about population topics. One of his lectures, eventually cast in the form of a lean and elegantly crafted article, was published in 1968 in *Science* under the arresting title "The Tragedy of the Commons." This article became one of the most cited papers in the social sciences. It was reprinted in more than a hundred collections of readings in many fields: including biology, sociology, public health, demography, political science, ecology, philosophy, ethics, and economics. Hardin followed it with an equally provocative essay, "Living on a Lifeboat" (1974). Metaphorically, the essay portrayed the world and nations, each separately, as lifeboats of limited capacity that cannot take new passengers without endangering the occupants. "For the foreseeable future," Hardin concluded his article, "survival demands that we govern our actions by the ethics of a lifeboat. Posterity will be ill served if we do not."

The "Commons" article owed something to Hardin's antiquarian interest in long-forgotten writings. Its core proposition drew on the work of a little-known English mathematician W. F. Lloyd, who showed in 1833 that the "freedom of the seas" had to be abandoned now that the supply of oceanic fish was dwarfed by the demands of an expanding human population. The oceanic fish stock was an "unmanaged commons." Applying this proposition to the contemporary world scene, Hardin argued that freedom requires population control, and called for a policy of "mutual coercion, mutually agreed upon."

See also: *Common Property Resources; Ecological Perspectives on Population; Population Policy.*

BIBILIOGRAPHY

SELECTED WORKS BY GARRETT HARDIN.

Hardin, Garrett. 1966. *Biology: Its Principles and Implications.* San Francisco: W. H. Freeman.

———. 1968. "The Tragedy of the Commons." *Science* 162: 1,243–1,248.

———. 1969. *Population, Evolution, and Birth Control: A Collage of Controversial Readings.* San Francisco: W. H. Freeman.

———. 1972. *Exploring New Ethics for Survival: The Voyage of the Spaceship Beagle.* New York: Viking Press.

———. 1973. *Stalking the Wild Taboo.* Los Altos, CA: W. H. Kaufmann.

———. 1974. "Living on a Lifeboat." *BioScience* 24 (10).

———. 1982. *Naked Emperors: Essays of a Taboo-Stalker.* Los Altos, CA: W. H. Kaufmann.

———. 1985. *Filters Against Folly: How to Survive Despite Economists, Ecologists, and the Merely Eloquent.* New York: Viking.

———. 1999. *The Ostrich Factor: Our Population Myopia.* New York: Oxford University Press.

PAUL DEMENY

HAYAMI, AKIRA

(1929–)

Born in Tokyo, historical demographer, economic historian, and Fellow of the Japan Academy, Akira Hayami was educated at Keio University. Subsequently, apart from a brief period at an ethnological institute, he lectured in economic history at that university until 1989—from 1967 as a professor. He has also held appointments at the International Research Center for Japanese Studies (1989) and at Reitaku University (1995). He was president of the Socioeconomic History Society, Japan (1991–1994) and vice-president of the International Economic History Association (1994–1998).

His first publications were on the economic history of Tokugawa Japan from 1603 to 1868. Since then, however, his major contribution has been to historical demography. Hayami first applied the methods of historical demography developed in France and the United Kingdom to Japanese data known as *shumon aratame-cho* (census-type annual listings of households and population). He drew attention to the wealth of information contained in those micro-data that could be used in the study of mortality, fertility, nuptiality, and the size and structure of households over several generations. He directed the collection and analysis of local population registers all over the country, but his own work focused mainly on two regions in central Japan. His investigations revealed that even allowing for the serious underenumeration of births and infant deaths in the registers, mortality in Tokugawa Japan was not high while marital fertility was moderate to low. He also found significant changes over time: a secular rise in the mean age at first marriage and a trend toward smaller households, which he associated with the growth of a market economy and intensive farming.

In 1995, he launched an international project on historical population registers in five European and Asian countries: Belgium, China, Italy, Japan, and Sweden. The purpose of the EurAsian project on Population and Family History (EAP) is to explore the ways in which pre-modern demography responded to resource constraints by looking at individual events in relation to the family life-cycle as well as regional circumstances. The EAP is planning to publish its research results in five volumes dealing with, respectively, mortality, reproductive culture, marriage, migration, and demographic systems.

See also: *Family Reconstitution; Henry, Louis; Historical Demography; Laslett, Peter.*

BIBLIOGRAPHY

SELECTED WORKS BY AKIRA HAYAMI.

Cornell, Laurel L., and Akira Hayami. 1986. "The *shumon aratame-cho:* Japan's Population Registers." *Journal of Family History* 11: 311–328.

Hayami, Akira. 2001. *The Historical Demography of Pre-modern Japan.* Tokyo, Japan: University of Tokyo Press.

van der Woude, Ad, Akira Hayami, and Jan de Vries, eds. 1990. *Urbanization in History: A Process of Dynamic Interactions.* Oxford: Clarendon Press.

SELECTED WORKS ABOUT AKIRA HAYAMI.

Saito, Osamu. 1995. "Historical Demography: Methodology and Interpretations." In *Historical Studies in Japan (VIII): 1988–1992,* ed. National Committee of Japanese Historians. Tokyo, Japan: Yamakawa Shuppansha.

OSAMU SAITO

HEALTH SYSTEMS

Health services, public and private, are a major sector of any national economy, and their organization and financing warrant close attention. Equally, the outputs of health systems need continual appraisal—especially in the light of new demands from aging populations and the burden of emerging diseases (notably AIDS) and also in view of widespread concern with persistent inequality in health status and access to health services in national populations.

In its *World Health Report 2000,* the World Health Organization (WHO) defined a health system as "all the activities whose primary purpose is to promote, restore or maintain health." Provision of health services, including traditional healers and medications, whether prescribed by a provider or not, are included in this definition, as are traditional public health activities such as health promotion and disease prevention. Road and environmental safety improvements (seatbelts, water management, and sanitation) are also included. Activities whose primary purpose is something other than health—for example general education—are excluded even though they often have important positive effects on health outcomes. The organizational responsibilities for health in government and donor agencies do not always align with health-system boundaries thus defined. Water and sanitation, for example, are usually managed by agencies responsible for public infrastructure rather than by health ministries, and investments in them are not usually counted as health expenditure.

Health systems vary significantly from country to country. The shape of a national health system often reflects societal values and views about the responsibilities of government for the health of citizens, but may also be the result of countries's responses to their changing demographic, epidemiological, and economic conditions. Health systems can differ in:

- How health care is financed—through taxes, payments to social or private insurance funds, or out-of-pocket payments or co-payments by consumers.

- How resources for health are managed and paid to providers—by governments through general or line-item budgets for providers, or by specialized payment schemes and contractual arrangements based on the number of patients and/or types of service provided.

- How health services are provided—through publicly owned and managed facilities, by private providers, or by some combination of these.

- The roles and responsibilities of different actors—including the public sector (as a financier, provider, or regulator), the private sector (including both for-profit and non-profit providers, insurance funds, professional associations and unions), and consumers.

Figure 1 illustrates the flow of resources in a health system (that of the former German Democratic Republic) in which health was financed mainly through taxes from individuals and enterprises (the flow along the upper left hand corner of the figure) to government, which distributed funds from general revenues to local health authorities, who then supported provision of services through a variety of government-run services (the right-hand side of the figure). Out-of-pocket expenditures by consumers were very limited (mainly for non-prescription medications), although in similar systems informal ("under the table") payments from patients to health care providers are often substantial. In contrast, the private sector plays a much larger role in the U.S. health system. In most countries, health systems combine a mix of public and private involvement in financing, fund management, provision, and regulation.

Assessments of health systems performance can employ a range of criteria, including:

- Health status of the population—conventional measures of mortality and morbidity, including life expectancy and the incidence

FIGURE 1

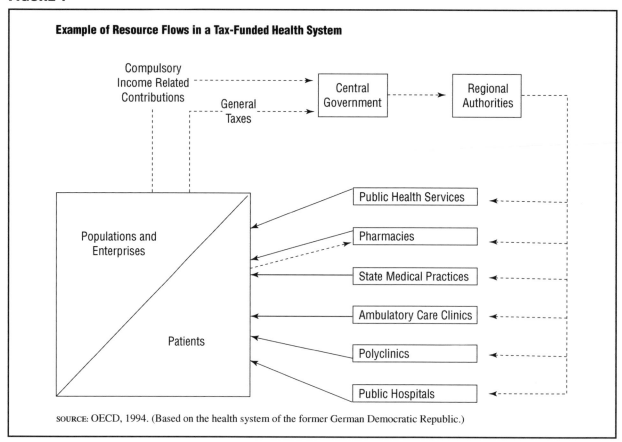

Example of Resource Flows in a Tax-Funded Health System

SOURCE: OECD, 1994. (Based on the health system of the former German Democratic Republic.)

and prevalence of diseases and disabilities. More complex measures may also be applied, such as the burden of disease, as expressed in terms of disability-adjusted life years (DALYs) or similar indexes that attempt to express a population's health using a single, comparable metric.

- Economics—the cost and cost-effectiveness of different health interventions, including the cost of gaining an additional year of healthy life as measured in DALYs, as well as the financial sustainability of particularly models of health financing and delivery, as affected, inter alia, by the changing demographic structure of the population, especially aging.

- Equity—the extent to which persons of differing income levels, including the poor, have access to needed health services or are protected from falling into poverty as the result of a personal or family medical crisis, or that all of those afflicted by a particular malady have a chance to obtain treatment.

- Consumer satisfaction with the quality and affordability of services, as measured through public-opinion surveys, exit interviews, etc.

Health reforms have been introduced in order to improve health system performance. The principal reform measures include:

- Changes in the way health care is financed: shifting from tax-based financing to cost recovery (user fees) and risk pooling (social and private insurance).

- Changes in the way services are organized, including changed roles for the public and private sectors (shifting from public financing and provision to public purchasing of privately provided services) and decentralization (shifting control over resources and personnel from central to local governments).

- Changes in the ways providers are paid (from government budgets for public provision to various modes of contracting with private providers—capitation, reimbursement schemes for specific types of treatments, performance-based contracting).

- Quality improvements (reorganization and redeployment of health personnel, changing the way in which medicines and other health-system inputs are purchased and distributed).

- Stewardship and accountability: introducing norms and reporting mechanisms for private providers, creating channels through which consumers and civil-society institutions can exercise oversight over health care.

Reforms are potentially beneficial but also contain risks. The effects of reform measures on reproductive health services, in particular, warrant close attention. Measures such as cost recovery may help to mobilize more resources for health care, but may also reduce access to needed reproductive health services by poor and vulnerable groups. Insurance schemes may lower the risks of being impoverished by most kinds of health emergency, but may not cover a life-threatening obstetric emergency. Integration into broader health programs of family planning and other priority services that previously had been funded as categorical programs may result in erosion of their priority status. Reproductive health advocates are active participants in the design and oversight of the reform process.

See also: *Disease, Burden of; Health Transition; Mortality Decline.*

BIBLIOGRAPHY

Hurst, Jeremy. 1992. *The Reform of Health Care: a Comparative Analysis of Seven OECD Countries.* Paris: Organization for Economic Cooperation and Development.

Murray, Christopher, and Alan Lopez, eds. 1996. *The Global Burden of Disease: a Comprehensive Assessment of Mortality and Disability from Diseases, Injuries, and Risk Factors in 1990 and Projected to 2020.* Cambridge, MA: Harvard University Press for World Health Organization and World Bank.

The World Development Report 1993: Investing in Health. New York: Oxford University Press for World Bank.

The World Health Report 2000, Health Systems: Improving Performance. Geneva: World Health Organization.

THOMAS W. MERRICK

HEALTH TRANSITION

The health transition is the latest in a series of secular transitions that demographers and other social scientists are expected to describe and explain. Its relative conceptual novelty means that its implications for demographic research, both historical and contemporary, remain unclear. John Caldwell, who introduced the concept of a "health transition" in 1990, hoped that that concept would encourage demographers to pay more attention to how people stay healthy while alive instead of focusing narrowly on how long they live. Of particular importance to him was how ordinary individuals in developing countries use knowledge to preserve or restore health and extend life at the household level. In this case data on education are central to tracking the health transition.

The Importance of the Health Transition

The idea of a health transition became very popular very quickly, partly because so many different fields of research are concerned with health trends and their implications for health policy. From an epidemiological perspective the idea of a global transition to better health involves tracking the courses of specific diseases. As long as infectious diseases (new and resurgent) are out of control, no global transition to better health will be possible. When health and general human welfare are equated, the growing number of refugees produced by wars and famines can make the idea of a global transition to better health seem premature. Different frameworks for conducting research invariably produce inconsistent and even contradictory perspectives on change and thus on the implications of a health transition for health policy.

Explicitly or implicitly, demographers generally assume that healthier individuals live longer than do sick ones, and thus populations with high life expectancy are healthier than those with low life expectancy. To the extent that mortality data track the health status of a population, the mortality transition effectively proxies any separate health transition. Caldwell's earliest demographic critics argued in this vein. At most, all that was needed was more specialized measures of mortality, such as infant mortality or maternal mortality, to highlight the importance of knowledge in the production of health during development.

However, demographers specializing in developed countries with high life expectancy were more receptive to the idea that there is more to health than death, especially at older ages. For several decades they have worked with epidemiologists and public health planners to develop measures that can be used to track the health status of a population without relying on mortality data but can be linked to those data (Manton and Land 2000). Measures such as active life expectancy (ALE) estimate the length of the average life lived free from disabilities and diseases that interfere with the activities of daily living (ADL). Disability-free life expectancy (DFLE) deals with the same problem. Other related measures include disability-adjusted life years (DALY) and quality-adjusted life years (QALY). Among the many implications of this research is that the health of the elderly can deteriorate even if life expectancy is stable or rising at older ages.

Criticisms of the New Approaches

Despite the potential utility of these new approaches to the measurement of a population's health status, they all have been criticized for being subjective and value-laden. For example, the way in which disabilities are perceived and measured differs from context to context, and in every context judgments must be made about various degrees of disability (mild, moderate, severe) before policy can become relevant. All these judgments reflect the interests of those who make them, especially when substantial monetary or other entitlements are involved. In contrast to disability, death is a relatively simple biological state. Its measurement is virtually free of economic and political influences, assuming that deaths are reported accurately.

The relationship between health and death, or morbidity and mortality, is not a new problem in demography. Leading Victorian statisticians debated fundamental theoretical issues and their policy implications before national death rates began to fall in

the 1870s. In 1837 Dr. William Farr argued that individuals born with less health (innate vitality) died earlier because they fell sick at earlier ages. Using this assumption, he surmised that the fall of infant and child mortality in England in the period 1755–1775 to 1813–1830, which he observed by using parish register data, meant that weaker infants were surviving to become relatively unhealthy, low-vitality adults. That is why England had higher adult death rates than Belgium or Sweden in the l830s. As Farr matured, his theories of mortality began to emphasize the role harsh environments could play in artificially accelerating the loss of health, thus causing premature (preventable) deaths that public health reforms could prevent without increasing the national burden of ill health.

Darwinian Interpretations

Unfortunately, Charles Darwin's theories gave a new scientific legitimacy to the idea that individuals were differentially frail or robust from birth and that nothing much could be done about it. The influential statistician Karl Pearson assumed that the process of culling, in which the frail die young, kept surviving adults relatively healthy. The fact that child mortality (persons age one to five) had been falling in England for several decades before 1900 explained why so many young men were rejected for military service in the first decade of the twentieth century. Females also were surviving to adulthood in poorer heath and thus were less able to bear children. This explained why birth rates were falling. To Pearson the well-intentioned campaigns to reduce infant death rates in England that began after 1900 would only result in the production of more and more physiologically frail, unhealthy adults who would be a burden to the country.

Inherent in this line of reasoning is the idea of an inverse health transition: As national life expectancy rises, the health status of the population decreases. Alternatively, as mortality falls, morbidity increases. Although this assumption has never dominated mainstream demography, its core ideas continue to reappear in different guises. In the same year that Caldwell introduced the concept of the health transition James Riley pointed out that as life expectancy continued to rise in the developed countries, so did most measures of morbidity. Indeed, as populations aged and chronic diseases replaced acute quickly killing diseases as the leading causes of death, the time spent by the living in states of ill health was bound to increase.

It is true that populations with low (or lower) life expectancy report less morbidity than do those with high (or higher) life expectancy levels. For example, in India people who live in Kerala State, which has the highest level of life expectancy, report more sickness than do people who live in states with low life expectancy levels such as Bihar. The United States has a higher level of life expectancy than does Kerala, but Americans report even higher levels of morbidity (see Figure 1).

Evaluations of Health

Fortunately, almost everyone who uses morbidity data from developed or developing countries recognizes that when people are asked to evaluate their own health, they draw on their knowledge of what good health means in the context in which they live. In some countries severe disabilities and certain diseases are consistent with reports of good health. In other countries any disease or disability, however mild, is equated with poor health.

Similar considerations affect comparisons of time off from work caused by sickness. In low-income countries the poor will work till they drop partly because taking time off from work is not subsidized in any way except by hard-pressed families that must pick up the slack or suffer the consequences. In high-income countries benefits are provided, and as they become more generous, workers take more time off from work. In general the inflation of morbidity as life expectancy rises is a form of cultural inflation, not a reflection of increasing frailty. In this case the term *cultural* includes how people have been taught to identify and respond to less than perfect states of health in conjunction with the amount of institutionalized support they receive for being sick.

Stressing the cultural inflation of morbidity (through its effects on reporting) does not mean denying the reality of adverse health trends. If people with diabetes are considered to live in a perpetually diseased state and diabetic persons live longer because insulin is available, saving their lives has increased the burden of illness. However, it can be argued that because of insulin they are not diseased, at least for many years. If Down's syndrome children are considered disabled, modern forms of care have greatly extended the life span of this disabled group.

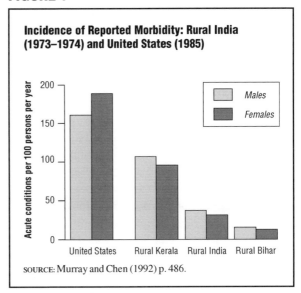

Incidence of Reported Morbidity: Rural India (1973–1974) and United States (1985)

SOURCE: Murray and Chen (1992) p. 486.

In the early twentieth century most Down's syndrome children died before the age of 20; a century later most live to old age. However, whether those surviving to old age should be considered intrinsically disabled or unhealthy during their extended lives, and thus a burden to society, is highly controversial.

Obesity continues to increase in the developed countries, and the individuals affected are at risk of developing various chronic diseases and/or disabilities in old age without dying earlier (above a certain threshold obese individuals do have an higher than average age-specific risk of dying). Even if national life expectancy is rising, it makes sense to argue that an increasingly overweight population is becoming a less healthy population.

However, weight is only one dimension of health, and the idea of a heath transition implicitly averages the many dimensions of health, some of which may be improving while others deteriorate. In the face of irreducible complexity, there are three strategies that can be adopted with respect to measuring health and thus reaching conclusions about the course of the health transition, including its relationship to mortality trends both in the past and in the present.

Three Strategies for Measuring Health

The first strategy is to continue assuming that for most research purposes health trends are adequately proxied by mortality data. In this case as long as life expectancy keeps rising, health is improving. This solution keeps demographic data at the center of health research but suggests that rising life expectancy is all that matters. Currently this strategy dominates the growing body of research on "health inequality" during economic development, in which measuring health inequalities between countries becomes little more than a matter of comparing life expectancy levels.

The second strategy is to observe health by measuring its loss in the form of sickness and disability by using data that are relatively culture-free. In this case the health transition becomes a doctor's transition; it is based on tracking forms of biological suboptimality that ordinary people may not perceive directly. Blood pressure is an obvious example. From this medicalized perspective on health, tracking the health transition would be done by doctors who were trained in the same medical tradition (Western scientific, or biomedicine) and examined otherwise comparable age cohorts at different points in time during the rise of life expectancy.

One study that approximates this ideal is Dora Costa's comparison of medical measures provided by doctors for the first generation of American men to reach age 65 in the twentieth century, with data for later cohorts over 65 at the end of the century. Based on some standard indicators relating to respiratory problems, valvular heart disease, arteriosclerosis, and joint and back problems, the prevalence of unhealthy chronic conditions seemed to decline by 66 percent (averaged over the selected indicators) over the course of the twentieth century. These data are reassuring in that they suggest that when cultural influences can be minimized, it is possible to observe health improving despite the fact that reported morbidity may be increasing as well.

The third strategy is to embrace the health transition in all its implicit complexity. This involves accepting the idea that data on both perceived change and physiological change are equally real and equally relevant to health policy. It also accords equality to micro-level and macro-level research. Micro-level, localized research is best for understanding how ordinary people acquire the knowledge necessary to produce health on a daily basis at any level of income (given that their knowledge is applied in contexts that support or discourage certain attitudes and practices). Macro-level research involves all the impersonal forms of change that influence sickness and disease in all contexts. For example, public health

can save lives without changing the knowledge and health-related behavior of ordinary people. Similarly, wars and famines can take lives that no amount of personal knowledge can save.

Conclusion

Doing justice to the health transition in its full complexity requires interdisciplinary research, but attempts at cooperation often are frustrated by the inability of experts from different fields to agree on conceptualization, research strategies, and measurement issues. Since demographers are not comfortable when research moves too far away from quantitative data and analysis, in all probability most will continue to use mortality data as a proxy for health trends and to treat the health transition as just another name for the mortality transition.

See also: *Caldwell, John C.; Disease, Burden of; Epidemiological Transition; Farr, William; Mortality Decline.*

BIBLIOGRAPHY

Caldwell, John. 1990. "Introductory Thoughts on Health Transition." In *What We Know about Health Transition: The Cultural, Social and Behavioral Determinants of Health,* ed. John Caldwall, Sally Findley, Pat Caldwell, Gigi Santow, Wendy Crawford, Jennifer Brand, and Daphne Broers-Freeman. Canberra: Australian National University Printing Service.

Cleland, John. 1990. "The Idea of the Health Transition." In *What We Know about Health Transition: The Cultural, Social and Behavioral Determinants of Health,* ed. John Caldwell, Sally Findley, Pat Caldwell, Gigi Santow, Wendy Crawford, Jennifer Brand, and Daphne Broers-Freeman. Canberra: Australian National University Printing Service.

Costa, Dora. 2000. "Understanding the Twentieth-Century Decline in Chronic Conditions among Older Men." *Demography* 37(2): 53–72.

Crimmons, E., Y. Saito, and D. Ingegneri. 1989. "Changes in Life Expectancy and Disability-Free Life Expectancy in the United States." *Population and Development Review* 15: 235–267.

Himes, Christine. 2000. "Obesity, Disease and Functional Limitation in Later Life." *Demography* 37: 73–82.

Horton, Richard. 1995. "Infection: The Global Threat." *New York Review of Books* April 6.

Johansson, Sheila R. 1991. "The Health Transition: The Cultural Inflation of Morbidity during the Decline of Mortality." *Health Transition Review* l: 39–68.

———. 1991. "Measuring the Cultural Inflation of Morbidity during the Decline in Mortality." *Health Transition Review* 2: 78–89.

———. 1996. "Doing 'Health' Research in an Unhealthy Research Environment." *Health Transition Review*, Supplement, 6: 371–384.

———. 2000. "Before the Health Transition: 'Health' and Health Policy in Victorian England and After." *Annales de Demographie Historique* 2: 109–132.

Manton, Kenneth, and Kenneth Land. 2000. "Active Life Expectancy Estimates for the U.S. Elderly Population: A Multidimensional Continuous-Mixture Model of Functional Change Applied to Completed Cohorts, 1982–1996." *Demography* 37(3): 253–265.

Murray, C., and L. Chen. 1992. "Understanding Morbidity Change." *Population and Development Review* 18: 481–503.

Murray, J. 2001. "Incentives and Absenteeism in Early Government Sickness Insurance Programs." Working Paper, Department of Economics, University of Toledo, Ohio.

Palloni, Alberto. 1989. *Sickness, Recovery and Death: A History and Forecast of Ill Heath.* Iowa City: University of Iowa Press.

———. 1990. "The Meaning of the Health Transition." In *What We Know about Health Transition: The Cultural, Social and Behavioral Determinants of Health,* ed. John Caldwall, Sally Findley, Pat Caldwell, Gigi Santow, Wendy Crawford, Jennifer Brand, and Daphne Broers-Freeman. Canberra: Australian National University Printing Service.

Riley, James. 1990. "Long Term Morbidity and Mortality Trends: Inverse Health Transitions." In *What We Know about Health Transition: The Cultural, Social and Behavioral Determinants of Health,* ed. John Caldwall, Sally Findley, Pat Caldwell, Gigi Santow, Wendy Crawford, Jennifer Brand, and Daphne Broers-Freeman. Canberra: Australian National University Printing Service.

Van de Walle, Etienne. 1990. "How do We Define Health Transition?" In *What We Know about Health Transition: The Cultural, Social and Behavioral Determinants of Health,* ed. John Caldwall, Sally Findley, Pat Caldwell, Gigi Santow, Wendy Crawford, Jennifer Brand, and Daphne Broers-Freeman. Canberra: Australian National University Printing Service.

Wilkinson, Richard. 1996. *Unhealthy Societies: The Affliction of Inequality.* London: Routledge.

S. Ryan Johansson

HENRY, LOUIS

(1911–1991)

Louis Henry was a French demographer who is considered the father of historical demography. Henry graduated from the Ecole Polytechnique in Paris in 1934 and served in the French army until 1945. In 1946 he joined the Institut National d'Études Démographiques (INED), which had been founded not long before that time by Alfred Sauvy (1898–1990), where he worked until his retirement in 1975. He also taught in many universities in France and abroad and was awarded a number of honorary doctorates.

Henry analyzed population trends in France and other European countries in the early postwar years for INED's journal *Population*, devising for that purpose improved tools of demographic analysis. That work led to an important treatment of interacting demographic phenomena ("D'un Problème Fondamental de l'Analyse Démographique," 1953) and to a book on marital fertility, *Fécondité des Marriages* (1953), in which he developed, in parallel with Norman Ryder in the United States, the concept of parity progression ratios, now a major tool of fertility analysis. Later his methodological innovations were brought together in *Démographie: Analyse et Modèles* (1972).

Henry also became interested in the level of fertility in populations in which birth control had not yet spread. He called such a regime "natural fertility." To find reliable evidence of such situations, he used data from the parish registers of pre-Revolutionary France (sixteenth through eighteenth centuries). The resulting analytical techniques, entailing "family reconstitution," were set out in a well-known manual, written with Michel Fleury, that was published in 1956. A pilot study of the village of Crulai in Normandy, a classic in historical demography, was published in 1958. In addition to analyses based on registration data, Henry made use of genealogical data.

The technique of family reconstitution from parish register data has been applied by countless historians in France and elsewhere. It took on even greater importance when it was used to reconstruct the total French population over the years 1670 to 1830. That project started in 1953, and the first aggregated results were published in a special issue of *Population* in 1975.

Those historical data also were used in the construction of models. Henry identified the key components of fertility (what later were termed the proximate determinants of fertility) and combined them in mathematical models to show how they result in age-specific or duration-specific marital fertility rates; he paid special attention to the analysis of birth intervals. His major papers on these issues have been translated into English (Henry 1972b).

Henry also developed models for nuptiality and various other analytical techniques.

See also: *Cohort Analysis; Demography, History of; Family Reconstitution; Historical Demography; Laslett, Peter; Ryder, Norman B.*

BIBLIOGRAPHY

SELECTED WORKS BY LOUIS HENRY.

Henry, Louis. 1953. *Fécondité des Mariages: Nouvelle Méthode de Mesure.* Paris: Institut National d'Études Démographiques.

———. 1967. *Manuel de Démographie Historique.* Paris: Librairie Droz, 1967.

———. 1972a. *Démographie: Analyse et Modèles.* Paris: Larousse. English translation: Edward Arnold, 1976; Spanish translation: University of Barcelona, 1976.

———. 1972b. *Selected Writings,* ed. Mindel Sheps and Evelyne Lapierre-Adamczyck. Amsterdam, New York: Elsevier.

SELECTED WORKS ABOUT LOUIS HENRY.

Fleury, Michel, and Louis Henry. 1956. *Manuel de Dépouillement et d'Exploitation de l'État Civil Ancien.* Paris: INED. Revised in 1965 and 1976.

Gautier, E., and Louis Henry. 1958. *La Population de Crulai: Paroisse Normande.* Paris: Institut National d'Etudes Démographiques.

HENRI LERIDON

HISTORICAL DEMOGRAPHY

It is conventional to draw a distinction between historical demography and demographic or population history. Historical demography, strictly defined, is the application of the array of conventional demographic methods to data sets from the past that are sufficiently accurate for analysis. Such data sets may take the form of vital records and censuses, but most frequently, particularly if produced before the nineteenth century (i.e., in *la période préstatistique*), would not have been created for the purposes of demographic enquiry. Parish registers, militia or tax lists, testamentary records, and genealogies have been the most prominent among the great variety of documentary sources used by historical demographers. Demographic history may subsume historical demography as a field of enquiry, but is more wide-ranging in its subject matter, being just as concerned with charting the impact of demographic processes on society and economy as on measuring and accounting for demographic change per se. For instance, demographic historians would be more interested in investigating the effects of massive demographic losses, such as the effects of the plague outbreaks in mid- fourteenth century Europe on the later medieval economy and values, or the consequences for New World civilizations of the introduction of Old World diseases into the Americas. Historical demographers would be more interested in tackling the technical problems of measuring and assessing the accuracy of estimates of the resulting mortalities associated with such catastrophic episodes or phases.

While the above definitional distinctions may seem clear cut, in practice the contrasts between the approaches and their practitioners can be quite muted. However, this discussion will not undertake a review of the history of demographic thought or techniques that form another set of considerations of demographic practice in the past. Most of the pioneering demographers who have been influential since the seventeenth century such as John Graunt, William Petty, Richard Cantillon, Johann Süssmilch, Adolphe Quételet, William Farr, Jacques Bertillon, Wilhelm Lexis, and Alfred Lotka were engaged in the development of technical means through which they could better understand the demography of their own times rather than developing a set of procedures for the study of specific demographic pasts. It will nonetheless be necessary to see how historical demography became integrated into the social sciences more generally and why a self conscious historical demography emerged in the quarter century after World War II.

Historical Development and the Role of Family Reconstitution

Historical demography secured a formal status first in France at the Institut National d'Études Démographiques (INED) where Louis Henry had begun research after World War II on contemporary fertility and fecundity. He was handicapped in his investigations of these matters since by the mid-twentieth century those states that collected the most reliable vital statistics possessed populations that were controlling their fertility and those that had what he termed "natural fertility" did not for the most part have well organized and accurate systems of vital registration. He was therefore drawn to records from the deeper European past.

First, Henry exploited genealogical sources of the Genevan bourgeoisie from the sixteenth to the seventeenth centuries and among other findings revealed that these families were already controlling their fertility using some form of birth control by the late seventeenth century. Subsequently in 1958, he made a truly path-breaking move when he used the events recorded in the parish register of the Normandy parish of Crulai to reconstruct the lives of the individual families resident in that community in the eighteenth century. The technique that he developed came to be known as family reconstitution and established a means of using data sets that had accumulated in the parochial registers of the Christian Church to calculate for the first time detailed and accurate measures of fertility, mortality, and nuptiality for the centuries that preceded state-based systems of census taking and vital registration.

Prior to Henry's innovation historical demography in the era that lacked censuses and vital registration had no obvious means of measuring demographic stocks and flows so essential for the calculation of crude and age-specific rates. Henry's method of reconstitution made it possible to devise a set of rules to determine the period of time during which a particular family might be regarded as under observation. The technique was quickly adopted and modified for work on English parish registers, which exist in large numbers from the late 1530s. E. A. Wrigley, an economic historian and geographer at Cambridge University, completed the first of these English studies on the Devon parish of Colyton in 1966. The findings from this study attracted much attention because it seemed that the parishioners of Colyton were limiting their fertility within marriage in the late seventeenth century and were also suppressing overall fertility by raising female marriage ages significantly.

In the subsequent three decades a large number of reconstitution studies from various European countries were completed using parish registers. The largest national samples still derive from France and England, but there are significant totals from Germany and a growing number from Spain and Scandinavia. One pervasive theme in these studies concerns the analysis of marital fertility. Levels of marital fertility proved to vary substantially even though the communities in question all displayed the characteristics of "natural fertility" (i.e., they showed no tendency toward parity dependent control or "stopping" behavior). For instance, marital fertility in Belgian Flanders was 40 percent higher than that of England in the eighteenth century, although the two regions are separated by only a few miles across the English Channel. Likewise marital fertility was almost 50 percent higher in Bavaria than it was in East Friesland in the eighteenth and nineteenth centuries. By enabling a comparison of the intervals between marriage and first birth with those between first and second birth, and comparison of inter-birth intervals following the birth of infants that died within the first year of life with those following births that survived at least through the first year of life, family reconstitution made it possible to conclude that the principal determinant of such fertility variations was the incidence and duration of breast feeding.

Family reconstitution also made it possible to scrutinize the findings of a seminal paper by John Hajnal on the distinctiveness of European marriage patterns. In the early phase of historical demography's emergence as a recognizable sub-discipline, the 1965 paper drew attention—principally on the basis of evidence in nineteenth century northern and western European censuses—to a marriage pattern characterized by late female marriage and a high proportion of women remaining permanently single. Such a pattern was apparently absent from all other major world regions. Family reconstitution allowed marriage ages to be calculated by linking individuals from their baptism to first marriage and showed that the geography of marriage sketched out by Hajnal had a deeper chronological presence and was detectable at least from the early seventeenth century and had not emerged as a result of social and economic changes downstream from or associated with rapid urbanization and industrialization after 1750.

Beyond Family Reconstitution and The Testing of Malthusian and Demographic Transition Theory

Family reconstitution provided remarkably detailed information about European populations in the *période préstatistique*. However, it was a technique that was not without certain shortcomings. It was extremely time-consuming to perform and required very well maintained parish registers to yield reliable results. Consequently even in relatively thoroughly researched settings such as England there are still fewer than 40 parishes out of some 10,000 that have been investigated demographically using this method; in France, a major project using family reconstitution overseen by Henry was based upon a sample of just one percent of 40,000 French rural parishes. The rules of family reconstitution result in the bulk of the demographic data accumulating around individuals who do not migrate and hence there is always the suspicion that the results might be biased toward the immobile, particularly in societies such as England with high rates of movement among parishes. This flaw also means that the demographic characteristics of highly mobile urban populations are far less well researched than those of rural and small town settings. But perhaps the most serious difficulty arises from the fact that family reconstitution does not make it possible to compute aggregate measures such as crude birth and death rates or indi-

ces of reproduction or natural increase. Searching for a solution to this problem loomed large in the research of the Cambridge Group for the History of Population and Social Structure in the 1970s and 1980s.

The Cambridge Group was the first center exclusively devoted to historical demographic research, notwithstanding the resources devoted to this field in Paris at INED and later in the École des Hautes Études en Sciences Sociales. In Cambridge the intellectual enquiry was principally energized by the desire to understand why the population in England had grown so much more rapidly over the eighteenth century than anywhere else in Europe. Family reconstitution, which had promised so much, could not provide a clear-cut answer to this highly significant question. Fundamentally a means was needed to provide information about population stocks that could be used to complement the data on flows that were provided by the events recorded in parish registers. A technique to accomplish this was devised in the late 1970s, initially termed "back projection" by James Oeppen, building upon pioneering work by Ronald D. Lee. The technique has been developed further and is known in the early twenty-first century as generalised inverse projection (GIP). The data requirements for the technique are not particularly demanding since only annual totals of births and deaths are needed, stretching backwards from a census of proven reliability—especially in accurately recording the death of persons at the very oldest ages. A valuable attribute of GIP is that all the estimates of demographic variables are constrained to be mutually consistent. GIP generates estimates of population totals and age structures at any earlier date, of fertility in the form of gross reproduction rates, estimates of expectation of life at birth and related sets of age-specific rates, and net migration rates. The technique has made it possible to generate long-run fertility and mortality series for England, Denmark, Scania, and Tuscany.

European countries vary considerably in the extent to which birth and death series may be assembled. For instance, in many Catholic countries the burials of children who died before they were of the age to receive communion were often not entered in the registers in the early decades of registration, making death series problematic. Such series have made it possible to test in specific contexts the applicability of the Malthusian model concerning the relationship between fertility and mortality and measures of per capita income. The English case has received most attention and as a result of the outputs from GIP it is possible to trace the size of the English population between the sixteenth and the nineteenth century and to compare it with a measure of real wages over the same period. Periods of rapid population growth were associated with significant declines in real wages. In fact, between 1541 and 1801 population growth rates up to 0.5 percent per annum did not reduce living standards, but once that rate was exceeded living standards fell. It is noteworthy that in the English case this economic-demographic relationship was disappearing just at the moment that T. R. Malthus published his famous *Essay* in 1798.

Not all of Malthus's predictions stand up to empirical testing. Real wages in England rose significantly between 1650 and 1750, but expectation of life at birth fell quite markedly. Fertility, driven by nuptiality changes, appeared to move much more consistently with real wages in the manner postulated by Malthus, particularly in his more optimistic second edition of the *Essay* published in 1803. In 1700 the English intrinsic population growth rate was very close to zero, but by the early decades of the nineteenth century the rate had risen to approximately 1.5 per cent, and over three-quarters of that growth could be attributed to a fall in the age of female marriage and a rising proportion ever married. Changes in marital and extra-marital fertility had little influence on the rate of population growth.

As a result of investigations of the kind carried out on the English demographic past historical demography moved to center stage in the debate over why the Industrial Revolution occurred and what its impact on demographic behavior had been. While this was a matter much discussed previously, it was not until historical demography had begun to generate reliable demographic data sets that economists acknowledged that the issues could be more clearly specified and historical economic-demographic relationships modeled formally.

Parish-register based demographic enquiry was only one strand in the demographic investigations of the Cambridge Group in the period from 1965 to 1985. Peter Laslett, the group's co-founder with Wrigley, pursued a linked enquiry into household and family demography and was concerned to construct patterns of household formation and population turnover. He came to realize that an essential

correlate of late marriage in north-west European settings was the propensity of young adults to leave their natal hearths in their early- to mid-teens and to circulate as servants in the households of persons to whom they were generally unrelated, before marriage. At marriage they would for the most part establish nuclear households in communities where neither bride nor groom had been born. This feature was used by Hajnal to draw out a major contrast in the marital and household formation dynamics of historic and near contemporary societies distinguished by what he termed "north-west European household formation" rules and those in which "joint household formation" rules prevailed. The latter were distinguished frequently by early marriage of women who moved directly from their household of birth to that of marriage and in which sons tended to marry and co-reside patrivirilocally until household fission took place at a later point in time. Such research helped to justify a mode of enquiry in which demographic research was undertaken in conjunction with simultaneous investigation of family and social structure, ensuring strong disciplinary connections with historical sociology and anthropology.

As the quantity of research accumulated it became apparent by the 1980s that eighteenth and nineteenth century European demographic patterns were also noteworthy for their geographical variability. England and some other parts of Britain had rapid demographic expansion after 1750, but population growth in France was much more constrained, with fertility drifting down as life expectancy moved upward to sustain near zero-growth conditions. In contrast in Sweden, where mortality was far more volatile from year to year, fertility changed little, but demographic growth in the early nineteenth century resulted from a significant rise in life expectancy. The Swedish case is of particular interest since it appears to meet far more effectively the image of the pattern of long-term demographic change associated with classic demographic transition theory. Furthermore, because Swedish demographic data from the mid-eighteenth century had long been available, Sweden was erroneously used as a paradigm case. The innovations in the use of early data sets have, however, changed researchers' sense of the demographic landscape of what was for long deemed stage I of classic transition theory. This stage is assumed in pre-modern societies to be distinguished by high mortality and high natural fertility. The latter was viewed as varying little both regionally and through time.

Classic transition theory also emphasized the role played by industrialization and associated urbanization and its resulting improvements in well-being and medical science. These socioeconomic changes were seen as instrumental in shifting mortality away from a high plateau to lower and more stable levels and leaving fertility at pre-modern levels so that rapid demographic growth ensued, before fertility was adjusted downwards. The European Fertility Project, set up by Ansley Coale at Princeton University in 1963, investigated the fall in marital fertility in Europe from the late nineteenth century. Using evidence from early national census and civil registration offices, it confirmed that overall fertility was highly variable, reflecting major regional contrasts in nuptiality and marital fertility. Parish-register based research has subsequently shown that this feature extended back into the sixteenth and seventeenth centuries. Furthermore, the European Fertility Project also showed that there was a very limited correlation between the levels of economic development and living standards in European countries on the one hand and the resort to fertility control by their populations on the other. Such evidence from historical demographers working on the pre-transition and transition periods suggested that there was little to be gained by treating these epochs as distinct demographic systems and constituted a realization which drew historical demography more firmly within the larger fold of demographic practice.

Recent Developments and Future Preoccupations

The 1970s and 1980s marked a "golden age" of historical demographic research. While major issues that concern the characteristics of pre-transitional fertility and nuptiality and Malthusian theory still have pride of place in the sub-discipline, the subsequent years have seen a broadening of research interests and, particularly, research contexts. The West European center of gravity of early demographic research with its concentration upon nuptiality and Malthusian notions as a framework for understanding demographic dynamics has been challenged by a growth in research on non-European, particularly Asian, demographic regimes in the past and exploitation of household registers and genealogies as key demographic sources in such settings which, unless

Christianized, lack parish registers. One theme, above all, has emerged suggesting that notwithstanding the prevalence in these areas of very early female marriage, population growth rates were generally no more rapid than those found in areas dominated by the European marriage regime. Extended breastfeeding, delayed starts to reproduction in marriage through spousal separation, abstinence, and abortion have been identified as means by which births were spaced out in China and Japan to produce total marital fertility rates that frequently fell below those found in Western Europe. Infanticide and child neglect often further constrained population growth. Researchers in these matters are now inclined to challenge a notion, prominent in the 1980s, that West European demographic growth rates were lower and more likely to have facilitated high savings levels, thereby facilitating longer term economic growth than would have been possible in areas of "joint household formation." A continued interest in further researching this theme is likely to dominate much future enquiry linking historical demography and the history of economic growth.

Use of population registers, both in East Asia and in some parts of Western Europe (in Sweden from 1750, in Netherlands, Belgium, and parts of Italy from the early- or mid-nineteenth century), is enabling a more sophisticated type of demographic research using event histories that make it possible to investigate demographic behavior both at the household and the individual level in a highly robust statistical fashion. However, the restricted geographical and chronological contexts within which this research method is feasible will likely limit the value of such research unless more effective means of creating longitudinal data sets can be achieved. Creation of such data sets would require linking censuses to the vital registration data that exist in large quantities for many societies both within and outside Europe from the beginning of the nineteenth century.

Research on mortality by historical demographers historically received far less attention than did investigations of nuptiality and fertility. Two highly distinctive positions dominated thinking on this topic: From the 1970s many argued that mortality was largely autonomous, being determined by the waxing and waning of epidemic disease and by climatic change, and was in no sense determined by human agency. Another argument claimed that mortality was largely determined by nutritional factors and only with the improvements in food supplies contingent upon rising agricultural productivity after 1750 did mortality decline as a result of growing resistance to infectious disease. British physician Thomas McKeown succeeded in promoting this latter view, particularly in medical circles.

Both positions regarding mortality in the past have been increasingly challenged as a result of growing realization that the inter- and intra-continental movements of population and the emergence of large metropolitan centers within emerging international trading systems had a major influence on levels of exposure and acquired resistance to infections—which in turn could lead to major changes in mortality levels, particularly among infants, children, and their mothers. Such influences were most likely responsible for the failure of model life tables based upon late-nineteenth and twentieth century population data to capture age-specific mortality patterns in historical populations. Those processes may also have been responsible for the existence of extended periods in the past when infant and child mortality could be seen to have worsened while the life chances of adults were static or improving.

Furthermore, McKeown's dismissal of the role of human intervention has been challenged by historians of public health who would argue that substantial declines in mortality arose from political interventions within urbanised societies in the late-nineteenth century that brought benefits to the poor as well as to the well nourished. New research on high and low status sections of European societies from the late Middle Ages has revealed very small differences in mortality levels and trends, especially after 1700 when adult life expectancies appear to have moved upward for all social status groups. There is growing evidence that adult female life expectancy in a substantial number of European countries has been moving upward in an unbroken fashion since about 1700 for all income groups.

Profitable research linking demographic patterns with anthropometric and paleodemographic investigation of skeletal remains and with data on human heights has been undertaken and there is considerable potential for more work of this kind over longer sweeps of time and in a variety of geographical contexts. The rising interest in adult mortality, particularly in declining mortality at the oldest ages, which is now regarded as the most dynamic demographic variable in many societies, has indirectly

impinged on historical demography. Historical demographers are searching for more accurate measurements of change in that component as well as seeking to better understand the factors that may have influenced adult longevity. They are making use of the techniques of event-history analysis. This growth area of historical investigation is undoubtedly a refection of interest in contemporary demographic developments and once again reveals how greatly the orientation of research on the demographic past is determined by contemporary demographic concerns.

See also: *Ancient World, Demography of; Cities, Demographic History of; Demography, History of; Family Reconstitution; Hayami, Akira; Health Transition; Henry, Louis; Household Composition; Laslett, Peter; Malthus, Thomas Robert; Paleodemography; Peopling of the Continents; Population Thought, History of; World Population Growth.*

BIBLIOGRAPHY

Bengtsson, Tommy, and M. Lindstrom. 2000. "Childhood Misery and Disease in Later Life: The Effects on Mortality in Old Age of Hazards Experienced in Early Life, Southern Sweden, 1760–1894." *Population Studies* 54: 263–277.

Fleury, Michel, and Louis Henry. 1965. *Nouveau manuel de dépouillement et d'exploitation de l'état civil ancien.* Paris: Institut National d'Études Démographiques.

Fogel, Robert W. 1994. "The Relevance of Malthus for the Study of Mortality Today: Long-run Influences on Health, Mortality, Labour-force Participation and Population Growth." In *Population, Economic Development and the Environment*, ed. Kerstin Lindahl-Kiessling and Hans Landberg. pp. 231–284. Oxford and New York: Oxford University Press.

Gautier, Étienne, and Louis Henry. 1958. *La population de Crulai, paroisse normande: Étude historique.* Institut National d'Études Démographiques, Travaux et Documents, Cahier No. 33. Paris: Presses Universitaires de France.

Gutmann, M. P., and G. Alter. 1993. "Family Reconstitution and Event-History Analysis." In *Old and New Methods in Historical Demography*, ed. David Reher and R. Schofield. pp. 159–181. Oxford and New York: Oxford University Press.

Hajnal, John. 1965. "European Marriage Patterns in Perspective." In *Population in History: Essays in Historical Demography,* ed. David V. Glass and D. E. C. Eversley. pp. 101–145. London: Arnold, and Chicago: Aldine.

———. 1982. "Two Kinds of Pre-industrial Household Formation System." *Population and Development Review* 8: 449–484.

Haines, Michael R., and Richard H. Steckel, eds. 2000. *A Population History of North America.* Cambridge and New York: Cambridge University Press.

Henry, Louis. 1956. *Anciennes familles genevoises: Etude démographique XVIe-XXe siècle. Travaux et Documents,* Cahier No 26. Paris: Institut National d'Etudes Démographiques.

Johansen, H. C. 2002. *Danish Population History 1600–1939.* Odense: University Press of Southern Denmark.

Knodel, John E. 1988. *Demographic Behaviour in the Past: A Study of Fourteen German Villages in the Eighteenth and Nineteenth Centuries.* Cambridge, Eng., and New York: Cambridge University Press.

Landers, John. 1993. "From Colyton to Waterloo: Mortality, Politics and Economics in Historical Demography." In *Rethinking Social History: English Society, 1570–1920, and Its Interpretation,* ed. Adrian Wilson. pp. 97–127. Manchester and New York: Manchester University Press.

Laslett, Peter, and Richard Wall, eds. 1972. *Household and Family in Past Time: Comparative Studies in the Size and Structure of the Domestic Group over the Last Three Decades in England, France, Serbia, Japan, and Colonial North America, with Further Materials from Western Europe.* London and New York: Cambridge University Press.

Lee, James Z., and Wang Feng. 1999. *One Quarter of Humanity: Malthusian Mythology and Chinese Realities.* Cambridge, MA, and London: Harvard University Press.

Lee, Ronald D. 1974. "Estimating Series of Vital Rates and Age Structure from Baptisms and Burials: A New Technique with Application to Pre-industrial England." *Population Studies* 28: 495–512.

Lee, Ronald D., and M. Anderson. 2002. "Malthus in State Space: Macro Economic-demographic Relations in English History, 1540 to 1870." *Journal of Population Economics* 15: 195–220.

Livi-Bacci, Massimo. 1991. *Population and Nutrition: An Essay on European Demographic History.* Cambridge, Eng., and New York: Cambridge University Press.

McKeown, Thomas. 1976. *The Modern Rise of Population.* London: Arnold.

Oeppen, James. 1993. "Back Projection and Inverse Projection: Members of a Wider Class of Constrained Projection Models." *Population Studies* 47: 245–267.

Saito, Osamu. 1996. "Historical Demography: Achievements and Prospects." *Population Studies* 50: 537–53.

Wrigley, E. A. 1966. "Family Reconstitution." In *An Introduction to English Historical Demography from the Sixteenth to the Nineteenth Century,* ed. E. A. Wrigley. pp. 96–159. London: Weidenfeld and Nicholson; New York: Basic Books.

Wrigley, E. A., R. Davies, J. Oeppen, and R. S. Schofield. 1997. *English Population History for Family Reconstitution 1580–1837.* Cambridge, Eng., and New York: Cambridge University Press.

Wrigley, E. A., and R. S. Schofield. 1981. *The Population History of England 1541–1871: A Reconstruction.* Cambridge, MA: Harvard University Press.

———. 1989. *The Population History of England 1541–1871: A Reconstruction.* 1st paperback edition with new introduction. Cambridge, Eng., and New York: Cambridge University Press.

Richard M. Smith

HIV-AIDS

See *AIDS*

HOLOCAUST

The word holocaust, derived from a term used in an early Greek translation of the Old Testament meaning a religious offering completely consumed by fire, has had several distinct usages in English. Since the seventeenth century or earlier it had been used to refer to any mass slaughter or disaster. In the late 1940s the term "The Holocaust" started to be used to refer collectively to the calamity that befell all those targeted and victimized by Nazi oppression from 1933 to 1945, particularly Jews, Gypsies (more properly known as Roma), various Slavic population groups, and the victims of eugenic killing programs. In time, the term was increasingly used to refer to the policies and programs aimed at the extermination of particular population groups individually, notably European Jewry and the Roma.

Subsequently, the word has also been used to refer to genocides or other major human rights abuses directed against other population groups in other parts of the world and in various epochs. Finally, the term came to be used by some to refer to any kind of disturbance seen as significant to the user. In effect, this is a return to the word's general meaning prior to World War II.

This varied usage of the term "The Holocaust," no doubt fueled by the various personal and collective tragedies associated with such events, has given rise to a series of debates about the uniqueness of the events themselves (see, for example, Rosenbaum, 2001). Is "The Holocaust," referring to the experience of European Jewry or the Roma, unique? Does it differ in kind from what happened to others in World War II or from mass killings at other times? The answers to these questions are complex and often contentious. In an important sense every genocide is unique and warrants its own terminology. Thus the Hebrew word *Shoah* is often used to refer to the Jewish Holocaust and the Roma word *Porrajmos* to refer to the Roma Holocaust. (One of the first modern uses of the term "Holocaust" was in Israel in 1947 as an English translation of the word *shoah*.) On the other hand, the experiences of European Jews and Roma between 1933 and 1945 are classic examples of genocide under international law.

According to Raul Hilberg's authoritative 1985 account of the Jewish Holocaust, the Holocaust was an extended "destruction process" that consisted of several steps: "definition, expropriation, concentration, and annihilation." The same phased process was roughly followed in the persecution of European Roma, the other group targeted for destruction solely on "racial" grounds.

Direct Holocaust mortality—in the sense of deaths resulting from explicit state policies and programs—had four major components:

1. Those killed as a result of various euthanasia programs beginning in late 1939;

2. Those killed by the *Schutzstaffel* (S.S.)—directed mobile killing teams (called *Einsatzgruppen*) that operated just behind the front lines as the German army advanced into the USSR, Soviet-occupied Poland, and the Baltic countries beginning in June 1941;

3. Those killed as a result of planned starvation or overwork in ghettos and concentration camps or other forced labor situations; and

4. Those killed in extermination camps (i.e., facilities designed explicitly for mass killings, the first of which began operations in December 1941) and during mass transports to such camps.

Some writers, including Yahuda Bauer, do not consider the euthanasia program to be part of the Holocaust. In any case, in terms of magnitude, most Holocaust deaths can be directly attributed to the extermination camps and the *Einsatzgruppen*.

The Role of Population Science and Population-Related Programs in the Holocaust

Population science intersected with the Holocaust in several ways. These include: the contributions of population-related "science" in shaping concerns about Jews and other target populations, and in providing legal and technical support for conducting various facets of the Holocaust; the direct incorporation of population data systems in Holocaust operations; and the use of demographic data and analysis by the perpetrators and those acting on behalf of the victims to document Holocaust losses.

Population data and analyses, discussions of population policies, and eugenic principles (then considered a well-established element of population science) all contributed in important ways to the intellectual and ideological milieu from which the Holocaust sprang. Perceived population problems and policies focused both on declining fertility in Europe within the context of nationalism, and on the threats posed by other countries or by groups, such as the Jews and the Roma, who were seen as racially alien. Indeed, in Europe in the 1920s and

1930s, and particularly in Germany, the "Jewish problem"—for which the Holocaust became "the final solution"—was frequently defined as a population problem. Solutions to the Jewish problem were also expressed in large part in terms of population-related governmental actions: marriage and fertility restrictions, forced migration, and ultimately programs of mass killing.

The eugenics movement not only provided an intellectual rationale for considering certain population groups to be inferior, even less than human, but also provided examples of how "sound eugenic principles" could be implemented through governmental action. For example, the Nazis established a forced sterilization program in Germany within months of taking power, explicitly citing the eugenics-based forced sterilization laws of the United States as a model. By the late 1930s the Nazi government took up the call of two German scholars for the "destruction of life unworthy of life" by instituting eugenically-justified forced euthanasia.

In 1940 and 1941 the forced euthanasia program expanded in scope from child euthanasia to include adults, and its coverage successively widened from the most severely medically disabled to eventually include all those institutionalized people who were unable to do productive work or who were members of "unworthy" races. Stimulated by the logistical challenges of such an expanded program, its managers developed the technology of mass killing (gas and cremation) subsequently used in the extermination camps. Moreover, beginning in 1941 the Nazis directly transferred equipment and staff from the euthanasia program to assist the *Einsatzgruppen* killing teams and in the establishment of the extermination camps.

Even seemingly-benign sectors of the population field became involved in the effort. For example, individual institutions often initiated euthanasia operations under the guise of statistical investigations. Similarly, a range of population data systems, including population registration systems and regular population censuses, were used to assist in the general planning of the Holocaust in several countries, as well as in the identification and targeting of individuals and families for deportation and of neighborhoods for mob violence.

Estimating the Toll

Two sets of demographers were attempting to document the progress of the Holocaust even while it was underway. Richard Korherr, a German demographer on the staff of Heinrich Himmler—head of the German secret police and the S.S.—was secretly commissioned in late 1942 to assess the decline in the European Jewish population on behalf of the perpetrators. Quite independently, between 1942 and 1945 several Jewish demographers were producing independent estimates of Holocaust-related Jewish losses, which were largely ignored. Estimates of Holocaust losses also were part of the pleadings and judgments during the course of the International War Crimes trials beginning in 1945.

Subsequently, many Holocaust scholars, including some with demographic expertise, have attempted to refine estimates of overall losses. Efforts at mortality estimation continued in the 1990s, in connection with a new series of reparation claims. Given the substantial uncertainties of definition and measurement involved, however, none of them offers persuasive grounds to abandon the estimate of about six million Holocaust deaths—the number cited by the perpetrators at Nuremberg, independently developed by victim advocates at the time, and accepted by the Nuremberg Tribunal itself.

See also: *Genocide.*

BIBLIOGRAPHY

Aly, Götz. 1999. *"Final Solution": Nazi Population Policy and the Murder of the European Jews.* London: Arnold.

Bauer, Yahuda. 2001. *Rethinking the Holocaust.* New Haven, CT: Yale University Press.

Browning, Christopher R. 1992. *The Path to Genocide: Essays on Launching the Final Solution.* Cambridge, Eng.: Cambridge University Press.

Friedlander, Henry. 1995. *The Origins of Nazi Genocide: From Euthanasia to the Final Solution.* Chapel Hill: The University of North Carolina Press.

Gutman, Israel, ed. 1990. *The Encyclopedia of the Holocaust.* New York: Macmillan.

Hilberg, Raul. 1985. *The Destruction of the European Jews,* revised and definitive edition. New York and London: Holmes and Meier.

Rosenbaum, Alan S., ed. 2001. *Is the Holocaust Unique? Perspectives on Comparative Genocide,* 2nd edition. Boulder, CO: Westview Press.

Seltzer, William. 1998. "Population Statistics, the Holocaust, and the Nuremberg Trials." *Population and Development Review* 24(3): 511–552.

WILLIAM SELTZER

HOMEOSTASIS

In the field of demography, the term *homeostasis* refers to the way in which populations control their long-term growth. Drawing on concepts of self-regulating systems in biology, demographic homeostasis usually is regarded as a phenomenon in which interrelated social, cultural, and economic institutions ensure that the long-term rate of population growth is close to zero. During the demographic transition of the last 200 years, there has been a huge expansion in the human population. In contrast, the centuries that preceded the transition were characterized by much more modest population growth. Thus, the study of homeostasis focuses primarily on the pre-transitional era. However, with the end of the demographic transition in sight during the twenty-first century, it is likely that homeostasis will become a topic of research interest in the future.

Terminology

For almost two centuries those trying to explain the nature of equilibrating mechanisms in populations have looked to the economist T. R. Malthus (1766–1834) for inspiration. Malthus proposed that competition between individuals is the basis of the equilibrating mechanism and that population balance can be arrived at through two possible means: the positive check of worsening mortality and the preventive check of reduced fertility.

The first edition of Malthus's *Essay* (1798), written in the style of a polemical pamphlet, with a limited exposition of theory and little supporting evidence, expressed this contrast with particular starkness and emphasized the positive check of mortality. Later, better-documented editions tended to stress the role of the preventive check through the mechanism of delayed marriage. In either case the model remained austere, with total population size being the key regulating element. Thus, the Malthusian model often is referred to as being based on

density dependence. Because it includes mechanisms by which countervailing forces work to keep a population in balance with its resource base, it sometimes is characterized as showing negative feedback. Both density dependence and negative feedback are features of population control systems that can be described as homeostatic. In fact, these terms are used so interchangeably in the context of population dynamics that they can be regarded as near synonyms.

There are two forms of evidence that suggest the existence of homeostatic mechanisms in human populations: the fact that observed growth has been near zero over most of human history and detailed assessments of the observed strength of homeostatic forces.

Slow Growth

Although the nineteenth and twentieth centuries saw a remarkable growth in human numbers (especially since around 1950), population growth over the greater part of human history must have been very close to zero. In light of the long duration of human prehistory, growth must have been close to zero during the Paleolithic era. Even the expansion of human numbers that took place with the development of agriculture, starting about 10,000 years ago, involved only marginally higher growth rates. As Joel E. Cohen puts it, "Before the several local inventions of agriculture, local human populations grew at long-term rates just above zero. Where agriculture was invented, local human populations grew ever so slightly faster" (Cohen, p. 32). However, events that occurred during this period cannot be quantitatively documented.

Although it most likely never will be possible to make reliable estimates of world population size before the last 200 years or so, there are some populations in which the ratio of facts to deductive reasoning is sufficiently favorable to make tolerably robust estimates of population growth for the last 2,000 years. The best documented of these cases are Europe and China, both of which show periods of growth, decline, and stagnation at various times during the last two millennia. Until the relatively recent past, however, even episodes of growth took place at modest rates compared with modern experience, and the growth rate over the very long run was extremely low. For example, the average annual growth rate in China from 2 to 1500 C.E. was in the neighborhood of 0.03 percent.

That long-term stability partly masks shorter-term fluctuations. In addition to explaining the factors leading to very slow growth, models of population change must consider the fluctuations. However, it is not easy to distinguish the cultural, economic, political, and environmental causes of such swings. Analyses of fluctuations in both European and Chinese history now generally emphasize nondemographic factors such as the degree of political stability and climatic change. In many cases periods of growth appear to be associated with eras of political stability, whereas times of generalized social unrest saw population declines. Possibly the most sophisticated analysis of this phenomenon is found in C. Y. Cyrus Chu and Ronald D. Lee (1994), who used data for China. Similarly, in Europe the demise of the Western Roman Empire appears to have been associated with a long-term decline in population size.

In contrast to the slow growth of settled populations, the potential for rapid growth clearly exists for all populations but seems to be realized only in some circumstances. In particular, rapid growth in pre-transitional populations appears to be restricted to places and eras where a population was able to settle new territory that previously was either not settled or thinly settled. Such expansions often were associated with the spread of alternative forms of farming or other technological innovations that allowed more effective exploitation of natural resources. A variation on this situation occurred in areas where catastrophic mortality from diseases introduced by new settlers devastated the indigenous population, effectively rendering the land thinly settled (Crosby 1986).

Tests of Homeostasis

Malthusian ideas and terminology are so widely employed in describing both long- and short-term population movements that it is common to find them used routinely in both historical and contemporary discussions of economic-demographic relations. However, the strength of these simple density-dependent mechanisms rarely has been tested for human populations. With European historical data, researchers are in a position to do this. Using European data, Lee (1987) has concluded that only a very small proportion (0.5 percent) of year-to-year changes in settled agricultural populations can be attributed to simple density-dependent mechanisms.

On a short-term basis this means that homeostasis is overwhelmed by a multitude of other factors. However, as Lee goes on to note, "It is essential to realise that as long as there is any trace at all of density dependence, no matter how weak, this tug, by its systematic persistence, comes to dominate human population dynamics over the long run, if not the short" (Lee 1987, p. 452). Thus, homeostatic mechanisms can be seen to operate in a long-term perspective, but they do this through such complex and indirect pathways that their effects are difficult to detect.

Socioeconomic Mechanisms

The potential for population growth must have been kept in check by powerful forces at most times. One potential force is, of course, high mortality and there is certainly evidence of spectacular mortality crises in the historical record. The return of bubonic plague to Europe in the middle of the fourteenth century, for example, is thought to have killed around a third of that continent's population. Even more dramatically, the arrival of Europeans in the Americas, Australia, and the Pacific islands led to the demographic collapse of indigenous populations. Such disasters may be attributed largely to the introduction of new diseases and the occurrence of so-called virgin-soil epidemics (Crosby 1986). However, they also may indicate the effects of the collapse of one form of social order and its replacement with another and even deliberate genocide.

In spite of the dramatic nature of such crises and their undoubted importance in the historical demography of the Americas, Australia, and the Pacific islands, it is not clear how significant events of this kind have been in regard to long-term demographic change in general. Historical evidence from Europe and Asia mostly indicates less extreme mortality and much less extreme fluctuations in population size, suggesting that control over fertility and opportunities for migration were more significant than was catastrophic mortality (Liu et al. 2001, Livi-Bacci 1993). The most persuasive interpretation of the data on long-term population growth, therefore, would seem to be that human societies developed regulatory mechanisms that kept long-run population growth rates close to zero.

The best-documented examples of these mechanisms come from Western Europe and East Asia. Although there was considerable local and regional variation in the nature of pretransitional demographic regimes, the overall range of experience seems broadly similar in the Asian and European populations that have been studied to date. Total fertility generally was in the range of four to six children (i.e., well below any theoretical maximum), whereas life expectancy at birth ranged between 20 and 40 years.

Although the overall ranges of mortality and fertility in Asian and European populations had much in common, that cannot be said for their social, economic, and cultural contexts. Different patterns of social behavior, as well as differences in ecological factors, disease environments, and political stability, shaped the demographic equilibriums, and both fertility and mortality were subject to different sets of determinants. For example, Asian marriage patterns generally bore no relation to the so-called West European model, in which both men and women married late and many people remained single. Similarly, deliberate infanticide, which was almost unknown in Europe, played a visible role in some parts of Asia. Patterns of sex-specific mortality also differed markedly between Western Europe and parts of Asia.

In all cases, however, it is clear that extensive systems of demographic and economic interaction and elaborate social conventions shaped the process of reproduction. Moreover, in addition to social norms, individuals and couples thought about and took action that affected their childbearing. This seems to be especially evident in China, where there is a long history of collective intervention in demographic matters of various kinds, including fertility. Thus, Zhongwei Zhao notes, "As early as the Tang (618 to 907 AD) and Song (960 to 1279 AD) periods, ideas and practice of limiting family size were already discussed and recorded in the works of some scholars" (Zhao, p. 214).

Origins

Consideration of these matters inevitably raises the question of how the institutions that underpin homeostasis arise and are sustained. Within demography there are two main schools of thought. One, which is found in the work of E. A. Wrigley (1978), stresses the role of unconscious rationality in generating homeostatic patterns. In this way of thinking, just as the "invisible hand" of classical economics guides markets even when individuals are unaware

of its presence, analogous forces steer social arrangements toward homeostatic equilibriums. The second school, most succinctly presented by Ron Lesthaeghe (1980), gives greater emphasis to conscious "short-term goal setting" on the part of the elite groups that set the prevailing moral guidelines and controlled the economic bases of society. According to this line of reasoning, these institutions are best seen as instruments of social control, and the equilibrating mechanisms also are viewed as methods of social differentiation.

An approach to the question of origins that links individuals and populations and has been influential in anthropology in recent years is the Darwinian evolutionary perspective, as seen in the work of Laura Betzig and her colleagues (1988). This approach draws on modern evolutionary ideas of "inclusive fitness" and "kin-selection" to investigate the role of evolutionary forces in determining human fertility patterns. A problem with a Darwinian approach is the manifestly Lamarckian nature of much cultural transmission, in which acquired characteristics are transmitted just as easily as inherited characteristics are. An unanswered question is how social institutions that favored low growth or homeostasis could have evolved in the absence of "group selection." As James W. Wood states, "It is very unlikely that special behavioral and institutional mechanisms have evolved *in order* to restrain population growth or regulate population size. But that does not mean that factors do not exist that have that effect, even if it is not the reason for their existence"(Wood, p. 101).

Alternatives

In contrast to Malthus's ideas of negative density dependence, Ester Boserup (1965, 1981) proposed that increasing population density stimulated technological progress in pre-transitional populations, leading to positive density dependence. Her ideas have been synthesized with those of Malthus by Lee (1986), who shows that both can be accommodated within a wider model of the interaction between population and economic growth. Lee's ideas have been developed by Wood (1998), who generalizes the "Malthus and Boserup model" to deal with a broad definition of well-being and explicitly considers the question of variance and population heterogeneity.

See also: *Demographic Transition, Evolutionary Demography; World Population Growth.*

BIBLIOGRAPHY

Betzig, Laura, Monique Borgerhoff Mulder, and Paul Turke, eds. 1988. *Human Reproductive Behaviour: A Darwinian Perspective.* Cambridge, Eng., and New York: Cambridge University Press.

Boserup, Ester. 1965. *The Conditions for Agricultural Growth: The Economics of Agrarian Change under Population Pressure.* Chicago: Aldine.

———. 1981. *Population and Technological Change: A Study of Long-Term Trends.* Chicago: University of Chicago Press.

Chu, C. Y. Cyrus, and Ronald D. Lee. 1994. "Famine, Revolt and the Dynastic Cycle: Population Dynamics in Historic China." *Journal of Population Economics* 7: 351–378.

Cohen, Joel E. 1995. *How Many People Can the Earth Support?* New York and London: Norton.

Crosby, Alfred W. 1986. *Ecological Imperialism: The Biological Expansion of Europe, 900–1900.* Cambridge, Eng., and New York: Cambridge University Press.

Galloway, Patrick R. 1986. "Long Term Fluctuations in Climate and Population in the Pre-Industrial Era." *Population and Development Review* 12: 1–24.

Lee, Ronald D. 1986. "Malthus and Boserup: A Dynamic Synthesis." In *The State of Population Theory: Forward from Malthus,* ed. David Coleman and Roger S. Schofield. Oxford and New York: Blackwell.

———. 1987. "Population Dynamics of Humans and Other Animals." *Demography* 24: 443–465.

Lesthaeghe, Ron. 1980. "On the Social Control of Human Reproduction." *Population and Development Review* 6: 527–548.

Liu, Ts'ui-jung, et al., eds. 2001. *Asian Population History.* Oxford and New York: Oxford University Press.

Livi-Bacci, Massimo. 1993. *A Concise History of World Population.* Oxford and New York: Blackwell.

Malthus, T. R. 1990. *An Essay on the Principle of Population,* (1798) ed. Patricia James. Cambridge, Eng., and New York: Cambridge University Press.

Wood, James W. 1998. "A Theory of Preindustrial Population Dynamics: Demography, Economy and Well-Being in Malthusian Systems." *Current Anthropology* 39: 99–135.

Wrigley, E. A. 1978. "Fertility Strategy for the Individual and the Group." In *Historical Studies of Changing Fertility,* ed. Charles Tilly. Princeton, NJ: Princeton University Press.

Zhao, Zhongwei. 1997. "Demographic Systems in Historic China: Some New Findings from Recent Research." *Journal of the Australian Population Association* 14: 201–232.

CHRIS WILSON

HOMICIDE AND SUICIDE

Homicide and suicide are significant public health problems that entail heavy social and economic costs. Intentional violence, self-directed and directed at others, was estimated by Christopher J. Murray and Alan D. Lopez to account in 1990 for 2.7 percent of the world's loss of disability-adjusted life years (DALYs), projected to rise to 4.2 percent in 2020.

In 1990, according to World Health Organization (WHO) data, the age-standardized suicide rate per 100,000 persons in 48 countries averaged 15.6 for males and 5.7 for females. Male rates ranged from a high of 52.2 in Hungary to a low of 0.1 in Egypt, and female rates from 17.5 in Sri Lanka to 0.5 in Bahrain. At roughly the same point in time, age-standardized homicide death rates ranged from 1 to 2 per 100,000 in most Western European countries to 9.9 per 100,000 in the United States and nearly 20 per 100,000 in Brazil and Mexico. The distributions used for age standardization are not dissimilar, and so the homicide and suicide death rates are roughly comparable. Although homicide mortality and homicide offender rates are conceptually different, they are often used interchangeably.

Suicide and especially homicide are of special interest insofar as they concern young persons. In virtually all societies the peak age of homicide mortality and commission lies in the range of 18 to 29 years, whereas the peak occurrence of suicide mortality is among the elderly. It is therefore of concern that in many countries, over time, the youth advantage (over the elderly) in terms of suicide rates has weakened and the youth disadvantage in terms of homicide rates has become more pronounced. Because other forms of mortality are low at young ages (in developed countries), suicide and homicide account for a large proportion of all young lives lost.

Suicide

Theories to explain national differences in suicide rates are biological, psychological, or social. The first seem to hold little water because of the huge cross-national variation in basic parameters such as the male–female suicide ratio. In most countries the male suicide rate exceeds the female; China appears to be the one significant exception. One reason that male suicide rates exceed female rates is that males of all ages are likely to choose more lethal methods of self-destruction. A venerable psychological theory holds that both suicide and homicide result from an undifferentiated violent impulse that is turned inward or outward, depending on social conditions. However, if this is so, one would expect suicide and homicide rates to be inversely correlated in an international cross section, whereas they are not.

This leaves social theory, in which the work of the sociologist Emile Durkheim continues to leave a heavy imprint. In basic Durkheimian theory suicide increases as social integration and social regulation—the extent to which behavior is governed by the group—decrease. More generally, Durkheim's hypothesis was that suicide rates vary inversely with the degree of involvement in social life. Subsequent researchers emphasized the impact of social status, which weakens external restraints and thus might be expected to be positively related to the propensity to kill oneself, and the virtuous role of "status integration," or the absence of role conflict. Suicide rates are positively correlated with gross domestic product (GDP) per capita in an international cross section; it might be argued that this is consistent with the Durkheimian hypothesis and its later elaborations. However, there is no correlation between the rate of economic growth in preceding decades and the suicide death rate even though one might expect rapid growth to be associated with the weakening of restraints and accelerated role change.

Differences in national suicide rates are large and stable over time. The most striking international pattern is that suicide rates in Muslim and Catholic countries are significantly lower for both men and women. Immigrants tend to retain the suicide rates of the country of origin. In the United States, Hispanic suicide rates are lower than European-American rates; the reasons cited include a greater role for the extended family, the Catholic religion, and fatalism. The suicide rate among African Americans is also lower than that among European Americans, a difference that has been variously ascribed to greater religiosity and the stronger role of the extended family among African Americans.

Suicides among elderly people are characterized by depression, often associated with acute or chronic illness and/or the loss of a spouse or companion. Another characteristic of elderly suicides is the high ratio of successful to attempted suicides. In most developed countries elderly suicide rates declined between the mid-1980s and mid-1990s after an increase in many of them in the previous decade.

This decline in elderly suicide stands in contrast to the trend in suicides among the young. In the United States age-specific suicide rates among adolescents and young adults (age 15 to 24) tripled between 1950 and 1995. Some of this increase may reflect greater willingness to label self-inflicted deaths among the young as suicide; however, there is little doubt that the data reflect a real phenomenon. As the young have fared worse than the old, males have fared worse than females. Whereas male suicide rates rose in most countries between 1970 and 1984, female suicide rates remained stable.

Homicide

Although experts dispute the particulars, there is little doubt that there has been a massive long-term decline in the prevalence of lethal interpersonal violence. Whereas homicide in advanced nations is largely confined to the poor, in premodern societies it was equally common over the entire social spectrum. The proposed explanation is that as development and modernization proceed, legal means of resolving disputes become available to those who have the resources to pursue them. In some countries declining homicide rates may be related to the long-term decline in the use of alcohol. Data for European countries for the period 1950–1995 show a strong positive relationship between alcohol sales and the homicide rate, with a greater impact on male than on female homicide. The association was especially strong in Northern Europe, with its culture of binge drinking.

Current theories of homicide stress the role of poverty. International cross-sectional analysis shows that homicide rates are positively correlated with the degree of income inequality, with the relationship strongest in wealthy democracies. This lends support to the relative deprivation theory of homicide, in which aggression is held to be spurred by a sense of frustration and relative poverty. A related result is that homicide rates are inversely correlated with the strength of welfare state institutions. Whereas in the United States the entry of the baby boom cohorts into adolescence during the 1960s was clearly reflected in rising aggregate homicide rates, the same compositional effect was not observed in the welfare states of Western Europe. However, work in the United States has shown that the statistical correlation between poverty and homicide persists even when measures of access to social capital, a variable not entirely distinct from the strength of the welfare state, are taken into account. There is also evidence, both from cross-sectional European studies and from U.S. time series that homicide mortality is linked to the weakening of traditional family structures.

Because its homicide rate is so high, the United States has been the focus of special attention. In the United States in 1990 the African-American homicide crude death rate was 38.8 per 100,000, the Hispanic-American crude rate was 15.5, and the European-American crude rate was 5.7. Roughly speaking, the trend in age-standardized U.S. homicide rates was a decline from the 1930s until the 1960s, followed by a rise until the 1990s and then a decline to levels not seen since the 1960s. Increases during the 1960s apparently reflect, in part, an effect by which relatively large cohorts of young persons experience higher homicide mortality than do relatively small ones. This would be consistent with the work of economist Richard Easterlin, who argues that relatively large cohorts fare worse along many dimensions than relatively small ones. The dramatic increase in U.S homicide rates during the 1980s and the equally dramatic decline during the 1990s were closely tied to gun deaths among black teenage males and the crack cocaine epidemic.

Homicide, Suicide, and Firearms

Much of the public health literature on homicide and suicide is concerned with the role of firearms, especially handguns. Studies relating gun control laws to homicide and suicide rates in the United States have tended to be inconclusive because the link between the legal regime and the actual preva-

lence of firearms is not strong either temporally or in cross section. International cross-sectional data, however, clarify the relationship. Firearm-related suicide and homicide rates vary markedly among countries, as do the proportions of homicide and suicide rates accounted for by firearms. The rate of household gun ownership is positively related to the gun-homicide death rate as well as to the proportion of homicides committed with a gun, and the corresponding correlations are even more significant for suicides. There are no inverse correlations between household gun ownership and the non-gun homicide and suicide death rates; that is, there are no offsetting substitution effects by which lower gun ownership might be associated with higher non-gun violent death rates. In cross-sectional international data, there is a significant positive correlation between firearm prevalence and the male youth suicide rate and an extremely strong correlation between firearm prevalence and the firearm youth suicide rate for males as well as females. In general, firearms accounted for a much higher proportion of male youth suicides than female youth suicides.

Conclusion

Homicide and suicide are not leading causes of death; however, they rank high on the list of causes of young persons' deaths. As an important source of potentially avoidable mortality, they merit close study by demographers, epidemiologists, public health experts, and others concerned with population health.

See also: *Crime, Demography of; Infanticide.*

BIBLIOGRAPHY

Blumstein, Alfred, Frederick P. Rivara, and Richard Rosenfeld. 2000. "The Rise and Decline of Homicide—and Why." *American Review of Public Health* 21: 505–541.

Cooney, Mark. 1997. "The Decline of Elite Homicide." *Criminology* 35(3): 381–407.

Johnson, Gregory R., Etienne G. Krug, and Lloyd B. Potter. 2000. "Suicide among Adolescents and Young Adults: A Cross-National Comparison of 34 Countries." *Suicide and Life-Threatening Behavior* 30(1): 74–92.

Killias, Martin. 1993. "International Correlations between Gun Ownership and Rates of Homicide and Suicide." *Canadian Medical Association Journal* 148(10): 1721–1725.

Krahn, Harvey, Timothy F. Hartnagel, and John W. Gartrell. 1986. "Income Inequality and Homicide Rates: Cross-National Data and Criminological Theories." *Criminology* 24(2): 269–295.

Krug, Etienne G., K. E. Powell, and L. L. Dahlberg. 1998. "Firearm-Related Deaths in the United States and 35 Other High- and Middle-Income Countries." *International Journal of Epidemiology* 27: 214–221.

Lester, David. 1997. "Suicide in an International Perspective." *Suicide and Life-Threatening Behavior* 27(1): 104–111.

MacKellar, F. Landis, and Masako Yanagasita. 1995. "Homicide in the U.S.: Who's at Risk?" *Population Trends and Public Policy* 21: 1–20.

Messner, Steven E., and Richard Rosenfeld. 1997. "Political Restraint of the Market and Levels of Criminal Homicide: A Cross-National Application of Institutional Anomie Theory." *Social Forces* 75(4): 1393–1416.

Murray, Christopher J., and Alan D. Lopez. 1996. *The Global Burden of Disease.* Cambridge, MA: Harvard University Press.

O'Brien, Robert, Jean Stockard, and Lynn Isaacson. 1999. "The Enduring Effects of Cohort Characteristics in Age-Specific Homicide Rates, 1960–1995." *American Journal of Sociology* 104(4): 1061–1095.

Pampel, Fred C., and Rosemary Gartner. 1995. "Age Structure, Socio-Political Institutions, and National Homicide Rates." *European Sociological Review* 11(3): 243–260.

Pampel, Fred C., and John B. Willamson. 2001. "Age Patterns of Suicide and Homicide Mortality Rates in High-Income Nations." *Social Forces* 80(1): 251–282.

Pearson, J. L., Y. Conwell, J. Lindesay, Y. Takahashi, and E. D. Caine. 1997. "Elderly Suicide: A Multinational View." *Aging and Mental Health* 1(2): 107–111.

Range, Lillian M., Mark M. Leach, Daniel McIntyre, Pamela B. Posey-Deters, Michelle S. Marion, Stacey H. Kovac, James H. Baños, and Joseph Vigiln. 1999. "Multicultural Perspectives on Suicide." *Aggressive and Violent Behavior* 4(4): 413–430.

Rosenfeld, Richard, Steven E. Messner, and Eric P. Baumer. 2001. "Social Capital and Homicide." *Social Forces* 80(1): 283–309.

Rossow, Ingeborg. 2001. "Alcohol and Homicide: A Cross-Cultural Comparison of the Relationship in 14 European Countries." *Addiction* 96(Supplement 1): S77–S92.

Stafford, Mark C., and Ralph A. Weisheit. 1988. "Changing Age Patterns of U.S. Male and Female Suicide Rate, 1934–1983." *Suicide and Life Threatening Behavior* 18(2): 149–163.

F. LANDIS MACKELLAR

HOUSEHOLD COMPOSITION

The United Nations Statistics Division defines a household as a residence unit that consists of one or more persons who make common provision for food and other essentials for living. Unlike a family, which comprises only persons related through blood, adoption, or marriage, a household may include members who are not related. While different concepts of household are sometimes adopted, the United Nations definition is widely used for both data collection and demographic research.

The household is one of the most important human socioeconomic institutions, with functions that vary both across regions and over time. In many historical populations, a household was not only a residence group but also a socioeconomic unit within which production, consumption, reproduction, early childhood socialization, and many other activities took place. Many of these functions are still important in contemporary households. It is this multifaceted character that makes the household an appealing subject of study to many social scientists.

Household composition is a description of the household according to certain characteristics of its membership, such as age, relationship to the head of the household, and number of marital pairs or nuclear families it contains. (A nuclear family is a married couple, or a couple—or a single parent—together with unmarried offspring.) In addition to indicating the household structure, these descriptions are useful in revealing why such residence groups are formed in a particular way, how they function in the society, and their socioeconomic consequences.

The investigation of household composition generally uses data from population censuses or sample surveys. In historical studies, census-type materials such as lists of inhabitants or household registers are frequently used. Family reconstitution data and genealogical records shed light on potential residential patterns, but they do not usually include information on household composition.

Historical research on household composition progressed rapidly in the second half of the twentieth century, and studies show remarkable variations in household composition prior to the twentieth century. As pointed out by John Hajnal and others, households in northwest Europe (encompassing the British Isles, the Low countries, German-speaking areas, northern France, and Scandinavia including Iceland but excluding Finland) were generally between four and five persons in size, included in most cases a single nuclear family, and rarely any more distant relatives, but might have non-relatives present. In eastern and southern Europe, in contrast, scholars have noted that it was common for the newly married to live with the parents of one of the spouses, and an appreciably higher proportion of households consisted of two or more married couples. In some Asian populations (e.g. China, India, Japan) the proportion of complex households—defined as those with one nuclear family plus other relatives or other nuclear families—was also considerably higher than in northern and western Europe.

Significant changes in household composition have taken place in many developed countries since the late nineteenth century. As a general trend, the household has become simpler in structure and smaller in size. In England, for example, between 1891 and 1981 the proportion of complex households fell from above 15 percent to less than 5 percent, and the proportion of single-person households increased from 7 percent to 22 percent. During the later part of this period, nonmarital cohabitation also rose rapidly: by the late 1980s, nearly a quarter of women aged 20 to 24 lived in such households. In Sweden, proportions of single-person households and of households comprising cohabiting couples were even higher. Similar changes were observed in most developed countries. The result of these trends has been a continual shrinkage in the average size of households, from around five persons per household at the end of the nineteenth century to two to three persons per household at the end of the twentieth century.

The transition in household composition has been directly related to the following factors. First, there has been a considerable change in people's reproductive behavior. During the twentieth century, in particular its second half, the proportion of women remaining childless increased and the level of fertility of those having children decreased. In many developed countries, the total fertility rate fell to well below the replacement level. As a result, the average number of children present in a household is much lower than in the past. Second, there has been a significant change in people's attitude toward marriage. Since the mid-twentieth century, non-marital cohabitation has been increasingly accepted by society. Divorce has become far more common, and there is less stigma attached to remaining single. All these changes contribute to the increase in single-person households, one-parent households, and consensual unions. Thirdly, there is also a noticeable decrease in propensities for coresidence between parents and their married children, and between nuclear family members and their distant relatives. Before the twentieth century, the proportion of complex households formed through such relationships was around 10 to 20 percent in England, and higher than this in many other countries; living arrangements of this kind were rare by the beginning of the twenty-first century. This change is partly a result of higher income levels and, among the elderly, improved health, allowing more people to live alone and independently when such an arrangement is preferred.

Similar trends have been found in some less-developed countries. In China and South Korea, for example, household size has also become smaller and its structure simpler in recent years. But the change in household composition in most less-developed countries has been slow and the pattern of change less clear. John Bongaarts found that in the 1990s, household size and composition in many of these countries were markedly different from those recorded in the developed countries, but similar to those observed in the second half of the nineteenth century in Europe and North America. As far as household size is concerned, the world is still very diverse: Average household size ranges from seven persons in Algeria and Oman to just above two persons in Sweden. In most of the less-developed countries, the average size of households is still between four and seven persons.

Examining household composition can reveal much about a society, but its limitations should not be ignored. The composition of a household identified from cross-sectional data is only a snapshot taken at a particular point in the process of household development. The dynamics of this process need to be studied to understand the household formation system and its outcomes. Furthermore, households are not socially isolated but exist within broader networks of kin and other social ties. Although the household is a fundamental unit, many socioeconomic activities take place in a wider context (e.g., a lineage or a group of kin-related households). Knowledge of these wider networks is important for a full understanding of household formation and composition.

See also: *Family: History; Family Life Cycle; Historical Demography; Laslett, Peter.*

BIBLIOGRAPHY

Bongaarts, John. 2001. "Household Size and Composition in the Developing World in the 1990s." *Population Studies* 55: 263–279.

Hajnal, John. 1983. "Two Kinds of Pre-Industrial Household Formation Systems." In *Family Forms in Historic Europe,* ed. Richard Wall, Jean Robin, and Peter Laslett. Cambridge, Eng.: Cambridge University Press.

Laslett, Peter. 1983. "Family and Household as Work Group and Kin Group: Areas of Traditional Europe Compared." In *Family Forms in Historic Europe,* ed. Richard Wall, Jean Robin, and Peter Laslett. Cambridge, Eng.: Cambridge University Press.

Lesthaeghe, Ron. 1995. "The Second Demographic Transition in Western Countries: An Interpretation." In *Gender and Change in Industrialized Countries,* ed. Karen Oppenheim Mason, and An-Margritt Jensen. Oxford: Clarendon Press.

United Nations. 1998. *Principles and Recommendations for Population and Housing Census (Revision 1).* New York: United Nations.

Wall, Richard. 2001. "The Transformation of the European Family across the Centuries." In *Family History Revisited: Comparative Perspectives,* ed. Richard Wall, Tamara Hareven, and Joseph Ehmer. Newark: University of Delaware Press.

Zhongwei Zhao

HUMAN ECOLOGY

Ecology in its most inclusive sense is the study of the relationship of organisms or groups of organisms to their environment. It perceives all life as a system of relationships that has been called the "web of life," of which every species forms a part. Human ecology is a branch of general ecology. It holds the view that humans, like all other organisms, are related to each other on the basis of a "struggle for existence" in an environment with finite limitations for supporting life. Struggle includes all activity (whether in competition, conflict, or cooperation) to survive and reproduce within these constraints.

Like every other species, humans must find a niche in their largely self-constructed web of life in order to gain a livelihood. In doing so they must make use of the resources and submit to the constraints imposed by the environment in which they find themselves. Unlike classical economics, which tends to view this process as one of individual adaptation, human ecologists insist on adaptation as a group: a collective phenomenon in which the main players are households, families, neighborhoods, and communities.

Environment
The environment is a sweeping concept that is defined to include all forces and factors external to an organism or group of organisms. The organism is responsive to the environmental conditions that are relevant to its needs and makes use of its existing technology. However, since the environment exists independently of any individual or species, it has no propensity to favor the needs of one organism or group of organisms (including humans) in preference to others. Consequently, in the short run humans must adapt to the conditions of the existing environment. In the long run they may modify ("build") the environment in ways that make life more secure and enjoyable. This too is a type of adaptation.

Because humans have genetic mental and physical capabilities for adaptation that far exceed those of any other animal, they are able to devise tools to assist in the exploitation of the environment in their struggle for survival. Furthermore, they have an unmatched ability to store past experience in memory and in a variety of records and possess a constructive imagination to guide their adaptive efforts. The magnitude of these differences from other animals is so great that it becomes the basis for a separate discipline of human ecology.

The exposition of human ecology as a distinct social science discipline is closely linked with the work of the sociologists Amos Hawley (b. 1910) and Otis Dudley Duncan (b. 1921).

All branches of ecology concur that adaptation is a group rather than an individual struggle. Membership in a compatible group is a condition of survival. Human ecology not only subscribes to this view but makes it a basic principle. In this view populations that occupy a particular sector of the environment (a habitat) adapt by organizing territorially delimited human communities. This is accomplished through the use of tools and technologies that derive from human ingenuity and cumulatively learned capabilities. The relationship of a population to its habitat is generally conceived as one of balance between human numbers and the opportunities for living.

Classical ecology sees three or four variable factors involved in the process of adjustment to the environment. Hawley postulates three: (1) population size, (2) the material or resource environment, and (3) the organization of the population. Within the third category Duncan distinguishes between social organization and technology to formulate the four-fold POET acronym of the "ecological complex": Ecological adjustment is a function of *population, organization, environment,* and *technology.*

Because demography is the study of population, there is much overlap in subject matter and research between human ecology and demography. Demography tends to be concerned with the renewal processes of large human population aggregates such as nation-states. Human ecology tends to focus on the detailed socioeconomic composition of population and its distribution over environments. It is an eclectic or "holistic" discipline that borrows freely from the theories and empirical research of such disciplines as sociology, evolutionary biology, economics, geography, demography, political science, and the physical sciences, integrating them with its own distinctive viewpoint. Some have characterized this viewpoint as social Darwinian.

Spatial Aspects of Ecological Organization

An important activity of all studies of ecology, particularly human ecology, is the portrayal by means of maps, graphs, and statistics of the distributions and densities of population in space. Mistakenly, some have defined human ecology solely or primarily as the descriptive study of spatial variations and patterns. However, the use of mapping and spatial analysis in studies of human ecology is guided by the more profound desire to understand ecological organization, interaction, and environmental adaptation. Ecology posits three basic factors to explain spatial patterning:

1. Interdependence among persons. People who depend on one another daily must be closer together than are those who exchange services less frequently.

2. Dependence on the physical environment. To gain its livelihood, a community must have access to raw materials, water, agricultural products, and other essential goods. In primitive situations this dependence is on the local habitat, and in more advanced societies it involves a wider sphere, via adjoining communities and particular ones located far away.

3. Friction of space. Technology facilitates the movement of goods, people, services, information, and money over substantial distances. Travel and transport of materials and persons from their place of origin to a desired destination require both time and energy, imposing "frictional" costs. The efficiency of transportation and communication measures this friction. Time and transport costs become important factors in determining the location of all types of firms and organization and also of private residence. Reduction in friction permits their wider scatter.

Urban, Rural, and Metropolitan Ecology

As commerce and industry develop, the larger centers (towns) become more dominant over settlements in the surrounding territory, and people travel there to exchange products and services. Such "central places" developed along convenient transportation points: rivers, seashores, or areas where favorable resources existed, at the intersection of routes (breaks in transportation). With advancing technology and population growth, the number of such dominant cities (to which the term *metropolis* is commonly applied) has multiplied manyfold. Moreover, as central places expand, they tend to spill over their legal boundaries into the adjacent territory, giving rise to increasingly diverse outlying satellite urban places and residential areas collectively known as suburbs or metropolitan rings.

Each city center interacts continuously with an extensive territory beyond its legal boundaries. The territory over which a particular center exercises dominance through a geographic division of labor is its hinterland. The intensity of interaction between the center and a point in the hinterland diminishes with distance from the center. The total community area may be divided into a primary area (daily commuting, retail shopping, intense interaction) and a secondary area of lesser dominance where many services are performed by local (subdominant) centers. The term *metropolitan area* (central city and its suburbs) is assigned to the former, and the term *metropolitan hinterland* to the latter. The outer boundary to this hinterland cannot be defined precisely; it is a zone within which the sphere of influence of one center is counterbalanced by the competing influence of an adjoining center, which varies for each of a wide range of indicators.

Under conditions of advanced technology manufacturing enterprises have considerable freedom in choosing a location. Location near the central business district may be unimportant for such an enterprise, particularly if its product is distributed nationwide or internationally. In contrast, retail and personal service enterprises are population-sensitive: They must locate near the sites where the people who consume their products and services live or work. More specialized units of this class, such as department stores, and stores selling narrower ranges of goods (jewelry, musical instruments, expensive clothing), as well as firms providing specialized financial, legal, or other professional services, seek a highly accessible location such as the city center or large outlying shopping centers. Single-purpose units such as filling stations, grocery stores, drugstores, laundries and dry cleaners, restaurants, churches, schools, and health facilities tend to settle in the neighborhoods to provide their clients with easy access.

Some very large metropolitan areas are renowned for serving a worldwide clientele, dominating other metropolitan centers. Familiar examples are New York, London, Paris, and Tokyo. Other large cities may be dominant within a nation or region. Still other metropolitan places may serve much smaller regional areas but provide linkages to the broader national and international network.

Although in industrialized countries a disproportionate share of the population may live in metropolitan areas and suburbs, by far the larger share of the physical environment consists of sparsely settled nonmetropolitan and rural areas. Some human ecologists cover all such categories; others tend to specialize, being primarily urban, suburban, or rural in their focus.

Ecological Change

A universal ecological process is temporal change, an irreversible alteration of an existing pattern of ecological relationships. Although most ecological processes tend to produce equilibrium and balance between interacting organizations and groups, change in ecological organization (whether as a result of small cumulative increments or sudden and drastic "shocks") is ever present. Change may come from alterations in population, the environment, technology, or social organization.

The principal mechanism of ecological change is nonrecurring spatial mobility. Recurrent mobility—habitual routine round-trip movements—produces little change. In fact, it promotes stability and equilibrium. One-way journeys (migration) signal ecological change. By studying the causes of migration, ecologists seek to study both the underlying causes and the resulting adjustment that occurs. It is important to know not only why migrants think they have moved but also the environmental conditions or characteristics that are present in cases where migration occurs and are lacking in cases where migration is absent or rare. The causes of migration may be categorized as "push" and "pull" factors: in their simplest forms, an excess of numbers in the area of origin and underpopulation in the area of destination.

The problem of overpopulation has long been a central concern of human ecologists. It exists in places where the number of persons in a given habitat is perceived to be excessive in relation to the opportunities for life and livelihood. Overpopulation may come about through sustained rapid population increase. However, it can also result from a temporary or long-term reduction in the food supply, the exhaustion of a natural resource, or the closing of a major local source of employment.

Some of these symptoms seem to be manifest in a substantial share of the world's living spaces, caused at least partially by the nature of global economic organization and regional disparities in fertility and population growth. Migration is technically a solution to overpopulation but raises other problems: It may be seen as threatening population balance in areas where a high level of prosperity has been achieved. Overpopulation may diminish as the conditions that generate it are corrected. A new phenomenon—underpopulation, or failure to maintain replacement—is also of interest to students of human ecology. Explaining this phenomenon, as for many other topics of human ecology, requires study of collectively held beliefs, opinions, and expectations.

Human Ecology and Collective Beliefs

In its classical formulation human ecology strongly discounted the influence of individual psychological phenomena on group behavior. More recently, there has been agreement that collective beliefs—beliefs shared by a large segment of a group—may underlie ecological changes that cannot be satisfactorily explained by environmental, organizational, or technological factors alone. Dominant beliefs about religion, economic organization (capitalist, collective), and status (class) exclusiveness as well as racial-ethnic preferences and antagonisms are examples.

See also: *Central Place Theory; Cities, Systems of; Lösch, August; Rural-Urban Balance.*

BIBLIOGRAPHY

Anderton, Douglas L., Richard E. Barrett, and Donald J. Bogue, eds. 1997. *The Population of the United States.* New York: Free Press.

Blau, Peter M., and Otis D. Duncan. 1978. *American Occupational Structure.* New York: Free Press.

Bogue, Donald J., and Elizabeth J. Bogue, eds. 1976. *Essays in Human Ecology.* Chicago, IL: Community and Family Study Center, University of Chicago.

Duncan, Otis D. 1983. *Metropolis and Region.* New York: AMS Press.

Duncan, Otis D., Howard Schuman, and Beverly Duncan. 1973. *Societal Change in a Metropolitan Community.* New York: Russell Sage Foundation.

Hawley, Amos H. 1950. *Human Ecology: A Theory of Community Structure.* New York: Ronald Press.

———. 1979. *Societal Growth: Processes and Implications.* New York: Free Press.

———. 1986. *Human Ecology: A Theoretical Essay.* Chicago, IL: University of Chicago Press.

DONALD J. BOGUE

HUNTER-GATHERERS

The term *hunter-gatherer* refers to an adaptation in which people subsist almost entirely on plants and prey they take in the wild. Except for some less self-reliant groups in the late twentieth century, hunter-gatherers produce nearly all the food they consume with gear of their own making, acquiring relatively little by means of trade. Therefore, the size, distribution, and density of hunter-gatherer populations are conditioned by the environments those peoples inhabit and the knowledge and technologies at their command and have varied dramatically over time in response to changes in both factors.

From the Pleistocene to the Holocene

The boundary between the Pleistocene (Ice Age) and Holocene (modern) epochs, about 11,600 B.P. (i.e., years before the present time), marks a major divide in this variability. The populations of archaic human hunter-gatherers of the Pleistocene (notably *Homo habilis, H. erectus,* and *H. neanderthalensis*) were presumably low as a consequence of their limited skills and intellectual abilities. Hunter-gatherer populations may have grown larger and denser after the emergence of anatomically modern humans in Africa (about 150,000 B.P.) and certainly did so after the appearance of the essentially modern behavior repertoire that signals the Upper Paleolithic (about 40,000 B.P.). However, despite essentially equal technological and intellectual abilities, Upper Paleolithic hunter-gatherer populations of the late Pleistocene never grew as large or dense as their Holocene counterparts. This was due to climate.

In comparison to the comparatively quiescent Holocene, Pleistocene climate changed frequently and abruptly, often going from nearly glacial to nearly interglacial conditions within a decade or two. Compounding this situation, atmospheric concentrations of carbon dioxide, which is essential to plant growth, were so low during the last 50,000 years of the Pleistocene that overall plant productivity and seed yields were only two-thirds of those in the Holocene. This combination of chaotic climatic change and low environmental productivity severely limited the opportunities of Pleistocene hunter-gatherers to develop stable, intensive adaptations capable of supporting large populations. As documented in the Middle East (Natufian culture) and Japan (Jomon culture), when rising carbon dioxide levels increased environmental productivity near the end of Pleistocene, a few hunter-gatherer groups developed more intensive and plant-dependent adaptations that supported larger and more sedentary populations. Rapid climate change, however, continued to limit these tendencies until the Holocene.

Responses to Climatic Change

Some hunter-gatherers responded almost instantly and in revolutionary ways to the onset of the stable, productive Holocene climatic regime. Jomon (Japan) hunter-gatherers intensified the use of plants, shellfish, and fish to support large, permanent settlements in a heavily populated landscape. Some hunter-gatherers in the Middle East, in contrast, shifted to part-time agriculture and began to compete for resources and space with the remaining hunter-gatherers, who were forced either to retreat and displace other hunter-gatherers or to work harder to glean more costly resources from shrunken territories.

Though its timing varies, this pattern of hunter-gatherer intensification eventually was repeated everywhere during the Holocene. The behavioral details differ depending on local resources, but the trend is always toward maximizing the rate at which these resources are acquired per unit of space, producing more nucleated, sedentary, and densely settled populations. This form of maximizing is a response to competition. Without competition, hunter-gatherers usually maximize the rate at which

resources are acquired per unit of time by minimizing the amount of time expended in their acquisition.

Time-minimizing hunter-gatherers are highly mobile, quickly leaving locations where resources have begun to diminish in search of others where returns are higher. Population growth increases the chances that another group has depleted these other prospective locations. This reduces the potential rewards of moving and increases the tendency to stay put and maximize the total amount of resources acquired from a smaller area by adding more costly roots, seeds, and small prey to the diet. In this way, the larger trajectory of hunter-gatherer intensification in the Holocene (including incipient agriculture) may be interpreted as a response to global population growth made possible by global climate change. The hunter-gatherers observed by anthropologists are representative of only the end of this trajectory, not of hunter-gatherers in general.

To illustrate this point, the population densities and maximum social group sizes of ethnographic hunter-gatherers are an order of magnitude larger, and their median and minimum territory sizes an order of magnitude smaller, than is likely for any time in the Pleistocene or early Holocene (Table 1). Ethnographic fertility and mortality more closely approximate values that seem reasonable for the late Pleistocene–early Holocene, although Pleistocene infant mortality probably was higher and total fertility probably was lower. In any case, the rapid population growth of some Eurasian hunter-gatherers almost immediately after the onset of the Holocene suggests that Pleistocene hunter-gatherers were capable of the same thing when rebounding from environmental disasters, growing rapidly at annual rates that may have ranged between 1 percent and 3 percent during short periods of optimal climate.

The Timing of Population Changes

The timing of hunter-gatherer intensification varies greatly within the Holocene. In contrast to their counterparts in Eurasia, where intensification occurred relatively early, hunter-gatherer populations in southern Africa, Australia, and much of North and South America remained relatively low well into the Holocene, rising rapidly to historically observed numbers only 3,000 or 4,000 years ago. Technology and environment seem lesser obstacles to these transformations than is the development of social

TABLE 1

Major Demographic Characteristics of Ethnographic Hunter-Gatherers

	Median	Maximum	Minimum	Sample Size	Source
Population					
Density (per square mile)	0.29	10.06	0.01	339	Binford 2001: Table 5.01
Total population	876	14,582	23	339	Binford 2001: Table 5.01
Total territory (square miles)	3,631	254,936	31	339	Binford 2001: Table 5.01
Social Group Size					
Smallest residential group	16	70	5.6	227	Binford 2001: Table 5.01
Largest residential group	46	650	19.5	297	Binford 2001: Table 5.01
Largest aggregation	158	1,500	42.0	213	Binford 2001: Table 5.01
Fertility and Mortality					
Males/100 females	100.0	230	30	93	Kelly 1995: Table 6-1
Total fertility rate*	5.50	8.50	0.81	42	Kelly 1995: Table 6-1
Birth interval (years)	3.3	5.4	2.3	11	Kelly 1995: Table 6-7
Mother's age at first birth (years)	19.3	22.8	15.9	9	Kelly 1995: Table 6-7
Mother's age at last birth (years)	35.0	39.0	26.3	10	Kelly 1995: Table 6-7
Weaning age (years)	2.5	4.5	1.0	30	Kelly 1995: Table 6-8
% mortality before first year	20.0	34.0	8.0	14	Kelly 1995: Table 6-9
% mortality before fifteenth year	42.0	61.0	6.0	23	Kelly 1995: Table 6-9

*Mean number of births per female

SOURCE: Binford (2001) and Kelly (1995).

conventions enabling the holding of land and hoarding of resources, without which individuals are insufficiently rewarded for the extra labor they must invest to intensify resource production. The many cases of late Holocene intensification make it clear that hunter-gatherer populations are probably always close to the limits imposed by environment, technology, and behavior but that the force of population growth is not a major source of innovations that breach those limits. (If it were, intensification would occur uniformly early.)

Simulations by Gary Belovsky (1988) and Bruce Winterhalder and colleagues (1988) show how hunter-gatherers and their resources are linked in a dynamic feedback cycle that makes population growth self-correcting. When resources are abundant, hunter-gatherer populations rise until resources are depleted, which causes the population to fall. As the population continues to fall, resources rebound, starting the cycle again. The whole cycle takes something like 90 years. Thus, hunter-gatherer populations are resource-limited but not static, and groups under the same limits may vary substantially in size, depending on which stage of this cycle they are in. These simulations also suggest that because intensive harvesting prevents resources from rebounding, hunter-gatherers who limit their foraging efforts will often maintain higher population densities than will hunter-gatherers who do not.

See also: *Environmental Impact, Human; Evolutionary Demography; Indigenous Peoples; Nomads; Prehistoric Populations.*

BIBLIOGRAPHY

Belovsky, Gary E. 1988. "An Optimal Foraging-Based Model of Hunter-Gatherer Population Dynamics." *Journal of Anthropological Archaeology* 7: 329–372.

Bettinger, Robert L. 2001. "Holocene Hunter-Gatherers." In *Archaeology at the Millenium*, ed. G. Feinman and T. D. Price. New York: Kluwer/Plenum.

Binford, Lewis R. 2001. *Constructing Frames of Reference: An Analytical Method for Archaeological Theory Building Using Ethnographic and Environmental Data Sets.* Berkeley: University of California Press.

Keeley, Lawrence H. 1988 "Hunter-Gatherer Economic Complexity and 'Population Pressure': A Cross-Cultural Analysis." *Journal of Anthropological Anthropology* 7: 373–411.

Kelly, Robert L. 1995 *The Foraging Spectrum: Diversity in Hunter-Gatherer Lifeways.* Washington, D.C.: Smithsonian Institution Press.

Winterhalder, Bruce, W. Baillargeon, F. Cappelletto, R. Daniel, and C. Prescott. 1988. "The Population Ecology of Hunter-Gatherers and Their Prey." *Journal of Anthropological Archaeology* 7: 289–328.

ROBERT L. BETTINGER

ISBN 0-02-865678-4